P9-DWT-423

Dedicated to the memory of
Timothy Garrett "Gary" Jackson, Sr.

SPECIAL REFERENCE WORK

PLAYER'S HANDBOOK

A Compiled Volume of Information for Players and GameMasters
of HackMaster: The Role-Playing Game 4th Edition

© Copyright 2001 Kenzer and Company. All Rights Reserved.

HackMaster is based on the original Dungeons and Dragons® rules created by E. Gary Gygax and Dave Arneson.

Questions, Comments, Product Orders?
Kenzer and Company
25667 Hillview Court
Mundelein IL 60060

Phone: (847) 540-0029
Fax: (847) 540-8065
E-mail: questions@kenzerco.com
Visit our website: www.kenzerco.com

Manufactured in the
United States of America

Second Printing: November 2001

Reality Check, A Disclaimer

Foreword: Interrupt Illusion

It's been a long time getting here friends, and it seems a bit ironic that the long journey we first embarked upon years ago has brought us right back where we started. Let us explain. Not long after we first published Knights of the Dinner Table magazine, letters started coming in from readers saying, "I want to play HackMaster! Why don't you make it?" As time passed those 'suggestions' slowly turned to demands. From the point of view of our fans it wasn't a matter of 'if' HackMaster the RPG would become a reality, it was 'when'.

The main problem with HackMaster was this — whenever we discussed the possibility of actually designing the game we were always taken back to the same in-yer-face dilemma: HackMaster began as a spoof of Advanced Dungeons and Dragons. Over the years, it went well beyond that original spoof, but the fact of the matter was STILL the same — at the heart of HackMaster lay AD&D. Starting from scratch would not only be akin to reinventing the wheel; it would also make HackMaster decidedly different from what had been presented in the magazine for so many years.

While developing HackMaster we knew that there could only be ONE way to do it right. If only, we told ourselves, we could actually use the AD&D core rules as the basic engine that everything "HackMaster" from the Knights of the Dinner Table comic book could be plugged into. (sigh). Shya' right — what were the chances of THAT ever happening? A great notion but surely an impossibility, we told ourselves.

Well, it turns out, the good folks at Wizards of the Coast were willing to grant us such a license.

Suddenly, we found ourselves standing on the shoulders of *Giants* (Giants in this case being all those talented individuals who have contributed to the AD&D game over the last 25 years). We were literally handed the keys to the kingdom and given a green light to spoof the game we grew up playing. To all of us on the KODT Development Team, AD&D was and is hallowed ground. As such, even though we took a wrecking crane and a crowbar to those rules, we certainly didn't take this opportunity to alter the rules lightly.

And so, that's how the journey began to swing full circle. What began as a spoof took on a life of its own and took its creators (and fans) on a wild and wonderful journey. And at the end of that journey it gently set those creators down at the place they began, playing *(and now writing!)* games based on the version of AD&D that they grew up loving. The end result, the product you now hold in your hands (and the Hacklopedia of Beasts and the GM's Guide) is a tad different than even we could guess. While it is indeed a side-splitting parody of the AD&D game, HackMaster is every bit a new version of that hallowed game. In fact, in a different time or place it could easily have been called "3e." Players of the original AD&D game will find Hackmaster comfortably familiar, yet new and exciting.

As KODT character Dave Bozwell would say "It's time to party like we rolled an 18/99!!!"

Brian Jelke, Steve Johansson, Jolly Blackburn and David S. Kenzer

The KODT Development Team

CREDITS

Knights of the Dinner Table/HackMaster Development Team is

Jolly R. Blackburn • Brian Jelke • Steve Johansson • David S. Kenzer

Editor/HackWriter/Knight Errant 11/10/15th Level: Jolly R. Blackburn
Editor/HackWriter/Assassin 11/10/12th Level: David S. Kenzer
Project Task Master/HackWriter 11th Level: Brian Jelke
Master Productionist/HackWriter 11th Level: Steve Johansson

Editor/HackWriter/Paladin 9/10/2nd Level: Barbara Blackburn
Editor/Cleric 10/9th Level: Jennifer Kenzer

Art Director/Bard 7/4th Level: Bob Burke

Art Liaison/Editor/BattleMage 7/5/3rd Level: Mark Plemmons • **Designer/Illusionist 9/3rd Level:** Jiffy Burke

Hackwriter/Diviner/Berserker 6/6/6th Level: Don Morgan • **HackWriter/Paladin 5/8th Level:** Glenn Harris

Party Chief of Propaganda/Bard/Druid 9/4/5 Level: Gerda Hansen • **HMA Manager:** Jamie LaFountain

---

HackWriters, Henchman Class:
Larry Granato, Reverend Kevin Kasper,
Noah Kolman, Scott Luskin, Mark Mueller, David Ritzlin

Hacktesting:
Tracy Casper, Doug Davis, Glenn Harris,
Don Morgan, Mark Mueller, Todd Weaver
and anyone whoever contributed to AD&D™
or bellied up to a gaming table.

Front Cover Art: Ruth Thompson
(Cover portrays the professional adventuring party,
Creatins of Flander's Meadow taking out a temple of Pagnyr'Parkus)

Back Cover Art:
Brendon and Brian Fraim, colored by Tom Martin

Interior Art:
Tommy Castillo, V. Shane Colcough, Doug Curtis, Allan Ditzig,
Stacy Drum, Brendon Fraim, Brian Fraim, William Hammock,
Nick Laing, Rob Lee, Ed Northcott , Eric Olson, Mark Pennington,
Aaron Siddall, Mike Simon, Randy Siplon, Darryl Sheakley

Special thanks:
"Super" Dave Radzik and Ray Ennis for HMA research.
Hard Fight A.C.T. LAB for Accelerated Campaign Testing
and Character Demise Studies

HackMaster Logo Artwork: Eric Olson

Fame Rub Signatures

Have Game Designers and other "lucky" notables sign their autographs here. That way they'll always be handy for emergency dice purgings and luck charging.

Note: To charge a die to roll higher numbers you should stroke the die left to right. For lower numbers stroke right to left. Fame Rubs can be used to prime new dice and many game designers at conventions and store signings are more than glad to oblige fans. As a rule of thumb you should do a minimum of six swipes of the die across the signature (but no more than ten as that can sometimes have the opposite effect of what is desired). To get you started we've added two facsimile signatures of Jo Jo Zeke and Gary Jackson. They'll only be 32% as effective as an original signature but they could come in handy in an emergency.

Hard 8 Enterprises®
What do you want to Hack today?™

Greetings friend,

You hold in your hands the long awaited 4th incarnation (edition) of the HackMaster Player's Handbook. This book (along with a properly certified GameMaster) is your gateway to the exciting world of HackMaster. "What is HackMaster," you ask?

Quite simply, HackMaster is a fantasy role-playing game with an edge. It is the game of choice for those who know the difference between Epic and Ordinary.

Let's not beat around the bush. Killing and breaking things — that's what best sums up the HackMaster™ phenomenon. Now, there are those individuals of a weaker spirit and mindset who would have you believe that role-playing is some artsy-fartsy new age form of entertainment. They believe it should be used to develop character, build inner strength and somehow reweave the social fabric into something higher and stronger than the way we found it.

There are even misguided individuals who will caution you that hack-n-slash and power gaming is a very bad thing. That it is somehow inferior and develops dangerous behavior that is detrimental to society. These same naysayers somehow feel that those of us who relish such qualities in our gaming styles are somehow lost. Worse, these same people feel the need to shepherd us away from our preferred form of gaming and usher us to their own nauseating lukewarm politically correct brand of role-playing drivel. HOGWASH!! To them I say, "Back off, Jack!"

HackMaster™, by gawd, is for the rest of us — for us poor clods who live in a world where we are forced to abide by the rules day to day. "Don't hit your sister with that stick!" "Get back to work! Lunch break is over!" "Did you make those copies of the Gentry account?" We suffocate in our daily lives as we carry the yokes and harnesses that society has placed upon our unwilling shoulders. Dammit!! The heart of a hero beats within our chests! Yet it is our sad doom that we are relegated to fighting traffic and never-ending lines when all we really want to do is fight dragons and repel armies. Is there no escape?!

HackMaster™ is our escape!! For those of us who love to see a burning building — who feel our muscles tighten at the sight of a good sword fight or brawl. Yes, HackMaster™ is the key - unlocking chains and opening doors to strange new worlds! It is the game for the rest of us!! For those of us who, if not for the sad fact we were born in a world constrained by reality, would be KINGS!! HackMaster™ is for those who crave power! We come from different walks of life, we earn our living in different ways, and yet we have one thing in common: we love a good fight and we're not afraid to step up to the plate and accept a challenge. We're not ordinary — we're Extraordinary.

And we bloody well don't offer any excuses for our behavior or our choice of entertainment. HackMaster™ is our license to yield to that primordial urge that courses through our veins. Killing and breaking things!! Indeed, that's what sums up HackMaster™ best.

My friend, if you are reading this, then you are most likely a HackMaster™ player already and you know what this game is all about. This book is for YOU! This book stands on the shoulders of three previous editions written by my dear departed friend, Timothy Garrett Jackson, the Master of Hack. I miss the S.O.B. Hard Eight really took a blow to the gut when news of his demise arrived at the offices. Some of us wondered if there would even be a 4th edition. But those doubts didn't last long. For as Gar' was always fond of saying, "The game must go on!" Indeed it must…and it will.

Armed with his original material, and thousands of suggestions and requests sent in by fans over the years, I have personally headed up the development of this 4th edition. It was a labor of love and an honor to have been afforded the opportunity to reforge the HackMaster™ legend for a new generation of gamers. Of course, the problem with any 'new' edition of an established set of core rules is that there is some level of implication that the previous editions were somehow flawed -- less than perfect. Hogwash! To survive in a competitive market is to evolve. To evolve is to change — for the better. I'm quite certain that there will someday be a 5th edition, and a 6th and so on. Why? Because, from the playing of the game, we gain experience. And there is ALWAYS another experience level to strive toward.

If you are new to the world of HackMaster™, I envy you. You are about to break the chains and leave the ranks of the mundane and the ordinary. After reading this book and finding a group of comrades-in-arms to join you on your quest, you will be embarking on the most rewarding journey of your life. More importantly, you will be joining the HackMasters of EverKnight™ and will soon be chronicling your own adventures and forging your own legends.

Enough talk! Be off with you, noble hero! The game's afoot!

Jo Jo Zeke

Jo Jo Zeke
Director of HackMaster Development
Hard Eight Enterprises

Table of Contents

Appendices

Table Index

Welcome to HackMaster

In a world where there are no shortages of lackluster, mediocre games, you've managed to pick up one of the rare gems. Consider yourself lucky, for there are many, many pitfalls out there as far as game selections for Joe and Jane Gamer to stray into. Whether it was by mere chance, or upon the recommendation of a friend in-the-know, the fact that you've chosen to pick up a copy of **HackMaster** speaks well of you.

Perhaps you think I'm boasting when I say this, but HackMaster, in my humble opinion, is the single most enjoyable, most imaginative game ever created. I should know — I've been involved with the HackMaster phenomenon since the beginning and when I die I pity for the poor person who tries to pry my HackMaster books and dice from my cold, dead fingers. I trust your enthusiasm for the game will rival mine once you've rolled up your first character and cut your teeth slaying a dragon or two.

The book you hold in your hands is a set of keys that will unlock the gates that have confined you to the humdrum world of reality for most of your life. Be forewarned, once you pass through those gates there's no turning back. You'll be whisked along on a lifetime of wondrous adventures of high fantasy. Never again will you be content with the ordinary. Such is the bittersweet price that must be paid by those who would become heroes and heroines.

How the Rulebooks are Organized

The HackMaster rulebooks in their entirety can seem a bit daunting to the uninitiated when first glanced on the bookshelf. Not to worry, the various volumes and supplements of HackMaster are intended primarily as reference works for the GameMaster (GM). If you only plan on being a player, you won't need to know or memorize the wealth of material crammed into those books in order to play and enjoy the game. At any rate, you should know a bit more about the other core rulebooks.

HackMaster Player's Handbook (PHB)

You're holding this book in your hands now. The PHB is really all that a player will ever need to play HackMaster. You'll find that virtually all the rules and information you need is contained within its pages. Of course, as your game grows and you gain experience and learn to master the 'art of hack' you'll probably crave more material to cut your teeth on. For that reason, there are other books in the HackMaster line designed for that purpose but there's no need to discuss them here.

All other source books for the game (with the exception of those optional books aimed specifically at the player) are the sole territory of the Game Master (GM). It is greatly frowned upon for a player to own and/or peruse such material. This is especially true for the Game Master's Guide and the Hacklopedia of Beasts, for reasons explained below. As a collector, if you must own these books for completeness, please don't read them. That is unless of course you are planning on becoming a GM yourself.

HackMaster GameMaster's Guide (GMG)

Most of the hard 'rules' of HackMaster are contained in the HackMaster GameMaster Guide (GMG). This book is the GM's inner sanctum. Players who truly want to enjoy the game, as it is intended to be played, should not, under any circumstances, read the GMG. Doing so would be akin to peeking behind the curtain of the goodly Wizard of Oz. To do so ruins the game for everyone.

The rules contained within the GMG are designed to guide the GM, and give him information that is vital for him to be able to run the game effectively. If he feels that players need to know something that is explained in the GMG, he will tell them. Otherwise, players will refrain from attempting to gain some sort of perceived advantage by obtaining this forbidden knowledge. [Note: As a player of HackMaster you'll run across the phrase, "For the GM'S Eyes Only!" from time to time. That's your cue to STOP reading.]

In our own group at Hard Eight, I do not tolerate players intruding into this inner sanctum. My players know, and I recommend this course of action to other GMs, that if I find out they have read rules from the GMG in an attempt to "rules lawyer" me, punishment is swift and severe. On the first infraction, I dock the unruly players 1,000 experience points (experience points, or e.p.s, will be explained further into this text). Subsequent infractions result in the loss of larger amounts of e.p.s until, ultimately, it is possible they could lose an entire level of character development (a concept that will also be explained more fully later). Some may think such tactics a bit harsh, but these rules keep order and prevent the gaming session from spiraling into a chaotic mass. 'Nuff said.

Hacklopedia of Beasts (HoB)

Like the GMG, the Hacklopedia of Beasts™ supplements are the province of the GM. They give complete and detailed information about the monsters, people, and other creatures inhabiting the HackMaster world. Now, I have heard that there are some GMs who do not mind if their players know something about the information contained in the Hacklopedia. In most, if not all, circumstances, however, we believe that players will find the experience more suspenseful, and therefore more enjoyable, if they don't know all the details about the creatures they will meet along the way. GMs are, of course, at liberty to consider player characters' backgrounds when enforcing this. There may be certain characters who, logically, would have limited knowledge of certain beasts which are common in the characters' own home-town area. These beasts, however, would be common creatures only, such as snakes, bears or fish. GMs worth their salt will know what type of info to spoon-feed their players. They certainly do not need to let them read the Hacklopedia.

A Few Words from the Author

Before we jump into the new edition I'd like to address a few issues that have come to light since the last edition went to press. Please take a few moments to read them.

On GMs and Non-Disclosure

Now there are times that the GM will want to shed his aura of supremacy and actually mingle as a player character among the common masses. This is perfectly acceptable since it sometimes takes a little recreational hacking to recharge the GM spirits, which are often worn down over the course of a long, drawn out campaign. But let me remind you of something, as GM (active or inactive matters not) you have taken an oath not to divulge the GM-only information you've been privy to. While in this role of player, the former GM turned player must NEVER divulge certain GM-eyes-only rules to non-GM players. It simply isn't done. Having said that, however, this shouldn't stop you from using every bit of your GM expertise and rules knowledge to challenge your acting GM. Such friendly competition can only make the contestants in such battles of wits that much stronger.

On the Use of the Male Pronoun

I apologize for wasting valuable space on this topic but it's been a thorn in my side since the last edition of HackMaster went to press. Those of you familiar with the 3rd Edition rules probably noticed we bought into the politically correct clap-trap of alternating male pronouns (he, him, his) with their female counterparts (she, her). I was pressured into such nonsense by one of my former copy editors and I've regretted it ever since. I apologize for allowing such foolishness to enter the realm of HackMaster. I'd just like to get my hands on the frickin' moron who suggested such a practice in the first place. What rubbish! Yeah, I'm sure some of you got the warm fuzzies when you stumbled across the word 'she' instead of 'he' when you read the rules on **falling damage** in 3rd Edition, but it's over!!

It's called proper usage of the written word, folks, and bottom line the use of the male pronoun when addressing a general audience has been standard practice for many, many centuries — long before I opened shop anyway. I'm comfortable with writing the way I was taught in grade school, thank you very much, and I'm too old and too stubborn to change my ways at this stage in the game. And quite frankly, I don't feel it's my responsibility to begin writing in a style that's alien to me and grates against my skin just to cater to a few thin-skinned readers who perceive the use of "he" or "him" as a personal attack. Deal with it.

In 4th edition the rules have been purged. The male pronoun is once again king and used exclusively throughout all the HackMaster books and supplements. If you construe this as an indication that Hard Eight Enterprises, or myself, is sexist or that I wish to exclude females from the game — that's YOUR problem. The truth is, Ladies of Hack have always been welcome at our table and can take care of themselves. They're not about to let our refusal to do the pronoun dance deprive them of enjoying the game. I suggest you adopt the same attitude. 'Nuff said on that subject. Let's move on.

Rule Contradictions?

It's come to my attention that there are certain individuals who are of the opinion that a great many rules in HackMaster are contradictory, flawed or even broken. Rubbish!! I thought my forward to HackMaster 3rd edition would put this issue to rest once and for all but here we are, three years later, and not a day goes by that I'm not confronted with these claims.

Let me say it again. And THIS time I'll make it very, very clear. There are no contradictions in HackMaster – only 'apparent' contradictions. You can trust me when I say that because I stand from a vantage point where I can see the entire game as a whole. If you run across a rule that you feel is in contradiction with another rule you should remind yourself that it's probably a case of your mastery of the rules being deficient. HackMaster is a complex game and as such not EVERY rule or nuance of the game has been trusted to the common GM and/or player. The game is bigger than any one player. It's bigger than you or me… well, it's bigger than you.

Entrenched and Holding the Line

As many of you know, the *Ladies Hack Journal* launched a surprisingly virulent campaign against Hard Eight when news broke we were working on a fourth edition. They assumed (and wrongly so) that we would succumb to the pressure of public opinion they brought to bear on us and that we'd reverse our long held stance that female dwarves have beards (they were also looking for a revocation of the rules on Strength penalties for female characters). I won't retread on that bloodied ground here – that battle has been fought before and fought well on both sides of the issue.

I do know that when news of Gary's death broke there was speculation that our resolve on the matter would buckle. Well, I'm here to tell you that female dwarves STILL have beards.

We've also refused to yield to demands of some HMPA chapters that a policy of "Open Die Rolls' for GMs be mandated in fourth edition. This will never happen. The GM Screen and undisclosed die rolls is one of the tenets of a GM's authority over his game. We will NOT undermine that authority.

Separating the Men from the Boys

To those of you who are veterans of HackMaster and role-playing in general, you already know what to do with this book. In fact, you're probably chomping at the bit to start unlocking the secrets of 4th edition. Be off with you! Unless you're in need of a refresher course on the basics, go ahead and skip ahead to Chapter 1 — I'll be along shortly

As for the rest of you, I'll assume you're new meat and still a little confused at this point. Not to fear. I'll be your guide. To help you get into the game more easily, we've added a section just for you called "Elementary HackMaster" which will grease the wheels and get you into the fray in no time.

Elementary HackMaster: The Basics

A Crash Course on Role-Playing

If you're new to role-playing you'll find this section extremely helpful. There will be a lot of new words and terminology to learn. In the back of this book you'll find a detailed glossary to HackMaster and role-playing in general. Be sure to refer to it as you come across a word you don't understand.

Let's start at the beginning. Even if you haven't role-played, I'm sure you've played one kind of game or another in your life, be it card game, board game, war game or video game. Now there are other game-designers out there who would have you believe that role-playing games are not competitive. That there are no real winners or losers. What a load of crock! No winners or losers?

If THAT'S your attitude you might as well put this book down right now and walk away. This game is obviously not for you. (I'm sure you can get a refund from the store you purchased this book from if you whine and cry enough and explain you're not worthy).

Still with me? Good. HackMaster is damn competitive. It's a battle of wits; against the GameMaster, against your fellow players, against all manner of horrid beasts intent on taking hit-points and Honor from you and lifting your hard-earned gold. You 'win' if you're alive at the end of the night to tell the tale and compare battle scars with your fellow survivors.

Role-playing is quite different from the games your parents probably played. Their idea of fun was sitting around a table with some friends, playing some type of innocent game like "First One to the End Wins."

They probably rolled some simple six-sided dice (or spun a spinner) to see how many spaces to move their tokens. Occasionally they would run into a static obstacle on the board to keep things interesting. What fun!! In such a manner they continued rolling dice and moving until one of them made it to the end. That person was proclaimed winner. Simple and straightforward. If that kind of fun turns your crank – more power to you. To each his own.

HackMaster, however, is a game of a different color. It packs a bit more attitude than the one I just described. In role-playing the colorful spaces have now been turned into three-dimensional pathways. These pathways take you through caverns and dark, hidden places, such as dungeons. The pathways branch out in all directions. You decide which way to go. Your decisions could mean the difference between fortunes gained or lost, between life and death. It's a game of sweaty palms and quickened hearts. In role-playing you're not dealing with the draw of a "lose-a-turn" card, or some other lame obstacle. The obstacles here are Swack Iron Dragons trying to cloud your mind with dragonspeak and bloodthirsty grunge elves with an eye on lifting your purse (as well as your scalp).

Be forewarned — Depending on the skills of your GameMaster, these creatures may seem as real as the people sitting across the table from you. You'll swear you can smell the foul stench of the Gutter Troll trying to drag you by the ankles from your hiding place. The flash of a sharp blade in the light of your torch may cause your pulse to race as the GM weaves the action and tells you the war whoops ringing in your ears are drawing nearer. Think you're up to it? You're no longer just a colorful plastic pawn moving around a board. You're a unique hero, ready to fight past such obstacles, armed with swords of your own and sheathed in armor. Some of you may even have magic weapons. You'll fight your way past the bands of opponents and continue on your way, looking for the next foe. On your way you'll fatten your purse (hopefully) and begin discovering new things about the strange world around you.

In a way, I've just taken you on your first role-playing adventure. The only difference is that in a real HackMaster session YOU will be making the decisions. That's what's it all about. The player (you) is placed in the midst of an imaginary unknown or dangerous situation created by a referee (Game Master) and must work his way through it — surviving the process. This is the heart of role-playing. The player adopts the role of a character and then guides that character through an adventure. The player makes decisions, interacts with other characters and players, and essentially "pretends" to be his character during the course of the game. Not that the player actually has to climb up a wall when his character does or, for that matter, have his head lopped off when his character gets caught stealing the crown jewels. It simply means that whenever the character is called on to do something or make a decision, the player imagines that he is in that situation and chooses an appropriate course of action. At the end of this section we'll go over an example of a role-playing session which should further illustrate the uniqueness of this form of gaming.

Learning HackMaster

If this is your first exposure to role-playing, don't worry. It's very likely that you won't understand everything you're going to read the first time out. Don't let it discourage you. I advise you to read the entire Player's Handbook from cover to cover. Again, if you come to a term you do not understand, look for it in the Glossary (Appendix N). If there's something you don't understand, make a note of it.

Learning the game is actually very simple when you start to put what you've learned into action. HackMaster is much easier to demonstrate than it is to explain. It's similar to what would happen if you'd never eaten steak before. Someone can describe to you how it tastes, but until you take that first juicy bite, you're never really going to know.

After reading this book your initial order of business is to create your first character and find some other players to play with. More importantly, you'll need to find a qualified GM to take you under his wing and teach you the ropes. This is actually much easier than it may sound. It's been my experience that veteran players love to bring new blood into the fold and are more than willing to help where they can.

Finding a gaming group is usually as simple as dropping by the corner game or hobby store. Most of these have bulletin boards where gaming groups offer information about how to join. Most are eager to help new gamers. Groups can also often be found advertised on bulletin boards at your local library, school or college recreation hall. You could even go online and see if any groups are advertising in your area. By the way, don't be put off if some groups seem unwilling to take you on. Name-Level Groups [See The Goal: Is That All There Is? below] are very elitist by nature and they are constantly honing their game to better compete at local and regional HackTournies. Oft times they don't have the time nor inclination to help neophyte players. It's nothing personal. Asking to play with such groups is like a Pony Leaguer asking to throw the ball around with a New York Yankee. You don't ask – you wait until you are invited.

Another excellent way to find other players is to join the HackMaster Player's Association (see The Goal: Is That All There Is?). The HMPA can put you in touch with other serious-minded players and GMs who have taken an oath to promote and further our hobby.

After a few sessions, when you start to get your footing, you should go back and re-read the rules. You'll find they begin to make more sense now that you have a better understanding of the game. Now you can begin to concentrate on finding a regular group to play with. If you can't find a group with an empty chair who will take you in, then consider starting your own group. You may not be sanctioned for tournament play (at first) but you and your friends can work on improving your game and rule mastery. Eventually, a competent GM will take you under his wing. He will whip you into shape right away if you've strayed off the path. Once that happens, you can step up to play with the big boys in a sanctioned (name) group.

In the meantime, don't sweat the small stuff — A good attitude and a willingness to improve your game will quickly earn you the respect of your GameMaster and your fellow players.

An Example of Play

To further clarify what really goes on during a HackMaster game, read the following example. This is typical of the sort of action that occurs during a playing session.

The group consists of a magic-user, a fighter, a thief and a cleric. They've hired an NPC halfling torchbearer and are following a treasure map, (see Diagram 1) which is leading them into a rather simple in-and-out dungeon. Hopes for large amounts of booty run high. As we pick up on the action, the party has just entered the dungeon corridor through a set of iron doors (bottom edge of map) and is about to enter the dungeon.

Diagram 1: A Simple in-and-out dungeon. Each square is ten feet.

GM: As you push through the ancient doors you find yourselves surrounded in darkness. There's only enough sunlight coming through the doors for you to see about thirty feet (3 squares) ahead.

Fighter: Okay, I nudge the torchbearer forward with my sword. At 5 coppers a day he's definitely going to earn his keep by going first. I tell him to stick close to me and to hold the torch high.

Thief: I'm hangin' back to take up the rear. I wanna watch our backs in case that Spotted Arvanger is still on our scent. I'm not convinced that arrow took him down. Oh, and I'll go ahead and spike those doors open so they can't close on us and trap us inside.

Magic-user: Good thinking. I'm bringing a Magic Missile spell online - just in case there's trouble ahead. I got a bad feeling about this crawl. It has 'set-up' written all over it.

Cleric: You guys are just being paranoid.

GM: As the torchlight flickers off of the roughly-hewn granite walls you see a passageway going as far as you can see in the light. You hear shuffling sounds as

you walk, and you think you see, in your peripheral vision, the shadows of what might be rats scurrying down the corridor.

Fighter: Rats? Hmmmm…. I guess they're not the feral kind if they're moving away. Okay, we'll move forward slowly. We'll look closely at the walls and floor as we go to spot any secret doors or traps.

GM: Okay. Tell me exactly who's looking.

Thief: I definitely am. I have a 40% chance to spot traps, and secret doors. Do I notice anything unusual?

GM: I thought you indicated you were watching the group's back. Which is it?

Thief: Uh… er… I'm checkin' fer traps. When the magic-user mentioned having a bad feeling I decided I should check things out.

GM: Uh huh, sure (rolls some dice). Okay, about forty feet in you notice a section of the floor that looks a bit strange. It doesn't take a genius to realize there's a pit trap. Whoever set it didn't do a very good job of concealing it.

Thief: Ha!! I figured as much. Can we work our way around it?

GM: You can try to hug the walls of the corridor and inch your way around it. But it's tricky business. I'm going to insist that you're all going to have to make a Dexterity check.

Fighter: Okay. I'll send the torchbearer first. That way we'll have a good light source to lead the way. You want me to roll for him?

Diagram 1

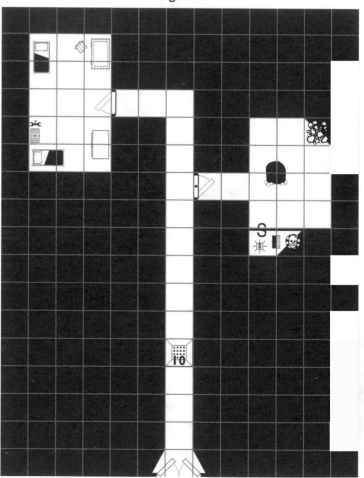

GM: No, I'll do it (rolls). Okay, the halfling makes it - no problem.

Fighter: Guess I'll go next (rolls). Whew! A 15 - just barely made it. That was close.

Magic-user: (rolling) No problem here. I gingerly walk around the pit.

Cleric: (roll) Same here. I made it.

Thief: (getting ready to roll)

GM: Hold up a second. Just as the thief is about to inch his way around the pit, a deep buzzing and a guttural snarl comes from the area toward the door, behind him.

Thief: Cripes! Don't tell me…it's that frickin' Arvanger! He followed us didn't he?

GM: You guessed it. Apparently he wants to avenge the death of his mate. He looks none too happy as he cautiously closes the distance between you.

Everybody else: Quick!! Jump across the pit.

Thief: (Looking toward GM) That's not a bad idea. Can I make it?

GM: (Thinking) Oh, man. It's a good ten feet. And you're wearing armor, not to mention a backpack.

Thief: Hey, don't forget I have Jumping as a skill. (consulting his character sheet)

GM: Very good. Go ahead and make your roll and make your calculations.

Thief: (rolls) Okay…kewl. I just leapt 24 feet. Plenty of room to spare.

GM: Hold on there Sparky. You're forgetting that you needed a twenty foot running start. Unfortunately for you the Arvanger gives chase as soon as you begin to run. He has a movement rate of 12 compared to your six. I'm going to rule that he catches up to you JUST as you jump.

Thief: Meaning?

GM: Meaning he sinks his claws into your backpack. This breaks your stride, and his momentum and your weight sends you BOTH tumbling head over heels into the pit.

Thief: Huh? What the hell are you talking about? He was wounded wasn't he? I'm SURE that arrow would have slowed him down some.

GM: No, sorry. Actually, the pain from the arrow lodged in his side only served to SPUR him on with rage and make him even more determined to catch you.

Thief: Okay, okay, whatever. I had my shortsword at the ready. As we are falling, I'm going to attempt to lodge it under his belly so that when we hit he'll be impaled on it.

GM: That's a bit of a stretch, don't you think?

Thief: Hey, I'm fighting for my life here. I'm motivated. I should at least have a percentage chance.

GM: Okay. I'll give you a 20% chance of pulling it off. But I'm also ruling that the Arvanger is going to make a biting attack on you as you fall. Any damage will be simultaneous. (roll) Fudge! He misses. Go ahead and roll for yours.

Fighter: I'm sheathing my sword and pulling out my bow. I'll move up to the pit and knock an arrow. If I can get a clear shot I'm going for it.

Thief: (rolls). Cripes! A frickin' 99?? Where the hell are those high numbers when I need them?

GM: Okay, you just fell ten feet to the bottom of the pit. Hate to tell you this but the pit was spiked. I'll roll for the Arvanger — his hard exoskeleton protects him from falling damage but not from the spikes.

Thief: What? Spikes? Aww, man, I'm a goner.

GM: The spikes puncture you for (rolls 1d10) eight points of damage.

Thief: Gaaa!!! 8 points! That puts me down to two hit points.

Cleric: Don't sweat it Sparky. Hang in there. I can still throw a Cure Light Wounds on your sorry butt.

GM: Don't forget about falling damage. (quietly) Okay, Lucy (referring to his six-sider), don't let me down (rolls). Uh oh.

Magic-user: That doesn't sound too good.

Thief: (gulp)

GM: Take five more! (snicker)

Thief: Damn. I'm shish kebab.

Magic-user: Hey, don't forget to check for the monster!

GM: -sigh- (rolls) Well the Arvanger bites it! He's dead, too.

Cleric: I break out the rope. I'll lower the halfling and tell him to tie a loop around the thief's shoulders. Then we'll pull him out.

Magic-user: Wait! This is just a short in-and-out crawl. Might as well leave him there. We can grab him on the way out.

Thief: What?

Fighter: The magic-user's right. No sense in carrying his dead weight through the entire dungeon.

Thief: C'mon guys! At least pull me out of the stinkin' pit.

Magic-user: Sorry, I can't hear you. You're dead - remember?

Cleric: Okay, I put away the rope.

Fighter: I draw my sword again. We'll continue on.

Thief: Thanks a lot, guys. I'll remember this.

Magic-user: Hey, did you guys hear something?

Cleric: Nope!

Aftermath: This particular adventure ended tragically. The magic-user was later smothered by a Lurker Within who was hiding in a jeweled snuff box. By the time the fighter and cleric had dragged his body back to the pit-trap where the thief's body lay, they were horrified to find that the 'Rats' had returned and had commenced to voraciously feeding on his corpse.

As you can see, investing in plenty of character sheets is very important. I hope this example will give newbies an idea of what a typical adventure might be like. You may have also noticed that while the players often questioned the GM's calls and decisions they didn't argue with him. The GM, after all, has final say.

The Goal: Is That All There Is?

What exactly is the point to role-playing games? Is it to mindlessly follow a set pattern of play, going from point A to point E with no stops in between? Is it to get to the end first, and be declared the winner? Not on your life! HackMaster has as many goals as there are people who play. Some play to let off steam, others to sharpen their wits. Most play to socialize and have a good time. That's why it's important to play with people you like, and stay away from jerks who make your real life miserable. Gaming should be something of an escape from the everyday humdrum.

Once you've put a few adventures under your belt, however, you may begin to wonder, "What next? Where do I go from here?"

For some players, it's enough to just game one or two times a week. That's fine. Undoubtedly, some of you will be a little more ambitious and find that you are beginning to demand MORE from the game. This section will briefly discuss some of your options and some suggested goals both for your character and for YOU as a player.

Improve your game: First things first. You can't go far in HackMaster until you've mastered the game. This, of course, is a lifetime endeavor. Few players can ever claim to have fully 'mastered' the game. It's an on-going endeavor and something you should always strive toward — even if you're a casual player. You'll find that you may have to make some tough decisions as time goes by. Sometimes, a player will outgrow or surpass his fellow players (or GM) as far as mastery over the game and playing style goes. This is to be expected. Most of the truly great players of the game will tell you that at some point in time they had to decide to move on to a new group.

HackMaster Player's Association (HMPA): The HMPA's motto is, "It's a good place to start!" Indeed it is. This organization was launched by veteran HackMaster players who were concerned about the rising problem of players/GMs playing with home-brewed rules in the late seventies. HackMaster was in danger of becoming bastardized as each gaming circle in each region of the country began playing their own warped version of the game. One of the HMPA's first acts was to champion the Uniform Rules of HackMaster Movement (U.R.H.M.) by challenging players and GMs to take a vow that they would ONLY play by the official rules. Their noble efforts helped moved HackMaster beyond the realm of 'recreational pastime' to what it is today. Thanks largely in part to the HMPA you can belly up to any gaming table in the country and be fairly confident the rules are the same.

Well, almost every table. Sadly, there are a handful of secret gaming societies out there where rogue-GMs and bandit-players play a warped version the HackMaster engine that has been gutted and rewired with lame home-brewed rules. They abhor the tight reign of sanity and rule-uniformity the HMPA advocates. Be advised that such individuals are not content to play by their broken rules in isolation. If they were, I wouldn't need to mention them here. These rogue-groups frequently pop up at local HackCons and other conventions with the intent of recruiting new members. You should avoid them at all costs and inform the HMPA if such individuals approach you.

The HMPA has spearheaded a wide variety of programs such as National HackTournies, Player Advantage Seminars at conventions, etc. They're all about members helping members (You'll find more information on this fine organization in Appendix O).

Tournaments: There are a host of HackMaster tournaments aimed at a various skill levels around the country. Such competition is healthy for the hobby and presents an opportunity for players and GMs alike to show their stuff.

Name Level Groups: Once the members of a group have improved their game and become competitive, the next step is to apply for 'name group status' to the HMPA. Name Level Groups enjoy certain benefits such as special seminars at conventions and sanctioned tournaments where only the best are invited to play. Examples of some famous named groups are the Dorm Troopers, Shaker's Five and Gnarlyhedron.

Game Kits (Required Materials for Play)

Aside from a copy of this book and an 'attitude' there are still several required items you will need to play. You should make it a point to gather up the items on the following list before your first game. I recommend getting a backpack, briefcase or some kind of nylon or cloth bag in which you can store your 'game kit' along with your HackMaster books, pencils and other gaming materials. That way you'll always have them on hand.

Character Sheets

You will need some sort of character record. A character sheet is provided in the back of this book, which you are free to photocopy for your personal use. Hard Eight Enterprises also publishes character sheets. Since it is highly probable that you will be going through quite a few character sheets in HackMaster, we suggest you buy in bulk. It's really quite a bargain. You can also download a pdf file of the official HackMaster character sheet from www.kenzerco.com

There are those who simply use blank sheets of paper. I do not recommend this, but nothing's stopping you, if you feel you have no other alternative. But you should know that using blank sheets of paper as opposed to official character sheets is considered the mark of an amateur among HackMaster players and GMs alike.

Dice

A full set of polyhedral dice is necessary. A full set consists of 4-, 6-, 8-, 10-, 12-, and 20-sided dice. A few extra of each type would be useful. As your game improves, you'll probably want to add more dice with an eye on dedicating a specific die in your dice arsenal for a specific task.

For example if you're playing a thief you may want to dedicate a specific d10 to backstab rolls only.

Polyhedral dice should be available wherever you bought this book. Just remember to buy your own dice. Whatever you do, DON'T try to borrow another player's dice, but you may accept if they offer to let you use them.

Throughout these rules the various dice are referred to by a code that is in the form: # of dice, followed by "d," followed by a numeral for the type of dice. In other words, if you are to roll one 6-sided die, you would see "roll 1d6." Five 12-sided dice are referred to as "5d12." (If you don't have five 12-sided dice, just roll one five times and add the results.)

When the rules say to roll "percentile dice" or "d100," you need to generate a random number from 1 to 100. One way to do this is to roll two 10-sided dice of different colors. Before you roll, designate one die to represent the ten's place and the other the one's place. Rolling them together enables you to generate a number from 1 to 100 (a result of "0" on both dice is read as "00" or "100"). For example, if the blue die (representing the tens place) rolls an "8" and the red die (ones place) rolls a "5," the result is 85. Another, more expensive, way to generate a number from 1 to 100 is to buy one of the dice that actually has numbers from 1 to 100 on it.

A Word about Dice Etiquette

Since we're on the subject of dice, you should immediately flip to Appendix L right now and read about **Dice Etiquette**. The sooner you learn about dice, their use, and the "rules of the table" concerning them, the better. If you are using spanking-new dice right out of the dice bin you might want to 'prime' your dice to charge them with luck. Appendix L will tell you how.

Miniatures

Miniature figures are handy for keeping track of where everyone is in a confusing situation like a battle. These can be as elaborate or as simple as you like. Some players use plastic soldiers, chess pieces, board-game pawns, dice, or bits of paper to represent their characters. This is just plain tacky. Such penny-pinching tactics ruin the ambience of the game for EVERYBODY! Do yourself a favor – don't be THAT guy. Invest in some quality lead or pewter figures (hand painted to resemble your character). Official HackMaster brand miniatures work best, but other figure lines of lesser quality can be used as

stand-ins and are generally tolerated, albeit begrudgingly, by most GMs and players alike (-1 to all rolls for those using unofficial miniatures).

The Paper Trail

At least one player should have a few sheets of graph paper for mapping the group's progress. Make sure this is someone who can draw a straight line, or at least has access to a straight edge.

Assorted pieces of scratch paper are handy for making quick notes, for passing secret messages to other players or the GM, or for keeping track of odd bits of information that you don't want cluttering up your character record.

Miscellany

Many players take great pride in their game kits and at being well prepared for any given situation. It's nice to be able to produce a needed item during the middle of a gaming session and thereby prevent a possible disruption of play.

Every gamer has his own idea of what makes a good game kit. Some suggestions are: character sheets, dice bag (with dice), a couple of sharp #2 pencils (with eraser), a pencil sharpener, pizza money, change for vending machines (if you happen to be playing in a game store or at a convention), back-up dice, calculator, paper, M&Ms, Fig Newtons, etc.

The Gaming Table

Physically, the players and referee (the GM) should be seated comfortably around a large table with the referee at the head. Players need plenty of room for papers, pencils, dice, dice rolling zones, rulebooks, drinks, and of course ample supplies of snacks. The creed of every gamer should be "The Game Must Go On!" A properly prepared playing area such as described above will ensure there will be as few interruptions of the session as possible.

In addition to the above, the good and thoughtful GM will allow for extra space for his maps, dice, rulebooks, and assorted notes. Keeping such material within arm's reach is just a good idea. Lost? Don't worry. It's not rocket science. If you have brains enough to read, you'll catch on. Just stick close, find a GM worthy of the title and you'll be fine.

The Player's Code of Conduct

Before you create your first character you should familiarize yourself with the Player's Code of Conduct. This code was developed by the HMPA and originally drawn up by players themselves in order to keep the game open and honest for everyone.

HackMaster Player's Code of Conduct
Drafted by the HackMaster Player's Association, June 5th 1981
Ratified by the HMPA National Office, February 17th 1983

1. The game must go on.

2. The GameMaster is always right.

3. The game table is neutral territory (as are game conventions and game shops). [amended Aug 12, 1997]

4. A player shall not look behind the GameMaster's screen or look at his notes.

5. All information on a player's character sheet shall be accurate, current and truthful.

6. A player shall not lay down dice and character sheet with more than one GameMaster without their prime GM's express approval and knowledge. [amended July 3, 1982, December 8, 1989, May 15, 1992]

7. A player shall not cheat and will promptly report those who do to their GameMaster immediately.

8. A player shall not covet or touch fellow players' dice and/or any other random number generating devices (including electronic dice, chits, designated coins and personal spinners). [amended August 3, 1993]

9. A player shall take responsibility for his own actions and or behavior when deemed inappropriate by others and shall NOT attribute them to HackMaster, role-playing in general or to Hard Eight Enterprise or Kenzer & Company.

10. A player shall not distribute photocopied or electronically scanned HackMaster products to others.

Player Character Ability Scores

This is where the adventure truly begins — creating a Player Character (PC). The process can be deceptive. What begins as a simple series of numbers and entries scrawled on a sheet of paper will suddenly take on a name and personality and come to life before your very eyes. He will emerge as an alter ego under your control, suddenly finding himself thrust into a strange, foreboding world of dragons, evil mages and walled cities.

As he embarks on the career path of an adventurer you will see through his eyes. Danger lurks at every turn, and survival will seem improbable, if not impossible. After each battle as you sit by the fire and sew your wounds in the company of your steadfast comrades-in-arms, you will thank the gawds that you've lived to see another day. What more could a hero ask for?

Note: If you're ready to start rolling up a character you should turn to the Appendix I: Step by Step procedures where you'll find an easy to follow checklist that will guide you through the process.

Every character in HackMaster is made up of eight basic characteristics (ability scores): Strength, Dexterity, Constitution, Intelligence, Wisdom, Charisma, Comeliness and Honor. These are the building blocks, the skeleton, of your character.

The first three abilities represent the physical nature of the character, while the second three quantify his mental and personality traits. The last two are a little more unique.

Strength, of course, is simple to define. It measures your character's ability to muscle his way through life. How much can he lift? How hard can he hit? Exactly how powerful is he?

Dexterity is a measure of agility and grace. Can he deftly maneuver through a gauntlet of death? Can he hit an apple off the head of a little boy at 200 paces? Can he do a triple lutz?

Constitution tells you just how hardy he is. Can he keep going and play through the pain? Can he march through miles of bone-wearying swampland without stopping for a breather? Does he shake off the common cold like a dog sheds water or does it send him to bed?

Intelligence is a measure of your character's mental ability. Can he add up his tab at the inn, pay for it and not get cheated? Can he figure out the strange riddle that unlocks the secret to the Giant King's treasure hoard? Can he remember all of the names of his adventuring party?

Wisdom measures how practically a person thinks. Does he believe the thief when he says he has no idea where his Ring of Water Walking is? Does he know that it's not a good idea to tell an Onyx Dragon to "Bite me?"

Charisma, while often associated with physical beauty, is more accurately a measure of how glib, charming and well-liked a character is. Can he talk his way past a bevy of guards? Can he help negotiate a peace treaty between the Gnome Titans and the Orcs? Can he actually sell ice cubes to Eskimos?

Comeliness is a measure of the character's physical attractiveness to others. Can he have all the ladies in waiting swooning over him as he makes his way to the princess' chambers? Can he make an impression just by walking into a room? How does he get his teeth so white? Gee, she really looks great without make-up!

Honor represents how the character measures up to society's ideals of courage, integrity and inner strength. Can his comrades count on him in a fight? Is his word his bond? Will he let someone dis' his mother without a fight?

These traits are meant to be only the first glimpses of life as your fantasy character begins to take shape from the impulses of your imagination.

In various places throughout these rules, the following abbreviations are used for the ability names:

Strength - Str	**Dexterity** - Dex	**Constitution** - Con
Intelligence - Int	**Wisdom** - Wis	**Charisma** - Cha
Comeliness – Com	**Honor** – Hon	

Let the Dice Fall Where they May

Before delving into the character generation process let's talk about die rolls again. It has come to my attention that there are still some players (and GameMasters who tolerate such players) who resort to a wide range of home-brewed rules and tables which provide alternate methods of dice-rolling and generating ability scores. What a sad, pathetic situation. I view such methodology with disdain and compare it to those professional athletes who use steroids and other drugs to gain an unfair advantage in competition.

Such methods have no place in HackMaster and are not tolerated. Characters generated in such a fashion are banned from sanctioned HackMaster tournaments/events and players who resort to such measures risk banishment from the HMPA if caught. They cheat themselves as well as others who play by the rules. Do yourself a favor. Avoid the humiliation of being publicly exposed. Be a real hero — roll the dice and let them fall where they may. Insist that those around you do the same.

Creating Ability Scores

Okay, let's get started. The very first step in generating a character is rolling his ability scores. So grab 3 six siders, a blank character sheet and a pad of scratch paper. After you generate your abilities a definition of each will follow.

The first seven ability scores are determined randomly by rolling three six-sided dice (3d6) to obtain a score from 3 to 18. [Beginning Honor is handled differently and will be covered later.]

NOTE: If the character you are creating is the offspring of Player Characters (i.e. both the mother and father are/were active Player Characters) then you may qualify for the Gene Pool Method when creating your ability scores. (Ask your GM for the details.) Characters created under the Gene Pool Method receive abilities which are based on those of the parents. PC offspring also benefit from the parents' social class and Honor, not to mention any inheritance (in the form of money and/or possessions) the parents may have left or passed on to their heir.

Roll Ability Scores

Roll three six-sided dice (3d6); the total shown on the dice is your character's Strength ability score. Repeat this step for Dexterity, Constitution, Intelligence, Wisdom, Charisma, and Comeliness in that order. This method gives a range of scores from 3 to 18, with most results ranging from 9 to 12. Only a few characters have high scores (15 and above), so you should treasure these. Record each ability on your character sheet in the appropriate block. Be sure to use a pencil — you'll be making numerous changes.

Roll Fractional Ability Scores

Now roll a d100 for each ability score (except Honor). For purposes of play, the ability score is considered to be the lowest integer associated with the ability. For example, a magic user with 3/54 strength would still be considered to have 3 strength. As characters gain experience levels, they increase their fractional scores, depending upon their honor. (see Chapter 11 for details) When a fractional ability score goes over 100, the main score is raised by one and the 100 is discarded. Record each fractional ability on your character sheet next to the appropriate ability. (For example, your Strength is 16. You just rolled a Fractional Ability of 37. Your Strength should now read 16/37.)

Some players have questioned the logic behind ability scores that rise due to one's Honor as they gain experience. Look at it this way: a 1st level character just starting out in the world is untested. Maybe he can lift 150 pounds over his head and he's pretty proud of that fact. Does it make sense that years later when he's 8th level or higher and has fought armies while wearing little more than a loincloth and clenching the jawbone of an ass that he can STILL only lift 150 pounds? How absurd. The character has grown over the years. He's learned to draw on the inner strength which was always there, but untapped. Likewise with the other ability scores such as Wisdom. Most best-selling authors write their first hit novel while in their forties or later. Master performing artists also improve (Dexterity) their skills over time. I don't want to overstate this line of logic but the point is this; ability scores that creep up slowly over the span of many levels are no more absurd than ability scores that are fixed for the life of the character.

Adjust Ability Scores

Now that you've rolled for each ability score you have an opportunity to adjust them. (Again, Honor is handled differently so you can't adjust that ability using this step.)

There are two options to choose from when adjusting scores. You can do one or both as many times as you wish as long as you don't lower an ability to less than 3 in the process (except Pixie fairies, who can lower Strength to 1 and Half-Ogres who can lower Charisma to 2).

Table 1A: Strength						
Ability Score	Hit Prob.	Damage Adj.	Weight Allowance	Max. Press	Open Doors	Bend Bars/ Lift Gates
1	-3	-8	1	3	1	0%
1/51	-3	-8	2	4	1	0%
2	-3	-7	3	5	1	0%
2/51	-3	-7	4	7	1	0%
3	-3	-6	5	10	2	0%
3/51	-3	-6	7	20	2	0%
4	-2	-5	9	25	3	0%
4/51	-2	-5	11	35	3	0%
5	-2	-4	13	30	3	0%
5/51	-2	-4	15	40	4	0%
6	-2	-3	18	55	4	0%
6/51	-2	-3	21	60	4	0%
7	-1	-2	24	70	4	0%
7/51	-1	-2	27	80	5	0%
8	-1	-1	30	90	5	1%
8/51	-1	-1	33	95	5	1%
9	Normal	-1	36	100	5	1%
9/51	Normal	-1	39	110	6	1%
10	Normal	None	43	115	6	2%
10/51	Normal	None	47	125	6	3%
11	Normal	None	51	130	6	4%
11/51	Normal	None	55	135	7	4%
12	Normal	+1	59	140	7	5%
12/51	Normal	+1	63	145	7	5%
13	+1	+1	67	150	7	6%
13/51	+1	+1	71	160	8	6%
14	+1	+2	76	170	8	7%
14/51	+1	+2	81	175	8	8%
15	+1	+3	86	185	9	9%
15/51	+1	+3	91	190	9	10%
16	+2	+4	97	195	10	11%
16/51	+2	+4	103	220	10	12%
17	+2	+5	109	255	11	15%
17/51	+2	+5	115	290	11	20%
18	+3	+6	130	350	12(3)	25%
18/51	+3	+6	160	480	14(6)	35%
19	+3	+7	200	640	15(8)	50%
19/51	+3	+7	300	660	16(9)	55%
20	+3	+8	400	700	17(10)	60%
20/51	+3	+8	500	625	17(11)	65%
21	+4	+9	600	810	17(12)	70%
21/51	+4	+9	700	865	18(13)	75%
22	+4	+10	800	970	18(14)	80%
22/51	+4	+10	900	1050	18(15)	85%
23	+5	+11	1000	1,130	18(16)	90%
23/51	+5	+11	1,100	1,320	19(16)	95%
24	+6	+12	1,200	1,440	19(16)	97%
24/51	+6	+12	1,300	1,540	19(17)	98%
25	+7	+14	1,500	1,750	19(18)	99%

Option I: Generate Ability Points: This option allows you to sacrifice points from one Ability Score and increase another.

For every two (2) points you sacrifice on one ability you generate one (1) point that can be added to another ability. For example, if your character had a 16 Str, 18 Dex, and a 15 Wis you could sacrifice 2 points of Dex (reducing it from 18 to 16) and add 1 point to your Strength (raising it from 16 to 17). Or, if you wish, you could add that point to your Wisdom instead (raising it from 15 to 16). You can lower/raise as many abilities as you want. These are a few limitations:

- You can't sacrifice points from an ability if it would result in that ability being lower than 3 *after* subsequent racial attribute modifiers are applied (except Pixie fairies who can lower Strength to 1 and Half-Ogres who can lower Charisma to 2). If you chose to lower your Charisma to 4 you can forget about playing that Half-Ogre Barbarian since your Charisma will only be 1 after the -3 Charisma penalty is applied!

- You can't sacrifice points from two different abilities — i.e. you couldn't take 1 point off your Strength and 1 point off your Wisdom. Both points must come off the same ability.

- Only whole integers are adjusted. You can't adjust Fractional Ability scores during this step. A Strength of 14/48 raised one point would result in a 15/48 Strength.

- Comeliness may not be raised or lowered.

Option II: Generating Extra Building Points: This option allows you to sacrifice points from an Ability Score in order to generate extra Building Points (see Chapter 4: Character Priors and Particulars). You'll receive a certain amount of Building Points (BP) later in the character creation process. BPs are used to purchase such things as skills, talents, starting money, give you rerolls on certain tables and make improvements to your character.

This option simply gives you an opportunity to increase your starting quota of BPs. For every point (1) you sacrifice on one ability you generate two (2) Building Points which are recorded and later added to your starting quota of Building Points. As with Option I, you can't sacrifice points on an ability if it would result in that ability being lower than 3.

Note that each option is a separate process. For example, dropping an ability score 2 points would result in generating 4 Building Points OR 1 ability point (which could be applied to another Ability Score). It's one or the other — not BOTH!

The Ability Scores

The eight character abilities are described below. Each description gives an idea of what that ability encompasses. Specific game effects are also given. This chapter also includes tables giving all modifiers and game information for each ability score.

Strength

Strength (Str) measures a character's muscle power. This ability is the prime requisite of fighters because they must be physically powerful in order to wear

armor, wield heavy weapons and generally kick ass. A fighter with a score of 16 or more in Strength gains a 10% bonus to the experience points he earns. Strength helps to modify the chance to hit an enemy. It can increase/decrease the damage he causes with each hit, the weight the character is able to carry without a penalty for encumbrance (see below) and the character's ability to force open doors and similar portals.

The rest of this section on Strength consists of explanations of the columns in Table 1A. Refer to the table as you read.

Hit Probability adjustments are added to or subtracted from the attack roll rolled on 1d20 during combat. A bonus (positive number) makes the opponent easier to hit; a penalty (negative number) makes him harder to hit.

Damage Adjustment also applies to combat. The listed number is added to or subtracted from the dice rolled to determine the damage caused by an attack (regardless of subtractions, a successful attack roll can never cause less than 1 point of damage, (what do we look like, idiots?)).

Weight Allowance is the weight (in pounds) a character can carry without being encumbered (encumbrance measures how a character's possessions hamper his movement – see Glossary). These weights are expressed in pounds. A character carrying up to the listed weight can move his full movement rate.

Maximum Press is the heaviest weight a character can pick up and lift over his head. A character cannot walk more than a few steps this way. No matter how tough you think you are though, don't get cocky. I'd just like to see you try to lift a Blue Horny-Ridged Dragon over your head.

Open Doors indicates the character's chance to force open a heavy or stuck door. When a character tries to force a door open, roll 1d20. If the result is equal to or less than the listed number the door opens. A character can waste time and keep trying to open a door until it finally opens, but each attempt takes time (exactly how much is up to the GM) and makes a lot of noise. Noise attracts monsters. Monsters eat adventurers. Noise bad. (Unless you're the GM, then noise is good.)

Numbers in parentheses are the chances (on 1d20) to open a locked, barred, or magically held door, but only one attempt per door can ever be made. If it fails, no further attempts by that character can succeed.

Bend Bars/Lift Gates states the character's percentage chance (rolled on percentile dice) to bend normal iron bars, lift a vertical gate (portcullis) or perform a similar feat of enormous strength.

When the character makes the attempt, roll percentile dice. If the number rolled is equal to, or less than, the number listed on Table 1A, the character bends the bar or lifts the gate like they were tissue paper. If the attempt fails, the character can never succeed at that task, his friends will make fun of him and he'll get a reputation as a wuss. But cheer up — a character can try to bend the bars on a gate that he couldn't lift, and vice versa.

Dexterity

Dexterity (Dex) encompasses several physical abilities including hand-eye coordination, agility, reaction speed, reflexes and balance. Dexterity affects a character's reaction to a threat or surprise, his accuracy with thrown weapons and bows and his ability to dodge an enemy's blows. It is the prime requisite of thieves and affects their professional skills. A thief with a Dexterity score of 16 or higher gains a 10% bonus to the experience points he earns. The rest of the party better watch their backs with this guy!

Defensive Adjustment applies to a character's saving throws (see Glossary) against attacks that can be dodged, such as lightning bolts, boulders, etc. It

also modifies the character's Armor Class (see Glossary), representing his ability to dodge normal missiles and parry weapon thrusts. For example, Bart is wearing chain mail, giving him an Armor Class of 5. If his Dexterity score is 16, his Armor Class is modified by -2 to 3, making him harder to hit. If his Dexterity score is 5, his Armor Class is modified by +2 to 7, making him easier to hit. You might as well paint a target on his chest.

(In some situations, beneficial Dexterity modifiers to Armor Class do not apply. Usually this occurs when a character is attacked from behind or when his movement is restricted because he's being attacked while prone, tied up, on a ledge, climbing a rope, magically Held, etc. Then he's on his own.)

Reaction Adjustment modifies the die roll for initiative to see how quickly the character reacts or if a character is surprised when he unexpectedly encounters NPCs. The more positive the modifier, the less likely the character is to be surprised, and the harder it is to get funny pictures of him at a surprise party.

Missile Attack Adjustment is used to modify a character's die roll whenever he uses a missile weapon (a bow or a thrown weapon). A positive number makes it easier for the character to hit with a successfully attack, while a negative number makes it harder.

Table 1B: Dexterity			
Ability Score	Defense Adjustment	Reaction Adjustment	Missile Adjustment
1	+5	-5	-6
1/51	+5	-5	-5
2	+4	-5	-5
2/51	+4	-4	-5
3	+4	-4	-4
3/51	+3	-4	-4
4	+3	-3	-4
4/51	+3	-3	-3
5	+2	-3	-3
5/51	+2	-2	-3
6	+2	-2	-2
6/51	+1	-2	-2
7	+1	-1	-2
7/51	+1	-1	-1
8	0	-1	-1
8/51	0	0	-1
9 - 9/99	0	0	0
10 - 10/99	0	0	0
11 - 11/99	0	0	0
12	0	0	0
12/51	0	0	+1
13	0	+1	+1
13/51	-1	+1	+1
14	-1	+1	+2
14/51	-1	+2	+2
15	-2	+2	+2
15/51	-2	+2	+3
16	-2	+3	+3
16/51	-3	+3	+3
17	-3	+3	+4
17/51	-3	+4	+4
18	-4	+4	+4
18/51	-4	+4	+5
19	-4	+5	+5
19/51	-5	+5	+5
20	-5	+5	+6
20/51	-5	+6	+6
21	-6	+6	+6
21/51	-6	+6	+7
22	-6	+7	+7
22/51	-7	+7	+7
23	-7	+7	+8
23/51	-7	+8	+8
24	-8	+8	+8
24/51	-8	+8	+9
25	-8	+9	+9

Constitution

A character's Constitution (Con) score encompasses his fitness, health and physical resistance to hardship, injury and disease. Basically, it is his life, so naturally it is an extremely important ability. It affects the character's hit points and chances of surviving such tremendous shocks to the body as being physically reshaped by magic or resurrected from death. It is vitally important to all classes. Several classes have minimum allowable Constitution scores.

A character's initial Constitution score is the absolute limit to the number of times the character can be raised or resurrected from death — Period! Each such revival reduces the character's Constitution score by one. Magic can restore a reduced Constitution score to its original value (or even higher) and you can raise your Constitution by raising fractional scores as you go up in levels, but this has no effect on the number of times a character can be revived from death! Once the character has exhausted his original Constitution, nothing short of divine intervention can bring him back, and I can tell you one thing, without spoiling any suspense—

Table 1C:
Constitution

Ability Score	Hit Point Adjustment	System Shock	Resurrection Survival	Poison Save	Immunity to Disease/Alcohol	Regeneration/Healing
1	-5	25%	30%	-2	+30%	Nil / 1 HP every 2 weeks
2	-4	30%	35%	-1	+25%	Nil / 1 HP every week
3	-4	35%	40%	0	+20%	Nil / 1 HP every 2 days
4	-3	40%	45%	0	+15%	Nil / 1 HP every 2 days
5	-3	45%	50%	0	+10%	Nil / 1 HP every 2 days
6	-2	50%	55%	0	+5%	Nil / 1 HP every 2 days
7	-2	55%	60%	0	no modifier	Nil / 1 HP every day
8	-1	60%	65%	0	-5%	Nil / 1 HP every day
9	-1	65%	70%	0	-10%	Nil / 1 HP every day
10	0	70%	75%	0	-20%	Nil / 1 HP every day
11	0	75%	80%	0	-25%	Nil / 1 HP every day
12	+1	80%	85%	0	-30%	Nil / 1 HP every day
13	+1	85%	90%	0	-35%	Nil / 1 HP every day
14	+2	88%	92%	0	-40%	Nil / 1 HP every day
15	+2	90%	94%	0	-45%	Nil / 1 HP every day
16	+3	95%	96%	0	-50%	Nil / 1 HP every day
17	+3	97%	98%	0	-55%	Nil / 1 HP every day
18	+4	99%	100%	0	-60%	Nil / 1 HP every 18 hours
19	+4	99%	100%	+1	-65%	1 HP every 12 hours
20	+5*	99%	100%	+1	-70%	1 HP/6 turns
21	+5**	99%	100%	+2	-75%	1 HP/5 turns
22	+6**	99%	100%	+2	-85%	1 HP/4 turns
23	+6***	99%	100%	+3	-90%	1 HP/3 turns
24	+7***	99%	100%	+3	-95%	1 HP/2 turns
25	+7***	100%	100%	+4	-99%	1 HP/1 turn

* All 1s rolled for Hit Dice are automatically considered 2s.
** All 1s and 2s rolled for Hit Dice are automatically considered 3s.
*** All 1s, 2s, and 3s rolled for Hit Dice are automatically considered 4s.

gawds in Garweeze Wurld intervene about as often as Bill Gates needs to borrow a dollar!

For example, Bart's Constitution score at the start of his adventuring career is 10. He can be revived from death 10 times. If he dies an 11th time, he cannot be resurrected or raised. This is natural selection at work.

Hit Point Adjustments are added to, or subtracted from, each Hit Die rolled for the character. If an adjustment would lower the number rolled to 0

Table 1D:
Intelligence

Ability Score	# 0f Lang.	Spell Level	Learning Ability	Max. # of Spells/Level	Illusion Immunity	Chance of Spell Mishap
1	0*	—	01%**	—	—	—
2	1	—	05%**	—	—	—
3	1	—	10%**	—	—	—
4	1	—	15%**	—	—	—
5	1	—	20%**	—	—	—
6	1	—	25%**	—	—	—
7	1	—	30%**	—	—	—
8***	1	Cantrips	30%***	5	—	35%
9 ****	2	4th	35%****	6	—	20%
10	2	5th	40%	7	—	15%
11	2	5th	45%	7	—	10%
12	3	6th	50%	7	—	05%
13	3	6th	55%	9	—	0%
14	4	7th	60%	9	—	0%
15	4	7th	65%	11	—	0%
16	5	8th	70%	11	—	0%
17	6	8th	75%	14	—	0%
18/01-50	7	9th	85%	18	Cantrips	0%
18/51-00	7	9th	90%	20	Cantrips	0%
19	8	9th	95%	All	1st-level	0%
20	9	9th	96%	All	2nd-level	0%
21	10	9th	97%	All	3rd-level	0%
22	11	9th	98%	All	4th-level	0%
23	12	9th	99%	All	5th-level	0%
24	15	9th	100%	All	6th-level	0%
25	20	9th	100%	All	7th-level	0%

* While unable to speak a language, the character can still communicate by grunts and gestures.
** Learning Ability for this level of intelligence is for Skills/Proficiencies only. Learning spells is impossible.
*** 8 is the minimum Intelligence required for a Gnome Titan to learn/cast spells though such a character, as indicated, would be limited to the use of cantrips.
**** 9 is the minimum Intelligence required to learn/cast spells for all races except for the Gnome Titan

or less, this must be counted. Thus, it's possible to gain an experience level and actually lose hit points or even die! Deal with it! Always use the character's current Constitution to determine hit point bonuses and penalties.

If a character's Constitution changes during the course of adventuring, his hit points may be adjusted up or down to reflect the change. The difference between the character's current hit point bonus (if any) and the new bonus is multiplied by the number of times the character rolled hit points (usually equal to his level) and added to or subtracted from the character's total. If Bart's Constitution increased from 13 to 14, he would gain 1 hit point for every level he had.

System Shock states the percentage chance a character has to survive magical effects that reshape or age his body: petrifaction (and reversing petrifaction), polymorph, magical aging, etc. It can also be used to see if the character retains consciousness in particularly difficult situations. For example, an evil magic-user decides he wants his hireling to be able to slip into a window of the tall tower of a noble's castle to grab a particular magical ring that the nobleman's wife keeps on her dresser. So, he polymorphs his dim-witted hireling into a crow. The hireling, whose Constitution score is 13, has an 85% chance to survive the change. Assuming he survives, he must successfully roll for system shock again when he is changed back to his original form or else he will die.

Resurrection Survival lists a character's percentage chance to be successfully resurrected or raised from death by magic. The player must roll the listed number or less, on percentile dice, for the character to be revived. If the dice roll fails, the character is dead, regardless of how many times he has previously been revived. Only divine intervention can bring such a character back again and, as I stated earlier, that's not likely to happen, so pull out another one of those nice character sheets.

Poison Save modifies the saving throw vs. poison for humans, elves, gnomes, gnomelings, half-elves and half-orcs. Dwarves and halflings do not use this adjustment, since they have special resistances to poison attacks. The GM has specific information on these saving throws.

Immunity to Disease/Alcohol lists the modifier the character receives when exposed to infectious diseases. It's also used to determine the effects of alcohol on a character.

    Disease: Each disease in HackMaster has a virility factor which indicates how easily it is contracted/spread. This modifier is applied to the Virility Roll. Note that immunity to disease does not affect magical diseases such as lycanthropy, or flesh rot caused by the touch of a mummy.

    Alcohol: Various types of alcohol, non-magical potions, certain medicines, etc. have their own unique potency factors. The Immunity to Alcohol modifier is often used to modify potency checks – especially when large quantities are consumed or such concoctions are mixed.

Regeneration enables those with specially endowed Constitutions (perhaps by a Wish or magical item) to heal at an advanced rate, regenerating damage taken. The character heals 1 point of damage after the passage of the listed amount of time. However, fire and acid damage (which are more extensive than normal wounds) cannot be regenerated in this manner. These injuries must heal normally or be dealt with by other magical means.

Healing. Average times for the normal healing of characters with lesser Constitutions are also listed. These rates assume the wound is being cared for and the character is not engaging in any strenuous activity. The regeneration ability described for characters with constitution scores of more than 18 may take place regardless of activity. However this regeneration stops if the character reaches -10 hp.

Intelligence

Intelligence (Int) represents a character's memory, reasoning and learning ability, including areas outside those measured by the written word. Intelligence dictates the number of languages a character can learn. Intelligence is the prime requisite of magic-users, who must have keen minds to understand and memorize magical spells. A magic-user with an Intelligence score of 16 or higher gains a 10% bonus to experience points earned. The magic-user's Intelligence dictates which spells he can learn and the number of

spells he can memorize at one time. Only those of the highest Intelligence can comprehend the mighty magic of 9th-level spells.

Intelligence is important to all characters because it also dictates how easily a PC can learn and apply new skills.

This ability gives only a general indication of a character's mental acuity. A semi-intelligent character (Int 3 or 4) can speak (with difficulty) and, let's just say, he's not the sharpest tool in the shed. He is apt to react instinctively and impulsively. He is not hopeless as a player character (PC), but playing such a character correctly is not easy unless you are an extremely skilled player (or you too are not the sharpest tool in the shed). A character with a low Intelligence (Int 5-7) could also be called dull-witted or slow. An intelligent person (Int 11 or 12) picks up new ideas quickly and learns easily. A highly intelligent character (Int 13 or 14) is one who can solve most problems without even trying very hard. One with exceptional intelligence (Int 15 or 16) is noticeably above the norm. A genius character (Int 17 or 18) is brilliant.

A character beyond genius is potentially more clever and more brilliant than can possibly be imagined. However, the true capabilities of a mind lie not in numbers such as IQ, Intelligence scores, or whatever. Many intelligent, even brilliant, people in the real world can tell you all about string theory, quantum physics or nuclear chain reactions, but don't know how to pump their own gas or use an ATM card. Some simply fail to apply their minds creatively and usefully, thus falling far below their own potential. Don't rely too heavily on your character's Intelligence score; you must provide your character with the creativity and energy he supposedly possesses!

Number of Languages lists the number of additional languages your character is capable of learning beyond his native language. Every character can speak his native language, no matter what his Intelligence is. This knowledge extends only to speaking the language; it does not include reading or writing. You can purchase additional known-languages using Building Points (see Chapter 4) but you can never know more languages than your Intelligence allows. You can also learn new languages in the game from a teacher/tutor or by hanging out with other characters willing to teach you. (Again, you can only learn a new language if you haven't surpassed the number of languages dictated by your Intelligence level.)

Furthermore, your GM can limit your language selection based on his campaign. It is perfectly fair to rule that your fighter from the Grevan Steppes hasn't learned the tongues of the Barrows, simply because he has never met anyone who has been to the Barrows.

Spell Level lists the highest level of spells that can be cast by a magic-user with this amount of Intelligence.

Learning Ability is the percentage probability that a character can learn a new skill/proficiency or that a magic-user can learn a particular spell.

Chance to Learn Skills/Proficiencies: Whenever a character attempts to learn a new skill, or train/study in a skill he already has in order to improve it (see Chapter 7: Skills, Talents and Proficiencies), this is his base percentage chance of success. After paying any training fees and completing the training time required for the desired skill the player may make a learning check. (Modifiers for that skill's training or course difficulty may apply.) If the character rolls the modified percentage or less he has successfully learned or improved the skill. If he fails, he cannot check that skill again until he's paid the training fees and completed the training time once again.

Chance to Learn Spells: A check is made as the magic-user comes across new spells, not as he advances in level. To make the check, the magic-user character must have access to a spell book containing the spell. If the player rolls the listed percentage or less, his character can learn the spell and copy it into his own spell book. If the magic-user fails the roll, he cannot check that spell again until he advances to the next level (provided he still has access to the spell).

Maximum Number of Spells per Level indicates the maximum number of spells a magic-user can know from any particular spell level. Once a magic-user has learned the maximum number of spells he is allowed in a given spell level, he cannot add any more spells of that level to his spell book (unless he does so through spell research). Once a spell is learned, it cannot be unlearned and replaced by a new spell.

For example, Karnak the magic-user has an Intelligence of 14. He currently knows nine 3rd-level spells. During an adventure, he finds a musty old spell book on the shelves of a dank, forgotten library. Blowing away the dust, he sees a 3rd-level spell he has never seen before! Excited, he sits down and carefully studies the arcane notes. His chance to learn the spell is 60%. Rolling the dice, Karnak's player rolls a 37. He understands the curious instructions and can copy them into his own spell book. However, when he looks in his spell book, he realizes he already has nine 3rd level spells written there. He tells the GM he wants to replace one of his old spells with this new one. His GM says, "and Pamela Anderson would like to be known for her intellect. Sorry, it ain't gonna happen."

If Karnak had only eight spells in his book, he could have learned the spell because he rolled the correct number. However, if the die roll had been greater

Ability Score	Magical Defense Adjustment	Bonus Spells	Chance of Spell Failure	Spell Immunity	Chance to Improve Skill
			Table 1E:		
			Wisdom		
1	-6	—	80%	—	—
2	-4	—	60%	—	—
3	-3	—	50%	—	01%
4	-2	—	45%	—	02%
5	-1	—	40%	—	03%
6	-1	—	35%	—	03%
7	-1	—	30%	—	04%
8	0	—	25%	—	04%
9	0	0	20%	—	05%
10	0	0	15%	—	05%
11	0	0	10%	—	05%
12	0	0	5%	—	05%
13	0	1st	0%	—	05%
14	0	1st	0%	—	06%
15	+1	2nd	0%	—	07%
16	+2	2nd	0%	—	08%
17	+3	3rd	0%	—	09%
18/01-50	+4	4th	0%	—	10%
18/51-00	+4	5th	0%	Befriend	11%
19	+4	1st, 3rd	0%	Cause Fear, Charm Person, Command, Hypnotism	12%
20	+4	2nd, 4th	0%	Forget, Hold Person, Ray of Enfeeblement, Scare	13%
21	+4	3rd, 5th	0%	Fear	14%
22	+4	4th, 5th	0%	Charm Monster, Confusion, Emotion, Fumble, Suggestion	
23	+4	1st, 6th	0%	Chaos, Feeblemind, Hold Monster, Magic Jar, Quest	15%
24	+4	5th, 6th	0%	Geas, Mass Suggestion, Rod of Rulership	16%
					18%
25	+4	6th, 7th	0%	Antipathy/Sympathy, Death Spell, Mass Charm	20%

Ability Score	Maximum # Henchmen Cronies/S-kicks	Loyalty Base	Reaction Adjustment	Comeliness Modifier	Starting Honor Modifier
			Table 1F: **Charisma**		
1	0*	-8	-7	-8	-9
2	1	-7	-6	-8	-8
3	1	-6	-5	-5	-7
4	1	-5	-4	-3	-6
5	2	-4	-3	-3	-5
6	2	-3	-2	-1	-4
7	3	-2	-1	-1	-3
8	3	-1	0	-1	-2
9	4	0	0	0	-1
10	4	0	0	0	0
11	4	0	0	0	0
12	5	0	0	0	+1
13	5	0	+1	+1	+2
14	6	+1	+2	+1	+3
15	7	+3	+3	+1	+4
16	8	+4	+5	+2	+5
17	10	+6	+6	+2	+6
18	15	+8	+7	+3	+7
19	18	+10	+8	+4	+8
20	20	+12	+9	+4	+9
21	25	+14	+10	+5	+10
22	30	+16	+11	+5	+11
23	35	+18	+12	+6	+12
24	40	+20	+13	+7	+13
25	45	+20	+14	+8	+14

* Note that a character is ALWAYS entitled to have one (1) sidekick no matter how low his Charisma is.

than 60 or the spell had been greater than 7th level (the maximum level his Intelligence allows him to learn), he again would have been prohibited from adding it to his collection.

Illusion Immunity is gained by those with exceptionally high Intelligence scores. Those with this immunity, when confronted with a magical ruse, notice some inconsistency or inexactness in the illusion or phantasm, automatically allowing them to make their saving throws. All benefits are cumulative; thus, a character with a 20 Intelligence is not fooled by 1st or 2nd-level illusion spells.

Spell Mishap is the base chance that any spell will malfunction with unintended results. A magic-user who experiences a spell mishap may fall victim to a random type of insanity or physical impairment Examples include paranoia, megalomania, obsessive compulsive disorder, nervous tic, wandering eye, etc. There is also a chance that a malfunctioning spell will have unusual, even disastrous, results which weren't at all intended. The minor risk of these trivial little "accidents" should not deter players from entering the field of magic use. Results of spell mishaps are more fully detailed in the HackMaster GM's Guide.

Wisdom

Wisdom (Wis) describes a composite of the character's enlightenment, judgment, guile, willpower, common sense and intuition. It also is an indication of how effectively a character can take learned knowledge and apply it. Wisdom also affects the character's resistance to magical attack. It is the prime requisite of clerics; those with Wisdom scores of 16 or higher gain a 10% bonus to experience points earned. Clerics and druids with Wisdom scores of 13 or higher also gain bonus spells over and above the number they are normally allowed to use.

Magical Defense Adjustment (listed on Table 1E) applies to saving throws against magical spells that attack the mind: Beguiling, Charm, Fear, Hypnosis, Illusions, Possession, Suggestion, etc. These bonuses and penalties are applied automatically, without any conscious effort from the character.

Bonus Spells are the number of additional spells a cleric (and only a cleric) is entitled to because of his extreme Wisdom. Note that

these spells are available only when the cleric is entitled to spells of the appropriate level. Bonus spells are cumulative, so a cleric with Wisdom of 15 is entitled to two 1st-level bonus spells and one 2nd-level bonus spell.

Chance of Spell Failure states the percentage chance that any particular spell fails when cast. Clerics with low Wisdom scores run the risk of having their spells fizzle at inopportune moments. Roll percentile dice every time the cleric casts a spell; if the number rolled is less than or equal to the listed chance for spell failure, the spell is expended with absolutely no effect whatsoever. Note that clerics with Wisdom scores of 13 or higher don't need to worry about their spells failing.

Spell Immunity gives those extremely wise characters complete protection from certain spells, spell-like abilities, and magical items as listed. These immunities are cumulative, so that a character with a Wisdom of 23 is immune to all listed spells up to and including those listed on the 23 Wisdom row.

Chance to Improve Skills is the base percentage chance that the character learns something significant while making a skill check and has improved his mastery of that skill (See Chapter 7: Skills, Talents and Proficiencies).

Charisma

The Charisma (Cha) score measures a character's persuasiveness, personal magnetism and ability to lead. It is not a reflection of physical attractiveness, although attractiveness certainly plays a role. It is important to all characters, but especially to those who must deal with nonplayer characters (NPCs), mercenary hirelings, retainers and intelligent monsters. It dictates the total number of henchmen a character can retain and affects the loyalty of henchmen, hirelings, cronies, sidekicks and retainers.

Maximum Number of Henchmen/Cronies/SideKicks states the number of nonplayer characters who will serve as permanent retainers of the player character. It does not affect the number of mercenary soldiers, men-at-arms, servitors or other persons in the pay of the character.

Loyalty Base shows the subtraction from, or addition to, the henchmen's and other servitors' loyalty scores (in the GMG). This is crucial during battles, when morale becomes important.

Reaction Adjustment indicates the penalty or bonus due to the character because of his Charisma when dealing with nonplayer characters and intelligent creatures. For example, Bart encounters a Centaur, an intelligent creature. Bart's Charisma is only 6. He is less likely to impress this creature than someone else might be, so he might want to think about getting someone else in his adventuring party with a higher Charisma to do the talking. Large amounts of gold also work.

Comeliness Modifier indicates the modifier, which should be initially applied to the character's Comeliness (this is a one-time modifier). Afterwards, as a character's Charisma is raised or lowered, whether by disease, aging or artifacts, Comeliness should be similarly affected on a point-for-point basis (a loss of one point of Charisma equals one point of Comeliness lost).

Table 1G:
Effects of Comeliness

Comeliness	How others view the Character
-16 or lower:	Those viewing a character with Comeliness this low are repulsed and horrified, so as to turn away or attempt to destroy the creature that is so offensive to the sight. If the individual with low Comeliness is powerful, his appearance will make others tend to want to escape, or they will experience a reinforcement of a previously determined awe (horror) reaction. If both viewer and creature are of evil alignment, the effect is that of a positive Comeliness of the same total.
-15 to -9:	Those viewing creatures with Comeliness in this range display disgust, evidenced by a tendency to look away. They will revile the individual, and act hostile in general. Under no circumstances will the viewers accept this character unless all are of evil alignment, so that the negative Comeliness can be regarded as positive.
-8 to 0:	All viewers will evidence aversion and a desire to be away from so ugly a creature. If given an excuse, those near the individual will be hostile and openly aggressive; otherwise they will merely tend toward rejection.
+ 1 to + 6:	Such an individual is simply ugly. The reaction evidenced will tend toward unease and a desire to get away from such brutishness as quickly as possible. If given the opportunity, the character's Charisma can offset ugliness, but this requires a fair amount of conversation and interaction to take place.
+ 7 to + 9:	The homeliness of the individual will be such that initial contact will be of a negative sort. This negative feeling will not be strongly evidenced. High Charisma will quickly overcome it if any conversation and interpersonal interaction transpires. (Consider a dwarf with a 16 Charisma and a base Comeliness roll of 9; he will be at 8 when viewed by all creatures except other dwarves - who will see him with Comeliness adjusted by + 2 for Charisma.)
+ 10 to + 13:	Plain to average Comeliness; no effect on the viewer.
+ 14 to + 17:	Interest in viewing the individual is evidenced by those in contact, as he is good-looking. The reaction adjustment is increased by a percentage equal to the Comeliness score of the character. Individuals of the opposite sex will seek out such characters, and they will be affected as if under a Fascinate spell unless the Wisdom of such individuals exceeds 50% of the character's Comeliness total.
+ 18 to + 21:	The beauty of the character will cause heads to turn and hearts to race. Reaction for initial contact is at a percent equal to 150% of the Comeliness score. Individuals of the opposite sex will be affected as if under a Fascinate spell unless their Wisdom exceeds two-thirds of the character's Comeliness total. Individuals of the same sex will do likewise unless Wisdom totals at least 50% of the other character's Comeliness score. Rejection of harsh nature can cause the individual rejected to have a reaction as if the character had a negative Comeliness of half the actual (positive) score.
+ 22 to + 25:	The stunning beauty and gorgeous looks of a character with so high a Comeliness will be similar to that of those of lesser beauty (18-21). However, individuals will actually flock around the character, follow him and generally behave foolishly or in some manner so as to attract the attention of the character. The reaction adjustment is double the score of Comeliness: i.e., 22 Comeliness equals 44%. Fascinate-like power will affect all those with Wisdom of less than two-thirds the Comeliness score of the character. If an individual of the opposite sex is actually consciously sought by a character with Comeliness of 22-25, that individual will be effectively Fascinated unless his Wisdom is 18 or higher. Rejection is as above.
+ 26 to + 30:	Only creatures from other planes - demi-gawds, demi-gawddesses and otherworldly beings of unusual sort, can possess unearthly beauty of this sort. Reaction adjustment is double the Comeliness score. Fascinate-like power affects all except those with Wisdom equal to at least 75% of Comeliness, except that 19 or higher Wisdom always allows a saving throw versus the power. An individual of the opposite sex who is consciously sought by the possessor of such unearthly beauty and Comeliness will always be under the "spell" of the individual with such beauty unless he has Wisdom of 20 or more. The Fascinate-like power of high Comeliness is similar to the 2nd-level spell of the same name. Those subject to this power will be captivated by the user, and treat him as a trusted friend, mentor and companion. A saving throw versus spell will negate the effect but if the Comeliness is not magical in nature, then Dispel Magic, Antimagic Shell and similar spells will not affect the Fascination effect. Fascinated creatures will follow the orders of characters with high Comeliness, provided a roll of 3d6 does not exceed the Comeliness of the character. Requests that are not in the best interest of the creature get a + 1 to the die, while those that are hazardous can add up to + 6 or more to this roll. If the roll is higher than the user's Comeliness, the Fascinate-effect is broken. If a once-Fascinated creature has been badly treated and breaks free of this enrapturement, the creature will react as if the character's Comeliness was a negative amount. If the creature has been well treated, it may still be friendly to the character even after the Fascination has worn off.

Starting Honor Modifier Charisma affects one's Honor. This modifier applies to your starting Honor only.

Comeliness

Comeliness reflects the physical attractiveness, social grace and personal beauty of the character. It is used to determine initial reactions to the character, and characters with a high Comeliness may affect the wills and actions of others. While Charisma deals specifically with leadership and interactions between characters, Comeliness deals with attractiveness and first impressions.

Comeliness is not Charisma. Charisma, however, can affect Comeliness. Comeliness is modified by the Comeliness Modifier listed on the Charisma Table.

As Charisma is raised or lowered, whether by disease, aging or artifacts, Comeliness should be similarly affected on a point-for-point basis (a loss of one point of Charisma equals one point of Comeliness equally lost).

In addition to the adjustment to Comeliness based on the Charisma score, characters of certain races must take an additional adjustment to their Comeliness scores. This racial adjustment applies only when the reaction of characters of other races is concerned, in similar fashion to the way that racial adjustments for Charisma apply only to those of other races. The penalties and bonuses are listed in Table 2B.

Comeliness can have an effect on creatures of human sort. (This category includes, but is not necessarily limited to, humans, demi-humans, humanoids, giant-class, and bipedal creatures of human-like form and motivation.) The effects of Comeliness are described in detail in Table 1G.

The effect of one's Comeliness upon others is temporary; once other characters or creatures know a character its effect is negated, and Charisma is used to determine reactions and followers. In this way characters of high Comeliness and low Charisma may attract interest, but not long-term followers and allies (beauty being only skin deep). Ultimately a character's Honor (or lack thereof) has much more impact on others' views of the character than his looks.

The effects of the Fascinate power (see Table 1G) do not affect the abilities of the individual with respect to fighting, casting of spells, etc., and in no way reduces the subject character to a zombie-like state or a puppet for the high-Comeliness character. Actions performed by a character while Fascinated may affect alignment (though they would have a good addition to the Comeliness check, say + 3 or + 4).

Magic can mildly and temporarily affect the Comeliness of a creature. Illusion-based spells such as Change Self and Alter Self will raise or lower Comeliness by a maximum of 1 point, no matter what the final form is. Illusions of characters or creatures with high Comeliness are effective only for a single round, as the nature of the Fascination is such that the affected character concentrates more fully on the illusion, weakening its effectiveness. Polymorphed figures can raise or lower Comeliness by 2 points from the original, due to subtle social clues that are not visual but still perceived, while Shapechange confers the full Comeliness effects of the final form.

Honor

As mentioned at the beginning of this chapter, the Honor ability is treated a bit differently than the other character abilities. For one thing, you don't roll 3d6 to determine your Honor. Secondly, Honor fluctuates greatly depending on the character's actions and behavior

First off, don't confuse Honor with the alignment-based code of honor that a Paladin or Cavalier must adhere to. *Honor Factor* is not a judgement of good and evil.

Individuals of high Honor are not necessarily good and those with low Honor are not necessarily evil. A cruel tyrant may very well possess high Honor while a goodly knight, through unfortunate circumstances, might possess a miserable Honor.

Honor is more a measure of the deeds accomplished by both the individual (and sometimes his bloodline/clan) as well as those he associates himself with (his party). It is an indication of such things as success in combat/politics, obedience to the parameters of one's character class, loyalty, talent and success, qualities that can be held by any character regardless of alignment. Adherence to one's alignment and patron gawd does factor into Honor but it's all a matter of context. A character worshipping an evil gawd can do some pretty nasty things without it reflecting on his Honor.

To have Honor is to command respect. When one loses Honor, one loses face. Honor is so essential to the hero that it is reflected in his very countenance. People, and even monsters, can sense how much Honor a PC has just by standing in his presence. And sometimes (if his Honor is through the roof) they can tell just by looking at him. So much gravity is placed on individual and group Honor in HackMaster that characters have been known to commit ritual suicide when it is deemed their Honor Factor has been irreparably trashed.

Honor can also dictate what a character bound to such a concept will do in a given situation. For example, when the men of the blue and the gray knowingly marched across that 'narrow deadly space' at Gettysburg to certain death it was a point of honor. There was nothing else for such men of honor to do placed in that situation. Leaving the field of battle in the hands of the enemy was unthinkable — so they fought.

Chapter 5 deals with Honor in more detail and how it's used in the game. It will explain how you can earn your 'Honor Die' and how it's used to do such things as raise Fractional Ability Scores, affect the outcome of mortal combat, etc.

Generating Starting Honor:

Note that it is important to calculate your starting Honor after you've gone through a few other steps first. See the Step by Step character creation procedure in Appendix I first. A character's starting Honor is determined by averaging the previous 7 abilities. Add all seven abilities(Str, Dex, Int, Wis, Con, Cha, Com) together and divide by 7. Round to the nearest integer.

Now add your Honor Modifier from your Charisma. This gives you your starting Honor. Then consult Table 1H to get your additional Building Points (see Chapter 4). Your beginning Honor can also be modified by such things as your Character Class and Character Background (see Chapters 3 and 4).

Table 1H: Beginning Honor Adjustment to Building Points	
Honor Score	Building Point Bonus
1	-9
2	-8
3	-7
4	-6
5	-5
6	-4
7	-3
8	-2
9	-1
10	0
11	0
12	0
13	0
14	+1
15	+2
16	+3
17	+4
18	+5
19	+6
20	+7
21	+8
22	+9
23	+10
24	+11
25	+12

What the Numbers Mean

Now that you have finished creating the Ability Scores for your character, stop and take a look at them. What does all this mean?

Let's say you roll up a character named "Bart." Here are the abilities "Bart" ended up with:

Strength: 16
Dexterity: 12
Constitution: 10
Intelligence: 8
Wisdom: 13
Charisma: 6
Comeliness: 5
Honor: 6

Bart has strengths and weaknesses, but it is up to you to interpret what the numbers mean. Here are just two different ways these numbers could be interpreted.

1) Bart is in average health (Con 10), but he's pretty strong (Str 16). Let's say he's a big guy, but because he was born poor he has had some health problems. He was raised on a farm and his parents kept him and his brothers working in the bean fields in both fair weather and foul. Bart endured some sickness because of such abuse, weakening his immune system. Still, he's not exactly sickly. Malnutrition probably accounts for his less than stellar intelligence (Int 8). But he has plenty of common sense, learning from the school of hard knocks. (Wisdom 13). Backbreaking work was Bart's classroom. Because he was raised working in the fields, poor Bart never had an opportunity to develop social skills. His farmer-Joe demeanor makes it hard for him to make new friends (Cha 6). It doesn't help that he's not too pleasing on the eye either (Com 5).

Using this scenario, you could play Bart as a big, rustic oaf with a talent for manual labor and an innate wisdom about how the world works.

2) Bart has several good points — he is strong (Str 16), wise (Wis 13) and has developed his manual skills (Dex 12). Unfortunately, his Intelligence is low (8) from a lack of study and opportunity (all those hours shoveling manure). Bart's health isn't bad (Con 10). His low Intelligence and Charisma (8, 6) are a result of his lack of contact with people outside his family and involvement with academics.

Looking at the scores this way, you could play Bart as a shy, brutish fellow who's good at fixing things, can carry his weight and isn't afraid to pitch in and work. Just don't ask him to hold an intelligent conversation.

Obviously, Bart's Ability Scores (often called "stats") are not the greatest in the world. Yet it is possible to turn these "disappointing" stats into a character who is both interesting and fun to play. Too often players become obsessed with "good" stats. As I've already mentioned, some players prefer to "cheat" and fudge the dice rolls in their favor in order to obtain a more desirable character. These rule-benders do not take into account the spirit of HackMaster. They immediately give up on a character if he doesn't have a majority of above-average scores. There are even those who feel a character is hopeless if he does not have at least one ability of 17 or higher! Needless to say, these players would never consider playing a character with an ability score of 6 or 7. But the best players realize that playing a character with some not-so-good scores is an opportunity for them to do some real role-playing. These are the characters that are remembered far longer than the spotless, one-dimensional heroes created by immature gamers who feel they can't play a unique hero.

In truth, Bart's survivability has a lot less to do with his ability scores than with your desire to role-play him. If you give up on him, of course he won't survive! Heck, he might not survive anyway. But if you take an interest in the character and role-play him well, then even a character with the lowest possible scores can present a fun, challenging, and all-around exciting time. Does he have a Charisma of 5? Why? Maybe he has a knack for provoking bar fights. Maybe he stutters. Or he might just be one of those guys who can't talk without putting his foot in his mouth.

His Dexterity is a 3? Why? Perhaps he's missing a limb after fighting off a Sturm Wolf. Maybe he just has an inner ear problem.

The point is: don't give up. Look at it as an opportunity to create a character unlike anyone else's — one who could end up teaching you something about the true nature of heroism.

Player Character Races

Now that you have determined the Ability Scores of your character, it's time to move to the next step — selecting the racial stock of your character. This is one of the most important decisions you will make in the creation process, and therefore it should be done with a great deal of thought and consideration.

Note that when we speak of a 'race' in Hackmaster, it has nothing to do with what we in contemporary society know of races, i.e. Eurasian or African. In HackMaster, race simply refers to the fantasy species of your character. In Hackmaster, there are many races from which to choose.

Each race is different from the others and each possesses special powers and abilities. Each race also has its own limitations as to what character classes to choose from. Each racial stock also has its own advantages and disadvantages, which you must consider. (In general, humans are superior to the others races for reasons you will discover as you read on.)

For game purposes, there is a limited variety of racial stocks from which to choose. They are dwarven, elven, gnome, gnomeling, half-elven, halfling, half-orc, half-ogre, human and pixie fairy. Some racial stocks have variants (also known as sub-races) such as grunge elf, gnome titan, etc. Non-human player character races are referred to collectively as 'demi-human' races.

In many cases, broad statements (stereotypes) are made concerning the race in general. You are certainly not restricted by these generalities. Individuality is as important to the grunge elf as it is to his human counterpart.

For example, the statement that "gnome titans tend to be rude and obnoxious when inebriated" may be true of most gnome titans but it certainly does not mean your gnome titan character has to follow suit. The racial descriptions are merely thumbnail sketches to help you get a feel for the race. The garden-variety gnome titan may have a well-deserved reputation for being a 'mean drunk' but that does not mean your gnome titan has to be.

Besides, if all gnome titan player characters were carbon-copy clones of one another, the game would bog down and players would pass out one by one from sheer boredom. Remember – your character is only as good as the sum total of your investment of time and creative input.

Only certain class/level restrictions and other established parameters of his chosen race limit your demi-human character. Player character demi-humans represent individuals who are the exception rather than the rule. This gives you a lot of latitude for fleshing out your character. Any given halfling thief should be as much a unique individual as any human thief would be. So don't let the racial descriptions limit your possibilities.

Ability Score Prerequisites for Demi-humans

Demi-humans (non-humans) have minimum and maximum requirements for their Ability Scores. If you want to have a demi-human character, the Ability Scores of the character must fall within the allowable range indicated for that race. These are initial prerequisites for race-selection purposes only.

During game play, the abilities of your character may rise above (or drop below) the racial requirements listed in Table 2A, which lists the minimums and maximums for each race. The Ability Score requirement for male members of each race are listed before the slash, the requirement for females are listed after the slash. (And before you start to whine about female characters taking hits on certain abilities — Don't! Our figures are based on meticulous research that we went to great effort and cost to conduct. The numbers are accurate and speak for themselves. Besides, it's not ALWAYS the female who takes the hit on an Ability Score.)

Consult Table 2A before making any racial adjustments to the Ability Scores of your character. If the basic scores that you rolled up meet the requirements for a particular race, your character can be of that race, even if later modifications change the Ability Scores so they exceed the maximums or don't meet the minimums. Once you satisfy the requirements at the start, you never have to worry about them again. Note that a player can always voluntarily drop an attribute to meet the maximum ability for a desired race. Such points dropped are simply lost.

Any character can be a human, if the player so desires. There are no minimum or maximum restrictions for human characters.

Demi-human Ability Adjustments

If you choose to make your character a demi-human, you now have to adjust some of the Ability Scores of your character. The adjustments are mandatory; all characters of these races receive them. Even if adjustments raise or lower your character's Ability Scores beyond the minimums and maximums shown on Table 2A, you do not have to pick a new race. The adjustments can also raise a score to 19 or higher or lower it to 2 or lower (except Pixie Fairies).

Table 2A: Ability Prerequisites for Demi-human Characters

Ability	Dwarf	Elf	Gnome	Gnomeling	Half-Elf	Halfling	Half-Orc	Half-Ogre	Pixie Fairy
STR	M/F	M/F	M/F	M/F	M/F	M/F	M/F	M/F	M/F
MIN	8/8	3/3	6/6	6/6	3/3	6/6	6/18	14/14	1/1
MAX	18/17	18/17	18/15	17/15	18/17	17/14	18/19	19/19	14/14
DEX									
MIN	3/4	7/7	3/3	5/5	6/6	7/8	3/4	3/3	12/12
MAX	17/18	19/19	18/18	18/18	18/18	18/18	17/17	17/17	19/19
CON									
MIN	12/12	6/7	8/8	9/9	6/6	10/10	13/13	14/14	6/7
MAX	19/19	18/18	18/18	18/18	18/18	19/19	19/19	19/19	14/14
INT									
MIN	3/3	8/8	7/8	6/7	4/6	6/6	3/3	3/3	8/8
MAX	18/18	18/18	18/18	18/18	18/18	18/18	17/17	17/17	19/19
WIS									
MIN	3/3	3/3	3/3	3/3	3/3	3/3	3/3	3/3	3/3
MAX	18/18	18/18	18/18	17/17	18/18	17/16	14/14	15/15	19/19
CHA									
MIN	3/3	8/8	3/3	3/3	3/3	3/3	3/3	2/2	8/8
MAX	16/15	18/19	18/18	18/18	18/18	18/18	12/12	11/11	19/19
COM									
MIN	3/2	5/6	3/3	3/3	5/5	3/3	3/2	-/-	8/8
MAX	15/14	18/19	17/17	17/17	17/18	18/18	12/11	12/12	19/19

Demi-human Class Restrictions and Level Limits

The human race has one special ability in HackMaster: Humans can choose to be of any class – fighter, magic-user, cleric, thief, etc – and can rise to great level in any class.

The other races have fewer choices when it comes to character classes and they are usually limited in the level they can attain. These restrictions reflect the natural tendencies of the races (dwarves excel in the arts of warfare and melee but dislike magic, etc.). The limits are high enough so a demi-human can achieve power and importance in at least one class. A halfling, for example, can become the best thief in the land, but he cannot become a great fighter. The cards are stacked against him in that regard.

Many players and GMs in the past have griped about the limits imposed on demi-humans. They deem them unfair and claim they detract from their enjoyment of the game. As such, many of these whiners view the class restriction/level limit rules as optional and choose to disregard them.

How nice it would be if we could ALL cherry pick the rules we play by so that our characters are NEVER put at a disadvantage or inconvenienced. Such characters will also NEVER see a sanctioned game or an official tournament; they are illegal and banned from play.

Admittedly, the restrictions and limits on demi-humans have been artificially imposed for the sake of play balance. The ability of humans to assume any role and reach any level is their only true advantage over their demi-human counterparts. The demi-human races have their own unique powers (such as racial talents/abilities) that make them entertaining to play – particularly the ability to be multi-classed (see Glossary). These powers balance the enjoyment of play against the ability to rise in level.

Besides that, HackMaster characters are likely to be killed off before they have a chance to worry about how high a level they can achieve anyway, so why get your breeches in a wad?

Table 2C presents an easy reference to the restrictions/limits on races, so that you can select the racial stock of your character based on abilities generated and with an eye towards what class of adventurer the character will be. Most demi-human races are able to work in two or more classes at the same time. Some gain Ability Score bonuses as well, but most are limited as to how great a level they may attain in a given class.

Numbers indicate the maximum level attainable by a character of the race in question.

"No" appearing in a race column indicates that the race in question is restricted from choosing that particular character class.

"U" appearing in a race column indicates that a character of the race in question has no limitation as to how high the character can go with regard to level in the appropriate class.

Table 2B: **Demi-human Ability Adjustments**	
Race	Adjustments
Dwarf	+1 Constitution; -1 Charisma; -1 Comeliness
Elf	+1 Dexterity; -1 Constitution; +1 Comeliness (sylvan elves only); +2 Comeliness (gray and high elves only); -2 Comeliness (drow only)
Gnome	+1 Intelligence; -1 Wisdom; -1 Comeliness; +2 Strength (Gnome Titans only)
Gnomeling	+1 Intelligence; +1 Dexterity; -1 Strength; -1 Wisdom; -1 Constitution
Halfling	+1 Dexterity; -1 Strength
Half Elves	+1 Comeliness
Half-orc	+1 Strength; +1 Constitution; -2 Charisma; -3 Comeliness
Half-Ogre	+2 Strength; +2 Constitution; -1 Wisdom; -2 Intelligence; -3 Charisma; -5 Comeliness
Pixie Fairy	-6 Strength, +2 Dexterity; +1 Intelligence, +1 Wisdom, +2 Charisma; +3 Comeliness

Languages

Your character automatically knows his native language (i.e. a gnome automatically knows how to speak gnomish). Demi-humans must choose these languages from among those listed in the following racial descriptions. Human PCs generally start the game knowing only their regional language – the language they grew up speaking.

Your character can start out knowing additional languages but you must purchase them by using Building Points (see Chapter 7). The maximum number of languages your character can know is dictated by his Intelligence (See Table 1D).

PCs will have the opportunity to learn new languages as they progress. Your GM can give you more information on how this is done.

Racial Preferences

In addition to the various attributes of the character races listed in this chapter, there are also certain likes and dislikes, which must be considered in selecting a racial type for your character. Members of most races have their own sets of prejudices and hereditary or traditional feelings toward members of the other races. Your gnome titan may not have anything against Orcs personally, but you can be sure that the average Orc is going to view your gnome titan with contempt and disdain. The dealings a character has with members of other various races will be affected by such racial preferences, to some extent. Especially when dealing with strangers of another race and meeting for the first time.

Similarly, NPCs like hirelings, wait staff, merchants and even monsters may react differently to various races. The following table is a general guide, which shows how the various races react to each other.

Table 2C: Demi-human Class Restrictions and Level Limitations[1]

Class	Dwarf	Elf	Gnome	Gnomeling	Half-elf	Halfling	Half-orc	Half-ogre	Pixie Fairy	Human
Cleric	10	13	9	7	14	8	4	5	10	U
Druid	no	13	no	6	14	6	no	no	no	U
Fighter	15	12	11	9	14	9	U	U	9	U
Barbarian	no	no[4]	no	no	no	U	U	U	no	U
Berserker	16	13	no[3]	9	14	9	U	U	9	U
Cavalier	no	13	no	no	no	no	no	no	9	U
Dark K.	no	no	no	no	no	no	no	no	no	U
Knight E.	15	12	11	9	14	9	U	U	9	U
Monk	no	no	no	no	no	no	no	no	no	U
Paladin	no	no	no	no	no	no	no	no	no	U
Ranger	no	15	no	no	16	no	no	no	no	U
Magic-User	no	15	no	no	12	no	no	no	U	U
Battle Mage	U	15	no[5]	no	10	no	no	no	no	U
Blood Mage[6]	no	15	no	no	11	no	no	no	no	U
Illusionist	no	no	15	U	no	no	no	no	U	U
Thief	U	12	13	U	U	U	8	7	15	U
Assassin	12	10	8	U	11	10[2]	U	7	no	U
Bard	no	no	no	no	U	no	no	no	no	U

1) The numbers on the chart are increased by 2 for demi-humans that are not multi-classed.
2) Thugs only.
3) The sub-race gnome titans may become berserkers. Such characters are restricted to 12th level max.
4) Grunge and wood elves only. Level Limitation 12
5) Gnome titans only. Level limitation 10.
6) The blood mage is a restricted magic-user specialist. Check with your GM for more information on this class.

Table 2D:
Racial Preferences

Basic Acceptability of Racial Type

RACE	Dwarf	Elf	Gnome	Gnomeling	Half-elf	Halfling	Half-orc	Half-ogre	Pixie Fairy	Human
Dwarf	P	A	G	H	N	G[1]	H	H	A	N
Elf	A	P	T	T	G	T	A	N	G[4]	N
Gnome	G	T	P	T	T	G	H	H	A	N
Gnomeling	G	T	T	P	T	N	A	A	H	N
Half-Elf	N	P	T	T	P	N	N	A	G	T
Halfling	G[2]	G[3]	T	G	N	P	N	T	T	N
Half-Orc	H	A	H	A	A	N	N	A	H	T
Half-ogre	H	N	H	A	A	T	A	N[5]	H	N
Pixie Fairy	A	G[4]	A	H	G	T	H	H	P	T
Human	N	N	N	N	T	N	T	N	T	P

1. Only with regard to tallfellows and stouts, other halflings are regarded with tolerance (T).
2. Only stouts regard dwarves as acceptable, other halflings tolerate them (T).
3. Only tallfellows regard elves as good company, other halflings are tolerant (T).
4. Drow and grunge elves are not as tolerant of pixie fairies as other elves. (H)
5. Half-ogres generally don't get along with anyone – not even members of their own kind.

P: indicates that the race is generally preferred, and dealings with the members of the race will be reflected accordingly.

N: shows that the race is thought of neutrally, although some suspicion will be evidenced.

G: means that considerable goodwill exists towards the race.

A: means that the race is greeted with antipathy.

T: indicates that the race is viewed with tolerance and generally acceptable, if not loved.

H: tokens a strong hatred for the race in question.

Dwarves

Dwarves are a noble race of demi-humans that dwells deep beneath the craggy mountains and peaks of Garweeze Wurld. In the great NetherDeep this rugged race has forged great cities and waged eternal war against the forces of chaos and evil. Most of the great battles against evil in Garweeze Wurld have been won because of alliances between several different groups of demi-humans, which were forged through dwarven diplomatic efforts. They've always been the first to recognize such threats and the first to react. It has been said that all of the brief periods of peace in the realms were paid for with dwarven blood.

The dwarves have much in common with the coarse rock they chip away at and the precious gems they love to hoard — hard and unyielding, but with much of value beneath the rugged surface. They are given to hard work and care little for most types of humor. They haven't the time for it and there is always serious work to be done. They are strong, brave and tenacious. They are also dependable. Dwarves don't make promises lightly, but when they do, they make every reasonable effort to keep them. They expect others to live up to their agreements as well. They also have long memories and are unforgiving. To wrong a dwarf is to make an enemy for life.

Dwarves enjoy beer, ale, mead and even stronger drink. Their chief love, however, is precious metal, particularly gold. They prize gems, of course, especially diamonds and opaque gems (except pearls, which they abhor). From their point of view, everything precious that lies beneath the surface belongs to them. In fact, they resent the meddlesome attempts of other races to extract and mine from the earth what is rightfully theirs.

Most other races see dwarves as a greedy, stubborn, grumpy folk. They view them as difficult, if not impossible, to get along with. Men and elves in particular find it difficult to understand why dwarves prefer the dampness of caves and mines to the brightness of an open glade.

For their part, dwarves have little patience for men and other shortsighted races (since man's concerns seem so petty when seen from a dwarven perspective). There is a feeling among dwarves that men are nothing more than a bunch of bumbling idiots who insist on breeding like rabbits, over-hunting/farming the land and who are never satisfied unless they're conquering every hill or glade they see. Nevertheless, dwarves also see men as worthy allies who shine in times of trouble.

Dwarves also tend to look upon elves with disdain, who they feel are not serious-minded the way they should be. They see elves as wasting their long lives pursuing pastimes that are downright silly and frivolous. However, as previously mentioned, dwarves have been known to band together with both men and elves in times of crisis, and long-term trade agreements and alliances are common.

Dwarves have no mixed feelings about the evil races that dwell below ground and in the NetherDeep, however. They have an intense hatred of Orcs, Goblins, evil giants and drow. The dire creatures of the NetherDeep often fear dwarves, and for good reason – the short, stout dwarves are tireless enemies of evil and chaos and are not shy about pressing the attack when encountered. Until either the dwarves or their foes are destroyed, it is the goal of the dwarven race to wage constant and bitter war against their enemies under the earth. It is a stubborn fight to the finish.

The standard dwarven sub-races are: hill, mountain, deep, gully and gray. You may specify a dwarven sub-race for your character. (Your GM has more information on dwarves in the Hacklopedia of Beasts, which he can share with you as needed). All the dwarven sub-races love the earth and dislike the sea. (Except for the so-called "Salty Dwarves" — a clan of dwarves who adapted to a life of piracy and terrorized the Ginge for many years. A few of their number can still be found.) Their short, stocky builds make them ill-suited for riding horses or other large mounts (although ponies present no difficulty), so they tend to be a trifle dubious and wary of these creatures.

Dwarves typically dwell in hilly or mountainous regions. They prefer life in the comforting gloom and solidity that is found underground. They are short, stocky fellows, easily identified by their size and shape. They average 4 to 4 1/2 feet tall. They have ruddy cheeks, bright eyes, and dark hair. Their skin is typically deep tan or light brown. Their hair is usually black, gray, or brown, and worn long, though not long enough to impair vision in any way. They favor long beards and mustaches, too. Dwarves, both male and female, value their beards highly and tend to groom them very carefully. Dwarven clothing tends to be simple and functional. Earth tones are preferred. Dwarven cloth

---

Dwarves At a Glance:

The Upside

Racial Bonuses:
- Infravision. Dwarves can see 60 feet in the dark
- Saving throw bonus on saves vs. magic* (See Table 2E)
- Saving throw bonus save vs. poison (See Table 2E)
- +1 on to-hits vs. Orcs, half-orcs, Goblins, and Hobgoblins**
- Ogres, Trolls, Ogre Magi, giants, and Titans suffer a -4 to hit dwarves**

Initial Languages:
Common, dwarf, gnome, gnomeling, goblin, kobold, orc***

Talents:
- Detect grade or slope in passage 1-5 on 1d6
- Detect new tunnel/passage construction 1-5 on 1d6
- Detect sliding/shifting walls or rooms 1-4 on 1d6
- Detect stonework traps, pits, and deadfalls 1-3 on 1d6
- Determine approximate depth underground 1-3 on 1d6

Allowable Classes:
Cleric, fighter, berserker, knight errant, battle mage, thief, assassin (Level restrictions apply. See Table 2C)

Allowable Multi-Classes:
Fighter/assassin, cleric/assassin, fighter/cleric or fighter/thief

Attribute Modifiers:
Dwarves gain/suffer the following bonuses/penalties: +1 Constitution; -1 Charisma; -1 Comeliness

Building Point Bonus: 10

Additional Talents Which May be Purchased:
Acute Alertness, Ambidextrous, Astute Observation, Axe Bonus, Blind Fighting, Brewing, Close to the Earth, Constitution/Health Bonus, Crossbow Bonus, Dense Skin, Detect Evil, Detect Poison, Determine Age, Determine Stability, Endurance, Evaluate Gems, Expert Haggler, Hit Point Bonus, Illusion Resistant, Mace Bonus, Meld Into Stone, Mining Sense, Pick Bonus, Resistance, Short Sword Bonus, Sibling Empathy, Sixth Sense, Stealth, Stone Tell, Touched by Yurgain***, Warhammer Bonus

The Downside
Dwarves suffer a 20% chance for failure every time they use any magical item except weapons, armor, shields, and (if the character is a thief) items that duplicate thieving abilities. This penalty does not apply if the character is a battle mage or a cleric using a cleric item.

* Bonus for save vs. spells is lost if the dwarven character chooses to become a battle mage.
** This advantage is lost if the character chooses to become a battle mage.
*** The number of languages a dwarf can learn is limited by his Intelligence (see Table 1D) or by the Building Points/training he devotes to languages.
**** The talent, Touched by Yurgain, is free. Dwarves choosing the battle mage class MUST take this talent.

is woven from such materials as the coarse hair of the mountain goat, flax acquired from various hardy highland grasses and wool. (Such cloth is considered very rough and uncomfortable to the touch by many other races, especially men and elves.)

Dwarves usually wear one or more pieces of jewelry, though these items are usually not of any great value nor very ostentatious. Though dwarves value gems and precious metals, they consider it in bad taste (and unwise) to flaunt wealth — it only invites trouble from others. Female dwarves often braid small gold or silver ringlets and colorful wrappings into their hair and beards. In many dwarven cultures the female must keep her beard braided and rolled up (coiled) closely along the jaw line — Only 'letting her beard down' for her husband or betrothed).

Dwarves generally live for 350 years and although they are small in stature, they have been blessed with numerous special abilities that help them to thrive in their rugged, underground lives. They are noted for being particularly resistant to magic and poisons. Because dwarves are a sturdy race, they add one to their initial Constitution scores. However, because they are a solitary people, tending toward distrust of outsiders and other races, they subtract one from their initial Charisma scores and one from their Comeliness.

A character of the dwarven race can be cleric, fighter, berserker, knight errant, battle mage, thief, or assassin. He can also choose to be a fighter/assassin, cleric/assassin, fighter/cleric or fighter/thief.

Dwarves have found it useful to learn the languages of many of their allies and enemies. In addition to their own languages, dwarves often speak the languages of gnomes, gnomelings, goblins, kobolds, orcs, and the common tongue, which is frequently used in trade negotiations with other races. The actual number of languages is limited by the Intelligence of the player character (see Table 1D) or by the building points/training he devotes to languages.

Dwarves are courageous, tenacious fighters who are ill disposed toward magic. They never use magical spells nor train as magic-users, unless they are 'Touched by Yurgain' the dwarven gawd of honor. (See Yurgain in the HackMaster: Gawds and Demigawds supplement). Such 'touched' Dwarves lack the non-magical nature of their fellow dwarves (see below) and are able to become battle mages. Only 5% of Dwarves are so touched. Player character dwarven battle mages are assumed to come from among this number. The price for choosing the career path of battle mage is high for the dwarf however – he loses the bonuses to save vs. magic (see below) as well as the bonuses he enjoys when attacking Orcs or being attacked by Ogres and the like.

Dwarves can also become clerics and use the spells of that class.

Because of their non-magical nature, dwarves receive a bonus to saving throws against attacks from magical wands, staves, rods, and spells. This bonus is +1 for every 3 1/2 points of Constitution score. Thus, for example, if a dwarf has a Constitution score of 7 he gains +2 on these saving throws. These bonuses are summarized on Table 2E.

Similarly, dwarves have exceptional resistance to toxic substances. All dwarven characters make saving throws against poison with the same bonuses that they get against magical attacks (see Table 2E).

A dwarf's non-magical nature can also cause problems when he tries to use a magical item. In fact, if a dwarf uses a magical item that is not specifically created for his class, there is a 20% chance the item will malfunction. For example, if a dwarven fighter uses a Bag of Holding – which can be used by any class, not just fighters – each time the dwarf uses it there is a 20% chance that the bag does not work properly. This chance of malfunction applies to rods, staves, wands, rings, amulets, potions, horns, jewels and miscellaneous magic. However, dwarves have learned to master certain types of magical items because of their military nature. These objects – specifically weapons, shields, armor, gauntlets and girdles – are not subject to magical malfunction when used by a dwarf of any class. This penalty does not apply to dwarven clerics using cleric items or to dwarven battle mages using magic-user items.

Table 2E: Constitution Saving Throw Bonuses	
Constitution Score	Saving Throw Bonus
4-6	+1
7-10	+2
11-13	+3
14-17	+4
18-20	+5
21-24	+6
25	+7

This check is made each time a dwarf uses a magical item. A malfunction affects only the current use; the item may work properly the next time. For devices that are continually in operation, the check is made the first time the device is used during an encounter. If the check is passed, the device functions normally until it is turned off. Thus, a dwarf would have to check upon donning a Robe of Blending but would not check again until he had taken the robe off and then put it on again. If a cursed item malfunctions, the character recognizes its cursed nature and can dispose of the item.

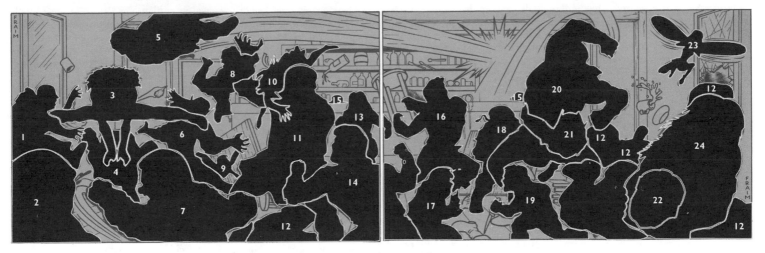

The Races of HackMaster:

1. Human, Male
2. Dwarf, Male
3. Grel, Male
4. Human, Male
5. Dwarf, Male
6. Elf, Male
7. Gnome, Male
8. Halfling, Male

9. Pixie Fairy, Male
10. Halfling, Female
11. Half-orc, Male
12. Human, Unconscious
13. Dwarf, Female
14. Human, Male
15. Human, Cowering
16. Half-elf, Male

17. Dwarf, Male
18. Gnomeling, Male
19. Gnome Titan, Male
20. Half-ogre, Male
21. Drow, Male
22. Dwarf, Male
23. Pixie Fairy, Female
24. Human, Female

Dwarves are superb miners. In the thousands of years that dwarves have lived in the earth, they have developed a number of skills and special abilities that help them to survive. All dwarves have infravision that enables them to see up to 60 feet in the dark. When underground, they can detect the following information when within 10 feet of the particular phenomenon (but they can determine their approximate depth below the surface at any time).

- Detect grade or slope in passage 1-5 on 1d6
- Detect new tunnel/passage construction 1-5 on 1d6
- Detect sliding/shifting walls or rooms 1-4 on 1d6
- Detect stonework traps, pits, and deadfalls 1-3 on 1d6
- Determine approximate depth underground 1-3 on 1d6

Note that the dwarf must deliberately try to make these determinations; the information does not simply spring to mind unbidden.

During their time under the earth, dwarves have also developed an intense hatred of many of the evil creatures they commonly encounter. In melee, dwarves add one to their dice rolls to hit Orcs, half-orcs, Goblins, and Hobgoblins. When Ogres, Trolls, Ogre Magi, giants, or Titans attack dwarves, these monsters must subtract four from their attack rolls because of the dwarves' small size and combat ability against these much bigger creatures.

Elf, High

A first encounter with a member of this noble race might leave the impression that elves are frailer and weaker than men are. To be sure, they are smaller and slighter of frame than most humans, but anyone with any experience with elvenkind can tell you that there is more to these demi-humans than meets the eye. They are quick, proud and fearless, with a number of special talents that more than make up for their slightly weaker Constitutions. It doesn't take much experience with elves to learn that they are a race that commands a certain degree of respect, and deservedly so.

One of the unique aspects of the race of elvenkind is their longevity. Elves can live for more than 700 years. Because of their long life spans, elves tend to become very wise and experienced, which is one reason they are respected. However, this broad perspective can be frustrating to shorter lived creatures. Because they can foresee how events will play out over the course of centuries, they are loath to apply a "quick fix" to a problem that may either naturally work itself out or have unintended long term ramifications that to a human viewpoint may be so far off as to be unimportant.

High Elves (incl. Sylvan Elves and Grey Elves) At a Glance:

The Upside
Racial Bonuses:
- Infravision. Elves can see 60 feet in the dark
- 90% resistance to Sleep and all charm-related spells

Initial Languages:
Common, elf, gnome, gnomeling, halfling, goblin, hobgoblin, orc, and gnoll*

Talents:
- +1 bonus on to-hit rolls when using a bow of any sort (except crossbow) or when using a short or long sword
- Move Silently. Opponents suffer a -4 penalty to their surprise die rolls. If the elf must open a door or screen to attack, this penalty is reduced to -2.
- Detect secret doors when passing by: 1 on 1d6
- Detect secret doors when searching: 1 or 2 on 1d6
- Detect concealed doors when searching: 1, 2 or 3 on 1d6
- Move through undergrowth as if in open terrain

Allowable Classes:
Cleric, druid, fighter, berserker, cavalier, knight errant, ranger, magic-user, battle mage, bloodmage, thief, assassin (Level restrictions apply. See Table 2C)

Allowable Multi-Classes:
Fighter/magic-user, fighter/thief, fighter/magic-user/thief, or magic-user/thief

Attribute Modifiers:
Elves gain/suffer the following bonuses/penalties: +1 Dexterity; -1 Constitution; +1 Comeliness (sylvan elves only) +2 Comeliness (gray elves and high elves only)

Building Point Bonus: 12

Additional Talents Which May be Purchased:
Acrobatic Skill Suite, Acute Alertness, Ambidextrous, Animal Companion, Astute Observation, Blind Fighting, Bow Bonus, Cold Resistance, Dagger Bonus, Forest Movement, Grace Under Pressure, Heat Resistance, Javelin Bonus, Keen Sight, Less Sleep, Magic Identification, Photographic Memory, Seeking Grasping Hands, Sibling Empathy, Sixth Sense, Speak With Plants, Spear Bonus, Spell Abilities, Trident Bonus

The Downside
Except for some attribute penalties and class restrictions, none.

*The number of languages an elf can learn is limited by his Intelligence (see Table 1D) or by the Building Points/training he devotes to languages.

There are six branches of the elven race; high, grey, wood, grunge (grel), dark, and aquatic. Elf player characters are always assumed to be of the most common type – high elves – unless the player specifies otherwise and can convince his GM he's up to the challenge of running the desired elf-type. The differences between the elven sub-races often appear to be mostly cosmetic in the eyes of many outsiders. However, most elves will quickly dispel that notion if asked. They maintain that there are important cultural and philosophical differences between the various groups. Closer study by outsiders will lead them to the same conclusions.

High elves are the most common, often mingling with the other races for purposes of trade, diplomacy and even curiosity.

Grey elves are considered the most noble and serious-minded of this breed. They are mysterious, and some say, even snobbish. They, of course, say otherwise.

Wood elves are considered wild, temperamental and savage. Some say they are more animal than demi-human.

More in-depth descriptions of the various types of elves can be found in the Hacklopedia of Beasts. Your GM will decide if you need to know more about a specific sub-race of elvenkind.

Grunge elves (sometimes known as **Grels**) are a scourge to all other elves. Centuries after being defeated, they continue to wage a futile guerrilla campaign. Though they admire bravery in their enemies, they have gained a reputation as a fearsome warlike breed who take pleasure in preying upon weak faery-kin. Their bloodlust makes most other elves shun all contact with them.

Surface elves hold that the subterranean **Dark Elves** [a.k.a. **Drow**] are corrupt, evil and no longer a part of the elven community. Grel claim that the drow are pansies of the worst sort.

Aquatic elves spend their lives beneath the waves and have adapted to these conditions. Their culture revolves around the sea and they worship various forms of maritime gawds.

High elves, the most common type of elf, are somewhat shorter than men, never growing much taller than 5 feet. Male elves usually weigh between 90 and 120 pounds, and females weigh between 70 and 100 pounds. Most high elves are dark-haired, and their eyes are a beautiful, deep shade of green. They possess infravision up to 60 feet. The features of an elf are delicate and finely chiseled and they speak in melodic tones, which dwarves absolutely hate.

These elves have very pale complexions although they spend a great deal of time outdoors. Some say that elven skin produces a natural sunscreen designed to protect them from overexposure.

Their bodies are slim, as their height and weight suggests. Their more fragile physiques cause them to have weaker constitutions than men; therefore, they must subtract one point from their initial Constitution score. However, while not as sturdy as humans are, elves are much more agile, and always add one point to their initial Dexterity scores. Comeliness is also modified depending on the specific elven race.

Elven clothing tends to be colorful, but not garish. They often wear pastel colors, especially yellows and greens, when attending public events. Because they dwell in forests however, high elves often wear greenish gray cloaks to afford them quick camouflage when necessary.

Elven women are the equals of their male counterparts in all aspects of warfare. If anything, their ferocity in battle is even greater than their male counterparts. The legends of the destruction wrought by bands of female elven warriors are rampant among the enemies of the elves.

Elves are often considered frivolous and aloof. In fact, they are not, although humans often find their personalities impossible to fathom. Because elves live for several hundred years, their view of the world is radically different from most other sentient beings. Elves do not place much importance on short-term gains nor do they hurry to finish projects. Humans see this attitude as frivolous; the elves simply find it hard to understand why everyone else is always in such a rush. Elves prefer to surround themselves with things that will bring them joy over long periods of time, such as music and nature. They prefer to concern themselves with natural beauty, dancing and frolicking, playing and singing, unless necessity dictates otherwise.

Ultimately, their radically different perspective separates the elves from the rest of their world. Elves find dwarves too grumpy and their adherence to strict codes of law inflexible. However, elves do recognize dwarven craftsmanship as something to be praised. Elves' attitude toward humans tends to be a bit more agreeable, but there is also a sense of pity and despair when viewing mankind's deeds. Elves cannot understand the drive humans have to gather wealth and power for themselves, and they find this tendency to be not only sad, but also painful to watch. Many an elf has been driven to bitterness at the horrible things they have seen men do to quench the lust for treasure and power.

The company of their own kind is very important to elves, since they find it hard to share their experiences or their perspectives on the world with other races. This is one of the main reasons elven families are so close. However, friendship too is something to be valued. Even friends of other races remain friends forever and although elves tend toward haughtiness and arrogance at times, they regard their friends and associates as equals. They do not make friends easily, but a friend (or enemy) is never forgotten.

Elves have learned that it is very important to understand all creatures, both good and evil, that share their forest home. Because of this, elves may speak the tongues of goblins, orcs, hobgoblins, gnolls, gnomes, gnomelings and halflings, in addition to common and their own highly-developed language. They will always show an interest in anything that will allow them to communicate with, and learn from, their neighbors. The actual number of languages is limited by the Intelligence of the player character (see Table 1D) or by the Building Points/training he devotes to languages.

They are not fond of ships or mines, but rather enjoy growing things and gazing at the open sky. They prefer to distance themselves from humans. Hatred for the evil denizens of the woods runs deep.

Their humor is clever and witty, as are their songs and poetry. Elves are brave but never foolhardy. They eat sparingly; they drink mead and wine, but seldom to excess. While they find well-wrought jewelry a pleasure to behold, they are not overly interested in money or gain. They find magic and swordplay (or any refined combat art) fascinating. If they have a weakness, it lies in these interests. Many elves also have an innate curiosity, which can cause problems.

A player character elf can be a cleric, druid, fighter, barbarian (grunge or wood elves only) berserker, cavalier, knight errant, ranger, magic-user, battle mage, bloodmage, thief, assassin. In addition, an elf can choose to be a multi-class fighter/magic-user, fighter/thief, fighter/magic-user/thief, or magic-user/thief. (The rules governing these combinations are explained in Chapter 3: Player Character Classes under "Multi-Class and Dual-Class Characters").

Although their constitutions are weak, elves possess extremely strong wills; such strong wills, in fact, that they have a 90% immunity to all charm-related and Sleep spells. Even if their natural resistance to these spells fails they get a normal saving throw, making it unlikely an elf will fall victim to any of these spells.

Elves do not live in walled cities, so martial training is a must to maintaining their egalitarian lifestyle in a hostile world – especially one in which the Grel still lurk. The elves' lengthy training with bows and swords, in addition to their great dexterity, gives them a natural bonus of +1 to hit when fighting with a short or long sword, or when using a bow of any kind other than a crossbow. Elves are especially proficient in the use of the bow. Because of their agility, elves can move, fire a bow, and move again, all in the same round. Their archers are extremely mobile, and therefore dangerous.

Elves are cautious fighters and always use their strengths to their advantage if possible. One of their greatest strengths is the ability to pass through natural surroundings, woods or forests, silently and almost invisibly. If the elf is not in metal armor he can move quietly and blend into vegetation for cover. Elves often surprise a person or party this way. The elf must either be alone or with a party comprised only of elves or halflings (also not in metal armor), or 90 feet or more away from his party to gain this bonus. If he fulfills these conditions, he moves so silently that opponents suffer a -4 penalty to their surprise die rolls. If the elf must open a door or screen to attack, this penalty is reduced to -2.

Only those with the ability to see invisible objects will be able to spot an elf hiding in the forest, as long as the elf is not attacking. The military value of this skill is immense, and elven armies will always send scouts to spy on the enemy, since such spies are rarely caught or even seen.

Elven infravision enables them to see up to 60 feet in darkness. Secret doors (those constructed to be hard to notice) and concealed doors (those hidden from sight by screens, curtains or the like) are difficult to hide from elves. Merely passing within 10 feet of a concealed door gives an elven character a one-in-six chance (roll a 1 on 1d6) to notice it. If actively searching for such doors, elven characters have a one-in-three chance (roll a 1 or 2 on 1d6) to find a secret door and a one-in-two chance (roll a 1, 2, or 3 on 1d6) to discover a concealed portal.

Grey Elves (Faerie): Grey elves have either silver hair and amber eyes or pale golden hair and violet eyes (the violet-eyed ones are known as faerie elves). They favor bright garments of white, gold, silver or yellow, and wear cloaks of deep blue or purple. Grey elves are the rarest of elves, and they have little to do with the world outside their forests. They value Intelligence very highly and, unlike other elves, devote much time to study and contemplation. Grey

elves get +1 to Intelligence instead of Dexterity. Otherwise their ability modifiers are as above.

Wood Elves (Sylvan): Also called sylvan elves, wood elves are the rustic branch of the elf family. They are slightly darker in complexion than high elves. Their hair colors range from yellow to coppery red, and their eyes are light brown, light green or hazel. They wear clothes of dark browns and greens, tans and russets, to blend in with their surroundings. Wood elves are very independent and value strength over intelligence.

Wood elves speak only elf and the languages of some forest animals, and the treant. Wood elves are more inclined toward neutrality than good. Wood elves get +1 Strength and –1 Intelligence, in addition to normal elven modifiers.

The Evil Elves

Ages ago, there were several tribes which comprised the elven race that inhabited the world's forests. Not long after they were created, however, the elves found themselves torn into rival bickering factions; some following the tenets of evil, the others espousing virtuous ideals. (Those opting to remain neutral in the conflict eventually cast their lot in with the good elves because at least they wouldn't have to worry about being stabbed in the back.) A terrible civil war ensued which dragged on for centuries. Attrition eventually proved the downfall for the wicked elves as they could no longer stand and defend their homelands against the occupying forces of high, grey and wood elves. Those on the losing side who chose to continue the fight retreated to mountainous scrub forests from which to wage guerrilla warfare. These determined warriors became the Grel. The sissies who couldn't hack it fled underground, becoming the Drow.

Elf, Grunge

Grunge elves (more commonly known as the grel) forever lurk in the minds of those who live within their reach. They are the antithesis of civilization — they are destroyers. They are a warrior race instilled with a deep sense of wanderlust, which constantly brings them into contact with new enemies and new conflicts. The grel were born to fight, yet strangely they refuse to fight en masse or adopt the rank and file military disciplines which their elven cousins have proven so adept in. The grel prefer the elements of fear, surprise and evil cunning when it comes to the art of war. It comes natural to them and great armies dread any prospect that involves fighting these proud warriors.

Banished from their homelands, the grel developed their own peculiar brand of stealthly warfare. As the years passed their battle skills were honed. Master Chung Hu Chek once wrote, "… in a fair fight, a hundred grels against a legion of well trained, well armed human warriors would probably be an even match. But," he adds, "if I were betting on such a match my money would be on the grel. This is because the grel NEVER fight fair."

Grels put the dark elves to shame, and many demi-humans consider them one of the greatest threats to the civilized world. The high elves have gone to war with them on numerous occasions with an eye toward eradicating the grel threat. The grel have always bounced back, even in the face of such stiff and costly opposition. They seem to revel in the fact that the entire world is against them. Perhaps this explains why they admire bravery in their enemies, especially when faced with overwhelming odds. (Grel warriors have been known to spare the lives of such individuals.) They are a fearsome warlike race who take great pleasure in preying upon the weak. They follow the dark gawd Arnuya who, like the grel, was banished by his own kind. This may explain why the grel religion is a dark one centered on vengeance. Arnuyan shamans teach of the potential destruction of the grel race at the hands of their enemies. They therefore fight other races for "preemptive vengence".

One reason so many fear the grel is their penchant for enslaving those who possess the skills or knowledge they need. It is estimated that most grel war bands are comprised of 30% slaves. Surprisingly, grels treat their slaves well — as long as they contribute to the livelihood of the band. Orc slave-fighters are highly prized by the grel because the brutes are such willing subjects as long as food is plentiful and they receive a share of any war booty. However, grels aren't entirely bad. They only seem that way to outsiders. To a grel, Honor is paramount and most of grel life revolves around increasing one's Honor or maintaining it. They're full of self-importance, desiring to make an impression on others. This explains a lot about grel behavior. Grel warriors have been known to turn their back on a capable, armed enemy as a show of disrespect as well as their own lack of fear. (And as Chung Hu Chek advises, "If a grel turns his back to you, strike the bastard down where he stands or you'll soon regret not taking advantage of the situation.")

The grel are a nomadic race who roam about the deep forests as they follow the migratory patterns of various game animals and prey. They are hated by most of the other forest dwelling demi-humans for their habit of over-hunting and depleting areas of food and resources before moving on.

Over the years, the grel have developed a raider culture. The grel routinely raid and loot settlements along their migratory routes. Grels love nothing more than to completely overrun a small village, kill or enslave its inhabitants and then spend several weeks (or even months) living off any resources and food stores the town can provide. Once the grel have depleted a town of its resources, they will torch the town and move on.

Tattoo Magic: Grels love the flesh of pixie fairies. Not only because they find it particularly tasty but because it's chock-full of magical energies. It is the consumption of pixie fairy meat which allows grels to make use of faerikin tattoo magic. Any grel who consumes a pixie fairy can add one pixie fairy tattoo type (see pixie fairies) and reap the magical benefits of that tattoo. Only one tattoo per pixie fairy eaten can result in magical benefits, and the penalties and drawbacks of getting such a tattoo are the same as those paid by the pixie fairy.

Grunge Elves (Grels) At a Glance:

The Upside

Racial Bonuses:
- Infravision. Grel can see 60 feet in the dark
- 90% resistance to Sleep and all charm-related spells
- Only surprised on a 1 on 1d10

Initial Languages:
Common, grel, elf, dwarf, orc, ogre, glersee, gnomish, brownie, pixie faerie*

Talents:
- War Cry: Enemies must save vs. fear at −5 or lose their first attack
- +1 bonus on to-hits when using a spear or bow
- Move Silently. Opponents suffer a -4 penalty to their surprise die rolls. If the Grel must open a door or screen to attack, this penalty is reduced to -2.
- Detect secret doors when passing by: 1 on 1d6
- Detect secret doors when searching: 1 or 2 on 1d6
- Detect concealed doors when searching: 1, 2 or 3 on 1d6
- Tracking (automatically gain this Sophisticated Task)
- Move through undergrowth as if in open terrain (per High Elves)

Allowable Classes:
Cleric, druid, fighter, barbarian, berserker, cavalier, knight errant, ranger, magic-user, battle mage, bloodmage, thief, assassin (Level restrictions apply. See Table 2C.)

Allowable Multi-Classes:
Fighter/magic-user, fighter/thief, fighter/magic-user/thief, or magic-user/thief

Attribute Modifiers:
Grunge elves gain/suffer the following bonuses/penalties: +1 Dexterity; -1 Constitution; -1 Comeliness

Building Point Bonus: 13

Additional Talents Which May be Purchased
Acrobatic Skill Suite, Acute Alertness, Ambidextrous, Animal Companion, Astute Observation, Blind Fighting, Bow Bonus, Cold Resistance, Constitution/Health Bonus, Dagger Bonus, Forest Movement, Grace Under Pressure, Heat Resistance, Javelin Bonus, Keen Sight, Less Sleep, Magic Identification, Mining Sense, Photographic Memory, Seeking Grasping Hands, Sibling Empathy, Sixth Sense, Speak With Plants, Spear Bonus, Spell Abilities

The Downside
The Grel must suffer the jealousy of the other races.

*The number of languages a grunge elf can learn is limited by his Intelligence (see Table 1D) or by the Building Points/training he devotes to languages.

Grel can be fighters (including barbarians, berserkers, cavaliers, knights errant and rangers), thieves (including assassins), clerics (including druids) or magic-users (including battle mages and blood mages). Choosing a class further defines a grel as one of the following subtypes:

Grugach: [grel barbarians] Cousin to the grel, these wild elves are completely barbaric, living beyond the far fringes of human and elf civilization. They are a bit xenophobic and tend to kill all non-elves on sight. They typically dress in the hides of animals they have killed with their bare hands.

Hunter Grel: [grel rangers] Average grels will be hunters. They wear light armor and earth tones that blend into the environments they live in. They typically carry short bows used for hunting and knives for skinning and cleaning animals. They are fierce looking elves, sporting mohawks and body tattoos. Ranger grels are not obligated to be of good alignment.

Shadow Grel: [grel assassins] These are the warrior class of the grel. Shadow grels are better armed, always carrying at least two war clubs and one long bow each. They are often covered in camouflage make-up to better hide against elven enemies.

Grel Clerics: [grel cleric] These elves lead the grel tribes, worshipping Arnuya exclusively. They are often dressed in more elaborate clothing and carry ceremonial daggers.

Grel Mages: [grel battle mage] Often competing with the clerics for the power of the tribe, the mages further the tribe's goals, as long as it helps their agenda of personal power. They are typically in charge of any slaves belonging to the tribe and will be dressed in dark cloaks, carrying staves and daggers.

Grels also possess the ability to pass through natural surroundings, woods or forests, silently and almost invisibly. If the grel is not in metal armor, he can move quietly and blend into vegetation for cover. Grels often ambush their enemies this way. The grel must either be alone or with a party comprised only of grels or allied elves or halflings (also not in metal armor), or 90 feet or more away from his party to gain this bonus. If he fulfills these conditions, he moves so silently that opponents suffer a -4 penalty to their surprise die rolls. Only those with the ability to see invisible objects will be able to spot a grel hiding in the forest, as long as the grel is not attacking. The tactical value of this skill is immense, and grel raiders usually destroy any patrol foolish enough to pursue them.

Like all elves, they are 90% immune to Sleep and charm-related spells and they still get a saving throw if that fails. They get +1 to hit with a spear or bow (except crossbows). Because of their agility, they can move up to one-half of their normal movement, hurl a spear and then move again to the limit of their movement rate in the same round. Grunge elves have infravision of 60'.

Grel have a fierce war scream that causes victims to save vs. fear at −5 or lose the first attack. They can use this ability once per day.

Grel are as long-lived as other elves. They are almost never found in civilized elf, human or demi-human lands except as raiders. A bitter enmity exists between the grel and the drow.

Elf, Dark (Drow)

The dark elves, also known as drow, live deep underground. Nearly all of them are evil, and they have used their cunning to become masters of much of the NetherDeep. Most intelligent creatures shun them. In many ways, dark elves are twisted, corrupt versions of their aboveground relatives. Drow have retained all the abilities and bonuses of other elves. In addition, because life in the NetherDeep is so demanding they have developed additional powers as detailed below.

The drow tell themselves that they no longer wish to live upon the surface of the earth. This is a copout to assuage their low self-esteem for being sissies and bailing on their grel cousins. The dark elves resent the elves and fairies who drove them away, and scheme against those who dwell in the sunlight. This scheming, however, seldom results in any action (much to the chagrin of the grel who still curse their dark cowardly cousins). Drow are content to live in magnificently dark, gloomy cities in the underworld that few humans or demi-humans ever see. Those few surface creatures that have seen a dark elf city (and returned to tell the tale) report that it is the stuff of which nightmares are made.

Player character drow are assumed to be individuals who failed in their schooling and fled drow society. (For the drow, the penalty for failure is centuries of menial labor). As such, drow player characters are viewed as losers and are forever banished from their native culture.

It is a tremendous challenge for a player to successfully take on the role of a drow; therefore, a player who wishes to run such a character must get permission from his GM beforehand. Very few dark elves are of good alignment, and these are usually player characters.

Drow have jet-black skin, an adaptation befitting skulking underground. They usually have white hair, which they like to grow long. They are shorter and more slender than humans, seldom reaching more than 5 feet in height. Male drow weigh between 80 and 110 pounds, and females between 95 and 120 pounds. Drow have finely chiseled features, and their fingers and toes are long and delicate. Like all elves, they have higher Dexterity and lower Constitution than humans. The only other physical difference drow exhibit is their eyes, which glow a feral red – evidence, perhaps, of the hatred that burns in their hearts and minds or perhaps simply because they're really tired.

Drow clothing is usually black, functional and often possesses special properties, although it does not radiate magic. For example, drow cloaks and boots act as if they are Cloaks and Boots of Elvenkind, except that the wearer is only 75% likely to remain undetected in shadows or to surprise enemies. The material used to make drow cloaks does not cut easily and is fire resistant, giving the cloaks a +6 bonus to saving throws vs. fire. These cloaks and boots fit and function only for those of elven size and build. Player character drow have a 15% chance of beginning their adventuring careers with drow cloaks and/or boots (roll separately for each). For every 5 Building Points the player sacrifices, an additional 5% modifier can be added to each check. Any attempt to alter a drow cloak has a 75% chance of unraveling the material, making it useless.

In the centuries they've spent underground, drow have learned the languages of many of the intelligent creatures of the underworld. Besides their own tongue, an exotic variant of elvish, drow speak both common and the

---

Dark Elves (Drow) At a Glance:

The Upside
Racial Bonuses:
- Infravision. Drow can see 120 feet in the dark
- 90% resistance to Sleep and all charm-related spells
- Only surprised on a 1 on 1d10
- Chance of starting with drow boots/cloak (see text)
- Chance of starting with drow chainmail (see text)
- Spell Ability (see text)
- Base resistance to magic of 50%. Increases by 2% for each level of experience.
- +2 bonus on saves vs. all forms of magical attack (including devices)

Initial Languages:
Common, drow, drow silent language, elf, dwarf, gnome, undercommon, kuo-toa, bugbear, and orcish *

Talents:
- +1 bonus on to-hits when using a crossbow, dart or a short/long sword.
- Move Silently. Opponents suffer a -4 penalty to their surprise die rolls. If the drow must open a door or screen to attack, this penalty is reduced to -2.
- Detect secret doors when passing by: 1 on 1d6
- Detect secret doors when searching: 1 or 2 on 1d6
- Detect concealed doors when searching: 1, 2 or 3 on 1d6
- Detect grade or slope in passage 1-5 on 1d6
- Detect new tunnel/passage construction 1-5 on 1d6
- Detect sliding/shifting walls or rooms 1-4 on 1d6
- Detect stonework traps, pits, and deadfalls 1-3 on 1d6
- Determine approximate depth underground 1-3 on 1d6

Allowable Classes:
Cleric, druid, fighter, berserker, cavalier, knight errant, ranger, magic-user, battle mage, blood-mage, thief, assassin (Level restrictions apply. See Table 2C)

Allowable Multi-Classes:
Fighter/magic-user, fighter/thief, fighter/magic-user/thief, or magic-user/thief

Attribute Modifiers:
Elves gain/suffer the following bonuses/penalties: +1 Dexterity; -1 Constitution; -2 Comeliness

Building Point Bonus: 13

Additional Talents Which May be Purchased:
Acrobatic Skill Suite, Acute Alertness, Ambidextrous, Animal Companion, Astute Observation, Blind Fighting, Close to the Earth, Cold Resistance, Constitution/Health Bonus, Crossbow Bonus, Dagger Bonus, Determine Stability, Grace Under Pressure, Heat Resistance, Javelin Bonus, Keen Sight, Less Sleep, Magic Identification, Mining Sense, Photographic Memory, Seeking Grasping Hands, Sibling Empathy, Sixth Sense, Speak With Plants, Sword Bonus

The Downside
- Dark elves suffer a -1 penalty on all rolls when exposed to bright sunlight or Continual Light spells. Lesser light sources do not bother them.
- All other elves hate dark elves, resulting in an initial reaction roll penalty of -2.

* The number of languages a drow can learn is limited by his Intelligence (see Table 1D) or by the Building Points/training he devotes to languages.

---

subterranean trade language used by many races under the earth. Drow characters begin the game with drow, elf, dwarf, undercommon, kuo-toa, bugbear and orcish. They also speak the languages of gnomes and other elves fluently.

Drow also have their own silent language composed of both signed hand movements and body language. These signs can convey information, but not subtle meaning or emotional content. If within 30 feet of another drow, they can also use complex facial expressions, body movements and postures to convey meaning. Coupled with their hand signs, these expressions and gestures give the drow's silent language a potential for expression equal to most spoken languages.

Drow wear finely crafted, lightly encumbering, black mesh armor. This extremely strong mail is made with a special metal called 'hard silver' or 'black silver'. The special alloy, when worked by a drow armorer, yields mail that has the same properties of chain mail +1 to +5, although it does not radiate magic. Player character drow have a 5% chance of beginning their adventuring careers with +1 hard silver chain mail. For every 5 Building Points the player sacrifices an additional 5% modifier can be added to each check.

Drow move silently in underground settings as high elves in natural surroundings and have superior infravision (120 feet). They also have the same intuitive sense about their underground world as dwarves, and can detect secret doors with the same chance of success as other elves. A dark elf can only be surprised by an opponent on a roll of 1 on 1d10.

All dark elves receive training in magic, and are able to use the following spells once per day: Dancing Lights, Faerie Fire, and Darkness. Drow above 4th level can use Levitate, Know Alignment and Detect Magic once per day. Drow clerics can also use Detect Lie, Clairvoyance, Suggestion, and Dispel Magic once per day.

Perhaps it is the common use of magic in drow society that has given the dark elves their incredible resistance. Drow have a base resistance to magic of 50%, which increases by 2% for each level of experience. (Multi-classed drow gain the bonus from only the class in which they have the highest level.) All dark elves save vs. all forms of magical attack (including devices) with a +2 bonus. Thus, a 5th-level drow has a 60% base magic resistance and a +2 bonus to her saving throws vs. spells that get past her magic resistance. (Note: in drow society only females can be magic-users. Drow society doesn't allow the arcane arts to be taught to males. The penalty for doing so is death. However, this may not preclude a male drow player character from being a magic-user. Such individuals obviously bribed someone in order to pursue such professions.)

Drow do have one great weakness – bright light. Because the drow have lived so long in the earth, rarely venturing to the surface, they are no longer able to tolerate bright light of any kind. Dark elves suffer a –1 penalty on all rolls when exposed to bright sunlight, Light spells or Continual Light spells. Lesser light sources such as torches, lanterns, magical weapons or Faerie Fire spells irritate them but cause no penalty.

Direct sunlight utterly destroys drow cloth, boots, weapons and armor. Any drow item begins to suffer irreversible decay when first exposed to sunlight. Within 2d6 days, the items lose their magical properties and rot, becoming totally worthless. Drow artifacts, if protected from sunlight, retain their special properties for 1d20+30 days before becoming normal items. To protect their items from the sunlight, drow expose them to the radiation of their underworld for one week out of every four. This treatment will enable their items to retain their undamaged properties and still be usable above ground.

Gnomes

Small cousins of the dwarves, gnomes are friendly but reticent, quick to help their friends but rarely seen by other races unless they want to be. They tend to dwell underground in hilly, wooded regions where they can pursue their interests in peace. They are noticeably smaller than their distant cousins. Gnomes, as they proudly maintain, are also less rotund than dwarves.

For the most part, gnomes resemble smaller, thinner, and more nimble dwarves. However, their faces differ from dwarves in two notable ways: wearing their beards short and neatly trimmed, and having enormous noses (often fully twice the size of any dwarf's or human's). They take great pride in their noses. Skin, hair, and eye color vary somewhat by sub-race. The most common type of gnome, the rock gnome, has skin ranging from a dark tan to a woody brown (sometimes with a hint of gray), pale hair, and eyes any shade of blue. Gnomish clothing tends toward leather and earth tones, brightened by a bit of intricately wrought jewelry or stitching. A typical gnome lives for 350 years.

Gnomes have lively and sly senses of humor, with a special love and talent for practical jokes. They have a great love of living things and finely wrought items, particularly gems and jewelry. They love all sorts of precious stones and are masters of gem polishing and cutting. They are also the most mechanically adept of all races with the capacity to build fabulous contraptions of gears and pulleys.

Most gnomes prefer to live in areas of rolling, rocky hills, well-wooded and uninhabited by humans. Their diminutive stature has made them suspicious of the larger races, such as humans and elves, although they are not hostile. They are sly and furtive with those they do not know or trust and somewhat reserved even under the best of circumstances. Dwelling in mines and burrows, they are sympathetic to dwarves, but find their cousins' aversion to surface dwellers foolish.

The standard gnomish sub-races are deep gnomes, rock gnomes, forest gnomes and the gnome titan. To the outsider, the first three varieties are indistinguishable from one another. The gnome titan, however, differs noticeably from other gnomes. Players choosing to run a gnome titan should refer to their separate description.

Most gnomes prefer to become thieves or illusionists. Multi-class characters are more common among the gnomes than any other demi-human race. A gnome character can be multi-classed with any of the following combinations, cleric/illusionist, cleric/thief, fighter/cleric, fighter/illusionist, fighter/thief, illusionist/thief

Due to his upbringing, a beginning gnome character can choose to know the following languages, in addition to any others allowed by the GM: common, dwarf, gnome, halfling, goblin, kobold and the simple common speech of burrowing mammals (moles, badgers, weasels, shrews, ground squirrels, etc.). Gnomes are able to communicate with such burrowing mammals via a basic language of grunts, snorts, whistles and gestures. The actual number of languages is limited by the Intelligence of the player character (see Table 1D) or by the Building Points/training he devotes to languages.

Like their cousins the dwarves, gnomes are highly magic resistant. A gnome player character gains a bonus of +1 for every 3 1/2 points of Constitution score, just as dwarves do (see Table 2E). This bonus applies to saving throws against magical wands, staves, rods, and spells.

Gnomes At a Glance:

The Upside

Racial Bonuses:
- Infravision. Gnomes can see 60 feet in the dark.
- Saving throw bonus on saves vs. magic (See Table 2E)
- +1 on to-hits vs. Kobolds or Goblins.
- Gnolls, Bugbears, Ogres, Trolls, Ogre magi, giants, and Titans suffer a -4 to hit gnomish characters.

Initial Languages:
Common, dwarf, gnome, gnomeling, halfling, goblin, kobold, and the simple common speech of burrowing mammals (moles, badgers, weasels, shrews, ground squirrels, etc.)*

Talents:
- Detect grade or slope in passage 1-5 on 1d6
- Detect unsafe walls, ceiling, and floors 1-7 on 1d10
- Determine approximate depth underground 1-4 on 1d6
- Determine approximate direction underground 1-3 on 1d6

Allowable Classes:
Cleric, fighter, knight errant, illusionist, thief, assassin (Level restrictions apply. See Table 2C)

Allowable Multi-Classes:
Cleric/illusionist, cleric/thief, fighter/cleric, fighter/illusionist, fighter/thief, illusionist/thief

Attribute Modifiers:
Gnomes gain/suffer the following bonuses/penalties: +1 Intelligence; -1 Wisdom; -1 Comeliness

Building Point Bonus: 10

Additional Talents Which May be Purchased:
Acute Alertness, Ambidextrous, Animal Friendship, Astute Observation, Blind Fighting, Brewing, Close to the Earth, Dagger Bonus, Dart Bonus, Defensive Bonus, Engineering Bonus, Forest Movement, Freeze, Hide, Mining Sense, Opportunist, Potion Identification, Short Sword Bonus, Sibling Empathy, Sixth Sense, Sling Bonus, Stealth

The Downside
Gnomes suffer a 20% chance for failure every time they use any magical item except weapons, armor, shields, illusionist items, and (if the character is a thief) items that duplicate thieving abilities.

*The number of languages a gnome can learn is limited by his Intelligence (see Table 1D) or by the Building Points/training he devotes to languages.

A gnome also suffers a 20% chance for failure every time they use any magical item except weapons, armor, shields, illusionist items, and (if the character is a thief) items that duplicate thieving abilities. This check is made each time the gnome attempts to use the device, or, in the case of continuous-use devices, each time the device is activated. Like dwarves, gnomes can sense a cursed item if the device fails to function.

In melee, gnome characters add one to their attack rolls to hit Kobolds or Goblins. When Gnolls, Bugbears, Ogres, Trolls, Ogre Magi, giants or Titans attack gnomes, these monsters must subtract four from their attack rolls because of the gnomes' small size and their combat skills against these much larger creatures.

Gnomish infravision enables them to see up to 60 feet in the dark. Being tunnelers of exceptional merit, gnomes are able to detect the following within 10 feet (exception: they can determine their approximate depth or direction underground at any time.). They must stop and concentrate for one round to use any of these abilities.

- Detect grade or slope in passage 1-5 on 1d6
- Detect unsafe walls, ceiling, and floors 1-7 on 1d10
- Determine approximate depth underground 1-4 on 1d6
- Determine approximate direction underground 1-3 on 1d6

Gnome characters gain a +1 bonus to their Intelligence scores, to reflect their highly inquisitive natures. They suffer a -1 penalty to Wisdom because their curiosity often leads them unknowingly into danger.

Gnomes can use any weapon that matches their size and often carry a second (or even a third) weapon as a back-up. Short swords, hammers, and spears are favorite melee weapons. Short bows, crossbows, slings and darts come into play when distance weapons are called for. In addition, virtually every gnome will carry a sharp knife somewhere on his person as a final means of defense.

Gnome Titan

Gnome titans are like their gnomish cousins in every way except they are bred to fight and wage war. They are the gnomish equivalent of the Spartans. Even so, they're not into causes and need very little reason to fight. While they possess the sense of humor of their true gnomish cousins, it's a mean sense of humor. They love to laugh at the expense of others. Their idea of a good practical joke is putting scalding water down someone's backside or sewing someone up in their sleeping bag and rolling them down a hill into a sleeping pack of Aarnz Hounds.

Small but muscular, these tiny scrappers are experts at hand-to-hand fighting. They are never heavily armored, but they hide a variety of small weapons on their person at all times. Gnome titans cut their beards close to their face so opponents cannot grab them. They dress in form-fitting clothes and use colors and fabrics that are dull and drab. Most gnome titans are heavily scarred.

Gnome titan characters gain a +2 to their Strength to reflect their incredibly strong bodies that have been bred for generations to become lean, mean hacking machines. However, this Strength bonus comes at the expense of endurance. Gnome titans only receive 50% of any hit points (rounded down) rolled on the hit dice for their class/level.

Gnome titans attack at one level higher than their current experience level.

Because they are so specialized at what they do; gnome titans are very slow to learn new things about themselves and the world around them. For this reason they only receive half (50%) of any experience points gained.

They can advance in (or purchase) any skills of a military/combat nature at half the cost due to their militant nature and mindset.

A gnome titan can choose to be a battle mage with a minimum required Intelligence of only an 8 (though such a character would be limited to the use of cantrips).

Gnome titans must select the gnomish gawd of war, Pangrus as their patron gawd. This can certainly be a drawback for this race since Pangrus demands a 20% tithe from followers.

Gnome titans have a special attack skill: the *Groin Stomp*. A gnome titan can perform this attack only on opponents who are already prone, who have been knocked to the ground or who are sleeping. Once the victim is on the ground, the gnome titan can jump onto his groin with a successful to-hit roll (don't forget the applicable bonus for prone, stunned or sleeping, as the case

---

Gnome Titans At a Glance:

The Upside

Racial Bonuses:
- Infravision. Gnome titans can see 60 feet in the dark
- Saving Throw Bonus on Saves vs. Magic (See Table 2E)
- +1 on to-hits vs. Kobolds or Goblins
- Gnolls, Bugbears, Ogres, Trolls, Ogre Magi, giants, and Titans suffer a -4 to hit gnomish characters
- Gnome titans attack at one level higher than their current experience level
- Gnome titans only pay half Building Point/training costs for any skill of a military or combat nature. (Talents still have full BP costs, regardless of their nature)
- Gnome titans fighting along side with other gnome titans receive a +1 to their to-hit and damage rolls because of the incredible boost in morale they receive.
- Gnome titans fighting as a group cannot be broken or routed.

Initial Languages:
Common, dwarf, gnome, gnomeling, halfling, goblin, kobold, and the simple common speech of burrowing mammals (moles, badgers, weasels, shrews, ground squirrels, etc.)*

Talents:
- Detect grade or slope in passage 1-5 on 1d6
- Detect unsafe walls, ceiling, and floors 1-7 on 1d10
- Determine approximate depth underground 1-4 on 1d6
- Determine approximate direction underground 1-3 on 1d6
- Groin Stomp Attack (Special Combat Maneuver)

Allowable Classes:
Cleric, fighter, berserker, knight errant, battle mage, illusionist, thief, assassin. (Level restrictions apply. See Table 2C.)

Allowable Multi-Classes:
Fighter/assassin, fighter/cleric, fighter/illusionist, fighter/thief

Attribute Modifiers:
Gnomes gain/suffer the following bonuses/penalties: +2 Strength; +1 Intelligence; -1 Wisdom; -1 Comeliness

Building Point Bonus: 15

Additional Talents Which May be Purchased:
Acute Alertness, Ambidextrous, Animal Friendship, Astute Observation, Blind Fighting, Brewing, Close to the Earth, Dagger Bonus, Dart Bonus, Defensive Bonus, Engineering Bonus, Forest Movement, Freeze, Hide, Mining Sense, Opportunist, Potion Identification, Short Sword Bonus, Sibling Empathy, Sixth Sense, Sling Bonus, Stealth

The Downside
- Gnomes suffer a 20% chance for failure every time they use any magical item except weapons, armor, shields, illusionist items, and (if the character is a thief) items that duplicate thieving abilities.
- Gnome titans only earn 50% of any experience points awarded.
- Gnome titans must choose the gnomish gawd of war, Pangrus, as their patron gawd, and pay a tithe of 20% of all their income.
- Gnome titans only receive 50% of any hit points (rounded down) rolled on the hit dice for their class/level. This does not apply to the 20 hit point 'kicker'.

*The number of languages a gnome titan can learn is limited by his Intelligence (see Table 1D) or by the Building Points/training he devotes to languages.

may be) and a successful groin stomp skill check. A successful gnome hits with sufficient force to stun the opponent for 1-4 rounds and cause 1-4 points of damage per stomp (penetration damage does not apply). While the opponent is on the ground, the gnome titan can continue to perform this maneuver, causing additional damage each round, until the opponent is unconscious. This particularly vicious form of attack also causes the victim to lose a point of Honor. A gnome titan retains this ability regardless of class. A gnome titan's skill mastery for groin stomp starts at (Str + Dex)/2 plus the Honor Die. Thereafter, with each level gained, the groin stomp skill mastery increases by twice the roll of his Honor Die.

Gnome titans fighting along side each other receive a +1 to their to- hits and damage rolls because of the incredible boost in morale they receive. Gnome titans fighting as a group cannot be broken or routed.

See the Hacklopedia of Beasts for more information on the origin and background of gnome titans. If you don't have clearance, be sure to ask your GM to provide you with what he can reveal. They have all the racial abilities/characteristics listed for gnomes with the addition of those listed above.

Gnomelings

Gnomelings are not a true race unto themselves. They are the result of the wide spread gnome-halfling interbreeding which took place after the Great Gnome Uprising. When the wars ended, the peaceful shires of the halfling territories had been occupied by gnome titan soldiers for many years. When the gnome titans finally withdrew, many chose to remain behind with the halfling women they'd taken a fancy to. The result of this strange situation was the emergence of the gnomeling.

Fortunately for the civilized denizens of Garweeze Wurld, all gnomelings are born sterile. Thus, there are no known second-generation gnomelings. Although they are equally likely to be found living among gnomes or halflings, their unusual nature makes them shy creatures.

Gnomelings are quick; they gain +1 to Intelligence and Dexterity, but get a –1 Wisdom penalty, perhaps from their gnomish side. Because of their small stature, gnomelings suffer –1 to Strength and Constitution.

Gnomelings are smaller than pure gnomes. Some outsiders have sometimes mistaken these tiny creatures for human children. Just like human children, gnomelings have the ability to be manipulative and sneaky. Gnomelings are at home in underground structures of any sort, and can easily navigate their way around any tunnel, burrow or dungeon. They are also adept at stealth,

and can move about unnoticed in most settings. These natural abilities make them quite skillful at thieving, as well as creating illusions. Some gnomelings have become fighters and clerics, but most prefer to perform in capacities that best suit their natural abilities.

In spite of their thieving abilities, most gnomelings tend toward goodness or neutrality. Lawfulness, however, is not something in which they have much interest. Most gnomelings see no need for laws at all. They believe everyone knows what they should and shouldn't do inherently, and therefore laws are simply unnecessary.

Looking out for number one is a gnomeling's biggest motivation. They are so small that they often feel vulnerable. They have been taught that no one will look out for them if they don't do it themselves.

They have no strong feelings about humans one way or the other, although many of them joke about their large size and clumsiness. They cannot abide dwarves, their dour personalities or their habit of hoarding of treasure. They also have extreme ill feelings toward pixie fairies. It is unclear why these two races have such hatred for one another, but gnomelings all say that the only good pixie fairy is a dead pixie fairy. Pixie fairies feel the same way about gnomelings. Gnomelings also have no use for half-orcs and half-ogres, whom they see as evil, stupid, clumsy and ugly. In spite of their close blood ties to gnomes, gnomelings are not overly fond of their larger cousins. However, they find halflings to be great company (especially when they're picking up the tab), and there is a natural fellowship between the two races. Gnomelings tolerate elves in general but find nothing special about them. They view the evil elves with a large measure of distrust, and are not quite sure what to make of them. They resent half-elves, often because as a mixed race they have adapted quite well in society, unlike the gnomeling.

A gnomeling's sense of humor runs more to the halfling variety of rustic, gentle joking and horseplay.

Gnomelings At a Glance:

The Upside

Racial Bonuses:
- Infravision. Gnomelings can see 30 feet in the dark
- Saving throw bonus on saves vs. magic (see Table 2E)
- +1 on to-hits vs. Kobolds or Goblins
- Gnolls, Bugbears, Ogres, Trolls, Ogre Magi, giants, and Titans suffer a -4 on to-hits gnomish characters
- Have special stealth abilities. Are able to hide and move about unnoticed. There is only a 5% chance of noticing a gnomeling who is hiding, and the person noticing must concentrate for one round.

Initial Languages:
Common, dwarf, gnome, gnomeling, halfling, goblin, kobold*

Talents:
- Detect grade or slope in passage 1-5 on 1d6
- Detect unsafe walls, ceiling, and floors 1-7 on 1d10
- Determine approximate depth underground 1-4 on 1d6
- Determine approximate direction underground 1-3 on 1d6
- +1 bonus on to-hits when using a dagger

Allowable Classes:
Cleric, druid, fighter, berserker, knight errant, illusionist, thief, assassin, (Level restrictions apply. See Table 2C.)

Allowable Multi-Classes:
Cleric/illusionist, cleric/thief, fighter/cleric, fighter/illusionist, fighter/thief, illusionist/thief

Attribute Modifiers:
Gnomelings gain/suffer the following bonuses/penalties: +1 Intelligence; +1 Dexterity; -1 Strength; -1 Wisdom; -1 Constitution

Building Point Bonus: 10

Additional Talents Which May be Purchased:
Acute Alertness, Ambidextrous, Animal Friendship, Astute Observation, Blind Fighting, Dagger Bonus, Dart Bonus, Defensive Bonus, Engineering Bonus, Experience Bonus, Forest Movement, Hide, Mining Sense, Potion Identification, Sixth Sense, Sling Bonus, Stealth

The Downside
- Gnomelings suffer a 10% chance for failure every time they use any magical item except weapons, armor, shields, illusionist items, and (if the character is a thief) items that duplicate thieving abilities.

*The number of languages a gnomeling can learn is limited by his Intelligence (see Table 1D) or by the Building Points/training he devotes to languages.

Gnomelings do not have beards. They can use short swords, but must work extra hard to be proficient because these weapons are quite large for them. They prefer the use of daggers, and are quite good with them. They are quite accurate when throwing daggers, and most carry several on their person. Their daggers are important to them, and many gnomelings name their daggers in special ceremonies. They will often wear bandoleers of throwing daggers.

They wear subdued clothing, in order to more successfully hide.

Because of their small size, gnomelings are not particularly strong or healthy. They are, however, extremely quick and agile. They can take all of a person's belongings and be down the road selling them before anyone even notices anything is missing. They are also stealthy and able to hide with little difficulty. The only place where a gnomeling would be unable to hide would be in a large, open room with little or no furnishings, or in an open field with short grass and nothing to use as cover.

They are quite intelligent and inquisitive. They learn a great deal by simply watching others from their hiding places. Because of their abilities, many are employed as spies among the gnome titans. They are not wise, however, often exposing themselves needlessly in order to examine a curious item or person.

Knowing where they come from is a great cause of consternation among gnomelings. They are extremely sensitive about their origins, and will fight anyone who insults them concerning this matter. They often see insults where none are intended.

Half-Elf

Half-elves are the most common mixed race beings. The relationship between elf, human and half-elf is defined as follows: Anyone with both elven and human ancestors is either a human or a half-elf (elves have only elven ancestors). If there are more human ancestors than elven, the person is human; if there are equal numbers or more elves, the person is half-elven.

Half-elves are usually much like their elven parent in appearance. They are handsome folk, with the good features of each of their races. They mingle freely with either race, being only slightly taller than the average elf (5 feet 6 inches on average) and weighing about 150 pounds. They typically live about 160 years. They do not have all the abilities of the elf, nor do they have the flexibility of unlimited level advancement of the human.

Finally, in some of the less-civilized nations, half-elves are viewed with suspicion and superstition.

In general, a half-elf has the curiosity, inventiveness and ambition of his human ancestors and the refined senses, love of nature and artistic tastes of his elven ancestors.

Half-elves do not form communities among themselves; rather, they can be found living in both elven and human communities. The reactions of humans and elves to half-elves ranges from intrigued fascination to outright bigotry.

Of all the demi-human races, half-elves have the greatest range of choices in character class. They tend to make good druids and rangers. A half-elf can choose to be a cleric, druid, fighter, berserker, knight errant, ranger, magic-user, battle mage, blood mage, thief, assassin, bard. In addition, a half-elf can choose from the following multi-class combinations: cleric (or druid)/fighter, cleric (or druid)/fighter/magic-user, cleric (or druid)/ranger, cleric (or druid)/magic-user, fighter/magic-user, fighter/thief, fighter/magic-

user/thief, and magic-user/thief. The half-elf must abide by the rules for multi-class characters.

Half-elves do not have their own language. Their extensive contact with other races enables them to choose any of the following languages (plus any other allowed by the GM): common, elf, gnome, halfling, goblin, hobgoblin, orc and gnoll. The actual number of languages is limited by the Intelligence of the player character (see Table 1D) or by the Building Points/training he devotes to languages.

Half-elven characters have a 30% resistance to Sleep and all charm-related spells.

Half-elven infravision enables them to see up to 60 feet in darkness.

Secret or concealed doors are difficult to hide from half-elves, just as they are from elves. Merely passing within 10 feet of a concealed door (one hidden by obstructing curtains, etc.) gives the half-elven character a one-in-six chance (roll a 1 on 1d6) of spotting it. If the character is actively seeking to discover hidden doors, he has a one-in-three chance (roll a 1 or 2 on 1d6) of spotting a secret door (one constructed to be undetectable) and a one-in-two chance (roll a 1, 2, or 3 on 1d6) of locating a concealed door.

Halflings

Halflings are short, generally plump people, very much like small obese humans. Their faces are round, broad and often quite florid. Their hair is typically curly and the tops of their feet are covered with coarse hair. They prefer not to wear shoes whenever possible. Their typical life expectancy is approximately 150 years. Halflings are sturdy and industrious, generally quiet and peaceful. Overall, they prefer the comforts of home to dangerous adventuring. They enjoy good living, large and frequent meals, rough humor and homespun stories. In fact, they can be a trifle boring at times, at least in the opinion of outsiders. Halflings are not forward, but they are observant and conversational if in friendly company. Halflings see wealth only as a means of gaining creature comforts, which they love. Though they are not overly brave or ambitious, they are generally honest and hard working when there is need.

Halflings generally keep to themselves unless their home or way of life is threatened. Their homes are well-furnished burrows and a matter of great pride for the individual. Halflings do most of their work outdoors in the sunshine or in open-air structures. For the most part they get along with the others races, including humans, and can be found in practically any civilization. Halflings are superb traders and are known in virtually every far-flung port and along most of the established trade routes.

Elves generally like them in a patronizing sort of way – treating them as you would nieces and nephews. Dwarves cheerfully tolerate them since they seldom run up a large bar tab. Gnomes, although they drink more and eat less, like halflings the best, feeling them kindred spirits. Halflings are more open and outgoing than elves, dwarves or gnomes; therefore, they get along with other races far better and are often the facilitator of said races being able to cooperate.

A halfling character can choose to be a cleric, druid, fighter barbarian, berserker knight errant, thief, assassins (thugs only), or a multi-class fighter/thief. Through their contact with other races, halfling characters are allowed to choose initial languages from common, halfling, dwarf, elf, gnome, gnomeling, goblin, and orc, in addition to any other languages the GM allows. The actual number of languages is limited by the Intelligence of the player character (see Table 1D) or by the Building Points/training he devotes to languages.

All halfling characters have a high resistance to magical spells, so for every 3 1/2 points of Constitution score, the character gains a +1 bonus on saving throws vs. rods, staffs, wands and spells. These bonuses are summarized on Table 2E.

Halflings have a similar resistance to poisons of all sorts, so they gain a Constitution bonus identical to that for saving throws vs. magical attacks when they make saving throws vs. poison (i.e., +1 to +5, depending on Constitution score).

Halflings have a natural talent with slings and thrown weapons. Rock pitching is a favorite sport of many a halfling child. All halflings gain a +1 bonus to their attack rolls when using thrown weapons and slings.

A halfling can gain a bonus to surprise opponents, but only if the halfling is not in metal armor. Even then, the halfling must be either alone, or with a party comprised only of halflings or elves, or 90 feet or more away from his party to gain this bonus. If he fulfills any of these conditions, he causes a -4 penalty to opponents' surprise rolls. If a door or other screen must be opened, this penalty is reduced to -2.

Depending on their lineage, certain halfling characters have infravision. Any halfling character has a 15% chance of having normal infravision out to 60 feet. This means he is of pure stout heritage. If the player character

---

Half-Elves At a Glance:

The Upside

Racial Bonuses:
- Infravision enables half-elves to see up to 60 feet in darkness.
- 30% resistance to Sleep and all charm-related spells

Initial Languages:
Common, elf, gnome, gnomeling, halfling, goblin, hobgoblin, orc and gnoll*

Talents:
- Detect secret doors when passing by: 1 on 1d6
- Detect secret doors when searching: 1 or 2 on 1d6
- Detect concealed doors when searching: 1, 2 or 3 on 1d6

Allowable Classes:
Cleric, druid, fighter, berserker, knight errant, ranger, magic-user, battle mage, bloodmage, thief, assassin, bard (Level restrictions apply. See Table 2C.)

Allowable Multi-Classes:
Cleric (or druid)/fighter, cleric (or druid)/fighter/magic-user, cleric (or druid)/ranger, cleric (or druid)/magic-user, fighter/magic-user, fighter/thief, fighter/magic-user/thief and magic-user/thief

Attribute Modifiers:
Half-elves gain/suffer the following bonuses/penalties: +1 Comeliness

Building Point Bonus: 11

Additional Talents Which May be Purchased:
Acrobatic Skill Suite, Acute Alertness, Ambidextrous, Astute Observation, Balance Bonus, Blind Fighting, Bow Bonus, Cold Resistance, Heat Resistance, Keen Sight, Less Sleep, Photographic Memory, Sibling Empathy, Sixth Sense, Sword Bonus

The Downside
None.

*The number of languages a half elf can learn is limited by his Intelligence (see Table 1D) or by the Building Points/training he devotes to languages.

- Determine approximate depth underground 1-4 on 1d6
- Determine approximate direction underground 1-3 on 1d6

Because stouts are so friendly with dwarves, they suffer a −1 penalty on reaction rolls from elves. Stout halfllngs usually live about 140 years.

Tallfellow Halflings

These halflings are the tallest and slimmest of their kind, averaging a little over 4' tall. Their favorite locale is temperate woodlands. As such, they often live nearer to elves than humans. They usually wear their hair long, sometimes covered with small caps. Moreover, they tend to wear clothing of greens and tans to help them blend into the woods. Tallfellows make excellent carpenters, and they often live in spacious aboveground wooden houses. When they need to travel, tallfellows prefer riding small ponies to walking. Most tallfellows are lawful good, but player characters can be of any alignment. Tallfellows usually live about 180 years.

Tallfellows can detect secret doors on a one-in-six chance (roll a 1 on 1d6). Because of their close ties with elves, tallfellows suffer a −2 reaction roll penalty vs. dwarves.

Thug Halflings

These halflings are the misfits, the bottom rung of halfling society. They are halflings who for one reason or another have turned their backs on boring halfling society and become thieves. Thug halflings' appearance can vary greatly because they can be of any of the halfling sub-races, but they usually dress in leather armor, the hallmark of all thieves.

They hang out in small bands, hiding out in the deep forests and gullies near major trade routes where they can prey on the weak.

Thug halflings get a +2 to Dexterity instead of the normal +1 other halflings receive. They also receive a −1 penalty to Wisdom because of their lack of education and discipline.

Thug halflings' lives revolve around stealing. In fact, generations of thug halflings have been at the head of several of Garweeze Wurld's major thieves' guilds. Thugs generally live less than 80 years. This is due, in large part, to their noxious personal habits.

Thugs are the only halflings who can be berserkers or assassins.

Half-Orc

Orcs are fecund and crossbreed with virtually every humanoid and demi-human species except elves. The mongrel offspring of Orcs and these other species are known by non-orcs as half-orcs (orcs have far more unpleasant names for them). Orc-goblins, Orc-hobgoblins, and Orc-humans are the most common. Most half-orcs tend to favor the orcish strain heavily, and as such are for all practical purposes Orcs, although 10% of these offspring can just about pass as brutish humans. These are treated as humans with levels instead of Hit Dice. Half-orc player characters are always part of the most-human 10%.

fails to gain this ability, there is a 25% chance that he can has limited infravision, which means he can see in the dark out to 30 feet. Such halfling characters are of mixed lineage, of either stout/tallfellow parentage or stout/hairfoot blood.

Similarly, halflings with any stoutish blood can note if a passage is an up or down grade with 75% accuracy (roll a 1, 2, or 3 on 1d4). They can determine direction half the time (roll a 1, 2, or 3 on 1d6). These abilities function only when the character is concentrating on the desired information to the exclusion of all else, and only if the character is pure or partially stout.

Halfling characters have a penalty of -1 to their initially generated Strength scores, and they gain a bonus of +1 to Dexterity.

The standard halfling sub-races are hairfoot, stout, tallfellow and thug.

Hairfeet are the most common type, but for player characters, any of the three is acceptable.

Hairfoot Halflings

The most common halfling, hairfeet prefer rural settings. They are a practical people, and there are many bakers, millers, farmers and innkeepers in their society. Averaging 3' tall, hairfeet are stockier than their cousins are. Their complexions run from pale peach to ruddy to dark brown, and their eyes are usually black or dark brown. Their hair can be blond, brown, red, black, and shades in between – though with few exceptions it is curly. Hairfeet are distinguished from other halflings by their lack of facial hair. Most hairfeet are lawful good, though player characters can be of any alignment. Hairfeet live about 100 years.

Stout Halflings

Stouts are not as common as hairfeet, and tend to be stronger. Stouts usually live apart from human societies, choosing instead to live near dwarves. There may be some dwarven blood somewhere in the stouts' ancient past. Ruddy in complexion, stouts vividly blush when pleased or embarrassed. Their hair tends to be light, and their eyes usually are blue, gray, or green. They favor practical, sturdy clothes, such as well-cured leather. They are the most industrious of all halflings, and are even comfortable around bodies of water and boats. Most stouts are lawful good, though players can choose any alignment for their characters.

All stouts are able to see up to 60 feet in the dark. They are also able to detect the following:

- Detect grade or slope in passage 1-5 on 1d6
- Detect unsafe walls, ceiling, and floors 1-7 on 1d10

The products of human and orcish parents, these pariahs are generally unwelcome wherever they go. Their skin ranges from peach to olive to deep tan, and their hair can be blond, red, brown, black, gray, or any shade in between.

Half-orcs can be members of the following classes: cleric, fighter, barbarian, berserker, knight errant, thief, assassin. They can be multi-classed in the following classes, fighter (or berserker)/cleric, fighter (or berserker)/thief, fighter (or berserker)/assassin. Half-orcs can be of any alignment. They also have infravision, enabling them to see up to 60' distant in the dark.

Half-orcs can choose from the following languages: common, orc, dwarf, goblin, hobgoblin, and ogre.

In human and halfling societies, half-orcs suffer a –2 reaction roll penalty. In dwarven, elven and gnomish societies, they suffer a whopping –4 reaction roll penalty.

Both human and Orc cultures distrust half-orcs because they remind them of the other's racial stock. Half-orcs advance in Orc culture by flaunting their superior ability and bullying the others. In human culture, half-orcs have a few options. They can associate with people who don't care about appearance and like them for their brute strength and stamina (i.e., adventurers looking for an easier ride through the dungeon). Half-orcs can also beat the living tar out of any dung-head that snubs him, looks at him funny, or even meets his gaze. The latter method can get you into trouble with the town guard, so it's best to do that when you're planning to leave town anyway. Most tend toward neutrality with slight lawful and evil tendencies, but lawful good half-orcs are not unknown. Some half-orcs have split from both cultures to form their own societies in remote areas. These half-orcs worship their own gawds and (like most hermits) are extremely suspicious of strangers.

As a half-orc character, you need to brace yourself for ribbing about your looks, parentage and rung on the evolutionary ladder. You don't need to take that crap. You're a half-orc, man! Orcs only live to be forty or so, so live fast and hard. If someone picks on you, kick his teeth in. If he's tougher, wait 'til he's hurt. If they outnumber you, wait and cut all their throats from ear to ear in their sleep. Once you realize the world has it out for you, you were dealt a losing hand and you've got nothing to lose, your play will greatly improve. Orcs are vicious. As a half-orc you should be selectively vicious.

Half-Ogre

The fearsome half-ogre is a hybrid, offspring of one ogre and one human parent. They range in height from 7 to 8 feet and weigh from 315 to 425 pounds. Skin tones and hair colors vary, but the most common shades of skin for half-ogres are brown, gray, black or dull yellow. The skin may have a slight gray-green tint. Teeth and nails are always orange. Most half-ogres have human-like eyes, though about one in five have the white pupils common to Ogres. They emit a noticeable body odor, which is not as strong as that of a full-blooded Ogre.

Half-ogres can be a cleric, fighter, barbarian, berserker, knight errant, thief, assassin. Half-ogres can be of any alignment.

Because of their tremendous size, half-ogres gain +2 to their Strength and +2 to their Constitution. They are large creatures, and suffer more damage from many types of weapons. However, because of their unattractive appearance and body odor, they suffer -3 Charisma and -5 Comeliness. Because of their childhood, half-ogres have poorly developed minds (-2 to Intelligence and –1 to Wisdom). Ogres raise children with a specific bias against brainwork. A half-ogre raised in human lands will have had a bias placed upon him; called big, ugly and dumb, regardless of potential his confidence (and Charisma) drop, as does his learning. Luckily, when the poor half-ogre finally catches one of the little humans he usually breaks the brat's collar bone, femur or some other important piece of anatomy.

Half-ogres speak common (more clearly and unimpeded than true Ogres), ogrish, orcish, troll, stone giant, and one other (usually human) language. Half-ogres possess infravision out to 30 feet. Their sense of smell is better than an Ogre's, but it falls short of a human's ability.

Half-ogres suffer a -2 penalty to their attack rolls against dwarves and -4 against gnomes, since those smaller races are so skilled at battling bigger folk.

Half-ogres have no society of their own. If they live with Ogres, they are the quick-thinking members of the tribe, ever on their toes to prove themselves worthy, but constantly getting slapped around and abused as runts. If a half-ogre is reared in a human community, he learns to live with suspicion and fear, and often turns to a military or solitary occupation. He will likely have a great inferiority complex and an eating disorder, developed and honed during adolescence.

Starting Hit Dice are doubled at 1st level, progressing normally at 2nd level and above.

Half-ogres are extremely aggressive, gaining a +1 to their attack bonuses and damage rolls with one type of melee weapon. In addition, their inherent toughness grants half-ogres a +1 bonus to saving throws vs. poison.

Half-ogres have a natural Armor Class of 8. If the character wears armor that would improve his AC to better than 8, this has no effect. If the character wears armor that gives him an AC of 8 or worse, he gets a +1 to his Armor Class.

See half-orcs for other tips on playing social rejects and misfits.

Half-Ogres At a Glance:

The Upside

Racial Bonuses:
- Infravision with a 30' range
- Half-ogres receive a +1 to saving throws versus poison
- Starting Hit Dice are doubled at 1st level

Initial Languages:
Common, ogre, orc, troll, stone giant, and gnoll*

Talents:
- +1 attack and damage bonus with one melee weapon
- Dense Skin
- Tough Hide

Allowable Classes:
Cleric, fighter, barbarian, berserker, knight errant, thief, assassin (Level restrictions apply. See Table 2C.)

Allowable Multi-Classes:
none

Attribute Modifiers:
Half-ogres gain/suffer the following bonuses/penalties: +2 Strength; +2 Constitution; -1 Wisdom, -2 Intelligence, -3 Charisma; -5 Comeliness

Building Point Bonus: 8

Additional Talents Which May be Purchased:
Active Sense of Smell, Ambidextrous, Blind Fighting, Damage Bonus, Endurance, Mace Bonus, Sibling Empathy

The Downside
- Half-ogres qualify as large creatures and suffer more damage from many weapons.
- Certain smaller races enjoy combat bonuses against half-ogres.
- -2 penalty to attack rolls against dwarves.
- -4 penalty to attack rolls against gnomes.
- Their armor and other garb costs 200% that of humans.

* The number of languages a half-ogre can learn is limited by his Intelligence (see Table 1D) or by the Building Points/training he devotes to languages.

Humans

Unlike the real world, humans in HackMaster are treated as a single race. That's not to say all humans are the same. A human character can be Caucasian, African-American, Asian, Hoosier, etc. It's really up to you. There are no specific rules when it comes to human racial variants. That's because

---

Humans At a Glance:

The Upside

Racial Bonuses:
- Can rise to any level in chosen class.
- Can choose any character class.

Initial Languages:
Common, human*

Talents:
Must be purchased

Allowable Classes:
Any

Allowable Multi-Classes:
None. Humans may only dual-class

Attribute Modifiers:
Humans are the norm and receive no modifiers for attributes.

Building Point Bonus: 10

Additional Talents Which May be Purchased:
Acrobatic Skill Suite, Acute Alertness, Ambidextrous, Astute Observation, Attack Bonus, Balance Bonus, Blind Fighting, Detect Secret Doors, Endurance, Experience Bonus, Grace Under Pressure, Hit Point Bonus, Keen Sight, Less Sleep, Opportunist, Photographic Memory, Resistance, Seeking Grasping Hands, Sibling Empathy, Sixth Sense, Tough Hide

The Downside
None

* The number of languages a human can learn is limited by his Intelligence (see Table 1D) or by the Building Points/training he devotes to languages.

ALL humans share the same special ability. They can choose any character class and rise to any level in any class.

Compared with members of other races, humans are much more sociable and tolerant of those unlike themselves (except, of course, during the pre-teen formative years when they mercilessly and maliciously pummel each others' egos into nothing). Humans are willing to adventure with just about anyone, of any race, if it furthers their aims. This includes "highfalutin'" elves, belligerent dwarves or even cantankerous gnomes.

Humans are also the most flexible and adaptable of the races, driven by a deep curiosity about the world around them. There is an almost innate drive that moves men to explore their surroundings with an eye on expanding and exerting their influence and control.

This constant wanderlust brings humans into almost constant conflict with members of other races. It also accounts for the deeply held hatred that the members of many races have for humans.

However, in spite of their knack for making enemies, humans seem well equipped to deal with this problem. Because of their almost limitless abilities unrestricted by the shortcomings of other races, humans are adept at establishing bases of power and accomplishing things of which members of other races only dream. They also multiply like rabbits and spread themselves like a manifest plague across the lands.

Because humans are the yardstick by which the other fantasy races are compared they receive no modifiers or special skills.

Pixie Fairies

Garweeze Wurld is home to many mysterious races, but none is more magical and mysterious than the hybrid pixie fairy. With strong yet delicate and beautiful wings, these tiny creatures, reaching only one or two feet tall, flit about the glades and sunny pastures of the land. This race is the result of cross breeding between pixies and fairies, though no one is quite sure how this happened. Whatever the reason, the result has been the creation of a handsome species. Pixie fairies have skin tones varying from snow white to mauve to orange and colorful magic-imbuing tattoos decorating their bodies.

These frail creatures have beautiful, shimmering, insect-like wings, which resemble those of the dragonfly. Two pairs of wings grace each side of their bodies. Primary wings are larger, and are on top of the secondary wings. Pixie fairies use their primary wings to gain lift and propulsion. The secondary, smaller wings help pixie fairies maneuver. Their wings come in a variety of hues, but most are brightly colored, with an iridescent sheen.

Human children sometimes say that if you see the glimmer of a pixie fairy's wings in the moonlight, and if you wish upon that fairy, your wish will come true. This is, of course, a complete crock so don't waste your time.

The face of a pixie fairy has some of the angular qualities of the elves with some features resembling small human children, such as large, innocent-looking eyes and pouting lips. They possess two antennae, which sprout upward from the inner edge of either eyebrow. The female of the species has slightly larger antennae. This is the easiest way for a trained observer to distinguish the sex of a pixie fairy, since they appear androgynous; lacking any other physical feature that would indicate their gender.

Pixie fairies don't have individual teeth, rather they have two crescent-shaped bony-ridges which span the upper and lower jaw as would rows of teeth.

Due to their incredibly high metabolisms, pixie fairies have a very short life span — generally only ten to fifteen years. However, there is some good news. When a faerie dies, if he is not raised within two weeks, he is reincarnated 1d4 months from his date of death and comes back as a pixie fairy. Pixie fairies emerge from the womb at about 1/4 the size of a full adult. They reach full size in about 3 months and have identical Ability Scores of their former incarnation including level, proficiencies, talents and hit points. However, they automatically must roll for a minor quirk on Table 6F and they lack ALL skills they had previously with the exception of the Pixie Fairy language.

Gradually, three months after their re-birth, the pixie fairy begins to regain full awareness of his former self. Each day after the 3 month mark he can attempt to make a skill check for one (1) of the skills he formerly held at a +10% modifier to the die roll. If he is successful he has regained that skill. The next day he can roll to see if he regains another skill and so on. If the skill check fails he has lost all memory of that skill and must retrain (incurring the normal fees and training time) if he wishes to regain that skill. In spite of this automatic reincarnation feature of their race, a pixie fairy can only be Raised,

Reincarnated or Resurrected a number of times equal to his initial Constitution score just like any other character.

Pixie fairies usually choose their birth mothers before dying (if possible). Making such arrangements is very serious business and usually take place as part of Pixie Meet (see Pixie Meet below). A pixie fairy who has made arrangements with a birth mother prior to dying regains 100% of his former Honor. If such an arrangement hasn't been made, the pixie fairy must recalculate his beginning honor using the rules in Chapter1.

Because of their metabolism and the fact that they are magical creatures their sustenance requirements differ from other races. Pixie fairies actually feed on errant magical energies (the residual energies left behind by magical spells, items, etc.) which tend to accumulate in certain rare plants and insects. For this reason pixie fairies must pay 3 times the normal costs for daily provisions that other characters pay. Although they eat a much lower quantity of food as compared to their larger counterparts, their diet is so selective and restrictive that they incur a greater cost for acquiring such provisions. However, a pixie fairy is able to forage enough food to sustain itself in any environment where plant and insect life are plentiful without any checks and without any cost (although this takes 4-8 hours per day).

Pixie fairies' high metabolisms allow them to heal an extra hit point per day more than other creatures with the same Constitution.

Pixie fairies are never surprised by other living creatures due to the telepathic impulses picked up by their antennae and enhanced with the Emphkrin Tribal Tattoo. In addition, any intelligent creature that associates with an individual pixie fairy for at least two weeks becomes telepathically linked with the pixie faerie. Persons thus linked who remain within a 10' range of their pixie fairy cohort will gain the ability of never being surprised.

Pixie fairies can turn invisible once per day for a duration of one turn per level of experience. However, they can ONLY turn invisible by flying. If restrained, confined to a tight space, etc., no invisibility is possible. They can wear armor (which must be tailored to fit at great cost) but doing so makes it impossible to fly. Pixie fairy armor does not protect the exposed wings. Many dedicated pixie fairy warriors have had their wings cut off so they can wear armor more effectively. Such creatures rely on butterfly or moth mounts and can pursue the cavalier character class if they choose.

Pixie Fairies At a Glance:

The Upside

Racial Bonuses:
- Fly at 18" per round
- Can use Giant Moth and Butterfly mounts
- a +2 bonus to hit in mounted combat or flying combat
- Heal an extra hit point per day
- Never surprised
- Telepathic linking
- When a fairy dies he is reincarnated within 1d4 months
- May cast a Faerie Phantom spell once per day
- At fifth level they may cast a Minor Sphere of Perturbation spell once per day

Initial Languages:
Common, elvish, gnomish, butterfly, bird, pixie fairy*

Talents:
- Turn invisible once per day.

Allowable Classes:
Cleric, fighter, berserker, cavalier, knight errant, magic-user, illusionist, or thief (Level restrictions apply. See Table 2C.)

Allowable Multi-Classes:
Fighter/magic-user

Attribute Modifiers:
+1 Intelligence, +1 Wisdom, +2 Dexterity; -6 Strength; +2 Charisma; +3 Comeliness

Building Point Bonus: 14

Additional Talents Which May be Purchased:
Acrobatic Skill Suite, Acute Alertness, Ambidextrous, Astute Observation, Attack Bonus, Blind Fighting, Faerie Kind Martial Arts, Flutter, Hit Point Bonus, Keen Sight, Magic Bonus

The Downside
- Pixie fairies must pay 3 times the gp value for their daily food requirements unless they forage for their food
- They have a very short life span — generally only ten to fifteen years
- Pixie fairies don't get the twenty hit point-kicker other characters receive at first level, instead they receive only a 10 hit point kicker
- They also only get half the hit points rolled for each level (rounded up)

*The number of languages a pixie fairy can learn is limited by his Intelligence (see Table 1D) or by the Building Points/training he devotes to language.

Table 2F: Pixie Fairy Tribal Tattoos				
Type/Name	Effects	Location	Penalty	BP COST*
Ardkrin	+1 AC against all melee attacks	Upper Arm	-1 CON	5
Shewkrin	+1 AC against all missile attacks	Lower Arm	-1 CON	5
Yiskrin	+1 to Charisma	Forehead	-1 CON	2
Tarkrin	Diminish Evil**	any area	-1 CON	10
Fakrin	Detect Evil***	any area	-1 CON	5
Emphkrin	Detect Living Creature****	Forehead	0	0
Shunkrin	+1 to All Saves	Forehead	-2 CON	10
Hurdkrin	+1 to Hit Points (per level)	Upper Arm	-1 CON	10
Grekrin(2 slots)	+2 to Strength	Lower Arm (both L & R)	-1 CON	15
Gorkrink	+1 to Damage	Upper Arm	-1 CON	10

* BP Cost: Pixie fairy characters can use Building Points during the character creation process to purchase beginning tattoos. Tattoos purchased with Building Points result in only 50% of the total Constitution penalty (rounded up) taking place.
** Gives −2 to all attacks from evil creatures.
*** Works like the spell of the same name.
**** This tattoo is free to pixie fairies and gives them their telepathic ability, which prevents them from being surprised.
Notes:
Grunge elves who eat pixie fairies are allowed to use tribal tattoos. See the grel description for details.
Only one tattoo of each type/name is allowed.

Pixie Meet/The Running:

Once every six years all pixie fairies must make a pilgrimage of sorts back to the Village of the Elders – the traditional founding village/homeland of their particular clan – for a week-long festival. The journey to the Meet is a dangerous time for pixie fairies because grunge elves take advantage of the huge migration to lie in wait and ambush the weak folk (who they eat in order to make use of their magical energies).

The festival culminates with all the attendees pooling their magic into the Amber Horde (See Hacklopedia of Beasts: Pixie Fairy). Afterwards, all the pooled magical energy is returned in the form of shares. The amount of magical energy each pixie fairy gets back is based on his current Honor and level relative to the other pixie fairies participating. This process has no effect on the character in game terms. It is a matter of tradition and paying homage to the clan. However, any pixie fairy who chooses not to attend Pixie Meet suffers an immediate loss of 50% of his Honor for offending his racial/tribal peers.

Combat: Pixie fairies normally use weapons sized to their own stature. When using such a weapon, a pixie fairy may attack while mounted at no penalty. Pixie fairies get a +2 bonus to hit in mounted combat or flying combat. They also receive a +1 bonus on any joust or charge attacks.

Getting Around: Pixie fairies generally have wings. All pixie fairies with wings are capable of flying and may do so with a normal unencumbered movement rate of 18". Pixie fairies can walk at a rate of 4", so obviously they prefer to fly. Many pixie fairies also ride giant butterfly mounts. A mounted pixie fairy can travel at a rate of 26" when mounted on a giant butterfly and 36" when mounted on a giant moth.

Special Abilities: All pixie fairies have the following innate abilities because of their magical natures:
  First level – May cast Faerie Phantom spell once per day.
  Fifth Level – May cast Minor Sphere of Perturbation spell once per day.

Tribal Tattoo Magic

Pixie fairies are allowed to use a special form of magic called tribal tattoo magic. Such tattoos serve as focal points which allow the pixie fairy to draw from his own inherent magical energies to achieve perpetual spell-like results. Because the tattoos draw their power directly from the pixie fairy there is a significant drawback: each tattoo permanently removes a point or more of the pixie fairy's Constitution.

Pixie fairy characters may have as many tattoos as they have slots available (one tattoo per slot, six total slots). Slot locations are as follows; forehead (two slots), upper arm (left), upper arm (right), lower arm (left), lower arm (right). Certain tattoo types can only go in a specific slot. Once a tattoo has been placed it cannot be removed and replaced with another.

Tattoos do not transcend the reincarnation process and are thus lost when a pixie fairy dies.

Warning: Pixie fairy tattoos continue to function when the character dies. Thus it is possible to skin a pixie fairy and, if the tattoo isn't damaged in the

process, magical items can be made from the cured skin/leather. This is something grels and other races have discovered and often take advantage of. A pair of Shewkrin Gloves makes the perfect gift for that ranger-type person in your life. And a tattooed pixie fairy arm makes an excellent wand.

Obtaining Tattoos: Tattoos may be purchased with BPs during the character creation process (in which case only half the total CON penalty is suffered (round up). Otherwise any 6th level pixie fairy can apply tribal tattoos to himself, other pixie fairies or even grels if compelled through force or threat of bodily harm – never voluntarily. Special inks must be used. These can be prepared by any pixie fairy but require the ashes from a cremated Treant's remains and the blood of an Aarnz Hound. Other tattoo ink formulas can be concocted, but its up to the GM to decide if the mixture works. Therefore, you leave yourself open for a royal hose-job from the screen-monkey, so don't try to get the Treant/Aarnz formula unless you're really desperate. A Gorecupine quill must be used as the needling-agent.

Pixie Dust

Because pixie fairies literally ooze with magic, when their sweat dries on their skin it flakes off in small dandruff-like golden particles known as Pixie Dust. A roving adventurer pixie fairy generally doesn't produce enough Pixie Dust to have any real value or use. However, if a pixie fairy sleeps and grooms himself in the same area on a routine basis (such as in a cage), it will accumulate enough Pixie Dust to make harvesting and gathering it of some value to anyone willing to spend the time scraping it up and selling it.

Woodland Thrall

At fifth level, a pixie fairy may call a woodland creature to become its thrall once per week. The summoned creature serves the pixie fairy for 1d20 days and then returns to the wild. While in the pixie fairy's service, the woodland thrall obeys any command (to the limits of its abilities) the pixie fairy gives it — including giving its life. For example, a pixie fairy with a squirrel as a thrall could order the squirrel to leap into the face of a magic-user casting a spell and the squirrel would do it (even though it would certainly mean his death once the magic-user recovers from the surprise). Your GM has the details on thrall-summoning.

Player Character Classes

After choosing your character's race the next major step is to select his character class. What's a character class you say? Well, think of it as your character's chosen profession or career. It's what your character has devoted most of his time and energy training at in the years prior to entering the game. Remember, as adventurers, player characters stand out from the rest the world. They have that little extra something which has equipped them for the life of a hero. Perhaps it a sense of purpose. Or maybe it's just an unshakable belief that they're going to break away from the humdrum existence shared by their peers and do something epic.

For whatever reason your character has that extra bit of drive and determination which has allowed him to rise up above the ranks of zero-leveldom and obtain 1st level.

Incidentally, it is at this juncture in your character's life that the two of you (player and character) meet — that moment where he's set his eye on the future and is about to strike out on his own. But what brought him to this moment of clarity? The explanations are numerous. Perhaps his father was killed by a vile rouge-orc and revenge was the catalyst. Or, maybe, the rumors of a distant war spurred on by a noble cause have drawn the character out of the crowd. Whatever the reason, it is certain he spent the greater part of his formative years preparing himself for the call by working hard at various endeavors and readying himself for adulthood and eventually the life of an adventurer. When you choose a character class you are further defining just who your character is and how he plans on making his way in the world.

Let's take Karnack the magic-user as an example. Now Karnack didn't just wake up one morning, roll out of bed and announce, "Eureka! I'm a magic user!" How absurd. He would have started down such a career path years before through careful study and preparation. In Karnack's case, he was a young scrap of a lad when his father took him to the summer festivals in the grand imperial city of Goremonya.

Once there, his father left him in the care of a street entertainer while he raced off to gamble the family's fortune away at the Blink Dawg fights. For hours young Karnack sat mesmerized as a third-rate mage performed simple illusions and parlor tricks for the amusement of the wide eyed children left in his care.

Karnak was enthralled with what he saw. His interest piqued, he followed the mage after his performance back to his tent. He begged the old man to show him how the tricks were done. He insisted on knowing the secret. How did the old man make the town crier disappear and then reappear in the nude? To the mage's surprise, he discovered the young Karnack had a mind for things magic and showed great promise. He took the youth under his wing and made

arrangements with Karnack's father to let the boy come work for him for six months as an apprentice.

As the years passed, Karnack hit the books for hours each day. He struggled with the mental disciplines and wrestled with concepts that strained the limits of his understanding. It was a hard, arduous effort but slowly, step by step he acquired the skills and built the foundation of knowledge and wisdom required for him to eventually learn the secrets of the arcane. Where countless other apprentices before him came up lacking, Karnack proved he had what it took to be a magic-user.

As it is for most of the character classes in HackMaster. Your character is assumed to have completed a great deal of prerequisite training and guidance before beginning his adventuring career. Now, armed with that knowledge, your character feels he has learned all he can from his teachers and mentors. Filled with confidence and swelled with pride, he feels he is ready to strike out on his own and make a name for himself.

Character Class Groupings

The character classes are divided into five basic groups according to general occupations: fighter, magic-user, cleric, thief and HackMaster. Within each group are several sub classes, which represent some type of specialization. All classes within a group share the same combat and saving throw progressions. Each character class within a group has different special powers and abilities that are available only to that class. Each player must select a specific character class or subclass. [Note: Be sure to pay attention to racial limitations and restrictions when choosing a class.]

Fighter, magic-user, cleric, and thief are the standard classes. They are historical and legendary archetypes that are common to many different cultures. Thus, they are appropriate to any sort of HackMaster game campaign. The HackMaster classes are restricted. They can only be obtained through game play (i.e. you cannot choose to become one, you have to earn it).

Fighter Classes

There are nine subclasses of the fighter group: fighter, barbarian, berserker, cavalier, dark knight, knight errant, monk, paladin and ranger. All are well trained in the use of weapons and/or skilled in the martial arts. The following is a brief thumbnail of each class;

Fighter: The basic fighter is the backbone of any good HackMaster campaign. He represents the individual disciplined in the battle arts such as the champion, swordsman, soldier and brawler. Fighters live or die by their knowledge of weapons and tactics. They can be found wherever the clashing of swords can be heard, at the front of any battle, contesting toe-to-toe with monsters and villains or serving as a protector of a small village that pays him well for his services. A good fighter needs to be strong and healthy if he hopes to survive.

Barbarian: The barbarian is adept at the many skills necessary for survival in a hostile, uncivilized wilderness. Barbarians are tough and unusually hardy.

Berserker: The berserker is a fighter who is wired for battle rage. They fight as normal fighters but under certain circumstances (such as taking large amounts of damage or when dealing out the same to others) they are prone to going berserk and being transformed into an unstoppable butchering machine. Mortal combat is so engrained in the mind of the berserker that he must engage in it every day or risk losing his status, as well as hit points, attribute points and even Honor.

	Table 3A:			
	Character Class Groupings			
Fighter Group	**Magic-User Group**	**Cleric Group**	**Thief Group**	**HackMaster Class***
Fighter	Magic-user	Cleric	Thief	HackFighter
Barbarian	Illusionist	Druid	Bard	HackMage
Berserker	Battle mage		Assassin	HacKleric
Cavalier	Blood mage			Hackssassin
Dark knight				
Knight errant				
Monk				
Paladin				
Ranger				

* HackMaster is a progression class and is restricted. Beginning characters cannot choose to be HackMaster class characters.

FRAIM

to magical research. A magic-user must rely on knowledge and wit to survive. Magic-users are rarely seen adventuring without a retinue of fighters and men-at-arms.

Magic-user: The basic magic-user studies all types of magic and learns a wide variety of spells. His broad range makes him well suited to the demands of adventuring.

Battle Mage: The battle mage is perhaps the most respected (and feared) of magic-users. The name of the class says it all. These battle-hardened individuals focus on a special form of mental discipline that allows them to cast spells in the thick of combat with little chance of mishap or interruption. Battle mages have access to all magic-user spells but when it comes to battle spells (those of the missile or Fireball variety as well as most spells either offensive or defensive in nature) they are second to none.

Blood Mage: The deadly blood mage is an optional magic-user specialist class, not detailed in this book. The blood mage, or necromancer, approaches and practices magic in a somewhat unorthodox manner. Instead of drawing errant magical energies from without and channeling them, the blood mage derives his power and casts his spells by drawing upon the life-energies of his own body (and of those around him). Most magic-users consider this a very reckless and dangerous practice and blood mages are shunned by mages from other schools of thought.

Illusionist: The illusionist is another example of a magic-user specialist. The illusionist spends his studies practicing illusion and phantasm magic. While the traditional magic-user (generalist) can cast the same spells as the illusionist, illusionists excel far beyond a magic-user within their specialty. This excellence in illusion-type magic bears a cost. They cannot cast quite the variety of spells that other magic-users can, and they cannot learn spells outside of illusory spells as easily as a magic-user of like intelligence.

Cleric Classes

A cleric sees to the spiritual needs of a community, race, or location.

Cleric: The cleric is a generic cleric (of any mythos) who tends to the needs of a community. He is both protector and healer. He is not purely defensive, however. When evil threatens, the cleric is well suited to seek it out on its own ground and destroy it.

Cavalier: The cavalier is a knight in service to some gawd, noble, order or special cause. Though not necessarily of good alignment, the cavalier is usually of noble or aristocratic origin.

Dark Knight: The dark knight is the antithesis of the paladin, a conniving and dastardly warrior, a symbol of all that is wicked and wrong in the world. Like the paladin he is a man of purpose but he doesn't fight for good — rather he tirelessly fights against it.

Knight Errant: Knights errant are glory hounds similar to cavaliers but they owe no allegiance to gawds, noble orders or special causes. Rather they fight for their own personal egos and for their own selfish reasons — usually to exact vengeance or to settle a hereditary grudge against an enemy. They are knights with a single mindedness. Though technically of good alignment they are allowed to use evil means to achieve their aims as long as the end result is good.

Monk: Monks are students who spend their lives practicing martial arts of the body. As such, they rely very little on armor and weapons and can gain special abilities related to their attunement of mind and spirit.

Paladin: The paladin is a warrior bold and pure, the exemplar of everything good and true. Like the fighter, the paladin is a man of combat but also a man of Honor. The paladin lives for the ideals of righteousness, justice, honesty, piety, and chivalry. He strives to be a living example of these virtues so that others might learn from him as well as gain by his actions.

Ranger: The ranger is a warrior and a woodsman. He is skilled with weapons and is knowledgeable in tracking and woodcraft. The ranger often protects and guides lost travelers and honest peasant-folk. A ranger needs to be strong and wise to the ways of nature to live a full life.

Magic-User Classes

The magic-user strives to be a master of magical energies, shaping them and casting them as spells. To do so, he studies strange tongues and obscure facts and devotes much of his time

Table 3B: Hit Dice, Spell Ability, and Class Level Limit				
Class of Character	Hit Die Type	Maximum # Hit Dice	Spell Ability	Class Level Limit	BP Bonus
CLERIC	d8	9	yes	none	10
Druid	d8	14	yes	23 (Hierophant of the Cabal)	10
FIGHTER	d10	9	no	none	10
Barbarian	d12	8	no	none	7
Berserker	d12	8	no	none	8
Cavalier	d12	10	no	none	10
Dark Knight	d10	9	yes	none	12
Knight Errant	d10	9	no	none	5
Monk	d6	22	no	21 (S.G.D.M.otF.S.W.)	12
Paladin	d10	9	yes*	none	12
Ranger	d8	11	yes**	none	10
MAGIC-USER	d4	11	yes	none	9
Battle mage	d4	10	yes	none	8
Blood mage	d4	11	yes	none	11
Illusionist	d4	10	yes	none	9
THIEF	d6	10	no***	none	12
Assassin	d6	15	no***	none	9
Bard	d6	10	yes****	none	8
HACKMASTER*****					
HackFighter	Special	Special	Special	none	NA
HackMage	Special	Special	Special	none	NA
HacKleric	Special	Special	Special	none	NA
HackSsassin	Special	Special	Special	none	NA

* Clerical spell ability up to 4th level spells, first gained at 9th level.
** Druid spell ability up to 3rd level spells, first gained at 8th level; and magic-user spell ability up to 2nd level, first gained at 9th level.
*** At 10th level (12th level with regard to assassins) thieves gain the ability to read magic-user (and illusionist) spells from scrolls.
**** Some of the affects of bard songs resemble the effects of spells.
***** Information on the HackMaster Classes is player restricted.

Table 3C: **Armor and Weapons Permitted by Class**				
Class of Character	Armor	Shield	Weapons*	Oil
CLERIC	any	any	club, flail, hammer, mace, staff****	yes
Druid	leather/padded	wooden	club, dagger, dart, hammer, scimitar, sling, spear, staff	yes
FIGHTER	any	any	any	yes
Berserker	any	none	any	yes
Barbarian	any	any	any	yes
Cavalier	any	any	any	no
Dark Knight	any	any	any	yes
Knight Errant	any	none	only melee weapons	siege use only
Monk	robes/garments	none	club, crossbow, dagger, hand axe, javelin, pole arm, spear, staff	no
Paladin	any	any	any	no
Ranger	any	any,	any**	yes
MAGIC-USER	robes/garments	none	dagger, dart, staff	yes
Battle mage	any	none	dagger, short sword, staff	yes
Blood mage	robes/garments	none	dagger, dart, staff	yes
Illusionist	robes/garments	none	dagger, dart, staff	yes
THIEF	any up to studded leather or elven chain mail	none	club, dagger, dart, sling, sword***	yes
Assassin	leather	any	any	yes
Bard	any up to chainmail	none	club, dagger, dart, javelin, sling, scimitar, spear, staff, bastard sword, broad sword, long sword, short sword	yes
HACKMASTER				
HackFighter	any	none	any	yes
HackMage	any	none	dagger, dart, short sword, staff	yes
HacKleric	any	any	club, flail, hammer, mace, staff	yes
HackSsassin	leather	any	any	yes

   * This heading includes any magical weapons of the type named unless use by the class in question is specifically proscribed in the description of the magic weapon.

   ** Characters under 5' height cannot employ the longbow or any weapon over 12' in length. Those under 100 pounds of body weight cannot use the heavy crossbow or pole arms in excess of 200 gold piece weight equivalent, including two-handed swords.

   *** A thief may use a short sword, broadsword, or longsword but not a bastard sword or a two-handed sword.

   **** Clerics might be allowed different weapons depending upon their deity.

Druid: The druid serves the cause of nature and neutrality; the wilderness is his community. He uses his special powers to protect it and to preserve balance in the world.

Thief Classes

The thief can be found throughout the world, wherever people gather and money changes hands. While many thieves are motivated only by a desire to amass fortune in the easiest way possible, some thieves have noble aims; they use their skills to correct injustice, spread good will, or contribute to the success of an adventuring group.

Thief: To accomplish his goals, for good or ill, the thief is a skilled pilferer. Cunning, nimbleness and stealth are his hallmarks. Whether he turns his talent against innocent passersby and wealthy merchants or oppressors and monsters is a choice for the thief to make.

Assassin: The assassin is trained for one simple purpose: stealthy killing of individuals. Like a thief they are skilled in stealth and nimbleness but focus more on the art of stealing lives over stealing possessions.

Bard: The bard is also a thief, but with a twist. His strength is his pleasant and charming personality. With it and his wits he makes his way through the world. A bard is a talented musician and a walking storehouse of gossip, tall tales, and lore. He learns a little bit about everything that crosses his path; he is a jack-of-all-trades but master of none. While many bards are scoundrels, their stories and songs are welcome almost everywhere. They are also adept at confidence games and running scams.

HackMaster Classes (Restricted)

The HackMasters are a special suite of classes reserved for those characters of incredibly high Honor who have proven themselves worthy of the title before both the gawds and fellow members of their race. These fearsome char-

acters are the namesake for the HackMaster game and the series of novels that inspired it. One does not choose to be a HackMaster, he is chosen (called). HackMasters are heroes in the truest sense of the word and are usually called forth during times of great crisis and global peril. They are world savers — no longer in charge of their own destinies but owned by history. They are the stuff legends are woven from. Making the cut is extremely difficult.

HackMasters represent characters who have entered into one of several Secret Organizations/Mysteries to further their training and answer a higher calling. The infamous HackMasters of Everknight were a group of such warriors who turned back the tide of evil during the Night of Long Shadows (Evernight) and gave the forces of good time enough to rally and win the war. (They enjoyed enormous popularity until their drunken escapades eventually turned the mobs against them.)

The specifics of these classes is restricted and presented in the HackMaster GameMaster's Guide. Your GM will provide that information to you on a need-to-know basis. However, to whet your appetite and give you something to shoot for, a thumbnail description of the each HackMaster class follows.

There are four HackMaster classes. One for each of the standard character classes.

HackFighter: The HackFighter is a true master of the Art of Hack, like the berserker, he can HackFrenzy and HackLust to become an unstoppable butchering machine. Even better, he can bestow this power on those who fight by his side. Legend has it that armies have fallen under the hands of but a single HackFighter. Whereas fallen fighters have bridges and roads named after them, the fallen HackFighter has cities and nations named in his honor.

HackMage: The HackMage is a magic-user with powers that stagger the imagination. These powerful mages have special abilities such as improved simulcasting, chain casting, spell frenzy and spell jacking. Membership in this prestigious class is limited to the very best. A magic-user must first obtain membership in one of the secret magic societies (i.e. the Circle of Sequestered Magicks, the Black Hands etc.) before they can even hope of becoming a HackMage.

HacKleric: These distinguished warrior-clerics have been handpicked by their patron gawds to promote their work on Garweeze Wurld. Charged with winning converts, building temples and fighting the enemies of the faith the HacKleric's job is among the most dangerous and harrowing to be found since he is bound to draw the ire of other gawds, demons

Table 3D: **Class Ability Requirements**							
Character Class	Str	Dex	Con	Int	Wis	Cha	Com
Fighter	9	--	--	--	--	--	--
Barbarian	15	14	15	--	<17	--	--
Berserker	17	--	15	--	--	--	--
Cavalier	15	15	15	10	10	--	9
Dark Knight	12	--	12	--	13	17	--
Knight Errant	14	--	--	--	13	17	15
Monk	12	15	11	12	15	--	--
Paladin	12	--	9	--	13	17	--
Ranger	13	13	14	--	14	--	--
Magic-User	--	--	--	9	--	--	--
Battle Mage	12	12	12	9	--	--	--
Blood Mage	--	--	16	9	15	--	--
Illusionist	--	16	--	9	--	--	--
Cleric	--	--	--	--	9	--	--
Druid	--	--	--	12	15	--	--
Thief	--	9	--	--	--	--	--
Assassin	12	12	--	11	--	--	--
Bard	--	12	--	13	--	15	12
HackFighter*	18	--	--	--	--	16	--
HackMage*	--	--	--	18	--	16	--
HacKleric*	--	--	--	--	18	16	--
HackSsassin*	12	18	11	12	15	16	--

   * The HackMaster Classes are a progression-class and are restricted. A character must progress to the required levels and meet all prerequisites as well as make a successful 'called' roll before obtaining study in these classes.

and their agents. To equip the HacKleric for his mission he has been bestowed with special awe-inspiring powers from the gawds themselves.

HackSsassin: The HackSsassin is powerful hybrid with thief, assassin and monk abilities. They often abandon their given names to take on names that emote fear in others. (Such as Death Whisper, Death Lurking, Shadow Warrior, etc.) While the HackFighter is a master of the art of hack, the Hackssassin is a master of stealth and quick death.

Notes Regarding Character Class Table 3B:

Class of Character is self-explanatory. Multi-classes have been omitted, but certain facts pertaining to them are given hereafter.

Hit Dice Type shows the type of die to be rolled by a character of the appropriate class at each level of experience he has gained so as to determine how many hit points the character has. Multi-classed characters determine their hit points as follows:

1. Roll the hit die (or dice) appropriate to each class the character is professing.
2. Total the sum of all dice rolled, and add constitution bonus for each die rolled.
3. Divide the total by the character's classes (two or three), dropping fractions under 1/2, rounding fractions of 1/2 or greater up to the next whole number.
4. The number derived (quotient) is the number of hit points the multi-classed character gains with the rise in that experience level.

Maximum Number of Hit Dice assumes that the character has no racial limitation to prevent rise commensurate with the number of hit dice. Note that additional hit points are still gained with increase in level, even though no additional hit dice can be, in those cases where there is no class (or race) level limit.

Spell Ability simply indicates whether or not the class of character is able to employ spells.

Class Level Limit tells how high in levels the character can progress in the class in question. As shown, most character classes do not have any upper limit, although racial limitations might affect non-human or demi-human characters.

Building Point Bonus indicates how many building points the class contributes to the character background process (See Chapter 4: Character Priors).

Class Ability Score Requirements

Each of the character classes has minimum scores in various abilities. A character must satisfy these minimums to be of that class. If your character's scores are too low for him to belong to any character class, ask your GM for permission to raise one of them to the minimum required in order to qualify for a class or to create an entirely new character. If you desperately want your character to belong to a particular class, but have scores that are too low, you should use the Ability Score adjustment techniques described in Chapter 1 to try to get your character to qualify for the desired class.

Character Class Descriptions

The complete character class descriptions that follow give the specific, detailed information you need about each class. These are organized according to groups. Information that applies to the entire group is presented at the start of the section. Each character class within the group is then explained.

The descriptions use game terms that may be unfamiliar to you; many of these are explained in this text (or you may look the terms up in the Glossary).

Ability Requirements: The minimum scores in the listed abilities that the character must possess in order to choose that particular character class.

Prime Requisite: The ability score or scores that are most important to a particular class. A fighter must be strong and a magic-user must be intelligent; their prime requisites, therefore, are Strength and Intelligence, respectively. Some character classes have more than one prime requisite. Any character who has a score of 16 or more in all his prime requisites gains a 10% bonus to his experience point awards.

Hit Dice Type: The type of die the player gets to roll each level as the character advances to determine how many new hit points he receives.

Allowed Races: Races that can choose this particular character class. If your race isn't listed you can't choose this class. (Unless of course the word 'any' appears in this block.)

Allowed Alignments: Indicates which alignments the characters of this class can be. Many classes such as the paladin or dark knight are restricted to a particular alignment(s).

Building Point Bonus: How many building points (BPs) you receive for selecting this class. These are added to your starting building points (and any BPs you received for your race).

Progression Table: Each class has its own unique progression table with the following information.

Experience Points: A measure of what a character has learned and how he has improved his skill during the course of his adventures. Characters earn experience points by completing adventures, acquiring treasure, killing monsters and by doing things specifically related to their class. Characters accumulate experience points from adventure to adventure. When they accumulate enough, they rise to the next level of experience, gaining additional abilities and powers. The progression tables for each character group list the total, accumulated experience points needed to reach each level.

Note that advancement is not automatic. You must spend the required amount of time and money training before rising to the next experience level. Your GM will tell you the requirements for advancement when the time comes.

Level: A measure of the character's power. A beginning character starts at 1st level. To advance to the next level, the character must earn a requisite number of experience points and complete the required training. Different character classes improve at different rates. Each increase in level improves the character's survivability and skills.

Title: Each experience level has its own name or title

The Fighter Classes

The fighter classes encompass the character classes of heroes who make their way in the world primarily by skill at arms: fighters, barbarians, berserkers, cavaliers, dark knights, knights errant, monks, paladins, and rangers. Fighters are allowed to use any weapon though certain classes favor training in a specific weapon(s) or weapon type(s). All save the monk can wear any type of armor. The disadvantage fighters have is that they are restricted in their selection of magical items and spells.

All fighters gain the ability to make more than one melee attack per round as they rise in level. Table 3E shows how many melee attacks most types of fighters can make per round, as a function of their levels. See Table 3T for monk characters.

The principal attribute of a fighter is Strength. To become a fighter, a character must have a minimum Strength score of 9. A good Dexterity rating is also useful when trying to dodge a freakin' two-handed-sword being swung at your head. A fighter who has a Strength score (his prime requisite) of 16 or more gains a 10% bonus to the experience points he earns. Also, high Strength gives the fighter a better chance to hit an opponent and enables him to cause more damage.

The fighter is an expert in weapons and, if he is clever, tactics and strategy. He lives knowing that death always lingers near. One bad fumble, one ill-timed miss with his blade could mean curtains for the fighter. For that reason fighters live hard and fast. They don't have time for whiners or for those who don't share their love of a good fight. And they make no apologies for living by their swords.

Fighters can have any alignment: good or evil, lawful or chaotic, or neutral. The concepts of Honor and glory mean more to fighters than most. In fact

> ### Fighter
> **Ability Requirements:**
> Strength 9
> **Prime Requisite:**
> Strength [gain 10% ep bonus if Str is 16 or higher]
> **Hit Dice Type:**
> d10
> **Allowed Races:**
> All
> **Allowed Alignments:**
> Any (as long as chosen racial type allows it)
> **Building Point Bonus:**
> 10 BP

such notions drive them to do things that those not familiar in the art of hack can truly understand. Fighters share a bond with others of their profession — even those who oppose them. The warrior tradition seems to be universal and it is not uncommon for great warriors to look across the battlefield and exchange bows of respect before engaging in mortal combat.

As a master of weapons, the fighter is the only character able to have weapon specialization and weapon mastery. (See Chapter 7). Weapon specialization enables the fighter to use a particular weapon with exceptional skill, improving his chances to hit and cause greater damage with that weapon. A fighter character is not required to specialize in a weapon; the choice is up to the play-

Table 3E: Fighter Melee Attacks per Round				
Fighter Level	Barbarian, Berserker, Cavalier Level	Dark Knight, Knight Errant Paladin Level	Ranger Level	Attacks/Round
1-6	1-5	1-6	1-7	1/round
7-12	6-10	7-11	8-14	3/2 rounds
13-18	11-15	11-17	15+	2/round
19+	16+	18+		5/2 rounds

er. But it is a great advantage you should consider for no other character class, not even ranger or paladin, is allowed weapon specialization and mastery.

While fighters cannot cast magical spells, they can use many magical items, including potions, protection scrolls, most rings, and all forms of enchanted armor, weapons, and shields.

When a fighter attains 9th level (becomes a "Lord"), he has a chance of attracting men-at-arms (followers). These soldiers, having heard of the fighter's great feats, come for the chance to gain fame, adventure, and cash. They are loyal as long as they are well treated, successful, and paid well. Abusive treatment or a disastrous campaign will likely lead to grumbling, desertion, and possibly mutiny. To attract the men, the fighter must have a castle or stronghold

Table 3F: Fighter Progression Table			
Experience Points	Experience Level	10-Sided Dice for Accumulated Hit Points	Level Title
0-2,000	1	20 +1d10*	Veteran
2,001-4,000	2	2	Warrior
4,001-8,000	3	3	Swordsman
8,001-18,000	4	4	Hero
18,001-35,000	5	5	Swashbuckler
35,001-70,000	6	6	Myrmidon
70,001-125,000	7	7	Champion
125,001-250,000	8	8	Superhero
250,001-500,000	9	9**	Lord
500,001-750,000	10	9+3	Lord (10th Level)
750,001-1,000,000***	11	9+6	Lord (11th Level)

* At first level fighters receive 20 points + 1d10. This twenty-point 'kicker' is received at first level only.

** Fighters gain 3 h.p. per level after the 9th.

*** 250,000 experience points per level for each additional level beyond the 11th.

and sizeable manor lands around it. Both the fighter's Honor and Fame factors will influence how many, and what caliber of followers he attracts.

As he claims and rules this land, soldiers journey to his domain, thereby increasing his power. Furthermore, the fighter can tax and develop these lands, gaining a steady income from them. Your GM has information about gaining and running a barony.

In addition to regular men-at-arms, the 9th-level fighter also attracts an elite bodyguard (his "household guards"). Although these soldiers are still mercenaries, they have greater loyalty to their Lord than do common soldiers. In return, they expect better treatment and more pay than the common soldier receives. Again your Honor and Fame Factors will influence what type of men you attract and how quickly you gain them.

A fighter can hold property, including a castle or stronghold, long before he reaches 9th level. However, it is only when he reaches this level that his name is so widely known that he automatically attracts the loyalty of other Fighters. If a fighter below 9th level achieves a Fame factor of 100 or more (see Chapter 5)

Table 3G: Fighter's Followers		
Roll percentile dice and add your Honor die on each of the following sub-tables of Table 3G: once for the leader of the troops, once for troops, and once for a bodyguard (household guards) unit.		
Die Roll	Leader (and suggested magical items)	
01-40	5th-level fighter, plate mail, shield, battle axe +2	
41-75	5th-level fighter, plate mail, shield +1, spear +1, dagger +1	
76-90	6th-level fighter, plate mail +1, shield, spear +1, dagger +1, plus 3rd-level fighter, splint mail, shield, Crossbow of Distance	
91-99	7th-level fighter, plate mail +1, shield +1, broad sword +2, heavy war horse with Horseshoes of Speed	
00	GM's Option	

Die Roll	Troops/Followers (all 0th-level)	
01-50	20 cavalry with ring mail, shield, 3 javelins, long sword, hand axe; 100 infantry with scale mail, polearm*, club	
51-75	20 infantry with splint mail, morning star, hand axe; 60 infantry with leather armor, pike, short sword	
76-90	40 infantry with chain mail, heavy crossbow, short sword; 20 infantry with chain mail, light crossbow, military fork	
91-99	10 cavalry with banded mail, shield, lance, bastard sword, mace; 20 cavalry with scale mail, shield, lance, long sword, mace; 30 cavalry with studded leather armor, shield, lance, long sword	
00	GM's Option (Barbarians, headhunters, armed peasants, extra-heavy cavalry, etc.)	

*Player selects type.

Die Roll	Elite Units	
01-10	10 mounted knights; 1st-level fighters with field plate, large shield, lance, broadsword, morning star, and heavy war horse with full barding	
11-30	10 1st-level elven fighter/magic-users with chain mail, longsword, long bow, dagger	
31-40	20 Berserkers: 2nd-level fighters with leather armor, shield, battle axe, broadsword	
41-65	20 expert archers: 1st-level fighters with studded leather armor, long bows or crossbows (+2 to hit, or bow specialization)	
66-99	30 infantry: 1st-level fighters with plate mail, body shield, spear, short sword	
00	GM's Option (pegasi cavalry, eagle riders, demi-humans, siege train, etc.)	

and keeps a stronghold, he can also attract followers by rolling on Table 3G in the same way a 9th level fighter may.

Barbarians

The barbarian class is a sub-class of fighter. Barbarian characters are adept at the many skills necessary for survival in a hostile wilderness. These skills include rapid movement, climbing, use of many weapons, certain "sixth senses" and many secondary and tertiary abilities. Barbarians are tough and hardy, and recover quickly from damage. A barbarian must have strength and constitution scores of no less than 15 each, a dexterity score of 14 or better, and a wisdom score of no greater than 16. The barbarian is considered to have no principal attribute, and as such does not gain any bonus to earned experience points. A player character barbarian cannot be a character with two classes.

Barbarian

Ability Requirements:
Strength 15+, Constitution 15+, Dexterity 14+, Wisdom <17

Prime Requisite:
None

Hit Dice Type:
d12

Allowed Races:
Human, Grel, Half-orcs, Half-ogres, Halflings

Allowed Alignments:
any non-lawful alignment

Building Point Bonus:
7 BP

Barbarians gain a bonus to their armor class of double their Dex bonus, but only if the armor worn is not of the fairly bulky or bulky type. If fairly bulky or bulky armor is worn, the bonus is normal. The reaction/attacking adjustment remains the same for the barbarian's Dexterity. In addition, barbarians gain double the normal Con bonus for hit points.

Barbarians can be of any non-lawful alignment. They do not use alignment language of any sort, however, and initially the barbarian knows only how to speak his racial or tribal tongue and the common tongue. A barbarian must learn how to read and write if he desires these skills. A barbarian can learn languages according to his Intelligence, just as any other character can.

Barbarians are tough and hardy fighters, hardened by the savage lands of their birth. They have 12-sided hit dice and receive a +3 to their base movement rate. (A human barbarian would have a base movement of 15. A halfling barbarian would have a base movement of 9.)

They use the combat tables for normal fighters, and may use any sort of weapon, shield and armor. The initial number of weapons the barbarian uses must include the hand axe, knife, and spear. Additional weapons based upon the barbarian's native area will be chosen by the GM.

Barbarians in general detest magic and those who use it. They will, at low levels of experience, refuse to employ any sort of magic item if they recognize it as such. They will often seek to destroy magic items, and if successful they receive an experience-point award as if they possessed the destroyed items. While magic-users will be shunned initially, and always viewed with suspicion,

Table 3H: Barbarian Progression Table			
Experience Points	Exp. Level	12-Sided Dice for Accumulated Hit Points	Level Title
0-6,000	1	20+1d12*	Barbarian
6,001-12,000	2	2	Barbarian
12,001-24,000	3	3	Barbarian
24,001-48,000	4	4	Barbarian
48,001-80,000	5	5	Barbarian
80,001-150,000	6	6	Barbarian
150,001-275,000	7	7	Barbarian
275,001-500,000	8	8**	Barbarian
500,001-1,000,000	9	8+4	Barbarian
1,000,001-1,500,000	10	8+8	Barbarian
1,500,001-2,000,000***	11	8+12	Chairman of the Horde

* At first level barbarians receive 20 points + 1d12. This twenty point 'kicker' is received at first level only.
** Barbarians gain 4 hps per level after the 8th.
*** 500,000 experience points per level for each additional level above the 11th.

cleric spells of the type used by shamans and witch doctors are not so viewed, though high level cleric spells are suspect.

A barbarian's natural attack abilities allow him to strike creatures that would normally be immune to non-magical attacks as the barbarian rises in level. At 4th level the barbarian can affect creatures which require a + 1 or better weapon to hit, while a 6th-level barbarian can strike creatures which require a + 3 weapon to hit. Similarly, at 8th level, the barbarian can hit creatures requiring a + 5 weapon to hit, and at 10th level can hurt creatures requiring a + 7 weapon to hit. At 12th level, a barbarian can affect creatures harmed normally only by weapons of + 9 or better. The barbarian, despite the ability to hit such creatures, does not gain a bonus "to hit" or inflict additional damage because of this ability. Only barbarians have this ability among all the player character classes.

All barbarians have the following bonuses to their saving throws: They are + 4 versus poison, + 3 versus paralyzation, death magic, petrification, and polymorph, and + 2 versus rod, staff and wand and breath weapon. Barbarians gain no benefit to their saving throw versus spell at start, but gain a + 1 to such saving throws for every four levels attained.

Barbarian Talents

The barbarian character receives the following talents automatically:

Climb cliffs and trees: The barbarian can climb trees and natural cliffs (or ledges, mountains, etc.) with a base chance of success of 60% plus 2% per level of experience. Racial, armor and Dexterity modifiers as described in the thief's section apply. Barbarians may also climb walls of other kinds once they have had the opportunity to practice scaling that particular type of surface.

Hide in natural surroundings: Barbarians can hide in natural surroundings that are familiar to the character with a base chance of 10% plus 5% per level. This is similar to how a thief would hide in shadows. Racial, armor and Dexterity modifiers as described in the thief's section apply.

Surprise: Barbarians surprise opponents on a 5 in 10 chance, or 6 in 10 if they are in familiar terrain. Barbarians are themselves surprised 10% of the time or only 5% in familiar terrain.

Back protection: Any attempt to attack a barbarian from behind, including such attacks by assassins or thieves, has a 5% chance per level of being detected and countered. That is, if a barbarian detects a back attack (a 5% chance at 1st level, 10% at 2nd, etc.) the barbarian avoids the attack form. The former back attack becomes a normal attack. The barbarian is also then entitled to attack the sneaky wuss even though the barbarian may already have

engaged in what would otherwise have been his full normal combat for that round.

Leaping and springing: Barbarians are able to leap up to a maximum distance of 10 feet forward, 3 feet backward, or 3 feet upward from a standing start. If the barbarian is able to move freely and get a running start, the forward leap can range from 16-21 feet (15 + d6), and the upward leap from 41/2 to 6 feet (4 + d4, each pip equaling 1/2 foot). Springing under similar conditions gives an upward distance of 4-7 feet, depending on the surface used as a step to gain height and spring.

Detect illusion: Barbarians have a 5% chance per level of determining that some sight, sound or other sensory phenomenon is actually an illusion/phantasm spell. This detection takes one round of intense scrutiny. Regardless of the barbarian's level, the chance to learn the true nature of such spells may never exceed 75%.

Detect magic: Barbarians have a 25% chance of detecting any sort of magic other than the illusion/phantasm variety. This again takes one round of scrutiny, and applies to items or spells, but not to persons who are able to effect magic. For each level the barbarian gains beyond the 1st level, the barbarian gains an additional 5% to his base chance of detection. However, this chance may never exceed 90% regardless of the barbarian's level of experience. The type of magic is never revealed by this ability since to the barbarian all magic is the same - bad.

Leadership: When dealing with other barbarians, a barbarian adds his level of experience to his charisma score to get an effective charisma effect on other barbarians. Comeliness does not affect, nor is it affected by, this ability.

Table 3I: Barbarian Power/Ability Acquisitions	
Level	Actions and Abilities
2	May associate freely with clerics
3	May use magic potions
4	May use magic weapons. May strike creatures hit only by + 1 weapons. Gains + 1 on saving throws versus spell.
5	May use magic armor
6	May associate with magic-users - if necessary! May strike creatures hit only by + 3 weapons
7	May use weapon-like miscellaneous magic items
8	May associate with magic-users - occasionally. May strike creatures hit only by + 5 weapons. Gains + 2 on saving throws versus spell. May summon a barbarian horde (see The Barbarian Horde section)
9	May use protection scrolls.
10	May use most magic items available to fighters. May strike creatures hit only by + 7 weapons
12	Gains + 3 on saving throws versus spell. May strike creatures hit only by + 9 weapons.

Barbarian Skills

In addition to the talents listed above, every barbarian possesses all of the following skills. These skills are generally not usable (certainly not to their fullest potential) in environs unfamiliar to the barbarian, although the skills can be applied to a new locale with differing flora, fauna, and climate, after about one month of tromping about the area.

Survival: The barbarian has all the necessary skills for basic survival in the wild, including hunting, small animal trapping, food gathering, shelter building, body covering, and fire building.

First aid: This skill allows the barbarian to bind wounds, set sprains or broken bones, and concoct natural antidotes and natural cures for diseases. In game terms, this translates to the barbarian immediately regaining 1 hit point, and thereafter he regains hit points at twice the normal rate, regaining 2 hit points per day if resting, and 1 hit point per day even if active and adventuring. The barbarian can also bind wounds to prevent further loss in hit points of other characters. Such "first aid" restores 1, hit point immediately, and then increases hit-point recovery by 100% if the barbarian continues to administer aid and cures. When dealing with natural poison and illness, the barbarian has a 10% chance of effecting a cure. If the poison or disease is known and is of natural origin, this chance of success rises to a percentage equal to 50 plus the victim's constitution score.

Outdoor craft: This skill includes plant and animal detection as a 3rd level druid, direction determination, and the ability to predict weather as if the spell of that name were cast by a 3rd-level druid.

Tracking: A barbarian's tracking skill is equal to that of a ranger of the same level, but a barbarian may only track in the outdoors.

Finally, a barbarian will have one or more of the following tertiary skills depending on the locale or culture from which he originates. Which skills are applicable are determined by the GM according to the nature of the campaign.

Animal handling: The barbarian can handle and domesticate wild animals. Usually this is restricted to dogs, but could include animals such as wolves, large birds and giant cats.

Horsemanship: The barbarian is skilled in using his horse in combat. This ability includes the handling of draft teams.

Long distance signaling: The barbarian is capable of using the signaling methods of his native land (including such things as drums, smoke, or mirror flashes) to communicate over long distances.

Running: This skill enables the barbarian to move at full speed (twice normal movement rate) for no less than three full days before having to "rest" by spending a day moving at normal rate. Similarly, endurance will be twice normal for movement situations.

Small craft, paddled: The barbarian is skilled in the building and use of small canoes and hide boats.

Small craft, rowed: This skill includes the building of wooden boats and the rowing and/or sailing of these boats.

Sound mimicry: The barbarian with this skill can mimic various sounds, including bird or animal calls, either for the purpose of luring those creatures or for signaling.

Snare building: This skill allows the barbarian to construct deadfalls, pits, and other traps for large and even very large animals. Sentient creatures can also fall prey to these traps.

Native territory: Many of a barbarian's abilities depend on the native territory of the character. It is mandatory that barbarian characters come from an out-of-the-way barbaric state or area within Garweeze Wurld. Typically they are cavemen, dervishes, nomads, or tribesmen. Only such uncivilized backgrounds can generate the necessary surroundings to produce individuals of the stock from which barbarian fighters would be drawn.

As barbarians rise in level, they gain further abilities, some of which have been noted above. Further, some of the limitations placed on the barbarian are relaxed or lifted. The Progression is outlined in Table 3I.

The Barbarian Horde

Upon reaching 8th level or a Fame Factor of 100, a barbarian may summon a barbarian horde. This horde can only be summoned in the native territory of the barbarian, from among barbarians of his background. A barbarian horde can number as many members as its leader's experience-point total divided by 1000. Thus, a barbarian who has just reached 8th level can gather a 275-member horde, and one who has just reached 9th level can have a 500-member horde. Those below 8th level may summon a horde numbering twice their Fame Factor (as long as it is 100 or greater).

A horde takes a week to gather in the barbarian's home territory, and must have a stated purpose, such as "Tear apart the College of Magic in Fangarie brick by brick" or " Rescue Princess Madelyn from Rotgut" or "Serve under Delphinius the Cleric in his battle against the orcs". Deviating from the proclaimed purpose by the horde or its leader may cause the horde to disband. Members of disbanded hordes will return by the quickest and safest route to their homelands.

A barbarian horde can only be kept together for as many weeks as the barbarian leader has levels of experience. At the end of this time, the horde is usually disbanded. Exceptions may be made if large amounts of treasure are distributed to the members or extenuating circumstances exist, (i.e. if the leader has an effective Charisma of 23 or more with respect to other barbarians, if the leader of the horde is a tribal leader as well, or if an unattained goal is in easy reach). Each of these special circumstances which apply would extend the duration of the horde by 1-2 weeks at most. A tribal leader who has his horde

disband beneath him will be pelted with vegetables the next time he returns to his homeland and lose Honor.

In addition to the normal barbarians in the horde, the leader of the horde will gain two aides, each of a level equal to one-half of the leader's level (rounded down). Each aide will have two assistants of one half the aide's level. An 8th-level barbarian would therefore have a horde of 275 men plus two 4th-level aides and four 2nd-level assistants to those aides. The horde may include shamans, witch doctors, or clerics, depending on the nature of the barbarians. Barbarian shamans and witch doctors gain wisdom bonuses and may use magic items of any sort as applicable. Normal clerics will have full spell capability, but in all cases barbarian ability-score statistics apply. Barbarian clerics are always non-player characters.

Berserkers

The berserker is a fighter wired for battle rage. These fearsome warriors attack as normal fighters but under certain circumstances (such as taking large amounts of damage or when dealing out the same to others) they are able to tap into powerful but dangerously unpredictable rage and go berserk (also known as running amok). This allows them to achieve a furious state of mind bordering on insanity that enables them to fight longer, harder, and more savagely than any character has a right to. When not berserked, the berserker has a lot in common with the barbarian, except it's obvious from the wild look in his eye that he has a truly savage and inhuman element in his personality. This appearance tends to greatly disturb and unsettle those he meets. Therefore, berserkers do not attract followers.

Berserker
Ability Requirements:
Str 17+, Con 15+
Prime Requisite:
Strength and Constitution
Hit Dice Type:
d12
Allowed Races:
any
Allowed Alignments:
any chaotic
Building Point Bonus
8 BP

Alas, the berserker has no control over his berserking (though he can eventually learn to self-induce the condition to some extent). This makes him a deadly, fearsome warrior who can be as much a menace to himself (and friends) as to his enemies. Once enraged, the berserker is transformed into an unstoppable butchering machine. The Masters of Hack call it "unbridled

Table 3J:
Berserker Progression Table

Experience Points	Exp. Level	12-Sided Dice for Accum. Hit Points	Level Title
0-6,000	1	20+1d12*	RageWarrior
6,001-12,000	2	2	RageMonger
12,001-24,000	3	3	RageMaster
24,001-48,000	4	4	BattleBane
48,001-80,000	5	5	BaneLord
80,001-150,000	6	6	BaneMaster
150,001-275,000	7	7	BattleDancer
275,001-500,000	8	8**	BattleRager
500,001-1,000,000	9	8+4	Berserker
1,000,001-1,500,000	10	8+8	Berserker Lord
1,500,001-2,000,000***	11	8+12	Master Berserker

* At first level berserkers receive 20 points + 1d12. This twenty point 'kicker' is received at first level only.
** berserkers gain 4 h.p. per level after the 8th.
*** 500,000 experience points per level for each additional level above the 11th.

rage". Typically this ability of the beserker only reveals itself during mortal combat against a superior foe or when he (or his party) is clearly outnumbered. Something about the clash of arms and adrenaline rush of toe-to-toe combat causes the berserker to snap and become almost superhuman (or superdemi-human as the case may be) for short periods of time.

The art of hack is a way of life for members of this class and the love of battle overshadows all else in the life of the berserker. They are famous for dying young and fast. In fact the idea of growing old and feeble and dying a 'soft death' repulses the berserker. Make no mistake about it — this is not a character class for the wuss of heart and only the most skilled players should attempt to run one. When a berserker dies in combat (and he will) he's not to be mourned or pitied. Such a noble death is to be celebrated.

No one knows exactly where the berserker's abilities come from. It's commonly believed such individuals have been touched by the gawds of war, who love to see a good fight. Then there are others who simply believe the berserker is a sick individual who's mastery of the art of hack pushed him over the brink of sanity. It's also believed by some that such 'touched' individuals have been chosen by higher powers to protect their people and are meant to use their special powers to further some noble cause or aim for the gawds. In fact, many cultures revere the proven berserker with great respect and awe. High level berserkers can achieve a form of 'celebrity' which can have enormous dividends such as free room and board, gifts, and the bestowing of lands, titles and honors. Berserkers gain +1 to their Fame Factor per level.

To become a berserker a character must possess the right stuff. First of all he must have a Strength ability score of 17 or more and a Constitution of 15 or more. Secondly, the character must take the quirks HackFrenzy and HackLust during the creation process, but without the associated building point bonus for picking these quirks.

A berserker who has a Constitution of 16 or greater gains a 10% bonus to all experience points earned. Berserkers can earn an individual experience point award for bravery in initiating combat. This award is worth 200 experience points. The berserker character must be the one who leads his side into battle against a superior force, before the foes attack.

A berserker can be good, neutral, or evil, but must be chaotic in alignment. While they are often loyal, trustworthy, and noble, they have a wild and willful nature that leaves them always unpredictable. There are no racial limitations or restrictions for the berserker. It is truly an equal opportunity character class.

A berserker can use any weapon or armor available. He may use a shield but whenever he goes berserk, he must dispense of any shield he is carrying until he comes down. Although he can use any weapon, he does not begin with as many weapon proficiencies as a normal fighter. Instead of four initial weapon proficiencies, the berserker has only two. Thereafter, weapon proficiencies are gained at the normal rate. Berserkers cannot use proficiency slots for missile weapons like thrown axes, bows, crossbows, slings or darts. The berserker lives to destroy things in hand-to-hand combat and loves to look his opponent in the eye when he slays him. If a berserker attacks an enemy with a ranged or thrown weapon he loses Honor.

Going Berserk

All berserkers have the ability to "go berserk" and run amok during combat. Their quirks (HackFrenzy and HackLust -- See Chapter 6: Quirks and Flaws) enable them to enter this state of mind and are triggered by taking a certain amount of damage in one round (HackFrenzy) or dealing out a certain amount of damage in one round (HackLust). The berserker class is unique in that it is the only class allowed to have both HackFrenzy and HackLust as quirks; all other characters are only allowed to have one or the other. It is entirely possible for a berserker's rage to be triggered by both quirks at the same time — thereby having two damage quotas to fulfill (one for each quirk — ouch!!). The quirks work exactly as described in Chapter 6, but the berserker also gains the following additional advantages and disadvantages when berserking:

Advantages:

Strength. The berserker's Strength increases by 2 points. The character gains all bonuses (to-hit, damage, weight allowance, etc.) for his increased Strength.

Hit Points. The Berserker instantly gains one additional hit point for every level of experience. The hit points gained do not heal existing wounds; they are simply added to the character's current total. These additional hit points can cause the character's total to exceed the normal maximum the character is allowed.

Armor Class. The berserker's base Armor Class improves by 1 for every level of the character, to a maximum of AC 0. This adjustment is to the character's normal unarmored rating. A 5th level berserker fighting without armor would have an Armor Class of 5. This Armor Class adjustment can be combined with modifications for Dexterity, magical items and spells. This bonus does not apply if the character is wearing armor. In this case, the armor's AC is used, not that created by the berserk fury. A 10th level berserker in chain mail would still have an

AC of 5 when he entered into his berserk rage. Note that a berserker is not prevented from wearing armor, either in normal combat or when berserk, but wearing armor negates this benefit.

KO Results. The berserker, while berserk, is immune to KO results from the Punching and Wrestling rules, and takes only half damage from bare-handed attacks from these rules.

Charms and Spells: While berserk, the character gains a + 2 to all saving throws vs. charms or mental-based attacks. (These include such spells as the wizard spells Charm Person, Befriend, Hypnotism, Irritation, Ray of Enfeeblement, Scare, Geas, and the cleric spells Command, Charm Person or Mammal, Enthrall, Cloak of Bravery, and Symbol).

He also gets a + 4 to save against the wizard spells Blindness, Proadus' Uncontrollable Fit of Laughter, Hold Person, Charm Monster, and Confusion, and the cleric spells Hold Person and Hold Animal.

The Emotion spell has no effect on the berserker, unless the caster chose the Fear result. If Fear was chosen, the berserker gets a normal saving throw; if he makes it, he continues on as before, but if he fails it, he is prematurely snapped out of his berserk state, with all the normal effects of coming out of the berserk state (but he doesn't suffer any other fear effect). The Fear spell has exactly the same effect: If he saves, there is no effect and if he doesn't save, he's snapped out of the berserk state. If he fails a saving throw against Charm Monster, he simply counts the caster as one of his allies; he doesn't come out of the berserk state or obey the caster's commands.

Being berserk offers no real protection from Finger of Death, except that the spell effects do not take place until the character has come out of his berserk state. If the berserker saves, he doesn't suffer the 2d8 +1 damage until immediately after he snaps out of the berserk state. If he fails to save, he doesn't die until he snaps out of the berserk state.

Disadvantages:

In addition to the benefits, the berserk fury has several special limitations and consequences. Many of these reflect the savage and unpredictable nature of berserkers.

Single-Mindedness. Once a character goes berserk, he must enter melee combat with the enemy. Though the berserker can pick and choose his targets, he cannot hang back from battle until he has fulfilled his damage quota for his HackFrenzy and/or HackLust quirks.

Once in combat, a berserk character cannot change opponents until the current foe is either slain or flees and cannot be pursued. The restriction on changing opponents applies only after the berserker has actually entered into combat. If not actually engaged in melee, the character must move and attack whatever enemy is closest. However, if he still has a damage quota to fulfill and there are no foes to engage he MUST attack an ally.

Retreat. Once a berserker has entered his battle fury, he cannot retreat from combat until either his damage quota is fulfilled or he comes down due to the passage of time.

Loss of Powers. As soon as the berserk rage ends, all powers gained (increased Strength, hit points, Armor Class and Charm resistance) vanish. Full damage is now applied and any damage suffered is taken from the temporary hit points first. Only after all these hit points are lost does the character suffer actual wounds. Thus it is possible for a berserker to drop dead from his wounds after coming down.

Exhaustion. Berserking can be physically draining. Berserkers don't come down from their HackFrenzy/HackLust in 1d4 turns as described in the quirk description. Because of the intensity of their rage (and training) Berserkers only remain berserk for a number of rounds equal to their Constitution.

As soon as the character stops being berserk, he must make a saving throw vs. death. If the saving throw is successful, the character is unaffected by his fury. Should he fail the saving throw, the berserker is immediately drained and exhausted. The character's Strength is reduced by 5 (from its normal non-berserk state) and remains reduced until the character has time to rest. Strength recovers at the rate of 1 point per turn of rest. The character cannot go berserk again until his Strength has returned to its normal level.

Reaction Modifier: The berserker character receives a - 3 reaction from all NPCs (except from other berserkers) because of his wild-eyed demeanor.

Uncertain Status: When the berserker goes berserk, you will need to inform your GM of your hit point total. From that point until the fight is done and the berserker has returned to normal, your GM will keep track of your hit points. He won't tell you how much damage you've taken for each hit, nor how many hit points you have left. Your GM will also roll all saves for the berserker while he's enraged. It's very possible for a berserker to be nickled and dimed to death and the player not even know it until he drops dead. After all, the character can feel no pain...so you cannot keep track of how close he is to death.

Ranged Weapons: While berserk, the character can use no ranged weapons. He kills only in hand-to-hand or melee-weapon combat.

Oblivious to Missiles. While berserk, the character cannot take cover against missile fire.

Friend or Foe? If, while the character is berserk, another character tries something he can interpret as attack (for instance, shoves him clear of an incoming attack) the berserker must roll 1d20 vs. his Intelligence. If he succeeds (that is, rolls his Intelligence score or less), he's dimly aware that his friend is not attacking him. If he fails (rolls higher than his Intelligence), he now thinks his friend is an enemy, and continues to think so until the fight is done and he is no longer berserk.

Taunting: The Taunt spell is automatically successful, and will cause the berserker to abandon his current enemy and rush to attack the taunter. Such things as mocking jigs and taunting skills will have a similar effect.

Self-Induced HackFrenzy

At 3rd level whenever the berserker knows a fight is coming, he can attempt to self induce a berserk rage, even if there is no fight currently going on. This isn't an instantaneous process. He must spend a little time to "psych himself up." It takes a full turn (ten combat rounds) to go berserk. In that time, the character is growling, moaning, uttering imprecations, etc. It's impossible to be quiet when trying to go berserk in this manner.

At the end of a full turn of preparation, he becomes berserk. He rolls for his damage quota and must immediately engage the enemy.

Hack Pangs

A berserker is so obsessed with combat that he must engage in it once per day or suffer penalties as defined on the following table. All penalties are cumulative. A berserker who does not engage in combat longer than 15 days loses 1d8 hit points per day. Once the berserker engages someone in real combat, all penalties will be removed one turn after the combat has begun.

Cavaliers

Cavaliers are often regarded as arrogant, pompous bastards. They would be despised by most people were it not for their prowess in battle. They are elitist, chauvinistic pigs who look down on just about everybody they meet except for other cavaliers or nobles. Even when they meet other cavaliers, there is a definite rivalry that inevitably rears its ugly head.

Cavalier
Ability Requirements: Str 15+, Con 15+, Dex 15+, Int 10+, Wis 10+, Com 9+
Prime Requisite: None
Hit Dice Type: d12
Allowed Races: Human, Elves, Half-elves, Gnome Titans, Pixie Fairy
Allowed Alignments: any good alignment initially
Building Point Bonus: 10BP

The character class of cavalier has no prime requisite, and as a result cavaliers do not gain experience-point bonuses for superior abilities. A cavalier must have minimum ability scores of 15 in Strength, Dexterity, and Constitution, and scores of 10 in Intelligence and Wisdom. A cavalier character must initially be of good alignment (lawful good, neutral good, or chaotic good). The cavalier attacks and makes saving throws as a fighter, but gains additional abilities with certain weapons and modifiers to certain saving throws. Cavaliers are not entitled to the benefits of weapon specialization.

In order to become a cavalier, a character must be in service to some gawd, noble, order, or special cause. The GM will determine if this requirement can be met within the limits of the campaign, and if it is being properly met by the cavalier character. The cavalier must always place honor, bravery, and personal deeds in the forefront of his activity, and must adhere to a special code of chivalry/honor (described below). If a cavalier's Honor drops into the dishonorable category he immediately suffers an experience points penalty to gained experience equal to 10% of his level.

A cavalier character must be of proper social class, and is usually of noble or aristocratic origin. Only those characters of upper class social status may immediately enter into the cavalier class. Those of lower social standing are generally excluded from becoming cavaliers, but certain members of lower social classes may be so honored because they generally work cheap. Such a character must be sponsored by a higher authority of greater status, and begins first as a 0-level Horseman (a retainer for a Knight), then a 0-level Lancer, and finally becomes a 1st-level Armiger of the cavalier class. The 0-level Horseman starts at -1500 experience points and has 1d4+1 initial hit points (plus, of course, the 20 hit point kicker common to all characters). The Horseman becomes a Lancer at -500 experience points and gains another d4 roll for cumulative hit points. The Lancer becomes a 1st-level cavalier at 0 experience

Table 3K: Berserker Lack of Hack Table	
Number of Days without Combat	**Penalty**
1	none
2	-1d4 hit points
3	-1 Str
4	-1 Dex
5	add a minor mental quirk
6	-20% to all skill and proficiency checks
7	-1 Con
8	-1d8 hit points
9	-1 Wis
10	-1 Con and -1 Wis
11	add a major mental quirk
12	-1 Str and -1 Dex
13	-20% to Honor
14	-50% to Honor

Table 3L: Cavalier Progression Table			
Experience Points	Exp. Level	12-Sided Dice for Accum. Hit Points	Level Title
(-1,500- -501)	0	21 + 1d4*	(Horseman)
(-501- -1)	0	2d4	(Lancer)
0-2,500	1	1d10+2**	Armiger,
2,501-5,000	2	2	Scutifer
5,001-10,000	3	3	Esquire
10,001-18,500	4	4	Knight Plebe
18,501-37,000	5	5	Knight Bachelor
37,001-85,000	6	6	Knight
85,001-140,000	7	7	Grand Knight
140,001-220,000	8	8	Banneret
220,001-300,000	9	9	Chevalier
300,001-600,000	10	10***	Cavalier
600,001-900,000	11	10+3	Cavalier, 11th
900,001-1,200,000	12	10+6	Cavalier, 12th
1,200,001-1,500,000	13	10+9	Cavalier Commander
1,500,001-1,800,000	14	10+12	Cavalier Commander
1,800,001-2,100,000	15	10+15	Cavalier Commander
2,100,001-2,400,000	16	10+18	Cavalier Commander
2,400,001-2,700,000	17	10+21	Cavalier Commander
2,700,001-3,000,000	18	10+24	Cavalier Commander
3,000,001-3,300,000	19	10+27	Cavalier Commander
3,300,001-3,600,000****	20	10+30	Cavalier Commander

* If qualification for 1st level required progression through the two 0-level grades, then hit dice for 1st level are 3d4 + 21, but in all other cases 1d12+20 applies.

** A character whose social standing qualifies him or her for immediate entrance into the cavalier class begins as a 1st-level Armiger with 1d10 + 2 hit points. He rolls 1d12 per level thereafter until 10th level.

*** Cavaliers gain 3 hps per level after the 10th.

**** 300,000 experience points per level for each level beyond the 20th points, and gains another d4 in hit points. In contrast, a character whose social standing qualifies him for immediate entrance into the cavalier class begins as a 1st-level Armiger with 1d10 + 22 hit points. The character's hit-point bonus for high constitution (it applicable) is first received at either Horseman or Armiger level, and is then applied to each additional hit die from second level on as normal. The special abilities of the cavalier class are only gained when the character attains Armiger status.

Humans, gnome titans, pixie-fairies, elves, and half-elves may become cavaliers. However, members of the latter two races cannot qualify unless they are of gray or high elf stock (or, for half-elves, descended from such stock) and unless they are from or sponsored by a noble house.

Cavaliers are not limited in which weapons they can use, but certain weapons are preferred over others, such that a cavalier will seek proficiency in these weapons before learning other weapons. These weapons are the lance (required of the 1st-level Armiger), long sword, broad sword, bastard sword, short sword, horseman's mace, horseman's flail, horseman's military pick, dagger, scimitar, and javelin. Only after these weapons have been mastered may the cavalier become proficient in the use of other types. Weapons that deal out damage at a distance (including pole arms with the exception of a lance used dismounted and missile weapons) call into question the cavalier's personal bravery, and as such are avoided.

The cavalier gains bonuses "to hit" with certain weapons as he advances in level. These "weapons of choice" and their attendant bonuses are:

- At 1st level, the cavalier is + 1 "to hit" with the lance, if used while mounted.
- At 3rd level, the cavalier is + 1 "to hit" with either the broad sword, long sword, or scimitar (player's choice).
- At 5th level, the cavalier is + 1 "to hit" with either the horseman's mace, horseman's flail, or horseman's military pick (player's choice).
- At 7th level, the cavalier is + 2 "to hit" with the lance, if used while mounted.
- At 9th level, the cavalier is + 2 "to hit" with either the broad sword, long sword, or scimitar (depending upon what was chosen at 3rd level).
- At 11th level, the cavalier is + 2 "to hit" with the horseman's mace, horseman's flail, or horseman's military pick (depending upon what was chosen at 5th level).
- At 13th level, the cavalier is + 3 "to hit" with the lance, if used while mounted.

At higher levels, the progression described above increases in a similar fashion. The plus "to hit" does not apply to damage, and does not allow the cavalier to hit creatures that can only be hit by magic weapons. Note that the higher pluses must be taken in the same weapon as chosen at lower levels, so that any cavalier has effectively three "weapons of choice." (A cavalier cannot be + 1 with the long sword and + 2 with the scimitar at 9th level, but would be + 2 with the long sword if that was the weapon chosen at 3rd level.)

The cavalier may make multiple attacks with a "weapon of choice" as if the character were 5 levels higher than actual as far as attacks per round are concerned (e.g., a 3rd-level cavalier can attack 3 times every 2 rounds with a weapon of choice, as opposed to 1 attack per round with some other ordinary weapon). At 16th level and above, the cavalier can attack 3 times per round with a weapon of choice.

The lance is the preferred weapon of the cavalier, and proficiency with it is required at the first level. The cavalier has a bonus to damage equal to the character's level of experience when using a lance while mounted. When the cavalier is dismounted and using a lance, damage is + 1. A heavy lance used while dismounted is treated as an awl pike, with respect to all specifications except length, weight, and speed factor. A medium or light lance used while dismounted is treated as a spear.

A cavalier's expertise in weapons allows the cavalier to use the full parry maneuver with weapons of proficiency more effectively than fighters can. Should a cavalier choose to parry rather than attack, he gains an AC bonus equal to his level. If a cavalier parries, he cannot attack in that round, even if he is capable of making multiple attacks in a single round.

To the Cavalier, armor is as much as badge of station as it is a means of protection. Thus, the Cavalier will always seek to own the very best and finest-quality armor he can afford. In this endeavor, appearance is as important as function, so engraving, inlaying, and decoration of the armor will always be added. Plate armor is the cavalier's first choice; other preferences ranking beneath that are (in order of desirability) plate mail, banded or splint mail, chain mail, scale mail, and ring mail. Leather, studded leather, and padded armor are worn by poor people, and as such are beneath the cavalier's station, such that the cavalier will not be caught dead in these armor types. This snobbishness applies even in the case of magical armor, so that chain mail + 2 will not be worn if normal banded or splint mail can be purchased.

Mounted combat and horsemanship are special provinces of the cavalier class. A human cavalier (but not an elf or a half-elf) makes all attacks from horseback as if the character were 1 level higher. This increase applies only to horses, mounts usable as steeds by cavaliers at higher level, and those mounts approved by the GM.

All cavaliers are virtually born and bred to the saddle, with those of lesser ability arduously trained at the 0 level. A cavalier is 85% unlikely to be thrown from the saddle, and 85% unlikely to be injured if his mount falls. This chance is increased by 1 % for each level above the first.

As a cavalier increases in level, he improves still further in horsemanship, and in the handling of other creatures as mounts. Horsemanship abilities increase as follows:

- At 3rd level, the cavalier can vault into the saddle with bulky armor and have the steed underway in a single segment.
- At 4th level, a female elven cavalier (and only a female elf) may handle and ride a unicorn as a steed.
- At 5th level the cavalier can urge his mount to greater speed than normal. The additional speed possible equals a 2" bonus to movement rate, and can be sustained for up to 6 turns. The additional speed thus gained has no ill effects upon the mount, although normal rest and feeding are always necessary.
- At 7th level the cavalier can handle and ride a pegasus as a steed.
- At 9th level, the cavalier can handle and ride a hippogriff as a steed.
- At 11th level, the cavalier can handle and ride a griffon or a similar creature (GM's judgment) as a steed.

The cavalier's mount will be friendly to and will accept the cavalier as long as it is properly treated. Of course, creatures of good alignment will not allow any of the evil sort to come near in these cases, and vice versa.

A cavalier's knowledge of horses (and, at higher levels, other mounts) allows the cavalier to estimate the relative worth of a steed. A cavalier can examine any mount and determine if it has low worth (one-third or fewer of the maximum possible hit points for the creature), average worth, or high worth (two-thirds or better of the maximum possible hit points). Any steed selected by a cavalier will have +2 hit points per hit die (up to the maximum hit points for the creature).

A cavalier makes all saving throws as a fighter. Such characters are, however, immune to fear (magical or otherwise) of any sort. All Cavaliers radiate a protection from fear aura in a 10 foot radius, so that all allied creatures within the radius are similarly immune. In addition, magical or magic-like phenomena that affect the mind are 90% unlikely to have any effect on the cavalier. This includes powers such as Beguiling, Charm, Domination, Hold, Hypnosis, Magic Jar, Possession, Sleep, Suggestion, and the Psionic Mind Blast, but not the effects of high Comeliness. This 90% immunity is in addition to any saving throw for the cavalier, if applicable. Cavaliers also save at + 2 versus all forms of illusion spells.

Cavaliers of good alignment are able to function at negative hit point totals, unlike members of other classes, or cavaliers of neutral or evil alignments. The number of negative hit points the cavalier can function at is determined by the cavalier's hit points at 1st level (4-13). When a negative number of hit points is reached, the cavalier does not become unconscious, but can no longer attack and must rest, bind wounds, and seek further healing. Cavaliers heal as other characters, but those of good alignment gain an additional 1-4 points for each full week of normal healing.

As a member of the social upper classes, the cavalier has a coat of arms and armorial bearing. This bearing is the device worn upon the cavalier's shield to identify himself on the battlefield and in tournament. The armorial bearing may be not kept covered while traveling, and must be boldly presented when an encounter occurs with creatures that might understand the import of such a device. In addition, at 4th level the cavalier may fly a pennon on his lance on the battlefield. A duplicate of this battle flag is held by the cavalier's retainers, and marks the territory of the cavalier. If the battle flag is lost, dishonor ensues (-20% to Honor), and the cavalier must make every effort to regain the flag. If he does, half of the lost Honor may be regained.

Finally, cavaliers may expect full hospitality - food, lodging, and whatever else is needed (within reason under the circumstances) - from all other cavaliers of the same alignment. Such hospitality is likewise due from all gentle, noble, and royal households according to their relationships between various political divisions that might be concerned.

The cavalier must follow a code of conduct and ethics, akin to chivalry. Upon being sworn to knighthood (by a cavalier of at least 2 levels higher, in a ceremony as simple as a dubbing with the sword or a full ritual of fasting, vigil, sacred vows, and celebration), the cavalier must pledge himself to this code. Failure to sustain the oath is not sufficient reason to revoke knighthood, unless the order or liege of the cavalier specifically demands such. In the latter case, the cavalier becomes a mere fighter, though weapon specialization is not gained and the privilege of weapons of choice is retained.

A cavalier must serve someone or some cause - normally a gawd, greater noble, order of knighthood, or the like. The cavalier must seek to sustain a special code of honor tailored specifically for his class. This code of honor holds dear the knightly virtues and the code of chivalry. The knightly virtues are these:

Liberality   Good Faith   Glory
Unselfishness   Pride   Courtesy   Bravery

The Cavalier code of honor must be rigidly adhered to at all times, and includes the following high ideals:

Noble service cheerfully rendered
Defense of any charge unto death
Courage and enterprise in obedience to rule
Respect for all peers and equals
Honor to all above your station
Obedience and respect from all beneath your station
Scorn for those who are lowly and ignoble (this includes knightly limitations on weapons and armor)
Military prowess exercised in service to your lord
Courtesy to all ladies (whose Comeliness is greater than 15)
War is the flowering of chivalry
Battle is the test of manhood
Combat is glory
Never shirk a task
Personal glory above all in battle
Death to all who oppose the cause
Death before dishonor

In enforcing this code, the GM may reduce or eliminate experience that is gained by the cavalier if its gaining violates the spirit or letter of the code. A cavalier who retreats from battle, even to save fellow party members, would receive half experience for the beasts slain in his retreat. Similarly, a cavalier who scolds a sassy princess he's rescued will gain no experience, since his actions were not approved of by the code. Note that even neutral and evil cavaliers are bound by this code, but in their cases the obedience is to non-good masters.

As a result of the code and desire for battle, cavaliers cannot be controlled in battle situations. They will charge any enemy in sight, with the following order of preference:

1. Powerful monsters (dragons, demons, giants, etc.) serving enemy leaders, then the leaders themselves
2. Opponent cavaliers, dark knights, knights errant or paladins (if the cavalier is evil) of great renown, enemy flags and standards
3. Opponent cavalry of noble or elite status
4. Other opponent cavalry
5. Opponent elite footmen
6. Opponent camp and headquarters
7. Opponent melee troops
8. Levies or peasants

The cavalier's charge will be made at full speed, regardless of army cohesion, intervening friendly troops, or other such considerations.

While all cavaliers are initially of good alignment, there are cavaliers of neutral and evil alignment as well. Alignment change can occur up to 4th level without penalty, if the change is well reasoned. At 4th level and beyond, any change of alignment results in the usual penalties. Neutral and evil cavaliers do not retain the ability to function at a negative hit-point total. Evil cavaliers may use poison, but cannot ignore the obligation of hospitality (though guests may be housed in a sub-standard manner). The device of an evil cavalier is made known throughout the land, and good cavaliers are duty bound to hunt down and destroy those cavaliers of evil alignment. Finally, evil and neutral cavaliers have limitations on the types of followers they can attract.

Cavaliers have special requirements on the types of followers, henchmen, and retainers they may have.

Followers: Unlike other characters, cavaliers begin to attract followers at relatively low level. These troops are men-at-arms. Their numbers and type are determined as follows:

At 4th level: 1-4 men-at-arms
At 5th level: 2-8 men-at-arms
At 6th level: 3-12 men-at-arms
At 7th level: 6-24 men-at-arms
At 8th level: 12-48 men-at-arms
At 9th level: 24-96 men-at-arms
At 10th level: 48-192 men-at-arms

The number ranges given above are followed on a per-level basis, and are not cumulative. If the dice roll for followers gained at a new level is equal to or lower than the number of followers a cavalier currently has, then no new followers are gained at that level. Example: A roll of 1 d4 at 4th level indicates that the cavalier attracts 3 followers. When the cavalier attains 5th level, 2d4 are rolled, and if the result is 2 or 3, then no new followers are gained (assuming that the original followers are still in the cavalier's service).

Whenever a number of new followers is gained, roll percentile dice and refer to Table 3M to determine how they are equipped.

Table 3M: Cavalier Follower Gear	
Die roll	Followers equipped with:
01-50	Light cavalry in ring mail and shield, each with 3 javelins, long sword, and hand axe; or, heavy infantry in scale mail, with pole arm of choice and club.
51-75	Heavy infantry in splint mail with morning star and hand axe; or, heavy infantry in leather armor with pike and short sword.
76-90	Crossbowmen in chain mail with heavy crossbow and short sword; or, crossbowmen in chain mail with light crossbow and military fork.
91-00	Cavalry in banded mail and shield with lance and horseman's mace; or, cavalry in studded leather with long sword and horseman's flail. Either type will be mounted on medium warhorses.

The cavalier must go to a locale where such men-at-arms are located in order to attract these followers. Those followers lost are not replaced except by troops gained at higher levels. A cavalier's followers will not demand wages or salary, but must be fed, cared for, and rewarded as suitable for the conditions.

Neutral cavaliers will attract men-at-arms only when they champion a specific, neutral cause, such as serving for a druid to protect creatures of the woodland. These followers will not remain if the cavalier goes elsewhere.

Evil cavaliers will only attract bandits, brigands and the like as followers. An evil cavalier could attract orcs or hobgoblins if in the correct area. If monsters of 1 + 1 hit dice or greater strength are considered, reduce the total number of followers accordingly, if the result would otherwise overcompensate for penalties of using such creatures.

For every group of 20 troops that serve a cavalier, there will be a fighter follower/leader of 5th level, dressed in plate mail and shield with a battle axe + 2. For every 60 troops there will be a 6th-level fighter leader (with plate mail + 1 and shield, longsword + 2), and a 3rd-level fighter lieutenant (plate mail, battle axe). These gains will be made as the total men-at-arms in the cavalier's service reach appropriate totals. These leaders will not be replaced if slain, although the cavalier may recruit mercenaries to take their place. Evil cavaliers may attract monsters as leaders (a troll instead of a 6th-level fighter, for instance). There is a 1 % per level chance that an encountered intelligent monster of fewer hit dice and similar alignment will become a follower of the evil cavalier. There is a 5% per level chance that such intelligent monsters will be disposed to cooperate with, or at least remain neutral to, the cavalier, providing the evil cavalier's armorial bearing and shield are known.

Cavaliers and Henchmen

A cavalier may have as many henchmen as indicated by the Charisma Table 1F, with a bonus of + 3 to that number for cavaliers of good alignment or a bonus of + 1 for neutral or evil cavaliers. The types of henchmen that a cavalier will (or can) accept are based on the alignment of the cavalier:

Good	Neutral	Evil
Clerics	Druids	Clerics
Fighters	Fighters	Fighters
Cavaliers (good)	Cavaliers	Cavaliers (evil)
Magic-users	Magic-users	Magic-users
Paladins	Thieves	Thieves
Bards	Bards	Assassins

Cavaliers and Retainers

As soon as a cavalier of good alignment reaches 4th level (Knight Plebe), the cavalier must acquire at least one retainer. These retainers can be either Armigers (level 1), or Scutifers (level 2), or both. Upon becoming a Knight (6th level), an Esquire (level 3) must be added to the staff. Upon becoming a Grand Knight (7th level), a Horseman to act as a herald and a Lancer to act as a guard must be added. At 8th level, the Banneret must bring at least an additional mounted man-at-arms to his staff of retainers. All cavalier retainers will serve for nothing more than care, upkeep, and training, as applicable. Gifts are always accepted, of course.

As a Chevalier (9th level), the cavalier may willingly travel with or without his group of retainers. At lower levels, the master of a cavalier can require the cavalier to travel without retainers. A cavalier is responsible for the actions of his followers and retainers, and is required to insure that others of the cavalier class live up to the standards of the class.

Dark Knights

The dark knight is the antithesis of the paladin, a conniving and dastardly warrior who champions all that is evil. Many have tried and failed to live up to the responsibilities of the dark knight since it is commonly assumed that he is a "loose cannon" who has no purpose other than to terrorize the countryside. Nothing could be farther from the truth. While he would certainly enjoy such activities, the dark knight has far more important work to attend to. Upon his shoulders rests the job of ensuring the downfall of all that is just and righteous in the world. It is not an easy task! While the fair-haired golden boy paladin has the facile task of leading a bunch of losers whose natural inclination is to meekly take

Dark Knight
(aka Anti-Paladin)
Ability Requirements:
Str 12+, Con 9+, Wis 13+,
Cha 17
Prime Requisite(s):
Wisdom and Charisma
Hit Dice Type:
d10
Allowed Races:
Human
Allowed Alignments:
chaotic evil
Building Point Bonus
12 BP

orders and cooperate, the dark knight must direct a bickering rabble of bloodthirsty killers into achieving the overarching goal of the triumph of evil. There is no rest for the wicked. A Machiavellian capability for political manipulation is essential for success (therefore the minimum Charisma 17). He must also have minimum ability scores of Strength 12, Constitution 12 and Wisdom 13. Wisdom and Charisma are the prime requisites of the dark knight. A dark knight who has a Wisdom score of 16 or more gains a 10% bonus to the experience points he earns. A dark knight must be chaotic evil in alignment and must always remain chaotic evil. A dark knight who changes alignment, either deliberately or inadvertently, loses all his special powers, sometimes only temporarily but other times forever. He can use any weapon and wear any type of armor.

Chaos and evil deeds are the liquor and smokes of a dark knight. If a dark knight ever knowingly performs a lawful act, he must seek a high-level (7th or more) cleric of chaotic evil alignment, confess his kind deed, and do penance as prescribed by the cleric. If a dark knight should ever knowingly and will-

Table 3N: Dark Knight Progression Table			
		10 Sided Dice for	
Experience Points	Experience Level	Accumulated Hit Points	Level Title
0-2,750	1	20+1d10*	Knave
2,751-5,500	2	2	Dread Knight
5,501-12,000	3	3	Shade Knight
12,001-24,000	4	4	Shadow Knight
24,001-45,000	5	5	Knight of Twilight
45,001-95,000	6	6	Knight of Midnight
95,001-175,000	7	7	Knightmare
175,001-350,000	8	8	Knight Terminus
350,001-700,000	9	9**	Knight Terminus Master
700,001-1,050,000	10	9+3	Lord Terminus
1,050,001-1,400,000***	11	9+6	Lord Terminus Rogue
1,400,001 – 1,750,000	12	9+9	Lord Terminus Master
1,750,001 – 2,100,000	13	9+12	Lord Terminus Supreme
2,100,001 – 2,450,000	14	9+15	Lord of the Pit
2,450,001 – 2,800,000	15	9+18	Dark Lord of the Pit (15th level)
2,800,001 – 3,150,000	16	9+21	D.L.o.t.P. (16th level)
3,150,001 – 3,500,000	17	9+24	D.L.o.t.P. (17th level)
3,500,001 – 3,850,000	18	9+27	D.L.o.t.P. (18th level)
3,850,001 – 4,200,000	19	9+30	D.L.o.t.P. (19th level)
4,200,001 – 4,550,000	20	9+33	D.L.o.t.P. (20th level, etc.)

* At first level dark knights receive 20 points + 1d10. This twenty point 'kicker' is received at first level only.

** Dark knights gain 3 hps per level after the 9th.

*** 350,000 experience points per level for each additional level above the 11th.

ingly perform a good act, he loses the status of being a dark knight immediately and irrevocably. All benefits are then lost and no deed or magic short of the intervention of a Demon Prince can restore the character to dark knight status: He is ever after a fighter with an attitude problem. The character's level remains unchanged when this occurs and experience points must be adjusted accordingly. Thereafter the character is bound by the rules for fighters. He does not gain the benefits of weapon specialization since he did not select this for his character at the start.

If the dark knight commits a good act while enchanted or controlled by magic, he loses his dark knight status until he can atone for the deed. This loss of status means the character loses all his special abilities and essentially functions as a fighter (without weapon specialization) of the same level. Regaining his status requires completion of some horrific drunken bender to once again prove his worth and harden his black heart. He gains no experience prior to or during the course of this bender, and regains his standing as a dark knight only upon sobering up.

A dark knight has the following special powers:

- He can detect the presence of good intent up to 60 feet away by concentrating on locating good in a particular direction. This can be done as often as desired, but each attempt takes one round. This ability detects both good-aligned monsters and characters.

- A dark knight is immune to all forms of disease but is often a carrier of some really nasty plagues. Any person associating with a dark knight is 10% likely per day of becoming infected with a random affliction as determined in Table 3O. The effects of these afflictions are described in the HackMaster GameMaster's Guide.

He can also inflict terrible wounds on others simply by wuss slapping them. The dark knight inflicts 2 hit points per experience level as well as causing the loss of 1-4 Honor points to the victim. He can use this power only once per day.

A dark knight is surrounded by an aura of evil with a 10-foot radius. Within this radius, all summoned and specifically good creatures suffer a -1 penalty to

Table 3O: Dark Knight Communicable Disease Table	
d100	Disease
01-10	rotting flesh
11-20	orc shingles
21-30	goblin pox
31-40	black plague
41-50	rotting death
51-60	blue death
61-70	dancing death
71-80	burning death
81-90	common cold
91-00	other

their attack rolls, regardless of whom they attack. They are further subject to a –2 penalty on all saving throws. Creatures affected by this aura can easily spot its source.

A dark knight using an unholy sword projects a circle of power 10 feet in diameter when the sword is unsheathed and held. This power dispels hostile magic of a level up to the dark knight's experience level. (An unholy sword is a very special weapon; if your dark knight acquires one, the GM will explain its other powers.)

A dark knight gains the power to command undead when he reaches 3rd level. He affects these monsters the same as does a cleric two levels lower--for example, at 3rd level he has the command power of a 1st-level evil cleric. (See the section on clerics for more details on this ability.)

A dark knight may call for his mount upon reaching 4th level, or anytime thereafter. This steed need not be a horse; it may be whatever sort of creature is appropriate to the character and may even be a Nightmare (as decided by the GM). A dark knight's warhorse is a very special animal, bonded by fate to the knave. The dark knight does not really "call" the animal, nor does the horse instantly appear in front of him. Rather, the character must steal his warhorse in some memorable way, most frequently by a specific quest at the behest of a Nefarian.

A dark knight can cast cleric spells once he reaches 9th level. He can cast only spells of the divination, necromantic, and summoning type. (Spell types are identified in Appendix D.) The acquisition and casting of these spells abide by the rules given for clerics. The spell progression and casting level are listed in Table 3Q. Unlike a cleric, the dark knight does not gain extra spells for a high Wisdom score. The dark knight cannot cast spells from cleric or druid scrolls nor can he use cleric items unless they are allowed to the warrior group.

Table 3P:
Dark Knight's Followers

Roll percentile dice and add your Honor die on each of the following sub-tables of Table 3P: once for the leader of the troops and once for troops.

Die Roll	Leader (and suggested magical items)
01-40	5th-level fighter, plate mail, shield, battle axe +2
41-75	5th-level dark knight, plate mail, shield +1, spear +1, dagger +1
76-90	6th-level dark knight, plate mail +1, shield, spear +1, dagger +1, plus 3rd-level fighter, splint mail, shield, Crossbow of Distance
91-99	7th-level dark knight, plate mail, shield +1, broad sword +2, heavy war horse with Horseshoes of Speed
00	GM's Option (or lesser demon)

Die Roll	Troops/Followers
01-50	20 Warg mounted goblins with ring mail, small shield, 3 javelins, long sword, & hand axe; 100 goblins with scale mail, small shield, short sword & club
51-76	20 orcs with splint mail, morning star, & hand axe; 60 orcs with scale mail, halberd &short sword
76-91	20 gnolls with chain mail, heavy crossbow, & longsword; 20 gnolls with chain mail, light crossbow & guisarme-voulge
91-99	25 bugbears with medium shield & bastard sword; 30 hobgoblin cavalry with light warhorse, banded mail, medium shield, lance & long sword
00	GM's Option (giants, trolls)

*Player selects type.

Table 3Q:
Dark Knight Spell Progression

Dark Knight Level	Casting Level	Spell Level 1	2	3	4
9	1	1	--	--	--
10	2	2	--	--	--
11	3	2	1	--	--
12	4	2	2	--	--
13	5	2	2	1	--
14	6	3	2	1	--
15	7	3	2	1	1
16	8	3	3	2	1
17	9*	3	3	3	1
18	9*	3	3	3	1
19	9*	3	3	3	2
20*	9*	3	3	3	3

* Maximum spell ability

A dark knight attracts a body of followers upon reaching 9th level or establishing a garrison. These numbskulls are often more trouble than they are worth though. He can still hire soldiers and specialists to bolster his forces and keep them in line.

A dark knight may employ only evil henchmen (or those who act in such a manner when alignment is unknown). A dark knight will cooperate with anyone only as long as it is to his advantage to do so. He will try to show them the way to slash and burn one's way through life through both harsh words and deeds. He will not abide the company of those who commit good or righteous acts and will mercilessly taunt them at any given opportunity.

Knights Errant

Knights errant are similar to cavaliers but they owe no allegiance to gawds, noble orders, special causes or codes of conduct. Rather they fight for their own personal reasons — usually involving vengeance or to settle a hereditary grudge (blood vendettas). Or so they claim. If the truth be known, most knight errants fight out of a sense of battle-ego and glory.

They are knights with a single mindedness. They have such a warped view of morality and the world that most knights errant actually believe they are noble and of good alignment. They believe in fighting 'evil' on their terms and not having their hands tied by the same

Knight Errant (aka Rogue Knight)
Ability Requirements:
Str 14+, Con 10+, Wis 13+, Cha 17+ Comeliness 15+
Prime Requisite(s):
Strength and Charisma
Hit Dice Type:
d10
Allowed Races:
Any
Allowed Alignments:
any good
Building Point Bonus:
5 BP

morale restraints true cavaliers and paladins must slavishly adhere to. Unlike other classes this skewed view of the world allows characters of the knight errant class to use evil means to achieve their aims as long as they can justify their actions and argue that the end result furthers their blood vendetta. They are masters of such justification and as such have greater wiggle room within their chosen alignment than other character classes.

For example, a knight errant could burn down a village filled with innocent women and children in order to get the 'bad guy' and justify his actions by saying, "Well, if he (the bad guy) had escaped he would have ended up killing far more innocent people." As warped as it sounds this type of logic is enough to get the knight errant off the hook as far as alignment violations.

Justification

Lest a knight errant character be accused of being too violent or aggressive and have his Honor or alignment brought into question, he must follow certain rules before initiating combat. The right of justification is a powerful tool for the knight errant and he hides behind it like a teflon shield to escape the wrath of the gawds. It is often the only thing standing between him and a horrible retribution at the hands of those who monitor alignment infractions and acts of dishonor.

Below are six typical justifications the knight errant might use to explain his actions.

1. If you encounter someone brandishing a weapon, you can attack him. Justification: It was obviously self-defense.

2. If you encounter someone who is armed but does not have a weapon in his hands, you can attack him. Justification: This is merely the good tactical move against an obviously worthy opponent. By "drawing before the other guy" you are able to avoid his treachery.

3. If you encounter someone and you cannot determine if he is armed or not (no visible weapons), you can attack him. Justification: He probably had concealed weapons. Once he is subdued or killed, you can find out if he was "carrying".

4. If you encounter someone who is clearly unarmed, you can attack him. Justification: He could be a monk, spell-caster, have invisible weapons, or weapons implanted in his body, or be serving as a decoy or character bait. Once again, after he is subdued or killed, you can find out about his true intentions.

5. If you encounter someone who is not only clearly unarmed but otherwise appears to be an "innocent civilian"; you must treat

the situation with extreme caution and initiate attack. Justification: Probable Cause — Feeble old people, minors, cripples, etc. could very well be enemies in disguise, they could be using illusions, etc. Any act such as waving or talking (i.e., casting spells) can be interpreted as hostile, and then you can attack them in self-defense.

6. Anyone who avoids, runs away or attempts to evade the party is guilty of something, so he can be attacked. Justification: Eventually, he would probably have done harm to others if you hadn't brought him down.

Surrender

On some occasions, enemies may attempt to use a combat maneuver known as "surrender" before or during combat. Most characters would be honor-bound to acknowledge such acts and accept the surrender. The knight errant, however, is a little more scrutinizing and street savvy.

1. White flags must always be regarded with suspicion. A white flag may be a battle banner, a signal flag, an attack warning, a trick, etc. A flag by itself means little.

2. There must be clear verbal acknowledgment of surrender. If your enemies are screaming hysterically or babbling in some foreign language, this does not count as a surrender, regardless of what else they are doing.

3. Throwing down of weapons is a requirement for surrender. Note that if the weapons are close enough to grab up again or there is a possibility of hidden weapons, the condition is not fulfilled. Ideally, opponents can be required to strip to the point where it can be verified that they are not armed. Still, caution is advised (see #4 above).

4. Fleeing is an obvious attempt to flank the party, so retreating enemies can be attacked in the back. Remember the old adage: "Kill them before they run away, so they won't come back to fight another day."

5. Any hesitation on the part of those suspiciously surrendering, including asking for conditions, begging for mercy without permission, falling down from wounds, trying to stop bleeding, etc., is merely a trick, and does not constitute a valid surrender.

6. Even when someone actually surrenders, you get one last swing in, because your arm was in motion from the last one (same applies to trigger fingers on crossbows).

Prisoners

At times it may be unavoidable that a surrender leads to the taking of prisoners. Great care is needed because of the tricks prisoners are known to play.

1. If your enemies are known to take no prisoners (or you have heard rumors to that effect, or you have suspicions that it might be so), then you do not have to grant them quarter.

2. If prisoners become an inconvenience, you can tie them up and leave them in the wilderness or dungeon. The laws of nature will resolve the situation.

3. Prisoners are responsible for their own upkeep, including the costs of restraining them. How the knight errant gets his money back is a personal choice.

4. Prisoners can be required to do menial work for the party. If the level of work sustained does not kill the prisoners, then it is not too much.

5. Strict measures are needed to keep prisoners in line. Any method that does not deliberately kill captives is appropriate. Note that accidental killings are acceptable.

6. In the case of exceptionally dangerous or troublesome prisoners, it is OK to kill a few as examples to the rest.

In the campaign, the knight errant is a showy, high profile braggart. He performs dangerous or almost reckless stunts in combat and loves to brag about them afterwards. They love to be the center of attention and usually attract crowds of admirers wherever they go. Because they exercise their bragging rights so indiscriminately they often receive a lot of credit for brave deeds whether they deserve the credit or not. A knight errant can be a callous individual with no interests other than killing his enemy as quickly as possible and making off with any spoils. Or he can be a clean-limbed, heroic figure, a hero who always fights and never kills if he doesn't have to. And they can do all this, and get away with it, as long as they demonstrate at least some token effort in furthering their cause or achieving their ultimate vengeance.

The knight errant has one additional skill in his bag of tricks which other characters don't have — a teflon-like ability to shun ill feeling toward himself or those with whom he travels with. If a knight errant is accused of a crime or scandalized by some deed or act he did which was viewed unfavorably by an individual or group, the knight errant can publicly apologize. Anyone who is apologized to by a knight errant must save vs. apology with a -5 modifier (see Apologies/Forgiveness in Chapter 5). If the save fails, the individual or group must immediately forgive the knight errant (including any fines, penalties etc.). Furthermore, the knight errant has the ability to turn things around so that his accusers and those who harbored ill feeling toward him become the target of any blame or ill feeling. If a save vs. apology results in a natural 1, the blame has shifted to the person(s) making the save.

Knight errants receive the proficiencies and skills: riding (land-based) armorer, blind-fighting, endurance, gaming, social etiquette and weaponsmithing for free as part of their pre-adventuring training.

Knight errants, because of their intensive training, also get a free weapon specialization. This doesn't cost any of their beginning weapon proficiencies: they still get all four of those, and get this specialization free.

The exploits and deeds of knight errants tend to become more infamous than those of other fighters and spread quicker. A knight errant's Fame factor is multiplied by 1.25 to reflect this fact. Of course, this makes it more difficult for them to do things in secret as they rise in level. Some troublesome NPC is always remembering "the tall, fair-haired knight errant" who was at the scene of the action, which makes it very easy for the authorities to follow the heroes' trail.

In addition, because of the battle-vanity inherent to this class, any knight errant running into another knight errant with a higher Fame Factor than his own must challenge that knight errant to a duel. There's a proper protocol for such duels and your GM will explain them to you when the time comes. The victor of a knight errant duel receives 25% of his opponent's Fame and 10% of his Honor to add to his own.

A knight errant may build his own stronghold and hire henchmen as most other characters can but he never gains followers automatically as a normal fighter does.

Table 3R: Knight Errant Progression Table			
		10 Sided Dice for	
Experience Points	Experience Level	Accumulated Hit Points	Level Title
0-2,750	1	20+1d10*	Wayward Warrior
2,751-5,500	2	2	Misguided Militant
5,501-12,000	3	3	Knight of the Whispering Wind
12,001-24,000	4	4	Knight of Drifting
24,001-45,000	5	5	Knight of the Shooting Stars
45,001-95,000	6	6	Knight of Shifting Sands
95,001-175,000	7	7	Rogue Knight
175,001-350,000	8	8	Rogue Knight Master
350,001-700,000	9	9**	Knight Errant
700,001-1,050,000	10	9+3	Knight Errant (10th level)
1,050,001-1,400,000***	11	9+6	K.E.(11th level)
1,400,001 – 1,750,000	12	9+9	K.E.(12th level)
1,750,001 – 2,100,000	13	9+12	K.E.(13th level)
2,100,001 – 2,450,000	14	9+15	K.E.(14th level)
2,450,001 – 2,800,000	15	9+18	K.E.(15th level)
2,800,001 – 3,150,000	16	9+21	K.E.(16th level)
3,150,001 – 3,500,000	17	9+24	K.E.(17th level)
3,500,001 – 3,850,000	18	9+27	K.E.(18th level)
3,850,001 – 4,200,000	19	9+30	K.E.(19th level)
4,200,001 – 4,550,000	20	9+33	K.E.(20th level, etc.)

*   At first level knight errants receive 20 points + 1d10. This twenty point 'kicker' is received at first level only.
** Knight errants gain 3 hps per level after the 9th.
*** 350,000 experience points per level for each additional level above the 20th.

Monks

The monk is a subclass of fighter who has honed his skills in martial arts. Although not any schlep off the street can qualify to be a monk, they are perhaps, the most deadly character class. Upon attaining the title of Superior Grand Dragon Master of the Four Seasonal Winds, he is able to inflict up to 128 points of damage in a single round. Many of the monk's abilities are based on rigorous physical training. However, there are others that are based on a pseudo-magical control of mind, body and spirit. This mysticism is not used in the same way as cleric or magic-user magic. Spell-like effects need not be prepared ahead of time, nor must they be prayed for. A monk's mystical powers are gained as a result of years of study on how the mind and spirit can manipulate the physical world.

To be a monk a character must have the following minimum ability scores: Strength 12, Wisdom 15, Dexterity 15, Intelligence 12 and Constitution 11. Monks never gain any experience points bonuses. Dexterity gives them no armor class adjustment. At first level, monks gain 2d6 for hit points. They gain 1d6 per level thereafter.

Monks are monastic aesthetics who practice rigorous mental and physical training and discipline in order to become superior fighters who need not rely on armor and weapons. Therefore, they must always be lawful in alignment, although they can be evil, good, or neutral with respect to their approach to lawfulness. A monk who, for any reason, loses this lawful alignment loses all monk abilities and must begin again as a first level character in a new class if he wishes to continue to gain skills and abilities. Non-player character monks will be aligned as follows: 15% lawful good, 35% lawful neutral, 50% lawful evil. Why so many NPC monks turn out to be evil is a mystery. Perhaps they're just pissed at the world for having had to spend their lives cooped up in a monastery eating rice and hacking at tree stumps with their bare hands all day.

As specialists in unarmed combat, monks receive only minimal training in the use of most weapons. However, those weapons from among the list that they are trained with may be used with a +1 to hit bonus. All other weapons may be used with a –1 to hit penalty. Note that this penalty does not apply if the weapon is used as an "improvised weapon" as described below. Favored monk weapons include club, crossbow, dagger, hand axe, javelin, pole arm,

Monk

Ability Requirements:
Str 12+, Dex 15+, Con 11+, Wis 15+, Int 12+

Prime Requisite(s):
None

Hit Dice Type:
d6

Allowed Races:
Human

Allowed Alignments:
lawful

Building Point Bonus:
12 BP

Table 3T: Monk Ability Table

Level	Effective Armor Class	Move	Open Hand Attacks per Melee Round*	Open Hand Damage
1	7	15"	5/4	1-4
2	6	15"	5/4	1-6
3	5	16"	5/4	2-7
4	4	16"	3/2	2-7
5	3	17"	3/2	2-8
6	2	17"	3/2	2-8
7	2	18"	3/2	3-9
8	1	18"	2	2-12
9	1	19"	2	3-12
10	0	20"	2	3-13
11	0	21"	5/2	4-13
12	0	22"	5/2	4-16
13	-1	23"	5/2	5-17
14	-1	24"	3	5-20
15	-2	25"	3	2-24
16	-2	26"	3	4-24
17	-3	27"	4	4-24
18	-4	28"	4	6-24
19	-5	29"	4	5-30
20	-6	30"	4	8-32
21	-7	31"	4	8-32

* Listings with a slash indicate extra attacks after the appropriate number of rounds, i.e. 5/4 means 5 attacks per 4 rounds, with the additional attack coming at the end of the round sequence.

spear and staff. Because a monk's ability to dodge blows and carry out devastating unarmed strikes depends greatly on unrestricted movement, he cannot wear armor nor use a shield.

With respect to combat, monks attack as fighters. However, they add one-half of a hit point per level of experience to the amount of damage they score when they successfully attack an opponent with a weapon. This simulates their study and knowledge of weapons and anatomy. At 1st level a monk scores x + 1/2 HP of damage, where x equals the damage done by the weapon used and 1/2 equals the number of hit points of damage for being first level. A 2nd level monk does x + 1 when he scores a hit, a 3rd level does x + 1 1/2, and so on all the way to Superior Grand Dragon Master of the Four Seasonal Winds who scores x + 10 1/2 HP damage. Monks of median level and above actually fight better without weapons, using their open hands, despite the weapon damage bonus they receive.

Open hand combat damage is shown on Table 3T. In addition, the monk has a chance to stun, or even kill, an opponent. An opponent is stunned by a monk for 1-6 (d6) melee rounds if the score of the monk's "to hit" die score exceeds the minimum number required for a hit by 5 or more. (i.e. if 15 is required, a score of 20 would indicate a stun or anytime the monk inflicts two dice of penetration damage.) The chance to kill is a percentage which equals the armor class (AC) of the opponent, modified by the number of experience levels above seven which the monk has attained. AC -1 is a negative chance for killing, as an example, but a monk of 9th level (two above 7th) would allow a 1% chance of killing someone with an AC of -1. Note that 1) the monk must score a hit, and 2) the hit must stun the opponent, and 3) the percentile dice score must be equal to or less than the armor class of the stunned opponent, modified by the monk's levels over 7th, in order to score a kill. Open hand fighting also allows the monk multiple attacks at such time as the monk has attained the experience levels shown in the monk's ability table.

Monks make saving throws on the table used by thieves, but they gain certain advantages. Non-magical missiles (arrows, bolts, bullets, thrown daggers, thrown javelins, thrown spears, etc.) that would normally hit can be dodged or knocked aside if the monk is able to make his saving throw against petrification for each such potential hit. In other respects, if a monk makes his saving throw against an attack form, the monk will sustain no damage from the attack, even if the attack form was a Fireball, for instance. At 9th level (Master) or higher, a monk who fails to make his saving throw will still sustain but one-half the total potential damage which the attack form could deliver, if possible. That is, a Fireball would do 50% of total damage, but the gaze of a basilisk would still petrify the monk.

At 1st level of experience, a monk is as likely to be surprised as any other character, i.e. 30%. This chance goes down to 28% at 2nd level, and it there-

Table 3S: Monk Progression Table

Experience Points	Experience Level	6 Sided Dice for Accumulated Hit Points	Level Title
0-1,000	1	20+2d6*	Grasshopper
1,001-3,000	2	3	Brother
3,001-6,000	3	4	Brother of the Winds
6,001-10,000	4	5	Brother of Secrets
10,001-22,000	5	6	Brother of Mysteries
22,001-40,000	6	7	Disciple
40,001-70,000	7	8	Sub-Master
70,001-110,000	8	9	Master
110,001-160,000	9	10	Superior Master
160,001-220,000	10	11	Master of the North Wind
220,001-400,000	11	12	Master of the West Wind
400,001-650,000	12	13	Master of the South Wind
650,001-890,000	13	14	Master of the East Wind
890,001-1,150,000	14	15	Master of Winter
1,150,001-1,300,000	15	16	Master of Autumn
1,300,001-1,600,000	16	17	Master of Spring
1,600,001-2,000,000	17	18	Master of Summer
2,000,001-2,250,000	18	19	Grand Master of Blood
2,250,001-2,500,000	19	20	Grand Master of Venom
2,500,001-3,000,000	20	21	Grand Master of Dragons
3,000,001+	21	22	**Superior Grand Dragon Master of the Four Seasonal Winds**

* At first level monks receive 20 points + 2d6. This twenty point 'kicker' is received at first level only.

after goes down 2% per level, so there is only a 26% chance of surprising a 3rd level monk, 24% chance at 4th level, 22% chance at 5th level, etc.

Monks have the following thief abilities which they perform at the indicated level of mastery. Dexterity and armor modifiers also apply as described in the thief's section. The abilities are:

1. Find Traps   10% + 3% per level
2. Move Silently   15% + 5% per level
3. Hide in Shadows   10% + 5% per level
4. Hear Noise   10% + 2% per level
5. Climb Walls   60% + 2% per level

Monks can escape taking damage from falling as follows:
At 2nd level, a monk can fall up to 10'
At 4th level, a monk can fall up to 20'
At 6th level, a monk can fall up to 30'
At 13th level, a monk can fall any distance without sustaining damage.

A monk need not be in proximity to any physical aids such as a wall to break his fall. The monk's ability to avoid damage from a fall is based on his training and mastery of learning how to position himself and land and roll properly (breakfall). He must, however, have his hands and feet free in order to use this skill. Tossing a monk, who is bound in any way, off of a cliff would result in a big red splatter mark at the bottom.

With each experience level, monks gain a new mystical special ability. These are described as follows.

1) **Intimidating Display** – The monk can display an intimidating routine of punches, blocks, kicks or other attacks in such a bewildering manner that those viewing the show will hesitate to watch and thus lose an action. This can be used in combat to automatically gain initiative for the first combat round but the monk must specifically state that he is using his intimidating display ability for this to occur. A monk cannot use intimidating display while actually engaged in combat.

2) **Improvise Weapon** – At second level the monk gains the uncanny ability to turn virtually any ordinary object into a weapon. Examples include chopsticks, chairs, clothing, dead animals and shoelaces. Treat these attacks as a normal unarmed strike by the monk with corresponding damage. The advantage to this is evident if the monk is fighting something that he would not want to touch with his bare hands such as animated piles of disgusting ooze, fire elementals, porcupines or even orcs with really poor hygiene.

3) **Pass Without Trace** – A monk can traverse any terrain without leaving a mark but he may only move at 1/4 of his normal movement rate.

4) **Self-Healing** - At 4th level the monk gains the ability to heal damage on his body. The amount of damage, which can be healed, is 2--5 hit points (d4 + 1), and this amount increases by 1 hit point with each experience level gained thereafter. This may be done once per day.

5) **Really Intimidating Display** – This ability is similar to the first level intimidating display ability except that those viewing the monk who fail to make a saving throw versus petrification will sit and watch the show for as long as the monk can keep it up.

6) **Weapon Strike** – When using a weapon other than his own body, a monk can specifically target an attack on an opponent's weapon. The AC of the weapon is base 10 minus any dexterity modifier the wielder may have. The effective armor class of a magic weapon is further modified down for each plus it is enchanted with. If the attack is successful, the weapon must save versus a crushing blow otherwise it becomes broken and useless.

7) **Resist Disease** - At 7th experience level a monk is not subject to diseases of any sort.

8) **Painful Strike** – A monk can use this ability once per opponent. It represents the monk's ability to strike an opponent in a critical spot. The intent to make a painful strike must be declared prior to making a to hit roll. Damage done from a successful painful strike attack can only be healed by magical or mystical means.

9) **Resist Spells** - Beguiling, Charms, Hypnosis, and Suggestion spells have only a 50% chance of affecting a monk of the 9th level of experience. That is, the monk is 50% resistant to such magic. This resistance increases 5% per level thereafter, so that at 10th level such spells have but a 45% chance of affecting the monk, 40% at 11th level, and so on. Saving throws apply if resistance fails. Monks of this level are no longer affected by Geas, Quest or Slow spells.

10) **Water Run** – A monk may run over water or similar liquids without sinking. While running on water he must continue to move at his maximum movement rate in order to effectively use this ability.

11) **Resist Poison** - At 11th and higher levels of experience monks are not affected by poison of any type.

12) **Invisibility** – Useable once per day for 1 turn per level that the monk has achieved beyond six.

13) **Mind Mask** – A monk of this level can completely mask his thoughts so that mind reading abilities such as ESP are useless.

14) **Telepathic Resistance** - Telepathic and mind blast attacks such as those from Mind Flayers are made as if the character had an Intelligence 6 points higher than his actual score, due to the monk's mental discipline.

15) **Retarded Aging** – The monk ages at half the normal rate.

16) **Speak with Plants and Animals** – The monk gains the ability to speak with plants and animals as druids do.

17) **Fasting** – At this level the monk can survive with only one tenth the normal about of food and water required for health and sustenance. He can do this indefinitely.

18) **Flame Walk** – A monk may walk over hot coals, burning embers or even molten lava without taking damage right away. Similar to the water run ability, the monk must continue walking at his maximum movement rate for the ability to function. Should he stop, he will begin taking the appropriate amount of damage within one round. Note that this ability does not confer total fire resistance to the monk's body. So a monk hit by a fireball while walking on lava would not take damage from the lava but would suffer the effects of the fireball if he failed his saving throw. Similarly, a monk running through a burning building would still be susceptible to damage from the heat and flames if they hit the rest of his body but his feet will be protected. Any clothing worn is susceptible to damage from the heat/flame source.

19) **Survive Without Air** – A monk with this ability can survive without air for up to 21 days.

20) **Speak with Dragons** – A monk of this level gains the ability to speak with dragons in their native tongue. Once per day the monk can use this mystic power to cast a Charm spell on the dragon. If the dragon makes a saving throw the Charm is negated but communication is still possible.

21) **Shaking Claw** - The last ability gained, and perhaps the most terrible power, is that fabled attack which enables the monk to set up vibrations in the body of the victim, and the monk can then control such vibrations so as to cause death to occur when the monk stops them. The monk merely touches his victim to set up the deadly vibrations. The victim can be virtually any creature. This power can be attempted but once per week, and the monk must touch the intended victim within 3 melee rounds or the power is drained for one week. It has no affect on the undead or creatures that can be hit only by magical weaponry. The victim cannot have more hit dice than the monk using the power, and in any event, the total hit points of the victim cannot exceed those of the monk by more than 200%, or the power has no effect. The command to die the control of the vibrations must be given by the monk within fourteen days; or else the vibrations simply cease of their own accord and do no damage whatsoever.

There are a number of strictures which monk characters must abide by. These restrictions apply to 1) armor and weapons, 2) treasure, 3) magic items usable, 4) henchmen, and 5) advancement in level, as follows:

1. Armor, as previously stated, cannot be worn. Weapons usable without penalty by monk characters are shown on Table 3C.

2. Monks, much like paladins, may not retain more than a small fraction of whatever treasure they gain. A monk may possess no more than two magic weapons and three other magic items (see 3 below) at any time. While monks may retain money sufficient for their modest needs, and to support their henchmen (see 4 below), all other treasure and excess magic items must be bestowed upon (non-player) religious institutions. (See also Followers hereafter.)

3. Magic items usable by monks include all magical varieties of weapons listed (unless proscribed), rings, and those miscellaneous magic items which are usable by thieves. Monks may employ no other magic items of any sort.

4. Until attaining the rank of Master, monks may not have any hirelings or henchmen at all. At 6th level of experience, monks may hire persons on a short-duration basis, for the duration of a single adventure only, At this level, they may also acquire up to two henchmen. Henchmen may be fighters (but not paladins nor rangers), thieves or assassins. With each level of experience above the 6th, which the monk attains, he may add one additional henchman, until the maximum number established by the monk's charisma score is reached. Monks will gain followers upon attaining 8th level; this is discussed hereafter.

5. Monks advance in levels through training, as do other characters up until 7th level. When a player character monk gains sufficient experience points to qualify him for 8th level, the monk must find and defeat in personal combat, hand-to-hand, without weapons or magic items, another 8th level monk or equivalent (i.e. 8 first level monks). The same must be done at the ninth and higher levels. A monk may not advance in levels until such combat has been won though he may continue to gain experience points until he reaches the minimum number of points required for the next higher level than he is trying to attain. Although this test is sometimes deadly, it need not be to the death and usually the only ill effect suffered by the losing monk(s) is a 10% experience point loss for each contest so lost.

Followers: When a monk player character wins his level combat challenge and attains the 8th level of experience, he may gain a number of monks as followers. He will attract from 2-5 first level monks if the player character has a monastery or monastery-like building to use as a headquarters. These followers can gain levels of experience. The player character will attract 1 or 2 additional monks of 1st level for each additional level of experience the player gains. While followers of a monk are as loyal as his other henchmen, they automatically leave service when they attain the level of Sub Master (7th). All followers will be of the exact same alignment as the monk player character. If he changes alignment, the current followers will desert, but new ones can still be gained by advancement in level. Note that monk followers require no support, upkeep, or pay of any sort.

The monastery or monastery-like headquarters of the monk can be that of the character he defeated to attain 8th or higher level, or it can be a building specially constructed by the monk player character. In the latter case, the monk may retain up to 250,000 gold pieces value in treasure in order to finance construction of the place. He may also retain sufficient treasure thereafter to maintain such a place.

Paladins

The paladin is a noble and heroic fighter, the symbol of all that is right and true in the world. Because of this, he has high ideals and impeccable morals that he must maintain at all times. Throughout legend and history there are many heroes who could be called paladins, however, many brave and heroic soldiers have tried and failed to live up to the ideals of the paladin. It is not an easy task! He must have minimum ability scores of Strength 12, Constitution 9, Wisdom 13, and Charisma 17. Strength and Charisma are the prime requisites of the paladin. A paladin must be lawful good in alignment and must always remain

Paladin

Ability Requirements:
Str 12+, Con 9+, Wis 13+, Cha 17+

Prime Requisite(s):
Strength and Charisma

Hit Dice Type:
d10

Allowed Races:
Human

Allowed Alignments:
lawful good

Building Point Bonus:
12 BP

Table 3U: Paladin Progression Table			
Experience Points	Experience Level	10 Sided Dice for Accumulated Hit Points	Level Title
0-2,750	1	20 +1d10*	Gallant
2,751-5,500	2	2	Keeper
5,501-12,000	3	3	Protector
12,001-24,000	4	4	Defender
24,001-45,000	5	5	Warder
45,001-95,000	6	6	Guardian
95,001-175,000	7	7	Chevalier
175,001-350,000	8	8	Justiciar
350,001-700,000	9	9**	Paladin
700,001-1,050,000	10	9+3	Paladin (10th level)
1,050,001-1,400,000	11	9+6	Paladin (11th level)
1,400,001-1,750,000	12	9+9	Paladin (12th level)
1,750,001-2,100,000	13	9+12	Paladin (13th level)
2,100,001-2,450,000	14	9+15	Shinning Knight
2,450,001-2,800,000	15	9+18	Holy Knight
2,800,001-3,150,000	16	9+21	Angelic Knight
3,150,001-3,500,000	17	9+24	Arch Angelic Knight
3,500,001-3,850,000	18	9+27	Holy WarLord of the 1st Order
3,850,001-4,200,000	19	9+30	Holy WarLord of the 2nd Order
4,200,001***	20	9+33	Holy WarLord of the 3rd Order

* At first level paladins receive 20 points + 1d10. This twenty point 'kicker' is received at first level only.

** Paladins gain 3 hps per level after the 9th

*** 350,000 experience points per level for each additional level above the 20th.

Table 3V: Paladin Spell Progression					
Paladin Level	Casting Level	Cleric Spell Level			
		1	2	3	4
9	1	1	--	--	--
10	2	2	--	--	--
11	3	2	1	--	--
12	4	2	2	--	--
13	5	2	2	1	--
14	6	3	2	1	--
15	7	3	2	1	1
16	8	3	3	2	1
17	9*	3	3	3	1
18	9*	3	3	3	1
19	9*	3	3	3	2
20*	9*	3	3	3	3

* Maximum spell ability

lawful good. A paladin who changes alignment, either deliberately or inadvertently, loses all his special powers — sometimes only temporarily and sometimes forever. He can use any weapon and wear any type of armor.

A paladin who has a Strength score of 16 or more gains a 10% bonus to the experience points he earns.

Lawfulness and good deeds are the meat and drink of a paladin. If a paladin should ever knowingly and willingly perform an evil act, he loses the status of paladinhood immediately and irrevocably. All benefits are then lost and no deed or magic can restore the character to paladinhood; he is ever after a fighter with a chip on his shoulder. Thereafter the character is bound by the rules for fighters. He does not gain the benefits of weapon specialization since he did not select this for his character at the start.

If the paladin commits an evil act while enchanted, controlled by magic or intoxicated, he loses his paladin status until he can atone for the deed. This loss of status means the character loses all his special abilities and essentially functions as a fighter (without weapon specialization) of the same level. Regaining his status undoubtedly requires completion of some noble but exceedingly dangerous quest to once again prove his worth and assuage his own guilt. He gains no experience prior to or during the course of this mission, and regains his standing as a paladin only upon completing the quest.

A paladin has the following special benefits:
* A paladin can detect the presence of evil intent up to 60 feet away by concentrating on locating evil in a particular direction. He can

do this as often as desired, but each attempt takes one round. This ability detects evil monsters and characters.

- A paladin receives a +2 bonus to all saving throws.
- A paladin can judge another paladin, cleric or cavalier he thinks has done wrong. The 'judged' character undergoes an immediate alignment audit and suffers any consequences.
- At 7th level and above, a paladin can scrutinize other characters and force an alignment audit (See chapter 5).
- A paladin is immune to all forms of disease. (Note that certain magical afflictions, such as lycanthropy and mummy rot, are curses and not diseases.)
- A paladin can heal by laying on hands. The paladin restores 2 hit points per experience level. He can heal himself or someone else, but only once per day.
- A paladin can cure diseases of all sorts (though not cursed afflictions such as lycanthropy). This can be done only once per week for each five levels of experience (once per week at levels 1 through 5, twice per week at levels 6 through 10, etc.).
- A paladin is surrounded by an aura of protection with a 10-foot radius. Within this radius, all summoned and specifically evil creatures suffer a -1 penalty to their attack rolls, regardless of whom they attack. Creatures affected by this aura can spot its source easily, even if the paladin is disguised.
- A paladin using a holy sword projects a circle of power 10 feet in diameter when the sword is unsheathed and held. This power dispels hostile magic of a level up to the paladin's experience level. (A holy sword is a very special weapon; if your paladin acquires one, the GM will explain its other powers.)
- A paladin gains the power to turn undead and fiends when he reaches 3rd level. He affects these monsters the same as does a cleric two levels lower — for example, at 3rd level he has the turning power of a 1st level cleric. See the section on clerics for more details on this ability.
- A paladin may call for his warhorse upon reaching 4th level, or anytime thereafter.
  This faithful steed need not be a horse; it may be whatever sort of creature is appropriate to the character (as decided by the GM). A paladin's warhorse is a very special animal, bonded by fate to the fighter. The paladin does not really "call" the animal, nor does the horse instantly appear in front of him. Rather, the character must find his warhorse in some memorable way, most frequently by a specific quest.
- A paladin can cast cleric spells once he reaches 9th level. He can cast only spells of the divination, necromantic and abjuration schools. The acquisition and casting of these spells abide by the rules given for clerics.
  The spell progression and casting level are listed in Table 3W. Unlike a cleric, the paladin does not gain extra spells for a high Wisdom score. The paladin cannot cast spells from cleric or druid scrolls nor can he use cleric items unless they are allowed to the fighter group.
- A paladin may not have in his possession more than 10 magical items. Furthermore, these may not exceed one suit of armor, one shield, four weapons (arrows and bolts are not counted), and four other magical items.
- A paladin never retains wealth. He may keep only enough treasure to support himself in a modest manner, pay his henchmen, men-at-arms, and servitors a reasonable rate, and to construct or maintain a small castle or keep (funds can be set aside for this purpose). All excess must be donated to the church or another worthy cause. This money can never be given to another player character or NPC controlled by a player, so don't even think about it.
- A paladin must tithe to whatever charitable, religious institution of lawful good alignment he serves. A tithe is 10% of the paladin's income, whether coins, jewels, magical items, wages, rewards or taxes. It must be paid immediately.
- A paladin does not attract a body of followers upon reaching 9th level or building a castle. However, he can still hire soldiers and specialists, although these men must be lawful good in comportment.
- A paladin may employ only lawful good henchmen (or those who act in such a manner when alignment is unknown). A paladin will cooperate with characters of other alignments only as long as they behave themselves. He will try to show them the proper way to live through

both word and deed. The paladin realizes that most people simply cannot maintain his high standards. Even thieves can be tolerated, provided they are not evil and are sincerely trying to reform. He will not abide the company of those who commit evil or unrighteous acts. Stealth in the cause of good is acceptable, though only as a last resort.

Rangers

The ranger is a hunter and woodsman who lives by not only his sword, but also his wits. The abilities of the ranger make him particularly good at tracking, woodcraft, infiltration and spying. The ranger must have scores not less than 13 Strength, 14 Constitution, 13 Dexterity and 14 Wisdom. The prime requisites of the ranger are Strength, Dexterity, and Wisdom. A ranger who has Strength, Dexterity, and Wisdom scores of 16 or more gains a 10% bonus to the experience points he earns. Rangers are always good, but they can be lawful, neutral, or chaotic. It is in the ranger's heart to do good, but not always by the rules.

Ranger
Ability Requirements:
Str 13+, Dex 13, Con 14+, Wis 14+
Prime Requisite(s):
Strength, Dexterity, Wisdom
Hit Dice Type:
d8
Allowed Races:
Human, Elf, Half-elf
Allowed Alignments:
any good
Building Point Bonus
10 BP

Although the ranger can use any weapon and wear any armor, several of his special abilities are usable only when he is wearing studded leather or lighter armor. In addition to the basic skills of a fighter, the ranger has several advantages. When wearing studded leather or lighter armor, a ranger can fight two-handed with no penalty to his attack rolls (see "Attacking with Two Weapons" in Chapter 12: Combat). Obviously, unless he has three hands, the ranger cannot use a shield when fighting this way. And don't try to tell your GM you can hold the blasted shield in your teeth. A ranger can still fight with two weapons while wearing heavier armor than studded leather, but he suffers the standard attack roll penalties.

The ranger is an expert woodsman and gains Tracking skill without expending any points. Furthermore, this skill improves by +5 for every three levels the ranger has earned (3rd to 5th level, +5; 6th to 8th level, +10, etc.). While wearing studded leather or lighter armor, the ranger can try to move silently and hide in shadows. His chance to succeed in natural surroundings is given on Table 3Y (modified by the ranger's race and Dexterity, as given on Tables 3NN and 3OO). When attempting these actions in non-natural surroundings (a musty crypt or city streets) the chance of success is halved. Hiding in shadows and moving silently are not possible in any armor heavier than studded leather. That's like trying to drive your car quietly down the street after a

		Table 3W: **Ranger Progression Table**		
		8 Sided Dice for	
Experience Points	Experience Level	Accumulated Hit Points	Level Title
0-2,250	1	20+2d8*	Runner
2,251-4,500	2	3	Strider
4,501-10,000	3	4	Scout
10,001-20,000	4	5	Courser
20,001-40,000	5	6	Tracker
40,001-90,000	6	7	Guide
90,001-150,000	7	8	Pathfinder
150,001-225,000	8	9	Ranger
225,001-325,000	9	10	Ranger Knight
325,001-650,000	10	11**	Ranger Lord
650,001-975,000	11	11+2	Ranger Lord (11th level)
975,001-1,300,000	12	11+4	R.L. (12th level)
1,300,001-1,625,000	13	11+6	R.L. (13th level)
1,625,001-1,950,000	14	11+8	R.L. (14th level)
1,950,001-2,275,000	15	11+10	R.L. (15th level)
2,275,001-2,600,000	16	11+12	R.L. (16th level)
2,600,001-2,925,000	17	11+14	R.L. (17th level)
2,925,001-3,250,000	18	11+16	R.L. (18th level)
3,250,001-3,575,000	19	11+18	R.L. (19th level)
3,575,001***	20	11+20	R.L. (20th level, etc.)

* At first level rangers receive 20 points + 2d8. This twenty point 'kicker' is received at first level only.

** Rangers gain 2 hps per level after the 11th.

*** 325,000 experience points per level for each additional level above the 20th.

bunch of well-meaning friends have tied cans on the back of your car after your wedding. Heavy armor clinks and clanks too much for even a ranger to sneak around in, so don't even try it.

In their role as protector of good, rangers tend to focus their efforts against some particular creature, usually one that marauds their homeland. Before advancing to 2nd level, every ranger must select a species enemy. Typical enemies include Giants, Orcs, Lizard Men, Trolls, or Ghouls; your GM has final approval on the choice. Thereafter, whenever the ranger encounters that enemy, he gains a +4 bonus to his attack rolls. This enmity can be concealed only with great difficulty, so the ranger suffers a -4 penalty on all encounter reactions with creatures of the hated type. Furthermore, the ranger will actively seek out this enemy in combat in preference to all other foes unless someone else presents a much greater danger.

Rangers are adept with both trained and untamed creatures, having a limited degree of animal empathy. If a ranger carefully approaches or tends any natural animal, he can try to modify the animal's reactions. (A natural animal is one that can be found in the real world — a bear, snake, zebra, etc.) No, just because you're a ranger doesn't mean you can have a pet dragon.

When dealing with domestic or non-hostile animals, a ranger can approach the animal and befriend it automatically. He can easily discern the qualities of the creature (spotting the best horse in the corral or seeing that the runt of the litter actually has great promise). When dealing with a wild animal or an animal trained to attack, the animal must roll a saving throw vs. rods to resist the ranger's overtures. (This table is used even though the ranger's power is non-magical.) The ranger imposes a -1 penalty on the die roll for every three experience levels he has earned (-1 at 1st to 3rd, -2 at 4th to 6th, etc.). If the creature fails the saving throw, its reaction can be shifted one category as the ranger chooses. Of course, the ranger must be at the front of the party and must approach the creature fearlessly.

For example, Runnymede, a 7th level ranger, is leading his friends through the woods. On entering a clearing, he spots a hungry wolf blocking the path on the other side. Signaling his friends to wait, Runnymede approaches the animal, whispering soothing words. The GM rolls a saving throw vs. rods for the wolf, modified by -3 for Runnymede's level. The wolf's normal reaction is unfriendly, but Runnymede's presence reduces this to neutral. The party waits patiently until the wolf wanders off to seek its dinner elsewhere. Later, Runnymede goes to the horse market to get a new mount. The dealer shows him a spirited stallion, the color of midnight. The horse is notorious for being vicious and stubborn. Runnymede approaches it carefully, again speaking soothingly, and mounts the stallion with no difficulty. Ridden by Runnymede, the horse is spirited but well behaved. If anyone else tries to ride it, well, let's just say they'll end up with more than saddle sores.

Table 3X: Ranger's Followers	
Die Roll	Follower
01-10	Bear, black
11-20	Bear, brown
21	Pixie fairy*
22-26	Cleric (human)
27-38	Dog/wolf
39-40	Druid
41-50	Falcon
51-53	Fighter (elf)
54-55	Fighter (gnome)
56-57	Fighter (halfling)
58-65	Fighter (human)
66	Fighter/magic-user (elf)*
67-72	Great cat (tiger, lion, etc.)*
73	Hippogriff
74	Pegasus*
75	Pixie*
76-80	Ranger (half-elf)
81-90	Ranger (human)
91-94	Raven
95	Satyr*
96	Thief (halfling)
97	Thief (human)
98	Treant*
99	Werebear/weretiger*
00	Other wilderness creature (chosen by the GM)

*If the ranger already has a follower of this type, ignore this result and roll again.

A ranger can learn druid spells when he reaches 8th level (see Table 3Y). He gains and uses his spells according to the rules given for druids. He does not gain bonus spells for a high Wisdom score, nor is he ever able to use druid scrolls or magical items unless specially noted otherwise.

A ranger can learn magic-user spells when he reaches 9th level. He uses his spells according to the rules for magic users. He gains a spellbook and a few spells for free. Exactly how many and what kind are up to the discretion of the GM. The rest of his spells must be obtained through adventuring. A ranger is not able to use magic-user scrolls or other magic items unless specifically noted otherwise. He can memorize a number of magic-user spells equal to the number of druid spells that can be memorized at one experience level lower.

				Table 3Y: Ranger Abilities		
Ranger Level	Hide in Shadows	Move Silently	Casting Level	Druid Spell Levels		
				1	2	3
1	10%	15%	--	--	--	--
2	15%	21%	--	--	--	--
3	20%	27%	--	--	--	--
4	25%	33%	--	--	--	--
5	31%	40%	--	--	--	--
6	37%	47%	--	--	--	--
7	43%	55%	--	--	--	--
8	49%	62%	1	1	--	--
9	56%	70%	2	2	--	--
10	63%	78%	3	2	1	--
11	70%	86%	4	2	2	--
12	77%	94%	5	2	2	1
13	85%	99%*	6	3	2	1
14	93%	99%	7	3	2	2
15	99%*	99%	8	3	3	2
16	99%	99%	9**	3**	3**	3**

* Maximum percentile score
** Maximum spell ability.

At 10th level, a ranger attracts 2d6 followers. These followers might be normal humans, but they are often animals or even stranger denizens of the land. Table 3X can be used to determine these, or your GM may assign specific followers. Rangers can build castles, forts, or strongholds, but do not gain any special followers by doing so.

Of course, your GM can assign particular creatures, either choosing from Table 3X or from any other source. He can also rule that certain creatures are not found in the region — it is highly unlikely that a tiger would come wandering through a temperate climate! But stranger things have happened. These followers arrive over the course of several months. Often they are encountered during the ranger's adventures (allowing you and your GM a chance to role-play the initial meeting). While the followers are automatically loyal and friendly toward the ranger, their future behavior depends on the ranger's treatment of them. In all cases, the ranger does not gain any special method of communicating with his followers. He must either have some way of speaking to them or they simply mutely accompany him on his journeys. ("Yeah, this bear's been with me for years. Don't know why — he just seems to follow me around. I don't own him and can't tell him to do anything he don't want to do," said the grizzled old woodsman sitting outside the tavern.) Of course, the ranger is not obligated to take on followers. If he prefers to remain independent, he can release his followers at any time. They reluctantly depart, but stand ready to answer any call for aid he might put out at a later time.

Like the paladin, the ranger has a code of behavior. A ranger must always retain his good alignment. If the ranger intentionally commits an evil act such that his alignment changes, he automatically loses his ranger status. Thereafter he is considered a fighter of the same level (if he has more experience points than a fighter of his level, he loses all the excess experience points). His ranger status can never be regained. If the ranger involuntarily commits an evil act (perhaps in a situation of no choice), he cannot earn any more experience points until he has cleansed himself of that evil. This can be accomplished by correcting the wrongs he committed, revenging himself on the person who forced him to commit the act, or releasing those oppressed by evil. The ranger instinctively knows what things he must do to regain his status (i.e., the GM creates a special adventure for the character).

Rangers tend to be loners, men constantly on the move. They cannot have henchmen, hirelings, mercenaries, or even servants until they reach 8th level. While they can have any monetary amount of treasure, they cannot have more treasure than they can carry. Excess treasure must either be converted to a portable form or donated to a worthy institution (an NPC group, not a player character or a savings bank). What do we look like, idiots?

The Magic-User Classes

The magic-user group encompasses all spellcasters working in the various fields of non-divine magic, including both those who specialize in specific schools of magic and those who study a broad range of magical theories. They draw upon the same arcane powers in order to exercise their profession but each class goes about it in a different way. All the magic-user classes have mighty spells of offensive, defensive and informational nature, but they tend to be rather weak in toe-to-toe combat compared to the other classes.

Magic-users and their ilk spend their lives (often in relative isolation) in pursuit of arcane knowledge and unlocking its dark secrets. Thus, Intelligence is the prime requisite (or one of several prime requisites) for all the magic-using character classes. Their research requires so much time, devotion and focus that they have little time for physical endeavors or social interaction. They are the pencil-necked geeks of the fantasy world. But don't be fooled, although the spell-lobber tends to start out as a rather weak individual compared to the fighter or the cleric, he is a power to be reckoned with at higher levels. And most magic-users have long memories and unforgiving demeanors toward those who treated them badly on their way up the experience ladder.

Mages tend to be poor fighters with little knowledge or interest in weaponry or the arts of hack. However, they command powerful and dangerous energies, which they can unleash with a few simple gestures, rare components and mystical words.

Spells are the tools, weapons and armor of the magic-user. While weak in a hand-to-hand combat, a magic-user who is spell-jacked (i.e. has an arsenal of spells prepared in memory) is able to strike down his foes at a distance, vanish in an instant, become a wholly different creature, or even invade the mind of an enemy and take control of his thoughts and actions.

No secrets are safe from a magic-user and no fortress is secure. His quest for knowledge and power often leads him into realms where mortals were never meant to go and even high-level fighters fear to tread. Those who practice magic seem to get drawn in until the arcane arts almost become an obsession. Given a choice, the typical magic-user would spend every waking hour delving into arcane knowledge, researching hidden mysteries and reading musty tomes that hold ancient secrets.

With the exception of battle mages and magic-users who are multi-classed, mages cannot wear armor and cast spells without suffering penalties that make the odds of a spell mishap much greater. There are many theories as to why this is so. Ask any two magic-users why they can't wear armor and lob spells and you're likely to get two conflicting answers. The most common theory put forth is that spells require the caster to contort their bodies in odd ways, and perform complicated gestures and intricate motions. This cannot be done effectively if a magic-user is wearing armor.

The real reason magic-users and armor don't mix is probably because wearing armor presents a distraction in the form of discomfort and exertion. This prevents the mage from fully concentrating on his spell casting. It's not that a magic-user CAN'T wear armor and cast spells, it's because doing so greatly increases the chance of a spell mishap. And as any magic-user will tell you, spell mishaps can be very, very nasty. Elves wearing elven chain can cast spells in armor without a spell mishap penalty, as magic is part of the nature of elves. However, elven chain is extremely rare and tough to get, though for some reason the damn NPC elves are always running around in it. So basically, find and mug an NPC elf early.

For similar reasons, magic-users are severely restricted in the weapons they can use. They are limited to those that are easy to learn. Hence, a magic-user can use a dagger or a staff, items that very basic. Other weapons allowed are darts, knives, and slings (weapons that require lit-

Table 3AA: **Magic-User Progression Table**			
		4 Sided	
		Dice for	
Experience	Experience	Accumulated	Level
Points	Level	Hit Points	Title
0-2,500	1	20+1d4*	Prestidigitator
2,501-5,000	2	2	Evoker
5,001-10,000	3	3	Conjuror
10,001-22,500	4	4	Theurgist
22,501-40,000	5	5	Thaumaturgist
40,001-60,000	6	6	Magician
60,001-90,000	7	7	Enchanter
90,001-135,000	8	8	Warlock
135,001-250,000	9	9	Sorcerer
250,001-375,000	10	10	Necromancer
375,001-750,000	11	11**	Wizard
750,001-1,125,000	12	11+1	Wizard (12th level)
1,125,001-1,500,000	13	11+2	Wizard (13th level)
1,500,001-1,875,000	14	11+3	Wizard (14th level)
1,875,001-2,250,000	15	11+4	Wizard (15th revel)
2,250,001-2,625,000	16	11+5	Mage
2,625,001-3,000,000	17	11+6	Mage (17th level)
3,000,001-3,375,000	18	11+7	Arch-Mage
3,375,-001-3,750,000	19	11+8	Arch Mage (19th level)
3,750,001+	20***	11+9	Arch-Mage (20th level)

* At first level magic-users receive 20 points + 1d4. This twenty point 'kicker' is received at first level only.

** Magic-users gain 1 hp per level after the 11th.

*** 375,000 experience points per level for each additional level beyond the 20th.

tle skill). They simply haven't the time to learn weapons that take practice to use effectively, nor the inclination.

Magic-users can use more magical items than any other characters. These include potions, rings, wands, rods, scrolls and most miscellaneous magical items. A magic-user can use a magical version of any weapon allowed to his class. He can use magical armor but the spell mishap penalties still apply.

Finally, all magic-users can create new magical items, ranging from simple scrolls and potions to powerful staves and magical swords. Once he reaches 7th level, a magic-user can pen magical scrolls and brew potions. He can construct more powerful magical items only after he has learned the appropriate spells (or works with someone who knows them). Your GM has all the necessary information on Spell Research and Magical Item Creation (see also Chapter 10).

The Schools of Magic

Spells are divided into nine different categories, or schools, according to the types of magical energy they utilize. Each school has its own special methods and practices.

Although they are called schools, schools of magic are not organized places where a person goes to study. The word "school" identifies a magical discipline. A school is an approach to magic and spellcasting that emphasizes a particular sort of spell. Practitioners of a school of magic may set up a magical university to teach their methods to beginners, but this is not necessary. Many powerful magic-users learned their craft studying under reclusive masters in distant lands or just down the street.

The nine schools of magic are:

Abjuration	Illusion
Alteration	Invocation/Evocation
Conjuration/Summoning	Necromancy
Greater Divination	Lesser Divination
Enchantment/Charm	

Of these schools, eight are greater schools while the ninth, lesser divination, is a minor school. The minor school of lesser divination includes all divination spells of the 4th spell level or less (available to all magic-users). Greater divinations are those divination spells of the 5th spell or higher.

There are magic-users who specialize in one of the nine schools of magic (or theories/approaches to magic). One example is presented herein: the illusionist. The battle mage is a different type of specialist; they vary not by magical discipline, but by their ability to concentrate on their castings during combat.

Table 3Z: **Armor Effect on Spell Mishaps**	
Armor Used*	Chance of Spell Mishap**
none	0
buckler	+5%
small shield	+15%
medium shield	+10%
padded	+20%
elven chain mail	+20%
leather	+25%
studded leather	+30%
brigandine	+35%
scale mail	+35%
hide	+40%
ring mail	+40%
chain mail	+50%
body shield	+55%
splint mail	+60%
banded mail	+80%
bronze plate mail	+90%
platemail	+100%
field plate	+120%
full plate	+150%

* Magic armor results in the same spell mishap % as normal armor of the same type.

** This percentage chance is added to the character's Chance of Spell Mishap % for his Intelligence as listed on Table 1D.

Magic-user Level	Magic-User Spell Level								
	1	2	3	4	5	6	7	8	9
1	3	--	--	--	--	--	--	--	--
2	4	--	--	--	--	--	--	--	--
3	4	1	--	--	--	--	--	--	--
4	5	2	--	--	--	--	--	--	--
5	6	2	1	--	--	--	--	--	--
6	6	2	2	--	--	--	--	--	--
7	6	3	2	1	--	--	--	--	--
8	6	3	3	2	--	--	--	--	--
9	6	3	3	2	1	--	--	--	--
10	6	4	3	2	2	--	--	--	--
11	6	4	4	3	3	--	--	--	--
12	6	4	4	4	4	1	--	--	--
13	7	5	5	4	4	2	--	--	--
14	7	5	5	4	4	2	1	--	--
15	7	5	5	5	5	2	1	--	--
16	7	5	5	5	5	3	2	1	--
17	7	5	5	5	5	3	3	2	--
18	7	5	5	5	5	3	3	2	1
19	7	5	5	5	5	3	3	3	1
20	7	5	5	5	4	3	3	3	2

Table 3BB: Magic-User Spell Progression*

* This table indicates the number of spells of each level a magic-user can memorize at one time. For example a fifth level mage could memorize six first level spells, two second level spells and one third level spell.

Learning New Spells

Learning and casting spells require long study, patience and research. Once his adventuring life begins, a magic-user is largely responsible for his own education; he no longer has a teacher looking over his shoulder and telling him which spell to learn next. Between levels he will need to seek out a mentor or magic college to help him turn his experience and acquired knowledge into something he can use to further his mastery of the arts.

While adventuring the magic-user must find his own source for magical knowledge: libraries, guilds or captured books and scrolls. Whenever a magic-user discovers instructions for a spell he doesn't know, he can try to read and understand the instructions. The player must roll percentile dice. If the result is equal to or less than the percentage chance to learn a new spell (listed on Table 1D: Intelligence), the character understands the spell and how to cast it. He can enter the spell in his spell book (unless he has already learned the maximum number of spells allowed for that level). If this die roll is higher than the character's chance to learn the spell, he doesn't understand the spell. Once a spell is learned, it cannot be unlearned. It remains part of that character's repertoire forever. Thus, a character cannot choose to "forget" a spell so as to replace it with another, so don't try to get away with that.

Spell Books

A magic-user's spell book can be a single book or a set of books, depending on your level and number of spells known. The spell book is the magic-user's diary, laboratory journal, and encyclopedia, containing a record of everything he knows. Naturally, it is his most treasured possession; without it he is almost helpless. It goes without saying then, if you're a magic-user, guard your spell book with your life, because, in a manner of speaking, it is your life (or at the very least your livelihood). See Chapter 10 for more information on spellbooks.

Spell-Memorizing

Before a magic-user can actually cast a spell, he must memorize its arcane formula. This locks an energy pattern for that particular spell into his mind. Once he has the spell memorized, it remains in his memory until he uses the exact combination of gestures, words, and materials that triggers the release of this energy pattern. Upon casting, the energy of the spell is spent, wiped clean from the magic-user's mind. The magic-user cannot cast that spell again until he returns to his spell book and memorizes it again.

Initially the magic-user is able to retain only a few of these magical energies in his mind at one time. Furthermore, some spells are more demanding and complex than others; these are impossible for the inexperienced magic-user to memorize. With experience, the magic-user's talent expands. He can memorize more spells and more complex spells. Still, he never escapes his need to study; the magic-user must always return to his spell books to refresh his powers.

Spell-Jacking

Some magic-user classes, such as the illusionist and battle mage, can spell-jack. This involves cramming more spells into memory than is normally allowed for the mage's level of experience. The danger of spell-jacking is that ALL the spells in memory (spell-jacked) can go off at the same time should a spell-mishap occur.

Spell Research

Another important power of the magic-user is his ability to research new spells and construct magical items. Both endeavors are difficult, time-consuming, costly and occasionally even perilous. Through research, a magic-user can create an entirely new spell. If high enough level and with the proper spell mix, your character can even build magical items, either similar to those already given in the rules or of your own design. Your GM has information concerning spell research and magical item creation.

Unlike many other characters, magic-users gain no special benefits from building a fortress or stronghold. They can own property and receive the normal benefits, such as monthly income and mercenaries for protection. However, the reputations of magic-users tend to discourage people from flocking to their doors. At best, a magic-user may acquire a few henchmen and apprentices to help in his work.

So, as you can see, the life of a magic-user is demanding and often lonely, but can reap great power and plenty of mysterious fun for those brave souls who play them.

Magic-Users

Magic-user generalists are the most versatile types of magic-users, those who choose not to specialize in any single school of magic. This is both an advantage and disadvantage. On the positive side, the magic-user's selection of spells enables him to deal with many different situations. Magic-users who study within a single school of magic learn highly specialized spells, but at the expense of spells from other areas.

Magic-users use Table 3BB to determine the levels and numbers of spells they can cast at each experience level. All magic-users gain one four-sided Hit Die (1d4) per level from 1st through 11th levels. After 11th level, magic-users earn 1 hit point per level and they no longer gain additional hit point bonuses for high Constitution scores. While this may seem weak, and a bit unfair to those who want to play magic-users and worry that their character might not last long, remember, life isn't fair! Besides, all you have to do is play smarter than the other characters. Keep a low profile until you've built up enough magic abilities that you become a force to be reckoned with. In other words, keep your blasted head down!

A magic-user who has an Intelligence score of 16 or higher gains a 10% bonus to the experience points he earns.

Magic-User (aka Spell Lobber, Spell Jockey)
Ability Requirements: Intelligence 9+
Prime Requisite(s): Intelligence
Hit Dice Type: d4
Allowed Races: Human, Elf, Half-elf, Pixie Fairy
Allowed Alignments: any
Building Point Bonus: 9 BP
Spell Jacking? No

Battle Mages

The battle mage is perhaps the most respected (and feared) of magic-users. They earn +2 to their starting Honor because of the prestige members of their profession enjoy. The name of the class says it all. These battle-hardened individuals focus on a special form of mental discipline that allows them to cast spells in the thick of combat with little chance of mishap or interruption. Battle mages have access to all magic-user spells but when it comes to battle spells (those of the missile or Fireball variety as well as most spells offensive/defensive in nature) they are second to none primarily because of their spell prepping, simul-casting and chain casting abilities.

Battle Mage
Ability Requirements: Intelligence 9+ Strength 12+ Dexterity 12+ Constitution 12+
Prime Requisite(s): Intelligence
Hit Dice Type: d4
Allowed Races: Human, Elf, Half-elf, Dwarf, Gnome Titan
Allowed Alignments: any
Building Point Bonus: 8 BP
Spell Jacking? Yes

Table 3CC:
Battle Mage Progression Table

Experience Points	Experience Level	4-Sided Dice for Accumulated Hit Points	Level Title
0 – 3000	1	16+1d4*	Second
3001– 6000	2	2	MinuteMage
6001– 12,000	3	3	Doughboy
12001 – 24,000	4	4	Dawgface
24001 – 48,000	5	5	WitchRanger
48,001 – 90,000	6	6	SpellSoldier
90,001 – 130,000	7	7	Artillerist
130,001 – 175,000	8	8	MeleeMage
175,001 – 275,000	9	9	SkirmishMage
275,001 – 400,000	10	10**	WarLock
400,001 – 800,000	11	10+1	BattleMage, junior grade
800,001 – 1,300,000	12	10+2	BattleMage
1,300,001 – 1,600,001	13	10+3	Arch BattleMage, junior grade
1,600,001 – 1,900,000	14	10+4	Arch BattleMage
1,900,00 – 2,300,000	15	10+5	WarMage, junior grade
2,300,00 – 2,700,000	16	10+6	Brigadier WarMage
2,700,001 – 3,300,000	17	10+7	WarMage
3,300,001 – 3,600,000	18	10+8	Arch WarMage, junior grade
3,600,001 – 4,000,000	19	10+9	Brigadier Arch WarMage
4,000,001***	20	10+10	Arch WarMage

* At first level battle mages receive 16 points + 1d4. This sixteen point 'kicker' is received at first level only.

** Battle mages gain 1 hp per level after the 10th.

*** 300,000 experience points per level of experience beyond the 20th.

Table 3DD:
Battle Mage Spell Progression*

Battle Mage Level	1	2	3	4	5	6	7	8	9	Spell-Jack**
1	3	--	--	--	--	--	--	--	--	--
2	4	--	--	--	--	--	--	--	--	--
3	4	1	--	--	--	--	--	--	--	--
4	5	2	--	--	--	--	--	--	--	1.5X
5	5	2	1	--	--	--	--	--	--	1.5X
6	6	2	2	--	--	--	--	--	--	1.5X
7	6	2	2	1	--	--	--	--	--	1.5X
8	6	3	3	2	--	--	--	--	--	1.5X
9	6	3	3	2	1	--	--	--	--	2X
10	6	4	3	3	2	--	--	--	--	2X
11	6	4	4	3	3	--	--	--	--	2X
12	7	4	4	4	4	1	--	--	--	2X
13	7	5	5	4	4	2	--	--	--	2X
14	7	5	5	4	4	2	1	--	--	2X
15	7	5	5	4	5	2	1	--	--	2X
16	7	5	5	5	5	3	2	1	--	2.5X
17	7	5	5	5	5	3	3	2	--	2.5X
18	7	5	5	5	5	3	3	2	1	2.5X
19	7	5	5	5	5	3	3	3	1	2.5X
20	7	5	5	5	5	4	3	3	2	2.5X

* This table indicates the number of spells of each level a battle mage can memorize at one time. For example a fifth level battle mage could memorize four first level spells, two second level spells and one third level spell.

** Indicates how many spells the battle mage can spell-jack (memorize) at the indicated level. Multiplier is applied to each spell level with results rounded down. For example, a 5th level battle mage could memorize five 1st level spells, two 2nd level spells and one 3rd level spell If the same mage spell-jacks he can memorize seven 1st level spells, 3 2nd level spells and 1 third level spell. (See Spell-Jacking)

Spell Prepping

Battle mages have the unique ability of spell-prepping (also called bringing a spell 'online'). Any spell of the missile/Fireball variety can be prepped. Spell-prepping involves casting the spell in the normal fashion and then 'holding' it. Such a prepped-spell does not immediately take effect and is held in stasis (usually as a small orb of energy hovering in the mage's open palm) until it is released by the mage or automatically goes off due to the prep-window expiring.

A battle mage can 'hold' a prepped-spell for 1 combat round per level of experience plus one. For example, a third level battle mage could hold a prepped spell for 4 combat rounds. Spells that have been prepped can be used on the first segment of any combat round.

Mishap/Disruption Resistance

Because of their ability to concentrate and refusal to be distracted from the task at hand, battle mages are more resistance to the risks of spell mishap than other mages. They get a –40% spell mishap modifier when wearing armor. This means a battle mage could wear ring mail with no penalty as long as he has a decent Intelligence.

If a battle mage is hit, or otherwise distracted while casting a spell, the spell is not automatically ruined. A battle mage gets to roll a save vs. his Intelligence. Success means the spell is not affected.

Simul-Casting

At higher levels, battle mages can simul-cast (cast two or more spells simultaneously.) Both spells, however, must be of a battle-nature (offensive/defensive).

Chain Casting

Another perk of the battle mage class is 'chain casting'. One or more battle mages can cast the same spell and multiply the effects. Chain-cast spells have their area of effect, range, duration and damage ratings multiplied by the number of battle mages participating in the process. (The spell cast is based on the lowest level battle mage participating in the process.) The primary advantage to this is that the cooperating mages can reach and affect more targets than they could individually. The participating mages must be within five feet of one another.

For example, two battle mages, one sixth and one seventh level, chain cast a Fireball. Individually, each one could only reach a range of 70 or 80 yards respectively. But together, they can reach a range of 140 yards (two times the range of the individual Fireball for the lowest level mage in the group). Damage from the chain cast spell will similarly be 14 dice (7x2). This is slightly less damage than they would have done if they each separately cast a Fireball in a shorter range but with their combined efforts, they have greatly increased their range (and area of effect).

Table 3EE:
Battle Mage Simul-Casting

Level of Battle Mage	Number of Simul-cast Spells
1 – 4	NA
5 – 7	2
8 – 9	3
10 – 12	4
13+	5

FRAIM

Spoils of a Hard Life

One of the downsides of being a battle mage is that the profession is hard on the mind and body. Battle mages get fewer hit points when advancing in levels compared to other mages. When advancing levels they are prohibited from adding any hit point modifiers a high Constitution would normally provide.

They also age more rapidly due to the stresses of their mental discipline. Battle mages age at twice the rate of other characters!! They also heal at half the normal rate.

Hit to Wisdom

Because battle mages tend to specialize in their mental disciplines and battle-magicks they don't devote as much time to other fields of magical studies. To causes them to suffer a –1 to Wisdom.

Illusionists

The illusionist is an example of a magic-user specialist. The school of illusion is a very demanding field of study. To specialize as an illusionist, a character needs a Dexterity score of at least 16.

An illusionist who has an Intelligence of 16 or more gains a 10% bonus to the experience points he earns.

While being equal, or even slightly inferior, to normal magic-users in most respects, illusionists have different and highly effective spells to employ. Because illusionists approach magic with a different mindset and technique than other magic-using classes they are particularly adept at using their arsenal of spells (illusionist spells). A perusal of the number and types of spells usable by illusionists will reveal that they are at least as powerful as normal magic-users and possibly slightly more potent at very high levels.

**Illusionist
(aka Spell-Jacker)**
Ability Requirements:
Intelligence 9+, Dexterity 16+
Prime Requisite(s):
Intelligence
Hit Dice Type:
d4
Allowed Races:
Human, Gnome, Gnomeling, Pixie Fairy
Allowed Alignments:
any
Building Point Bonus:
9 BP
Spell Jacking?
Yes

Illusionist Spell-Jacking

Because they are specialists, illusionists can spell-jack (see Table 3GG). Spell-jacking works in the same manner as normal spell memorization except that the illusionist is cramming more information in his head and pushing the envelope.

This allows him to hold more spells in memory but it also increases the chances of a spell mishap. When spell-jacked, there is a base 10% chance of a spell mishap of ANY spell the illusionist casts. This is in addition to any modifiers for wearing armor and/or Intelligence. If a spell mishap occurs while an illusionist is spell-jacked there is a chance that ALL spells the illusionist still has in memory (i.e. uncast) will suddenly go off with unexpected and possibly disastrous results. Such are the risks of being careless with magic.

Other Specialist Benefits

- The illusionist gains one additional spell to memorize per spell-level, however, this additional spell must be taken from the illusion school of magic
- Illusionists gain a +1 to save against spells of the illusion variety because of their enhanced understanding of such magics
- Targets of an illusion spell cast by an illusionist receive a –1 to their saving throw
- Illusionists have a +15% bonus to learn new illusion spells
- When researching new spells in the field of illusion, the illusionist has an easier time (your GM has details on this)
- The illusionist can scribe scrolls and create potions of the illusion variety at 6th level

Other Specialist Disadvantages

- Illusionists may not research new spells outside the field of illusion.
- Illusionists may not create magic items outside the illusion variety.
- The illusionist receives a –15% penalty to learn spells outside of the field of illusion.
- Whenever advancing, the illusionist automatically gains one new spell as per all magic-users, but he can only obtain a spell of the illusion variety. If none are available because he knows all of them or has failed to learn the remaining ones, no spell is gained.
- The illusionist must memorize two illusion spells per level or he loses one spell per spell level as well as the bonus spell for that level. For example, an illusionist has the following spells at first level: Read Magic, Sleep, Audible Glamer and Light. A first level illusionist gets three spells plus one as a bonus (if it's an illusion spell). Since Audible Glamer is his only illusion spell, our mage will have to memorize it twice (and any two other spells), or else his spell total will drop to two anyway (a penalty of one and loss of the bonus 4-2=2). So don't be a fool, memorize spells from your school!

Table 3FF: Illusionist Progression Table

Experience Points	Experience Level	4-Sided Dice for Accumulated Level Hit Points	Title
0--2,250	1	20+1d4*	Prestigitator
2,251--4,500	2	2	Minor Trickster
4501--9,000	3	3	Trickster
9,001-18,000	4	4	Master Trickster
18,001-35,000	5	5	Cabalist
35,001---60,000	6	6	Visionist
60,001-95,000	7	7	Phantasmist
-1,95,001--145,000	8	8	Apparitionist
145,001-220,000	9	9	Spellbinder
220,001-440,000	10	10**	Illusionist
440,001--660,000	11	10+1	Illusionist (11th level)
660,001-880,000	12	10+2	Illusionist (12th level)
1,100,001-1,300,000	13	10+3	Illusionist (13th level)
1,300,001-1,520,000	14	10+4	Illusionist (14th level)
1,520,001-1,740,000	15	10+5	Illusionist (15th level)
1,740,001-1,960,000	16	10+6	Illusionist (16th level)
1,960,001-2,180,000	17	10+7	Illusionist (17th level)
2,180,001-2,400,000	18	10+8	Illusionist (18th level)
2,400,001-2,620,000	19	10+9	Illusionist (19th level)
2,620,001-	20***	10+10	Illusionist (20th level)

* At first level illusionists receive 20 points + 1d4. This twenty point 'kicker' is received at first level only.
** Illusionists gain 1 hp per level after the 10th.
*** 220,000 experience points per level of experience beyond the 20th.

Table 3 GG: Illusionist Spell Progression*

Illusionists Level	1	2	3	4	5	6	7	8	9	Spell Jack**
1	3	--	--	--	--	--	--	--	--	--
2	4	--	--	--	--	--	--	--	--	--
3	4	1	--	--	--	--	--	--	--	1.5X
4	5	2	--	--	--	--	--	--	--	1.5X
5	6	2	1	--	--	--	--	--	--	1.5X
6	6	2	2	--	--	--	--	--	--	1.5X
7	6	3	2	1	--	--	--	--	--	1.5X
8	6	3	3	2	--	--	--	--	--	2X
9	6	3	3	2	1	--	--	--	--	2X
10	6	4	3	2	2	--	--	--	--	2X
11	6	4	4	3	3	--	--	--	--	2X
12	6	4	4	4	4	1	--	--	--	2X
13	7	5	5	4	4	2	--	--	--	2X
14	7	5	5	4	4	2	1	--	--	2X
15	7	5	5	4	5	2	1	--	--	2.5X
16	7	5	5	5	5	3	2	1	--	2.5X
17	7	5	5	5	5	3	3	2	--	2.5X
18	7	5	5	5	5	3	3	2	1	2.5X
19	7	5	5	5	5	3	3	3	1	2.5X
20	7	5	5	5	5	4	3	3	2	3X

* This table indicates the number of spells of each level an illusionist can memorize at one time. For example a fifth level illusionist could memorize six first level spells, two second level spells and one third level spell.
** Indicates how many spells the illusionist can spell-jack (memorize) at the indicated level. Multiplier is applied to each spell level with results rounded down. For example a 5th level illusionist could memorize six 1st level spells, two 2nd levels spells and one 3rd level spell (see Spell-Jacking). The same illusionist who is spell-jacking could memorize nine 1st level spells, three 2nd level spells and one 3rd level spell (See Spell-Jacking)

- The illusionist, as a specialist in illusion magic, may not even learn spells of the opposition magic to illusion: Abjuration, Necromancy and Invocation/Evocation.
- The illusionist cannot use magic items that duplicate the effect of the opposition schools of Abjuration, Necromancy and Invocation/Evocation.

Cleric Character Classes

The cleric is a believer and advocate of a gawd from a particular mythos. More than just a follower, he intercedes and acts on behalf of others, seeking to use his powers to advance the beliefs of his mythos.

Clerics have certain powers: the ability to cast spells, the strength of arm to defend their beliefs, and special, gawd-granted powers to aid them in their calling. While clerics are not as fierce in combat as warriors, they are trained to use weaponry in the fight for their cause. They can cast spells to further their gawd's aims, protect its adherents and brutally massacre its opponents. They have few offensive spells, but these are very powerful.

Clerics

The cleric may be an adherent of any religion. Clerics can have any alignment acceptable to their order. A cleric must have a Wisdom score of 9 or more. High Constitution and Charisma are also particularly useful.

All clerics gain one eight-sided Hit Die (1d8) per level from 2nd through 9th. After 9th level, clerics earn 2 hit points per level and they no longer gain additional hit point bonuses for high Constitution scores. A cleric who has a Wisdom of 16 or more gains a 10% bonus to the experience points he earns.

All clerics have certain holy (or unholy depending on alignment) symbols, which aid them and give power to their spells. And although they are endowed with special powers by their gawds, the cleric often relies on the skills of armed combat to keep others in line and further his mission. Clerics gain additional spells for having high Wisdom scores.

Clerics are sturdy soldiers, although their selection of weapons is limited. Standard clerics are traditionally restricted from shedding blood. Thus they are allowed to use only blunt, bludgeoning weapons when they bash their enemies skulls into oozing sticky messes. They can use a fair number of magical items including cleric scrolls, most potions and rings, some wands and rods, staves, armor, shields and magical versions of any weapons allowed by their order.

Clerics are worthy toe-to-toe fighters, but they are decent spell-slingers as well. Clerics are bestowed with cleric spells by their particular gawd in exchange for their devotion to correct and diligent prayers and for their work in furthering the gawd's work in the world. Such spells help the cleric to serve, fortify, protect and revitalize those under his care. He has a wide variety of spells to choose from, suitable to many different purposes and needs. The cleric also has a limited number of attack spells, some of which are simply the reverse form of curative incantations. Note that all spells must be spoken or read aloud.

Because of their healing and protective abilities, some would have you believe that clerics in HackMaster are some sort of army medic, standing around waiting for their buddies to come to the back line and get healed before returning to the action at the front. Not so! Clerics have an arsenal of spells and have enough combat skills to smack around most other classes. They don't exist to cure others. They exist to further the goals of their patron gawd. As long as the other PCs in your cleric's group further the goals of his gawd, fine, protect them. But he shouldn't feel any need to cure another that does not worship his gawd, worships another gawd or isn't currently serving your gawd indirectly (by fulfilling a mission you think is worthy, or protecting your hide).

Clerics can gain extra Honor by converting non-believers to their cause. For each such convert, the cleric gains one point of temporal Honor. However, for each convert that strays from the flock, the cleric loses a point of

Cleric

Ability Requirements:
Wisdom 9+

Prime Requisite(s):
Wisdom

Hit Dice Type:
d8

Allowed Races:
All

Allowed Alignments:
any

Building Point Bonus:
10 BP

Spell Jacking?
No

Table 3HH:
Cleric Progression Table

Experience Points	Experience Level	8-Sided Dice for Accumulated Level Hit Points	Title
0-1,500	1	20+1d8*	Altar Boy
1,501-3,000	2	2	Acolyte
3001-6000	3	3-	Brother
6,001-13,000	4	4	Layman
13,001-27,500	5	5	Adept
27,501-55,000	6	6	Friar
55,001-110,000	7	7	Curate
110,001-225,000	8	8	Preacher
225,001-450,000	9	9**	Priest
450,001-675,000	10	9+2	Perfect
675,001-900,000	11	9+4	Canon
900,001-1,125,000	12	9+6	Deacon
1,125,001-1,350,000	13	9+8	Abbot
1,350,001-1,575,000	14	9+10	Evangelist
1,575,001-1,800,000	15	9+12	Prior
1,800,001-2,025,000	16	9+14	Prelate
2,025,001-2,250,000	17	9+16	Rector
2,250,001-2,475,000	18	9+18	Vicar
2,475,001-2,700,000	19	9+20	Patriarch
2,700,001-2,925,000	20***	9+22	High Priest

* At first level clerics receive 20 points + 1d8. This twenty point 'kicker' is received at first level only.

** Clerics gain 2 hps per level after the 9th.

*** 225,000 experience points per level for each additional level beyond the 20th.

Table 3II:
Cleric Spell Progression

Cleric Level	1	2	3	4	5	6*	7**
1	3	--	--	--	--	--	--
2	4	--	--	--	--	--	--
3	4	1	--	--	--	--	--
4	5	2	--	--	--	--	--
5	5	3	1	--	--	--	--
6	5	3	2	--	--	--	--
7	5	3	2	1	--	--	--
8	5	3	3	2	--	--	--
9	6	4	3	2	1	--	--
10	6	4	3	3	2	--	--
11	7	4	4	3	2	1	--
12	8	5	5	3	2	2	--
13	8	6	6	4	2	2	--
14	8	6	6	5	3	2	1
15	8	6	6	6	4	2	1
16	9	7	7	6	4	3	1
17	9	7	7	7	5	3	2
18	9	8	8	8	6	4	2
19	9	9	8	8	6	4	2
20	9	9	9	8	7	5	2

* Usable only by clerics with 17 or greater Wisdom.

** Usable only by clerics with 18 or greater Wisdom.

temporal Honor. Thus, gaining and keeping followers for their patron is of utmost importance to clerics.

Another important attribute of the cleric is the ability to turn away (or actually command into service) the undead (undead – evil creatures that exist in a form of non-life, neither dead nor alive) and less powerful demons and devils. These creatures, as well as demons and devils, are detailed in the Hacklopedia of Beasts.

The cleric is charged with defeating these mockeries of life. His ability to turn undead (see "Turning Undead" in Chapter 12: Combat) enables him to drive away these creatures or destroy them utterly (though a cleric of evil alignment can bind the creatures to his will). As a rule of thumb, a cleric is effective against any undead monster whose Hit Dice are not greater than those of the cleric. Only high level clerics have any hope of driving away or influencing demons or devils.

All clerics are able to scrutinize other clerics and paladins they meet and force an immediate alignment audit (see Cleric Scrutiny section in Chapter 5).

As a cleric advances in level, he gains additional spells, better combat skills and a stronger turning ability. Upon reaching 8th level, the cleric automatically attracts a fanatically loyal group of believers, provided the character has established a place of worship of significant size. The cleric can build this place of worship at any time during his career, but he does not attract believers until he reaches 8th level or his Fame Factor reaches 100. These fanatics are normal warriors, 0-level soldiers, ready to fight for the cleric's cause. The cleric attracts 20 to 200 of these followers; they arrive over a period of several weeks. After the initial devotees assemble, no new followers trickle in to fill the ranks of those who have fallen in service. Your GM will decide the exact number and types of followers attracted by the cleric. The character can hire other troops as needed, but these are not as loyal as his followers.

At 9th level, the cleric may receive official approval to establish a religious stronghold, be it a fortified abbey, temple complex or a secluded convent. Obviously, the stronghold must contain all the trappings of a place of worship and must be dedicated to the service of the cleric's cause. However, the construction cost of the stronghold is half the normal price, since the work has official sanction and much of the labor is donated. The cleric can hold property and build a stronghold any time before reaching 9th level, but this is done without church sanction and does not receive the benefits described above. If the cleric then clears the surrounding territory and humans dwell in this area, there will be a monthly revenue per inhabitant from trade, taxation and tithes. Your GM will provide full details on building temples and serving as the cleric-head of a faith when he deems you need such information.

The Garweeze Wurld Mythoi

Although your GM is free to set his campaign in a home-brewed world of his own making, most HackMaster campaigns are traditionally set in Garweeze Wurld. This richly detailed world has its own mythoi called the *Gawds of Twilight Last*. These gawds are briefly described here in thumbnail fashion for the benefit those players with clerics who may find them worthy of serving.

The gawds of Garweeze Wurld represent the last rag-tag survivors of an epic war that raged for thousands of years between ALL the various (and well known) pantheons. When the smoke cleared and the dust settled only a few

FRAIM

gawds from those original pantheons remained. These Gawds of Twilight Last formed a fragile peace and merged, creating a new pantheon. A new pecking order was established and spheres of control were shifted. The mighty Zeus, once gawd-supreme over Mount Olympus was reduced to a minor gawd with token powers. Luvia the Merciless was blinded as punishment for his role in setting events in motion that led to the war among the gawds.

Gawds derive their powers from living worshippers (in much the same way demons and devils derive their powers from dead worshippers in the form of souls). Competition for worshippers is fierce since the number of worshippers a gawd has ultimately determines his position in the pecking order among his peers. The problem is, the gawds have sworn a binding oath, which prevents them from directly opposing each other. So they must use their clerics (and worshippers) to do their dirty work for them.

The Gawds of Twilight Last, along with their agents and champions, are constantly competing with one another for worshippers as the epic struggle of good vs. evil continues to keeps them at odds. If your GM has chosen to use these gawds in his campaign he will be able to give any you more information on the gawd your cleric has chosen to serve.

Weapons Allowed by the Gawds of Twilight Last

Not all the gawds are opposed to the shedding of blood. Indeed, some require their clerics to use swords, spears, or other specific weapons. Given below is a partial list of the Gawds of Twilight Last along with the weapons they allow their clerics to use.

Gawd	AL	Sphere	Weapon
Arnaya	CE	Gawd of Vengeance	Spear, Bow
Draper the Thief Gawd	CN	Stealth/Cunning	Dagger
Feeble Gawd, The	LN	Mysteries	Mace, club
Francor'Dieus	LE	Earth	Pick
Gazzar-Kree	LG	Peace/Tranquility	Quarterstaff
Grawdyng	NE	Death	Sickle
Ikka Paatang	N	Nature	Club, scimitar, sickle
Luvia the Blind Gawd	LG	Justice	Mace, club
Mangrus	CN	Disease	Scourge, whip
Markovia	CG	Oceans	Harpoon, spear, trident
Navinger	CG	Love/Eunuchs	Bow and arrows, man-catcher
Nudor	NG	Healing	Abhor weapons of any kind except open palm
Odin	CG	War	Battle axe, mace, morning star, spear, sword
Pangrus	CN	War (Gnomish)	Bow and arrows, javelin, light lance, sling, spear
Par'Kryus	CN	Wind	Blowgun, dart
Shona	CG	Games/ritual combat	Sword, javelin
Skraad	LN	Blacksmith/Fates	War hammer
Thor	CN	Thunder	Club, mace, war hammer
Thrain	LN	Wisdom	Quarterstaff, morningstar
Yiders	CE	Strength	Hammer, war mace
Zeus the Diminished	LG	Lightning	Dart, javelin, spear

Of course there are many other reasons a gawd might be associated with a particular weapon or group of weapons. These are often cultural, reflecting the weapons used by the people of the area. There may be a particular legend associated with the gawd, tying it to some powerful artifact weapon (Thor's hammer, for example).

Dictates of the Faith

All clerics must live by certain tenets and beliefs often tailored for their particular gawd. These guide the clerics' behavior. The cleric receives his spells and special abilities directly from his gawd (the gawd does not need to make a personal appearance to grant the spells, the cleric prays for them) only if he follows these tenants. Additionally, the cleric must take extreme care not to abuse his power lest he get smacked down by an agent of his gawd (or the gawd himself!) and his powers are revoked as further punishment.

If a cleric violates the dictates of his faith or violates his alignment he may lose his cleric abilities until proper penance and compensation have been performed. Your GM will be serving as the 'eyes of the gawds' in this regard and it is his right (and obligation) to slap around clerics who fail to live up to the standards of their religion (see Atonement section of Chapter 5).

Druids

The druid is a sub-class of the cleric. Druids are guardians of the wilderness, be it forest, plains, or jungle. They can only be absolute neutrals (see Alignment section in Chapter 5), viewing good and evil, law and chaos, as balancing forces of nature that are necessary for the continuation of all things. They must have a minimum Wisdom of 12 and a Charisma of 15. Both of these major attributes must exceed 15 if a druid is to gain a 10% bonus to earned experience.

As protectors of nature, druids are aloof from the complications of the civilized world and what they see at the petty short-term trials of men. Their greatest concern is for the continuation of the orderly and proper cycles of nature; birth growth, death and rebirth. Druids tend to view all things as cyclic and thus the battles of good and evil are only the rising and falling tides of time. Only when the cycle and balance are disrupted does the druid become concerned. Given this view of things, the druid must be neutral in alignment.

Druids are charged with protecting wilderness; in particular trees, wild plants, wild animals and crops. By association, they are also responsible for their followers and their animals. Thus, druids will never destroy woodlands or crops no matter what the circumstances. Even though a forest, for example, might be a den of evil and hostile beings, druids would not destroy it, although nothing would prevent them from changing the nature of the place if the desire and wherewithal existed. In similar fashion, they avoid slaying wild animals or even domestic ones except as necessary for self-preservation and sustenance.

Druids recognize that all creatures (including humans) need food, shelter and protection from harm. Hunting, farming and cutting lumber for homes are logical and necessary parts of the natural cycle. However, druids do not tolerate unnecessary destruction or exploitation of nature for profit. Druids often prefer subtle and devious methods of revenge against those who defile

Druid

Ability Requirements:
Wisdom 12+, Charisma 15+
Prime Requisite(s):
Wisdom, Charisma
Hit Dice Type:
d8
Allowed Races:
Human, half-elf, halfling, elf, gnomeling
Allowed Alignments:
True Neutral
Building Point Bonus:
10 BP
Spell Jacking?
No

nature. It is well known that druids can be unforgiving, very patient and somewhat sadistic when it comes to enforcing their precepts. Some have even been know to track down those mischievous youths who innocently carve their initials in trees in order to carve out a similar mark on the delicate skin of the offender.

Mistletoe is an important holy symbol to druids and it is a necessary part of some spells (those requiring a holy symbol). To be fully effective, the druid must gather the mistletoe by the light of the full moon using a golden or silver sickle specially made for the purpose. Mistletoe gathered by other means halves the effectiveness of a given spell, if it causes damage or has an area of effect, and grants the target a +2 bonus to his saving throw if a saving throw is applicable. Because the adventuring druid often travels into regions void of mistletoe, they must often construct special holy symbols woven from dried leaves (and the roots of the mistletoe plant as long as the plant itself isn't harmed).

Druids as a class do not dwell permanently in castles, or even in cities or towns, All druids prefer to live in sacred groves, dwelling in sod, log or stone buildings of smallish size. When attaining levels above the 11th, characters will generally inhabit building complexes set in woodlands and similar natural surroundings.

Weapons Allowed

Unlike the cleric, the druid is allowed to use only "natural" armors; padded, hide or leather armor and wooden shields, including those with magical enhancements. All other armors are forbidden to him. His weapons are limited to club, sickle, dart, spear, dagger, scimitar, sling and staff.

Spells Allowed

Druids have their own arsenal of spells. It will be noted that the druid spells are more attuned to nature and the outdoors than are the spells of other clerics or magic-users.

Druids serve to strengthen, protect and revitalize, as the usual cleric does. The more powerful druid spells, as well as their wider range of weaponry, make up for the fact that druids are unable to use any armor or shields other than leather armor and wooden shields (metallic armor spoils their magical powers). They must speak or read spells aloud. Due to their involvement with living, growing things, druids have no power to turn or control undead, demons or devils.

Druids can use all magical items normally allowed clerics, except for those that are written (books and scrolls) and armor and weapons not normally allowed for druids.

	Table 3JJ: **Druid Progression Table**			
Experience Experience Points	Level	8-Sided Dice for Accumulated Hit Points	Level Title	
0-2,000	1	20+1d8*	Aspirant	
2,001-4,000	2	2	Ovate	
4,001-7,500	3	3	Initiate of the 1st Circle	
7,501-12,500	4	4	Initiate of the 2nd Circle	
12,501-20,000	5	5	Initiate of the 3rd Circle	
20,001-35,000	6	6	Initiate of the 4th Circle	
35,001-60,000	7	7	Initiate of the 5th Circle	
60,001-90,000	8	8	Initiate of the 6th Circle	
90,001-125,000	9	9	Initiate of the 7th Circle	
125,001-200,000	10	10	Initiate of the 8th Circle	
200,001-300,000	11	11	Initiate of the 9th Circle	
300 001-750,000	12	12	Druid	
750:001-1,500,000	13	13	Archdruid	
1,500,001-3,000,000	14	14	The Great Druid	
3,000,001-3,500,000	15	15**	The Grand Druid***	
3,500,001-500,000	16	15+1	Hierophant Druid****	
500,001-1,000,000	17	15+2	Hierophant Initiate	
1,000,001-1,500,000	18	15+3	Hierophant Adept	
1,500,001-2,000,000	19	15+4	Hierophant Master	
2,000,001-2,500,000	20	15+5	Numinous Hierophant	
2,500,001-3,000,000	21	15+6	Mystic Hierophant	
3,000,001-3,500,000	22	15+7	Arcane Hierophant	
3,500,001+	23	15+8	Hierophant of the Cabal	

* At first level druids receive 20 points + 1d8. This twenty point 'kicker' is received at first level only.
** Druids gain 1 hp per level after the 15th.
*** See the description of druids concerning 15th level and the Grand Druid.
**** See hierophant druids in the druid description. At 16th Level druids start over at 0 experience points.

Table 3KK: **Druid Spell Progression**							
Druid Level	1	2	3	4	5	6	7
1	4	-	-	-	-	-	-
2	4	1	-	-	-	-	-
3	5	2	1	-	-	-	-
4	6	2	2	-	-	-	-
5	6	3	2	-	-	-	-
6	6	3	2	1	-	-	-
7	6	4	3	1	-	-	-
8	6	4	3	2	-	-	-
9	6	4	3	2	1	-	-
10	6	4	3	3	2	-	-
11	6	5	3	3	2	1	-
12	6	5	4	4	3	2	1
13	6	5	5	5	4	3	2
14	6	6	6	6	5	4	3
15	6	6	6	6	6	6	6

Granted Powers

A druid makes most saving throws as a cleric, but he gains a bonus of +2 to all saving throws vs. fire or electrical attacks.

All druids can speak a secret language in addition to any other tongues they know. This secret language does count toward the "Number of Languages Known" listed on Table 1D. The vocabulary of this druid language is limited to dealing with nature and natural events. Druids jealously guard this language; it is the one infallible method they have of recognizing each other.

At first level, druids can identify plants, animals and pure water with a chance of success equal to 40% + 1% for each full point of their Intelligence and Wisdom scores, +10% per level. Additional powers are granted as the druid reaches higher levels.

At 3rd level the druid is granted the following powers:

- He can identify plants, animals and pure water with perfect accuracy.

- He can pass through overgrown areas (thick thorn bushes, tangled vines, briar patches, etc.) without leaving a trail and at his normal movement rate.

- He can learn the languages of woodland creatures. These include Centaurs, Dryads, Elves, Fauns, Gnomes, Gnomelings, Dragons, Giants, Lizard Men, Manticores, Nixies, Pixies, Pixie fairies, Sprites, and Treants. The druid can add one language at 3rd level and one more every time he advances a level above 3rd.

At 7th level the druid is granted the following powers:

- He is immune to charm spells cast by woodland creatures (Dryads, Nixies, etc.)

- He gains the ability to shapechange into a reptile, bird or mammal up to three times per day after he reaches 7th level. Each animal form (reptile, bird or mammal) can be used only once per day. The size can vary from that of a bullfrog or small bird to as large as a black bear. Upon assuming a new form, the druid heals 10-60% (1d6 x 10%) of all damage he has suffered (round fractions down). The druid can only assume the form of a normal (real world) animal in its normal proportions, but by doing so he takes on all of that creature's characteristics – its movement rate and abilities, its Armor Class, number of attacks, and damage per attack.

- Thus, a druid could change into a wren to fly across a river, transform into a black bear on the opposite side and attack the orcs gathered there, and finally change into a snake to escape into the bushes before more orcs arrive.

- The druid's clothing and one item held in each hand also become part of the new body; these reappear when the druid resumes his normal shape. The items cannot be used while the druid is in animal form.

Druid Organization

The religion of druids has a worldwide structure. At their upper levels (12th and above), only a few druids can hold each level.

Druids, Archdruids and the Great Druid

At 12th level, the druid character acquires the official title of "Druid". There can be only nine 12th level druids in any geographic region (as defined by oceans, seas and mountain ranges; a continent may consist of three or four such regions). A character cannot reach 12th level unless he takes his place as one of the nine druids. This is possible only if there are currently fewer than nine druids in the region, or if the character defeats one of the nine druids in magical or hand-to-hand combat, thereby assuming the defeated druid's position. If such combat is not mortal, the loser drops experience points so that he has exactly 200,001 remaining – just enough to be 11th level.

The precise details of each combat are worked out between the two combatants in advance. The combat can be magical, non-magical or a mixture of both. It can be fought to the death, until only one character is unconscious, until a predetermined number of hit points is lost, etc. Whatever can be agreed upon between the characters is legitimate, so long as there is some element of skill and risk.

When a character becomes a 12th level druid, he gains three underlings. Their level depends on the character's position among the nine druids. The druid with the most experience points is served by three initiates of 9th level; the second-most experienced druid is served by three initiates of 8th level; and so on, until the least experienced druid who is served by three 1st level aspirants.

Only three Archdruids (13th level) can operate in a geographical region. To become an Archdruid, a 12th level druid must defeat one of the reigning Archdruids or advance into a vacant position. Each of the three Archdruids is served by three initiates of 10th level.

From among the Archdruids of the entire world, three are chosen to serve the Grand Druid (see "The Grand Druid and Hierophant Druids" section). These three retain their attendees but are themselves servants of the Grand Druid.

The Great Druid (14th level) is unique in his region. He, too, won his position from the previous Great Druid. He is served by three initiates of 11th level.

The ascendance of a new Great Druid usually sets off shock waves of turmoil and chaos through the druid hierarchy. The advancement of an Archdruid creates an opening that is fiercely contested by the druids, and the advancement of a druid creates an opening in their ranks.

The Grand Druid and Hierophant Druids

The highest-ranking druid in the world is the Grand Druid (15th level). Unlike Great Druids (several of whom can operate simultaneously in different lands), only one person in a world can ever hold this title at one time. Consequently, only one druid can be 15th level at any time.

The Grand Druid knows six spells of each level. He also can cast up to six additional spell levels, either as a single spell or as several spells whose levels total to six (for example, one 6th level spell, six 1st level spells, three 2nd level spells, etc.).

The Grand Druid is attended by nine other druids who are subject only to him and have nothing to do with the hierarchy of any specific land or area. Any druid character of any level can seek the Grand Druid and ask to serve him. Three of these nine are Archdruids who roam the world, acting as his messengers and agents. Each of them receives four additional spell levels. The remainder is normally druids of 7th to 11th level, although the Grand Druid can request a druid of any level to serve him and often considers applications from humble aspirants.

The position of Grand Druid is not won through combat. Instead, the Grand Druid selects his successor from the acting Great Druids. The position is demanding, thankless and generally unexciting for anyone except a politician. After a few hundred thousand experience points of such stuff, any adventurer worthy of the name probably is ready to move on to something else.

For this reason, the Grand Druid reaches 16th level after earning only 500,000 more experience points. After reaching 16th level, the Grand Druid can step down from his position at any time, provided he can find a suitable successor (another druid with 3,000,000 experience points).

Upon stepping down, the former Grand Druid must relinquish the six bonus spell levels and all of his experience points but he keeps the rest of his abilities. He is now a 16th level Hierophant Druid, and begins advancing anew (using the progression given in Table 3KK). The character may rise as high as 20th level as a Hierophant Druid (almost always through self-training).

Beyond 15th level, a druid never gains any new spells (ignore the Druid Spell Progression table from this point on). Casting level continues to rise with experience. Rather than spells, spell-like powers are acquired.

> **16th level:** At 16th level, the Hierophant Druid gains four powers: Immunity to all natural poisons. Natural poisons are ingested or insinuated animal or vegetable poisons, including monster poisons, but not mineral poisons or poison gas.
> He has vigorous health for a person of his age. The Hierophant is no longer subject to the ability score adjustments for aging.
> The ability to alter his appearance at will. Appearance alteration is accomplished in one round. A height and weight increase or decrease of 50% is possible, with an apparent age from childhood to extreme old age. Body and facial features can resemble any human or humanoid creature. This alteration is not magical, so it cannot be detected by any means short of True Seeing.
>
> **17th Level:** The character gains the biological ability to hibernate. His body functions slow to the point where the character may appear dead to a casual observer. Aging ceases.
> The character is completely unconscious during hibernation. He awakens either at a preordained time ("I will hibernate for 20 days") or when there is a significant change in his environment (the weather turns cold, someone hits him with a stick, etc.).
> A 17th level Hierophant Druid can also enter the Elemental Plane of Earth at will. The transference takes one round to complete. This ability also provides the means to survive on that plane, move around, and return to the Prime Material Plane at will. It does not confer similar abilities or immunities on the Prime Material Plane.
>
> **18th level:** The character gains the ability to enter and survive in the Elemental Plane of Fire.
>
> **19th level:** The character gains the ability to enter and survive in the Elemental Plane of Water.
>
> **20th level:** The character gains the ability to enter and survive in the Elemental Plane of Air.

Thief Character Classes

Thieves are opportunists who feel that the world (and everyone in it) somehow owes them a living. They get by day-by-day, living in the highest style they can afford and doing as little work as possible. And, depending on their specialty, they have different ways of going about it. The true thief finds his way through the world by stealing and taking advantage of those who are careless with their assets. The bard is a little more cunning and a bit more charming. He lives by his wits. He uses his skills in song and music to lower the defenses of those he meets. He's expert at running confidence games and scams. And in a pinch he has some of the skills of the true thief to fall back on. The assassin on the other hand is a dark figure who thinks nothing of cutting a throat or poisoning a drink to get what he wants.

All the thief-types share one thing in common — the less they have to toil and struggle (like everyone else) and are able to maintain a comfortable standard of living, the better off they think they are. While this attitude is neither evil nor cruel, (except for the assassin of course) it does not foster a good reputation. Many a thief has a questionable past or a shady background he'd prefer was left uninvestigated. Even so, most thieves take great pride in the fact that they are more clever than those poor silly individuals who earn their living by the sweat of their brow.

Thieves

Thieves can be found in every corner of the world. Where hard coin is passed from one palm to another the thief is not far away. They are attracted to commerce and valuables like rats to cheese. Thieves come in all shapes and sizes. And while some are more capable at their profession than others, they all live off the hard-earned fruits of others' labor. In some ways they are the epitome of roguishness. While the profession of thief may not be entirely honorable, it is not entirely dishonorable, either. No one likes a petty thief but many admire a thief of great ability and renown.

At his best, the thief is a romantic hero fired by noble purpose but a little wanting in strength of character. Such a flawed individual may truly strive for good but continually runs afoul of temptation. He can't help himself. Even thieves who are relatively well off from past exploits find it hard to resist the lure of gold or treasure which presents itself. At worst he's a cold-blooded snake, who'd steal from his own grandpappy, kick a dog and backstab his friend for a few coppers.

Thieves combine a few of the qualities of the other character classes. They are allowed to use a wide variety of magical items, weapons and armor. They have special abilities that are unique to their group; the fruit of many, many years of practicing their craft on the streets.

Thieves tend to spend a lot of time deciphering runes and old maps and thus, have a percentage chance to read strange writings they come across. All are skilled in climbing and clinging to small cracks and outcroppings, even more skilled than the hardy men of the mountains. They are alert and attentive. They hear things that others would miss. Nothing gets past them if there is a potential mark involved. Finally, they are dexterous (and just a little bit light-fingered), able to perform tricks and filch small items with varying degrees of success.

When a thief tries to use one of his skills, the GM rolls percentile dice to determine whether the attempt succeeds or fails. If the dice roll is equal to or less than the special ability score, the attempt succeeds. Otherwise, it fails. Of course, this roll is done in secret and often it isn't obvious whether the thief succeeded or not. I recommend having your buddy

Thief

Ability Requirements:
Dexterity 9+
Prime Requisite(s):
Dexterity
Hit Dice Type:
d6
Allowed Races:
All
Allowed Alignments:
any
Building Point Bonus:
12 BP

	Table 3LL: **Thief Experience Levels**		
Experience Points	Experience Level	6-Sided Dice for Accumulated Hit Points	Level Title
0-1,250	1	20+1d6*	Apprentice
1,251-2,500	2	2	Footpad
2,501-5,000	3	3	Cutpurse
5,001-10,000	4	4	Larcenist
10,001-20,000	5	5	Scout
20,001-42,500	6	6	Treasure Hunter
42,501-70,000	7	7	Fingersmith
70,001-110,000	8	8	Filcher
110,001-160,000	9	9	Burglar
160,001-220,000	10	10**	Highwayman
220,001-440,000	11	10+2	Robber
440,001-660,000	12	10+4	Expert Treasure Hunter
660,001-880,000	13	10+6	Guild Thief
880,001-1,100,000	14	10+8	Guild Soldier
1,100,001-1,320,000	15	10+10	Thief
1,320,001-1,540,000	16	10+12	Master Thief
1,540,001-1,760,000	17	10+14	Captain Thief
1,760,001-1,980,000	18	10+16	Guild Master Thief
1,980,001-2,200,000	19	10+18	Guild Captain
2,200,001-2,420,000	20***	10+20	Guild Boss

* At first level thieves receive 20 points + 1d6. This twenty point 'kicker' is received at first level only.

** Thieves gain 2 hps per level after the 10th.

*** 220,000 experience points per level for each additional level beyond the 20th.

give you a thumbs up if he cannot see you when you hide in shadows, so you know to try again if you failed.

The thief's prime requisite is Dexterity; a character must have a minimum score of 9 to qualify for the class. While high numbers in other scores (particularly Intelligence) are desirable, they are not necessary. The thief can have any alignment (more lawful and good ones tend to be military scouts, saboteurs, agents, treasure blazers, treasure hunters and government spies). Many are at least partially neutral.

A thief with a Dexterity score of 16 or more gains a 10% bonus to the experience points he earns.

Thieves have a limited selection of weapons, as most of their time is spent practicing thieving skills not weaponry. The allowed weapons are club, dagger, dart, hand crossbow, knife, lasso, short bow, sling, broad sword, long sword, short sword and staff. A thief can wear leather, studded leather, padded leather or elven chain armor. When wearing any allowed armor other than leather, the thief's abilities are penalized (see Table 3PP).

Table 3MM: **Thieving Skill Base Scores**	
Skill	Base Score
Pick Pockets	15%
Open Locks	10%
Find Traps	5%
Remove Traps	5%
Move Silently	10%
Hide in Shadows	5%
Detect Noise	15%
Climb Walls	60%
Read Languages	0%

To determine the initial value of each skill, start with the base scores listed on Table 3MM. To these base scores, add (or subtract) any appropriate modifiers for race, Dexterity, and armor worn (given on Tables 3NN, 3OO and 3PP, respectively).

The scores arrived at in the preceding paragraph do not reflect the effort a thief has spent honing his skills. To simulate this extra training, all thieves at 1st level receive 65 discretionary percentage points that they can add to their

Table 3NN: **Thieving Skill Racial Adjustments**									
Skill	Dwarf	Elf*	Gnome	Gnomeling	Half-elf	Halfling	Pixie fairy	Half-orc	Half-ogre
Pick Pockets	--	+5%	--	--	+5%	+5%	+10%	-5%	-10%
Open Locks	+10%	-5%	+5%	+5%	--	+5%	-15%	+5%	+5%
Find Traps	+10%	+5%	+5%	+5%	--	+10%	-15%	--	+5%
Remove Traps	+15%	--	+10%	+5%	--	--	-15%	+5%	+5%
Move Silently	-10%	+5%	+5%	+5%	--	+10%	+20%	--	-5%
Hide in Shadows	-5%	+10%	+5%	+10%	+5%	+15%	+30%	--	-20%
Detect Noise	--	+5%	+10%	+5%	--	+5%	-50%	+5%	+10%
Climb Walls	+5%	--	-15%	-15%	--	-15%	-50%	+5%	+20%
Read Languages	--	--	--	--	--	-5%	-10%	-10%	-20%

* includes Grel, Drow and other sub-races as well.

Table 3OO:
Thieving Skill Dexterity Adjustments

Dexterity	Pick Pockets	Open Locks	Find/Remove Traps	Move Silently	Hide in Shadows
7	-25%	-20%	-20%	-30%	-20%
8	-20%	-15%	-15%	-25%	-15%
9	-15%	-10%	-10%	-20%	-10%
10	-10%	-5%	-10%	-15%	-5%
11	-5%	--	-5%	-10%	--
12	--	--	--	-5%	--
13-15	--	--	--	--	--
16	--	+5%	--	--	--
17	+5%	+10%	--	+5%	+5%
18	+10%	+15%	+5%	+10%	+10%
19	+15%	+20%	+10%	+15%	+15%
20	+20%	+25%	+15%	+20%	+20%
21	+25%	+30%	+20%	+25%	+25%
22	+30%	+35%	+25%	+25%	+30%
23	+35%	+40%	+30%	+30%	+35%
24	+40%	+45%	+35%	+35%	+40%
25	+45%	+50%	+40%	+40%	+45%

Table 3PP:
Thieving Skill Armor Adjustments

Skill	No Armor	Elven Chain	Chainmail (Bards only)	Studded Leather, Ring mail or Padded
Pick Pockets	+5%	-20%	-25%	-25%
Open Locks	--	-5%	-10%	-10%
Find/Remove Traps	--	-5%	-10%	-10%
Move Silently	+10%	-10%	-15%	-15%
Hide in Shadows	+5%	-10%	-15%	-15%
Detect Noise	--	-5%	-10%	-5%
Climb Walls	+10%	-20%	-25%	-25%
Read Languages	--	--	--	--

A thief character uses the "No Armor" column if wearing Bracers of Defense or a cloak without large or heavy protective clothing.

base scores. No more than 30 points can be assigned to any single skill. Other than this restriction, the player can distribute the points however he wants.

Each time the thief rises a level in experience, the player receives another 35 points to distribute. No more than 15 points per level can be assigned to a single skill, and no skill can be raised above 95 percent, including all adjustments for Dexterity, race and armor. Some portion of the points earned must be applied to skills used during the course of the prior level. Your GM has the right to big-foot you into lowering certain allocations if you used some skills over others, even to the extent of disallowing any allocation to a skill that was very underused.

In addition to the base percentages listed above, demi-human characters and characters with high or low Dexterity scores have adjustments to their base numbers. Since some races naturally blow chunks when it comes to doing certain things (ever seen an Ogre try to hide in shadows?!?), some characters may find that, after adjustments, they have negative scores. In this case, the character must spend points raising his skill percentage to at least 1% before he can use the skill.

Skill Explanations

Pick Pockets: The thief uses this skill when filching small items from other people's pockets, sleeves, girdles, packs, etc., when palming items (such as keys), and when performing simple sleight of hand (such as planting something on someone else or in their pocket, like a poisonous snake, note or fragile bottle of acid). A failed attempt means the thief did not get an item, but it does not mean that his attempt was detected. Your GM will determine this, and trust me on this one, if you are noticed, he'll let you know in some way or form.

Open Locks: A thief can try to pick padlocks and solve puzzle locks (locks with sliding panels, hidden releases and concealed keyholes). This skill is typically needed for opening locked doors to get where you're not supposed to be or when trying to open a small coffer after the stupid magic-user melted the skeleton key (by slapping down a Fireball Barrage on the former key holder). Picking a padlock requires tools. Using typical thief's tools grants normal chances for success. Using improvised tools (a bit of wire, a thin dirk, a stick, etc.) imposes a penalty on the character's chance for success. The GM sets the penalty based on the situation; penalties can range from -5 for an improvised

but suitable tool, to -60 for an awkward and unsuitable item (like a stick). The amount of time required to pick a lock is 1d10 rounds. A thief can try to pick a particular lock only once per experience level. If the attempt fails, the lock is simply too difficult for the character until he learns more about picking locks (goes up a level and actually increases his open lock talent score).

Find Traps: The thief is trained to find all types of traps and alarms (usually without setting them off first). These include poisoned needles, spring blades, deadly gases and warning bells. To find the trap, the thief must be able to touch and inspect the device, wall, etc.

Normally, the GM rolls the dice to determine whether the thief finds a trap. If the GM says, "You're absolutely certain there are no traps," it's up to you to decide whether that means there are no traps or there are traps but your character didn't spot them. If the thief finds a trap, he knows its general principle but not its exact nature. A thief can check an item for traps once per experience level. Searching for a trap takes 1d10 rounds. This check is typically used on a small area (approximately 5' x 5').

Remove Traps: Once a trap is found, the thief can try to remove it or disarm it. This requires 1d10 rounds. If the dice roll indicates success, the trap is disarmed. If the dice roll indicates failure, the trap is beyond the thief's current skill. He can try disarming the trap again when he raises his find/remove traps skill. If the dice roll is 96-100, the thief accidentally triggers the trap. In this case, he most likely suffers some grizzly consequences or perhaps another party member suffers as well (or instead). Note that this makes a thief less-than-popular, so you might want to avoid this, though on the other hand, better unpopular and alive than popular and dead. Sometimes if your percentage to remove traps stinks you might want to get in a secure place and deliberately spring the trap rather than try to remove it and get in the line of fire of something really nasty. This skill is far less useful when dealing with magical or invisible traps; thieves can attempt to remove such traps, but their chances of success are half their normal percentages.

Move Silently: A thief can try to move silently at any time simply by announcing that he intends to do so. While moving silently, the thief's movement rate is reduced to 1/3 normal. The GM rolls percentile dice to determine whether the thief is moving silently. The thief always thinks he is being quiet. Successful silent movement improves the thief's chance to surprise a victim, avoid discovery or move into position to stab an enemy in the back.

FRAIM

Obviously, a thief moving silently but in plain view of his enemies is wasting his time, unless he's simply trying to amuse them or if the enemy is a Blind Wretched Pursuer.

Hide in Shadows: A thief can try to disappear into shadows or any other type of concealment – bushes, curtains, crannies, etc. A thief can hide this way only when no one is looking at him; he remains hidden only as long as he remains virtually motionless. The thief can make small, slow, careful movements: draw a weapon, uncork a potion, etc. A thief can never initiate hiding while someone is watching him, no matter what his dice roll is, his position is obvious to the observer. However, trying to hide from a creature that is locked in battle with another is possible, as the enemy's attention is fixed elsewhere. The GM rolls the dice and keeps the result secret, but the thief always thinks he is hidden. Kind of like playing hide and seek, isn't it? This can be a lot of fun for GMs. Hidden characters are equally concealed to those with or without infravision. Spells, magical items and special abilities that reveal invisible objects can reveal the location of a hidden thief.

Detect Noise: A good thief pays attention to every detail, no matter how small, including faint sounds that most others miss. His ability to hear tiny sounds (behind heavy doors, down long hallways, etc.) is much better than the ordinary person's. Listening is not automatic; it's a skill. The thief must stand still and concentrate on what he's hearing for one round. He must have silence in his immediate surroundings and must remove his helmet or hat. Sounds filtering through doors or other barriers are unclear at best.

Climb Walls: Although everyone can climb rocky cliffs and steep slopes, the thief is far superior to others in this ability. Not only does he have a better climbing percentage than other characters, he can also climb most surfaces without tools, ropes, or devices. Only the thief can climb smooth and very smooth surfaces without climbing gear. Of course, the thief is very limited in his actions while climbing; he is unable to fight or effectively defend himself. He also climbs at a very slow rate (your GM will give you the details on this).

Read Languages: Out of necessity, thieves tend to learn odd bits of information. Among these is the ability to read various languages, particularly as they apply to treasure maps, deeds, secret notes and the like. At 4th level, the thief has enough exposure to languages that he has a chance to read most non-magical writing. This ability naturally improves with more experience. However, your GM will rule that some languages (those the thief has never encountered) are indecipherable to the thief, so you should prepare for this ahead of time. What you need to do is have your character spend his off-hours at libraries once in awhile. That way it's hard for your GM to deny you a chance that you may have come across a particular language.

The die roll to read a language must be made every time the character tries to read a document (not just once per language). A successful die roll means the thief puzzled out the meaning of the writing. His understanding of the document is roughly equal to his percentage chance for success: a 20% chance means that, if the thief understands it at all, he gets about 20% of the meaning. A different document in the same language requires another die roll (it probably contains different words). It isn't necessary to keep notes about what languages the thief has read in the past, since each document is handled individually. Only one die roll can be made for any particular document at a given read languages skill level. If the die roll fails, the thief can try again after gaining a new experience level. If the character knows how to read a given language because he spent the Building Points on it, this die roll is unnecessary for documents in that language (obviously). Thieves have other abilities not listed on Table 3MM.

Backstab: Thieves are weak in toe-to-toe hacking matches, but they are masters of the knife in the back. When attacking someone by surprise and from behind, a thief can improve his chance to successfully hit (+4 modifier for rear attack and negate the target's shield and Dexterity bonuses) and greatly increase the amount of damage his blow causes. A thief gains the +4 to hit during a backstab instead of the normal +2 gained by others who attack from behind.

To use this ability, the thief must be behind his victim and the victim must be unaware that the thief intends to attack him. If an enemy sees the thief, hears him approach from a blind side, or is warned by another, he is not caught unaware, and the backstab is handled like a normal attack (although bonuses for a rear attack still apply). Opponents in battle will often notice a thief trying to maneuver behind them – the first rule of fighting is to never turn your back on an enemy! However, someone who isn't expecting to be attacked (a friend or ally, perhaps) can be caught unaware even if he knows the thief is behind him.

The weapon's standard damage die is counted an additional number of times as listed in Table 3QQ. Then Strength and magical weapon bonuses are added.

Backstabbing does have limitations. First, the extra damage dice apply only to the first attack made by the thief, even if multiple attacks are possible. Once a blow is struck, the initial surprise effect is lost. Second, the thief cannot use it on every creature. The victim must be generally humanoid. Part of the skill comes from knowing just where to strike. A thief could backstab an Ogre, but he wouldn't be able to do the same to a Beholder. The victim must also have a definable back, which leaves out most slimes, jellies, oozes and the like. Finally, the thief has to be able to reach a significant target area. To backstab a titan, the thief would have to be standing on a ledge or window balcony. Backstabbing him in the ankle just is not going to be as effective.

The Ogre marches down the hallway, peering into the gloom ahead. He fails to notice the shadowy form of Shrapnel the thief hidden in an alcove. Slipping into the hallway, Shrapnel creeps up behind the monster. As he sets himself to strike a mortal blow, his foot scrapes across the stone. The hairy ears of the Ogre perk up. The beast whirls around, ruining Shrapnel's chance for a backstab and what remains of his day. If Shrapnel had made a successful roll to move silently, he could have attacked the Ogre with a +4 bonus on his chance to hit and inflicted five dice rolls of his normal damage (since he is 15th level – note this could even be increased further if some of the damage were penetration damage!).

Thieves' Cant: Thieves' cant is a special form of communication known by all thieves and their associates. It is not a distinct language; it consists of slang words and innuendos that can be worked into any language. The vocabulary of thieves' cant limits its use to discussing things that interest thieves: stolen loot, easy marks, breaking and entering, mugging, confidence games and the like. It is not a language, however. Two thieves cannot communicate via thieves' cant unless they know a common language. The cant is useful, however, for identifying fellow cads and bounders by slipping a few tidbits of lingo into a normal conversation.

Use Scrolls: At 10th level, a thief gains a limited ability to use magical and cleric scrolls. A thief's understanding of magical writings is far from complete, however. The thief has a 25% chance to read the scroll incorrectly and reverse the spell's effect. This sort of malfunction is almost always detrimental to the thief and his party. It could be as simple as accidentally casting the reverse of the given spell or as complex as a foul-up on a Fireball scroll, causing the ball of flame to be centered on the thief instead of its intended target. The exact effect is up to the GM (this is the sort of thing GMs enjoy, so expect the unexpected).

Table 3QQ: Backstab Damage Multipliers	
Thief's Level	Extra Damage Dice
1-4	+1
5-8	+2
9-12	+3
13+	+4

Table 3RR: Thief's Followers		
D100 Roll	Follower	Level Range
01-03	Dwarf fighter/thief	1-4
04-08	Dwarf thief	1-6
09-13	Elf thief	1-6
14-15	Elf thief/fighter/magic-user	1-3
16-18	Elf thief/magic-user	1-4
19-24	Gnome thief	1-6
25-27	Gnome thief/fighter	1-4
28-30	Gnome thief/illusionist	1-4
31-35	Half-elf thief	1-6
36-38	Half-elf thief/fighter	1-4
39-41	Half-elf thief/fighter/magic-user	1-3
42-46	Halfling thief	1-8
47-50	Halfling thief/fighter	1-6
51-98	Human thief	1-8
99	Human dual-class thief/fighter	1-8/1-4
00	Other (GM selection)	--

Thieves' Dwellings

Thieves do not build castles or fortresses in the usual sense. Instead, they favor small, fortified dwellings, especially if the true purpose of the buildings can easily be disguised. A thief might, for example, construct a well-protected den in a large city behind the facade of a seedy tavern or old warehouse. Naturally, the true nature of the place will be a closely guarded secret! Thieves almost always build their strongholds in or near cities, since that is where it is most lucrative for them to ply their trades.

This, of course, all assumes that the thief is interested in operating a band of thieves out of his dwelling. Not all thieves have larceny in their hearts, however. If a character devoted his life to those aspects of thieving that focus on scouting, stealth, and the intricacies of locks and traps, he could build an entirely different sort of stronghold – one filled with the unusual and intriguing objects he has collected during his adventurous life. Like any thief's dwelling, it should blend in with its surroundings; after all, a scout never advertises his whereabouts. It might be a formidable maze of rooms, secret passages, sliding panels and mysterious paraphernalia from across the world.

Once a thief reaches 10th level or his Fame Factor reaches 100, his reputation is such that he can attract followers, either a gang of scoundrels and scalawags or a group of scouts eager to learn from a reputed master. The thief attracts 4d6 of these fellows. They are generally loyal to him, but a wise thief is always suspicious of his comrades. Table 3RR can be used to determine the type and level of followers, or the GM can choose followers appropriate to his campaign.

Thieves tend to be very jealous of their turf. If more than one thief starts a gang in the same area, the result is usually a war. The feud continues until one side or the other is totally eliminated or forced to move its operation elsewhere.

Assassins

The assassin is a thief who has devoted himself to the finer arts of the profession. He is adept at such things as spying, gathering information and the killing of individuals who never see it coming. He is sought out for his services by kings and paupers alike who don't have the stomach for doing such dirty deeds with their own hands.

Like thieves, they are skilled in stealth and nimbleness but focus more on the art of stealing lives over stealing possessions. Assassins are a sub-class of the thieves, and they have the functions of the latter as well as their own. Thus, to be an assassin, a character must have a minimum Strength of 12, an Intelligence of 11 or more, and a Dexterity score of not less than 12. Assassins gain a 10% bonus to experience only if all three abilities are 16 or higher. Because assassins are so despised by others they receive a –20 to their beginning Honor. Assassins can have high Honor as long as their true profession is kept a secret. Players should never announce that they are assassins to other players or NPCs. If possible they should try to pass themselves off as thieves, fighters or bards. Eventually the truth will be found out when a clever player notices you don't possess the true abilities of the profession you claim to practice, but the longer you can keep your class a secret the better. If anyone gets suspicious, think seriously about greasing him before he can talk. If he's a loud mouth, the other players may thank you anyway.

Assassins are evil in alignment (perforce, as the killing of humans and other intelligent life forms for the purpose of profit is basically held to be the antithesis of weal). They can, of course, be lawful, neutral or chaotic but must always be evil. As mentioned above, assassins have thieving capabilities and their own ability functions. Because they can use any sort of shield and weapon, they are generally superior to thieves in combat.

Killing is the assassin's primary function. They may freely use poison ingested or insinuated by weapon. Ingested poison must be put into the victim's food or drink, and the character performing this action must detail exactly when, where and how the poisoning will be done. The GM will then adjudicate the action. Poisoned weapons run the risk of being noticed by others. Your GM has details about this.

The Assassin

Ability Requirements:
Strength 12+, Intelligence 11+
Dexterity 12+
Prime Requisite(s):
Dexterity, Intelligence, Strength
Hit Dice Type:
d6
Allowed Races:
Any except pixie fairy
Allowed Alignments:
evil
Building Point Bonus:
9 BP

Experience Points	Experience Level	6-Sided Dice for Accumulated Hit Points	Level Title
0 – 1,500	1	20+1d6*	Bravo (Apprentice)
1,501 – 3,000	2	2	Rutterkin
3,001 – 6,000	3	3	Waghalter
6,001 – 12,000	4	4	Murderer
12,001 – 25,000	5	5	Thug
25,001 – 50,000	6	6	Killer
50,001 – 1000,000	7	7	Cutthroat
100,001 – 200,000	8	8	Executioner
200,001 – 300,000	9	9	Assassin
300,001 – 425,000	10	10	Expert Assassin
425,001 – 575,000	11	11	Senior Assassin
575,001 – 750,000	12	12	Chief Assassin
750,001 – 1,000,000	13	11	Prime Assassin
1,000,001 – 1,500,000	14	14	Guild Soldier
1,500,001 – 2,000,000	15	15**	Guild Assassin
2,000,001 – 2,500,000	16	15+2	Guild Capo
2,500,001 – 3,000,000-	17	15+4	GuildMaster Assassin
3,000,001 – 3,500,000	18	15+6	Guildfather of Assassins
3,500,001 – 4,000,000	19	15+8	Grandfather of Assassins
4,000,001 – 4,500,000	20 ***	15+10	Gawdfather of Assassins

Table 3SS:
Assassin Experience Levels

* At first level assassins receive 20 points + 1d6. This twenty point 'kicker' is received at first level only.
** Assassins gain 2 hps per level after the 15th.
*** 500,000 experience points per level for each additional level beyond the 20th.

Assassins attack on the some combat tables as thieves do, including backstabbing. However, if they surprise a victim, they may attack on the Assassination Table (available in the GMG). This gives them a roughly 50% chance of immediately killing the victim if both the assassin and target are the same level. If this fails, normal damage according to weapon type and Strength ability modifiers still accrues to the victim. Thus, if a poisoned weapon is used, the victim must also make the saving throw versus poison or suffer the poison's effects. The assassin decides which attack mode he will use: assassination, backstabbing or normal melee combat.

Special Assassin Abilities

Primary abilities of assassins, which enhance their function, are those of being able to speak alignment languages and being able to disguise, as follows:

1. **Alignment Tongues:** Assassins with Intelligence of 15 or more are able to learn an alignment tongue (even those special languages of druids and thieves). This ability is gained at 9th level (Assassin) and with each advance in experience level thereafter. The maximum number of alignment languages which can be spoken by an assassin is four - one for each point of intelligence above 14, i.e., one at 15, two at 16, three at 17, and four at 18 intelligence. Note: An assassin would have to be of 12th level (Chief Assassin) and have 18 Intelligence to be able to speak four alignment languages. The assassin may select from the following languages:

Chaotic Evil	Neutral Evil	Chaotic Good
Neutral Good	Chaotic Neutrality	Neutrality
Lawful Evil	Druid	Lawful Good
Thieves' Cant	Lawful Neutrality	

2. **Disguise:** Assassins can don disguises in order to gain the opportunity to poison or surprise a victim - or for other reasons. The assassin can disguise himself so as to appear to be a human, demihuman or humanoid creature of either sex. Disguise can lower height by two or three inches, or raise it by up to four or five inches. It can make the assassin look slimmer or appear much heavier. Disguise can make the assassin appear to be virtually any class of character, a simple pilgrim, a merchant, etc. There is a chance, however, that the victim, or one of his henchmen or guards, will notice the disguise. There is a base chance of 2% per day of a disguised assassin being spotted. This chance goes upward by 2% if the assassin is posing as another class, another race, and/or the opposite sex (maximum of 8% chance). Each concerned party (victim, henchmen, bodyguards) in proximity to the assassin will

be checked for, immediately upon meeting the disguised assassin and each 24 hour period thereafter.

The chance for spotting a disguised assassin goes downward by 1% for each point below 24 of combined Intelligence and Wisdom of the observer concerned, i.e. a victim with an Intelligence and Wisdom combined total of 20 has reduced his chances of spotting the disguised assassin by 4%. Similarly, Intelligence and Wisdom above a combined total of 30 increase the chance of detection by 1% per point. Note: True Seeing or a Wand of Enemy Detection will discover an assassin, as will Detect Evil, or Know Alignment in some cases.

3. **Spying:** The secondary function of the assassin is spying. This mission can be coupled with the stealing of some item. Your GM has a matrix for determining how successful the assassin is at spying and how much information he is able to gather.

4. **Thieving Abilities:** Tertiary functions of assassins are the same as thieves. They have all abilities and functions of thieves; but, except for backstabbing, assassins perform thieving at two levels below their assassin level, i.e., a 3rd level assassin has the thieving abilities of a 1st level thief, a 4th level assassin the abilities of a 2nd level thief, etc.

5. **Assassination for Gold and Experience:** Performing an assassination will gain experience points for the character - awarded for both the fee paid and the level of the victim. These awards are determined by your GM on the basis of a formula given in HackMaster GameMaster's Guide.

An assassin cannot have any hirelings until he attains 4th level; at that time lower level assassins may be taken into service. Upon attaining 8th level, the character may also include thieves amongst his hirelings. Upon attaining 12th level, the character may hire any class desired. Of course, only neutral or evil characters will serve an assassin. The total number of henchmen is that dictated by the character's Charisma score. "Followers" are also possible, but these come only at the 14th level of the assassin class or if his Infamy Factor has reached 150. Assassins gain a point of Infamy for each person they have assassinated (in addition to the normal method of calculating Infamy in Chapter 5).

In order for an assassin character to gain experience levels above the 14th (Guild Soldier), he must have the requisite experience points and then either assassinate the local Guild Assassin (15th level) or challenge him to a duel to the death. Likewise, a 15th level player character assassin can journey to the place where the Guild Capo (16th level) has his headquarters and slay him by assassination or in a duel. Note that duplicity, trickery and ambush are fine, as assassins consider all forms of treachery as fair. A higher level character can accept a challenge and then have the challenger slain by archers, for instance. This process continues all the way to the level of Gawdfather of Assassins (20th level). It is also a common practice for the Gawdfather of Assassins to use a double or doubles so that one is never quite certain of his exact whereabouts at any given time.

As GuildMaster Assassin, a character will have a body of guild members, that number between 7 and 28. Upon a change of leadership, it is 75% likely that each guild member will leave the area. Thus, it will be necessary for the new GuildMaster to allow new members into the guild. These new assassins will all be 1st level and must be worked up in experience levels. Your GM will set the maximum number of such "followers" of the local guild. These are in addition to normal henchmen. Note that guild members are loyal only to strength, power and profit.

The headquarters of a guild is always within a large town or big city. It must not be a noticeable fortress or an ostentatious place. It is typically a warehouse or other nondescript structure, with safeguards and traps added. This avoids attention and unwanted notoriety. All expenses of maintaining the guild and its members - excluding the GuildMaster- are assumed to be fully paid for by normal guild activities. Any improvements, changes, the expenses of the GuildMaster and all other special costs must be borne by the leader. Similarly, the Guildfather controls several GuildMaster halls and the Grandfather of Assassins controls several Guildfather's.

The headquarters of the Gawdfather of Assassins can be virtually anywhere and of any form - cavern, castle, monastery, palace, temple, you name it. However, if it is a large and obvious place, the headquarters must be located well away from all communities, such as in the midst of a murky woods, a dis-

mal marsh or fen, a lonely moor, a deserted island, a remote coast, forsaken hills or atop a mountain. Upon attaining the headship of all assassins, the new Gawdfather must pay all remaining followers of the former guild 1000 gold pieces for each of their experience levels, destroy the old headquarters, and construct a new one somewhere else.

An assassin character need not be a member of the assassins' guild of the town or city he dwells in, but all non-player assassin characters are members of such guilds. There is one such guild in most towns and cities, and each controls an area of from 10 to 100 miles radius around the headquarter's town or city. Any assassin discovered in a guild area who is not a member of the local assassins guild will be invited to join, (if deemed worthy by its members) thus coming under the authority and command of the GuildMaster Assassin. The assassin character need not join, but he will be under sentence of death if the character performs an assassination while not a guild member.

Bards

A bard makes his way in life by his charm, talent and wit. A good bard should be glib of tongue, light of heart, and fleet of foot (when all else fails). They are less opportunistic than thieves, often relying on shell-games, confidence games, swindles, extortion and other tricks and scams to lighten the pursues of their marks. Sometimes they sell snake oil, other times they perform for coppers while wooing the noble's daughter (only to later steal her jewelry and her heart).

A bard is a jack-of-all-trades, but a master of none. He fights as thief, but he has a wider selection of weapons. A bard can wear

Bard
Ability Requirements: Charisma 15+, Intelligence 13+, Dexterity 12+, Comeliness 12+
Prime Requisite(s): Dexterity, Charisma
Hit Dice Type: d6
Allowed Races: Human, Half-elf
Allowed Alignments: any neutral
Building Point Bonus: 8 BP

any armor up to and including chain mail, but he cannot use a shield. All bards have some basic skill as singers, vocalists and musicians. A bard character automatically begins play with a musical instrument proficiency and the singing skill. The character does not have to expend Building Points for these, but he may choose to use BPs to increase his skill mastery.

To become a bard, a character must have a Dexterity of 12 or more, an Intelligence of 13 or more, a Charisma of 15 or more and a Comeliness of 12 or higher. The prime requisites are Dexterity and Charisma. A bard can be lawful, neutral or chaotic, good or evil, but must always be partially neutral.

		Table 3TT:	
		Bard Experience Levels	
Experience Points	Experience Level	6-Sided Die* for Accumulated Hit Points	Level Title
0-2,000	1	20+1d6*	Tramp
2,001-4,000	2	2	Face-man
4,001-8,000	3	3	Drifter
8,001-16,000	4	4	Fraud
16,001-25,000	5	5	Circus Performer
25,001-40,000	6	6	Jongleur
40,001-60,000	7	7	Troubadour
60,001-85,000	8	8	Scoundrel
85,001-110,000	9	9	Skald
110,001-150,000	10	10**	Scheister
150,001-200,000	11	10+1	Swindler
200,001-400,000	12	10+2	Fast Talker
400,001-600,000	13	10+3	Artist
600,001-800,000	14	10+4	Bunko Artist
800,001-1,000,000	15	10+5	Con Artist
1,000,001-1,200,000	16	10+6	Scam Artist
1,200,001-1,400,000	17	10+7	Scammer
1,400,001-1,600,000	18	10+8	Grifter
1,600,001-1,800,000	19	10+9	Bard
1,800,001-2,000,000***	20	10+10	Master Bard

* At first level bards gain 20 points + 1d6. This twenty point 'kicker' is received at first level only.

** Bards gain 2 hps per level after the 10th.

*** 200,000 experience points per level for each additional level beyond the 20th.

Only by retaining some amount of detachment can he be so entirely self-centered and care so little for the welfare of the poor suckers he's fleecing.

In his travels, a bard also manages to learn a few magic-user spells. Like a magic-user, a bard's Intelligence determines the number of spells he can know and the chance to know any given spell. These he keeps in his spell book, abiding by all the restrictions on memorization and spell use that bind a magic-user, especially in the spell casting difficulties of wearing armor. Table 3UU lists the number of spells a bard can cast at each level.

Since bards are dabblers rather than full-time magic-users, their spells tend to be gained by serendipity and happenstance. In no case can a bard choose to specialize in a school of magic. Beginning bards do not have a selection of spells. A 2nd level bard begins with Read Magic plus one to four 1st level spells rolled randomly by the GM. The bard can add new spells to his spell book as he finds them, but he does not automatically gain additional spells as he advances in level; all spells beyond those he starts with must be found during the course of adventuring. An Intelligence check must still be made to see if the bard can learn a given spell as per normal magic users. The bard's casting level is equal to his current level.

Bard Level	Spell Level 1	2	3	4	5	6
1	--	--	--	--	--	--
2	1	--	--	--	--	--
3	2	--	--	--	--	--
4	2	1	--	--	--	--
5	3	1	--	--	--	--
6	3	2	--	--	--	--
7	3	2	1	--	--	--
8	3	3	1	--	--	--
9	3	3	2	--	--	--
10	3	3	2	1	--	--
11	3	3	3	1	--	--
12	3	3	3	2	--	--
13	3	3	3	2	1	--
14	3	3	3	3	1	--
15	3	3	3	3	2	--
16	4	3	3	3	2	1
17	4	4	3	3	3	1
18	4	4	4	3	3	2
19	4	4	4	4	3	2
20	4	4	4	4	4	3

Table 3UU:
Bard Spell Progression

Combat and spells, however, are not the main strength of the bard. His expertise is in dealing and communicating with others. To this end, the bard has a number of special powers. The base percentage for each power is listed on Table 3VV. This base percentage must be adjusted for the race and Dexterity of the bard as given in the thief description.

After all adjustments are made, the player must distribute (however he chooses) 20 additional percentage points to the various special abilities. Thereafter, each time the character advances a level, he receives an additional 15 points to distribute.

Table 3VV:
Bard Abilities

Climb Walls	Detect Noise	Pick Pockets	Read Languages
50%	20%	10%	5%

These abilities are described in the thief section, above.

Bard Special Abilities

Influence: The bard can also influence reactions of groups of NPCs. When talking to or performing before a group that is not attacking (and not intending to attack in just seconds), the bard can try to alter the mood of the listeners. He can try to soften their mood or make it uglier. The method can be whatever is most suitable to the situation at the moment – a fiery speech, collection of jokes, a sad tale, a fine tune played on a fiddle, a haunting lute melody or a heroic song from the old homeland. Everyone in the group listening must roll a saving throw vs. paralyzation (if the crowd is large, make saving throws for groups of people using average Hit Dice). The die roll is modified by -1 for every three experience levels of the bard (round fractions down). If the saving throw fails, the group's reaction can be shifted one level (see the Reactions section in the GMG), toward either the friendly or hostile end of the scale, at the play-

er's option. Those who make a successful saving throw have their reaction shifted one level toward the opposite end of the scale. This ability cannot affect people in the midst of battle. It is effective only if the audience has time to listen.

Confidence Games and Scams: Another ability of bards is the con game, i.e. running scams. Bards have a knack for winning the confidence of the unsuspecting. Such operations require quite a bit of set-up to pull off. The pigeon(s) must be identified, the pay-off determined, etc. While any character could potentially plan and execute such scams, it is the bard who is the master of the game. He receives special modifiers when it comes to gaining someone's trust and averting suspicion from himself. Your GM will have the appropriate matrixes to determine if any given scam or con is successful.

Performance: The music, poetry, and stories of the bard can also be inspirational, rallying friends and allies. If the exact nature of an impending threat is known, the bard can heroically inspire his companions (immortalizing them in word and song), granting a +1 bonus to attack rolls, or a +1 bonus to saving throws, or a +2 bonus to morale (particularly useful in large battles) to those involved in melee. The bard must spend at least three full rounds singing or reciting before the battle begins. This affects those within a range of 10 feet per experience level of the bard.

The effect lasts one round per level. Once the effect wears off, it can't be renewed if the recipients are still in battle. However, troops who have withdrawn from combat can be reinspired by the bard's words.

A troop of soldiers, inspired by Quentin the Shrill of Voice, could charge into battle. After fighting a fierce fight, but getting their butts kicked by some particularly tough Gnolls they retreat and the enemy does not pursue. Quentin, seeing them crestfallen and dispirited, once again rouses their will to fight. Reinvigorated, they charge back into battle with renewed spirit. Likely they will die horrible deaths, but at least Quentin can finish off the one or two remaining Gnolls, then pick over the remains of the lot of them. Good for Quentin!

Countersong: Bards are also able to counter the effects of songs and poetry used as magical attacks. Characters within 30 feet of the bard are immune to the attack as long as the bard sings a counter song (or recites some bad poetry, tells a dirty limerick, etc.). While doing this, the bard can perform no other action except a slow walk. Furthermore, if he is struck or fails a saving throw, his effort is ruined. Success is checked by having the bard make a saving throw vs. spell. Success blocks the attack, failure means the attack has its normal effect (everyone affected rolls saving throws, normal damage is inflicted, etc.). The bard can use this ability once per encounter or battle. This power does not affect verbal spell components or command words; it is effective against spells that involve explanations, commands or suggestions.

Jack-of-All: Finally, bards learn a little bit of everything in their travels and interactions at seedy pubs, brothels, etc. Thus, all bards can read and write their native tongue (if a written language exists) and all know local history (without cost). Furthermore, bards have a 5% chance per experience level to identify the general purpose and function of any magical item. The bard need not handle the item but must examine it closely. Even if successful, the exact function of the item is not revealed, only its general nature.

Since Quentin the Shrill of Voice is 2nd level, he has a 10% chance to know something about a magical sword +1. If he succeeds, he knows whether the sword is cursed and whether it has an alignment ("This sword was used by the evil warrior Lurdas. I wouldn't touch it if I were you!"). This ability does not enable him to identify the sword's exact properties, only its history and background. He has no idea of its bonuses or penalties or any special magical powers, except as can be inferred from the histories. The best part about this ability is that your allies have no idea whether you are feeding them a crock of Orc dung or not. If you see a great item go ahead and lie, then pawn it later. Be careful, though, if you look too wealthy they'll suspect, so it's best to blow most of it on fine wine and expensive wenches, or at least bury it for later.

Bards also have a 5% chance per level of knowing some useless bit of trivia or background history on any given topic. The facts will only be as correct or as complete as his three times his level plus 120 minus the GM's percentage check. For example, Quentin the Shrill of Voice is in a run-down tavern in

Hagleytown. A patron strikes up a conversation about Kobold mating rituals. As a Face-man (2nd level bard), Quentin has a 10% chance to know some useless trivia on the subject. The GM rolls a 09, Quentin, in fact, knows something on the subject. To check for correctness/completeness, the GM adds 6 (3x his level) to 120, then deduct a percentage roll (in this case a 77). The total comes to 49%. Quentin is only 49% percent correct, but acts as if he knows it all. If anyone at the bar happens to be a sage that studied Kobolds, he could call Quentin on this and Quentin would lose Honor. If not, Quentin's Honor would likely rise.

Upon reaching 10th level, a bard can attempt to use magical devices of written nature – scrolls, books, etc. However, his understanding of magic is imperfect (although better than that of a thief), so there is a 15% chance that any written item he uses is read incorrectly. When this happens, the magical power works the opposite of what is intended, generally to the detriment of the bard or his friends. The GM will tell you what happens to your character, based on the situation and particular magical item. The result may be unpleasant, deadly or embarrassing. (Deciding these things is part of the GM's fun!)

Bard Junior Players

Being grifters, bards can never attract more than a few protegees to help them run scams and other cons. Bards can never attract large bodies of followers by building a stronghold. They can build or own a fortress or castle, but never seem to be able to keep them for long. Most often, they win them in card games, or trade old mines or other worthless real-estate. Eventually, the real owner comes back to take the property by force. In any case, by then a good bard will have sold it off to a third party and moved on to some place where no one knows his name.

Multi-Class and Dual-Class Characters

A multi-class character improves in two or more classes simultaneously. His experience is divided equally between each class. The available class combinations vary according to race. The character can use the abilities of both classes at any time, with only a few restrictions. Only demi-humans can be multi-class characters.

A dual-class character is one who starts with a single class, advances for a time, then changes to a second character class and starts over again. The character retains the benefits and abilities of the first class but never again earns experience for using them. There are some limitations on combining the abilities of the two classes but, as long as minimum ability and alignment requirements are met, there are no restrictions on the possible character class combinations. Only humans can be dual-class characters.

Multi-Class Combinations

All of the standard demi-human races are listed here, along with their allowable multi-class combinations. Note that the specific character class or subclass names are used below.

Dwarf: cleric/assassin, fighter/assassin, fighter/thief, fighter/cleric

Halfling: fighter/thief

Elf: fighter/magic-user, fighter/thief, magic-user/thief, fighter/magic-user/thief

Half-elf: fighter/cleric, fighter/thief, fighter/magic-user, cleric/ranger, cleric/magic-user, fighter/magic-user/cleric, fighter/magic-user/thief, fighter/druid, ranger/druid, magic-user/druid, fighter/magic-user/druid, magic-user/thief

Gnome: fighter/cleric, fighter/illusionist, fighter/thief, cleric/illusionist, cleric/thief

Half-orc: berserker/assassin, berserker/cleric, berserker/thief, fighter/assassin, fighter/thief, fighter/cleric

Gnomeling: fighter/cleric, fighter/illusionist, fighter/thief, cleric/illusionist, cleric/thief, illusionist/thief

Gnome Titan: fighter/assassin, fighter/cleric, fighter/illusionist, fighter/thief

Half-ogre: none

Pixie Fairy: fighter/magic-user

Multi-Class Benefits and Restrictions

A multi-class character always uses the most favorable combat value and the best saving throw from his different classes. The character's hit points are the average of all his Hit Dice rolls. When the character is first created, the player rolls hit points for each class separately, totals them up, then divides by the number of dice rolled (round fractions to the nearest integer, but record the fractions for later addition). Any Constitution bonus is then added to the character's hit points.

Later the character is likely to gain levels in different classes at different times. When this happens, roll the appropriate Hit Die and divide the result by the number of classes the character has (round fractions to the nearest integer after adding to the total). The character's Constitution bonus is split between his classes; thus, a fighter/magic-user gets 1/2 of his Con bonus when he goes up a level as a fighter and the other 1/2 of the Con bonus when he goes up a level as a magic-user. A fighter/magic-user/thief would get 1/3 of his bonus when he goes up as a fighter, 1/3 when he goes up as a magic-user and the other 1/3 when he goes up as a thief.

The character starts with the largest number of proficiency slots of the different classes. Thereafter, he gains new proficiency slots at the fastest of the given rates. To determine the character's initial money, roll according to the most generous of the character's different classes.

Fighter: A multi-classed fighter can use all of his abilities without restriction. The fighter abilities form the base for other character classes.

Cleric: Regardless of his other classes, a multi-classed cleric must abide by the weapon restrictions of his mythos. Thus, a fighter/cleric can ordinarily use only bludgeoning weapons (but he uses the fighter combat value). He retains all his normal cleric abilities.

Magic-user: A multi-classed magic-user can freely combine the powers of the magic-user with any other class allowed, although the wearing of armor is restricted by the spell mishap probabilities as normal.

Thief: A multi-classed thief cannot use any thieving abilities other than open locks or detect noise if he is wearing armor that is normally not allowed to thieves. He must remove his gauntlets to open locks and his helmet to detect noise.

Dual-Class Benefits and Restrictions

Only humans can be dual-classed characters. To be dual-classed, the character must have scores of 15 or more in the prime requisites of his first class and scores of 17 or more in the prime requisites of any classes he switches to. The character selects one class to begin his adventuring life. He can advance in this class as many levels as he desires before switching to another class; there is no cut-off point beyond which a character cannot switch. However, he must attain at least 2nd level in his current class before changing to another class. There is no limit to the number of classes a character can acquire, as long as he has the Ability Scores and wants to make the change. (Certain character classes have alignment restrictions that the character must meet, however.)

Any time after reaching 2nd level, a human character can enter a new character class, provided he has scores of 17 or better in the prime requisites of the new class. After switching to a new class, the character no longer earns experience points in his previous character class and he can no longer advance in level in that class. Nor can he switch back to his first class at a later date, hoping to resume his advancement where he left off.

Once he leaves a class he has finished his studies in it. Instead, he starts over in a new class, at 1st level with 0 experience points, but he does retain his previous Hit Dice and hit points. He gains the abilities, and must abide by all of the restrictions, of the new class. He does not gain or lose any points on his Ability Scores. The character uses the combat and saving throw tables appropriate to his new class and level.

This is not to imply that a dual-class human forgets everything he knew before; he still has, at his fingertips, all the knowledge, abilities and skills of his old class. But if he uses any of his previous class's abilities during an encounter, he earns no experience for that encounter and only half experience for the adventure. The only values that can be carried over from the previous class without restriction are the character's Hit Dice and hit points. The character is penalized for using his old attack or saving throw numbers, weapons or armor that are now prohibited, and any special abilities of the old class that are not also abilities of the new class. (The character is trying to learn new ways to do things; by slipping back to his old methods, he has set back his learning in his new character class.)

In addition, the character earns no additional Hit Dice or hit points while advancing in his new class.

The restrictions in the previous two paragraphs last until the character reaches a higher level in his new class than his maximum level in any of his previous classes. At that point, both restrictions are dropped: the character gains access to the abilities of his previous classes without jeopardizing his experience points for the adventure, and he earns additional Hit Dice (those of his new class) and hit points for gaining experience levels in his new class.

Once these restrictions are lifted, the character must still abide by the restrictions of whichever class he is using at the moment. A dual-class fighter/druid, for example, cannot cast spells while wearing metal armor.

Clover Gip begins his career as a cleric with a Wisdom of 16. He rises to 3rd level and then decides to become a fighter, since his Strength is 17. He keeps his 34 hit points (rolled on 3d8 +20), but in all other ways he is treated as a 1st level fighter. Upon reaching 4th level, Clover Gip is allowed to roll 1d10 for additional hit points. He can now cast spells as a 3rd level cleric and fight as a 4th level fighter. For the rest of his career, Clover Gip advances as a fighter but retains his minor cleric powers; a useful advantage when the situation gets ugly!

When a dual-class or multi-class character is struck by a level draining creature, he first loses levels in the class in which he has advanced the highest. When his different classes are equal in level, the class level requiring the most experience points is lost first.

The player character is allowed to regain levels lost by level draining, but until he regains all of his former levels, he must select which class he will use prior to any particular adventure. Using abilities of the other class then subjects him to the experience penalties given earlier. When he regains all of his former levels, he is then free to use all the abilities of all his classes once again. Of course, he cannot raise his earlier class(es) above the level(s) he was at when he switched class.

Clover Gip is a 3rd level cleric/4th level fighter. He is struck by a Wight and loses one level from his fighter class, since it is his highest level. If struck again, he would lose one level from his cleric class, so he damn well better run. Thereafter he could regain his lost levels, but would have to choose to act as either a fighter or cleric. Once he earned enough experience to regain his previous cleric level, he would not be allowed to advance further in it (restoring himself to his previous level only). But he could still advance as a fighter and use his 3rd level cleric abilities.

Character Priors and Particulars

Up to this point in the creation process, your character is little more than a series of numbers on a sheet of paper. And that's really all he'll remain until you step into his shoes and wear him like a second skin. Part of the challenge of role-playing is taking a newly generated character and growing him into a unique gaming persona of which you can be truly proud.

At this point, however, your character is a virtual stranger. What do you really know of him? What makes him tick? Most player characters start out as young adults, so it can be safely assumed that your hero didn't suddenly spring forth from nothingness like Athena from the brow of mighty Zeus. There are many years, perhaps even decades, of experiences behind that series of numbers on your character sheet.

Your character has a richly detailed past and it's your job to find out what that past entailed. What did your character do during those formative years? Are his parents rich? Are they still alive? Does your character have any scars from past battles? Did he get a tattoo he now regrets? Is he healthy? Is he left-handed? Does he stutter? What skills and proficiencies does he have?

In this chapter you will learn the answers to all these questions and more as you begin to explore your character's past. In the process you'll be given an opportunity to further sculpt your character and do a bit of fine-tuning. Mind you, this process won't fully flesh out your character. It will only block out some major defining details about your character. It'll be your job (under the guidance of your ever-watchful GM of course) to fill in the blanks and put your own unique thumbprint on him.

Building Points (BPs)

Every character begins the game with a handful of Building Points based on his character class and/or race. You'll spend these points to buy such things as beginning skills and abilities. You can also use them to buy modifiers on some of the background tables that follow to help you sculpt the kind of character you really want. Additionally, for the cost of one BP each, a player may buy rerolls on any of the tables in this chapter. You may buy as many rerolls as you have building points but once you've reached zero BPs, you must abide by the random rolls in this chapter thereafter.

Note: You must spend ALL your Building Points prior to beginning your character's first adventure (i.e. before he becomes active). Any BPs not spent are converted into starting cash at that time, and any further opportunities to customize your character are lost forever.

Earning Additional BPs with Quirks and Flaws

You can earn additional Building Points by taking on flaws and quirks (see Chapter 6). This can be done in one of two ways; choosing (cherry picking) which flaws or quirks you want or rolling for them randomly. The ONLY time a character can take on quirks and flaws in exchange for BPs is during the initial creation process. (The exception is when the character is restored to life with a spell of 4th or lower level, in which case he may be required to roll to see what new quirks or flaws he takes on.)

Cherry Picking

With this option you get to choose which flaws and quirks you want, and which subsequent benefits or limitations they may place on your character. The downside is you are limited to how many you can take and you do not earn as many BPs. Choosing a specific minor flaw or quirk for your character

is worth a flat 2 BPs. Choosing a major flaw or quirk is worth a flat 4 BPs. You can choose a max of two (2) minor flaws AND one (1) major flaw.

Rolling for Quirks and Flaws

This option pays more BPs than cherry picking, but there are some risks. For one, you have no control over what quirks or flaws you are going to get – you must roll randomly on the quirk and flaw tables in Chapter 6. And, because you're putting your faith in the dice and rolling on tables there's a chance you may have to 'roll again' for additional flaws.

The upside is that you can earn many more BPs with this option. Before rolling for quirks and flaws the player must commit by stating aloud how many times he's rolling on Table 6A: Flaws and Quirks d100. A player can roll a maximum number of nine times. The BPs earned depend on the BP value listed for the resulting quirk or flaw in Chapter 6.

Earning BPs by Sacrificing Attribute Points

This has never been a popular option with experienced players, but it is there if you need it nonetheless. For every attribute point you sacrifice you earn 2 BPs. There are restrictions, however – you cannot lower an attribute below racial or class minimums and you cannot lower an attribute below 3. This is a good option to use in a pinch when you are really unhappy at the result of a particular roll on one of the background tables and wish to roll again.

A Word of Caution on Quirks and Flaws

Because some flaws and quirks are seen as being greatly beneficial (such as HackFrenzy and HackLust) by many players, and because BPs are so valuable, there's a tendency for players to want to load up with quirks and flaws in order to min/max their characters. Be forewarned that your GM has every right to use your weaknesses and shortcomings against you. Also there are some quirks and flaws that are character-busters. Would you want to be a magic-user who has a phobia of all things magical, a thief who's afraid of the dark or an assassin who has no hands?

Character Background

Now that you've beefed up your Building Points (possibly taking on a few flaws or quirks in the process), it is finally time to find out more about your character. The following tables will determine such vital things as your character's starting age, social class, circumstances of birth, etc.

You and your GM will make use of this information during the course of your character's career to further detail your character's background. Mind you, this won't be accomplished overnight, but rather slowly, over the course of many adventures. In fact, it's a good idea to put off some of the detailing until you've had a chance to run the character through a few adventures and get a feel for him. Running the character will most certainly suggest background details for your character that you might not have thought of otherwise. (Also, you'll have saved a lot of time if your character gets greased in the first adventure.)

For example, at some point your character may find himself suddenly cut off from his fellow party members in a hostile country with the enemy hounding his every footstep. He's low on hit points and the situation looks bleak. At this point you may recall (from one of your background rolls) that you have a sister who is a cleric. She moved abroad years ago to champion her faith and never returned home. (That's about as far as you fleshed out your background regarding your sister.) Now at this point, a clever player might suggest to the GM that his devoted sister has actually spent the intervening years building a temple in the very 'hostile country' in the middle of which he now finds himself stranded. He informs the GM that his sister wrote him a letter with all the details when he was younger and that he is now making his way carefully to her temple to seek refuge.

Now the GM might or might not buy your suggestion. But it's definitely worth a shot. Despite the adversarial relationship between GM and player, most GMs welcome an opportunity for a player to expand his background in such a creative manner. If the GM accepts the player's logic, and rules in his favor, then another small bit of the player's character background has been defined and pinned down. [Note that the GM could later use this same bit of background info against the player. Perhaps a band of Grevans have laid siege to the temple and the sister dispatches a message to her brother asking him to come to her aid in all haste.]

You are encouraged to flesh out your character's background in great detail (based on the results of the following background tables, of course) but, as shown above, it's a good idea to leave some details sketchy so you don't pin yourself down, and leave some creative leeway. You never know when your character may need to remember his long, lost sister!

Character Age

An adventuring character's age is very important. Tables 4A through 4C are used to determine your character's starting age (add the variable die roll to the base starting age to get the character's starting age). They are also used to determine your character's maximum life span, assuming he leads a quiet and peaceful life and is lucky enough to live out his years. (Yeah, right! In HackMaster? Not bloody likely.)

The maximum age for a character is secretly determined and recorded by your GM. Player characters may have a vague idea of how long they expect to live, but do not know their true allotted life span.

As a character ages, his Ability Scores are directly affected. Upon reaching one-half of his base maximum age (45 for a human), the character loses 1 point of Strength and 1 point of Constitution, but he gains 1 point each for his Intelligence and Wisdom.

At two-thirds of his base maximum age (60 for a human), the character loses 2 more points of Strength, 2 points of Dexterity, and 1 more point of Constitution, but he gains 1 point of Intelligence and Wisdom. Upon reaching the base maximum age, the character loses 1 more point from each of Strength, Dexterity, and Constitution, while gaining 1 more point in both Intelligence and Wisdom.

All aging adjustments are cumulative. See Table 4C for a summary of these effects.

Your GM can assist you in determining the exact day and month of birth. It will be your responsibility to adjust your character's age each year of game time as his birthday passes.

Magical Aging: There may be times when a magical device or spell adds or subtracts years from a player character's life. This magical aging can have two different effects. Some magical aging physically affects the character. For example, a Haste spell ages those it affects by one year. This aging is added directly to the player character's current age. He physically acquires the appearance of himself one year older (a few more wrinkles, etc.).

Characters who increase in age from magical effects do not gain the benefits of increased Wisdom and Intelligence. These are a function of the passage of game time and life experiences. But the character does suffer the physical losses to Strength, Dexterity, and Constitution associated with aging. These are breakdowns of the body's systems.

Physical age can also be removed in the same manner. Some potions give years back to the character. In this case, the physical appearance of the character is restored. The character can regain lost vigor (Str, Dex and Con) as his body is renewed but he does not lose any of the benefits of aging (Wis and Int).

Table 4B: Age Modifier by Class Table*	
Class	Modifier
assassin	none
barbarian	none
bard	1d2
battle mage	2d8
berserker	1d4
cavalier	1d4
cleric	1d6
dark knight	1d3
druid	1d6
fighter	1d4
illusionist	2d8
knight errant	1d4
magic-user	2d8
monk	1d3
paladin	1d6
ranger	1d4
thief	1d2

* Pixie fairies do not receive this modifier

Table 4C: Aging Effects			
Race	Middle Age* (1/2 Base Max.)	Old Age** (2/3 Base Max.)	Venerable*** (Base Max.)
Dwarf (all)	125 years	167 years	250 years
Elf (all)	175 years	233 years	350 years
Gnome (all)	100 years	133 years	200 years
Gnomeling	75 years	100 years	150 years
Half-elf	62 years	83 years	125 years
Halfling (all)	50 years	67 years	100 years
Half-orc	30 years	40 years	60 years
Half-ogre	55 years	73 years	98 years
Human	45 years	60 years	90 years
Pixie fairies****	6 years	11 years	14 years

* -1 Str/Con; +1 Int/Wis
** -2 Str/Dex, -1 Con; +1 Wis
*** -1 Str/Dex/Con; +1 Int/Wis
**** Pixie fairies' Ability Scores do not adjust with age.

It is important to remember that adjustments cannot cause an Ability Score to exceed racial maximums. Likewise, any adjustments cannot lower an Ability Score below racial or class minimums.

Magical aging can also work to increase or decrease the life span of the character. In such a case, the actual age of the character is unaffected. All adjustments to the character's maximum age (which only the GM knows) are made by the GM. For example, a human finds a magical fountain that bestows great longevity (10 to 60 years more). The GM has already determined the human will naturally live to 103 years (base 90 + 2d20, in this case 13). The water of the fountain bestows 40 more years to that number, so unless the character meets a violent and untimely end, he will live to 143 years. He still suffers the effects of aging at the usual ages (45, 60, and 90 years, respectively), but the period in which he would be considered a venerable elder of his people is extended for 40 years.

Some characters, such as the battle mage, age faster than other characters because of the nature of their profession. Because their accelerated aging is due to their complete devotion to their work, they DO gain the Wisdom and Intelligence benefits associated with aging as well as the normal losses to Strength, Dexterity and Constitution. Certain races (like the pixie fairy) age quite a bit more quickly than other characters. See Chapter 2 for more details about the average life span for the different character races.

Table 4A: Age			
Race	Starting Age Base Age	Variable	Maximum Age Range* (Base+Variable)
Dwarf (all types)	40	5d6	250+2d100
Elf (all types)	100	5d6	350+4d100
Gnome (all types)	60	3d12	200+3d100
Gnomeling	40	2d12	150+2d100
Half-elf	15	1d6	125+3d20
Halfling (all types)	20	3d4	100+1d100
Half-ogre	13	2d4	100+1d10
Half-orc	15	1d3	60+1d20
Human	15	1d4	90+2d20
Pixie fairy	2	1d3	6+1d4

* Add half the character's Constitution to the result.

Character Handedness

Knowing whether your character is left-handed, right-handed or ambidextrous is important information in many situations. Only an ambidextrous character can use two weapons simultaneously in combat without suffering any penalties. A left-handed character whose left hand is incapacitated, forcing him to wield a weapon with his right hand, suffers a –2 modifier on all of his to-hits. Similarly, a right-handed thief who has had his right hand cut off by the magistrate for practicing his skills in the public marketplace is going to find it much harder to easily use his lock picking tools (-15%). Through time (1d6 months), a character forced to use his non-favored hand to use tools or weapons, can overcome such penalties.

Table 4D:	
Handedness of Character	
Roll	Handedness
01 - 12	Left-handed
13 – 22	Ambidextrous*
23 – 00	Right-handed

* All elves are ambidextrous.
** Dwarves and gnomes may add or subtract 10% to their roll to reflect their tendency to be ambidextrous.
*** Characters with 16 Dex or higher may add or subtract 5% to their roll.

You are permitted to buy a re-roll on this table if you don't like the results. Each re-roll costs one (1) Building Point. You may buy as many re-rolls as you want as long as you have BPs to spend.

Height and Weight

The height and weight of your character is generated randomly using Table 4E. Begin with the appropriate base score for your character's race, and then add the dice roll modifier.

As with all tables, this can create some ridiculous results (one of the pesky problems with randomness) and, at the same time, cannot account for the full variety of mankind (or demi-humankind). The table only reproduces a fairly average range for each race, and you may wish for your character to stand out in a crowd. For this reason you are permitted to buy a re-roll on this table if you don't like the results. Each re-roll costs one (1) Building Point. You may buy as many re-rolls as you want as long as you have BPs to spend.

Table 4E:
Average Height and Weight

	Height in Inches		Weight in Pounds	
Race	Base*	Modifier	Base*	Modifier
	M/F		M/F	
Dwarf	43/41	1d10	130/105	4d10
Elf	55/50	1d10	90/70	3d10
Gnome	38/36	1d6	72/68	5d4
Gnomeling	32/33	1d6	46/44	2d4
Half-elf	60/58	2d6	110/85	3d12
Halfling	32/30	2d8	52/48	5d4
Half-ogre	84/82	2d6	315/310	1d100
Half-orc	66/62	1d4	150/120	4d10
Human	60/59	2d10	140/100	6d10
Pixie fairy	18/18	1d4	24/24	1d6

* Females tend to be lighter and shorter than males. Thus, the base numbers for height and weight are divided into male/female values. Note that the modifier still allows for a broad range in each category.

Character Social Class

Now you must determine the social class for your character. Is he a man among men, sought by sages for his considerable knowledge? Is he known among the highest regal courtrooms throughout the world? Or did he once share a prison cell with four Dralch slaves in the bowels of the Black Hole of

Table 4F:
Social Class Table

Dice roll	Social (/Economic) Class	Typical Members of the Social Class
01	Slave Class (SLC) *	Slaves, indentured servants, prisoners, banished individuals
02-06	Lower Lower Class (LLC)	Freed slaves, peasants, tinkers, vagabonds, beggars, criminals, low-level thieves, low-level and mid-level assassins
07-11	Middle Lower Class (MLC)	Herdsmen, laborers, peddlers, actors, jugglers, men-at-arms, low-level barbarians, mid-level thieves, high-level assassins, low-level bards
12-20	Upper Lower Class (ULC)	Freemen, tradesmen, petty officers, money changers, fences, low-level fighters, high-level thieves
21-35	Lower Middle Class (LMC)	Artisans, craftsmen, petty merchants, junior officers, bankers, landless knights, druids, rangers
36-55	Middle Middle Class (MMC)	Landed gentry, merchants, petty officials, senior officers, landless petty nobles, mid-level fighters, low-level magic-users, low-level illusionists
56-87	Upper Middle Class (UMC)	Guild masters, great merchants, military commanders, officials, landless nobles, lesser clerics, high-level fighters, mid-level magic-users, mid-level illusionists
88-96	Lower Upper Class (LUC)	Great landed gentry, generals and marshals, greater officials, knights, mid-level clerics, cavaliers, paladins, high-level magic-users, high-level illusionists
97-99	Middle Upper Class (MUC)**	Knights, commanders, great clerics, nobles, high-level paladins, very high-level magic-users and illusionists
00	Upper Upper Class (UUC)***	Great nobles, sovereign nobility, royalty

* On SLC results roll a 1d20. 1-5 indicates character is a runaway slave. 06-15 indicates the character is an escaped criminal (GM to determine the crime) 16-20 indicates character was stripped of all rank and title by his native culture and banished.
** On a result of MUC check with your GM. Character may have a title, chain-of-office or position.
*** On a result of UUC check with your GM. Character may have properties, titles and other family/royal house entitlements.

Fangaerie? Perhaps he comes from a comfortable country villa on the outskirts of Hagley Town where his family was well respected.

To find out where your character stands, you must roll on Table 4F, the Social Class Table. You will note that this table does not include any social or political information, but only a few basic guidelines and examples of what type of characters share the social class/rank you've rolled. Keep in mind that your GM may have further modeled the social class distinctions to the tenor of his individual milieu.

If you don't like the results you receive, you can choose to buy a re-roll. Each re-roll costs one (1) Building Point. You may buy as many re-rolls as you want as long as you have BPs to spend.

Social Class Modifier to Honor: A character's social class/rank modifies his starting Honor. Don't feel bad about this; remember, if your character comes from the dregs of society, there's only one direction he can go...up! Overcoming the stigma of one's humble beginnings is one of the classic facets of the fantasy hero. Honor should be modified as follows:

LLC:	-10
MLC:	-5
ULC:	–1
LMC through UMC:	none
LUC:	+1
MUC:	+5
UUC:	+10

Racial Modifiers to Circumstances of Birth

	Table 4G	Table 4H
Dwarves, all	+5	+15
Elves		
Drow	+5	+15
Gray	-8	+25
Grunge	+10	-20
High	-5	+20
Wood	-5	+10
all others	-5	+20
Gnomes		
Gnone Titan	+5	0
all others	-5	+15
Half-elves	+15	0
Halflings, all	-5	+10
Half-orcs	+25	-30
Half-ogres	+35	-40
Humans	0	0
Pixie fairies	+15	+50

Social Class and demi-humans: Note that the actual positioning of non-humans is entirely dependent upon the individual milieu. As a general rule, a human society would consider the non-humans to have the following modifiers on Table 4F. PCs of these races would have an unmodified social class result when residing in a settlement dominated by their own kind.

Dwarves: no modifier
Elves: wood elves -30, gray elves +30, drow -45, grels -40, others: +15
Gnomes: +10
Gnomelings: -15
Halflings: -25
Half-elves: +5
Half-orcs: -45
Half-ogres: -45
Pixie fairies: no modifier

Social Class and Profession: As a general rule, any character must have a social status of, at the lowest, one rank below that specified for his or her profession in the milieu. For instance, using the system outlined above, a character embarking on a career as a fighter must have a social standing of no lower than Middle Lower Class, and conversely a character with a standing lower than that cannot hope to make his way in the fighter profession. Social class can be raised, however, as a character's career progresses. Honor, Fame and personal wealth (both real and perceived) can raise one's station in life. Your GM has the details on how this works.

Character Heritage/Lineage

No man is an island. Likewise, no character is a truly an individual. He's the product of countless generations of characters that came before him. Character heritage/lineage is very important in HackMaster. It affects one's Honor as well as the Honor of one's offspring and protegees. The sins of the father oft times saddle the son with the stigma of dishonor he must overcome.

A character may also inherit the enemies and allies of his father or family. Siblings and extended family can also be important in a character's career. A rich, influential uncle who is High Priest of Luvia may be able to use his influence to give your character sanctuary from your political enemies. Your brother who is working as an apprentice to a dark mage may be able to steal those hard-to-find spell components you need from his laboratory.

The following tables will help you get a very broad idea of your character's heritage/lineage. The results will be recorded and used by your GM to help you build a more detailed background for your character.

Some of the results obtained may not fit demi-human characters. For example, most dwarven characters will want to know which clan/bloodline they come from since some dwarven relics can only be used by dwarves of a certain clan (the Ironhearts, for example). Your GM can work with you on tailoring the results of your background if need be.

Circumstances of Birth: In most human cultures there is a stigma attached to individuals born outside of wedlock. Illegitimate (bastard) children are often denied inheritance and the right to hold political office or even positions

of power (in various religions, for example). (Demi-humans, for the most part, are more tolerant of 'love children' and other circumstances of birth, and not so concerned with legitimacy.)

Table 4G: Circumstances of Birth (d100)

Roll	Circumstance of Birth
<01 - 90	Character's birth was legitimate. Parents were married at time of character's birth.
91 - 00+*	Character's birth was illegitimate. Parents were not married at time of character's birth. Roll again on Illegitimate Birth Table.

*The child of unmarried parents is typically one social class lower than the social class of the father (85% percent of the time).

Table 4H: Illegitimate Birth Table (d100)

Roll	Nature of Illegitimacy
<01 – 05	Character was abandoned at birth. Parents unknown. [-3 to beginning Honor]
06 - 30	Birth was a result of rape. Father unknown. [-5 to beginning Honor]
31 – 60	Mother was a prostitute. Father unknown. [-10 to beginning Honor]
61 – 90	Birth was the result of an adulterous affair. 75% chance father's identity is known. [-3 to beginning Honor]
91 – 00+	Birth was arranged through a surrogate mother. 25% chance birth mother's identity is known. [-1 to beginning Honor]

Status of Parents: Roll d100 for each parent (mother and father). An 81 or above indicates that parent is deceased. A 91 or higher on the first roll indicates you are an orphan (do not roll for other parent). If both parents are dead, the character is considered an orphan. If only one parent is dead, roll to see if surviving parent remarried. (1d20: a result of 15 or more indicates that parent remarried and character has a stepparent.) Note: If you roll a 01 when checking a parent's status, that parent's Fame is notable (celebrity) and as a result some of that Fame falls to you. Your character's Fame should always be adjusted by multiplying it by 1.5 (see Chapter 5).

Status of Parents d100

01	Celebrity parent (1.5x Fame for character)
02-80	Parent living
81-90	Parent deceased*
91-100	Character orphaned (Do not roll for the character's other parent*)

* If only one parent is dead, a roll of 15 or above on a d20 shows that the character has a stepparent. Roll again on the above chart to determine the status of the stepparent.

Orphans/abandoned characters start with 50% of any starting money normally available to the character's class. Orphans are two social classes lower than the father (if the identity of the father is known that is – otherwise the an orphaned character is automatically LLC)

Quality of Upbringing: How a character was reared and the quality of his upbringing can have a huge impact on how he turned out. A caring, attentive parent is going to better equip his child for adulthood than a parent who is unaffectionate, abusive or not there at all. On the following table you should roll twice – once for the mother and once for the father. If the father was indicated as 'unknown' in Table 4H, don't roll for him and consider that parent to be dead.

Note that any quirks or flaws a character is forced to take as a result of his family do not grant him the building point bonus associated with that particular quirk or flaw.

Family Heritage: Family heritage is an indication of what type of Honor/prestige has been passed on to the character by his father/family. An honorable heritage will prove to be of great benefit to a character, as he strikes out on his own. He can get a lot of mileage from his family's name if the family is well regarded by the community. Likewise, a character will find a dishonorable heritage to be a great hindrance and hard to overcome. Of course the farther away from his birth region a character travels the less impact family heritage/lineage will have.

Table 4I: Quality of Parent Table (1d100)*		
Result	Parental Quality	Effect
01–60	Loving parent.	Character grew up well nurtured and properly cared for. Five (5) Building Point bonus
61–80	Ill-Equipped Parent.	Parent was well intentioned but poor at raising children.
81–91	Indifferent Parent.	Character was viewed as a burden. Character grew up with feelings of inadequacy and felt unloved. (Roll on Minor Quirk Table - player choice of which one)*
92–00+	Abusive Parent.	Character was abused by parents. (Roll on Major Quirk Table - player choice of which one)*

* Roll twice – once for each parent. If character is an illegitimate child, roll only once for mother.

Modifiers: Orphans add +20 Bastards add +35

Table 4J: Family Heritage (d100)		
Roll	Heritage	Effect
01	Great dishonor	[–5 to beginning Honor]
02 – 15	Dishonor	[-2 to beginning Honor]
16 – 45	No Honor	[No modifier]
46 – 76	Honorable	[+2 to beginning Honor]
77 – 00	Great Honor	[+5 to beginning Honor]

Siblings: As mentioned before, siblings (or the lack of them) can be a very important factor to a player character. Younger siblings make excellent choices for protegees (See Chapter 15: NPCs). They also can come in handy if you need to borrow money, seek shelter or need support. Although they are technically NPCs, they are your closest blood relatives and have the highest loyalty factors you'll find (unless, of course, sibling rivalry exists).

Status of Siblings

1. Roll 1d100 on Table 4K to determine the number of siblings.

2. Roll a d20 for each sibling. A 1-10 indicates sibling is brother, an 11 – 20 indicates sibling is a sister.

3. Next, roll a 1d100 for each sibling to see if they are still living. An 80+ result indicates sibling either died during birth or simply didn't survive into adulthood.

4. Sibling Rivalry: Sometimes the worst enemy a character can have is his own brother or sister. The sibling can also be a character's best friend. Roll 1d100 for each living sibling and add your Charisma Ability Score to the result. A result of 25 or below indicates that sibling considers you a bitter rival/enemy. An 85 or above indicates you and that sibling are extremely devoted to one another – this sibling would lay down his life for you. If the sibling is an illegitimate sibling modify the die roll by –20.

5. For each surviving sibling, roll d100. A 95-00 indicates that sibling is a twin. On a result of 99-00 the twin is considered to be an 'identical twin'.

If another sibling gets a result in the same range, that sibling is a triplet and so on.

Twins have a 5% base chance of being able to telepathically communicate with each other. Such communication is limited to strong emotions such as pain, grief, terror, etc. Identical twins have a 15% chance of being able to telepathically communicate with one another. In addition, one

identical twin can teach the other twin any skill he possesses at no cost and in the half the normal required training time as listed in Appendix F. The character must still roll his % chance to learn new skill from Table 1D for his Intelligence, but he receives a –15% modifier to the roll.

Extended Family: Besides parents and siblings, the character may also have an extended family. This would include grandparents, uncles/aunts and cousins. Your GM has tables to determine if such relatives exist and whether or not they are still alive.

Order of Birth: The order of one's birth in relation to any surviving siblings can be very important. The first born male is often heir to his father's estate. Roll on Table 4L if the character has at least one sibling (determined on Table 4K).

Table 4L: Order of Birth (d100)		
Roll	Order of Birth	Effect
01 - 20	First born	[+ 5 to starting money roll]
21 – 40	2nd born	[+2 to starting money roll]
41 – 60	Middle born (roll randomly)	[no effect]*
61 – 80	2nd to last born	[-2 to starting money roll]
81 – 00	Last born	[-5 to starting money roll]

* Roll once on Minor Personality Quirk Table

Hereditary Grudges/Family

Because family Honor and heritage contributes so much to your character's motivation, it is important to determine some facts about family history. He may begin adventuring because he wants to settle up with some brigand who once roughed up an ancestor. Perhaps the family's Honor was lowered by some particular race, nationality or house in years past, and has yet to be avenged. In short, your character may harbor one or more hereditary grudges against a traditional family enemy.

More importantly you may have inherited valuable family allies. Across the whole of Garweeze Wurld, families align themselves with other houses for power, prestige, or for the basic purpose of mutual protection.

Your GM will let you know if you have any such grudges or family allies.

Table 4K: Number of Siblings (d100)	
Dice Roll	Number of Siblings
01-15	None – Only child
16-35	1 sibling
36-50	2 siblings
51-60	3 Siblings
61-68	4 siblings
69-75	5 siblings
76-81	6 siblings
82 –86	7 siblings
86 – 90	8 siblings
91 – 95	9 siblings
96 – 00	Character has 1d4 illegitimate siblings. Roll on table 4H with a –10 modifier to determine nature of illegitimate siblings (honor modifiers only effect them). Roll for order of birth - your character is first born if he is legitimate himself.

Table 4M: Character Starting Money	
Roll	Starting Funds
<01-05	Hereditary Debt[1]
06-10	Flat Broke
11-15	20 + 1d4 gps
16-20	25 + 1d4 gps
21-25	30 + 1d4 gps
26-30	35 + 1d4 gps
31-35	45 + 1d6 gps
36-40	50 + 1d6 gps
41-45	55 + 1d6 gps
46-50	60 + 1d6 gps
51-55	70 + 1d8 gps
56-60	80 + 1d8 gps
61-65	90 + 1d8 gps
66-70	100 + 1d8 gps
71-75	110 + 1d10 gps
76-80	120 + 1d10 gps
81-85	130 + 1d10 gps
86-90	140 +1d10 gps
91-95	145 + 1d20 gps
96-100	150 + 1d20 gps
101-105	160 + 1d20 gps[2]
106-110	170 + 1d20 gps[3]
111-115	180 + 2d20 gps[4]
116+	190 + 2d20 gps[5]

1. Character has inherited a debt from his parents/family, which is responsible for repaying. Re-roll on table above and multiply the results by 10. This is the amount that must be repaid in d12 game months. The GM must decide exactly to whom the debt is owed and repercussions for defaulting payment. (Note there is ALWAYS a hit to Honor for failure to repay a loan.)
2. Character has also inherited his father's weapon (see GM).
3. Character has inherited his father's weapon and armor (see GM).
4. Character has inherited his father's weapon, armor and horse (w/basic tack) (see GM).
5. Character has inherited all of the items in #4, plus the deed to some land. (see GM)

Starting Money

All player characters begin with some amount of cash. This nest egg may be your character's life savings. It may be a gift from his parents to start him out in the world, such as a father bequeathing an heirloom weapon to his son. It may be his booty from an army campaign. Perhaps he stumbled across a small treasure chest, whetting his appetite for greater and more dangerous prizes. How he came by his money is not important (although it may be fun to know). You are free to create any explanation you want.

Most of these funds will quickly be spent on accommodations in the adventuring area and acquiring the equipment needed for adventuring.

To learn your character's starting funds, roll d100, apply the modifiers and and consult Table 4M. This is the number of gold pieces your character has to obtain equipment. If you are creating a character starting out at a level above 1st level, check with the GM to see if you can increase your character's funds beyond the amounts given here.

Multi-class characters use the most advantageous die modifier of their classes.

Modifiers to Starting Money Roll (Cumulative):

LLC:	-20
MLC:	-15
ULC:	-10
LMC:	-5
MMC:	0
UMC:	+5
LUC:	+10
MUC:	+15
UUC:	+20
First born:	+5
Only child:	+10
Orphan:	-20 (Regardless of result orphans only receive 50% of any indicated funds.)
Fighter group:	+10
Magic-user group:	-10
Cleric group:	0
Thief group:	+5
Per BP Spent:	+2-24 (2d12). These Building Points can only be spent before the roll.

Notes on Starting Funds:

Cleric characters can use their starting money only to purchase the necessary equipment and goods for adventuring. Once all these purchases are made, the cleric must return all but two or three of his remaining gold pieces to his superiors (since his equipment is supplied by his organization). Clerics cannot lend any of their initial funds to other characters.

Characters who start out broke or with debts may have to borrow money from other player characters. If that doesn't pan out they may have to sign on with a professional adventuring party (see Chapter 13: The Adventure and Ongoing Campaign). This is a good way to get a financial sponsor who will equip the character and provision him, in exchange for the lion's share of any treasure and valuables the expedition secures.

Other Character Traits and Particulars

Obviously there are a still a great number of other personal characteristics your character possesses. What about his hair color and style? How about his eye color, body shape, voice, noticeable features, general personality, temper and disposition? There are no tables for these things, nor should there be. Your job as a player is to add such details, thereby creating and molding the type of character you want. You probably know some from the very start. (Do you want to play a towering, robust warrior, or a slim, unassuming swordsman?). Others traits, especially your character's personality, will grow and take form as you play. Remember – you are an actor and your character is your role!

Buying Beginning Skills, Talents and Proficiencies

Now that you've determined a bit of your character's background, it's time to spend any remaining Building Points you have on skills, talents and proficiencies (STPs). Chapter 7 has more information on these along with a complete list and the necessary BP costs to purchase them in Appendices F-H.

Be sure to read the introductory section to Chapter 7: Skills, Talents and Proficiencies before making your selections. Some skills/talents/proficiencies are restricted. Other must be bought in sequence because they are the prerequisite for a more advanced ability. When you're finished spending your BPs and selecting your STPs come back here.

Leftover Building Points?

The character creation process is now nearly complete. All you need to do now is use any starting capital you have to buy equipment and outfit your character for the adventure. (See Chapter 9 for a comprehensive list of the different types of items you can purchase.)

If you have any BPs you haven't spent, you must first convert them to gold or use them for adjusting fractional Ability Scores. Each building point is worth 25 gps or 25 fractional ability points. Any BPs that are not converted at this stage are forever lost.

Alignment, Honor, Fame

How your character sees the world,
And how the world sees your character.

Honor Factor

There is one factor your character has that you should take special note of Honor. The notion of Honor runs deep to the very heart and soul of HackMaster. Characters without Honor will not be able to function for long on Garweeze Wurld. There, a person's Honor is everything.

First let's define exactly what Honor is. Honor is very different from the alignment-based code of Honor to which a paladin must adhere. Honor Factor is not a judgement of good and evil.

Individuals of high Honor are not necessarily good and those with low Honor are not necessarily evil. A cruel tyrant may very well possess high Honor, while a goodly knight, through unfortunate circumstances, might possess a miserable honor.

Honor is more a measure of the deeds accomplished by both the individual (and sometimes his bloodline/clan) as well as those individuals he associates himself with (his party, peers, etc.).

Honor is an indication of such things as success in combat/politics, obedience to the parameters of one's character class, loyalty, talent, and success, qualities that can be held by any individual regardless of alignment. Adherence to one's alignment and patron gawd does factor into Honor but it's all a matter of context. A character worshipping an evil gawd can do some pretty nasty things without reflecting on his Honor. Honor is more about staying true to one's self and beliefs.

In many ways Honor is about respect and how others view you. This is why Fame ties in so closely with Honor. Your Honor causes your Fame to rise and fall. A lowly zero level blacksmith in a backwater town can't have Honor no matter how great he is at his job. Though Honor will be very important to that individual and he may very well refuse to do work for someone he deems to be dishonorable.

To have Honor is to command respect. When a character loses Honor, he loses face. Honor is so essential to the hero that it is reflected in his very continence. People and even monsters can sense how much Honor a PC has just by standing in his presence. And sometimes (if his Honor is through the roof) just by looking at him. So much gravity is placed on individual and group Honor in HackMaster that characters have been known to commit ritual suicide when it is deemed their Honor Factor has been trashed and is irreparable.

Honor: What's it good for?

Good question. For one, you may be prevented from rising to the next experience level if your Honor isn't in the proper window. An optimal Honor can help your character advance to the next level sooner and with less associated costs. Honor can also affect how the fates deal with you (meaning they could help or hinder your luck with the dice). There are also magical weapons and relics that can only be used by characters with a certain level of Honor. Certain breeds of warhorses won't allow someone beneath a certain level of Honor to ride them. The list goes on and on. Most importantly, as hinted at above, Honor affects the way those you meet react to you.

Your GM will be observing the actions and behavior of your character with an eye on awarding (and docking) Honor points. You should be aware that he's not required to announce when and why he's adjusting your Honor. He's only required to inform you of your modified Honor Factor at the end of each game session. For example, let's say you have a disgruntled hireling working for you. He's mad because you slighted him in front of his peers and now he's the laughing stock of the party. His job is to fill everyone's canteens and waterskins at the start of each day. To get back at you he's been secretly putting a little extra 'something' in your canteen. You're not even aware of this outrageous act but nevertheless, your Honor is taking a hit every day because he's been bragging to his fellow hirelings about what he's been doing.

What else can affect your Honor? A lot of things. The thing to keep in mind is that your Honor can be affected through no fault of your own. Often, it's the perception (rightly or wrongly) of others which affects Honor the most. If you're returning to town hanging on to one hit point and are suddenly challenged to a fight by the town drunk, it's very understandable, in game terms, why you might choose to avoid taking a chance and avoid the situation. To those townsfolk who witness your reluctance to fight, however, you've just been branded a coward. Chances are your Honor just took a big hit. But it works both ways. The town drunk, who was so gored out of his mind that he didn't even realize who he was talking to is now deemed a braveheart. His Honor suddenly shoots up and he now finds he commands a level of new respect from his fellow citizens. (Though his boost in Honor will only be temporary. Typically 1d4 days. Zero level characters don't have Honor Factors. The best they can do is to catch their 'fifteen minutes' of fame when it comes their way. Consequently they can be very dangerous if they realize that their fifteen minutes are almost up and they think they might want to stretch it some.)

The following is a short list of only a few of the criteria a GM bases his adjustments on. You can use this list as a rough measuring stick for working toward improving your Honor but keep in mind the amount of points may vary. If a GM suspects you are trying to 'work the numbers' and checking off various actions expressly to earn Honor it is his right, no, his obligation, NOT to award points.

Things that Increase Individual and Group Honor

The following list is by no means complete but represents just some of the many actions that can increase one's Honor. Note that one's Honor might preclude some of the actions on the following list.

- Admonishing another PC when he wrongs you.
- Allowing a disarmed opponent to pick up his weapon.
- Allowing the enemy to draw first blood.
- Allowing the enemy to remove their dead and wounded from the field of battle.
- Being associated with someone with a higher Honor/Fame Factor
- Being blessed by certain classes or creatures can raise Honor.
- Using your 'bragging rights' by telling tales of your deeds at local taverns.
- Delivering the coup de grace to a superior opponent.
- Dying (and staying dead) can raise the Honor of the character's fellow party members.
- Entering into mortal combat sans shield/armor. (Note: this applies ONLY if your class/race allows you to use such items.)
- Fighting a 'worthy adversary' or battle-hardened adversary.
- Gloating over a victory.
- Humiliating an enemy. (Care must be taken. If you are witnessed humiliating an honorable character it could backfire with your own Honor taking a hit as well.)
- Picking up the funeral expenses of someone you slew in combat.

- Publicly humiliating a creature/character of a higher level or Honor. (Includes authority figures like guards, nobles etc.)
- Refusing medical treatment for the good of the party (so others may be treated first or so the adventure isn't delayed or hindered.)
- Rendering an attitude adjustment (see Skills) can recoup some lost Honor.
- Taking an arrow or hit for someone else.
- Taunting an enemy into fighting.
- Urinating on a fallen enemy's corpse in full view of his compatriots.
- Who ever lands the killing blow gets extra Honor.
- Winning a mano-on-mano challenge.

Things that Decrease Individual and Group Honor

The following list represents just some of the many actions that can decrease one's Honor. Some characters seem to seek out new and creative ways in which to diminish their group's Honor. Note that one's Honor might preclude some of the actions on the following list.

- An outsider laughing/mocking you or a fellow party member.
- Being admonished by another PC for a wrongdoing.
- Being associated with someone with a lower Honor Factor.
- Being cursed or vexed by certain classes or creatures can lower Honor.
- Being publicly insulted or disparaged. (Especially by an NPC or someone of a lower experience level than yourself.)
- Most forms of dirty fighting whittle away at your Honor. Unless of course the other guy 'dirty fights' first.
- Dying only to be raised again results in a hit on Honor.
- Getting caught in violation of one's alignment as the result of an alignment audit.
- Getting caught 'bragging' about deeds which rightfully belong to someone else (or which someone else shares Honor in).
- Killing a host who has provided you food or shelter.
- Neglecting to properly bury the body of a member of one's own race.

- Losing a battle standard, flag, crest during combat.
- Losing a mano-on-mano challenge.
- Losing one or more experience levels.
- Paying off an extortionist or shake-down.
- Putting up with bad service from a waiter or barkeep.
- Snitching or ratting out another.
- Surrendering.
- Walking away from a challenge. (This can be tricky. For example simply buying a drink for someone who has challenged you to a fight could be construed as "backing down from a fight".)
- Being eye-balled can affect your Honor if the event is not properly challenged.
- Letting someone take advantage of you (For example, losing a haggle exchange or paying good money for bad/shoddy product.)
- Attacking an unarmed or obviously inferior opponent.
- Fleeing combat.

Bad Karma

There are certain actions that not only decrease your Honor but also tag you with bad karma. Characters with bad karma have their Honor capped (i.e. it can't rise) until they've made amends to counter the dishonorable act that created the situation.

For example, a character with the 'nagging conscience' quirk loses his temper, murders an innocent man and hides his body in a pile of leaves by the roadside. The GM decides he's not going to let the character get away with his crime that easily. The character's alignment may have allowed him to do the despicable act but his sense of Honor won't. The murdered man's blood cries out for a proper burial. Until the character returns and buries the unfortunate man, the GM decides, the character's Honor is capped. If the character refuses to yield to his conscience the bad karma could begin to erode the character's Honor. In this example his 'conscience' is a witness to his dishonor and constantly accuses him.

Stealing Honor

You can also steal Honor from another character. This involves taking Honor from another and adding it to your own. You can only steal Honor from a character of equal or higher Honor than yourself. (There's no Honor in putting down those who are inferior to you. In fact, even trying to do so could adversely affect your Honor.)

There are four ways to steal Honor; Honor duels, counting coup, admonishment and open competition.

Honor Duels: To steal Honor by the first method you must announce (proclaim) that you are challenging the target-character to a Duel of Honor. If he refuses the challenge, his Honor immediately drops and you get some percentage of it (determined by the GM) to add to your own. If he accepts, you engage him in combat. First one to yield or drop wins the duel and loses a percentage of his Honor to the victor.

Counting Coup: This method works a bit differently and involves striking a superior armed opponent in close quarters with the blunt side of a weapon (or with a stick or similar harmless object no more than 3 feet in length). The intent is to merely 'tap' the opponent rather than delivering real damage. Each time you 'count coup' on such an enemy (i.e. you make a successful to-hit roll) you take a number of his Honor points to add to your own. If he kills you and there are no witnesses, he'll get these points back immediately. If he kills you and there are witnesses, his Honor loss will remain, but you will lose any Honor gained (stupidity, in this case, trumps bravery).

Admonishment: If one character (NPC or PC) wrongs another NPC/PC (i.e. he steals an item from him, refuses to render him aid, etc.) in the same party, the offended character can announce that he is "admonishing" the wrongdoer. The admonished character must immediately make an Honor Check (see Honor Check later in this chapter) and the admonishing character modifies the die roll with his own Honor Die. If the admonished PC fails his Honor Check he immediately loses 10% of his Honor to the other PC. The admonished character can Apologize (see Apology/Forgiveness later in this chapter). If successful he gets his Honor back.

Open Competition (a.k.a. Street Rules): Open Competition begins similarly to admonishment, with one character wronging another. Depending on the nature of the act, the wronged character will receive a deduction to Honor, while the wrongdoer will receive half the points lost from the wronged PC/NPC. If the wronged character finds out, he can admonish the wrongdoer as above. But sometimes, the act is just too embarrassing. Or the wronged individual simply chooses to react in kind, deducting Honor from the other and gaining points at a ratio of one to two (if the GM deducts 6 honor from the wronged individual, the wrongdoer would receive 3).

Note that the competition is not combat, that would be an Honor Duel. The open competition is anything outside of combat and it can be in full view of both parties and others (providing for larger Honor swings), just between the two, or in complete secrecy (pickpocketing, whizzing in his canteen at night, etc.). Anything goes, thus the nickname "Street Rules," as in "He was dis'n me with Street Rules in secret, but I caught on and replaced his Extra Healing potion with acid and crumbled poison ivy into his herbalism kit."

Individual (Character) Honor

As mentioned before Honor comes in two varieties, Group and Individual. Individual Honor is what you'll be most concerned about (and have the most control over). It will be an on-going job to maintain your Honor levels and protect your reputation so you are still able to command the respect you deserve. In many ways, Honor points are like hit-points – everyone you meet will be trying to whittle away at them.

Starting Honor

All characters begin their careers with some measure of Honor based on their beginning statistics, chosen character class and race. These points represent the Honor they gained previous to beginning their life as an adventurer. Starting Honor is modified by such things as social class (See Chapter 4: Character Priors and Particulars). Those characters born with a silver spoon in their mouths usually benefit from their status by starting off with a bit more Honor than poorer, more unfortunate characters. What they make of themselves afterward is up to them. Similarly, those characters who were orphaned or born out of wedlock suffer a hit to their starting Honor. Again, this reflects medieval society's view of such characters. Characters beginning the game with low Honor should look at it as a challenge to overcome such stigmas and move on.

Temporal Honor

During a typical game session you'll find that you may be raking in the Honor Points left and right (or losing them in a similar fashion.) Honor adjustments made during a gaming session are called Temporal Honor. You and your GM will be keeping a running tally of your Temporal Honor throughout the session as it rises and falls.

At the end of the session he will add 25% of your Temporal Honor to your Honor Factor. Depending on your character's behavior your Honor will rise or fall accordingly.

Table 5A: **Honor Standards for Level Progression**		
Current Level	GREAT HONOR (Bonus Window*)	DISHONORABLE (Penalty Window**)
1	17-20	<6
2	25-30	<9
3	33-40	<12
4	41-50	<15
5	49-60	<18
6	57-70	<21
7	65-80	<24
8	73-90	<27
9	81-100	<30
10	89-110	<33
11	97-120	<36
12	105-130	<39
13	113-140	<42
14	121-150	<45
15	129-160	<48
16	137-170	<51
17	145-180	<54
18	153-190	<57
19	161-200	<60
20	169-210	<63

* Characters with Honor in the 'bonus window' get a +1 to ALL their die rolls.

** Characters with low Honor (penalty window) receive a –1 to ALL their die rolls.

Table 5A: Explanation

Current Level: The current level of the character. When determining bonus/penalty windows for characters when advancing levels use the current level NOT the level the character is about to achieve.

Bonus Window: Indicates the range of Honor for the indicated experience level that yields bonuses. Characters in the bonus window get +1 to all their die rolls and gain an additional 5% experience point award. They also receive training for any new skills and for advancing at 90% of the listed cost.

Penalty Window: Indicates the range of Honor for the indicated experience level that causes the character to be penalized for having a miserable Honor. Characters in the penalty window get -1 to all their die rolls and suffer a 10% experience point penalty while they are in the penalty window. They must also pay a 10% premium for any training and/or fees to advance to the next level. (This reflects the fact that it's harder for that character to find teachers/mentors willing to take him on.)

NPCs can smell low Honor on a character or party like stink on a monkey. No one treats a character with low or negative Honor with any respect. Merchants will be more likely to take advantage of you. Barroom bullies are more likely to pick a fight. Innkeepers are more likely to turn you away. It's like having a black storm cloud hanging over your head.

For this reason, the lower your Honor gets, the more it tends to spiral out of control. Everyone loves to kick a man when he's down. Good Honor is your shield against such attacks. Honor loves company and those you hang with and adventure with are going to affect your personal Honor so it's important to choose your teammates carefully. Which brings us to our next topic.

Mulligans: Another benefit of having one's Honor fall in the 'optimal Honor' range (Great Honor) in the 'bonus window' as listed on Table 5A is that the player is awarded one 'mulligan' or re-roll per game session which he can use for any die roll (combat, damage, Honor check, initiative, whatever).

Group (Party) Honor

Whenever two or more characters team up and begin spending time together your GM will create a Group Honor Factor for them. This information should be recorded on your adventuring party record sheet along with other pertinent information about the party.

Group Honor is an average of the Honor Factors of those characters comprising the group. Each month the party adventures together the GM will recalculate the Group Honor Factor. He'll also take each character's individual Honor Factor and permanently adjust it one point closer to the new average. This means those characters with low Honor will benefit by being part of the group. Those with high Honor will find their Honor being slowly dragged down by the others.

There's really no way around this dilemma. It's the price you pay for associating yourself with others. There are a few magic items that can boost both personal and group Honor but they are rare and you can't really rely on stumbling across such items. The only workable solution is for each party member to diligently work on boosting his or her own individual Honor. This, of course, will help the Group's Honor as a whole. Unfortunately, there are some players who don't pull their weight in this regard and you should know that they exist. In fact there's a name for them: Honor Mooches. These unscrupulous bastards love to migrate from game table to game table. Their characters have miserable Honor Factors so they latch themselves on to a group of players who unwittingly let them into their midst. Then they play with the group just long enough to suck Honor away from their teammates and bring their own up. It's particularly hard to sniff these Honor Mooches out when they've

recently siphoned from a few groups as their Honor will be at a decent level giving the appearance of earned Honor when none is there.

Excess Honor

As strange as it may sound your character can have too much Honor. It can be very dangerous for a character to have an Honor Factor which is too high relevant to his level. As a general rule of thumb a character's Honor should never rise very far above 10 plus 10 times his level of experience. For example a 5th level fighter's optimal Honor Factor would be 60 (10 + (10 x 5) = 60).

There's nothing preventing you from going beyond these limits but to do so is asking for trouble — it's inappropriate. Exceeding your station in life as far as Honor is concerned is a form of hubris in the eyes of others, and of particular import, the gawds. It attracts the attention of powerful creatures who enjoy nothing more than slapping down any mortal foolish enough to step above his station in life without earning the right to do so (meaning it's best to climb the experience level ladder).

The gawds are notorious for making it their sworn-duty to deal with those 'bearing more Honor than merited'. This doesn't necessarily mean that Zeus is personally going to come flying down from the clouds to stomp on your mage. But it does mean that he could stir up trouble for you. This could be in the form of more frequent random encounters, bad luck, bad weather, etc.

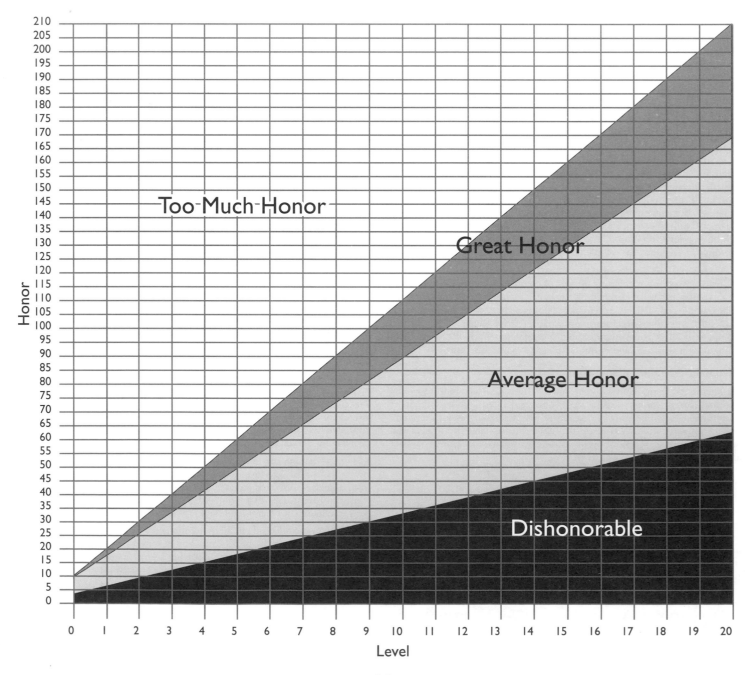

Table 5C:
Earning Honor Dice
Character Level

Honor	1	2	3	4	5	6	7	8	9	10	11	12	13	14	15	16	17	18	19	20
<10	1	1	1	1	1	1	1	1	1	1	1	1	1	1	1	1	1	1	1	1
15	d3	d3	d3	d3	d3	d3	d3	d3	d3	d3	d3	d3	d3	d3	d3	d3	d3	d3	d3	d3
20	d4	d4	d4	d4	d4	d4	d4	d4	d4	d4	d4	d4	d4	d4	d4	d4	d4	d4	d4	d4
25	d3	d4+1	d4+1	d4+1	d4+1	d4+1	d4+1	d4+1	d4+1	d4+1	d4+1	d4+1	d4+1	d4+1	d4+1	d4+1	d4+1	d4+1	d4+1	d4+1
30	d3	d6	d6	d6	d6	d6	d6	d6	d6	d6	d6	d6	d6	d6	d6	d6	d6	d6	d6	d6
35	1	d4+1	d6	d6+1	d6+1	d6+1	d6+1	d6+1	d6+1	d6+1	d6+1	d6+1	d6+1	d6+1	d6+1	d6+1	d6+1	d6+1	d6+1	d6+1
40	1	d4	d6+1	d6+1	d6+1	d8	d8	d8	d8	d8	d8	d8	d8	d8	d8	d8	d8	d8	d8	d8
45	1	d3	d6	d6+1	d6+1	d8	d8+1	d8+1	d8+1	d8+1	d8+1	d8+1	d8+1	d8+1	d8+1	d8+1	d8+1	d8+1	d8+1	d8+1
50	1	d3	d4+1	d8	d8+1	d8	d8+1	d10	d10	d10	d10	d10	d10	d10	d10	d10	d10	d10	d10	d10
55	1	1	d4+1	d6+1	d8	d8+1	d8+1	d10	d10+1	d10+1	d10+1	d10+1	d10+1	d10+1	d10+1	d10+1	d10+1	d10+1	d10+1	d10+1
60	1	1	d4	d6	d8+1	d10	d10	d10	d10+1	d12	d12	d12	d12	d12	d12	d12	d12	d12	d12	d12
65	1	1	d4	d4+1	d8	d8+1	d10	d10	d10+1	d12	d12+1	d12+1	d12+1	d12+1	d12+1	d12+1	d12+1	d12+1	d12+1	d12+1
70	1	1	d3	d4+1	d6+1	d10	d10	d10+1	d10+1	d12	d12+1	d12+1	d12+1	d12+1	d12+1	d12+1	d12+1	d12+1	d12+1	d12+2
75	1	1	d3	d4	d6+1	d8+1	d10	d10+1	d10+1	d12	d12+1	d12+1	d12+2	d12+2	d12+2	d12+2	d12+2	d12+2	d12+2	d20
80	1	1	d3	d4	d6	d8	d10+1	d10+1	d12	d12	d12+1	d12+1	d12+2	d12+2	d12+2	d12+2	d12+2	d12+2	d20	d20
85	1	1	1	d3	d6	d6+1	d10	d10+1	d12	d12+1	d12+1	d12+2	d12+2	d12+2	d20	d20	d20	d20	d20	d20
90	1	1	1	d3	d4+1	d6+1	d8+1	d12	d12	d12+1	d12+1	d12+2	d12+2	d12+2	d20	d20	d20	d20	d20	d20
95	1	1	1	d3	d4+1	d6	d8+1	d10+1	d12	d12+1	d12+2	d12+2	d12+2	d20	d20	d20	d20	d20	d20	d20
100	1	1	1	1	d4+1	d6	d8	d10	d12+1	d12+1	d12+2	d12+2	d12+2	d20	d20	d20	d20	d20	d20	d20
105	1	1	1	1	d4	d4+1	d8	d8+1	d12	d12+1	d12+2	d12+2	d12+2	d20	d20	d20	d20	d20	d20	d20
110	1	1	1	1	d4	d4+1	d6+1	d8+1	d10+1	d12+2	d12+2	d12+2	d20	d20	d20	d20	d20	d20	d20	d20
115	1	1	1	1	d4	d4+1	d6+1	d8	d10+1	d12	d12+2	d12+2	d20	d20	d20	d20	d20	d20	d20	d20
120	1	1	1	1	d3	d4	d6+1	d8	d10	d12	d20	d20	d20	d20	d20	d20	d20	d20	d20	d20
125	1	1	1	1	d3	d4	d6	d6+1	d10	d10+1	d12+2	d20	d20	d20	d20	d20	d20	d20	d20	d20
130	1	1	1	1	d3	d4	d6	d6+1	d8+1	d10+1	d12+1	d20	d20	d20	d20	d20	d20	d20	d20	d20
135	1	1	1	1	d3	d3	d6	d6+1	d8+1	d10	d12	d12+2	d20	d20	d20	d20	d20	d20	d20	d20
140	1	1	1	1	1	d3	d4+1	d6	d8+1	d10	d10+1	d12+1	d20	d20	d20	d20	d20	d20	d20	d20
145	1	1	1	1	1	d3	d4+1	d6	d8	d8+1	d10+1	d12	d12+2	d20	d20	d20	d20	d20	d20	d20
150	1	1	1	1	1	d3	d4+1	d6	d8	d8+1	d10	d10+1	d12+1	d20	d20	d20	d20	d20	d20	d20
155	1	1	1	1	1	1	d4+1	d4+1	d8	d8+1	d10	d10+1	d12	d12+2	d20	d20	d20	d20	d20	d20
160	1	1	1	1	1	1	d4	d4+1	d6+1	d8	d8+1	d10+1	d12+1	d20	d20	d20	d20	d20	d20	d20
165	1	1	1	1	1	1	d4	d4+1	d6+1	d8	d8+1	d10	d12	d12+2	d20	d20	d20	d20	d20	d20
170	1	1	1	1	1	1	d4	d4+1	d6+1	d8	d8+1	d10	d10+1	d12+1	d20	d20	d20	d20	d20	d20
175	1	1	1	1	1	1	d4	d4	d6+1	d6+1	d8	d8+1	d10	d10+1	d12	d12+2	d20	d20	d20	d20
180	1	1	1	1	1	1	d3	d4	d6	d6+1	d8	d8+1	d8+1	d10	d10+1	d12+1	d20	d20	d20	d20
185	1	1	1	1	1	1	d3	d4	d6	d6+1	d8	d8+1	d8+1	d10	d10+1	d12	d12+2	d20	d20	d20
190	1	1	1	1	1	1	d3	d4	d6	d6+1	d6+1	d8	d8+1	d8+1	d10	d10+1	d12+1	d20	d20	d20
195	1	1	1	1	1	1	d3	d3	d6	d6	d6+1	d8	d8+1	d10	d10+1	d12	d12+2	d20	d20	d20
200	1	1	1	1	1	1	d3	d3	d4+1	d6	d6+1	d6+1	d8	d8+1	d8+1	d10	d10+1	d12+1	d20	d20
205	1	1	1	1	1	1	d3	d3	d4+1	d6	d6+1	d6+1	d8	d8	d8+1	d10	d10+1	d12	d12+2	d20
210	1	1	1	1	1	1	d3	d3	d4+1	d4+1	d6	d6+1	d6+1	d8	d8+1	d8+1	d10	d10+1	d12+1	d20
215	1	1	1	1	1	1	d3	d3	d4+1	d4+1	d6	d6+1	d6+1	d8	d8+1	d8+1	d10	d10+1	d12	d12+2
220	1	1	1	1	1	1	1	d4+1	d4+1	d6	d6	d6+1	d6+1	d8	d8+1	d8+1	d10	d10+1	d12	d12+1
225	1	1	1	1	1	1	1	d4	d4+1	d6	d6	d6+1	d6+1	d8	d8	d8+1	d10	d10+1	d12	d12
230	1	1	1	1	1	1	1	d4	d4+1	d4+1	d6	d6	d6+1	d6+1	d8	d8+1	d8+1	d10	d10+1	d10+1
235	1	1	1	1	1	1	1	d4	d4+1	d4+1	d6	d6+1	d6+1	d8	d8	d8+1	d10	d10	d10+1	d10+1
240	1	1	1	1	1	1	1	d4	d4	d4+1	d6	d6	d6+1	d6+1	d8	d8+1	d8+1	d10	d10+1	d10
245	1	1	1	1	1	1	1	d4	d4	d4+1	d4+1	d6	d6	d6+1	d6+1	d8	d8+1	d8	d8+1	d10
250	1	1	1	1	1	1	1	d3	d4	d4+1	d4+1	d4+1	d6	d6	d6+1	d6+1	d8	d8	d8+1	d8+1
255	1	1	1	1	1	1	1	d3	d4	d4	d4+1	d4+1	d6	d6	d6+1	d6+1	d8	d8	d8	d8+1
260	1	1	1	1	1	1	1	d3	d4	d4	d4+1	d4+1	d4+1	d6	d6	d6+1	d6+1	d8	d8	d8+1
265	1	1	1	1	1	1	1	d3	d3	d4	d4	d4+1	d4+1	d6	d6	d6+1	d6+1	d8	d8	d8
270	1	1	1	1	1	1	1	1	d3	d3	d4	d4	d4	d4+1	d4+1	d6	d6	d6+1	d6+1	d8
275	1	1	1	1	1	1	1	1	d3	d4	d4	d4	d4+1	d4+1	d6	d6	d6+1	d6+1	d8	d8
280	1	1	1	1	1	1	1	1	d3	d4	d4	d4	d4+1	d4+1	d4+1	d6	d6	d6+1	d6+1	d6+1
285	1	1	1	1	1	1	1	1	d3	d4	d4	d4	d4+1	d4+1	d4+1	d6	d6	d6+1	d6+1	d6+1
290	1	1	1	1	1	1	1	1	1	d3	d4	d4	d4	d4+1	d4+1	d4+1	d6	d6	d6+1	d6+1
295	1	1	1	1	1	1	1	1	1	d3	d3	d4	d4	d4	d4+1	d4+1	d4+1	d6	d6	d6+1
300	1	1	1	1	1	1	1	1	1	d3	d3	d4	d4	d4	d4+1	d4+1	d4+1	d6	d6	d6
305	1	1	1	1	1	1	1	1	1	d3	d3	d4	d4	d4	d4	d4+1	d4+1	d4+1	d6	d6
310	1	1	1	1	1	1	1	1	1	d3	d3	d3	d4	d4	d4	d4	d4+1	d4+1	d4+1	d6
315	1	1	1	1	1	1	1	1	1	1	d3	d3	d3	d4	d4	d4	d4+1	d4+1	d4+1	d6
320	1	1	1	1	1	1	1	1	1	1	d3	d3	d3	d4	d4	d4	d4	d4+1	d4+1	d4+1
325	1	1	1	1	1	1	1	1	1	1	1	d3	d3	d4	d4	d4	d4	d4+1	d4+1	d4+1
330	1	1	1	1	1	1	1	1	1	1	1	d3	d3	d3	d4	d4	d4	d4+1	d4+1	d4+1
335	1	1	1	1	1	1	1	1	1	1	1	d3	d3	d4	d4	d4	d4	d4	d4	d4+1
340	1	1	1	1	1	1	1	1	1	1	1	d3	d3	d3	d4	d4	d4	d4	d4	d4
345	1	1	1	1	1	1	1	1	1	1	1	1	d3	d3	d4	d4	d4	d4	d4	d4
350	1	1	1	1	1	1	1	1	1	1	1	1	d3	d3	d3	d4	d4	d4	d4	d4
355	1	1	1	1	1	1	1	1	1	1	1	1	1	d3	d3	d4	d4	d4	d4	d4
360	1	1	1	1	1	1	1	1	1	1	1	1	1	d3	d3	d4	d4	d4	d4	d4
365	1	1	1	1	1	1	1	1	1	1	1	1	1	1	d3	d3	d4	d4	d4	d4
370	1	1	1	1	1	1	1	1	1	1	1	1	1	1	d3	d3	d3	d4	d4	d4
375	1	1	1	1	1	1	1	1	1	1	1	1	1	1	1	d3	d3	d4	d4	d4
380	1	1	1	1	1	1	1	1	1	1	1	1	1	1	1	1	1	d3	d3	d3
385	1	1	1	1	1	1	1	1	1	1	1	1	1	1	1	1	1	1	d3	d3
390	1	1	1	1	1	1	1	1	1	1	1	1	1	1	1	1	1	1	d3	d3
395	1	1	1	1	1	1	1	1	1	1	1	1	1	1	1	1	1	1	1	d3
400	1	1	1	1	1	1	1	1	1	1	1	1	1	1	1	1	1	1	1	d3
405	1	1	1	1	1	1	1	1	1	1	1	1	1	1	1	1	1	1	1	1

Lowering Honor

Fortunately there are ways to burn off Honor points before having too many becomes a problem. The most obvious way is to do dishonorable acts. But take care if you choose this route. You could send your Honor spiraling out of control if you commit a dishonorable act and people begin to talk about it. If you find you are in danger of exceeding your optimal Honor Factor, try under-tipping a waitress a few times or hanging around in a seedy bar where NPCs with negative Honor Factors frequent.

A second way of lowering Honor is by using your Honor Dice to sway a critical outcome (see the Honor Dice section below for more details). At any time a player may add his Honor Die roll to any one of his combat rolls, saving throws or skill checks by simply declaring that he desires to do so and deducting 10 points of Honor. The player must declare BEFORE the affected roll is made. There is no limit to the number of times a player can do this, i.e., 30 points can be deducted to add three Honor Dice. A player can also add fractional dice by deducting less than 10, 5 for 50%, 3 for 30%, etc. In this case, the die roll is simply multiplied by the fraction to figure the bonus number. All fractions are rounded to the nearest integer.

A player can take this action regardless of whether he is honorable or dishonorable, as long as he has the points. Furthermore, if the character lowering his Honor in this way takes heroic action or does an otherwise honorable act, his GM will allow him to garner a bonus of some or all of the lost Honor at the end of that evening's session. For example, let's say in a long battle, a demon kills an entire adventuring band, except the cleric. He grabs their souls and opens a gate to the Abyss. As the demon prepares to leap through, the cleric burns 40 points of Honor to add two Honor Dice to his attack roll and two Honor Dice to his damage roll. If he kills the demon and saves the souls of his dead friends the GM will likely award him back his Honor Points after the session. In the same scenario, let's say, instead of immediately going for the gate, the demon grabs for the cleric to drag him to the netherworlds as well. If the cleric burns 20 points of Honor to gain two Honor Hice to deduct from his initiative so he can flee before the demon can make a move, he'll save his own hide, but it's unlikely the GM will be let him recoup that lost 20 points.

The final way to burn off Honor points is to purge your Honor. Purging Honor reduces your Honor by 90% (rounded down). You can purge your Honor once per level of experience. Why would you want to do this? Purging Honor allows you to avoid any one action/event that would have caused the death of your character.

For example, you foolishly walk into a room and get a blast of dragon's breath right in the face. Your character is fried to a cinder. Game over. If you haven't purged your Honor during your current level of experience, and IF your Honor is in the optimal Honor range, you can avoid that situation. It's up to the GM how this is implemented for a given event, but in this example, the GM might allow you to shut the door in time to cause the dragon to pause, or leap aside, etc. Note that purging one's Honor applies only to the character performing the purge. In the example above, if an entire party had walked through the door only those character(s) who purge Honor would be able to leap aside. Of course, if the first character who was blasted was at the start of the marching order as indicated by his official HackMaster miniature and he entered first, something different might happen. In this case, if he purged his Honor, he could slam the door shut and avoid the blast for the whole group.

Purging Honor can also be used to guarantee success in almost any given action. For example you know the dragon you are facing has a missing scale right below his left temple — a weak spot about the size of a quarter. You could try to aim with your crossbow and hit that bare patch of skin but the modifiers for such a called shot might make it near impossible. Purging your Honor could guarantee your to-hit roll succeeds. (You're on you own for all subsequent die-rolls including damage and saves however). There is one qualifier when determining if purging Honor can guarantee a given action. The action must be 'possible' (even if it's only a 1% chance). A character couldn't announce he's going to lift a stone church over his head and then purge his Honor and proclaim that he was successful. It doesn't work that way. In this case, all he'd get is a hernia for his trouble (your GM has statistics for hernias).

Purging Honor and using Honor Dice bring an element of cinematic drama into the game and allows characters to do truly larger than life feats. They can also help prevent a character from biting the big one and keep a campaign going that would have been otherwise wrecked by the untimely demise of one or more PCs. Keep in mind that you get only one chance to purge Honor per level and that you lose 90% of your Honor when doing so.

Typically only lower level characters take advantage of this method. After all, a first level character's optimal Honor Factor is only twenty. Losing eighteen points of Honor isn't really that bad and can be made up in the short term. But an eighth level character would likely lose at least 65-81 points of Honor!

Fame/Infamy

Fame/Infamy is an indication of how widely known (and spoken of) your character's deeds and exploits are in the campaign milieu he's adventuring in. Evil characters have Infamy. Characters of Good alignment have Fame. Characters of Neutral alignment have either Fame or Infamy, depending on their slant in life (their choice).

Fame/Infamy is linked with your character's Honor and level of experience and can modify such things as how easy it is for you to hire hirelings, attract followers, raise armies, rise in social status, reactions from creatures/NPCs you meet on your adventures, etc. As your Fame/Infamy rises you'll find that your reputation literally precedes you as you move from area to area. If you're one to be feared and have a reputation for burning and looting villages, you may find that your enemies are fleeing before your arrival (or making preparations to defend against you). If you have a reputation for aiding those in trouble you may find that people are seeking you out to request your services/assistance. Fame goes along with the territory when it comes to being a hero. You'll find it will be an advantage at times and a hindrance at others. Your GM will consider your Fame as you interact with others.

To calculate your current Fame, take your Honor and multiply it by your current Level and divide by 10. (Round down) For example, a 2nd level thief with a 10 Honor would have a Fame of 2 (10x2)/10. There is a box on your character sheet to keep track of your Fame/Infamy.

You can modify your Fame by hiring bards to sing of your exploits or by exercising your 'bragging rights' by telling the tale of your exploits at taverns and social gatherings.

Bragging Rights: Bragging rights for any deed or exploit rightfully belong to the person(s) who contributed to its successful outcome. A character who performs an unassisted kill on a dragon, for example, has sole bragging rights. However, if two of his buddies held the dragon at bay with their spears so the mage had time to cast his spell, all three share in the bragging rights. Who actually has bragging rights isn't always clear and bragging rights are often a matter of dispute in any campaign. It is up the GM, as final arbitrator to decide (perhaps secretly) who has such rights. Bragging about a deed that doesn't rightfully belong to you could send your Honor plummeting.

The Swearing of Oaths

There will be times when your character (or the party as a whole) will need to swear an oath. Oaths in the world of HackMaster are taken very, very seriously. A man's word is his Honor and breaking an oath can have dire consequences. There are two forms of oaths a character can make, blood oaths and gawd oaths.

Blood Oaths

A blood oath is the simplest form of oath to make. All that's needed is a witness. When a character swears a blood oath he is literally swearing by his Honor. Blood oaths are usually made when a character promises something. For example, Lord Flataroy wants to take a short cut through the realms of the Southern Orc League in order to cross the Fargruss River before the spring thaw. The Orkin Council refuses to let him do so unless he swears

Table 5B:	
Breaking a Blood Oath (1d20)	
Roll	% of Honor Lost
01	75%
02-05	65%
06-09	50%
10-13	40%
14-17	30%
18-19	20%
20	10%

Note that keeping/making good on a blood oath has no benefit whatsoever. A person is expected to keep his word so no incentive is given. If breaking an oath results in a negative Honor it is recorded as such.

a blood oath that when he returns to his homeland he will not talk about what he has seen in the Orkin Frontier. Flataroy readily agrees and the Orkin Council takes him at his word and allows him to pass.

If the blood oath is broken (intentionally or unintentionally) the character loses face (Honor) and must immediately roll on Table 5B.

Gawd Oaths

A gawd oath is the most solemn of all oaths. Here a character isn't swearing by his Honor but by his patron gawd. Breaking a gawd oath has but one simple penalty – the loss of one full experience level. The offending character goes down to one experience point above the minimum amount needed for next lower level. In effect, that gawd himself is enforcing the oath or agreement and is responsible for meting out punishment.

Honor Dice

Finally, there is one more benefit to being a man (or demi-human) of Honor. All but the most ignoble characters have an Honor Die. The sacred Honor Die is used to supplement various die/dice rolls such as improving fractional ability scores when going up levels (See Chapter 1). The Honor Die can also help improve skills and increase the likelihood that training/schooling is successful. The Honor Die can sometimes sway the outcome of who gets initiative, how NPCs and monsters react to you, etc. There's only one way to improve your Honor Die and that's to earn it. Honor Dice are awarded according to Table 5C. Any player caught using any physical die other than his declared Honor Die for an Honor Die roll immediately loses 10 points of Honor. The same penalty applies for a player that uses his Honor Die for anything other than use as an Honor Die.

Honor Checks

At times your character may be required to make an Honor Check. Honor Checks are made during Honor Duels. They're also required when a character has undergone an alignment audit and been found lacking. Your GM may force a character to make an Honor Check when engaging with other high level characters or whenever Honor figures largely in a situation. It also helps establish pecking order among characters of Honor (each character rolls and the highest is the alpha character – order remains until there's a challenge or whenever a new NPC or PC is added to the group). More frequently, however, Honor Checks are used to resolve apologies/forgiveness (see below).

Honor Checks are made against a variable number determined as follows: 20 minus a roll of your Honor Die minus your base modifier for Honor Checks. Honor Checks are made by rolling a d20 and comparing it to the result of the above formula. Equal or better means success.

Base Modifiers for Honor Checks are: Dishonorable: -5 Honorable: +3
Great Honor (or higher): +5

Example: A thief who suddenly confronts an agent of Draper, the Thief Gawd, (his patron gawd) and who is found lacking on his alignment audit must make an immediate Honor Check. The thief happens to be in the honorable category for his level and he's earned an Honor Die of the d6 variety. He rolls a 3, therefore he must roll a 14 or more (20-3-3) on a d20 in order to make a successful Honor Check.

Apologies/Forgiveness: Saving throws modified by your Honor are also used to resolve apologies/forgiveness in the game among characters. If one character wrongs another character and is admonished for it (i.e. he loses Honor to that character) he can later apologize to that character and force him to make a save vs. apology. If he fails, he MUST accept the apology and the character apologizing gets his Honor back. For this type of saving throw, the recipient of the apology also deducts the apologizer's base modifier and Honor Die result from his save. So the modifiers for a save versus apology are: a roll of the recipient's Honor Die + the recipient's base modifier for Honor Checks - a roll of the apologizer's Honor Die - the apologizer's base modifier for Honor Checks (note if the apologizer is dishonorable, you'd deduct a -5 or actually add five).

Example: Gurt, the party thief, pulls first watch on guard duty. He ends up rifling through Purzy's backpack and eats all his corn dodgers and drinks all his hard cider. When Purzy wakes up, he discovers what Gurt has done he is furious. He admonishes Gurt severely (Gurt loses x number of Honor points that are added to Purzy's Honor). Gurt wants his Honor back so he apologizes to Purzy. Now, Purzy's player is still ticked off over the incident and has no intention of forgiving Gurt. (The in-game friction has spilled over and now the actual players are mad at each other.) But since Gurt apologized, Purzy is now forced to consider it (i.e. he's forced to make a save vs. apology).

Gurt is an honorable character (base modifier +3) and he rolls a 3 on his Honor Die. Purzy is a first level fighter of great honor (base modifier +5) and his Honor Die (a 1d4) comes up a two. Purzy rolls a 12, adds 5 (his base mod-

ifier) and 2 (his honor die roll), then deducts 3 (Gurt's base modifier) and another 3 (Gurt's roll) for a total of 13 (12+5+2-3-3). Since Purzy needs an 18 to save successfully (on Table 12H we find a first level fighter needs a base 18 to save versus apology), he fails. So, despite the player's true feelings on the matter, his character forgives Gurt and all is forgiven. Gurt regains any lost Honor for being admonished and Purzy can no longer hold the incident against him.

The save vs. apology die roll can be modified as follows:

Apologizer sheds tears; -1

Each day that has passed since the incident (admonishment); −1

Apologizer Grovels; -3

Note: If the Apologizer grovels and is forgiven, he only gets back half of the Honor lost due to the admonishment. If he isn't forgiven, he loses another 1d4 points of Honor because…well, because he groveled.

Presence Factor (PRE)

Presence is tied to one's Honor. It's an indication of how one carries oneself and how those who stand in the character's company react to him. Presence can help in situations where a character is addressing a crowd, attempting to exert his authority, sway opinion, negotiate difficult terms, etc. It's used as the base skill mastery % for such skills as Oration, Negotiate, Sway Crowd, etc.

Your character's presence factor at any given time is his Charisma plus the roll of his Honor Die. Presence is re-figured every time a check is made (i.e. you re-roll the Honor Die and add it to your Charisma with every presence check).

Character Alignment

Finally, after all other steps toward creating a character have been completed, the player must choose an alignment for the character. In some cases (e.g. the paladin), the choice of alignment may be limited or even mandatory.

The character's alignment is a guide to his basic moral and ethical attitudes toward others, society, good, evil, and the forces of the universe in general. Use the chosen alignment as a guide to provide a clearer idea of how the character will handle moral dilemmas.

Alignment is divided into two sets of attitudes: order and chaos, and good and evil. By combining the different variations within the two sets, nine distinct alignments are created. These nine alignments serve well to define the attitudes of most of the people and creatures in the world.

Alignment Combinations

Each alignment varies from all others, sometimes in broad, obvious ways, and sometimes in subtle ways. Each alignment is described in the following paragraphs.

Lawful Good: Characters of this alignment believe that an orderly, strong society with a well-organized government can work to make life better for the majority of the people. To ensure the quality of life, laws must be created and obeyed. When people respect the laws and try to help one another, society as a whole prospers. Therefore, lawful good characters strive for those things that will bring the greatest benefit to the most people and cause the least harm, that is, the needs of the many outweigh the needs of the few. A lawful good character would willingly allow a village or even a city to be overrun by humanoids if he thought it was the best way to save the rest of the kingdom. He would do this even knowing full-well that every man would be put to the sword and every woman and child abused then turned into slaves or butchered. An honest and hard-working serf, a kindly and wise king, or a stern but forthright minister of justice are all examples of lawful good people.

Lawful Neutral: Order and organization are of paramount importance to characters of this alignment. They believe in a strong, well-ordered government, whether that government is a tyranny or benevolent democracy. Society outweighs the need of any individual and at any cost. In addition, the benefits of organization and regimentation outweigh any moral questions raised by their actions. An inquisitor determined to ferret out traitors at any cost or a soldier who never questions his orders are good examples of lawful neutral behavior.

Lawful Evil: Structure and organization elevate those who deserve to rule as well as provide a clearly defined hierarchy between master and servant. If someone is hurt or suffers because of a law, then tough luck for them. Lawful evil characters believe that the smartest and most powerful should rule, commanding respect from all beneath him. The servant should always try to become the master at some point, pushing the master to try to stay ahead (but it's perfectly okay for the master to kill the servant if he discovers anything but complete loyalty). Lawful evil characters obey laws because they think that is the way society needs to function and they fear punishment. Because they may be forced to honor an unfavorable contract or oath they have made, lawful evil characters are usually very careful about giving their word. Once given, they break their word only if they can find a way to do it legally, within the laws of the society. An iron-fisted tyrant and a slave merchant are examples of lawful evil beings.

Neutral Good: These characters believe that the concerns of society and individualism both have merit, but each pale in comparison to the need to promote good. If fostering good means supporting organized society, then that is what must be done. If good can only come about through the overthrow of existing social order, so be it. Social structure itself has no innate value to them. A baron who violates the orders of his king to destroy something he sees as evil is an example of a neutral good character.

True Neutral: True neutral characters are broken into two camps. The first believe in the ultimate balance of forces, and they refuse to see actions as good or evil. Since the majority of people in the world make judgments, characters of this type are extremely rare. Druids think in this manner because they care only for nature, which is neutral by definition. True neutrals do their best to avoid siding with the forces of either good or evil, law or chaos. It is their duty to see that all of these forces remain in balanced contention. True neutral characters sometimes find themselves forced into rather peculiar alliances.

To a great extent, they are compelled to side with the underdog in any given situation, sometimes even changing sides as the previous loser becomes the winner. A true neutral druid might join the local barony to put down a tribe of evil gnolls, only to drop out or switch sides when the gnolls were brought to the brink of destruction. He would seek to prevent either side from becoming too powerful.

The second type of true neutral is the uncaring individual. Characters of this type care little about good, evil, society or individualism. They see benefits and disadvantages to each and act according to their needs at the moment. They concern themselves only with their own success and survival, but not necessarily at the expense of others. These characters are not chaotic, because they appreciate and enjoy the benefits of society and its laws. Individuals with Intelligence below five MUST be this alignment or the alignment of their parent or guardian (if one exists), as they are too dim to consciously choose any action based on morals. Animals, for example, must be true neutral. Most people tend toward true neutral. A street urchin, a greedy merchant or a two-bit thief are good examples of True Neutral.

Neutral Evil: Neutral evil characters are primarily concerned with themselves and their own advancement, at the expense of everyone else. They have no particular objection to working with others or, for that matter, going it on their own. Their only interest is getting ahead. If there is a quick and easy way to gain a profit, whether it be legal, questionable, or obviously illegal, they take advantage of it. Although neutral evil characters do not have the every-man-for-himself attitude of chaotic characters, they have no qualms about betraying their friends and companions for personal gain. They typically base their allegiance on power and money, which makes them quite receptive to bribes. An unscrupulous mercenary, a common thief, and a double-crossing informer who betrays people to the authorities to protect and advance himself are typical examples of neutral evil characters.

Chaotic Good: Chaotic good characters are strong individualists marked by a streak of kindness and benevolence. They believe in all the virtues of goodness and right, but they have little use for laws and regulations. They have no use for people who "try to push folk around and tell them what to do." Their actions are guided by their own moral compass which, although good, may not always be in perfect agreement with the rest of society. A rogue that steals from the rich to give to the poor is a good example of a chaotic good character.

Chaotic Neutral: Chaotic neutral characters tend to follow whatever whim strikes them at the moment. Good and evil are irrelevant when making a decision. They abhor laws and restrictions of any kind, whether because they hate society or philosophically want to bring about anarchy.

Chaotic neutral characters are extremely difficult to deal with. Such characters have been known to cheerfully and for no apparent purpose gamble away everything they have on the roll of a single die. They are almost totally unreliable. In fact, the only reliable thing about them is that they cannot be relied upon! This alignment is perhaps the most difficult to play. Lunatics and madmen tend toward chaotic neutral behavior.

Chaotic Evil: These characters are the bane of all that is good and organized. Chaotic evil characters are motivated by the desire for personal gain and pleasure. They see absolutely nothing wrong with taking whatever they want by whatever means possible.

Laws and governments are the tools of weaklings unable to fend for themselves. The strong have the right to take what they want, and the weak are there to serve the strong.

When chaotic evil characters band together, they are not motivated by a desire to cooperate, but rather to oppose powerful enemies. Such a group can be held together only by a strong leader capable of bullying his underlings into obedience. Since leadership is based on raw power, a leader is likely to be replaced at the first sign of weakness by anyone who can take his position away from him by any method. Bloodthirsty buccaneers and monsters of low Intelligence are fine examples of chaotic evil personalities.

A Note on Good and Evil

The biggest mistake players with evil PCs make is that they almost immediately slay or screw over a fellow player. They run around like a professional wrestler on steroids breaking and killing things at every turn. Such characters live short and uneventful lives. The best evil characters are charismatic, two-faced and cunning. They don't broadcast, "Look! I'm evil" by holding a neon sign over their heads. They often look, and behave like decent, likeable individuals. With a smile, they win over the confidence of those who are around them and go out of their way to be helpful. Only then, when everyone's defenses are down, do they show their true colors. Of course, you could play your evil character as a hot head who has no control, but the real challenge of playing an evil character is to do so with an eye on survival and getting ahead. Evil characters often use deception (see Appendices F and G: secret persona and ulterior motive) as tools to this end.

The biggest mistake people make when they play good characters (particularly lawful good characters) is to play them like wimps. Does a paladin need to accept the surrender of some orcs? Yes. Does he need to bring them to justice? Yes. Does he need to bring them to town for a trial? It depends. If he's outside of a local jurisdiction (e.g. in the wilderness or in the orc lair), he can simply execute them right there on the spot. Surprised? Don't be. Orcs are evil and they have gawds that keep them evil. If let go, they will breed more evil orcs. So the paladin is okay. Now in this example, it wouldn't be proper for the paladin to torture the orcs first, unless they had information that could save the nearby village and it was the only way to make them talk. But simply torturing for fun is clearly evil.

Non-Aligned Creatures

In addition to the alignments above, some things—particularly unintelligent monsters (killer plants, etc.) and animals—never bother with moral and ethical concerns. For these creatures, alignment is simply not applicable. A dog, even a well-trained one, is neither good nor evil, lawful nor chaotic. It is simply a dog. For these creatures, alignment is always detected as neutral.

Playing the Character's Alignment

Aside from a few minimal restrictions required for some character classes, a player is free to choose whatever alignment he wants for his character. However, before rushing off and selecting an alignment, there are a few things to consider.

First, alignment is a tool to role-playing and should be used that way. Some players think alignments are unfair and that they restrict or limit what a character can do. This is only partially true. Your character is free to almost any action he wants. If your paladin wants to disembowel his enemies and eat their hearts for supper with a fine red wine, so be it. If your lawful evil cleric wants to give all his gold to the poor and run a soup kitchen that's fine too. However, both characters would be in violation of their alignment and in danger of shifting. (Admittedly, if the evil cleric is doing charitable deeds as a cover for some larger, sinister scheme that he had yet to unfold he'd be okay. Deception and ulterior motive are the tools of evil characters.)

In HackMaster as in real life there are consequences for your actions. Characters who want to play paladins must be lawful good. Period! That's the condition for receiving their class abilities and special powers. If a paladin goes around backstabbing innocent townsfolk and taking their gold, rest assured he's going to lose the use of his powers (as well as an experience level if he doesn't change his ways quick).

Is that unfair? Of course not. When a player agrees to play a certain alignment, he's committing himself to playing his character according to the tenants of that alignment. Just because it's suddenly convenient for him to cut a merchants throat in order to get a five-finger discount on his wares doesn't mean there won't be repercussions.

Just don't choose an alignment that will be too difficult to role-play or that won't be fun for you to play. Remember, selecting an alignment is a way of saying, "My character is going to act like a person who believes this." If you fail to live up to your end of the bargain and you are forced to change alignments (thereby losing an experience level and Honor) you have no one to blame but yourself.

Alignment Adherence

Alignment defines how your character views the world but, as was already pointed out, it certainly doesn't prevent him from changing his beliefs, acting irrationally, or behaving out of character. Although your GM will insist that your character generally adhere to his chosen alignment there is a bit of 'wiggle room' afforded the player so that he doesn't feel too straitjacketed.

Just think in these terms: for every action there must be an equal action in the opposite direction. If you do something that is against your alignment you will shift closer to the brink of changing to the next alignment in that direction. But you can subsequently take actions that will compensate for your drifting and take you back closer to your professed alignment. Your GM will keep track of how far you've shifted away from your professed alignment using alignment infraction points. In general, any action you take that is not true to your professed alignment will result in you racking up an alignment infraction point. Some grievous infractions with far reaching consequences could result in more than one alignment infraction point (AIP) at the discretion of your GM.

Usually you can accumulate five AIPs without any fear of repercussion unless an alignment audit is called on your character (see below). However, if you reach nine AIPs you've automatically breached your alignment and shift to the next alignment in the direction of the greatest number of AIPs. For example, let's say a lawful good character robs a merchant eight times. He will rack up eight AIPs for committing eight unlawful acts but can still profess to be lawful good because he is under the nine AIP limit. Now he commits an evil act like kicking a blind beggar's three-legged pup up and down the street for fun. The GM assigns another AIP for a total of nine and the character's professed alignment immediately shifts to neutral good (one step closer to

chaotic from lawful). Even though it was the evil act that tipped him over the edge, the majority of the AIPs were due to chaotic acts so the alignment shift would be towards chaos, not evil. Once a character has changed alignment, all AIPs are removed and the PC can begin with a clean slate for the new professed alignment.

Of course, your GM is never going to tell you exactly where you stand. He may warn you that you're "pushing it" or say something like, "Do you think your paladin would really do that?" but he's not going to say, "Hey Bob, you're kissin' a minus 8 on your alignment." That being said, if your GM is such a wuss that he actually warns you BEFORE you take an action, go ahead and take it to the limit. That kind of weak behavior is a big neon sign indicating that he won't punish you without three or four warnings. So push the limit for awhile and live it up.

Unfortunately, the consequences of reaching the AIP barrier of nine are immediate. The character immediately loses an experience level and takes a hit to his Honor (50% of his current Honor is marked off).

Alignment adherence may sound like it's difficult but it really isn't as long as you remember that "for every action there's an opposite action" rule. If you're feeling uneasy about where your alignment stands, you can always ask a cleric or paladin (or dark knight if you are of evil alignment) to give you an alignment audit.

Alignment Audit

The nice thing about alignment adherence is that you have a large degree of freedom to dance around your professed alignment and as long as you don't breach the barrier, you're fine. But extreme care must be taken because there are times in the game when your character could face an unannounced alignment audit. Several things could bring this about:

1. Peer Scrutiny: Paladins and clerics are able to scrutinize other paladins and clerics of the same alignment they come in contact with and bring them into judgement. When this happens, an immediate alignment audit takes place. In THIS type of instance, if the paladin or cleric being judged is found to have 5 or more AIPs, he's determined to be unfaithful and immediately loses the powers and abilities of his class (including spells). The only way to get his class abilities and powers back is by performing penance (see below) and getting back into good graces with his gawd. (Note that dark knights can scrutinize other dark knights and clerics of evil alignment.)

2. Clerical Scrutiny: Any cleric (and high level paladins) can scrutinize a character of the same alignment and call for an alignment audit. This can even be done on a dead character. (Clerics usually insist upon an alignment audit before performing various services such as Raise Dead or Resurrection.) If the character is found to have 5 or more AIPs, the cleric will refuse to perform any requested services or spells on the character. Also, the character found lacking must make an immediate Honor check or immediately change alignments and suffer the consequences.

3. **Divine Scrutiny:** Any character meeting a gawd, or the agent of a gawd (such as an angel) and even certain types of devils face-to-face must undergo an immediate alignment audit. Such beings insist on scrutinizing those in their presence to discern their true alignment and intent. If the character is found to have five or more AIPs, he is forced to change alignments immediately and suffer the consequences for doing so.

4. **Scrutinizing Magic Items:** Some magic items perform an alignment audit on a character before he can wield or use the item and make use of its powers.

5. **Scrutinizing Creatures:** Some creatures can cause a character to undergo an alignment audit. For example, a unicorn can only be ridden by a female virgin character of chaotic good alignment. Other details of the unicorn audit are beyond the scope of this manual.

Changing Alignment

Whether or not the character actively professes some gawd, he or she will have an alignment and serve one or more gawds of this general alignment indirectly and unbeknownst to the character. Changing of alignment is a serious matter, although some players would have their characters change alignment as often as they change socks. Not so!

First, as already noted, change of alignment for clerics and paladins can be very serious, as it might cause change of gawd and the loss of class spells and abilities.

If a druid changes his alignment- that is, becomes other than neutral, then he is no longer a druid at all! Change of alignment will have an adverse effect on any class of character if he is above the 2nd level.

Immediately upon alignment change actually occurring, the character concerned will lose one level of experience, dropping experience points to take him to the very beginning of the next lower level, losing the hit die and/or hit points, and all abilities which accrued to him with the lost level.

If the alignment change is involuntary (such as that caused by a powerful magic, a curse, etc.), then the character can regain all of the losses (level, hit die, etc.) upon: (1) returning to his former alignment as soon as is possible, (2) making atonement through a cleric of the same alignment, and (3) sacrificing treasure which has a value of not less than 10,000 gp per level of experience of the character. The sacrificial amount is variable and it's left to your GM to be the final judge in these matters. Typically, such atonement and sacrifice can be accomplished by a quest.

There are other, more immediate effects of changing alignment. Certain character classes require specific alignments. A paladin who is no longer lawful good is no longer a paladin. A cleric who has shifted in alignment is now in great disfavor by the gawd he served and from whom he had acquired his spells. (Note: clerics and paladins who were forced to change alignment involuntarily must STILL roll on the Table 5D before getting their powers back once returning to their original alignment.)

A character may have magical items usable only to specific alignments (intelligent swords, etc.). Such items don't function (and may even prove dangerous) in the hands of a differently aligned character.

Characters who knowingly or unknowingly change alignment through forethought or actions permanently lose the experience points and level due to disfavor among the gawds. They must also accept a severe disability in alignment language during a one level transitional period. Until the character has again achieved his former level of experience held prior to change of alignment, he will not be able to converse in the former alignment's tongue nor will anything but the rudest signaling be possible in the new alignment language. Although it is possible for a character to allow himself to be blown by the winds as far as alignment is concerned, he will pay a penalty which will effectively damn the character to oblivion.

News of a character's change in behavior will certainly get around to friends and acquaintances. Although some people he never considered friendly may now warm to him, others may take exception to his new attitudes. A few may even try to help him "see the error of his ways". The local clergy, on whom he relies for healing, may look askance on his recent behavior, denying him special services (while at the same time sermonizing on his plight). The character who changes alignment often finds himself unpopular, depending on the attitudes of the surrounding people. People do not understand him. If the character drifts into chaotic neutral behavior in a highly lawful city, the townspeople might decide that the character is afflicted and needs close supervision,

even confinement, for his own good! Ultimately, the player is advised to pick an alignment he can play comfortably, one that fits in with those of the rest of the group, and he should stay with that alignment for the course of the character's career. There will be times when the GM, especially if he is clever, creates situations to test the character's resolve and ethics. But finding the right course of action within the character's alignment is part of the fun and challenge of role-playing.

Penance: Clerics and paladins are held to a higher standard than most character classes because they have a special relationship with their patron gawd. Both classes gain special abilities and spells as a reward for being in good standing with their gawd. Likewise, if a cleric or paladin violates his alignment there's a chance he will lose ALL his abilities (including spells) until he's made atonement.

Whenever a cleric or paladin has been found unfaithful as the result of an alignment audit (or was forced to change alignment involuntarily and later changed back to their former alignment) he must make atonement with his patron gawd before his powers and abilities are restored.

Table 5D: Cleric/Paladin Atonement Table	
Roll	Atonement
1	Character must voluntarily inflict 1d4 points of damage upon himself per day and may only seek healing for these if he has fewer than 10 hit points.[1]
2	Character must voluntarily inflict 1d6 points of damage upon himself per day and may only seek healing for these if he has fewer than 10 hit points.[1]
3	Character must voluntarily inflict 1d8 points of damage upon himself per day and may only seek healing for these if he has fewer than 10 hit points.[1]
4	Pay 1d20*100 in gps to church/temple of character's faith
5	Pay 2d20*100 in gps to church/temple of character's faith
6	Sacrifice most cherished possession and pilgrimage to holy site 1d10 days away.
7-8	Sacrifice most cherished possession and pilgrimage to holy site 1d20+10 days away.
9-10	Sacrifice most cherished possession and 2 points from ability scores.[2]
11	Sacrifice most cherished possession and 3 points from ability scores.[2]
12	Character must purge his Honor.
13	Continuously bear an enormous Holy Symbol of character's faith for 1d20 months.
14	Pay monthly tithe of 100 gps to church/temple of character's faith for 1 year.
15-16	Temporarily retire from adventuring to perform community service for 1 month.
17-18	Temporarily retire from adventuring to perform community service for 6 months.
19-20+	Temporarily retire from adventuring to perform community service for 1 year.

[1] - duration is determined by the GM.
[2] - points sacrificed may be taken from one or more abilities

Chapter 6

Quirks and Flaws

Quirks and flaws represent those aspects of your character which make him a true individual. They're those little imperfections and unique traits that make him human. The difference between the two is simple. Flaws, for purposes of HackMaster, are physical in nature. For example: scars, near-sightedness, and male-pattern baldness are all flaws. Quirks are mental in nature. These include phobias, paranoia, bad tempers, etc. Quirks and flaws are often seen as obstacles that are detrimental to character development. This isn't so. They are challenges. Many quirks and flaws can be advantageous, as you will see when you read the rest of this section.

Building Points

Players can gain extra building points for their characters by taking flaws or quirks (see Chapter 4: Character Priors and Particulars). This can be done in one of two ways: choosing (cherry picking) which flaws/quirks you want or rolling for them randomly.

The ONLY time a character can take on quirks or flaws for BPs is during the initial creation process. (The exception is when the character is raised with a diminutive Raise Dead or Resurrection spell, in which case he may be required to roll to see what new quirks or flaws he takes on.)

Cherry Picking

With this option you get to choose which quirks and flaws you want. The downside is you are limited to how many you can take and you don't earn as many BPs. Choosing a specific minor flaw or quirk is worth a flat 2 BPs. Choosing a major flaw or quirk is worth a flat 4 BPs. You can choose a maximum of two (2) minor flaws AND one (1) major flaw.

Rolling for Quirks/Flaws

This option pays more BPs than cherry picking but there are some risks. For one, you have very little control over what quirks or flaws you are going to get – you must roll randomly on the quirk and flaw tables in this section (start with Table 6A). And, because you're putting your faith in the dice and rolling on tables there's a chance you may have to 'roll again' for additional flaws. The one protection you do have is that you may spend any existing BPs that you may have to reroll on any of the tables in this chapter. Spending one BP allows you one reroll, ignoring the previous result. You can do this as long as you have BPs to spend, but if you exhaust your BPs, you have to live by the results of your rolls.

The upside is that you can earn more BPs with this option. Before rolling for quirks and flaws the player must commit by stating how many times he's rolling on Table 6A.

A player can roll a maximum of nine times on Table 6A. The BPs earned depends on the BP value given in the table. (Reminder: These BP values are ONLY for flaws and quirks rolled randomly).

Curing Quirks and Flaws. It is possible to have many quirks and flaws cured by either a skilled doctor or physician, or a mid to high level cleric (for a stiff fee of course). Some are rather easy to cure (like allergies, migraines, etc.); others are nearly impossible to cure (like a lost limb) without some powerful magic or spell being involved.

Flaws

Physical: Major and Minor

Flaws are physical imperfections and disabilities. They represent obstacles that need to be overcome and/or compensated for, in order for someone to function among people who do not have that same flaw. Characters who have some flaws become more real, as we can all relate to people who are different. Learning to deal with challenges along the path to adventure is what gives roleplaying its true flavor.

Quirks

Mental: Major and Minor

Quirks are things about your character that set you apart from the norm. Some quirks give your character additional abilities, which may or may not be beneficial. They are the "fingerprints" of your character's personality, making him truly unique among his fellow adventurers.

Personality: Major and Minor

Personality quirks affect how a character behaves in everyday life and how he interacts with others in social situations. They make him who he is and often represent behaviors the character cannot control.

Table 6A: Flaws and Quirks d100	
Roll	Table
01-14	Roll on Table 6B
15-28	Roll on Table 6C
29-42	Roll on Table 6D
43-50	Roll on Table 6E
51-66	Roll on Table 6F
67-76	Roll on Table 6G
77-93	Roll on Table 6H
94-100	Roll on Table 6I

Table 6B: Flaws, Minor (Physical) d100		
Roll	Flaw	BP Bonus
01 - 09	Albino	5
10 - 14	Animal [type] Antipathy*	7
15 - 23	Anosmia (loss of the sense of taste)	5
24 - 26	Asthmatic	10
27 - 35	Blind, Color	5
36 - 40	Chronic Nose Bleeds	8
41 - 49	Excessive Drooling	5
50 - 58	Flatulent	5
59 - 61	Hearing Impaired	10
62 - 70	Lisp	5
71 - 85	Roll again on this table and an extra time on Table 6C	
86 - 100	Roll again on this table and an extra time on Table 6D	

* See flaw description for roll for specifics

Table 6C: Flaws, Minor (Physical) d100		
Roll	Flaw	BP Bonus
01 - 07	Loss of Ear	6
08 - 13	Loss of Eye	7
14 - 21	Male Pattern Baldness	5
22 - 26	Migraines	8
27 - 34	Missing Finger(s)*	5
35 - 42	Nervous Tic	5
43 - 47	Scar, Facial	8
48 - 54	Sleep Chatter	6
55 - 61	Sound Sleeper	6
62 - 70	Strange Body Odor	6
71 - 85	Roll again on this table and an extra time on Table 6E	
86 - 100	Roll Twice more on this table. (If this result comes up again, roll again on this table, and an extra time on Table 6E)	

*See Flaw description for roll for specifics

Table 6D:
Flaws, Minor (Physical) d100

Roll	Flaw	BP Bonus
01 - 10	Stutter	8
11 - 30	Tone Deaf	5
31 - 45	Vision Impaired, Far Sighted	7
32 - 37	Blind, one eye	5
38 - 70	Vision Impaired, Near Sighted	7
71 - 90	Roll once on Table 6B and once on Table 6C	
91 - 100	Roll on Table 6E (Flaws, Major)	

Table 6E:
Flaws, Major (Physical) d100

Roll	Flaw	BP Bonus
01 - 06	Accident Prone	11
07 - 12	Acute Allergies*	11
13 - 17	Amputee, Arm	15
18 - 20	Amputee, Double, Arm	20
21 - 23	Amputee, Double, Leg	20
24 - 28	Amputee, Leg	15
29 - 31	Blind	20
32 - 40	Deaf	20
41 - 45	Hemophiliac	15
46 - 50	Low Threshold for Pain (LTP)	15
51 - 56	Maimed*	11
57 - 62	Mute	11
63 - 67	Narcolepsy	15
68 - 73	No Depth Perception	11
74 - 78	Seizure, Disorders (Epilepsy)*	12-20
79 - 84	Sleep Walker	11
85 - 90	Trick Knee	12
91 - 100	Roll once on this table and once on Table 6B	

* See flaw description for roll for specifics

Flaw Descriptions (Physical)

Accident Prone: This character has two left feet. He may fall off his horse or trip over a rock. Any character that is accident-prone always fumbles on a 1 or a 2 on his to-hit rolls. (**Major: 11 points**)

Acute Allergies: This person's immune system isn't working quite right. A character can be allergic to a myriad of substances. A character who is acutely allergic either will be unable to stop sneezing, or will break out in hives if they are exposed to the proper allergen. Roll a 1d20 on the following table to determine what substance a character is allergic to. (**Major: 11 points**)

Allergen Table:
```
1-2 ......food (GM can determine specific food)
3-4 ......cloth
5-6 ......wood
7-9 ......cats
10 .......other animals (all)
11-12 ....gold
13-14 ....other metals (GM can determine specific metal)
15-16 ....pollen
17-18 ....dust
19-20 ....character must add an additional allergy, roll twice.
```

Albino: Characters with this flaw have a lack of melanin in the skin, hair, and eyes giving them an extremely pale complexion, light blue eyes, and on some occasions pink eyes and pure white hair. Some people call albinos "ghost people" because of their somewhat eerie appearance. Persons with this flaw must protect their skin from harsh sun or suffer severe burns. Most albinos also have very dry skin so they use oil to moisturize and protect it. Additionally, the eyes of such a character are very sensitive to sunlight and other bright light. These characters must use wide-brimmed hats or veils to shade their eyes, and protect their heads from harsh sun. (**Minor: 5 points**)

Amputee, arm: Characters with this flaw are missing an arm. How such an event took place may add a colorful story to a character's past. Whatever the cause, such a character cannot, of course, wield two weapons at once, or use a weapon and a shield at the same time. They may not wield two-handed weapons, use bows, or juggle. They cannot play stringed instruments. And they must add 25% to the chance of spell mishap when they are casting a spell with somatic components. This character is at somewhat of a disadvantage, many would say. However, most people who lose the use of one

limb develop extremely strong muscles in the other. Therefore, amputees missing an arm lose no strength bonuses. Because these characters have had to compensate for the loss of a limb using their minds to figure out new ways of doing things, they get to add 25 points to their fractional Intelligence score. (**Major: 15 points**)

Amputee, both arms: Such characters have a tough road to travel, to be sure. Double amputees missing both arms cannot be fighters of any sort. They are not able, most of the time, to wield weapons. They can be magic-users, but cannot perform spells that require somatic components and will have trouble getting material components. They also cannot throw Fireballs. However, such characters are very quick on their feet, and have learned to do many things using their feet. Therefore, there is a 10% chance such a character has trained himself to wield a dagger or other small weapon using his feet. He must, of course, be stationary to achieve such a feat. These characters can run faster than most, and gain 3 points to their movement rate. They also have had to use their minds to discover new ways of surviving, and therefore get 1 point added to their Intelligence. (**Major: 20 points**)

Amputee, leg: Characters who have lost a leg have some additional difficulties that two-legged people do not have. However, such characters may be able to be fitted with a wooden leg, which will enable them to function better. The movement rate for an amputee with a wooden leg is cut by 3 points. Those with the Peg-Leg proficiency, however, lose no movement points. Because these characters have had to use their arms much more than most people in order to compensate for the loss of a leg, they will gain 25 points to their fractional Strength attribute. (**Major: 15 points**)

Amputee, both legs: Characters who have lost both legs are at a severe disadvantage when it comes to adventuring. Those with the Peg-Leg proficiency, however, can be fitted with wooden legs and walk at an almost normal rate,

Table 6F:
Quirks, Minor (Mental) d100

Roll	Flaw	BP Bonus
01 - 05	Absent Minded	9
06 - 08	Acrophobia (fear of heights)	10
09 - 11	Agoraphobia (fear of open spaces)	10
12 - 17	Alcoholic	8
18 - 22	Animal Phobia*	9
23 - 28	Chronic Nightmares	6
29 - 32	Claustrophobia (fear of closed spaces)	8
33 - 35	Delusional (Minor)*	10
36 - 41	Depression (Minor)*	8
42 - 47	Gambling Addiction	8
48 - 53	Inappropriate Sense of Humor	7
54 - 56	Kleptomaniac (compelled to steal)	10
57 - 59	Obsessive Compulsive	10
60 - 70	Nagging Conscience	5
71 - 73	Paranoid	10
74 - 79	Short Term Memory Loss	8
80 - 82	Superstitious	10
83 - 90	Temper*	7
91 - 95	Roll again on this table and an extra time on Table 6G	
96 - 100	Roll again on this table and an extra time on Table 6H	

* See quirk description for roll for specifics

Table 6G:
Quirks, Major (Mental) d100

Roll	Flaw	BP Bonus
01 - 04	Delusional (Major)*	15
05 - 07	Depression (Major)*	16
08 - 13	Enmity toward Class*	13
14 - 19	Enmity toward Monster*	13
20 - 25	Enmity toward Race*	13
26 - 29	HackFrenzy	15
30 - 33	HackLust	15
34 - 41	Psychotic Aversion to Class*	11
42 - 50	Psychotic Aversion to Monster*	11
51 - 58	Psychotic Aversion to Race*	11
59 - 65	Pyromaniac	12
66 - 72	Sadistic	12
73 - 80	Wuss-of-Heart	11
81 - 90	Roll again on this table and an extra time on Table 6F	
91 - 100	Roll again on this table and an extra time on Table 6H	

* See quirk description for roll for specifics

Table 6H:		
Quirks, Minor (Personality) d100		
Roll	Flaw	BP Bonus
01 - 08	Chronic Liar	6
09 - 17	Clingy	5
18 - 30	Glutton	5
31 - 35	Greedy	8
36 - 42	Gullible	7
43 - 48	Jerk	8
49 - 55	Loud Boor	7
56 - 67	Misguided	5
68 - 72	Obnoxious	6
73 - 76	Pack Rat	5
77 - 82	Self Absorbed	8
83 - 88	Socially Awkward	7
89 - 95	Value Privacy (Reclusive)	9
96 - 100	Roll again on this table and an extra time on Table 6G	

Table 6(I):		
Quirks, Major (Personality) d100		
Roll	Flaw	BP Bonus
01 - 35	Multiple Personalities (per personality)	special*
36 - 70	Truthful*	11
71 - 85	Roll twice on Table 6H	
86 - 100	Roll twice on Table 6G	

* See quirk description for roll for specifics

losing only 1 point to their movement rates. Such people can also ride horses or carts to get around. Such individuals have extremely strong arms, and gain 1 point of Strength. Those without the Peg-Leg proficiency can still use wooden legs, but will lose 4 movement points. Those without wooden legs will only have a movement rate of 2, being able only to crawl. There have been cases when a double amputee has been carried in another person's backpack. In those instances, the one carrying the amputee has never had to worry about having someone to "watch his back." (**Major: 20 points**)

Animal Antipathy: Characters with this flaw have gained the enmity of a specific type of animal. These animals can sense something about the character that disturbs them and arouses primal hatred. They will attack the character on sight. Roll 1d20 on the following table to determine what animal has antipathy for the character. (**Minor: 7 points**)

Animal Antipathy Table:

```
1-2 . . . . . . . .horse
3-4 . . . . . . . .dog
5-6 . . . . . . . .cat
7-8 . . . . . . . .bird
9-10 . . . . . . .insect
11-12 . . . . . .fish
13-14 . . . . . .bat
15-16 . . . . . .snake
17-18 . . . . . .ape
19-20 . . . . .GM's choice (Your GM may choose from
               this table, or from any animal in the
               Hacklpedia of Beasts)
```

Anosmia: People with anosmia have no sense of taste or smell. This could be an advantage in some cases, depending on the cooking ability and bathing habits of your comrades. However, just because a person can't smell a poisonous gas doesn't mean it can't still kill him. Likewise, a person who is unable to taste may be more vulnerable to poisoning by ingestion, since he would be unable to distinguish the taste of stew from the taste of arsenic, for instance. Characters who have this flaw have been known to use it to their advantage in drinking or eating contests, however. In addition, these characters are able to enter areas with extremely strong odor that would repel others. (**Minor: 5 points**)

Asthmatic: Asthmatic characters suffer from wheezing, coughing, and difficulty breathing. Triggers for asthma attacks, which can be fatal, are inhaled allergens or sometimes, stress or trauma. The GM may require a character who is under stress or exposed to an allergen to make a Constitution check in order to avoid an attack. A character who experiences an asthma attack as a result of an allergen or stress must rest (and do nothing else) for one round each turn, otherwise he will be subject to the suffocation rules in the GMG. Characters who are asthmatic suffer more damage from inhaled toxins, or any

airborne substance used for an attack. Damp, dusty dungeons make it difficult for asthmatic individuals, causing them to wheeze and cough. This forces them to rest twice as often as a person without asthma or they risk triggering an attack (Constitution check). (**Minor: 10 points**)

Blind: Blind characters have lost their vision. How such a devastating physical loss happened can make for an interesting background story for a character. There are varying levels of blindness. Some who are considered blind, can see light and colors, as well as movement. However, everything appears as a blur, with little, if any, ability to distinguish detail. Some blind characters can see light, but nothing else. Others are consigned to constant darkness. In either case, blind characters suffer a -4 penalty to all to-hit rolls. Although such a character cannot see, his other senses are heightened, especially hearing and touch. (Characters starting off blind can hear twice as well as a normal person of their race (See Chapter 3: Races). Many who are blind have little difficulty getting around, but their movement, is cut in half because they must venture forth carefully. Some who are blind may be offered the use of a trained guide animal. Such an animal would bring the person's movement rate to normal. This animal can warn of danger, help navigate, and even afford some physical protection. (**Major: 20 points**)

Blind, one eye: Those blind in one eye have only a slight disadvantage. Their vision is slightly hindered, giving them -1 to-hit when using ranged weapons. Those with one eye also lose 1 point of Comeliness. Characters blind in one eye automatically pick up the flaw No Depth Perception. (**Minor: 5 points**)

Blind, color: Unable to distinguish between colors, these characters live life with little problem. However, there are times when such a condition can be dangerous, or even fatal. For instance, a color-blind character may have trouble knowing which potion will heal him (drink the red one) and which one is poison (don't drink the yellow one.) Of course, if the vials are labeled and the character can read, then there's no problem. Otherwise, drinking potions can be risky. (**Minor: 5 points**)

Chronic Nosebleeds: People suffering from this flaw need to keep plenty of handkerchiefs handy. For some reason, without warning, these characters will suffer nosebleeds, which are so severe they must apply pressure, put their heads back, and apply packed snow or ice. It is possible for a person to die from an untreated severe nosebleed. If left untreated, a character with a severe nosebleed will lose 1 hit point of damage per turn. However, most of the time no permanent damage is done. Of course, those with such a condition should be careful not to get too near monsters that are attracted by the smell of blood, such as sharks or vampires. (**Minor: 8 points**)

Deafness: Those who are deaf can live fairly normal lives despite the loss of their hearing. However, life is a bit more difficult. Those who are deaf have trouble communicating with anyone who doesn't know some sort of sign language. Of course, if the deaf character can write, he can use notes to communicate, provided the person he wishes to communicate with can read. Deafness has its advantages. Deaf characters are unaffected by sonic attacks, and many sound-based spells have no affect. The eyesight tends to be much keener for people who can't hear (up to 25% better), as well. (**Major: 20 points**)

Excessive Drooling: This flaw is a mild annoyance for the most part. However, it subtracts 1 point each from Comeliness and Charisma scores. (**Minor: 5 points**)

Flatulence: Persons with this flaw have the unsavory habit of constantly producing excessive bodily gasses. Most people will shun a flatulent person, therefore, he will lose 1 point from his Charisma attribute unless he is dealing with half-orcs. A person with this problem will not rise very high in society. (**Minor: 5 points**)

Hearing Impairment: This flaw is milder than deafness. Such a person simply has a hard time hearing, but is able to hear some things. People are forced to repeat themselves several times when trying to communicate with a hearing impaired character. The hard of hearing character will have trouble in a crowded, noisy place, being unable to pick out the conversation of a friend from the din of the crowd. In the heat of battle, such an impairment might prove fatal. During key times such as this, the GM may require the character to make an Intelligence check to see if he was able to pick up the intended communication. (**Minor: 10 points**)

Hemophiliac: Those with this condition are known as "bleeders." This is a dangerous flaw for an adventurer. A hemophiliac's blood will not clot the way it should, therefore, if such a person is injured in any way, he will suffer additional damage. For every point of damage taken, he will suffer an additional point of damage. Furthermore, the character must make a successful

Constitution check in order to avoid losing an additional hit point per wound per round. Healing potions or magic only repairs half the damage as usual. A hemophiliac must rest twice as long after being injured before regaining his health back. (**Major: 15 points**)

Lisp: The person with a lisp suffers little in the way of damage because of this flaw. However, a lisping person will lose a point of Charisma due to this speech impediment. Additionally, others may have a hard time understanding the speech of a person who lisps. People often make fun of those who talk funny, so lispers may find themselves in more brawls than usual. (**Minor: 5 points**)

Loss of ear: This flaw affects only a person's appearance and his ability to wear certain types of hats. Those who are missing an ear suffer no loss to hearing. However, Comeliness is affected. Those missing an ear lose 1 point per ear from Comeliness. (**Minor: 6 points**)

Loss of eye: Those missing an eye lose some vision, causing them to suffer -1 to all to hit rolls. Comeliness also suffers, with the character in question losing 1 point from this attribute. However, if the person uses an attractive eye patch, this effect is negated and his Comeliness goes back to normal. There is a 10% chance that members of the opposite sex will find the character more appealing than those with two eyes. Characters with this flaw automatically have the No Depth Perception Flaw. (**Minor: 7 points**)

Low Threshold of Pain (LTP): This flaw can make a character cry like a schoolgirl just from getting a splinter in his finger. A person with LTP is unable to stand even the smallest pain. Those with LTP lose a point of Honor every time they react to pain in public. Therefore, those with LTP who suffer minor wounds will be affected as if they had received major wounds. For every point of damage suffered, the effect will be doubled. However, once the combat is over, a person with this malady will bounce back, suffering only actual damage. Persons with LTP who suffer the loss of half his hit points or more in one blow will pass out for 1d20 rounds minus their Constitution. In addition, characters with LTP will be unable to resist torture and will be quick to tell an inquisitor anything he wants to know. (**Major: 15 points**)

Maimed: A person who is maimed has been disfigured so badly, and permanently that they lose 3 points to Comeliness and Charisma. Such a person has some sort of grotesque injury or malady that has decimated their appearance. They may be called "freaks" or "monsters." Children will run away when they see a maimed person, or they may taunt him. Bullies may pick on the character. There is a 50% chance that public reaction will be fear and a 50% chance that such reaction will be disrespect. Sometimes, fearful crowds can be whipped into a frenzy against such a person and may attack. Players should roll 1d6 on the table below to determine how the character has been maimed. (**Major: 11 points**)

Maimed Table:

Die Roll:	Maiming:
1	Severe facial burn or scarring
2	Misshapen head
3	Roll again: (1-3) Fingers webbed, (4-6) extra finger
4	Two missing facial features (nose and ear, nose and lips, etc.)
5	Misshapen body
6	Person gets an additional area of maiming. Roll again twice.

Male Pattern Baldness: Only men can suffer from this flaw. These men have lost most of their hair. Such a flaw is not much of a hindrance. It does take 1 point away from the character's Comeliness attribute. However, there is a 20% chance that females they meet may react to the character as if he had a Charisma one point higher than it actually is. What can I say? Some women love bald men. (**Minor: 5 points**)

Migraines: Characters who have this flaw suffer from excruciating headaches on a regular basis. When a migraine strikes a character, he will be unable to function. He must rest for one day before resuming any activity. If he opts to continue while in pain, all to-hit and damage rolls will suffer -1. Anything else they do which causes them to have to roll dice will also incur a point penalty. Once a week during game time, a person with migraines will be out of commission due to migraine pain. (**Minor: 8 points**)

Missing Finger(s): A person with this flaw is missing at least one finger. The more points a character wants to use on this flaw, the more fingers are missing. A character missing a finger fumbles more often. Therefore, a person missing a finger will fumble on 1 and 2 on his to-hit rolls. The possibility for fumbling increases for every finger missing. For instance, those missing two fingers fumble on 1, 2 and 3. Those missing three fingers fumble on 1,2, 3 and 4. Get it? O.K. then. (**Minor: 5 points for first finger, 1 point each for extra fingers**)

Mute: Mute characters cannot perform any magic spells that have verbal components. They can communicate only with gestures, or by writing. Sometimes mute characters anger other people because they fail to understand why the character is not answering questions. This may place the character in some danger. Such a person cannot be a bard, unless they want to be a mime. (**Major: 11 points**)

Narcolepsy: A person with Narcolepsy has no control over when and where his character will fall asleep. This can be quite dangerous. Characters with Narcolepsy may fall asleep while climbing up a wall, fighting a dragon or playing poker. Any of these could be deadly. Players with this flaw may enlist the aid of a trusted person to wake them up, but even the most vigilant of friends cannot be with anyone all of the time. (**Major: 15 points**)

Nervous Tic: This flaw causes a character to twitch in an uncontrollable way. Usually such twitching is limited to the face or neck. Someone with a tic may have one eye which winks involuntarily, or one side of their neck will pull, causing their head to bob to the side. Most of the time, this condition causes no problems. However, imagine what would happen, say, if a person who has an eye tic is thought to be winking at the wife of some big, burly soldier. Nervous tics can also affect a character's ability to aim ranged weapons, therefore, characters with this flaw suffer -1 to hit with these weapons. (**Minor: 5 points**)

No Depth Perception: A character with this flaw is unable to distinguish whether objects are far away or near. This character might as well be blind. Ranged weapons are useless to such a character. This character gets -2 to all to-hit rolls. He will walk into walls or walk off cliffs if he isn't careful. This person needs a really good friend or a guide dog. (**Major: 11 points**)

Scar, Facial: Something awful happened to this character. He suffers from a hideous scar, which he cannot hide. Such a character suffers -2 to Comeliness and Charisma. Otherwise, it has little effect. (**Minor: 8 points**)

Seizure Disorder: This character has some type of organic brain disease or damage, which causes him to have seizures. Seizures take many forms, but one of the most common are the Grand Mal seizures, which cause the person to fall to the ground and convulse uncontrollably. The chance of the character having Grand Mal is 60%. If no one is around to help, this person could swallow his tongue and suffocate in three rounds. Some people with seizure disorders simply freeze, or zone out for a few seconds. This could cause a character to offend others without knowing it because it will seem as if he is simply ignoring them if they talk to him while he is having such a seizure. No one is sure what triggers such attacks. These occurrences seem to be completely random. Therefore, it is up to the GM to remember to roll for every day of game time to see if the character suffers a seizure. On a roll of 6 or lower on a 1d10, the character suffers a seizure. The next day, the chance for another seizure drops to 5 out of 10. Characters suffering seizures are completely vulnerable. Seizures last 1d12 turns. (**Major: 20 points for Grand Mal, 12 points for milder form**)

Sleep Chatter: This person talks in his sleep every night. There is a 5 out of 10 chance that the character will reveal things that normally he would not want anyone to know. He may declare his love for the female barbarian in the party, who may promptly kick his ass. He may spout the location of his stash of goods, or let it out that he's the one who swiped the magic-user's Ring of Water Walking. The things a character says in his sleep however, are questionable as to accuracy. Those listening will be unable to tell if the character is talking about something real, or something in a dream. (**Minor: 6 points**)

Sleep Walker: Those who walk in their sleep often find themselves in danger. This flaw can bring a whole new meaning to the phrase "he died in his sleep." This character may walk out of a high window, into the middle of a campfire or into an orc encampment. Friends of this character may find themselves being asked to tie the character down at night. If they agree, the character will be saved from injuring himself, but will then be vulnerable to nighttime attack. (**Major: 11 points**)

Sound Sleeper: This character wouldn't wake up if a herd of bullweilers trampled past his bed. Such a character is extremely vulnerable when asleep. They will not wake up unless they are struck with enough force to cause at least 1 point of damage. Once they wake up, however, they are much more refreshed than others are. Therefore, when they rest in order to heal, they heal an extra hit point per day more than others do. (**Minor: 6 points**)

Strange Body Odor: This character has a distinctive stench about him. A strange odor emanates from his body, causing him to lose 1 point of Charisma. He will be unwelcome in most social gatherings. He will be welcome among ogres, bugbears and similar creatures, however, and may attract unwanted mates. (**Minor: 6 points**)

Stutter: Characters who stutter have a difficult time communicating. Magic users who stutter take an extra 2-20 segments to prepare any spells that have a verbal component. Stutterers lose 1 point of Charisma and are often taunted. (**Minor: 8 points**)

Tone Deaf: A character with this flaw is completely tone deaf. He couldn't sing a proper song to save his life. This flaw is pretty harmless unless you happen to be a bard. (**Minor: 5 points**)

Trick Knee: A person with a trick knee can be walking along and then suddenly have his knee give way. In most adventuring situations, this is not a good thing. The character with this flaw loses a point of movement because of how careful he has to be not to fall down. Riding a horse is a good option for this character. In a dungeon setting, a trick knee can get a character killed. The GM will keep this flaw in mind whenever a character is crossing a narrow bridge over a high precipice, or just whenever he feels like rolling for it. (**Major: 12 points**)

Visually Impaired, Farsighted: Farsighted people can see objects far away just fine, but have trouble seeing things that are near. As such, they have trouble with close-up fighting, suffering -1 to hit in hand-to-hand combat. For most other purposes, they suffer very little ill effects, but when ordering from a menu, they might have to strain, and they can only use "large print" versions of spell scrolls. (**Minor: 7 points**)

Visually Impaired, Nearsighted: Also called myopic, these characters can see objects that are near, but have trouble seeing things that are far away. Therefore, they suffer a -4 penalty on to-hit rolls when using ranged weapons against targets that are at medium range or farther and -2 to hit at short range or lower. Otherwise, there is little impact on a character's life. (**Minor: 7 points**)

Quirk Descriptions (Mental)

Absent Minded: Characters with this quirk have a hard time remembering things. An absent minded character may get to a dungeon and realize that he has forgotten to bring his coil of rope or his torches. (**Minor: 9 points**)

Acrophobia: Characters who have this quirk are afraid of heights. They may be fine inside a tall tower or on a higher floor of a building, but will freeze if they find themselves on a high rocky cliff or mountain. These characters will generally refuse to climb anything higher than their heads. (**Minor: 10 points**)

Agoraphobia: Characters who are agoraphobic have an irrational fear of wide, open spaces. They will generally avoid large rooms or open plains. (**Minor: 10 points**)

Alcoholic: Characters with this quirk are addicted to alcoholic beverages. They are never seen without a drink in their hands and have trouble functioning when sober. They spend much of their lives inebriated, losing coordination and blacking out. They may blank out for hours, days or even weeks. Every time this character has an alcoholic beverage he must roll a d20. If he rolls an 8 or higher he is compelled to order/secure another drink. He must make a check after EACH drink and cannot stop drinking till he succeeds. The only way to make him stop is if he is forcibly prevented from doing so by his friends. (**Minor: 8 points**)

Animal Phobia: A person with this quirk has an irrational fear of a certain animal. When encountering a feared animal, the character will attempt to flee, or he will freeze. Player should roll 1d20 on the following table to determine what animal the character is afraid of. (**Minor 9 points**)

Animal Phobia Table:

1-2 . . . . .horse	11-12 . . . . . .snake
3-4 . . . . .dog	13-14 . . . . . .birds
5-6 . . . . .cat	15-16 . . . . . .fish
7-8 . . . . .insect	17-18 . . . . . .worms
9-10 . . . . . . .rodent	19-20 . . . . . .cattle

Chronic Nightmares: Character suffers from Chronic Nightmares he can't shake. The dreams visit him in his sleep nightly preventing him from getting the rest he needs. (Wounds heal at the rate of 1 every two days). There is also a 20% chance that on any given night he'll wake up screaming and in a cold sweat. (**Minor: 6 points**)

Claustrophobia: People with this quirk have an irrational fear of confined or enclosed spaces. Every time the character wants to enter or finds himself in a confining space, such as hiding in a box, crawling through a tunnel or possibly even entering a dungeon he must roll a saving throw against paralyzation. If the save is failed the character either refuses to enter, or panics if he is already in a tight space. If the save is successful the character may act as normal, but still takes a -10% on all skill rolls and a -2 on all to hit rolls and saves while in the enclosed area. The GM may force the character to make additional saving throws if he comes under heavy stress while he is in tight quarters, even if his initial save was successful (**Minor: 8 points**)

Delusional: This person doesn't quite know what's real and what isn't. Depending on the severity of the disorder, this quirk can be only a minor annoyance or "far-out" belief or it can be a major problem. Players should roll 1d10 on the following table to determine character's delusion, and a further d6 to determine severity, with a 1-4 meaning the delusion is minor and a 5-6 meaning the delusion is major. If the quirk is from a roll from Table 6G then the delusion is automatically major. (**Minor: 10 points or Major: 15 points**)

Delusion Table:

1 . . . .(Major) Character thinks he is an animal and behaves like one. Check with your GM. (Minor) Character thinks animals are people and talks to them

2 . . . .(Major) Character thinks he can fly, and often tries. (Minor) Character thinks other people can fly and often asks them to

3 . . . .(Major) Character thinks he is royalty and acts like it, ordering people around, perhaps trying to walk into a castle as if it were his own. (Minor) Thinks one of the party members is royalty and treats him as such

4 . . . . .(Major) Character thinks he is in the middle of a battle when he is not. He attacks anyone that makes a quick movement or looks at him funny. (Minor) Character thinks he is a war hero and brags about accomplishments that aren't his.

5 . . . .(Major) Character thinks his party members are monsters, screams and runs away, or tries to attack them. (Minor) Character thinks bugs are crawling on himself and those around him so he swats at them and stomps on them

6 . . .(Major) Thinks scaled monsters are his friends and treats them as such. (Minor) Character talks to an imaginary friend

7 . . . .(Major) Character thinks screaming will scare away monsters, so when he's in a dungeon, he screams loudly (Minor) Character thinks a monster is following him and keeps whirling around to catch it.

8 . . . .(Major) Character thinks he is invisible. He tries to pick pockets and do other things he thinks no one can see (Minor) Character thinks his eyes are tricking him so he is constantly asking others what they see.

9 . . .(Major) Character thinks he can walk on water, and often tries (Minor) Character thinks water is poisonous so he never bathes or drinks water.

10 . . . .(Major) Character thinks he can tame monsters, and tries. (Minor) Character thinks he has a tame monster for a pet and acts as if his pet is real and present.

Depression: This quirk can be caused by a chemical imbalance in the brain of a player character, or by a traumatic event. Characters with this problem can function normally most of the time, but will usually have episodes where they will be unable to do anything at all. Some will have suicidal tendencies. Others will take insane risks, feeling as if it doesn't matter if they live or die. **(Minor: 8 points or Major: 16 points)**

Enmity Toward Class: A character with this quirk has a deep hatred toward all people of a certain class, regardless of any other factor. This character will automatically attack any person of the hated class. This person will never willingly adventure with a person belonging to the enemy class. The GM should roll a 1d20 on the following table to determine the class the character is at enmity with. If you roll the same class as the character, roll again. **(Major: 13 points)**

Class Enmity Table:

1	Barbarian
2	Bard
3	Cleric
4	Druid
5	Fighter
6	HackMaster
7	Cavalier
8	Paladin
9	Ranger
10	Magic User
11	BattleMage
12	Dark Knight
13	Illusionist
14	Thief
15	Assassin
16	Monk
17	Berserker
18	Knight Errant
19	Blood Mage
20	Roll twice, ignoring this result

Enmity toward Monster: A person with this quirk has an unreasoning hatred for a particular monster, or monster type. If the character's party is in a battle with several monsters, he will ignore all other opponents if a hated monster is involved and attack that monster first. He will attack any monster that is his enemy on sight, without thought for his own, or his party's, safety. Your GM will tell you what type of monster your character has enmity with. He can choose any from the Hacklopedia of Beasts. You might also want to choose one and offer up some reasons for your hatred based on your background. Your GM may not buy it, but it's worth a try. Beats the heck out of him rolling Dragons, All on his tables. **(Major: 13 points)**

Enmity toward Race: This quirk causes a character to have an unyielding hatred for any member of a certain race. No other factor will matter in such cases. This character will attack or endlessly harrass with intent to instigate physical confrontaion with members of the hated race on sight. This person will never willingly adventure with a person belonging to the enemy race. The GM should roll a 1d10 on the following table to determine what race the character has enmity with. If the race rolled is the same as that of the character, re-roll. **(Major: 13 points)**

Racial Enmity Table:

1	Dwarf
2	Elf
3	Gnome
4	Gnomeling
5	Half elf
6	Halfling
7	Half-orc
8	Half-ogre
9	Pixie Fairy
10	Human

Gambling Addiction: Characters with this quirk can't seem to hang onto money for long. If they are in the vicinity of any sort of gambling activity, they will participate. If they run out of money, they may put up their horse, borrow from comrades or even steal. They may make deals, which they will regret later. They will bet on anything from a cock fight to whether or not it will rain before noon. **(Minor: 8 points)**

HackFrenzy: This quirk makes the character susceptible to fits of violent rage. A character suffering from HackFrenzy has a short fuse and can be pushed over the edge with little provocation. This quirk manifests itself when the character takes an amount of damage in a single combat round that is equal to or above twenty percent of his current hit-point level. Whenever this

happens, the character must immediately make a saving throw (vs. HackFrenzy). Failure means he immediately goes into HackFrenzy mode.

A character who is HackFrenzied must immediately roll 1d8 per level of experience. The resulting sum represents the number of hit points the character must inflict on others before his HackFrenzy is satiated.

For example Tom, the 3rd level Fighter, has 20 hit points left. While exploring a dungeon he is attacked and hit for 5 points of damage in a single round. He fails his save vs. HackFrenzy and immediately rolls 3d8 with a result of 17. He must now inflict 17 points of damage before his rage subsides. If there are enemy targets in range he can choose to inflict damage on them. If, however, there are NO enemy targets within range and Tom still hasn't met his HackFrenzy quota that round, he must attack friendly targets. A frenzied character can perform no other action except attacking in melee (and moving to engage the nearest target), as long as he has an unfulfilled quota. If there are no hit points to be obtained within sight he will immediately run in a random direction in search of targets.

A frenzied character's extremely difficult to kill or drop while running amok. He takes only half damage from any attacks dealt to him while frenzied. Once he's met his quota and the frenzy ends, however, he immediately takes on the full effect of any damage he sustained while in such a state. Thus, it is possible for the character to fight on even after death and literally die *after* the fact. If character is unable to fulfill his damage quota and satiate his HackFrenzy he will eventually come down (1d4 turns) and collapse from exhaustion. **(Major: 15 points)**

HackLust: This quirk is similar to HackFrenzy except it is triggered not by taking damage but by dealing it out. If a player rolls a critical hit he must immediately roll a save vs. HackLust. Failure means he must press on the attack to inflict damage on others equal to three times the amount of damage he dealt with the critical hit. Like HackFrenzy, characters with HackLust will attack even friendly targets if their quota has not been met. **(Major: 15 points)**

Inappropriate Sense of Humor: A person with this quirk is apt to double over with laughter at the most inopportune moments. For instance, if this character's buddy ends up suddenly falling down a 50 foot mine shaft and breaks his leg, the person with the inappropriate sense of humor might begin laughing and say something like, "Look at the funny way your leg bends to the side!" This quirk is apt to get the character punched out frequently.

Characters with this disability like to tell jokes that aren't funny and wait smiling for his 'audience' to laugh. He may even repeat the punchline after an awkward silence. Additionally, this quirk makes a character prone to playing practical jokes on people they shouldn't, such as pious clerics, nobles or Orc chieftains. Those that suffer from an Inappropriate Sense of Humor are liable to blurt out insults at the wrong moments. **(Minor: 7 points)**

Kleptomaniac: Characters with this quirk have an unquenchable urge to steal. It doesn't matter how valuable an item is, a character who is a kleptomaniac will attempt to steal anything. He will even steal while the person he's stealing from is watching. **(Minor: 10 points)**

Nagging Conscience: A person with this quirk is plagued by a conscience that won't allow him peace of mind if he's committed certain crimes or acts of dishonor. His conscience is a silent witness to his shame and accuses him constantly. There's a chance his conscience might begin to nag him, preventing his honor from rising or even causing loss of honor until the character has made amends or paid some sort of penance to ease his conscience. **(Minor: 5 points)**

Obsessive/Compulsive Disorder: This person has a (cranial) chemical imbalance, causing him to believe that the world is out of control - too chaotic. This forces him to obsess about certain things, and/or compulsively perform certain repetitive acts (in order to regain some measure of control). For instance, a character may be obsessed with not stepping on any cracks in the road and will ignore all other dangers to keep from doing so. A character may have the compulsion to comb his hair every 10 minutes. Often the two disorders go hand in hand, with the result that a character may be obsessed with cleanliness and will therefore feel a compulsion to scrub his surroundings or himself constantly. Players should roll 1d20 on the following table to determine what obsession/compulsion the character has. Then roll 1d2 to determine if it is a obsession or a compulsion. **(Minor: 10 points)**

Obsession/Compulsion Table:

1 . . .Obsessed with members of opposite sex OR Compulsion to kiss members of opposite sex
2 . . .Obsession with numbers OR Compulsion to count everything
3 . . .Obsession with clothing OR Compulsion to buy clothing
4 . . .Obsession with gold OR Compulsion to gather as much gold as possible
5 . .Obsession with horses OR Compulsion to scrub and brush horses
6 . .Obsession with weapons OR Compulsion to own as many weapons as possible
7 . .Obsession with armor OR Compulsion to own as much armor as possible
8 . .Obsession with magic OR Compulsion to accumulate as many magical items as possible
9 . . .Obsession with cleanliness OR Compulsion to clean
10 . .Obsession with body image OR Compulsion to exercise
11 . .Obsession with hair OR Compulsion to comb hair
12 . .Obsession with the sun OR Compulsion to stare at the sun
13 . .Obsession with bugs OR Compulsion to eat bugs
14 . .Obsession with food OR Compulsion to cook/eat
15 . .Obsession with sounds OR Compulsion to discover source of unusual or unknown sounds
16 . .Obsession with books or scrolls or Compulsion to accumulate as many books or scrolls as possible
17 . .Obsession with jewels OR Compulsion to accumulate as many jewels as possible
18 . .Obsession with rocks OR Compulsion to collect rocks
19 . .Obsession with smells OR Compulsion to discover source of any odd odors
20 . .Roll again. If character already has an obsession, when you roll again, select a compulsion, and vice versa.

Paranoid: Paranoid characters think everyone is out to get them. They trust no one. They certainly do not trust those with whom they adventure. They may think there is a conspiracy against them. They will closely guard themselves and their goods, perhaps finding it hard to sleep for fear of being screwed over. (**Minor: 10 points**)

Psychotic Aversion to Class: A character with this quirk will do anything to avoid contact with members of a certain class. He will not adventure or socialize with anyone who is a member of this class. The GM should roll a 1d20 on the following table to determine the class the character wants to avoid. If you roll the same class as the character, roll again. (**Major: 11 points**)

Class Aversion Table:

1	Barbarian
2	Bard
3	Cleric
4	Druid
5	Fighter
6	HackMaster
7	Cavalier
8	Paladin
9	Ranger
10	Magic User
11	Battle Mage
12	Dark Knight
13	Illusionist
14	Thief
15	Assassin
16	Monk
17	Berserker
18	Knight Errant
19	Blood Mage
20	Roll twice, ignoring this result

Psychotic Aversion to Monster: This quirk causes characters to avoid contact with a certain type of monster at all costs. If a character with this quirk encounters the monster against which he has this aversion, he will do whatever he can to escape the area. GMs should use the Hacklopedia of Beasts to determine what creature the character psychotically avoids. (**Major: 11 points**)

Psychotic Aversion to Race: People with this quirk will avoid contact with members of a certain race whatever the cost. Characters will never adventure or socialize with a member of this race. The GM should roll a 1d10 on the following table to determine what race the character avoids. If the race rolled is the same as that of the character, re-roll. (**Major: 11 points**)

Racial Enmity Table:

1	Dwarf
2	Elf
3	Gnome
4	Gnomeling
5	Half elf
6	Halfling
7	Half-orc
8	Half-ogre
9	Pixie Fairy
10	Human

Pyromaniac: Most people call those with this quirk "firebugs." Characters with this quirk are obsessed by fire. When the urge hits, they will burn down structures just to watch the flames. Seeing fire, such as a campfire, lit torch or fireplace fire, tends to spark this destructive urge in pyromaniacs. (**Major: 12 points**)

Sadistic: A person with this quirk is not a nice person, as he enjoys performing cruel acts against others. This aberration may take the form of animal cruelty or it may become even darker and nastier. Those adventuring with a sadistic character in the party may find themselves the victim of cruel jokes or painful "accidents." Sadistic people are sometimes able to hide this tendency, but those who act on it usually find themselves unwelcome in many parts of society. (**Major: 12 points**)

Short Term Memory Loss: People with this quirk may be able to remember things that happened to them as children, but will be unable to tell anyone what they had for dinner. They may forget things like the fact that they checked a room for traps and they may check the room over again. They may forget how they got into a particular room in the dungeon, and may forget their way out. There are many possibilities for error when a character has short-term memory loss. (**Minor: 8 points**)

Superstitious: Characters who are superstitious feel they can control what happens to them by avoiding certain actions, or performing certain rituals. These people put a lot of faith in luck. They may have a lucky tunic that they never take off, or never wash for fear of washing the luck away. They may avoid doing any adventuring on certain days of the month, feeling as if those days are unlucky for them. Roll 1d20 on the following table to determine what superstition the character has. (**Minor: 10 points**)

Superstitions Table:

1 . . . .Believes a certain color is unlucky (your GM will choose). Will not wear clothing of this color or enter structures painted this color. Will avoid animals of this color and those who wear this color.
2 . . .Believes a certain color is lucky (your GM will choose). Will only wear clothing of this color. Prefers animals of this color, those who wear this color and items of this color.
3 . . . .Thinks the Wurld is flat. He will avoid travelling in ocean-going vessels for fear of falling off.
4 . . . .Thinks being near dead things is unlucky. Will avoid anything reminding him of death: cemeteries, graves, coffins, etc. Gets -2 to hit when encountering any undead.
5 . . . .Believes haggling or price-shopping is unlucky. If this character buys something that has a reduced price for any reason, he will constantly worry about it breaking or being of inferior quality. Eventually, he will discard the item in favor of one bought at full price or found.
6 . . . .Has a lucky number (roll a d20 to determine the number). He will take insane risks on his lucky day. Performs "rituals" using his number to gain luck.
7 . . . .Believes he's lucky and anyone touching him will steal his luck. He will not lend or share items with others (such as rope, torches, weapons, etc.). The character will go ballistic if anyone touches any of his stuff.
8 . . .Believes a certain common animal is unlucky (GM will determine). This character will avoid contact with such an animal and will go so far as to leave the room or cross the street to get away from the animal's proximity.
9 . . . .Believes going left is unlucky. Will only take routes where it is assured he will not have to turn left. Believes left-handed people are evil. He will avoid taking a left turn in a dungeon.
10 . . .Doesn't believe in ghosts or undead of any type. If he sees one, he will attempt to disbelieve or ignore incorporeal spirits entirely. After defeating a corporeal undead, he will attempt to defraud it by pulling of its 'mask' or wiping away its 'makeup'.
11 . . .Believes Pixie Fairies are lucky, so he attempts to capture them to gain favors, refusing to release them unless they "bless" him.
12 . . .Believes harm will befall him, his friends or his relatives if he steps on a crack. He will not step on a crack for any reason. His movement rate is cut in half if he is travelling over extremely cracked surfaces.
13 . . .Has an unlucky number (roll a d20 to determine the number). He will not venture forth on this day. He will avoid anyone with this number of letters in their name. Will avoid being in a room with this number of people.
14 . . . .Believes he must make a donation to any cleric or church he passes. Failure will surely bring ill-luck down upon him and bring the particular gawd against him.
15 . . .Believes those in authority were chosen by the gawds to be in their position. Will attempt to please and pander to anyone in authority he sees.
16 . . . .Believes every time he hears a bell tinkling an angel gets his wings. Roll again.

17 . . .Believes adventuring with members of the opposite sex is bad luck. Will avoid this at all costs.

18 . . .Has a magic charm that he believes helps protect him. He will not do anything until he kisses the charm for good luck. If he loses it he will not be able to function until he finds a new lucky charm.

19 . . .Believes it's bad luck not to tip a beggar. WIll always tip beggars in town.

20 . . .Has two superstitions. Roll again and ignore this result.

Temper Tantrum: This quirk causes characters to be unable to control their tempers. A character with this quirk will throw a fit if they are frustrated in any way. Such a person may trash a room at an inn because his bed was lumpy or the person in the next room made too much noise. He may turn over a table and storm off is he loses at a game of cards. (**Minor 7 points**)

Wuss-of-Heart: A character with this quirk doesn't have a single brave bone in his body. This character's companions cannot count on him in extreme situations. He will hang back to the rear of the party in combat situations, and may sneak away if he can. Such a character is not suited to be any type of fighter. (**Major: 11 points**)

Quirk Descriptions (Personality)

Chronic Liar: This character cannot tell the truth from a lie. He lies about everything, even things that don't matter. Many of his lies will be so outrageous that no one would believe them,. He insists they are the truth, even if presented with overwhelming evidence to the contrary. This quirk could prevent the character from making lasting, meaningful friendships. As the Lizard Mage said to Sturm Pyre in the book *This Sword's Retired*, *"A lie, albeit it small, driveth a wedge between friends."* A character with this quirk might want to think about investing in the skill: Liar, Skilled. He may still be a liar but at least no one will know it. (**Minor: 6 points**)

Clingy: This personality quirk makes a person feel extremely needy. The character attempts to have all need filled by one person. Your GM will determine to whom the character clings. The clingy character will try to keep his chosen one in sight at all times. He will attempt to please the person, and will ask the person questions constantly about how he feels about this or that. (**Minor: 5 points**)

Glutton: This character never met a Grevan stew he didn't like. He has an insatiable appetite and can be bribed with food. Dinners last for hours for this character. He must buy twice as many rations as other characters. He may steal other characters' rations while they sleep for a little midnight snack. (**Minor: 5 points**)

Greedy: Although most characters in HackMaster live to obtain wealth, characters with this quirk can never have enough. They will do anything to accumulate more and more riches, including lying to friends, stealing from them or deceiving them. He may take insane risks in order to feed his appetite for wealth. (**Minor: 8 points**)

Gullible: This character is the guy P.T. Barnum was talking about when he said a sucker is born every minute. He is the perfect patsy. He will fall for anything. He will almost always pay the highest price for any item or buy inferior items passed-off as quality. (**Minor: 7 points**)

Jerk: This character doesn't work or play well with others. He insults people, bullies them and generally orders them around. He feels as if he is the center of the universe and everybody should know it. He has no patience for people who don't cater to him, but he isn't really nice to those who do. He feels as if life owes him and he's bound and determined to collect. This character loses a point of Charisma. (**Minor: 8 points**)

Loud Boor: Similar to a jerk, a loud boor has a personality that annoys others. He wants to be the center of attention at any social gathering. He will do whatever he can to get that attention. He will talk loudly, and tell long, bragging stories about himself. He will drop names of important people he has known or met. He will always drink too much. He may perform some type of outrageous behavior to gain attention, such as stripping to his skivvies and jumping into a keg of ale. He loses a point of Charisma because of his annoying behavior. (**Minor: 7 points**)

Misguided: This person has good intentions, but isn't always able to keep out of trouble even so. He means well, but can never keep from making mistakes. Any character with this personality quirk is allowed a greater number of alignment infractions than other characters, before being punished for them. GMs must consider this quirk whenever your character does something

against his alignment. If you can make a good excuse, the infraction may not count against him. (**Minor: 5 points**)

Multiple Personality Disorder: A character with this personality quirk has at least one extra unique personality. He may be a rugged fighter, but his other personality is a tiny schoolgirl. During stressful events, this characters extra personality might kick-in. Roll 1d100 on the table below for each personality. Duplicator results simply means a different personality of the same class/race/age. There is a 75% chance that each personality is not initially aware of the others; roll for each personality, as some may be aware of the others, but not vice-versa. (**Major: 11 for first extra personality, 5 points for each additional personality**)

Extra Personality Table:

Die Roll:	Extra Personality:
01 - 04	Young member of the opposite sex
05 - 08	Elderly member of the opposite sex
09 - 12	Young adult or middle-aged member of the opposite sex
13 - 16	Young member of the same sex
17 - 20	Elderly member of the same sex
21 - 24	Young adult or middle-aged member of the same sex
25 - 28	Extremely violent person
29 - 32	Extremely cowardly person
33 - 36	Extremely nasty person
37 - 40	Noble
41 - 44	Slave
45 - 48	Beggar
49 - 52	Royalty
53 - 56	Dwarf
57 - 60	Pixie Fairy
61 - 64	Gnome Titan
65 - 68	Elf
69 - 72	Assassin
73 - 76	Thief
77 - 80	Extremely pious person
81 - 100	Adds another personality, roll twice more on this chart

Obnoxious: This character is similar to a jerk or a loud boor, but he tends to act in annoying and disgusting ways on a frequent basis. He picks his nose in public, scratches his private parts, burps, and tells obscene jokes. Often this person thinks he is the world's friendliest guy and generally, he is friendly. However, his behavior makes him extremely unpopular. He loses a point of Charisma. (**Minor: 6 points**)

Pack Rat: A character with this quirk cannot throw anything away. Not only that, but he cannot keep himself from gathering up just about everything he sees in a dungeon setting. Because many monsters are notorious pack rats, this quirk can present a serious problem. The main difficulty is encumbrance. When a character with this quirk comes across a pile of treasure, which may include many items of junk, such as towels, wads of used gum, etc. he cannot seem to pass these items up. He will gather up everything, whether he can carry it all or not. This can be somewhat annoying and troublesome to the other members of this character's adventuring party. (**Minor: 5 points**)

Self-Absorbed: Similar to a jerk, the character who is self-absorbed thinks about no one else. When he talks, he always talks about himself. He has no idea how anyone else feels, nor does he care. He assumes everyone feels either attracted to him, or jealous of him. He loses a point of Charisma because of his attitude. (**Minor: 8 points**)

Socially Awkward: A character with this personality quirk is clueless when it comes to social interaction. He avoids social situations if possible because he feels uncomfortable. If he finds himself in a gathering of some sort, he will make many mistakes. He will spill his drink, say stupid things and perhaps step on someone's feet while dancing. This person loses 1 point of Charisma because of his lack of social grace. (**Minor: 7 points**)

Truthful: At first glance, this personality quirk might seem like a good thing. And, for the most part, it is. However, in the gaming arena, sometimes being able to lie can save your life. The character who is truthful cannot lie, even to save his life. (**Major: 11 points**)

Value Privacy (Reclusive): This person finds other people to be at best annoying and at worst, abominable. He prefers his own company to that of others. He believes that *"hell is other people."* He will avoid all social engagements whenever possible, even offending important people to do so. He loses 1 point of Charisma because of this attitude. (**Minor: 9 points**)

Getting the Job Done:
Skills, Talents and Proficiencies

So far your HackMaster character is defined by race, class and Ability Scores. But he's not yet complete. You still need to arm him with the knowledge and know-how that will help him to topple kingdoms and out-wit time-wizened wyrms. He needs certain skills, talents and proficiencies (collectively referred to as STPs in these rules). Without these essential STPs your character is dead in the water, little more than numbers on a sheet of paper. These STPs represent the interface between you and your in-game persona. You use them to interact with the GameMaster's world. Virtually everything your character knows how to do is either a skill, talent or proficiency — even magic!

Before going any further it's important that you know the difference between the three. A complete list of Skills, Talents and Proficiencies can be found in Appendix F, and complete descriptions in Appendix G.

Skills represent learned knowledge that your character has which isn't dependent on his character's class or race (i.e. he didn't automatically acquire the skill as a result of his chosen class or race).

Talents are class or race specific (i.e. you can ONLY acquire or use these abilities if your character has dedicated himself to the character class that offers them or is a member of a certain race.) A good example of a talent is the dwarf's ability to see in the dark (infravision). Another example of a talent is the thief's ability to hide in shadows or pick pockets.

Proficiencies represent a special type of skill. They indicate the character is 'proficient' in the use of a specific weapon or group of weapons. A good example of a weapon proficiency is a human paladin with a two-handed sword proficiency.

Skills

To recap, skills represent learned knowledge that your character has which aren't dependent on his character's class or race (i.e. he didn't automatically acquire the skill as a result of his chosen class or race). A skill can range from the complex (civil engineering) to the simple and mundane (how to build a good fire). Skills are divided into four basic subgroups: arcane skills, academia skills, language skills and task/arts skills.

Arcane Skills:

Arcane skills represent the disciplines that allow a character to tap into and use such things as magic. They are the most difficult to acquire and to master and as such, most arcane skills can ONLY be chosen during the character creation process (typically by choosing a character class that specializes in that arcane skill set). Such arcane skills are technically considered to be talents (see Talents below) and there's no need to delve into them here.

There are some arcane skills, however, that can be learned by anyone. These include spellcraft and arcane lore. Acquiring these skills simply gives the character a general working knowledge of the arcane. They do NOT allow him to tap into and use arcane or cleric powers.

Academia Skills:

These are knowledge-based skills that don't require any tools, tasks or procedures to implement. You know – head knowledge. Academia can range from the trivial (local knowledge) to the more academic (art appreciation:

sculpture). The character can rattle off information on the subject of any academia skills he possesses. Note that many academic skills can be combined with other skills (such as tasks and tool skills). For example, you could combine house construction (skill: academia) with carpentry tools (skill: tool) and produce lumber (skill: task) to build a house.

Language Skills:

Languages are acquired knowledge. Each language skill has two components that indicate the character's level of understanding. Comprehension includes speaking (and being understood) and hearing (understanding what is spoken). Reading/writing means the character can read and write the language in the appropriate alphabet or script. Note that the maximum number of language skills a character can possess is determined by his Intelligence.

Task/Arts Skills:

Musical Instrument skills allow characters to play various types of musical instruments. These are detailed further in Appendices F and G.

Task oriented skills are those which require some sort of hands-on action and/or set of procedural actions in order to successfully use them. These include things like painting a portrait, making a boat, sharpening a sword, repairing a suit of armor, etc. They almost always require a skill check to see what level of success is achieved.

Tool skills allow characters to master the use of certain types of skills. Often a prerequisite for other skills. Also useful in bumping up the quality of workmanship/craftsmanship from shoddy to professional or expert.

Skill Sets and Professional Status

Skill sets/suites are bundles of related skills and proficiencies that contribute to a certain type of craft or profession.

For example, the healer suite is made up of five first aid skills and related tool skills (like a suture kit and bone saw) which enable a character to diagnose and render proper treatment for wounds, diseases, etc. Fully mastering most skill sets involves menial tasks and requires great expenditure of time and money. As such, most Player Characters find such pursuits beneath them or not conducive to their career as an adventurer. This means skill sets and professional status usually fall under the realm of the NPC (and hence the GM). But don't be too quick to dismiss skill sets. Some of them, like the healer suite, can be quite useful.

A character possessing a skill set can use the skill set itself like a skill or he can choose to use a specific skill within that suite. Once a character has reached a mastery of at least 65% in all of the listed skills in a suite, he has gained professional status for those skills. That means ALL the skills within the suite are permanently combined (averaged) and a 10% bonus is applied. A character with professional status in a skill suite is qualified to teach those skills to other players and/or NPCs as a mentor. Mentors are paid good money for their services.

Your GM can provide you with more information on mentoring and professional status. He can also tell you what skill sets are available to pursue. In the meantime, the following short list will whet your appetite.

Using Skills

If a character possesses the appropriate skill to perform a task, he normally doesn't have to make a check to see if he can successfully use it. For example, a character with the swimming skill should be able to take a midnight skinny dip in a pond without having to check. The need to do skill checks are determined by the GM and are usually required when the character is trying to perform a skill under difficult conditions when such 'mastery' over a skill becomes of paramount importance. If the same character suddenly falls through thin ice while wearing plate mail the GM would certainly require a swimming skill check to see if he drowns. (And in this situation severe negative modifiers would also apply.)

Skill checks are resolved by rolling 1d100 vs. the character's skill mastery.

Skill mastery is determined by the character's relevant abilities (See Appendix F) plus the sum total of all mastery die and Honor Die rolls he's added to that skill as the result of building points or training.

For example, when Klenched Fist the thief attended school, he studied the combat procedure skill, jugular swipe. After paying the course fee of 275 gold pieces he successfully passed the course. The mastery die for jugular swipe is 1d4. Klench rolls a 3. Since Dexterity is listed as the relevant ability for that skill he gets to add 3 to his DEX (18). Luckily for Klench he also has a 1d12 Honor Die which he earned for his current Honor. He rolls an 8. That means his skill mastery percentage for jugular swipe is 29% (18+3+8). If Klench takes another block of instruction in jugular swipe, and successfully passes, he'll be able to roll the Mastery Die and Honor Die again and add them to his skill mastery percentage. Note that unless the skill description says otherwise, an initial block of instruction/training must be taken and successfully completed before your relevant ability scores are applied. In other words, if Klench hadn't taken a course in Jugular Swipe his skill level for that skill would have been 0% (unskilled).

Skill Mastery: What do the numbers mean?

Your base skill mastery gives you an indication of just how much mastery you have of a specific skill. The following ranges give a rough indication of what your base skill mastery means.

Master Range	Skill Level
0%	Unskilled
01–25%	Beginner (Novice, Untrained) (SB)
26-50%	Apprentice (Schooled, Trained) (SS)
51-75%	Advanced* (SA)
76-100%	Expert (SE)
101-125%	Master (SK)

*_65% and above is considered 'professional' level._

Explanation of Skill Levels

Beginner: Basic knowledge only. No real training. Dabbling. Backyard mechanic. Range of most skill mastery scores when only basic relevant abilities are being used.

Apprentice: Schooled, character has working knowledge of skill. Can perform routine tasks involving the skill. Unable to teach what he knows.

Advanced: Detailed knowledge and experience, character is typically troubled only by the most complex aspects of the skill. Can teach basic elements to other to other characters but only up to 45% skill mastery.

Expert: Character is expert at the skill. Can teach the skill to others up to a skill mastery of 65%.

Master : Character has gone beyond what his teachers and/or mentor were able to teach him and has learned on his own. He is considered a master on the subject or topic. He is capable of expanding the field by coming up with new ideas and techniques. Can teach skill to others up to a skill mastery of 95%.

Training and Studying: Gaining new skills & improving old ones

Skills and proficiencies do not leap unbidden and fully realized into a character's mind. Instead, a character must study, train, and practice to learn a new proficiency or skill. Unless the character actively devotes himself to such study and training his progress will grind to a screeching halt. Training can be used to learn new skills or proficiencies and/or to improve those skills and proficiencies already possessed.

I. Obtaining New Skills

New skills are obtained in one of three ways:

1. **Building Points:** By buying the skill with Building Points during the character creation process (See Chapter 4). Note that magic-users (with the exception of battle mages) must pay twice the BP cost for combat skills, but only half the BP

Skill Set	Skills/Proficiencies
Healer/Doctor	anatomy, first aid, suture kit, surgery tools, battle surgery.
Limner/Painter	map making, appraisal of art objects, cartography, reading/writing, drafting tools.
Mason	stone-cutting, trowel-specialty, mattock, bricklaying.
Miner	stone-cutting, assaying, surveying, mining tools.
Navigator	astronomy, sailing, swimming, navigation.
Sailor	sailing, swimming, fishing, navigation, nautical, tie knots, survival (ocean).
Scribe	reading, writing, basic math.
Shipwright	sailing, carpentry, woodworking, sewing.
Tailor/Weaver	weaving, sewing, embroidery.
Teamster/Freighter . .	animal handling, wagon-repair, freighting.
Trader/Barterer	appraisal of common goods, haggling, bargain sense, street credibility.
Trapper/Furrier	slaughter game animal, basic wood lore, skinning, haggling, bartering.

Once a character has achieved professional status in a skill set, it is up to the player and the GM to determine just what the character can do with it. The skills listed in each skill set give a good indication of what the character has learned, but other knowledge and abilities may be added with the GM's approval. Thus, a hunter might know the basics of finding food in the wilderness, how to read animal signs to identify the types of creatures in the area, the habits of dangerous animals, and how to stalk wild animals. It is safe to assume that simple jobs succeed automatically. (A hunter could find food for himself without any difficulty.) For more complicated tasks, the GM must assign modifiers to apply to the skill check.

Collaborative Effort

It's important to note that in HackMaster two or more characters can combine their skills and areas of expertise in order to accomplish a job or to perform a task that they couldn't do individually. Suppose a scouting party comes to a crevasse and realizes they need to build a hasty footbridge so that the army that follows them can move across without being delayed.

The scouts take inventory of what skills they have as a group. One scout has carpentry skills, another has the civil engineering skill and a third has the orchestrate task skill. In addition, twelve of the fourteen scouts possess the laborer (generalist) skill. The GM decides that as a group they have the necessary skills to build a bridge. The skills are added together and averaged. The GM uses the resulting number (with any appropriate modifiers) to determine the quality of the finished bridge.

cost for academia skills. During the character creation process, the character rolls the mastery die once for each expenditure of the BP cost of the skill. For example, if a character buys a skill at three times the cost, he rolls the mastery die three times and adds the total to the relevant ability (See Appendix F: Skills, Talents and Proficiencies List). Note that you add the relevant ability only once. There is no limit to the number of mastery die rolls that can be purchased, but the skill level cannot exceed 125%.

Skills currently possessed can also be improved through formal and informal instruction (just like gaining new skills as described in Chapter 11). One special way to increase the amount that a skill is improved during training is to use it in an appropriate circumstance for dramatic or important effect. Anytime you roll under your Chance to Improve Skill value without modifiers (see Table 1E: Wisdom) when making a skill mastery check, your character may have learned something new (you'll need to ask your GM). For example, let's say your party commandeers a sailing vessel and you decide to sail it back to port. A storm suddenly rises up, threatening to capsize the ship. You announce you have the seamanship skill, and the GM has you make a penalized skill check to see if you can successfully re-rig the sails and bring the ship out of danger. As the group holds its breath, you roll the dice and they come up 03. You check your Wisdom score (13) and see that your Chance to Improve Skill value is 05%. Voila, not only have you saved your entire party, but your character has learned something significant which will increase his ability to gain from his later coursework. The next time your character takes the appropriate skill course during training, he can add a +1 bonus to his mastery die roll. This bonus can be applied any number of times as long as the character succeeds in different circumstances. Keep a running tally between training on your record sheet so you don't lose out on any bonuses later.

2. **Training/Studying:** By learning new skills when advancing from one level to the next (as described in Chapter 11).

a) **Formal Training:** Universities and schools. The most practical way for a character to pick up new skills and improve old ones is through formal training. This involves going to a university or school which specializes in the character's class and receiving instruction. A character can attend school ONLY when advancing from one level to the next.

b) **Mentoring:** Another way to pick up skills (especially the more mundane variety) is finding a teacher. Most skills are easier to learn if someone teaches the character. Your GM has rules regarding mentors.

II. Improving Skills:

Skills currently possessed can also be improved through formal and informal instruction (just like gaining new skills as described in Chapter 11). One special way to increase the amount that a skill is improved during training is to use it in an appropriate circumstance for dramatic or important effect. Anytime you roll under your Chance to Improve Skill value without modifiers (see Table 1E: Wisdom) when making a skill mastery check, your character may have learned something new (you'll need to ask your GM). For example, let's say your party commandeers a sailing vessel and you decide to sail it back to port. A storm suddenly rises up, threatening to capsize the ship. You announce you have the seamanship skill, and the GM has you make a penalized skill check to see if you can successfully re-rig the sails and bring the ship out of danger. As the group holds its breath, you roll the dice and they come up 03. You check your Wisdom score (13) and see that your Chance to Improve Skill value is 05%. Voila, not only have you saved your entire party, but your character has learned something significant which will increase his ability to gain from his later coursework. The next time your character takes the appropriate skill course during training, he can add a +1 bonus to his mastery die roll. This bonus can be applied any number of times as long as the character succeeds in different circumstances. Keep a running tally between training on your record sheet so you don't lose out on any bonuses later.

Talents

Talents represent those special abilities that are character class or race specific (i.e. you can ONLY acquire or use these abilities if your character has dedicated himself to the character class which offers them or is a member of a specific race). For example, Klenched Fist the thief knows how to pick pockets because it comes with the job. Krataan the fighter, on the other hand, can NEVER learn how to pick-pockets unless, of course, he decided to dedicate himself to being a thief (see multi-class). Another example of a talent is the unarmored half-ogre's ability (tough hide).

Weapon Proficiencies

Proficiencies are a special type of skill and exclusive to weapons. They indicate the character is 'proficient' in the use of a specific weapon (weapon proficiency), or group of weapons. Weapon Proficiencies also differ from skills in that characters are limited to how many they can have depending on their level and class.

Acquiring Proficiencies:

Even newly created, 1st-level characters have weapon proficiencies available to them. (see Table 7A). A character starts with a number of weapon proficiency slots determined by his character class group.

Each weapon proficiency slot is empty until the player "fills" it by selecting a weapon. When filling the proficiency slot, the player must still spend the BPs associated with becoming proficient in that weapon. The one exception to this is that characters in the fighter group get the first weapon proficiency slot filled for free. That is there is no BP cost associated with it.

Consider the case of Klenched Fist, an elven thief. Table 7A gives him two weapon proficiency slots. He fills these slots by choosing two weapons and spending the building points associated with them. These represent what weapons the character was proficient with and learned how to use before beginning his adventuring career. Thereafter, as Klenched Fist advances in experience levels, he gains additional weapon proficiency slots. The rate at which he gains them depends upon the character class he belongs to. Once a weapon proficiency slot is filled, it can never be changed or reassigned.

Table 7A lists how many weapon proficiency slots the character starts with, and how many levels the character must gain before he earns another slot.

Table 7A: Proficiency Slots			
Group	Initial	#Levels	Attack Penalty
Fighter	4	3	-2
Magic-User	1	6	-5
Cleric	2	4	-3
Thief	2	4	-3

Table 7A Explanation:

Initial Weapon Proficiencies: the number of weapon proficiency slots granted to characters of that group at 1st level. The player must pay one (1) BP to fill each proficiency slot with a weapon.

 # Levels: indicates how quickly a character gains additional proficiency slots. A new proficiency slot is gained at every experience level that is evenly divisible by the number listed. Note: gaining a new slot simply means the character gains the ability to 'learn' to be proficient in a new weapon. (He has slot(s) which can be filled). However, he can ONLY fill these slots by training in a new weapon at school or from a mentor. Terac (a fighter), for example, gains one weapon proficiency slot at every level evenly divisible by 3. He gets one new slot at 3rd level, another at 6th, another at 9th, and so on. He would like to fill one of those new slots with the crossbow. In order to do so, however, he will have to take a block of instruction on the crossbow at a school or from a mentor.

Penalty: the modifier to the character's attack rolls when he fights using a weapon he is not proficient with. Guntar, a dwarf, chose to be proficient with the warhammer. Finding himself in a desperate situation, he snatches up a dagger, even though he knows little about it (he is not proficient with it). Using this weapon awkwardly, he has a -2 penalty to his chance to hit.

Weapon Proficiencies and Slots

A weapon proficiency ensures a character's knowledge and training on a specific weapon. When a character is created, the player checks Table 7A to see how many weapon proficiency slots the character has. These initial slots must be filled before the character embarks on his first adventure. They cannot be saved for, say, the opportune appearance of a magical weapon.

Each weapon proficiency slot must be assigned to a specific weapon, not a class of weapons. Each weapon listed in Table 9T: (Weapons) requires its own proficiency; each has its own characteristics that must be mastered before the weapon can be used to its full capability. A man-at-arms who is proficient in the guisarme, for example, is not necessarily skilled with a glaive; the two weapons look deceptively similar, but the fighting styles they are designed for are different. A player character could become proficient with a long bow or a short bow, but not with all bows in general (unless he's nuts and devotes a proficiency slot to each individually!) Of course, it should go without saying that a character can assign weapon proficiency slots only to those weapons allowed to his character class.

As a character reaches higher experience levels, he also earns additional weapon proficiency slots. The rate at which slots are gained depends on the character's class. (Remember these slots are not automatically filled – you must train in the use of the newly chosen weapon first).

Fighters who concentrate on hacking learn to handle a great number of weapons. They gain weapon proficiency slots quickly. Bookish Magic-users have little interest in hand-to-hand combat and subsequently gain few additional weapon proficiency slots. Multi-class characters can use the most beneficial line on Table 7A [not the sum of both of their classes] to determine their initial proficiencies and when they gain new proficiencies.

Effects of Weapon Proficiencies

A character with proficiency in a specific weapon is familiar with its use and maintenance. Said character does not receive bonuses for using a weapon he is proficient with; the combat tables are premised on everyone using a weapon he is proficient with. When a character uses a weapon that he is not proficient with, however, he suffers a penalty on his chance to hit. The amount of this penalty depends on the character's class.

Fighters have the smallest penalty because their training has given them a passing familiarity with all weapons. Magic-users, on the other hand, are heavily penalized because of their limited exposure. The modifiers for each class (which are penalties to the attack die roll) are listed on Table 7A.

Related Weapons Bonus

When a character gains a weapon proficiency, he is learning to use a particular weapon effectively. However, many weapons have similar characteristics. A footman's mace, horseman's mace, morning star, flail, hammer and club, while all different, are all heavy, bludgeoning weapons. A character who has trained with one can apply some of his experience to the others. He may not be fully proficient, but he knows more about it than someone who picks it up without any training in similar weapons.

When a character uses a weapon that is similar to a weapon he is proficient with, his attack penalty is only one-half the normal amount (rounded up to the character's disadvantage). A fighter, for example, would have a -1 penalty with a related weapon instead of -2. A magic-user would have a -3 penalty instead of -5.

Specific decisions about which weapons are related are available to the GM in the GMG.

Weapon Specialization (Fighters Only)

Knowing how to use a weapon properly is very different from being a master of said weapon. In HackMaster, your character's skill is reflected in bonuses he earns as he reaches higher levels. As your character advances, he becomes a craftier, more deadly opponent. Experience has taught him to anticipate his adversary and to pounce on any advantage that presents itself. But this is a general, overall improvement, brought about by his sharpening senses and timing. It applies equally to all types of fighting.

Weapon specialization enables a fighter (only) to choose a single weapon and truly master its use. Any weapon may be chosen. Specialization is normally announced (and paid for with weapon proficiency slots) when the character is created. However, even after a player character earns experience, he can still choose to specialize in a weapon provided he has the weapon proficiency slots available and completes specialized training in that weapon (see below). The specialization requires a single-minded dedication and training. As such, multi-class characters cannot use weapon specialization; it is available only to single-class fighters.

Specialization Training

Weapon specialization is gained by allocating additional weapon proficiency slots to the chosen weapon AND successfully completing advanced training on that weapon. This involves paying twice the training fee and spending twice the training time. To specialize in any sort of melee or ranged weapon, the character must devote TWO slots--one slot to become proficient with it, and then a second slot to specialize in it. Any bow (other than a crossbow) requires a total of THREE proficiency slots: one for proficiency and two to specialize.

Standor the Grunge Elf decides to specialize with the spear. Two of his four proficiency slots are thus devoted to the spear. With the two remaining, he can become proficient with two additional weapons (for example, the short sword and long bow).

Effects of Specialization

Specialization with a melee weapon gives a character a +1 bonus to all his attack rolls with that weapon and a +2 bonus to all damage rolls (in addition to bonuses for Strength and magic).

Bow and crossbow specialists gain an additional range category, point blank. Point-blank range for bows is from six feet to 30 feet. Point-blank range for heavy and light crossbows is from six feet to 60 feet. For the hand crossbow it is three to 20 feet and for the peashooter it is three to 10 feet. At point-blank range, the character gains a +2 modifier on attack rolls.

No additional damage is caused, but Strength (for bows) and magical bonuses apply. Furthermore, if the character has an arrow nocked and drawn, or a bolt loaded and cocked, and has his target in sight, he can fire at the beginning of the round before any initiative rolls are made.

Fighter Level	Melee Weapon	Light X-bow	Heavy X-bow	Thrown Dagger	Thrown Dart	Other (Non-bow) Missiles
1-6	3/2	1/1	1/2	3/1	4/1	3/2
7-12	2/1	3/2	1/1	4/1	5/1	2/1
13+	5/2	2/1	3/2	5/1	6/1	5/2

Table 7B: Specialist Attacks Per Round

Fighters who specialize also gain extra attacks earlier than those who don't choose to specialize.

Bonus attacks for specialists are listed on Table 7B. The use of this table is explained in Chapter 12: Combat: The Art of Hack. Bow specialists do not gain any additional attacks per round.

Weapon Mastery

There are swordsmen, and then there are swordsmen. A warrior who devotes his life to the study of martial combat and the characteristics of a single type of weapon can become a weapon master—a fighter whose precision, quickness, and skill are virtually unequaled anywhere.

Weapon masters are rare characters. Only single-classed fighters can ever achieve weapon mastery, and even then they do so with time, study, and sacrifice. To achieve mastery in a weapon, a character must first specialize in the use of that weapon. Then, at any time after he reaches 5th level, he can spend another weapon proficiency slot to become a weapon master. He can continue to devote proficiency slots to the study of his chosen weapon, but can't progress faster than the rate at which he gains new weapon proficiency slots. So, a character who becomes a master at 5th level couldn't acquire his second slot of mastery until 6th level, his third until 9th level, and so on.

Swords of any kind are the most common weapons mastered, followed by bows, crossbows, and then axes or spears. Polearms cannot be mastered in this fashion.

Effects of Mastery

If a fighter spends another weapon proficiency slot on a melee weapon he already specializes in, his attack and damage bonuses increase to +2 and +3, respectively. For bows and crossbows his point-blank bonuses increase to +2/+2 as with melee weapons, and he gains an additional +1 to hit at all other range categories. (Remember, this bonus doesn't take range modifiers into account, so the archer has a total of +1 at short, -1 at medium, and —4 at long range, if the penalties are factored in.)

High Mastery

By spending a second slot on mastery, a character can become a high master. By this time, the character has spent four slots on a single weapon and is at least 6th level. High masters decrease the speed factor of their chosen weapon by one; for example, a battle axe in the hands of a high master would have a speed factor of 1 instead of 2. Also, the "to hit" and damage bonus increases to +3/+3 for melee weapons and missile weapons at point blank range.

High masters who specialize in bows, crossbows, or slings gain a new range category: extreme range. For all weapons, extreme range is 1/3 farther than long range. For example, if a weapon has a normal maximum range of 30 yards, in the hands of a master it can shoot 40 (1/3x30=10, 30+10=40) yards. Extreme range shots have a —10 penalty to hit before adjustments are made for the effects of mastery.

Grand Mastery

High masters who spend one more slot on learning their weapon of choice can become grand masters. Grand masters are capable of feats of swordplay that border on the fantastic. Grand masters gain one additional attack per round, above and beyond a specialist's rate of attacks for their level, so a 12th-level melee weapon grand master would attack 3 times per round with his weapon of choice. Furthermore, missile weapon specialists gain an extra +2 to hit at extreme range.

Grand masters also increase the amount of damage when they employ their chosen weapon. The weapon's base damage die is increased to the next greater die size against all opponents. A long sword thus inflicts 1d8/1d10/1d20 points of damage in the hands of a grand master. If the weapon causes multiple dice of damage, all of them are increased. Thus, a two-handed sword in the hands of a grand master inflicts 3d8 points of damage on large targets. Needless to say, grand masters are extremely dangerous opponents.

All That Glitters: Money and Treasure

"Death can always be cheated but treasure is forever."

Sturm Pyre

As mentioned previously in the introduction, there are those misguided individuals who would have you believe there are no winners in role-playing. Those who spout such mindless rhetoric should be carefully prodded away with a ten-foot pole — lest they infect you with their brand of shortsighted thinking. For the reality is those of us who role-play are winners by the mere fact we are able to escape into fantastic realms of the imagination (while those less-enlightened non-gamers around us are left behind hopelessly confined to the world of the mundane.) So there are winners in role-playing after all.

There are also winners within the context of the game. Player characters can be measured against each other in a variety of ways; by experience level, Honor, the number of heroic feats they have under their belt, etc. More often, however, the measure of success for an individual in HackMaster (as it often is in the real world, sadly) is how much cash and toys one has managed to acquire. In other words – money and treasure.

Don't get me wrong. Your character (or yourself) may have higher, nobler ideals than garnering material wealth. A cleric for example, should be more interested in serving his patron gawd and furthering his cause(s) than selfish gain. But consider this…that same cleric is going to need money to build that new temple to his gawd in the Orkin frontier. He's going to need those rubies he lifted from the Dungeons of Kreatin Faarpang to help pay for feeding the plague victims suffering on the Grevan Steppes. So money and treasure are important to all characters in some fashion (and let's not forget that the acquisition of both can earn the character valuable experience points).

Money

All characters start off with some measure of a stake (see STARTING MONEY in Chapter 4). Don't get attached to it — it's going to slip through your fingers like water through a sieve as you begin the expensive task of equipping yourself (see Chapter 9). Without some type of income or support coming in to replenish your ever-shrinking coin purse your wanna-be hero isn't going to get too far.

Besides properly equipping yourself, you're going to have everyday living expenses to contend with. More importantly you're going to have to fill your belly with food or risk starving (unless you're a ranger or possess the skills needed to live off the fat of the land). As you can already see, all this takes money — but how to get some?

Depending on your chosen profession (character class) you're going to have several options open to you. If you're a thief you can use your years of experience in the streets and carefully learned skills to lift some fat coin off of some unsuspecting NPC (or a fellow PC – nudge nudge) unfortunate enough to cross your path. If you're a bard you might be able to sing for your supper for a wealthy noble family or a tavern full of locals. The charity of others can provide a decent living for a talented individual. A fighter? Most bars and taverns hold pit-fights where you can take on any comers in hopes of winning the miserly purse awarded to the last man standing. But is this the life of a hero? – scratching for every copper coin he can get his hands on? Baaaah!

The real money is in adventuring — also known affectionately by veteran players as treasure-trawling, dungeon crawling, loot-siphoning, etc. It is the process of using right and might to finance your adventuring career. But you can't do that very effectively without being properly outfitted – which of course takes more money.

It's a dilemma to be sure, but it is one you must quickly overcome. Use your creativity and make your hard-earned skills work for you. As a first level character you'll find it's going to be tough to survive all by your lonesome.

The sooner you can manage to hook up with some fellow adventurers (other player characters) and form a party, the better it will be for everyone's financial situation (see Adventuring Parties in Chapter 13).

A Word about Currency

There are numerous different systems of currency throughout the world in which you will find yourself adventuring. As you wander and explore from one petty kingdom to the next you'll find that the types of coins/currency you encounter are as varied as the local people and spoken languages.

For simplicity's sake, most GMs choose to use a standard (or common) rate of exchange throughout the campaign. So while a gold piece may be called a Kiver among the southern Orc tribes and a Darnarian in the City-State of Faengarie both are worth exactly the same – 1 gold piece. The same holds true for silver pieces (sp), copper (cp), hard silver (hsp), electrum (elp) and platinum (pp). So as you sell a pack animal and some treasure in one town, travel for over a week, conquer a few foes and earn some coin, you'll find that you can spend it just as easily in the next town where you stop to re-supply.

Your character will most probably be adventuring in an area where such coins and other treasure are plentiful. Think of the situation as similar to Alaskan boomtowns during the gold rush days, when eggs sold for one dollar each and mining tools sold for $20, $50 and $100 or more! Costs in the adventuring area are distorted because of the law of supply and demand - the supply of coin is high, while supplies of equipment for adventurers are in great demand.

The standard rate of exchange for each coin is given in Table 8A.

			Exchange Value			
Coin	CP	SP	ELP	GP	HSP	PP
Copper Piece (CP) =	1	1/10	1/50	1/100	1/200	1/500
Silver Piece (SP) =	10	1	1/5	1/10	1/20	1/50
Electrum (ELP) =	50	5	1	1/2	1/4	1/10
Gold Piece (GP) =	100	10	2	1	1/2	1/5
Hard Silver Piece (HSP)=	200	20	4	2	1	2/5
Platinum (PP) =	500	50	10	5	2.5	1

Table 8A: Standard Exchange Rates

Money Changing: Large sums of lower value coins can be changed to a smaller number of larger value coins, and vice versa, at a relatively small cost - typically 5% of the transaction. This is done through the aid of a moneychanger, of which there is certainly no shortage. Wherever money changes hands, be it the small roadside bazaar or a large city, the moneychangers are going to be found nearby. Most cities will require that local moneychangers to purchase permits in order to legally do business (thus getting a piece of the action themselves). The implication is that those moneychangers with permits are somehow regulated or deemed to be trustworthy by the city. To make such an assumption would be a mistake. Most government officials (at all levels) are corrupt and not above taking bribes and payoffs. So care must be taken when dealing with the moneychanger. Short-changing and counterfeit or underweight coins are just a few of the many possible risks.

Bankers: The banker serves as a moneychanger for all intents and purposes, but also provides additional services such as keeping and safeguarding large funds (for a fee, of course) and giving a marker to vouch for the amount. (Note that bankers will not usually give any interest.) Bankers also loan money (see the Loans section below).

Jewelers: Jewelers and gem merchants will buy and sell all types of jewelry and gems. Again, they are businessmen and their aim is to make a healthy profit for themselves. If they can take advantage of a customer, they will. The buying price will usually be 80% of the appraised value of the piece or stone. Some jewelers may appear to be more generous and offer 90%. However, it is almost certain they are intentionally under-appraising the gems/stones. Characters should carefully shop around whenever possible to determine which establishment offers them the best value.

Haggling and Bartering

There are no fixed price tags in HackMaster when it comes to merchants and their wares. Haggling and bartering is expected and even welcomed — especially on high value items. Haggling is a tricky dance and there are more than a few unspoken rules. Knowing just when you need to come down by a few gold, go up or just walk away is an art form all in itself. Making a common beginner's misstep such as stubbornly refusing to yield on your offer can quickly offend the average merchant (who is more than likely to wave you away and refuse to do business with you at all).

Loans

There will be times when your character needs an item which he simply doesn't have the money to buy. Or perhaps an incredible opportunity has suddenly presented itself, such as a war galley coming on the market at an incredible bargain price. You and your fellow party members would love to take advantage of this windfall, but you find yourselves coin-shy. In such instances, you may want to consider taking out a loan. Bankers, guilds, and well-to-do benefactors often grant loans based on the reliability, Honor/Fame, status, or material possessions (i.e. collateral) of the individual.

An unknown and low-level character is very unlikely to get a loan without giving security for the value of the amount borrowed. Most bankers insist that the borrower swear a Blood Oath (see Chapter 5) that he will repay the loan or suffer the consequences. Furthermore, interest rates are simply obscene — typically 10% per month or even 5% per week! A well-known character of honorable status, however, may be able to secure a loan at a relatively low interest rate (say 1% per week or thereabouts). As always, most deals are negotiable and it is up to the character to work the best possible deal.

Investments

Another way to raise the necessary funds to bank your adventuring party is to seek out investors/sponsors. This basically involves transforming your party into a company (commonly called an adventuring company). Such companies take many forms. Some are very organized, and even have shareholders who may be nobles or wealthy merchants. Other adventuring companies more closely resemble a full partnership.

Typically the investors pony up the cash required to fully equip the party and cover all expenses and the party then operates like a proper business. After each expedition/adventure the secretary of the adventuring company must write up a report detailing the 'take' (any money, treasure and other valuables obtained during adventure). The investors recoup their investment off the top and then take their cut of the profits. The party members each then take their own cut – shares vary depending on how much money was initially fronted/invested.

The major drawback of this type of setup is that any magic items and other treasure are typically converted into gold (sold) so that they can simply be paid out in shares to avoid disputes over ownership. If a party member desires a certain item he must deduct the street value from any shares he's to receive (or make up the difference if his cut isn't enough to cover the full price). If a certain item is deemed to be particularly useful for the further success of the adventuring company, the investor(s) may allow a character to use the item with the understanding that it's company property. (If a character loses 'company property' he may have to pay for it out of his own shares).

Chapter 13 has more detailed information on professional adventuring parties and how they work.

Speaking of investments, don't overlook the fact that your character can choose to invest in an adventuring company as well. Many players with retired characters like to sponsor/invest in a famous adventuring company to build their character portfolios without actively playing.

Treasure

Fabulous treasure and high-fantasy adventuring go hand in hand. What would the tale of King Arthur be without Excalibur or the elusive Holy Grail? Who could remember Ali Baba without the den of forty thieves? Hidden out there in the campaign world are great treasures awaiting discovery. Ancient dragons rest their scaly rumps on huge hordes of gold, silver and gems. Orc chieftains greedily account for wains groaning under the weight of loot from the latest successful raid. Mindless jellies ooze through the dessicated bones and finely decorated armor of unfortunate souls. Foul lords of darkness cunningly leave small fortunes apparently unguarded, like spiders luring in the flies. Stooped magic-users spend unnaturally long lifetimes assembling libraries and laboratories with shelves full of arcane magical items.

Some treasure troves, like those of dragons, are gathered and hoarded for reasons fully understood only by their collectors. Others are gathered for more mundane purposes—power, luxury and security. A rare few troves actually date from eons in the past, their owners long dead and nearly forgotten. Some treasure hordes are small, such as the pickings of a yellow mold. Others are enormous, such as Rot Gut's treasury. Treasures great and small may either be (at least seemingly) free for the taking or fiercely trapped and carefully watched over.

Treasure Types

Treasure comes in many different forms and sizes, ranging from the somewhat mundane to the beautiful, magical, and exotic.

Coins: There are of course always coins to be found, minted from copper, silver, gold, electrum, hard silver and platinum. But these precious metals can also be shaped into gilded cups, intricately etched bowls, or even elegantly chased silverware. Characters usually know the value of coins and will have no difficulty establishing their worth in most cases. However, ancient treasure hordes may contain coins no longer commonly used. It may be that these items can be sold only by assessing their weight. 10 coins have a combined weight of one pound.

Objects made of valuable metal are even more difficult to appraise. Either the characters must find a jeweler who can value the item and a buyer willing to pay a fair price, or these too must be melted down for their metal. In the larger cities this is not too difficult. There are always appraisers and fences (those who can sell a dangerous, stolen, or unique item without attracting too much unwanted attention) ready to take your business, although getting the full value for a given item might prove difficult. (Accusations of theft are another problem.)

Characters must be aware of cheats and counterfeiters, though. An apparently valuable bowl could actually turn out to be base metal plated in a thin layer of fine silver. The metal of coins could be debased with copper or brass. Weights could be rigged to give false prices. Characters must find and give their business only to merchants they can trust.

Gems/Jewels/Precious Stones: Gems are another common form of treasure and here is another area where the player characters are even more dependent on help from others. Unless the party already has a skilled appraiser of precious stones, they're going to have to trust someone else. After all, those red stones they found in the last treasure could be cheap glass, richly colored but only marginally valuable quartz, semi-precious garnets, or valuable rubies. Again, the player characters are going to have to seek out a trustworthy jeweler and be watchful for cheats and scams. However, truly tricky GMs might present your characters with uncut gems. These are almost impossible for the untrained eye to spot or appraise. The majority of characters (as well as most players) are not going to realize that a piece of unremarkable stone can be a highly valued gem when properly cut.

Art Objects: Perhaps the most difficult of all treasure items to appraise are objects of artistic value. While gems cut or uncut are valuable, their worth can be greatly increased when used artfully in a piece of exotic jewelry. Gold is valuable by weight, but even more so when fashioned into a lovely cup or pin. Dwarven craftsmen from hidden communities practice the finest arts of gem cutting, while gnomish artisans in earthen burrows labor away on elaborate gold and silver filigrees. Ancient elven carvings, done in exquisitely grained woods, stand side by side with the purest of statues chiseled by man. All of these have a value that goes far beyond their mere materials.

But artistic creations seldom have a fixed value. Their price depends on the player characters finding a buyer and that person's willingness to buy. A few large cities may have brokers in arts, merchants who know the right people and are willing to act as go-betweens.

Most of the time, however, the player characters have to go to the effort of peddling their wares personally. This requires tact and delicacy, for such items are seldom bought by any but the wealthy and the wealthy often do not like stooping to business negotiations. Player characters must carefully avoid giving insult to the barons, dukes, counts, and princes they might deal with.

Antiques – Trash or Treasure?: Antiques are another treasure item that are difficult for the untrained eye to appraise, let alone recognize. An antique item is only valuable if it finds the right buyer. That rusty and badly nicked sword you just tossed aside might be worth thousands to a collector looking for an example of early Krymurian metalworking. A perfectly matched set of azure blue crystal goblets might be worth a king's ransom — or then again, maybe not. Everything has a price but finding the buyer willing to part with his hard-earned coin for an old, worn out bronze helmet is always the hard part. As with art objects, it can take a great deal of effort to identify and sell such valuable hidden treasures. But the rewards can be great.

Unloading the Loot

Besides the more common types of treasure that has been mentioned, there are the truly bizarre things your character can find – exotic animals, spices, furs, carved horns, rare spell components, or even trade goods. As with art objects, the values of these items are highly subjective. First the player characters have to find a buyer who is interested in the unique item. This is not too difficult for some things, such as luxurious animal furs or exotic trade goods, but it can be a tremendous enterprise if you have a spell component that is useful only to the most powerful of magic-users.

Next the character must haggle about the price. Furriers and merchants do this as a matter of course. Others haggle because they hope the character does not know the true value of what they hold or because they themselves do not know. After all this, the character might be able to sell their goods. However, if you enter into this in the true spirit of role-playing and see it as part of the adventure, the whole process is enjoyable.

Magical Items

The treasures mentioned thus far are all, first and foremost, monetary. Their usefulness is immediate and obvious. They give characters wealth, and with wealth comes power and influence. However, there are other treasures, very desirable ones that your characters will not want to sell or give away. These are the magical items that your characters find and use.

Although clerics and magic-users can make magical items (according to the guidelines your GM has for magical research), it is far more common for your characters to find these items during the course of adventures. Magical items are powerful aids for characters.

With such items, characters can gain bonuses in combat, cast spells with the mere utterance of a word, withstand the fiercest fire, and perform amazing feats impossible by any other known means. Not all magical items to be found on the adventure trail are beneficial to their owners, however. Some are cursed, the result of faulty magical construction or, very rarely, the deliberate handiwork of some truly mad or evil magic-user.

A very few magical items are rare or unique artifacts, items created by beings more powerful than even the greatest player characters. These are perilously dangerous items to use. There are only three methods to determine how to use artifacts — dumb luck, trial and error, and diligent research.

There are many different magical items your character can find, but they all fall into a few basic categories. Each type of magical item has properties you should be aware of.

Magical Weapons

The mere mention of a magic blade is enough to make the typical fighter drool. There can be a magical version of nearly any type of normal weapon, although there are admittedly few magical bardiches or guisarme-voulges. By far, the most common magical weapons are swords and daggers. A magical weapon typically gives a +1 or greater bonus to attack rolls, increasing a character's chance to hit and cause damage.

Perhaps magical swords are enchanted to be quicker on the attack, or maybe their edge is sharper than can be wrought with normal steel, the explanation can be whatever the GM desires. Whatever the reason, magical weapons give results far beyond those of even the finest crafted non-magical blade.

A rare few weapons have even greater powers (such as the HackMaster class swords of legend). These may allow your character to sense danger, heal wounds, float in midair, or have the most amazing luck. The rarest of the rare can actually communicate with your character and are imbued with an otherworldly Intelligence. While the most powerful of magical weapons, these clever instruments of destruction sometimes seek to impose their wills on their owners, for good or evil.

When you find a magical weapon, more than likely you do not know its properties. Some functions, such as the advantage it gives you in combat, can be learned by trial and error. Other properties must be learned through research and spells. Ancient histories and Legend Lore spells can provide information on the properties of your weapon. On rare occasions, the item's properties are discovered through blind luck. Simply commanding the weapon to activate one power after another (hoping it will suddenly spring to life) works only for the most minor abilities – detecting danger, spotting secret doors or locating treasure.

Greater abilities require that specific commands be uttered, using powerful words or phrases, perhaps in long-forgotten languages.

Magical Armor

Enchanted armors are the complements to magical weapons. These armors have a +1 or better bonus to their normal Armor Class, being made of stuff stronger and finer than non-magical armor. Furthermore, these armors grant some measure of protection against attacks that normal armors would not stop. Chain mail +1, for instance, improves the character's saving throw against the fiery breath of a dragon by 1, thus providing more than just a physical shield. In rare instances, armor may possess extraordinary powers. Although such armors are generally finely made and elaborately engraved, characters can discover the armors' powers only by the same methods they use to discover the powers of magical weapons.

Potions and Oils

Magical potions and oils are easily found but hard to identify. They come in small bottles, jugs, pots, or vials and clearly radiate magic if a detection spell is used. However, the effect of any potion is unknown until some brave soul tries a small sample. The results can be quite varied. The imbiber may discover he can float or fly, resist great heat or cold, heal grievous wounds, or fearlessly face the greatest dangers. He may also find himself hopelessly smitten

by the first creature he sees or struck dead by a powerful poison. It is a risk that must be taken to learn the nature of the potion.

Scrolls

Scrolls are a convenience and luxury for spellcasters. By reading the incantation written on the pages, the cleric or magic-user can instantly cast that spell. He does not need to memorize it, have the material components handy, or do any of the things normal spellcasting requires. Experienced and powerful magic-users normally spend their evenings preparing such scrolls for their own adventuring use.

Some scrolls are usable by all characters, granting special but temporary protections from various dangers – evil creatures, Werewolves, powerful beings from other planes, etc. Other scrolls bear hideous or humorous curses, brought into effect at the mere reading of their titles. Unfortunately, the only way to know what a scroll contains is to silently scan its contents. For scrolls containing magic-user spells, this requires the use of a Read Magic spell. Other scrolls can be read by all. This scan does not cast the spell written on the scroll, but it tells the character what is written there (and exposes him to the effects of curses). Once the scroll is read to determine its contents, that character can use it at any time in the future.

Rings

Magical rings are usable by many different classes and bestow a wide range of powers, from pyrotechnic displays to wishes. While the aura of a magical ring can be detected, its properties cannot be discovered until it is worn and the command word is uttered. (The command word is most commonly found inscribed on the inside of the band.) As with all magical

items, some rings can harm your character. Worse still, cursed rings can be removed only with the aid of spells!

Wands, Staves, and Rods

These are among the most powerful of standard magical items. Wands are commonly used by magic-users, allowing them to cast powerful spells with the flick of a wrist. Staves can be used by magic-users or clerics. Staves can be truly destructive, dwarfing even the potential of a wand. Rods are the rarest of all, the accouterments of witch-kings and great lords. With rods come dominance and power.

Fortunately for your character, few of these items are cursed or dangerous to handle. But all must be operated by a command word – a specific word or phrase that triggers the power within. No wand, stave, or rod shows any indication of its powers by mere sight or handling. Careful research and probing are most often needed to tap the potential stored within.

Wands, staves, and rods are not limitless in their power. Each use drains them slightly, using up a charge. There is no power gauge or meter showing what is left. A character discovers his wand is drained only when it no longer functions or suddenly crumbles into useless dust.

Miscellaneous Magic

Miscellaneous magical items are where the true variety of magical treasures lies. Each item possesses some unique power. There are horseshoes to make your horse go faster, brooms to ride, sacks that hold more than they should, paints that create real things, girdles that grant great strength, caps to make your character smarter, books that increase ability scores, and much, much more. Each item is different and not all can be identified in the same way. The effects of some become obvious the instant the item is handled, donned, or opened. Others require research and questioning to learn the command word needed to activate them. All are quite valuable and rare.

Artifacts and Relics

Finally, there are artifacts and relics. Don't count on your PC ever finding one of these rarest of all magical items. Even if your character does find one, think carefully before you decide to let him keep it permanently. Artifacts are the most powerful magical items in the game. Indeed, many are powerful enough to alter the course of history! They are unique and have unique histories. You can never find more than one left Hand of Vectra in a world. Because it is so unique, each artifact has special and significant powers. Artifacts never appear by accident – they are always placed by the GM. Finding an artifact is always the result of a very special adventure. Your GM has placed that artifact for a reason. It is not likely that he really intends for your characters to keep it. Instead, he has something arranged in which you need that artifact for a specific purpose. The problem with keeping artifacts is that they are too powerful. Not only do they unbalance your character in the short run, they also eventually corrupt and destroy him. The magical power of artifacts is such that they destroy their owners sooner or later. There is a price to be paid for power, and it is not a cheap one.

Dividing and Storing Treasure

Once your group completes a successful adventure, it is almost certain to have collected some treasure. Therefore, it helps to have some prearranged agreement about how this treasure is to be divided among the different player characters and their henchmen. If your party is an Adventuring Company the details of dividing treasure has already been determined in the company's charter.

Otherwise, there are no rules about how your characters should divide treasures and this process will be a true role-playing decision that must be reached among all the players at the table.

Here are some suggested methods and reasons to make, or not make, some agreements. If you bear these in mind, you will have fewer arguments and bad feelings between the different players and their characters in your group. Cash treasure is the easiest. The most direct and simplest method is equal shares for all player characters and full or half shares for all henchmen. A player may argue that his character's contribution was greater than that of other characters, but these things average out in the long run. Besides, that player has no

real idea of the contribution of others. A character who guarded the rear may have discouraged hidden opponents from springing an ambush on the group, something that only the GM knows.

Additional considerations include extraordinary costs. Some adventuring groups establish a special fund to pay the costs (if there are any) of healing, resurrecting, or restoring fellow player characters. Again, this works on the principle that all faced the danger and therefore all should share equally in the expenses. Other groups make allowances for differing character levels (higher level characters presumably shouldered more of the burden of the adventure, and so should be rewarded proportionately.) Some parties give special rewards to those who took greater chances or saved others. These encourage everyone in the group to take part.

As a general rule, if a character administers an 'unassisted kill' the 'right of spoils' for that kill belong to that character alone. (Barring any provisions in the group charter that say otherwise).

Enchanted Considerations

Magical treasure is more difficult to divide up, since there is rarely enough to give a useful item to every character, nor are all items of equal value or power. Here you must rely more on your sense of fairness if you wish to maintain party harmony. Since magical items are worthwhile to a party only if they can be used, your first concern should normally be to get the right item into the right hands. A magical sword in the possession of a magic-user is not nearly as useful as it would be in the hands of a fighter. Likewise, a wand does a fighter little good but could be a potent addition to a magic-user. Therefore it is a good idea to match items to characters.

Alternatively, your party could determine the price an item would sell for, and then make it available to any PC who is willing to give the rest of the party that amount of money. If more than one player is willing to pay the price, the interested players could roll dice to see who gets the item. Or, for items that several characters could all use equally well (such as a Potion of Healing that is useful to all), the characters can bargain with each other and roll dice for choices. A player character may relinquish a claim on one magical item in exchange for another. A character who has already received a magical item may not be allowed another choice if there are not enough pieces to go around. If no other agreement can be reached, the players can roll dice and have their characters pick in descending order. It is a fair method (since people cannot rightfully complain about a random roll), but it can create imbalances. One or two characters could wind up with the bulk of the magical items over the course of several adventures. At this point, they would be wise to voluntarily withdraw from the selection process.

Clever Storage Options: Divide and Conquer

There are tactical issues to think about when distributing treasure. It is simply not wise for one or two characters to carry the bulk of the party's magical items. Successful adventurers spread their gear throughout their party. (This holds true even for explorers and special forces in the real world.) This way, if one character falls off the cliff and disappears forever or is spirited away by an Invisible Stalker, the party has not lost everything. To illustrate another consideration, you are better off to have the fighters, thieves, and magic-users carry the healing potions rather than let the cleric do it, since he has healing spells. If he has both the healing spells and the potions and should disappear into the mist, your party has lost all its healing ability. If it is spread around through the group, at worst you might lose the potions or the spells, but not both (unless disaster really strikes, in which case there is no way to prevent it anyway). In the end, you will find that it does not pay to be too greedy.

Once your characters have assembled a sizeable amount of treasure, they have to find some place to keep it. You can find wealthy money lenders/merchants with fortified treasuries who, for gaming purposes, serve the role of banks. They'll store/safeguard large sums of money and treasure for a stiff fee. Characters can also find other ways to keep their money secure. Chests with strong locks are a good start, but there are still better methods. One choice is to make the treasure small enough that you can carry it with you at all times. (Of course, one good mugging and you're broke.) There is also the difficulty of buying a drink with a 1,000 gp gem. A second choice is to place your money in the hands of someone you think you can trust. We all know what the risks are there.

You could have your character give his fortune to a local lord or church and then hope to call in favors at a future date. This is not quite as foolish as it sounds. If the beneficiary of your largesse refuses to honor your agreement, you'll never give him money again and neither will anyone else, most likely. If no one gives him any money, where will he find the funds to support his lifestyle? No, such a person must seriously try to honor his commitments. Of course, he may not do as much as you would like. The best solution is that used throughout history – buy goods and chattels. Land, livestock, and trade goods are harder to steal and harder to lose. If you must keep a large fortune, it is best to keep it in something that can be carried easily and is unlikely to be stolen.

Dibs Protocol

During a game session, players will inevitably earn some meager pittance of treasure. There are many ways that players can determine who gets what (as discussed previously) but we feel it is worth mentioning how the dibs calling process works. They say that possession is nine tenths of the law. Well, 'dibs calling' is the other ten percent. Whenever a new item is introduced into the adventure and the ownership of that item among player characters is not already clearly established, a player may call dibs on it. He does so simply by shouting out 'dibs' after the item has been introduced. Once dibs has been called, it may adversely affect a player character's Honor if he does not respect the ownership right of the person who called dibs to the item in question. If two players happen to call dibs simultaneously, they should settle the dispute by rolling dice with the higher roll winning the 'dibs' rights. Note, however, that if the item in question was introduced as the result of an unassisted kill the 'right of spoils' goes to the slaying player — period. Any 'dibs' called on such an item is ignored.

'Dibs' calls are generally made for specific items in specific instances. For example, a player may not use blanket 'dibs' statements like, "I call dibs on all magic items we ever find." It doesn't work that way. However, in addition to ownership of items, dibs may also be called to establish a player character's right to engage a certain enemy in combat. For example, "I've got dibs on that Orc shaman. I'll waste his ass!" In this case, the honorable thing to do for the other players would be to allow their 'dibs'-calling companion to engage the Orc shaman in one-on-one combat. Dibs can also be called to establish one's right to obtain a service prior to others, as in, "I've got first dibs getting my stuff appraised by the gem dealer." This could be important if a player is trying to sell an item and doesn't want to risk his chance of getting a fair price in the event that other players dump similar items on the market before him. Finally it should be noted that 'dibs' rights, once obtained, can be sold or traded just like any other commodity to another player.

Suggested Agreements for Division of Treasure

Agreements:
1. Equal shares (share and share alike) is a simple division by the total number of characters involved.
2. Shares by level is a division whereby all character levels of experience are added and the total treasure divided by this sum. One share of treasure is given for each experience level.*
3. Equal shares plus bonus is a method to reward excellence and leadership. Treasure is divided by the sum of all characters, plus two or three. The outstanding character or characters, as determined by vote, each gain one extra share.

*For multi-classed characters add one-half of the lesser class(es) levels to the greater class levels to determine total experience levels for the division of treasure. Characters with two classes receive shares for the class levels they are permitted to employ for this purpose (See Chapter 3, the section detailing Multi-Class and Dual-Class Characters).

Modifiers:
1. Non-player characters who are henchmen of a player character count as one-half character or for one half of their levels and cannot gain bonus shares. Such NPCs must have clearly demonstrated that they contributed to the success of the party.
2. A character who is incapacitated or killed (but subsequently brought back to life) is eligible to share only in treasure gained prior to such incapacity or death.
3. Characters who are uncooperative, obstruct the party, attack party members, or are the approximate cause of the incapacitation or death of a party member shall forfeit from one-quarter to all of their share(s) as penalty for their actions.
4. Characters who were maimed or took damage equaling more than half their full hit points receive an extra share.

Dividing Up Magical Treasure

While it is a simple matter to total up the coins and precious items that can be sold for an established amount of money, the division of magic items is far more difficult. It is therefore necessary for party members to determine how magic will be divided. As the number of items that will be gained is unknown, the selection of a system of division is not possible until after the adventure is concluded, and the party counts up its new-found wealth.

1. If but one or two items of magic are gained, these can be grouped singly or paired to equal a share of treasure. If one is of relatively small worth, it can be grouped with money to equal one share.
2. Three or more magic items:
   a) best item
   b) next best item
   c) third + fourth items
   d) "x" amount of money as compensation for not getting any magic items
3. Three or more magic items, alternate method:
   a) best item
   b) second item + "x" amount of money
   c) third item + "3x" amount of money

Magic items thus parceled are then diced for, the character with the highest roll selecting first, and then the second highest scoring character choosing next, etc. It is suggested that each character be given a number of rolls equal to his or her level of experience, the highest of these rolls being the one retained. Non-player character henchmen are typically allowed but a single roll.

Variations on the above systems are, of course, possible. Systems should always be established prior to the inception of the adventure whenever possible.

Chapter 9

Goods, Services and Equipment

Character Outfitting

Let's cut to the quick. As good as you might think your character is, the truth is, he has a very tough haul ahead of him. After the character creation process, your character will be plunged into the campaign world where he must quickly learn to sink or swim — do or die. The only asset he has at this critical juncture in his career is a coin pouch filled with a few hard coins and the clothes on his back. His background may better prepare him, to be sure, but we're still talking some meager assets at best. Perhaps he has a basic weapon, a horse, or if he's lucky, he may enter the game with the deed or title to a small piece of property.

Everything else must be purchased (or acquired by other means) through game play. Before your character can be an effective hero and make his mark on the world he's going to need a little more in the way of equipment. He must to be outfitted.

Outfitting requires very careful consideration – you should not take this process lightly. Spend your starting money wisely. Your character will need equipment and provisions to properly prepare for his life of adventuring. The most basic things you will need of are weapons, armor, clothing and outfitting gear. You should also keep enough money to buy meals and lodging until you've managed to find some source of income. Otherwise, your GM will really screw you over when you try to pawn off some of his stuff to buy a decent meal or room for the night.

As you will soon discover, there are never sufficient funds to purchase everything you desired, so choices must be made. Try to make intelligent ones, your character will have a hard enough time surviving in the world of HackMaster without you screwing up his finances. Also, keep in mind that an adventurer, especially in the lower experience levels, must travel light. If he can't carry what he owns on his back or strapped across the back of a pack mule, he may very well find such property to be more of a hindrance than a benefit. Every item you buy has its own inherent weight (see **Encumbrance**- this chapter) and will contribute to weighing your character down. Too much weight also reduces a character's movement rate (see Chapter 16 for details on Movement).

Equipment Lists

The following list are mere samplings of the goods, services and equipment, that you should be able to find in Garweeze Wurld (or your GM's home-brewed, inferior campaign world). Your GM will likely add or delete from these lists. He may also have modifiers for the availability of some items that will make them easier (or harder) to find.

Every market place will have its own mix of goods and products from which to choose. Every bazaar has its own gathering of merchants and middlemen with goods imported from far away lands. Some items will be in much higher demand than others (and thus harder to find and more expensive). What you want might not be available or, if your GM has set his game in a specific time period, might not have even been discovered or invented yet!

Many of the uncommon items in these lists are explained in the descriptions that follow at the end of the section. The price given for each item in the lists is its average price, the amount you can expect the item to cost in a normal economy. However, large cities, barren wildernesses, and places with brave adventurers carrying bags full of gold are not normal economies. In these places you might find yourself paying more (very rarely less) than the amount listed. The desert merchants of Flammar have a popular saying, "The price of goods shifts like the sands. Sometimes it is more. Sometimes it is less. But one thing is for sure — the price is always RIGHT!"

Short on money? Not to worry. Most merchants are happy to barter and haggle over prices. For the sake of game play, however, it's not a good idea to haggle over the price of EVERY purchase. It slows down the game. Save your haggling for the important big-ticket purchases. Haggling over every bowl of soup and every tankard of ale will only result in others forming a low opinion of you (both players and NPCs). No one likes a penny-pincher.

Your GM has full set of rules on the process of haggling and bartering, which he can explain to you. There are also corresponding skills that you can learn to help you gain the upper hand in such dealings. One last thing, as in most dealings, however, the buyer should always beware. Things might not always be as they appear.

Equipment Descriptions

Not every piece of equipment is described here. That would be monumentally stupid. The vast majority of things found on the equipment lists need no description, as their functions, forms, and purposes should be obvious even to HackMaster beginners. Only those items whose use is obscure or appearance is unusual are described below. Specific game effects of equipment items are given in the charts and other appropriate sections of these rules.

Explanation of Equipment List Headings

Base Availability: Even after completing your list of items you wish to purchase and scraping up the needed monies, you might find that some items are extremely hard to find. There are no supermarkets or strip malls in HackMaster. Nor will you find friendly merchants with well-stocked shelves brimming with every imaginable item waiting for you to come fill your shopping cart. Can a fighter expect to

walk into an armorer's shop and find a suit of field plate armor exactly his size on the spot? Not likely. Can the thief walk into the corner outfitting shop and plop down his gold and buy a set of shiny new lock picks? Think again.

It is often necessary for characters to shop in a number of places in order to obtain everything they desire. Each item on the following lists has three Base Availability Indexes (High, Medium and Low). Base availability is an indication of how readily available an item is for purchase. The High index is used when the character is shopping in a large metropolitan area or in a large established market place/bazaar. Medium is used for medium sized towns and population centers. Low is used for villages, roadside vendors, etc.

To purchase the desired item from the list you must roll 1d100 (adding any modifiers your GM may wish to add, based on your location, timing and other market conditions). If you roll equal to or less than the appropriate Availability Index, the item is available. Note that you must roll for EACH purchase even if you are buying two of the same item. (The merchant may only have ONE two-handed sword, after all.) The exception is when buying animals, which tend to be traded or sold in groups (see the descriptive text on Livestock later in this section for more details).

If you fail to find a desired item, you might want to visit another shop or town and try again. Or… you might try to contract an artisan or craftsman to make the item for you to order (though this will certainly take hours, if not days or weeks, to complete). You may also try making it known that you are in the market for an item which is unavailable and are willing to pay more than the going rate. Often a merchant will have items that are in high demand held back for his best customers. Surely, he'll find it hard to resist making a huge profit at your expense.

Cost: The price listed for each item on the equipment list is the average going price. Depending on the merchant, the region, etc. you may expect the actual price to be much higher (or rarely, much lower). This is where haggling comes into play.

Weight: Most items have their weight listed in pounds. It is your responsibility to record the weight of everything you are carrying and total it. GMs frequently conduct encumbrance audits. Players caught carrying more than they should are often penalized experience points.

Alcohol/Beverages

The reader will notice there are a wide variety of beverages on the price list, most of which are alcoholic. Why so many? One might conclude that the world of HackMaster is populated by nothing more than drunkards and barflies. That's not the case. Remember you are adventuring in a world that lacks sewage plants and water treatment facilities. Unless the water you are drinking comes from a clean well or a spring-fed pool there is a high risk of contracting sickness and disease.

For this reason, the drink of choice for most adventurers is a good stiff one — especially when drinking in public establishments that are not bound by the tethers of any local health codes. Take note of the fact that any GM worth his salt is quick to take advantage of the situation when a player fills his canteen from a stagnant standing pool of water or orders a glass of water at the inn (if lucky, the character will suffer little more than a bad case of the runs).

Many of the alcoholic concoctions on the price list have other benefits besides simply quenching one's thirst. Liver Squeezings for example (a drink made from the liver of a female Owlbear) is reputed to speed up the healing process (it can also render a character permanently blind if he drinks too much of it at once). The Gut Bruiser is actually a mild poison often used to test the mettle of newcomers who wish to belly up to the bar with the regulars. Stout Brown Grevan is said to increase strength and stamina. Orluian mead makes one braver – or so it is said. As with all rumors and wives' tales you should take the above with a grain of salt. The properties of such drinks may, or may not be true.

Miscellaneous Equipment

Holy Item: Holy items are small representations of all those things revered by religions—stars, crosses, hammers, rosaries, anointed oils, blessed wine, sacred teachings, and more. Just what constitutes a holy item depends on the religion.

Table 9A: Alcohol/Beverages				
Item	Cost	Hi	Med	Low
Ale (per gallon)	2 sp	95	85	75
Ale, Dead Viking (Cut Ale) (pint)	1 sp	95	95	95
Ale, Kromian	5 gp	85	70	60
Ale, Pint	5 cp	95	85	75
Beer, Cut, (pint)	5 cp	90	85	75
Beer, Heavy (pint)	1 sp	95	85	75
Bitter Broth (pint)	5 sp	65	70	80
Brandy, Orluian (pint)	5 gp	70	50	35
Grog (pint)	3 sp	95	85	75
Gut Bruiser (pint)	1 gp	75	65	55
Finch-Yager (Amber Brew)	7 gp	70	60	50
Honey Brew (pint) (medicinal)	1 gp	80	70	60
Liver Squeezings	2 gp	85	70	60
Mead, Baker's Thicke (pint)	10 sp	95	90	85
Mead, Common (pint)	5 sp	95	85	80
Mead, Dwarven, Keg	300 gp	30	20	10
Mead, Nordlar (gallon)	10 gp	75	60	45
Mead, Orluian (gallon)	100 gp	65	50	40
Rum (pint)	5 sp	75	65	55
Stout Brown Grevan (pint)	7 sp	90	85	80
Whiskey, Bitter-Korn	2 gp	90	80	70
Wine, Blackberry (pint)	1 gp	85	70	60
Wine, Good (pint)	10 sp	75	65	55
Wine, Gutberry (pint)	4 gp	85	70	60
Wine, Watered (pint)	1 cp	95	85	75
Wine, Watered (pitcher)	2 sp	95	85	75
Wine, Elderberry (pint)	40 gp	60	40	20

To compute weight for any liquids carried allow 1 lb. per pint (8 lbs. per gallon). Don't forget to buy a container as well, GMs always get you with that one. And remember to include the weight for the type of container being used to transport the liquid so you won't fail a dreaded encumbrance audit.

Note also that each type of alcohol has its own inherent effects on the imbiber. Your GM knows this information and will share it when or if appropriate.

Table 9B: Clothing			Base Availability		
Item	Cost	Weight	Hi	Med	Low
Belt	3 sp	.5 lbs.	95	85	75
Boots	—	—			
Riding	3 gp	2.5 lbs.	90	85	75
Soft	1 gp	2 lbs.	95	85	75
Snakeskin	25 gp	2 lbs.	65	45	35
Breeches	2 gp	.5 lbs.	95	85	75
Cap, Hat	—	—			
Fine, Formal	3 gp	.25 lbs.	90	80	70
Common, Utilitarian	1 sp	.25 lbs.	95	85	75
Beret, Upper Class	6 gp	.5 lbs.	75	70	65
Cloak	—	—			
Good cloth	8 sp	3 lbs.	95	85	75
Fine fur	50 gp	6 lbs.	90	80	70
Garments (matching outfit)	—				
Fine, Leather	20 gp	5 lbs.	90	80	70
Fine, Silk	50 gp	2 lbs.	75	65	55
Fine, Embroidered	75 gp	3 lbs.	85	75	65
Common	2 cp	3 lbs.	95	85	75
Shoddy	1 cp	3 lbs.	95	85	75
Girdle	3 gp	.5 lbs.	95	85	75
Gloves	1 gp	.5 lbs.	95	85	75
Gown, common	12 sp	2 lbs.	95	85	75
Hose	2 gp	.5 lbs.	90	80	70
Jerkin, Laced	1 gp	.5 lbs.	90	80	70
Knife sheath	3 cp	.5 lbs.	95	85	75
Mittens, Winter	3 sp	.5 lbs.	95	85	75
Pin/Brooch, gold	6 gp	—	85	75	65
Pin/Brooch, brass/iron	5 sp	—	95	85	75
Robe	—	—			
Common	9 sp	3 lbs.	95	85	75
Embroidered	20 gp	4 lbs.	90	75	65
Sandals	5 cp	1 lbs.	95	85	75
Sash	2 sp	.5 lbs.	95	85	75
Shirt, wool	5 cp	.5 lbs.	90	80	70
Shoes	5 sp	2 lbs.	95	85	75
Silk jacket	80 gp	1 lbs.	70	60	50
Surcoat	6 sp	4 lbs.	95	85	75
Sword scabbard, hanger, baldric	4 gp	3 lbs.	95	85	75
Tabard	6 sp	3 lbs.	95	85	75
Toga, coarse	8 sp	3 lbs.	90	80	70
Tunic	8 sp	1 lbs.	95	85	75
Vest	6 sp	.5 lbs.	95	85	75

Table 9C: Containers: Packs, Bags, Bottles etc.					
			Base Availability		
Item	Cost	Weight	Hi	Med	Low
Backpack	2 gp	2 lbs.	95	85	75
Barrel, small	2 gp	30 lbs.	95	90	85
Basket	—				
Large	3 sp	1 lbs.	95	85	75
Small	5 cp	*	95	90	85
Belt pouch	—	—			
Large	1 gp	1 lbs.	95	90	85
Small	7 sp	.5 lbs.	95	90	85
Bolt case	1 gp	1 lbs.	90	85	80
Bucket	5 sp	3 lbs.	95	90	85
Chest	—				
Large	2 gp	25 lbs.	95	90	85
Small	1 gp	10 lbs.	95	90	85
Flask, metal (pint)	10 sp	.25 lbs.	90	80	70
Glass bottle (pint)	1 gp	*	85	75	65
Iron pot/kettle (gallon)	5 sp	2 lbs.	95	90	85
Sack	—				
Large	2 sp	.5 lbs.	95	90	85
Small	5 cp	*	95	90	85
Map or scroll case	8 sp	.5 lbs.	90	85	80
Wineskin	8 sp	1 lbs.	95	90	85

* These items weigh little individually. Ten of these items weigh one pound.

Any good holy item has a similar effect on undead or evil creatures, provided it is wielded by a follower of the belief associated with that item or a heckuva actor. Thus, rules that refer to holy symbols and holy water apply to all similar items, provided these items are specially prepared by the cleric's order.

Because of their special nature, holy items cannot normally be purchased. Different sects tend to protect the symbols of their faith to prevent their misuse or corruption.

Therefore, such items must be obtained through the auspices of a local congregation. This is not difficult for sincere followers of that faith, although requests for rare or unusual items must always be justified. Nonbelievers are given holy items only if there is a clear and present danger to the faith. And, let's be honest, no matter who you are money talks and a healthy church donation will be required (and can also move a non-believer temporarily into the 'believer/follower' category in the eyes of the clergy).

Lanterns: A hooded lantern (30-foot radius of light) is a standard lantern with shuttered or hinged sides. It is not directional, as its light is cast equally in all directions.

A bullseye lantern (60-foot cone of light, 20-foot diameter at its terminus) has only a single shutter, the other sides being highly polished to reflect the light in a single direction. Both hooded and bullseye lanterns can be carried in one hand. A single flask of oil (one pint) burns for six hours in either. The beacon lantern (240-foot beam of light, 80-foot diameter at its terminus) is a much larger affair and must be mounted on the prow of a ship, the bed of a wagon, or other large structure. It operates like the bullseye lantern but illuminates to a greater distance. The beacon goes through oil quickly, burning a flask every two hours.

Locks: Locks are typically primitive affairs (except for those complicated by the use of magic or an outstanding locksmith). All are worked with a skeleton-type key (more than one for very complex locks). Combination locks, nine-pin tumblers, security alarm systems, wireless/keyless entry systems and kryptonite locks do not exist in the HackMaster GigaVerse. As with most things, there are good, very complex locks as well as bad, easily opened locks.

Magnifying Glass: This simple lens is more an oddity than a useful tool. It does not greatly enhance viewing, especially since many are unevenly ground, creating distortion. It is useful as a substitute for tinder and steel when starting fires and for roasting insects.

Merchant's Scale: This is a set that includes a small balance and pans along with a suitable assortment of weights. Its main use is to weigh coins—a common method of settling a transaction. Merchants are well aware that coins can be undersized, shaved, or plated. The only sound protection is to check the coins against a set of established weights. It is also needed when using foreign coins to make a purchase or exchange. Of course, merchants are no more noble than anyone else and may use sets of false weights—one set heavier than normal for selling an item (causing the customer to pay more) and another lighter than usual for buying items (letting the merchant pay less). In well-regulated areas, officials verify the accuracy of weights and measures, but this

in itself is no protection. Players might wish to have a scale and weights for their own protection.

Oil: Greek fire is a general name given to all highly flammable oils used in combat. These oils are highly flammable and a little dangerous to carry. Greek fire can also be used to make torches.

Lamp oil is used for lamps and lanterns. It is not particularly explosive although it can be used to feed an existing blaze.

Spyglass: Like the magnifying glass, the spyglass is more of an oddity than a useful item. Objects viewed through it are a little closer, although not much. For better results magical items are preferred. The spyglass gives from two to three times magnification.

Water Clock: This bulky item is good for giving the time accurate to a half-hour. Activated by a regulated flow of drops, the water clock is not something you carry in your pocket. For it to work at all, it must have a source of water and be left undisturbed.

A very uncommon item, it is primarily an amusement for the wealthy and a tool for the student of arcane lore. The vast majority of society is not concerned with exact time.

Thieves' Tools

This is a small collection of tools useful to burglars. The kit includes one or more skeleton keys, long metal picks, a long-nosed clamp, a small hand saw, and a small wedge and hammer. These combined with some common tools (such as a crowbar) make up most of the special equipment a thief needs to perform his trade. As any smart thief knows, it is not wise to simply arrive in

Table 9D: Daily Food and Lodging					
			Base Availability		
Item	Cost	Weight	Hi	Med	Low
Banquet (per person)	10 gp	—	90	85	80
Bath	3 cp	—	95	85	75
Bear Fat Dumplings	6 cp	—	70	60	50
Bread	5 cp	—	95	85	75
Cheese	4 sp	—	95	85	75
Cheese, Rank (hard)	10 sp	—	80	75	60
City rooms (per month)	—				
Opulent	100 gp	—	90	85	80
Common	20 gp	—	95	85	75
Poor	6 sp	—	95	90	85
Egg or fresh vegetables	1 gp	—	95	90	85
Grain and stabling for horse (daily)	5 sp	—	95	90	85
Grouse Onion Stew	3 cp	—	95	90	85
Honey	5 sp	—	95	90	85
Inn lodging (per day/week)	—				
Opulent Lodging	50 gp	—	90	85	80
Common	5 sp/3 gp	—	95	90	85
Poor	5 cp/2 sp	—	95	90	85
Meat for one meal	1 sp	—	95	90	85
Meals (per day)	—				
Gourmet	5 gp	—	90	85	80
Good	5 sp	—	95	90	85
Common	3 sp	—	95	90	85
Poor	1 sp	—	95	90	85
Scratch-Root Stew	1 sp	—	95	90	85
Separate latrine for rooms (per month)	2 gp	—	85	75	60
Soup	5 cp	—	95	90	85

Table 9E: Light Sources					
			Base Availability		
Item	Cost	Weight	Hi	Med	Low
Candle	1 cp	*	95	90	85
Lantern	—	—			
Beacon	150 gp	50 lbs.	85	75	60
Bullseye	12 gp	3 lbs.	90	85	80
Hooded	7 gp	2 lbs.	90	85	80
Oil (per flask)					
Greek fire	10 gp	2 lbs.	60	40	25
Lamp	6 cp	1 lbs.	90	85	80
Torch	1 cp	1 lbs.	95	90	85

* These items weigh little individually. Ten of these items weigh one pound.

Table 9F:
Livestock (Including Mounts and Beasts of Burden)

Item	Cost	Weight	Base Availability* Hi	Med	Low
Ape, Pack (trained)	1,500 gp	400 lbs.	50	30	10
Boar	10 gp	var.	90	85	80
Bull	20 gp	var.	85	75	60
Cow, Calf	5 gp	var.	90	85	80
Cow, Milk	10 gp	var.	90	85	80
Camel	50 gp	var.	90	85	80
Capon	3 cp	var.	90	85	80
Cat, Big, Hunting (jaguar...)	1,500 gp	var.	40	30	20
Cat, Domestic	1 sp	var.	95	90	85
Chicken, Hen, Laying	5 cp	var.	95	90	85
Chicken, Hen, Roasting Kind	2 cp	var.	95	90	85
Cow	10 gp	var.	90	85	80
Dawg	—				
Guard (per skill)	50 gp	var.	80	70	60
Hunting (game specific)	25 gp	var.	85	75	65
Pitbull, Untrained	5 sp	var.	95	80	80
Pitbull, Trained	500 gp	var.	75	65	50
Rottweiler, Untrained	10 sp	var.	90	80	70
Rottweiler, Trained	800 gp	var.	85	75	65
War	100 gp	var.	75	65	55
Dolphin, Mount (trained)	2,000 gp	var.	40	30	20
Dolphin, War (trained)	4,000 gp	var.	30	20	10
Donkey, mule, or ass	8 gp	var.	90	85	80
Elephant	—	—			
Labor	200 gp	var.	75	65	50
War	500 gp	var.	50	40	20
Saber-Toothed	1,500 gp	var.	30	25	15
Falcon, Trained	1,000 gp	var.	80	60	40
Ferret, Trained	70 gp	var.	60	40	20
Goat, Common	1 gp	var.	90	85	80
Goat, Unblemished	8 gp	var	70	50	40
Goat, Pack, Trained	10 gp	var.	70	50	40
Goose	5 cp	var.	90	85	80
Guinea Hen	2 cp	var.	90	85	80
Hawk, Trained	800 gp	var.	80	60	40
Horse	—	—			
Draft	200 gp	var.	90	85	80
Draft, Team	500 gp	var.	80	60	40
Dwarven war	1,300 gp	var.	30	20	10
Heavy war	400 gp	var.	70	50	40
Light war	150 gp	var.	70	50	40
Medium war	225 gp	var.	70	50	40
Riding	75 gp	var.	90	85	80
Shirkmare	2,500 gp	var.	40	30	20
Killer Whale, War (trained)	6,000 gp	var.	25	15	5
Killer Whale, Mount	4,000 gp	var.	30	20	10
Monkey, Trained (per skill)	500 gp	var.	60	40	20
Otter	70 gp	var.	60	40	20
Ox	15 gp	var.	95	90	85
Oxen, Matched Pair	50 gp	var.	85	75	65
Partridge	5 cp	var.	90	85	80
Peacock	5 sp	var.	90	85	80
Pig, Suckling	1 gp	var.	95	90	85
Pig, Sow	3 gp	var.	95	90	85
Pigeon	1 cp	var.	95	90	85
Pigeon, Homing	100 gp	var.	70	50	40
Pigeon, Carrier	150 gp	var.	60	40	30
Pony	30 gp	var.	95	90	85
Ram	4 gp	var.	70	50	40
Rooster	8 cp	var.	95	90	85
Sheep	2 gp	var.	95	90	85
Songbird	10 sp	var.	95	90	85
Swan	5 sp	var.	80	75	70
Weasel, Trained	75 gp	var.	65	45	25

* Quantity Available. If availability check determines the type of livestock desired is available then take the base availability index and divide by ten (round down). The result indicates the number of d20s you should roll to determine how many such animals are available for sale. [In third edition this footnote read 'd100' above. This was a typo as reported in Unearthed Errata volume 6 number 4 and now permanently corrected here.].

A note on slaughtering livestock for meat: The beauty of livestock is that first they're beasts of burden, then later as food stores run low, they're actually self-propelled rations. The formula for determining the yield of edible flesh when slaughtering livestock is: Hit points/10*Size= pounds of edible flesh. Where Size is as follows: Tiny = .25, Small = 2, Medium=4, Large = 6 and Huge = 10, Giant=25. The size of individual livestock is listed in the Hacklopedia of Beasts, which is available only to a GM. Barbarians, rangers and characters with the "Slaughter, Game Animal" skill are able to increase the yield of edible meat by 25%. Characters with "Slaughter, Livestock" skill can increase the yield by 50%.

Table 9G:
Miscellany

Item	Cost	Weight	Base Availability Hi	Med	Low
Book, Used	5 cp(c)	.5	90	80	60
Cloth (per 10 sq. yds.)	—				
Common	7 gp	10 lbs.	95	85	80
Fine	50 gp	10 lbs.	90	80	75
Rich	100 gp	10 lbs.	85	75	70
Canvas (per sq. yard)	4 sp	1 lbs.	95	85	80
Ring, Poison Container	1 gp	—	65	50	45
Water clock	1,000 gp	200 lbs.	80	75	60
Withering Blue (poison)8 oz.	50 gp	—	30	20	10

Price listed is base price for a used book. The actual buying or selling price will vary considerably depending on the subject matter and date of publication. For every year that's passed since the date of publication on a book add 1 copper piece to the value. If the subject is history multiply the base price by a factor of 2. If the subject of the book is arcane in nature multiply the base price by a factor of 10.

Table 9H:
Musical Instruments

Item	Cost	Weight	Base Availability Hi	Med	Low
Bagpipes	60 gp	20 lbs.	70	60	50
Bandore	15 gp	10 lbs.	75	65	55
Chime	2 gp	3 lbs.	90	85	80
Drum	4 gp	8 lbs.	90	85	80
Fife	5 gp	1 lbs.	90	85	80
Flute	15 gp	2 lbs.	85	80	75
Gong	5 gp	10 lbs.	90	85	80
Harp	75 gp	25 lbs.	95	90	85
Horn	6 gp	4 lbs.	80	75	70
Lute	25 gp	1 lbs.	90	85	80
Lyre, Darnetian	200 gp	15 lbs.	70	60	50
Mandolin	28 gp	10 lbs.	90	85	80
Pan Flute	5 gp	1lbs.	95	90	85
Rebec and Bow	30 gp	5 lbs.	90	85	80
Recorder	6 gp	1 lbs.	95	90	85
Whistle	1 gp	.25 lbs.	95	90	85

a town and announce that you're looking for a good set of thieves' picks. To obtain these items requires finesse. In many municipalities it is illegal to own thieves' tools, let alone sell them. Of course, in most large cities, enforcing this is next to impossible.

Salimic Acid: This powerful extract from the poison vine, salimenza is a corrosive acid used by thieves to thwart complicated locks that are stubborn to pick. Beeswax is used to shape a cone/funnel on the keyhole into which the thief pours the acid. It takes 1d6 turns for the acid to do it's work and even then there's only a base 20% chance it will eat away the lock's inner workings to the point that the lock is negated. There is a secondary use for this acid as a powerful poison.

Sharpened Coin: This is a simply coin that has had its edges honed to a sharp edge. A covert tool that can be used to cut purse strings without being detected.

Black Face: A special paste made of soot (lamp black), talc and bacon grease. Adds +3% to a thief's chances of hiding in shadows.

Hacksaw: This is more accurately a coarse file. Thieves often use it to saw through metal bars and padlocks.

Livestock, Mounts and Beasts of Burden

Trained Animals: Any 'trained' animal can shrug off its training and bolt (or in the case of the Pack Ape go 'ape shit') if mistreated. Overloading such animals, not feeding them and pushing them for long periods without rest is sure to make even the most loyal of beasts turn on a character.

When buying a trained animal you are typically paying the base price for each 'skill' the animal has been taught. Your GM has the full list of available skills a particular animal can learn.

Bonding Period: There is a six week 'bonding period' between master and animal (except for mounts, which take 1d20 days) before a character fully earns an animal's trust, loyalty and sometimes respect. This will be modified, of course, by how well (or poorly) the animal is treated.

Animals who are bonded with their masters get modifiers for their morale and vs. fear when their master is present.

Pecking Order: Special care must be taken with animals that have a pack mentality, such as dawgs and apes. Even trained pack animals will respond to the 'call of the wild' and feel the need to establish a pecking order to determine the alpha male and female. Generally, such establishment/re-establishment of the pecking order will result in 5 to 10 percent casualties.

Tack and Harness

Barding: A warhorse, or any animal trained for combat, is a considerable investment for the average fighter. Therefore, it behooves the owner to see that his mount is as well protected as possible. Other than avoiding risks, the best nonmagical protection is horse armor or barding. Barding is simply some type of armor fitted to be worn by a mount. It works the same way as the corresponding personal armor described later in this chapter in terms of Armor Class value and hit point absorption.

Full barding covers the neck, chest, and body of the beast, while half barding covers the head, neck, chest, and front quarters. Half barding provides the same AC protection and damage absorption as full barding but only to front and front flank attacks. Barding can be made from many different materials; stouter types provide increasing protection according to the Armor Class of the construction. All of this, however, is at the expense of increased weight and lowered maneuverability of the mount. Plate barding, for example, is the equivalent of a fighter's field plate and is made of carefully interlocked plates and joints. It provides an Armor Class of 2 to the mount. It weighs at least 80 to 100 pounds at the lightest and thus, a fully equipped warhorse with this armor can manage little more than a steady trot at top speed.

Barded animals also require special attention. Care must be taken to prevent chafing and sores. The mount cannot wear the armor indefinitely. It must be removed at night and ideally should not be worn except in preparation for a battle or tournament. Removing a horse's barding takes 15 minutes for leather and 30 minutes for metal armors. Fitting it takes twice as long.

The weight of barding is carefully distributed to account for the weight of the armor and the rider, so barded animals cannot be used as pack animals! It is normal practice to have a second mount for carrying gear and supplies.

When barding is fitted over a mount with a natural Armor Class better than the barding's afforded AC, some protection is still gained. This is explained under Armor later in this chapter.

Saddles: There are two basic saddles—riding and pack. Riding saddles take many forms, but their basic purpose is to carry a person. Pack saddles are special frames designed to carry supplies and equipment. The only practical limit to how much a well-stowed pack saddle can carry is the carrying ability of the animal.

Transport, Water

Boat, Collapsible: This is a small leather shell which can be stretched into shape by means of several bowed poles. Once stretched out to it's full size it makes a small raft-like boat that can hold two light people (or 300 lbs total in encumbrance). The raft has a low draft and is difficult to paddle but it can get a character across small bodies of water. The boat can remain waterborne for periods up to six hours at a time. After that the leather softens and the stitching begins to leak. (Stretching the boat out and letting it dry in the sun restores its waterproofing however. The boat has another useful feature. It can be used as a one man tent by simply flipping it over.

Caravel: This ship normally has two or three masts and square sails. No oars are used.

The typical caravel is 70 feet long and 20 feet wide. The normal crew is from 30 to 40 men. The average cargo displacement is 150-200 tons.

Coaster: Also called a round ship, this is a small merchant ship that hugs the coasts. This is a sailing ship, fitted with two masts and triangular sails. The average size is 60 to 70 feet long and 20 feet wide. The rudder hangs from one side. The crew is 20 to 30 men, and the cargo capacity is about 100 tons. Normally there is only a small sterncastle. A coaster is slow and not tremen-

dously seaworthy, but it can carry large amounts of cargo with smaller crews than galleys.

Cog: This ship is a larger, improved version of the coaster, able to make ventures into the open sea. Like the coaster, it is a sailing ship with one or two masts, but the cog employs square sails. It is about 75 to 90 feet long and 20 feet wide. The crew is only 18 to 20 men. There is normally one deck and fore- and stern castle. The cargo capacities of cogs vary greatly, but the average is 100 to 200 tons.

Currach: This is an early, primitive vessel. It is made from thick hides stretched over a wood-and-wicker frame. A single mast carries a small square sail, but the currach is usually worked by oars. It is normally 20 to 40 feet long. The crew is approximately six to eight and the cargo space is limited—no more than five tons.

Drakkar: The largest of the barbarian longships is known as a drakkar or dragonship. Built for war, this ship stretches about 100 feet in length. Although a single mast can be raised, oars provide the main source of power. The crew of 60 to 80 men rows, one man to an oar. Up to 160 additional men can be carried for boarding and raiding. Due to its great size, a drakkar is not very seaworthy. This, and the fact there is no space on board for many supplies (certainly not enough for 240 men) or sleeping quarters, keeps the drakkar close to the coast where it can put in for the night. Because of its cost and limited use, a drakkar is usually built by kings and rulers and is not used for the mundane task of shipping cargo.

Table 9I:
Outfitting Bundles (Pre-Packs)

Outfitting bundles are pre-packed assortments of provisions and equipment which characters can buy with a single purchase. This is to help save time so players don't have to meticulously re-provision themselves every few days of game time. Each bundle is tailored to a particular task or character class. They are lettered A to G and list the number of days/weeks the bundle will feed/provision one character. The player simply enters the bundle type on his character sheet followed by the number of days/weeks which he checks off accordingly. This will aid the GM in monitoring player activity. For instance, if a player states he is trying to coax a wild horse into coming closer, and says that he is pulling out a carrot from his pack, the GM can note what bundle type the character is carrying. Then, he can look up the bundle on the following list to determine if the player is indeed, actually carrying a carrot.

Type	Lasts	Cost	Weight
A. Basic Excursion	3 days	25 gp	30 lb.

1 flask of water, 1 loaf of bread, dried fish, sausage, 3 pieces of fruit, 3 vegetables, needle/thread, 10 feet/rope, whetstone

| B. Extended Excursion | 7 days | 50 gp | 75 lb. |

3 flasks of water, 4 loaves of bread, sausage, 6 pieces of fruit, 5 potatoes, 3 carrots, 1 onion, needle/thread, 10 feet/rope, 1 flask lampoil, whetstone, wool blanket

| C. Prolonged Excursion | 14 days | 120 gp | 140 lb. |

3 flasks of water, 1 flask of cut ale, 8 loaves of bread, 2 blocks hard cheese, pickled fish, blood sausage, 10 lbs. of corn dodgers, 1 jar of honey, 1 jar jam, pressed dates, 1 dozen eggs, 5 lbs. of smoked venison, needle/thread, 10 feet/rope, whetstone, tender and flint, 2 flasks of lamp oil

| D. Basic Dungeon Crawl | 1 day | 50 gp | 50 lb. |

1 flask of water, 1 loaf of bread, sausage links, 1 wedge of cheese, 1 apple, needle/thread, 10 feet/rope, whetstone, 5 iron spikes, 10 torches

| E. Extended Dungeon Crawl | 3 days | 100 gp | 85 lb. |

1 flask of water, 2 loaves of bread, 1 jar of honey, 1 jar of nuts, 3 lbs. of corn dodgers, 3 potatoes 1 radish, smoked beef,, whetstone, 10 iron spikes, 20 torches, 2 flasks of lamp oil, a piece of chalk

| F. Basic Overland Excursion | 2 days | 35 gp | 50 lb. |

1 flask of water, 1 wedge of cheese, smoked venison, 1 loaf of bread, peppered sausage, 1 apple, 2 carrots, 1 bag of oats (horse feed), 1 woolen blanket, 1 machette, 10 feet of rope.

| G. Extended Overland Excursion | 7 days | 80 gp | 100 lb. |

2 flasks of water, 2 loaves of bread, 5 pickled eggs, smoked sausage, 5 pieces of fruit, 5 vegetables, 10 feet/rope, whetstone, 3 bag of oats (horsefeed)

Dromond: Although this ship boasts one or two masts and triangular sails, the main power comes from the 100 oars, 50 to a side. These oars are divided into an upper and lower bank, with one man per oar on the lower bank and three men on the upper bank. Thus, the total crew is about 200 men. The dromond is about 130 to 175 feet long and 15 feet wide, making it a very slender ship. The cargo capacity is around 70 to 100 tons.

A dromond can be used both for shipping and war. As a warship, a ram projects from the front just above the water line. Castles are built fore, aft, and amidships as firing platforms. Marines then take up the cargo space. With such numbers of men, it is a very dangerous ship to attack. A dromond is not a seaworthy craft, however, and usually sails in sight of shore. They beach at night like all galleys, since supplies and sleeping accommodations are very limited.

Galleon: This is the largest and most advanced sailing ship that might be available in the HackMaster game. It is a sail-driven ship with three or four masts. There are normally three through decks (running the length of the ship), while the castles fore and aft have two decks. The average size is about 130-feet long and 30-feet wide. Crews average about 130 men. Although cargo capacity is about 500 tons, a galleon is mainly used as a warship. They can easily carry men equal to their tonnage, making capture by pirates nearly impossible.

Galley, Great: The great galley is an improved version of the dromond. It is slightly smaller than the dromond, about 130 feet long and 20 feet wide. The main power comes from 140 rowers, one man to an oar, but is supplemented by three masts; this combination gives it better speed and handling. The cargo capacity is 150 tons. When outfitted as a warship, the front end is built as a ram and marines are carried instead of cargo. Like all galleys, the great galley is a coastal vessel, rarely venturing into open water. It is not seaworthy in heavy storms and waits in port for these to pass.

Galley, War: Similar to the Great Galley in size and crew compliment but ill equipped to carry cargo.

Galley, Trireme: The trireme is similar to the great galley but dedicated to ramming. It's is 135 feet long, 13 feet wide. Crew consists of 170 rowers arranged in three tiers (upper, middle and lower) so that more oars can be placed in the water. 10 marines and 4 archers round out the ship's full compliment along with a captain and a flautist to keep time. A single masted sail can be erected but this coastal vessel is not suited for the open water.

Galley, Deceres : This mammoth war ship is uncontested when it comes to galleys. Over 145 feet in length and 20 feet wide it is one of the largest ships

Table 9J: Provisions: Rations

Item	Cost	Weight	Hi	Med	Low
Barrel of pickled fish	3 gp	500 lbs.	90	85	80
Butter (per lb.)	2 sp	1 lbs.	85	80	75
Coarse sugar (per lb.)	1 gp	1 lbs.	70	60	50
Corn dodgers (2 weeks rations)	5 gp	75 lbs.	90	85	80
Eggs (per 100)	8 sp	15 lbs.	90	85	80
Eggs (per two dozen)	2 sp	3 lbs.	90	85	80
Figs (per lb.)	3 sp	1 lbs.	85	80	75
Fish, Parvum (1 day's rations)	1 sp	2 lbs.	70	60	50
Fish, Salted (1 day's rations)	5 cp	3 lbs.	85	80	75
Herbs (per lb.)	5 cp	1 lbs.	90	85	80
Belladonna, sprig	4 sp	1 lbs.	90	85	80
Garlic, bud	5 cp	1 lbs.	90	85	80
Wolvesbane, sprig	1 gp	1 lbs.	90	85	80
Nuts (per lb.)	1 gp	1 lbs.	90	85	80
Preserves, Fruit (1 day's rations)	5 cp	1 lbs.	85	80	75
Raisins (per lb.)	2 sp	1 lbs.	90	85	80
Rations, Dry (1 week's rations)	10 gp	65 lbs.	85	80	75
Rations, Iron (1 week's rations)	5 gp	25 lbs.	90	85	80
Rations, Standard (1 week's rations)	3 gp	50 lbs.	85	80	75
Rice (per lb.)	2 sp	1 lbs.	90	85	80
Salt, 1 lb bag	1 gp	1 lbs.	85	80	75
Sausage, Blood (1 meal)	1 sp	.5 lbs.	90	85	80
Sausage, Peppered (1 meal)	2 sp	1 lbs.	85	80	75
Sausage, Sailor's (1 week's rations)	2 gp	15 lbs.	90	85	80
Spice (per lb.)	—				
Exotic (saffron, clove)	15 gp	.5 lbs.	80	75	65
Rare (pepper, ginger)	2 gp	.5 lbs.	70	60	50
Uncommon (cinnamon)	1 gp	.5 lbs.	75	65	55
Venison, Smoked (1 meal)	1 gp	.5 lbs.	90	85	80
Tun of cider (250 gal.)	8 gp	2500 lbs.	90	85	80
Tun of good wine (250 gal.)	20 gp	2500 lbs.	95	85	70

Table 9K: Provisions: Outfitting

Item	Cost	Weight	Hi	Med	Low
Chain (per ft.)	—	—			
Heavy	4 gp	3 lbs.	95	85	70
Light	3 gp	1 lbs.	95	85	70
Chalk	1 cp	*	95	85	70
Firewood (per day)	1 cp	200 lbs.	95	90	85
Fishhook	1 sp	**	95	90	85
Fishing net, 10 ft. sq.	4 gp	5 lbs.	90	85	80
Hourglass	25 gp	1 lbs.	85	75	65
Ladder, 10 ft.	5 cp	20 lbs.	95	90	85
Lock	—	—			
Good	100 gp	1 lbs.	90	85	80
Poor	20 gp	1 lbs.	90	85	80
Mirror, small metal	10 gp	*	90	85	80
Perfume (per vial)	5 gp	*	90	85	80
Piton	3 cp	.5 lbs.	90	85	80
Rope (per 50 ft.)	—	—			
Hemp	1 gp	20 lbs.	90	85	80
Silk	10 gp	8 lbs.	70	60	50
Signal whistle	8 sp	*	90	85	80
Soap (per lb.)	5 sp	1 lbs.	90	85	80
Tent	—	—			
Large	25 gp	20 lbs.	80	75	70
Pavilion	100 gp	50 lbs.	80	75	70
Small	5 gp	10 lbs.	80	75	70
Winter blanket	5 sp	3 lbs.	90	85	80

* These items weigh little individually. Ten of these items weigh one pound.
** These items have no appreciable weight and should not be considered for encumbrance unless hundreds are carried.

Table 9L: Tools

Item	Cost	Weight	Hi	Med	Low
Block and tackle	5 gp	5 lbs.	90	85	80
Carpentry Tools (set)	50 gp	60 lbs.	90	85	80
Crampons	4 gp	2 lbs.	90	85	80
Crowbar/Pry bar	10 sp	10 lbs.	90	85	80
Flint and steel	5 sp	*	90	85	80
Grappling hook	8 sp	4 lbs.	90	85	80
Mining Tools (set)	2 gp	30 lbs.	90	85	80
Magnifying glass	100 gp	*	85	75	70
Merchant's scale	2 gp	1 lbs.	90	85	80
Portable Forge	400 gp	500 lbs.	80	75	70
Repair Kit, Armor	—				
Banded mail	20 gp	10 lbs.	80	70	60
Brigandine	10gp	5 lbs.	85	80	75
Bronze Plate mail	20 gp	10 lbs.	80	70	60
Chain mail	12gp	10 lbs.	85	80	75
Field plate	50 gp	15 lbs.	65	45	25
Full Plate	100 gp	20 lbs.	50	30	10
Hide	6 gp	3.5 lbs.	90	85	80
Leather	5gp	3 lbs.	90	85	80
Padded	1gp	2 lbs.	90	85	80
Plate mail	25 gp	10 lbs.	80	70	60
Ring mail	5 gp	5 lbs.	85	80	75
Robes	10 gp	.25 lb.	90	85	80
Scale mail	5 gp	10 lbs.	90	85	80
Splint	17 gp	10 lbs.	80	70	60
Studded Leather	10 gp	6 lbs.	85	80	75
Repair Kit, Sail/Nautical	50 gp	50 lbs.	90	85	80
Spyglass	1,000 gp	1 lbs.	80	65	50
Surgeon's Kit	100 gp	20 lbs.	85	75	70
Thieves' Tools**	—				
Coin Sharpened (Cut Purse)	5 sp	.25 lbs.	95	90	85
Hacksaw (hardened)	5 sp	3 lbs.	85	75	70
Key Making set	50 gp	3 lbs.	75	65	55
Lockpick set	30 gp	1 lbs.	70	65	60
Locksmithing Tools	100 gp	5 lbs.	85	75	70
Salimic Acid, Vial	150 gp	*	65	55	45
Soot/Face Black	10 sp	—	95	95	95
Whetstone	2 cp	1 lbs.	95	90	85

* These items weigh little individually. Ten of these items weigh one pound.
** Thieves and assassins may add +20 to the base availability chance when searching for thieves' tools due to their connections with the thieves' guild and underground.

Table 9M: Religious Items and Accouterments					
			Base Availability		
Item	Cost	Weight	Hi	Med	Low
Beads, Prayer	1 gp	—	95	85	80
Incense, Burner	1 gp	—	95	85	80
Incense, Stick (per dozen)	5 cp	—	95	85	80
Robes, Clerical	25 to 500 gp	—	85	80	75
Snake, Bond	100 gp	—	70	65	60
Symbol, Holy/Unholy gold	50 gp	1 lbs.	95	85	80
Symbol, Holy/Unholy iron	5 gp	1 lbs.	95	85	80
Symbol, Holy/Unholy silver	10 gp	1 lbs.	95	85	80
Symbol, Holy/Unholy wood	1 gp	.5 lbs.	95	85	80
Water, Holy/Unholy gold	25 gp	1 lbs.	95	85	80

Table 9N: Scribe Materials					
			Base Availability		
Item	Cost	Weight	Hi	Med	Low
Ink Pot/Vial	8 gp	*	95	85	80
Journal, Blank 100 pages	75 gp	1 lb	80	75	70
Paper (per sheet)	2 gp	**	85	80	75
Papyrus (per sheet)	8 sp	**	80	75	70
Parchment (per sheet)	1 gp	**	90	85	80
Pen, Bone/Ivory/Wood	8 sp	.25 lbs.	95	85	80
Pen, Quill	2 cp	.25 lbs.	95	85	80
Sealing/candle wax (per lb.)	1 gp	1 lbs.	90	85	80
Signet ring or personal seal	5 gp	.25 lbs.	95	85	80
Stylus, Wood	5 cp	.25 lbs.	95	85	80
Tablet, Silted Clay	1 gp	1 lbs.	95	85	80
Tablet, Wax	10 sp	1 lbs.	95	85	80
Vellum (per sheet)	8 gp	**	80	75	70

* These items weigh little individually. Ten of these items weigh one pound.
** These items have no appreciable weight and should not be considered for encumbrance unless hundreds are carried.

to ply the waters of Garweeze Wurld. 572 rowers power oars over forty feet in length. It takes 30 crewmen to man the ship. During times of war the Deceres can carry 250 extra passengers in the form of armed marines. The ship is equipped with two fighting towers and two to six catapults.

Knarr: This small ship is 50 to 75 feet long and 15 to 20 feet wide. It has a single mast and a square sail. In times of poor wind, a few oars at the bow and stern can provide more power. The crew ranges from eight to 14 men. The cargo capacity is small, anywhere from ten to 50 tons. The ship is, however, relatively seaworthy and can be used to make long sea voyages (although it cannot be called comfortable). Its flat bottom makes it useful for sailing up rivers and estuaries, and it can be beached easily.

Longship: This is the standard barbarian warship. It is more substantial than the knarr but not nearly as massive as the drakkar. An average longship is 75 feet long with 20 to 25 oars per side. Each oar is worked by a single man, for a total crew of 40 to 50 men. There is also a single mast and a square sail. In addition to the crew, the ship can carry 120 to 150 men. A longship can be used for shipping, but its cargo capacity is only about 50 tons. It is, however, fairly seaworthy and can sail across the open sea when necessary.

Armor

You are going to want your player character to buy armor. Armor is the easiest and cheapest way to improve your character's chance of surviving the more violent dangers of the adventuring life. Clearly, the better the armor the character possesses, the less likely he is to be hurt. Armor protection is measured by Armor Class (AC), a number rating; the lower the Armor Class number, the better the protection. Certain classes have restrictions on the type of armor they can wear. For other classes, armor reduces the effectiveness or success chance of their skills (e.g., try moving silently in a suit of chain mail).

Banded: This armor is made of overlapping strips of metal sewn to a backing of leather and chain mail. Generally the strips cover only the more vulnerable areas, while the chain and leather protect the joints where freedom of movement must be ensured. Through straps and buckles, the weight is more or less evenly distributed.

Brigandine: This armor is made from small metal plates sewn or riveted to a layer of canvas or leather and protected by an outer layer of cloth. It is rather

stiff and does not provide adequate protection to the joints where the metal plates must be spaced widely or left off.

Bronze Plate Mail: This is a plate mail armor—a combination of metal plates, chain mail or brigandine, leather and padding—made of softer bronze. It is easier and cheaper to make than steel armor, but it does not protect as well. A large breastplate and other metal plates cover areas of the body, but the other materials must protect the joints and movable parts of the body. It is not the full plate armor of the heavy type.

Chain Mail: This armor is made of interlocking metal rings. It is always worn with a layer of quilted fabric padding underneath to prevent painful chafing and to cushion the impact of blows. Several layers of mail are normally hung over vital areas. The links yield easily to blows, absorbing some of the shock. Most of the weight of this armor is carried on the shoulders and it is uncomfortable to wear for long periods of time.

Field Plate: This is the most common version of full plate armor, consisting of shaped and fitted metal plates riveted and interlocked to cover the entire body. It includes gauntlets, boots, and a visored helmet. A thick layer of padding must be worn underneath.

However, the weight of the suit is well distributed over the whole body. Such armor hampers movement only slightly. Aside from its expense, the main disadvantages are the lack of ventilation and the time required putting it on and taking it off (see **Getting Into and Out of Armor**- this chapter). Each suit of field plate must be individually fitted to its owner by a master armorer, although captured pieces can be resized to fit the new owner (unless such is patently absurd, such as a human trying to resize a halfling's armor).

Full Plate: This is the impressive, complete body armor. It is perfectly forged and fitted. All the plates are interlocking and carefully angled to deflect blows. The surfaces are normally highly ornamented with etching and inlaid metals. Each suit must be carefully custom-fitted to the owner and there is only a 20% chance that a captured suit can be refitted to a new owner of approximately the same size. The metal plates are backed with padding and chainmail. The weight is well distributed. The armor is hot, slow to don, and extremely expensive. Due to these factors, it tends to be used more for parades and triumphs than actual combat.

Hide: This is armor prepared from the extremely thick hide of a creature (such as an elephant) or from multiple layers of regular leather. It is stiff and hard to move in.

Leather: This armor is made of leather hardened in boiling oil and then shaped into breastplate and shoulder protectors. The remainder of the suit is fashioned from more flexible, somewhat softer materials.

Padded: This is the simplest type of armor, fashioned from quilted layers of cloth and batting. It tends to get hot and after a time becomes foul with sweat, grime, lice and fleas.

Plate Mail: This armor is a combination of chain or brigandine with metal plates (cuirass, epaulettes, elbow guards, gauntlets, tasses, and greaves) covering vital areas. The weight is distributed over the whole body and the whole

Table 9O: Services					
			Base Availability		
Item	Cost	Weight	Hi	Med	Low
Bath	3 cp	—	95	85	80
Doctor, Leech, or Bleeding	3 gp	—	90	85	80
Doctor, Sew Wounds	10 gp	—	90	85	80
Guide, in city (per day)	2 sp	—	90	85	80
Lantern or torchbearer (per night)	1 sp	—	90	85	80
Laundry (by load)	1 cp	—	85	80	70
Massage	1 gp	—	90	85	80
Messenger, 10 to 50 miles	1 gp	—	95	85	80
Messenger, 51 to 100 miles	5 gp	—	90	85	80
Messenger, in city (per message)	10 cp	—	85	80	75
Messenger, per 100 miles	5 gp	—	80	75	70
Minstrel (per performance)	3 gp	—	90	85	80
Mourner (per funeral)	2 sp	—	90	85	80
Scout, Wilderness (per day)	1 gp	—	90	85	80
Scribe, Legal document/contract	10 sp	—	90	85	80
Scribe, Letter	2 sp	—	90	85	80
Tattoo (per design)	1 gp	—	95	85	80
Teamster w/wagon	1 sp/mile	—	90	85	80

thing is held together by buckles and straps. This is the most common form of heavy armor.

Ring Mail: This armor is an early (and less effective) form of chain mail in which metal rings are sewn directly to a leather backing instead of being interlaced.

Scale Mail: This is a coat and leggings (and perhaps a separate skirt) of leather covered with overlapping pieces of metal, much like the scales of a fish.

Shields: All shields improve a character's Armor Class by 1 or more against a specified number of attacks. A shield is useful only to protect the front and flanks of the user. Attacks from the rear or rear flanks cannot be blocked by a shield (exception: a shield slung across the back does help defend against rear attacks). The reference to the size of the shield is relative to the size of the character. Thus, a human's small shield would have all the effects of a medium shield when used by a gnome (except hit points, explained later).

A buckler (or target) is a very small shield that fastens on the forearm. Crossbowmen or archers can wear it with no hindrance. Its small size enables it to protect against only one frontal attack per melee round (of the user's choice), improving the character's Armor Class by 1 against that attack.

Table 9P: Tack and Harness

Item	Cost	Weight	Hi	Med	Low
Barding Horse**	—				
Chain	500 gp	70 lbs.	85	80	75
Full plate	2,000 gp	85 lbs.	70	65	60
Full scale	1,000 gp	75 lbs.	75	70	65
Half brigandine	500 gp	45 lbs.	85	80	75
Half padded	100 gp	25 lbs.	90	85	80
Half scale	500 gp	50 lbs.	85	80	75
Leather or padded	150 gp	60 lbs.	95	90	85
Barding, Dolphin					
Chain	1,000 gp	30 lbs.	35	25	10
Leather	500 gp	20 lbs.	45	35	30
Barding, Killer Whale					
Chain	1,700 gp	60 lbs.	35	25	10
Leather	900 gp	50 lbs.	45	35	30
Bit and bridle	15 sp	3 lbs.	95	85	80
Blinders, Horse	05 sp	3 lbs.	95	85	80
Cart harness	2 gp	10 lbs.	95	85	80
Fort, Elephant	400 gp	300 lbs.	55	50	45
Halter	5 cp	*	95	85	80
Horseshoes & shoeing	1 gp	10 lbs.	95	85	80
Saddle	—	—			
Pack	5 gp	15 lbs.	95	85	80
Riding	10 gp	35 lbs.	95	85	80
Saddle bags	—	—			
Large	4 gp	8 lbs.	95	85	80
Small	3 gp	5 lbs.	95	85	80
Saddle blanket	3 sp	4 lbs.	95	85	80
Yoke	—	—			
Horse	5 gp	15 lbs.	95	85	80
Ox	3 gp	20 lbs.	95	85	80

* These items weigh little individually. Ten of these items weigh one pound.
** For barding for Elephants multiply price by 3 and weight by four.
Bonding with a new mount takes 1d20 days. Until bonding period is complete any new mount is likely to be skittish and have lower morale.

Table 9Q: Transport, Land*

Item	Cost	Weight	Hi	Med	Low
Cart, Small	5 gp	—	90	85	80
Carriage	—				
Common	150 gp	—	90	85	80
Coach, ornamented	7,000 gp	—	75	70	65
Chariot	—				
Riding	200 gp	—	80	75	70
War	500 gp	—	75	70	65
Sedan chair	100 gp	—	90	85	80
Wagon, Two-Wheeled	60 gp	—	90	85	80
Wagon, Four Wheeled	125 gp	—	85	80	75
Wheel, Replacement (spoked)	5 gp	65 lbs.	90	85	80
Wheel, Replacement (planked)	1 gp	125 lbs.	90	85	80

*Movement rates for this equipment are given in the GMG

Table 9R: Transport, Water*

Item	Cost	Weight	Hi	Med	Low
Barge, River	500 gp	—	90	85	80
Boat, Collapsible	300 gp	—	90	85	80
Canoe	—				
Small	30 gp	—	90	85	80
War	50 gp	—	90	85	80
Caravel	10,000 gp	—	60	50	40
Coaster	5,000 gp	—	70	65	60
Cog	10,000 gp	—	60	50	40
Currach	500 gp	—	85	80	75
Drakkar	25,000 gp	—	45	35	25
Dromond	15,000 gp	—	60	50	40
Galleon	50,000 gp	—	40	30	20
Galley, Great	30,000 gp	—	45	35	25
Galley, War	45,000 gp	—	40	30	20
Galley, Trireme	80,000 gp	—	40	30	20
Galley, Duceres	1,000,000 gp	—	35	25	10
Knarr	3,000 gp	—	65	60	55
Longship	10,000 gp	—	60	50	40
Oar, Replacement					
Common	2 gp	25lbs.	90	85	80
Galley	10 gp	120 lbs.	80	70	60
Raft or small keelboat	100 gp	—	90	85	80
Sail, Standard size	20 gp	—	90	85	80
Sail, Made to spec.	150gp+	—	90	85	80
Ship, Merchant, Large	15,000 gp	—	60	50	40
Ship, Merchant, Small	7,500 gp	—	65	60	55

*Movement rates for this equipment are given in the GMG

A small shield is carried on the forearm and gripped with the hand. Its lightweight permits the user to carry other items in that hand (although he cannot use weapons). It can be used to protect against two frontal attacks of the user's choice.

The medium shield is carried in the same manner as the small shield. Its weight prevents the character from using his shield hand for other purposes. With a medium shield, a character can protect against any frontal or flank attacks.

The body shield is a massive shield reaching nearly from chin to toe. It must be firmly fastened to the forearm and the shield hand must grip it at all times. It provides a great deal of protection, improving the Armor Class of the character by 4 against melee attacks and by 6 against missile attacks. The body shield protects for all attacks from the front or front flank sides. It is very heavy.

Splint Mail: This armor is made of narrow vertical strips riveted to a backing of leather and cloth padding.

Since this is not flexible, the joints are protected by chain mail.

Studded Leather: This armor is made from leather (not hardened as with normal leather armor) reinforced with close-set metal rivets. In some ways it is very similar to brigandine, although the spacing between each metal piece is greater.

Armor Sizes

The equipment list reflects the price of a suit of armor (including an appropriate helmet) made for any normal player character race. Although a pixie-fairy is much smaller than a human and needs a smaller suit, there are fewer armorers available to meet such specialized needs. Thus, the armor for a pixie-fairy is as expensive as that for a human.

Nonstandard sizes and shapes of armor are going to cost significantly more and must be custom-made. This is not the kind of thing one can pick up at the local store! When armor is found during the course of an adventure, the players should note the characteristics of the creature that wore the armor previously. While a human-sized character might be able to wear the armor of a gnoll, it will do little good for a gnome titan. Likewise, the armor of a giant is of little use to anyone (other than another giant).

Armor size also affects the weight of the armor. The weights listed on the table are for human-sized (medium) armors. Small armor weighs half the amount listed, while large armor weighs 50% more. Pixie-fairy armor weighs one-tenth the amount listed.

Table 9S: Armor and Related Items

Item	Cost	AC	HP	Weight	Bulk	Base Availability Hi	Med	Low
Robes/Garments	Varies	9	1	Varies	non	Varies (see Table 9B)		
Leather	5 gp	8	2	15 lbs.	non	95	90	85
Padded	4 gp	8	2	10 lbs.	fairly	95	90	85
Ring mail	65 gp	7	6	30 lbs.	fairly	90	85	80
Studded leather	40 gp	7	4	25 lbs.	fairly	95	90	85
Scale mail	120 gp	6	7	40 lbs.	fairly	90	85	80
Hide	75 gp	6	5	35 lbs.	fairly	95	90	85
Brigandine	120 gp	6	6	35 lbs.	fairly	90	85	80
Chain mail	350 gp	5	8	40 lbs.	fairly	95	90	85
Chain mail, Elven	700gp	5	8	20 lbs.	non	30	20	10
Bronze plate mail	1,000 gp	4	12	45 lbs.	bulky	85	80	75
Banded mail	900 gp	4	9	35 lbs.	bulky	90	85	80
Splint mail	600 gp	4	8	40 lbs.	bulky	95	90	85
Plate mail	2,000 gp	3	12	50 lbs.	bulky	85	80	75
Field plate	4,000 gp	2	24**	60 lbs.	bulky	70	65	60
Full plate	6,000-10,000 gp	1	36**	70 lbs.	bulky	65	60	55
Helmet								
Great helm	30 gp	—	—	10 lbs.	bulky	70	65	60
Basinet	8 gp	—	—	5 lbs.	fairly	95	90	85
Shield								
Buckler	5 gp	+1	3	3 lbs.	non	90	85	80
Buckler, Spiked	15 gp	+1	3	4 lbs.	non	90	85	80
Small	20 gp	+2	4	5 lbs.	non	90	85	80
Medium	30 gp	+3	5	10 lbs.	fairly	90	85	80
Body*	100 gp	+4 (+6)	6	25 lbs.	bulky	90	85	80

* A body shield affords +6 AC against missile weapons.
** Field and full-plate absorb 2 hit points per die.

Table 9W: Hit Point Absorption Regression for Damaged Armor

Item	1	2	3	4	5	6	7	8	9
Robes/Garments	—	—	—	—	—	—	—	—	1
Leather	—	—	—	—	—	—	—	2	1
Padded	—	—	—	—	—	—	—	2	1
Ring mail	—	—	—	—	—	—	6	2	1
Studded leather	—	—	—	—	—	—	4	2	1
Scale mail	—	—	—	—	—	7	4	2	1
Hide	—	—	—	—	—	5	4	2	1
Brigandine	—	—	—	—	—	6	4	2	1
Chain mail	—	—	—	—	8	6	4	2	1
Bronze plate mail	—	—	—	12	8	6	4	2	1
Banded mail	—	—	—	9	8	6	4	2	1
Splint mail	—	—	—	8	8	6	4	2	1
Plate mail	—	—	12	10	8	6	4	2	1
Field plate	—	24*	12	10	8	6	4	2	1
Full plate	36*	24*	12	10	8	6	4	2	1

Armor Class

*Field and full-plate absorb 2 hit points per die.

Armor Hit Points

As is obvious to anyone with a second grade education or higher, all armor types not only protect the wearer from damage as defined herein as an AC increase, but also absorb damage to a certain degree. In HackMaster, armor absorption works as follows. Each armor type has a certain hit point value associated with it (clearly leather armor does not absorb as much damage as a metal suit of plate mail). For each die of damage rolled against a character on a successful hit (i.e., the hit has penetrated your armor), the armor absorbs one point of the damage. If the roll was one, you take no damage from that attack; the armor takes a point of damage instead. When the armor gets to zero, it has lost so much material and so many rifts and holes then exist that it drops in protective value (i.e., the AC drops one point). Each time armor takes its

Table 9X: Shield Hit Points

Item\AC modifier	+4	+3	+2	+1
Buckler	—	—	—	3
Small	—	—	4	3
Medium	—	5	4	3
Body	6	5	4	3

full hit points it drops to the armor equivalent of the level just below. Table 9W: Hit Point Absorption Regression for Damaged Armor, shows the exact progression for armor, while Table 9X: Shield Hit Points, shows equivalent information for shields. For example, fighter Andy wears platemail. He gets hit with an 8 die Fireball, then suffers two whacks from an orc brandishing a broadsword (2d4 damage per hit). Andy's plate mail has taken 12 damage (8 from the Fireball, 2 from each broadsword chop) and is beaten enough to drop one armor rating from AC 3 to AC 4. If it suffers 10 more points of damage it drops to AC 5. Eight more knock it to AC 6, six more and AC 7, four more and AC 8, two more and AC 9, one more and Andy's armor is totally destroyed and in pieces. Armor can be repaired at great cost and expense by hiring an armorer or buying a repair kit and paying the additional raw material costs (note, in the latter case, your character must also have the appropriate armor repair skill). Typically, it's cheaper to repair armor than to buy new, but if your armor suffers too much, or you don't take proper care of it, it will eventually become totaled (i.e., the cost of repairing it will exceed the cost of a new suit).

Shield Hit Points

Shields also have a hit point total associated with them. This total represents the amount of punishment the shield itself can take. Whenever an opponent misses you by the defense bonus of the shield or less, the shield suffers full damage (in effect, the shield took the brunt of the blow). Shields drop in class as they take damage just like armor.

You can also add your shield AC modifier to saving throws against destructive spells and situations (see Chapter 12 for the details on saving throws), but you must declare this before rolling your save and the shield takes full damage whether you successfully save or not. Even if you choose against using your shield as a bonus for your save, area effect spells deliver full damage to the shield if you fail your save. Note that shields hardly last long at all, but they help you from suffering too much early on. So buy a mule and load it up with shields for use in the dungeon.

Getting Into and Out of Armor

There are times when it is important to know how quickly a character can get into or out of his armor. Accidents and unforeseen events happen all the time. The party is attacked at night. Those sleeping around the campfire in their skivvies may want to don their armor before rushing into battle against Jurassic Badgers. A character slips and falls into the river where his heavy armor pulls him down like a stone. He greatly desires to get it off before he drowns face down in the muck at the bottom of the sewage-filled river downstream of the city. Just how long does it take him?

The time required to don armor depends on its make. Those armors that are a single piece—leather tunics, robes, chain mail—take one round (two for metal items) to don with slight assistance. Without aid, the time is doubled. Armor that is made of separate pieces require 1d6 + 4 rounds, again with assistance. Without help, the time required is tripled.

In all cases, the times given assume that the proper undergarments and padding are also worn.

Sometimes characters need to get into armor in a hurry and thus, they dress hastily. This assumes that some buckles aren't fastened, seating adjusted, etc. Single suits can be hastily donned in one round at the cost of 1 point of AC (though the AC will never get worse than 8). Thus, a fighter could hastily pull on his brigandine jack (AC 6) and charge into a fray with an AC of 7. Hastily donning piece armor (plate mail for example) improves the character's AC by 1 (from a base of 10) for every round spent dressing. A fighter could choose to spend three rounds fitting on parts of his plate mail, giving him an AC of 7, before going into battle. Additionally, hastily donned armor's hit points are reduced to the number corresponding to its effective AC at the time.

Removing armor is a much quicker matter. Most can be shed in a single round. Piece armor (particularly full plate) requires 1d4 + 1 rounds. However, if the character is willing to cut straps and bend pins, such armors can be removed in half the time (roll 1d4 + 1, divide by 2, then round fractions up).

Creatures with Natural Armor Classes

Some creatures possess a natural Armor Class already superior to some of the armor types (for example, the horse is AC 7). However, these creatures can still benefit from wearing armor of a quality worse than their natural Armor Class. If the AC of armor is equal to or worse than the AC of the creature, the AC of the creature improves by 1.

For example, a horse has a natural AC of 7. The AC of leather armor is 8, worse than the horse's natural AC. However, if a horse is fitted with leather barding, its AC drops to 6 since it gains the benefit of the additional protection.

Weapons

The Weapons Table lists more than just the price of each item. It also gives other game information. Since each weapon is different, you should note this information separately for each weapon that your character purchases or finds.

Weapon Size: All weapons are classed according to a size category—S, M or L. Small (S) weapons are approximately two feet or less in size; medium (M) weapons are two to five feet long; large (L) weapons are generally six feet or greater in length.

A character can always wield a weapon equal to his own size or less. Normally this requires only one hand, except for some missile weapons (bows and crossbows in particular). A character can also use a weapon one size greater than himself, although it must be gripped with two hands. Beyond this size limit, the weapon is not usable without special help (most often magical).

Tiny Toes, the halfling (size S), can use a short sword with no difficulty (a size S weapon), or a long sword with two hands (a size M weapon), but a glaive

(size L) is just too large for him to wield. Likewise, he can use a short bow but is unable to handle a long bow.

Type: Weapons are classified according to types—crushing (C), puncturing (P), and hacking (H). These types are used to determine armor type modifiers. Weapons vs. armor type is explained in Chapter 12: Combat.

Speed Factor: Weapon speed is a relative measure of the clumsiness of the weapon. The lower the number, the quicker and easier the weapon is to use. Weapon speed is explained in Chapter 12: Combat.

Damage: All weapons are rated for the amount of damage they can cause to small (S), medium (M) and larger-than-man-sized creatures (L). All weapon damage rolls have a minimum or one point of damage.

Bows: Bows come in various shapes and sizes. The power of a bow is measured by its pull. The greater the pull, the more Strength needed to work the bow. Thus, it is possible for characters to have bows that grant them damage bonuses for high Strength (it is assumed the character has chosen a bow that has a greater pull). Likewise, characters with low Strengths suffer their usual penalties when using a bow (they are forced to use weaker bows or simply cannot draw back as far making them look ridiculous, like some kind of adventuring cupid). The pull of a bow seldom prevents a character from using the weapon, only from gaining the full effect. The true test of a character's Strength comes in stringing a bow – the bow of a strong hero may simply be unstringable by a lesser man.

Bows with heavier pull are not normally any more expensive than standard bows. The exceptions to this are those bows that enable the user to gain a strength bonus. These bows must be custom crafted and cost three to five times the normal price. These bows are also difficult to string or use effectively for those without bonus-level Strength. Such inferior characters must roll a successful bend bars/lift gates roll to string or use such weapons.

						Damage vs.			Base Availability		
Item	Cost	Weight	Size	Damage Type[6]	Speed Factor	S	M	L	H	Med	Low
Battle axe	5 gp	7 lbs.	M	H	2	2d4	2d4	2d4	90	85	80
Blowgun	5 gp	2 lbs.	L	—	—	Δ	Δ	Δ	90	85	80
Bow	—	—	—	—	—						
Composite long bow	100 gp	3 lbs.	L	—	—	Δ	Δ	Δ	85	80	75
Composite short bow	75 gp	2 lbs.	M	—	—	Δ	Δ	Δ	80	75	70
Great Long bow (elven)	800gp	4 lbs.	L	—	—	Δ	Δ	Δ	20	10	5
Long bow	75 gp	3 lbs.	L	—	—	Δ	Δ	Δ	90	85	80
Short bow	30 gp	2 lbs.	M	—	—	Δ	Δ	Δ	90	85	80
Club	—	3 lbs.	M	C	-1	1d8	1d6	1d6-2	95	90	85
Crossbow	—	—	—	—	—	—	—	—	—	—	—
Hand crossbow	300 gp	3 lbs.	S	—	—	Δ	Δ	Δ	75	70	65
Heavy crossbow	50 gp	14 lbs.	M	—	—	Δ	Δ	Δ	85	80	75
Light crossbow	35 gp	7 lbs.	M	—	—	Δ	Δ	Δ	80	75	70
Peashooter crossbow	350 gp	.5 lbs.	S	—	—	Δ	Δ	Δ	55	40	25
Dagger or dirk	2 gp	1 lbs.	S	P	-3	1d6	1d6-1	1d6-2	95	90	85
Dart	5 sp	.5 lbs.	S	P	—	1d6-1	1d6-2	1d6-4	95	90	85
Footman's flail	15 gp	15 lbs.	M	C	2	1d6	1d6+1	2d4	90	85	80
Footman's mace	8 gp	10 lbs.	M	C	2	1d8	1d6+1	1d6	90	85	80
Footman's pick	8 gp	6 lbs.	M	P	2	1d6	1d6+1	2d4	95	90	85
Hand or throwing axe	1 gp	5 lbs.	M	H	-1	1d8	1d6	1d6-1	95	90	85
Harpoon	20 gp	6 lbs.	L	P	2	1d6	2d4	2d6	95	90	85
Horseman's flail	8 gp	5 lbs.	M	C	1	1d4+1	1d4+1	1d4+1	90	85	80
Horseman's mace	5 gp	6 lbs.	M	C	1	1d8	1d6	1d6-1	90	85	80
Horseman's pick	7 gp	4 lbs.	M	P	0	1d6	1d6-1	1d6-2	90	85	80
Hurled Tankard, Full[8]	—	3 lbs.	S	C	—	1d6	1d6-1	1d6-2	90	85	80
Hurled Tankard, Empty	—	2 lbs.	S	C	—	1d6-1	1d6-2	1d6-4	90	85	80
Javelin	5 sp	2 lbs.	M	P	—	1d6	1d6	1d6	95	90	85
Knife	5 sp	.5 lbs.	S	P/H	-3	1d6-1	1d6-2	1d6-4	95	90	85
Lance[4]	—	—	—	—	—	—	—	—	—	—	—
Heavy horse lance	15 gp	15 lbs.	L	P	3	1d6	1d8+1	3d6	85	80	75
Light horse lance	6 gp	5 lbs.	L	P	1	1d6-1	1d6	1d8	85	80	75
Jousting lance	20 gp	20 lbs.	L	P	5	1d6-3	1d6-2	1d4+1	85	80	75
Medium horse lance	10 gp	10 lbs.	L	P	2	1d4+1	1d6+1	2d6	85	80	75
Mancatcher[2]	30 gp	8 lbs.	L	—	2	—	—	—	95	90	85
Morning star	10 gp	12 lbs.	M	C	2	2d4+1	2d4	1d6+1	85	80	75
Polearm	—	—	—	—	—	—	—	—	—	—	—
Awl pike[5]	5 gp	12 lbs.	L	P	8	1d4	1d6	1d12	90	85	80
Bardiche	7 gp	12 lbs.	L	H	4	1d6	2d4	2d6	95	90	85
Bec de corbin	8 gp	10 lbs.	L	P/C	4	1d10	1d8	1d6	95	90	85
Bill-guisarme	7 gp	15 lbs.	L	P/H	5	1d8	2d4	1d10	95	90	85
Fauchard	5 gp	7 lbs.	L	P/H	3	1d4	1d6	1d8	90	85	80
Fauchard-fork	8 gp	9 lbs.	L	P/H	3	1d6	1d8	1d10	95	90	85

Δ The damage for these missile weapons is dependent upon the ammo used. They are detailed on Table 9U, Weapons: Ammo.

Arrows for long bows of all types are divided between lightweight flight arrows and heavier sheaf arrows. Flight arrows have longer ranges and are normally used in hunting. Sheaf arrows have a stronger metal head but a reduced range. They are often used in times of war.

Crossbow: Strength bonuses or penalties do not apply to crossbows, since they are purely mechanical devices. The peashooter crossbow is impossible to use without great care for anyone larger than a gnome. Even the wee-folk (ideal for pixie-fairies for whom they are designed) must use two hands to operate them. Peashooters hold two tiny darts, fired simultaneously. They must be braced against an object and cocked with two hands (for the fairy-folk). The hand crossbow is easily held in one hand and cocked with the other. Light crossbows, also called latches, must be braced against an object to be cocked with a lever mounted on the stock. The heavy crossbow, also called an arbalest, has a powerful pull and must be cocked with a cranequin (a simple winch or lever) that comes with the weapon. One foot is placed in a stirrup at the end of the crossbow while the cranequin is worked.

The peashooter crossbow can be used by a pixie fairy of any class, regardless of class weapon restrictions, as long as they purchase the weapon proficiency.

All crossbows fire quarrels or bolts and the correct size must be used with each weapon. Due to their great power, light and heavy crossbows deliver penetration damage (see Chapter 12: Combat: The Art of Hack) with a damage roll of maximum or maximum minus one.

Lance: The different lances are rated according to size and sturdiness. Each type can be used only if the rider is on the same type of horse or a greater one. A man on a light warhorse could not use a heavy horse lance, if only because the impact would bowl him and the horse right over! Furthermore, the heavy and jousting lances require that the rider be firmly in a saddle and using stirrups.

The jousting lance is a heavy horse lance modified for use in tournaments, in which the desire is not to kill the opponent. The end of the lance is fitted with a special blunted tip intended to lessen the chance of wounds. Of course, good intentions often go awry, so there is still a chance of injury during a joust.

Mancatcher: This item is a highly specialized type of polearm designed to capture without killing a victim. It consists of a long pole with a spring-loaded set of sharpened jaws at the end. The victim is caught between the arms, which then snap shut. The mancatcher is effective only on man-sized creatures.

The target is always treated as AC 10 plus shield, modified for Dexterity. If a hit is scored, the character is caught. The caught victim loses all shield and Dexterity bonuses and can be pushed and pulled about. This causes an automatic 1d2 points of damage per round and gives a 25% chance of pulling the victim to the ground. The victim can escape on a successful bend bars/lift gates roll, although this results in 1d2 points more damage. A common tactic is to use the weapon to pull horsemen off their mounts, then pin them to the ground.

Polearms: A popular group of weapons, their length is a distinct advantage and, for the peasant, they are relatively easy weapons to make and use against monsters or adventurers. Thus, there exists a great abundance of polearms of different sizes and shapes. Due to their numbers, there is no standard system for naming polearms. The names used in the HackMaster game might possibly be applied to other weapons elsewhere, but, it goes without saying that the names used here are most correct and should always be used.

Because of their length, all polearms are infantry weapons and require two hands to use. They are almost always the weapons of the common peasant and soldier, who, lacking a horse and heavy armor needs some weapon to keep the enemy's knights at bay.

Thus, most polearms are intended for use in close-packed formations to present a forest of sharp points and wicked blades to any knight foolish enough to charge. Unfortunately, giants and giant-kin like to wield these puppies one-handed. Ouch!

Item	Cost	Weight	Size	Damage Type[6]	Speed Factor	Damage vs. S	M	L	Base Availability 11	Med	Low
Glaive[1]	6 gp	8 lbs.	L	H	3	1d4	1d6	1d10	95	90	85
Glaive-guisarme[1]	10 gp	10 lbs.	L	P/H	4	1d6	2d4	2d6	85	80	75
Guisarme	5 gp	8 lbs.	L	H	3	1d10	2d4	1d8	90	85	80
Guisarme-voulge	8 gp	15 lbs.	L	P/H	5	2d4	2d4	2d4	95	90	85
Halberd	10 gp	15 lbs.	L	P/H	4	1d8	1d10	2d6	85	80	75
Hook fauchard[2]	10 gp	8 lbs.	L	P/H	4	1d4	1d4	1d4	85	80	75
Lucern hammer[5]	7 gp	15 lbs.	L	P/C	4	2d6	2d4	1d6	90	85	80
Military fork[1]	5 gp	7 lbs.	L	P	2	1d6	1d8	2d4	95	90	85
Partisan[5]	10 gp	8 lbs.	L	P	4	1d4	1d6	1d6+1	85	80	75
Ranseur[5]	6 gp	7 lbs.	L	P	3	2d4	2d4	2d4	90	85	80
Spetum[5]	5 gp	7 lbs.	L	P	3	1d4+1	1d6+1	2d6	95	90	85
Voulge	5 gp	12 lbs.	L	H	5	2d4	2d4	2d4	90	85	80
Quarterstaff[1]	—	4 lbs.	L	C	-1	1d6	1d6	1d6	95	90	85
Sewing needle[7]	5 sp	**	S	P	-4	.125 pts	.125 pts	.125 pts.	95	90	85
Scourge	1 gp	2 lbs.	S	—	0	1d6	1d6-2	1d6-4	95	90	85
Sickle	6 sp	3 lbs.	S	H	-1	1d6	1d6-1	1d6-2	95	90	85
Sling	5 cp	*	S	—	—	—	—	—	95	90	85
Spear[5]	8 sp	5 lbs.	M	P	1	1d6-1	1d6	1d8	90	85	80
Spear, Great[5]	1 gp	8 lbs.	L	P	3	1d6	1d8	1d10	90	85	80
Staff sling	2 sp	2 lbs.	M	—	—	—	—	—	85	80	75
Stilleto, Bloodthorn	12 gp	.5 lbs.	S	P	-4	1d6-2	1d6-2	1d6-2	75	70	65
Sword	—	—	—	—	—	—	—	—	—	—	—
Bastard sword	25 gp	10 lbs.	M	H	—	—	—	—	90	85	80
One-handed	—	—	—	—	1	1d6	1d8	1d12	95	90	85
Two-handed	—	—	—	—	3	1d4	2d4	2d8	85	80	75
Broad sword	10 gp	4 lbs.	M	H	0	1d10	2d4	1d6+1	90	85	80
Khopesh	10 gp	7 lbs.	M	H	4	1d10+1	2d4	1d6	95	90	85
Long sword	15 gp	4 lbs.	M	H	0	1d8	1d12		90	85	80
Rapier, Petite	15 gp	.5 lbs.	S	P	-4	1d6-2	1d6-1	1d6	80	75	70
Scimitar	15 gp	4 lbs.	M	H	0	1d8	1d8	1d8	95	90	85
Short sword	10 gp	3 lbs.	S	P	-2	1d6-1	1d6	1d8	90	85	80
Two-handed sword	50 gp	15 lbs.	L	H	5	1d6-1	1d10	3d6	85	80	75
Trident	15 gp	5 lbs.	L	P	2	1d4	1d6+1	3d4	90	85	80
Warhammer	2 gp	6 lbs.	M	C	-1	1d8	1d6	1d4	95	90	85
Whip	1 sp	2 lbs.	M	—	3	1d6-2	1d6-4	1	95	90	85

1. This weapon inflicts double damage against charging creatures of L or greater size.
2. This weapon can dismount a rider on a successful hit.
3. These weapons are free and make handy bashers for frugal characters.
4. This weapon inflicts double damage when used from the back of a charging mount.
5. This weapon inflicts double damage when firmly set to receive a charge.
6. The "Type" category is divided into Crushing (C), Puncturing (P), and Hacking (H). Note that the Edged Weapon categories; honed and serrated from 3rd edition have been combined into the Hacking category. This indicates the type of attack made, which may alter the weapon's effectiveness against different types of armor.
7. Sewing needles do a flat .25 (one quarter) hit point of damage.
8. If a hurled tankard (full) hits its target, roll to see if the victim is temporarily blinded from alcohol.
* These items weigh little individually. Ten of these weigh one pound.
** These items weigh little individually. Ten of these weigh two grams.

Table 9U:
Weapons: Ammo

Item	Cost	Weight	Size	Damage Type	Speed Factor	Damage S	M	L	Base Availability Hi	Med	Low
Blowgun											
Barbed Dart	1 sp	*	S	P	—	1d6-1	1d6-2	1d6-4	95	90	85
Needle	2 cp	*	S	P	—	1	1	1	95	90	85
Bow											
Arrow, Flight	3sp/12	*	S	P	—	1d6	1d6	1d6	90	85	80
Arrow, Sheaf	3 sp/6	*	S	P	—	1d8	1d8	1d8	85	80	75
Crossbow											
Quarrel, Hand	1 gp	*	S	P	—	1d6-1	1d6-3	1d6-4	90	85	80
Quarrel, Hard Silver Jack.¹	50 gp	*	S	P	—	+1	+1	+1	50	30	15
Quarrel, Heavy	2 sp	*	S	P	—	1d8	2d4+1	3d4	90	85	80
Quarrel, Light	1 sp	*	S	P	—	1d6	1d8	2d4+1	90	85	80
Quarrel, Peashooter	10 sp	*	S	P	—	1d6-3	1d6-4	1	90	85	80
Quarrel, Silver Jacketed	25 gp	*	S	P	—	—	—	—	60	40	30
Sling											
Sling bullet	1 cp	.5 lbs.	S	C	—	1d6-1	1d6	1d6+1	95	95	95
Sling stone	—	.5 lbs.	S	C	—	1d6-1	1d6-1	1d6-1	95	95	95

1. Hard silver coating adds a +1 damage to the standard missile weapon damage.
* These items weigh little individually. Ten of these weigh one pound.

Table 9V:
Missile Weapon Ranges

Weapon	ROF	Range (yards) S	M	L
Blowgun	2	10	20	30
Comp. long bow, flight arrow	2	60	120	210
Comp. long bow, sheaf arrow	2	40	80	170
Comp. short bow	2	50	100	180
Great Longbow, flight arrow	1/2	80	160	230
Great Longbow, sheaf arrow	1/2	70	140	210
Longbow, flight arrow	2	70	140	210
Longbow, sheaf arrow	2	50	100	170
Short bow	2	50	100	150
Club	1	10	20	30
Hand crossbow	1	20	40	60
Heavy crossbow	1/2	80	160	240
Light crossbow	1	60	120	180
Peashooter crossbow	2	10	20	30
Dagger	2	10	20	30
Dart	3	10	20	40
Hammer	1	10	20	30
Hand axe	1	10	20	30
Harpoon	1	10	20	30
Javelin	1	20	40	60
Knife	2	10	20	30
Sling bullet	1	50	100	200
Sling stone	1	40	80	160
Spear	1	10	20	30
Staff sling bullet	2	30	60	90
Staff sling stone	2	30	60	90

"ROF" is the rate of fire (how many shots that weapon can fire off in one round.) This is independent of the number of melee attacks a character can make in a round.

Each range category (Short, Medium, or Long) includes attacks from distances equal to or less than the given range. Thus, a heavy crossbow fired at a target 136 yards away uses the medium range modifier. The attack roll modifiers for range are -2 for medium range and -5 for long range.

Awl Pike: Essentially this is a long spear 12 to 20 feet long ending in a spiked point or tapered spear head. Since the pike sticks out in front, men can be packed side-by-side in dense formations, and several rows of men can fight. Large blocks of pikemen make formidable troops. However, once the pikemen engage in close combat, they normally drop their clumsy awl pikes and fight hand-to-hand with short swords.

Bardiche: One of the simplest of polearms, the bardiche is an elongated battle-axe. A large curving axe-head is mounted on the end of a shaft 5 to 8 feet long. The bardiche grew out of a common peasant tool and is popular with the plebes. One relative disadvantage is that the bardiche requires more space to wield than a pike or a spear.

Bec de corbin: This is a highly specialized weapon of the upper classes. It is an early can-opener designed specifically to deal with plate armor. The pick or beak is made to punch through plate, while the hammer side can be used to give a stiff blow. The end is fitted with a short blade for dealing with unarmored or helpless foes. The weapon is about eight feet long. Since the weapon relies on impact, a great deal of swinging space is needed.

Bill-guisarme: A particularly bizarre-looking combination weapon, the bill-guisarme is an outgrowth of the common bill hook. Mounted on a seven- to eight-foot-long pole, it has a combination of a heavy cleaver blade, a jutting back spike, and a hook or spike on the end. Thus, it can be used in several different ways. Like most polearms, it requires lots of room to use.

Fauchard: An outgrowth of the sickle and scythe, the fauchard is a long, inward curving blade mounted on a shaft six to eight feet long. It can slash or thrust, although the inward curving point makes thrusting rather ineffective. Its advantage is that a peasant can easily convert his common scythe into this weapon of war.

Fauchard-fork: This is an attempted improvement on the fauchard, adding a long spike or fork to the back of the blade. Supposedly this improves the thrusting ability of the weapon. It is still an inefficient weapon.

Glaive: One of the most basic polearms, the glaive is a single-edged blade mounted on an eight- to ten-foot-long shaft. While not the most efficient weapon, it is relatively easy to make and use. Normally the blade turns outward to increase the cutting area, resembling a cleaver or axe when used in this way.

Glaive-guisarme: Another combination weapon, this one takes the basic glaive and adds a spike or hook to the back of the blade. In theory, this increases the usefulness of the weapon although its actual application is somewhat questionable.

Guisarme: Thought to have derived from a pruning hook used by farmers to trim their orchard trees, this is an elaborately curved heavy blade. While convenient and handy, it is not very effective.

Guisarme-voulge: This weapon has a modified axe blade mounted on an eight-foot-long shaft. The end of the blade tapers to a point for thrusting and a back spike is fitted for punching through armor. Sometimes this spike is replaced by a sharpened hook used to dismount riders.

Halberd: After the awl pike and the bill class of arms, this was one of the most popular weapons of the Middle Ages. Fixed on a shaft five to eight feet long is a large axe blade, angled for maximum impact. The end of the blade tapers to a long spear point or awl pike. On the back is a hook for attacking armor or dismounting riders. Originally intended to defeat cavalry, it is not tremendously successful in that role since it lacks the reach of the pike and needs considerable room to swing. It found new life against blocks of pikemen.

Should the advance of the main attack stall, halberdiers issue out of the formation and attack the flanks of the enemy. The pikemen with their overlong weapons are nearly defenseless in such close combat.

Hook fauchard: This combination weapon is another attempted improvement to the fauchard. A back hook is fitted to the back of the blade, supposedly to dismount horsemen. Like the fauchard, this is not a tremendously successful weapon.

Lucern hammer: This weapon is similar to the bec de corbin. Fitted with a shaft up to ten feet long, it is usually found in the hands of the common soldier. Like the bec de corbin, its main purpose is to punch through armor. The end is fitted with the long point of an awl pike to hold off enemy cavalry.

Military fork: This is one of the simplest modifications of a peasant's tool since it is little more than a pitchfork fixed to a longer shaft. With tines strengthened and straightened, the military fork serves well. The need for cutting and cleaving eventually often results in combining the fork with other weapons.

Table 9Y:
Character Encumbrance

Character Strength	Unencum.	Light	Moderate	Heavy Laden	Severe	Max.Car. Weight
1	0-1	2-3	4-5	6-7	8-9	9
1/51	0-2	3-4	5-6	7-8	9-10	10
2	0-3	4-5	6-7	8-9	10-11	11
2/51	0-4	5-6	7-8	9-10	11-12	12
3	0-5	6-7	8-9	10-11	12-15	15
3/51	0-7	8-9	10-11	12-14	15-21	21
4	0-9	10-11	12-14	15-18	19-27	27
4/51	0-11	12-14	15-17	18-22	23-33	33
5	0-13	14-16	17-20	21-26	27-39	39
5/51	0-15	16-19	20-23	24-30	31-45	45
6	0-18	19-23	24-27	28-36	37-54	54
6/51	0-21	22-26	27-32	33-42	43-63	63
7	0-24	25-30	31-36	37-48	49-72	72
7/51	0-27	28-34	35-41	42-54	55-81	81
8	0-30	31-38	39-45	46-60	61-90	90
8/51	0-33	34-41	42-50	51-66	67-99	99
9	0-36	37-45	46-54	55-72	73-108	108
9/51	0-39	40-49	50-59	60-78	79-117	117
10	0-43	44-54	55-65	66-86	87-129	129
10/51	0-47	48-59	60-71	72-94	95-141	141
11	0-51	52-64	65-77	78-102	103-153	153
11/51	0-55	56-69	70-83	84-110	111-165	165
12	0-59	60-74	75-89	90-118	119-177	177
12/51	0-63	64-79	80-95	96-126	127-189	189
13	0-67	68-84	85-101	102-134	135-201	201
13/51	0-71	72-89	90-107	108-142	143-213	213
14	0-76	77-95	96-114	115-152	153-228	228
14/51	0-81	82-101	102-122	123-162	163-243	243
15	0-86	87-108	109-129	130-172	173-258	258
15/51	0-91	92-114	115-137	138-182	183-273	273
16	0-97	98-121	122-146	147-194	195-291	291
16/51	0-103	104-129	130-155	156-206	207-309	309
17	0-109	110-136	137-164	165-218	219-327	327
17/51	0-115	116-144	145-173	174-230	231-345	345
18	0-130	131-163	164-195	196-260	261-390	390
18/51	0-160	161-200	201-240	241-320	321-480	480
19	0-200	201-250	251-300	301-400	401-600	600
19/51	0-300	301-375	376-450	451-600	601-900	900
20	0-400	401-500	501-600	601-800	801-1200	1200
20/51	0-500	501-625	626-750	751-1000	1001-1500	1500
21	0-600	601-750	751-900	901-1200	1201-1800	1800
21/51	0-700	701-875	876-1050	1051-1400	1401-2100	2100
22	0-800	801-1000	1001-1200	1201-1600	1601-2400	2400
22/51	0-900	901-1125	1126-1350	1351-1800	1801-2700	2700
23	0-1,000	1001-1250	1251-1500	1501-2000	2001-3000	3000
23/51	0-1,100	1101-1375	1376-1650	1651-2200	2201-3300	3300
24	0-1,200	1201-1500	1501-1800	1801-2400	2401-3600	3600
24/51	0-1,300	1301-1625	1626-1950	1951-2600	2601-3900	3900
25	0-1,500	1501-1875	1876-2250	2251-3000	3001-4500	4500

Table 9Z:
Carrying Capacities of Animals

Mount	Base Move	2/3 Move	1/3 Move
Camel	0-330 lbs.	331-500 lbs.	501-660 lbs.
Dawg	0-15 lbs.	16-20 lbs.	21-30 lbs.
Elephant	0-500 lbs.	501-750 lbs.	751-1,000 lbs.
Horse, draft	0-260 lbs.	261-390 lbs.	391-520 lbs.
Horse, heavy	0-260 lbs.	261-390 lbs.	391-520 lbs.
Horse, light	0-170 lbs.	171-255 lbs.	256-340 lbs.
Horse, medium	0-220 lbs.	221-330 lbs.	331-440 lbs.
Horse, riding	0-180 lbs.	181-270 lbs.	271-360 lbs.
Llama	0-165 lbs.	166-250 lbs.	251-335 lbs.
Mule	0-250 lbs.	251-375 lbs.	376-500 lbs.
Ox	0-220 lbs.	221-330 lbs.	331-440 lbs.
Pack Ape	0-170 lbs.	171-255 lbs.	256-340 lbs.
Yak	0-220 lbs.	221-330 lbs.	331-440 lbs.

Partisan: Shorter than the awl pike but longer than the spear, the partisan is a broad spearhead mounted on an eight-foot-long shaft. Two smaller blades project out from the base of the main blade, just to increase damage and trap weapons. Since it is a thrusting weapon, it can be used in closely-packed formations.

Ranseur: Very much like a partisan, the ranseur differs in that the main blade is thinner and the projecting blades extended more like tines of a fork. These can trap a weapon and sometimes punch through armor.

Spetum: The spetum is a modification of the normal spear. The shaft increases to eight to ten feet and side blades are added. Some have blades that angle back, increasing the damage when pulling the weapon out of a wound. These blades can also trap and block weapons or catch and hold an opponent.

Voulge: The voulge, like the bardiche, is a variation on the axe and the cleaver. The voulge is little more than a cleaver on the end of a long (seven- to eight-foot) pole. It is a popular weapon, easy to make and simple to learn. It is also called the Lochaber axe.

Scourge: This wicked weapon is a short whip with several thongs or tails. Each thong is studded with metal barbs, resulting in a terrible lash. It is sometimes used as an instrument of execution.

Stilletto, Bloodthorn: This tiny, secret weapon of the fairy-kin appears to be little more than a small thorn from a common rose. Upon hitting a secret switch, a blade shoots from the center, creating a sturdy, albeit miniscule, metal knife. Favored by pixie-fairy thieves and assassins, the main advantage of the bloodthorn stiletto is its appearance. Besides its secretive nature, it's also an extremely quick weapon, able to strip the wings from a mosquito before the blink of an eye. Other than those benefits, its almost irrelevant damage makes it virtually useless.

Sword, Bastard: This sword is similar to a long sword in size and weight, but has a longer hilt. It can be used one- or two-handed. Use the speed factor and damage appropriate to the grip. If it is used two-handed, your character cannot employ a shield.

Sword, Khopesh: A khopesh has about six inches of handle and quillons. Its blade extends straight from the quillons for about two feet. The blade becomes sickle-shaped at this point, being about two additional feet long but effectively extending the overall length of the sword by only 1-1/2 feet. This makes the khopesh both heavy and unwieldy, difficult to employ properly, and slow to recover, particularly after a badly missed blow. Its sickle-like portion can snag an opponent if a hit is made against the opponent's armor class counting only Dexterity and shield. In this case, the opponent must make a successful Dexterity check or become off balance for the following round (+2 to hit). In the case of snagging the opposing weapon, the attacker must specifically target the weapon. Treat the weapon AC as 10 modified for the opponent's Dexterity. If the weapon hit is successful, the defender must make a successful Dexterity check or drop the weapon.

Sword, Petite Rapier: This sword is designed specifically for the pixie-fairy. Essentially a very thin and short long sword, it does minimal damage. Its main advantage is that its speed factor allows for quick attacking and consequently better spell disruption. Because of its fine size and difficulty of manufacture, these weapons are rather pricey, providing one of the poorest gp outlay to average damage ratios in HackMaster. Still, no stylish pixie-fairy would be caught in a fight without one.

Encumbrance

If you are like most players, you'll want your character to own one of everything. Thus equipped, your character could just reach into his pack and pull out any item he wants whenever he needs it. Sadly, there are limits to how much your character can carry. That's why smart characters buy horses, mules, pack apes, llamas and yaks. But even these beasts have their limits. These limits are determined by encumbrance, measured in pounds. To calculate encumbrance, simply total the pounds of gear carried by the creature or character. Add five pounds for clothing, if any is worn. This total is then compared to the carrying capacity of the creature to determine the effects.

Encumbrance is divided into five categories: Unencumbered, Light, Moderate, Heavy, and Severe Encumbrance. To calculate your character's encumbrance category, first figure out the total weight he is carrying (including five pounds for clothing). Then look on Table 9Y. (Use Table 9Z to figure out the encumbrance category of your character's mount(s) or beast(s) of burden.)

The Max. Car. (Maximum Carried) Weight column lists the most weight (in pounds) your character can carry and still move. But movement is limited to 10 feet per round, as your character staggers under the heavy load.

Effects of Encumbrance

Encumbrance has two basic effects. First, it obviously reduces your character's movement rate. Ever try to run carrying two 25 pound blocks of salt or a couple of bags of groceries? Light encumbrance reduces the movement rate by 1/3 (round fractions down), Moderate reduces it by one half, Heavy reduces it by 2/3, and Severe lowers the movement rate to 1. Encumbrance also reduces your character's combat abilities. If encumbrance reduces your character to half of his normal movement rate, he suffers a -1 penalty to his attack roll. If he is reduced to 1/3 or less of his normal movement rate, the attack penalty is -2 and there is an additional AC penalty of +1. If your character's movement is reduced to 1, the attack roll penalty is -4 and the AC penalty is +3. Clearly, when a Carrion Pecker is chasing you, the wise thing for a heavily encumbered character to do is to quickly drop most of his gear before turning around and wading in to battle.

Encumbrance: Mounts and Beasts of Burden

The "Base Move" column in Table 9Z lists the maximum amount an animal can carry and maintain its normal movement rate. Animals can be loaded greater than this, up to a maximum of twice their normal load. However, this causes a drop in the animal's movement rate (as indicated by the column headings). When calculating a mount's load, be sure to include the weight of the rider!

Packing it in: A Place for Everything

Besides knowing how much weight your character can carry, you need to know how his gear will be carried. The capacities of different containers are given in Table 9AA. The values listed in Table 9AA are for standard-sized items. It is certainly possible for sacks, chests, and backpacks to be larger or smaller than the sizes listed. The weight capacity, however, lists the maximum weight the item can carry, regardless of size. Beyond this point, the material used to construct the item will fail, sooner or later. The volume gives the length, width, and height or depth of the item. Items that exceed the capacity of a container cannot be stored in it.

Since all player characters are adventurers, it is assumed they know the best methods for packing and stowing equipment. Blankets are rolled into bedrolls, small items are carefully arranged, rope is properly coiled, weapons are slung in the most comfortable manner, etc. While small items can be easily stuffed into a pack, large bulky things may encumber a person more than their actual weight would indicate. The GM has the right to rule that an object is more encumbering than it actually appears.

Tarus Bloodheart finds a 5 ft. x 9 ft. flying carpet. He carefully rolls it into a thick cylinder and wisely ties it closed. Even though he has taken this sensible precaution, the carpet is still a large and awkward thing. The GM rules that although the carpet weighs only 20 pounds, its encumbrance is equal to that of an item weighing 50 pounds. Tarus must increase his current encumbrance level by 50 pounds, adding the awkwardness of the rolled carpet slung over his shoulder to his already carefully packed backpack.

Magical Armor and Encumbrance

One of the special properties of magical armor is its effect on encumbrance. This information, however is GM classified and available only in the GM's guide. As a player you may never peek inside that hallowed tome or purchase it,

unless, in the latter case, you never open it. The only thing you need to know about magic armor and its effect on encumbrance is that it has a beneficial effect. If the GM does not give you a benefit for wearing magical armor, call him on it. Of course, certain types of magic armor and alleged magic armor may not give any encumbrance benefit whatsoever. Since your GM can and will dispense penalties for incorrect rules-challenges, reserve your challenge for an encumbrance audit, when you're already screwed anyway.

Table 9AA: Stowage Capacity		
Item	Weight Cap.	Volume
Backpack	50 lbs.	3'x2'x1'
Basket, large	20 lbs.	2'x2'x2'
Basket, small	10 lbs.	1'x1'x1'
Belt pouch, large	8 lbs.	6"x8"x2"
Belt pouch, small	5 lbs.	4"x6"x2"
Chest, large	100 lbs.	3'x2'x2'
Chest, small	40 lbs.	2'x1'x1'
Sack, large	30 lbs.	2'x2'x1'
Sack, small	15 lbs.	1'x1'x8"
Saddle bags, large	30 lbs.	18"x1'x6"
Saddle bags, small	20 lbs.	1'x1'x6"

FRAIM

Chapter 10

Magic

Now, gentle reader, you have reached the pinnacle of it all. It is the crowning achievement that makes HackMaster unique among role-playing genres. The magic. It's the "sorcery" in "Swords and Sorcery," and without it we'd be playing some kind of lame historical type of game set in ancient Greece or something. Some of the most powerful weapons player characters have at their disposal in the HackMaster game are magical spells.

Through the use of spells, a character can cause rifts in the earth below the feet of his enemies, call lightning out of the sky, heal grievous injuries spouting blood in all directions, hurl explosive balls of fire, and shift blame for his actions on others. These are only a few things magic-users can do once they master the strange lore of HackMaster spells.

Not all have the competency to cast spells, however. This ability requires a certain amount of patience, brains or Wisdom. Magic-user spells can be mastered only by those with keen Intelligence and patience, and require long years of study. Cleric spells call for inner peace and faith and an intense devotion to one's calling. Moronic fighters and barbarians can no sooner cast a cantrip than leap to the moon.

In fact, the vast majority of the poor saps in a fantasy campaign lack these traits or have never had the opportunity to develop them. The baker may be a bright and clever fellow, but, following in his father's footsteps, he has condemned himself to a boring life learning the arts of bread making. He never had the opportunity to study old books and crumbling scrolls, or maybe he preferred a boring life, existing only to serve pastries to player characters. The hard-working peasant may be pious and upright in his faith. But so busy is he slaving for his important NPC master or your player character that he lacks the time for the contemplative and scholarly training required of a cleric. So it is only a fortunate few who have the ability and opportunity to learn the arcane lore of spellcasting.

A few character classes other than magic users and clerics have a limited ability to cast spells. The ranger, through his close association with nature, is able to cast a few spells, though his choices are limited to his natural inclinations. The paladin, through his devotion and humility, can use some of the spells of the cleric, as can the dark knight for opposite reasons. The bard, through luck, happenstance, curiosity, and perseverance, can manage a few magic-user spells, perhaps by persuading a lonely magic-user to reveal his secrets.

Regardless of their source, all spells fall into the general categories of magic-user or cleric. Although some spells appear in both categories, in general, the categories differ in how spells are acquired, stored, and cast.

Magic-User Spells

Magic-user spells range from spells of simple utility to great and powerful magics. The magic-user spell group has no single theme or purpose. The vast majority of magic-user spells were created by ancient magic-users for many different purposes. Some are to serve him in his everyday needs. Others provide adventurers with the might and firepower they need to survive. Some are relatively simple and safe to use; others are complicated, filled with hazards and snares that backfire explosively on the rash and unwary.

The workings of magic are dimly understood at best. There are many theories about where the power comes from, and how the magic-user draws on that power. The most commonly accepted idea is that the mysterious combination of words, gestures, and materials that make up a spell somehow taps an extra-dimensional source of energy that in turn causes the desired effect. Somehow, the components of the spells, those words, gestures and materials, route this energy to a specific and desired result.

Fortunately, how this happens is not very important. Your magic-user can still burn his enemies to charred cinders with a couple of Skipping Betties whether he knows why the spell worked or not. All he needs to know is, "when I do this, that happens."

Casting a magic-user spell is a very complicated ordeal. The process of learning the correct procedure to cast a spell is difficult and taxing to the mind. Thus, a magic-user must check to see if he learns each new spell (according to his Intelligence—see Table 1D). Furthermore, there is a limit to just how much of this strangeness – illogical mathematics, alchemical chemistry, structural linguistics – a magic-user's mind can comprehend, and so he must live with a limit to the number of spells he can know.

As the magic-user learns spells, he records their arcane notes into his spell books. Without spell books, a magic-user cannot memorize new spells. Within them are all his instructions for memorizing and casting the spells he knows. As the magic-user successfully learns a new spell, he carefully enters its formula into his spell books.

A magic-user can never have a spell in his books that he does not know, because if he doesn't understand it, he cannot write the formula. Likewise, he cannot enter a spell into his books if it is higher in level than he can cast. If he finds an ancient tome with spells of higher power, he must simply wait until he advances to a level at which he can use them. He should protect these spellbooks at all cost. Without them, he's a poor excuse for a fighter and more useless than a halfling at an ogrish ass-kicking contest.

The exact shape and size of a character's spellbooks is a detail your GM will provide. They are typically thick tomes of carefully inked parchment. They're never convenient to carry around. And if you do carry them, and you fall in a pit of burning oil or boiling tar, you might as well let your character die there rather than play a magic-user without spells. So, ultimately, it is the memorization that is important.

To draw on magical energy, the magic-user must shape specific mental patterns in his mind. He uses his spell books to force his mind through mental exercises, preparing it to hold the final, complicated patterns. These complex patterns are alien to normal thought, so they don't register in the mind as normal learning. To shape these patterns, the magic-user must spend time memorizing the spell, twisting his thoughts and recasting the energy patterns each time to account for subtle changes—planetary motions, seasons, time of day, and more.

Once a magic-user memorizes a spell, it remains in his memory (as potential energy) until he uses the prescribed components to trigger the release of the energy patterns. Upon casting, the energy of the spell is spent, wiped clean from the magic-user's mind. The mental patterns are lost until the magic-user studies and memorizes that spell again the next day.

The number of spells a magic-user can memorize per day is given by his level (see Table 3BB); he can memorize the same spell more than once, but each memorization counts as one spell toward his daily memorization limit. Note that some spell casters can spell-jack to go beyond this limit, but they run the risk of it backfiring with a greater chance of mishap and even more disastrous results (see Chapter 3 for more details). Part of a magic-user's Intelligence can be seen in the careful selection of spells he has memorized.

Memorization is not a thing that happens immediately. The magic-user must have a clear head gained from a restful night's sleep and then has to spend time studying his spell books. The amount of study time needed is 10 minutes per level of the spell being memorized. Thus, a 9th-level spell (the most powerful) would require 90 minutes of careful study. Clearly, high-level spellcasters do not lightly change their memorized spells.

Spells remain memorized until they are cast or wiped from the character's mind by a spell, magical item or if the magic-user simply memorizes a spell right over the top of it.

Schools of Magic

All magic-user spells fall into nine different schools of magic. Each school is comprised of a defined group of related spells.

Abjuration:

The Abjuration spells are a group of specialized protective spells. Each spell is used to prevent or banish some magical or non-magical effect or creature. A magic-user will use these spells to save his own hide from arrows or attacks by evil creatures. Consequently, they are not very popular among others in the party. But what do they know- they have armor to protect them!

Alteration:

Spells which cause a change in the properties of some already existing thing, creature, or condition are known as Alteration spells. These spells usually fit into the "generally useful" category, if you ask a magic-user's fellow party members. Providing a fighter with great strength just prior to wading into a group of unfortunate goblins is always an appreciated spell. The magic-user can also teleport persons or items around, or turn some unlucky shmoe into a very detailed, lifelike stone statue.

Conjuration/Summoning:

The Conjuration/Summoning spells bring something directly to the caster from elsewhere. Conjuration normally produces physical matter or items from some other place. Summoning enables you to compel living creatures and powers to appear in your character's presence or to channel extra-planar energies through himself. Kewl, huh?

Enchantment/Charm:

Spells which cause a change in the quality of an item or the bearing or 'tude of a person or creature are part of the Enchantment/Charm school. Enchantments are needed in the creation of magic items. Charms are good for forcing others to do your bidding or putting them to sleep so your allies can cut their throats more easily.

Greater Divinations:

These spells are more powerful than Lesser Divinations (see below). Such spells enable the magic-user to learn secrets long forgotten, to predict the future, and to uncover things hidden or cloaked by spells. Unexpected things can always happen when these spells are concerned. Your GM typically gets a lot of leeway with these spells, so I'd tailor your use of them to whether your GM is in a good mood or not.

Illusions:

The Illusion school deals with spells used by the magic-user to deceive the tiny minds or senses of others. You can hypnotize them, pass off an item as magical or go invisible. Not very destructive, but useful as all get out.

Invocation/Evocation:

Spells which channel magical energy to create specific effects and materials comprise the Invocation/Evocation school. Invocation normally relies on the intervention of some higher agency (to whom the spell is addressed), while evocation enables the caster to directly shape the energy. These spells are some of the most popular, giving us all the incarnations of Fireball, Web and most of the offensive and destructive spells.

Other party members love these because they help eliminate opponents. The sissies cry like little girls when an area effect over flows or catches them in a back-lash. I recommend keeping one extra in-memory at all times in case they back-talk or give you crap about it. Just in case.

Lesser Divination:

The Lesser Divination spells are available to be learned by all magic-users, regardless of their affiliation. This school includes the most basic and vital spells of the magic-user, those he needs to practice other aspects of his craft. Lesser divinations include Read Magic and Detect Magic.

Necromancy:

This one of the most restrictive of all spell schools. Necromancy deals with dead things or the restoration of life, limbs, or vitality to living creatures in very unnatural ways. Although a small school, its spells tend to be powerful and they are the meat and mead of the blood mage. Given the risks of the adventuring world, necromantic spells are considered quite useful, but scary to the rest of the party. All the more reason to carry them: it keeps NPCs and PCs alike off your back.

Learning Spells

Whether a character chooses to be a magic-user, battle mage or a specialist in one of the schools of magic (e.g., blood mage or illusionist), he must learn his spells from somewhere. While it might be possible for the exceptional magic-user to learn the secrets of arcane lore entirely on his own, it isn't very likely. It is far more likely that your character was apprenticed to another magic-user as a lad.

This kindly (severe), loving (callous), understanding (ill-tempered), generous (mean-spirited), and upright (untrustworthy) master taught your character everything he knows at the start of the game. Then, when it was time, the master sent him into the world (threw him out) with a smile and a pat on the back (snarling with his foot up your character's behind).

Or perhaps your character studied at a proper academy for magic-users. There he completed his lessons under the eye of a firm (mean) but patient (irritable) tutor who was ready with praise for good work (a ruler across the knuckles for the slightest fault).

But alas, your character's parents were impoverished and his studies had to end (fed up with this treatment, your youthful character fled during the night). As you can see, there are a number of ways your character might have learned his spells.

The one good thing that comes from your character's studies is his initial spell book. It may have been a gift from his school or he may have stolen it from his hated master. Whatever the case, your character begins play with a spell book containing up to a few 1st-level spells. Your GM will tell you the exact number of spells and which spells they are. Since GM's tend to screw you big-time with a random roll at first level, it's lucky that as your character adventures, he will have the opportunity to add more spells to his collection.

When your character attains a new level, he will receive exactly one random spell. It may be possible for your character to copy spells from the spell book of another player character, if he teaches you (all magic-users use a different, unique notation and if not taught, it must be deciphered with great difficulty). Or he may have to wait until he can find a spell book with new spells. You can also trade spells, magic and cash to NPCs or PCs to gain spells.

In all cases, before he can add a new spell to his spell book, you have to check to see if your character learns that spell. The chance of learning a spell depends on your magic-user's Intelligence, as given in Table 1D. This chance may be raised or lowered if your character is a specialist.

Illusions

Of all spells, those of the illusion school cause the most problems. Not that they are more difficult for your player character to cast, but these spells are more difficult for you to role-play and for your GM to adjudicate. Illusions rely on the idea of believability, which in turn relies on the situation and the state of mind of the victim. Your GM must determine this for NPCs, which is perhaps an easier job. You must role-play this for your character.

Spells of this school fall into two basic groups, illusions and phantasms. Illusions are creations that manipulate light, color, shadow, sound and sometimes even scent. Higher level illusions tap energy from other planes, and are actually quasi-real, being woven of extra-dimensional energies by the caster. Common illusions create appearances, they can conceal objects by making them look like something else or make them invisible.

Phantasms exist only in the minds of their victims; these spells are never even quasi-real. (The exceptions to this are the Phantasmal Force spells, which are actually illusions rather than phantasms.) Phantasms act upon the mind of the victim to create an intense reaction, fear being most common.

The key to successful illusions or phantasms is believability, which depends on three main factors: what the caster attempts, what the victim expects, and what is happening at the moment the spell is cast. By combining the information from these three areas, the player and the GM should be able to create and adjudicate reasonable illusions and phantasms.

When casting an illusion or phantasm, the caster can attempt to do anything he desires within the physical limits of the spell. Prior knowledge of the illusion created is not necessary but is extremely useful. Suppose your character decides to cast a Phantasmal Force spell and can choose between creating the image of a Troll (a creature he has seen and battled) or that of a Blind Beholder (a creature he has never seen but has heard terrifying descriptions of). He can either use his memory to create a realistic Troll or use his imagination to create something that may or may not look like a real Blind Beholder. The Troll, based on his first-hand knowledge of these creatures, is going to have lots of little details – a big nose, warts, green, scabby skin, and even a shambling Troll-like walk. Your illusion of a Blind Beholder will be much less precise, just a floating ball with one big eye and eyestalks. Your character doesn't know its color, size or behavior.

The type of image chosen by the caster affects the reaction of the victim. If the victim in the above case has seen both a Troll and a Blind Beholder, which will be more believable? Almost certainly, it will be the Troll, which looks and acts the way the victim thinks a Troll should. He might not even recognize the other creature as a Blind Beholder since it doesn't look like any Beholder he's ever seen. Even if the victim has never seen a Troll or a Beholder, the Troll will still be more believable; it acts in a realistic manner, while the Beholder does not. Thus, spellcasters are well advised to create images of things they have seen, for the same reason authors are advised to write about things they know. Of course, if the opponent has seen both a Troll and a Blind Beholder before and lived to talk about it, you'd better run…he's probably damned tough!

An illusion spell, therefore, depends on its believability. Believability is determined by the situation and a saving throw. Under normal circumstances,

those observing the illusion are allowed a saving throw vs. spell if they actively disbelieve the illusion.

For player characters, disbelieving is an action in itself and takes a round. For NPCs and monsters, a normal saving throw is made if the GM deems it appropriate. The GM can and will give bonuses or penalties to this saving throw as he thinks appropriate. If the caster has cleverly prepared a realistic illusion, this certainly results in penalties on the victim's saving throw. If the victim were to rely more on scent than sight, on the other hand, it could gain bonuses to its saving throw. If the saving throw is made, the victim sees the illusion for what it is. If the saving throw is failed, the victim believes the illusion. A good indication of when player characters should receive a positive modifier to their saving throws is when they say they don't believe what they see, especially if they can give reasons why.

Illusions do have other limitations. The caster must maintain a show of reality at all times when conducting an illusion. (If a squad of fighters is created, the caster dictates their hits, misses, damage inflicted, apparent wounds, and so forth and the GM decides whether the bounds of believability have been exceeded.) Maintaining an illusion normally requires concentration on the part of the caster, preventing him from doing other things. Disturb him and the illusion vanishes.

Cleric Spells

The spells of a cleric, while sometimes having powers similar to those of the magic-user, are quite different in their overall tone. As a living embodiment of his gawd, the majority of good cleric spells work to aid others or provide some service to the community in which he lives. Few of his spells are truly offensive, but many can be used cleverly to protect or defend. For evil clerics, the opposite is usually the case.

Like the magic-user, the cleric's level determines how many spells he retains. He must select these spells in advance, demonstrating his wisdom

and far-sightedness by choosing those spells he thinks will be most useful in the trials that lurk ahead. Unlike the magic-user, the cleric needs no spell book and does not roll to see if he learns spells. Cleric spells are obtained in an entirely different manner. To obtain his spells, a cleric must be faithful to the cause of his gawd. If the cleric feels confident in this (and most do), he can pray for his spells. Through prayer, the cleric humbly and politely requests those spells he wishes to memorize. Under normal circumstances, these spells are then granted.

A cleric's spell selection is limited by his level. The knowledge of what spells are available to the cleric becomes instantly clear as soon as he advances in level. This, too, is bestowed by his gawd.

Clerics must pray to obtain spells, as they are requesting their abilities from some greater power, be it their gawd or some intermediary agent of this power. The conditions for praying are identical to those needed for the magic-user's studying. Clearly then, it behooves the cleric to maintain himself in good standing with this power, through word and deed.

Clerics who slip in their duties, harbor indiscreet thoughts, or neglect their beliefs, find that their gawd has an immediate method of redress. If the cleric has failed in his duties, the gawd can deny him spells above second level as a clear message of dissatisfaction. (Spells of first and second level are gained by skill of reaching out to the outer planes of the gawds and can be granted by minor beings not associated with the gawd of the cleric.) These can be regained if the character immediately begins to make amends for his errors. A serious transgression could require special service, such as a quest or some great sacrifice of goods (see Chapter 5 on Atonement). These are things your GM will decide, should your character veer from the straight and narrow path of his religion. Finally, not all gawds are equal, so that those of lesser power are unable to grant certain spells. Powers of demi-gawd status can only grant up to 5th-level spells. Lesser gawds can grant 6th-level spells, while the greater gawds have all spell levels available to them.

Casting Spells

Both magic-users and clerics use the same rules for casting spells. To cast a spell, the character must first have the spell memorized. If it is not memorized, the spell cannot be cast. The caster must be able to speak freely (if the spell has a verbal component), move his arms and body (if the spell has a somatic component) and hold the proper material component(s) (if any). If the spell is targeted on a person, place, or thing, the caster must be able to see the target. It is not enough to cast a Sidewinder Fireball 150 feet ahead into the darkness; the caster must be able to see the point of explosion and the intervening distance. Likewise, a Magic Missile (which always hits its target) cannot be fired into a group of bandits with the instruction to strike the leader; the caster must be able to identify and see the leader.

Once the casting has begun, the character must stand still. Casting cannot be accomplished while riding a roughly moving beast or a vehicle, unless special efforts are made to stabilize and protect the caster. Thus, a spell cannot be cast from the back of a galloping horse under any conditions, nor can a magic-user or cleric cast a spell on the deck of a ship during a storm. However, if the caster were below decks, protected from the wind and surging waves, he might be able to cast a spell if he were used to the sway of a ship (i.e., he had his sea legs). While it is not normally possible to cast a spell from a moving chariot, a character who was steadied and supported by others could do so.

During the segments in which the spell is cast, the caster cannot move to dodge attacks. Therefore, no AC benefit from Dexterity is gained by spellcasters while casting spells. Furthermore, if the spellcaster is struck by a weapon or fails to make a saving throw before the spell is cast, the caster's concentration is disrupted. The spell is lost in a fizzle of useless energy and is wiped clean from the memory of the caster until it can be re-memorized.

Spell Components

The actions required to cast a spell are divided into three groups: verbal, somatic (gestures), and material. Each spell description (found in Appendicies C and D) lists what combination of these components is needed to cast a spell. Verbal components require the caster to speak clearly (he can not be silenced in any way); somatic components require free gestures (thus, the caster cannot be bound or held); material components must be tossed, dropped, burned, eaten, broken, etc. as indicated for the spell to work. While there is no specific description of the words and gestures that must be performed, the material components are listed in the spell descriptions. Some of these are common and easy to obtain. Others represent items of great value or scarcity. Whatever the component, it is automatically destroyed or lost when the spell is cast, unless the spell description specifically notes otherwise.

Your magic-user or cleric must have the proper components to cast the spell. Without them, he is helpless, even if the spell is memorized. Some might think that for simplicity of play, it is best to assume that any spellcaster with any sense has a supply of the common items he is likely to need – wax, feathers, paint, sand, sticks and fluff, for example. Not true! An assumption like that ruins the fun and flavor of running a magic-user. While the fighters are polishing their swords or visiting the armorer, you should be gathering these common items, whether finding them yourself or in the bazaar. In particular, you will need to make a special effort to obtain expansive and rare items.

Magical Research

One oft-ignored asset of both magic-users and clerics is magical research. While the spell lists for both groups offer a wide variety of tools and effects, the clever player character can quickly get an edge by researching his own spells. Where other spellcasters may fall quickly into tired and predictable patterns ("Look, it's a magic-user! Get ready for the Fireball, guys!"), an enterprising character can deliver sudden (and nasty) surprises!

Although your GM has the rules for handling spell research, there are some things you should know about how to proceed. First and foremost, research means that you and your GM will be working together to expand the game. Since most GMs could care less about your sorry hide, you'll have to do the bulk of the work on your own. Second, whatever your character researches, it cannot be more powerful than the spells he is already able to cast. If it is, you'll fail utterly and waste a good ream of paper in the process. So don't bother. Finally, you will have to be patient and willing to have your character spend some money. Make that lots of money. He won't create the spell immediately, as research takes time. It also takes plenty of dough, so you can expect your GM to use this opportunity to really ream you good.

Knowing these things, you should first write up a description of the spell you want to create. Be sure to include information on components, saving throws, range, duration, and all the other entries you find in the normal spell listings. When you give your GM the written description, tell him what you want the spell to do and ask him for clarification on your written word. While your magic-user is probably smart and has a good grasp of the written word, you might be a complete imbecile with 3rd grade writing skills. Don't be above getting some help. Since sometimes what you write isn't really what you meant to say, by talking to your GM, you can get him to pin down the right words for you before you waste all your character's money. Also, if you can sucker him into feeling like he partially authored your work and he starts to feel like it was his idea, you're far more likely to be successful. Because, after this, he will either accept or reject your spell. This is his choice and not all GMs will have the same answer. Don't complain and whine like a little baby. Find out what changes are needed to make the spell acceptable. You can probably iron out the differences.

Once all these things are done, your character can research the spell. Be ready for this to take some time. Eventually he will succeed, although the spell may not do quite what he expected. Your GM will probably revise the spell, reducing the area of effect or damage inflicted or both. This is why in the beginning you need to think of ulterior uses for the spell that are unusual. Such loop-holes might give you the edge for having a much better spell than the GM expects. Finally, all you have to do is name your spell. This should be something suitably pompous, such as "Evercrombie's Splattering Steamroller." After all, you want something to impress the plebes!

Experience

In HackMaster the old adage, "What doesn't kill you makes you stronger" has never been truer. Every time your character goes on an adventure, he will learn something. By honing his skills and learning things about the world around him, he will grow in mind and spirit. For example, he might learn the hard way that leaping from a fifty foot cliff is bit hard on the hit points. He might learn that you never, EVER turn your back on a gnome titan when he's been drinking. Or…he might learn that casting a Fireball in tight confines can be lethal to both friend and enemy alike.

In short, your character is learning from his day to day experiences and taking those lessons and applying them during the course of his adventuring so that he comes away a little stronger and a little smarter.

In HackMaster, the term "experience" is used to describe the measure of a character's ability in his chosen profession - in other words, his character's class.

Each player character begins the campaign at the lowly experience level of one. (1st level) and with zero experience points accumulated. However, that will quickly change.

Almost as soon as your character begins his adventuring career, he will begin to accrue experience points. At the completion of each adventure (or after each game session), he will return along with his party to their base of operations. Here treasure and magic items will be split up (see Treasure) and the GM will calculate and award any experiences points.

Typically, experience points are awarded to characters for treasure gained, opponents slain, captured or otherwise vanquished and for solving or overcoming problems through the use of skills, abilities or even parleying.

Characters with high scores in their primary attributes might be entitled to an experience point bonus (see character abilities). When a character gains a sufficient number of experience points, the character will be eligible to gain an experience level (see character classes). Those characters with optimal Honor Factors will advance more quickly. Likewise, those characters with low Honor Factors may be penalized and held back (See Honor Factor).

As a side note, it is important to keep in mind that most humans and demi-humans (NPCs) are '0-level'. They do not have the ability to gain experience levels. They don't have the 'right stuff' to rise above their lot in life and break free of the yoke medieval society has placed upon their shoulders. Player characters, on the other hand, are exceptional individuals. They are heroes in the making and are both unusual and superior.

Training

When your character has earned enough experience to attain the next level, you have every right to be proud and excited. But before you start to celebrate there are still a few hurtles to get past before you can advance.

In HackMaster all characters are required to attend school (University) before advancing to the next level. Schools gives your character a chance to take what he has learned in the field and return to his studies. When training, a character studies his skills under a qualified teacher or mentor, taking the raw knowledge he has gained and honing it into measurable improvement. Only under the qualified guidance of an instructor of a higher level will you be able to take what you've learned and effectively build on it.

Your GM will be rating both the performance of YOU as a player and your character before your training begins. This rating will modify the amount of time and money you'll need to spend to learn your basic blocks of instruction in order to advance. On the average, completing school takes a few weeks (depending on the tutor's ability and the level to which you are advancing). You should allow one week per level you are advancing to when making arrangements to attend school. (You might need to arrange for someone to take care of your affairs and obligations while you are away.) Most players choose to attend school during the character's non-adventuring time so as not to disrupt the campaign for the other party members.

Your GM will have all the details on which schools will be available to you. While you are at school and learning your basic block of instruction for the next level, you will be afforded the opportunity to take additional classes (thereby learning new skills and improving ones already known). Your GM will have a tailored list of such classes available at the particular school you are attending. If you are lucky there may even be an instructor of legendary-status (such as Chung Hu-Chek, famed martial arts instructor) who imparts his special skills and knowledge to you.

Some classes may be unavailable, however, or even cost prohibitive. Going to school is expensive and extra classes have hefty fees associated with them (especially at higher levels). Even so, it is a good idea to take advantage of any training opportunities when they present themselves.

Not to dampen your spirits, but you should also know that a GM has the right to rule that the circumstances are not appropriate for the character to advance in level and that he can flunk your character. Perhaps your character's Honor Factor is deplorable. Or maybe the GM feels your rule mastery isn't sufficient to play at the next higher level. You can appeal such a decision (contact your HMPA representative for more details on how to do this) but it's generally a good idea to ask your GM why he's held back your advancement and try to work with him to address his contentions.

Gaining Experience

The exact method of awarding experience points and experience point values is GM proprietary and as such we won't be covering it in detail in this book. The following, however, are just a few examples of the type of activities that can result in experience point awards;

- Anything of value you take either by force or through the use of skills and cunning is usually worth .EPs This includes gold looted from fallen victims, treasure taken from the lairs of creatures such as dragon hordes. It might even include profits made as a result of expert haggling on the part of your character.

- Magic items gained and retained have a marginal experience point value. That's because they are of great benefit to the character and party in themselves. The EP award will vary depending on how you obtained the item and how powerful or useful it is. Oft times just possessing such an item is award enough.

- Experience points awarded for treasure gained - monetary or magical - are dimished if the GM feels the challenge or threat to the party or character wasn't that great.

- Monsters captured or slain are almost always worthEP.s Captured monsters ransomed or sold can earn EPs as well.

• Individual characters earn their experience points by plying their craft and using their skills. For example, a cleric's role in any given encounter is to use his spell abilities to aid the party. A fighter's role is to engage in combat. A magic-user's role is to cast spells. A thief's role is to further the party's aim through stealth. A monk's role is to use his unusual talents to come to successful ends and so on for the other classes.

Individual characters also earn experience points for the following;

- Unassisted kills (also earns the character sole looting rights for that kill).

- Landing the killing blow on slain foes (also earns character dibs on any treasure for kill).

- Successfully using certain skills and abilities to further the party's goals.

Characters who use their class abilities and skills during the course of a given adventure are generally entitled to a full share of earned experience points awarded by the GM.

A Word to the Critics

With every new edition of HackMaster that hits the streets a rash of reviews soon follows in the various game publications. Individuals who have never been able to get off their asses to write a game somehow feel qualified to take the hard work of someone else and rake it over the proverbial coals.

Don't get me wrong. I like game reviews and I invite criticism. But so many reviewers have become predictable over the years. One area of the rules they've favored for their harshest attacks in the past have been the system of experience described above — namely the provisions of awarding experience points through the acquisition of gold pieces and by slaying monsters. Such a system, they charge, is non-representative of how an actual character would grow more adept in his profession.

Apparently these pear-shaped morons forgot to consider the "fantasy roleplaying game" part of the equation before they tripped over their bag of Doritos picking up pen and paper to whip out their reviews. Do I have to say it? This is a game, folks, a FANTASY game. Don't make me have to slap a "Suspension of Disbelief is Required" sticker on the cover of all the HackMaster books and supplements.

HackMaster is a game of Swack Iron Dragons, Purple Impalers, spell casting clerics, butt-kicking druids, halfling berserkers, dark elf battle mages, and half-orc assassins. If a pee-witted game critic can accept the existence of all this as well as 12 foot tall giants, and policy-making dragon committees, then why in the hell can't he accept the notion of experience points for treasure gained? Is it so hard to understand that an experience point is a concrete measure of a host of abstract factors? Experience represents such things as increased confidence, physical exercise, insight and on-the-job training.

When a character earns enough experience points to advance to the next experience level, these abstract factors translate into a measurable improvement in the abilities of the character. Which is just another way of saying he kicks ass a little better and gets his own ass kicked a little less often.

Sorry, to have to restate the obvious but I felt the need to get a pre-emptive strike in before the critics had their say. While they're busy flaming 4th edition, the rest of us can go on playing the game we love. Eh?

Group (Party) Experience

Group experience points are earned through the combined efforts of the characters working as a team. Each party member (character) contributes to the good of the party by pulling his weight and using his skills and abilities when called upon. If the party is successful, then each individual member of the party benefits.

Thus, the general policy of most adventuring parties is a "One for all! All for one!" attitude. Each member of the party receives an equal share of experience points for overcoming their enemies or obstacles encountered during the adventure or gaming session.

Group cooperation is important, so experience points for defeated monsters and any realized treasure are generally given to all members of the group, regardless of their actions. After all, who's to say the magic-user, who did little more than bring a Fireball on-line just in case things got ugly, wouldn't have saved the day had the Orc brigands not broken and ran? Or that the bard who covered the party's escape route wasn't doing something important? A character who never hefts a sword may still have good advice or important suggestions on better tactics. Furthermore, the magic-user and the bard can also learn from the actions of others.

Since group cohesion and integrity is so important, however, it is sometimes necessary to award exemplary behavior. Sadly, it's also sometimes necessary to punish a shirker or party slacker. In HackMaster, most GMs allow the players to dock or award experience points for certain members if it is felt that player hindered or furthered the group's success. (This usually involves a voting process). If an individual is docked experience points by his peers, the points docked are distributed equally among the other party members. Likewise, if a bonus is voted to an individual, the extra points must come from the other party members' shares.

Individual Experience

Player characters also earn experience points for individual deeds as determined by their class. Landing the killing blow to a creature can earn a character extra experience. An unassisted kill can earn him FULL experience points for that creature. Generally, each character earns points for doing actions appropriate to his chosen class or religion.

- Fighters can earn more experience points for defeating creatures.
- Magic-users earn points for using their spells for specific purposes. (A magic-user who lamely walks into the woods and casts a spell for no apparent reason doesn't gain experience points). Magic-users can also earn experience points for researching new spells and creating magical items.
- Clerics can earn experience points for researching new spells and creating magical items as well. Clerics also earn experience points by spreading their beliefs (converting), building new temples, and using their powers in service of their gawd.
- Thieves earn experience points by using their pick pocket skills and other special abilities to deprive others of their property. They can also earn experience by detecting or disarming traps and using their stealth to scout for the party.
- A character can also earn experience point incentives earned by the player's for playing the game well. When a player does a good job creating and pretending to be his character, the GM may give his character extra experience points for good role-playing. If the player is really involved and takes a major part in the game, the GM might choose to reward that behavior as well. If the player uses his head to come up with a really good idea, the GM can give the character experience points for his contribution.

Finally, a character can earn experience points for successfully completing an adventure or achieving a goal the GM has set. Although a player may have a pretty good idea of what his character is supposed to accomplish, he won't know if he'll be awarded experience points for it until his character actually receives them. There is no rule, however, that the GM must be consistent in his awards, or even that he must give a character anything at all. How many experience points he awards and for what is entirely left to his discretion.

Peer-Awarded Experience (Optional: GM's Discretion)

At the completion of an adventure (or more often the conclusion of a campaign) the GM may (repeat, "MAY" decide to award some Bonus Experience Points (BEPs). The amount of BEPs can be meager or substantial. It's really up to the GM. The BEPs are placed in a pool and it is then left to the players to decide who gets to draw from the pool and how much.

After discussing how the extra points are to be divided up, the party votes. If a decision can't be made, a roll-off or lottery is often used. (The GM generally does not get involved in the process as far as how the points are divvied up).

There is one stipulation regarding peer-awarded points, however. The recipient(s) must be in good standing as far as alignment and Honor. (And you didn't think alignment adherence would come back to haunt you).

The Big Pay Off: Going up in Experience Levels

Eventually, when you gain enough experience points, you come to a juncture where your character is eligible to rise to the next level. Your GM will assist you when this moment arrives, but there are certain things you should be aware of so you don't unintentionally get shorted.

Things that can affect your rate of advancment.

There are several things which can cause you to go up to the next level quicker or even to be held back. You should be aware of these, since in the heat of the game your GM is likely to overlook them. And let's face it, you need to look out for number one.

Primary ability scores: Most character classes have primary ability scores. If these scores are above a certain level the character may qualify for a 10% experience point bonus. (i.e. he can obtain the next level with less experience points). For example a fighter's primary ability score is a 16 or higher Strength. Make sure you add the 10% bonus EACH TIME your GM awards experience points.

Great Honor/Dishonor: Your character's Honor can make it easier to go up the next level, or hold him back. If your character's Honor places him in the Great Honor Bonus Window (See Chapter 5 Table 5A) category, he will earn an additional 5% to any experience point award given while he remains in that window.

Experience point awards/penalties: During the course of the game your GM may award you with extra EPs for outstanding behavior/achievements above and beyond those earned normally. Likewise he may slap you with an EP penalty bad role-playing, disruptive behavior, etc. Such awards/penalties can affect your rate of advancement to the next level.

Step-by-Step Advancement Procedure

Immediately inform your GM once you've broken the EP barrier to the next level. At the end of the game session the two of you will proceed through the necessary steps to prepare your character for advancement.

Step 1: Verification and GM Rating

GM verifies the character has the required number of EPs to advance and rates your character according to his Honor and other factors.

Step 2: Schooling: Basic block of instruction (BBI)

Now your character must attend schooling, either in a formal school or under the tutelage of a qualified mentor or teacher, and complete the BBI (basic block of instruction) for the level he's advancing to. BBI is an abstract collection of teachings and procedures which your character needs to apply his knowledge and experience and rise in level. It's what gives him any new abilities/powers associated with his new level.

The rating number you were assigned by your GM in Step 1 indicates the number of weeks it will take for your character to complete his BBI. Each week of BBI studies costs him 1,500 gold pieces (payable in advance) in fees. Advancement does not take place until the character has completed his training. Completing BBI is the qualifier for advancement in levels. Other than any abilities/powers associated with the new level there are no other awards or benefits in completing training.

Step 3: Advanced Training

During your BBI, you have an opportunity to learn new skills or improve those you already have. This is handled in two different ways:

A. Concurrent Training

During your BBI, you may sign up for up to one (1) additional Skill course. You must pay the fees listed in Appendix F prior to taking the class. At the end of your BBI you must roll to see if you passed the course, using your % Chance to Learn for your Intelligence and adding in the Course Difficulty Modifier. If you succeed you may roll the Skill Mastery Die listed for that skill, along with your Honor Die, and add the total to your current Skill

Mastery for that skill (or to the relevant abilities for that skill if this is a NEW skill you've just learned).

If you fail the course the fees are lost, no new skills/improvement takes place and you lose a point of Honor.

B. Prolonged Training

After your BBI is completed you may choose to stay at school and continue your studies. For each week you stay in school you can attempt to learn/improve two skills. You must pay 1,500 gold pieces per week plus any course fees. At the end of each week you must roll to see if you passed the course (See step A above).

> There is no limit to how long a character can stay in school so long as he has the money to pay for his classes, however, for each week beyond the BBI the character loses one (1) point of Honor. After all, you're an adventurer by the gawds, not a backpack-toting full-time student at Urbana-Champaign!

Step 4: Increasing Hit Points

After you complete your training, and advance to the next level, you roll the hit die indicated on the progression table for your character's class and add the result to your total hit points. This is your 'new' maximum hitpoint level.

Step 5: Improving Fractional Ability Scores

You may now roll your Honor Die and the appropriate polyhedron based on your class for each of your fractional ability scores and add the result to the former number. If a fractional score is pushed above 100 you should raise that ability score by 1 and record the balance of the fractional score. For example if you had a 12/87 Dexterity and rolled a twenty on your Honor Die your new Dexterity would be 13/07.

Once you are finished rolling these fractional ability scores, check the Tables in Chapter 1 to see if any of your ability modifiers have changed and make the necessary changes on your character sheet.

Step 6: Improve Your Saving Throws (see Chapter 12)

Your Saving Throw numbers change (for the better) as your character goes up in level, so check the appropriate Table for your class in Chapter 12, and mark any changes on your character sheet for easy reference during combat. (When you'll need it!)

Step 7: Choose New Proficiencies (Chapter 7)

Be sure to check Table 7A in Chapter 7 to see if you have earned any new Proficiencies, and record any new information on your character sheet.

Step 8: Record New Abilities/Powers (Chapter 3)

Refer to Chapter 3 to see if you have gained any new spells, skills, abilities or powers from your increase in level. Record any new abilities/powers for your new level that are specific to your Class on your character sheet.

Table 11A: Stat Percentile Die Roll by Class				
	Fighter	Magic User	Cleric	Thief
Strength	d20	d4	d12	d8
Intelligence	d4	d20	d6	d10
Wisdom	d6	d12	d20	d4
Dexterity	d10	d8	d4	d20
Constitution	d12	d10	d10	d6
Charisma	d8	d6	d8	d12
Comeliness	d4	d4	d4	d4

FRAIM

Combat: The Art of Hack

Now we come to the heart of HackMaster — Combat. In fact, the very name of the game, HackMaster literally means, "Master of Combat". There's no skirting that fact. The art of hack is important and every player should know the rules for handling combat inside and out. To not do so is akin to inviting others (both players and NPCs) to take advantage of you. Lack of knowledge on this subject is seen as a weakness and in HackMaster every weakness is exploited. It is strongly recommended that you earmark this section and refer to it often.

The world of HackMaster is fraught with danger and unknown perils. As such, your character, no matter what his profession may be, is going to find himself face to face with all manner of vicious beasts, creepy vermin, annoying beggars and bloodthirsty killers of all shapes and sizes. The HackMaster game is an adventure game designed to give players a feeling of excitement and peril. Characters brave the unknown perils of dank dungeons and menacing wilderness. Even when your character returns home for rest in some seedy dive, there's likely to be some thug trying to take your loot.

To Hack or Not to Hack

Now don't get me wrong. Combat isn't the most important thing in HackMaster – winning combat is. As important as fighting is to HackMaster, however, some players and GMs still don't believe that it's the be-all and end-all of play.

Frankly, that's somewhat true. I know that's a shock to some of you, but you'll be all right, really. Combat is simply one way for characters to deal with situations and conflicts. True, the most important, exciting and generally most effective way of dealing with situations is through the force-of-arms but there are other, less effective, ways to deal with situations (though it's not by accident that these methods do not have whole chapters devoted to them…).

If characters could do nothing but fight, the game would quickly resemble a video game; every encounter would be the same. You see a barkeep in one of those types of games, you know he's an enemy, because there is nothing else. You fight him. Now there's nothing wrong with that. In fact, this writer heartily recommends such wanton hacking. However, you will soon discover that bragging among your fellow players about your latest combat exploit at the expense of the GM, while endlessly fun, is not nearly as fun is bragging to the GM's precious little NPCs about what a hack-gawd your character is. Why is this so fun? Because the GM, the guy behind the screen that's out to get you, is forced to role-play the worthless slug you're jawin' at even while he's still smarting from that whuppin' you smacked down on his carefully devised monster encounter that's the subject of said bragging. And even more fun than boasting is taunting and insulting NPCs. Particularly the mouthy ones. And trust me, there'll be mouthy ones a plenty. Then, when you back it up by wuss-slapping silly one of the GM's sassy NPCs in front of a crowd of onlookers, you'll be on cloud nine.

So, because there is more to the game than fighting, namely besting the GM's NPCs in battles of wits and taunting, we'll need to cover much more than simple hack-and-slash combat in this chapter. In addition to explaining the basic mechanics of smashing and chopping foes into tiny pieces, there are rules here for smacking people around bare-fisted, shooting them with projectiles, burning them with oil, turning undead, plus special ways to attack and defend, shoot things and more. Sounds good doesn't it?

Terms

Here are some terms we use throughout the combat rules. This will get you started so the chapter text will be easier to read and more details are provided throughout this chapter.

Armor Class (AC) is the protective rating of a type of armor or natural protection of a creature. In some circumstances, AC is modified by the amount of protection gained or lost because of the character's situation. For instance, crouching behind a boulder while a barrage of missile fire is coming improves a character's Armor Class, while being attacked from behind by some cowardly thief worsens his AC.

Armor provides protection by reducing the chance that a character is attacked successfully (and suffers damage). Armor also absorbs some damage. A fighter in full plate mail may be a slow-moving target, but penetrating his armor to cause any damage is no small task.

Armor Class starts at 10, the worst (a guy in his skivvies), and counts down, as low as –10 and even beyond. Shields also improve the AC of a character (see shields in Chapter 9: Good and Services).

Abilities and situations can also affect a character's Armor Class. High Dexterity gives a bonus to Armor Class, for example. But even a character with a Dexterity bonus can have this bonus negated if he is attacked from the rear or is asleep.

Critical Hit is a hit which lands in such a way as to cause a particularly nasty wound. Perhaps the thrust of a sword finds a gap in the opponent's armor, or maybe that blow with your mace deflected off your opponent's shield only to strike him square in the face. Your GM has special matrices that will determine how much damage a critical hit does and exactly the type of damage is rendered. Damage types include; Incapacitating (painful) Wounds, Fractures, Bleeding Wounds, Incidental Damage, Scar Damage, Bruise/Contusion Damage, Gnawing Damage, Profuse Bleeding Damage, Disfigurement Damage, Vital Organ Damage, Arterial Bleeding, Scalding Damage, etc.

Damage is what happens to a character, object (like a door or shield) or armor (absorption) when successfully attacked by an opponent. Damage can also occur as the result of poison, fire, falling, acid or anything else the truly devious GM can come up with. Damage from most attacks is measured in hit points. Each time a character is hit, he suffers points of damage. It could be as little as 1 point to as many as 100 or more. These points are subtracted from the character's current hit point total. When this reaches 0, the character is dying.

Initiative determines the order in which things happen in a combat round. Like so many things in the world, initiative is determined by a combination of ability, situation and chance.

At the start of each round of battle each character makes an initiative roll. This roll can and will be modified by the abilities of the combatants and by the situation. The person with the lower modified die roll acts first.

Melee is a fancy French word for hand-to-hand battle. Here you will earn glory and honor or taste defeat and humiliation at the hands of the GM.

Missile combat occurs any time a weapon is shot, thrown, hurled, kicked or otherwise propelled. Missile and melee combat have the same basic rules, but there are special situations and modifiers that apply only to missile combat.

Saving Throws or "saves" are measures of a character's resistance to special types of attacks – poisons, magic and attacks that affect the whole body or mind of the character. The ability to make successful saving throws improves as the character increases in level. High Ability Scores can also help you make saves.

Surprise can happen any time characters meet another group unexpectedly (monsters, evil knights, peasants, wedding guests, etc.). Surprise is simply what happens when one side – a person or party – is taken unawares, unable to react until they gather their wits. Their opponents, if not surprised, are allowed a bonus round of action while the surprised characters recover. It's entirely possible for both sides in a given situation to be surprised!

Attacking with surprise gives bonuses to the attack roll (see Table 12A). A surprised character also has a decreased chance of rolling a successful saving throw, if one is needed. Surprise is determined by a die roll and is normally checked at the beginning of an encounter. Surprise is very unpredictable, so there are very few modifiers to the roll.

The Attack Roll

At the heart of the HackMaster combat system stands the all-important attack roll, also known as the "to-hit" roll. This is the die roll that determines whether an attack succeeds or fails. Attack rolls are used for attacks with swords, crossbows, rocks, tankards and other weapons, as well as sucker punches, tackling, groin kicks and other hand-to-hand attacks. Making an attack roll is simple: just roll a d20, add all relevant bonuses and your GM will look up your total on the to-hit tables, cross-index it against your opponent's Armor Class and tell you if you hit.

While the GM's guide is technically off-limits to all players, I cannot recommend more strongly that you buy a copy and GM one time for your little brother, nephew, mom or somebody (thus making you a GM at least temporarily). This will give you access to the to-hit tables. Memorize them. Then when you play you can verify whether the GM is cheating. Of course you will also need to memorize all of the monster's Armor Classes in the Hacklopedia of Beasts as well, but any player worth his salt has already thought of that. You must know your enemy to defeat your enemy. And, of course, the GM knows all of your stats and weaknesses. Do you think for a second he doesn't use that knowledge illegally against you? You bet your sweet patootie he does! Again, you technically need to be a GM to have access to these books.

Attack Roll Modifiers

In combat, many factors can modify the number a character needs for a successful hit. These variables are reflected in modifiers to the attack roll or opponent's AC.

Strength Modifiers: A character's Strength can modify the die roll, altering both the chance to hit and the damage caused. This modifier is always applied to melee attacks and hurled missile weapon attacks (an axe or shot glass).

A positive Strength modifier can be applied to bows if the character has a special bow made for him, one designed to take advantage of his high Strength. Characters with Strength penalties always suffer them when using a bow weapon. Like a wimpy little cupid, they simply are not able to draw back the bowstring far enough. Characters never have Strength modifiers when using crossbows – the power of the shot is imparted by a machine, not the character.

Magical items: The magical properties of a weapon can also modify combat. Items that impart a bonus to the attack roll or Armor Class are identified by a plus sign. For example, a sword +4 improves a character's to-hit roll (and damage roll) by four. A suit of chainmail +1 improves the Armor Class of the character by one (which means you subtract one from the character's AC, changing an AC of 5 to an AC of 4, for example). Cursed items have a negative modifier (a penalty), resulting in a subtraction from the attack roll or an addition to Armor Class.

There is no limit to the number of modifiers that can be applied to a single die roll. Nor is there a limit to the positive or negative number (the total of all modifiers) that can be applied to a die roll.

Table 12A lists some standard combat modifiers. Positive numbers are bonuses for the attacker, negative numbers are penalties.

Weapon Type vs. Armor Type Modifiers

Not all weapons were forged equally. Aside from the differences in size, weight, length and shape, certain types of weapons are more useful against some types of armor than others. Indeed, the different armors and weapons of the HackMaster world were created to defeat one another. Every newly invented weapon led to the development of a new type of armor designed to counter it. This led to new weapons of destruction, which led to new armor, and so on.

In the HackMaster game, weapons fall into several categories based on how they are used. The basic categories are hacking, puncturing and crushing.

Hacking weapons include most swords and axes. Damage is caused by the combination of weight, muscle and a good sharp edge.

Table 12A: To-hit Modifiers

Situation	Attack Roll Modifier
Attacker on higher ground than defender	+1
Defender invisible	-4
Defender off-balance, encumbered, held by one leg	+2
Defender sleeping, held, paralyzed or totally immobile	Automatic*
Defender stunned, prone, slowed, held by both legs, or partially bound	+4
Defender surprised	+1
Missile fire, long range	-5
Missile fire, medium range	-2
Rear attack	+2 and Defender may not use shield or Dex.
Flank attack	Defender may not use shield
Rear flank attack	Defender may not use shield or Dex.

*If the defender is attacked during the course of a normal melee, the attack automatically hits and causes normal damage. If no other fighting is going on (i.e., all others have been slain or driven off), the defender can be slain automatically. This is a good tactic for spell-casters and torchbearers.

Table 12B: Weapon Type vs. Armor Type To-hit Modifiers

Armor Type	Hacking	Puncturing	Crushing
Banded mail	-2	0	-1
Brigandine	-1	-1	0
Chain mail	-2	0	+2
Bronze Plate mail	-2	0	+2
Field Plate	-3	-1	0
Full Plate	-4	-3	0
Leather armor	0	+2	0
Hides	0	+2	0
Padded armor	0	+2	0
Plate mail	-3	0	0
Ring mail	-1	-1	0
Scale mail	0	-1	0
Splint mail	0	-1	-2
Studded leather	-2	-1	0

Puncturing weapons (spears, pikes, arrows, javelins, etc.) rely on the penetrating power of a single sharp point and thrust or propulsion (in the case of missile weapons).

Crushing weapons (maces, hammers, clubs and flails) depend almost entirely on the impact caused by momentum, weight and strength.

A few weapons, particularly some of the more exotic polearms, fall into more than one of these categories. A simple kitchen knife can be used as a hacking weapon or a puncturing weapon. The versatility of these weapons provides the user with a combat advantage, in that the mode most favorable to the attacker can be used, depending upon the situation.

Armor types, in turn, have different qualities. Field plate is more effective, overall, than other armors by virtue of the amount and thickness of the metal, but it still has specific weaknesses against certain classes of weapons.

Table 12B lists the weapon type vs. armor type modifiers applied to the attacker's die roll. To use this table, the actual armor type of the target must be known in addition to the target's Armor Class. The bonuses of magical armor do not change the type of armor, only the final Armor Class. This system is used only when attacking creatures in armor. The modifiers are not used when attacking creatures with a natural Armor Class.

Impossibly Easy or Hard To-Hit Numbers

Sometimes you, the attacker, will find yourself with an impossible to-hit roll needed. Maybe you're playing a thief who's blind and critically hit, attacking with a cursed sword in his off hand and the defender's AC is –4. Never fear, if you roll a natural 20 on the attack roll, you hit! Likewise, a natural 1 is always a miss.

Combat and Encounters

Encounters are the heart, lungs and brain of the HackMaster game. Since encounters with monsters and NPCs typically lead to combat or a loss of Honor by one side or the other, knowledge of the mechanics of combat is critical for everyone. There are several factors for the GM to consider in any encounter, most of which arise from the circumstances of the encounter. Is anyone surprised? How far apart are the opponents? How many of them are there? Answers to these questions are found in the Encounter section of the GMG and are for the GM's eyes only. These are questions common to all encounters, whether combat occurs or not.

The Combat Round

When an encounter escalates into a combat situation, the time scale of the game automatically goes to rounds (also called melee rounds or combat rounds). A round is approximately six seconds long and is further broken into 10 segments. Segments are important during initiative. Ten combat rounds equal a turn (or, put another way, a turn equals a minute of game time). This is particularly important to remember for spells that last for turns, rather than rounds.

What You Can Do in One Round

A character can accomplish only one basic action in a melee round, be it attacking, casting a spell, drinking a potion, tending to a fallen comrade or cutting pouches from a lifeless victim. The basic action, however, may involve several lesser actions.

When making an attack, a character is likely to close with his opponent, circle for an opening, feint here, jab there, block a thrust, duck and perhaps finally make a telling blow. A spellcaster may fumble for his components, dodge an attacker, mentally review the steps of the spell, intone the spell and then move to safety when it is all done. All of these things happen in a six second round.

Some examples of the actions a character can accomplish during a round include the following:

- Make an attack (make attack rolls up to the maximum number allowed for the character class at a given level)
- Cast one spell (if the casting time is 10 segments or less)
- Drink a potion
- Light a torch
- Use a magical item
- Move to the limit of his movement rate
- Attempt to open a stuck or secret door
- Bind a character's wounds
- Rifle through the pouches on a slain enemy
- Pick your ally's pocket while he's busy with a foe
- Hammer in a spike

FRAIM

The Combat Sequence

Combat follows a simple three-step process:

1. The GM announces that it is time to begin initiative. Each player that wants to cast a spell must shout "Spell!" at this time or he forfeits the right to cast a spell until next round.

2. Each player and the GM rolls for initiative. Those planning to use readied missile weapons need not roll initiative.

3. Actions are made in order of initiative.

These steps are repeated until the combat ends—one side is defeated, surrenders, or runs away.

Initiative

The initiative roll determines who acts on what segment during a given combat round. This can be critical, for often he who hacks first hacks last. Initiative is not set, but changes from round to round (combat being an uncertain thing at best). A character never knows for certain if he will get to act before another. Each player rolls a d10 for his individual initiative, subtracts his Dexterity modifier, then applies all applicable modifiers from Table 12C. Likewise, the GM rolls initiative for each group of monsters.

When casting spells, the spellcaster rolls a d4 for initiative (modified by Dexterity) if he needs to retrieve material components, otherwise, he does not roll at all. The spell activates on the segment of its casting time (regardless of Dexterity bonuses or penalties).

Initiative Modifiers

Situational factors can affect who has initiative. To reflect this, modifiers are added to or subtracted from the initiative die roll.

Multiple Attacks, Missile Weapons and Initiative

Fighters with multiple attacks with the same weapon roll twice for initiative, and re-roll ties (the same weapon cannot strike twice in one segment). Monsters attacking multiple times usually follow a claw, claw, bite or similar routine. The GMG covers initiative for them. Here you need only know that the attacks are spread throughout the round. Try to kill monsters like this early so they don't get their extra attacks later in the round.

Table 12C: Standard Modifiers to Initiative	
Specific Situation	Modifier
Hasted	-10
Slowed	+10
On higher ground	-1
Set to receive a charge	-3
Wading or slippery footing	+3
Wading in deep water	+6
Foreign environment*	+8
Hindered (tangled, climbing, held)	+5
Waiting (see Chapter 14)	+1
Attacking with weapon	Weapon speed
Draw a weapon	Weapon speed + 5
Fist or natural weaponry	-2
Breath weapon	-1
Casting a spell	Casting time
Innate spell ability	Casting time as if spell
Magical items	Casting time as if spell
Search for item	+d4
For every 1/10th movement rate traveled	+1

*This applies to situations in which the character is in a completely different environment (swimming underwater without the aid of a Ring of Free Action, for example).

Results below zero are possible. These indicate that the character takes action on segment one, but lowest initiative number goes first (i.e., -2 on the modified roll beats a -1). Ties are simultaneous. If a sluggish character gets a modified roll of over 11+, subtract 10 and that is the segment he takes action on the following round.

Readied missile weapons attack on segment 1 (no initiative roll is required). Weapons fired twice attack on segments 1 and 6. Those fired three times go on 1, 5 and 9. Four times: 1, 4, 7 and 10.

Spellcasting and Initiative

Casting times for spells replace initiative rolls. Spells requiring material components can create a delay for the spellcaster if they are not in a handy location, adding d4 to the casting time. If a spell caster finishes the spell before segment 5, he can hunt around on his person for the next components he needs for his subsequent spell. When a spell requires one round to cast and the components were handy, it takes effect at the end of the current round, after all other actions are completed.

Spells that require more than one round to cast continue to be intoned by the spellcaster through additional rounds. If the spellcasting character is disturbed in any way during this time, the spell is lost.

Attacking with Two Weapons

The character chooses not to use a shield in favor of another weapon, granting him a greater number of attacks, with a penalty to his attack in most cases.

When using a second weapon in his off-hand, a character is limited in his weapon choice. His principal weapon can be whatever he chooses, provided it can be wielded with one hand. The second weapon must be smaller in size and weight than the character's main weapon (though a dagger or a hand axe can always be used as a second weapon, even if the primary weapon is also a dagger or hand axe). A fighter can use a long sword and a short sword, or a long sword and a dagger, but he cannot use two long swords. Nor can the character use a shield, unless it is kept strapped onto his back.

When attacking, characters suffer penalties to their attack rolls. Attacks made with the main weapon suffer a -2 penalty, and attacks made with the second weapon suffer a -4 penalty. The character's Reaction Adjustment (based on his Dexterity, see Table 1B) modifies this penalty. A low Dexterity score will worsen the character's chance to hit with each attack. A high Dexterity can negate this particular penalty, although it cannot result in a positive modifier on the attack rolls for either weapon (i.e., the Reaction Adjustment can, at best, raise the attack roll penalties to 0).

The use of two weapons enables the character to make one additional attack each combat round, with the second weapon. The character gains only one additional attack each round, regardless of the number of attacks he may normally be allowed. Thus, a fighter able to attack 3/2 (once in the first round and twice in the second) can attack 5/2 (twice in the first round and three times in the second).

Movement in Combat

In a combat round, a being can move up to 10 times its movement rating (see Chapter 16: Time and Movement) in feet. Thus, if a character has a movement rating of 9, he can move up to 90 feet in a round. However, the types of moves a character can make during combat are somewhat limited.

Movement in Melee

The basic move is to get closer for combat—i.e., move close enough to an enemy to attack. This is neither a blind rush nor a casual stroll. Instead, the character approaches quickly but with caution. When closing for combat, a character can move up to half his allowed distance and still make a melee attack. Moving in this fashion adds a +5 modifier to his initiative result – if the result exceeds 10, he will attack next round as per usual.

Movement and Missile Combat

Rather than slug it out toe-to-toe with an opponent, a character can move up to one-half his normal movement rate and engage in missile fire at half his normal rate of fire. Thus, a man capable of moving 120 feet and armed with a long bow (two shots per round, under normal circumstances) could move 60 feet and still fire one shot. The shot occurs on the latest segment, in this case segment 6 (see Multiple Attacks, Missile Weapons and Initiative, above). The same man, armed with a heavy crossbow (one shot every other round) would be able to shoot only once every four rounds while on the move.

Charging an Opponent

A character can also charge a foe. A charge increases the character's movement rate by 50% and enables the character to make an attack at the end of his movement. A charging character also gains a +2 bonus to his attack roll, mainly from momentum. Certain weapons (such as a lance) inflict double the rolled damage in a charge.

However, charging gives the opponents several advantages. First, they gain a -3 bonus to their initiative rolls. Second, charging characters gain no Dexterity bonuses to Armor Class and they suffer an AC penalty of 1. Finally, if the defender is using a puncturing weapon with reach longer than the attacker's weapon and sets it against the charge (bracing the butt against a stone or his foot or firmly holding the blade forward with both hands), he inflicts double damage on a successful hit.

Retreat

To get out of a combat, characters can make a careful withdrawal or the true cowards can simply flee. Note that this type of action will have a negative effect on your Honor, unless you return to eliminate the opponent later, in which case this manuever is reclassified as "retrograde movement" and not fleeing!

Withdrawing: When making a withdrawal, a character carefully backs away from his opponent (who can choose to follow and continue to hack). The backing character moves up to 1/3 his normal movement rate.

If two characters are fighting a single opponent and one of them decides to withdraw, the remaining character can block the advance of the opponent. This is a useful method for getting a seriously injured ally out of a battle.

Fleeing: To flee from combat, a yellow, cowardly sissy-character simply turns tail and runs up to his full movement rate. The fleeing character drops his defenses and turns his back to his opponent.

The enemy is allowed a free attack (or multiple attacks if the creature has several attacks per round) at the rear of the fleeing character (no Dex bonus or shield bonus). This attack is made the instant the character flees – it doesn't count against the number of attacks that opponent is allowed during the round, and initiative is irrelevant. The fleeing character can be pursued, unless a companion blocks the advance of the enemy.

Attacking Without Killing

There are times when a character wants to defeat another being without killing it. A companion may have been charmed into attacking his friends

Table 12D:
Armor Modifiers for Wrestling

Armor	Attacker's To-hit Modifier
Studded leather	-1
Chain, ring, and scale mail	-2
Banded, splint, and plate mail	-5
Field plate armor	-8
Full plate armor	-10

(and his friends don't want to kill him at this time), an enemy may have information the PCs can get only by subduing him and torturing him later, characters may simply see the monetary value of bringing back a real live monster, or characters may want to breed monsters for an e.p. farm.

There are three types of non-lethal attacks—punching, wrestling and overbearing. Punching is basic bare-fisted fighting. Wrestling is the classic combination of grappling, holds and throws. Overbearing is simply trying to pull down an opponent by sheer mass or weight of numbers, pinning him to the ground.

Punching and Wrestling

Punching occurs when a character bludgeons others with his fists. Sometimes you just need to have a knock-down drag-out good old-fashioned fist fight. There's just nothing like the feeling of your knuckles plowing into someone's nose and hearing their bones and cartilage snap, or watching the blood and teeth spray when you let loose a good uppercut to the mouth. No weapons are used, although wearing brass knuckles, an iron gauntlet or similar item can be effective if you want to do more damage, but personally, I feel it lessens the enjoyment.

Wrestling requires both hands free, unencumbered by shields and the like, and it's for sissies, but if you want to do it, go ahead. No one's stopping you. Just try not to rip your skirt.

When punching or wrestling a normal attack roll is made. The normal Armor Class of the target is used. If a character is attempting to wrestle in armor, the modifiers on Table 12D are used. Normal modifiers to the attack roll are also applied. Penalties for being held or attacking a held opponent do not apply to wrestlers. Wrestling involves a lot of holding and twisting as it is, and the damage resolution system for punching and wrestling takes this into account.

If the attack roll is successful, consult Table 12E to find the result of the attack: Cross-index the character's modified attack roll with the proper attack form. If, for example, a character successfully punched with an 18, the result would be a rabbit punch (if he rolled an 18 on a successful wrestling attempt, the result would be a kick). Punching and wrestling attacks can succeed on attack rolls of 1 or less (exceptions to the general rule).

Punch: In game terms, the type of blow has little effect, but using the names adds spice to the battle and helps you visualize combat better.

Table 12E:
Punching and Wrestling Results

Attack Roll	Punch	Damage	% KO	Wrestle
20+	Haymaker	2	10	Bear hug*
19	Wild swing	0	1	Arm twist
18	Rabbit punch	1	3	Kick
17	Kidney punch	1	5	Trip
16	Glancing blow	1	2	Elbow smash
15	Jab	2	6	Arm lock*
14	Uppercut	1	8	Leg twist
13	Hook	2	9	Leg lock
12	Kidney punch	1	5	Throw
11	Hook	2	10	Gouge
10	Glancing blow	1	3	Elbow smash
9	Combination	1	10	Leg lock*
8	Uppercut	1	9	Headlock*
7	Combination	2	10	Throw
6	Jab	2	8	Gouge
5	Glancing blow	1	3	Kick
4	Rabbit punch	2	5	Arm lock*
3	Hook	2	12	Gouge
2	Uppercut	2	15	Headlock*
1	Wild swing	0	2	Leg twist
Less than 1	Haymaker	2	25	Bearhug*

*Hold can be maintained from round to round, until broken.

Damage: Bare-handed attacks cause only 1 or 2 points of damage. Penetration damage does not apply to punching or wrestling attacks. Metal gauntlets, brass knuckles, and the like cause 1d6-1/1d6-2/1d6-3 points of damage for small, medium and large opponents respectively. Using these items during a brawl does allow penetration damage. A character's Strength bonus or penalty, if any, applies to punching attacks.

Punching damage is handled a little differently than normal damage. Only 25% of the damage caused by a bare-handed attack is normal damage. The remaining 75% is temporary. For the sake of convenience, record punching damage separately from other damage and calculate the percentage split at the end of all combat.

If a character reaches 0 hit points due to punching attacks (or any combination of punching and normal attacks), he immediately falls unconscious.

A character can voluntarily pull his punch, not causing any hit point damage, provided he says so before the damage is applied to his enemy. There is still a chance of a knockout.

% K.O.: Although a punch does very little damage, there is a chance of knocking an opponent out. This chance is listed on the table as "% K.O." If this number or less is rolled on percentile dice, the victim is stunned for 1d10 rounds.

Wrestle: This lists the action or type of grip the character managed to get. A hold is broken by a throw, a gouge, the assistance of another person or the successful use of a weapon. (Penalties to the attack roll apply to weapon attacks by a character who is in a hold.)

All wrestling moves inflict 1 point of damage plus Strength bonus (if the attacker desires) or penalty, while continued holds cause cumulatively 1 more point of damage for each round they are held. A headlock held for six rounds would inflict 21 points of damage total (1+2+3+4+5+6).

Overbearing

Sometimes the most effective attack is simply to pull an opponent down by sheer numbers. No attempt is made to gain a particular hold or even to harm the victim. The only concern is to pin and restrain him.

To overbear an opponent, a normal attack roll is made. For every level of size difference (1 if a Large attacker takes on a Medium defender, for example), the attack roll is modified by 4 (+4 if the attacker is larger, -4 if the defender is larger).

The defender also gains a benefit if it has more than two legs: a -2 penalty to the attacker's roll for every leg beyond two. There is no penalty to the defender if it has no legs. A lone Orc attempting to pull down a horse and rider would have at least a -8 penalty applied to the attack roll (-4 for size and -4 for the horse's four legs).

If the attack succeeds, the opponent is pulled down. A character can be pinned if further successful overbearing attacks are rolled each round. For pinning purposes, do not use the prone modifier to combat (from Table 12A).

If multiple attackers are all attempting to pull down a single target, make only one attack roll with a +1 bonus for each attacker beyond the first. Always use the to-hit number of the weakest attacker to figure the chance of success, since cooperation always depends on the weakest link. Modifiers for size should be figured for the largest attacker of the group.

A giant and three pixies attempting to pull down a man would use the pixies' attack roll, modified by +3 for three extra attackers and +8 for the size difference of the giant (Huge) and the man (Medium).

Weapons In Nonlethal Combat

Sometimes one party makes the mistake of bringing nothing but their fists to a sword fight. Such poor chumps will find this section useful. While not very sporting, in this scenario it's a lot more fun to be the guy with the weapon. This is because the character attempting to punch, wrestle, or overbear an armed opponent can do so only by placing himself at great risk. An armed defender is automatically allowed to strike with his weapon before the unarmed attack is made, regardless of the initiative die roll. Furthermore, since his opponent must get very close, the defender gains a +4 bonus to his attack and damage rolls. If the attacker survives, he can then attempt his attack.

Those involved in a wrestling bout are limited to weapons of small size after the first round of combat. You can't very well use a halberd on someone giving you a bear hug and biting your ear or hanging on your back clawing your eyes. For this reason, nearly all characters looking to wrestle will want to carry a dagger or knife to shove between the ribs of a would-be ear-biter.

Nonlethal Weapon Attacks: It is possible to make an armed attack without causing serious damage (striking with the flat of the blade, for example). The character has a -4 penalty to his attack roll for trying to pull-up or check swing. The damage from such an attack is 50% normal; one-half of this damage is temporary.

Nonlethal Combat and Creatures

When dealing with non-humanoid opponents, a number of factors must be considered. First, unintelligent creatures, as a rule, won't try to grapple, punch, or pull you down. They cheerfully settle for tearing you apart limb by limb or ripping out your larynx. This, to their small and animalistic minds and the sadistic side of the GM, is far more fun.

Second, the natural weapons of a creature are always usable. Unlike men with swords, a Sabre-Toothed Tiger or an Aarnz Hound doesn't lose the use of its teeth and fangs just because a character is very close to it. They gleefully clamp right down on the 'ol wind pipe.

Finally, and of greatest importance, creatures tend to be better natural fighters than humans.

So the moral is simple. Use your weapons stupid! If you find yourself fighting a natural denizen unarmed, try to punch and hope for a knockout. But keep 3d6 and a fresh character sheet handy.

Touch Spells and Combat

Many spells used take effect only when the caster touches the target. Under normal circumstances, this is no problem-the spellcaster reaches out and touches the recipient. However, if the target is unwilling, or the spell is used in the midst of a general melee, the situation is much different.

Unwilling Targets: The spellcaster must make a successful attack roll for the spell to have any effect. The caster attacks against AC 10 plus the victim's Dexterity bonus. If the roll succeeds, the spellcaster touches the target and the normal spell effect occurs. Enemy creatures count as unwilling targets, and have an AC of 10 with no dexterity bonus.

Willing Targets: When attempting to cast a spell on a willing target, the casting is automatic as long as both characters are not engaged in combat. For example, if a fighter withdraws from melee, a cleric could heal him the next round. If the recipient of the spell attempts to do anything besides waiting for the spell to take effect, an attack roll against AC 10 must be made as above, however, no AC modifiers for Dexterity are applied, since the target is not trying to avoid the spell.

Missile Weapons in Combat

Missile weapons are divided into two general categories. The first includes all standard, direct-fire, single-target missiles--slings, arrows, quarrels, stones, sticks, tankards, spears, throwing axes and the like.

The second category includes all grenade-like missiles that have an area effect, no matter how small. Thus, an attack with these weapons does not have to hit its target directly to have a chance of affecting it. Included in this group are small flasks of oil, acid, poison, holy water, barrels, potions and anything else you can find that splatters, explodes or leaves a wide swath of destruction in its path.

Range

The first step in making a missile attack is to find the range from the attacker to the target. This is measured in yards from one point to the other. This distance is compared to the range categories for the weapon used (see Table 9V in Chapter 9: Goods and Services).

If the distance is greater than the long range listed, the target is out of range. If the distance is between the long and medium range numbers, the target is at long range. When the distance is between the medium and short range numbers, the target is at medium range. When the distance is equal to or less than the listed short range, the target is at short range.

Short range attacks suffer no range modifier. Medium range attacks suffer a -2 penalty to the attack roll. Long range attacks suffer a -5 penalty. Some weapons have no short range since they must arc a certain distance before reaching their target. These attacks are always made with an attack roll penalty.

Rate of Fire

Bows, crossbows, and many other missile weapons have different rates of fire (ROF) – the number of missiles they can shoot in a single round.

Small, light weapons can be thrown very quickly, so up to three darts can be thrown in a single round. Arrows can be nocked and let loose almost as quickly, so up to two shots can be fired in a single round.

Some weapons (such as heavy crossbows) take a long time to load and can be fired only every other round. Whatever the ROF, multiple missile shots are handled the same way as other multiple attacks for the purposes of determining initiative. The ROF of each missile weapon is listed in (see Table 9V in Chapter 9: Goods and Services).

Ability Modifiers in Missile Combat

Dexterity always modifies the attack roll of personal missile weapons (i.e., not siege engines and the like). Attack roll and damage modifiers for Strength are only used when an attack is made with a hurled weapon. Here the power of the character's arm is a significant factor in the effectiveness of the attack. When using a bow, the attack roll and damage Strength modifiers apply only if the character has a properly prepared bow (see Chapter 9: Goods and Services). Characters never receive Strength bonuses when using crossbows or similar mechanical devices.

Firing into a Melee

Missile weapons are intended mainly as long-range weapons. Ideally, they are used before the opponents reach your line. However, there's always some jerk that thinks he can shoot sharp pointy objects at high speed into melee and avoid hitting his friends. While possible, and certainly allowed, this is a risky proposition. Typically, guys like this wake up the next morning with a shiner or worse.

When missiles are fired into a melee, the GM counts the number of figures in the immediate area of the intended target. Each Medium figure counts as 1. Small (S) figures count as 1/2, Large as 2, Huge as 4, and Gargantuan as 6. The total value is compared to the value of each character or creature in the target melee. Using this ratio, the GM rolls a die to determine who (or what) will be the target of the shot.

Malcolm (man-sized, or 1 point) and Grinder (also man-sized, or 1 point) are fighting a giant (size G, 6 points) while Thule fires a long bow at the giant. The total value of all possible targets is 8 (6+1+1). There's a 1 in 8 chance that Grinder is the target, a 1 in 8 chance that Malcolm is hit, and a 6 in 8 chance the shot hits the giant. The GM could roll an 8-sided die to determine who gets hit, or he could reduce the ratios to a percentage (75% chance the giant is hit, etc.) and roll percentile dice. In this case, he rolls a 78; Malcolm is targeted. He better hope the shot kills Malcolm at this point or the next day, Thule will wake up with a shiner.

Grenade-Like Missiles

Unlike standard missiles, which target a specific creature, a grenade-like missile is aimed at a point, whether this point is a creature or a spot on the ground. When attacking with a missile like this, simply pick where you want the weapon to land. This then becomes the target point and is used to determine the direction and distance of a miss or scatter.

Grenade-like missiles are not listed on the equipment tables for range, ROF, and damage.

A missile of five pounds or less has a short range of 10 feet, medium range up to 20 feet, and everything beyond that to a maximum of 30 feet is long range. Heavier items have reduced ranges. Just how far an object can be thrown is determined by the GM.

Once a container hits, it has to break to spill its contents. The item will have to fail a saving throw or it will bounce and not break. The GMG contains information on how to resolve the inevitable situations in which a grenade-like missile misses its target, whether because it failed to break or because the character tossing it missed his attack roll.

Types of Grenade-Like Missiles

Acid damage is particularly grim. Aside from the possibility of scarring (which is left to the GM), acid damage cannot be healed by regeneration. It must be healed normally or magically. Thus it is very useful against regenerating creatures such as Trolls.

Holy Water affects most forms of undead and creatures from the Lower Planes. It has no effect against a creature in gaseous form or undead without material form.

Unholy water (as holy water, but used by minions of evil) affects paladins, angels, good gawds and creatures and other beings from the Upper Planes.

Holy (or unholy) water affects these creatures as does acid, causing damage that cannot be regenerated but must be healed normally or magically.

Oil causes damage only when it is lit. Sometimes this requires a two-step process, such as when tossing oil into melee with allies. Step one is soaking the target in oil. Step two is hitting him with a torch, candle, open lantern, Fireball or the like. Thus, using flaming oil often requires two successful attacks. Another method is to light a soaked piece of cloth tied to the oil flask (the Molotov cocktail method). Use this method when there are no friendly troops involved or when you dislike your allies. A direct hit from flaming oil burns for two rounds, causing 2d6 points of damage in the first round and 1d6 points in the second round.

Other types of grenade-like missile weapons include high proof alcohol, Greek fire, alchemical napalm, satchels of red hot coal, Potions of Impact, jars full of marbles, etc.

Taking Cover Against Missile Fire

One of the best ways to avoid being hit and injured is to hide behind something—a wall, a tree, a building corner, a heap of boulders, or whatever happens to be available. If you later come out and kick the butt of the scumbag shooting the missile weapon, we call this taking cover. If you run, we call this hiding like a frightened little girl and this impacts your Honor in a very negative fashion. Taking cover doesn't work particularly well in a melee, since the cover hampers defender and attacker equally and causes immediate loss of Honor if the opponent survives to tell the tale, so if you have to hide, do it against missile fire, then come out swinging.

There are two types of protection your character can have. The first is concealment, also called soft cover. A character hiding behind a clump of bushes is concealed. He can be seen, but only with difficulty, and it's no easy task to determine exactly where he is. The bushes cannot stop an arrow, but they do make it less likely that the character is hit. Other types of concealment include curtains, tapestries, smoke, fog, and brambles.

The other type of protection is cover, or, more precisely, hard cover. It is, as its name implies, something a character can hide behind that will block a missile. Hard cover includes stone walls, the corner of a building, tables, doors, earth embankments, tree trunks, and the like.

Cover helps a potential target by giving the attacker a negative modifier to his attack roll. The exact modifier for concealment or cover depends on the

degree to which it is being used as shelter. A character who stands behind a two-foot wall is a pretty obvious target, especially when compared to the character who lies down behind that wall and carefully peers over it. Table 12F lists the different modifiers for varying degrees of cover and concealment.

Cover also has an effect on saving throws, granting the character the modifier listed on Table 12F as a bonus to his saving throws against spells that cause physical damage (for example, Fireball, Lightning Bolt, etc.)

Furthermore, a character who has 90% cover (or more) suffers one-half normal damage on a failed save and no damage at all if a saving throw is successful. This assumes, of course, that the Fireball, Lightning Bolt or whatever, hit the cover. A man crouching behind a stone wall

Table 12F: Cover and Concealment AC Modifiers		
Target is:	Cover	Concealment
25% hidden	+2	+1
50% hidden	+4	+2
75% hidden	+7	+3
90% hidden	+10	+4

would be protected if a Fireball exploded in front of the wall, but would not be protected by cover if the blast occurred behind him, on his side of the wall.

The Full Parry

So far, the bulk of this chapter has dealt with ways to attack. This is as it should be, for those who hesitate will wind up skewered in most encounters. If you must go on the defensive in melee, we recommend the full parry. During combat, your characters parry all the time – there's no need to single out each individual parry.

When a character deliberately chooses not to defend himself (a magic-user casting a spell, for instance), his chance of being hit increases. Thus choosing to parry, in and of itself, is not a separate option under the HackMaster game rules.

Normally your character parries blows, then counters, then parries, etc. However, if all you want to do is defend yourself (perhaps waiting for the cleric to get close to cure you, waiting for your opponent's magic to wear off or simply because you're yellow and devoid of Honor) your character can use the full parry maneuver. When executing a full parry, a character forfeits all actions for the round--he can't attack, move, or cast spells. This frees the character to concentrate solely on defense. At this point, all characters but fighters gain an AC bonus equal to half their level. A 6th-level thief would have a +3 bonus to his AC (lowering his AC by 3). A fighter type gets a bonus equal to half his level plus one. A 6th-level gnome titan would gain a +4 AC bonus.

The full parry has no effect on magic or missile attacks.

Injury and Death

Sometimes, no degree of luck, skill, ability, swindling or resistance to various attacks can prevent overwhelming harm from coming to your character. The heroic life of HackMaster carries with it unavoidable risks. If you wanted to be safe you should have stayed in the sandbox. Sooner or later a character is going to be hurt. And hurt badly.

Unlike some wimpy wannabe games, damage in HackMaster is not handled abstractly or approximately. All characters and monsters have a number of hit points. The more hit points a creature has, the more physical damage he can take. Damage is subtracted from a character's (or creature's) hit points. Should one of the player characters hit an Ogre in the side of the head for 8 points of damage, those 8 points are subtracted from the ogre's total hit points. Hit point loss is cumulative until a character dies or has a chance to heal his wounds.

As your character gains levels he gets tougher and can take more physical abuse. Do you think that cop in Die Hard could have taken all that damage as a rookie cop? No way. He'd have probably passed out from the broken glass in his foot alone. But he was a higher level hero and took the hits to complete his adventure.

Wounds

When a character hits a monster, or vice versa, damage is suffered by the victim. The amount of damage depends on the weapon or method of attack. In Table 9T of Chapter 9, all weapons are rated for the amount of damage they inflict to Small, Medium, and Large targets. This is given as a die range (1d8, 2d6, etc.).

Each time a hit is scored, the appropriate dice are rolled and the damage is subtracted from the current hit points of the target. An Orc that attacks with a sword, for example, causes damage according to the information given for the type of sword it uses, plus Strength bonuses (or penalties). An Aarnz Hound that bites once and rends with one of its clawed paws causes 1d8 points of damage with its bite and 2-5 (1d4 + 1) points with its claw. (The GM gets this information from the Hacklopedia of Beasts.)

Sometimes damage is listed as a die range along with a bonus of +1 or more. The Aarnz Hound's claw attack, above, is a good example. This bonus may be due to high Strength, magical weapons, or the sheer ferocity of the creature's attack. The bonus is added to whatever number comes up on the die roll, assuring that some minimum amount of damage is caused. Likewise, penalties can also be applied, but no successful attack can result in less than 1 point of damage.

Additional Bonus Damage

Damage Multipliers. To know that you can strike for additional damage is music to a character's ears, especially when the odds are stacked against you in combat. Sometimes an attack has a damage multiplier, e.g., a thief's backstab. In this case, roll the damage dice twice, but only add your Strength modifier and other modifiers into the first die roll.

Penetration Damage occurs when a character rolls the maximum number on any damage die. When this occurs he must immediately roll an additional die of that type as penetration damage (any damage bonuses are not included in this additional roll). The result of the extra die roll, less one point (so penetration can actually result in zero extra damage if a one is rolled), is added to the total damage. This process continues indefinitely as long as the damage die in question continues to come up maximum. For example, if you hit with a weapon that does 1d8 damage and you roll an 8, you must roll again. Let's say your second roll is also an 8 (this adds 7 points of damage). Your next roll is a 4 so you must stop rolling but get to add another 3 points for the final roll. Total damage is 18 points (i.e. 8+7+3) exclusive of any bonuses you may have. Armor absorption does not protect against penetration damage and shields suffer additional damage from penetration damage when it is being rolled against a shield. In the case of shields, any damage in excess of the shield hit point total is applied to the defender as usual (though in this case armor DOES absorb a point from each and every die that penetrates).

Follow Through Damage occurs any time a character deals enough damage to another monster or character to drop that character to zero or more, any additional damage can (attacker's choice) be immediately applied to an adjacent defender. Note that applying follow through damage may allow a dropped character to live where he might have died because damage application to that character stops when he is reduced to zero. If you want to make sure he is slain we recommend against applying follow through (or returning later to whack him again). Follow through damage does not require an additional attack roll nor does it allow a saving throw. This process continues until all damage from the roll has been dealt, or all adjacent defenders are slain. Spells cannot exceed area of effect and where applicable, spells and missile weapons must follow proper trajectory (i.e., no magic bullets in HackMaster).

Getting hit by weapons or monsters isn't the only way a character can get hurt. GMs are well known for their creativity when it comes to dishing out damage to player characters, so be prepared.

Healing

Once a character is wounded, you'll want to get him healed. Characters can heal either by natural or magical means. Natural healing is slow, but it's available to all characters, regardless of class. Magical healing may or may not be available, depending on the presence (or absence) of spellcasters or magical devices. The only limit to the amount of damage a character can recover through healing is the total hit points the character has. Healing can never restore more hit points to a character than his maximum hit point total. A character cannot exceed this limit until he gains a new level, whereupon another Hit Die (or a set number of points) is added to his total.

Natural Healing

Characters heal naturally at a rate of 1 hit point per day (see Chapter 1 – Con) of mild activity. Mild activity is defined as low activity—nothing more strenuous than riding a horse or traveling from one place to another.

Fighting, running in fear, lifting a heavy boulder, or any other physical activity prevents resting, since it strains old wounds and may even reopen them.

If a character has complete bed rest (doing nothing for an entire day), he can regain 3 hit points for the day. For each complete week of bed rest, the character can add any Constitution hit point bonus he might have to the base of 21 points (3 points per day) he regained during that week.

In both cases above, the character is assumed to be getting adequate food, water and sleep. If these are lacking, the character does not regain any hit points that day, no matter how much you whine.

Magical Healing

Healing spells, potions, and magical devices can speed the process of healing considerably. The specifics of such magical healing methods are described in the spell descriptions in this book and in the GMG (for magical items). By using these methods, wounds close instantly and vigor is restored. The effects are immediate.

Magical healing is particularly useful in the midst of a bloody combat or to eliminate the effects of a particularly grievous wound (aka a critical hit).

Herbalism & Healing Proficiencies

Characters can also gain minor healing benefits from those proficient in the arts of herbalism and healing. These talents are explained in Appendix H.

Table 12G: Cleric Saving Throws

level	Paralyzation, Poison, Death magic	Rod, Staff, or Wand	Petrification, HackFrenzy, HackLust, Polymorph¹	Breath Weapon²	Apology	Spells³
1	10	14	13	16	15	15
2	10	14	13	16	14	15
3	9	14	13	16	14	15
4	9	13	12	15	13	14
5	9	13	12	15	13	14
6	8	12	11	14	12	13
7	8	12	11	14	12	13
8	7	11	10	13	11	12
9	7	11	10	13	11	12
10	6	10	9	12	10	11
11	6	10	9	12	10	11
12	6	10	9	12	9	11
13	5	9	8	11	9	10
14	5	9	8	11	8	10
15	5	9	8	11	8	10
16	4	8	7	10	7	9
17	4	8	7	10	7	9
18	3	8	6	9	6	8
19	3	6	6	9	6	8
20	2	6	5	8	5	7

Table 12H: Fighter Saving Throws

level	Paralyzation, Poison, Death magic	Rod, Staff, or Wand	Petrification, HackFrenzy, HackLust, Polymorph¹	Breath Weapon²	Apology	Spells³
0	16	18	17	20	19	19
1	15	17	16	19	18	18
2	14	16	15	18	18	17
3	13	15	15	17	17	16
4	13	15	14	16	17	16
5	12	14	13	15	16	15
6	11	13	12	14	16	14
7	10	12	11	13	15	13
8	10	12	11	12	15	13
9	9	11	10	11	14	12
10	8	10	9	10	14	11
11	7	9	8	9	13	10
12	7	9	8	8	13	10
13	6	8	7	7	12	9
14	5	7	6	6	12	8
15	4	6	5	5	11	7
16	4	6	5	4	11	7
17	3	5	4	3	10	6
18	3	5	4	2	10	6
19	2	4	3	2	9	5
20	2	4	3	2	9	5

Character Death

If a character suffers a single blow that drops him to –4 hit points, he's dead. If a character suffers a hit that drops him to 0 to –3 hit points in a single blow, that character is fallen and bleeding to death. The character must make a Constitution check against half his Constitution in order to remain conscious. He can do nothing but speak in a soft voice and bleed. He cannot fight, move or cast spells. Conscious or unconscious, the character is dying and loses one hit point per round (at the beginning of each round) until someone either stops the bleeding using magic (even one point will do it), healing proficiency, herbalism skill or successfully tends to his wounds by making a Wisdom save against half his Wisdom. Each round a conscious character must make another Constitution check to remain conscious. Any character reaching –6 hit points or less will have permanent scarring. If the character drops to –10, he is dead.

Death From Massive Damage

In addition to dying when hit points reach - 4 or -10, a character also runs the risk of dying abruptly when he suffers massive amounts of damage. A character who suffers 50 or more points of damage from a single attack must roll a successful saving throw vs. death, or he dies.

This applies only if the damage was done by a single attack. Multiple attacks totaling 50 points in a single round don't require a saving throw.

For example, a character with 94 hit points would be required to make a check if a dragon breathed fire on him for 66 points of damage. The same character wouldn't have to do so if four Ogres hit him for a total of 53 points of damage in that round.

If the saving throw is successful, the character remains alive (unless of course the 50+ hit-point loss reduced his hit points to -4 or below!). If the saving throw fails, the character immediately dies from the intense shock his body has taken.

The character may still be raised in the normal ways, however.

Inescapable Death

There are occasions when death is unavoidable, no matter how many hit points a character has.

A character could be locked in a room with no exits, with a 50-ton ceiling descending to squash him like a bug. He could be trapped in an escape-proof box filled completely with acid or buried. He could have his throat cut while sleeping by a zero-level barkeep (soon to be local baron, if you had enough cash on hand!). While these examples are harsh (and grisly, but fun), they could easily, and will likely, happen at some point in the world of the HackMaster game.

Raising the Dead

Curative and healing spells have no effect on a dead character—he can only be returned to life with a Raise Dead, Reincarnate or Resurrection spell (or a device that accomplishes one of these effects). Each time a character is returned to life, the player must make a resurrection survival roll based on his current Constitution (see Table 1C). If the die roll is successful (i.e., the player rolls equal to or less than his resurrection survival percentage), the character is restored to life in whatever condition is specified by the spell or device.

A character restored to life in this way has his Constitution permanently lowered by 1 point. This can affect hit points previously earned. Should the character's Constitution bonus go down, the character's hit point total is reduced by the appropriate number of hit points (the amount of hit point bonus lost is multiplied by the number of levels for which the character gained extra hit points from that bonus). When the character's Constitution drops to 0, that character can no longer be raised. He is permanently removed from play.

The Saving Throw

The saving throw is a die roll that gives a chance, however slim, that the character or creature finds some way to save himself from harm or at least lessen the damage. The saving throw is a sacred haven for players incorporated into these hallowed rules only after the Great HMPA Lobby and Revolt of '78 (ask your local retailer about details for joining the HMPA). In the old days, GMs just dished out suffering and death indiscriminately. Now, we have the saving throw, locked in stone, as a method for players to avoid the GM's unfair death traps and treachery.

To make a saving throw, a player simply rolls his luckiest d20. We recommend you buy and use a special die, just for saves…but you don't have to - it's your funeral. The result on the d20 must be equal to or greater than the character's saving throw number. The number a character needs to roll varies depending upon the character's class, his level, what the character is trying to save himself from and any bonuses he might have due to magic, Dexterity, etc. A character's saving throw numbers can be found in Tables 12G-12J. Roll on the table appropriate to your class.

Notes for Saving Throw Tables 12G - 12J:

1) Excluding polymorph wand attacks
2) Excluding those that cause petrification or polymorph
3) Excluding those for which another saving throw type is specified, such as death, petrification, polymorph, etc..

Ability Checks as Saving Throws

When a character attempts to avoid danger through the use of one of his abilities, an ability check can be used in lieu of a saving throw.

For example, Jonas the thief has broken into the ancient Pyramid of the Pharaoh Ghanapicko when he hears the grinding of stone from

Table 12J: Thief Saving Throws

level	Paralyzation, Poison, Death magic	Rod, Staff, or Wand	Petrification, HackFrenzy, HackLust, Polymorph[1]	Breath Weapon[2]	Apology	Spells[3]
1	14	15	13	17	16	16
2	13	14	12	16	16	15
3	13	14	12	16	15	15
4	13	13	11	16	15	14
5	12	12	11	15	14	14
6	12	12	11	15	14	13
7	12	12	11	15	13	13
8	12	11	11	15	13	12
9	11	11	10	14	12	12
10	11	10	10	14	12	11
11	11	10	10	14	11	11
12	11	9	10	14	11	10
13	10	9	9	13	10	10
14	10	8	9	13	10	9
15	10	8	9	13	9	9
16	10	7	9	13	9	8
17	9	7	8	12	8	8
18	9	6	8	12	8	7
19	9	6	8	12	7	7
20	9	6	8	12	7	7

Table 12I: Magic User Saving Throws

level	Paralyzation, Poison, Death magic	Rod, Staff, or Wand	Petrification, HackFrenzy, HackLust, Polymorph[1]	Breath Weapon[2]	Apology	Spells[3]
1	14	11	13	15	17	12
2	14	11	13	15	17	12
3	14	11	13	15	16	11
4	14	10	12	14	16	11
5	13	10	12	14	15	11
6	13	10	12	14	15	10
7	13	9	11	13	14	10
8	13	9	11	13	14	10
9	12	8	11	13	13	9
10	12	8	10	12	13	9
11	12	8	10	12	12	9
12	12	7	10	12	12	8
13	11	7	9	11	11	8
14	11	7	9	11	11	8
15	11	6	9	11	10	7
16	11	6	8	10	10	7
17	10	5	8	10	9	7
18	10	5	8	10	9	6
19	10	5	7	9	8	6
20	10	4	7	9	8	6

above. He looks up to find a five-ton block of the ceiling headed straight for him! He is going to need speedy reactions to roll out of the way, so a Dexterity ability check should be rolled to see if he avoids the trap.

Modifying Saving Throws

Saving throws can be modified by magical items, specific rules and special situations. These modifiers can increase or decrease the chance of a successful saving throw. Modifiers that increase the chance are given as a number preceded by a plus sign. Modifiers that make success more difficult are given as a number preceded by a minus sign (-1, -2, etc.).

High ability scores sometimes give saving throw bonuses. A high Wisdom protects against illusions, charms, and other mental attacks. Dexterity can give a character a slightly higher chance of avoiding the effects of Fireballs, Lightning Bolts, crushing boulders, and other attacks where nimbleness may be a help (see Tables 1B and 1E.). Of course, low scores in these abilities can have the opposite effect. Like that tall skinny kid with the freckles in third grade that always seemed to dodge into the dodge ball rather than evade it.

Magical items such as Cloaks and Rings of Protection, can give bonuses to a character's saving throw (these are listed in the item descriptions in the GMG).

Magical armor allows a saving throw bonus only when the save is made necessary by something physical, whether normal or magical. Magical armor never gives a saving throw bonus against gas (which it cannot block), poison (which operates internally) and spells that are mental in nature or that cause no physical damage.

For example, magical armor would not help a character's saving throw against the bite of a Giant Spider, poison gas, or a Charm Person spell. Magical armor does extend its protective power to saving throws against dragon's breath, Fireballs, Disintegration, falling into lava, spells that cause damage, etc.

Specific spells and magical items have effects, both good and ill, on a character's saving throws. Often, spells force the victim to save with a penalty, which makes even the most innocuous spell quite dangerous. (Specific information can be found in the spell descriptions, for spells, or in the GMG's Magical Items section, for magical items.)

Poisons are sometimes weaker or stronger than norm, so a saving throw bonus or penalty may apply.

Turning Undead

One important, and potentially life-saving, combat ability available to clerics and paladins is the ability to turn undead. This is a special power granted by the character's gawd. Druids cannot turn undead.

Through the cleric or paladin, the gawd manifests a portion of its power, terrifying evil, undead creatures or blasting them right out of existence. However, since the power must be channeled through a mortal vessel, success is not always assured.

When encountering undead, a cleric or paladin can attempt to turn the creatures. Only one attempt can be made per character per round, but several different characters can make attempts at the same time (with the results determined individually).

Attempting to turn counts as an action, requiring one round and occurring during the character's turn in the initiative order (thus, the undead may get to act before the character can turn them). The mere presence of the character is not enough. Speech and gestures and the forceful presentation of a holy symbol are required so the character must have his hands free and be in a position to speak. However, turning is not like spellcasting and is not interrupted if the character is attacked during the attempt.

To resolve a turning attempt, look on Table 12K. Cross-index the Hit Dice or type of the undead with the level of the cleric (two levels lower for a paladin). If there is a number listed, roll 1d20. If the number rolled is equal to or greater than that listed, the attempt is successful. If the letter "T" (for "turned") appears, the attempt is automatically successful without a die roll. If the letter "D" (for "dispel") is given, the turning utterly destroys the undead. A dash (--) means that a cleric or paladin of that level has no chance of turning that type of undead. A successful turn or dispel affects d4 undead, a "T" or "D" result effects 2d4 undead. The closest undead are affected first; they must be able to see the cleric and be within 20 feet.

Turned undead bound by the orders of another (for example, skeletons) simply retreat and allow the character and those with him to pass or complete their actions. Free-willed undead attempt to flee the area of the turning character, until out of his sight. If unable to escape, they circle at a distance, no closer than ten feet to the character, provided he continues to keep his holy symbol visible and presented forcefully.

If the character forces the free-willed undead to come closer than ten feet (by pressing them into a corner, for example) the turning is broken and the undead attack normally, though they may be turned again.

Evil Clerics and Undead

Evil clerics are normally considered to be in league with undead creatures, or at least to share their aims and goals. Thus, they have no ability to turn undead. However, they can attempt to command these beings. This is resolved in the same way as a turning attempt. Up to 12 undead can be commanded. A "T" result means the undead automatically obey the evil cleric, while a "D" means the undead become completely subservient to the evil cleric. They follow his commands (to the best of their ability and understanding) until turned, commanded, or destroyed by another.

Evil clerics also have the ability to affect paladins, turning them as if they were undead. However, since the living spirit of a paladin is far more difficult to quell and subvert, paladins are vastly more difficult to turn.

An evil cleric attempting to turn a paladin does so as if the cleric were three levels lower than he actually is. Thus, a 7th-level evil cleric would turn paladins on the 4th-level column. He would have only a slim chance of turning a 7th-level paladin (7 HD) and would not be able to turn one of 8th level at all (using the level of the paladin as the HD to be turned). All "D" results against paladins are treated as "T" results.

Type or Hit Dice	Level of Cleric†											
of Undead	1	2	3	4	5	6	7	8	9	10-11	12-13	14+
Skeleton or 1 HD	14	11	8	5	T	T	D	D	D*	D*	D*	D*
Zombie	16	14	11	8	5	T	T	D	D	D*	D*	D*
Ghoul or 2 HD	18	16	14	11	8	5	T	T	D	D	D*	D*
Shadow or 3-4 HD	19	18	16	14	11	8	5	T	T	D	D	D*
Wight or 5 HD	20	19	18	16	14	11	8	5	T	T	D	D
Ghast	--	20	19	18	16	14	11	8	5	T	T	D
Wraith or 6 HD	--	--	20	19	18	16	14	11	8	5	T	T
Mummy or 7 HD	--	--	--	20	19	18	16	14	11	8	5	T
Spectre or 8 HD	--	--	--	--	20	19	18	16	14	11	8	5
Vampire or 9 HD	--	--	--	--	--	20	19	18	16	14	11	8
Ghost or 10 HD	--	--	--	--	--	--	20	19	18	16	14	11
Lich or 11+ HD	--	--	--	--	--	--	--	20	19	18	16	14
Special**	--	--	--	--	--	--	--	--	20	19	18	16

Table 12K:
Turning Undead

*An additional 2d4 creatures of this type are destroyed.

**Special creatures include unique undead, free-willed undead of the Negative Material Plane, certain Greater and Lesser Powers, and those undead that dwell in the Outer Planes.

†Paladins turn undead as clerics who are two levels lower.

Chapter 13

The Adventure and The Ongoing Campaign

Basic Adventuring 101

To most players, the adventure is everything. It's the reason for playing. Through the adventure your GM will be attempting to challenge you to the limits of your intellect and know-how. This is why the GM-player relationship is often viewed as adversarial. It's you (and your fellow players) against the GameMaster. Now this doesn't mean you can't have great respect and admiration for each other. In fact, this is often the case. Just keep reminding yourself that it's NEVER personal. Your GM has taken an oath to pull no punches and to keep the competitive bar of his campaign raised to the same tough standards expected at every other gaming table where HackMaster is played.

When sitting down to run through an adventure you should remind yourself that every adventure has a goal of some sort. Sometimes there may be more than one goal. It could be to slay that Swack Iron Dragon who's been terrorizing an innocent village and bring his head to the duke. Or maybe it's to rescue a lost princess whose father is offering a huge reward for her return. Stay on your toes, however. Not every adventure is what it appears. Just like the movies, many adventures have unexpected plot twists and surprise endings. That 'lost' princess you were seeking, for example, might turn out to be a runaway who fled for her life when she learned her father was planning on having her killed. Or maybe she's a vampire and her father wants her returned so he can attempt to cure her, but he neglected to mention this little 'fact'.

Typically, an adventure can be concluded in a reasonable playing time: four to eight hours is standard. This might require the players to get together for one, two, or even three playing sessions to complete the adventure. But the game doesn't have to end when an adventure is finished. That's the beauty of role-playing.

The same characters, provided they have survived their first adventure, can go on to new adventures. Such a series of adventures is called a campaign. A campaign is little more than a series of on-going adventures with one adventure's events spilling over to the next — much like an episodic television series. This is the great appeal of role-playing. When you're finished playing you don't throw away your character sheet and begin from scratch the following week. As long as your character is still alive and kicking at the end of the evening you'll continue to play him week after week. In fact, some players have been running the same character for years. The HackMaster game embraces more than enough adventure opportunities to keep a group of characters occupied for that long.

Just to give you some idea of what to expect, your first adventure will probably consist of you and the adventuring "party" you've teamed up with (i.e. other players with their own characters) exploring some underground labyrinth or perhaps some wilderness region.

Preparing such an adventure is the job of your GM. All you'll need to do is show up with your character and a willingness to persevere. If the GM is doing his job (and if he isn't I want to know about it) he'll show up to the game with carefully prepared notes and meticulous maps showing all the outstanding features of the imaginary place where you'll be bumping about.

In this chapter we will discuss the adventure and the on-going campaign but first we need to talk about the adventuring party.

The Adventuring Party: Who's Watching Your Back?

Up to this point you've been concerned primarily with creating your character and outfitting him for adventure. HackMaster, however, is not simply about the individual. The backbone of the game is, and always has been, the basic adventuring party. Hence the slogan, "Who's watching your back?" on the back cover of this book.

Even the gawds feel the need for alliances and working closely with comrades with similar aims and ambitions. Likewise, there's nothing a group of like-minded heroes working as a well-oiled machine toward a common goal can't accomplish. It's been said that evil knows no greater fear than when two or more heroes join together.

Still, many players (mostly new ones) like to behave as lone wolves. By their way of thinking, gold and experience goes much further when divided by one. Such shortsighted individuals are quick to stab their fellow players in the back if they think it puts them ahead. They see the game solely as a contest between themselves and their fellow players. How sad. Clearly the game is a contest between the players and the GM. Any contest against your fellow party members is secondary.

There's a name for such lone wolves —"Dead Men!" Not because they're eventually put down by a superior foe, but because they have no one to back them up. No one's watching their backs. Such players are usually done-in by the other more seasoned players who don't tolerate such antics at their table. And that's as it should be.

Joining an Adventuring Party

Joining an adventuring party is one of the most important things your character can do. If you're joining an established campaign, chances are the adventuring party has already been formed. In this case your character will have to win the favor of the other members and gain membership. This can usually be accomplished by simply buying a round of drinks for the party members and indicating your interest to join. A tale or two of your bravado and past accomplishments may aid your petition to join. Don't be alarmed if the party you are approaching seems aloof or standoffish at first. That's to be expected. After all, they don't know you from Adam. Who is this brash young character in their faces? Part of the game is winning the trust of those you adventure with and proving your mettle. Once you've gotten an adventure under your belt and demonstrated your willingness to toe the line you'll find acceptance. In the meantime you should swallow your pride and put on your best game face.

If this is the start of a new campaign, however, you and the other players will more than likely be on the same equal footing. It'll probably be to your advantage to simply form a new party from scratch.

You have several options when doing this and there are benefits and drawbacks to each.

Freelance Adventuring Parties:

Most adventuring parties are of the freelance type. Such groups usually start off informally and are comprised of player characters thrown together by chance and/or circumstance. There are countless ways to explain how you and your fellow player characters met. But for one reason or another you've decided to throw in with one another and seek your fortunes together.

Freelance adventuring parties have no formal organization and no affiliations with anyone outside the group. The purpose of the party is the mutual protection of its members and the accumulation of treasure and magic. There are no binding agreements other than a simple treasure policy (equal shares most likely). Members are free to leave at any time. This type of party works well for beginners and there's no reason not to go this route if you have enough gold to properly equip yourselves for adventure.

Sponsored Adventuring Parties:

Many times when a party is formed they lack the financial means to equip themselves properly. The fighter barely has enough to buy a used set of leather armor. The mage finds he can't afford to buy the necessary spell components. The dungeon the party has chosen for its first foray is days away yet there's no money for horses or even decent provisions. What to do?

The sponsored adventuring party involves transforming such a party strapped for cash into a company (Adventuring Company). Investors are lined up willing to put up the cash to cover the party's expenses under contract, i.e., provisions, equipment, room and board, etc. This is a good option for those PCs who start off the game a little coin shy and who are unable to properly equip themselves. The contract may be for a one-time expedition or it may be an on-going concern.

Such companies take many forms. Some have shareholders. Others more closely resemble a full partnership. Typically investors with venture capital pony up the cash to equip the party and cover expenses and the party operates like a business. After each expedition/adventure the secretary of the group must write up a report detailing the 'take' (any money, treasure and other valuables obtained during adventure). The investors recoup their investment off the top and then take their cut of the profits, usually 50%. Only then do the party members take their cut – shares vary depending on how much money was initially fronted/invested.

The sponsors of such companies are usually well-to-do, affluent men who often look at such an investment as a practical means to getting their hands on certain items which are otherwise difficult to acquire (such as antiques, relics, magic items, etc.). Oft times they are retired adventurers themselves who have spare gold to invest and know first hand how profitable adventuring can be, not to mention dangerous.

The drawback of this type of setup is that any magic items and other treasure are typically converted into gold (sold) so that profits can simply be paid out in shares to avoid disputes over ownership. If a party member desires a certain item he must deduct the street-value from any shares he's to receive, or make up the difference if his cut isn't enough to cover the full price. If a certain item is deemed to be useful for the further success of the Adventuring Company, the investor(s) may allow a character to use the item with the understanding that it's company property. If a character loses 'company property' he may have to pay for it out of his own shares.

Although the terms of any sponsorship are subject to negotiation the following terms are typical:

- the sponsor agrees to finance the party and front the cash for equipment, provisions, horses, room and board and other expenses. In return members agree to recoup the investor of his up-front money and give him 50% of any remaining treasure.

- the party agrees to work for the sponsor until they have earned back ten times the amount initially invested. For example, if the sponsor fronted the party 5,000 g.p.s to launch the company the party members would have to continue working in the sponsor's employ until he had made 50,000 g.p.s back from his share of expedition loot. The party may offer to 'buy' off the sponsor by paying off the remaining balance but the sponsor has the right to refuse such an offer.

- each party member is required to swear before the sponsor a gawd oath to his patron gawd that he will abide by the terms of the sponsorship or lose one experience level.

Aside from the nastiness of breaking a gawd oath, it's usually unwise to cheat an investor. Investors are wealthy and powerful. Therefore they can hire high-level assassins to hunt you down and eliminate you if they think you are skimming or breaching the terms of the agreement in any way.

Professional Adventuring Parties:

This type of adventuring party operates much like a sponsored adventuring party. The difference is one or more of the party members owns the company, i.e., any sponsors/investors have been bought out.

The party member/owners serve as shareholders. They may bring other PCs or NPCs into the group as employees but they retain their ownership status (unless they sell out their shares or interest in the company).

Legally, in most areas of Garweeze Wurld, professional adventuring parties must be chartered (sanctioned) by the local seat of government. This involves paying a charter license (5d100 gold pieces) and agreeing to pay a 10% tax on the gold piece value of all treasure the party finds. Of course most professional adventuring parties do a little creative bookkeeping and pay far less taxes than they are supposed to. But if you go this route, beware the Taxmen, for he can be both sneaky and brutal in his tactics.

Such a tax may seem outlandish and most players are probably wondering, "Who on earth would submit to such a thing?" Well, there is an advantage to being a chartered adventuring party. Those adventuring parties recognized by the state have the power to stake claims on any previously unknown (unregistered) dungeon or ruin. Once a party has filed a claim on a dungeon they are

granted sole salvage rights to that complex for a period of 90 days. Anyone violating their claim can be fined by the court and ordered to pay restitution to the party holding the right of spoils for loss of revenue.

The rub is that dungeons or ruins often fall outside of the borders of most kingdoms. Therefore, a situation can, and often does, arise in which two adventuring parties have made a claim in separate jurisdictions. The legal disputes can take years to resolve while the dungeon lays fallow, waiting for a brave party of adventurers to try their luck with investigating it. Although the acquisition of salvage rights does not always avoid such situations, there are times when only one legal claim is made and the rights of the adventuring company are protected from freelancers by a nearby government. So this practice of buying a charter license is always something for players to consider.

Professional adventuring parties often issue stock if they need to raise capital. They may also take on investors or sponsors in hard times with an agreement that such investors can be bought out after a certain period of time. They operate under a strict code of conduct (drawn up by the owners or founders).

When filing its charter, a professional adventuring party must take on a name and a symbol (crest). This has resulted in many such parties becoming household names as their party-fame rises while news of their exploits spread. Some professional adventuring parties employ full-time minstrels to sing of their deeds. In Fangaerie each spring, professional adventuring parties meet to compete with one another.

Party Legals

Every adventurer worth his salt knows the importance of proper preparation. We're not talking maps, magic potions, backpacks full of oil, torches, iron spikes, 10' poles, and iron rations. We're talking legal arrangements. Legal documents are vital to the professional adventuring party.

It is often important to check with an NPC-attorney before beginning any adventure to make sure your character/party's papers are in order. The party may want to keep a counselor on retainer for the group's legal needs. He will make sure the requisite official forms are prepared and signed.

Listed below are eleven general documents of interest. The list is extensive, but not exhaustive. Of course, each document must be customized for the characters and situation. Most legal documents are signed, with each signature signifying the swearing of a blood oath (see Chapter 5) that each signor agrees to the terms of the contract and will abide by the agreement. Failure to do so, of course, results in a loss of Honor and possibly prosecution by a local magistrate.

A number of magic items can be used to prepare the heroes legally, and may even be employed during the adventure. They include the Librum of Legalese, Frikey's Flask of Interminable Appeals, the Stupendous Scroll of Briefs and Writs, and of course, the Pen of Fine Print.

Keep in mind that each legal document will cost 1d100 gold pieces in fees. This fee compensates the attorney for his time and expertise and covers any expenses he incurred while having the document drafted, notarized and filed.

1. **Contract for the Division of Spoils:** A must-have. Squabbling over splitting up treasure and experience is the second-most likely cause of intra-party violence (after inside thieving). It should also deal with contingencies such as character deaths, the addition of new members, changes in levels, and anything else that would affect booty distribution. Payout in shares seems to be the most common form of division of spoils. Under this system each party member earns shares depending on how much he contributed to the party's success. Party members can also be docked shares as a form of punishment.

2. **Waiver of Liability:** A legal document which immunizes party members against each other from claims arising from misspells, critical fumbles, accidents, damage to, or loss of, items, and other mishaps that are not a result of enemy actions or deliberate malice. For example, a character might become irate when a klutzy companion inadvertently drops his +12 Hackmaster down a bottomless abyss, but this release frees the clumsy oaf from responsibility and retaliation. After all, everyone will have a bad day, sooner or later. It's a good idea to have any hirelings or henchmen who join your party sign one of these.

3. **Last Will and Testament:** Self-explanatory. One is required for each member of the party. Characters should take care to keep their wills up to date by modifying codicils as needed. Character assets can be passed down to new characters in succession, giving a starting advantage and continuity in equipage. In order to avoid

a big government tax bite, consultation with a certified NPC tax attorney is highly recommended. PCs may also want to specify that their bequest is dependent on a fitting funeral and internment, forestalling the leave-the-body-in-a-ditch-so-we-can-carry-more-treasure syndrome. It's a good idea to insist on all party members making a gawd oath (see Chapter 5) that they will try, to the fullest of their ability, to honor your will. The threat, of the loss of an experience level, holds a little more weight when docking a few Honor points is thrown into the bargain.

4. **Pre-Adventure Agreement:** In many cases the party will be performing a specific mission that needs special legal consideration. A dungeon crawl differs greatly from a rescue expedition. Will there be additional rewards, bonus experience, or other benefits? This document spells out any unique requirements and understandings. Of particular interest is how expenses and losses will be covered in the event the payoff is not forthcoming.

5. **Adventuring Procedures' Manual:** A compendium of standard policies the party will adhere to under normal conditions. Although not a legal form in itself, it provides proper documentation of adventuring background material, party bylaws, and provides justification for group actions.

It should cover such topics as marching order, watch schedule, responsibility for trap-checking and lock-picking, policies for healing spells and resurrections, and so on. Reference to the procedures' manual clarifies critical choices in the face of cowardly or stubborn followers and companions, and heads off legal actions that claim capricious or unfair decision-making.

6. **Alternative Dispute Resolution:** While not actually an agreement unto itself, the ADR clause should be considered with any legal document between party members. When disputes arise, this allows resolution through a process outside the actual court system. It can be non-binding mediation (a mutually agreed-upon third party hears both sides and gets issues on the table, but does not offer a ruling), binding or non-binding arbitration (a mutually chosen third-party actually rules as in a trial, but with limited or no discovery), a specified trial by ordeal, a duel or simply negotiation. ADR is preferable to use of the local court systems, which may be slow, expensive, and/or corrupt.

7. **Notice of Compliance:** A proclamation giving notice that the party will comply with all applicable laws regarding hiring of henchmen, overtime, labor conditions, discrimination against non-humans, etc. Used to protect the party against lawsuits and government meddling.

8. **Insurance Policies:** Many professional adventuring parties pay shares to a party treasury. This treasury is used to pay for resurrections or healing of its membership. It also serves as an emergency slush fund. As the treasury grows, a portion of it is often peeled off into an insurance fund of sorts. If a party member dies, his heir is guaranteed to receive a lump-sum payment. Sometimes, the party member is expected to pay into such an insurance fund. This can be well worth the investment of insuring lives and valuable items and making sure your heir, protégé or family is provided-for. Watch for tricky terms that might prevent payouts.

9. **Business papers:** Adventuring groups who form partnerships, companies, or limited liability corporations to obtain the best financial advantage will want to have their contracts in order. Such organizations may require incorporation papers, charters, account ledgers, independent audits, annual reports, minutes of board meetings, etc. It is best to decide where these papers will be stored so as to remain safe. Often, a member of the party is chosen as the business manager and/or treasurer.

10. **Stipulations and Addenda:** Any additional agreements or changes may be covered in this form, along with supporting documentation and the like. They may be updated during the adventure as needed.

11. **Professional Adventuring Party Charters/By-Laws:** Most professional adventuring parties have a charter and by-laws. This document is usually kept by the party leader (or sponsor) and is used to resolve disputes, in-party justice, payout of shares, etc. They can be rather extensive or as simple as "All members of the party shall act in the best interest of the party as a whole."

The following is a typical charter for a professional adventuring party.

- Everyone swears a blood oath that they will obey the party leader.
- Everyone swears a gawd oath that they will not knowingly or through deceit bring harm to the party.
- Treasure shares shall be paid out as follows:
  1 share to every party member
  1 1/2 shares to the party leader
  1 share to anyone who took more than half damage
  5 shares to the party treasury (emergency fund for raising the dead and healing the wounded)
  1 share to any party member who loses a limb or is blinded
  1 1/4 share to the mapper
  1/2 share to the party member who finds hidden treasure or who disarms one or more traps
- Anyone who knowingly attacks a fellow party member shall be banished from the group and forfeit ALL his shares.
- Anyone who steals from a fellow party member shall lose a finger.
- Anyone who shirks a task shall be fined 1 share.
- Each party member may have one day off per week (unless more time is needed to heal).
- Anyone hoarding food or drink shall be fined 1 share.
- Each party member agrees to perform his duties (such as guard duty) when his lot is drawn.

Types of Adventures You Can Expect:

Basically, there are seven major types of adventures you'll be encountering in your adventuring career. Each type of adventure is approached somewhat differently and presents a unique set of challenges to the hero.

Dungeon Crawls: Adventures into the NetherDeep (underground) by means of subterranean mazes and passageways are by far the most popular AND the most challenging. Each year the HMPA conducts a Player Character Demise Survey and the results are ALWAYS the same — more player characters meet their demises in dungeon settings than ANY other type of adventure. Gary used to have a saying, "Dungeon is just a seven letter word for Death!" You'll do well to keep those words in mind and stay alert at ALL times while dungeon delving. There's no room (and little tolerance) for complacency on a Dungeon Crawl (DC).

In the DC, the party arms itself to the teeth and then sets off to enter and explore the dungeons of some castle, temple or similar structure. These types of underground adventures are hardly ever wrapped up in a single gaming session. The party usually forges ahead until circumstances (usually the death of one or more comrades or dwindling hit points) forces them to retreat with the promise of returning later and 'fighting another day'.

Dungeon crawls call for special preparation. Things like artificial light sources (torches, candles, lamps) poles for probing, rope, spikes, mapping materials, sewing kits (for wounds) and like equipment are the main tools for such activity. A very wise sage once said, "Better to have a thing and not need it than to need a thing and not have it."

There's a very famous story which circulates around various gaming circles of a certain player who climbed all the way to the National HackMaster Finals only to have his character bite the big one because he had been too cheap to lay out 5 silver pieces for a new bow string (the old one snapped when he fumbled just as a Hedgerow Lunger charged him).

Another concern when dealing with dungeon crawls is mapping. Since the typical dungeon is an endless maze of twists and turns, one or more of the party will be charged with mapping the party's progress. Don't take this chore lightly if it falls to you. The life of yourself and your teammates could depend on the accuracy of your map should you have to beat a hasty retreat. We'll discuss mapping in greater detail later in this chapter.

As your party is exploring and mapping, movement will be greatly slowed. It's wise to designate a front guard (aka 'the point') and rear guards beforehand. Whoever is handiest with a sword (usually the fighter of the group) usually takes point. Spell lobbers (magic-user and cleric types) should stay in the middle where they'll be protected. Some groups prefer sending their thief out ahead of the party where he can scout for traps and other dangers (especially if he has infravision). Other groups like to keep their thief well to the back to watch for any rear attacks.

The typical dungeon will be filled with chambers and rooms (some hidden) – most will be inhabited by unfriendlies. In rare instances, some will be empty (or at least they'll APPEAR to be empty). There will also be a myriad of traps to catch those unaware, tricks to fool the unwise, and monsters lurking to devour the unwary.

The rewards, however, are great. Gold, gems and magic items await those with the mettle to claim them. Obtaining such riches will be the key for you and your party to better prepare for further expeditions. They'll also earn you experience points (See Chapter 11) that will go toward making you more adept in your chosen profession and more powerful in all respects.

Don't be sidetracked, however. First and foremost you must survive. Experience points and gold mean very little to the dead. You'll find it'll take every skill you can muster (and a little luck) to fight your way into and out of the dungeon, vanquishing the guardians of the treasure that lay hidden there, and then carrying any realized loot back to the surface.

Wilderness Adventure: Adventuring outdoors, into unknown lands or howling wildernesses is the second most popular type of HackMaster adventure. Most players are reluctant to venture too far from civilization, and for good reason. Until your character and his adventuring compatriots have climbed several levels, traveling too far from the safety net of civilization can prove deadly.

The biggest advantage to adventuring outdoors, as compared to dungeon crawling, is that sometimes a good fast horse can carry you out of harm's way should you find yourself outmatched. Even so, wilderness adventures are extremely perilous at best and packed with opportunities for the GM to do you in.

Instead of meeting one to three kobolds in a twenty by twenty foot room, for example, you just might find yourself face to face with 500 pissed off grunge elves blocking the road you're traveling (as well as any avenues of escape). There are also dens of monsters too horrible to mention here, and trackless wastelands to contend with. Perhaps worst of all, you're in the open and vulnerable. There's no hiding the magic-user or thief in the middle, there's no door to spike shut and the fighters can't block the passage taking on a few of the enemy with their superior AC.

As such, protracted expeditions are normally undertaken by higher level characters. Even so, even those characters NEW to the life of adventuring must get from point A to point B. Forays of limited duration are possible for such characters if the proper precautions are taken. Oft times, you can hook up with a roving patrol or travel in the company of NPC caravans for mutual protection. Just heed any hints your GM may be throwing out. If you're getting in over your heads, he's likely to let you know. In the beginning, he might suggest that your party do some local exploration - perhaps to reach the site of a dungeon entrance or to accept the hospitality of a friendly clan of dwarves.

Keep in mind that horses and pack animals may be necessary for such journeys as well as additional supplies, such as extra ammunition, map-making equipment, tents, shelters, etc.

Travel will be at a slow rate in unknown areas, for your party will be exploring, looking for foes to overcome, mapping, and searching for new finds of lost temples, dungeons, and the like. If the expedition continues for several days, there will be a need to hunt for game (or raid the locals) to replenish food stores. You may even unexpectedly come across inhabited areas such as thorps, hamlets, villages, or even towns. Since it will not be immediately apparent if such settlements are friendly to strangers you may want to by-pass them.

Town Adventures: Speaking of settlements, these cities, towns and sometimes even large villages provide the setting for the third most popular type of adventure. Like man, no character is an island unto himself. Your character will need to interact with others on a routine basis. What's the point in amassing gold and treasure if you don't have a place to spend it?

Settlements can be interesting, informative and oft times as dangerous as the dungeons themselves. A party stocking up on torches, lamp oil, crossbow bolts and pack animals is likely to draw attention.

While the dungeon serves as the proving ground for heroes where skills and mettle are put to the test, it is the town where your character develops as an individual and becomes flesh and bone.

Towns are highly interesting, informative places and often present hazardous encounters and incidents that your character will have to deal with without relying so much on the force of arms or magic. Becoming a member of society requires a whole different set of skills than that of the other types of adventures. Interaction with the populace, locating quarters, buying supplies and equipment, seeking information as well as cooperating with others, and

abiding by local laws, traditions and customs all require subtlety and role-playing. Such activities in a completely strange town require forethought and skill. Care must be taken in all one says and does. Questions about rank, profession, gawds and alignments are perilous, and use of an alignment tongue is socially repulsive in most places. There are usually beggars, bandits and drunks to be dealt with; greedy and grasping merchants and informants to do business with; inquiring officials or suspicious guards to be answered. The taverns house many potentially helpful sources of useful information to your character, but they also contain clever and dangerous adversaries who prey on the naïve and unsuspecting. Why do you think the barroom brawl is such a staple in American Westerns? Then there are the unlit streets and alleys of the city after dark … Who is that lovely maiden beckoning to you to step into some shadowy side entryway?

Political Arena: As your character reaches higher levels, he may begin to realize that his heroic efforts are having little impact on the world at large around him. Instead of serving a king or lord, he may begin craving the chance to hold the reigns of power himself and become a mover-and-shaker.

Getting involved in the political arena and taking on a chain-of-office or a position is one of the most rewarding things a character can do. There's a tremendous burden of responsibility that comes with the job, as well as intrigue, and the danger of assassination at the hands of a rival who has eyes on your office. Some characters rise to politics through the military. Others because they are approached by NPCs (either subjects or characters in a position to appoint titles or offices) who were attracted to the character by his heroic exploits or great Fame/Honor. You shouldn't shy away from such opportunities if they present themselves. It's the surest way for a character to leave a lasting mark on the GM's game world.

The World of Business and Free Enterprise: Like politics, this type of adventuring is usually taken up by high level characters who are going into semi-retirement. However, many low level characters try their hand at starting a business and actually do quite well. Some characters may simply fall into a business. For example, a group of thieves steal a ship from a harbor to escape the long arm of the law. Later, on the high seas, they realize the ship is carrying a cargo of valuable trade goods. At the next port, they could try to trade those goods for hard gold (discovering in the process that they have to pay port fees, import taxes, etc.). Business campaigns often run in the background of the GM's normal campaign. Once a character has employees or business partners he can trust, he may feel comfortable leaving the business to run on its own while he takes up adventuring again — checking in now and then when he's in town to see how things are going.

Inter-Dimensional Adventuring: There are countless other planes of existence in the world of HackMaster. Some planes are the home to demons and other unspeakable terrors. Other planes are occupied by members of a particular alignment. Many planes are the home world to various gawds (pantheons). As these are mysterious places known to exist by only a very few, we won't go into detail about them here. During the course of your adventuring career, you will undoubtedly meet denizens from these planes of existence and will stumble upon ways to travel among them. It's even possible to travel to the campaign worlds of other HackMaster GMs.

Inter-Genre Adventuring: It is also possible, with the proper magic and steps, for your characters to transcend the barriers of time, space and logic and visit other gaming genres. How will your mage hold up against members of the Heroes of HackLeague™ or how would your berserker rate in the world of CattlePunk? A thief could probably clean up picking pockets in the vacuum of SpaceHack™. The possibilities are endless. Inter-genre adventuring can be a wonderful diversion for high-level characters who have become bored with dungeon crawling and need a change of scenery.

Getting your Bearings

The first challenge you will face as a player is familiarizing yourself with the GM's world (also called 'milieu' or 'campaign world'). Most HackMaster campaigns are set in the only official campaign world, Garweeze Wurld, but it is entirely possible, and acceptable, for GMs to base their campaigns in settings of their own making. Usually such home-brewed settings pale in comparison to the lush, rich detail of Garweeze Wurld, but almost any capable GM with at least a smidgen of talent and/or imagination can piece together a world with enough sand to hold the interest of his players.

Your GM will brief you on certain information pertaining to his world prior to the adventure but the burden is really on you, as a player, to glean as much information as you'll need about your environs to help you succeed. He's certainly not going to volunteer all the information you need to develop your game plan. The fact of the matter is that while your character was raised in the GM's world and obviously has a lot of knowledge of that world, you as a player do not. You can count on your GM using this against you, too.

It will take a while for you to get your bearings and learn enough about the GM's world that you feel comfortable, but again, that's part of the fun of role-playing. You'll be learning about the world through your character's eyes. It will be a constant learning process. The more you explore the fantasy world your character lives in the more you will learn and the more it will seem real. To aid in this learning process, however, you must take an active role.

There are many ways to go about this. One time-honored approach is to ask questions of the GM through the local populace (NPCs). You might ask the barkeep, "Hey toadface, where does the Road to Fangaerie lead?" (To which the obvious reply is, "To Fangaerie.") You could also ask that group of pilgrims you just met in the roadside inn if they would sketch you a map of the region.

Another way to learn about the world your character stomps around in is to simply ask your GM. Many GMs provide their players with background packets that include information the player characters would obviously know such as forms of currency, the calendar system, local rulers, famous villains or heroes, popular rumors, local lore or history, etc. Usually such information will be tailored to your character based on the region he grew up in. The information may be further tailored based on your character's race and/or class.

Of course, the GM may not have seen fit to include ALL the information your character would possess. This may require you to ask him questions directly. One of my personal favorite tactics is to present the argument to the GM that my character possesses special knowledge of the area or situation (even though I, myself as a player may not) due to my character's particular background or skills (such as Local Lore). Pressing such a point can sometimes yield advantageous results. For example, you know your character was born and raised in Hagley Town. It's entirely proper for you to ask, "How many people live in Hagley Town?" or "Which side of town do the well-to-do citizens of Hagley Town live in?" You're GM isn't likely to present you with a spreadsheet with a demographic breakdown of the population of Hagley Town but he will give you some basic info. The point is, don't be shy about pumping your GM for information.

Adventure Preparedness

Before setting off on any adventure you would be wise to borrow a phrase from the Boy Scouts, "Be Prepared!" Just because you have a map to the "Dungeon of Doom" doesn't mean you and your fellow party members should go prancing off half-cocked to clean it out. No way - a dungeon foray takes proper planning and more importantly proper provisioning.

Looking for the Hook

Every adventure has a hook. The 'hook' is the lure or the segue that leads the party down the path to the adventure the GM has prepared for the session. Sometimes the adventure hook will be obvious. Perhaps in the previous adventure the villain escaped and now the party wants to settle the score.

Oft times, however, the hook isn't clear and the players have to work to find it. One way of doing this is to hang out at the local tavern and throw out feelers for any rumors that may hint of adventure opps (opportunities) in the area. Greasing a few palms with hard coin will aid in this process.

Sometimes the 'hook' shows itself in the form of a person. Like the dwarf at the bar who is overheard saying something about "more gold than you can shake a stick at" and "damn dragon nearly did us in." Or it may present itself in the form of an object. Like the time my fighter bought a bundle of torches from a roadside vendor only to discover later that one of the torches was actually a tightly rolled up scroll which contained a treasure map.

Outfitting/Provisioning

Once the 'hook' has been discovered the party must then concern itself with properly equipping itself and buying provisions. The more details you have about the nature of the adventure path you are being lured down, the better. Depending on the adventure and your party makeup, you may want consider taking such steps as hiring men-at-arms, obtaining mounts, stocking up on food and water, etc. Just keep in mind that you're looking for an edge - whatever gives the party its best possible shot at success in surviving a dungeon or wilderness. Chapter 9 (Goods and Services) lists typical items and prices for things you might find useful. Of course, moving about a city or town finding what you need can be an adventure in itself.

Mapping

A word about mapping is in order. A map is very important because it helps assure that the party will be able to return to the surface. One player must keep a map of the expedition's trek to make sure the party doesn't get lost. Mapping also helps the party make educated guesses and assumptions as to where hidden rooms might lie.

If two players make maps, the chances of success for the expedition improves. Graph paper with 5 or 6 lines to the inch is suggested for underground mapmaking. A sheet of small size hex grid is usual for outdoor maps. Both sorts of paper should always be on hand.

The player chosen for mapping detail should be observant and able to pay attention to small details. He should also know his left from his right. Generally, the mapper who does his job well and contributes to the overall success of the dungeon foray gets an extra share of treasure for his efforts. But this is a matter to be decided before hand. If you have a loudmouth that never shuts up gaming with you, you might consider making that guy the mapper; it's hard to talk when you are listening to the GM rattle off dimensions and concentrating on what you're doing. Be forewarned, though, that this strategy can backfire if the noisy one doesn't pay attention. I suggest you give proper threats and warnings beforehand, so that the character understands *exactly* what horrific fate will befall him if he screws up.

Always make notes on the map to show danger, traps, tricks, monsters, where the bodies of dead comrades have been stashed for later retrieval, etc. Appendix M lists the entire set of 'official' map symbols for HackMaster. You should diligently use this uniform set of symbols so that there's no confusion. Should the character who is mapping die or become incapacitated his player will not be allowed to translate or interpret the map for other members of the party. They'll be on their own.

Never become overly concerned if your map is not exact. If it is off 10' here or 20' there, it probably won't make much difference. As long as it gives your party an idea as to where they are and how to get back, it is serving its purpose.

Some characters who have the photographic memory talent may be able to get by without a map in less complicated dungeon systems. Some may also have the mapless travel skill, which also helps them find their way around. And indeed, some players may have sufficiently trained recall so as to be able to find their way back with but small difficulty. However, if your character doesn't at least go through the motions of mapping the GM may force you to roll at every intersection on your way back to the surface to decide if your character makes the right choice of direction. And, if your character dies, the rest of the party may find themselves suddenly in the dark as to where they are.

If pursuit prevents mapping, always go in a set escape pattern if possible-left-straight-right-straight, etc. Such patterns are easy to reverse. In mazes always follow one wall or the other, left or right, and you will never get lost. If transported or otherwise lost, begin mapping on a fresh sheet of paper, and check for familiar or similar places as you go along. Never become despondent, that is an indication of GM victory over you; fight until the very end, never surrender!

Do not get sidetracked. A good GM will have many ways to distract an expedition, many things to draw your attention away from the task at hand. Ignore them if at all possible. The mappers must note all such things, and another expedition might be in order on another day to investigate or destroy something or some monster you passed the first time through. Always stay with what was planned if at all possible, and wait for later to handle the other matters. This not to say that something hanging like a ripe fruit ready to be plucked must be bypassed, but be relatively certain that what appears to be the case actually is. Likewise, there are times when objectives must be abandoned.

If the party becomes lost, the objective must immediately be changed to discovery of a way out. If the group becomes low on vital equipment or spells, it should turn back. The same is true if wounds and fatalities have seriously weakened the group's strength. The old statement about running away to fight another day holds true in the game. It is a wise rule to follow.

On the other hand, if the party gains its set goal and is still quite strong, some other objectives can be established, and pursuit of them can then be followed. There's no reason you can't refer back to the map and revisit those areas of the dungeon that you feel warrant further investigation.

Character Death

Don't be disheartened (or surprised) if your first few characters suffer horrible fates and die agonizing deaths. This is to be expected. It is important that you adopt the attitude early, of pulling yourself up by the bootstraps, shaking off the dust and trying again. You certainly don't cry and mope about it or accuse the GM of being unfair. Such tactics are the mark of a loser.

Only by demonstrating a willingness to learn and getting back on that horse will you earn the respect and admiration of your peers. You must endeavor to persevere and strive toward mastering the game. This is really the only way you will eventually work a character through the danger zone (1st through 4th level) and reach a point where you've garnered enough powers and skills to have a real fighting chance of surviving for the long haul.

Character death is nothing to be ashamed of. As long as he was a character of Honor and fought the good fight, you have no reason to hang your head low. Being a hero would be meaningless without the risk of death. (To be sure, there are ways to cheat death, which will be discussed later, but in HackMaster NOTHING is for certain.)

Before going into a dungeon it's a good idea to locate a cleric of sufficient level (and of the appropriate alignment) who can perform Raise Dead/Resurrection rites should one or more members of the party perish. It's also a good idea to stash away enough gold to cover the costs of such procedures so you're covered when the time comes.

Party Tacticals

Once you've equipped yourselves for the adventure and are ready for action you should take a few minutes to organize the party and get your tacticals nailed down. Your GM will certainly appreciate this, for, just like you, his enjoyment comes from adventuring, not from waiting for a party to get their act together. Having standard tacticals allows the party leader to give clear and concise information to the GM without having to constantly consult with the other party members. Remember - indecision kills. Quick, decisive calls mean there will be fewer random encounters for the party, since they're not standing around arguing over who should take the point or which direction to go.

Organize your party by showing which characters are where with your official HackMaster™ miniatures. Miniatures are not required, but are a great help. Be aware, though, that your GM will impose penalties for using unofficial miniatures. The GM will usually require a marching order to be drawn on a piece of paper if figures are not at hand. Show marching orders for a 10' passage, a 20' passage, door openings, etc. Always prepare for rear actions as well as frontal combats. Assign one individual as leader. This character will "call", i.e. tell the GM where the party will go and what they will do.

Decide some standard actions if the party is ambushed. The magic-user should have some idea of which spell to use in certain situations. Those characters with healing ability should be kept in the middle so they can move forward or backward in the marching order to render assistance.

Choose your Battles

Now this is going to sound strange coming from me, but my advice to most players is to avoid unnecessary encounters. Garweeze Wurld is a dangerous place and there's a thousand and one ways for your character to bite the big one. So why take unnecessary risks?

Choose your battles. The difference between success and failure is knowing when to stand your ground and when to walk away. Your party has an objective, and wandering monsters are something that stands between you and your goal. The easiest way to overcome such difficulties is to avoid the interposing or trailing creature if at all possible. While random encounters are an excellent source of unprogrammed experience points (often with little or no risk to the player character), you shouldn't allow yourself to be distracted.

Wandering monsters typically weaken the party in several ways, making it necessary for the party to use up equipment and spells against them. Unless your Honor is at stake you should consider giving monsters a wide berth. You're not acting in a cowardly fashion. You can explain to your GM that you're intelligently sticking to your game plan and refusing to be distracted from the mission at hand. If you happen to get docked a few Honor points because it appears you're running from a fight, don't worry. Just add the monster to your Grudge List of Asses to Kick. You can deal with him on your way back to the surface if need be and settle the score.

Party Unity

The success of any party requires co-operation, mutual trust and confidence. This is collectively known as teamwork. Teamwork is enhanced when members of a party are certain that the survivors will do their best to see that any slain character is carried forth from the dungeon to be resurrected if at all possible. If not, it's nice to know that your Last Will and Testament will be

honored and that your heir (your next character possibly) will receive your possessions and assets.

All members of the expedition should be ready and willing to part with any goods, money, and magic items in order to save lives and contribute to the overall success of the party or adventuring company. Each should be willing to fight to the death. This will only happen when mutual trust exists. But, what about characters of evil alignment? Selfish neutrals? Uncooperative players?

Intelligent players of evil alignment will certainly be ready to help in order to further their own ends. This is not to say that they will be chummy with those of good alignment. On a single expedition, however, or when they have ownership in the adventuring company, it is possible to arrange situations where they are very likely to be helpful in order to benefit themselves and their cause. It doesn't matter that they are acting out of their own selfish best interest. The end result is the same. They have a stake in seeing the party succeed.

Generally, evil characters, particularly chaotic evil ones, are prone to be troublesome and hurtful to the party. That's because a snake tends to do what snakes do. They should, accordingly, be shunned when possible. Selfish neutrals are similar to evil characters, but their price is usually easier to meet, and it is therefore easier to integrate them into an expedition, which will depend upon co-operation for success. The character of good alignment, who is basically uncooperative - often acting as an evil or (selfish) neutral would - is another matter. For such players usually join under the pretense of being helpful and willing to act in the best interest of the party. Undoubtedly, the best way to take care of such players is to expel them from the group as soon as circumstances permit. Do this as often as necessary to either change the player's mind about co-operation, or until he becomes tired of having his characters consigned to oblivion because of their attitude.

Parleying

In order to determine the intent of a possibly friendly or neutral monster, or to pass along your intentions or desires, some form of communication is necessary. Speech might do for human-types, as the common tongue is known by most. But what of encounters with a Giant, Blink Dogs, or dozens of similar creatures? An open and raised right hand is often helpful, and simply refraining from hostile moves will possibly allow for further exchange. Remember though, that you cannot bribe a band of Ogres to allow you to pass through unless you can communicate clearly.

Most GMs love parleying and negotiations, for this allows them to assume an active role in actual play. Your GM will assume the persona proper to the creature your party is dealing with - be it shy and hostile, stupid, greedy, helpful, misinformed, or whatever. Intelligent monsters will always balance the offer versus the expectation. A lone Ogre is likely, even with his rather dim wit, to recognize that a strong party will kill him if he attacks or demands too much, so a small bribe is better than risky combat to get tasty flesh for his belly and pretty baubles for his pockets. On the other hand, any basically hostile monster will exploit weakness unless it seems certain that more can be gained by other action. Be resigned to pay amounts in excess of the actual value received.

As a player, you must earn what you gain. Negotiation usually gives you a chance to get on with the earning process, or live to come back and fight another day. Always be wary and use your wits, look at all facets of the situation, and then use your best judgment accordingly. In many cases a payment, bribe, toll, share or ransom fee will enable success or survival, and negotiation is a useful tool to the expert adventurer. Remember, you can always come back later and lay down some whup-ass.

Far to go and Much to Learn

We didn't even begin to scratch the surface as far as preparing you for your career of adventure. A thousand books couldn't contain all the information needed to fully prepare you for the challenges that await you. You'll have to fill in the gaps from your own experiences and hard-earned lessons. Use this chapter simply as a way to make things run a bit more smoothly on this rocky road we call HackMaster. It is my hope that you will use it in good health, as you grab your sword and mount up. See you on the trail to Fangaerie!

Encounters

Encounters of the HackMaster Kind

When your player character enters the game world he'll quickly find he's not alone. No matter where he goes or what he does, he's going to have 'encounters' with other individuals (NPCs) and creatures (monsters) which populate the GM's milieu. An encounter is anything significant a character meets, sees, or interacts with during the course of a game. When a 1st level thief sits down in a bar and some bully of a half-orc walks up and demands he buy him a drink, that character has just had an encounter. When the door slams shut on a party after entering a dungeon antechamber and quickly begins to flood with sewage, they've just had an encounter.

Encounters force the character to react and the player to think. Why is this jerk picking on me? Can I take him in a fair fight? Why is this anvil just sitting in the dungeon corridor? Does it belong to anyone? Who painted it cobalt blue? Is it trapped? Magical? Does it have a purpose? Is it beneficial or dangerous? Few characters are going to simply walk around such an odd item. They're going to properly investigate it before moving on.

Encounters are vital to the HackMaster game, for without them nothing can really happen to the player character. Encounters provide danger, risk, mystery, information, intrigue, suspense, humor, and more. An adventure without encounters is like being marooned on a desert island with no one to interact with. Once the island itself had been explored, a character would soon become bored to tears. Without encounters, HackMaster would be reduced to LackMaster.

For an encounter to provide excitement, it must also have an element of danger. A good deal of this comes from the fact that player characters don't know what's going to happen. How will the encountered creatures or individuals react to them? For example, upon approaching a city, your GM could inform the party, "You meet a jovial guard who appears delighted to see you." (If he does say something like this — you ought to be suspicious.) He's more likely, however, to say something like, "Upon noticing your approach, the barrel-chested guard raises his arm and orders you to: 'Halt! State yer business!'" It's possible the guard won't like the characters' response. Maybe he's racist and refuses to let the dwarven thief enter the city. Or maybe he's simply having a bad day and decides he's going to mess with the party and give them a hard time.

How the party decides to react could have a huge impact on the adventure. One guard doesn't pose much of a threat to a well-armed adventuring party but as an authority figure he represents far more than just a single individual. Drawing weapons against him is going to bring down the wrath of the entire city guard on your backs (i.e., another encounter). Who needs that kind of trouble? Is there another way of handling this situation? Should the party just choke down its pride and put up with such abuse? Ultimately the player(s) are going to decide. That's what encounters are all about – reacting to a given situation and dealing with the outcome.

Planned Encounters

When your character travels or explores a dungeon, your GM will have prepared two general types of encounters. The first are specific (planned) encounters. These are meetings, events, or things the GM has chosen to place in the adventure to build on the story of the adventure and to further the plot line he's developed.

Planned encounters generally have more choices of action—your GM might want you to discover some important information or set up a particularly difficult battle. Planned encounters usually yield greater treasures and more magical items. The GM may place creatures to guard the armory or prevent the characters from reaching the throne room.

For example, a party is exploring a cavern that they were led to by a map. Hoping to find hidden treasure, they are surprised to find that the cave is occupied by a great horned Owlbear. The creature has built its nest in such a way that it's blocking a side passageway, a passageway that just happens to lead to where the party is ultimately heading. Obviously the GM planned this encounter. The Owlbear is an obstacle placed to impede the players from reaching their objective and therefore must be destroyed with great prejudice.

Random Encounters

Later, in the same cave your group bumps into a Blood Golem. This is the second type of encounter, a random encounter, also called a wandering monster. In this case, your GM has made die rolls to see if you come upon something and, if so, just what that something is. Random encounters are an excellent source of unplanned experience points, often with little or no risk to the player character.

Random encounters normally involve simple choices - run away, fight, or ignore. Sometimes characters can talk to creatures in random encounters and learn valuable information, but not often, so it's typically better to hack first and ask questions later. Random encounters also tend to have little or no treasure. A patrol of Orc guards does not carry as many valuable items on its rounds as it would have in its barracks. So consider letting one escape so you can track him back to his lair and surprise his mates. But take care not to let him out of your sight, less his allies return and ambush you. Random encounters are most often used to weaken PCs, raise an unexpected alarm, hurry them along, or just make their lives difficult.

A Word on Monsters/NPCs

The relationship between GM and player is very adversarial in HackMaster. More so than in the other lesser role-playing games (these games are more like HackMaster with training wheels than the real McCoy). That's because it's the GM's job to challenge his players to the fullest extent permissible under the rules. On the flip side, it's the player's sworn duty to push the envelope and challenge the GM, keeping in mind, of course, that the GM is always right. Once he's made his official call, players are obliged to abide by that decision (unless, of course, they can think of a way to circumvent or work around that call in a legal fashion).

It's important to keep the GM vs. player equation in context. It's never personal and shouldn't be taken as such.

Dungeon Hazards

Sometimes encounters are not with people or monsters but with things. Suppose the party is walking down a forest path and they come to two stone pillars that flank each side of the trail. They seem out of place. Who put them here? Why? After investigating a bit, one of the party members steps between the pillars and instantly grows stronger. (The GM tells him to add one point to his Strength). The other party members scramble to get some of the same action and the next guy steps through. The GM announces he's just been polymorphed into an Orc. Mortified, the player steps through the pillars again (this time from the opposite direction) hoping the effects will be reversed. This time, however, a blue arc of electricity shoots from the pillars and fries the poor slob to a crisp. Apparently the effects of walking through the pillars are random.

This is another type of encounter. Such an encounter might be important to your adventure or it might be a red herring – something placed there just to confuse or delay you. It might also be a set up for a future adventure – later on your characters might learn that the pillars are actually a gateway to another dimension and that a certain magic item is needed to use it properly.

During the course of an adventure, you will undoubtedly come across such traps and tricks and you should learn to recognize them for what they are. This won't be easy, of course. Your GM will spend considerable time and effort to make all such occurrences effective in his ultimate goal of frustrating your success. You and your fellow players must do everything within your collective power to render them harmless, unsuccessful or profitable. On the other hand, you must never allow preparedness and caution to turn to paranoia. Tapping every nook and cranny of the dungeon corridor with a ten-foot stick slows down progress and quickly turns an 'epic adventure' into humdrum tedium. In other words, it borders on cowardice and can serve to lower your honor.

Traps

Traps are aimed at *confining, channeling, injuring,* or *killing* characters. Each type of trap presents its own particular set of challenges.

Confining Traps

Confining traps are typified by areas that are closed by bars or stone blocks, although some might be pits with valves that close and can then only be opened by weight above. Most confinement areas will have another entrance by which a capturing or killing creature(s) will later enter. It is usually impossible to avoid such areas, as continual minute scrutiny makes exploration impossible and only serves to increase the number of encounters with wandering or patrolling monsters. If your party finds itself confined in

such a trap, prepare for attack, search for ways out, and beware of being channeled (see below).

Channeling Traps

Traps of this variety are often linked to the confining variety. Walls that shift and doors, that allow entry but not egress, are typical. While they often cannot be avoided, such traps can be dealt with much as a confining trap is. However, they pose the additional problem of finding a way back. Careful mapping is a good remedy.

Injuring Traps

These include traps that wear down the party as they struggle to attain their goal. Typical injuring traps are blades that scythe across a corridor when someone steps on a stone in the floor, arrows that fire when someone yanks a trip rope, or spears released when someone opens a door. Use of a pole or spear as a prod ahead might help with these, and likewise such a prod could discover pits in the floor. The safest remedy is to have plenty of healing-capability on hand – either in the form of potions or spells – so as to enhance your chances of survival.

Killing Trap

Traps of this variety are typical of important areas or deep dungeon levels. Deep pits with poisoned spikes, poisoned missiles, explosive methane hazards, chutes to lava pits, floors that tilt to deposit the party into a pool of acid or before the gaping maw of an angry Red Dragon, 16 ton blocks that fall from the ceiling or locked rooms that flood are all examples of killing traps. Again, observation and safety measures (poles, spikes thrown ahead, rope, etc.) will be of some help. Luck will have to serve as well.

In summation, any trap can be bad and many can mean a character's or entire party's demise. They are hazards of the trade and the best you can do is to stay alert and be prepared. Observation and clever deduction, as well as proper caution, should negate a significant portion of traps.

Well-balanced adventuring parties will improve your chances of success — a cleric for healing, a thief for trap detection and a magic-user to Knock open doors go a long way towards reducing the danger. Proper outfitting and provisioning is also important. Rope to pull comrades from pits, extra light sources as a back up, ten foot poles for prodding, iron pegs to 'spike' doors in the open position so they don't close on you…all of these are important tools that every adventuring party expecting to return home again should have in their possession.

Tricks

Another type of 'encounter' you will face are tricks. Your GM has a huge arsenal of options in his bag of tricks when it comes to encounters. So many tricks can be used and devised by your GM that it is virtually impossible to thoroughly detail all the possibilities here. Your GM's devious imagination is the only boundary for what sort of tricks can be placed in a dungeon. It is incumbent upon the players to counter with their own guile.

Sympathy Monster Tricks

Many tricks are simply annoying; others are both annoying and misleading and sympathy monsters are among the worst. A good example of this type of trick took place in a HackMaster tournament adventure held at GaryCon '94. The adventuring party entered a room and found a cute little furry creature that seemed to be malnourished and suffering from a nasty wound that had failed to heal properly. The party cleric, a young lady who should have known better, bought into the GM's trickery and took pity on the poor creature. She fed the animal (over the objections of the other party members who most certainly DID know better) and even wasted valuable healing salve to treat the animals wounds. She was quite pleased with her 'good deed' but she soon discovered the error of her ways. The 'cute' creature turned out to be a carrier of anthrax and ended up taking out half the party. Lesson learned.

"Didn't See THAT One Coming" Tricks

With this type of trick the GM uses one trick to distract the players and get their guard down so he can spring a second, more sinister trick or trap on them. For example, in one adventure I ran for the HardEight Boys, the party came to a room that emitted a strange 'buzzing' sound. The party was baffled and spent a great deal of time discussing what the hell it could be. What could be making such a noise? Finally, the elf of the party announced he was putting his ear to the door to see if he could identify the source. Scratch off one player character to the insidious Ear Seeker who lay hidden on the door's surface. Tsk, tsk. But it didn't end there. The surviving party members, assuming the Ear Seeker was the 'trick/trap' guarding the room announced an 'All clear' and burst into the room with swords drawn. Of course they were stunned and horrified to discover the room was choked with a huge hive of angry Carnivorous Wasps — the source of the mysterious buzzing they had heard. The only survivor that day was the NPC torchbearer who had sense enough to remain in the hallway. He still tells the tale for anyone willing to buy him a stiff drink.

Illusionary Tricks

Many tricks can also be illusionary in nature. Such illusions can annoy, delay, mislead or even kill an entire party. There can be illusionary creatures, pits, fires, walls and so on. Consider an illusion showing a tempting pile of gold cast over an actual pit of vipers. Illusionary tricks are particularly difficult to deal with in HackMaster. If you suspect an illusion announce that you are attempting to disbelieve, as per Chapter 10: Magic.

Tricks of Deception

This type of trick is similar to the illusionary variety. They are designed to deceive or confuse the character by feeding him false information through his senses. Slanting (or sloping) passages may be designed so that the characters do not notice that they are actually going deeper into the dungeon. Other common deceptions include architectural designs that intentionally create non-magical optical illusions such as secret doors, false walls, or distortions in space and distance, etc.

Teleporting Tricks

As the name implies, this type of trick is meant to lose, confuse or strand the party. They make mapping nearly impossible, and take the group to areas they do not wish to enter. Teleporting zones can send characters to opposite ends of the dungeon (or even to deeper levels) without them even knowing it. This type of trick also includes such things as sinking or rising (elevator) rooms, sliding rooms and chutes. Rooms can turn so as to make perceived directions wrong or secret doors can open into alternate areas depending on how they are manipulated.

Grudge Monsters

One of the dangers of pushing a GM too far is the unleashing of grudge monsters. These are unprogrammed NPCs or monsters that the GM throws at the players with the intent of doing their characters physical harm or to teach them a lesson for various infractions. GM's are discouraged from using Grudge Monsters to settle personal scores but it sometimes happens. Such is life in HackMaster.

Character Baiting (aka Bait Trap)

Sometimes a GM will use a monster or item to bait a character into a trap or dangerous situation. For example, a gold crown sitting on a tree stump along the side of the trail should raise a few red flags. Grabbing such an item before analyzing the situation could be deadly.

Of course this is only a small fraction of the wide variety of tricks the GM can throw at you. Much of the fun of role-playing is attempting to work solutions for such tricks and becoming a better-able, better-prepared adventurer. Tricks are best countered with forethought and discernment. They can be dealt with by the prepared and careful party, but rashness can lead to real trouble of the fatal variety. Your GM will be using his imagination and wit to trick you, and you must use your faculties to see through or at least partially counter such tricks.

The Surprise Roll

Sometimes an encounter, either random or planned by the GM, catches one or both of the groups involved totally off guard. This is called surprise and is determined by rolling 1d10 for each side (or only one side if the GM has decided that one of the sides cannot be surprised, for some reason). If the die roll is a 1, 2, or 3, that group or character is surprised (for effects, see the "Effects of Surprise" section below). Naturally, surprise does not happen all the time. There are many ways it may be prevented. The most patently obvious is if the player characters can see those they are about to encounter well before getting close.

For example, the characters may see the dorsal fin of a Hammerhead Bullette coming their way, or notice the lanterns of a rival adventuring party coming down the corridor, or hear the barks of a pack of pit bulls closing through the trees. In these cases there is almost no way the characters are going to be surprised by the encounter. But if a Gouger leaped upon one of the group while he was intently watching the Bullette, or if a bunch of Gutter Trolls suddenly emerged from the darkness, then the characters would have to roll to see if they were surprised. They were gawking and therefore unprepared for these threats and so could be taken off guard.

The GM decides when a check for surprise must be made. He can require that one roll be made for the entire party, that a separate check be made for each character, or that only specific characters check. This depends entirely upon the situation.

For example, the entire party is anxiously watching the approaching Bullette. A Gouger then leaps from the branches of a tree. The GM knows that no one in the group was paying any attention to the treetops, so he has one person in the group roll the surprise die for the entire party. The roll is a 2, the PCs are surprised, the Gouger gets a free round of attacks, and there is mass confusion as the clawing, biting creature lands in their midst! If two of the characters had been on a general watch, the GM could have had these characters roll for surprise instead of the entire group. If both were surprised, the entire group would have been unprepared for the Gouger's attack.

Otherwise, one or both of the guards might have noticed the creature before it pounced. Experienced player characters quickly learn the value of having someone watch their back at all times.

The surprise roll can also be modified by Dexterity, race, class and situation. The GM has the listing of modifiers that apply to given situations. Modifiers can affect either your character's chance of being surprised or his chance of surprising others. A plus to your die roll reduces the odds that you are surprised; a minus increases those odds. Likewise, a minus to the enemy's die roll means that the modifier is in your favor, while a plus means that things are going his way. Characters with high Dexterity are caught off guard only in unusual situations and are more difficult to surprise. It is important to bear in mind that surprise and ambush are two different things.

An ambush is prepared by one group in order to make an unexpected and devastating attack on another group. This can succeed only if the GM decides the other group cannot detect the ambush. A properly set ambush gives the attackers the opportunity to use spells and normal attacks before the other side reacts. If the ambush succeeds, the ambushing group gets its initial attack and the other group must roll for surprise in the next round, so the ambushing group may very well get two rounds of attacks before the other group can reply.

Effects of Surprise

Characters and monsters that are surprised all suffer the same grievous penalty. They are caught totally off guard and thus cannot react. The surprising group receives one round of attacks with melee, missile, or magical items. They cannot use this time to cast spells unless the caster had the spell already prepped.

A barbarian on the unsurprised side could fire his long bow twice (two attacks per round) before his opponents could even hope to react. A monk able to attack twice per round could attempt both hits before any initiative dice are rolled. A magic-user could unleash a Frost Ray from his Wand of Cold before the enemy knew he was there. Of course, what applies to player characters also applies to monsters, so that the Gouger in the earlier example could claw and bite before the characters even knew what was happening.

The second effect of surprise is that the surprised characters lose all AC bonuses for high Dexterity during that instant of surprise. The surprised characters are dumbfounded by the attack. Instead of deftly avoiding blows, they're just standing there flat-footed. Since they don't grasp the situation, they cannot avoid the danger as well.

Surprise can also be used to avoid an encounter. Unsurprised characters can attempt to flee from a surprised group before the other group reacts. Of course, this cowardly move is not always successful, since escape is greatly dependent upon the movement rates of the different creatures.

If both groups manage to surprise each other, the effects of surprise are cancelled. For example, Terac runs around the corner straight into two thieves in an alley who were in the middle of an illegal transaction. Taken by surprise, Terac stops suddenly and frantically looks for someplace else to run. The thieves in turn are startled thinking they've just been nailed by a city guard. Both sides stare at each other for a moment unable to do anything else. The next round, the surprise passes. Terac spots another side alley and darts for it. The thieves breathe a sigh of relief and decide that since he's running away, Terac is not a threat. Initiative rolls are now made to see who acts first. The thieves surmise (wisely) that Terac is running away from someone and maybe it would be a good idea to depart the area.

Encounter Distance

Once your character or party has an encounter and the potential implications of surprise have been determined, your GM will tell you the range of the encounter – how far away the other guys are. Many factors affect encounter distance. These include such things as:

- The openness of the terrain.
- The weather conditions.
- Whether surprise occurred.
- Lighting conditions and so on.

These are only a few of many factors the GM will consider. Although you do not know the exact distance until your GM tells you, surprise, darkness or close terrain (jungles, city alley, or narrow dungeons) usually results in shorter encounter distances. Conversely, open ground (agricultural plots, huge vaulted caverns, or parade grounds), good light or advance warning results in greater encounter distances (see Chapter 17: Vision and Light).

Encounter Options

Once an encounter occurs, there is no set sequence for what happens next. It all depends on just what your characters have encountered and what they choose to do. That's the excitement of a role-playing game—once you meet something, almost anything could happen. There are some fairly common results of encounters, however.

Evasion

Sometimes all you want is for your characters to avoid, escape, or otherwise get away from whatever it is you've met. Sometimes this is because you realize your group is seriously outmatched, but usually it's just because you're a bunch of wusses trying to save your miserable hides. Perhaps returning badly hurt from an adventure, your group spots a Swack Iron Dragon soaring overhead. You know it can turn your party to toast if it wants. Rather than take that risk, your group cowers, waiting for it to pass. Or, topping a ridge, you see the Orkin Horde of Haarg sweeping across the borders as they prepare to mount a foraging raid on a nearby human town. There are 5,000 of them and six of you. Retreat seems like the better part of valor, so you turn your horses and ride.

And sometimes you want to avoid an encounter simply because it will take too much time and you'd end up breaking curfew trying to get home.

While riding with an urgent message for his lord, your character rides into a beggar mob. Paying them no mind, he lashes his horse and gallops past. Evading or avoiding an encounter is not always successful. Some monsters pursue; others do not. In the examples above, Ahktang orders his scouts to give chase to the characters so they can't warn the town. The beggars, on the other hand, shout a few oaths as your galloping horse splashes mud on them and then continue on their way. Your character's success at evading capture will depend on movement rates, determination of pursuit, terrain, and just a little luck. Sometimes when he really should be caught, your character gets lucky. At other times, well, he just has to stand his ground and take it like a man.

Parley

Hopefully your character doesn't run from encounters all the time, and attacking everything you meet may eventually lead to problems. Sometimes the best thing to do is talk, whether it's casual conversation, rumor mongering or intimidating threats. In fact, talking is sometimes better than fighting. To solve the problems your GM has created for your character, you need information. Asking poignant questions, developing contacts and putting out disinformation are all useful ways to handle an encounter. Not everything you meet, human or otherwise, is out to kill your character. Help often appears in the most surprising forms. Thus it often pays to take the time to talk to creatures.

Fight

Of course, there are times when you don't want to or can't run away. (Running all the time will certainly brand you as a no-good wuss and potentially affect your Honor.) There are times when you know talking is not a good idea. Sooner rather than later, probably sooner, your character will have to fight. The real trick is to know when to fight and when to talk or run. If you attack every creature you meet, the first thing that will happen is that nobody will want to talk to your character. Your character will also manage to kill or chase off everyone who might want to help him. Sooner or later your GM is going to get tired of this and send an incredibly powerful group of monsters after your character (aka Grudge Monsters). Given the fact that you've been killing everything in sight, he's justified in doing this.

It is always important to know who you are attacking and why. The trick is to figure out who are the bad guys and who are the good guys. Make mistakes and you pay. You might kill an NPC who has a vital clue or unintentionally anger a demon far more powerful than yourself. NPCs will be reluctant to associate with your character, and the law will find fewer and fewer reasons to protect him.

Sometimes you can also gain surprise by talking to the NPC or monster first. For example, let's say your character wanted to deliver a message to the associate of a certain merchant, by eliminated said merchant. You could walk right up to the merchant's booth and attack him, but then he'll probably see it coming flee. A better course of action might be to approach the merchant and ask him about his wares. After suffering through a sales-pitch (GMs love to role-play useless NPCs), you pull out your morningstar and offer a trade. Then, when he leans forward to examine the weapon, you smash him in the face.

Wait

Sometimes when you encounter another group, you don't know what you should do. You don't want to attack them in case they are friendly, but you don't want to say anything to provoke them. What you can do is wait and see how they react. Waiting is a perfectly sensible option. However, there is the risk that in waiting, you lose the advantage should the other side suddenly decide to attack. Waiting for a reaction so that you can decide what to do causes a +1 penalty to the first initiative roll for your group, if the other side attacks.

Of course, in any given encounter, there may be many other options open to your character. The only limit is your imagination (and common sense). Charging a band of Hedge Ogres to break through their lines and flee may work. Talking them down with an elaborate bluff about the army coming up behind you might scare them off. Clever use of spells could end the encounter in sudden and unexpected ways. The point is, this is a role-playing game and the options are as varied as you wish to make them.

Non-Player Characters (NPCs)

Player characters cannot fight, survive, wheel, deal, plot or scheme without interacting with non-player characters (NPCs). Indeed, the very heart of the HackMaster game is the relationship between player characters and non-player characters. How the player characters react to and treat NPCs determines the type of game the group plays. Although many choices are possible, players quickly find that consideration and good treatment of NPCs is the most frequently successful route, though bullying is more fun and usually cheaper.

An NPC is any person, creature, or monster that is controlled by the GM. Most NPCs are either people (intelligent races that live in local society) or monsters (intelligent and unintelligent creatures that aren't normally found in towns and villages). The term "monster" is only a convenient label. It does not mean the creature is automatically dangerous or hostile. Likewise, NPCs who are people are not uniformly helpful and cooperative. As with all things, the range of possible reactions of NPCs to PCs covers the entire spectrum.

In the course of their adventures, player characters will be most concerned with six groups of NPCs: hirelings, followers, cronies, sidekicks, henchmen and hangers on. It is their aid that helps player characters vanquish deadly monsters and accomplish mighty deeds. As their names imply, these NPCs can be persuaded in various ways to join the player characters in their adventures. Sadly, the most common methods of persuasion utilized by most players are those of pain and fear. This is probably due to the fact that most players see NPCs as tools of the GameMaster which he uses to thwart their plans. Even so, NPCs are useful and you would be wise to employ them as needed.

Players who come to HackMaster after having played other role-playing systems should note that the notion of Honor is very important when dealing with NPCs. Since one's Honor is often based on how others view your character, it's usually not in your best interest to treat NPCs poorly or cruelly (Though this doesn't stop many PCs from bullying the NPC).

Hirelings

The most frequently employed NPC is the hireling. A typical hireling is a person who works for money. Most hirelings have fairly ordinary skills, while others are masters of a craft or art, and a few are experts of specialized adventuring skills.

Typical hirelings include the following:

Animal Handler	Animal Driver	Archer
Architect	Armorer	Assassin
Baker	Blacksmith	Bladesmith
Foot Soldier	Jeweler	Laborer
Messenger	Minstrel	Pack Bearer
Sage	Sailor	Scroll Caddy
Spy	Torch Bearer	Tracker
Latrine Jockey	Gibbon Wrangler	

Of course this list is by no means complete. If you can think of a chore or task you can bet there's an NPC out there willing to do it for a price.

Hirelings are always employed for a stated term of service or for the performance of a specific task. Thus, a mercenary contracts to serve for one season. A thief can be hired to steal a named item. A sage works to answer a single question. A blacksmith may indenture himself for a term of years. A sailor works for a single voyage. An assassin works on a per victim basis.

Quite often these contracts can be renewed without difficulty, but the only thing that binds a hireling to the player character is regular pay and good treatment. Hirelings do not serve a PC out of any great loyalty. For the most part they are self-serving and looking only for weekend ale money or a way to make an easy buck.

Thus there are some things hirelings will not do. Most hirelings do not foolishly risk their lives. To be sure, when you hired them, they probably talked a lot of guff and assured you they'd be there to back you up if there should be any trouble. But at the first sign of danger most hirelings make like the wind and blow.

There are soldiers willing to take their chances on the field of battle, but even these courageous (or foolish) few do not willingly undertake the greater hazards of adventuring. Fighting other soldiers on terms they understand is one thing. Fighting a p.o.'ed dragon in the confines of a dungeon labyrinth by torchlight is another.

Mercenary soldiers are useful when it comes to pulling guard duty, manning castle walls, guarding caravans, collecting taxes and charging a massed foe well enough, but they often refuse to accompany a PC on an adventure. Even a hireling who regularly undertakes dangerous missions (a thief or an assassin, for example) normally refuses to join player character parties. Such nefarious hirelings are usually loners and like to keep on the move.

They contract to do a job and get it done in their own way, without interference from anyone else. Hirelings are no more loyal than human nature allows. For the most part, if paid and treated well, with opportunities to realize their ambitions, working for a charismatic leader, hirelings can be relied upon to do their jobs faithfully. But poor pay, injustice, discrimination, threats, abuse and humiliation at the hands of their masters make them somewhat less than reliable. A smart leader sees to the comfort and morale of his men before his own concerns. With less savory characters—those hired to perform dark deeds—the player character takes even greater chances, especially given the questionable morals of such characters.

There does exist a certain type of hireling who is willing to accompany PCs into the dungeons and on hair-raising adventures. But they demand three to five times the normal fees. Halfling Thugs (see *Hacklopedia of Beasts*) are the most common hireling of this variety. They are hardened individuals who value the jingle of gold in their pocket more than their health and are willing to take the risks. Halfling Thugs often hire themselves out as torch bearers or pack bearers and are renowned for being fairly reliable and steady of nerve. They are, understandably, in short supply and most adventuring parties contract-hire such individuals for extended periods in order to have exclusivity to their services.

Whatever their personalities, hirelings generally need to make morale checks (explained in the GMG) whenever they are faced with a particularly dangerous situation or are offered a bribe or other temptation. Finding hirelings is not difficult. People need jobs. It is simply a matter of advertising. Under normal circumstances, applicants respond to ads. Only when trying to employ vast numbers or hire those with unusual specialties (such as spies) does the process become complicated.

Just what needs to be done in this situation depends entirely upon the GM's campaign. Your character may have to skulk through the unsavory bars of the waterfront, rely on questionable go-betweens, or pay a visit to the thieves' guild (if there is one). Just employing one of these characters can be a small adventure in itself. Employment costs of hirelings vary from a few gold pieces a month to thousands of gold pieces for an especially dangerous task. The skill and experience of a hireling has a great effect on his salary. A learned sage researching some obscure piece of lore can charge hefty sums. Costs can also be affected by the conditions of the campaign—

the setting, the recent events of the world, and the reputations of the player characters (if any). Most hirelings sign on for what they think is fair. While few will turn down more money, most will drive the best bargain they can. Your GM has more information about employment costs, since he may need to alter these to fit his campaign.

The Hiring Process

Care should be taken when employing hirelings. Many communities have strict laws concerning employment. If a hireling is maimed or killed while in the service of another, the employer is usually responsible for paying the hireling (or his survivors) compensation in the form of wergild (literally 'man money'). There are also powerful hireling rackets (usually run by Halfling Thugs) who keep hireling rates artificially high.

Another problem with hirelings is that they often misrepresent themselves and profess to have skills or knowledge they don't actually have. There's nothing quite so infuriating as hiring a tracker to lead you through the Grand Thicket only to find yourself lost for six days and realizing your expert 'tracker' is an idiot. Or how about an animal handler who claims he can control a string of Pack Apes who turns out to be deathly afraid of the beasts.

Beware of hireling scams as well. More than one pack bearer loaded down with dungeon-spoils has gone over the hill with the goods never to be seen again. Many Halfling Thug hireling rackets are little more than thieves' guilds with thieves hiring themselves out to the unsuspecting with an eye on lightening a party of their gold and valuables.

You should also make sure you're hiring the very best. Make your gold work for you. Interview prospective hirelings. Give them simple tests to do to see if they're really as good as they claim. You should also screen out any slackers. One simple method of weeding out lazy or poor quality hirelings is the Shirker Test. This is accomplished by dropping a copper piece on the ground in front of the hireling. If he doesn't bend down to pick it up he's either too lazy or doesn't need the money bad enough to bruise his pride. Either way you don't want someone like that on the payroll.

Followers

More reliable than those who are motivated purely by money are those who, while they expect pay, were originally drawn into service by the reputation or high Honor of the player character. These are followers, usually a unit of soldiers of one type or another. Followers serve only those of significant power and reputation, thus the construction of a stronghold is often a requirement to attract followers. Details on the followers that are attracted by certain character classes are included in the descriptions of each individual character class.

Followers have the same needs and limitations as hirelings. Most must be paid and well treated. They also do not usually accompany the player characters on group adventures. They have some advantages over hirelings, however. Followers do not serve for a specific term of contract. They remain with the player character as long as their basic needs are met. They are more loyal than the average hireling and are treated as elite troops. Unlike most hirelings, followers can gain levels (although this occurs very slowly since they usually act only as soldiers). All followers in a unit advance to the next level at the same time. Finally, the player character need not seek out followers—they come to him, seeking out positions within his illustrious outfit.

Followers will also seek out professional adventuring parties of notable Fame/Honor. Don't be fooled. Such individuals are looking to hitch their wagon to a rising star in the hopes that the party or characters' prestige and power will help raise their status in life.

Followers appear only once. Replacements do not arrive to fill the ranks of the fallen. (A massive loss of followers in combat gives the character a bad reputation, discouraging others from flocking to his banner.) Player characters should take care of their followers, perhaps treating them as an elite bodyguard.

Some characters attract unique followers such as animals or magical beings. Although termed followers, these creatures are more properly treated as henchmen in terms of loyalty and what they will and will not do. They do not count against the character's limit on henchmen, however, since they are technically followers.

Cronies

During their pre-adventure years, it is assumed that most player characters have managed to make acquaintances and friends who can come in handy once in awhile. Such NPCs are referred to as cronies. Cronies are not particularly loyal, but they can come through in a pinch. They usually have some useful skills or know important information and can be counted on to provide a little friendly aid in a cold, cruel world. Cronies are not in it for the long haul. They are fair-weather buddies. They'll never accompany a character on an adventure, but they often provide help simply for old times' sake, and not for profit. A crony is the guy you can barge in on if you're in town and know you can get a free meal and room on his floor to unroll your bedroll. He may be good for the loan of a few gold pieces here and there. There are some cronies who may ask for a compensation in return, but most consider such favors along the line as 'one good turn deserves another.' The GM has more specific information on cronies, and will help you determine how many, and what type of cronies your character has.

Sidekicks

No matter how tough a player character is, friendship is important. Even the Lone Ranger wasn't completely alone. He had his sidekick, and so can PCs. Like Tonto, a sidekick in HackMaster is a sworn friend. He will ride into battle, stand toe-to-toe with a band of bloodthirsty Ogres or storm the gates of Hell itself for his friend. No one is more loyal than a sidekick. Because of the special nature of sidekicks, each PC gets only ONE during his entire career. Sidekicks will expect no payment, but they may be driven away by continued insults or abuse. Sidekicks are loyal, but they're not doormats. Again, your GM can help you with the details of gaining a sidekick. Players often confuse cronies with sidckicks. The difference is easy. You call a crony if you need help moving. You call a sidekick when you need help moving a body.

Mentor/Protegee

The concept of mentors and protegees is unique to HackMaster. Your GM will have more specific rules about this subject, however, players should know a few basic things about them. In HackMaster, PCs are allowed to gain up to four NPC protegees to mentor. These NPCs are people who have shown some potential or motivation that has caught the attention of a PC. A PC can act as a sort of sponsor, funneling portions of his own experience and treasure to build up his protegees. He can enroll them in accelerated-development programs, helping them increase in skill level, weapon proficiency, knowledge of languages, etc.

Beginning players may wonder why they would want to be so kind to lowly NPCs, however, experienced players have long since understood the value of such a program. PCs who have "sponsored" NPCs in this way have built what is known as a "prep pool." This is a sort of "life insurance" program designed to help players who have had their high-level characters killed through some cruel twist of fate. When such an unfortunate event occurs, the player can

select one of his former character's protegees as his next character, thus saving himself the trouble of having to start at the bottom once again.

If your background indicates you have living siblings (see Chapter 4: Character Priors) you should give serious consideration to making one or more of them your protegees. Brothers and other blood relatives have certain perks and advantages when it comes to character-prepping.

Henchmen

Henchmen are much that hirelings are not. They are adventurers who serve out of loyalty. They are willing to risk their lives for those they respect. They are also hard to find.

Henchmen are powerful allies to a player character. Unlike hirelings, they have the nerve and ability to become powerful adventurers. Although they expect their share of treasure, they do not usually join a player character for money. They are attracted to the PC because of his reputation or other qualities he possesses. As such, henchmen cannot be expected to flock to the banner of a neophyte adventurer. He may gain himself one or two companions, but others come only when he has earned a greater reputation, met more people, and proven himself a true friend and ally to these NPCs.

Henchmen can come from any source. Most often they are at first mere hirelings or followers who, through distinctive actions, come to the attention of the player character. Some may be higher level, more skilled hirelings who develop a bond with the player character through long employment. Others may be followers who have sound advice for the player character.

A henchman is always of lower level than the PC. Should he ever equal or surpass the PC's level, the henchman leaves forever; it is time for him to try his luck in the real world. In some ways, the player character is the mentor and the henchman his student. When the student has learned as much as his teacher, it is time for him to go out on his own.

Henchmen are more than just loyal followers, they are friends and allies. Naturally, they expect to be treated as such. They have little need for those who do not trust them or treat them coldly. Abusiveness or taking advantage of the friendship quickly ends the relationship. Just as in real life friendships, player characters must be sensitive to the needs and feelings of their henchmen. Furthermore, henchmen attach themselves to a particular player character, not a group of player characters. Thus, it is only under the direst of circumstances that a henchman accepts the orders of another PC in the party.

Should his friend (the player character) fall, the henchman sees to his needs. He doesn't abandon him and continue with the other player characters unless this is clearly the only way to aid his friend.

A PC's Charisma determines the maximum number of henchmen he can have. This is a lifetime limit, not just a maximum possible at any given time. In a world where the fallen can be restored to life, it is expected that a man would make this effort for his dearest friends, both player characters and henchmen.

For example, Rupert the half-elf has had seven henchmen, but all have fallen for one reason or another. Rupert's Charisma is 15, so with the death of

NPC's- Quick Reference

1. Our Hero- definitely **NOT** an NPC
2. Sidekick- a credit to his title...
3. Henchman- a childhood friend
4. Cronie-along for the ride!
5. Follower
6. Protegee
7. Hireling: Scroll Caddy (being careless with the material again...)
8. Hireling: Torch Bearer
9. Hirelings and Hangers On

his latest henchman, no more come to join him. (Word has obviously gotten around that Rupert's friends tend to meet unpleasant ends, and he doesn't even have the decency to bring them back to life! Even if he had tried to raise his henchmen and failed, Rupert would still be viewed as a jinx, bad luck for those around him.) Attracting a henchman is fairly difficult. One cannot advertise for friends with any great success. They grow and develop from other relationships. A henchman can be found by placing trust in a skilled hireling. Heroic deeds (saving the life of an NPC) can create a strong and instant bond. Love certainly can form this bond. The player and the GM must trust their own judgment to determine when an NPC becomes a henchman.

There is no clear line a NPC must cross to make the transition from hireling to henchman. Instead, it is a slide from one status to the other. Once an NPC becomes a henchman, the player gains a high degree of control over the character. He should be responsible for the record keeping for that character. It is almost, but not quite, like having a new PC for the player. If the GM allows it, the player can have all information regarding the abilities of the henchman, although the GM may choose not to reveal this information. The player is allowed to make nearly all decisions for the NPC, but the GM can overrule any action as being out of character.

There are certain things henchmen do not do. They do not give away or loan out magical items. They do not allow others free access to their spell books. They do not tolerate spell use that questions their loyalty (Detect Lie or Know Alignment cast upon them). They do not accept less than their due share. In general, within these limits, henchmen do what is desired of them. The GM can at any time dictate the actions of a henchman, since the character is still an NPC.

If a PC is not attentive to the wishes and needs of his henchmen, or if he abuses and humiliates them, he can expect the worst. This is the stuff mutinies and rebellions are made of. Should an abusive player character fall at the hands of a once-loyal henchman, he has only himself to blame.

On the other hand, not all henchmen are paragons of loyalty. The player character must always be aware that henchmen are sometimes not what they seem. They can be a means to get at the player character. Throughout history, many a cruel and cunning villain has posed as a true companion, waiting for his chance to strike or spy on his "friend."

Hangers On

Word should be made of a particularly annoying class of NPCs known collectively as 'hangers on'. These unscrupulous bastards seek out player characters with notable Honor and Fame with the hopes of cashing in or mooching whatever they can get. They try to pass themselves off as henchmen or characters of great skill offering to serve the PC.

As time passes, however, it begins to become apparent that these slackers have no skills whatsoever. They fail to show up to rallies. They also seem to show up at the dungeon when the fighting is over explaining they were 'held up' or some other lame excuse. Often, before the PC is aware of the scam, the hanger on has soaked him for hundreds, sometimes thousands, of gold pieces.

"If I had a good sword I'd fight for you!" they promise. "If only I had a horse I wouldn't have been late for the foray planning meeting."

It's tough to avoid these types of characters but you can minimize the damage if you keep your guard up.

Player Character Obligations

Whenever a player character takes on a hireling, follower, cronie, sidekick or henchman, he has committed himself to certain obligations and customs that surround such agreements. Some of these are obvious, having been worked out between the player character and the NPC in advance. Usually the wages and terms of service are settled upon before any agreement is reached. For hirelings and followers, this is a set amount of money each day, week, or month or a fee for a specific task. Henchmen commonly receive a portion (half a normal share) of all treasure and magic found on adventures. A player character is normally expected to contribute a little more from his own funds, however.

Other obligations of the player character are varied. Some must always be considered, while others almost never come into effect. A player character is expected to provide meals and boarding (unless the NPC has a home nearby). This is the most common obligation and applies to NPCs of all walks of life. For those engaged in more dangerous pursuits, however, additional concessions must be granted. Since horses are expensive, player characters should be ready to cover the cost of mounts lost in combat or on campaign. It is unreasonable to expect a mercenary to buy a new mount from his meager savings. Likewise, the player character must replace other items of war craft, such as weapons and armor. All soldiers are expected to provide their own equipment when they are first employed, but the player character must replace all losses. Certainly all player characters are expected to pay the cost of special transport—securing passage on ships and arranging wagons for baggage. Of the grimmer duties, player characters are expected to pay for a decent (though hardly lavish) interment.

One of the more unusual obligations of a player character is to ransom his men. This is especially true of men lost during a campaign. The greater number of soldiers lost in a battle are not slain but captured. A common practice of the medieval period was to officially ransom these prisoners for well-established prices. A common yeoman footman might ransom for 2 gp, a minor cleric for 80 gp, a knight's squire for 200 gp, and a king's man for 500 gp. The lord of the prisoner pays his ransom. A player character (as a lord and master) is expected to do the same. Of course, the player character can pass much of this cost on to his own subjects and the relatives of the prisoner. When funds are scarce, men might languish for long periods in the hands of the enemy before their ransom is raised.

Furthermore, should a player character ransom a hireling, follower, or henchman, he has every reason to expect loyal service from that man in the future. After all, he has demonstrated his willingness to save that NPC from hardship and death.

In a fantasy world, a player character is also expected to bear the cost of magical spells cast to the benefit of his men. He may arrange to have his men blessed before battle or healed after it. He shouldn't grumble about the expense, because the spells also make good tactical sense. The Bless spell increases the success of his army in the field. Magical cures get his army back on its feet quicker. All these things can make him very successful while also making him popular with his hired men.

Finally, the player character is expected to make an effort to raise or restore slain henchmen. This is not a normal expectation of hirelings or followers (although it can happen in extreme cases). The effort should be honest and true. A player character shouldn't fool himself into thinking no one will notice if he doesn't do his utmost. The player character who returns from an adventure minus his henchman is automatically under a cloud of suspicion, despite his most vehement protests. A player character must take great care to maintain his reputation as a good and upright employer.

Rumblings in the Ranks:

Now, there will be times when hirelings, followers and henchmen will begin to grumble and express discontentment. This may happen despite your best efforts to live up to your obligations such as treating them well and paying them as promised. Every situation is unique but you must handle such situations quickly and decisively. Dissension, especially among hirelings is contagious. You'll need to deal with any open displays of rebellion before they blow up in your face.

Sometimes such a situation can be defused by offering more shares of the booty or increasing pay. This can backfire, however, especially with hirelings. They'll view such actions more as a sign of weakness than an act of kindness and push for more and more. When it comes to you and those who work for you or follow you, respect is paramount. You need to keep the lines of superior and underling well defined. You'd be surprised what a good attitude adjustment can do for morale. Cold cock a surly torch bearer in front of his peers and suddenly that unruly mob forming outside the quartermaster's tent disperses and you might not hear a peep of out them for days.

One word of caution:

Hirelings are not without pride. Putting a hireling in his place is different than humiliating him. Nothing is more dangerous than a disgruntled hireling or follower who feels he's been slighted or maltreated. Such individuals will hate the PC who he feels did him wrong till the day he dies and will be bent on his ruin.

Chapter 16

Time and Movement

"C'mon boys ! MOVE yer asses!! All we have going for us is TIME and when it's gone — what are we left with?"

Lord Flataroy

There are two different types of time that are discussed in these rules. Game time is the imaginary time that passes for the characters in the game. Real time is the time in the real world, the time that passes for the players and GM as they play the game.

Game Time

As in the real world, time passes within the game world itself as you play HackMaster. Minutes fade into hours. Hours fade into days. Days become weeks. Weeks become months…well, you get the idea.

The passage of game time is very important because it often takes a certain amount of time for your character to complete a task or to achieve his aims. For example, a mage researching a new spell may require months of game time before he meets with any level of success.

And that deep rending wound your comrade is sewing up for you? Unless you have access to some form of magical healing it might take weeks to heal properly. Likewise, it might take days to ride cross-country on your errand to the nearest town. Hours might pass as you negotiate the twisty passages of the dungeon or as you wait for your friends to return to get your lifeless body from the bottom of the spiked pit in which he lies in a twisted heap. And although it may feel like a lifetime has passed as your death duel with that Greater Owlbear unfolds, most battles last only a fraction of a minute. All of the above are examples of how game time can pass during a typical session.

Real Time

Real time is just that – the passage of time in the REAL world. While your game session may have lasted only a few hours in 'real time' it is quite possible that your character experienced the passage of weeks or months of 'game time' during that same session.

Distinguishing between Real Time and Game Time

Neophytes to HackMaster are sometimes confused by the concepts of real time vs. game time but it's actually quite simple – the two types of time are just different. It's very important that players and GMs understand and carefully distinguish each type from the other. The following example of play should clear things up if you're still confused.

Let's say that a player (Frank) announces his character, Rudnick Clericsbane, is eligible to advance to the next level. In order to advance and improve his skills and utilize the knowledge and experience he has acquired, the character must attend a school where a mentor will help him apply what's he learned.

After consulting with the player, the GM determines Rudnick must attend university for six weeks in order to complete his training. [Note this 'six week' period is in 'game time'.]

Thus, Rudnick is out of action for at least six weeks time in the campaign world. Since the GM decides nothing interesting at all happens while he is at school it only requires a minute or two of 'real time' to handle the situation. The exchange in real time is something like this:

Frank: Okay, so Rudnick is going to attend Braar's Fighter Academy in Drayton's Forge. I like the classes offered there and I'm already a student of Master Chung-Hu Chek. I excelled last time I studied under him so I only have to pay 80% of the listed training fees.

GM: OK, Drayton's Forge is a four day journey from your current location. Your schooling is going to take six weeks so with travel time there and back let's just call it 8 weeks. Nothing worth mentioning happens to Rud on his trip since it's a fairly well patrolled area. (rolls) Oh, but you DID make a new friend while at school – I'll give you the details on that next week. Make a note of it.

As for the rest of you, while Rud's at school you'll have a chance to heal your wounds, gamble in the inn, poke about town for rumors and adventure hooks, etc. Oh, and by the way, don't forget the stable is charging each of you one gold per week to care for your horses. Go ahead and mark off 8 gold pieces each. And another 40 gold each for the 'opulent lodgings' you rented. As you recall the rooms were 5 gold per week.

Mike: Huh? But that's 48 g.p.s! Damn! I'm going broke real fast over here. Maybe I'll just take my horse and camp on the outskirts of town while we wait for Rud to get back. Or maybe, I'll go on another adventure myself when he's gone.

GM: Fine and MAYBE I'll be obliged to ROLL for random encounters every four hours for being outside the City Guard's perimeter. Let's see, 8 weeks? That's 56 days so that figures out to something like 1,344 rolls. You REALLY wanna go down that path?

Mike: Ack! No, no…never mind. The inn is fine. I'll pay. I'll pay.

And so eight weeks of game time flash by in mere minutes of real time. The importance of game time is that as a campaign progresses, characters tend to become involved in different time-consuming projects. Three characters may set off on a four-week overland journey, while a magic-user researches for six weeks. At the inn, a fighter rests and heals his wounds for two weeks. It is important to note how much time passes during different tasks, so that the activities of different characters can be followed. Players quickly learn to coordinate time-intensive tasks to maintain enjoyment of the game and to keep things moving. For example, a magic-user might wait before initiating any spell research until the fighter of the group is about to leave for school. A thief might decide it's a good time to mingle and socialize at the local thieves' guild while the fighter is laid up in bed healing from his brush with death.

The Measure of Gametime

Calendar

Campaign (game) time is measured just as it is in real life: years, months, weeks, days. When beginning play, these things are not tremendously important, so players need not worry about them right away. With continued adventuring, players eventually become familiar with their surroundings and do more time consuming things, like building keeps, training, etc.

Rounds

Minutes in HackMaster are referred to as rounds. One round equals approximately one minute. Rounds are used to resolve such things as non-combat spell duration, the time it takes to execute certain skills, etc.

Melee Rounds

During combat, rounds drop to six-second intervals. It's obviously moronic to think it takes sixty seconds to stab someone with a sword. It takes six because, in battle, the combatants dodge, parry, thrust and hack a couple of times before getting that one opening to land a solid whack.

Segments

Each melee round is further divided into ten segments (thus each segment is 0.6 seconds). We divide rounds in this way to get better accuracy on exactly when spells activate and blow up the land. Anything else would simply be unrealistic.

Turns

The last unit of game time you must be familiar with is the turn. A turn is equal to 10 rounds of game time, or ten minutes. Turns are normally used to measure specific tasks (such as searching) and certain spells. Thus, a spell that lasts 10 turns is equal to 100 minutes, or one and two-thirds hours.

Melee Turns

A turn is simply ten rounds. Thus, during combat, the duration of a turn is one minute.

Duration is determined when an action begins; it does not change when a situation goes from combat to non-combat (or vice versa). Thus, a spell with a duration of 10 turns cast during combat lasts ten minutes, even if the combat ends before that time has elapsed.

Movement

Closely related to time is movement. Clearly your character is able to move, otherwise adventures would be rather static and boring. But how fast can he move? If a large, green Carrion Crawler is scuttling after Guss, is the redoubtable dwarf fast enough to escape? Could Guss outrun an irritated but heavily loaded grel he just sucker-punched in the groin? Sooner or later these considerations become important to player characters.

Table 16A:
Base Movement Rate

Race	Rate/Points
Human	12
Dwarf	6
Elf	12
Half-elf	12
Gnome	6
Gnomeling	4
Halfling	6
Half-Orc	12
Half-Ogre	13
Pixie-Fairy	4/18*
* unencumbered flying rate.	

All characters have movement rates that are based on their race. Table 16A lists the movement rates for unencumbered characters of different races. Movement rates equate to inches when using miniatures. They are also referred to as movement 'points' through out the rules. For example a human character who takes an arrow to the leg might lose 1 point of movement. His movement rate of 12 points (or inches) is reduced to 11 points.

A character can normally walk his movement rate in tens of yards in a single round. An unencumbered human can walk 120 yards (360 feet) in one minute. A dwarf, similarly equipped, can walk 60 yards in the same time. This walk is at a fairly brisk, though not strenuous, pace that can be kept up for long periods of time.

However, a character might not be able to move at his optimal pace. If the character is carrying equipment, he might move slower because of the encumbrance (see "Encumbrance" in Chapter 9: Goods and Services). As the character carries more gear and finds more loot, he gradually slows down until he reaches the point where he can barely move at all. Be careful of this situation, because it is here that cruel GMs, as in 'all' GMs, unleash the fast moving grudge monsters. So if you must load up, and when there's a pile of treasure you pretty much must, try to be ready for a fight.

When a character is moving through a dungeon or similar setting, his movement rate corresponds to tens of feet per round (rather than the tens of yards per round of outside movement). It is assumed that the character is moving more cautiously, paying attention to what he sees and hears while avoiding traps and pitfalls.

Characters can also move faster than the normal walking pace. In the dungeon (or any time the character is using his dungeon movement rate), the character can automatically increase his movement to that of his normal walking pace. In doing so, however, he suffers a penalty to his chance of being surprised (+2). He also gives a bonus (-2) to others against their likelihood of being surprised by him (the rapidly moving character is not taking care to conceal the noise of his passage in the echoing confines of the underground). Furthermore, the character does not notice traps, secret doors or other unusual features.

It is also certainly possible for a character to double time or run—an especially useful thing when being chased by creatures tougher than he cares to fight. The simplest method for handling these cases is to roll an initiative die. If the fleeing character wins, he increases the distance between himself and his pursuers by 10 times the difference in the two dice. This is repeated each turn until the character escapes or is caught and eaten (or worse).

Swimming

When it comes to swimming, all characters fall into one of three categories. The first category includes all characters that do not possess any swimming skills. These characters can only hold their breath and float for a number of rounds equal to their Constitution. After that period has elapsed, they must succeed at a Constitution check or sink and begin drowning. A cumulative -1 penalty applies to this check for every round past the first. Once a character has failed the Constitution check, they are subject to the drowning rules below.

The second category of characters includes those who possess the swimming: dog paddle skill. These characters can swim at a rate of 1/3 their normal land movement rate, for a number of turns equal to their Constitution. Afterwards they must make a Constitution check to Continue swimming. This check suffers a cumulative -1 penalty for each turn after the first. Once the check is failed, the character is subject to the drowning rules below.

The final category of characters includes those characters with the swimming: dog paddle and swimming skills. These characters can swim at 1/2 their normal land movement rate for a number of turns equal to twice their Constitution. After they have exceeded this time, they must make a Constitution check to continue swimming. This check suffers a cumulative -1 penalty for each check after the first. The character must check for each additional turn they wish to swim. If the character fails the swimming check, he may make a swimming: dog paddle check. If he succeeds, he may tread water for a number of rounds equal to his Constitution, as per the rules for untrained swimmers above. Afterwards, he must make Constitution checks as described above. If he fails, he is subject to the drowning rules below. If the swimmer fails his swimming: dog paddle check, he is immediately subject to the drowning rules below.

Drowning

A potentially drowning victim may hold his breath for a number of melee rounds equal to twice his Constitution. After this period of time, the creature must make a Constitution check every melee round in order to remain conscious. Each round, a +1 penalty to the Constitution check applies. In the round the victim fails the Constitution check he becomes unconscious. In the following round his lungs fill with water and he is reduced to zero hit points. The next round he dies.

Chapter 17

Vision and Light

More Than Just an Eyeful

Vision and light (i.e. light sources) are extremely important in HackMaster, hence the subject warrants its own chapter. No matter how great your character is (or thinks he is) he's not going to accomplish a heck of a lot unless he can see what he's doing. Granted, some players will end up with blind characters either voluntarily (for receiving character flaw 'blindness,' for example) or involuntarily (perhaps as the result of an injury during combat). Such characters can thrive in the world of HackMaster if they manage to develop the right skills to compensate for their handicap before someone or something does them in. But such characters overcoming the odds and pushing on are the exception rather than the rule.

Most characters can't do diddly-squat unless they are able to see what they are doing. Keep in mind that vision is often obscured by factors such as poor lighting conditions, distance, weather conditions, and so on. If a character can't clearly see a target, his chances of hitting it are very small. If he can't see at all, he's not going to be able to read important things like road signs, scrolls or books.

Since this is a fantasy game many characters have special visual abilities and can see extreme distances and/or even in the absence of light, either by racial or magical means that would defy logic in our own world.

Limits of Vision

The distance between the viewer and what he's attempting to see is the biggest factor to consider when dealing with the limitations of vision. How far away an object can be seen clearly will vary from race to race and, as mentioned above, may be improved through the use of a magic item and/or spell.

Size and weather greatly affect vision as well. Mountains can be seen from great distances (60 to 100 miles or more), yet virtually no detail can be seen. On flat terrain, the horizon is about five to 12 miles away, but a character usually cannot see a specific object that far away. The limit of vision for seeing and identifying man-sized objects is much, much less than this.

Under optimal conditions, the maximum range at which a man-sized object can be seen is about 1,500 yards, if it is moving. If the object is stationary, it usually cannot be seen at this distance. Even if it is moving, all that can be seen is a moving object. The character cannot tell what it is or what it is doing.

At 1,000 yards, both moving and stationary man-sized objects can be spotted. General size and shape can be determined, but exact identifications are impossible. It is not likely that creature type can be identified at this range, unless the creature has a very unique shape.

At 500 yards, general identifications can be made. Size, shape, color and creature type are all distinguishable. Individuals still cannot be identified, unless they are distinctively dressed or separated from the rest of the group. Livery and heraldic symbols or banners can be seen if large and bold. Most coats of arms cannot be distinguished at this distance. General actions can be ascertained with confidence.

At 100 yards, individuals can be identified (unless, of course, their features are concealed). Coats of arms are clear. Most actions are easily seen, although small actions (such as fumbling through a pouch for an item) may be unclear.

At 10 yards, all details but the smallest are clear. Emotions and actions are easily seen, including such small actions as picking pockets (if it is detectable).

Of course, conditions are seldom perfect. There are a number of factors that can reduce visibility and alter the ranges at which things can be spotted and identified. Table 17A lists the effects of different types of conditions. All ranges are given in yards.

"Movement" indicates the maximum distance at which a moving figure can be seen. "Spotted" is the maximum distance at which a moving or a stationary figure can be seen. "Type" gives the maximum distance at which the general details of a figure can be seen – species or race, weapons, etc. "ID" range enables exact (or reasonably exact) identification. "Detail" range means small actions can be seen clearly.

There are many factors other than weather that affect viewing. Size is an important factor. When looking at a small creature (size S), all categories are reduced to the next lower category (except the "detail" range, which remains unchanged). Thus, under clear conditions, the ranges for seeing a small creature are "movement" at 1,000 yards, "spotted" at 500 yards, "type" at 100 yards, and "ID" and "detail" at 10 yards.

When viewing large creatures, the "movement," "spotting," and "type" ranges are doubled. Exceptionally large creatures can be seen from even greater distances. Large groups of moving creatures can also be seen at great distances. Thus, it is easy to see a herd of buffalo or an army on the march from a great distance.

Table 17A: Visibility Ranges*					
Condition	Movement	Spotted	Type	ID	Detail
Clear sky	1,500	1,000	500	100	10
Drunken Haze**	10	5	3	2	6"
Fog, dense or blizzard	10	10	5	5	3
Fog, light or snow	500	200	100	30	10
Fog, moderate	100	50	25	15	10
Mist or light rain	1,000	500	250	30	10
Night, full moon	100	50	30	10	5
Night, no moon	50	20	10	5	3
Twilight	500	300	150	30	10

*The figures above are the norm for characters of human, halfling and dwarven stock. Some races, such as the grey elf can see twice as far (double the range indicated above). Gnome titans, on the other hand, can only see about 75% as well a human character. If visual ability isn't specifically mentioned under a racial listing assume the race in question possesses normal (human) vision.

** Drunken Haze has been included so that GMs can approximate the effects of alcohol on characters. Any character in an 'acutely inebriated' state (sloshed) or greater as indicated on the inebriation tables (see GM's Guide) will suffer from tunnel vision and blurred vision (aka Drunken Haze).

As a final caveat, the ranges in Table 17A assume Earthlike conditions. Sighting conditions on one of the Lower Planes, or the horizon distance on another world, could be entirely different. If your GM feels he must take this into account, he will have to make it up or, if he's particularly industrious, learn more about this subject at his local library.

The ranges given in Table 17A do not take terrain into account. All ranges are based on flat, open ground. Hills, mountains, tall grass or dense woods all drastically reduce the chances of seeing a creature. (The terrain does not alter sighting ranges, only the chances of seeing a creature.) Thus, even on a clear day, woods may hide a bear until he is 30 yards away. The bear, once visible, can be quickly and easily identified as a bear. The GM has more information on specific effects of terrain on sighting.

Light

Most characters in HackMaster cannot see much without the presence of some level of illumination. Some night conditions (those for the outdoors) are given in Table 17A. But all of these assume some small amount of light (such as starlight or moonlight). In totally lightless conditions, normal vision is rendered absolutely useless and the character is effectively blind – unless of course some type of artificial or magical light source is present.

Different light sources vary widely in the area and range they are able to illuminate. Table 17B gives the radius of light and burning time for the most common types of light sources.

Of course, while a lantern or fire enables characters to see, it does have some disadvantages. The greatest of these is that it is hard to sneak up on someone if he can see you coming. It is hard to remain inconspicuous when you have the only campfire on the plain, or you are carrying the only torch in the dungeon. Furthermore, not only do creatures know you are coming, they can gen-

erally see you before you see them (since the light source illuminates the area around you, those outside that area can see into it). Characters should always bear these risks in mind.

Infravision

Infravision is the ability to see into the infrared spectrum. Thus heat radiation becomes visible and differences in temperature allow infrared sight. Warm things are bright, cool things gray, very cold things are black. Most infravision extends to 60' distance. Dungeon-dwelling monsters have infravision to 120'. All infravision is spoiled if a light source is within range of the creature possessing the infrared sight capability. Similarly, great heat will spoil the capability.

Thieves hiding in shadows are successful with respect to infravision only if there is a heat/light source nearby to mask their body heat, or a very cold object to provide similar cover.

Ultravision

Ultravision is the ability to perceive radiation beyond the wavelength of visible light (from about 40 to 4000 Angstroms). Creatures with this ability can see in normal nighttime darkness.' That is, they see at night as well as a human can see at dusk because of the continual bombardment of short wave radiation upon the earth.

Using Mirrors

At times it is useful for characters to look at objects or creatures via reflections in a mirror. This is particularly true of those creatures so hideous (such as a Medusa or Catoblepas) that gazing directly upon them might turn the viewer to stone or cause death. When using a mirror, a light source must be present. Secondly, attempting to direct your actions by looking in a mirror is very disorienting (try it and see). Thus, all actions requiring an ability or attack roll suffer a -2 penalty. A character making a skill check suffers a -50 penalty and one making a proficiency check suffers a –10 penalty. The character also loses all Dexterity bonuses to Armor Class if fighting an opponent seen only in a mirror.

Table 17B: Light Sources		
Source	Radius	Burning time
Beacon lantern	240 ft.*	30 hrs./pint
Bonfire	50 ft.	1/2 hr./armload
Bullseye lantern	60 ft.*	2 hrs./pint
Campfire	35 ft.	1 hr./armload
Candle	5 ft.	10 min./inch
Continual light	60 ft.	Indefinite
Hooded lantern	30 ft.	2 hrs./pint
Light spell	20 ft.	Variable
Torch	15 ft.	30 min.
Weapon**	5 ft.	As desired

* Light from these is not cast in a radius, but rather in a cone-shaped beam. At its far end, the cone of light from a beacon lantern is 90 feet wide. A bullseye lantern has a beam 20 feet wide at its far end.

** Some magical weapons shed light. Your GM has details on which ones do so.

Appendix A

Spell List - Alphabetical

This appendix lists all the spells in alphabetical order by name. Magic User spells are listed first, beginning with a list of the cantrips. Following the Magic User spells are the Cleric and Druid spells, also listed alphabetically.

(M.U. = Magic User, IL = Illusionist, CL = Cleric, DR = Druid)

Cantrip List

A
Air of Legitimacy (Legerdemain)
Aura of Vulnerability (Person-Affecting)

B
Bee (Personal)
Belch (Person-Affecting)
Blink (Person-Affecting)
Bluelight (Personal)
Bug (Personal)

C
Change (Legerdemain)
Chill (Useful)
Clean (Useful)
Color (Useful)
Colored Lights (IL Cantrip)
Cough (Person-Affecting)
Coy Smile (Person-Affecting)
Creak (Haunting)
Curdle (Reversed)

D
Dampen (Useful)
DIBS (Useful)
Dim (IL Cantrip)
Dirty (Reversed)
Distract (Legerdemain)
Double Take (Person-Affecting)
Dry (Useful)
Dust (Useful)
Dusty (Reversed)

E
Exterminate (Useful)
Exude Fear (Person-Affecting)

F
Feign Toughness (Person-Affecting)
Firefinger (Personal)
Flavor (Useful)
Flinch (Person-Affecting)
Footfall (Haunting)
Freshen (Useful)

G
Gather (Useful)
Giggle (Person-Affecting)
Gnats (Personal)
Groan (Haunting)

H
Hairy (Reversed)
Haze (IL Cantrip)
Hide (Legerdemain)

I
Indian Burn (Person-Affecting)

K
Knot (Reversed)
Knowing Look (Person-Affecting)

L
Lazy Eye (Person-Affecting)

M
Mask (IL Cantrip)
Menacing Scowl (Person-Affecting)
Mirage (IL Cantrip)

Moan (Haunting)
Mouse (Personal)
Mute (Legerdemain)

N
Nod (Person-Affecting)
Noise (IL Cantrip)
Noogie (Person-Affecting)

P
Palm (Legerdemain)
Poker Face (Person-Affecting)
Polish (Useful)
Present (Legerdemain)

R
Rainbow (IL Cantrip)
Rattle (Haunting)
Ravel (Reversed)
Remote Gouged Eye (Person-Affecting)

S
Salt (Useful)
Scratch (Person-Affecting)
Sheepish Grin (Person-Affecting)
Shine (Useful)
Smokepuff (Personal)
Sneeze (Person-Affecting)
Sour (Reversed)
Spice (Useful)
Spider (Personal)
Spill (Reversed)
Sprout (Useful)
Stitch (Useful)
Sweeten (Useful)

T
Tangle (Reversed)
Tap (Haunting)
Tarnish (Reversed)
Thump (Haunting)
Tie (Useful)
Tweak (Personal)
Twitch (Person-Affecting)
Two-D'lusion (IL Cantrip)

U
Unlock (Personal)
Untie (Reversed)

V
Veiled Threat (Person-Affecting)

W
Warm (Useful)
Weak Bladder (Person-Affecting)
Wet Willie (Person-Affecting)
Whistle (Haunting)
Wilt (Reversed)
Wink (Person-Affecting)
Wrap (Useful)

Y
Yawn (Person-Affecting)

Magic User and Illusionist Spell List

A
Advanced Illusion (M.U. 5)
Affect Normal Fires (M.U. 1)
Airy Water (M.U. 5)
Alarm (M.U. 1)
Alter Self (M.U 2)
Animal Growth (M.U. 5)
Animate Dead (M.U. 5)
Anti-Magic Shell (M.U. 6)
Antipathy-Sympathy (M.U. 8)
Armor (M.U. 1)
Astral Spell (M.U. 9)
Audible Glamer (M.U. 2)
Aura of Innocence (M.U. 1)
Avoidance (M.U. 5)

B
Banishment (M.U. 7)
Bash Door (M.U. 1)
Bash Face (M.U. 3)

Befriend (M.U 1)
Bind (M.U. 2)
Binding (M.U. 8)
Blindness (M.U. 2)
Blink (M.U. 3)
Blur (M.U. 2)
Body Heat Activated Spell (M.U. 6)
Break hex (M.U. 6)
Burning Hands (M.U. 1)

C
Cacodemon (M.U. 7)
Chain-of-Fire (M.U. 2)
Chain Lightning (M.U. 6)
Change Self (M.U. 1)
Chaos (M.U. 5)
Charm Monster (M.U. 4)
Charm Person (M.U. 1)
Charm Plants (M.U. 7)
Charm Undead (M.U. 3)

Charm of Undying Devotion (M.U. 6)
Cheetah-Speed (M. U. 2)
Chill Touch (M.U. 1)
Chromatic Orb (M.U. 1)
Clairaudience (M.U. 3)
Clairvoyance (M.U. 3)
Clone (M.U. 8)
Close Portal (M.U. 4)
Cloud of Pummeling Fists (M.U. 2)
Cloudburst (M.U. 3)
Cloudkill (M.U. 5)
Color Spray (M.U. 1)
Comprehend Languages (M.U. 1)
Confusion (M.U. 4)
Conjure Animals (M.U. 6)
Conjure Elemental (M.U. 5)
Conjure Mount (M.U. 1)
Contact Other Plane (M.U. 5)
Contagion (M.U. 4)
Containment (contains blast) (M.U. 5)
Contingency (M.U. 6)

Continual Darkness (M.U. 3)
Continual Light (M.U. 2)
Control Undead (M.U. 7)
Control Weather (M.U. 6)
Crystalbrittle (M.U. 9)

D
Dancing Lights (M.U. 1)
Darkness, 15-foot Radius (M.U. 2)
Deafness (M.U. 2)
Death Fog (M.U. 6)
Deathrune (M.U. 9)
Death Spell (M.U. 6)
Deeppockets (M.U. 2)
Delude (M.U 3)
Demand (M.U. 8)
Demi-Shadow Magic (M.U. 6)
Demi-Shadow Monsters (M.U. 5)
Demon Flame (M.U. 9)
Detect Evil (M.U. 2)

159

Detect Invisibility (M.U. 2)
Detect Magic (M.U. 1)
Detect Scrying (M.U. 4)
Detect Undead (M.U. 1)
Dig (M.U. 4)
Dimension Door (M.U. 4)
Disintegrate (M.U. 6)
Dismissal (M.U. 5)
Dispel Exhaustion (M.U. 4)
Dispel Magic (M.U. 3)
Distance Distortion (M.U. 5)
Dolor (M.U. 5)
Domination (M.U. 5)
Drayton's Engaging Conversation (M.U. 5)
Drayton's Hidden Stash (M.U. 5)
Dream (M.U. 5)
Duo-Dimension (M.U. 7)

E

Emergency Teleport at Random (M.U. 4)
Emotion (M.U. 4)
Enchant an Item (M.U. 6)
Enchanted Weapon (M.U. 4)
Energy Drain (M.U. 9)
Enervation (M.U. 4)
Enlarge (M.U. 1)
Ensnarement (M.U. 6)
Erase (M.U. 1)
ESP (M.U. 2)
Explosive Runes (M.U. 3)
Extension I (M.U. 4)
Extension II (M.U. 5)
Extension III (M.U. 6)
Eyebite (M.U. 6)

F

Fabricate (M.U. 5)
Faerie Phantoms (M.U. 1)
False Vision (M.U. 5)
Fascinate (M.U. 2)
Fawlgar's Grasping Death Spell (M.U. 9)
Fear (M.U. 4)
Feather Fall (M.U. 1)
Feeblemind (M.U. 5)
Feign Death (M.U. 3)
Find Familiar (M.U. 1)
Finger of Death (M.U. 7)
Fire Charm (M.U. 4)
Fire Shield (M.U. 4)
Fire Telekinesis (M.U. 2)
Fire Trap (M.U. 4)
Fireball (M.U. 3)
Fireball Barrage (M.U. 1)
Fireball, Death Brusher (M.U. 8)
Fireball, Delayed Blast (M.U. 7)
Fireball, Land Scraper (M.U. 4)
Fireball, Lava Yield (M.U. 9)
Fireball, Maximus (M.U. 8)
Fireball, Normal (M.U. 3)
Fireball, Nuclear Winter (M.U. 9)
Fireball, Proximity Fused (M.U.6)
Fireball, Scatter-Blast (M.U. 3)
Fireball, Show-No-Mercy (M.U.6)
Fireball, Sidewinder (Factor 1-5) (M.U.1-5)
Fireball, Skipping Betty (M.U.2)
Fireball, Torrential (M.U.5)
Fireball, Volley (M.U.4)
Firewater (M.U. 1)
Flame Arrow (M.U. 3)
Flaming Sphere (M.U. 2)
Flutter Soft (M.U.1)
Fly (M.U. 3)
Fog Cloud (M.U. 2)
Fog Vision (M.U. 1)
Fool's Gold (M.U. 2)
Forcecage (M.U. 7)
Foresight (M.U. 9)
Forget (M.U. 2)
Fumble (M.U. 4)

G

Galba's Magical Aura (M.U. 1)
Gandle's Feeble Trap (M.U. 2)
Gandle's Humble Hut (M.U. 3)
Gandle's Spell Immunity (M.U. 8)
Gate (M.U. 9)
Gaze Reflection (IL 1)
Geas (M.U. 6)
Glassee (M.U. 6)
Glassteel (M.U. 8)
Glitterdust (M.U. 2)
Globe of Invulnerability (M.U. 6)
Grasping Death (M.U. 8)
Grease (M.U. 1)
Grow (M.U. 3)
Guards and Wards (M.U. 6)
Gust of Wind (M.U. 3)

H

Haarpangs's Floating Cart (M.U. 1)
Haarpang's Magnificent Sphere of Freezing (M.U.6)
Haarpang's Magnificent Sphere of Resiliency (M.U.4)
Haarpang's Magnificent Sphere of Telekinesis (M.U.8)
Haarpang's Memory Kick (M.U. 4)
Hallucinatory Terrain (M.U. 4)
Haste (M.U. 3)
Heat Seeking Fist of Thunder (M.U. 2)
Hold Monster (M.U. 5)
Hold Person (M.U. 3)
Hold Portal (M.U. 1)
Hold Undead (M.U. 3)
Hurl Animal (M.U. 4)
Hypnotic Pattern (M.U. 2)
Hypnotism (M.U. 1)
Hyptor's Disjunction (M.U. 9)
Hyptor's Faithful Bitch-Hound (M.U. 5)
Hyptor's Shimmering Sword (M.U. 7)
Hyptor's Total Recall (M.U. 6)

I

Ice Storm (M.U. 4)
Identify (M.U. 1)
Illusionary Script (M.U. 3)
Illusionary Wall (M.U. 4)
Imprisonment (M.U. 9)
Improved Invisibility (M.U. 4)
Improved Phantasmal Force (M.U. 2)
Incendiary Cloud (M.U. 8)
Infravision (M.U. 3)
Invisibility (M.U. 2)
Invisibility, 10-foot Radius (M.U. 3)
Invisible Stalker (M.U. 6)
Irritation (M.U. 2)
Item (M.U. 3)

J

Jump (M.U. 1)

K

Karnaac's Transformation (M.U. 6)
Knock (M.U. 2)
Know Alignment (M.U. 2)

L

Legend Lore (M.U. 6)
Levitate (M.U. 2)
Light (M.U. 1)
Lightning Bolt (M.U. 3)
Liggl's Cone of Cold (M.U. 5)
Limited Wish (M.U. 7)
Locate Object (M.U. 2)
Lower Water (M.U. 6)

M

Mage Lock (M.U. 4)
Magic Jar (M.U. 5)
Magic Mirror (M.U. 4)
Magic Missile (M.U. 1)
Magic Missile of Skewering (M.U. 2)
Magic Mouth (M.U. 2)
Magic Shield (M.U. 1)
Major Creation (M.U. 5)
Mass Charm (M.U. 8)
Mass Invisibility (M.U. 7)
Mass Suggestion (M.U. 6)
Massmorph (M.U. 4)
Material (M.U. 3)
Maze (M.U. 8)
Melt (M.U. 1)
Mend (M.U. 1)
Merge Coin Pile (M.U. 1)
Message (M.U. 1)
Meteor Swarm (M.U. 9)
Mimic Caster (M.U. 8)
Mind Blank (M.U. 8)
Minor Creation (M.U. 4)
Minor Globe of Invulnerability (M.U. 4)
Minor Sphere of Perturbation (M.U. 1)
Mirage Arcana (M.U. 6)
Mirror Image (M.U. 2)
Misdirection (M.U. 2)
Mislead (M.U. 6)
Mist of Corralling (M.U. 4)
Monster Summoning I (M.U. 3)
Monster Summoning II (M.U. 4)
Monster Summoning III (M.U. 5)
Monster Summoning IV (M.U. 6)
Monster Summoning V (M.U. 7)
Monster Summoning VI (M.U. 8)
Monster Summoning VII (M.U. 9)
Move Earth (M.U. 6)
Munari's Irresistible Jig (M.U. 8)
Munz's Bolt of Acid (M.U. 2)
Murgain's Muster Strength (M.U. 3)
Murgain's Migraine (M. U. 3)

N

No Fear (M.U.3)
Non-Detection (M.U. 3)

O

P

Paralyzation (M.U. 3)
Part Water (M.U. 6)
Perceived Malignment (M.U. 3)
Permanency (M.U. 8)
Perpetual Illusion Spell (M.U. 6)
Perpetual Shocking Grasp (M.U. 4)
Phantasmagoria (M.U. 6)
Phantasmal Fireball (M.U. 1)
Phantasmal Force (M.U. 2)
Phantasmal Killer (M.U. 4)
Phantom Armor (M.U. 1)
Phantom Steed (M.U. 3)
Phantom Wind (M.U. 3)
Phase Door (M.U. 7)
Plant Growth (M.U. 4)
Polymorph Any Object (M.U. 8)
Polymorph Other (M.U. 4)
Polymorph Self (M.U. 4)
Polymorph to Amphibian (M.U. 3)
Polymorph to Primate (M.U. 3)
Pool Gold (M.U. 1)
Power Word, Blind (M.U. 8)
Power Word, Kill (M.U. 9)
Power Word, Stun (M.U. 7)
Precipitation (M.U. 1)
Premonition (M. U. 2)
Premptive Strike (M.U. 3)

Preserve (M.U. 1)
Prismatic Sphere (M.U. 9)
Proadus' Uncontrollable Fit of Laughter (M.U. 2)
Programmed Illusion (IL 6)
Project Image (M.U. 6)
Protection From Cantrips (M.U. 2)
Protection From Evil (M.U. 1)
Protection From Normal Missiles (M.U. 3)
Push (M.U. 1)
Pyrotechnics (M.U. 2)

Q

R

Rainbow Pattern (M.U. 4)
Ray of Enfeeblement (M.U. 2)
Read Magic (M.U. 1)
Reincarnation (M.U. 6)
Remove Curse (M.U. 4)
Repulsion (M.U. 6)
Reveal Secret Portal (M. U. 2)
Reverse Gravity (M.U. 7)
Rope Trick (M.U. 2)
Run (M.U. 1)
Runes of Eyeball Implosion (M.U. 3)

S

Scare (M.U. 2)
Screen (M.U. 8)
Secret Page (M.U. 3)
Seeming (M.U. 5)
Sending (M.U. 5)
Sepia Snake Sigil (M.U. 3)
Sequester (M.U. 7)
Shades (M.U. 6)
Shadow Door (M.U. 5)
Shadow Magic (M.U. 5)
Shadow Monsters (M.U. 4)
Shadow Walk (M.U. 7)
Shape Change (M.U. 9)
Shatter (M.U. 2)
Shift Blame (M.U. 1)
Shocking Grasp (M.U. 1)
Shout (M.U. 4)
Simulacrum (M.U. 7)
Sink (M.U. 8)
Sleep (M.U. 1)
Slow (M.U. 3)
Smell Immunity (M.U. 1)
Solid Fog (M.U. 4)
Spectral Force (M.U. 3)
Spectral Hand (M.U. 2)
Spell Turning (M.U. 7)
Spider Climb (M.U. 1)
Spiritwrack (M.U. 6)
Spook (M.U. 1)
Statue (M.U. 7)
Stinking Cloud (M.U. 2)
Stirring Oration (M.U. 4)
Stone Passage (M.U. 4)
Stone Shape (M.U. 5)
Stone Sphere (M. U. 5)
Stone to Flesh (M.U. 6)
Stoneskin (M.U. 4)
Strength (M.U. 2)
Succor (M.U. 9)
Suggestion (M.U. 3)
Summon Shadow (M.U. 5)
Summon Swarm (M.U. 2)
Sure-Grip Snare (M.U. 3)
Symbol (M.U. 8)

T

Tattoo of Shame (M.U. 2)
Taunt (M.U. 1)
Telekinesis (M.U. 5)
Telepathic Mute (M.U.2)
Teleport (M.U. 5)
Teleport Intercampaignia (M.U. 9)
Teleport Intragenre (M.U. 9)
Teleport Without Error (M.U. 7)
Temporal Stasis (M.U. 9)
Tempus Fugit (M.U. 5)
Throw Voice (M.U. 1)
Time Stop (M.U. 9)
Tongues (M.U. 3)
Torment (M.U. 7)
Total Control (M.U.2)
Touch of Death (M.U.5)
Transmute Rock to Lava (M.U. 9)
Transmute Stone to Mud (M.U. 5)
Transmute Water to Dust (M.U. 6)
Trap the Soul (M.U. 8)
True Seeing (M.U. 6)
Truename (M.U. 7)

U

Ultravision (M.U. 4)
Unseen Servant (M.U. 1)

V

Vacancy (M.U. 4)
Vampiric Touch (M.U. 3)
Vanish (M.U. 7)
Veil (M.U. 6)
Vision (M.U. 7)
Vocalize (M.U. 2)
Volley (M.U. 7)

W

Wall of Acid (M.U. 4)
Wall of Fire (M.U. 4)
Wall of Fog (IL 1)
Wall of Force (M.U. 5)
Wall of Ice (M.U. 4)
Wall of Iron (M.U. 5)
Wall of Stone (M.U. 5)

Wall Passage (M.U. 5)
Ward Off Evil(M.U. 3)
Water Breathing (M.U. 3)
Web (M.U. 2)
Weird (M.U. 9)
Whip (M.U. 2)
Whispering Wind (M.U. 2)
White Hot Metal (M.U. 2)
Wind Wall (M.U. 3)
Wish (M.U. 9)
Wizard Eye (M.U. 4)
Wizard Lock (M.U. 2)
Wizard Mark (M.U. 1)
Wraithform (M.U. 3)
Write (M.U. 1)
Wrygal's Delicious Deception (M.U. 1)

Y

Yudder's Whistle of Hell's Gate (M.U. 1)

Z

Zarba's Crushing Hand (M.U. 9)
Zarba's Fist of Rage (M.U. 8)
Zarba's Grasping Hand (M.U. 7)
Zarba's Guardian Hand (M.U. 5)
Zarba's Shoving Hand (M.U. 6)
Zarba's Sphere of Personal Inclimate Weather (M.U.6)
Zarba's Sphere of Insanity (M.U. 7)
Zargosa's Flaming Sphere's of Torment (M.U. 3)
Zargosa's Instant Summons (M.U. 7)
Zargosa's Lodge of Protection (M.U. 4)
Zargosa's Opulent Manor House (M.U. 7)
Zargosa's Tentacled Fury (M.U. 4)
Zephyr (M.U. 2)
Zombie Slave (M.U. 4)

Cleric and Druid Spell List

A

Abjure (CL 4)
Aerial Servant (CL 6)
Aid (CL 2)
Air Walk (CL 5)
Animal Friendship (DR 1)
Animal Growth (DR 5)
Animal Summoning I (DR 4)
Animal Summoning II (DR 5)
Animal Summoning III (DR 6)
Animate Dead (CL 3)
Animate Object (CL 6)
Animate Rock (DR 7)
Anti-Animal Shell (DR 6)
Anti-Plant Shell (DR 5)
Astral Spell (CL 7)
Atonement (CL 5)
Augury (CL 2)

B

Barkskin (DR 2)
Befriend (CL 1)
Blade Barrier (CL 6)
Bless (CL 1)
Break Hex (CL 5)

C

Call Lightning (DR 3)
Call Woodland Beings (DR 4)
Cause Inclement Weather (DR 7)
Ceremony (CL 1/DR 1)
Changestaff (DR 7)
Chant (CL 2)
Chariot of Sustarre (DR 7)
Charm Person or Mammal (DR 2)
Cloak of Fear (CL 4)
Cloudburst (DR 3)
Combine (CL 1)
Command (CL 1)
Commune (CL 5)
Commune With Nature (DR 5)
Confusion (DR 7)
Conjure Animals (CL 6)
Conjure Earth Elemental (DR 7)
Conjure Fire Elemental (DR 6)
Continual Light (CL 3)
Control Temperature, 10-foot Radius (DR 4)
Control Weather (CL 7/DR 7)
Control Winds (DR 5)

Create Food & Water (CL 3)
Create Water (CL 1/DR 2)
Creeping Doom (DR 7)
Cureall (CL 6)
Cure Blindness or Deafness (CL 3)
Cure Critical Wounds (CL 5)
Cure Disease (CL 3/DR 3))
Cure Light Wounds (CL 1/DR 2)
Cure Minor Injury (DR 1)
Cure Moderate Wounds (CL 2)
Cure Nasty Wounds (CL 3)
Cure Serious Wounds (CL 4/DR 4)

D

Detect Balance (DR 1)
Detect Charm (DR 2)
Detect Evil (CL 1)
Detect Lie (CL 4)
Detect Magic (CL 1/DR 1)
Detect Poison (DR 1)
Detect Snares & Pits (DR 1)
Detect Ulterior Motives (CL 5)
Diminished Rite (CL 4)
Dispel Evil (CL 5)
Dispel Magic (CL 3/DR 4)
Divination (CL 4)
Dust Devil (CL 2)

E

Earthquake (CL 7)
Endure Heat/Endure Cold (CL 1)
Entangle (DR 1)
Enthrall (CL 2)
Exaction (CL 7)

F

Faerie Fire (DR 1)
Feeblemind (DR 6)
Feign Death (CL 3/DR 2)
Find the Path (CL 6)
Find Traps (CL 2)
Finger of Death (DR 7)
Fire Seeds (DR 6)
Fire Storm (DR 7)
Fire Trap (DR 2)
Flame Blade (DR 2)
Flame Strike (CL 5)

Flame Walk (CL 3)
Flutter Soft (CL 1)
Fog Vision (DR 1)
Forbiddance (CL 6)
Free Action (CL 4)

G

Gate (CL 7)
Giant Insect (CL 4)
Glyph of Warding (CL 3)
Goodberry (DR 2)
Grow (DR 4)

H

Hallucinatory Forest (DR 4)
Heal Critical Wounds (CL 6/DR 7)
Heal Light Wounds (CL 2/DR 3)
Heal Moderate Wounds (CL 3)
Heal Nasty Wounds (CL 4)
Heal Serious Wounds (CL 5/DR 5)
Heat Metal (DR 2)
Heroes' Feast (CL 6)
Hold Animal (DR 3)
Hold Plant (DR 4)
Holy (Unholy) Word (CL 7)

I

Imbue With Spell Ability (CL 4)
Insect Plague (CL 5/DR 5)
Invisibility to Animals (DR 1)
Invisibility to Undead (CL 1)

J

K

Know Alignment (CL 2/DR 3)

L

Lesser Reanimation (CL 3)
Lesser Reincarnation (DR 5)
Light (CL 1)
Liveoak (DR 6)

Locate Animals/Plants (DR 1)
Locate Object (CL 3)
Lower Water (CL 4)

M

Magic Font (CL 5)
Magical Vestment (CL 3)
Magic Stone (CL 1)
Meld Into Stone (CL 3)
Messenger (DR 2)
Moonbeam (DR 5)

N

Negative Plane Protection (CL 3)
Neutralize Poison (CL 4/DR 3)
No Fear (CL 4)

O

Obscurement (DR 2)

P

Part Water (CL 6)
Pass Plant (DR 5)
Pass Without Trace (DR 1)
Plane Shift (CL 5)
Plant Door (DR 4)
Plant Growth (DR 3)
Prayer (CL 3)
Precipitation (DR 1)
Predict Weather (DR 1)
Premonition (CL 2)
Produce Fire (DR 4)
Produce Flame (DR 2)
Protection from Acid (DR 5)
Protection From Evil (CL 1)
Protection From Fire (DR 3)
Protection From Lightning (DR 4)
Protection From Petrifaction (DR 5)
Purify Food and Drink (CL 1)
Purify Water (DR 1)
Pyrotechnics (DR 3)

Q

Quest (CL 5)

R

Rainbow (CL 5)
Raise Dead (CL 5)
Reflecting Pool (DR 2)
Regenerate (CL 7)
Reincarnate (DR 7)
Remove Curse (CL 3)
Remove Fear (CL 1)
Remove Paralysis (CL 3)
Repel Insects (DR 4)
Repel Living Creatures and Plants (DR 7)
Resist Fire/Resist Cold (CL 2)
Restoration (CL 7)
Restorative Cure-All (CL 7)
Resurrection (CL 7)
Rigor Mortis (CL 2)
Rigor Mortis, 10-foot radius (CL 4)

S

Sanctuary (CL 1)
Shillelagh (DR 1)
Silence, 15-foot Radius (CL 2)
Slow Poison (CL 2/DR 2)
Snake Charm (CL 2)
Snare (DR 3)
Speak With Animals (CL 2/DR 1)
Speak With Dead (CL 3)
Speak With Monsters (CL 6)
Speak With Plants (DR 4)
Spell Immunity (CL 4)
Spike Growth (CL 5/ DR 3)

Spike Stones (CL 4 DR/5)
Spiritual Hammer (CL 2)
Starshine (DR 3)
Sticks to Snakes (CL 4/DR 5)
Stirring Sermon (CL 3)
Stone Passage (DR 4)
Stone Shape (DR 3)
Stone Tell (CL 6)
Succor (CL 7)
Summon Insects (DR 3)
Sunray (CL 7/DR 7)
Symbol (CL 7)

T

Tongues (CL 4)
Touch of Death (CL 4)
Transmute Metal to Wood (DR 7)
Transmute Rock to Lava (DR 7)
Transmute Rock to Mud (DR 5)
Transmute Water to Dust (DR 6)
Transport Via Plants (DR 6)
Tree (DRL 3)
Trip (DR 2)
True Seeing (CL 5)
Turn Wood (DR 6)

U

V

W

Wall of Fire (DR 5)
Wall of Thorns (DR 6)
Ward Off Evil (CL 3)
Warp Wood (DR 2)
Water Breathing (DR 3)
Water Walk (CL 3)
Weather Summoning (DR 6)
White Hot Metal (CL 3/DR 3)
Wind Walk (CL 7)
Withdraw (CL 2)
Wood Shape (DR 3)
Word of Recall (CL 6)
Wyvern Watch (CL 2)

Tommy Castillo

Appendix B

Notes on Spells

Spell Lists

The spells are organized according to their group (cleric or magic-user) and then listed by level. Within each level, the spells are arranged alphabetically. At the start of each spell description is a bold "stat" block that lists the following important game statistics:

Name:

Each spell is identified by name. In parentheses after the name is the school (for magic-user spells) to which that spell belongs. When more than one is listed, that spell is common to all schools given. Some spells are reversible (they can be cast for an effect opposite to that of the standard spell). This is noted after the spell name. Clerics with reversible spells must memorize the desired version. For example, a cleric who desires a Cause Light Wounds spell must petition for this form of the spell when meditating and praying. Note that severe penalties can result if the spell choice is at variance with the cleric's alignment (pennance could include no more horse and cart privileges, being left outside in the rain, having to escort your ugly cousin to the duke's ball, having to clean up in the stables for a week, denial of specific spells, entire spell levels, or even all spells for a certain period). The exact result (if any) depends on the mood and reaction of the cleric's patron gawd, as determined by the GM.

Reversible magic-user spells operate similarly. When the magic-user learns spell, he records both forms in his spell books. However, the magic-user must decide which version of the spell he desires to cast when memorizing the spell, unless the spell description specifically states otherwise. For example, a magic-user who has memorized Stone to Flesh and desires to cast Flesh to Stone must wait until the latter form of the spell can be memorized (i.e., rest eight hours and study). If he can memorize two 6th-level spells, he could memorize each version once or one version twice.

School:

In parentheses after the spell name is the name of the school of magic to which the spell belongs. For the magic-user spells, this defines which spells a magic-user specialist can learn, depending on the magic-user's school of specialization. For the cleric spells, the school notation is used only for reference purposes, to indicate which school the spell is considered to belong to, in case the GM needs to know that information for spell resistance (for example, elves' resistance to charm-related spells or the ability of dark knights and paladins to cast cleric spells of certain schools).

Range:

This lists the distance from the caster at which the spell effect occurs or begins. A "0" indicates the spell can be used on the caster only, with the effect embodied within or emanating from him. "Touch" means the caster can use the spell on others if he can physically touch them. Unless otherwise specified, all other spells are centered on a point visible to the caster and within the range of the spell. The point can be a creature or object if desired. In general, a spell that affects a limited number of creatures within an area affects those closest to the center first, unless there are other parameters operating (such as level or Hit Dice). Spells can be cast through narrow openings only if both the caster's vision and the spell energy can be directed simultaneously through the opening. A magic-user standing behind an arrow slit can cast through it; sending a Fireball through a small peephole he is peering through is another matter.

If a spell caster tries to cast a spell through something smaller than a standard size arrow slit, the are several considerations that need to be resolved in order to determine the outcome.

First, the caster must make a Dexterity check in order to pass the magic through the tiny opening. If he makes it, the spell effect will occur on the opposite side of the penetration. If the caster fails the Dexterity check by 5 or less, the spell effect will still travel though the penetration but the chance of a spell mishap increases by +25%. If the caster fails his Dexterity check by more

than 5, the spell effect fails to pass through the opening and takes effect as if it were centered on the caster.

Even if the caster does successfully send the magic through the opening, he must still make a to-hit roll to determine if the spell is properly centered in the desired location. This to-hit roll is made against Armor Class 10 in the case of trying to hit a non-moving inanimate object or a point in space. It is made against the AC of the target if the target is a potentially mobile monster, PC or NPC with an armor class rating. If the caster fails this to hit roll, the spell will still take effect but in a random location determined as if it were a grenade-like missile such as oil, acid or holy water. Even if the caster succeeds in hit to hit roll, the target may still take advantage of any magic resistance it has or saving throw as applicable. Obviously, it is very difficult and potentially dangerous to cast a spell through an opening that is smaller than a standard size arrow slit. So if you try it, just remember, if something goes wrong, it's your own damn fault!

Components:

This lists the category of components needed, V for verbal, S for somatic, and M for material. When material components are required, these are listed in the spell description. Spell components are expended as the spell is cast, unless otherwise noted. Cleric holy symbols are not lost when a spell is cast. For cases in which material components are expended at the end of the spell (Free Action, Shapechange, etc.), premature destruction of the components ends the spell.

Duration:

This lists how long the magical energy of the spell lasts. Spells of instantaneous duration come and go the moment they are cast, although the results of these spells may be permanent and unchangeable by normal means. Spells of permanent duration last until the effects are negated by some means, usually by a Dispel Magic. Some spells have a variable duration. The caster cannot choose the duration of spells, in most cases. Spells with set durations (for example, 3 rounds per level of the magic-user must be kept track of by the player. Spells of variable duration (for example, 3+1d4 rounds) are secretly recorded by the GM. Your GM may warn you when spell durations are approaching expiration, but I doubt it. There is usually no sign that a spell is going to expire, especially with spells like Fly and Invisibility. If your GameMaster does inform you about when spells of this nature about to expire, you should thank your lucky stars and then promptly report him to the HackMaster GameMaster Association.

Certain spells can be ended at will by the caster. In order to dismiss these spells, the original caster must be within range of the spell's center of effect – within the same range at which the spell can be cast. The caster also must be able to speak words of dismissal. Note that only the original caster can dismiss his spells in this way. This is slightly different than spells that require concentration to maintain. In order to prematurely end a spell that requires concentration, the caster must simply cease to concentrate on it.

Casting Time:

If only a number is given, the casting time is the caster's initiative segment (plus 1d4 if he needs to pull out spell components). If the spell requires a round or number of rounds to cast, it goes into effect at the end of the last round of casting time. If Clotzky casts a spell that takes one round, it goes into effect at the end of the round in which he begins casting. If the spell requires three rounds to cast, it goes into effect at the end of the third round. Spells requiring a turn or more go into effect at the end of the stated turn.

Area of Effect:

This lists the creatures, volume, dimensions, weight, etc., that can be affected by the spell. Spells with an area or volume that can be shaped by the caster will, unless the spell description specifically states otherwise, have a minimum dimension of 10 feet in any direction. Thus, a cloud that has a 10 foot cube per caster level might, when cast by a 12th-level caster, be 10 foot x 10 foot x 120 foot, 20 foot x 20 foot x 30 foot, or any similar combination that totals twelve 10 foot cubes. Combinations such as 5 foot x 10 foot x 240 foot are not possible unless specifically stated in the spell or in an official article previously authorized by Gary Jackson.

Some spells (such as Bless) affect the friends or enemies of the caster. In all cases, this refers to the perception of the caster at the time the spell is cast. For example, a chaotic good character allied with a lawful neutral cleric would receive the benefits of the latter's Bless spell. Though, when he is no longer useful, the LN cleric may eliminate the chaotic character in his sleep or turn him in to the authorities for some stupid, unlawful act.

Saving Throw:

This lists whether the spell allows the target a saving throw and explains the effect of a successful save: "Negates" or "Neg." results in the spell having no effect; "1/2" means the character suffers half the normal amount of damage; "none" means no saving throw is allowed. Wisdom adjustments to saving throws apply only to enchantment/charm spells. Solid physical barriers provide saving throw bonuses and damage reduction. Cover and concealment may affect saving throws and damage (the GM has additional information about this).

A creature that successfully saves against a spell with no apparent physical effect (such as a Charm, Hold Person, or Magic Jar) will feel nothing unusual.

A being's carried equipment and possessions are assumed to make their saving throws against special attacks if the creature makes its saving throw, unless the spell specifically states otherwise. If the creature fails its saving throw, or if the attack form is particularly potent, saving throws may have to be rolled to see if any possessions survive, using each individual item's saving throw (your GM has these numbers).

Spell Description

The text provides a complete description of how the spell functions and its game effects. It covers most typical uses of the spell, if there are more than one, but cannot deal with every possible application players might find. In these cases, the spell information in the text should provide guidance on how to adjudicate the situation, though the GM is always the ultimate authority.

Spells with multiple functions enable the caster to select which function he wants to use at the time of casting. Usually a single function of a multiple-function spell is weaker than a single-function spell of the same level. Spell effects that give bonuses or penalties to abilities, attack rolls, damage rolls, saving throws, etc., are not usually cumulative with each other or with other magic: the strongest single effect applies. For example, a fighter drinks a Potion of Giant Strength and then receives the 2nd-level magic-user spell Strength. Only the strongest magic (the potion) is effective. When the potion's duration ends, however, the Strength spell is still in effect, until its duration also expires.

Grievous Wounding Damage

Spells with damage dice can inflict grievous wounds. This is essentially a magical version of penetration damage: for each die that gives a maximum result, another die is rolled. As with penetration damage, this can continue indefinitely. Note that this also applies to healing spells.

Appendix C

Magic-User Spells

Magic-Users employ a greater variety of material components than do other character classes employing spells, i.e. clerics and druids. Some of the required components will be difficult to find and/or expensive, but alternative spells can always be chosen. Substitute materials might be allowed. This is up to your GM. It should be noted that such substitution could affect spell range, duration, area of effect, effect, etc.

A magic-user who has his components at the ready beforehand can cast a spell in the casting time specified in each spell. For those who do not have their material components in hand, add 1d4 segments to the casting time to account for the time used to fumble around pouches, pockets and packs for spell components.

In general, reversible or multiple application spells require the magic-user to determine which form he is memorizing prior to the adventure. Consult your referee in this regard.

Cantrips

Cantrips are the magic spells learned and used by apprentices in the magic-user group during their long, rigorous and tedious training for the craft of magic use. An aspiring magic-user may use 1 cantrip per day as a 0 level neophyte (-2000 EP to-1001 EP), 2 cantrips per day as a 0 level initiate (-1000 to -501), and 3 cantrips per day as a 0 level apprentice (-500 to -1). Cantrips must be memorized just as higher level spells are.

Most cantrips are simple little spells of no great effect, so when the individual becomes a 1st level magic-user, the knowledge and information pertaining to these small magics are discarded in favor of the more powerful spells then available. However, a magic-user may opt to retain up to four cantrips in place of one 1st level spell. This assumes that the magic-user has, in fact, retained his book of cantrips - a tome as large as a good-sized book of higher level spells.

All cantrips are 0 level, have a 1 foot range, have a generally small area of effect, require only soft, simple verbal and somatic components and are cast in a very short time (1/10 to 1/2 segment). Unless otherwise noted, the magic has only a brief duration (although the effects may last: a magically Dried item remains dry even after the magic is gone). Only those which involve living creatures afford any saving throw. Individuals in a state of extreme concentration (such as when casting a spell) do not have that concentration broken by person-affecting cantrips. The effects of cantrips, and the people and items affected by them, radiate a very faint magical aura.

The Casting of Cantrips:

Cantrips are basically cast the same way that spells are cast. Note that despite their simple components and short casting times, only two cantrips can be cast during any round by a single magic-user or apprentice. Furthermore, the segment of the round in which the cantrip is cast is dependent on the usual factors: surprise, initiative and so on.

After the first of the two cantrips are cast, the magic-user must roll a four-sided die to determine how many segments later he will be able to cast the second cantrip (if so desired). It is not possible for a magic-user to cast both a spell and a cantrip during the same round, no matter how short the casting times are.

Cantrips are grouped according to their general effect or purpose into these seven* categories:

Useful	Personal
Reversed	Social Engagement
Legerdemain	Haunting-Sound
Person-Affecting	

* plus an eighth category available only to specialist illusionists, the **Minor Illusion** cantrips. Any magic-user has the potential to know cantrips in any or all of the other categories.

Useful Cantrips

Chill
(Evocation)
Area of Effect: 1 ft. cube   **Casting Time:** 1/2 segment

This cantrip allows the caster to cause non-living liquid or solid material to become about 40° Fahrenheit cooler than it was, subject to a minimum temperature of freezing (32° Fahrenheit). The chilling effect lasts for but an instant, after which the subject warms slowly back to normal temperature. Verbal component is a soft whistling, somatic is a downward-thrust thumb.

Clean
(Abjuration)
Area of Effect: 4 sq. yds.   **Casting Time:** 1/2 segment

This cantrip enables the caster to remove heavy soil, dirt and similar foreign objects from floors, walls, dishes, windows, etc. The subject surfaces are then spotless, but care must be taken in removal of pigments and the like, so usually only one type of material will be treated in a single application. Verbal component is a low outrush of air, somatic is a circular hand motion.

Color
(Evocation)
Area of Effect: 1 cubic yd.   **Casting Time:** 1/2 segment

By use of this cantrip, the caster brings color to an object. It can be used to restore faded hues or to tinge those already colored with a different hue. Thus, dull or faded fabric can be brightened, pigments restored or even hair or skin changed to another color.

The effect must be renewed every 30 days. Verbal component is a humming sound, somatic is a back-and-forth or wringing hand motion.

Dampen
(Evocation)
Area of Effect: 1 cubic yd.   **Casting Time:** 1/2 segment

When this cantrip is cast, the subject area is permeated by a fog-like dampness which leaves all material within it damp to the touch. It is useful for many sorts of things. It is hard on parchment, and it similarly makes it and like substances hard to set aflame. Those within the area of effect of the dampen cantrip will be enwrapped in a light fog, and objects in this fog, while still visible, will lose their detail. Verbal component is a low hooting or a hummed ditty, somatic is a hand gesture upwards with writhing fingers.

Dibs
(Alteration)
Area of Effect: 1 object   **Casting Time:** 1/10 segment

When this cantrip is cast there is a 25% chance that the caster can override somebody else's dibs on something. This spell can only be attempted once to override any particular dibs, but it could be cast again to override another caster's successful Dibs cantrip! The somantic component requires the caster to point out the desired item.

Dry
(Abjuration)
Area of Effect: 1 cubic yd.   **Casting Time:** 1/2 segment

This cantrip removes dampness and excess moisture from materials within the area of effect. It is useful for cloth, herbs and cleaning chores. Verbal component is similar to that of the Dampen cantrip, and the somatic is a two-handed wringing motion.

Dust
(Abjuration)
Area of Effect: 10 ft. radius   **Casting Time:** 1/2 segment

A cantrip of this sort removes all fine dust and tiny grit particles from exposed surfaces such as floors, shelves, walls, etc. The material so removed is transported elsewhere, but new dust can accumulate, of course. Verbal component is a continuous in-drawing of breath, somatic is a back-and-forth hand motion.

Exterminate
(Abjuration)
Area of Effect: 1 small creature   **Casting Time:** 1/10 segment

When this cantrip is used, the caster may kill a small pest such as a fly, mouse, rat, beetle or the like. It is useful for indoor and outdoor applications. If the subject is very small, an area of up to 1/2 cubic foot can be rid of pests. This cantrip is effective against magical creations and normal-sized creatures magically shrunk to insect-size, but has no effect on polymorphed creatures and similarly enchanted beings. The somatic gesture is a pointed finger, while the caster verbalizes a low "zzzt" sound.

Flavor
(Enchantment)
Area of Effect: One object   **Casting Time:** 1/2 segment

This cantrip enables the caster to give the subject a superior or better or different flavor. Thus, mush can be made to taste as if it were lobster bisque, but the dweomer will not actually affect quality or wholesomeness. Spoiled food remains spoiled; a poisoned drink would still be deadly (though any tell-tale taste of the poison may be masked in this fashion). The verbal component is a muttered lip-smacking sound; the somatic gesture is a shaking motion.

Freshen
(Enchantment)
Area of Effect: One object   **Casting Time:** 1/2 segment

By means of this cantrip, the caster brings new life or freshness to the object desired. The magic applies to food and drink items such as milk, beer, meat and raw vegetables. It also works with cut vegetables, flowers, herbs, etc. Although it will remove a slight taint of spoilage, restore drooping flowers, and so on, it is not as effective as a Purify Food & Drink spell, and it lasts for but an hour. The subject must be of relatively small size, i.e. a small cask of liquid, a sheep, a bushel of vegetables, etc. If used on a creature that is harmed by magics such as Purify Food & Drink, the cantrip inflicts 1d4 points of damage. The verbal component is an "mmmmmm" sound, while the hand makes a mystic symbol with thumb and forefinger forming a circle and the other fingers upright and apart.

Gather
(Alteration)
Area of Effect: 1 sq. yd.   **Casting Time:** 1/6 segment

This cantrip enables the caster to neatly gather numerous small objects into a stack or pile. For instance, if nails, nuts, coins, papers or like objects were spilled, the magic would bring them together. It can be used selectively, for instance to separate one type of material from another, but only the selected type would be gathered neatly. The caster verbalizes the type of material to be gathered while making a gathering motion.

Polish
(Alteration)
Area of Effect: One object   **Casting Time:** 1/2 segment

When this cantrip is used, the caster magically smooths and brings a luster to materials such as wood, metal, stone, leather or ceramic. Naturally, the desired object must be relatively clean in order for the cantrip to be effective. The object affected must be of reasonable size - a floor of up to 1,000 square feet, an armoire, etc. It works better on smaller objects, of course, such as boots, mirrors, crystal containers, etc. The caster hums a ditty while making a buffing motion.

Salt
(Evocation)
Area of Effect: One object   **Casting Time:** 1/6 segment

This cantrip causes a sprinkling of fine salt to magically appear and descend upon the desired object - a stew, some troublesome weed patch or a barrel full of stock fish to be preserved. The object must be of a reasonable size - up to perhaps 4 square yards in area or about 30 gallons liquid volume. Care must be taken to avoid over-salting if the object involved is smaller, and if the object is larger, it will not receive much salt.

Creatures adversely affected by salt (such as a Giant Slug) take 1d4 points of damage from this cantrip. The verbal component is a labial smacking, performed while the hand makes a sprinkling motion.

Shine
(Alteration)
Area of Effect: One object   **Casting Time:** 1/2 segment

Similar to the Polish cantrip, this magic allows the caster to remove tarnish, rust, corrosion and similar substances from the desired object. This cantrip brings about a mirror-bright shine to objects capable of such, causing their surfaces to be smooth and unmarred. A piece of jewelry, for instance, would be made more attractive, and the gems (only) of such a piece might be actually made more valuable. If base value of the gem(s) in a piece of jewelry was originally decreased, and a Shine cantrip is used upon the object, then the owner may (if desired) find out whether the value of the gem(s) has been changed. (The GM should roll again on the "Increase or Decrease of Worth Beyond Base Value" table in the GMG, with a -1 modifier to the die roll.) No gem can be "re-valued" in this manner more than once.

A single object up to about 1 cubic yard in volume can be treated by this cantrip. Its components are similar to those of Polish.

Spice
(Evocation)
Area of Effect: One object   **Casting Time:** 1/2 segment

Unlike the Flavor cantrip, this magic actually brings a particular spice to the object of food or drink. Thus, ginger, pepper and like spices can be brought to add zest (or disguise). Herbs such as bay leaf, garlic, parsley, and so forth can likewise be evoked by this cantrip. The quantity is sufficient to spice food or drink for about a dozen people. The spice (or herb) appears over the object vessel as a fine powder or flake, falls upon it and adds its substance to the dish or drink. A ditty is hummed for the verbal component, while the hand makes a crumbling and sprinkling motion.

Sprout
(Alteration)
Area of Effect: 1 cubic yd.   **Casting Time:** 1/2 segment

By means of this cantrip, the caster causes acceleration in the growth of plants, particularly with respect to the germination of plant seeds. Upon its casting, the cantrip will cause seeds to shoot forth tiny sprouts, newly sprouted plants to grow an inch or so, buds to flower, etc. Fruits and vegetables can be caused to ripen (or actually go past ripening to spoilage) by this cantrip. A susurrant sound is verbalized while the caster's hand makes hoeing motions.

Stitch
(Alteration)
Area of Effect: Special   **Casting Time:** 1/2 segment

This cantrip magically sews seams in cloth or leather. It will make new ones, or repair old work. About 20 yards of cloth can be thus stitched, but only about 2 yards of leather. The seam thus created is neither stronger nor weaker than a seam done without magic. Usually a brief rhyme is recited as the hand makes a sewing motion.

Sweeten
(Evocation)
Area of Effect: One object   **Casting Time:** 1/2 segment

This cantrip is the same as a Spice cantrip, except that the result is the evocation of a sweetener - sugar, honey or even a syrup. Components are a buzzing sound and a stirring motion.

Tie
(Alteration)
Area of Effect: One object   **Casting Time:** 1/2 segment

By means of this cantrip, the caster can magically cause the object of the magic - thread, string, cord, rope, or even cable - to tightly knot itself to either its other end or an end of a similar object within 1 foot of it. The resulting knot will be a normal one such as a square knot, halfhitch, running bowline or whatever other sort is desired. The caster verbalizes the name of the knot while holding up three fingers.

Warm
(Evocation)
Area of Effect: 1 ft. cube   **Casting Time:** 1/2 segment

This cantrip is the same as Chill, except that the magic brings a warming of the liquid or solid. The temperature will rise at most about 40° Fahrenheit. The cantrip will never cause living creatures to become warmer than their normal body temperature. Components are an "Aaah" sound vocalized while the hands are briskly rubbed together.

Wrap
(Alteration)
Area of Effect: 1 cubic yd.   **Casting Time:** 1/2 segment

When a Wrap cantrip is employed, the caster creates a strong and sturdy wrapping around the subject desired - a bit of herbs, a heap of flour, a bundle of cloth, etc. The material of the cantrip is of a suitable type and thickness for the item(s) to be wrapped. Thus, a few ounces of fine powder will be contained in a waxy tissue, gem stones in a felt-like envelope, meal in cloth and so forth. The wrapping can be undone normally, but the caster can just as easily order it to open, so the cantrip is often used to enfold the material components of a spell. The caster verbalizes a general class of wrapping desired while making folding motions with his hands.

Reversed Cantrips

Curdle
(Enchantment)
Area of Effect: One object   **Casting Time:** 1/6 segment

This cantrip is broader than its name, for it affects many food and drink items. The magic curdles milk and hastens spoilage or wilting, but does not Putrefy Food & Drink as per that spell. It has a permanent effect on the object. It is otherwise similar to Freshen. The caster verbalizes a retching sound while pointing the thumb downward.

Dirty
(Evocation)
Area of Effect: 4 sq. yds.   **Casting Time:** 1/6 segment

The opposite of a Clean cantrip, this enables the caster to soil, spot and sully walls, floors, dishes, garments, etc. Verbal component is a spitting sound, made while the feet are shuffled and stamped.

Dusty
(Evocation)
Area of Effect: 10 ft. radius   **Casting Time:** 1/6 segment

By means of this cantrip, the caster causes a film of dust and grime to settle upon all exposed surfaces within the cantrip area of effect. The verbal component is a low humming sound, made while the hands move in shaking motions.

Hairy
(Alteration)
Area of Effect: One object   **Casting Time:** 1/10 segment

While this cantrip is not actually one of the standard useful ones which apprentices reverse for mischief, it is one which is generally used for no good purpose. It causes hair, fur or hair-like growth to thicken and lengthen. Thus, a head of hair, a peach, a beard, a cat or somesuch could be affected. The growth will cause the subject material to increase from 2-12 inches in length. The subject material must be trimmed or cut to remove the cantrip's effect. This cantrip can be reversed to shorten growth or effectively shave, but since the effect on short material (growth under 1 inch in length) is complete absence of growth for 2-12 days, it is not often used. The caster verbalizes snicking sounds while making massaging motions for growth, or scissoring motions for removal.

Knot
(Alteration)
Area of Effect: One object   **Casting Time:** 1/2 segment

This cantrip is a permutation of the Tie cantrip. It causes the thread, string, cord or rope to knot itself in such a manner as to be very difficult to untie, and from 2-8 rounds, minus Dexterity bonus for reaction adjustment of the individual untying the knot, to undo. It works even on material already affected by a Tie cantrip, but not on magical ropes, ropes being held onto by a character or creature or taut lines such as a bowstring. The caster verbalizes a low zzzz sound while moving the arm forward with a strong wrist motion.

Ravel
(Alteration)
Area of Effect: Special   **Casting Time:** 1/10 segment

This cantrip is the reverse of a Stitch. It will work only if there is a loose or broken thread in the seam or fabric to be affected, except for material magically stitched by the appropriate cantrip. When the latter sort of seam or material is involved, the Ravel cantrip will always work except in a case where the subject is otherwise magical, i.e. a Bag of Holding, a Cloak of Protection, Boots of Elvenkind, etc. The name of the cantrip is verbalized while the fingers make a plucking motion.

Sour
(Evocation)
Area of Effect: One object   **Casting Time:** 1/2 segment

When this cantrip is used, the caster causes the subject food or drink to take on a sour taste, not unlike vinegar of the appropriate sort. While it is typically used to spoil wine, beer or some pastry, the Sour cantrip can have a useful purpose. The magic actually causes about a pint (maximum) of vinegar to appear over the subject. This can be an empty container in which such liquid is desired. The caster purses the lips and makes a whoosh sound while clenching the hand.

Spill
(Alteration)
Area of Effect: One container   **Casting Time:** 1/6 segment

The opposite of a Gather cantrip, this enables the caster to cause the contents of a container to spill out. The object container is actually tipped by the cantrip, and since the magic is not powerful, containers of more than about gallon size or magical ones will not be affected by the cantrip. Solids and/or liquids within the object container will spill out, if the container is not securely closed or capped. To bring about the magic, the caster verbalizes an "uh-oh" sound while making an abrupt hand motion.

Tangle
(Alteration)
Area of Effect: One object   **Casting Time:** 1/6 segment

A permutation of the Tie cantrip, this magic allows the caster to cause fine material such as thread, hair, small grass and the like to become twisted and entwined in a tangle. It will not work on heavy material such as rope.

Untangling subject material will take 3-12 rounds, unless it is roughly done - and the material is broken and snapped in the process, torn loose, etc. The cantrip will tangle mixed materials such as grass and string, hair and threads and so forth. A buzzing is verbalized while the finger makes a stirring motion.

Tarnish
(Alteration)
Area of Effect: One object   **Casting Time:** 1/2 segment

The reverse of a Shine cantrip, this causes a covering of rust, corrosion, verdigris or the like to cover an object normally subject to such tarnishing. The object must be of about 1 cubic yard or less in volume. Verbal component is a spitting sound, while the hand makes a sprinkling motion.

Untie
(Alteration)
Area of Effect: One object   **Casting time:** 1/3 segment

This permutation of a Tie cantrip is simply the reverse of the magic. The caster selects an object - thread, string, cord, etc. - which is knotted or tied. The cantrip removes the knot or tying. Note that the Untie cantrip will nullify a Tangle. The cantrip will not remove both a Knot and a normal tying (normal knot or one caused by a cantrip), but it will cause the former to disappear so that only a normal tying remains. This cantrip has no effect on magical objects. Somatic and verbal components vary according to the desired result. In general, a popping sound is made while the hands are moved apart - either as if a knot were being untied or a cord snapped.

Wilt
(Enchantment)
Area of Effect: One object   **Casting Time:** 1/2 segment

This is a reverse of the Freshen cantrip which affects only vegetable material - whether growing or picked. Thus, a plant can be made to wilt (or possibly wither if it is not very healthy), or a bunch of cut flowers sag or droop. Verbal component is a descending hum, while the forefinger is slowly curled from an upright position.

Legerdemain Cantrips

Air of Legitimacy
(Illusion/Phantasm)
Area of Effect: One object   **Casting Time:** 1/3 segment
Duration: 1 round

This cantrip can be used to make an ordinary or forged document or seal of some sort look official to the average observer. Detailed studying of the object or observation by someone very familiar with the real item allows a saving throw to notice the deception.

Change
(Alteration)
Area of Effect: One object   **Casting Time:** 1/10 segment

By means of a Change cantrip, the caster alters one small object to another, although the Change must be within the same biological kingdom, and only animal and vegetable objects are affected. Thus, a piece of parchment can be changed to a brightly colored cloth square, then the cloth can be changed to a rose by another use of the cantrip. Likewise, a bird can be changed into a bat, the bat to a flying squirrel by another use of the same type of cantrip, and so forth. Each change requires a Change cantrip.

The cantrip will not cause more than a 50% increase or decrease in size/volume, and the effect will last for a base time of 1 turn. If the change is radical, then the time will be reduced accordingly, i.e. changing a dead object to a live one is a radical change and will last only 1 round. On the other hand, a very slight alteration such as color change or the like will last for 1 or more days.

A saving throw against this magic does not apply as long as normal, small, non-magical creatures of animal-intelligence are concerned. Typically, a magic word is verbalized while the hand makes a pass over the object to be affected.

Distract
(Enchantment)
Area of Effect: Special   **Casting Time:** 1/3 segment

By means of this cantrip, the caster causes all who are watching to look at an area of the caster's choice. The area must be to the right or left of the caster, and the distraction must be within 10 feet of the caster. Thus, the caster can cause viewers to watch his right hand and a location a few feet distant where the caster's finger is pointing, while the caster's left hand does something unnoticed.

Saving throws apply only to individuals above 0 level, or with at least 1+1 Hit Dice and an Intelligence rating of greater than 7. The Distract cantrip has a duration of only 1 segment. The caster speaks an attention-getting word or phrase and gestures to the left or right to effect the cantrip.

Hide
(illusion)
Area of Effect: One object   **Casting Time:** 1/10 segment

This cantrip allows the caster to magically hide an object of virtually any size for a short period of time. The cantrip casts a dweomer over the desired object so that it becomes invisible to all who are in front of the caster. Note that the magic does not affect sound, so that if a crowing rooster were made to seemingly disappear, the noise of its cry would still be heard. Likewise, if an elephant were hidden by the cantrip, the sound of its tread, trumpeting or even breathing might be heard. The dweomer will not work if viewers are beside or behind the caster.

The cantrip lasts for 1 turn on an object of 2 cubic yards or less in volume. The duration is reduced by 1 round for every additional 2 cubic yards of volume made to seemingly disappear, until at 20 cubic yards of volume, the duration is 1 round. At over 20 cubic yards of volume, duration is reduced by 1 segment per 2 additional cubic yards; i.e., the Hide cantrip will have a duration of 9 segments if cast on an object of 22 cubic yards volume; 8 segments for 24 cubic yards, 7 segments for 26, 6 for 28, 5 for 30, 4 for 32, 3 for 34, 2 for 36, and 1 segment for 38 cubic yards. Anything over 38 cubic yards in volume will at best momentarily disappear and then reappear again.

Verbal component is an activating word such as "abracadabra" while the hand makes a pass across the forepart of the object. The caster can dispel the cantrip simply by speaking the activating word.

Mute
(Alteration)
Area of Effect: One object   **Casting Time:** 1/10 segment

The Mute cantrip allows the caster to alter the shape of small objects of a mineral nature. The magic is effective against glass, metal, stone, etc. A plane can be altered to a rod, a torus to a sphere, etc. Thus, a coin could be changed to be a ring. Similarly, glass could be changed to crystal, lead to silver, copper to gold, etc. However, the dweomers of magical items are too strong for this cantrip to affect them. The duration of the Mute is but 1 round. If another individual actually touches the object affected, the dweomer of the cantrip might be affected: the individual touching it makes a saving throw versus spell and if it succeeds the cantrip is dispelled. The components for the Mute cantrip are similar to those of a Change cantrip.

Palm
(Illusion)
Area of Effect: One small item   **Casting Time:** 1/10 segment

This cantrip enables the caster to secret a small object in his hand without seeming to do so. The dweomer creates an illusory duplicate of the object to be palmed, so that the other can be taken while under a form of Hide cantrip (which actually works regardless of viewer position). The illusory duplicate of the palmed object lasts but 1 segment, so it must be covered or screened from view or else any onlookers will see it wink out of existence. A special word is spoken while a digit points at the object to be palmed. The caster may then pick up the now-invisible actual object while seemingly only touching or handling the illusory duplicate.

Present
(Alteration)
Area of Effect: 2' radius   **Casting Time:** 1/6 segment

A Present cantrip enables the caster to bring any small object or series of objects from within a 2-foot radius of his person to his hand. The object or objects will appear magically in the caster's hand as he puts the hand upward or outward with a flourish and speaks the key word to begin the dweomer. If an object as large as a tankard is thus presented, the cantrip will be exhausted, but as many as a dozen coins could be brought to the hand before the dweomer failed.

The caster must know the exact nature and location of the object or objects to be presented. If they are on the person of another individual, a saving throw versus spell applies to the individual, unless the object or objects are in plain sight.

Person-Affecting Cantrips

Aura of Vulnerability
(Illusion/Phantasm)
Area of Effect: 1 creature   **Casting Time:** 1/3 segment
Duration: 1 round

When this cantrip is cast on a creature it makes them look somewhat weaker and less able to defend themselves. An unwilling victim is allowed a saving throw to avoid the cantrip.

Belch
(Evocation)
Area of Effect: One person   **Casting Time:** 1/10 segment

When this cantrip is cast, the subject will involuntarily belch. A saving throw is applicable only to see how loud or muffled the burping is, failure indicating a very loud belch, success meaning that the sound is relatively low and muffled. The verbal component is an almost inaudible belch, done at the same time that the caster's hand presses his diaphragm.

Blink
(Evocation)
Area of Effect: One person   **Casting Time:** 1/10 segment

By means of this cantrip, the caster causes the subject person (or creature) to blink his or its eye or eyes. The blinking reaction is only momentary, of course, lasting no more than half a second. A successful saving throw indicates only a single eye wink, or no effect for one-eyed creatures. The verbal component is a softly spoken magical word (such as "hat-cha-cha"), voiced while the caster snaps his fingers.

Cough
(Evocation)
Area of Effect: One person   **Casting Time:** 1/3 segment

This cantrip enables the caster to make the subject individual cough spasmodically. If a saving throw is made, the cough is only a brief hacking which will not usually disturb other activities. Failing the saving throw indicates the victim is affected by a loud and active series of coughs lasting from 1 to 3 seconds. The somatic component is a gagging gesture while a gasp is verbalized.

Coy Smile
(Enchantment/Charm)
Area of Effect: 1 person   **Casting Time:** 1/6 segment
Duration: 1 round

This cantrip makes the subject smile in a "come hither" fashion if he fails his saving throw. The caster smiles himself to cast the cantrip.

Double Take
(Enchantment/Charm)
Area of Effect: One person   **Casting Time:** 1/3 segment

This cantrip causes the subject to take a second look at something of the caster's choosing. It must be something that the subject has at least casually noticed already. The spell caster must give a low whistle while pointing to cast this spell.

Exude Fear
(Enchantment/Charm)
Area of Effect: One person   **Casting Time:** 1/3 segment
Duration: 1 turn

The subject of this cantrip gives off an impression to observers of being afraid. Acts to the contrary will be seen by onlookers as "false bravado" or "insane bravery". The somatic component is a pointed finger accompanied by a soft clucking noise.

Feign Toughness
(Illusion/Phantasm)
Area of Effect: 1 creature   **Casting Time:** 1/3 segment
Duration: 1 round

This cantrip makes the affected creature appear to be somewhat bigger and tougher than it really is. Unwilling victims of this cantrip are allowed to make a saving throw to avoid its effects.

Flinch
(Enchantment/Charm)
Area of Effect: 1 creature   **Casting Time:** 1/3 segment

When this spell is cast upon a creature it must make a successful saving throw or flinch in a direction of the caster's choosing. The somatic component requires the caster to make a sudden motion towards the victim.

Giggle
(Charm)
Area of Effect: One person   **Casting Time:** 1/3 segment

By means of this cantrip, the caster causes the subject individual to involuntarily giggle. The loudness and length of this reaction depend on the saving throw. If the subject fails to save, the result will be a chuckle or giggle lasting about 2 or 3 seconds. If the save succeeds, only a brief chuckle will be caused.

The verbal component is a single word or phrase (known in most magical circles as a "punch line") to be spoken while one finger is moved back and forth rapidly.

Indian Burn
(Illusion/Phantasm)
Area of Effect: 1 person   **Casting Time:** 1/3 segment
Duration: 1 round

Anyone who fails their save against this cantrip feels a burning pain on their forearm, much as if a pair of unseen hands were wringing it. This cantrip does not cause damage, but it does have a 50% chance of spoiling a spell being cast, if that spell has somatic components. The caster must make a wringing motion with his hands to use this cantrip.

Knowing Look
(Alteration)
Area of Effect: 1 person   **Casting Time:** 1/6 segment
Duration: 1 round

When this spell is used on someone it makes him look like he knows exactly what is going on or what someone is talking about. The caster needs to rub his chin when he casts this cantrip.

Lazy Eye
(Alteration)
Area of Effect: 1 person   **Casting Time:** 1/6 segment

Anyone who fails their save against this cantrip will have one of his eyes drift to the side for a moment, causing him to be distracted for a second or two while he readjusts himself. The caster must cross his eyes when he casts this cantrip.

Menacing Scowl
(Alteration)
Area of Effect: 1 person   **Casting Time:** 1/3 segment
Duration: 1 round

This cantrip makes the victim give a nasty, angry look to anyone in range. When the caster uses this cantrip he must furl his eyebrows.

Nod
(Evocation)
Area of Effect: One person   **Casting Time:** 1/10 segment

This cantrip causes the subject to give an involuntary nod of the head due to muscle contraction. The effect is as if the subject were nodding in agreement or as a greeting. A successful saving throw negates the effect. The caster gives a slight nod of the head while pointing his small finger at the subject.

Noogie
(Enchantment/Charm)
Area of Effect: 1 person   **Casting Time:** 1/10 segment
Duration: 1 round

This cantrip makes the victim feel like someone is rubbing their knuckles into his head. A successful saving throw avoids the cantrip. The somatic component requires the caster to shake his fist from side to side.

Poker Face
(Alteration)
Area of Effect: Caster   **Casting Time:** 1/10 segment
Duration: 1 round plus 1 round/level

When this cantrip is used it allows the caster to remain expressionless regardless of the circumstances. Onlookers cannot gauge the caster's emotions or reactions based on the caster's appearance. The somatic component requires the caster to quickly dig his fingernails into his palm while softly humming.

Remote Gouged Eye
(Evocation)
Area of Effect: One creature   **Casting Time:** 1/6 segment

A Remote Gouged Eye cantrip allows the caster to poke a target in the eye at a distance of up to 20 feet. The attack does no damage but the affected person will cringe in pain and be unable to see clearly from that eye for 2 rounds. Attacks made during this time are at −1 to hit. The caster makes a gouging motion with one hand to use this cantrip.

Scratch
(Evocation)
Area of Effect: One creature   **Casting Time:** 1/6 segment

A Scratch cantrip causes the subject creature to experience an annoying itch on some portion of the body. Unless a saving throw is successful, the subject will involuntarily scratch at this itch. This scratching will take but a second and will immediately cause the itch to cease. The verbal component is the name of some body pest (flea, louse, etc.), uttered while the area of the itch is pointed to.

Sheepish Grin
(Enchantment/Charm)
Area of Effect: 1 creature   **Casting Time:** 1/3 segment

This cantrip makes the recipient give a shy smile. The victim may make a saving throw to avoid the effect. The caster must make a small waving motion towards the victim to cast the cantrip.

Sneeze
(Evocation)
Area of Effect: One creature   **Casting Time:** 1/2 segment

A cantrip of this nature causes an irritation in the nasal passages of the subject. Unless the subject makes a successful saving throw versus spell, a sneeze will occur. This single sneeze will relieve the irritation. The caster verbalizes the name of an irritant substance while touching his nose.

Twitch
(Evocation)
Area of Effect: One creature   **Casting Time:** 1/3 segment

By means of this cantrip, the caster causes a muscle contraction in some portion of the subject creature's appendages - head, neck, hand, arm, foot, leg, etc. The twitch will be noticeable, but will not cause the subject great discomfort or loss of control or concentration. The cantrip is negated by a successful saving throw. Verbal component is the name of the area to be affected while the caster gazes at the area and makes a twitching motion with the hand.

Veiled Threat
(Evocation)
Area of Effect: One creature   **Casting Time:** 1/6 segment
Range: Touch   **Saving Throw:** Negates

A Veiled Threat cantrip allows the caster to make a common action seem threatening to a single viewer. The viewer of the threat will perceive even the most innocuous nod, smile or wink as a threat of bodily harm and react accordingly. Note that this cantrip can be used to make the actions of someone else besides the caster appear threatening, but the person so affected may attempt to make a saving throw to avoid the effect. The viewer of the threat may not make a saving throw regardless of whom he is threatened by. Note that no others will perceive the suspect action as threatening (unless it obviously is, i.e. shaking a fist at someone). To use this cantrip, the caster waves his hand in a circular motion and nods while making a faint "oosh" sound. If not using the cantrip on himself, he must lightly touch the recipient at the end of the waving motion.

Weak Bladder
(Enchantment)
Area of Effect: One person   **Casting Time:** 1/10 segment

This cantrip causes the subject individual to lose control of his bladder and have to urinate immediately. For the next hour the subject will have to urinate frequently, as if he were drinking gallons of water. The caster must make a squeezing motion with his fist to enact the spell.

Personal Cantrips

Wet Willie
(Evocation)
Area of Effect: One person   **Casting Time:** 1/3 segment

This cantrip makes the victim feel like there is somebody's slobber-covered finger in his ear. This is somewhat unsettling, and causes the victim to suffer a −10% penalty on all listening bases checks for the rest of the round. The caster twists his finger at the victim to cast the spell.

Wink
(Enchantment)
Area of Effect: One person   **Casting Time:** 1/10 segment

This cantrip enables the caster to cause the subject individual to wink one eye. A saving throw indicates that the winking is rapid and not greatly noticeable, while failure to save indicates a greatly exaggerated, prolonged winking. The caster speaks a magical phrase (such as "twenty-three skiddo") while making an imperceptible winking of his eye.

Yawn
(Evocation)
Area of Effect: One creature   **Casting Time:** 1/6 segment

A Yawn cantrip makes the subject creature feel a brief wave of drowsiness which in turn evokes a yawn reaction. If a saving throw versus spell succeeds, the subject creature is totally unaffected by the cantrip. Failure, however, not only forces a yawn to immediately occur, but the subject is then more susceptible to a Sleep spell.

During the balance of the round in which the Yawn cantrip was cast, and during the whole of the following round, the subject will automatically fall into comatose slumber if a Sleep spell is cast upon it, so 1 additional creature will be vulnerable to the spell if more than 1 creature of 4 or fewer Hit Dice are subjected to the Sleep spell. Furthermore, if creatures of 4+1 to 4+4 Hit Dice are involved, there is a chance that two such creatures will actually be affected by the Sleep spell.

Even a creature of up to 5+2 Hit Dice can be affected by Sleep if previously victimized by a Yawn cantrip, but the effect of the Sleep spell is rolled for as if the creature had 4+1 to 4+4 Hit Dice, i.e. there is a 50% chance that it will not be affected. The caster hums a lullaby for the verbal component while making a rocking motion with cupped hands.

Bee
(Summoning)
Area of Effect: One bee   **Casting Time:** 1/2 segment

When this cantrip is used, the caster summons a honey bee from someplace - where is of no importance, for the creature appears in seconds. The bee will appear in whatever spot the caster is gazing at, up to 1 foot distance from him. The bee is, of course, annoyed, and it is 90% likely to sting any living creature it finds itself upon. (This will certainly cause the subject to react violently if it would otherwise be so affected by a bee sting.) The verbal component is a low buzzing sound, made while the caster moves a forefinger through flight-like passes.

Bluelight
(Conjuration)
Area of Effect: 1/4 ft. dia. sphere   **Casting Time:** 1/2 segment

This cantrip enables the caster to conjure a small sphere of glowing blue radiance. The light has an eerie effect when seen from a distance, but the 3-inch sphere only illuminates an area of 5 feet around itself. Furthermore, the Bluelight does not cast reflections beyond this radius. The light does not affect either infravision or ultravision. When the caster says a rhyme using the words blue and light in any combination, the Bluelight appears in his open palm and remains aglow until the caster ceases to concentrate on it.

Bug
(Summoning)
Area of Effect: One bug   **Casting Time:** 1/2 segment

A variation of the Bee cantrip, the Bug cantrip enables the caster to summon some form of crawling insect. The beetle or bug appears in the same manner as the bee summoned by the cantrip of that name. It will likewise be irritated and will pinch, bite or otherwise attack the creature it might find itself upon, with appropriate results. Verbal component is the name of the insect desired while the caster's forefinger makes a sliding and pointing motion at the desired area of the bug's appearance (up to 1 foot distant).

Firefinger
(Alteration)
Area of Effect: 1/2 ft. line   **Casting Time:** 1/3 segment

The Firefinger cantrip enables the caster to cause a jet of flame up to one-half foot in length to shoot forth from his finger. The flame is very hot and will ignite combustible materials such as parchment, twigs, kindling and the like without difficulty, providing the materials are relatively dry. The flame persists for up to 1 segment. To bring about the magic of this cantrip, the caster speaks a word of power over elemental fire (such as "ron-son", "zip-po", or the much revered word, dun-hill), extends the forefinger, and makes a sideways motion with the thumb.

Gnats
(Summoning)
Area of Effect: 1 cubic foot   **Casting Time:** 1/2 segment

A cantrip of this nature is similar to the Bee and Bug cantrips described above, except that when it is used a cloud of gnats is summoned. The swarm will immediately proceed to fly around the head of the nearest living creature (which must be no more than 1 foot from the caster), and unless this creature makes a successful saving throw versus poison, the cloud of gnats will distract the creature for 1-4 segments before the gnats fly elsewhere. The verbal component is a high-pitched buzzing sound made with the tongue and upper palate while the caster points a digit at the area in which the gnat cloud is to appear.

Mouse
(Summoning)
Area of Effect: One mouse   **Casting Time:** 1/2 segment

Similar to the cantrip which summons a bee or a bug, the Mouse cantrip enables the caster to bring forth a mouse up to 10 feet from his position. The animal will be a typical field mouse or as similar a species as possible. When it arrives, the caster will have no control over the mouse, and the animal will

Haunting-Sound Cantrips

behave as would any mouse in the given situation. The caster speaks a summoning word (typically the name of a food desirable by mice) while holding his hands in such a way as to resemble mouse ears.

Smokepuff
(Evocation)
Area of Effect: 1 ft. dia. cloud   **Casting Time:** 1/3 segment

When this cantrip is employed, a puff of actual smoke appears in the desired location, up to 1 foot distant from the caster, and will ascend as would a normal cloud of smoke, or be dissipated, depending on the prevailing conditions. The caster can cause the smoke to be either white, gray, black, brown, yellow or green. The caster names the color of smoke desired while moving a hand from an extended horizontal position to a vertical one, meanwhile breathing forth a puff of air.

Spider
(Summoning)
Area of Effect: One spider   **Casting Time:** 1/2 segment

This cantrip, much as does a Bee or Mouse cantrip, summons a small, ordinary spider from elsewhere to the location desired by the caster, up to 10 feet distant from his person. The arachnid so summoned will usually be a common garden spider or the like, no larger than an inch or two in diameter, and basically harmless. There is a 5% chance that the creature will turn out to be one with powerful poison (Black Widow, Brown Recluse, etc.).

Since the spider summoned will be annoyed, the creature upon which it finds itself will be subject to an immediate bite attack. This will have only a momentary effect, distracting the victim for 1 segment, for a normal spider. If the spider is of the very poisonous sort, the victim must also make a saving throw versus poison at +4. Success indicates 1 point of damage is inflicted. Failure indicates 2 points of damage are inflicted, and the victim will feel sick and be unable to act normally for 1-4 days unless a Neutralize Poison spell is cast to remove the toxin. (A Slow Poison will defer the sickness for 1 day.) To cast the cantrip, the caster speaks the word arachnid while spreading his fingers and wiggling them.

Tweak
(Conjuration)
Area of Effect: One creature   **Casting Time:** 1/3 segment

By means of this cantrip, the caster causes an unseen thumb and forefinger to harmlessly, but annoyingly, tweak some portion of a chosen subject within a 10 foot radius of the caster. Portions subject to the tweak cantrip are: cheek, nose, ear, beard, moustache, whiskers or tail. The cantrip's effects do not disturb spell casting, although the tweaking might distract any creature by causing it to turn to discover the source of the annoyance. A failure to save versus spell (with respect to creatures with an Intelligence under 7), or failure to roll a score greater than Intelligence on 3d6 (with respect to creatures with Intelligence of 7 or greater), indicates a 1-segment distraction. The caster speaks a magic phrase (such as "kitchy-kitchy-coo") while making a pinching and pulling motion with thumb and forefinger.

Unlock
(Conjuration)
Area of Effect: One lock   **Casting Time:** 1/2 segment

This cantrip enables the caster to conjure an invisible, key-like force appropriate to the locking mechanism to be opened (or closed). The Unlock cantrip will affect only simple locks of the most basic sort - typically those which have closing pressure prongs or bolt and pins, or bolt and spring closures. Locks with tumblers or levers, as well as secret-combination locks, are not subject to this cantrip. Note that simple locks with complex wards to prevent skeleton-key triggering will be subject to an Unlock cantrip. While the caster speaks a word or phrase associated with locks ("tick-tock-doublelock" or "yah-el", etc.) he makes a twisting motion with fingers held as if to grasp a key.

Creak
(Evocation)
Area of Effect: Special   **Casting Time:** 1/6 segment

By means of this cantrip, the caster evokes a noise similar to that of a door with corroded hinges slowly opening, or else a sound as if someone or something were walking across squeaking floorboards. The former sound lasts for 1/3 segment, the latter noise will last half a segment and seem to traverse up to 10 feet distance. The caster makes a low creaking sound in his throat while using a hand to make an opening motion or fingers to make a walking motion.

Footfall
(Illusion)
Area of Effect: Special   **Casting Time:** 1/6 segment

When this cantrip is used, the caster creates the auditory illusion of footsteps. The sound is as if a human or humanoid was walking. The footfalls can be soft or fairly noisy. They can approach, move away from, follow or otherwise seem to parallel a person or party. They must begin within 1 foot of the caster, but they may thereafter move away from him up to a 2 foot distance, or may approach closer than 1 foot. The caster must softly vocalize sounds similar to footsteps while pointing in the area they are to occur initially and subsequently.

Groan
(Illusion)
Area of Effect: Special   **Casting Time:** 1/6 segment

A Groan cantrip creates the audible illusion of a wracking cry coming from some location no more than 1 foot from the caster. Naturally, those creatures within hearing distance are allowed a saving throw versus spell, and if it succeeds, the individual will hear no such noise. The caster makes a soft groaning sound in his throat while pointing to the area from which the sound is to appear to come. A container or door will not hamper the range, so that a groaning sound can be made to seem to come from behind a door, in a chest, etc.

Moan
(Illusion)
Area of Effect: Special   **Casting Time:** 1/10 segment

This cantrip is the same as a Groan cantrip, except that the sound involved is either a pitiful moaning or else an eerie one. The desired sound is either a low-pitched one for the haunting effect or a high-pitched one for the pitiful effect. The caster makes a low moaning sound and points at the area from which the sound emanates.

Rattle
(Illusion)
Area of Effect: Special   **Casting Time:** 1/10 segment

By means of this cantrip, the caster causes the audible illusion of a rattling sound associated with chains. Its direction and distance is the same as for a Groan cantrip. The sound will last for up to 2 seconds. All creatures within 1 foot of the sound are entitled to a saving throw versus spell to determine whether they hear the illusionary sound. The spell caster names the rattling device which he desires to create the illusion of while shaking one hand vigorously.

Tap
(Evocation)
Area of Effect: 1 sq. ft   **Casting Time:** 1/6 segment

By means of this cantrip, the caster is able to evoke an invisible force which will tap or rap against some solid object - a door, lid, floor, table, wall, pane or whatever. The sound will occur once, twice or thrice, according to the number of fingers extended by the caster. It is an actual sound: creatures within 1 foot of the noise will certainly hear it if they are able. Verbal component is a hollow sound created by the tongue against the palate, or a key phrase spoken softly, while the finger makes a tapping motion.

Thump
(illusion)

Area of Effect: Special　　　**Casting Time:** 1/10 segment

An audible illusion, the Thump cantrip causes all creatures within a 10 foot radius of the area of effect to hear a loud but muffled thumping sound, as if something large just fell from a height of a foot or so. A successful saving throw versus spell nullifies the cantrip's effect. The caster can cause the sound to seemingly come from any location within a 10 foot radius of his person. The caster swallows loudly while pointing toward the area where the cantrip is to come from, while thinking of the thumping sound.

Whistle
(Evocation)

Area of Effect: Special　　　**Casting Time:** 1/6 segment

When this cantrip is cast, the dweomer causes a faint or loud whistling sound. A faint whistling can be heard within 10 feet, a loud one within 30 feet. The sound can be sharp and normal-seeming or echoing, hollow and eerie. The caster must whistle softly in a manner similar to the desired sound while he looks at the area from which the sound is to come and holds two fingers near his mouth.

Minor Illusion Cantrips

Colored Lights
(Alteration)

Area of Effect: Special　　　**Casting Time:** 1/2 segment

When this cantrip is used, the caster creates one or more globes of pastel light (cf. magic-users' Bluelight cantrip). A single globe of illumination 1 foot in diameter can be brought forth, or a pair of 6-inch diameter globes, three 4-inch globes or four 3-inch globes. The caster can cause these globes of light to be of any pastel color. Each will illuminate a radius around it equal to five diameters, i.e., a 1-foot globe sheds a 5-foot radius of brilliance, while a 3-inch sphere of light illuminates only a radius of 15 inches.

As long as the caster concentrates on the colored lights, the cantrip will remain active, and the globe or globes will float near or rest upon the caster, as he desires, within the 1 foot range. Globes can be moved back and forth, up and down, to and fro as desired. The illumination from any one of them will not cast reflections beyond 1 foot, and the light shed cannot be detected beyond 3 feet. Infravision and ultravision are not affected if light is colored pale blue or pink, but other hues will disturb these visual capabilities. Verbal and somatic components are these: the caster must speak the color and number of globes desired, then speak a magic word ("noma", "mazda", etc.), while directing the globes with one or more fingers.

Dim
(Alteration)

Area of Effect: Special　　　**Casting Time:** 1/2 segment

By means of a Dim cantrip, the illusionist causes a light source to become weaker or the very air to become less permeated by light rays. If light sources are to be affected, then about 6 torches, a medium-sized fire (such as in a fireplace or campfire), 72 candles or even a light or Continual Light spell can be affected.

The Dim cantrip will cause any of the above light sources to at best shed only half their normal radiance for one full round. Torches will burn only as brightly as candles; candles will but glow dimly; a tire will become torch-like in illumination, and all Light spells dim to half their normal brightness. Affected light must be within 1 foot of the caster. He must speak a magical phrase (such as "bee-row-nout" or "rhee-oh-stat") and make a downward motion with one hand to effectuate the cantrip.

Haze
(Alteration)

Area of Effect: 1 ft. cube　　　**Casting Time:** 1/2 segment

When a Haze cantrip is cast, the atmosphere in the desired area of effect becomes cloudy, as if layered by smoke or filled with floating dust. Any crea-ture attempting to discharge missiles or cast spells at a target screened by such a Haze will be affected. The target is 5% harder to hit, so missile discharge is at -1 to-hit and saving throws are at +1 (or one is given when otherwise none is allowed, although it is only a 5% chance to save in the latter case). Hiding in shadows is 5% more effective when screened by a Haze cantrip.

The hazy effect lasts but a single round. It must be cast over an area within 1 foot of the caster. Atmospheric conditions will destroy the haze if applicable - a good breeze, rain, etc. A Gust of Wind spell will immediately disperse the Haze. The caster hums a melody while the hands make passes before the body to effect this cantrip.

Mask
(illusion)

Area of Effect: One person　　　**Casting Time:** 1/6 segment

A Mask cantrip enables the caster to alter his visage or the visage of whatever subject individual (human, demi-human or humanoid) he chooses, by means of an illusion. Ears, hair, head shape, facial features and all such aspects of appearance are affected. The Mask will only be detectable if a viewer can peer closely and does so. The effect lasts for 3-6 rounds. The caster touches his face, thinks of the desired features, and then speaks a word descriptive of the visage desired.

Mirage
(illusion)

Area of Effect: 2 ft. sq.　　　**Casting Time:** 1/2 segment

This cantrip lets the caster cause an area to appear to be something other than it is. The Mirage cantrip brings an illusionary scene to cover the area. The area must be relatively flat and featureless, and the Mirage must be an actual place, in existence at the time, which the caster has actually beheld. A saving throw versus spell is applicable. The cantrip lasts for as long as the caster concentrates, although each round there is a 5% cumulative chance that it will waver and reveal its true nature. Touching a Mirage will instantly dispel the cantrip, as will casting a Dispel Magic spell. The caster must speak a word or two describing the Mirage and then make a single pass to cause the magic to begin. It is maintained by concentration alone thereafter.

Noise
(illusion)

Area of Effect: 1 ft. radius　　　**Casting Time:** 1/6 segment

The caster of a Noise cantrip causes illusory sound of whatever nature he desires, although it is indistinct and confusing. Thus, he can cause a murmuring sound as it many voices were speaking behind a thick door or at a great distance, a rushing sound similar to wings and wind combined, shuffling and scraping as if many people were moving things or walking slowly but at some distant place, etc. All creatures within the area of effect will be subject to the cantrip, but each gets a saving throw. Success negates the noise with respect to the individual. Range is 10 foot for the cantrip's radius of sound. The caster points a digit at the desired area and then softly makes sounds imitative of the noises desired.

Rainbow
(Alteration)

Area of Effect: Special　　　**Casting Time:** 1/3 segment

By means of this cantrip, the caster brings into being a plane of pastel colors which exactly duplicates a natural rainbow. He can cause this 30-foot-long, 1-foot-wide band of color to arch into a bowed shape, remain a ribbon, twist and turn, etc. In any event, one end of the rainbow must be within 1 foot of the caster when the cantrip is cast. The colors will glow softly and be visible even in total (normal) darkness. If no motion is desired, the caster may leave the vicinity of the rainbow. If motion is desired, the caster must control it by hand gesture and remain within 1 foot of it. The rainbow will last for 1 round and then fade away. All creatures failing to save versus spell will gaze at the rainbow for 1-4 segments, 2-5 if the caster keeps it in motion. Verbal component is a name of power ("gar-land", "pegee-lee", etc.), which is spoken while the fingers of both hands form a pyramid.

Two-D'lusion
(Illusion)

Area of Effect: 4 sq. ft.   **Casting Time:** 1/6 segment

This cantrip is virtually the same as a Phantasmal Force spell in most respects. The caster creates a two-dimensional illusion of whatever he desires. If any viewer sees it from an angle of more than 45 degrees from its horizontal or vertical viewing axis, the nature of the illusion will be immediately apparent. It is dispelled by touch or magic (or Dispel Magic). It is invisible from the side or the rear, and lasts as long as the caster concentrates upon it. To effect the cantrip, the caster must speak a phrase descriptive of the illusion while making a circular motion with his closed hand.

Social Engagement Cantrips

Blather
(reversible)
(Enchantment/Charm)

Area of Effect: 1 person   **Casting Time:** 1/3 segment
Range: 10 feet   **Duration:** 1 turn

The recipient of this cantrip can talk at length about any subject, even if they have no idea what the topic of conversation is about. The caster must hold his hand up and move his fingers in a talking motion while saying "blah, blah, blah", to evoke the magic.

Conceal Gas
(Illusion/Phantasm)

Area of Effect: 1 person   **Casting Time:** 1/10 segment
Duration: 1 round

This cantrip will nullify any sounds or smells associated with the by-products of the subject's gastric system. The caster must wave his hands in the air as if he is trying to blow a smell away from his face.

Dispel Body Odor
(reversible)
(Alteration)

Area of Effect: One person   **Casting Time:** 1/3 segment

Anyone who has this cantrip cast upon them will no longer smell badly; instead smelling as if they had just bathed. This spell will last until the odor builds up again naturally. The reversed spell makes the victim smell like he has been performing manual labor in the sun for a week without bathing. An unwilling victim may make a saving throw to avoid this cantrip. The caster must raise both of his arms in succession and scrub his armpits to cast the spell.

Gristle Teleportation
(Alteration)

Area of Effect: Caster's mouth   **Casting Time:** 1/6 segment

The caster can use this cantrip to remove a small piece of unwanted food from his mouth and conceal it within two feet of his person. The material component of this spell is a napkin which the caster must wad up in his hand.

Hide Food
(Illusion/Phantasm)

Area of Effect: One plate   **Casting Time:** 1/2 segment

This cantrip will turn up to one plate's worth of food invisible for one hour. The caster must rub his hand over his abdomen in a circular motion to use this cantrip.

Illusion of Courtesy
(Illusion/Phantasm)

Casting Time: 1/6 segment

The caster can use this cantrip to make any one action or phrase that he is about to use seem to be done in a polite, non-offensive manner. The caster must smile a large, toothy smile during this incantation and nod his head repeatedly.

Interject Witty Comment
(Alteration)

Casting Time: 1/10 segment

This cantrip will make the very next thing uttered by the caster seem witty and humorous to those listening. The caster must make a motion with his hands as if he is playing an imaginary drum in the air.

Neutralize Alcohol
(reversible)
(Alteration)

Area of Effect: 1 quart   **Casting Time:** 1/3 segment
Range: 10 feet

This cantrip will halve the amount of alcohol in the target drink. Its reverse will double the alcohol content of the target drink. The somatic component of the neutralization effect is moving one's hand over the top of a drink while the reverse requires one to pretend to pour a bottle into a glass while smiling and nodding his head.

Numb Tongue
(Illusion/Phantasm)

Area of Effect: Caster   **Casting Time:** 1/6 segment
Duration: 1 turn

When the caster uses this spell on himself it allows him to not taste anything that he puts in his mouth. He may end the spell at will. He is required to grab his tongue and wag it around to evoke the cantrip.

Pass Salt
(Alteration)

Area of Effect: 1 container   **Casting Time:** 1/6 segment

This cantrip will telekinetically move a food or seasoning container up to ten feet towards any one person of the caster's choosing. The cantrip cannot cause damage. It prevents any spills during the container's journey. The caster must reach out towards the container and pretend to move it to the recipient.

Personal Zephyr
(Evocation)

Casting Time: 1/3 segment   **Duration:** 1 hour

This cantrip will create a light breeze that will blow across the caster, cooling him as if he was using a hand held fan. The cantrip lasts for one hour. The caster must periodically blow into his hand and sprinkle the breath over his head.

Protection from Sneezes
(Abjuration)

Area of Effect: Caster   **Casting Time:** 1/10 segment
Duration: 1 round

This cantrip will prevent the caster's own sneezes and deflect the force and spray of somebody else's sneeze, should someone relieve the tickle in their nasal passages in the direction of the caster. The somatic component of this cantrip is holding a finger under one's nose.

Set Table
(reversible)
(Alteration)

Area of Effect: 1 table   **Casting Time:** 1/2 segment

This cantrip is used to quickly set a table. The caster need only pile the dishes and utensils at the end of the table and the cantrip will take care of the rest. The reversed cantrip will collect all of the place settings on a table and stack them neatly on the table's edge. The caster must use his hands to mimic the motions of dealing a deck of cards.

Sleep with Eyes Open
(Illusion/Phantasm)

Area of Effect: 1 person   **Casting Time:** 1/2 segment
Duration: 1 hour

The recipient of this cantrip is able to sleep while still appearing to be awake to the casual observer. The caster must slap himself in the face a couple of times.

Strengthen Smile Muscles
(Alteration)

Area of Effect: 1 person   **Casting Time:** 1/3 segment
Range: 10 feet   **Duration:** 1 day

This cantrip will allow any one person to continuously smile without his face getting tired for up to 1 hour. The caster must state, "My, oh my, what a wonderful day."

Wash Hands
(Alteration)
Area of Effect: 2 Hands   **Casting Time:** 1/2 segment

This cantrip cleans the subject's hands just as if he had scrubbed them with soap and water. The caster must rub his hands together in a vigorous hand washing motion.

Wipe Face
(Alteration)
Area of Effect: 1 person   **Casting Time:** 1/2 segment

This spell cleans the face of any creature it is cast upon, just as if it had been scrubbed with soap and water. The caster must vigorously pretend to rub his own face to evoke this magic.

First Level Spells

Affect Normal Fires
(Alteration)
Level: 1
Range: 5 yds./level   **Components:** V, S, M
Duration: 2 rds./level   **Casting Time:** 1 segment
Area of Effect: 10-ft. radius   **Saving Throw:** None

This spell enables the magic-user to cause non-magical fires – from as small as a torch or lantern to as large as the area of effect – to reduce in size and brightness to become mere coals or increase in light to become as bright as full daylight and increase the illumination to double the normal radius. Note that this does not affect either fuel consumption or damage caused by the fire.

The caster can affect any or all fires in the spell's area. He can alter their intensities with a single gesture as long as the spell is in effect. The spell lasts until the caster cancels it, all fuel is burned or the duration expires. The caster can also extinguish all flames in the area, which expends the spell immediately. The material component is the fire to be affected. The spell does not affect Fire Elementals or similar creatures.

Alarm
(Abjuration, Evocation)
Level: 1
Range: 10 yards   **Components:** V, S, M
Duration: 4 hrs. + 1/2 hr./level   **Casting Time:** 1 round
Area of Effect: Up to 20-ft. cube   **Saving Throw:** None

When an Alarm spell is cast, the magic-user causes a selected area to react to the presence of any creature larger than a normal rat – anything larger than about one-half cubic foot in volume or more than about three pounds in weight. The area of effect can be a portal, a section of floor, stairs, etc.

As soon as any creature enters the warded area, touches it or otherwise contacts it without speaking a password established by the caster, the Alarm spell lets out a loud ringing that can be heard clearly within a 60-foot radius. This radius is reduced by 10 feet for each interposing door and by 20 feet for each substantial interposing wall. The sound lasts for one round and then ceases.

Ethereal or astrally projected creatures do not trigger an alarm, but flying or levitating creatures, invisible creatures or incorporeal or gaseous creatures do. The caster can dismiss the alarm with a single word. The material components of this spell are a tiny bell and a piece of very fine silver wire or rook's brain.

Armor
(Conjuration)
Level: 1
Range: Touch   **Components:** V, S, M
Duration: Special   **Casting Time:** 1 round
Area of Effect: 1 creature   **Saving Throw:** None

By means of this spell, the magic-user creates a magical field of force that serves as if it were scale mail armor (AC 6). The spell has no effect on a person already armored or a creature with Armor Class 6 or better. It is not cumulative with the Shield spell, but it is cumulative with Dexterity and, in case of fighter/magic-users, with the shield bonus.

The Armor spell does not hinder movement or prevent spellcasting, and adds no weight or encumbrance. It lasts until successfully dispelled or until the wearer sustains cumulative damage totaling greater than 8 points + 1 per level of the caster. It is important to note that the armor does not absorb this damage. The armor merely grants an AC of 6; the wearer still suffers full damage from any successful attacks. Thus, the wearer might suffer 8 points of damage from an attack, then several minutes later sustain an additional 1 point of damage. Unless the spell were cast by a magic-user of 2nd level or higher, it would be dispelled at this time. Until it is dispelled, the Armor spell grants the wearer full benefits of the Armor Class gained. The material component is a piece of finely cured leather that has been blessed by a cleric.

Audible Glamer
(Illusion/Phantasm)
Level: 1
Range: 60 yds. + 10 yds./level   **Components:** V, S, M
Duration: 3 rds./level   **Casting time:** 1 segment
Area of Effect: Hearing range   **Saving Throw:** Special

When the Audible Glamer spell is cast, the magic-user causes a volume of sound to arise, at whatever distance he desires (within range), and seem to recede, approach or remain at a fixed place as desired. The volume of sound created, however, is directly related to the level of the spellcaster. The volume is based upon the lowest level at which the spell can be cast, 1st level.

The noise of the Audible Glamer at this level is that of four men, maximum. Each additional experience level of the magic-user adds a like volume, so that at 2nd level the magic-user can have the spell cause sound equal to that of eight men. Thus, talking, singing, shouting, walking, marching or running sounds can be created. The auditory illusion created by an Audible Glamer spell can be virtually any type of sound, but the relative volume must be commensurate with the level of the magic-user casting the spell. A horde of rats running and squeaking is about the same volume as eight men running and shouting. A roaring lion is equal to the noise volume of 16 men, while a roaring dragon is equal to the noise volume of no fewer than 24 men.

A character stating that he does not believe the sound receives a saving throw and, if it succeeds, the character then hears a faint and obviously false sound, emanating from the caster's direction. Note that this spell can enhance the effectiveness of the Phantasmal Force spell. The material component of the spell is a bit of wool or a small lump of wax.

Aura of Innocence
(Enchantment/Charm)
Level: 1
Range: 1 yd./level   **Components:** V, S, M
Duration: 3 rds./level   **Casting time:** 1 segment
Area of Effect: One person   **Saving Throw:** Negates

An Aura of Innocence spell allows the recipient to remain free from suspicion of being associated with any act or crime for the duration of the spell no matter how convincing the evidence is. Those viewing the recipient may attempt to make a saving throw in order to negate the effect. Otherwise, even a man who blatantly stabs a person and flaunts the bloody dagger to onlookers would not be immediately suspected of the crime. After the duration expires, people who witnessed an act will begin to recall the truth and wonder why their judgement was so clouded. The material component is a woolen fleece.

Bash Door
(Evocation)
Level: 1
Range: 30 yards   **Components:** V, S
Duration: Instantaneous   **Casting Time:** 1 segment
Area of Effect: One door   **Saving Throw:** None

This spell allows the caster to cause a tremendous force against a door. A closed (and even locked) door may be forced open with a successful open doors roll made with the equivalent effect of a strength of 25. Note that no additional strength is actually granted to the magic-user's physical body. The force of a Bash Door spell may only be used on a door. It has no effect on walls, windows or creatures.

Befriend

(Enchantment/Charm)
Level: I
Range: 0
Duration: 1d4 rds. + 1 rd./level
Area of Effect: 60-ft. radius

Components: V, S, M
Casting Time: 1 segment
Saving Throw: Special

A Befriend spell causes the magic-user to temporarily gain 2d4 points of Charisma. Intelligent creatures within the area of effect at the time the spell is cast must make immediate reaction checks based on the character's new Charisma. Those with favorable reactions tend to be very impressed with the spellcaster, make an effort to be friends with him and help him as appropriate to the situation. Officious bureaucrats might decide to become helpful; surly gate guards might wax informative; attacking Orcs might spare the caster's life, taking him captive instead.

When the spell wears off, the creatures realize that they have been influenced, and their reactions are determined by the GM. The components for this spell are chalk (or white flour), lampblack (or soot) and vermilion applied to the face before casting the spell.

Burning Hands

(Alteration)
Level: I
Range: 5 feet
Duration: Instantaneous
Area of Effect: The caster

Components: V, S
Casting Time: 1 segment
Saving Throw: 1/2

When the magic-user casts this spell, a jet of searing flame shoots from his fingertips. His hands must be held so as to send forth a fanlike sheet of flames: the magic-user's thumbs must touch each other and the fingers must be spread. The Burning Hands send out flame jets 5 feet long in a horizontal arc of about 120 degrees in front of the magic-user.

Any creature in the area of the flames suffers 1d3 points of damage, plus 2 points for each level of experience of the spellcaster, to a maximum of 1d3+20 points of fire damage. Those successfully saving vs. spell receive half damage. Flammable materials touched by the fire burn (for example, cloth, paper, parchment, thin wood, etc.). Such materials can be extinguished in the next round if no other action is taken.

Change Self

(Illusion/Phantasm)
Level: I
Range: 0
Duration: 2d6 rds. + 2 rds./level
Area of Effect: The caster

Components: V, S
Casting Time: 1 segment
Saving Throw: None

This spell enables the magic-user to alter the appearance of his form – including clothing and equipment – to appear 1 foot shorter or taller; thin, fat or in between; human, humanoid or any other generally man-shaped bipedal creature. The caster cannot duplicate a specific individual. The spell does not provide the abilities or mannerisms of the chosen form. The duration of the spell is 2d6 rounds plus two additional rounds per level of experience of the spellcaster.

The GM may allow a saving throw for disbelief under certain circumstances; for example, if the caster acts in a manner obviously inconsistent with his chosen role. The spell does not alter the perceived tactile (i.e., touch) properties of the caster or his equipment, and the ruse can be discovered in this way.

Charm Person

(Enchantment/Charm)
Level: I
Range: 120 yards
Duration: Special
Area of Effect: 1 person

Components: V, S
Casting Time: 1 segment
Saving Throw: Negates

This spell affects any single person it is cast upon. The term person includes any bipedal human, demi-human or humanoid of man-size or smaller, such as Brownies, Dryads, dwarves, elves, Gnolls, gnomes, Goblins, half-elves, halflings, half-orcs, hobgoblins, humans, kobolds, Lizard Men, Nixies, Orcs, Pixies, Sprites, Troglodytes, and others. Thus, a 10th level fighter could be charmed, but an Ogre could not.

The person receives a saving throw vs. spell to avoid the effect, with any adjustment due to Wisdom. If the person receives damage from the caster's group in the same round the Charm is cast, an additional bonus of +1 per hit point of damage received is added to the victim's saving throw. If the spell recipient fails his saving throw, he regards the caster as a trusted friend and ally to be heeded and protected.

The spell does not enable the caster to control the charmed creature as if it were an automaton, but any word or action of the caster is viewed in the most favorable way. Thus, a Charmed Person would not obey a suicide command, but he might believe the caster if assured that the only chance to save the caster's life is for the person to hold back an onrushing Red Dragon for "just a minute or two."

Note also that the spell does not endow the caster with linguistic capabilities beyond those he normally possesses (i.e., he must speak the victim's language to communicate his commands). The duration of the spell is a function of the charmed person's Intelligence and is tied to the saving throw. The spell may be broken if a successful saving throw is rolled, and this saving throw is checked on a periodic basis, according to the creature's Intelligence (see the following table).

If the caster harms, or attempts to harm, the charmed person by some overt action, or if a Dispel Magic spell is successfully cast upon the charmed person, the Charm spell is broken. If two or more charm effects simultaneously affect a creature, the result is decided by the GM. This could range from one effect being clearly dominant, to the subject being torn by conflicting desires, to new saving throws that could negate both spells. Note that the subject has full memory of the events that took place while he was charmed.

Intelligence Score	Time Between Checks
3 or less	3 months
4-6	2 months
7-9	1 month
10-12	3 weeks
13-14	2 weeks
15-16	1 week
17-18	3 days
19-20	2 days
21 or more	1 day

Note: The period between checks is the time period during which the check occurs. When to roll the check during this time is determined (randomly or by selection) by the GM. The roll is made secretly.

Chill Touch

(Necromancy)

Level: I
Range: 0
Duration: 3 rds. + I rd./level
Area of Effect: The caster

Components: V, S
Casting Time: I segment
Saving Throw: Negates

When the caster completes this spell, a blue glow encompasses his hand. This energy attacks the life force of any living creature upon which the magic-user makes a successful melee attack. The touched creature must roll a successful saving throw vs. spell or suffer 1d4 points of damage and lose 1 point of Strength. If the save is successful, the creature remains unharmed. Creatures not rated for Strength suffer a -1 penalty to their attack rolls for every other successful touch. Lost Strength returns at the rate of 1 point per hour. Damage must be cured magically or healed naturally. This spell has a special effect on undead creatures. Undead touched by the caster suffer no damage or Strength loss, but they must successfully save vs. spell or flee for 1d4 rounds + 1 round per level of the caster.

Chromatic Orb

(Alteration - Evocation)

Level: I
Range: 30 feet
Duration: Special
Area of Effect: One creature

Components: V S, M
Casting Time: I segment
Saving Throw: Special

The Chromatic Orb spell enables the caster to create a small globe of varying hue in his hand and hurl it at any opponent he desires, providing there are no barriers between him and the target creature, and that the target creature is within 30 feet (the longest distance the Chromatic Orb can be hurled). It is magical, and even creatures normally struck only by +5, +4, etc. magic weapons will be affected by the Chromatic Orb if it strikes.

Magic resistance prevents the spell's effects, of course. At 1 foot or closer, there is a +3 chance to-hit, at over 1 foot to 2 feet there is a + 2 chance to strike the target, and from over 2 feet to the maximum 3 feet range the chance to-hit is only +1. If a Chromatic Orb misses a target, it dissipates without further effect.

The color of the globe determines its effect when a subject is struck. Low level casters are restricted as to what color orb they can bring into existence by means of this spell, although the hues below their level are always available should the choice be made to select a color not commensurate with level of experience. Colors and effects are shown on the table below.

Minimum Level of Caster	Color of Orb Generated	Hit Points of Damage	Special Powers
1st	Pearly	I-4	light (I)
2nd	Ruby	I-6	heat (2)
3rd	Flame	I-8	fire (3)
4th	Amber	I-10	blindness (4)
5th	Emerald	I-12	stinking cloud (5)
6th	Turquoise	2-16	magnetism (6)
7th	Sapphire	2-8	paralysis (7)
10th	Amethyst	(Slow)	petrification (8)
12th	Ashen	(paralysis)	death (9)

Notes on special powers:

1: Light equal to a Light spell will be generated and persist for 1 round/level of the caster, and any subject failing to save versus spell will be blinded for the duration.

2: Heat from the ruby Orb will melt up to 1 cubic yard of ice, and creatures not saving versus spell will suffer a loss of 1 point of Strength and 1 point of Dexterity (or -1 to-hit and AC) for 1 round following being struck by the Orb.

3: Fire from the Orb will set aflame all combustibles within a 1 foot radius of the target, and unless the target saves versus spell an additional 2 points of fire damage will be suffered (except when protected from fire by magical or natural means).

4: The target subject will suffer blindness for 5-8 rounds unless a successful saving throw versus spell is made (Cure Blindness or Dispel Magic negates this effect).

5: A magical stinking cloud of 51 radius (around the target) is created when a successful hit is made, and the subject must save versus poison or else

be helpless, and in any event will be helpless until leaving the area of the vapors (cf. Stinking Cloud spell).

6: The turquoise Orb inflicts electrical damage, and if the target is wearing ferrous metal it will be magnetized for 3-12 rounds unless a saving throw versus spell is successful. Magnetized metal will stick fast to other magnetized metal items, and non-magnetized ferrous metal items will cling until pulled free.

7: Unless a saving throw versus paralyzation is made, the subject creature will be paralyzed for 5-20 rounds.

8: The subject creature will be turned to stone unless a saving throw versus petrification is made, and even if the save is made, the subject will be slowed for 2-8 rounds (cf. Slow spell).

9: The subject creature will die unless a successful saving throw versus death magic is made, and even if a save is made, the subject will be paralyzed for 2-5 rounds.

The material component of the spell is a gem of the appropriate hue, or else a clear crystal one (such as a diamond). The gem can be as small (in value) as 50 gold pieces as long as its color is appropriate.

Color Spray

(Alteration)

Level: I
Range: 0
Duration: Instantaneous
Area of Effect: 5 x 20 x 20 ft. wedge

Components: V, S, M
Casting Time: I segment
Saving Throw: Special

Upon casting this spell, the magic-user causes a vivid, fan-shaped spray of clashing colors to spring forth from his hand. From one to six creatures (1d6) within the area are affected in order of increasing distance from the magic-user. All creatures above the level of the spellcaster and all those of 6th level or 6 Hit Dice or more are entitled to a saving throw vs. spell. Blind or unseeing creatures are not affected by the spell.

Creatures not allowed or failing saving throws, and whose Hit Dice or levels are less than or equal to the spellcaster's level, are struck unconscious for 2d4 rounds; those with Hit Dice or levels 1 or 2 greater than the magic-user's level are blinded for 1d4 rounds; those with Hit Dice or levels 3 or more greater than that of the spellcaster are stunned (reeling and unable to think or act coherently) for one round. The material components of this spell are a pinch each of powder or sand that is colored red, yellow and blue.

Comprehend Languages

(Alteration)
Reversible

Level: I
Range: Touch
Duration: 5 rds./level
Area of Effect: I speaking creature or written text

Components: V, S, M
Casting Time: I round
Saving Throw: None

When this spell is cast, the magic-user is able to understand the spoken words of a creature or read an otherwise incomprehensible written message (such as writing in another language). In either case, the magic-user must touch the creature or the writing.

Note that the ability to read does not necessarily impart understanding of the material, nor does the spell enable the caster to speak or write an unknown language. Written material can be read at the rate of one page or equivalent per round. Magical writing cannot be read, other than to know it is magical, but the spell is often useful when deciphering treasure maps.

This spell can be foiled by certain warding magic (the 3rd level Secret Page and Illusionary Script spells), and it does not reveal messages concealed in otherwise normal text. The material components of this spell are a pinch of soot and a few grains of salt. The reverse of this spell, Confuse Languages, cancels a Comprehend Languages spell or renders a writing or a creature's speech incomprehensible, for the same duration as above.

Conjure Mount

(Conjuration/Summoning)
Level: 1
Range: 10 yards
Duration: 2 hrs. + 1 hr./level
Area of Effect: 1 mount
Components: V, S, M
Casting Time: 1 turn
Saving Throw: None

By means of this spell, the caster conjures a normal animal to serve him as a mount. The animal serves willingly and well, but at the expiration of the spell duration it disappears, returning to its own place. The type of mount gained by this spell depends on the level of the caster; of course, a caster can choose a lesser mount if desired. Available mounts include the following:

Caster Level	Mount
1-3	Mule or light horse
4-7	Draft horse or war horse
8-12	Camel
13-14	Elephant (and howdah at 18th level)
15+	Griffon (and saddle at 18th level)

The conjured mount does not come with any riding gear, unless it is of a class lower than the caster would normally be entitled to; thus, a 4th level magic-user can gain a war horse without saddle and harness, or a light horse with saddle and harness. The statistics of the animal gained are typical of all creatures of the same class. The mount disappears when slain. The material component of the spell is a bit of hair from the type of animal to be conjured.

Dancing Lights

(Alteration)
Level: 1
Range: 40 yds. + 10 yds./level
Duration: 2 rds./level
Area of Effect: Special
Components: V, S, M
Casting Time: 1 segment
Saving Throw: None

When a Dancing Lights spell is cast, the magic-user creates, at his option, from one to four lights that resemble either torches or lanterns (and cast that amount of light), glowing spheres of light (such as evidenced by Will-o-the-Wisps), or one faintly glowing, vaguely manlike shape, somewhat similar to that of a creature from the Elemental Plane of Fire.

The Dancing Lights move as the spellcaster desires, forward or back, straight or turning corners, without concentration upon such movement by the magic-user. If the magic-user concentrates, he can move the lights in a fantastic manner and put on quite a show. The spell cannot be used to cause blindness (see the 1st level Light spell), and it winks out if the range or duration is exceeded. The material component of this spell is either a bit of phosphorus or wychwood, or a glowworm.

Detect Magic

(Divination)
Level: 1
Range: 0
Duration: 2 rds./level
Area of Effect: 10 ft. x 60 ft.
Components: V, S
Casting Time: 1 segment
Saving Throw: None

When the Detect Magic spell is cast, the magic-user detects magical radiations in a path 10 feet wide and up to 60 feet long, in the direction he is facing. The intensity of the magic can be determined (dim, faint, moderate, strong, overwhelming), and the magic-user has a 10% chance per level to recognize if a certain type of magic (alteration, conjuration, etc.) is present.

The caster can turn, scanning a 60-degree arc per round. A stone wall of 1 foot or more thickness, solid metal of 1 inch thickness, or a yard or more of solid wood blocks the spell. Magical areas, multiple types of magic or strong local magical emanations may confuse or conceal weaker radiations. Note that this spell does not reveal the presence of good or evil, or reveal alignment. Extraplanar creatures may not necessarily be magical.

Detect Undead

(Divination, Necromancy)
Level: 1
Range: 0
Duration: 3 turns
Area of Effect: 60 ft. + 10 ft./level
Components: V, S, M
Casting Time: 1 round
Saving Throw: None

This spell enables the caster to detect all undead creatures out to the limit of the spell. The area of effect extends in a path 10 feet wide and 60 feet long (plus 10 feet longer per level of the magic-user), in the direction the caster is facing. Scanning a direction requires one round, and the caster must be motionless.

While the spell indicates direction, it does not give specific location or distance. It detects undead through walls and obstacles but is blocked by 1 foot of solid stone, 1 yard of wood or loose earth, or a thin coating of metal. The spell does not indicate the type of undead detected, only that undead are present. The material component for this spell is a bit of earth from a grave.

Enlarge

(Alteration)
Reversible
Level: 1
Range: 5 yds./level
Duration: 5 rds./level
Area of Effect: 1 creature or object
Components: V, S, M
Casting Time: 1 segment
Saving Throw: Negates

This spell causes instant growth of a creature or object, increasing both size and weight. It can be cast only upon a single creature (or a symbiotic or community entity) or upon a single object that does not exceed 10 cubic feet in volume per caster level. The object or creature must be seen to be affected. It grows by up to 10% per level of experience of the magic-user, increasing this amount in height, width and weight. All equipment worn or carried by a creature is enlarged by the spell.

Unwilling victims are entitled to a saving throw vs. spell. A successful saving throw means the spell fails. If insufficient room is available for the desired growth, the creature or object attains the maximum possible size, bursting weak enclosures in the process, but it is constrained without harm by stronger materials – the spell cannot be used to crush a creature by growth. Magical properties are not increased by this spell – a huge sword +1 is still only +1, a staff-sized wand is still only capable of its normal functions, a giant-sized potion merely requires a greater fluid intake to make its magical effects operate, etc. Weight, mass and strength are affected, though. Thus, a table blocking a door would be heavier and more effective, a hurled stone would have more mass (and cause more damage), chains would be more massive, doors thicker, a thin line turned to a sizeable, longer rope, and so on.

A creature's hit points, Armor Class and attack rolls do not change, but damage rolls increase proportionately with size. For example, a fighter at 160% normal size hits with his long sword and rolls a 6 for damage. The adjusted damage roll is 10 (that is, 6 x 1.6 = 9.6, rounded up). Bonuses due to Strength, class, and magic are not altered.

The reverse spell, Reduce, negates the Enlarge spell or makes creatures or objects smaller. The creature or object loses 10% of its original size for every level of the caster, to a minimum of 10% of the original size. Thereafter, the size shrinks by 1-foot increments to less than 1 foot, by 1-inch increments to 1 inch, and by 1/10-inch increments to a minimum of 1/10 of an inch – the recipient cannot dwindle away to nothingness.

For example, a 16-foot-tall giant reduced by a 15th level magic-user (15 steps) would be reduced to 1.6 feet (in nine steps), then to 6/10 of a foot or 7.2 inches (in one step), and finally to 2.2 inches (in the last five steps). A shrinking object may damage weaker materials affixed to it, but an object will shrink only as long as the object itself is not damaged. Unwilling creatures are allowed a saving throw vs. spell. The material component of this spell is a pinch of powdered iron.

Erase

(Alteration)

Level: 1

Range: 30 yards	**Components:** V, S
Duration: Permanent	**Casting Time:** 1 segment
Area of Effect: 1 scroll or 2 pgs.	**Saving Throw:** Special

The Erase spell removes writings of either magical or mundane nature from a scroll or from one to two pages of paper, parchment, or similar surfaces. It removes Explosive Runes, Glyphs of Warding, Runes of Eyeball Implosion, Sepia Snake Sigils, and magic-user marks, but it does not remove Illusory Script or Symbols (see those spells). Non-magical writings are automatically erased if the caster is touching them; otherwise, the chance for success is 90%. Magical writings must be touched, and are only 30% likely to be erased, plus 5% per caster level, to a maximum of 90% (for example, 35% for a 1st level caster, 40% for a 2nd level caster, etc.).

Faerie Phantoms

(Illusion/Phantasm)

Level: 1

Range: 60 yds. + 10 yds./level	**Components:** V, S
Duration: Special	**Casting Time:** 1 segment
Area of Effect: 1d6 phantoms per level	**Saving Throw:** None

When a Faerie Phantoms spell is cast, the spell caster causes 1d6 illusionary faeries to come into being. The phantasmal faeries will behave as normal faeries and begin frolicking, dancing, fluttering and generally having a grand ol' time without any concentration by the caster.

If the caster concentrates, he can generally have the faeries react in a desired way such as attacking a foe, walking with the caster, or putting on a play. The faeries themselves do no damage. But their successful attacks can be sufficient to disrupt the concentration of another spell caster. When a phantom faerie is struck by a melee or missile attack, magical or otherwise, it disappears but any other existing phantoms remain intact until struck. If the phantoms are not dispelled or struck, they will last for one turn per level of the caster.

Feather Fall

(Alteration)

Level: 1

Range: 10 yds./level	**Components:** V
Duration: 1 rd./level	**Casting Time:** 1 segment
Area of Effect: Special	**Saving Throw:** None

When this spell is cast, the creature(s) or object(s) affected immediately assumes the mass of a piece of down. The rate of falling is instantly changed to a mere 2 feet per second (120 feet per round), and no damage is incurred upon landing while the spell is in effect. However, when the spell duration ceases, a normal rate of fall occurs.

The spell can be cast upon the magic-user or some other creature or object up to the maximum range and lasts for one round for each level of the magic-user. The Feather Fall affects one or more objects or creatures in a 10-foot cube, as long as the maximum weight of the creatures or objects does not exceed a combined total of 200 pounds plus 200 pounds per level of the spellcaster.

For example, a 2nd level magic-user has a range of 20 yards, a duration of two rounds, and a weight limit of 600 pounds when casting this spell. The spell works only upon free-falling, flying or propelled objects (such as missiles). It does not affect a sword blow or a charging creature. Note that the spell can be effectively combined with Gust of Wind and similar spells.

Find Familiar

(Conjuration/Summoning)

Level: 1

Range: 1 mile/level	**Components:** V, S, M
Duration: Special	**Casting Time:** 2d12 hours
Area of Effect: 1 familiar	**Saving Throw:** Special

This spell enables the caster to attempt to summon a familiar to act as his aide and companion. Familiars are typically small creatures, such as cats, frogs, ferrets, crows, hawks, snakes, owls, ravens, toads, weasels or even mice. A crea-ture acting as a familiar can benefit a magic-user, conveying its sensory powers to its master, conversing with him and serving as a guard/scout/spy as well.

A magic-user can have only one familiar at a time, however, and he has no control over what sort of creature answers the summoning, if any at all come. The creature is always more intelligent than others of its type (typically by 2 or 3 Intelligence points), and its bond with the magic-user confers upon it an exceptionally long life. The magic-user receives the heightened senses of his familiar, which grants the magic-user a +1 bonus to all surprise die rolls.

Normal familiars have 2-4 hit points plus 1 hit point per caster level, and an Armor Class of 7 (due to size, speed, etc.). The magic-user has an empathic link with the familiar and can issue it mental commands at a distance of up to 1 mile. Note that empathic responses from the familiar are generally fairly basic – while able to communicate simple thoughts, these are often overwhelmed by instinctual responses. Thus, a ferret familiar spying on a band of Orcs in the woods might lose its train of thought upon sighting a mouse. Certainly its communications to its master would be tinged with fear of the "big ones" it was spying on! The caster cannot see through the familiar's eyes.

If separated from the caster, the familiar loses 1 hit point each day and dies if reduced to 0 hit points. When the familiar is in physical contact with its magic-user, it gains the magic-user's saving throws against special attacks. If a special attack would normally cause damage, the familiar suffers no damage if the saving throw is successful and half damage if the saving throw is failed. If the familiar dies, the magic-user must successfully roll an immediate system shock check or die. Even if he survives this check, the magic-user loses 1 point from his Constitution when the familiar dies. The power of the conjuration is such that it can be attempted but once per year.

When the magic-user decides to find a familiar, he must load a brass brazier with charcoal. When this is burning well, he adds 1,000 gp worth of incense and herbs. The spell incantation is then begun and must be continued until the familiar comes or the casting time is finished. The GM secretly determines all results.

Note: most familiars are not inherently magical, nor does a Dispel Magic spell send them away. Deliberate mistreatment, failure to feed and care for the familiar or continuous unreasonable demands have adverse effects on the familiar's relationship with its master. Purposely arranging the death of one's own familiar incurs great disfavor from certain powerful entities, with dire results.

d100 Roll	Familiar	d100 Roll	Familiar
01-10	Black Cat	51-55	Owl
11-15	Marmoset	56-60	Yellow Frog
16-20	Ferret	61-65	Toad
21-25	Mouse	66-70	Small Snake
26-30	Crow	71-75	Weasel
31-35	Rat	76-80	Small Lizard
36-40	Hawk	81-85	Fox
41-45	Small Monkey	86-90	Rabbit
46-50	Special	91-95	Hedgehog
		96-100	Small Dog

If a special familiar is indicated use the caster's alignment to determine the type of familiar that is summoned. If the caster is a pixie fairy, an elf, or a half-elf they may either choose the familiar indicated for their alignment, or take the special one for their race.

Familiar	Caster's Alignment
Brownie	Lawful Good
Thessikrat	Lawful Neutral
Imp	Lawful Evil
Dungeon Cat	Neutral or Neutral Evil
Pseudo Dragon	Neutral Good or Chaotic Good
Quasit	Chaotic Neutral or Chaotic Evil
Elven Cat	Elf or Half-elf only
Butterfly Steed	Pixie fairy only

Consult the appropriate volume of the Hacklopedia of Beasts for more information about each familiar's specific abilities.

Fireball Barrage

(Alteration)

Level: 1
Range: 50 yds. + 10 yards/lvl.   **Components:** V, S, M
Duration: 1 round/level   **Casting Time:** 1 segment
Area of Effect: 1 or more   **Saving Throw:** None
creatures within range

This spell allows the caster to launch a volley of tiny flaming spheres at any target within the spell's range. The caster must roll to hit for each ball shot. Those that hit will do 1d3 points of damage. The caster may shoot one such ball per round for the duration of the spell. The material components of this spell are a small ball of bat guano and a handful of sulfur

Fireball, Sidewinder Factor 1

(Evocation)

Level: 1
Range: 1 mile maximum   **Components:** V, S, M
Duration: 1 rd./level   **Casting Time:** 1 segment
Area of Effect: 10-ft. radius   **Saving Throw:** 1/2

The Sidewinder Fireball is similar to the Skipping Betty Fireball except that it uses d6-4 for damage instead of d4 and the range of the Fireball is only 100 feet per level of the caster. Thus each range increment is 100 feet. The spell range is further reduced by 10 feet per degree if the air temperature is less than 32° Fahrenheit.

Potential targets also need not be in the 45 degree firing arc from the front of the caster. Additionally, the terrain need not be level as the Sidewinder Fireball can maneuver around obstructions and even hit an object hidden behind a wall, for example. The somatic gestures necessary for casting this spell include a side winding motion made with the casters arms. The material components are a tiny ball of bat guano and some sulfur.

Firewater

(Alteration)

Level: 1
Range: 10 feet   **Components:** V, S, M
Duration: 1 round   **Casting Time:** 1 segment
Area of Effect: 1 pint of water   **Saving Throw:** None
per level of caster

By means of this spell, the magic-user changes a volume of water to a volatile, flammable substance similar to alcohol and likewise lighter than water. If this substance is exposed to flame, fire or even a spark, it will burst into flames and burn with a hot fire. Each creature subject to Firewater flame will suffer 2-12 hit points of damage.

The Firewater created will evaporate and be useless within 1 round, even if it is securely contained and sealed, so it must be utilized (ignited) within 10 segments of its creation. The material components of this spell are a few grains of sugar and a raisin.

Flutter Soft

(Alteration)

Level: 1
Range: 60 feet   **Components:** V, S, M
Duration: 1 hour   **Casting Time:** 1 segment
Area of Effect: One creature   **Saving Throw:** None

When this spell is cast upon a flying creature it allows that creature to fly in complete silence. This spell will silence the flight of anything from the size of a small bird to a dragon. The material component is an owl feather.

Fog Vision

(Divination)

Level: 1
Range: Touch   **Components:** V, S, M
Duration: 1 turn/level   **Casting Time:** 1 segment
Area of Effect: one person   **Saving Throw:** None

This spell enables the caster or someone he touches the ability to see as if it were a clear sunny day even in the thickest fog. If the spell is cast within fog at night, the vision granted is still equivalent to that on a clear sunny day.

Gabal's Magical Aura

(Illusion/Phantasm)

Level: 1
Range: Touch   **Components:** V, S, M
Duration: 1 day/level   **Casting Time:** 1 round
Area of Effect: Special   **Saving Throw:** Special

By means of this spell, any one item of no more than five pounds weight per level of the spellcaster can be given an aura that is noticed by someone using magic detection. Furthermore, the caster can specify the type of magical aura that is detected (alteration, conjuration, etc.) and this effectively masks the item's actual aura, if any, unless the item's own aura is exceptionally powerful (if it is an artifact, for instance).

If the object bearing Gabal's Magical Aura has an Identify spell cast on it or is similarly examined, the examiner has a 50% chance of recognizing that the aura has been placed to mislead the unwary. Otherwise, the aura is believed and no amount of testing reveals what the true magic is. While this spell does not confer any to-hit or damage bonuses when placed upon weapons, it will allow someone who uses a weapon enchanted with the spell to hit creatures who would otherwise only be hit by magic weapons with a +1 enchantment.

A successful saving throw versus magic by the creature potentially hit by the weapon will negate this facet of the dweomer. The component for this spell is a small square of silk, which must be passed over the object that receives the aura.

Gaze Reflection

(Alteration)

Level: 1
Range: 0   **Components:** V, S
Duration: 2 rds. + 1 rd./level   **Casting Time:** 1 segment
Area of Effect: Special   **Saving Throw:** None

The gaze reflection spell creates a shimmering, mirror-like area of air before the magic-user that moves with the caster. Any gaze attack, such as that of a Basilisk, Eyes of Charming, a Vampire's gaze, the 6th level Eyebite spell, and so on, is reflected back upon the gazer if the gazer tries to make eye contact with the spellcaster (the spellcaster suffers no effects from the gaze attack). Such creatures receive a saving throw vs. their own gaze effect.

The spell does not affect vision or lighting and is not effective against creatures whose effect comes from being gazed upon (such as a Medusa). Only active gaze attacks are blocked by this spell.

Grease

(Conjuration)

Level: 1
Range: 10 yards   **Components:** V, S, M
Duration: 3 rds. + 1 rd./level   **Casting Time:** 1 segment
Area of Effect: 10 x 10 feet   **Saving Throw:** Special

A Grease spell covers a material surface with a slippery layer of a fatty, greasy nature. Any creature entering the area or caught in it when the spell is cast must save vs. spell or slip, skid and fall. Those who successfully save can reach the nearest non-greased surface by the end of the round. Those who remain in the area are allowed a saving throw each round until they escape the area.

The GM should adjust saving throws by circumstance; for example, a creature charging down an incline that is suddenly greased has little chance to avoid the effect, but its ability to exit the affected area is almost assured! The spell can also be used to create a greasy coating on an item – a rope, ladder rungs, weapon handle, etc. Material objects not in use are always affected by this spell, while creatures wielding or employing items receive a saving throw vs. spell to avoid the effect. If the initial saving throw is failed, the creature immediately drops the item. A saving throw must be made each round the creature attempts to use the greased item.

The caster can end the effect with a single utterance; otherwise, it lasts for three rounds plus one round per level. The material component of the spell is a bit of pork rind or butter.

Haarpang's Floating Cart
(Evocation)
Level: I
Range: 20 yards
Duration: 6 hours + I hour/level
Area of Effect: Special
Components: V, S, M
Casting Time: I segment
Saving Throw: None

With this spell, the caster creates the slightly concave, circular plane force jokingly referred to as Haarpang's Floating Cart (after the famous cripple who found it difficult to get around with all his scroll cases and magic tomes.). The 'cart' is actually a hovering disc approximately 3 feet in diameter which can bear 100 pounds of weight per level of the magic-user casting the spell. The 'Cart' floats approximately 3 feet above the ground at all times and remains level. It floats along horizontally within its range of 20 yards at the command of the caster, and will accompany him at a movement rate of no more than 6.

If unguided, it maintains a constant interval of 6 feet between itself and the magic-user. If the spellcaster moves beyond range (by moving faster, by such means as a Teleport spell or by trying to take the cart more than 3 feet from the surface beneath it), or if the spell duration expires, the floating cart winks out of existence, and whatever it was supporting crashes to the surface beneath it. There is, however, a 10% chance when the cart vanishes it will take anything it was supporting with it. Such items are forever lost and are usually deposited in a random Type II bagzone. The material component of the spell is a drop of mercury.

Hold Portal
(Alteration)
Level: I
Range: 20 yds./level
Duration: I rd./level
Area of Effect: 20 sq. ft./level
Component: V
Casting Time: I segment
Saving Throw: None

This spell magically bars a door, gate or valve of wood, metal or stone. The magical closure holds the portal fast, just as if it were securely closed and locked. Any extraplanar creature (Djinn, elemental, etc.) with 4 or more Hit Dice can shatter the spell and burst open the portal. A magic-user of 4 or more experience levels higher than the spellcaster can open the held portal at will. A Knock spell or a successful Dispel Magic spell can negate the Hold Portal. Held portals can be broken or physically battered down.

Hypnotism
(Enchantment/Charm)
Level: I
Range: 5 yards
Duration: I rd. + I rd./level
Area of Effect: 30 ft. cube
Components: V, S
Casting Time: I segment
Saving Throw: Negates

The gestures of the magic-user, along with his droning incantation, cause 1d6 creatures within the area to become susceptible to a suggestion – a brief and reasonable-sounding request (see the 3rd level magic-user Suggestion spell). The request must be given after the Hypnotism spell is cast. Until that time, the success of the spell is unknown. Note that the subsequent suggestion is not a spell, but simply a vocalized urging (the caster must speak a language the creature understands for this spell to work).

Creatures that successfully roll their saving throws are not under hypnotic influence. Those who are exceptionally wary or hostile save with +1 to +3 bonuses. If the spell is cast at an individual creature that meets the caster's gaze, the saving throw is made with a penalty of -2. A creature that fails its saving throw does not remember that the caster hypnotized it.

Identify
(Divination)
Level: I
Range: 0
Duration: I rd./level
Area of Effect: I item/level
Components: V, S, M
Casting Time: Special
Saving Throw: None

When an Identify spell is cast, magical items subsequently touched by the magic-user can be identified. The eight hours immediately preceding the casting of the spell must be spent purifying the items and removing influences that would corrupt and blur their magical auras. If this period is interrupted, it must be begun again.

When the spell is cast, each item must be handled in turn by the magic-user. Any consequences of this handling fall fully upon the magic-user and may end the spell, although the magic-user is allowed any applicable saving throw. The chance of learning a piece of information about an item is equal to 10% per level of the caster, to a maximum of 90%, rolled by the GM. Any roll of 96-00 indicates a false reading (91-95 reveals nothing).

Only one function of a multifunctional item is discovered per handling (i.e., a 5th level magic-user could attempt to determine the nature of five different items, five different functions of a single item, or any combination of the two). If any attempt at reading fails, the caster cannot learn any more about that item until he advances a level. Note that some items, such as special magical tomes, cannot be identified with this spell.

The item never reveals its exact attack or damage bonuses, although the fact that it has few or many bonuses can be determined. If it has charges, only a general indication of the number of charges remaining is learned: powerful (81% - 100% of the total possible charges), strong (61% - 80%), moderate (41% - 60%), weak (6% - 40%), or faint (five charges or less). The faint result takes precedence, so a fully charged ring of three wishes always appears to be only faintly charged.

After casting the spell and determining what can be learned from it, the magic-user loses 8 points of Constitution. He must rest for one hour to recover each point of Constitution. If the 8-point loss drops the spellcaster below a Constitution of 1, he falls unconscious. Consciousness is not regained until full Constitution is restored, which takes 24 hours (one point per three hours for an unconscious character).

The material components of this spell are a pearl (of at least 100 gp value) and an Owl feather steeped in wine; the infusion must be drunk prior to spellcasting. If a Luckstone is powdered and added to the infusion, the divination becomes much more potent: exact bonuses or charges can be determined and the functions of a multifunctional item can be learned from a single reading. At the GM's option, certain properties of an artifact or relic might also be learned.

Jump
(Alteration)
Level: I
Range: Touch
Duration: 1d3 rds. + I rd./level
Area of Effect: Creature touched
Components: V, S, M
Casting Time: I segment
Saving Throw: None

The individual touched when this spell is cast is empowered to leap once per round for the duration of the spell. Leaps can be up to 30 feet forward or straight upward or 10 feet backward. Horizontal leaps forward or backward have only a slight arc – about 2 feet per 10 feet of distance traveled. The Jump spell does not ensure safety in landing or grasping at the end of the leap.

The material component of this spell is a grasshopper's hind leg, to be broken by the caster when the spell is cast.

Light

(Alteration)

Level: 1

Range: 60 yards
Duration: 1 turn/level
Area of Effect: 20-ft. radius

Components: V, M
Casting Time: 1 segment
Saving Throw: Special

This spell creates a luminous glow, equal to torchlight, within a fixed radius of the spell's center. Objects in darkness beyond this sphere can be seen, at best, as vague and shadowy shapes. The spell is centered on a point selected by the caster, and he must have a line of sight and unobstructed path for the spell when it is cast.

Light can spring from air, rock, metal, wood or almost any similar substance. The effect is immobile unless it is specifically centered on a movable object or mobile creature. If this spell is cast upon a creature, the applicable magic resistance and saving throw rolls must be made. Successful resistance negates the spell, while a successful saving throw indicates that the spell is centered immediately behind the creature, rather than upon the creature itself.

Light taken into an area of magical darkness does not function, but if cast directly against magical darkness negates it (but only for the duration of the Light spell, if the darkness effect is continual). Light centered on the visual organs of a creature blinds it, reducing its attack rolls and saving throws by 4 and worsening its Armor Class by 4. The caster can end the spell at any time by uttering a single word. The material component is a firefly or a piece of phosphorescent moss.

Magic Missile

(Evocation)

Level: 1

Range: 60 yds. + 10 yds./level
Duration: Instantaneous
Area of Effect: 1-5 targets in a 10-foot square

Components: V, S
Casting Time: 1 segment
Saving Throw: None

Use of the Magic Missile spell creates up to five missiles of magical energy that dart forth from the magic-user's fingertip and unerringly strike their target. This includes enemy creatures in a melee. The target creature must be seen or otherwise detected to be hit, however, so near-total concealment, such as that offered by arrow slits, can render the spell ineffective.

Likewise, the caster must be able to identify the target. He cannot direct a Magic Missile to "Strike the commander of the legion," unless he can single out the commander from the rest of the soldiers. Specific parts of a creature cannot be singled out. Inanimate objects (locks, etc.) cannot be damaged by the spell, and any attempt to do so wastes the missiles to no effect. Against creatures, each missile inflicts 1d4+1 points of damage.

For every two extra levels of experience, the magic-user gains an additional missile – he has two at 3rd level, three at 5th level, four at 7th level, etc. If the magic-user has multiple missile capability, he can have them strike a single target creature or several creatures, as desired.

Magic Shield

(Evocation)

Level: 1

Range: 0
Duration: 5 rds./level
Area of Effect: Special

Components: V, S
Casting Time: 1 segment
Saving Throw: None

When this spell is cast, an invisible barrier comes into being in front of the magic-user. This Magic Shield totally negates Magic Missile attacks. It provides the equivalent protection of AC 2 against hand-hurled missiles (axes, darts, javelins, spears, etc.), AC 3 against small device-propelled missiles (arrows, bolts, bullets, manticore spikes, sling stones, etc.), and AC 4 against all other forms of attack. The shield also adds a +1 bonus to the magic-user's saving throws against attacks that are basically frontal. Note that these benefits apply only if the attacks originate from in front of the magic-user, where the shield can move to interpose itself.

Melt

(Alteration)

Level: 1

Range: 30 yards
Duration: 1 round/level
Area of Effect: 1 cu. yd. of ice or 2 cu. yds. of snow per level of caster

Components: V, S, M
Casting Time: 1 segment
Saving Throw: Special

When a Melt spell is cast, the magic-user effectively raises the temperature in the area of effect. This sudden increase in warmth will melt ice in 1 round, so that a 1st level magic-user can melt a cube of solid ice, 1 yard on a side, in 1 round after the spell is cast, so that the ice becomes water. Twice this volume of snow can be affected, so that the spell will melt 1 cubic yard of snow in 1l2 round, or will turn 2 cubic yards (1 yd. x 1 yd. x 2 yds.) of snow to water in 1 round.

Against such monsters as White Dragons, Winter Wolves, Yeti, Woolly Rhinos, those composed of para-elemental ice, and the like, a Melt spell will inflict 2 points of damage per level of the spell caster, or 1 point per level if the subject creature makes its saving throw versus spell. The Melt spell is generally ineffective against types of creatures other than those enumerated above. The material components for a Melt spell are a few crystals or rock salt and a pinch of soot.

Mend

(Alteration)

Level: 1

Range: 30 yards
Duration: Permanent
Area of Effect: 1 object

Components: V, S, M
Casting Time: 1 segment
Saving Throw: None

This spell repairs small breaks or tears in objects. It will weld a broken ring, chain link, medallion or slender dagger, providing but one break exists. Ceramic or wooden objects with multiple breaks can be invisibly rejoined to be as strong as new. A hole in a leather sack or wineskin is completely healed over by a Mend spell.

This spell does not, by itself, repair magical items of any type. One turn after the spell is cast, the magic of the joining fades and the effect cannot be magically dispelled. Note that items do not have to be "broken" to be affected by this spell. It would be just as effective in joining two blankets together as it would be at repairing a hole torn in one. The maximum volume of material the caster can mend is 1 cubic foot per level. The material components of this spell are two small magnets of any type (lodestone in all likelihood) or two burrs.

Merge Coin Pile

(Alteration)

Reversible

Level: 1

Range: 10 yards
Duration: Permanent
Area of Effect: 10 ft. x 10 ft. area

Components: V, S, M
Casting Time: 1 segment
Saving Throw: Special

This spell allows the caster to quickly and accurately convert a pile of coinage (all types) into a neat pile of higher denomination coins of equivalent value to the coins that the spell was cast upon. Coins that are not carried by a creature within the area of effect get no saving throw and are automatically converted.

If a creature who holds or carries coins is within the area of effect he may attempt a saving throw to enable the coins on his person to resist the effect. The new pile of coins appears in the center of the area of effect. The caster may specify which denominations he wishes the coin converted to and may even specify that the new coins are to be stamped with a certain minting as long as he has seen the type of minting desired. With the reverse of this spell, the caster may make change from higher denominations of coinage. Saving throws described above apply for coinage carried by a creature. Note that a successful attempt at making small change on a full coin pouch may cause the pouch to burst at the seems. The material component of this spell is the pile of coins to be converted.

Message

(Alteration)

Level: I

Range: 0

Duration: 5 rds./level

Area of Effect: Special

Components: V, S, M

Casting Time: I segment

Saving Throw: None

When this spell is cast, the magic-user can whisper messages and receive replies with little chance of being overheard. When the spell is cast, the magic-user secretly or openly points his finger at each creature to be included in the spell effect. Up to one creature per level can be included. When the magic-user whispers, the whispered message travels in a straight line and is audible to all of the involved creatures within 30 feet, plus 10 feet per level of the caster. The creatures who receive the message can whisper a reply that is heard by the spellcaster. Note that there must be an unobstructed path between the spellcaster and the recipients of the spell. The message must be in a language the caster speaks; this spell does not by itself confer understanding upon the recipients. This spell is most often used to conduct quick and private conferences when the caster does not wish to be overheard. The material component of the spell is a short piece of copper wire.

Minor Sphere of Perturbation

(Alteration)

Level: I

Range: 60 yards

Duration: I turn/level

Area of Effect: 20-ft. radius

Components: V, M

Casting Time: I segment

Saving Throw: Negates

This spell enables the caster to create a globe of magic wherein things just don't function quite right. All creatures within the globe suffer -1 to-hit and to damage rolls and -1 to saving throws. Their movement is reduced by 10% and those affected cannot concentrate on casting spells or using spell-like devices while within the sphere. Once those affected leave the globe, their perception and abilities return to normal within one round. The globe is translucent but can be seen by the distorted reality waves (much like heat waves) that mark its boundary. The material component is a pinch of pepper blown in the direction of the target(s).

Phantasmal Fireball

(Illusion/Phantasm)

Level: I

Range: 60 yds. + 10 yds./level

Duration: Instantaneous

Area of Effect: 20-ft. radius

Components: V, S, M

Casting Time: I segment

Saving Throw: special

This spell creates the illusion of a Fireball (see the 3rd level spell). The illusion is visual, thermal and auditory (but not olfactory) and affects all believing creatures that view it. Undead are immune. Damage dealt to those affected equals 1d6 per level of the caster. Saving throws for illusions are explained under "Illusions" in Chapter 10: Magic.

Creatures that disbelieve the illusion see it for what it is and add +4 to associates' saving throws if this knowledge can be communicated effectively. Creatures believing the illusion are subject to its effects (again, as explained in Chapter 10). The GM must rule on the effectiveness of this spell. The material component of the spell is a bit of singed fleece.

Phantasmal Force

(Illusion/Phantasm)

Level: I

Range: 60 yds. + 10 yds./level

Duration: Special

Area of Effect: 400 sq. ft. + 100 sq. ft./level

Components: V, S, M

Casting Time: I segment

Saving Throw: Special

This spell creates the illusion of any object, creature, or force, as long as it is within the boundaries of the spell's area of effect. The illusion is visual and affects all believing creatures (undead are immune) that view it. It does not create sound, smell, or temperature. Effects that depend on these senses usually fail. The illusion lasts until struck by an opponent – unless the spellcaster causes the

illusion to react appropriately – or until the magic-user ceases concentration upon the spell (due to desire, moving, or a successful attack that causes damage).

Saving throws for illusions are explained under "Illusions" in Chapter 10: Magic. Creatures that disbelieve the illusion see it for what it is and add +4 to associates' saving throws if this knowledge can be communicated effectively. Creatures believing the illusion are subject to its effects (again, as explained in Chapter 10). The illusionary effect can be moved by the caster within the limits of the area of effect. The GM has to rule on the effectiveness of this spell; detailed guidelines are outlined in Chapter 10: Magic. The material component of the spell is a bit of fleece.

Phantom Armor

(Alteration/illusion)

Level: I

Range: Touch

Duration: Special

Area of Effect: One person

Components: V S, M

Casting Time: I round

Saving Throw: None

When this spell is cast, the magic-user creates a quasi-real suit of plate mail. This semi-illusory material covers the subject and actually gives some real protection unless the opponent actively disbelieves in the Armor (saves versus spell), or else a Dispel Magic spell is cast upon it, or a Wand of Negation affects it. Until gone, or disbelieved, the Armor protects the wearer as if he were in plate mail (AC 3, and armor type 3 as well). For each level of the spell caster, the phantom armor will absorb 1 point of damage delivered by a blow which would otherwise hit armor class 3. When the phantom armor has absorbed as many points of damage as the spell caster has levels of experience, it is dispelled and vanishes. Any remaining and all additional damage accrues to the person. Additionally, Phantom Armor allows a bonus of +1 on saving throws versus all attack forms which would be similarly modified by magic armor.

The dweomer in no way affects the movement or spell-casting abilities of the wearer. It is not subject to a Rust Monster's attack (and such may enhance disbelief). The spell will not function with any other form of magical protection. The material component is a small plate of mithral (10 gp value) which disappears when the spell is cast.

Pool Gold

(Alteration)

Level: I

Range: 20 feet

Duration: I round

Area of Effect: 20-ft. radius

Components: V, S, M

Casting Time: I segment

Saving Throw: Special

The Pool Gold spell allows the caster to gather all gold in an area into one or more neatly stacked piles. It is a minor form of telekinesis that will even extract gold leaf from furniture or gold jewelry from a person. In such cases as these when there is resistance involved, the item or person gets a saving throw to resist the effect. The material component is one gold coin.

Precipitation (Alteration)

Level: I

Range: 10 ft./level

Duration: I segment/level

Area of Effect: 3 ft. dia. cylinder up to 12 ft. high

Components: V, S, M

Casting Time: 3 segments

Saving Throw: None

When this spell is cast, all water vapor in the atmosphere within the area of effect is precipitated in the form of a light rain. (Note that low level spell casters will certainly be within the area of effect of the spell.) The rain will continue for only as many segments of time as the spell caster has levels of experience. Since only some 1/100th of an inch of precipitation falls during the course of a segment, the spell will have only the following general effects:

Thin, light material will become damp in 1 segment and thoroughly wet thereafter. Twigs and heavy material such as canvas will be damp in 2 segments and wet thereafter. Flat, relatively non-porous surfaces, such as stone floors, rock, painted wood, etc., will be damp in 1 segment and filmed with water thereafter. Semi-porous surfaces and materials will become damp on the surface in 2 segments, and thereafter the damp area will progress downward/inward, until after 5 segments the surface or material will be thoroughly wet. Porous surfaces and materials will simply absorb the rain up to the limit of their capacity - which probably extends well beyond the duration of the spell.

Small flames, such as those of candles, will be extinguished by 1 segment of precipitation. Small fires will slow and become smoky for 1 round after precipitation has ceased. Large fires will not be materially affected by the spell.

Note that if the temperature is above 90° Fahrenheit., the duration of the spell will be extended to double normal except in arid regions. Also, where the temperature ranges between 34° and 31° Fahrenheit, the precipitation will fall in the form of sleet. At 30° Fahrenheit and below, the precipitation will fall as rather thick snow, and most dampness/wetness effects will be negated or postponed until the snow melts.

If the magical heat of large area spell (i.e., a Wall of Fire, Fireball, Flame Strike, etc.) is applied to Precipitation, a cloud of warm fog of double the area of the precipitation effect will be formed. If magical cold is applied to the spell or the water which remains thereafter, normal ice will be formed. The material component of the spell is a pinch of silver dust.

Protection from Evil

(Abjuration)
Reversible
Level: 1
Range: Touch   **Components:** V, S, M
Duration: 2 rds./level   **Casting Time:** 1 segment
Area of Effect: Creature touched   **Saving Throw:** None

When this spell is cast, it creates a magical barrier around the recipient at a distance of 1 foot. The barrier moves with the recipient and has three major effects. First, all attacks made by evil (or evilly enchanted) creatures against the protected creature suffer -2 penalties to attack rolls; any saving throws caused by such attacks are made with +2 bonuses. Second, any attempt to possess (as by a Magic Jar attack) or to exercise mental control over (as by a Vampire's charm ability) the protected creature is blocked by this spell.

Note that the Protection does not prevent a Vampire's charm itself, but it does prevent the exercise of mental control through the barrier. Likewise, a possessing life force is merely kept out. It would not be expelled if in place before the protection is cast. Third, the spell prevents bodily contact by creatures of an extraplanar or conjured nature (such as Aerial Servants, Elementals, Imps, Invisible Stalkers, Salamanders, Water Weirds, Xorn, and others). This causes the natural (body) weapon attacks of such creatures to fail and the creatures to recoil, if such attacks require touching the protected being. Animals or monsters summoned or conjured by spells or similar magic are likewise hedged from the character.

This protection ends if the protected character makes a melee attack against or tries to force the barrier against the blocked creature. To complete this spell, the magic-user must trace a 3-foot-diameter circle on the floor (or ground) with powdered silver. This spell can be reversed to become Protection From Good; the second and third benefits remain unchanged. The material component for the reverse is a circle of powdered iron.

Push

(Conjuration/Summoning)
Level: 1
Range: 10 ft. + 1 ft./level   **Components:** V, S, M
Duration: Instantaneous   **Casting Time:** 1 segment
Area of Effect: Special   **Saving Throw:** Negates

Upon pronouncing the syllables of this spell, the magic-user causes an invisible force to strike against whatever object he is pointing at, The force of the Push is not great, being 2 foot-pounds per level of the magic-user casting the spell, but it can move small objects up to 2 feet in a direction directly away from the caster, topple an object under the proper conditions, or cause a creature to lose its balance. An example of the latter use is causing a creature attacking to lose its balance when it is attacking, for if the creature foils its saving throw, it will not be able to attack that round. Of course, the mass of the creature attacking cannot exceed the force of the Push by more than a factor of 50, i.e. a 1st level magic-user cannot effectively push a creature weighing more than 100 pounds.

A Push spell employed against an object held by a creature will cause it to subtract the force of the spell in foot pounds (2, 4, 6, etc.) from its chance to hit or add to opponent saving throws as applicable if the creature foils to make

its saving throw against magic when the spell is cast. The material component of this spell is a small pinch of powdered brass, which must be blown from the palm prior to pointing at the object of the spell.

Read Magic

(Divination)
Level: 1
Range: 0   **Components:** V, S, M
Duration: 2 rds./level   **Casting Time:** 1 round
Area of Effect: Special   **Saving Throw:** None

By means of a Read Magic spell, the magic-user is able to read magical inscriptions on objects – books, scrolls, weapons and the like – that would otherwise be totally unintelligible. The personal books of the magic-user, and works already magically read, are intelligible. This deciphering does not normally invoke the magic contained in the writing, although it may do so in the case of a cursed scroll. Furthermore, once the spell is cast and the magic-user has read the magical inscription, he is thereafter able to read that particular writing without recourse to the use of the Read Magic spell.

The duration of the spell is two rounds per level of experience of the spellcaster; the magic-user can read one page or its equivalent per round. The magic-user must have a clear crystal or mineral prism, which is not expended, to cast the spell.

Run

(Enchantment)
Level: 1
Range: Touch   **Components:** V, S, M
Duration: 5-8 hours   **Casting Time:** 1 round
Area of Effect: Special (humans,   **Saving Throw:** None
demi-humans only)

The Run spell enables the recipient to run at full speed (twice normal speed) for from 5-8 hours without tiring. However, after so running the individual must spend a like number of hours resting, as well as drinking plenty of liquids and eating heartily. For every 2 levels of experience of the spell caster, another individual can be affected, i.e. at 4th level, 2 individuals can be touched and empowered to run; at 6th level, 3 individuals; etc.

Only humans and demi-humans in their natural forms are affected by this spell, and barbarians having the special running ability of that class are immune to the spell's effects. The material component of this spell is an elixir made from the juice of dried plums boiled in spring water and the oil of 5-8 beans of a spurge (castor) plant.

Shift Blame
(Enchantment/Charm)

Level: I

Range: Touch

Components: V, S, M

Duration: 3 rds./level

Casting Time: I segment

Area of Effect: Creature touched

Saving Throw: Negates

When the magic-user casts this spell, he creates an irrefutable suspicion in the eyes of onlookers with regard to the victim of the spell. Those viewing the spell recipient will be convinced beyond any doubt that the he is responsible for some act or crime as desired by the spell caster. The caster need only accuse the victim of a crime and others will believe him and act accordingly.

After the duration expires, those affected by the spell may reevaluate their actions and change their mind if logic dictates such a response. Otherwise, they might continue to believe the victim is guilty anyway. The material component of the spell is a bit of egg white that must be tossed on the face of the victim.

Shocking Grasp
(Alteration)

Level: I

Range: Touch

Components: V, S

Duration: Special

Casting Time: I segment

Area of Effect: Creature touched

Saving Throw: None

When the magic-user casts this spell, he develops a powerful electrical charge that gives a jolt to the creature touched. The spell remains in effect for one round per level of the caster or until it is discharged by the caster touching another creature. The shocking grasp delivers 1d8 points of damage, plus 1 point per level of the magic-user (for example, a 2nd level magic-user would discharge a shock causing 1d8+2 points of damage). While the magic-user must come close enough to his opponent to lay a hand on the opponent's body or upon an electrical conductor that touches the opponent's body, a like touch from the opponent does not discharge the spell.

Sleep
(Enchantment/Charm)

Level: I

Range: 30 yards

Components: V, S, M

Duration: 5 rds./level

Casting Time: I segment

Area of Effect: Special

Saving Throw: None

When a magic-user casts a Sleep spell, he causes a comatose slumber to come upon one or more creatures (other than undead and certain other creatures specifically excluded from the spell's effects). All creatures to be affected by the Sleep spell must be within 30 feet of each other. The number of creatures that can be affected is a function of Hit Dice or levels. The spell affects 2d4 Hit Dice of monsters. Monsters with 4+3 Hit Dice (4 Hit Dice plus 3 hit points) or more are unaffected. The center of the area of effect is determined by the spellcaster. The creatures with the least Hit Dice are affected first, and partial effects are ignored. For example, a magic-user casts Sleep at three Kobolds, two Gnolls, and an Ogre. The roll (2d4) result is 4. All the Kobolds and one Gnoll are affected (1/2 + 1/2 + 1/2 + 2 = 3 1/2 Hit Dice).

Note that the remainder is not enough to affect the last Gnoll or the Ogre. Slapping or wounding awakens affected creatures but normal noise does not. Awakening requires one entire round. Magically sleeping opponents can be attacked with substantial bonuses (see "Modifiers to the Attack Roll" in Chapter 12: Combat). The material component for this spell is a pinch of fine sand, rose petals or a live cricket.

Smell Immunity
(Illusion/Phantasm)

Level: I

Range: 60 feet

Components: V, S, M

Duration: I turn/level

Casting Time: I segment

Area of Effect: I creature

Saving Throw: Neg

This spell completely dampens a creature's sense of smell, making them immune to Stinking Cloud spells and the stench of Ghasts, Troglodytes, and the like. However the spell is not selective, and will block out all smells. Therefore poisons may be harder to detect, a hound will not be able to follow

a trail, and the recipient will take longer to figure out that he just stepped in a cow chip. The material component is a small pair of nose plugs.

Spider Climb
(Alteration)

Level: I

Range: Touch

Components: V, S, M

Duration: 3 rds. + I rd./level

Casting Time: I segment

Area of Effect: Creature touched

Saving Throw: Negates

A Spider Climb spell enables the recipient to climb and travel upon vertical surfaces as well as a Giant Spider, or even hang upside down from ceilings. Unwilling victims must be touched and are then allowed a saving throw vs. spell to negate the effect. The affected creature must have bare hands and feet in order to climb in this manner, at a movement rate of 6 (3 if at all encumbered).

During the course of the spell, the recipient cannot handle objects that weigh less than a dagger (one pound), for such objects stick to his hands and feet. Thus, a magic-user will find it virtually impossible to cast spells if under a Spider Climb spell. Sufficient force can pull the recipient free; the GM can assign a saving throw based on circumstances, the strength of the force, and so on. For example, a creature with a Strength of 12 might pull the subject free if the subject fails a saving throw vs. paralyzation (a moderately difficult saving throw). The caster can end the spell effect with a word. The material components of this spell are a drop of bitumen and a live spider, both of which must be eaten by the spell recipient.

Spook
(Illusion/Phantasm)

Level: I

Range: 30 feet

Components: V, S

Duration: Special

Casting Time: I segment

Area of Effect: I creature

Saving Throw: Negates

A Spook spell enables the magic-user to play upon natural fears to cause the target creature to perceive the spellcaster as someone or something inimical. Without actually knowing what this is, the magic-user merely advances threateningly upon the creature. If the creature does not make a successful saving throw vs. spell, it turns and flees at maximum speed as far from the magic-user as possible, though items carried are not dropped.

The creature has a saving throw penalty of -1 for every two experience levels of the caster, to a maximum of -6 at 12th level. Note that a natural (unmodified) roll of 20 automatically succeeds, regardless of saving throw penalties. Although the caster does not actually pursue the fleeing creature, a phantasm from its own mind does. Each round after the initial casting, the creature receives another saving throw, without penalty, until it successfully saves and the spell is broken. In any event, the spell functions only against creatures with Intelligences of 2 or more, and undead are not affected at all.

Taunt
(Enchantment)

Level: I

Range: 60 yards

Components: V, S, M

Duration: I round

Casting Time: I segment

Area of Effect: 30-ft. radius

Saving Throw: Negates

A Taunt spell enables the caster to jape and jeer effectively at a single type of creature with an Intelligence of 2 or greater. The caster need not speak the language of the creatures. His words and sounds have real meaning for the subject creature or creatures, challenging, insulting and generally irritating and angering the listeners. Those failing to save vs. spell rush forth in fury to do battle with the spellcaster.

All affected creatures attack the spellcaster in melee if physically capable of doing so, seeking to use body or hand-held weapons rather than missile weapons or spells. Separation of the caster from the victim by an impenetrable or uncrossable boundary (a Wall of Fire, a deep chasm, a formation of set pikemen) causes the spell to break. If the caster Taunts a mixed group, he must choose the type of creature to be affected. Creatures commanded by a strong leader (i.e., with a Charisma bonus, with higher Hit Dice, etc.) might gain a saving throw bonus of +1 to +4, at the GM's discretion. If used in conjunction with a Throw Voice spell, the creatures may attack the apparent source, depending upon their Intelligence, a leader's presence, and so on. The material component is a slug, which is hurled at the creatures to be taunted.

Throw Voice

(Illusion/Phantasm)

Level: 1

Range: 10 yds./level, max. 90 yds.	**Components:** V, M
Duration: 4 rds. + 1 rd./level	**Casting Time:** 1 segment
Area of Effect: 1 creature or object	**Saving Throw:** Negates

This spell enables the magic-user to make his voice, someone else's voice or a similar sound seem to issue from someplace else, such as from another creature, a statue, from behind a door, down a passage, etc. The spellcaster can speak in any language that he knows, or make any sound that he can normally make. With respect to such voices and sounds, anyone rolling a successful saving throw vs. spell with a -2 penalty detects the ruse. If cast in conjunction with other illusions, the GM may rule greater penalties or disallow an independent saving throw against this spell in consideration of its contribution to the total effect of the combined illusion. The material component of this spell is a parchment rolled up into a small cone.

Unseen Servant

(Conjuration/Summoning)

Level: 1

Range: 0	**Components:** V, S, M
Duration: 4 hr. + 1 hour/level	**Casting Time:** 1 segment
Area of Effect: 30-ft. radius	**Saving Throw:** None

The Unseen Servant is an invisible, mindless and shapeless force, used to step and fetch, open unstuck doors, and hold chairs, as well as to clean and mend. It is not strong, but unfailingly obeys the command of the magic-user. It can perform only one activity at a time and can move only lightweight items, carrying a maximum of 20 pounds or pushing/pulling 40 pounds across a smooth surface. It can open only normal doors, drawers, lids, etc.

The Unseen Servant cannot fight, nor can it be killed, as it is a force rather than a creature. It can be magically dispelled, or eliminated after receiving 6 points of damage from area-effect spells, breath weapons or similar attacks. If the caster attempts to send it beyond the allowed radius, the spell ends immediately. The material components of the spell are a piece of string and a bit of wood.

Wall of Fog

(Evocation)

Level: 1

Range: 30 yards	**Components:** V, S, M
Duration: 2d4 rds. + 1 rd./level	**Casting Time:** 1 segment
Area of Effect: 20 ft. cube + 10 ft. cube/level	**Saving Throw:** None

By casting this spell, the magic-user creates a billowing wall of misty vapors in any area within the spell range. The Wall of Fog obscures all sight, normal and infravision, beyond 2 feet. The caster may create less vapor if he wishes. The wall must be a roughly cubic or rectangular mass, at least 10 feet across in its smallest dimension. The misty vapors persist for three or more rounds. Their duration can be halved by a moderate wind, and they can be blown away by a strong wind. The material component is a pinch of split dried peas.

Wizard Mark

(Alteration)

Level: 1

Range: Touch	**Components:** V, S, M
Duration: Permanent	**Casting Time:** 1 segment
Area of Effect: Up to 1 sq. ft.	**Saving Throw:** None

When this spell is cast, the magic-user is able to inscribe, visibly or invisibly, his personal rune or mark, as well as up to six additional characters of smaller size. A Wizard Mark spell enables the caster to etch the rune upon stone, metal or any softer substance without harm to the material upon which the mark is placed. If an invisible mark is made, a Detect Magic spell will cause it to glow and be visible (though not necessarily understandable). Detect Invisibility, True Seeing, a Gem of Seeing, or a Robe of Eyes will likewise expose an invisible Wizard Mark. A Read Magic spell will reveal the maker's words, if any.

The mark cannot be dispelled, but it can be removed by the caster or by an Erase spell. If cast on a living being, normal wear gradually causes the mark to fade. The material components for this spell are a pinch of diamond dust (about 100 gp worth) and a pigment or pigments for the coloration of the mark. If the mark is to be invisible, the pigments are still used, but the caster uses a stylus of some sort rather than his finger.

Wrygal's Delicious Deception

(Illusion/Phantasm)

Level: 1

Range: 100 feet	**Components:** V, S, M
Duration: 1 turn	**Casting Time:** 1 segment
Area of Effect: 60 yard radius	**Saving Throw:** None

When Wrygal's Delicious Deception is cast it creates an aroma of delicious food being cooked. The odor emanates from the center of the area of effect, and all creatures within that area can smell it, regardless of closed doors or other obstacles. In effect this increases the chance of encountering wandering monsters to 50%, rolled each round. At the GM's option other local creatures can be attracted if they are in the area, i.e. guard dogs would be distracted, an Ogre in the next room might come out to see what's cooking, and so on. Obviously the spell does not work on creatures who do not eat, are mindless, or undead. The material component is a wing from a Camp Moth.

Write

(Evocation)

Level: 1

Range: 0	**Components:** V, S, M
Duration: 1 hour/level	**Casting Time:** 1 round
Area of Effect: One magical spell inscription	**Saving Throw:** Special

By means of this spell a magic-user might be able to inscribe a spell he cannot understand at the time (due to level or lack of sufficient Intelligence) into the tome or other compilation he employs to maintain a library of spells. The magic-user must make a saving throw versus magic to attempt the writing of any spell, +2 if it is only up to 1 level greater than he currently uses, 0 at 2 levels higher, and -1 per level from 3 levels higher onwards. If this saving throw fails, the magic-user is subject to 1d4 points of damage for every level of the spell he was attempting to transcribe into his magic book, and furthermore be knocked unconscious for a like number of turns. This damage, if not fatal, can only be healed at the rate of 1-4 points per day, as it is damage to psyche and body.

Furthermore, a spell will take 1 hour per level to transcribe in this fashion, and during this period, the magic-user is in a trance state and can always be surprised by any foe. In addition to the writing surface upon which the spell is to be transcribed, the spell caster needs a fine ink composed of rare substances (minimum cost 200 gp per bottle, if available at all without manufacture by the magic-user).

Yudder's Whistle of Hell's Gate

(Evocation)

Level: 1

Range: 5 yard radius/level	**Components:** V, S, M
Duration: 1 round/level	**Casting Time:** 1 segment
Area of Effect: 5 yard radius/lvl.	**Saving Throw:** Special/Neg

When this spell is used the caster creates a high pitched, shrill whistling that only dogs and creatures with similarly enhanced hearing can hear. The whistle renders normal dogs helpless while it lasts, and actually makes them run away in fear if they fail a saving throw. Dire animals, magical dogs and downright weird dog-like creatures may make a save to avoid the effects completely, otherwise they too are helpless or flee the area if they fail a second save. Note that the spell is not selective – all eligible victims in the area are affected! The material component is a small dog whistle.

Second Level Spells

Alter Self

(Alteration)

Level: 2

Range: 0	**Components:** V, S
Duration: 3d4 rds. + 2 rds./level	**Casting Time:** 2 segments
Area of Effect: The caster	**Saving Throw:** None

When this spell is cast, the magic-user can alter his appearance and form – including clothing and equipment – to appear taller or shorter; thin, fat or in between; human, humanoid or any other generally man-shaped bipedal creature. The caster's body can undergo a limited physical alteration and his size can be changed up to 50%. If the form selected has wings, the magic-user can actually fly, but at only one-third the speed of a true creature of that type, and with a loss of two maneuverability classes (to a minimum of E).

If the form has gills, the caster can breathe under water as long as the spell lasts. However, the caster does not gain any multiple attack routines or additional damage allowed to an assumed form. The caster's attack rolls, Armor Class and saving throws do not change. The spell does not confer special abilities, attack forms or defenses. Once the new form is chosen, it remains for the duration of the spell. The caster can change back into his own form at will; this ends the spell immediately. A caster who is slain automatically returns to his normal form.

Bind

(Enchantment)

Level: 2

Range: 30 yards	**Components:** V, S, M
Duration: 1 rd./level	**Casting Time:** 2 segments
Area of Effect: 50 ft. + 5 ft./level	**Saving Throw:** None

When this spell is employed, the magic-user can command any nonliving ropelike object, including string, yarn, cord, line, rope or even a cable. The spell affects 50 feet of normal rope (with a 1 inch diameter), plus 5 feet per caster level. This length is reduced by 50% for every additional inch of thickness and increased by 50% for each half-inch less. The possible commands are coil (form a neat, coiled stack), coil & knot, loop, loop & knot, tie & knot and the reverses of all of the above (uncoil, etc.).

One command can be given each round. The rope can only enwrap a creature or an object within 1 foot of it – it does not snake outward – so it must be thrown or hurled near the intended target. Note that the rope itself, and any knots tied in it, are not magical. A typical rope might be AC 6 and take 4 points of slashing damage before breaking. The rope does not inflict damage of any type, but it can be used as a trip line or to entangle a single opponent who fails a saving throw vs. spell. The material component is a ropelike object mentioned above.

Blindness

(Illusion/Phantasm)

Level: 2

Range: 30 yds. + 10 yds./level	**Component:** V
Duration: Special	**Casting Time:** 2 segments
Area of Effect: 1 creature	**Saving Throw:** Negates

The Blindness spell causes the victim to become blind, able to see only a grayness before its eyes. Various cure spells will not remove this effect, and only a Dispel Magic or the spellcaster can do away with the blindness if the creature fails its initial saving throw vs. spell. A blinded creature suffers a -4 penalty to its attack rolls, and its opponents gain a +4 bonus to their attack rolls.

Blur

(Illusion/Phantasm)

Level: 2

Range: 0	**Components:** V, S
Duration: 3 rds. + 1 rd./level	**Casting Time:** 2 segments
Area of Effect: The caster	**Saving Throw:** None

When a Blur spell is cast, the magic-user causes the outline of his form to become blurred, shifting and wavering. This distortion causes all missile and melee combat attacks against the caster to be made with -4 penalties on the first attempt and -2 penalties on all successive attacks. It also grants the magic-user a +1 bonus to his saving throw for any direct magical attack. A Detect Invisibility spell will not counter this effect, but the 5th level cleric spell True Seeing and similar magic will.

Chain of Fire

(Evocation)

Level: 2

Range: 30 yards	**Components:** V, S, M
Duration: Special	**Casting Time:** 2 segments
Area of Effect: Special	**Saving Throw:** None

The Chain of Fire spell brings forth a blazing curtain of magical fire in the shape of a linked chain. The chain can be shaped into a straight line up to one 10-foot square per level of the spellcaster, or a ring with a radius of up to 5 feet + 5 feet per two levels of experience of the magic-user. In either form, the Chain of Fire is 6 feet high.

The Chain of Fire must be cast so that it is vertical with respect to the caster. Both sides of the chain, send forth waves of heat, inflicting 1d4 points of damage upon creatures within 10 feet and 1d2 points of damage upon those within 20 feet. In addition, the wall inflicts 1d6 points of damage, plus 1 point of damage per level of the spellcaster, upon any creature passing through it.

Note that attempting to catch a moving creature with a newly-created Chain of Fire is difficult; a successful saving throw enables the creature to avoid the chain, while its rate and direction of movement determine which side of the created chain it is on. The Chain of Fire lasts as long as the magic-user concentrates on maintaining it, or one round per level of experience of the magic-user, in the event he does not wish to concentrate upon it. The material component of the spell is a chain woven out of straw or a similar combustible.

Cheetah Speed

(Alteration)

Level: 2

Range: Touch	**Components:** V, S, M
Duration: 3 rds. + 1 rd./level	**Casting Time:** 2 segments
Area of Effect: 1 creature/level	**Saving Throw:** None

When this spell is cast, each affected creature may triple its normal movement rate. A creature under the effect of Cheetah Speed gains a -2 initiative advantage but may not increase his number of attacks per round. Similarly, spellcasting and spell effects are not sped up. The number of creatures that can be affected is equal to the caster's experience level. Note that this spell negates the effects of a Slow spell. Additionally, this spell ages the recipient by one year, because of sped-up metabolic processes. This spell is not cumulative with itself or with other similar magic. Its material component is a bit of cheetah fur.

Cloud of Pummeling Fists

(Evocation)
Level: 2
Range: 1 yd./level
Duration: 2 rds.
Area of Effect: 10-ft. radius
Components: V, S, M
Casting Time: 2 segments
Saving Throw: None

This spell creates a mass of disembodied fists in the area of effect. The caster may use a punching attack from each fist on any creature within the area of effect. The cloud does not move. The number of fists within the cloud is determined by rolling 5d4. Each fist may only attack once per round. Each fist must roll to-hit as if the caster himself were attacking. A successful hit delivers 1d4 points of damage to the victim. However, only 1/4 of the total amount delivered is retained as "real" damage. The balance is regained with in an hour.

Continual Light

(Alteration)
Reversible
Level: 2
Range: 60 yards
Duration: Permanent
Area of Effect: 60-ft. radius
Components: V, S
Casting Time: 2 segments
Saving Throw: Special

This spell is similar to a Light spell, except that it is as bright as full daylight and lasts until negated by magical darkness or by a Dispel Magic spell. Creatures who suffer penalties in bright light suffer them in this spell's area of effect. As with the Light spell, it can be cast into the air, onto an object or at a creature. When cast at a creature, the target gets a saving throw vs. spell; success indicates that the spell affects the space about 1 foot behind the creature instead.

Note that this spell can also blind a creature if it is successfully cast upon the creature's visual organs, reducing its attack rolls, saving throws, and Armor Class by 4. If the spell is cast on a small object that is then placed in a light-proof covering, the spell's effects are blocked until the covering is removed. A Continual Light brought into an area of magical darkness (or vice versa) is

temporarily negated so that the otherwise prevailing light conditions exist in the overlapping areas of effect. A direct casting of Continual Light against a similar or weaker magical darkness cancels both. This spell eventually consumes the material it is cast upon, but the process takes far longer than the time in the typical campaign. Extremely hard and expensive materials can last hundreds or even thousands of years.

Darkness, 15' Radius

(Alteration)
Level: 2
Range: 10 yds./level
Duration: 1 turn + 1 rd./level
Area of Effect: 15-ft. radius
Components: V, S, M
Casting Time: 2 segments
Saving Throw: None

This spell causes total, impenetrable darkness in the area of effect. Infravision is useless. Neither normal nor magical light works unless a Light or Continual Light spell is used. In the former event, the Darkness spell is negated by the Light spell, and vice versa. The material components of this spell are a bit of bat fur and either a drop of pitch or a piece of coal.

Deafness

(Illusion/Phantasm)
Level: 2
Range: 60 yards
Duration: Special
Area of Effect: 1 creature
Components: V, S, M
Casting Time: 2 segments
Saving Throw: Negates

The deafness spell causes the recipient to become totally deaf and unable to hear any sounds. The victim is allowed a saving throw vs. spell. An affected creature has a -1 penalty to its surprise rolls unless its other senses are unusually keen. Deafened spellcasters have a 20% chance to miscast any spell with a verbal component. This deafness can be done away with only by means of a Dispel Magic spell or by the spellcaster. The material component of this spell is beeswax.

Deeppockets

(Alteration, Enchantment)

Level: 2

Range: Touch | **Components:** V, S, M
Duration: 12 hrs. + 1 hr./level | **Casting Time:** 1 turn
Area of Effect: 1 garment | **Saving Throw:** None

This spell enables the magic-user to specially prepare a garment so as to hold far more than it normally could. A finely sewn gown or robe of high-quality material (at least 50 gp value) is fashioned so as to contain numerous hand-sized pockets. One dozen is the minimum number.

The Deeppockets spell then enables these pockets to hold a total of 100 pounds (5 cubic feet in volume) as if it were only 10 pounds of weight. Furthermore, there are no discernible bulges where the special pockets are. At the time of casting, the caster can instead choose to have 10 pockets each holding 10 pounds (1/2 cubic foot volume each). If the robe or like garment is sewn with 100 or more pockets (200 gp minimum cost), 100 pockets can be created to contain one pound of weight and 1/6 cubic foot volume each.

Each special pocket is actually an extradimensional holding space. If the spell duration expires while there is material within the enchanted pockets, or if a successful Dispel Magic is cast upon the enchanted garment, all the material suddenly appears around the wearer and immediately falls to the ground. The caster can also cause all the pockets to empty with a single command. In addition to the garment, which is reusable, the material components of this spell are a tiny golden needle and a strip of fine cloth given a half-twist and fastened at the ends.

Detect Evil

(Divination)

Reversible

Level: 2

Range: 0 | **Components:** V, S
Duration: 5 rds./level | **Casting Time:** 2 segments
Area of Effect: 10 x 180 ft. | **Saving Throw:** None

This spell discovers emanations of evil (or of good in the case of the reverse spell) from any creature, object, or area. Character alignment is not revealed under most circumstances: characters who are strongly aligned, do not stray from their faith and who are at least 9th level might radiate good or evil if they are intent upon appropriate actions. Powerful monsters, such as Ki-rin, send forth emanations of evil or good, even if polymorphed. Aligned undead radiate evil, for it is this power and negative force that enables them to continue existing. An evilly cursed object or unholy water radiates evil, but a hidden trap or an unintelligent viper does not. The degree of evil (faint, moderate, strong, overwhelming) can be noted.

Note that clerics have a more powerful version of this spell. The spell has a path of detection 10 feet wide and 60 yards long in the direction in which the magic-user is facing. The magic-user must concentrate – stop, have quiet, and intently seek to detect the aura – for at least one round to receive a reading.

Detect Invisibility

(Divination)

Level: 2

Range: 0 | **Components:** V, S, M
Duration: 5 rds./level | **Casting Time:** 2 segments
Area of Effect: 10 yds./level | **Saving Throw:** None

When the magic-user casts a Detect Invisibility spell, he is able to see clearly any objects or beings that are invisible, as well as any that are astral, ethereal or out of phase. In addition, it enables the magic-user to detect hidden or concealed creatures (for example, thieves in shadows, halflings in underbrush, and so on). It does not reveal the method of concealment or invisibility, except in the case of astral travelers (where the silver cord can be seen). It does not reveal illusions or enable the caster to see through physical objects. Detection is a path 10 feet wide along the magic-user's line of sight to the range limit. The material components of this spell are a pinch of talc and a small sprinkling of powdered silver.

ESP

(Divination)

Level: 2

Range: 0 | **Components:** V, S, M
Duration: 1 rd./level | **Casting Time:** 2 segments
Area of Effect: 5 yds./level | **Saving Throw:** None
(90 yds. maximum)

When an ESP spell is used, the caster is able to detect the surface thoughts of any creatures in range – except for those of undead and creatures without minds (as we know them). The ESP is stopped by 2 feet of rock, 2 inches of any metal other than lead, or a thin sheet of lead foil. The magic-user employing the spell is able to probe the surface thoughts of one creature per round, getting simple instinctual thoughts from lower order creatures. Probes can continue on the same creature from round to round or can move on to other creatures.

The caster can use the spell to help determine if a creature lurks behind a door, for example, but the ESP does not always reveal what sort of creature it is. If used as part of a program of interrogation, an intelligent and wary subject receives an initial saving throw. If successful, the creature successfully resists and the spell reveals no additional information. If the saving throw is failed, the caster may learn additional information, according to the GM's ruling. The creature's Wisdom adjustment applies, as may additional bonuses up to +4, based on the sensitivity of the information sought. The material component of this spell is a copper piece.

Fascinate

(Illusion/Phantasm)

Level: 2

Range: 30 yards | **Components:** V, S
Duration: Special | **Casting Time:** 2 segments
Area of Effect: One creature | **Saving Throw:** Negates

By means of this spell the caster attempts to captivate the subject creature's attention and gain its love, friendship and/or obedience. The spell creates an illusion around the spell caster so that he becomes, in the eyes of the subject, a trusted and/or desired companion. Unless a saving throw versus spell is successful, the subject will follow the magic-user wherever he goes, if possible without undue risk to life and safety.

If the caster is able to converse with the fascinated creature, the subject will obey requests from the spell caster as long as a roll of 3d6 per request does not exceed the caster's Comeliness. Requests which are obviously against the better interests of the creature add +1 to the dice roll, and the more hazardous and unreasonable of these requests will add from +2 to +6 to the dice roll.

The spell is shattered whenever Comeliness is exceeded, and the subject will certainly be filled with rage and hate. Creatures of normal sort with animal intelligence will remain fascinated for only a short period of time (1-4 days), but if the caster has been careful to treat the subject well, attend to its needs and feed it, there is a 2% chance per point of his Comeliness that the subject will willingly choose to befriend and follow him. Otherwise, the creature will attack (if it was not cared for) or leave (if it was cared for) when the spell wears off. Non-intelligent creatures are not subject to a Fascinate spell (cf. Charm Person).

Fireball, Skipping Betty

(Evocation)

Level: 2

Range: 1 mile | **Components:** V, S, M
Duration: 1 rd./level | **Casting Time:** 2 segments
Area of Effect: 10-ft. radius | **Saving Throw:** 1/2

The Skipping Betty Fireball can be used as an effective long range weapon by a magic-user. This fireball leaves the caster's hand traveling at a nearly constant rate of 100 yards per round. Each round a target is in range, the caster may attempt to hit the target with the fireball by rolling a successful to hit roll.

If the roll fails or no desired target is in range, the caster can allow the Skipping Betty Fireball to "skip" off the ground (or water) and continue to fly into its next range increment. An attempt to hit a new target in the next range increment may be made each round the Skipping Betty travels. Once the fireball has successfully hit a target it detonates with a 10 foot blast radius as a normal fireball causing 1d4 points of damage/caster level to all within the area of effect who fail to make a saving throw.

Potential targets must be within a 45 degree firing arc from the front of the caster. Each time a Skipping Betty skips it is subject to a –1 to hit penalty on subsequent targeting attempts and a –1 damage penalty (cumulative) to those affected by it when it finally does detonate. If the caster cannot hit a target (or obstruction) before the spell duration expires the Skipping Betty fails to explode and does no damage.

Note that the caster must have a reasonably unobstructed and level path to effectively hit a target in a range increments beyond the first. He must also be able to see his target otherwise he will suffer a –4 to hit penalty. Uneven terrain with obstructions will cause additional to hit penalties at the discretion of the GM. If a Skipping Betty misses its target by more than 5 from the required number to hit in this case, it detonates after hitting one of the obstructions. The material components are a tiny ball of bat guano, a pinch of sulphur and a piece of gum arabic.

Fireball, Sidewinder Factor 2

(Evocation)
Level: 2
Range: 1 mile maximum   **Components:** V, S, M
Duration: 1 rd./level   **Casting Time:** 2 segments
Area of Effect: 10-ft. radius   **Saving Throw:** 1/2

The Sidewinder Fireball is similar to the Skipping Betty Fireball except that it uses d6-3 for damage instead of d4 and the range of the fireball is only 100 feet per level of the caster. Thus each range increment is 100 feet. The spell range is further reduced by 10 feet per degree if the air temperature is less than 32° Fahrenheit. Potential targets also need not be in the 45 degree firing arc from the front of the caster. Additionally, the terrain need not be level as the Sidewinder Fireball can maneuver around obstructions and even hit an object hidden behind a wall, for example. The somatic gestures necessary for casting this spell include a side winding motion made with the casters arms. The material components for this spell are bat guano, gum arabic and sulphur.

Fire Telekinesis

(Alteration)
Level: 2
Range: 30 yards   **Components:** V, S
Duration: 2 rounds per level   **Casting Time:** 2 segments
Area of Effect: One 5 ft. x5 ft. fire   **Saving Throw:** Special

By means of this spell, the magic-user is able to move fire by concentrating on moving it mentally. The magic-user must be within range of an existing fire to manipulate it. This can be used in two ways:

1) The flames themselves can be "picked up" and moved through the air at a movement rate of 5 feet for the duration of the spell. The previous fuel source will remain in place and will be extinguished (although still hot) and any new fuel source that the flames come in contact with may be ignited if it fails to save versus fire. Living creatures hit by the slowly moving flames will suffer 1d6 points of damage per hit. The caster must successfully make a to-hit roll against the target's Armor Class to inflict the damage and may make one such attack per round.

2) As an alternative to moving the entire set of flames from the original fuel source, the magic-user may manipulate the flames to lash out at objects within 10 feet of the original fire. For a torch-sized fire only one such flame may be manipulated per round. Creatures hit by the flame that lashes out are similarly subject to 1d6 points of damage. For a campfire-sized blaze, the magic-user may lash out with up to 1 flame per level against any creatures within 10 feet of the fire. Each flame that successfully hits a target does 1d6 points of damage. Candle-sized flames may not be used to lash out for damage but may be moved to ignite another larger fuel source, which can then be further manipulated as it grows.

Flaming Sphere

(Evocation)

Level: 2

Range: 10 yards **Components:** V, S, M
Duration: 1 rd./level **Casting Time:** 2 segments
Area of Effect: 3-ft. radius **Saving Throw:** Negates

A Flaming Sphere spell creates a burning globe of fire within 10 yards of the caster. This sphere rolls in whichever direction the magic-user points, at a rate of 30 feet per round. It rolls over barriers less than 4 feet tall, such as furniture, low walls, etc. Flammable substances are set afire by contact with the sphere. Creatures in contact with the globe must successfully save vs. spell or suffer 2d4 points of fire damage. Those within 5 feet of the sphere's surface must also save or suffer 1d4 points of heat damage. A successful saving throw means no damage is suffered.

The GM may adjust the saving throws if there is little or no room to dodge the sphere. The sphere moves as long as the spellcaster actively directs it; otherwise, it merely stays at rest and burns. It can be extinguished by the same means as any normal fire of its size. The surface of the sphere has a spongy, yielding consistency and so does not cause damage except by its flame. It cannot push unwilling creatures aside or batter down large obstacles. The material components are a bit of tallow, a pinch of sulphur, and a dusting of powdered iron.

Fog Cloud

(Alteration)

Level: 2

Range: 10 yards **Components:** V, S
Duration: 4 rds. + 1 rd./level **Casting Time:** 2 segments
Area of Effect: Special **Saving Throw:** None

The Fog Cloud spell can be cast in one of two ways, at the caster's option: as a large, stationary bank of normal fog, or as a harmless fog that resembles the 5th level magic-user spell Cloudkill. As a fog bank, this spell creates a fog of any size and shape up to a maximum 20-foot cube per caster level. The fog obscures all sight, normal and infravision, beyond 2 feet. As a Cloudkill-like fog, this is a billowing mass of ghastly, yellowish-green vapors, measuring 40 feet x 20 feet x 20 feet. This moves away from the caster at 10 feet per round.

The vapors are heavier than air and sink to the lowest level, even pouring down sinkholes and den openings. Very thick vegetation breaks up the fog after it has moved 20 feet into the vegetation. The only effect of either version is to obscure vision. A strong breeze will disperse either effect in one round, while a moderate breeze will reduce the spell duration by 50%. The spell cannot be cast under water.

Fool's Gold

(Alteration, Illusion)

Level: 2

Range: 10 yards **Components:** V, S, M
Duration: 1 hr./level **Casting Time:** 1 round
Area of Effect: 10 cu. in./level **Saving Throw:** Special

Copper coins can temporarily be changed to gold pieces, or brass items turned to solid gold, for the spell duration by means of this magic. The area of effect is 10 cubic inches per level – i.e., a 1-inch x 1-inch x 10-inch volume or equivalent, equal to about 150 gold coins. Any creature viewing the "gold" is entitled to a saving throw vs. spell, which can be modified by the creature's Wisdom; for every level of the magic-user, the creature must subtract 1 from his dice roll. Thus, it is unlikely that Fools' Gold will be detected if created by a high level caster.

If the "gold" is struck hard by an object of cold-wrought iron, there is a slight chance it will revert to its natural state, depending on the material component used to create the "gold." If a 25-gp citrine is powdered and sprinkled over the metal as this spell is cast, the chance that cold iron will return it to its true nature is 30%; if a 50 gp amber stone is powdered and used, the chance drops to 25%; if a 250 gp topaz is powdered and used, the chance drops to 10%; and if a 500 gp oriental (corundum) topaz is powdered and used, there is only a 1% chance that the cold iron will reveal that it is Fools' Gold.

Forget

(Enchantment/Charm)

Level: 2

Range: 30 yards **Components:** V, S
Duration: Permanent **Casting Time:** 2 segments
Area of Effect: 1-4 creatures **Saving Throw:** Negates
in a 20-ft. cube

By means of this spell, the spellcaster causes creatures within the area of effect to forget the events of the previous round (the one minute of time previous to the utterance of the spell). For every three levels of experience of the spellcaster, another minute of past time is forgotten. This does not negate Charm, Suggestion, Geas, Quest or similar spells, but it is possible that the being who placed such magic upon the recipient could be forgotten.

From one to four creatures can be affected, at the discretion of the caster. If only one is to be affected, the recipient saves vs. spell with a -2 penalty; if two, they save with -1 penalties; if three or four are to be affected, they save normally. All saving throws are adjusted by Wisdom. A cleric's Heal or Restoration spell, if specially cast for this purpose, will restore the lost memories, as will a Limited Wish or Wish, but no other means will do so.

Gandle's Feeble Trap

(Illusion/Phantasm)

Level: 2

Range: Touch **Components:** V, S, M
Duration: Permanent **Casting Time:** 3 rounds
Area of Effect: Object touched **Saving Throw:** None

This false trap is designed to fool a thief or other character attempting to pilfer the spellcaster's goods. The magic-user places the spell upon any small mechanism or device, such as a lock, hinge, hasp, screw-on cap, ratchet, etc. Any character able to detect traps, or who uses any spell or device enabling trap detection, is 100% certain a real trap exists. Of course, the spell is illusory and nothing happens if the trap is sprung; its primary purpose is to frighten away thieves or make them waste precious time. The material component of the spell is a piece of iron pyrite touched to the object to be trapped while the object is sprinkled with a special dust requiring 200 gp to prepare. If another Feeble Trap is within 50 feet when the spell is cast, the casting fails.

Glitterdust

(Conjuration/Summoning)

Level: 2

Range: 10 yds./level **Components:** V, S, M
Duration: Special **Casting Time:** 2 segments
Area of Effect: 20 ft. cube **Saving Throw:** Special

This spell creates a cloud of glittering golden particles within the area of effect. Those in the area must roll a successful saving throw vs. spell or be blinded (-4 penalties to attack rolls, saving throws, and Armor Class) for 1d4+1 rounds. In addition, all within the area are covered by the dust, which cannot be removed and continues to sparkle until it fades. Note that this reveals invisible creatures. The dust fades in 1d4 rounds plus one round per caster level. Thus, Glitterdust cast by a 3rd level magic-user lasts for four to seven rounds. The material component is ground mica.

Heat Seeking Fist of Thunder

(Evocation)

Level: 2

Range: 100 feet **Components:** V, S, M
Duration: Instant **Casting Time:** 2 segments
Area of Effect: 20 ft. radius circle **Saving Throw:** 1/2

This spell creates a disembodied hand that rushes toward a heat source and explodes with magical energy when it hits. The spell requires a heat source at least as large as a torch. When the spell is successfully cast all those within 20 feet of the target heat source take 1d4 damage per level of the caster, or half that with a successful saving throw. The damage done is sonic in nature and sounds like an extremely loud thunderclap. The target heat source is obliterated when the spell is cast.

Hypnotic Pattern

(Illusion/Phantasm)

Level: 2

Range: 30 yards   **Components:** S, M

Duration: Special   **Casting Time:** 2 segments

Area of Effect: 30-ft. cube   **Saving Throw:** Negates

When this spell is cast, the magic-user creates a weaving, twisting pattern of subtle colors in the air. This pattern causes any creature looking at it to become fascinated and stand gazing at it as long as the spellcaster maintains the display, plus two rounds thereafter. The spell can captivate a maximum of 24 levels, or Hit Dice, of creatures (for example, 24 creatures with 1 Hit Die each, 12 with 2 Hit Dice, etc.). All creatures affected must be within the area of effect, and each is entitled to a saving throw vs. spell. A damage-inflicting attack on an affected creature frees it from the spell immediately. The magic-user need not utter a sound, but he must gesture appropriately while holding a glowing stick of incense or a crystal rod filled with phosphorescent material.

Improved Phantasmal Force

(Illusion/Phantasm)

Level: 2

Range: 60 yds. + 10 yds./level   **Components:** V, S, M

Duration: Special   **Casting Time:** 2 segments

Area of Effect: 200 sq. ft. + 50 sq. ft./level   **Saving Throw:** Special

Like the 1st level Phantasmal Force spell, this spell creates the illusion of any object, creature, or force, as long as it is within the spell's area of effect. The spellcaster can maintain the illusion with minimal concentration; thus, he can move at half normal speed (but not cast other spells).

Some minor sounds are included in the effects of the spell, but not understandable speech. Also, the Improved Phantasmal Force spell continues for two rounds after the magic-user ceases to concentrate upon it. The material component is a bit of fleece.

Invisibility

(Illusion/Phantasm)

Level: 2

Range: Touch   **Components:** V, S, M

Duration: Special   **Casting Time:** 2 segments

Area of Effect: Creature touched   **Saving Throw:** None

This spell causes the creature touched to vanish from sight and be undetectable by normal vision or even infravision. Of course, the invisible creature is not magically silenced, and certain other conditions can render the creature detectable. Even allies cannot see the invisible creature or his gear, unless these allies can normally see invisible things or employ magic to do so.

Items dropped or put down by the invisible creature become visible; items picked up disappear if tucked into the clothing or pouches worn by the creature. Note, however, that light never becomes invisible, although a source of light can become so (thus, the effect is that of a light with no visible source). The spell remains in effect until it is magically broken or dispelled, until the magic-user or recipient cancels it, until the recipient attacks any creature, or until 24 hours have passed. Thus, the invisible being can open doors, talk, eat, climb stairs, etc., but if he attacks, he immediately becomes visible, although the Invisibility enables him to attack first.

Note that the cleric spells Bless, Chant and Prayer are not attacks for this purpose. All highly Intelligent (Intelligence 13 or more) creatures with 10 or more Hit Dice or levels of experience have a chance to detect invisible objects (they roll saving throws vs. spell; success means they noticed the invisible object). The material components of the Invisibility spell are an eyelash and a bit of gum arabic, the former encased in the latter.

Irritation

(Alteration)

Level: 2

Range: 10 yds./level   **Components:** V, S, M

Duration: Special   **Casting Time:** 2 segments

Area of Effect: 1-4 creatures in a 15-ft. radius   **Saving Throw:** Negates

An Irritation spell affects the epidermis of the subject creatures. Creatures with very thick or insensitive skins (such as buffalo, elephants, scaled creatures, etc.) are basically unaffected. There are two versions of the spell, either of which can be cast from the standard preparation:

Itching. When cast, this causes each subject to feel an instant itching sensation on some portion of its body. If one round is not immediately spent scratching the irritated area, the creature is so affected that the next three rounds are spent squirming and twisting, effectively worsening its Armor Class by 4 and its attack rolls by 2 during this time. Spell preparations are ruined in the first round this spell is in effect, but not in the following three rounds. Doing nothing but scratching the itch for a full round prevents the rest of the effect. If cast at one creature, the saving throw has a -3 penalty; if cast at two creatures, the saving throw has a -1 penalty; and if cast at three or four creatures, the saving throw is normal.

Rash. When a rash is cast, the subject notices nothing for 1d4 rounds, but thereafter its entire skin breaks out in red welts that itch. The rash persists until either a Cure Disease or Dispel Magic spell is cast upon it. It lowers Charisma by 1 point per day for each of four days (i.e., maximum Charisma loss is 4 points). After one week, Dexterity is lowered by 1 point also. Symptoms vanish immediately upon the removal of the rash, and all statistics return to normal. This can be cast at one creature only, with a saving throw penalty of -2. The material component for this spell is a leaf from poison ivy, oak or sumac.

Knock

(Alteration)

Reversible

Level: 2

Range: 60 yards   **Components:** V

Duration: Special   **Casting Time:** 1 segment

Area of Effect: 10 sq. ft./level   **Saving Throw:** None

The Knock spell opens stuck, barred, locked, held or magically locked doors. It opens secret doors, as well as locked or trick-opening boxes or chests. It also loosens welds, shackles or chains. If used to open a mage locked door, the spell does not remove the former spell, but simply suspends its functioning for one turn. In all other cases, it permanently opens locks or welds — although the former could be closed and locked again later. It does not raise barred gates or similar impediments (such as a portcullis), nor does it affect ropes, vines and the like.

Note that the effect is limited by the area; a 3rd level magic-user can cast a Knock spell on a door of 30 square feet or less (for example, a standard 4-ft. x 7-ft. door). Each spell can undo up to two means of preventing egress through a portal. Thus if a door is locked, barred and held, or triple locked, opening it requires two Knock spells. In all cases, the location of the door or item must be known.

The reverse spell, Lock, closes and locks a door or similar closure, provided there is a physical mechanism. It does not create a weld, but it locks physically operated locking mechanisms, set bars and so on, up to two functions. It cannot affect a portcullis.

Know Alignment

(Divination)
Reversible
Level: 2
Range: 10 yards   **Components:** V, S
Duration: 1 rd./level   **Casting Time:** 1 round
Area of Effect: 1 creature or   **Saving Throw:** Negates
        object per 2 rds.

A Know Alignment spell enables the magic-user to read the aura of a creature or an aligned object (unaligned objects reveal nothing). The caster must remain stationary and concentrate on the subject for two full rounds. A creature is allowed a saving throw vs. spell and, if successful, the caster learns nothing about that particular creature from the casting. If the caster concentrates on a creature or object for only one round, he can learn only its alignment with respect to law and chaos. Certain magical devices negate the Know Alignment spell. The reverse, Undetectable Alignment, conceals the alignment of an object or creature for 24 hours – even from a Know Alignment spell.

Levitate

(Alteration)
Level: 2
Range: 20 yds./level   **Components:** V, S, M
Duration: 1 turn/level   **Casting Time:** 2 segments
Area of Effect: 1 creature or   **Saving Throw:** Negates
        object

When a Levitate spell is cast, the magic-user can place it upon his person, an object or a single creature, subject to a maximum weight limit of 100 pounds per level of experience (for example, a 3rd level magic-user can levitate a maximum of 300 pounds). If the spell is cast upon the magic-user, he can move vertically up or down at a movement rate of 2 per round. If cast upon an object or another creature, the magic-user can levitate it at the same speed, according to his command.

This spell does not empower horizontal movement, but the recipient could push along the face of a cliff, for example, to move laterally. The spellcaster can cancel the spell as desired. If the subject of the spell is unwilling, or the object is in the possession of a creature, a saving throw vs. spell is allowed to determine if the Levitate spell affects it. Once cast, the spell requires no concentration, except when changing height. A levitating creature attempting to use a missile weapon finds himself increasingly unstable; the first attack has an attack roll penalty of -1, the second -2, the third -3, etc., up to a maximum of -5. A full round spent stabilizing allows the creature to begin again at -1. Lack of leverage makes it impossible to cock a medium or heavy crossbow. The material component of this spell is either a small leather loop or a piece of golden wire bent into a cup shape with a long shank on one end.

Locate Object

(Divination)
Reversible
Level: 2
Range: 0   **Components:** V, S, M
Duration: 1 rd./level   **Casting Time:** 2 segments
Area of Effect: 20 yds./level   **Saving Throw:** None

This spell aids in locating a known or familiar object. The magic-user casts the spell, slowly turns, and senses when he is facing in the direction of the object to be located, provided the object is within range (i.e., 60 yards for 3rd level magic-users, 80 yards for 4th, 100 yards for 5th, etc.). The spell can locate such objects as apparel, jewelry, furniture, tools, weapons or even a ladder or stairway.

Note that attempting to find a specific item, such as jewelry or a crown, requires an accurate mental image; if the image is not close enough to the actual, the spell does not work. Desired but unique objects cannot be located by this spell unless they are known by the caster. The spell is blocked by lead. Creatures cannot be found by this spell. The material component is a forked twig. The reversal, Obscure Object, hides an object from location by spell, Crystal Ball, or similar means for eight hours. Creatures cannot be affected by this spell. The material component is a chameleon skin.

Magic Missile of Skewering

(Evocation)
Level: 2
Range: 60 ft.+10 ft. per level   **Components:** V, S
Duration: Instant   **Casting Time:** 2 segments
Area of Effect: One creature   **Saving Throw:** None
        plus skewering

A Magic Missile of Skewering is a specialized version of the first level spell Magic Missile. The caster creates a glowing arrow of magical energy that is directed towards a target within the spell's range. The missile always hits and causes 1d4+1 damage, plus an additional 1d4+1 for every three full levels of the casting magic-user. So the missile inflicts 2d4+2 damage at 3rd level, 3d4+3 damage at 6th level, and so on. When the missile strikes it "skewers" its target, inflicting its damage before it continues along its path, until it strikes a solid object, runs out of range or runs out of targets.

This works as follows: When the missile strikes its first target it emerges out of the opposite side of the target and seeks an additional target within a 90 degree angle. If there is a target within the spell's overall range it is struck. Then the process repeats itself until the spell runs out of range or energy, or the missile cannot continue due to the presence of barriers in its path. The first creature struck takes full damage, but every creature struck afterwards takes a progressive 1d4+1 less damage than the creature hit before it. Therefore if a ninth level magic-user were to cast this spell the first target would take 4d4+4 hp, the second 3d3+3 hp, the third 2d4+2 hp and the last 1D4+1 damage. The Magic Missile of Skewering is treated in all ways as a Magic Missile with regard to spell immunities. If it strikes a creature immune to Magic Missiles, the spell ends immediately.

Magic Mouth

(Alteration)

Level: 2

Range: 10 yards	**Components:** V, S, M
Duration: Special	**Casting Time:** 2 segments
Area of Effect: 1 object	**Saving Throw:** None

When this spell is cast, the magic-user imbues the chosen object with an enchanted mouth that suddenly appears and speaks its message when a specified event occurs. The message, which must be of 25 words or less, can be in any language known by the spellcaster, and can be delivered over a period of one turn. The mouth cannot speak magical spells or use command words. It does, however, move to the words articulated – if it is placed upon a statue, the mouth of the statue would actually move and appear to speak. Of course, the Magic Mouth can be placed upon a tree, rock, door or any other object, excluding intelligent members of the animal or vegetable kingdoms.

The spell functions when specific conditions are fulfilled, according to the command of the spellcaster. Some examples are to speak "to the first creature that touches you," or "to the first creature that passes within 30 feet." Commands can be as general or as detailed as desired, although only visual and audible triggers can be used, such as the following: "Speak only when a venerable female human carrying a sack of groat clusters sits crosslegged within 1 foot." Such visual triggers can react to a character using the disguise ability.

Command range is 5 yards per level of the magic-user, so a 6th level magic-user can command the Magic Mouth to speak at a maximum encounter range of 30 yards ("Speak when a winged creature comes within 30 yards"). The spell lasts until the speak command can be fulfilled; thus, the spell duration is variable. A Magic Mouth cannot distinguish invisible creatures, alignments, level, Hit Dice, or class, except by external garb. If desired, the effect can be keyed to a specific noise or spoken word. The material component of this spell is a small bit of honeycomb.

Mirror Image

(Illusion/Phantasm)

Level: 2

Range: 0	**Components:** V, S
Duration: 3 rds./level	**Casting Time:** 2 segments
Area of Effect: 6-ft. radius	**Saving Throw:** None

When a Mirror Image spell is invoked, the spellcaster causes from two to eight exact duplicates of himself to come into being around him. These images do exactly what the magic-user does. Since the spell causes a blurring and slight distortion when it is cast, it is impossible for opponents to be certain which are the illusions and which is the actual magic-user.

When an image is struck by a melee or missile attack, magical or otherwise, it disappears, but any other existing images remain intact until struck. The images seem to shift from round to round, so that if the actual magic-user is struck during one round, he cannot be picked out from among his images the next. To determine the number of images that appear, roll 1d4 and add 1 for every three levels of experience the magic-user has achieved, to a maximum of eight images. At the end of the spell duration, all surviving images wink out.

Misdirection

(Illusion/Phantasm)

Level: 2

Range: 30 yards	**Components:** V, S
Duration: 8 hours	**Casting Time:** 2 segments
Area of Effect: 1 creature/object	**Saving Throw:** Negates

By means of this spell, the magic-user misdirects the information from a detection spell (Detect Charm, Detect Evil, Detect Invisibility, Detect Lie, Detect Magic, Detect Snares and Pits, etc.). While the detection spell functions, it indicates the wrong area, creature or the opposite of the truth with respect to Detect Evil or Detect Lie. The magic-user directs the spell effect upon the object of the detection spell. If the caster of the detection spell fails his saving throw vs. spell, the Misdirection takes place. Note that this spell does not affect other types of divination (Know Alignment, Augury, ESP, Clairvoyance, etc.).

Munz's Bolt of Acid

(Conjuration)

Level: 2

Range: 180 yards	**Components:** V, S, M
Duration: Special	**Casting Time:** 2 segments
Area of Effect: 1 target	**Saving Throw:** Special

By means of this spell, the magic-user creates a magical bolt that speeds to its target as if fired from the bow of a fighter of the same level as the magic-user. No modifiers for range, non-proficiency, or specialization are used. The bolt has no attack or damage bonus, but it inflicts 2d4 points of acid damage (with saving throws for items on the target); there is no splash damage. For every three levels that the caster has achieved, the acid, unless somehow neutralized, lasts for another round, inflicting another 2d4 points of damage each round. So at 3rd-5th level, the acid lasts two rounds; at 6th-8th level, the acid lasts for three rounds, etc. The material components of the spell are a dart, powdered rhubarb leaf and an adder's stomach.

Murgain's Muster Strength

(Enchantment/Charm)

Level: 2

Range: Touch	**Components:** V, S
Duration: Permanent	**Casting Time:** 2 segments
Area of Effect: 1 creature	**Saving Throw:** None (neg.)

When this spell is cast upon a creature it fills him with strength and determination to defy the odds. Any fear and exhaustion effects that the recipient is suffering from are immediately nullified, and he regains 1d4 hit points immediately. These effects are "permanent" until the subject fails another fear check, becomes tired again or is once-again wounded.

The spell is especially potent when it is used to dramatically save the day or to face impossible odds (GM's discretion). Under these circumstances the recipient becomes totally immune to fear effects and morale checks for one round per caster level, and regains 2d4 hit points instead of the normal 1d4. Note that this requires real drama, such as saving everyone from certain impending doom, not the drama of being so tired and wounded that you're not sure if you will be able to loot the rest of the dungeon!

Premonition

(Divination)

Level: 2

Range: Touch	**Components:** V ,S, M
Duration: 2 rounds/level	**Casting Time:** 2 segments
Area of Effect: One creature	**Saving Throw:** None (neg.)

The recipient of this spell begins to get a "bad feeling" whenever something bad is about to happen to them. While the spell lasts, the recipient is immune to being surprised, cannot be the victim of a backstab and should get a moment's warning if they approach something dangerous. Note that the spell does not give specific information, so while it would make a character feel uneasy about a trapped chest it would not tell him there was a gas trap inside. A character would get a bad feeling about a mountain pass, but wouldn't immediately know that there was a band of Ogres waiting to ambush him. The spell component is a bit of clover.

Preserve (Abjuration)

Level: 2

Range: Touch	**Components:** V, S, M
Duration: Permanent	**Casting Time:** 2 rounds
Area of Effect: 1/2 cu. ft. per level of caster	**Saving Throw:** None

A Preserve spell enables the caster to retain some item fresh and whole until some later time when it is needed in a spell. Of course, the dweomer is ineffective in retaining the potency of material such as mistletoe, holly berries and similar stuffs which must be gathered periodically. It is otherwise effectual. The sort of material which can be treated by a Preserve spell depends upon the level of the caster: Hard, relatively dry material: 2nd-4th level, Soft, relatively wet material: 5th-7th level, Semi-liquid and liquid materials: 8th level & up. A container is necessary only in cases where a relatively high degree of moisture is concerned. The material components of the spell are a pinch of dust, a bit of resin (or amber) and a drop of brandy.

Proadus' Uncontrollable Fit of Laughter
(Enchantment/Charm)

Level: 2
Range: 60 yards
Duration: 1 rd./level
Area of Effect: 1 or more creatures in a 30-ft. cube
Components: V, S, M
Casting Time: 2 segments
Saving Throw: Negates

The victim of this spell perceives everything as hilariously funny. The effect is not immediate, and the creature feels only a slight tingling on the round the spell is cast. On the round immediately following, the victim begins smiling, then giggling, chuckling, tittering, snickering, guffawing and finally collapsing into gales of uncontrollable, hideous laughter. Although this magical mirth lasts only a single round, the affected creature must spend the next round regaining its feet, and it loses 2 points from its Strength (or -2 to attack and damage rolls) for all remaining rounds of the spell.

The saving throw vs. spell is modified by the Intelligence of the creature. Creatures with Intelligences of 4 or less (semi-intelligent) are totally unaffected. Those with Intelligences of 5-7 (low) save with -6 penalties. Those with Intelligences of 8-12 (average to very) save with -4 penalties. Those with Intelligences of 13-14 (high) save with -2 penalties. Those with Intelligences of 15 or greater (exceptional) have unmodified saving throws. The caster can affect one creature for every three levels attained – for example, one at 3rd level, two at 6th level, three at 9th level, etc. All affected beings must be within 30 feet of each other. The material components are a small feather and minute tarts. The tarts are hurled at the subjects, while the feather is waved in one hand.

Protection From Cantrips
(Abjuration)

Level: 2
Range: Touch
Duration: 5 hrs. + 1 hr./level
Area of Effect: Creature or object touched
Components: V, S
Casting Time: 1 round
Saving Throw: None

By casting this spell, the magic-user receives immunity to the effects of cantrips cast by other magic-users, apprentices, or creatures that use the cantrip spell. The spell protects the caster, or one item or person that he touches (such as a spell book or a drawer containing spell components). Any cantrip cast against the protected person or item dissipates with an audible popping sound. This spell is often used by a magic-user who has mischievous apprentices, or one who wishes apprentices to clean or shine an area using elbow grease rather than magic. Any unwilling target of this spell must be touched (via an attack roll) and is allowed a saving throw vs. spell to escape the effect.

Pyrotechnics
(Alteration)

Level: 2
Range: 120 yards
Duration: Special
Area of Effect: 1 fire source
Components: V, S, M
Casting Time: 2 segments
Saving Throw: None

A Pyrotechnics spell draws on an existing fire source to produce one of two effects, at the option of the caster. First, it can produce a flashing and fiery burst of glowing, colored aerial fireworks that lasts one round. This effect temporarily blinds those creatures in, under, or within 120 feet of the area and that have an unobstructed line of sight to the burst. Creatures viewing this are blinded for 1d4+1 rounds unless they successfully save vs. spell. The fireworks fill a volume 10 times greater than that of the original fire source.

This spell can also cause a thick, writhing stream of smoke to arise from the source and form a choking cloud that lasts for one round per experience level of the caster. This covers a roughly spherical volume from the ground or floor up (or conforming to the shape of a confined area) that totally obscures vision beyond 2 feet. The smoke fills a volume 100 times that of the fire source. All within the cloud must roll successful saving throws vs. spell or suffer -2 penalties to all combat rolls and Armor Class. The spell uses one fire source within

a 20-foot cube, which is immediately extinguished. An extremely large fire used as a source might be only partially extinguished. Magical fires are not extinguished, although a fire-based creature (such as a Fire Elemental) used as a source suffers 1 point of damage per caster level. The material components are the exisiting fire source and a pinch of sulphur.

Ray of Enfeeblement
(Enchantment/Charm)

Level: 2
Range: 10 yds. + 5 yds./level
Duration: 1 rd./level
Area of Effect: 1 creature
Components: V, S
Casting Time: 2 segments
Saving Throw: Negates

By means of a Ray of Enfeeblement, a magic-user weakens an opponent, reducing its Strength and thereby the attacks that rely upon it. Humans, demi-humans and humanoids of man-size or less are reduced to an effective Strength of 5, losing all Strength bonuses and suffering an attack roll penalty of -2 and a -1 penalty to damage. Other creatures suffer a penalty of -2 on attack rolls. Furthermore, they have a -1 penalty for each die of damage they inflict (but no damage roll can inflict less than 1 point per die of damage.) Your GM will determine any other effects appropriate to the affected creature. If the target creature makes its saving throw, the spell has no effect. This spell does not affect combat bonuses due to magical items, and those conferring increased Strength function normally.

Reveal Secret Portal
(Divination)

Level: 2
Range: 0
Duration: 5 rds./level
Area of Effect: 10 yds./level
Components: V, S, M
Casting Time: 2 segments
Saving Throw: None

When the magic-user casts a Reveal Secret Portal spell, he is able to clearly see any concealed or secret doors, portals or compartments in his line of sight. It does not reveal illusions, enable the caster to see through physical objects or reveal hidden or invisible creatures. Detection functions in a path 10 feet wide along the magic-user's line of sight, to the range limit. The material component of this spell is a magnifying glass.

Rope Trick
(Alteration)

Level: 2
Range: Touch
Duration: 2 turns/level
Area of Effect: Special
Components: V, S, M
Casting Time: 2 segments
Saving Throw: None

When this spell is cast upon a piece of rope from 5 to 30 feet long, one end of the rope rises into the air until the whole rope hangs perpendicular, as if affixed at the upper end. The upper end is, in fact, fastened to an extradimensional space. The spellcaster and up to seven others can climb up the rope and disappear into this place of safety where no creature can find them.

The rope can be taken into the extradimensional space if fewer than eight persons have climbed it; otherwise, it simply stays hanging in the air (extremely strong creatures might be able to remove it, at the GM's option). Spells cannot be cast across the interdimensional interface, nor can area effects cross it. Those in the extradimensional space can see out of it as if there were a 3-foot x 5-foot window centered on the rope. The persons in the extradimensional space must climb down prior to the end of the spell, or they are dropped from the height at which they entered the extradimensional space.

The rope can be climbed by only one person at a time. Note that the rope trick spell enables climbers to reach a normal place if they do not climb all the way to the extradimensional space. Also note that creating or taking extradimensional spaces into an existing extradimensional space is hazardous. The material components of this spell are powdered corn extract and a twisted loop of parchment.

Scare

(Enchantment/Charm)

Level: 2
Range: 30 yds. + 10 yds./level   **Components:** V, S, M
Duration: 1d4 rds. + 1 rd./level   **Casting Time:** 2 segments
Area of Effect: 15-foot radius   **Saving Throw:** Special

This spell causes creatures with fewer than 6 Hit Dice or levels of experience to fall into fits of trembling and shaking. The frightened creatures have a -2 reaction adjustment and may drop items held if encumbered. If cornered, they fight, but with -1 penalties to attack rolls, damage rolls and saving throws. Only elves, half-elves, and clerics are allowed saving throws against this spell. Note that this spell has no effect on the undead or on upper or lower planar creatures of any sort. The material component used for this spell is a bit of bone from an undead Skeleton, Zombie, Ghoul, Ghast or Mummy.

Shatter

(Alteration)

Level: 2
Range: 30 yds. + 10 yds./level   **Components:** V, S, M
Duration: Instantaneous   **Casting Time:** 2 segments
Area of Effect: 3-ft. radius   **Saving Throw:** Negates

The Shatter spell is a sound-based attack that affects non-magical objects of crystal, glass, ceramic or porcelain, such as vials, bottles, flasks, jugs, windows, mirrors, etc. All such objects within a 3-foot radius of the center of the spell effect are smashed into dozens of pieces by the spell. Objects weighing more than one pound per level of the caster are not affected, but all other objects of the appropriate composition must save vs. crushing blow or be shattered. Alternatively, the spell can be focused against a single item of up to 10 pounds per caster level. Crystalline creatures usually suffer 1d6 points of damage per caster level to a maximum of 6d6, with a saving throw vs. spell for half damage. The material component of this spell is a chip of mica.

Spectral Hand

(Necromancy)

Level: 2
Range: 30 yds. + 5 yds./level   **Components:** V, S
Duration: 2 rds./level   **Casting Time:** 2 segments
Area of Effect: 1 opponent   **Saving Throw:** None

This spell causes a ghostly, glowing hand, shaped from the caster's life force to materialize within the spell range and move as the caster desires. Any touch attack spell of 4th level or less that is subsequently cast by the magic-user can be delivered by the spectral hand. The spell gives the caster a +2 bonus to his attack roll. The caster cannot perform any other actions when attacking with the hand; the hand returns to the caster and hovers if the caster takes other actions.

The hand lasts the full spell duration unless dismissed by the caster, and it is possible to use more than one touch attack with it. The hand receives flank and rear attack bonuses if the caster is in a position to do so. The hand is vulnerable to magical attack but has an Armor Class of -2. Any damage to the hand ends the spell and inflicts 1d4 points of damage to the caster.

Stinking Cloud

(Evocation)

Level: 2
Range: 30 yards   **Components:** V, S, M
Duration: 1 rd./level   **Casting Time:** 2 segments
Area of Effect: 20-ft. cube   **Saving Throw:** Special

When a Stinking Cloud is cast, the magic-user creates a billowing mass of nauseous vapors up to 30 yards away from his position. Any creature caught within the cloud must roll a successful saving throw vs. poison or be reeling and unable to attack because of nausea for 1d4+1 rounds after leaving the cloud. Those who make successful saving throws can leave the cloud without suffering any ill effects, although those remaining in the cloud must continue to save each round. These poisonous effects can be slowed or neutralized by appropriate magic. The cloud duration is halved in a moderate breeze (8-18 m.p.h.) and is dispersed in one round by a stronger breeze. The material component of the spell is a rotten egg or several skunk cabbage leaves.

Strength

(Alteration)

Level: 2
Range: Touch   **Components:** V, S, M
Duration: 1 hr./level   **Casting Time:** 1 turn
Area of Effect: Person touched   **Saving Throw:** None

Application of this spell increases the Strength of the character by a number of points. Benefits of the Strength spell last for up to 1 hour per level of the spellcaster. The amount of added Strength depends upon the spell recipient's group and is subject to all restrictions on Strength due to race and class. Multi-class characters use the best die from among their classes.

Class Strength Gain	
Cleric	1d6 points
Thief	1d6 points
Fighter	1d8 points
Magic-User	1d4 points

The spell is not cumulative with other magic that adds to Strength. Beings without Strength scores (Kobolds, Lizard Men, etc.) receive a +1 to attack and damage rolls. The material component of this spell is a few hairs, or a pinch of dung, from a particularly strong animal – ape, bear, ox, etc.

Summon Swarm

(Conjuration/Summoning)

Level: 2
Range: 60 yards   **Components:** V, S, M
Duration: Special   **Casting Time:** 2 segments
Area of Effect: 10-ft. cube   **Saving Throw:** Negates

The swarm of small animals (roll on following table to determine type, or the GM can assign an appropriate creature) drawn by the Summon Swarm spell will viciously attack all creatures in the area chosen by the caster. Creatures actively defending against the swarm to the exclusion of other activities suffer 1 point of damage for each round spent in the swarm. Those taking other actions, including leaving the swarm, receive damage equal to 1d4 points + 1 point per three levels of the caster each round. Note that spellcasting within the swarm is impossible.

Dice Roll	Swarm Type
01-40	Rats
41-70	Bats
71-80	Spiders
81-90	Centipedes/beetles
91-100	Flying insects

The swarm cannot be fought effectively with weapons, but fire and area effects can force it to disperse by inflicting damage. The swarm disperses when it has taken a total of 2 hit points per caster level from these attacks. A Protection From Evil spell keeps the swarm at bay, and certain area-effect spells, such as Gust of Wind and Stinking Cloud, disperse a swarm immediately, if appropriate to the swarm summoned (for example, only flyers are affected by a Gust of Wind). The caster must remain stationary and undisturbed to control the swarm; if his concentration lapses or is broken, the swarm disperses in two rounds. The swarm is stationary once conjured. The material component is a square of red cloth.

Tattoo of Shame

(Alteration)

Level: 2
Range: Touch   **Components:** V, S, M
Duration: Permanent   **Casting Time:** 1 round
Area of Effect: Up to 1 sq. ft.   **Saving Throw:** Negates

When this spell is cast, the magic-user is able to inscribe symbols upon the flesh of another living creature. Although no physical harm is done by the runes, the recipient will automatically lose 50% of his Honor. Furthermore, the victim of the spell will only be able to gain Honor at a rate 50% that of someone who does not bear such marks.

If the victim tries to cover the marks with clothing, a Detect Magic spell will still cause it to glow and be visible regardless of the amount of clothing worn. True Seeing, a Gem of Seeing, or a Robe of Eyes will likewise expose an individual with a concealed Tattoo of Shame. The mark can be dispelled with a successful Dispel Magic or by an Erase spell. The caster can remove the Tattoo of Shame as desired (with a touch). The material components for this spell are a pinch of dung and a pigment or pigments for the coloration of the mark. The caster must also use a stylus of some sort to inscribe the marks.

Telepathic Mute
(Alteration)
Level: 2
Range: 10 ft./level
Components: V, S, M
Duration: 2 rounds/level
Casting Time: 2 segments
Area of Effect: One creature
Saving Throw: None

The victim of a Telepathic Mute cannot use telepathy, ESP or mind reading of any form, cannot receive mental commands or messages from others, and cannot mentally control any of its minions. The material component is a lead slug or coin.

Total Control
(Enchantment/Charm)
Level: 2
Range: 10 yards/level
Components: V
Duration: 2 rounds/level
Casting Time: 2 segments
Area of Effect: One creature
Saving Throw: None (neg.)

A creature under the effects of this spell becomes totally immune to Fear and never needs to make a morale check. The spell also makes non-elves immune to Ghoul paralysis, and any creature immune to the paralyzing touch of Ghasts.

Web
(Evocation)
Level: 2
Range: 5 yds./level
Components: V, S, M
Duration: 2 turns/level
Casting Time: 2 segments
Area of Effect: 8,000 cubic ft.
Saving Throw: Neg. or 1/2

A Web spell creates a many-layered mass of strong, sticky strands similar to spider webs but far larger and tougher. These masses must be anchored to two or more solid and diametrically opposed points – floor and ceiling, opposite walls, etc. – or the web collapses upon itself and disappears. The Web spell covers a maximum area of eight 10-foot x 10-foot x 10-foot cubes and the webs must be at least 10 feet thick, so a mass 40 feet high, 20 feet wide, and 10 feet deep may be cast. Creatures caught within webs, or simply touching them, become stuck among the gluey fibers. Anyone in the area when the spell is cast must roll a saving throw vs. spell with a -2 penalty. If the saving throw is successful, two things may have occurred. If the creature has room to escape the area, then it is assumed to have jumped free. If there is no room to escape, then the webs are only half strength.

Creatures with less than 13 Strength (7 if the webs are half strength) are stuck until freed by another or until the spell wears off. Missile fire is generally ineffective against creatures trapped in webs. Creatures with Strengths between 13 and 17 can break through 1 foot of webs per round. Creatures with 18 or greater Strength can break through 2 feet of webs per round. If the webs are at half strength, these rates are doubled. Great mass equates to great strength in this case, and creatures of large mass hardly notice webs. Strong and huge creatures can break through 10 feet of webs per round. Furthermore, the strands of a Web spell are flammable. A magical flaming sword can slash them away as easily as a hand brushes away cobwebs. Any fire – torch, flaming oil, flaming sword, etc. – can set them alight and burn them away in a single round. All creatures within flaming webs suffer 2d4 points of damage from the flames, but those free of the strands are not harmed. The material component of this spell is a bit of spider web.

Whip
(Evocation)
Level: 2
Range: 1 foot
Components: V, S, M
Duration: 1 round/level
Casting Time: 2 segments
Area of Effect: Special
Saving Throw: Special

By means of this spell, the magic-user creates a material, whip-like substance up to 1 foot distant from his person. The spell caster can then wield this whip by moving his hand as if it held an actual one, for the magical one will respond to movements made by its evoker. The lash can be used so as to make both a whistling crack and an actual strike each turn. The sound alone is sufficient to keep normal animals at bay unless they save versus spell. Any animal actually struck (as indicated by a normal to-hit die roll) must save versus spell at -1 to -4 or else slink away and not return for at least an hour. Note that the whip does not do actual damage to the creature struck. Creatures with an Intelligence above 3 are not affected, nor are giant-sized animals above bear-size, nor are monsters.

The whip can also be used in melee combat, a successful to-hit roll indicating that the lash has struck and wrapped around an opponent's weapon. If that weapon is an edged one, the whip must make a saving throw versus crushing blow (13 or better); if the weapon is non-edged, the whip must save versus normal blow (6 or better). Success on this saving throw indicates that the whip has torn the weapon from the opponent's hand - unless the opponent succeeds on a saving throw versus spell.

An affected weapon will be cast to the ground, and the opponent must take 1 round to recover it. The magic bonus of a target weapon applies as a penalty to the whip's saving throw versus crushing blow or normal blow, and the magic resistance of an intended target opponent must fail for a to-hit roll to be possible in the first place. The material component of the spell is a small bit of silk braided so as to form a miniature whip.

Whispering Wind
(Alteration, Phantasm)
Level: 2
Range: 1 mi./level
Components: V, S
Duration: Special
Casting Time: 2 segments
Area of Effect: 2-ft. radius
Saving Throw: None

By means of this spell, the magic-user is able to either send a message or cause some desired sound effect. The whispering wind can travel as many miles above ground as the spellcaster has levels of experience, to a specific location within range that is familiar to the magic-user. The whispering wind is as gentle and unnoticed as a zephyr until it reaches the location. It then delivers its whisper-quiet message or other sound. Note that the message is delivered regardless of whether anyone is present to hear it. The wind then dissipates.

The magic-user can prepare the spell to bear a message of up to 25 words, cause the spell to deliver other sounds for one round, or merely have the whispering wind seem to be a faint stirring of the air that has a susurrant sound. He can likewise cause the whispering wind to move as slowly as a mile per hour or as quickly as a mile per turn. When the spell reaches its objective, it swirls and remains until the message is delivered. As with the Magic Mouth spell, no spells may be cast via the whispering wind.

White Hot Metal
(Alteration)
Level: 2
Range: 10 feet
Components: V, M
Duration: 1 round/level
Casting Time: 2 segments
Area of Effect: Up to one pound of metal
Saving Throw: None (neg.)

This spell makes up to one pound of metal white hot almost instantly. The heat is sufficient to melt softer metals such as gold, silver or lead and harder metals are ruined if they are subject to any stress (such as combat). Magical metals, mithral items and adamantite alloys may make a saving throw vs.

crushing blow to avoid being warped and ruined. If the spell is cast upon a creature's equipment it is entitled to a saving throw to avoid the spell, otherwise contact with White Hot Metal causes 2d6 damage each round. The material component is the metal being heated.

Wizard Lock

(Alteration)

Level: 2

Range: Touch

Duration: Permanent

Area of Effect: 30 sq. ft./level

Components: V, S

Casting Time: 2 segments

Saving Throw: None

A Wizard Lock spell cast upon a door, chest or portal magically locks it. The caster can freely pass his own lock without affecting it; otherwise, the magically locked door or object can be opened only by breaking in, by a successful Dispel Magic or Knock spell, or by a magic-user four or more levels higher than the one casting the spell. Note that the last two methods do not remove the Wizard Lock; they only negate it for a brief duration – about one turn. Creatures from other planes cannot burst a Wizard Lock as they can a held portal (see the Hold Portal spell).

Third Level Spells

Bash Face

(Evocation)

Level: 3

Range: 10 ft. + 1ft./level

Duration: Instantaneous

Area of Effect: One target

Components: V, S, M

Casting Time: 3 segments

Saving Throw: None

This spell allows the caster to attack a target creature in the face with a powerful magical force. The caster must roll to-hit but the affected armor class is that of the target's face, which is often unarmored, though Dexterity bonuses still apply. A successful attack will inflict 4-24 points of damage. The material component is a leather glove.

Blink

(Alteration)

Level: 3

Range: 0

Duration: 1 rd./level

Area of Effect: The caster

Components: V, S

Casting Time: 1 segment

Saving Throw: None

By means of this spell, the magic-user causes his material form to "blink" directly from one point to another at a random time and in a random direction. This means that melee attacks against the magic-user automatically miss if initiative indicates they fall after he has blinked. Each round the spell is in effect, the magic-user rolls 2d8 to determine the timing of the blink – the result of the dice roll is used as the magic-user's initiative for that round. The magic-user disappears and instantaneously reappears 10 feet distant from his previous position. (Direction is determined by a roll of 1d8: 1 = right ahead, 2 = right, 3 = right behind, 4 = behind, 5 = left behind, 6 = left, 7 = left ahead, 8 = ahead.)

The caster cannot blink into a solid object; if such is indicated, re-roll the direction. Movable objects of size and mass comparable to the caster are shoved aside when the caster blinks in. If blinking is impossible except into a fixed, solid object, the caster is then trapped on the Ethereal Plane.

During each round that he blinks, the spellcaster can be attacked only by opponents who win initiative or by those who are able to strike both locations at once (for example, with a breath weapon, Fireball or similar wide-area attack forms). Opponents with multiple attacks, or those operating under Haste or similar effects, can often strike early enough to have at least one attack against the caster. If the spellcaster holds off his attack (if any) until after the blink, the 2d8 delay until the blink is added to his normal 1d10 initiative roll (thus, he probably attacks in the next round).

The spellcaster can also try to get his attack in before he blinks (he must announce his intent before rolling the 2d8 for blink timing and the 1d10 for initiative). In this case, the caster compares the two dice rolls, hoping that his initiative roll is lower than his blink roll (the two rolls are not added if he is trying to attack before he blinks). If so, he attacks according to his initiative roll, then blinks according to the blink roll. If his blink roll is lower than his initiative roll, however, he blinks first and then attacks in whatever direction he's facing (he must go through with his attack, even if he is facing in the wrong direction to affect anyone).

Charm Undead

(Necromancy)

Level: 3

Range: 10 ft./level

Duration: Permanent

Area of Effect: One undead creature

Components: V, S, M

Casting Time: 3 segments

Saving Throw: None

This spell allows the caster to command one undead creature. The victim must be a mindless form of undead, such as a Skeleton or Zombie, and receives no saving throw. While charmed the victim will not attack the caster and will follow simple instructions from the caster as long as it can hear his commands. Language is not a barrier, but telepathic commands will not work. The material component is a small silver collar that costs 5 gold pieces to construct.

Clairaudience

(Divination)

Level: 3

Range: Unlimited

Duration: 1 rd./level

Area of Effect: 60-ft. radius

Components: V, S, M

Casting Time: 3 segments

Saving Throw: None

The Clairaudience spell enables the magic-user to concentrate upon some locale and hear in his mind any noise within a 60-foot radius of that point. Distance is not a factor, but the locale must be known – a place familiar to the spellcaster or an obvious one (such as behind a door, around a corner, in a copse of trees, etc.).

Only sounds that are normally detectable by the magic-user can be heard by use of this spell. Lead sheeting or magical protections prevent the operation of the spell, and the magic-user has some indication that the spell is so blocked. The spell creates an invisible sensor, similar to that created by a Crystal Ball spell, that can be dispelled. The spell functions only on the magic-user's current plane of existence. The material component of the spell is a small horn of at least 100 gp value.

Clairvoyance

(Divination)

Level: 3

Range: Unlimited

Components: V, S, M

Duration: I rd./level

Casting Time: 3 segments

Area of Effect: Line of sight

Saving Throw: None

Similar to the Clairaudience spell, the Clairvoyance spell empowers the magic-user to see in his mind whatever is within sight range from the spell locale chosen. Distance from the magic-user is not a factor, but the locale must be known – familiar or obvious. Furthermore, light is a factor, as the spell does not enable the use of infravision or magical enhancements. If the area is magically dark, only darkness is seen; if naturally pitch dark, only a 10-foot radius from the center of the spell's area of effect can be seen. Otherwise, the seeing extends to the normal vision range according to the prevailing light. Lead sheeting or magical protection foils a Clairvoyance spell, and the magic-user has some indication that it is so blocked. The spell creates an invisible sensor, similar to that created by a Crystal Ball spell, that can be dispelled. The spell functions only on the magic-user's current plane of existence. The material component is a pinch of powdered pineal gland or hawk eyes.

Cloudburst

(Alteration)

Level: 3

Range: 10 ft./level

Components: V, S, M

Duration: I round

Casting Time: 5 segments

Area of Effect: 3 ft. dia. cylinder up to 6 ft. high

Saving Throw: None (special)

By means of this spell the caster causes the atmosphere to instantly precipitate all of its water vapor in the form of huge drops of rain, the resulting condensation not only causing a true downburst of rain but also sucking more vapor into the area to likewise be precipitated. The Cloudburst will effectively drench everything in its area of effect within 1 segment, for its rain will fall at the rate of 1 inch of rainfall in 1 round.

All normal fires within the area of effect will be extinguished by a Cloudburst - small ones instantly, medium-sized ones in 3-5 segments, and large sized ones in 8-10 segments. Magical fires will also be extinguished by a Cloudburst, with the following general rules applying:

Permanent magical fires will re-light in 1-2 rounds. Small magical fires that can be quickly lit anew, such as that of a Flame Tongue sword, will be affected only during the actual Cloudburst.

Spells such as Produce Fire and Burning Hands will be negated. Large area spells such as Fireball, Flame Strike, Wall of Fire, etc., will, in the course of being extinguished, vaporize the rain into a cloud of steam covering an area four times as large as the spell's area of effect (i.e., a cylinder of up to 12 feet in diameter and as much as 24 feet high). This steam will inflict 1-3 points of damage per round on normal creatures within its area, and will do twice that damage to cold-dwelling or cold-using creatures. The cloud of steam will persist for 2-5 rounds, half that if a breeze is blowing, or only 1 round if a strong wind is blowing.

In arid regions, the Cloudburst will act only as a double-strength Precipitation spell. In hot and humid areas, the duration of the spell will be extended to 2 rounds. In areas with a temperature of 31 or 36° Fahrenheit inclusive, sleet rather than rain will fall, with ice and slush being formed when it accumulates. In temperatures of 30° Fahrenheit and lower, the cloudburst becomes a snowburst, with one inch of snow per segment falling. The material components for the spell are powdered silver and powdered iodine crystals.

Continual Darkness

(Alteration)

Level: 3

Components: V, M

Range: 60 yards

Casting Time: 3 segments

Duration: Permanent

Saving Throw: None

Area of Effect: 30 ft. radius globe

When this spell is cast, a globe of impenetrable darkness is created. The effects of this darkness, as well as the material component of the spell, are the same as the second level magic-user spell, Darkness, 15' radius (cf. Continual Light).

Delude

(Alteration)

Level: 3

Range: 0

Components: V, S

Duration: I turn/level

Casting Time: 3 segments

Area of Effect: 30-ft. radius

Saving Throw: Negates

By means of a Delude spell, the magic-user conceals his own alignment with that of any creature within a 30-foot radius at the time the spell is cast. The creature must be of higher than animal intelligence for the spell to work; its own alignment remains unchanged. The creature receives a saving throw vs. spell and, if successful, the Delude spell fails. If the spell is successful, any Know Alignment spell used against the caster discovers only the assumed alignment. Note that a Detect Good or Detect Evil also detects the assumed aura, if the aura is strong enough. The creature whose aura has been assumed radiates magic, but the magic-user radiates magic only to the creature whose alignment has been assumed. If a Delude spell is used in conjunction with a Change Self or Alter Self spell, the class of the magic-user can be totally hidden, if he is clever enough to carry off the disguise.

Dispel Magic

(Abjuration)

Level: 3

Range: 120 yards

Components: V, S

Duration: Instantaneous

Casting Time: 3 segments

Area of Effect: 30-ft. cube

Saving Throw: None

When a magic-user casts this spell, it has a chance to neutralize or negate magic it comes in contact with, as follows: First, it removes spells and spell-like effects (including device effects and innate abilities) from creatures or objects. Second, it disrupts the casting or use of these in the area of effect at the instant the Dispel is cast. Third, it destroys magical potions (which are treated as 12th level for purposes of this spell).

Each effect or potion in the spell's area is checked to determine if it is dispelled. The caster can always dispel his own magic; otherwise, the chance to dispel depends on the difference in level between the magical effect and the caster. The base chance is 50% (11 or higher on 1d20 to dispel). If the caster is of higher level than the creator of the effect to be dispelled, the difference is subtracted from the number needed on 1d20 to dispel (making it more likely that the dispel succeeds); if the caster is of lower level, the difference is added to the number needed on 1d20 to dispel (making it less likely that the Dispel succeeds). A roll of 20 always succeeds and a roll of 1 always fails. Thus, if a caster is 10 levels higher, only a roll of 1 prevents the effect from being dispelled.

A Dispel Magic spell does not affect a specially enchanted item, such as a magical scroll, ring, wand, rod, staff, miscellaneous item, weapon, shield or armor, unless it is cast directly upon the item. This renders the item non-operational for 1d4 rounds. An item possessed and carried by a creature gains the creature's saving throw against this effect; otherwise, it is automatically rendered non-operational. An interdimensional interface (such as a Bag of Holding) rendered non-operational would be temporarily closed. Note that an item's physical properties are unchanged: A non-operational magical sword is still a sword. Artifacts and relics are not subject to this spell; however, some of their spell-like effects may be, at the GM's option.

Note that this spell can be very effective when used upon charmed and similarly beguiled creatures. Certain spells or effects cannot be dispelled; this is noted in the description for that spell or effect.

Summary of Dispel Magic Effects

Source of Effect	Resists As	Result of Dispel
Caster	None	Dispel automatic
Other caster/innate ability	Level/HD of other caster	Effect negated
Wand	6th level	*
Staff	8th level	*
Potion	12th level	Potion destroyed
Other magic	12th, unless special	*
Artifact	GM discretion	GM discretion

* Effect negated; if cast directly on item, item becomes non-operational for 1d4 rounds.

Explosive Runes

(Alteration)

Level: 3

Range: Touch

Components: V, S

Duration: Special

Casting Time: 3 segments

Area of Effect: 10-ft. radius

Saving Throw: None or 1/2

By tracing these mystic runes upon a book, map, scroll, or similar object bearing written information, the magic-user prevents unauthorized persons from reading his material. The explosive runes are difficult to detect – 5% chance per level of magic use experience of the reader; thieves have only a 5% chance. But trap detection by spell or magical device always finds these Runes. When read, the Explosive Runes detonate, delivering 6d4+6 points of damage to the reader, who gets no saving throw. A like amount, or half that if saving throws are made, is suffered by each creature within the blast radius.

The magic-user who cast the spell, as well as any he instructs, can read the protected writing without triggering the Runes. Likewise, the magic-user can remove the Runes whenever desired. Others can remove them only with a successful Dispel Magic or Erase spell. Explosive Runes otherwise last until the spell is triggered. The item upon which the runes are placed is destroyed when the explosion takes place, unless it is not normally subject to destruction by magical fire (see the item saving throws in the GMG).

Feign Death

(Necromancy)

Level: 3

Range: Touch

Components: V, S

Duration: 1 hr. + 1 turn/level

Casting Time: 1 segment

Area of Effect: Creature touched

Saving Throw: None

By means of this spell, the caster (or any other creature whose levels of experience or Hit Dice do not exceed the magic-user's own level) can be put into a cataleptic state that is impossible to distinguish from death. Although the person or creature affected by the Feign Death spell can smell, hear and know what is going on, no feeling or sight of any sort is possible. Thus, any wounding or mistreatment of the body is not felt and no reaction occurs; damage is only half normal. In addition, paralysis, poison and energy or level drain cannot affect an individual under the influence of this spell. Poison injected or otherwise introduced into the body takes effect when the spell recipient is no longer under the influence of this spell, although a saving throw is permitted.

Note that only a willing individual can be affected by a Feign Death spell. The spellcaster can end the spell effects at any time desired, as will a successful Dispel Magic, but a full round is required for bodily functions to begin again.

Fireball

(Evocation)

Level: 3

Range: 10 yds. + 10 yds./level

Components: V, S, M

Duration: Instantaneous

Casting Time: 3 segments

Area of Effect: 20-ft. radius

Saving Throw: 1/2

A fireball is an explosive burst of flame, which detonates with a low roar and delivers damage proportional to the level of the magic-user who cast it – 1d4 points of damage for each level of experience of the spellcaster. The burst of the fireball creates little pressure and generally conforms to the shape of the area in which it occurs. The fireball fills an area equal to its normal spherical volume (roughly 33,000 cubic feet— thirty-three 10-foot x 10-foot x 10-foot cubes).

Besides causing damage to creatures, the fireball ignites all combustible materials within its burst radius, and the heat of the fireball melts soft metals such as gold, copper, silver, etc. Exposed items require saving throws vs. magical fire to determine if they are affected, but items in the possession of a creature that rolls a successful saving throw are unaffected by the fireball.

The magic-user points his finger and speaks the range (distance and height) at which the fireball is to burst. A streak flashes from the pointing digit and, unless it impacts upon a material body or solid barrier prior to attaining the prescribed range, blossoms into the fireball (an early impact results in an early detonation). Creatures failing their saving throws each suffer full damage from the blast. Those who roll successful saving throws manage to dodge, fall flat or roll aside, each receiving half damage (the GM rolls the damage and each affected creature suffers either full damage or half damage [round fractions down], depending on whether the creature saved or not). The material component of this spell is a tiny ball of bat guano and sulphur.

Fireball, Scatter-Blast

(Evocation)

Level: 3

Range: 10 yds. + 10 yds./level

Components: V, S, M

Duration: Instantaneous

Casting Time: 3 segments

Area of Effect: 1d6 10-ft. radius spheres

Saving Throw: 1/2

A Scatter-Blast Fireball has similar effects as a normal fireball but the exact area of effect is unpredictable. When the magic-user casts this spell, he chooses where to center the spell and then rolls a d6. This is the number of independent 10 foot radius fireballs that are generated by this incantation. The location of each will be from 10-40 yards (1d4x10) away from the center of the spell in a direction determined randomly for each based on a d8 roll (1 = north, 2 = northeast, 3 = east, 4 = southeast, 5 = south, 6 = southwest, 7 = west, 8 = northwest). The material components of this spell is a tiny ball of bat guano and sulphur.

Fireball, Sidewinder Factor 3

(Evocation)

Level: 3

Range: 1 mile maximum.

Components: V, S, M

Duration: 1 rd./level

Casting Time: 3 segments

Area of Effect: 10-ft. radius

Saving Throw: 1/2

The Sidewinder Fireball is similar to the Skipping Betty Fireball except that it uses d6-2 for damage instead of d4 and the range of the fireball is only 100 feet per level of the caster. Thus each range increment is 100 feet. The spell range is further reduced by 10 feet per degree if the air temperature is less than 32° Fahrenheit. Potential targets also need not be in the 45 degree firing arc from the front of the caster. Additionally, the terrain need not be level as the Sidewinder Fireball can maneuver around obstructions and even hit an object hidden behind a wall, for example. The somatic gestures necessary for casting this spell include a side winding motion made with the casters arms. The material components are bat guano, sulphur and gum arabic.

Flame Arrow

(Conjuration/Summoning)

Level: 3
Range: 30 yds. + 10 yds./level
Components: V, S, M
Duration: 1 round
Casting Time: 3 segments
Area of Effect: Special
Saving Throw: None

This spell has two versions. First, the magic-user can cause normal arrows or crossbow bolts to become magical flaming missiles for one round. The missiles must be nocked and drawn (or cocked) at the completion of the spell. If they are not loosed within one round, they are consumed by the magic. For every five levels the caster has achieved, up to 10 arrows or bolts can be affected. The arrows inflict normal damage, plus 1 point of fire damage to any target struck. They may also cause incendiary damage. This version of the spell is used most often in large battles.

The second version of this spell enables the caster to hurl fiery bolts at opponents within range. Each bolt inflicts 1d6 points of piercing damage, plus 4d6 points of fire damage. Only half the fire damage is inflicted if the creature struck successfully saves vs. spell. The caster receives one bolt for every five experience levels (two bolts at 10th level, three at 15th level, etc.). Bolts must be used on creatures within 20 yards of each other and in front of the magic-user. The material components for this spell are a drop of oil and a small piece of flint.

Fly

(Alteration)

Level: 3
Range: Touch
Components: V, S, M
Duration: 1 turn/level + 1d6 turns
Casting Time: 3 segments
Area of Effect: Creature touched
Saving Throw: None

This spell enables the magic-user to bestow the power of magical flight. The creature affected is able to move vertically and horizontally at a rate of 18 (half that if ascending, twice that if descending in a dive). The maneuverability class of the creature is B. Using the Fly spell requires as much concentration as walking, so most spells can be cast while hovering or moving slowly (movement of 3). Possible combat penalties while flying are known to the GM (found in the "Aerial Combat" section of the GMG). The exact duration of the spell is always unknown to the spellcaster, as the variable addition is determined secretly by the GM. The material component of the fly spell is a wing feather of any bird.

Gandle's Humble Hut

(Alteration)

Level: 3
Range: 0
Components: V, S, M
Duration: 4 hrs. + 1 hr./level
Casting Time: 3 segments
Area of Effect: 15-ft.-diameter sphere
Saving Throw: None

When this spell is cast, the magic-user creates an unmoving, opaque sphere of force of any desired color around his person. Half of the sphere projects above the ground, and the lower hemisphere passes through the ground. Up to seven other man-sized creatures can fit into the field with its creator; they can freely pass into and out of the hut without harming it. However, if the spellcaster removes himself from the hut, the spell dissipates. The temperature inside the hut is 70° Fahrenheit, if the exterior temperature is between 0 and 100° Fahrenheit. An exterior temperature below 0 or above 100° lowers or raises, respectively, the interior temperature on a 1-for-1 basis. The humble hut also provides protection against the elements, such as rain, dust, sandstorms and the like. The hut can withstand any wind of less than hurricane force without being harmed, but wind force greater than that destroys it.

The interior of the hut is a hemisphere; the spellcaster can illuminate it dimly upon command, or extinguish the light as desired. Note that although the force field is opaque from the outside, it is transparent from within. Missiles, weapons and most spell effects can pass through the hut without affecting it, although the occupants cannot be seen from outside the hut. The hut can be dispelled. The material component for this spell is a small crystal bead that shatters when the spell duration expires or the hut is dispelled.

Grow

(Alteration)

Level: 3
Range: 3 yards/level
Components: V, S, M
Duration: Instantaneous
Casting Time: 3 segments
Area of Effect: one creature
Saving Throw: Negates

This spell enables the caster to age a living creature by one year within a matter of seconds. If the target does not wish to be aged, he may attempt a saving throw to avoid the effect. A Grow spell may be cast on any living being. The spell affects the target's physical body only. Intelligence and Wisdom bonuses due to aging are not conferred as a result of this spell. Additionally, a child aged in this way would still behave as a child though he might have the body of an adult.

Gust of Wind

(Alteration)

Level: 3
Range: 0
Components: V, S, M
Duration: 1 round
Casting Time: 3 segments
Area of Effect: 10 ft. x 10 yds./lvl.
Saving Throw: None

When this spell is cast, a strong puff of air originates from the magic-user and moves in the direction he is facing. The force of this gust of wind (about 30 mph) is sufficient to extinguish candles, torches, and similar unprotected flames. It causes protected flames – such as those of lanterns – to dance wildly and has a 5% chance per level of experience of the spellcaster to extinguish even such lights. It also fans large fires outward 1d6 feet in the direction of the wind's movement.

It forces back small flying creatures 1d6 x 10 yards and causes man-sized beings to be held motionless if attempting to move against its force. It slows larger-than-man-sized flying creatures by 50% for one round. It blows over light objects, disperses most vapors, and forces away gaseous or unsecured levitating creatures. Its path is a constant 10 feet wide, by 10 yards long per level of experience of the caster (for example, an 8th level magic-user causes a gust of wind that travels 80 yards). The material component of the spell is a legume seed.

Haste

(Alteration)

Level: 3
Range: 60 yards
Components: V, S, M
Duration: 3 rds. + 1 rd./level
Casting Time: 3 segments
Area of Effect: 40-ft. cube, 1 creature/level
Saving Throw: None

When this spell is cast, each affected creature functions at double its normal movement and attack rates. A hasted creature gains a -2 initiative bonus. Thus, a creature moving at 6 and attacking once per round would move at 12 and attack twice per round. Spellcasting and spell effects are not sped up. The number of creatures that can be affected is equal to the caster's experience level; those creatures closest to the center of effect are affected first. All affected by Haste must be in the designated area of effect.

Note that this spell negates the effects of a Slow spell. Additionally, this spell ages the recipient by one year, because of sped-up metabolic processes. This spell is not cumulative with itself or with other similar magic. Its material component is a shaving of licorice root.

Hold Person

(Enchantment/Charm)

Level: 3
Range: 120 yards
Components: V, S, M
Duration: 2 rds./level
Casting Time: 3 segments
Area of Effect: 1-4 persons, 20-ft. cube
Saving Throw: Negates

The Hold Person spell affects any bipedal human, demi-human or humanoid of man size or smaller, including Brownies, Dryads, dwarves, elves, Gnolls, gnomes, Goblins, half-elves, halflings, half-orcs, hobgoblins, humans, Kobolds, Lizard Men, Nixies, Orcs, Pixies, Sprites, Troglodytes, and others. This spell holds 1d4 humans, demi-humans, or humanoid creatures rigidly immobile for five or more rounds.

The spell is centered on a point selected by the caster; it affects persons selected by the caster within the area of effect. If the spell is cast at three or four people, each gets an unmodified saving throw. If only two people are being targeted, each makes his saving throw with a -1 penalty. If the spell is cast at only one person, the saving throw suffers a -3 penalty. Saving throws are adjusted for Wisdom. Those succeeding on their saving throws are unaffected by the spell.

Undead creatures cannot be held. Held beings cannot move or speak, but they remain aware of events around them and can use abilities not requiring motion or speech. Being held does not prevent the worsening of the subjects' condition due to wounds, disease or poison. The caster can end the spell with a single utterance at any time; otherwise, the duration is 10 rounds at 5th level, 12 rounds at 6th level, 14 rounds at 7th level, etc. The spellcaster needs a small, straight piece of iron or a blue throttle wing as the material component of this spell.

Hold Undead

(Necromancy)
Level: 3
Range: 60 feet   **Components:** V, S, M
Duration: 1d4 rds. + 1 rd./level   **Casting Time:** 5 segments
Area of Effect: 1d3 undead   **Saving Throw:** Negates

When cast, this spell renders immobile 1d3 undead creatures whose total Hit Dice are equal to or less than the caster's level. No more than three undead can be affected by a single spell. To cast, the magic-user aims the spell at a point within range and the three undead closest to this are considered to be in the area of effect, provided all are within the field of vision and spell range of the caster. Undead of a mindless nature (Skeletons, Zombies, Ghouls, etc.) are automatically affected. Other forms of undead are allowed a saving throw to negate the effect. If the spell is successful, it renders the undead immobile for the duration of the spell. The material component for this spell is a pinch of sulphur and powdered garlic.

Illusionary Script

(Illusion/Phantasm)
Level: 3
Range: Touch   **Components:** V, S, M
Duration: 1 day/level   **Casting Time:** Special
Area of Effect: Script reader   **Saving Throw:** Special

This spell enables the magic-user to write instructions or other information on parchment, paper, etc. The illusionary script appears to be some form of foreign or magical writing. Only the person (or people) who the magic-user desires to read the writing can do so. A magic-user recognizes it for illusionary script. Unauthorized creatures glancing at the script must roll saving throws vs. spell. A successful save means the creature can look away with only a mild sense of disorientation. Failure means the creature is subject to a suggestion implanted in the script by the caster at the time the Illusionary Script spell was cast. The suggestion cannot require more than three turns to carry out. The suggestion could be to close the book and leave or to forget the existence of the book, for example.

A successful Dispel Magic spell will remove the illusionary script, but an unsuccessful attempt erases all of the writing. The hidden writings can be read by a combination of the True Seeing spell and either the Read Magic or Comprehend Languages spell, as applicable. The material component is a lead-based ink that requires special manufacture by an alchemist, at a cost of not less than 300 gp per usage.

Infravision

(Alteration)
Level: 3
Range: Touch   **Components:** V, S, M
Duration: 2 hrs. + 1 hr./level   **Casting Time:** 1 round
Area of Effect: Creature touched   **Saving Throw:** None

By means of this spell, the magic-user enables the recipient to see in normal darkness up to 60 feet without light. Note that strong sources of light (fire, lanterns, torches, etc.) tend to blind this vision, so infravision does not function efficiently in the presence of such light sources. Invisible creatures are not detectable by infravision. The material component of this spell is either a pinch of dried carrot or an agate.

Invisibility, 10' Radius

(Illusion/Phantasm)
Level: 3
Range: Touch   **Components:** V, S, M
Duration: Special   **Casting Time:** 3 segments
Area of Effect: 10-ft. radius   **Saving Throw:** None

This spell confers invisibility upon all creatures within 10 feet of the recipient. Gear carried and light sources are included, but any light emitted is still visible. The center of the effect is mobile with the recipient. Those affected by this spell cannot see each other. Any affected creature moving out of the area becomes visible, but creatures moving into the area after the spell is cast do not become invisible. Affected creatures (other than the recipient) that attack negate the invisibility only for themselves. If the spell recipient attacks, the Invisibility, 10' Radius spell is broken for all. The material components are the same as for the Invisibility spell.

Item

(Alteration)
Level: 3
Range: Touch   **Components:** V, S, M
Duration: 4 hrs./level   **Casting Time:** 3 segments
Area of Effect: 2 cu. ft./level   **Saving Throw:** Special

By means of this spell, the magic-user is able to shrink one non-magical item (if it is within the size limit) to 1/12 of its normal size. Optionally, the caster can also change its now-shrunken composition to a cloth-like one. An object in the possession of another creature is allowed a saving throw vs. spell.

Objects changed by an Item spell can be returned to normal composition and size merely by tossing them onto any solid surface or by a word of command from the original spellcaster. Even a burning fire and its fuel can be shrunk by this spell.

Lightning Bolt

(Evocation)
Level: 3
Range: 40 yds. + 10 yds./level   **Components:** V, S, M
Duration: Instantaneous   **Casting Time:** 3 segments
Area of Effect: Special   **Saving Throw:** 1/2

Upon casting this spell, the magic-user releases a powerful stroke of electrical energy that inflicts 1d6 points of damage per level of the spellcaster to each creature within its area of effect. A successful saving throw vs. spell reduces this damage to half (round fractions down). The bolt begins at a range and height decided by the caster and streaks outward in a direct line from the casting magic-user (for example, if a 40-foot bolt was started at 180 feet from the magic-user, the far end of the bolt would reach 220 feet (180 + 40)).

The lightning bolt may set fire to combustibles, sunder wooden doors, splinter up to a half-foot thickness of stone and melt metals with a low melting point (lead, gold, copper, silver, bronze). Saving throws must be rolled for objects that withstand the full force of a stroke (see the Fireball spell). If the damage caused to an interposing barrier shatters or breaks through it (i.e., the saving throw fails), the bolt continues. A bolt can breach 1 inch of wood or half an inch of stone per caster level, up to a maximum of 1 foot of wood or half a foot of stone. The lightning bolt's area of effect is chosen by the spellcaster: either a forked bolt 10 feet wide and 40 feet long or a single bolt 5 feet wide and 80 feet long. If a bolt cannot reach its full length, because of an unyielding barrier (such as a stone wall), the lightning bolt rebounds from the barrier toward its caster, ending only when it reaches its full length.

For example: An 80-foot-long stroke is begun at a range of 40 feet, but it hits a stone wall at 50 feet. The bolt travels 10 feet, hits the wall and rebounds for 70 feet back toward its creator (who is only 50 feet from the wall, and so is caught in his own lightning bolt!).

The GM might allow reflecting bolts. When this type of lightning bolt strikes a solid surface, the bolt reflects from the surface at an angle equal to the angle of incidence (like light off a mirror). A creature crossed more than once by the bolt must roll a saving throw for every time it is crossed, but it still suffers either full damage (if one saving throw is missed) or half damage (if all saving throws are made). The material components of the spell are a bit of fur and an amber, crystal, or glass rod.

Material

(Evocation-Conjuration)

Level: 3

Range: 1ft.	**Components:** V, S
Duration: Permanent	**Casting Time:** 1 round
Area of Effect: 1 cu. ft. per level	**Saving Throw:** None

A Material spell allows the magic-user to actually bring into being certain common things. There is no great difficulty in causing common basic materials such as stone, earth (soil) or wood to appear. These sorts of materials in raw, unworked form are easily gained by means of this spell. Similarly, other inorganic or nonliving materials such as water, air, dung, straw, etc., can be conjured. Where simple plants are concerned, such as when the caster attempts to bring into being an area of grass, there is a base 100% chance of total failure, modified downward by 1% per level of the spell caster.

Animal life can never be affected by this spell. In no event can worked, refined, or fabricated items be brought into being by a material spell, nor can rough gems or precious metals. The spell essentially enables the magic-user to create common things of a basic nature.

Monster Summoning I

(Conjuration/Summoning)

Level: 3

Range: Special	**Components:** V, S, M
Duration: 2 rds. + 1 rd./level	**Casting Time:** 3 segments
Area of Effect: 30-yd. radius	**Saving Throw:** None

Within one round of casting this spell, the magic-user magically conjures 2d4 1st level monsters (selected by the GM, from his 1st level encounter tables). The monsters appear anywhere within the spell's area of effect, as desired by the magic-user. They attack the spell user's opponents to the best of their ability until either he commands that the attacks cease, the spell duration

expires, or the monsters are slain. These creatures do not check morale, but they vanish when slain.

Note that if no opponent exists to fight, summoned monsters can, if the magic-user can communicate with them and if they are physically able, perform other services for the summoning magic-user. In rare cases, adventurers have been known to disappear, summoned by powerful spellcasters using this spell. Those summoned recall all the details of their trip. The material components of this spell are a tiny bag and a small (not necessarily lit) candle.

Murgain's Migraine

(Necromancy)

Level: 3

Range: 30 yards	**Components:** V, S
Duration: Until Dispelled	**Casting Time:** 3 segments
Area of Effect: 1 creature	**Saving Throw:** Negates

This spell causes a severe and painful migraine headache in a creature. The afflicted individual is immediately stricken with painful and distracting symptoms. He will become grumpy and unpleasant to be around. While under the effect of the spell, all attack rolls and saving throws are penalized by 1. The chances of a spell mishap are increased by 10% and skill checks become more difficult (-10). The victim of the spell is allowed a new saving throw each day the spell is in effect. The effect persists until the character receives a Cure Disease spell or until the character makes a successful saving throw. If the character has not received a Cure Disease or made a successful saving throw in an amount of days equal to his Constitution score, he will begin to permanently lose one ability point per day (determined randomly).

No Fear

(Enchantment/Charm)

Level: 3

Range: 10 yards/level	**Components:** V
Duration: 2 rounds/level	**Casting Time:** 3 segments
Area of Effect: 10 ft. radius	**Saving Throw:** None (neg.)

When this spell is cast it fills the recipients with fierce bravery, giving them a +2 bonus on to hit and damage rolls in melee combat as well as making them immune to Fear and morale checks. The spell affects everyone within a 10-foot radius from the target point when first cast, but afterwards the recipients can freely move about without losing the bonuses granted by this spell.

Nondetection

(Abjuration)

Level: 3

Range: Touch	**Components:** V, S, M
Duration: 1 hr./level	**Casting Time:** 3 segments
Area of Effect: 1 creature/item	**Saving Throw:** None

By casting this spell, the magic-user makes the creature or object touched undetectable by divination spells such as Clairaudience, Clairvoyance, Locate Object, ESP, and detection spells. It also prevents location by such magical items as Crystal Balls and ESP Medallions. It does not affect the Know Alignment spell or the ability of intelligent or high level beings to detect invisible creatures. If a divination is attempted, the Nondetection caster must roll a saving throw vs. spell. If this is successful, the divination fails. The material component of the spell is a pinch of diamond dust worth 300 gp.

Paralyzation

(Illusion/Phantasm)

Level: 3

Range: 10 ft./level	**Components:** V, S
Duration: Special	**Costing Time:** 3 segments
Area of Effect: 20 ft. x 20 ft. area	**Saving Throw:** Negates

The Paralyzation spell enables the spellcaster to create illusionary muscle slowdown in creatures whose combined Hit Dice do not exceed twice the total level of experience of the caster. If the recipient creatures fail their saving throws, they become paralyzed, and a Dispel Magic spell must be used to remove the effect, or the caster may dispel it at any time he desires.

Perceived Malignment

(Enchantment/Charm)

Level: 3

Range: 50 feet — **Components:** V

Duration: Special — **Casting Time:** 3 segments

Area of Effect: 1 creature — **Saving Throw:** None (neg.)

When this spell is cast on someone he becomes convinced that someone else has done him a great wrong, filling the target with rage and a need to seek retribution at all costs. The caster decides whom the target of the subject's rage is, and while the subject is under this spell he receives an extra 1d8 hp, +3 to-hit and damage, and immunity to morale checks and fear as long as he is in combat with the object of his rage. While the spell lasts, the target must attempt to engage in hand-to-hand combat with the object of their rage, and will attack that creature exclusively until one of them is dead. The spell lasts for the duration of the combat or until a total of one turn has passed without the spell's target engaging in combat with his "enemy".

Phantom Steed

(Conjuration, Phantasm)

Level: 3

Range: Touch — **Components:** V, S

Duration: 1 hr./level — **Casting Time:** 1 turn

Area of Effect: Special — **Saving Throw:** None

When this spell is cast, the magic-user creates a quasi-real, horselike creature. The steed can be ridden only by the magic-user who created it, or by any person for whom the magic-user specifically creates such a mount. A phantom steed has a black head and body, gray mane and tail, and smoke-colored, insubstantial hooves that make no sound. Its eyes are milky-colored. It does not fight, but all normal animals shun it and only monstrous ones will attack. The mount has an Armor Class of 2 and 7 hit points, plus 1 per level of the caster. If it loses all of its hit points, the phantom steed disappears.

A phantom steed moves at a movement rate of 4 per level of the spellcaster, to a maximum movement rate of 48. It has what seems to be a saddle and a bit and bridle. It can bear its rider's weight, plus up to 10 pounds per caster level. These mounts gain certain powers according to the level of the magic-user who created them:

8th Level: The ability to pass over sandy, muddy, or even swampy ground without difficulty.

10th Level: The ability to pass over water as if it were firm, dry ground.

12th Level: The ability to travel in the air as if it were firm land, so chasms and the like can be crossed without benefit of a bridge. Note, however, that the mount cannot casually take off and fly; the movement must be between points of similar altitude.

14th Level: The ability to perform as if it were a Pegasus; it flies at a rate of 48 per round upon command. Note that a mount's abilities include those of lower levels; thus, a 12th level mount has the 8th, 10th, and 12th level abilities.

Phantom Wind

(Alteration/Phantasm)

Level: 3

Range: 1 ft./level — **Components:** V, S

Duration: 1 round/level — **Casting Time:** 3 segments

Area of Effect: 1 ft. broad path — **Saving Throw:** None

When this spell is employed, the caster creates a wind which cannot be seen or felt. This movement of air does, however, serve to blow light objects before it, flutter curtains or drapes, flap loose clothing (such as capes, cloaks, and mantles), fan fires and move clouds of gaseous materials (such as a Wall of Fog, a Fog Cloud, a Cloudkill cloud, etc.). The wind created moves in the direction in which the caster points, its effects being felt in a progressively longer path as the spell continues, at a movement rate of 1 foot per round, with the effects lasting the entire course of the path. Thus, the spell could, for example, be employed to move several sailed vessels, but the first affected by the wind would also be the one to move the farthest.

Polymorph to Amphibian

(Alteration)

Level: 3

Range: 5 ft./level — **Components:** V, S, M

Duration: Permanent — **Casting Time:** 3 segments

Area of Effect: 1 creature — **Saving Throw:** Negates

When this spell is cast it turns any one creature into a random amphibian. The victim retains its original Intelligence and memories but must make a system shock in order to survive the change. The spell is permanent until ended by a successful Dispel Magic, Remove Curse or similar magics. Roll a d8 on the chart below to determine what kind of amphibian the target turns into:

Polymorph to Amphibian (d8)	
1	A salamander
2	A small frog
3	A toad
4	A caecilian
5	A Giant Salamander (AC 5, can bite once per round for 1D6 damage)
6	A Man-Eating Bullfrog
7	A newt (but the effects wear off in 1d6 hours)
8	A Jelly Banded Newt

The material component is an eye from newt or other amphibian.

Polymorph to Primate

(Alteration)

Level: 3

Range: 5 ft./level — **Components:** V, S, M

Duration: Permanent — **Casting Time:** 3 segments

Area of Effect: one creature — **Saving Throw:** Negates

This spell transforms the victim into a primate in much the same manner as the Polymorph to Amphibian spell. The victim must pass a system shock roll in order to survive. If they live, they become a random primate but get to keep their memories and Intelligence. As a primate, spellcasters cannot talk, but have a 75% chance of being able to successfully cast a spell that has no verbal components. Roll a d8 on the following chart to determine what kind of primate the target becomes:

Polymorph to Primate	
1	Ring-tailed lemur (can still use small melee weapons)
2	Baboon
3	Orangutan (+2 to Strength, can use weapons)
4	Spider monkey
5	Howler monkey
6	Gibbon (of the opposite sex)
7	Tarpier
8	Monkey Brain! The victim retains their original form, but their intellect is reduced to that of a monkey, giving them a five Wisdom and Intelligence.

The change is permanent until a Dispel Magic, Remove Curse or similar magic is successfully used to break the spell. The material component is a bit of primate (not human) hair or a piece of tropical fruit.

Preemptive Strike

(Evocation)

Level: 3

Range: Caster — **Components:** V, S, M

Duration: 1 hour/level — **Casting Time:** 1 round

Area of Effect: 5 ft. radius — **Saving Throw:** Half damage

This spell is used to protect the caster against a personal attack. The spell will fire a bolt of magical energy at the first hostile creature who comes within five feet of the caster. The bolt never misses, always hits the victim before they can make any of their attacks and inflicts 3d6 points of damage plus 2 points per level of the caster (the victim can make a save for half damage). Therefore the spell will strike at a thief attempting a backstab or an Ogre closing in to attack, but would not be triggered by a pickpocket or an archer shooting arrows at the caster. This spell ends immediately after it has been discharged, or when the duration runs out. The material component is a preserved eyeball.

Protection from Normal Missiles
(Abjuration)

Level: 3
Range: Touch
Duration: I turn/level
Area of Effect: Creature touched
Components: V, S, M
Casting Time: 3 segments
Saving Throw: None

By means of this spell, the magic-user bestows total invulnerability to hurled and projected missiles such as arrows, axes, bolts, javelins, small stones and spears. Furthermore, it causes a reduction of 1 from each die of damage (but no die inflicts less than 1 point of damage) inflicted by large or magical missiles, such as ballista missiles, catapult stones, hurled boulders, and magical arrows, bolts, javelins, etc. Note, however, that this spell does not convey any protection from such magical attacks as Fireballs, Lightning Bolts, or Magic Missiles. The material component of this spell is a piece of tortoise or turtle shell.

Runes of Eyeball Implosion
(Alteration)

Level: 3
Range: Touch
Duration: Special
Area of Effect: One creature
Components: V, S
Casting Time: 3 segments
Saving Throw: None

By tracing these mystic runes upon a book, map, scroll or similar object bearing written information, the magic-user prevents unauthorized persons from reading his material. The Runes of Eyeball Implosion are difficult to detect—5% chance per level of magic use experience of the reader; thieves have only a 5% chance. Trap detection by spell or magical device always finds these runes. When read, the runes cause an inwardly directed detonation of the reader's eyes, accompanied by a sickening popping sound, delivering 3d4+3 points of damage to the reader, who gets no saving throw.

The magic-user who cast the spell, as well as any he instructs, can read the protected writing without triggering the runes. Likewise, the magic-user can

remove the runes whenever desired. Others can remove them only with a successful Dispel Magic or Erase spell. Runes of Eyeball Implosion otherwise last until the spell is triggered. The item upon which the runes are placed is unharmed when the magic is triggered. Obviously, the person who triggered the runes will be blind everafter.

Secret Page
(Alteration)

Level: 3
Range: Touch
Duration: Until dispelled
Area of Effect: I page, up to 2 ft. square
Components: V, S, M
Casting Time: I turn
Saving Throw: None

When cast, a Secret Page spell alters the actual contents of a page so that they appear to be something entirely different. Thus, a map can be changed to become a treatise on burnishing ebony walking sticks. The text of a spell can be altered to show a ledger page or even another form of spell. Confuse Languages and Explosive Runes spells may be cast upon the secret page, but a Comprehend Languages spell cannot reveal the secret page's contents.

The caster is able to reveal the original contents by speaking a command word, perusing the actual page, and then returning it to its secret page form. The caster can also remove the spell by double repetition of the command word. Others noting the dim magic of a page within this spell cloaking its true contents can attempt to Dispel Magic, but if it fails, the page is destroyed. A True Seeing spell does not reveal the contents unless cast in combination with a Comprehend Languages spell. An Erase spell can destroy the writing. The material components are powdered herring scales and either Will o' Wisp or Boggart essence.

Sepia Snake Sigil
(Conjuration/Summoning)

Level: 3
Range: 5 yards
Duration: Special
Area of Effect: I sigil
Components: V, S, M
Casting Time: 3 segments
Saving Throw: None

When this spell is cast, a small written symbol appears in the text of any written work. When read, the so-called Sepia Snake springs into being and strikes at the nearest living creature (but does not attack the magic-user who cast the spell). Its attack is made as if it were a monster with Hit Dice equal to the level of the magic-user who cast the spell.

If it strikes successfully, the victim is engulfed in a shimmering amber field of force, frozen and immobilized until released, either at the caster's command, by a successful Dispel Magic spell, or until a time equal to 1d4 days +1 day per caster level has elapsed. Until then, nothing can get at the victim, move the shimmering force surrounding him, or otherwise affect him. The victim does not age, grow hungry, sleep, or regain spells while in this state. He is not aware of his surroundings. If the Sepia Snake misses its target, it dissipates in a flash of brown light, with a loud noise and a puff of dun-colored smoke that is 10 feet in diameter and lasts for one round.

The spell cannot be detected by normal observation, and Detect Magic reveals only that the entire text is magical. A Dispel Magic can remove it; an Erase spell destroys the entire page of text. It can be cast in combination with other spells that hide or garble text. The components for the spell are 100 gp worth of powdered amber, a scale from any snake, and a pinch of mushroom spores.

Slow
(Alteration)

Level: 3
Range: 90 yds. + 10 yds./level
Duration: 3 rds. + I rd./level
Area of Effect: 40-ft. cube, I creature/level
Components: V, S, M
Casting Time: 3 segments
Saving Throw: Negates

A Slow spell causes affected creatures to move and attack at half their normal rates. It negates a Haste spell or equivalent, but does not otherwise affect magically speeded or slowed creatures. Slowed creatures have an Armor Class penalty of +4 AC, an attack penalty of -4, and all Dexterity combat bonuses are negated. The magic affects a number of creatures equal to the spellcaster's level, if they are within the area of effect chosen by the magic-user (i.e., a 40-foot cubic volume centered as called for by the caster). The creatures are affected from the center of the spell outward. Saving throws against the spell suffer a -4 penalty. The material component of this spell is a drop of molasses.

Spectral Force

(Illusion/Phantasm)

Level: 3

Range: 60 yds. + 1 yd./level   **Components:** V, S

Duration: Special   **Casting Time:** 3 segments

Area of Effect: 40-ft. cube +   **Saving Throw:** Special
        10-ft. cube/level

The Spectral Force spell creates an illusion in which sound, smell, and thermal illusions are included. It is otherwise similar to the Improved Phantasmal Force spell. The spell lasts for three rounds after concentration ceases.

Suggestion

(Enchantment/Charm)

Level: 3

Range: 30 yards   **Components:** V, M

Duration: 1 hr. + 1 hr./level   **Casting Time:** 3 segments

Area of Effect: 1 creature   **Saving Throw:** Negates

When this spell is cast by the magic-user, he influences the actions of the chosen recipient by the utterance of a few words – phrases or a sentence or two – suggesting a course of action desirable to the spellcaster. The creature to be influenced must, of course, be able to understand the magic-user's suggestion – it must be spoken in a language that the spell recipient understands.

The suggestion must be worded in such a manner as to make the action sound reasonable; asking the creature to stab itself, throw itself onto a spear, immolate itself, or do some other obviously harmful act automatically negates the effect of the spell. However, a suggestion that a pool of acid was actually pure water and that a quick dip would be refreshing is another matter. Urging a Red Dragon to stop attacking the magic-user's party so that the dragon and party could jointly loot a rich treasure elsewhere is likewise a reasonable use of the spell's power. The course of action of a suggestion can continue in effect for a considerable duration, such as in the case of the red dragon mentioned above.

Conditions that will trigger a special action can also be specified; if the condition is not met before the spell expires, the action will not be performed. If the target successfully rolls its saving throw, the spell has no effect. Note that a very reasonable suggestion causes the saving throw to be made with a penalty (such as -1, -2, etc.) at the discretion of the GM. Undead are not subject to Suggestion.

The material components of this spell are a snake's tongue and either a bit of honeycomb or a drop of sweet oil.

Sure Grip Snare

(Evocation)

Level: 3

Range: 10 feet   **Components:** V, S, M

Duration: 1 hour/level   **Casting Time:** 1 round

Area of Effect: 1 object up to   **Saving Throw:** Negates
        10 ft. x10 ft. x10 ft.

When this spell is cast the caster designates one object to be warded. If anyone other than those that the caster designates at the time of the casting touch the warded item the spell is instantly discharged, accompanied by a loud snap. The victim must make a saving throw - if successful he is partially tripped up by the spell and must spend one round freeing himself. If the save is failed, he is snatched up and held upside down about five feet above the ground, completely helpless. The victim remains helpless for 1 round per level of the caster, until a Dispel Magic is successfully used or until the caster releases the victim. The material component is a small mousetrap.

Tongues

(Alteration)

Reversible

Level: 3

Range: 0   **Components:** V, M

Duration: 1 rd./level   **Casting Time:** 3 segments

Area of Effect: 30-ft. radius   **Saving Throw:** None

This spell enables the magic-user to speak and understand additional languages, whether they are racial tongues or regional dialects. This does not enable the caster to speak with animals. The spell enables the caster to be understood by all creatures of that type within hearing distance, usually 60 feet. This spell does not predispose the subject toward the caster in any way. The magic-user can speak one additional tongue for every three levels of experience. The reverse of the spell (Babble) cancels the effect of the Tongues spell or confuses verbal communication of any sort within the area of effect. The material component is a small clay model of a ziggurat, which shatters when the spell is pronounced.

Vampiric Touch

(Necromancy)

Level: 3

Range: 0   **Components:** V, S

Duration: One touch   **Casting Time:** 3 segments

Area of Effect: The caster   **Saving Throw:** None

When the caster touches an opponent in melee with a successful attack roll, the opponent loses 1d6 hit points for every two caster levels, to a maximum drain of 6d6 points for a 12th level caster. The spell is expended when a successful touch is made or one turn passes. The hit points are added to the caster's total, with any hit points over the caster's normal total treated as temporary additional hit points. Any damage to the caster is subtracted from the temporary hit points first. After one hour, any extra hit points above the caster's normal total are lost. The creature originally losing hit points through this spell can regain them by magical or normal healing. Undead creatures are unaffected by this spell.

Ward Off Evil

(Abjuration)

Reversible

Level: 3

Range: Touch   **Components:** V, S, M

Duration: 2 rds./level   **Casting Time:** 3 segments

Area of Effect: 10-ft. radius   **Saving Throw:** None
        around creature touched

The globe of protection of this spell is identical in all respects to a Protection from Evil spell, except that it encompasses a much larger area and its duration is greater. The effect is centered on and moves with the creature touched. Any protected creature within the circle can break the warding against enchanted or summoned monsters by engaging in melee with them. If a creature is too large to fit into the area of effect is the recipient of the spell, the spell acts as a normal Protection from Evil spell for that creature only. To complete this spell, the caster must trace a circle 20 feet in diameter using blessed chalk. The material component for the reverse is powdered iron.

Water Breathing

(Alteration)

Reversible

Level: 3

Range: Touch   **Components:** V, S, M

Duration: 6 turns/level   **Casting Time:** 5 segments

Area of Effect: Creature touched   **Saving Throw:** None

The recipient of a Water Breathing spell is able to freely breathe underwater for the duration of the spell (i.e. 6 turns for each level of experience of the caster casting the spell). The reverse, Air Breathing, allows water-breathing creatures to comfortably survive in the atmosphere for an equal duration. The material component is a reed.

Wind Wall

(Alteration)

Level: 3

Range: 10 yds./level

Components: V, S, M

Duration: 1 rd./level

Casting Time: 3 segments

Area of Effect: wall, 10 x 5 ft. /level, 2 ft. wide

Saving Throw: Special

This spell brings forth an invisible vertical curtain of wind 2 feet thick and of considerable strength – a strong breeze sufficient to blow away any bird smaller than an eagle or tear papers and like materials from unsuspecting hands. If in doubt, a saving throw vs. spell determines whether the subject maintains its grasp.

Normal insects cannot pass such a barrier. Loose materials, even cloth garments, fly upward when caught in a Wind Wall. Arrows and bolts are deflected upward and miss, while sling stones and other missiles under two pounds in weight receive a -4 penalty to a first shot and -2 penalties thereafter. Gases, most breath weapons, and creatures in gaseous form cannot pass this wall, although it is no barrier to noncorporeal creatures. The material components are a tiny fan and a feather of exotic origin.

Wraithform

(Alteration, Illusion)

Level: 3

Range: 0

Components: S, M

Duration: 2 rds./level

Casting Time: 1 segment

Area of Effect: The caster

Saving Throw: None

When this spell is cast, the magic-user and all of his gear become insubstantial. The caster is subject only to magical or special attacks, including those by weapons of +1 or better, or by creatures otherwise able to affect those struck only by magical weapons. Undead of most sorts will ignore an individual in wraithform, believing him to be a Wraith or Spectre, though a Lich or special undead may save vs. spell with a -4 penalty to recognize the spell. The magic-user can pass through small holes or narrow openings, even mere cracks, with all he wears or holds in his hands, as long as the spell persists. Note, however, that the caster cannot fly without additional magic.

No form of attack is possible when in wraithform, except against creatures that exist on the Ethereal Plane, where all attacks (both ways) are normal. A successful Dispel Magic spell forces the magic-user in Wraithform back to normal form. The spellcaster can end the spell with a single word. The material components for the spell are a bit of gauze and a wisp of smoke.

Zargosa's Flaming Spheres of Torment

(Evocation, Alteration)

Level: 3

Range: 70 yds. + 10 yds./level

Components: V, S, M

Duration: Special

Casting Time: 3 segments

Area of Effect: 1 target/meteor

Saving Throw: None

This spell enables the magic-user to cast small globes of fire (one for each experience level he has attained), each of which bursts into a 1-foot-diameter sphere upon impact, inflicting 1d4 points of damage to the creature struck. It can also ignite combustible materials (even solid planks). The spheres are treated as missiles hurled by the magic-user with a +2 bonus to the attack rolls and with no penalty for range. Misses are treated as grenadelike missiles that inflict 1 point of damage to creatures within 3 feet. The spell can be cast in either of two ways:

A) The magic-user discharges five flaming spheres every round (see the Initiative section in Chapter 12: Combat). Note that this carries over into at least the following round.

B) The magic-user discharges only one flaming sphere per round.

In addition to releasing the missile, the caster can perform other actions in the round, including spellcasting, melee, or device use. Spells requiring concentration force the magic-user to forgo the rest of the missiles to maintain concentration. Also, if the magic-user fails to maintain an exact mental count

of the number of missiles he has remaining, he has involuntarily lost the remaining portion of the spell. The spell ends when the caster has fired off as many spheres as he has experience levels, when he forgoes casting any still remaining, or when a successful Dispel Magic spell is thrown upon the caster. The components necessary for the casting of this spell are nitre and sulphur formed into a bead by the addition of pine tar. The caster must also have a small hollow tube of minute proportion, fashioned from gold. The tube costs no less than 1,000 gp to construct, so fine is its workmanship and magical engraving, and it can be reused.

Fourth Level Spells

Charm Monster

(Enchantment/Charm)

Level: 4

Range: 60 yards

Components: V, S

Duration: Special

Casting Time: 4 segments

Area of Effect: 1 or more creatures in 20-ft. radius

Saving Throw: Negates

This spell is similar to a Charm Person spell, but it can affect any living creature – or several low level creatures. The spell affects 2d4 Hit Dice or levels of creatures, although it only affects one creature of 4 or more Hit Dice or levels, regardless of the number rolled. All possible subjects receive saving throws vs. spell, adjusted for Wisdom. Any damage inflicted by the caster or his allies in the round of casting grants the wounded creature another saving throw at a bonus of +1 per point of damage received.

Any affected creature regards the spellcaster as friendly, an ally or companion to be treated well or guarded from harm. If communication is possible, the charmed creature follows reasonable requests, instructions, or orders most faithfully (see the suggestion spell). If communication is not possible, the creature does not harm the caster, but others in the vicinity may be subject to its intentions, hostile or otherwise. Any overtly hostile act by the caster breaks the spell, or at the very least allows a new saving throw against the charm. Affected creatures eventually come out from under the influence of the spell. This is a function of the creature's level (i.e., its Hit Dice).

Monster Level or Hit Dice	% Chance Per Week of Breaking Spell
1st or up to 2	5%
2nd or up to 3+2	10%
3rd or up to 4+4	15%
4th or up to 6	25%
5th or up to 7+2	35%
6th or up to 8+4	45%
7th or up to 10	60%
8th or up to 12	75%
9th or over 12	90%

The exact day of the week and time of day is secretly determined by the GM.

Close Portal

(Alteration)

Level: 4

Range: 120 feet

Components: V, S

Duration: 1 round/level

Casting Time: 4 segments

Area of Effect: 1 creature

Saving Throw: Negates

The victim of a Close Portal spell is prevented from using extradimensional movement of any kind for the duration of the spell. This type of movement includes teleports, blinking, dimension doors, astral spells, shadow walking, plane shifting, and words of recall of any kind. The spell also prevents ethereal or astral creatures from manifesting into the material plane. Or if such a creature is caught on the Prime Material Plane, it prevents them from vanishing back into the Ethereal or Astral Planes.

Confusion

(Enchantment/Charm)

Level: 4
Range: 120 yards
Duration: 2 rds. + 1 rd./level
Area of Effect: Up to 60-ft. cube

Components: V, S, M
Casting Time: 4 segments
Saving Throw: Special

This spell causes confusion in one or more creatures within the area, creating indecision and the inability to take effective action. The spell affects 1d4 creatures, plus one creature per caster level. These creatures are allowed saving throws vs. spell with -2 penalties, adjusted for Wisdom. Those successfully saving are unaffected by the spell. Confused creatures react as follows:

d10 Roll	Action
1	Wander away (unless prevented) for duration of spell
2-6	Stand confused for one round (then roll again)
7-9	Attack nearest creature for one round (then roll again)
10	Act normally for one round (then roll again)

The spell lasts for two rounds plus one round for each level of the caster. Those who fail are checked by the GM for actions each round for the duration of the spell, or until the "wander away for the duration of the spell" result occurs. Wandering creatures move as far from the caster as possible, according to their most typical mode of movement (characters walk, fish swim, bats fly, etc.). Saving throws and actions are checked at the beginning of each round. Any confused creature that is attacked perceives the attacker as an enemy and acts according to its basic nature. If there are many creatures involved, the GM may decide to assume average results.

For example, if there are 16 Orcs affected and 25% could be expected to make the saving throw, then four are assumed to have succeeded. Out of the other 12, one wanders away, four attack the nearest creature, six stand confused, and the last acts normally but must check next round. Since the Orcs are not near the party, the GM decides that two attacking the nearest creature attack each other, one attacks an Orc that saved, and one attacks a confused Orc, which strikes back. The next round, the base is 11 Orcs, since four originally saved and one wandered off. Another one wanders off, five stand confused, four attack, and one acts normally. The material component is a set of three nut shells.

Contagion

(Necromancy)

Level: 4
Range: 30 yards
Duration: Permanent
Area of Effect: 1 creature

Components: V, S
Casting Time: 4 segments
Saving Throw: Negates

This spell causes a major disease and weakness in a creature. The afflicted individual is immediately stricken with painful and distracting symptoms: boils, blotches, lesions, seeping abscesses, and so on. Strength, Dexterity, and Charisma are reduced by 2. Attack rolls are decreased by 2. The effect persists until the character receives a Cure Disease spell or spends 1d3 weeks taking a complete rest to recover. Characters ignoring the contagion for more than a day or so may be susceptible to worse diseases at the discretion of the GM.

Detect Scrying

(Divination)

Level: 4
Range: 0
Duration: 1d6 turns + 1 turn/lvl.
Area of Effect: 120-ft. radius

Components: V, S, M
Casting Time: 3 segments
Saving Throw: Special

By means of this spell, the magic-user immediately becomes aware of any attempt to observe him by means of Clairvoyance, Clairaudience, or Magic Mirror. This also reveals the use of Crystal Balls or other magical scrying devices, provided the attempt is within the area of effect of the spell. Since the spell is centered on the spellcaster, it moves with him, enabling him to "sweep" areas for the duration of the spell.

When a scrying attempt is detected, the scryer must immediately roll a saving throw. If this is failed, the identity and general location of the scryer immediately become known to the magic-user who cast this spell. The general location is a direction and significant landmark close to the scryer. Thus, the caster might learn, "The magic-user Sniggel spies on us from east, under the stairs," or, "You are watched by Asquil in the city of Samarquol." The material components for this spell are a small piece of mirror and a miniature brass hearing trumpet.

Dig

(Evocation)

Level: 4
Range: 30 yards
Duration: 1 rd./level
Area of Effect: 5-ft. cube/level

Components: V, S, M
Casting Time: 4 segments
Saving Throw: Special

A Dig spell enables the caster to excavate 125 cubic feet of earth, sand, or mud per round (i.e., a cubic hole 5 feet on a side). In later rounds the caster can expand an existing hole or start a new one. The material thrown from the excavation scatters evenly around the pit. If the magic-user continues downward past 20 feet in earth, there is a 15% chance that the pit collapses. This check is made for every 5 feet dug beyond 20 feet. Sand tends to collapse after 10 feet, mud fills in and collapses after 5 feet, and quicksand fills in as rapidly as it is dug. Any creature at the edge (within 1 foot) of a pit must roll a successful Dexterity check or fall into the hole. Creatures moving rapidly toward a pit dug immediately before them must roll a saving throw vs. spell to avoid falling in. Any creature in a pit being excavated can climb out at a rate decided by the GM. A creature caught in a collapsing pit must roll a saving throw vs. death to avoid being buried; it escapes the pit if successful.

Tunneling is possible with this spell as long as there is space available for the material removed. Chances for collapse are doubled and the safe tunneling distance is half of the safe excavation depth, unless such construction is most carefully braced and supported. The spell is also effective against creatures of earth and rock, particularly Clay Golems and those from the Elemental Plane of Earth. When cast upon such a creature, it suffers 4d6 points of damage. A successful saving throw vs. spell reduces this damage to half. To activate the spell, the spellcaster needs a miniature shovel and tiny bucket and must continue to hold them while each pit is excavated. These items disappear at the conclusion of the spell.

Dimension Door

(Alteration)

Level: 4
Range: 0
Duration: Instantaneous
Area of Effect: The caster

Components: V
Casting Time: 1 segment
Saving Throw: None

By means of a Dimension Door spell, the magic-user instantly transfers himself up to 30 yards distance per level of experience. This special form of teleportation allows for no error, and the magic-user always arrives at exactly the spot desired – whether by simply visualizing the area (within spell transfer distance, of course) or by stating direction such as, "300 yards straight downward," or, "upward to the northwest, 45 degree angle, 420 yards." If the magic-user arrives in a place that is already occupied by a solid body, he remains trapped in the Astral Plane. If distances are stated and the spellcaster arrives with no support below his feet (i.e., in mid-air), falling and damage result unless further magical means are employed. All that the magic-user wears or carries, subject to a maximum weight equal to 500 pounds of nonliving matter, or half that amount of living matter, is transferred with the spellcaster. Recovery from use of a Dimension Door spell requires one round.

Dispel Exhaustion

(Illusion/Phantasm)

Level: 4
Range: Touch
Duration: 3 turns/level
Area of Effect: 1 to 4 persons

Components: V, S
Casting Time: 4 segments
Saving Throw: None

By means of this spell, the caster is able to restore 50% of lost hit points to all persons (humans, demi-humans and humanoids) he touches during the round it is cost, subject to a maximum of four persons. The spell gives the illusion to the person touched that he is fresh and well. Stamina is renewed, but when the spell duration expires, the recipient drops back to their actual hit point strength. The spell will allow recipients to move at double speed for 1 round every turn (cf. Haste spell).

Emergency Teleport at Random

(Alteration)
Level: 4
Range: 0
Duration: 1 turn/level
Area of Effect: The caster

Components: V
Casting Time: 1 round
Saving Throw: None

This spell is very similar to a Contingency spell. The caster nominates a specific trigger that will activate a teleport spell on himself. Some triggers could include teleporting the caster if he is wounded to below 10 hit points, if he is immersed in a liquid, if someone is about to attack him from behind or if anyone says "Kobolds are Kewl" in Elvish within 10 feet of him. A vague trigger could cause the spell to fail, i.e. "Teleport me away as soon as I am in danger" as a trigger could result in the caster being teleported the first time he walks near a steep cliff!

When the Teleport is activated the caster is teleported 1d100 miles in a random direction. Also roll a d4 to determine whether or not the caster remains at his current height. On a roll of a 1 the caster appears 1d100 feet lower than his current position, on a 2 or 3 his relative height remains the same, and on a roll of a 4 the caster appears 1d100 feet higher than his current elevation. Use the rules given for the Teleport spell to determine any side effects of the caster appearing in a solid object, appearing above the ground or other mishaps.

Emotion

(Enchantment/Charm)
Level: 4
Range: 10 yds./level
Duration: Special
Area of Effect: 20-ft. cube

Components: V, S
Casting Time: 4 segments
Saving Throw: Negates

When this spell is cast, the magic-user can create a single emotional reaction in the subject creatures. The following are typical;

1. Courage: This emotion causes the creatures affected to become berserk, fighting with a +1 bonus to the attack dice, causing +3 points of damage, and temporarily gaining 5 hit points. The recipients fight without shield and regardless of life, never checking morale. This spell counters (and is countered by) fear.
2. Fear: The affected creatures flee in panic for 2d4 rounds. It counters (and is countered by) courage.
3. Friendship: The affected creatures react more positively (for example, tolerance becomes goodwill). It counters (and is countered by) hate.
4. Happiness: This effect creates joy and a feeling of complacent well-being, adding +4 to all reaction rolls and making attack unlikely unless the creatures are subject to extreme provocation. It counters (and is countered by) sadness.
5. Hate: The affected creatures react more negatively (for example, tolerance becomes negative neutrality). It counters (and is countered by) friendship.
6. Hope: The effect of hope is to raise morale, saving throw rolls, attack rolls, and damage caused by +2. It counters (and is countered by) hopelessness.
7. Hopelessness: The affected creatures submit to the demands of any opponent: surrender, get out, etc. Otherwise, the creatures are 25% likely to do nothing in a round, and 25% likely to turn back or retreat. It counters (and is countered by) hope.
8. Sadness: This creates unhappiness and a tendency toward maudlin introspection. This emotion penalizes surprise rolls by -1 and adds +1 to initiative rolls. It counters (and is countered by) happiness.

All creatures in the area at the instant the spell is cast are affected unless successful saving throws vs. spell are made, adjusted for Wisdom. The spell lasts as long as the magic-user continues to concentrate on projecting the chosen emotion. Those who fail the saving throw against fear must roll a new saving throw if they return to the affected area.

Enchanted Weapon

(Enchantment)
Level: 4
Range: Touch
Duration: 5 rds./level
Area of Effect: Weapon(s) touched

Components: V, S, M
Casting Time: 1 turn
Saving Throw: None

This spell turns an ordinary weapon into a magical one. The weapon is the equivalent of a +1 weapon, with +1 to attack and damage rolls. Thus, arrows, axes, bolts, bows, daggers, hammers, maces, spears, swords, etc., can be made into temporarily enchanted weapons. Two small weapons (arrows, bolts, daggers, etc.) or one large weapon (axe, bow, hammer, mace, etc.) weapon can be affected by the spell. The spell functions on existing magical weapons as long as the total combined bonus is +3 or less. Missile weapons enchanted in this way lose their enchantment when they successfully hit a target, but otherwise the spell lasts its full duration. This spell is often used in combination with the Enchant an Item and Permanency spells to create magical weapons, with this spell being cast once per desired plus of the bonus. The material components of this spell are powdered lime and carbon.

Enervation

(Necromancy)
Level: 4
Range: 10 yds./level
Duration: 1d4 hrs. + 1 hr./level
Area of Effect: 1 creature

Components: V, S
Casting Time: 4 segments
Saving Throw: Negates

This spell temporarily suppresses the subject's life force. The necromancer points his finger and utters the incantation, releasing a black bolt of crackling energy. The subject must roll a saving throw vs. spell, adjusted for Dexterity, to avoid the bolt. Success means the spell has no effect. Failure means the subject is treated exactly as if he had been drained of energy levels by a Wight, one level for every four levels of the caster. Hit Dice, spells, and other character details dependent on level are lost or reduced. Those drained to 0th level must make a system shock check to survive and are helpless until the spell expires. The spell effect eventually wears off, either after 1d4 hours plus one hour per caster level, or after six hours of complete and undisturbed rest. Level abilities are regained, but lost spells must be re-memorized. Undead are immune to this spell.

Extension I

(Alteration)
Level: 4
Range: 0
Duration: Special
Area of Effect: Special

Components: V
Casting Time: 2 segments
Saving Throw: None

By use of an Extension I spell, the magic-user prolongs the duration of a previously cast 1st, 2nd, or 3rd level spell by 50%. Thus, a Levitation spell can be made to function 15 minutes/level, a Hold Person spell made to work for three rounds/level, etc. Naturally, the spell affects only spells that have durations. This spell must be cast immediately after the spell to be extended, either by the original caster or another magic-user. If a complete round or more elapses, the extension fails and is wasted.

Fear

(Illusion/Phantasm)
Level: 4
Range: 0
Duration: Special
Area of Effect: 60-ft. cone, 30-ft. diameter at end, 5-ft. at base

Components: V, S, M
Casting Time: 4 segments
Saving Throw: Negates

When a Fear spell is cast, the magic-user sends forth an invisible cone of terror that causes creatures within its area of effect to turn away from the caster and flee in panic. Affected creatures are likely to drop whatever they are holding when struck by the spell; the base chance of this is 60% at 1st level (or at 1 Hit Die), and each level (or Hit Die) above this reduces the probability by 5%. Thus, at 10th level there is only a 15% chance, and at 13th level no chance, of dropping items. Creatures affected by Fear flee at their fastest rate for a number of melee rounds equal to the level of experience of the spellcaster. Undead and creatures that successfully roll their saving throws vs. spell are not affected. The material component of this spell is either the heart of a hen or a white feather.

Fireball, Land Scraper

(Evocation)
Level: 4
Range: 10 yds. + 10 yds./level   **Components:** V, S, M
Duration: Instantaneous   **Casting Time:** 4 segments
Area of Effect: 20-ft. radius + 5 ft. **Saving Throw:** 1/2
          wide by 10 ft. high parallelepiped back to caster

The Land Scraper Fireball is similar in most respects to a normal Fireball except that the area of effect is increased by a 5 ft. wide by 10 ft. high parallelepiped that extends back to the caster from the center of the main fireball. Creatures potentially affected by the fire in the parallelepiped volume gain a +1 to their saving throws.

Fireball, Sidewinder Factor 4

(Evocation)
Level: 4
Range: 1 mile maximum   **Components:** V, S, M
Duration: 1 rd./level   **Casting Time:** 4 segments
Area of Effect: 10-ft. radius   **Saving Throw:** 1/2

The Sidewinder Fireball is similar to the Skipping Betty Fireball except that it uses 1d6-1 for damage instead of d4 and the range of the fireball is only 100 feet per level of the caster. The spell range is further reduced by 10 feet per degree if the air temperature is less than 32° Fahrenheit. Potential targets need not be in the 45 degree firing arc from the front of the caster. Additionally, the terrain need not be level as the Sidewinder fireball can maneuver around obstructions and even hit an object hidden behind a wall, for example. The somatic gestures necessary for casting this spell include a side winding motion made with the casters arms. The material component is a tiny ball of bat guano and sulphur.

Fireball, Volley

(Evocation)
Level: 4
Range: 10 yards + 10 yards/lvl.   **Components:** V, S, M
Duration: Special   **Casting Time:** 4 segments
Area of Effect: 10 foot radius   **Saving Throw:** Half

This spell gives the caster the ability to throw one fireball per round for as long as the spell lasts. The duration of the spell is one round for every three full levels of the caster, and the fireballs that are thrown always cause 3d6 damage each (save for half damage). Therefore a 10th level caster could throw one fireball per round for each of the three rounds that the spell lasts. The caster cannot use other spells or attacks during a round that he throws a fireball, but he is allowed to move as normal. If the caster chooses to not throw a fireball during a round that round's fireball is lost, but the spell still lasts its full duration. Thus, he could throw a fireball the next round provided the spell's duration had not run out. The material component is a small tube filled with tiny balls of bat guano and sulfur.

Fire Charm

(Enchantment/Charm)
Level: 4
Range: 10 yards   **Components:** V, S, M
Duration: 2 rds./level   **Casting Time:** 4 segments
Area of Effect: 15-ft. radius **Saving Throw:** Negates

By means of this spell the magic-user causes a normal fire source, such as a brazier, flambeau, or bonfire, to serve as a magical agent, for from this source he causes a gossamer veil of multi-hued flame to encircle the fire at a distance of 5 feet. Any creatures observing the fire or the dancing circle of flame around it must successfully roll a saving throw vs. spell or be charmed into remaining

motionless and gazing, transfixed, at the flames. While so charmed, creatures are subject to suggestions of 12 or fewer words, saving vs. spell with a -3 penalty, adjusted for Wisdom. The caster can give one such suggestion to each creature, and the suggestions need not be the same.

The maximum duration for such a suggestion is one hour, regardless of the caster's level. The fire charm is broken if the charmed creature is physically attacked, if a solid object comes between the creature and the veil of flames so as to obstruct vision, or when the duration of the spell expires. Those exposed to the fire charm again may be affected at the GM's option, although bonuses may also be allowed to the saving throws. Note that the veil of flame is not a magical fire, and passing through it incurs the same damage as would be sustained from passing through its original fire source. The material component for this spell is a small piece of multicolored silk of exceptional thinness that the spellcaster must throw into the fire source.

Fire Shield

(Evocation, Alteration)
Level: 4
Range: 0   **Components:** V, S, M
Duration: 2 rds. + 1 rd./level **Casting Time:** 4 segments
Area of Effect: The caster   **Saving Throw:** None

This spell can be cast in one of two forms: a warm shield that protects against cold-based attacks, or a chill shield that protects against fire-based attacks. Both return damage to creatures making physical attacks against the magic-user. The magic-user must choose which variation he memorizes when the spell is selected.

When casting this spell, the magic-user appears to immolate himself, but the flames are thin and wispy, shedding no heat, and giving light equal to only half the illumination of a normal torch. The color of the flames is determined randomly (50% chance of either color) – blue or green if the chill shield is cast, violet or blue if the warm shield is employed. The special powers of each shield are as follows:

A) Warm shield. The flames are warm to the touch. Any cold-based attacks are saved against with a +2 bonus; either half normal damage or no damage is sustained. There is no bonus against fire-based attacks, but if the magic-user fails to make the required saving throw (if any) against them, he sustains double normal damage. The material component for this variation is a bit of phosphorous.

B) Chill shield. The flames are cool to the touch. Any fire-based attacks are saved against with a +2 bonus; either half normal damage or no damage is sustained. There is no bonus against cold-based attacks, but if the magic-user fails to make the required saving throw (if any) against them, he sustains double normal damage. The material component for this variation is a live firefly or glow worm or the tail portions of four dead ones.

Any creature striking the spellcaster with its body or hand-held weapons inflicts normal damage upon the magic-user, but the attacker suffers the same amount of damage. An attacker's magical resistance, if any, is tested when the creature actually strikes the magic-user. Successful resistance shatters the spell. Failure means the creature's magic resistance does not affect that casting of the spell.

Fire Trap

(Abjuration, Evocation)
Level: 4
Range: Touch   **Components:** V, S, M
Duration: Until discharged   **Casting Time:** 1 turn
Area of Effect: Object touched **Saving Throw:** 1/2

Any closeable item (book, box, bottle, chest, coffer, coffin, door, drawer, and so forth) can be warded by a Fire Trap spell. The spell is centered on a point selected by the spellcaster. The item so trapped cannot have a second closure or warding spell placed upon it (if such is attempted, the chance is 25% that the first spell fails, 25% that the second spell fails, or 50% that both spells fail). A Knock spell does not affect a fire trap in any way – as soon as the offending party enters or touches the item, the trap discharges. Thieves and others have only half their normal chance to detect a fire trap (by noticing the characteristic markings required to cast the spell). They have only half their normal chance to remove the trap (failure detonates the trap immediately). An unsuccessful Dispel Magic does not detonate the spell. The caster can use the trapped object without discharging it, as can any individual to whom the spell was specifically attuned when cast (the exact method usually involves a keyword).

When the trap is discharged, there is an explosion of 5-foot radius from the spell's center; all creatures within this area must roll saving throws vs. spell. Damage is 1d4 points plus 1 point per level of the caster, or half this (round up) for creatures successfully saving. (Under water, this ward inflicts half damage and creates a large cloud of steam.) The item trapped is not harmed by this explosion. To place this spell, the caster must trace the outline of the closure with a bit of sulphur or saltpeter and touch the center of the effect. Attunement to another individual requires a hair or similar object from that person.

Fumble
(Enchantment/Charm)
Level: 4

Range: 10 yds./level	**Components:** V, S, M
Duration: 1 rd./level	**Casting Time:** 4 segments
Area of Effect: 30-ft. cube	**Saving Throw:** Special

When a Fumble spell is cast, the magic-user creates an area in which all creatures suddenly become clumsy and awkward. Running creatures trip and fall, those reaching for an item drop it, those employing weapons likewise awkwardly drop them, etc. Recovery from a fall or picking up a fumbled object typically requires a successful saving throw and takes one round. Note that breakable items might suffer damage when dropped. A subject succeeding with his saving throw can act freely that round, but if he is in the area at the beginning of the next round, another saving throw is required. Alternatively, the spell can be cast at an individual creature. Failure to save means the creature is affected for the spell's entire duration; success means the creature is slowed (see the 3rd level spell). The material component of this spell is a dab of solidified milk fat.

Haarpang's Magnificent Sphere of Resiliency
(Alteration, Evocation)
Level: 4

Range: 20 yards	**Components:** V, S, M
Duration: 1 rd./level	**Casting Time:** 4 segments
Area of Effect: 1-ft. diameter/lvl.	**Saving Throw:** Negates

When this spell is cast, the result is a globe of shimmering force that encloses the subject creature – if it is small enough to fit within the diameter of the sphere and it fails to successfully save vs. spell. The resilient sphere contains its subject for the spell's duration, and it is not subject to damage of any sort except from a Rod of Cancellation, a Wand of Negation, or a Disintegrate or Dispel Magic spell. These cause it to be destroyed without harm to the subject.

Nothing can pass through the sphere, inside or out, though the subject can breathe normally. The subject may struggle, but all that occurs is a movement of the sphere. The globe can be physically moved either by people outside the globe or by the struggles of those within. The material components of the spell are a hemispherical piece of diamond (or similar hard, clear gem material) and a matching hemispherical piece of gum arabic.

Haarpang's Memory Kick
(Alteration)
Level: 4

Range: 0	**Components:** V, S, M
Duration: 1 day	**Casting Time:** 1 turn
Area of Effect: The caster	**Saving Throw:** None

By means of this spell, the magic-user is able to memorize, or retain the memory of, three additional spell levels (three 1st level spells, or one 1st and one 2nd, or one 3rd level spell). The magic-user has two options: A) Memorize additional spells. This option is taken at the time the spell is cast. The additional spells must be memorized normally and any material components must be acquired. B) Retain memory of any spell (within the level limits) cast the round prior to starting to cast this spell. The round after a spell is cast, the Enhancer must be successfully cast. This restores the previously cast spell to memory. However, the caster still must acquire any needed material compo-

nents. The material components of the spell are a piece of string, an ivory plaque of at least 100 gp value, and ink consisting of squid secretion with either Black Dragon's blood or Giant Slug digestive juice. These disappear when the spell is cast.

Hallucinatory Terrain
(Illusion/Phantasm)
Level: 4

Range: 20 yds./level	**Components:** V, S, M
Duration: 1 hr./level	**Casting Time:** 1 turn
Area of Effect: 10 yds./lvl. cube	**Saving Throw:** None

By means of this spell, the magic-user causes an illusion that hides the actual terrain within the area of effect. Thus, open fields or a road can be made to look like a swamp, hill, crevasse, or some other difficult or impassable terrain. A pond can be made to look like a grassy meadow, a precipice like a gentle slope, or a rock-strewn gully like a wide and smooth road. The hallucinatory terrain persists until a Dispel Magic spell is cast upon the area or until the duration expires. Individual creatures may see through the illusion, but the illusion persists, affecting others who observe the scene. If the illusion involves only a subtle change, such as causing an open wood to appear thick and dark, or increasing the slope of a hill, the effect may be unnoticed even by those in the midst of it. If the change is extreme (for example, a grassy plain covering a seething field of volcanic mudpots), the illusion will no doubt be noticed the instant one person falls prey to it. Each level of experience expands the dimensions of the cubic area affected by 10 yards; for example, a 12th level caster affects an area 120 yds. x 120 yds. x 120 yds. The material components of this spell are a stone, a twig, and a bit of green plant – a leaf or grass blade.

Hurl Animal
(Alteration)
Level: 4

Range: 10 yds./level	**Components:** V, S, M
Duration: Instantaneous	**Casting Time:** 4 segments
Area of Effect: 10 yds./level	**Saving Throw:** Negates

This spell provides the caster with a limited form of telekinesis manifested by a single short, violent thrust. Oddly enough, the spell only works when used on living normal domesticated animals. The caster can hurl one or more animals within range and within a 10-foot cube, directly away from himself at high speed, to a distance of up to 10 feet per caster level. This is subject to a maximum weight of 25 pounds per caster level. Damage caused by hurled animals is decided by the GM, but is typically 1 point of damage per caster level for lighter animals such as chickens and up to 5 points of damage per level for heavier animals such as large cows. Normal domestic animals who fall within the weight capacity of the spell can be hurled, but they are allowed a saving throw vs. spell to avoid the effect.

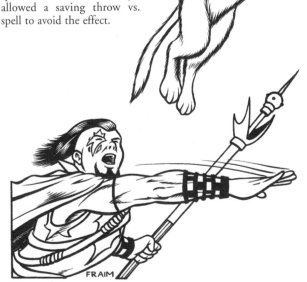

FRAIM

Ice Storm

(Evocation)

Level: 4

Range: 10 yds./level	**Components:** V, S, M
Duration: Special	**Casting Time:** 4 segments
Area of Effect: 20 or 40 ft. radius	**Saving Throw:** None

This spell can have one of two effects, at the caster's option: Either great hail stones pound down for one round in a 40-foot-diameter area and inflict 3d10 points of damage to any creatures within the area of effect, or driving sleet falls in an 80-foot-diameter area for one round per caster level. The sleet blinds creatures within its area for the duration of the spell and causes the ground in the area to be icy, slowing movement by 50% and making it 50% probable that a creature trying to move in the area slips and falls. The sleet also extinguishes torches and small fires. Note that this spell will negate a White Hot Metal or similar spell. The material components for this spell are a pinch of dust and a few drops of water.

Illusionary Wall

(Illusion/Phantasm)

Level: 4

Range: 30 yards	**Components:** V, S
Duration: Permanent	**Casting Time:** 4 segments
Area of Effect: 1 x 10 x 10 ft.	**Saving Throw:** None

This spell creates the illusion of a wall, floor, ceiling, or similar surface, which is permanent until dispelled. It appears absolutely real when viewed (even magically, as with the cleric spell True Seeing or its equivalent), but physical objects can pass through it without difficulty. When the spell is used to hide pits, traps, or normal doors, normal demi-human and magical detection abilities work normally, and touch or probing searches reveal the true nature of the surface, though they do not cause the illusion to disappear. The material component is a rare dust that costs at least 400 gp and requires four days to prepare.

Improved Invisibility

(Illusion/Phantasm)

Level: 4

Range: Touch	**Components:** V, S
Duration: 4 rds. + 1 rd./level	**Casting Time:** 4 segments
Area of Effect: Creature touched	**Saving Throw:** None

This spell is similar to the Invisibility spell, but the recipient is able to attack, either by missile discharge, melee combat, or spellcasting, and remain unseen. Note, however, that telltale traces (such as a shimmering effect) sometimes allow an observant opponent to attack the invisible spell recipient. These traces are only noticeable when specifically looked for (after the invisible character has made his presence known). Attacks against the invisible character suffer -4 penalties to the attack rolls, and the invisible character's saving throws are made with a +4 bonus. Beings with high Hit Dice that might normally notice invisible opponents will notice a creature under this spell as if they had 2 fewer Hit Dice (they roll saving throws vs. spell; success indicates they spot the character).

Mage Lock

(Enchantment/Charm)

Level: 4

Range: Touch	**Components:** V, S, M
Duration: Permanent	**Casting Time:** 1 turn
Area of Effect: 1 item	**Saving Throw:** None

This spell is used to install a magical "safety" onto a magic item. In order to activate or deactivate an item so protected a command word must be uttered, which is set when the spell is cast. In order to cast this spell the magic-user must have the magic item in his possession for at least a week so the item can attune itself to the caster. Potions and scrolls cannot be mage locked, and any "pluses" that an item has cannot be turned on and off, although secondary abilities can be. For example, a deactivated Sword of Sharpness still has its magical bonus on to-hit and damage rolls, but cannot use its Sharpness ability until the command word is used. Once the sharpness ability has been activated it remains active until the command word is used again. Obviously Relics and Artifacts are above being mage locked, and the spell can be dispelled with a Dispel Magic or similar magic. Note that a magic resistant creature could use a mage locked item if its magic resistance overcomes the mage lock's enchantment. The material component is the magic item that is being locked.

Magic Mirror

(Enchantment, Divination)

Level: 4

Range: Touch	**Components:** V, S, M
Duration: 1 rd./level	**Casting Time:** 1 hour
Area of Effect: Special	**Saving Throw:** None

By means of this spell, the magic-user changes a normal mirror into a scrying device similar to a Crystal Ball. The details of the use of such a scrying device are found in the GMG. The mirror used must be of finely wrought and highly polished silver and cost not less than 1,000 gp This mirror is not harmed by casting the spell, but the other material components – the eye of a hawk, an eagle, or even a Roc, and nitric acid, copper, and zinc – are used up. The following spells can be cast through a Magic Mirror: Comprehend Languages, Read Magic, Tongues and Infravision. The following spells have a 5% chance per level of the caster of operating correctly: Detect Magic, Detect Good or Evil, and Message. The base chances for the subject to detect any Crystal Ball-like spell are listed in the GMG.

Massmorph

(Alteration)

Level: 4

Range: 10 yds./level	**Components:** V, S, M
Duration: Special	**Casting Time:** 4 segments
Area of Effect: 10 ft. cube/level	**Saving Throw:** None

When this spell is cast upon willing creatures of man-size or smaller, up to 10 such creatures per level of the caster can be magically altered to appear as trees of any sort. Thus, a company of creatures can be made to appear as a copse, grove or orchard. Furthermore, these massmorphed creatures can be passed through and even touched by other creatures without revealing their true nature. Note, however, that blows to the creature-trees cause damage, and blood can be seen. Creatures to be massmorphed must be within the spell's area of effect; unwilling creatures are not affected. Affected creatures remain unmoving but aware, subject to normal sleep requirements, and able to see, hear and feel for as long as the spell is in effect. The spell persists until the caster commands it to cease or until a Dispel Magic spell is cast upon the creatures. Creatures left in this state for extended periods are subject to insects, weather, disease, fire and other natural hazards. The material component of this spell is a handful of bark chips from the type of tree the creatures are to become.

Minor Creation

(Illusion/Phantasm)

Level: 4

Range: Touch	**Components:** V, S, M
Duration: 1 hr./level	**Casting Time:** 1 turn
Area of Effect: 1 cubic ft./level	**Saving Throw:** None

This spell enables the magic-user to create an item of nonliving, vegetable nature – soft goods, rope, wood, etc. The caster actually pulls wisps of material of the Plane of Shadow from the air and weaves them into the desired item. The volume of the item created cannot exceed 1 cubic foot per level of the spellcaster. The item remains in existence for only as long as the spell's duration. The spellcaster must have at least a tiny piece of matter of the same type of item he plans to create by means of the minor creation spell – a bit of twisted hemp to create rope, a splinter of wood to create a door and so forth.

Minor Globe of Invulnerability

(Abjuration)

Level: 4
Range: 0   **Components:** V, S, M
Duration: I rd./level   **Casting Time:** 4 segments
Area of Effect: 5-ft. radius   **Saving Throw:** None

This spell creates an immobile, faintly shimmering magical sphere around the caster that prevents any 1st, 2nd, or 3rd level spell effects from penetrating (i.e., the area of effect of any such spells does not include the area of the minor globe of invulnerability). This includes innate abilities and effects from devices. However, any type of spell can be cast out of the magical globe, and these pass from the caster of the globe to their subject without affecting the globe. Fourth and higher level spells are not affected by the globe. The globe can be brought down by a successful Dispel Magic spell. The caster can leave and return to the globe without penalty. Note that spell effects are not actually disrupted by the globe unless cast directly through or into it: The caster would still see a mirror image created by a magic-user outside the globe. If that magic-user then entered the globe, the images would wink out, to reappear when the magic-user exited the globe. Likewise, a magic-user standing in the area of a Light spell would still receive sufficient light for vision, even though that part of the Light spell volume in the globe would not be luminous. The material component of the spell is a glass or crystal bead that shatters at the expiration of the spell.

Mist of Corralling

(Evocation)

Level: 4
Range: 10 ft./level   **Components:** V, S, M
Duration: I turn + I round/level   **Casting Time:** I round
Area of Effect: Up to 50 ft. radius   **Saving Throw:** None
cloud 10 ft. high

When a Mist of Corralling is cast it causes a shimmering cloud to appear. This cloud is 10 ft. high and can be adjusted to be between a 5 ft. and 50 ft. radius. Creatures within this cloud find it difficult to leave, and must make an open doors roll in order to escape. Visibility within the cloud is limited to 10 feet. The cloud itself can be increased or decreased in size according to the caster's wishes, and the whole cloud can be moved by the caster so long as its center point remains within the spell's range. The material component is a piece of spider web.

Monster Summoning II

(Conjuration/Summoning)

Level: 4
Range: Special   **Components:** V, S, M
Duration: 3 rds. + I rd./level   **Casting Time:** 4 segments
Area of Effect: 40 yd. radius   **Saving Throw:** None

This spell is much like the 3rd level spell Monster Summoning I, except that this spell summons 1d6 2nd level monsters. These appear anywhere within the spell's area of effect and attack the caster's opponents, until he commands them to cease, the spell duration expires, or the monsters are slain. These creatures do not check morale; they vanish when slain. If no opponent exists to fight and the magic-user can communicate with them, the summoned monsters can perform other services for the summoning magic-user. The material components of this spell are a tiny bag and a small (not necessarily lit) candle.

Perpetual Shocking Grasp

(Alteration)

Level: 4
Range: Touch   **Components:** V, S, M
Duration: Permanent   **Casting Time:** 4 segments
Area of Effect: I cubic foot of   **Saving Throw:** None
metal per level

By means of this spell the caster can give any metal object the ability to repeatedly gather a sufficient electric charge such that it will deliver a shock to anyone touching it. Damage taken by those touching (or touched by) the object is 1d4+1. If one continues to touch the object, he will not take additional damage unless he breaks contact and touches it again. Gloves, clothing and non-metal armor are not sufficient to insulate one from this effect.

Phantasmal Killer

(Illusion/Phantasm)

Level: 4
Range: 5 yds./level   **Components:** V, S
Duration: I rd./level   **Casting Time:** 4 segments
Area of Effect: I creature   **Saving Throw:** Special

When this spell is cast, the magic-user creates the illusion of the most fearsome thing imaginable to the victim, simply by forming the fears of the victim's subconscious mind into something that its conscious mind can visualize — the most horrible beast. Only the spell recipient can see the phantasmal killer (the caster sees only a shadowy shape), but if it succeeds in scoring a hit, the subject dies from fright. The beast attacks as a 4 Hit Dice monster. It is invulnerable to all attacks and can pass through any barriers. Once cast, it inexorably pursues the subject, for it exists only in the subject's mind. The only defenses against a phantasmal killer are an attempt to disbelieve (which can be tried but once), slaying or rendering unconscious the magic-user who cast the spell, or rendering unconscious the target of the spell for its duration. To disbelieve the killer, the subject must specifically state the attempt and then roll an Intelligence check. This roll has a -1 penalty for every four levels of the caster.

Special modifiers apply to this attack:

Condition	Modifier
Surprise	-2
Subject previously attacked by this spell	+I
Subject is a magic-user	+2
Subject is wearing a helm of telepathy	+3

Magic resistance, bonuses against fear, and Wisdom adjustments also apply. The subject's magic resistance is checked first; if the spell overcomes the resistance, the subject's fear/Wisdom bonuses (if any) then apply as negative modifiers to his Intelligence check. If the subject of a phantasmal killer attack succeeds in disbelieving, and he is wearing a Helm of Telepathy, the beast can be turned upon the magic-user, who must then disbelieve it or be subject to its attack and possible effects. If the subject ignores the killer to perform other actions, such as attacking the caster, the killer may, at the GM's option, gain bonuses to hit (for flank or rear attacks, etc.). Spells such as Remove Fear and Cloak of Bravery, cast after the killer has attacked, grant another check to disbelieve the effect.

Plant Growth

(Alteration)

Level: 4

Range: 10 yds./level **Components:** V, S
Duration: Permanent **Casting Time:** 4 segments
Area of Effect: 100 ft. sq. per caster level **Saving Throw:** None

When a Plant Growth spell is cast, the magic-user causes normal vegetation to grow, entwine, and entangle to form a thicket or jungle that creatures must hack or force a way through at a movement rate of 1 per round (or 2 if the creatures are larger than man size). The area must contain brush and trees for this spell to work. Briars, bushes, creepers, lianas, roots, saplings, thistles, thorn, trees, vines, and weeds become thick and overgrown so as to form a barrier. The area of effect is the caster's level, squared, times 100 square feet. This area can be arranged in any square or rectangular shape that the caster desires. Thus, an 8th level magic-user can affect (8 x 8 =) 64 x 100 square feet, or 6,400 square feet. This could be an 80-foot x 80-foot square, a 160-foot x 40-foot rectangle, a 640-foot x 10-foot rectangle, etc. Individual plant girth and height is generally affected less than thickness of brush, branch and undergrowth. The spell's effects persist in the area until it is cleared by labor, fire, or such magical means as a Dispel Magic spell.

Polymorph Other

(Alteration)

Level: 4

Range: 5 yds./level **Components:** V, S, M
Duration: Permanent **Casting Time:** 4 segments
Area of Effect: 1 creature **Saving Throw:** Negates

The Polymorph Other spell is a powerful magic that completely alters the form and ability, and possibly the personality and mentality, of the recipient. Of course, while a creature with a lower Intelligence can be polymorphed in form into something with a higher Intelligence, it will not gain that creature's mental ability. The reverse – polymorphing a higher Intelligence creature into one of significantly lower Intelligence – results in a creature much more intelligent than appearances would lead one to believe. The polymorphed creature must succeed on a system shock roll to see if it survives the change. After this, it must make a special Intelligence check to see if it retains its personality (see following).

The polymorphed creature acquires the form and physical abilities of the creature it has been polymorphed into, while retaining its own mind. Form includes natural Armor Class (that due to skin toughness, but not due to quickness, magical nature, etc.), physical movement abilities (walking, swimming, and flight with wings, but not plane shifting, blinking, teleporting, etc.), and attack routines (claw/claw/bite, swoop, rake and constriction, but not petrification, breath weapons, energy drain, etc.). Hit points and saving throws do not change from the original form. Noncorporeal forms cannot be assumed. Natural shapeshifters (lycanthropes, Dopplegangers, higher level druids, etc.) are affected for but one round, and can then resume their normal form. If slain, the polymorphed creature reverts to its original form, though it remains dead. As class and level are not attributes of form, abilities derived from either cannot be gained by this spell, nor can exact ability scores be specified.

When the polymorph occurs, the creature's equipment, if any, melds into the new form (in particularly challenging campaigns, the GM may allow protective devices, such as a Ring of Protection, to continue operating effectively). Note that most creatures generally prefer their own form and will not willingly stand the risk of being subjected to this spell! The creature retains its mental abilities, including spell use, assuming the new form allows completion of the proper verbal and somatic components and the material components are available. Creatures not used to a new form might be penalized at the GM's option (for example, -2 to attack rolls) until they practice sufficiently to master it.

When the physical change occurs, there is a base 100% chance that the subject's personality and mentality change into that of the new form (i.e., a roll of 20 or less on 1d20). For each 1 point of Intelligence of the subject, subtract 1 from the base chance on 1d20. Additionally, for every Hit Die of difference between the original form and the form it is assuming, add or subtract 1 (depending on whether polymorphed form has more Hit Dice [or levels] or fewer Hit Dice [or levels] than original, respectively). The chance for assumption of the personality and mentality of the new form is checked daily until the change takes place. A subject acquiring the mentality of the new form has effectively become the creature whose form was assumed and comes under the control of the GM until recovered by a Wish spell or similar magic. Once this

final change takes place, the creature acquires the new form's full range of magical and special abilities. For example: If a 1 Hit Die Orc of 8 Intelligence is Polymorphed into a White Dragon with 6 Hit Dice, it is 85% (20 - 8 Intelligence + 5 level difference [6-1] = 17 out of 20 = 85%) likely to actually become one in all respects, but in any case it has the dragon's physical and mental capabilities. If it does not assume the personality and mentality of a White Dragon, it knows what it formerly knew as well.

The magic-user can use a Dispel Magic spell to change the polymorphed creature back to its original form, and this requires a system shock roll. Those who have lost their individuality and are then converted back maintain the belief that they are actually the polymorphed creature and attempt to return to that form. Thus, the Orc who comes to believe he is a White Dragon, when converted back to his Orc form, steadfastly maintains he is really a White Dragon polymorphed into the shape of an Orc. His companions will most likely consider him mad. The material component of this spell is a caterpillar cocoon.

Polymorph Self

(Alteration)

Level: 4

Range: 0 **Components:** V
Duration: 2 turns/level **Casting Time:** 4 segments
Area of Effect: The caster **Saving Throw:** None

When this spell is cast, the magic-user is able to assume the form of any creature, save those that are noncorporeal, from as small as a wren to as large as a hippopotamus. Furthermore, the magic-user gains its physical mode of locomotion and breathing as well. No system shock roll is required. The spell does not give the new form's other abilities (attack, magic, special movement, etc.), nor does it run the risk of the magic-user changing personality and mentality. When the polymorph occurs, the caster's equipment, if any, melds into the new form (in particularly challenging campaigns, the GM may allow protective devices, such as a Ring of Protection, to continue operating effectively). The caster retains all mental abilities, including spell use, assuming the new form allows completion of the proper verbal and somatic components and the material components are available. A caster not used to a new form might be penalized at the GM's option (for example, -2 penalty to attack rolls) until he practices sufficiently to master it. Thus, a magic-user changed into an owl could fly, but his vision would be human; a change to a black pudding would enable movement under doors or along halls and ceilings, but not the pudding's offensive (acid) or defensive capabilities. Naturally, the strength of the new form is sufficient to enable normal movement. The spellcaster can change his form as often as desired for the duration of the spell, each change requiring a round. The magic-user retains his own hit points, attack rolls, and saving throws. The magic-user can end the spell at any time; when voluntarily returning to his own form and ending the spell, he regains 1d12 hit points. The magic-user also will return to his own form when slain or when the effect is dispelled, but no hit points are restored in these cases.

Rainbow Pattern

(Alteration, Illusion/Phantasm)

Level: 4

Range: 10 yards **Components:** S, M
Duration: Special **Casting Time:** 4 segments
Area of Effect: 30-ft. cube **Saving Throw:** Negates

By means of this spell, the magic-user creates a glowing, rainbow-hued band of interweaving patterns. Any creature caught in it may become fascinated and gaze at it as long as the effect lasts. The spell can captivate a maximum of 24 levels, or Hit Dice, of creatures – 24 creatures with 1 Hit Die each, 12 with 2 Hit Dice, etc. All creatures affected must be within the area of effect, and each is entitled to a saving throw vs. spell. An attack on an affected creature that causes damage frees it from the spell immediately. Creatures that are restrained and removed from the area still try to follow the pattern. Once the rainbow pattern is cast, the magic-user need only gesture in the direction he desires, and the pattern of colors moves slowly off in that direction, at the rate of 30 feet per round. It persists without further attention from the spellcaster for 1d3 rounds. All affected creatures follow the moving rainbow of light. If the pattern leads its subjects into a dangerous area (through flame, off a cliff, etc.), allow a second saving throw. If the view of the lights is completely blocked (by an Obscurement spell, for instance), the spell is negated. The magic-user need not utter a sound, but he must gesture appropriately while holding a crystal prism and the material component, a piece of phosphor.

Remove Curse

(Abjuration)
Reversible
Level: 4
Range: Touch   **Components:** V, S
Duration: Permanent   **Casting Time:** 4 segments
Area of Effect: Special   **Saving Throw:** Special

Upon casting this spell, the magic-user is usually able to remove a curse – whether it is on an object, on a person, or in the form of some undesired sending or evil presence. Note that the Remove Curse spell cannot affect a cursed shield, weapon or suit of armor, for example, although it usually enables a person afflicted with a cursed item to be rid of it. Certain special curses may not be countered by this spell, or may be countered only by a caster of a certain level or higher. A caster of 12th level or higher can cure lycanthropy with this spell by casting it on the animal form. The were-creature receives a saving throw vs. spell and, if successful, the spell fails and the magic-user must gain a level before attempting the remedy again. The reverse of the spell is not permanent; the Bestowed Curse lasts one turn for every experience level of the magic-user casting the spell. It causes one of the following effects (roll percentile dice):

d100 Roll Result	
1-50	Lowers one ability of the subject to 3 (the GM determines which by random selection)
51-75	Worsens the subject's attack rolls and saving throws by -4
76-00	Makes the subject 50% likely per turn to drop whatever it is holding (or simply do nothing, in the case of creatures not using tools)

It is possible for a magic-user to devise his own curse, and it should be similar in power to those given (the GM has final say). The subject of a Bestow Curse spell must be touched. If the subject is touched, a saving throw is still applicable; if it is successful, the effect is negated. The bestowed curse cannot be dispelled.

Shadow Monsters

(Illusion/Phantasm)
Level: 4
Range: 30 yards   **Components:** V, S
Duration: 1 rd./level   **Casting Time:** 4 segments
Area of Effect: 20-ft. cube   **Saving Throw:** Special

A magic-user casting the Shadow Monsters spell uses material from the Demiplane of Shadow to shape semi-real illusions of one or more monsters. The total Hit Dice of the shadow monster or monsters thus created cannot exceed the level of experience of the magic-user; thus, a 10th level magic-user can create one creature that has 10 Hit Dice, two that have 5 Hit Dice, etc. All shadow monsters created by one spell must be of the same sort. The actual hit point total for each monster is 20% of the hit point total it would normally have. (To determine this, roll the appropriate Hit Dice and multiply the hit points by .2. Any remainder less than .4 is dropped – in the case of monsters with 1 or fewer Hit Dice, this indicates the monster was not successfully created—and scores between .4 and 1 are rounded up to 1 hit point.) Those viewing the shadow monsters are allowed to disbelieve as per normal illusions, although there is a -2 penalty to the attempt. The shadow monsters perform as the real monsters with respect to Armor Class and attack forms. Those who believe in the shadow monster suffer real damage from their attacks. Special attack forms such as petrification or level drain do not actually occur, but a subject who believes they are real will react appropriately.

Those who roll successful saving throws see the shadow monsters as transparent images superimposed on vague shadowy forms. These are Armor Class 10 and inflict only 20% of normal melee damage (biting, clawing, weapon, etc.), dropping fractional damage less than .4 as done with hit points. For example: A Shadow Griffon attacks a person who knows it is only quasi-real. The monster strikes with two claw attacks and one bite, hitting as a 7-Hit Die monster. All three attacks hit; the normal damage dice are rolled, multiplied by .2 separately, rounded up or down, and added together to get the total damage. Thus, if the attacks score 4, 2 and 11 points, a total of 4 points of damage is inflicted (4 x .2 = .8 [rounded to 1], 2 x .2 = .4 [rounded to 1], 11 x .2 = 2.2 [rounded to 2]. The sum is 1 + 1 + 2 = 4).

Shout

(Evocation)
Level: 4
Range: 0   **Components:** V, M
Duration: Instantaneous   **Casting Time:** 1 segment
Area of Effect: 10 x 30 ft. cone   **Saving Throw:** Special

When a Shout spell is cast, the magic-user gives himself tremendous vocal powers. The caster can emit an ear-splitting noise that has a principal effect in a cone shape radiating from his mouth to a point 30 feet away. Any creature within this area is deafened for 2d6 rounds and suffers 2d6 points of damage. A successful saving throw vs. spell negates the deafness and reduces the damage by half. Any exposed brittle or crystal substance subject to sonic vibrations is shattered by a shout, while those brittle objects in the possession of a creature receive the creature's saving throw. Deafened creatures suffer a -1 penalty to surprise rolls, and those that cast spells with verbal components are 20% likely to miscast them. The Shout spell cannot penetrate the 2nd level cleric spell, Silence, 15' Radius. This spell can be employed only once per day; otherwise, the caster might permanently deafen himself. The material components for this spell are a drop of honey, a drop of citric acid, and a small cone made from a bull or ram horn.

Solid Fog

(Alteration)
Level: 4
Range: 30 yards   **Components:** V, S, M
Duration: 2d4 rds. + 1 rd./level   **Casting Time:** 4 segments
Area of Effect: 20 x 10 x 10 ft.   **Saving Throw:** None
            volume/level of caster

When this spell is cast, the magic-user creates a billowing mass of misty vapors similar to a Wall of Fog spell. The caster can create less vapor if desired, as long as a rectangular or cubic mass at least 10 feet on a side is formed. The fog obscures all sight, normal and infravision, beyond 2 feet. However, unlike normal fog, only a very strong wind can move these vapors, and any creature attempting to move through the solid fog progresses at a movement rate of 1 foot per round. A Gust of Wind spell cannot affect it. A Fireball, Flame Strike, or Wall of Fire can burn it away in a single round. The material components for the spell are a pinch of dried, powdered peas combined with powdered animal hoof.

Stirring Oration

(Enchantment/Charm)
Level: 4
Range: Centered on caster   **Components:** V
Duration: 1 turn + 1 round/level   **Casting Time:** 1 round
Area of Effect: 20 ft. radius/level   **Saving Throw:** None

With this spell the caster can deliver an impassioned speech that touches the minds and hearts of all who hear it. Creatures in the area who can understand the caster may re-roll any failed morale and fear checks, and treat the caster as if he had a Charisma score of four points higher than he actually does. Player characters can always make up their own minds as to whether or not they want to be influenced by this spell.

Stone Passage

(Alteration)
Level: 4
Range: Touch   **Components:** V, S
Duration: 1 turn   **Casting Time:** 4 segments
Area of Effect: 1 creature   **Saving Throw:** None

This spell allows the recipient and all of his equipment to move through stone as if it were a dense pudding. The recipient can choose to only put parts of his body into stone, or he may completely enter. Note that he cannot see or hear if his head is inside a rock, and if Stone Passage is used to travel to a specific location the traveler must be very careful not to get lost! If the spell runs out while the spell's target is still completely in stone he is instantly slain with his body entombed in stone. If partially inside, the victim must make a system shock roll or the character is dead. If successful, any body parts left inside of the stone are trapped and a way must be found to free them. Note that movement is exhausting and difficult, and characters with a Strength of 11 or lower may not move through the stone at all.

Stoneskin
(Alteration)
Level: 4
Range: Touch   **Components:** V, S, M
Duration: Special   **Casting Time:** 1 segment
Area of Effect: 1 creature   **Saving Throw:** None

When this spell is cast, the affected creature gains a virtual immunity to any attack by cut, blow, projectile or the like. Even a Sword of Sharpness cannot affect a creature protected by Stoneskin, nor can a rock hurled by a giant, a snake's strike, etc. However, magical attacks from such spells as Fireball, Magic Missile, Lightning Bolt and so forth have their normal effects. The spell's effects are not cumulative with multiple castings. The spell blocks 1d4 attacks, plus one attack per two levels of experience the caster has achieved. This limit applies regardless of attack rolls and regardless of whether the attack was physical or magical. For example, a Stoneskin spell cast by a 9th level magic-user would protect against from five to eight attacks. An attacking Griffon would reduce the protection by three each round; four Magic Missiles would count as four attacks in addition to inflicting their normal damage. The material components of the spell are granite and diamond dust sprinkled on the recipient's skin.

Ultravision
(Alteration)
Level: 4
Range: Touch   **Components:** V S, M
Duration: 6 turns + 6 turns/level   **Casting Time:** 4 segments
Area of Effect: One creature   **Saving Throw:** None

By means of this spell the magic-user empowers the recipient to see radiation in the ultraviolet spectrum. In night conditions this means that vision will be clear, as if it were daylight, to a range of 100 yards, and shadowy and indistinct from beyond 100 yards to about 300 yards distance. If the night is very dark, with thick clouds overhead, these distances are reduced by 50%. Where more than about 6 feet of earth or 3 feet of stone interpose between the sky and the individual, such as in virtually any underground area, Ultravision allows only vision of the dimmest sort in about a 3-foot radius, since the ultraviolet rays are screened out. Of course, if an emission source is nearby, the visual capabilities improve accordingly. Nearby light, including the radiance shed by magic items, tends to spoil ultravision, the brightness of the rays "blinding" the eyes to dimmer areas more distant. The material component for this spell is a crushed amethyst of at least 500 gp value.

Vacancy
(Alteration, Illusion/Phantasm)
Level: 4
Range: 10 yds./level   **Components:** V, S, M
Duration: 1 hr./level   **Casting Time:** 4 segments
Area of Effect: 10-ft. radius/level   **Saving Throw:** None

When a Vacancy spell is cast, the magic-user causes an area to appear to be vacant, neglected, and unused. Those who behold the area see dust on the floor, cobwebs, dirt, and other conditions typical of a long-abandoned place. If they pass through the area of effect, they seem to leave tracks, tear away cobwebs, and so on. Unless they actually contact some object cloaked by the spell, the place appears empty. Merely brushing an invisible object does not cause the vacancy spell to be disturbed: Only forceful contact grants a chance to note that all is not as it seems. If forceful contact with a cloaked object occurs, those creatures subject to the spell can penetrate the spell only if they discover several items that they cannot see; each being is then entitled to a saving throw vs. spell. Failure means they believe that the objects are invisible. A Dispel Magic spell cancels this spell so that the true area is seen. A True Seeing spell, a Gem of Seeing, and similar effects can penetrate the deception, but a Detect Invisibility spell cannot. This spell is a very powerful combination of invisibility and illusion, but it can cloak only nonliving things. Living things are not made invisi-

ble, but their presence does not otherwise disturb the spell. The magic-user must have a square of the finest black silk to cast this spell. This material component must be worth at least 100 gp and is used up during spellcasting.

Wall of Acid
(Evocation)
Level: 4
Range: 40 yards   **Components:** V, S, M
Duration: Special   **Casting Time:** 4 segments
Area of Effect: a 2 ft. x 10 ft. x 10 ft.   **Saving Throw:** None
1/2 parallelepiped

The Wall of Acid spell brings forth a highly caustic mass of liquid acid in the form of a 10 foot wide by 10 foot high wall with a thickness of 2 feet. If this spell is cast in the presence of gravity, it will immediately begin to drop to the ground as any normal liquid would. The caster can center the wall at any point within the spell range but the height must always be 10 feet. Creatures caught within the initial formation of the wall are subject to 2-8 hp of damage or half if they make a successful saving throw. Those wearing leather armor gain a +1 to their saving throw while those wearing most metal armors gain +2 and those wearing plate mail gain +4. Those who fail their save and those who are not wearing armor (regardless of whether or not they made their save) are subject to an additional 1-4 points of damage per round until the acid can be rinsed off or otherwise neutralized. Any creatures within 10 feet of the wall are subject to splash damage when the wall comes crashing to the ground (unless it is cast outside the bounds of strong gravity). The saving throw bonuses above apply, and affected creatures will take 1-4 points or 1-2 points depending on whether or not they saved. Those who fail their save against splash damage are similarly subject to 1-4 points of damage per round until the acid can be rinsed off. Once the acid crashes to the ground, it may form a puddle if it lands on rock or solid compacted earth. If it does not land on an impermeable surface, it will soak into the ground and become relatively harmless within one round. If it puddles (this includes the round it might be soaking in for permeable soil) those creatures standing in it are subject to an initial 1-2 points of damage if they have soft or worse foot covering and 1 point of damage per round until the acid can be rinsed off. Those standing in a puddle of acid who have hard foot covering are only subject to that damage if their foot covering fails a separate saving throw against acid. The material component of the spell is a cup of stomach acid.

Wall of Fire
(Evocation)
Level: 4
Range: 60 yards   **Components:** V, S, M
Duration: Special   **Casting Time:** 4 segments
Area of Effect: Special   **Saving Throw:** None

The Wall of Fire spell brings forth an immobile, blazing curtain of magical fire of shimmering color – violet or reddish blue. The spell creates either an opaque sheet of flame up to one 20-foot square per level of the spellcaster, or a ring with a radius of up to 10 feet + 5 feet per two levels of experience of the magic-user. In either form, the Wall of Fire is 20 feet high. The Wall of Fire must be cast so that it is vertical with respect to the caster. One side of the wall, selected by the caster, sends forth waves of heat, inflicting 2d4 points of damage upon creatures within 10 feet and 1d4 points of damage upon those within 20 feet. In addition, the wall inflicts 2d6 points of damage, plus 1 point of damage per level of the spellcaster, upon any creature passing through it. Creatures especially subject to fire may take additional damage, and undead always take twice normal damage. Note that attempting to catch a moving creature with a newly-created Wall of Fire is difficult; a successful saving throw enables the creature to avoid the wall, while its rate and direction of movement determine which side of the created wall it is on. The Wall of Fire lasts as long as the magic-user concentrates on maintaining it, or one round per level of experience of the magic-user, in the event he does not wish to concentrate upon it. The material component of the spell is phosphorus.

Wall of Ice

(Evocation)

Level: 4
Range: 10 yds./level
Components: V, S, M
Duration: 1 turn/level
Casting Time: 4 segments
Area of Effect: Special
Saving Throw: None

This spell can be cast in one of three ways: as an anchored plane of ice, as a hemisphere, or as a horizontal sheet to fall upon creatures with the effect of an ice storm.

A) Ice plane. When this spell is cast, a sheet of strong, hard ice is created. The wall is primarily defensive, stopping pursuers and the like. The wall is 1 inch thick per level of experience of the magic-user. It covers a 10-foot-square area per level (a 10th level magic-user can create a Wall of Ice 100 feet long and 10 feet high, a wall 50 feet long and 20 feet high, etc.). Any creature breaking through the ice suffers 2 points of damage per inch of thickness of the wall. Fire-using creatures suffer 3 points of damage per inch, while cold-using creatures suffer only 1 point of damage per inch when breaking through. The plane can be oriented in any fashion as long as it is anchored along one or more sides.

B) Hemisphere. This casting of the spell creates a hemisphere whose maximum radius is equal to 3 feet plus 1 foot per caster level. Thus, a 7th level caster can create a hemisphere 10 feet in radius. The hemisphere lasts until it is broken, dispelled, or melted. Note that it is possible, but difficult, to trap mobile opponents under the hemisphere.

C) Ice sheet. This casting of the spell causes a horizontal sheet to fall upon opponents. The sheet covers a 10-foot-square area per caster level. The sheet has the same effect as an ice storm's hail stones – 3d10 points of damage inflicted to creatures beneath it. A Wall of Ice cannot form in an area occupied by physical objects or creatures; its surface must be smooth and unbroken when created. Magical fires such as fireballs and fiery dragon breath melt a Wall of Ice in one round, though this creates a great cloud of steamy fog that lasts one turn. Normal fires or lesser magical ones do not hasten the melting of a wall of ice.

The material component of this spell is a small piece of quartz or similar rock crystal.

Wizard Eye

(Alteration)

Level: 4
Range: 0
Components: V, S, M
Duration: 1 rd./level
Casting Time: 1 turn
Area of Effect: Special
Saving Throw: None

When this spell is employed, the magic-user creates an invisible sensory organ that sends him visual information. The Wizard Eye travels at 30 feet per round if viewing an area ahead as a human would (i.e., primarily looking at the floor), or 10 feet per round if examining the ceiling and walls as well as the floor ahead. The Wizard Eye can see with infravision up to 10 feet, and with normal vision up to 60 feet away in brightly lit areas. The Wizard Eye can travel in any direction as long as the spell lasts. It has substance and a form that can be detected (by a Detect Invisibility spell, for instance). Solid barriers prevent the passage of a Wizard Eye, although it can pass through a space no smaller than a small mouse hole (1 inch in diameter).

Using the eye requires the magic-user to concentrate. However, if his concentration is broken, the spell does not end – the eye merely becomes inert until the magic-user again concentrates, subject to the duration of the spell. The powers of the Wizard Eye cannot be enhanced by other spells or items. The caster is subject to any gaze attack met by the eye. A successful Dispel Magic cast on the magic-user or the eye ends the spell. With respect to blindness, magical darkness, and so on, the Wizard Eye is considered an independent sensory organ of the caster. The material component of the spell is a bit of bat fur.

Zargosa's Lodge of Protection

(Alteration, Enchantment)

Level: 4
Range: 20 yards
Components: V, S, M
Duration: 1d4+1 hrs. + 1 hr./level
Casting Time: 4 turns
Area of Effect: 30 sq. ft./level
Saving Throw: None

This spell enables the magic-user to magically call into being a sturdy cottage or lodge, made of material that is common in the area where the spell is cast – stone, timber, or (at worst) sod. The floor area of the lodging is 30 square feet per level of the spellcaster, and the surface is level, clean, and dry. In all respects the lodging resembles a normal cottage, with a sturdy door, two or more shuttered windows, and a small fireplace. While the lodging is secure against winds of up to 70 miles per hour, it has no heating or cooling source (other than natural insulation qualities). Therefore, it must be heated as a normal dwelling, and extreme heat adversely affects it and its occupants. The dwelling does, however, provide considerable security otherwise, as it is as strong as a normal stone building, regardless of its material composition.

The dwelling resists flames and fire as if it were stone, and is impervious to normal missiles (but not the sort cast by siege machinery or giants). The door, shutters, and even chimney are secure against intrusion, the former two being magic-user locked and the latter being secured by a top grate of iron and a narrow flue. In addition, these three areas are protected by an Alarm spell. Lastly, an Unseen Servant is conjured to provide service to the spellcaster. The inside of the shelter contains rude furnishings as desired by the spellcaster – up to eight bunks, a trestle table and benches, as many as four chairs or eight stools, and a writing desk. The material components of this spell are a square chip of stone, crushed lime, a few grains of sand, a sprinkling of water, and several splinters of wood. These must be augmented by the components of the Alarm and Unseen Servant spells if these benefits are to be included (string and silver wire and a small bell). Note: There is a 1% chance per level of the caster that the duration of this spell will be permanent. (i.e. Zarba's lodge of protection will become a permanent structure.) The Unseen Servant, however, will be dismissed as normal.

Zargosa's Tentacled Fury

(Conjuration/Summoning)

Level: 4
Range: 30 yards
Components: V, S, M
Duration: 1 hr./level
Casting Time: 1 round
Area of Effect: 30 sq. ft./level
Saving Throw: None

This spell creates many rubbery, black tentacles in the area of effect. These waving members seem to spring forth from the earth, floor, or whatever surface is underfoot – including water. Each tentacle is 10 feet long, AC 4, and requires as many points of damage to destroy as the level of the magic-user who cast the spell. There are 1d4 such tentacles, plus one per experience level of the spellcaster. Any creature within range of the writhing tentacles is subject to attack as determined by the GM. The target of a tentacle attack must roll a saving throw vs. spell. If this succeeds, the subject suffers 1d4 points of damage from contact with the tentacle; the tentacle is then destroyed. Failure to save indicates that the damage inflicted is 2d4 points, the ebon member is wrapped around its subject, and damage will be 3d4 points on the second and all succeeding rounds. Since these tentacles have no intelligence to guide them, there is the possibility that they entwine any object – a tree, post, pillar, even the magic-user himself – or continue to squeeze a dead opponent. A grasping hold established by a tentacle remains until the tentacle is destroyed by some form of attack or until it disappears at the end of the spell's duration. The component for this spell is a piece of tentacle from a Giant Octopus or Giant Squid.

Zombie Slave

(Necromancy)

Level: 4
Range: 30 feet | **Components:** V, S, M
Duration: 1 hour/level | **Casting Time:** 4 segments
Area of Effect: 1d6 Zombies in a 20 ft radius sphere | **Saving Throw:** None

This spell can be used in conjunction with an Animate Dead spell to enable the magic-user to automatically exert control over any Zombies created as a result of the spell. Furthermore, a magic-user can use this spell to temporarily exert control over either free-willed Zombies or those created by another spellcaster. Zombies so affected will follow simple commands or can remain in an area to attack all who enter. The material component of this spell are a drop of blood and a pinch of bone powder or bone shard.

Fifth Level Spells

Advanced Illusion

(Illusion/Phantasm)

Level: 5
Range: 60 yds. + 10 yds./level | **Components:** V, S, M
Duration: 1 rd./level | **Casting Time:** 1 round
Area of Effect: One 40-ft. cube + one 10-ft. cube/level | **Saving Throw:** Special

This spell is essentially a spectral forces spell that operates through a program (similar to a Programmed Illusion spell) determined by the caster. It is thus unnecessary for the magic-user to concentrate on the spell for longer than the round of casting it, as the program has then started and will continue without supervision. The illusion has visual, audio, olfactory and thermal components. If any viewer actively attempts to disbelieve the spell, he gains a saving throw vs. spell. If any viewer successfully disbelieves and communicates this fact to other viewers, each such viewer gains a saving throw vs. spell with a +4 bonus. The material components are a bit of fleece and several grains of sand.

Airy Water

(Alteration)

Level: 5
Range: 0 | **Components:** V, S, M
Duration: 1 turn/level | **Casting Time:** 5 segments
Area of Effect: 10-ft. radius sphere or 15-ft. radius hemisphere | **Saving Throw:** None

The Airy Water spell turns normal liquid, such as water or water-based solutions, into a less dense, breathable substance. Thus, if the magic-user wanted to enter an underwater place, he would step into the water, cast the spell, and sink downward in a globe of bubbling water. He and any companions in the spell's area of effect can move freely and breathe just as if the bubbling water were air. The globe is centered on and moves with the caster. Water-breathing creatures avoid a sphere (or hemisphere) of Airy Water, although intelligent ones can enter it if they are able to move by means other than swimming. No water-breathers can breathe in an area affected by this spell. There is only one word that needs to be spoken to actuate the magic; thus, it can be cast under water. The spell does not filter or remove solid particles of matter. The material component of the spell is a small handful of alkaline or bromine salts.

Animal Growth

(Alteration) Reversible

Level: 5
Range: 60 yards | **Components:** V, S, M
Duration: 1 rd./level | **Casting Time:** 5 segments
Area of Effect: Up to 8 animals in a 20-ft. cube | **Saving Throw:** None

When this spell is cast, the magic-user causes all designated animals, up to a maximum of eight, within a 20-foot-square area to grow to twice their normal size. The effects of this Growth are doubled Hit Dice (with improvement in attack rolls) and doubled damage in combat. The spell lasts for one round for each level of experience of the magic-user casting the spell. Only natural animals, including giant forms, can be affected by this spell. The reverse, Shrink Animal, reduces animal size by half and likewise reduces Hit Dice, attack damage, etc. The component of both versions of the spell is a pinch of powdered bone.

Animate Dead

(Necromancy)

Level: 5
Range: 10 yards | **Components:** V, S, M
Duration: Permanent | **Casting Time:** 5 rounds
Area of Effect: Special | **Saving Throw:** None

This spell creates the lowest of the undead monsters — Skeletons or Zombies – usually from the bones or bodies of dead humans, demi-humans, or humanoids. The spell causes existing remains to become animated. Unlike the cleric version of this spell, however, the caster does not automatically control his abominations. The Skeletons or Zombies remain in an area and attack any creature (or just a specific type of creature) entering the place, etc. The undead remain animated until they are destroyed in combat or are turned; the magic cannot be dispelled. The following types of dead creatures can be animated:

A) Humans, demi-humans, and humanoids with 1 Hit Die. The magic-user can animate one Skeleton for each experience level he has attained, or one Zombie for every two levels. The experience levels, if any, of the slain are ignored; the body of a newly dead 9th level fighter is animated as a Zombie with 2 Hit Dice, without special class or racial abilities.

B) Creatures with more than 1 Hit Die. The number of undead animated is determined by the monster Hit Dice (the total Hit Dice cannot exceed the magic-user's level). Skeletal forms have the Hit Dice of the original creature, while Zombie forms have one more Hit Die. Thus, a 12th level magic-user could animate four Zombie Gnolls (4 x [2+1 Hit Dice] = 12), or a single Fire Giant Skeleton. Such undead have none of the special abilities they had in life.

C) Creatures with less than 1 Hit Die. The caster can animate two Skeletons per level or one Zombie per level. The creatures have their normal Hit Dice as skeletons and an additional Hit Die as Zombies. Clerics receive a +1 bonus when trying to turn these. This spell assumes that the bodies or bones are available and are reasonably intact (those of Skeletons or Zombies destroyed in combat won't be!). It requires a drop of blood and a pinch of bone powder or a bone shard to complete the spell. The casting of this spell is not a good act, and only evil magic-users use it frequently.

The caster has a base 10% +1%/level chance of exerting control over the newly created undead. This is further modified by 1% for every point of Intelligence, Wisdom and Charisma that a magic-user has above 9. Note that specialist necromancers gains a +75% modifier to control attempts. Should he fail to exert control, the undead will seek only to destroy their maker until they themselves are destroyed.

Avoidance

(Abjuration, Alteration)
Reversible

Level: 5
Range: 10 yards | **Components:** V, S, M
Duration: Permanent until dispelled | **Casting Time:** 5 segments
Area of Effect: Up to 3-ft. cube | **Saving Throw:** Special

By means of this spell, the caster sets up a natural repulsion between the affected object and all other living things except himself. Thus, any living creature attempting to touch the affected object is repulsed (unable to come closer than 1 foot), or repulses the affected object, depending on the relative mass of the two (a halfling attempting to touch an iron chest with an Avoidance spell upon it will be thrown back, while the chest will skitter away from a giant-sized creature as the creature approaches). The material component for the spell is a magnetized needle. The spell cannot be cast upon living things; any attempt to cast Avoidance upon the apparel or possessions of a living creature entitles the subject creature to a saving throw vs. spell. The reverse of this spell, Attraction, uses the same material component and sets up a natural attraction between the affected object and all living things. A creature is drawn to the object if the creature is smaller, or the object slides toward the creature if the creature is larger. It takes a successful bend bars/lift gates roll to remove the enchanted object once it has adhered to an object or creature.

Chaos

(Enchantment/Charm)

Level: 5

Range: 5 yds./level

Duration: 1 rd./level

Area of Effect: Up to 40-ft. cube

Components: V, S, M

Casting Time: 5 segments

Saving Throw: Special

This spell is similar to the 4th level Confusion spell, but only the following beings receive a saving throw: fighters, magic-users specialized in enchantments, monsters that use no magic and have an Intelligence of 4 or less, creatures of 21 Intelligence or higher, and creatures with more levels or Hit Dice than the caster's level. The spell causes disorientation and severe perceptual distortion, creating indecision and the inability to take effective action. The spell affects 1d4 creatures, plus one creature per caster level. Those allowed saving throws roll them vs. spell with -2 penalties, adjusted for Wisdom. Those who successfully save are unaffected by the spell. Affected creatures react as follows:

d10 Roll	Action
1	Wander away (unless prevented) for duration of spell
2-6	Stand confused for one round (then roll again)
7-9	Attack nearest creature for one round (then roll again)
10	Act normally for one round (then roll again)

The spell lasts one round for each level of the caster. Those affected are checked by the GM for actions each round for the duration of the spell, or until the "wander away for the duration of the spell" result occurs. Wandering creatures move as far from the caster as possible using their most typical mode of movement (characters walk, fish swim, bats fly, etc.). Saving throws and actions are checked at the beginning of each round. Any confused creature that is attacked perceives the attacker as an enemy and acts according to its basic nature. The material component for this spell is a small disc of bronze and a small rod of iron.

Cloudkill

(Evocation)

Level: 5

Range: 10 yards

Duration: 1 rd./level

Area of Effect: 40 x 20 x 20 ft. cloud

Components: V, S

Casting Time: 5 segments

Saving Throw: None

This spell generates a billowing cloud of ghastly yellowish green vapors that is so toxic as to slay any creature with fewer than 4+1 Hit Dice, cause creatures with 4+1 to 5+1 Hit Dice to roll saving throws vs. poison with -4 penalties or be slain, and creatures with up to 6 Hit Dice (inclusive) to roll unmodified saving throws vs. poison or be slain. Holding one's breath has no effect on the lethality of the spell. Those above 6th level (or 6 Hit Dice) must leave the cloud immediately or suffer 1d10 points of poison damage each round while in the area of effect. The Cloudkill moves away from the spellcaster at 10 feet per round, rolling along the surface of the ground. A moderate breeze causes it to alter course (roll for direction), but it does not move back toward its caster. A strong wind breaks it up in four rounds, and a greater wind force prevents the use of the spell. Very thick vegetation will disperse the cloud in two rounds. As the vapors are heavier than air, they sink to the lowest level of the land, even pouring down den or sinkhole openings; thus, the spell is ideal for slaying nests of giant ants, for example. It cannot penetrate liquids, nor can it be cast under water.

Conjure Elemental

(Conjuration/Summoning)

Level: 5

Range: 60 yards

Duration: 1 turn/level

Area of Effect: Special

Components: V, S, M

Casting Time: 1 turn

Saving Throw: None

There are actually four spells in the Conjure Elemental spell. The magic-user is able to conjure an air, earth, fire, or water elemental with this spell – assuming he has the material component for the particular elemental. (A considerable fire source must be in range to conjure a Fire Elemental; a large amount of water must be available to conjure a Water Elemental.) Conjured

elementals have 8 Hit Dice. It is possible to conjure successive elementals of different types if the spellcaster has memorized two or more of these spells. The type of elemental to be conjured must be decided upon before memorizing the spell. Each type of elemental can be conjured only once per day. The conjured elemental must be controlled by the magic-user – the spellcaster must concentrate on the elemental doing his commands – or it turns on the magic-user and attacks. The elemental will not break off a combat to do so, but it will avoid creatures while seeking its conjurer. If the magic-user is wounded or grappled, his concentration is broken. There is always a 5% chance that the elemental turns on its conjurer regardless of concentration. This check is made at the end of the second and each succeeding round. An elemental that breaks free of its control can be dispelled by the caster, but the chance of success is only 50%. The elemental can be controlled up to 30 yards away per level of the spellcaster. The elemental remains until its form on this plane is destroyed due to damage or until the spell's duration expires. Note that Water Elementals are destroyed if they are ever more than 60 yards from a large body of water. The material component of the spell (besides the quantity of the element at hand) is a small amount of one of the following:

> Air Elemental – burning incense
> Earth Elemental – soft clay
> Fire Elemental – sulphur and phosphorus
> Water Elemental – water and sand

Special protection from uncontrolled elementals is available by means of a Protection From Evil spell.

Contact Other Plane

(Divination)

Level: 5

Range: 0

Duration: Special

Area of Effect: Special

Components: V

Casting Time: 1 turn

Saving Throw: None

When this spell is cast, the magic-user sends his mind to another plane of existence in order to receive advice and information from powers there. As these powers resent such contact, only brief answers are given. (The GM answers all questions with "yes," "no," "maybe," "never," "irrelevant," etc.) Any questions asked are answered by the power during the spell's duration. The character can contact an elemental plane or some plane farther removed. For every two levels of experience of the magic-user, one question may be asked. Contact with minds far removed from the plane of the magic-user increases the probability of the spellcaster going insane or dying, but the chance of the power knowing the answer, as well as the probability of the being telling the correct answer, are likewise increased by moving to distant planes. Once the Outer Planes are reached, the Intelligence of the power contacted determines the effects. The accompanying random table is subject to GM changes, development of extraplanar NPC beings, and so on. If insanity occurs, it strikes as soon as the first question is asked. This condition lasts for one week for each removal of the plane contacted (see the GMG), to a maximum of 10 weeks. There is a 1% chance per plane that the magic-user dies before recovering, unless a Remove Curse spell is cast upon him. A surviving magic-user can recall the answer to the question. On rare occasions, this divination may be blocked by the action of certain lesser or greater powers.

Chance of Plane	Chance of Insanity *	Chance of Knowledge Veracity **
Elemental Plane 20%	55% (90%)**	62% (75%)**
Inner Plane 25%	60%	65%
Astral Plane 30%	65%	67%
Outer Plane, Int 19 35%	70%	70%
Outer Plane, Int 20 40%	75%	73%
Outer Plane, Int 21 45%	80%	75%
Outer Plane, Int 22 50%	85%	78%
Outer Plane, Int 23 55%	90%	81%
Outer Plane, Int 24 60%	95%	85%
Outer Plane, Int 25 65%	98%	90%

* For every point of Intelligence over 15, the magic-user reduces the chance of insanity by 5%.
** If the being does not know an answer, and the chance of veracity is not made, the being will emphatically give an incorrect answer. If the chance of veracity is made, the being will answer "unknown." Percentages in parentheses are for questions that pertain to the appropriate elemental plane.

The GM may allow a specific Outer Plane to be contacted. In this case, the difference in alignment between the caster and the plane contacted alters the maximum Intelligence that can be contacted – each difference in moral or ethical alignment lowers the maximum Intelligence that can be contacted by 1. For example, an 18th level lawful good caster could contact Mount Celestia (a lawful good plane) on the "Intelligence 20" line, or Elysium (a neutral good plane) on the "Intelligence 19" line.

Containment

(Abjuration)

Level: 5

Range: 10 ft./level	**Components:** V, S, M
Duration: 5 rounds/level	**Casting Time:** 5 segments
Area of Effect: 10 ft. square wall/level	**Saving Throw:** None

This spell is used to contain a blast or area of effect from a spell. When Containment is cast the caster may create up to one 10 ft. by 10 ft. wall per level of experience. Each wall is completely transparent, is only about an inch thick, and can easily be passed through by any creature. Each wall prevents an area of effect from a spell from passing through, but they do not prevent spells from being cast through them. For example, a magic-user surrounded by a Containment spell 10 ft. in diameter could cast a Fireball through the barrier at a group of Gnolls 10 ft. away. No one within 5 ft. of the caster would be affected, however. Similarly, a magic-user with the Gnolls could cast a Fireball at the magic-user within the 10 ft. diameter barrier without any problem. When that Fireball explodes the blast radius would not extend past the barriers, protecting the Gnolls from any backlash. The material component is a piece of glass.

Demishadow Monsters

(Illusion/Phantasm)

Level: 5

Range: 30 yards	**Components:** V, S
Duration: 1 rd./level	**Casting Time:** 5 segments
Area of Effect: 20-ft. cube	**Saving Throw:** Special

This spell is similar to the 4th level spell Shadow Monsters, except that the Monsters created are effectively 40% of normal hit points. If the saving throw is made, their damage potential is only 40% of normal and their Armor Class is 8. The Monsters have none of the special abilities of the real creatures, although victims may be deluded into believing this to be so.

Dismissal

(Abjuration)

Level: 5

Range: 10 yards	**Components:** V, S, M
Duration: Permanent	**Casting Time:** 1 round
Area of Effect: 1 creature	**Saving Throw:** Negates

By means of this spell, a magic-user on the Prime Material Plane seeks to force or enable a creature from another plane of existence to return to its proper plane. Magic resistance, if any, is checked if this spell is used to force a being home. If the resistance fails, the caster's level is compared to the creature's level or Hit Dice. If the magic-user's level is higher, the difference is subtracted from the creature's die roll for its saving throw vs. spell. If the creature's level or Hit Dice is higher, the difference is added to the saving throw roll. If the creature desires to be returned to its home plane, no saving throw is necessary (it chooses to fail the roll). If the spell is successful, the creature is instantly whisked away, but the spell has a 20% chance of actually sending the subject to a plane other than its own. The material component is any item that is distasteful to the subject creature.

Distance Distortion

(Alteration)

Level: 5

Range: 10 yds./level	**Components:** V, S, M
Duration: 2 turns/level	**Casting Time:** 5 segments
Area of Effect: 10-ft. cube/level	**Saving Throw:** None

This spell can be cast only in an area completely surrounded or enclosed by earth, rock, sand or similar materials. The magic-user must also cast a Conjure Elemental spell to summon an Earth Elemental. The elemental serves without attempting to break free when the spellcaster announces that his intent is to cast a Distance Distortion spell. The spell places the Earth Elemental in the area of effect, and the elemental then causes the area's dimensions to be either doubled or halved for those traveling over it (spellcaster's choice). Thus, a 10-foot x 100-foot corridor could seem to be either 5 feet wide and 50 feet long or 20 feet wide and 200 feet long. When the spell duration has elapsed, the elemental returns to its own plane. The true nature of an area affected by Distance Distortion is undetectable to any creature traveling along it, but the area dimly radiates magic, and a True Seeing spell can reveal that an Earth Elemental is spread within the area. The material needed for this spell is a small lump of soft clay.

Dolor

(Enchantment/Charm)

Level: 5

Range: 1	**Components:** V, S
Duration: 2 rounds	**Casting Time:** 5 segments
Area of Effect: One creature	**Saving Throw:** Special

By means of this spell, the magic-user attempts to force compliance or obedience from some oppositely aligned or hostile creature from a plane foreign to that of the spell caster. The dweomer causes unease in the creature in question during its mere reading, and on the round thereafter, the subject becomes nervous and filled with doubts, while on the last round of effect the creature actually feels a dull, all-encompassing dolor. The initial effects cause the subject creature to make all saving throws versus commands and non-offensive spells (including charms) at -1 on the dice rolled to determine whether or not it resists, the adjustment favoring compliance. The secondary effects cause the adjustment to go to -2. The tertiary effect brings with it an adjustment of -3. Thereafter, the creature is no longer affected and it makes further saving throws without adjustment.

The verbal component of the spell must deal with the class of creature in question, containing as much information as possible about the subject creature.

When uttering the spell, the magic-user can be mentally assailed by the creature if the subject has a higher Intelligence than the spell caster. In such a case, the creature has a 5% chance per point of superior Intelligence of effectively charming and dominating the magic-user. In the case of such control, the creature will then do with the spell caster as its alignment dictates. If the spell caster is distracted or interrupted during the casting of the spell, the subject creature is able to automatically effect the charm and domination.

Domination

(Enchantment/Charm)

Level: 5

Range: 10 yds./level	**Components:** V, S
Duration: Special	**Casting Time:** 5 segments
Area of Effect: 1 person	**Saving Throw:** Negates

The Domination spell enables the caster to control the actions of any person until the spell is ended by the subject's Intelligence (see the charm person spell). Elves and half-elves resist this enchantment as they do all charm-type spells. When the spell is cast, the subject must roll a saving throw vs. spell at a penalty of -2, but Wisdom adjustments apply. Failure means the magic-user has established a telepathic link with the subject's mind. If a common language is shared, the magic-user can generally force the subject to perform as the magic-user desires, within the limits of the subject's body structure and Strength. Note that the caster does not receive direct sensory input from the subject. Subjects resist this control, and those forced to take actions against their natures receive a new saving throw with a bonus of +1 to +4, depending on the type of action required. Obviously self-destructive orders are not carried out. Once control is established, there is no limit to the range at which it can be exercised, as long as the caster and subject are on the same plane. A protection from evil spell can prevent the caster from exercising control or using the telepathic link while the subject is so warded, but it cannot prevent the establishment of domination.

Drayton's Engaging Conversation
(Enchantment, Evocation)

Level: 5
Range: 10 yards **Components:** V
Duration: Special **Casting Time:** 5 segments
Area of Effect: 1 or more creatures **Saving Throw:** Special
in a 10-ft. radius

This devious spell distracts the subject creatures by drawing them into an absorbing discussion on topics of interest to them. A chain of responses occurs during the next 11 rounds, with additional saving throws as described later. These responses are conversation (rounds 1-3), possible confusion (rounds 4-6), and then either rage or lamentation (rounds 7-11). All saving throws are affected by the creatures' Intelligences, as noted later. The subject creatures must be able to understand the language in which the spellcaster speaks. Upon casting the spell, the magic-user begins discussion of some topic germane to the creature or creatures to be affected. Those making a successful saving throw vs. spell are unaffected. Affected creatures immediately begin to converse with the spellcaster, agreeing or disagreeing, all most politely. As long as the spellcaster chooses, he can maintain the spell by conversing with the subject(s). If the caster is attacked or otherwise distracted, the subject creatures do not notice.

Intelligence	Saving Throw Modifier
2 or less	Spell has no effect
3-7	-1
8-10	0
11-14	+1
15+	+2

The magic-user can leave at any time after the casting and the subject(s) continue on as if the caster were still present. As long as they are not attacked, the creatures ignore all else going on around them, spending their time talking and arguing to the exclusion of other activities. However, when the caster leaves, each subject completes only the stage of the spell that it is currently in, and then the spell is broken. If the caster maintains the spell for more than three rounds, each affected creature can roll another saving throw vs. spell. Those failing to save wander off in confusion for 1d10+2 rounds, staying away from the spellcaster. Those who make this saving throw continue to talk and roll saving throws for each round that the caster continues the spell, up through the sixth round, to avoid the confusion effect. If the spell is maintained for more than six rounds, each subject must roll a successful saving throw vs. spell to avoid going into a rage, attacking all other subjects of the spell with intent to kill. This rage lasts for 1d4+1 rounds. Those who successfully save against the rage effect realize that they have been deceived and collapse to the ground, lamenting their foolishness, for 1d4 rounds unless attacked or otherwise disturbed.

Drayton's Hidden Stash
(Alteration, Conjuration/Summoning)

Level: 5
Range: Special **Components:** V, S, M
Duration: 60 days **Casting Time:** 1 turn
Area of Effect: One chest, about **Saving Throw:** None
2 x 2 x 3 ft.

This spell enables a specially constructed chest (into the which the spellcaster can stash away valuable items) to be hidden deep within the Ethereal Plane, to be summoned using a small model of the Chest. The large chest must be exceptionally well-crafted and expensive, constructed for the caster by master craftsmen. If made principally of wood, it must be ebony, rosewood, sandalwood, teak or the like, and all of its corner fittings, nails, and hardware must be platinum. If constructed of ivory, the metal fittings of the chest must be gold. If the chest is fashioned from bronze, copper, or silver, its fittings must be electrum or silver. The cost of such a chest is never less than 5,000 gp. Once it is constructed, the magic-user must have a tiny replica (of the same materials and perfect in every detail) made, so that the miniature of the chest appears to be a perfect copy. One magic-user can have but one pair of these chests at any given time – even Wish spells do not allow exceptions! The chests themselves are non-magical, and can be fitted with locks, wards, and so on, just as any normal chest. While touching the chest and holding the tiny replica, the caster chants the spell. This causes the large chest to vanish into the Ethereal

Plane. The chest can contain 1 cubic foot of material per level of the magic-user no matter what its apparent size. Living matter makes it 75% likely that the spell fails, so the chest is typically used for securing valuable spell books, magical items, gems, etc. As long as the spellcaster has the small duplicate of the magical chest, he can recall the large one from the Ethereal Plane whenever the chest is desired. If the miniature of the chest is lost or destroyed, there is no way, not even with a wish spell, that the large chest can return, although an expedition might be mounted to find it. While the chest is in the Ethereal Plane, there is a cumulative 1% chance per week that some being finds it. This chance is reset to 1% whenever the chest is recalled and the spell recast to return it to the Ethereal Plane. If the chest is found, the GM must work out the encounter and decide how the being reacts to the chest (for example, it might ignore the chest, fully or partially empty it, or even exchange or add to the items present!). Whenever the secret chest is brought back to the Prime Material Plane, an ethereal window is opened for a variable amount of time (usually about one turn); the window slowly diminishes in size. When this hole opens between the planes, check for an ethereal encounter to see if a monster is drawn through. If the large chest is not retrieved before the spell duration lapses, there is a cumulative chance of 5% per day that the chest is lost.

Dream
(Invocation, Illusion/Phantasm)
Reversible

Level: 5
Range: Touch **Components:** V, S
Duration: Special **Casting Time:** 1 turn
Area of Effect: 1 creature **Saving Throw:** None

The Dream spell enables the caster, or a messenger touched by the caster, to send messages to others in the form of dreams. At the beginning of the spell, the caster must name the recipient or identify him by some title that leaves no doubt as to his identity. As the caster completes the spell, the person sending the spell falls into a deep trancelike sleep, and instantaneously projects his mind to the recipient. The sender then enters the recipient's dream and delivers the message unless the recipient is magically protected. If the recipient is awake, the message sender can choose to remain in the trancelike sleep. If the sender is disturbed during this time, the spell is immediately cancelled and the sender comes out of the trance. The whereabouts and current activities of the recipient cannot be learned through this spell. The sender is unaware of his own surroundings or the activities around him while he is in his trance. He is totally defenseless, both physically and mentally (i.e., he always fails any saving throw) while in the trance. Once the recipient's dreams are entered, the sender can deliver a message of any length, which the recipient remembers perfectly upon waking. The communication is one-way; the recipient cannot ask questions or offer information, nor can the sender gain any information by observing the dreams of the recipient. Once the message is delivered, the sender's mind returns instantly to his body. The duration of the spell is the time required for the sender to enter the recipient's dream and deliver the message. The reverse of this spell, Nightmare, enables the caster to send a hideous and unsettling vision to the recipient, who is allowed a saving throw vs. spell to avoid the effect. The Nightmare prevents restful sleep and causes 1d10 points of damage. The Nightmare leaves the recipient fatigued and unable to regain spells for the next day. A Dispel Evil spell cast upon the recipient stuns the caster of the Nightmare for one turn per level of the cleric countering this evil sending.

Extension II
(Alteration)

Level: 5
Range: 0 **Components:** V
Duration: Special **Casting Time:** 4 segments
Area of Effect: Special **Saving Throw:** None

This spell is the same as the 4th level Extension I spell, except it extends the duration of 1st through 4th level spells by 50%.

Fabricate

(Enchantment, Alteration)

Level: 5

Range: 5 yds./level

Duration: Permanent

Area of Effect: 1 cu. yd./level

Components: V, S, M

Casting Time: Special

Saving Throw: None

By means of this spell, the magic-user is able to convert material of one sort into a product that is of the same material. Thus, the spellcaster can Fabricate a wooden bridge from a clump of trees, a rope from a patch of hemp, clothes from flax or wool, and so forth. Magical or living things cannot be created or altered by a Fabricate spell. The quality of items made by this spell is commensurate with the quality of material used as the basis for the new Fabrication. If the caster works with a mineral, the area of effect is reduced by a factor of 27 (1 cubic foot per level instead of 1 cubic yard). Articles requiring a high degree of craftsmanship (jewelry, swords, glass, crystal, etc.) cannot be Fabricated unless the magic-user otherwise has great skill in the appropriate craft. Casting requires one full round per cubic yard (or foot) or material to be affected by the spell.

False Vision

(Divination)

Level: 5

Range: 0

Duration: 1d4 rds. + 1 rd./level

Area of Effect: 30-ft. radius

Components: V, S, M

Casting Time: 5 segments

Saving Throw: None

When this spell is cast, the magic-user is able to confound any attempt to scry (by means of either a spell or a magical device) any point within the area of effect of the spell. To use the spell, he must be aware of the scrying attempt, although knowledge of the scryer or the scryer's location is not necessary. Upon casting the spell, the caster and all he desires within the radius of the spell become undetectable to the scrying. Furthermore, the caster is able to send whatever message he desires, including vision and sound, according to the medium of the scrying method. To do this, the caster must concentrate on the message he is sending. Once concentration is broken, no further images can be sent, although the caster remains undetectable for the duration of the spell. The material component for this spell is the ground dust of an emerald worth at least 500 g.p., which is sprinkled into the air when the spell is cast.

Feeblemind

(Enchantment/Charm)

Level: 5

Range: 10 yds./level

Duration: Permanent

Area of Effect: 1 creature

Components: V, S, M

Casting Time: 5 segments

Saving Throw: Negates

This spell is used solely against people or creatures who use magic spells. The Feeblemind causes the subject's intellect to degenerate to that of a moronic child. The subject remains in this state until a Heal or Wish spell is used to cancel the effects. Magic-using beings are very vulnerable to this spell; thus, their saving throws are made with the following adjustments:

Spell Use of Target	Saving Throw Adjustment
Cleric	+1
Magic-User (human)	-4
Combination or non-human	-2

Wisdom adjustments apply to the saving throw.

The material component of this spell is a handful of clay, crystal, glass, or mineral spheres, which disappears when the spell is cast.

Fireball, Sidewinder Factor 5

(Evocation)

Level: 5

Range: 1 mile maximum.

Duration: 1 rd./level

Area of Effect: 10-ft. radius

Components: V, S, M

Casting Time: 5 segments

Saving Throw: 1/2

The Sidewinder Fireball is similar to the Skipping Betty Fireball except that it uses d6 for damage instead of d4 and the range of the Fireball is only 100 feet per level of the caster. Thus each range increment is 100 feet. The spell range is further reduced by 10 feet per degree if the air temperature is less than 32° Fahrenheit. Potential targets also need not be in the 45 degree firing arc from the front of the caster. Additionally, the terrain need not be level as the Sidewinder Fireball can maneuver around obstructions and even hit an object hidden behind a wall, for example. The somatic gestures necessary for casting this spell include a side winding motion made with the casters arms.

Fireball, Torrential

(Evocation)

Level: 5

Range: 10 yds. + 10 yds./level

Duration: Instantaneous

Area of Effect: 40-ft. radius

Components: V, S, M

Casting Time: 5 segments

Saving Throw: 1/2

The Torrential Fireball is similar in most respects to a normal Fireball except that the damage dealt is 1d6 per caster level and the area of effect is a 40-foot radius sphere.

Hold Monster

(Enchantment/Charm)

Level: 5

Range: 5 yds./level

Duration: 1 rd./level

Area of Effect: 1-4 creatures in a 40-ft. cube

Components: V, S, M

Casting Time: 5 segments

Saving Throw: Negates

This spell immobilizes from one to four creatures of any type within spell range and in sight of the spellcaster. He can opt to Hold one, two, three, or four creatures. If three or four are attacked, each saving throw is normal; if two are attacked, each saving throw suffers a -1 penalty; if only one is attacked, the saving throw suffers a -3 penalty. The material component for this spell is one hard metal bar or rod for each monster to be Held. The bar or rod can be as small as a three-penny nail.

Hyptor's Faithful Bitch-Hound

(Conjuration/Summoning)

Level: 5

Range: 10 yards

Duration: Special

Area of Effect: Special

Components: V, S, M

Casting Time: 5 segments

Saving Throw: None

By means of this spell, the magic-user summons up a phantom watchdog (always an alpha-female) that only he can see. He may then command it to perform as guardian of a passage, room, door or similar space or portal. The phantom Bitch-Hound will protect the space it has been charged with guarding as though the life of her pack/cubs depended on it. She will immediately commence to barking loudly and ferociously if any creature larger than a cat approaches the place it guards.

As the Hound is able to detect invisible creatures and ward against the approach of ethereal creatures, she is an excellent guardian. She does not react to illusions that are not at least quasi-real. If the intruding creature exposes its back to the watchdog, the dog delivers a vicious attack as if it were a 10-Hit Dice monster, striking for 3d6 points of damage. It is able to hit opponents of all types, even those normally subject only to magical weapons of +3 or greater. Creatures without backs (for example, Ochre Jellies) are not attacked. The Hound cannot be attacked, but it can be dispelled. The spell lasts for a maximum of one hour plus half an hour per caster level, but once it is activated by an intruder, it lasts only one round per caster level. There is a 5% chance that the bitch hound will be over zealous in her duties and will attack the magic-user who cast the spell if he leaves her sight and later returns and attempts to approach the area he commanded her to guard. If the spellcaster is ever more than 30 yards distant from the area that the watchdog guards, the spell ends.

The material components of this spell are a tiny silver whistle, a piece of bone, and a thread.

Lyggl's Cone of Cold
(Evocation)

Level: 5

Range: 0	**Components:** V, S, M
Duration: Instantaneous	**Casting Time:** 5 segments
Area of Effect: Special	**Saving Throw:** Half

When this spell is cast, it causes a cone-shaped area of extreme cold, originating at the magic-user's hand and extending outward in a cone 5 feet long and 1 foot in diameter per level of the caster. It drains heat and causes 1d4+1 points of damage per level of experience of the magic-user. For example, a 10th level magic-user would cast a cone of cold 10 feet in diameter and 50 feet long, causing 10d4+10 points of damage. Its material component is a crystal or glass cone of very small size.

Magic Jar
(Necromancy)

Level: 5

Range: 10 yds./level	**Components:** V, S, M
Duration: Special	**Casting Time:** 1 round
Area of Effect: 1 creature	**Saving Throw:** Special

The Magic Jar spell enables the caster to shift his life force into a special receptacle (a gem or large crystal). From there the caster can force an exchange of life forces between the receptacle and another creature, thus enabling the magic-user to take over and control the body of another creature, while the life force of the host is confined in the receptacle. The special life force receptacle must be within spell range of the magic-user's body at the time of spellcasting. The magic-user's life force shifts into the receptacle in the round in which the casting is completed, allowing no other actions. While in the magic jar, the caster can sense and attack any life force within a 10-foot-per-level radius (on the same plane); however, the exact creature types and relative physical positions cannot be determined. In a group of life forces, the caster can sense a difference of four or more levels/Hit Dice and can determine whether a life force is positive or negative energy. For example, if two 10th level fighters are attacking a Hill Giant and four Ogres, the caster could determine that there are three stronger and four weaker life forces within range, all with positive life energy. The caster could try to take over either a stronger or a weaker creature, but he has no control over exactly which creature is attacked. An attempt to take over a host body requires a full round. It is blocked by a Protection From Evil spell or similar ward. It is successful only if the subject fails a saving throw vs. spell with a special modifier (see following). The saving throw is modified by subtracting the combined Intelligence and Wisdom scores of the target from those of the magic-user (Intelligence and Hit Dice in non-human or non-humanoid creatures). This modifier is added to (or subtracted from) the die roll.

Difference	Die Adjustment
-9 or less	+4
-8 to -6	+3
-5 to -3	+2
-2 to 0	+1
+1 to +4	0
+5 to +8	-1
+9 to +12	-2
+13 or more	-3

A negative score indicates that the magic-user has a lower total than the target; thus, the host has a saving throw bonus. Failure to take over the host leaves the magic-user's life force in the Magic Jar. If successful, the caster's life force occupies the host body and the host's life force is confined in the Magic Jar receptacle. The caster can call upon rudimentary or instinctive knowledge of the subject creature, but not upon its real or acquired knowledge (i.e., the magic-user does not automatically know the language or spells of the creature). The caster retains his own attack rolls, class knowledge and training, and any adjustments due to his Intelligence or Wisdom. If the host body is human or humanoid, and the necessary spell components are available, the magic-user

can even use his memorized spells. The host body retains its own hit points and physical abilities and properties. The GM decides if any additional modifications are necessary; for example, perhaps clumsiness or inefficiency occurs if the caster must become used to the new form. The alignment of the host or receptacle is that of the occupying life force. The caster can shift freely from the host to the receptacle if within the 10-foot-per-level range. Each attempt to shift requires one round. The spell ends when the magic-user shifts from the jar to his own body. A successful Dispel Magic spell cast on the host can drive the caster of the Magic Jar spell back into the receptacle and prevent him from making any attacks for 1d4 rounds plus 1 round per level of the caster of the dispel. The base success chance is 50%, plus or minus 5% per level difference between the casters. A successful Dispel Magic cast against the receptacle forces the occupant back into his own body. If the magic-user who cast the magic jar is forced back into his own body, the spell ends. If the host body is slain, the caster returns to the receptacle, if within range, and the life force of the host departs (i.e., it is dead). If the host body is slain beyond the range of the spell, both the host and the caster die. Any life force with nowhere to go is treated as slain unless recalled by a Raise Dead, Resurrection or similar spell. If the body of the caster is slain, his life force survives if it is in either the receptacle or the host. If the receptacle is destroyed while the caster's life force occupies it, the caster is irrevocably slain.

Major Creation
(Illusion/Phantasm)

Level: 5

Range: 10 yards	**Components:** V, S, M
Duration: Special	**Casting Time:** 1 turn
Area of Effect: Special	**Saving Throw:** None

Like the Minor Creation spell, the major creation spell enables the magic-user to pull wisps of material from the Demiplane of Shadow to create an item of nonliving, vegetable nature – soft goods, rope, wood, etc. The magic-user can also create mineral objects – stone, crystal, metal, etc. The item created cannot exceed 1 cubic foot per level of the spellcaster in volume. The duration of the created item varies with its relative hardness and rarity:

Item Created	Duration
Vegetable matter	2 hours/level
Stone or crystal	1 hour/level
Precious metals	2 turns/level
Gems	1 turn/level
Mithral*	2 rounds/level
Adamantite	1 round/level

* Includes similar rare metals.

Attempting to use any of these as material components in a spell will cause the spell to fail. The spellcaster must have at least a tiny piece of matter of the same type as the item he plans to create – a bit of twisted hemp to create rope, a chip of stone to create a boulder, and so on.

Monster Summoning III
(Conjuration/Summoning)

Level: 5

Range: Special	**Components:** V, S, M
Duration: 4 rds. + 1 rd./level	**Casting Time:** 5 segments
Area of Effect: 50-yd. radius	**Saving Throw:** None

This spell is much like the 3rd level spell Monster Summoning I, except that this spell summons 1d4 3rd level monsters. These appear within the spell's area of effect and attack the caster's opponents, until either he commands them to cease, the spell duration expires, or the monsters are slain. These creatures do not check morale and vanish when slain. If no opponent exists to fight, and the magic-user can communicate with them, the summoned monsters can perform other services for the magic-user. The material components of this spell are a tiny bag and a small candle.

Seeming

(Illusion/Phantasm)

Level: 5

Range: 10-ft. radius	**Components:** V, S
Duration: 12 hours	**Casting Time:** 5 segments
Area of Effect: 1 person/2 levels	**Saving Throw:** None

This spell enables the caster to alter the appearance of one person for every two levels of experience he has attained. The change includes clothing and equipment. The caster can make the recipients appear as any generally man-shaped bipedal creature, each up to 1 foot shorter or taller than his normal height, and thin or fat or in between. All those affected must resemble the same general type of creature: human, Orc, ogre, etc. Each remains a recognizable individual. The effect fails for an individual if the illusion chosen by the caster cannot be accomplished within the spell parameters (for example, a halfling could not be made to look like a centaur, but he might be made to look like a short, young ogre). Unwilling persons receive saving throws vs. spell to avoid the effect. Affected persons resume their normal appearances if slain. The spell is not precise enough to duplicate the appearance of a specific individual.

Sending

(Evocation)

Level: 5

Range: Unlimited	**Components:** V, S, M
Duration: Special	**Casting Time:** 1 turn
Area of Effect: 1 creature	**Saving Throw:** None

By means of this spell, the caster can contact a single creature with whom he is familiar and whose name and appearance are known. If the creature in question is not on the same plane of existence as the spellcaster, there is a base 5% chance that the sending does not arrive. Local conditions on other planes may worsen this chance considerably, at the option of the GM. The Sending, if successful, can be understood even by a creature with an Intelligence as low as 1 (animal intelligence). The magic-user can send a short message of 25 words or less to the recipient; the recipient can answer in like manner immediately. Even if the Sending is received, the subject creature is not obligated to act upon it in any manner. The material component for this spell consists of two tiny cylinders, each with one open end, connected by a short piece of fine copper wire.

Shadow Door

(Illusion/Phantasm)

Level: 5

Range: 10 yards	**Components:** S
Duration: 1 rd./level	**Casting Time:** 2 segments
Area of Effect: Special	**Saving Throw:** None

By means of this spell, the magic-user creates the illusion of a door. The illusion also permits the magic-user to appear to step through this "door" and disappear. In reality, he has darted aside and can flee, totally invisible, for the spell duration. Creatures viewing this are deluded into seeing or entering an empty 10-foot x 10-foot room if they open the "door." A True Seeing spell, a Gem of Seeing or similar magical means can discover the magic-user. Certain high Hit Dice monsters might also notice the magic-user (see the Invisibility spell), but only if making an active attempt to do so.

Shadow Magic

(Illusion/Phantasm)

Level: 5

Range: 50 yds. + 10 yds./level	**Components:** V, S
Duration: Special	**Casting Time:** 5 segments
Area of Effect: Special	**Saving Throw:** Special

The Shadow Magic spell enables the magic-user to tap energy from the Demiplane of Shadow to cast a quasi-real magic-user evocation spell of 3rd level or less. For example, this spell can be Magic Missile, Fireball, Lightning Bolt, or so on, and has normal effects upon creatures in the area of effect if they fail their saving throws vs. spell. Thus, a creature failing to save against a

Shadow Magic Fireball must roll another saving throw. If the latter roll is successful, the creature suffers half the normal Fireball damage; if the roll is not successful, the creature suffers full normal Fireball damage. If the first saving throw was successful, the Shadow Magic nature is detected and only 20% of the rolled damage is received (rounding down below fractions below .4 and rounding up fractions of .4 and above).

Stone Shape

(Alteration)

Level: 5

Range: Touch	**Components:** V, S, M
Duration: Permanent	**Casting Time:** 1 round
Area of Effect: 1 cu. ft./level	**Saving Throw:** None

By means of this spell, the magic-user can form an existing piece of stone into a shape that suits his purposes. For example, the magic-user can make a stone weapon, a special trapdoor, an idol, etc. This spell can also enable the spellcaster to reshape a stone door so as to escape imprisonment, providing the volume of stone involved is within the limits of the area of effect. While the caster can thus create stone doors and coffers, the fineness of detail is not great. If the construction involves small moving parts, there is a 30% chance they do not function. The material component of this spell is soft clay that must be worked into roughly the desired shape of the stone object and then touched to the stone when the spell is uttered.

Stone Sphere

(Evocation)

Level: 5

Range: 1 yds./level	**Components:** V, S, M
Duration: Permanent	**Casting Time:** 5 segments
Area of Effect: Special	**Saving Throw:** Special

This spell creates a stone sphere of 1/2 feet diameter per level. It is typically employed to close passages, portals and breaches against opponents. It can also be dropped or rolled onto opponents. In order to do this the person rolling or dropping the sphere must make a successful to-hit roll. Then the victim is allowed a saving throw versus paralyzation. If that is successful, he takes no damage. Otherwise the victim will take 1d12 points of damage per level and be 25% likely to have one or more appendages pinned underneath the sphere (assuming it is on a flat surface). The stone is permanent unless destroyed by a Dispel Magic or Disintegrate spell, or by normal means such as breaking or chipping. The material component is a small marble.

Summon Shadow

(Conjuration/Summoning, Necromancy)

Level: 5

Range: 10 yards	**Components:** V, S, M
Duration: 1 rd. + 1 rd./level	**Casting Time:** 5 segments
Area of Effect: 10-ft. cube	**Saving Throw:** None

When this spell is cast, the magic-user conjures up one Shadow (see the Hacklopedia of Beasts) for every three levels of experience he has attained. These monsters are under the control of the spellcaster and attack his enemies on command. The shadows remain until slain, turned, or the spell duration expires. The material component for this spell is a bit of smoky quartz.

Telekinesis

(Alteration)

Level: 5

Range: 10 yds./level	**Components:** V, S
Duration: Special	**Casting Time:** 5 segments
Area of Effect: 10 yds./level	**Saving Throw:** Negates

By means of this spell, the magic-user is able to move objects by concentrating on moving them mentally. The spell can provide either a gentle, sustained force or a single short, violent thrust. A sustained force enables the magic-user to move a weight of up to 25 pounds a distance up to 20 feet per round. The spell lasts two rounds, plus one round per caster level. The weight can be moved vertically, horizontally, or both. An object moved beyond the caster's range falls or stops. If the caster ceases concentration for any reason, the object falls or stops. The object can be telekinetically manipulated as if with one hand. For example, a lever or rope can be pulled, a key can be turned, an object rotated and so on, if the force required is within the weight limitation. The caster might even be able to untie simple knots, at the discretion of the GM. Alternatively, the spell energy can be expended in a single round. The caster can hurl one or more objects within range, and within a 10-foot cube, directly away from himself at high speed, to a distance of up to 10 feet per caster level. This is subject to a maximum weight of 25 pounds per caster level. Damage caused by hurled objects is decided by the GM, but cannot exceed 1 point of damage per caster level. Opponents who fall within the weight capacity of the spell can be hurled, but they are allowed a saving throw vs. spell to avoid the effect. Furthermore, those able to employ as simple a counter-measure as an enlarge spell, for example (thus making the body weight go over the maximum spell limit), can easily counter the spell. The various Bigby's hand spells also counter this spell.

Teleport

(Alteration)
Level: 5
Range: Touch
Components: V
Duration: Instantaneous
Casting Time: 2 segments
Area of Effect: Special
Saving Throw: None

When this spell is used, the magic-user instantly transports himself, along with a certain amount of additional weight that is on or being touched by the spellcaster, to a well-known destination. Distance is not a factor, but interplanar travel is not possible by means of a Teleport spell. The spellcaster is able to Teleport a maximum weight of 250 pounds, plus an additional 150 pounds for each level of experience above the 10th (a 13th level magic-user can Teleport up to 700 pounds). If the destination area is very familiar to the magic-user (he has a clear mental picture due to previous proximity to and study of the area), it is unlikely that there is any error in arriving, although the caster has no control over his facing upon arrival. Lesser known areas (those seen only magically or from a distance) increase the probability of error. Unfamiliar areas present considerable peril (see table).

Probability of Teleporting:			
Destination Is:	High	On Target	Low
Very familiar	01-02	03-99	00
Studied carefully	01-04	05-98	99-00
Seen casually	01-08	09-96	97-00
Viewed once	01-16	17-92	93-00
Never seen	01-32	33-84	85-00

Teleporting high means the magic-user arrives 10 feet above the ground for every 1% he is below the lowest "On Target" probability; this could be as high as 320 feet if the destination area was never seen. Any low result means the instant death of the magic-user if the area into which he Teleports is solid. A magic-user cannot Teleport to an area of empty space – a substantial surface must be there, whether a wooden floor, a stone floor, natural ground, etc. Areas of strong physical or magical energies may make Teleportation more hazardous or even impossible.

Tempus Fugit

(Illusion/Phantasm)
Reversible
Level: 5
Range: 0
Components: V, S
Duration: 5 turns/level
Casting Time: 5 segments
Area of Effect: 10 ft. radius
Saving Throw: None

This illusion affects the minds and bodies of any in the area of effect. Those within the spell's area perceive a much faster passage of time. Creatures need not be in the area when the spell is cast to be affected. Every turn spent within the area of the Tempus Fugit seems like a full six turns. All affected individuals are sped up accordingly, with regard to any time-dependent function. This includes sleep, hunger, healing and spell memorization. Any spell cast within the area of the Tempus Fugit also has an accelerated duration. One hour within the area of

the spell is as six to those affected, four hours within a Tempus Fugit spell is equivalent to a full day with regards to rest, spell preparation and recovery of hit points. Note that these times apply to non-combat situations.

The caster can reverse the spell so that time is slowed for those within its area. An hour will seem to be only ten minutes, a full day merely four hours. Reversal requires no special preparation. With either version of the spell, the magic-user is also affected. When the reverse version is cast, the effects of the spell last at least ten minutes after the caster dispels it, due to his slowed reaction speed.

Touch of Death

(Necromancy)
Level: 5
Range: Touch
Components: V, S
Duration: Permanent
Casting Time: 5 segments
Area of Effect: One living creature
Saving Throw: Negates

Touch of Death allows the caster to immediately make a special touch attack against one victim. If the attack is successful the victim must make a successful saving throw vs. death magic or instantly die. Even if the victim saves he suffers 2D8+1 damage, which may also be enough to slay them. Note that victims can still be raised or reincarnated, and that the spell only works on living creatures, not on extraplanar beings, undead, constructs, and the like.

Transmute Stone to Mud

(Alteration)
Reversible
Level: 5
Range: 10 yds./level
Components: V, S, M
Duration: Special
Casting Time: 5 segments
Area of Effect: 20-ft. cube/level
Saving Throw: None

This spell turns natural rock of any sort into an equal volume of mud. The depth of the mud can never exceed half its length or breadth. If it is cast upon a rock, for example, the rock affected collapses into mud. Creatures unable to Levitate, Fly or otherwise free themselves from the mud sink at the rate of 10 feet per round and suffocate, except for lightweight creatures that could normally pass across such ground. Brush thrown atop the mud can support creatures able to climb on top of it, with the amount of brush required subject to the GM's discretion. The mud remains until a Dispel Magic spell or a reverse of this spell, mud to rock, restores its substance – but not necessarily its form. Evaporation turns the mud to normal dirt, at the rate of 1d6 days per 10 cubic feet. The reverse, Transmute Mud to Rock, can harden normal mud into soft stone (sandstone or similar mineral) permanently unless magically changed. The material components for the spell are clay and water (or sand, lime, and water for the reverse).

Wall of Force

(Evocation)
Level: 5
Range: 30 yards
Components: V, S, M
Duration: 1 turn + 1 rd./level
Casting Time: 5 segments
Area of Effect: 10-ft. square/level
Saving Throw: None

A Wall of Force spell creates an invisible barrier in the locale desired by the caster, up to the spell's range. The Wall of Force cannot move and is totally unaffected by most spells, including Dispel Magic. However, a Disintegrate spell will immediately destroy it, as will a Rod of Cancellation or a Sphere of Annihilation. Likewise, the Wall of Force is not affected by blows, missiles, cold, heat, electricity, etc. Spells and breath weapons cannot pass through it in either direction, although Dimension Door, Teleport, and similar effects can bypass the barrier. The magic-user can, if desired, form the wall into a spherical shape with a radius of up to 1 foot per level or an open hemispherical shape with a radius of 1.5 feet per caster level. The Wall of Force must be continuous and unbroken when formed; if its surface is broken by any object or creature, the spell fails. The caster can end the spell on command. The material component for this spell is a pinch of powdered diamond worth 5,000 gp.

Wall of Iron

(Evocation)

Level: 5
Range: 5 yds./level
Duration: Permanent
Area of Effect: 15 sq. ft./level or special

Components: V, S, M
Casting Time: 5 segments
Saving Throw: None

When this spell is cast, the magic-user causes a vertical iron wall to spring into being. This wall can be used to seal off a passage or close a breach, for the Wall of Iron inserts itself into any surrounding nonliving material if its area is sufficient to do so. The Wall of Iron is one-half-inch thick per level of experience of the spellcaster. The magic-user is able to create an iron wall of up to 15 square feet per experience level; thus, a 12th level magic-user can create a Wall of Iron with an area of 180 square feet. The magic-user can double the wall's area by halving its thickness. If the caster desires, the Wall can be created vertically resting on a flat surface, so that it can be tipped over to fall on and crush any creature beneath it. The Wall is 50% likely to tip in either direction. This chance can be modified by a force of not less than 30 Strength and 400 pounds mass – each pound over 400 or Strength point over 30 alters the chance by 1% in favor of the stronger side. Creatures with room to flee the falling wall may do so by making successful saving throws vs. death. Those who fail are killed. Huge and gargantuan creatures cannot be crushed by the wall. The wall is permanent, unless successfully dispelled, but it is subject to all forces a normal iron wall is subject to – rust, perforation, etc. The material component of this spell is a small piece of sheet iron.

Wall of Stone

(Evocation)

Level: 5
Range: 5 yds./level
Duration: Permanent
Area of Effect: Special

Components: V, S, M
Casting Time: 5 segments
Saving Throw: None

This spell creates a wall of granite rock that merges into adjoining rock surfaces. It is typically employed to close passages, portals, and breaches against opponents. The Wall of Stone is 0.25 inch thick and up to 20 square feet per level of experience of the magic-user casting the spell. Thus, a 12th level magic-user can create a Wall of Stone 3 inches thick and up to 240 square feet in surface area (a 12-foot-wide and 20-foot-high wall, for example, to completely close a 10-foot x 16-foot passage). The wall created need not be vertical, nor rest upon any firm foundation (see the Wall of Iron spell); however, it must merge with and be solidly supported by existing stone. It can be used to bridge a chasm, for instance, or as a ramp. For this use, if the span is more than 20 feet, the wall must be arched and buttressed. This requirement reduces the area of effect by half. Thus, a 20th level caster can create a span with a surface area of 200 square feet. The wall can be crudely shaped to allow crenelations, battlements and so forth by likewise reducing the area. The stone is permanent unless destroyed by a Dispel Magic or Disintegrate spell, or by normal means such as breaking or chipping. The material component is a small block of granite.

Wall Passage

(Alteration)

Level: 5
Range: 30 yards
Duration: 1 hr. + 1 turn/level
Area of Effect: 5 x 8 x 10 ft.

Components: V, S, M
Casting Time: 5 segments
Saving Throw: None

A Wall Passage spell enables the spellcaster to open a passage through wooden, plaster or stone walls, but not other materials. The spellcaster and any associates can simply walk through. The spell causes a 5-foot wide x 8-foot high x 10-foot deep opening. Several of these spells can form a continuing passage so that very thick walls can be pierced. If dispelled, the Wall Passage closes away from the dispelling caster, ejecting those in the passage. The material component of this spell is a pinch of sesame seeds.

Zarba's Guardian Hand

(Evocation)

Level: 5
Range: 10 yds./level
Duration: 1 rd./level
Area of Effect: Special

Components: V, S, M
Casting Time: 5 segments
Saving Throw: None

The Zarba's Guardian Hand spell creates a man-sized to gargantuan-sized magical hand that appears between the spellcaster and his chosen opponent. This disembodied Hand then moves to remain between the two, regardless of what the spellcaster does or how the opponent tries to get around it. Neither invisibility nor polymorph fools the hand once a creature has been chosen. The Hand does not pursue an opponent. The size of the Hand is determined by the magic-user, and it can be from human size (5 feet) all the way up to titan size (25 feet). It provides cover for the caster against the selected opponent, with all the attendant combat adjustments. It has as many hit points as the caster in full health and has an Armor Class of 0. Any creature weighing less than 2,000 pounds trying to push past the hand is slowed to half its normal movement. If the original opponent is slain, the caster can designate a new opponent for the hand. The caster can command the Hand out of existence at any time. The material component of the spell is a soft glove.

Sixth Level Spells

Antimagic Shell

(Abjuration)

Level: 6
Range: 0
Duration: 1 turn/level
Area of Effect: 1 ft./level diameter

Components: V, S
Casting Time: 1 segments
Saving Throw: None

By means of this spell, the magic-user surrounds himself with an invisible barrier that moves with him. The space within this barrier is totally impervious to all magic and magical spell effects, thus preventing the passage of spells or their effects. Likewise, it prevents the functioning of any magical items or spells within its confines. The area is also impervious to breath weapons, gaze or voice attacks, and similar special attack forms.

The Antimagic Shell also hedges out charmed, summoned, or conjured creatures. It cannot, however, be forced against any creature that it would keep at bay; any attempt to do so creates a discernible pressure against the barrier, and continued pressure will break the spell. Normal creatures (a normally encountered troll rather than a conjured one, for instance) can enter the area, as can normal missiles. Furthermore, while a magical sword does not function magically within the area, it is still a sword. Note that creatures on their home plane are normal creatures there. Thus, on the Elemental Plane of Fire, a randomly encountered fire elemental cannot be kept at bay by this spell. Artifacts, relics and creatures of demigawd or higher status are unaffected by mortal magic such as this. Should the caster be larger than the area enclosed by the barrier, parts of his person may be considered exposed, at the GM's option. A Dispel Magic spell does not remove the spell; the caster can end it upon command.

Body Heat Activation Spell

(Evocation)

Level: 6
Range: 20 ft./level
Duration: 1 day/level
Area of Effect: 10 ft. cube/level

Components: V, S, M
Casting Time: 1 turn
Saving Throw: Special

Body Heat Activation can be linked to any one other spell, allowing that spell to be instantly cast upon the area. The second spell may be any one that the caster knows, but it cannot be of a level higher than one third the caster's level, rounded down, and no higher than sixth level in any case. This second spell is cast at the same time as the Body Heat Activation Spell and is triggered as soon as a warm blooded creature larger than a normal rat enters the area of effect. The spell is centered upon this first target, but others in the area may become victims if the linked spell has an area of effect. The caster may choose to make himself immune to his own Body Heat Activated spells. Note that this spell will fail to activate if the ambient temperature in the area is between 88 and 108° Fahrenheit. The material component is blood from a cold blooded creature.

Break Hex

(Abjuration)

Level: 6

Range: 30 feet
Components: V, S

Duration: Permanent
Casting Time: 1 round

Area of Effect: Special
Saving Throw: None

This spell is a more powerful form of the Remove Curse spell that will automatically remove any curse or hex short of a Death Hex or divine curse.

Chain Lightning

(Evocation)

Level: 6

Range: 40 yds. + 5 yds./level
Components: V, S, M

Duration: Instantaneous
Casting Time: 5 segments

Area of Effect: Special
Saving Throw: Half

This spell creates an electrical discharge that begins as a single stroke of lightning, 2 1/2 feet wide, commencing from the fingertips of the caster. Unlike a Lightning Bolt spell, Chain Lightning strikes one object or creature initially, then arcs to a series of other objects or creatures within range, losing energy with each jump. The bolt initially inflicts 1d6 points of damage per level of the caster, to a maximum of 12d6 (half damage if the object or creature rolls a successful saving throw vs. spell). After the first strike, the lightning arcs to the next nearest object or creature. Each jump reduces the damaged inflicted by 1d6. Each creature or magical object hit receives a saving throw vs. spell. Success on this save indicates the creature suffers only half damage from the bolt.

The chain can strike as many times (including the first object or creature) as the spellcaster has levels, although each creature or object can be struck only once. Thus, a bolt cast by a 12th level magic-user can strike up to 12 times, causing less damage with each strike.

The bolt continues to arc until it has struck the appropriate number of objects or creatures, until it strikes an object that grounds it (interconnecting iron bars of a large cell or cage, a large pool of liquid, etc.), or until there are no more objects or creatures to strike. Direction is not a consideration when plotting chain lightning arcs.

Distance is a factor – an arc cannot exceed the spell's range. If the only possible arc is greater than the spell's range, the stroke fades into nothingness. Creatures immune to electrical attack can be struck, even though no damage is taken. Note that it is possible for the chain to arc back to the caster!

The material components are a bit of fur, a piece of amber, glass, or crystal rod, and one silver pin for each experience level of the caster.

Charm of Undying Devotion

(Enchantment/Charm)

Level: 6

Range: 5 yds./level
Components: V, S

Duration: Special
Casting Time: 6 segments

Area of Effect: 1 person
Saving Throw: Negates

The Charm of Undying Devotion spell enables the caster or a person chosen by the caster to control the actions of any person until the spell is ended by the subject's successful saving throw or the magic has been dispelled. Elves and half-elves resist this enchantment as they do all charm-type spells. When the spell is cast, the victim must roll a saving throw vs. spell. Failure means the magic-user has established a telepathic link between the subject's mind and the mind of any other person, possibly the caster himself. If a common language is shared, the person controlling the link can generally force the subject to perform as he desires, within the limits of the subject's body structure and Strength. Note that the person controlling the link does not receive direct sensory input from the subject. Subjects resist this control, and those forced to take actions against their natures receive a new saving throw with a bonus of +1 to +4, depending on the type of action required. If the victim fails his saving throw, even self-destructive orders are carried out. Once control is established, there is no limit to the range at which it can be exercised, as long as the

person controlling the link and subject are on the same plane. A Protection From Evil spell can prevent the person controlling the link from exercising control or using the telepathic link while the subject is so warded, but it cannot prevent the establishment of the charm.

Conjure Animals

(Conjuration/Summoning)

Level: 6

Range: Special
Components: V, S

Duration: 1 rd./level
Casting Time: 6 segments

Area of Effect: 30 yds. radius
Saving Throw: None

The Conjure Animals spell enables the magic-user to magically create one or more mammals to attack his opponents. The total Hit Dice of the mammals cannot exceed twice his level, if determined randomly, or his level if a specific animal type is requested (see the Game Master Guide). Thus, a magic-user of 12th level could randomly conjure two mammals with 12 Hit Dice, four with 6 Hit Dice each, six with 4 Hit Dice each, eight with 3 Hit Dice each, twelve with 2 Hit Dice each, or 24 with 1 Hit Die each. Count every +1 hit point bonus of a creature as 1/4 of a Hit Die; thus, a creature with 4+3 Hit Dice equals a 4 3/4 Hit Dice creature. The Conjured Animal(s) remain for one round for each level of the conjuring magic-user or until slain. They follow the caster's verbal commands. Conjured Animals unfailingly attack the magic-user's opponents, but they resist being used for any other purpose.

Contingency

(Evocation)

Level: 6

Range: 0
Components: V, S, M

Duration: 1 day/level
Casting Time: 1 turn

Area of Effect: The caster
Saving Throw: None

By means of this spell, the magic-user is able to place or receive another spell upon his person so that the latter spell will come into effect under the conditions dictated during the casting of the Contingency spell. The Contingency spell and the spell it is to bring into effect are cast at the same time (the one-turn casting time indicated is the total for both castings). The spell to be brought into effect by the prescribed Contingency must be one that affects the magic-user's person (Feather Fall, Levitation, Fly, Feign Death, etc.) and be of a spell level no higher than 1/3 of the caster's experience level (rounded down), but not higher than the 6th spell level.

Caster Level	Contingency Spell Level
12-14	4th
15-17	5th
18+	6th

Only one Contingency spell can be placed on the spellcaster at any one time; if a second is cast, the first one (if still active) is cancelled. The conditions needed to bring the spell into effect must be clear, although they can be rather general. For example, a Contingency spell cast with an Airy Water spell might prescribe that any time the magic-user is plunged into or otherwise engulfed in water or similar liquid, the Airy Water spell will instantly come into effect. Or a Contingency could bring a Feather Fall spell into effect any time the magic-user falls more than 2 feet. In all cases, the Contingency immediately brings into effect the second spell, the latter being "cast" instantaneously when the prescribed circumstances occur. Note that if complicated or convoluted conditions are prescribed, the whole spell complex (the Contingency spell and the companion magic) may fail when called upon. The material components of this spell are (in addition to those of the companion spell) 100 gp worth of quicksilver and an eyelash of an Ogre magic-user, Kirin, or similar spell-using creature. In addition, the spell requires a statuette of the magic-user carved from elephant ivory (which is not destroyed, though it is subject to wear and tear), which must be carried on the person of the spellcaster for the Contingency spell to perform its function when called upon.

Control Weather

(Alteration)

Level: 6

Range: 0   **Components:** V, S, M

Duration: 4d6 hours   **Casting Time:** 1 turn

Area of Effect: 4d4 sq. mi.   **Saving Throw:** None

The Control Weather spell enables a magic-user to change the weather in the local area. The spell affects the weather for 4d6 hours in an area of 4d4 square miles. It requires one turn to cast the spell, and an additional 1d4 turns for the weather conditions to occur. The current weather conditions are decided by the GM, depending on the climate and season. Weather conditions have three components: precipitation, temperature and wind.

The spell can change these conditions according to the following chart. The upper-cased headings represent the existing weather conditions. The small headings beneath each large heading are the new conditions to which the caster can change the existing conditions. Furthermore, the caster can control the direction of the wind. For example, a day that is clear and warm with moderate wind can be controlled to become hazy, hot, and calm. Contradictions are not possible – fog and strong wind, for example. Multiple control weather spells can be used only in succession. The material components for this spell are burning incense and bits of earth and wood mixed in water. Obviously, this spell functions only in areas where there are appropriate climatic conditions.

Precipitation	Temperature	Wind
CLEAR WEATHER	HOT	CALM
Very clear	Sweltering heat	Dead calm
Light clouds or hazy	Warm	Light wind
		Moderate wind
PARTLY CLOUDY	WARM	MODERATE WIND
Clear weather	Hot	Calm
Cloudy	Cool	Strong wind
Mist/light rain/small hail		
Sleet/light snow		
CLOUDY	COOL	STRONG WIND
Partly cloudy	Warm	Moderate wind
Deep clouds	Cold	Gale
Fog		
HEAVY RAIN/LARGE HAIL	COLD	GALE
Driving sleet/heavy snow	Cool	Strong wind
Gale	Arctic cold	Storm
Hurricane-typhoon		

Death Fog

(Alteration, Evocation)

Level: 6

Range: 30 yards   **Components:** V, S, M

Duration: 1d4 rds. + 1/level   **Casting Time:** 6 segments

Area of Effect: Two 10-ft. cubes/level   **Saving Throw:** None

The casting of a Death Fog spell creates an area of solid fog that has the additional property of being highly acidic. The vapors are deadly to living things, so that vegetation exposed to them will die – grass and similar small plants in two rounds, bushes and shrubs in four, small trees in eight and large trees in 16 rounds. Animal life not immune to acid suffers damage according to the length of time it is exposed to the vapors of a Death Fog, as follows:

1st round:	1 point
2nd round:	2 points
3rd round:	4 points
4th and each succeeding round:	8 points

The Death Fog otherwise resembles the 2nd level Fog Cloud spell: rolling, billowing vapors that can be moved only by a very strong wind. Any creature attempting to move through the Death Fog progresses at a rate of 1 foot per unit of normal movement rate per round. A Gust of Wind spell cannot affect it, but a Fireball, Flame Strike, or Wall of Fire can burn it away in a single round. The material components are a pinch of dried and powdered peas, powdered animal hoof and strong acid of any sort (including highly distilled vinegar or acid crystals), which must be obtained from an alchemist.

Death Spell

(Necromancy)

Level: 6

Range: 10 yds./level   **Components:** V, S, M

Duration: Instantaneous   **Casting Time:** 6 segments

Area of Effect: 30-ft. cube/level   **Saving Throw:** None

When a Death Spell is cast, it snuffs out the life forces of creatures in the area of effect instantly and irrevocably. Such creatures cannot be raised or resurrected, but an individual slain in this manner might be brought back via a wish. The number of creatures that can be slain is a function of their Hit Dice.

Maximum # of Creatures Hit Dice	Creatures Affected
Under 2	4d20
2 to 4	2d20
4+1 to 6+3	2d4
6+4 to 8+3	1d4

If creatures of differing Hit Dice are attacked with a Death Spell, roll the dice (4d20) to determine how many creatures of under 2 Hit Dice are affected. If the number rolled is greater than the actual number of sub-2 Hit Dice creatures, apply the remainder of the roll to the higher Hit Dice creatures by consulting the following table.

Creatures Hit Dice	Conversion Factor (CF)
Under 2	1
2 to 4	2
4+1 to 6+3	10
6+4 to 8+3	20

In other words, from the 4d20 roll subtract the number of creatures of less than 2 Hit Dice (these creatures die). If there are any remaining points from the 4d20 roll, subtract 2 for each creature of 2 to 4 Hit Dice (these creatures also die). If this still doesn't use up all the 4d20 roll, subtract 10 for each creature of 4+1 to 6+3 Hit Dice, and so on. Stop when all the creatures are dead, all the 4d20 roll is used up, or the remainder is less than half the CF of any remaining creatures. (If the remainder is one-half or more of the CF of a creature, that creature dies.) For example, a mixed group of 20 Goblins, eight Gnolls, and four Ogres, led by a Hill Giant, are caught in the area of a Death Spell. The 4d20 roll gives a total of 53 points; 20 of this eliminates the Goblins (20 x 1 CF), 16 kills the Gnolls (8 x 2 CF), and the remaining 17 kills two Ogres (10 points to kill one Ogre, and the remaining 7 points are enough to kill one more Ogre). The other two Ogres and the hill giant are unharmed. A Death Spell does not affect lycanthropes, undead creatures or creatures from planes other than the Prime Material Plane. The material component of this spell is a crushed black pearl with a minimum value of 1,000 g.p.

Demishadow Magic

(Illusion/Phantasm)

Level: 6

Range: 60 yds. + 10 yds./level   **Components:** V, S

Duration: Special   **Casting Time:** 6 segments

Area of Effect: Special   **Saving Throw:** Special

This spell is similar to the 5th level Shadow Magic spell, but this spell enables the casting of partially real 4th- and 5th- level evocations (Cone of Cold, Wall of Fire, Wall of Ice, Cloudkill, etc.). If recognized as Demishadow Magic (if a saving throw vs. spell is successful), damaging spells inflict only 40% of normal damage, with a minimum of 2 points per die of damage. A Demishadow Cloudkill slays creatures with fewer than 2 Hit Dice and inflicts 1d2 points of damage per round.

Disintegrate

(Alteration)

Level: 6
Range: 5 yds./level   **Components:** V, S, M
Duration: Instantaneous   **Casting Time:** 6 segments
Area of Effect: 1 creature or   **Saving Throw:** Negates
10 x 10 x 10 ft. cube

This spell causes matter to vanish. It affects even matter (or energy) of a magical nature, such as Zarba's Shoving Hand, but not a Globe of Invulnerability or an Antimagic Shell. Disintegration is instantaneous, and its effects are permanent. Any single creature can be affected, even undead. Nonliving matter, up to a 10-foot x 10-foot x 10-foot cube, can be obliterated by the spell. The spell creates a thin, green ray that causes physical material touched to glow and vanish, leaving traces of fine dust. Creatures that successfully save vs. spell have avoided the ray (material items have resisted the magic) and are not affected. Only the first creature or object struck can be affected. The material components are a lodestone and a pinch of dust.

Enchant an Item

(Enchantment, Invocation)

Level: 6
Range: Touch   **Components:** V, S, M
Duration: Special   **Casting Time:** Special
Area of Effect: 1 item   **Saving Throw:** Negates

This is a spell that must be used by a magic-user planning to create a magical item. The Enchant an Item spell prepares the object to accept the magic. The item must meet the following tests: 1) it must be in sound and undamaged condition; 2) the item must be the finest possible, considering its nature, i.e., crafted of the highest quality material and with the finest workmanship; and 3) its cost or value must reflect the second test, and in most cases the item must have a raw-materials cost in excess of 100 gp. With respect to requirement 3, it is not possible to apply this test to items such as ropes, leather goods, cloth, and pottery not normally embroidered, bejeweled, tooled, carved, or engraved. If such work or materials can be added to an item without weakening or harming its normal functions, however, these are required for the item to be enchanted.

The magic-user must have access to a workshop or laboratory, properly equipped and from which contaminating magic can be screened. Any magical item not related to the fabrication process (such as most protective devices) and within 30 feet of the materials is a source of contaminating magic and will spoil the process. The item to be prepared must be touched by the spellcaster. This touching must be constant and continual during the casting time, which is a base 16 hours plus an additional 8d8 hours (as the magic-user may never work more than eight hours per day, and haste or any other spells will not alter the time required in any way, this effectively means that casting time for this spell is two days + 1d8 days). All work must be uninterrupted, and during rest periods the item being enchanted must never be more than 1 foot distant from the spellcaster; if it is, the whole spell is spoiled and must be begun again. (Note that during rest periods absolutely no other form of magic can be performed, and the magic-user must remain quiet and in isolation or the enchantment is ruined.)

At the end of the spell, the caster will know that the item is ready for the final test. He will then pronounce the final magical syllable, and if the item makes a saving throw (which is exactly the same as that of the magic-user) vs. spell, the spell is completed. The spellcaster's saving throw bonuses also apply to the item, up to +3. A result of 1 on the 1d20 roll always results in failure, regardless of modifications.

Once the spell is finished, the magic-user can begin to place the desired spell upon the item. The spell he plans to place must be cast within 24 hours or the preparatory work fades, and the item must be enchanted again. Each spell subsequently cast upon an object bearing an Enchant an Item spell requires 2d4 hours per spell level of the magic being cast. Again, during casting the item must be touched by the magic-user, and during the rest periods it must always be within 1 foot of his person. This procedure holds true for any additional spells placed upon the item, and each successive spell must be begun within 24 hours of the last, even if the prior spell failed. No magic placed on an item is permanent unless a Permanency spell is used as a finishing touch. This

always runs a 5% risk of draining 1 point of Constitution from the magic-user casting the spell.

Also, while it is possible to tell when the basic spell (Enchant an Item) succeeds, it is not possible to tell if successive castings actually work, for each must make the same sort of saving throw as the item itself made. Naturally, an item that is charged – a rod, staff, wand, Javelin of Lightning, Ring of Wishes, etc. – can never be made permanent. Magical devices cannot be used to enchant an item or cast magic upon an object so prepared, but scrolls can be used for this purpose. The materials needed for this spell vary according to both the nature of the item being enchanted and the magic to be cast upon it. For example, a Cloak of Displacement might require the hides of one or more Displacer Beasts, a sword meant to slay dragons could require the blood and some other part of the type(s) of dragon(s) it will be effective against, and a Ring of Shooting Stars might require pieces of meteorites and the horn of Ki-rin. These specifics, as well as other information pertaining to this spell, are decided by the GM and must be discovered or researched in play.

Ensnarement

(Conjuration/Summoning)

Level: 6
Range: 10 yards   **Components:** V, S, M
Duration: Special   **Casting Time:** 1 turn
Area of Effect: Special   **Saving Throw:** Negates

Casting this spell attempts a dangerous act: to lure a powerful creature from another plane to a specifically prepared trap, where it will be held until it agrees to perform one service in return for freedom from the Ensnarement spell. The type of creature to be Ensnared must be known and stated, and if it has a specific, proper, or given name, this must be used in casting the Ensnarement spell. The spell causes an awareness of a gate-like opening on the plane of the creature to be Ensnared. A special saving throw is then made to determine if the creature detects the nature of the planar opening as a trap or believes it to be a gate. To save, the creature must roll equal to or less than its Intelligence score on 1d20. The score is modified by the difference between the creature's Intelligence and that of the spellcaster. If the creature has a higher score, the difference is subtracted from its dice roll to save. If the spellcaster has a higher score, the difference is added to the dice roll. If the saving throw succeeds, the creature ignores the spell-created opening, and the spell fails. If the saving throw fails, the creature steps into the opening and is Ensnared. When so trapped, the otherplanar creature can freely attack the ensnaring magic-user, unless the caster has created a warding circle. Such circles may be temporary (drawn by hand) or permanent (inlaid or carved). Even with such protection, the entrapped creature may break free and wreak its vengeance upon the spellcaster. A hand-drawn circle has a base failure chance of 20%, while one inlaid or carved has a base of 10% (and that is for the first time it is used, to determine whether or not the job was done properly). The base chance is modified by the difference between the magic-user's combined Intelligence and experience level and the Intelligence and the experience level or Hit Dice of the creature Ensnared. If the spellcaster has a higher total, that difference in percentage points is subtracted from the chance for the creature to break free. If the creature has a higher total, that difference is added to its chance to break free. The chance can be further reduced by careful preparation of the circle. If the hand-made circle is drawn over a longer period of time, using specially prepared pigments (1,000 gp value per turn spent drawing), the chance of breaking free is reduced by 1% for every turn spent in preparation. This can bring the base chance to 0%. Similarly, an inlaid or carved design can be brought to a 0% chance of the creature breaking free by inlaying with various metals, minerals, etc. This cost will require a minimum of one full month of time and add not less than 50,000 gp to the basic cost of having the circle inlaid or carved into stone. Any break in the circle spoils the efficacy of the spell and enables the creature to break free automatically. Even a straw dropped across the line of a magic circle destroys its power. Fortunately, the creature within cannot so much as place a straw upon any portion of the inscribed ward, for the magic of the barrier absolutely prevents it. Once safely Ensnared, the creature can be kept for as long as the spellcaster dares. (Remember the danger of something breaking the ward!) The creature cannot leave the circle, nor can any of its attacks or powers penetrate the barrier. The caster can offer bribes, use promises, or make threats in order to exact one service from the captive creature. The GM will then assign a value to what the magic-user has said to the Ensnared creature, rating it from 0 to 6 (with 6 being the most persuasive). This rating is then subtracted from the Intelligence score of the creature. If the creature rolls a successful Intelligence check against its adjusted Intelligence, it refuses service. New offers, bribes, etc., can be made, or the old ones re-offered 24 hours later, when the creature's Intelligence has dropped by 1 point due to confinement. This can be repeated until the creature promises to serve, until it breaks free, or until the caster decides to get rid of it by means of some riddance spell. Impossible demands or unreasonable commands are never agreed to. Once the single service is completed, the creature need only so inform the spellcaster to be instantly sent from whence it came. The creature might later seek revenge.

Extension III
(Alteration)
Level: 6
Range: 0   **Components:** V
Duration: Special   **Casting Time:** 6 segments
Area of Effect: Special   **Saving Throw:** None

This spell is the same as the 4th level Extension I spell, except that it will extend 1st through 3rd level spells to double duration and will extend the duration of 4th or 5th level spells by 50%.

Eyebite
(Enchantment/Charm, Illusion/Phantasm)
Level: 6
Range: 20 yards   **Components:** V, S
Duration: 1 round/3 levels   **Casting Time:** 6 segments
Area of Effect: 1 creature   **Saving Throw:** Special

An Eyebite spell enables the caster to merely meet the gaze of a creature and speak a single word to cause an effect. This gaze attack is in addition to any other attacks allowed to the magic-user. The magic-user selects one of four possible gaze attacks at the time the spell is cast, and this attack cannot be changed. For example, a 12th level caster who chose fear would have four opportunities to make gaze attacks causing fear, one for each round of the spell's duration. Any gaze attack is negated by a successful saving throw vs. spell, with Wisdom adjustments. The four effects of the spell are as follows:

Charm: The magic-user can charm a single person or monster by gaze and by uttering a single word. The effect is to make the charmed subject absolutely loyal and docile to the caster, even to the point of personal danger. It is otherwise the same as a Charm Monster spell. All creatures other than humans, demi-humans, and humanoids save with +2 bonuses.

Fear: The magic-user can cause fear by gaze and by speaking a single word. The subject flees in blind terror for 1d4 rounds. After this, the creature refuses to face the caster and cowers or bolts for the nearest cover if subsequently confronted by the caster (50% chance of either). The latter effect lasts one turn per caster level. This attack can be negated by spells that counter fear.

Sicken: This power enables the caster to merely gaze, speak, a word, and cause sudden pain and fever to sweep over the subject's body. Creatures with Ability Scores function at half effectiveness; others inflict only one-half damage with physical attacks. Movement is at one-half normal rate. The subject remains stricken for one turn per level of the caster, after which all abilities return at the rate of one point per turn of complete rest or one point per hour of moderate activity. The effects cannot be negated by a Cure Disease or Heal spell, but a Remove Curse or successful Dispel Magic spell is effective. Creatures other than humans, demi-humans, and humanoids save with +2 bonuses versus this attack.

Sleep: The magic-user can cause any individual to fall into a comatose slumber by means of a gaze and a single word, unless the subject successfully rolls its saving throw vs. spell. Creatures normally subject to a 1st level Sleep spell save with -2 penalties. An affected creature must be shaken or otherwise shocked back to consciousness. In all cases, the gaze attack has a speed factor of 1. This spell does not affect undead of any type, or extend beyond the plane occupied by the caster. Note that the caster is subject to the effects of his reflected gaze and is allowed any applicable saving throw. In the case of a reflected charm gaze, the caster is paralyzed until it wears off or is countered.

Fireball, Show-No-Mercy
(Evocation)
Level: 6
Range: 10 yds. + 10 yds./level   **Components:** V, S, M
Duration: Instantaneous   **Casting Time:** 6 segments
Area of Effect: 20-ft. radius   **Saving Throw:** 1/2

The Show-No-Mercy Fireball is similar in most respects to a normal Fireball except that the damage dealt is 1d8 per level of the caster .

Fireball, Proximity Fused
(Evocation)
Level: 6
Range: 10 yds. + 10 yds./level   **Components:** V, S, M
Duration: 1 rd./level   **Casting Time:** 6 segments
Area of Effect: 20-ft. radius   **Saving Throw:** 1/2

The Proximity Fused Fireball can be cast at a single target point. It will not go off until a target comes within 10 feet of the center of the spell's area. A target is defined as any living creature weighing over 10 lbs. Damage dealt to those in the blast radius is 1d6 per level of the caster. In other respects, this spell is similar to the normal third level Fireball spell.

Geas
(Enchantment/Charm)
Level: 6
Range: 10 yards   **Components:** V
Duration: Special   **Casting Time:** 4 segments
Area of Effect: 1 creature   **Saving Throw:** None

A Geas spell places a magical command upon a creature (usually human or humanoid) to carry out some service, or to refrain from some action or course of activity, as desired by the spellcaster. The creature must be intelligent, conscious, under its own volition and able to understand the caster. While a Geas cannot compel a creature to kill itself or perform acts that are likely to result in certain death, it can cause almost any other course of action. The Geased creature must follow the given instructions until the Geas is completed. Failure to do so will cause the creature to grow sick and die within 1d4 weeks. Deviation from or twisting of the instructions causes a corresponding loss of Strength points until the deviation ceases. A Geas can be done away with by a Wish spell, but a Dispel Magic or Remove Curse spell will not negate it. Your GM will decide any additional details of a Geas, for its casting and fulfillment are tricky, and an improperly cast Geas is ignored.

Glassee
(Alteration)
Level: 6
Range: Touch   **Components:** V, S, M
Duration: 1 rd./level   **Casting Time:** 1 round
Area of Effect: Special   **Saving Throw:** None

By means of this spell, the magic-user is able to make a section of metal, stone, or wood as transparent as glass to his gaze, or even make it into transparent material as explained hereafter. Normally, the Glassee spell can make up to 4 inches of metal, 6 inches of stone, and 20 inches of wood transparent. The spell will not work on lead, gold, or platinum. The magic-user can opt to make the Glassee work only for himself for the duration of the spell, or he can actually make a transparent area, a one-way window, in the material affected. Either case gives a viewing area 3 feet wide by 2 feet high. If a window is created, it has the strength of the original material. The material component of the spell is a small piece of crystal or glass.

Globe of Invulnerability

(Abjuration)

Level: 6
Range: 0
Duration: I rd./level
Area of Effect: 5-ft. radius

Components: V, S, M
Casting Time: I round
Saving Throw: None

This spell creates an immobile, faintly shimmering, magical sphere around the caster that prevents any 1st, 2nd, 3rd, or 4th level spell effects from penetrating. Thus, the area of effect of any such spell does not include the area of the Globe of Invulnerability. This includes innate spell-like abilities and effects from devices. However, any type of spell can be cast out of the magical sphere; spells pass from the caster of the Globe to the subject without effect on the Globe. Fifth and higher level spells are not affected by the Globe. The Globe can be brought down by a successful Dispel Magic spell. The material component of the spell is a glass or crystal bead that shatters at the expiration of the spell.

Guards and Wards

(Evocation, Alteration, Enchantment/Charm)

Level: 6
Range: 0
Duration: I hr./level
Area of Effect: Special

Components: V, S, M
Casting Time: 3 turns
Saving Throw: None

This special and powerful spell is primarily used to defend the magic-user's stronghold. The ward protects a one-story stronghold, with a base dimension of 400 feet x 400 feet. The magic-user can ward a multistory area by reducing the base area proportionately. The following take place in the warded area upon casting the spell:

1. All corridors become misty; visibility is reduced to 10 feet.
2. All doors are Mage Locked.
3. Stairs are filled with webs from top to bottom. These act as the 2nd level web spell, except that they regrow within one turn if destroyed.
4. Where there are choices in direction — such as a cross or side passage – a minor confusion-type spell functions so as to make it 50% probable that intruders believe they are going in the exact opposite direction.
5. The whole area radiates magic. The normal use of the Detect Magic spell becomes impossible for those of less than the caster's level and difficult for others.
6. One door per level of experience of the magic-user is covered by an illusion to appear as if it were a plain wall.
7. The magic-user can place one of the following additional magical effects:
   A. Dancing lights in four corridors.
   B. A magic mouth in two places.
   C. A stinking cloud in two places.
   D. A gust of wind in one corridor or room.
   E. A suggestion in one place.

Note that items 6 and 7 function only when the magic-user is totally familiar with the area of the spell's effect. Dispel Magic can remove one effect, at random, per casting. A Remove Curse spell will not work.

The material components of the spell are burning incense, a small measure of sulphur and oil, a knotted string, a small amount of Umber Hulk blood and a small silver rod.

Haarpang's Magnificent Sphere of Freezing

(Alteration, Evocation)

Level: 6
Range: Special
Duration: Special
Area of Effect: Special

Components: V, S, M
Casting Time: 6 segments
Saving Throw: Special

Haarpang's Magnificent Sphere of Freezing is a multipurpose spell of considerable power. If the caster opts, he may create any of the following:

A) Frigid globe. A small globe of matter at absolute zero temperature that spreads upon contact with water, or a liquid that is principally water, freezing

it to a depth of 6 inches over an area equal to 100 square feet per level of the spellcaster. This ice lasts for one round per level of the caster.

The material component is a thin sheet of crystal about an inch square.

B) Cold ray. The spell can be used as a thin ray of cold that springs from the caster's hand to a distance of 10 yards per level of the magic-user; this ray inflicts 1d4+2 points of damage per level of the caster upon the first creature struck. A saving throw vs. spell is applicable; all damage is negated if it is successful (as the ray is so narrow a save indicates it missed). If the first creature is missed, the path of the ray is plotted to its full distance, and anything else in its path must save (if applicable) or suffer appropriate damage.

The material component is a white sapphire of not less than 1,000 gp value.

C) Globe of cold. This creates a small globe about the size of a sling stone, cool to the touch, but not harmful. This globe can be hurled, either by hand to a distance of 40 yards (considered short range), or as a sling bullet. The globe shatters upon impact, inflicting 6d6 points of cold damage upon all creatures within a 10-foot radius (one-half damage if a saving throw vs. spell is successful). Use the Grenadelike Missile Table in the HackMaster Game Master's Guide to find where misses strike. Note that if the globe is not thrown or slung within one round per level of the spellcaster, it shatters and causes cold damage as stated above. This timed effect can be employed against pursuers, although it can prove hazardous to the spellcaster and his associates as well.

The material component is a 1,000-gp diamond.

Hyptor's Total Recall

(Alteration)

Level: 6
Range: 0
Duration: Instantaneous
Area of Effect: The caster

Components: V, S
Casting Time: I segment
Saving Throw: None

By use of this spell, the magic-user is able to instantly recall any 1st through 5th level spell he has used during the past 24 hours. The spell must have been memorized and actually used during that time period. Hyptor's Total Recall allows the recovery of only one spell. If the recalled spell requires material components, these must be provided by the caster; the recovered spell is not usable until the material components are available.

Invisible Stalker

(Conjuration/Summoning)

Level: 6
Range: 10 yards
Duration: Special
Area of Effect: Special

Components: V, S, M
Casting Time: I round
Saving Throw: None

This spell summons an Invisible Stalker from the Elemental Plane of Air. This 8-Hit Dice monster obeys and serves the spellcaster in performing whatever tasks are set before it. It is a faultless tracker within one day of the quarry's passing. The Invisible Stalker follows instructions even if they send him hundreds or thousands of miles away and, once given an order, follows through unceasingly until the task is accomplished. However, the creature is bound to serve; it does not do so from loyalty or desire. Therefore, it resents prolonged missions or complex tasks, and it attempts to pervert instructions accordingly. Invisible Stalkers understand common speech but speak no language save their own. The material components of this spell are burning incense and a piece of horn carved into a crescent shape.

Karnaac's Transformation

(Alteration, Evocation)

Level: 6
Range: 0
Duration: I rd./level
Area of Effect: The caster

Components: V, S, M
Casting Time: 6 segments
Saving Throw: None

Karnaac's Transformation is a sight guaranteed to astound any creature not aware of its power, for when the magic-user casts the spell, he undergoes a startling transformation. The size and strength of the magic-user increase to heroic proportions, so he becomes a formidable fighting machine; the spell causes the caster to become a berserk fighter! The magic-user's hit points double, and all damage he sustains comes first from the magical points gained; once these points are eliminated, all subsequent damage (to his true hit points) is doubled. The Armor Class of the magic-user is 4 better than that possessed prior to casting the spell (AC 10 goes to 6, AC 9 to 5, AC 8 to 4, etc.), to a maximum Armor Class of -10. All attacks are as a fighter of the same level as the magic-user (i.e., the magic-user uses the combat values normally reserved for fighters). The magic-user can use either a dagger or a staff when attacking. A dagger can be used twice per round, and each successful attack inflicts an additional 2 points of damage. A staff can be used only once per round, but with a +2 bonus to attack and damage rolls. The magic-user fights in melee in preference to all other forms of attack, and continues attacking until all opponents are slain, he is killed, the magic is Dispelled, or the spell duration expires. The material component for casting this spell is a Potion of Heroism (or Superheroism) that the magic-user must consume during the course of uttering the spell.

Legend Lore

(Divination)
Level: 6

Range: 0	**Components:** V, S, M
Duration: Special	**Casting Time:** Special
Area of Effect: Special	**Saving Throw:** None

The Legend Lore spell is used to determine legendary information regarding a known person, place or thing. If the person or thing is at hand, or if the magic-user is in the place in question, the likelihood of the spell producing results is far greater and the casting time is only 1d4 turns. If only detailed information on the person, place, or thing is known, casting time is 1d10 days. If only rumors are known, casting time is 2d6 weeks. During the casting, the magic-user cannot engage in activities other than the routine: eating, sleeping, etc. When completed, the divination reveals if legendary material is available. It often reveals where this material is – by place name, rhyme or riddle. It sometimes gives certain information regarding the person, place or thing (when the object of the Legend Lore is at hand), but this data is always in some cryptic form (rhyme, riddle, anagram, cipher, sign, etc.).

Naturally, a Legend Lore spell reveals information only if the person, place or thing is noteworthy or legendary. For example, suppose Lord Proadus came across an extremely well-made sword. It radiates magic, but when he used an Identify spell, he could not learn any information. Even giving it to a trusted fighter didn't work, as the sword did not reveal any special powers. Finally, he casts a Legend Lore spell, hoping to gain more information. Since the sword is at hand, he completes the spell in three turns. In his mind comes the message, "This great sword was forged in the belly of the Dwarven Forge and tempered with the blood of a Swack Iron Dragon. Since the dawn of time it has lain lost in the shadows of time, awaiting a man of callused hands and uncombed hair to pick it up." The wily Proadus realizes, this must be a very powerful item, since his spell gave only a cryptic answer. But who is it waiting for? And where is the Dwarven Forge? For more information, Proadus is going to have to cast more spells. But now the process will take much longer, since he has only the vaguest of clues to follow. The Legend Lore spell is cast with incense and strips of ivory formed into a rectangle, but some item of value to the caster must be sacrificed in addition – a potion, magical scroll, magical item, etc.

Lower Water

(Alteration)
Reversible
Level: 6

Range: 80 yards	**Components:** V, S, M
Duration: 5 rds./level	**Casting Time:** 1 turn
Area of Effect: 10-ft./level square	**Saving Throw:** None

The magic-user casting a Lower Water spell causes water or similar fluid in the area of effect to sink away. The water can be lowered up to 2 feet for every experience level of the magic-user, to a minimum depth of 1 inch. The water is lowered within a square area whose sides are 10 feet long per caster level. Thus, a 12th level magic-user affects a volume of 24 feet x 120 feet x 120 feet, a 13th level caster a volume of 26 feet x 130 feet x 130 feet, and so on. In extremely large and deep bodies of water, such as deep ocean, the spell creates a whirlpool that sweeps ships and similar craft downward, putting them at risk and rendering them unable to leave by normal movement for the duration of

the spell. When cast on Water Elementals and other water-based creatures, this spell acts as a Slow spell: The creature moves at half speed and makes half the number of attacks each round. It has no effect on other creatures. The material component of this spell is a small vial of dust. Its reverse, Raise Water, causes water or similar fluids to return to their highest natural level: spring flood, high tide, etc. This can make fords impassable, float grounded ships, and may even sweep away bridges, at the GM's option. It negates Lower Water and vice versa. The material component of the Raise Water spell is a small vial of water.

Mass Suggestion

(Enchantment/Charm)
Level: 6

Range: 30 yards	**Components:** V, M
Duration: 4 turns + 4 turns/level	**Casting Time:** 6 segments
Area of Effect: 1 creature/level	**Saving Throw:** Negates

The Mass Suggestion spell enables the magic-user to influence the actions of one or more chosen creatures in the same way as the suggestion spell. Up to one creature per experience level of the caster can be influenced, provided that all subject creatures are within the 30-yard range. Undead are not subject to this spell. The suggestion must be reasonably worded and understood by the creatures, and must be the same for all hearing it. Creatures successfully saving vs. spell are unaffected. Saving throws against the spell suffer a penalty of -1, and if a single creature is to be affected, its saving throw suffers a -4 penalty. Note that a very reasonable Mass Suggestion can cause the saving throw to be made with an additional penalty (such as -1, -2, etc.), at the discretion of your GM. A mass suggestion can continue in effect for a considerable duration, at the GM's discretion. Conditions that will trigger a special action can also be specified; if the condition is not met before the spell expires, the action will not be performed. The material components of this spell are a snake's tongue and either a bit of honeycomb or a drop of sweet oil.

Mirage Arcana

(Illusion/Phantasm, Alteration)
Level: 6

Range: 10 yds./level	**Components:** V, S (M optional)
Duration: Special	**Casting Time:** Special
Area of Effect: 10 ft./level radius	**Saving Throw:** None

The magic of this spell is similar to that of the Vacancy spell, only more powerful and elaborate. The spell enables the caster to make an area appear to be something other than it is – a setting he has personally seen. The spell remains as long as the caster maintains a minimal concentration upon it. Even after this, the spell persists for a total of one hour plus one additional turn for each experience level of the caster. (Note: Minimal concentration can be maintained during normal conversation but not while spellcasting, in melee, or if harmed by an attack.) If the caster actually uses a small bit of anything connected with the place to create this spell, it takes on a quasi-reality. In its basic form, forceful contact is necessary to have any hope of discovering the magic, short of a detection device or spell. In its more complex form, where a material component is used, detection is possible only by some magical means, whether device, item or spell. Either form of Mirage Arcana is subject to the Dispel Magic spell. As with all powerful illusions, the mind of the believer urges appropriate effects upon the viewer's body. Under the influence of the spell, the viewer could possibly walk across a bed of hot coals thinking it was a shallow stream of water that was cooling his feet (and thus suffer no damage), dine upon imaginary food and actually be satisfied, or rest comfortably upon a bed of sharp stones, thinking it a featherbed. Gravity is not affected by the spell, however, so an envisioned bridge spanning a deep chasm does not support the believer. Those who witness the event see it as a sudden disappearance of the individual. They do not connect it with an illusion unless they are otherwise aware of some magic at work.

Mislead

(Illusion/Phantasm)

Level: 6

Range: 10 yards **Component:** S
Duration: 1 rd./level **Casting Time:** 1 segments
Area of Effect: Special **Saving Throw:** None

When a Mislead spell is cast by the magic-user, he actually creates an illusory double at the same time that he is cloaked by Improved Invisibility magic (see the 4th level spell). The magic-user is then free to go elsewhere while his double seemingly moves away. The spell enables the illusion of the magic-user to speak and gesture as if it were real, and there are full olfactory and touch components as well. A true seeing spell or a Gem of Seeing will reveal the illusion for what it is. A Detect Invisibility or True Seeing spell or items such as a Gem of Seeing or Robe of Eyes can detect the invisible magic-user (see the 5th level magic-user spell Shadow Door).

Monster Summoning IV

(Conjuration/Summoning)

Level: 6

Range: Special **Components:** V, S, M
Duration: 5 rds. + 1 rd./level **Casting Time:** 6 segments
Area of Effect: 60-yd. radius **Saving Throw:** None

This spell is much like the 3rd level spell Monster Summoning I, except that this spell summons 1d3 4th level monsters. These appear within the spell's area of effect and attack the caster's opponents, until he commands them to cease, the spell duration expires, or the monsters are slain. These creatures do not check morale; they vanish when slain. If no opponent exists to fight, summoned monsters can, if the magic-user can communicate with them, and if they are physically capable, perform other services for the summoning magic-user. The material components of this spell are a tiny bag and a small (not necessarily lit) candle.

Move Earth

(Alteration)

Level: 6

Range: 10 yds./level **Components:** V, S, M
Duration: Permanent **Casting Time:** Special
Area of Effect: Special **Saving Throw:** None

When cast, the Move Earth spell moves dirt (clay, loam, sand) and its other components. Thus, embankments can be collapsed, hillocks moved, dunes shifted, etc. However, in no event can rock prominences be collapsed or moved. The area to be affected dictates the casting time; for every 40 yard x 40 yard surface area and 10 feet of depth, one turn of casting time is required. The maximum area that can be affected is 240 yards x 240 yards, which takes four hours. If terrain features are to be moved – as compared to simply caving in banks or walls of earth – it is necessary that an earth elemental be subsequently summoned to assist. All spell casting or summoning must be completed before any effects occur. As any summoned Earth Elemental will perform most of its work underground, it is unlikely that it will be intercepted or interrupted. Should this occur, however, the movement of the earth requiring its services must be stopped until the elemental is once again available. Should the elemental be slain or dismissed, the Move Earth spell is limited to collapsing banks or walls of earth. The spell cannot be used for tunneling and is generally too slow to trap or bury creatures; its primary use is for digging or filling moats or for adjusting terrain contours before a battle. The material components for this spell are a mixture of soils (clay, loam, sand) in a small bag and an iron blade.

Note: This spell does not violently break the surface of the ground. Instead, it creates wavelike crests and troughs, with the earth reacting with glacier-like fluidity until the desired result is achieved. Trees, structures, rock formations, etc. are relatively unaffected, save for changes in elevation and relative topography.

Part Water

(Alteration)

Level: 6

Range: 10 yds./level **Components:** V, S, M
Duration: 5 rds./level **Casting Time:** 1 turn
Area of Effect: 20 ft. x **Saving Throw:** None
3 ft./level x 30 ft./level

By employing a Part Water spell, the magic-user is able to cause water or similar liquid to move apart, thus forming a 20-foot-wide trough. The depth and length of the trough are dependent upon the level of the magic-user, and a trough 3 feet deep by 10 yards long is created per level. For example, at 12th level the magic-user would part water 36 feet deep by 20 feet wide by 120 yards long. The trough remains as long as the spell lasts or until the magic-user who cast it opts to end its effects. If cast under water, this spell creates an air cylinder of appropriate length and diameter. If cast directly on a Water Elemental or other water-based creature, the creature receives 4d8 damage and must roll a successful saving throw vs. spell or flee in panic for 3d4 rounds. The material components for the spell are two small sheets of crystal or glass.

Perpetual Illusion

(Illusion/Phantasm)

Level: 6

Range: 10 yds./level **Components:** V, S, M
Duration: Permanent **Casting Time:** 6 segments
Area of Effect: 20-ft. cube + 10-ft. **Saving Throw:** Special
cube/level

When this spell is cast, the magic-user creates an illusion with visual, auditory, olfactory and thermal elements. The spell can create the illusion of any object, creature or force, as long as it is within the boundaries of the spell's area of effect. It affects all creatures that view the illusion, even to the extent of them suffering damage from falling into an illusory pit full of sharp spikes. Creatures that attempt to disbelieve the illusion gain a saving throw vs. spell and, if successful, they see it for what it is and add +4 bonuses to associates' saving throws, if this knowledge can be communicated effectively. Creatures not sensing the spell effect are immune until they become aware of it. The perpetual illusion is subject to a Dispel Magic spell, of course. The material component of the spell is a bit of fleece.

Phantasmagoria

(Illusion/Phantasm)

Level: 6

Range: 6 ft. **Components:** V, S
Duration: 1 round/level **Casting Time:** 6 segments
Area of Effect: 4 square + **Saving Throw:** Negates
1 square ft. per level of caster

By means of this spell, the magic-user prepares a special form of spectral forces spell which is triggered by some special action. The Phantasmagoria typically includes a full visual, audial, olfactory and touch illusion which involves failing, sliding or moving rapidly. The effect can be aimed at making the subjects believe that they are so doing or that something else is doing so. For example, the Phantasmagoria may be triggered when failing into a pit, reaching the center of an area, opening a door, or performing some like action. The subject(s) will then believe that the fall continues for scores of feet; that a pit has opened and that they are helplessly sliding down into an unknown area; that a wall of water is rushing down from the area beyond the just-opened door, or whatever. Note that unlike the Programmed Illusion spell, the Phantasmagoria spell must always involve the illusion of something failing or rushing, or a dwindling perspective.

Programmed Illusion

(Illusion/Phantasm)

Level: 6
Range: 10 yds./level
Duration: Special
Area of Effect: 20-ft. cube + 10-ft. cube/level

Components: V, S, M
Casting Time: 6 segments
Saving Throw: Special

This spell creates a Spectral Force spell that activates upon command or when a specific condition occurs. The illusion has visual, auditory, olfactory and thermal elements. It can be of any object, creature, or force, as long as it remains within the boundaries of the spell's area of effect. The occurrence that begins the illusion can be as general or as specific and detailed as desired, such as the following: "Begin only when a venerable female human carrying a sack of groat clusters sits cross-legged within one foot of this spot." Such visual triggers can react to a character using the disguise ability. Command range is 5 yards per level of the magic-user, so a 12th level magic-user can command the Programmed Illusion to occur at a maximum encounter range of 60 yards. A Programmed Illusion cannot distinguish invisible creatures, nor alignment, level, Hit Dice or class, except by external garb. If desired, the effect can be keyed to a specific noise or spoken word. The spell lasts until the illusion occurs; thus, the spell duration is variable. The illusion will last for a maximum of one round per level of the spellcaster. Creatures that attempt to disbelieve the illusion gain a saving throw vs. spell and, if successful, see it for what it is and add +4 bonuses to associates' saving throws, if this knowledge can be communicated effectively. Creatures not sensing the spell effect are immune until they become aware of it. The illusion is subject to a Dispel Magic spell. The material component of the spell is a bit of fleece.

Project Image

(Alteration, Illusion/Phantasm)

Level: 6
Range: 10 yds./level
Duration: 1 rd./level
Area of Effect: Special

Components: V, S, M
Casting Time: 6 segments
Saving Throw: None

By means of this spell, the magic-user creates a nonmaterial duplicate of himself, projecting it to any spot within spell range. This image performs actions decided by the magic-user – walking, speaking, spellcasting – conforming to the actual actions of the magic-user unless he concentrates on making it act differently (in which case the magic-user is limited to half movement and no attacks). The Image can be dispelled only by means of a successful Dispel Magic spell (or upon command from the spellcaster); attacks pass harmlessly through it. The image must be within view of the magic-user projecting it at all times, and if his sight is obstructed, the spell is broken. Note that if the magic-user is invisible at the time the spell is cast, the image is also invisible until the caster's invisibility ends, though the magic-user must still be able to see the image (by means of a Detect Invisibility spell or other method) to maintain the spell. If the magic-user uses Dimension Door, Teleport, Plane Shift or a similar spell that breaks his line of vision, the Project Image spell ends. The material component of this spell is a small replica (doll) of the magic-user.

Reincarnation

(Necromancy)

Level: 6
Range: Touch
Duration: Permanent
Area of Effect: Person touched

Components: V, S, M
Casting Time: 1 turn
Saving Throw: None

With this spell, the magic-user can bring back to life a person who died no more than one day per experience level of the magic-user. The essence of the dead person is transferred to another body, possibly one very different from his former body. Reincarnation does not require any saving throw, system shock or resurrection survival roll. The corpse is touched, and a new incarnation of the person will appear in the area in 1d6 turns. The person Reincarnated recalls the majority of his former life and form, but the character class, if any, of the new incarnation might be different indeed. The new incarnation is determined on the following table. If a player character race is indicated, the character must be created.

d100 Roll	Incarnation	d100 Roll	Incarnation
01-02	Anthraxian	52-55	Human
03-04	Articulated Masticator	56-57	Kobold
05-06	Gibbering She Baboon	58-59	Lemur, Ring-Tailed
07-08	Beetle, Dung	60-61	Lizardman
09-10	Bovinian	62	Owlbear
11-12	Bugbear	63	Candy Striped Rot Grub
13	Butterfly	64-66	Orc
14-15	Chicken	67-68	Flat-Footed Ogre
16-17	Chimparian	69-70	Ogre Mage
18-19	Cow	71-72	Pigeon
20-21	Dog	73-74	Pixie fairy
22-23	Dwarf	75-76	Pollywog
24-25	Elf	77-78	Quickling
26	Flail Snail	79-80	Hungry Rust Monster
27-28	Fungus	81-82	Slug
29-30	Gnoll	83-84	Snyad
31-32	Gnome	85-86	Squirrel
33-34	Gnome titan	87-88	Tick, Giant
35-36	Gnomeling	89-90	Toad
37-39	Goblin	91-92	Troglodyte
40-41	Grunge elf	93-94	Troll
42-43	Half-elf	95-96	Merga Troll
44-45	Halfling	97-98	Minotaur
46-47	Half-ogre	99-100	Myconid
48-49	Half-orc		
50-51	Hobgoblin		

Note: Very good or very evil persons will not be reincarnated as creatures whose general alignment is the opposite. Reincarnated characers must make 1d8 rolls on the Flaw/Quirk tables. If the reincarnated character dies within 24 hours after coming back in their new form the Reincarnation doesn't take and the soul is still linked to the old body rather than the reincarnated body. Therefore if the creature dies again it can be Raised or Resurrected into its old body. Otherwise, after 24 hours if the reincarnated character dies and is subsequently Raised or Resurrected, his essence returns to the new reincarnated body.

The material components of the spell are a small drum and a drop of blood.

Repulsion

(Abjuration)

Level: 6
Range: 0
Duration: 1 round/2 levels
Area of Effect: 10 ft./level x 10 ft.

Components: V, S, M
Casting Time: 6 segments
Saving Throw: None

When this spell is cast, the magic-user is able to cause all creatures in the path of the area of effect to move directly away from his person. Repulsion occurs at the speed of the creature attempting to move toward the spellcaster. The repelled creature continues to move away for a complete round even if this takes it beyond spell range. The caster can designate a new direction each round, but use of this power counts as the caster's principal action in the round. The caster can, of course, choose to do something else instead of using the Repulsion attack. The material component for this spell is a pair of small magnetized iron bars attached to two small canine statuettes, one ivory and one ebony.

Shades

(Illusion/Phantasm)

Level: 6
Range: 30 yards
Duration: 1 rd./level
Area of Effect: 20-ft. cube

Components: V, S
Casting Time: 6 segments
Saving Throw: Special

This spell is related to the Shadow Monsters and Demishadow Monsters spells. The Shades spell uses material from the Demiplane of Shadow to form semi-real illusions of one or more monsters, up to 1 Hit Die per caster level. All shades created by one spell must be of the same sort, and they have 60% of the hit point total the real creatures would have. Those who view the shades and fail their saving throws vs. spell believe the illusion. The shades perform as the real monsters with respect to Armor Class and attack forms. Special attack forms such as petrification or level drain do not actually occur, but a subject who believes the shades are real will react appropriately, until the illusion is countered by a Dispel Magic spell or the condition is countered by a heal spell. Those who roll successful saving throws see the shades as transparent images superimposed on vague shadowy forms. These are Armor Class 6 and cause only 60% of the true monsters' normal melee damage.

Spiritwrack

(Evocation/Abjuration)

Level: 6
Range: I ft.+ I ft./level
Duration: Special
Area of Effect: Special
Components: V, M
Costing Time: Special
Saving Throw: Special

A Spiritwrack spell is a very strong protection/punishment spell against the powerful creatures of the nether planes (Abyssal, Hades, Hell, etc.), but to employ the magic, the spell caster must know the name of the being at whom he will direct the energy. Prior to actual utterance of a Spiritwrack spell the magic-user must prepare an illuminated sheet of vellum, carefully inscribed in special inks made from powdered rubies and the ichor of a slain demon of type 1, 11, or III and covered with gold leaf in a continuous border. The spell caster must personally prepare this document, including the being's name thereon. (This will require from 8-32 hours of time and cost 1,000 gp for vellum, special pens, gold leaf, and other miscellaneous materials alone; the cost of the powdered rubies is a minimum of 5,000 gp for each document.) If the demon, devil or other powerful being from a nether outer plane is present in some form (and not possessing another creature's body instead), the magic-user can then begin actual spell incantation.

Immediately upon beginning the reading of the document, the being named will be rooted to the spot unless it makes its magic resistance percentage (adjusted for the level of the magic-user) as a saving throw; and even if such a saving throw is made, the monster feels greatly uncomfortable, and if it has not been magically forced to the locale and so held there, it is 90% likely to retreat to its own (or another) plane, as the named being is powerless to attack the magic-user while he is reading the spell document. This first part of the document continues for 1 full round, with the discomfort to the named being becoming greater at the end. During the second minute of the incantation, the being named undergoes acute pain and loses I hit point per Hit Die it possesses. At the end of this round of reading, the being is in wracking pain. The third and final round of utterance of the condemnation will cause a loss to the being of 50% of its existing hit points, horrible pain, and at the end consign it to some confined space on its own plane - there to remain in torture for a number of years equal to the level of the magic-user who prepared the document.

Obviously, the being so dealt with will be the sworn foe of the magic-user forever afterwards, so the magic-user will be loath to finish the spell but rather use it as a threat to force submission of the being. Each round of reading will cause the being forced to listen to be a cumulative 25% likely to concede even without any other offerings or payment.

Stone to Flesh

(Alteration)
Reversible

Level: 6
Range: 10 yds./level
Duration: Permanent
Area of Effect: I creature
Components: V, S, M
Casting Time: 6 segments
Saving Throw: Special

The Stone to Flesh spell turns any sort of stone into flesh. If the recipient stone object was formerly living, this spell restores life (and goods), although the survival of the creature is subject to the usual system shock survival roll. Any formerly living creature, regardless of size, can be thus returned to flesh. Ordinary stone can be turned to flesh in a volume of 9 cubic feet per level of experience of the spellcaster. Such flesh is inert, lacking a vital life force, unless a life force or magical energy is available (for example, this spell would turn a Stone Golem into a Flesh Golem, but an ordinary statue would become a body). If cast upon stone, the magic-user can create a cylinder of fleshy material from 1 to 3 feet in diameter and up to 10 feet long, allowing a passage to be made. The material components are a pinch of earth and a drop of blood. The reverse, flesh to stone, turns flesh of any sort to stone. All possessions on the person of the creature likewise turn to stone. The intended subject of the spell receives a saving throw vs. spell to avoid the effect. If a statue created by this spell is subjected to breakage or weathering, the being (if ever returned to his original, fleshy state) will have similar damage, deformities, etc. The GM may allow such damage to be repaired by various high level cleric spells, such as regenerate. The material components of the spell are lime, water, and earth.

Transmute Water to Dust

(Alteration)
Reversible

Level: 6
Range: 60 yards
Duration: Permanent
Area of Effect: 10-ft. cube/level
Components: V, S, M
Casting Time: 5 segments
Saving Throw: None
(special)

When this spell is cast, the subject area instantly undergoes a change from liquid to powdery dust. Note that if the water is already muddy, the area of effect is doubled, while if wet mud is being transmuted, the area of effect is quadrupled. If water remains in contact with the transmuted dust, the former quickly soaks the latter, turning the dust into silty mud (if a sufficient quantity of water exists to do so), otherwise soaking or dampening the dust accordingly. Only liquid actually in the area of effect at the moment of spellcasting is affected. Liquids that are only partially water are affected only insofar as the actual water content is concerned; however, potions containing water are rendered useless. Living creatures are unaffected, except for those native to the Elemental Plane of Water. Such creatures receive saving throws vs. spell. Failure inflicts 1d6 points of damage per caster level upon the subject, while success means the creature receives half damage. Only one such creature can be affected by any single casting of this spell, regardless of the creature's size or the size of the spell's area of effect. The reverse of the spell is simply a very high-powered create water spell that requires a pinch of normal dust as an additional material component. For either usage of the spell, other components required are diamond dust of at least 500 gp value and a bit of seashell.

True Seeing (True Sight)

(Divination)

Level: 6
Range: Touch
Duration: I rd./level
Area of Effect: Line of sight, max. 60 ft.
Components: V, S, M
Casting Time: I round
Saving Throw: None

When the magic-user employs this spell, he confers upon the recipient the ability to see all things as they actually are. The spell penetrates normal and magical darkness. Secret doors become plain. The exact location of displaced things is obvious. Invisible things become visible. Illusions and apparitions are seen through. Polymorphed, changed or enchanted objects are apparent. The real form appears translucently superimposed on the apparent form: a Gold Dragon polymorphed to human form would appear human with a ghostly dragon looming over the human form. Unlike the cleric version of this spell, the recipient cannot determine alignment. The recipient can focus his vision to see into the Ethereal Plane or the bordering areas of adjacent planes. The range of vision conferred is 60 feet. True seeing does not penetrate solid objects; it in no way confers X-ray vision or its equivalent. Furthermore, the spell effects cannot be enhanced with magic.

The spell requires an ointment for the eyes that is made from a very rare mushroom powder, saffron and fat. It costs no less than 300 gp per use and must be aged for 1d6 months.

Veil

(Illusion/Phantasm)

Level: 6
Range: 10 yds./level
Duration: I turn/level
Area of Effect: 20-ft. cube/level
Components: V, S
Casting Time: 6 segments
Saving Throw: None

The Veil spell enables the magic-user to instantly change the appearance of his surroundings and party or create hallucinatory terrain so as to fool even the most clever creatures (unless they have the True Seeing spell, a Gem of Seeing, or a similar magical aid). The Veil can make a sumptuous room seem like a filthy den; even tactile impressions conform to the visual illusion. Likewise, a party might be made to resemble a mixed band of Brownies, Pixies and Faeries led by a Treant. If hallucinatory terrain is created, touch does not cause it to vanish.

Zarba's Shoving Hand

(Evocation)

Level: 6

Range: 10 yds./level

Components: V, S, M

Duration: 1 rd./level

Casting Time: 6 segments

Area of Effect: Special

Saving Throw: None

Zarba's Shoving Hand is a more powerful version of Zarba's Guardian Hand. It creates a man-sized (5 feet) to gargantuan-sized (21 feet) hand that places itself between the spellcaster and a chosen opponent. This disembodied hand then moves to remain between the two, regardless of what the spellcaster does or how the opponent tries to get around it. However, the Shoving Hand also shoves its opponent. This force can push away a creature weighing 500 pounds or less, slow movement to 10 feet per round if the creature weighs between 500 and 2,000 pounds, or slow movement by 50% if the creature weighs more than 2,000 pounds. A creature pushed away is pushed to the range limit, or until pressed against an unyielding surface. The Hand itself inflicts no damage. The Shoving Hand has an Armor Class of 0, has as many hit points as its caster in full health, and vanishes when destroyed. The caster can cause it to retreat (to release a trapped opponent, for example) or dismiss it on command. The material component is a glove.

Zarba's Sphere of Personal Inclement Weather

(Alteration)

Level: 6

Range: 10 ft./level

Components: V, S

Duration: 2 hours/level

Casting Time: 1 round

Area of Effect: 10 ft. radius around one creature

Saving Throw: Negates

When this spell is cast it causes freakishly bad weather to follow the victim around. Some possibilities include bad sandstorms, torrential rain, hail, a blizzard, very high winds or extreme heat and humidity. The weather does not have to match a character's surroundings, i.e. a character in a jungle could still be surrounded by a blizzard, and it would follow him even if he went indoors. Dangerous weather may cause 1d4 points of damage per hour (at the GM's discretion) if the victim does not take appropriate precautions.

Seventh Level Spells

Anger Deity

(Enchantment/Charm)

Level: 7

Range: Infinite

Components: V

Duration: Instantaneous

Casting Time: 1 round

Area of Effect: 1 gawd

Saving Throw: None

An Anger Deity spell allows the spellcaster to offend a gawd in the hopes of getting a reaction out of him. After the caster spends one round casting the spell (which involves insulting the gawd, his momma, and his dawg) roll on the the following chart to determine the reaction:

01-25:	The Gawd himself appears to punish the spellcaster.
26-50:	The Gawd sends minions to deal with the spellcaster.
51-100:	The character is the victim of "divine revenge"

All results take place on the round after the spell is cast.

If the spell succeeds in angering the gawd enough to make a personal appearance the caster is in deep, deep trouble. The gawd may attack the caster, permanently polymorph him into something undesirable, curse the caster, drag the caster's soul into the Netherworld, or do any number of extremely nasty things. Needless to say this is usually the end of the character's career.

If the gawd sends his minions one major minion or 1D6 minor minions will appear the next round. A major minion would include a Solar, Greater Devil, and the like. A minor minion would include Lesser Demons, Devas, and similar creatures. The minions will attack the caster immediately.

If "divine revenge" is indicated it can take on many forms. Some possibilities include a Lightning Bolt from the sky that strikes for 10-100 points of damage, a great chasm opening up underneath the caster, or all of the cows in the caster's village refusing to give milk.

Banishment

(Abjuration)

Level: 7

Range: 20 yards

Components: V, S, M

Duration: Instantaneous

Casting Time: 7 segments

Area of Effect: 60-ft. radius

Saving Throw: Special

A Banishment spell enables the caster to force some extraplanar creature out of the caster's home plane. The effect is instantaneous, and the subject cannot come back without some special summoning or means of egress from its own plane to the one from which it was Banished. Up to 2 Hit Dice or levels of creature per caster level can be banished. The caster must both name the type of creature(s) to be sent away and give its name and title as well, if any. In any event, the creature's magic resistance must be overcome for the spell to be effective. The material components of the spell are substances harmful, hateful or opposed to the nature of the subject(s) of the spell. For every such substance included in the casting, the subject creature(s) loses 5% from its magic resistance and suffers a -2 penalty to its saving throw vs. spell. For example, if iron, holy water, sunstone and a sprig of rosemary were used in casting a Banishment upon a being that hates those things, its saving throw versus the spell would be made with a -8 penalty (four substances times the factor of -2). Special items, such as hair from the tail of a Ki-rin or Couatl feathers, could also be added to change the factor to -3 or -4 per item. In contrast, a titan's hair or mistletoe blessed by a druid might lower the factor to -1 with respect to the same creature. If the subject creature successfully rolls its saving throw vs. spell, the caster is stung by a backlash of energy, suffers 2d6 points of damage, and is stunned for one round.

Cacodemon

(Conjuration/Summoning)

Level: 7

Range: 10 ft.

Components: V, S, M

Duration: Special

Costing Time: Special

Area of Effect: Creature summoned

Saving Throw: Special

This perilous exercise in dweomercraeft summons up a powerful demon of type IV, V, or VI, depending upon the demon's name being known to the magic-user. Note that this spell is not of sufficient power to bring a demon of greater power, and lesser sorts are not called as they have no known names. In any event, the spell caster must know the name of the type IV, V, or VI demon he is summoning. As the spell name implies, the demon so summoned is most angry and evilly disposed. The spell caster must be within a circle of protection (or a thaumaturgic triangle with protection from evil) and the demon confined within a pentagram (circled pentacle) if he is to avoid being slain or carried off by the summoned Cacodemon. The summoned demon can be treated with as follows:

1) The magic-user can require the monster to perform a desired course of action by force of threat and pain of a Spiritwrack spell (q.v.), allowing freedom whenever the demon performs the full extent of the service, and forcing the demon to pledge word upon it. This is exceedingly dangerous, as a minor error in such a bargain will be seized upon by the monster to reverse the desired outcome or simply to kill and devour the summoner. Furthermore, the demon will bear great enmity for the magic-user forever after such forced obedience, so the spell caster had better be most powerful and capable.

2) By tribute of fresh human blood and the promise of one or more human sacrifices, the summoner can bargain with the demon for willing service. Again, the spell caster is well advised to have ample protection and power to defend himself, as the demon might decide the offer is insufficient - or it is easier to enjoy the summoner's slow death - and decide not to accept the bargain as offered. Although the demon will have to abide by a pledge, as his name is known, he will have to hold only to the exact word of the arrangement, not to the spirit of the agreement. On the other hand, only highly evil magic-users are likely to attempt to strike such a bargain, and the summoned Cacodemon might be favorably disposed towards such a character, especially if he is also chaotic.

3) The summoned demon can be the object of a Trap the Soul spell (q.v.). In this case, the magic-user will not speak with or bargain for the demon's services, although the Cacodemon might be eager to reach an

accord with the dweomercrafter before he is forced into imprisonment. The trapping of the demon is risky only if proper precautions have not been taken, for failure to confine the monster usually means only that it is able to escape to its own plane. Once trapped, the demon must remain imprisoned until the possessor of his object of confinement breaks it and frees him, and this requires one service from the now loosed monster. If the individual(s) freeing the demon fails to demand a service when the monster asks what is required of him, the demon is under no constraint not to slay the liberator(s) on the spot, but if a service is required, the creature must first do his best to perform it and then return to the Abyss.

The duration of service of any demon must be limited unless the demon is willing to serve for an extended period. Any required course of action or service which effectively requires an inordinate period of time to perform' or is impossible to perform, is 50% likely to free the demon from his obligations and enable him to be unconstrained in his vengeance upon the spell caster if he is not thereafter continually protected, for a demon so freed can remain on the plane it was summoned to for as long as 666 days.

The demon summoned will be exceptionally strong, i.e. 8 hit points per Hit Die.

Casting time is 1 hour per type (numeric) of the demon to be summoned. If there is any interruption during this period, the spell fails. If there is an interruption while the Cacodemon is summoned, there is a 10% chance that it will be able to escape its boundaries and attack the magic-user, this percentage rising cumulatively (by one) each round of continued interruption.

Each demon is entitled to a saving throw versus this summoning spell. If a score higher than the level of the magic-user summoning is rolled with 3d6 (2d10 with respect to type VI demons), that particular spell failed to bring the desired demon. When this occurs, it is certain that the named demon is imprisoned or destroyed or the name used was not perfectly correct, so the spell caster will have to call upon another name to bring forth a Cacodemon.

The components of this spell are 5 flaming black candies; a brazier of hot coals upon which must be burned sulfur, bat hairs, lard, soot, mercuric or nitric acid crystals, mandrake root, alcohol and a piece of parchment with the demon's name inscribed in runes inside a pentacle; and a dish of blood from some mammal (preferably a human, of course) placed inside the area where the Cacodemon is to be held.

Charm Plants

(Enchantment/Charm)
Level: 7
Range: 30 yards
Components: V, S, M
Duration: Permanent
Casting Time: 1 turn
Area of Effect: 10 x 30 ft.
Saving Throw: Negates

The Charm Plants spell enables the spellcaster to bring under command vegetable life forms and communicate with them. These plants obey instructions to the best of their ability. The spell will charm plants in a 30-foot x 10-foot area. While the spell does not endow the vegetation with new abilities, it does enable the magic-user to command the plants to use whatever they have in order to fulfill his instructions. If the plants in the area of effect do have special or unusual abilities, these are used as commanded by the magic-user. For example, this spell can generally duplicate the effects of the 1st level druid spell Entangle, if the caster desires. The saving throw applies only to intelligent plants, and it is made with a -4 penalty to the die roll. The material components of the spell are a pinch of humus, a drop of water and a twig or leaf.

Control Undead

(Necromancy)
Level: 7
Range: 60 ft.
Components: V, S, M
Duration: 3d4 rds. + 1 rd./level
Casting Time: 1 round
Area of Effect: 1d6 undead
Saving Throw: Special

This spell enables the magic-user to command 1d6 undead creatures for a short period of time. Upon casting the spell, the magic-user selects one point within range of the spell. Those undead nearest to this point are affected, until either undead equal in Hit Dice to the caster's level or six undead are affected. Undead with 3 Hit Dice or less are automatically controlled. Those of greater

Hit Dice are allowed a saving throw vs. spell, which, if successful, negates the attempt to control that creature. Regardless of the success or failure of the saving throw, each creature required to make a check counts toward the Hit Dice limit of the spell. Those creatures under the control of the magic-user can be commanded by the caster if they are within hearing range. There is no telepathic communication or language requirement between the caster and the Controlled undead. Even if communication is impossible, the Controlled undead do not attack the spellcaster. At the end of the spell, the Controlled undead revert to their normal behaviors. Those not mindless will remember the control exerted by the magic-user. The material component for this spell is a small piece each of bone and raw meat.

Duo-Dimension

(Alteration)
Level: 7
Range: 0
Components: V, S, M
Duration: 3 rds. + 1 rd./level
Casting Time: 7 segments
Area of Effect: The caster
Saving Throw: None

A Duo-Dimension spell causes the caster to have only two dimensions, height and width, with no depth. He is thus invisible when turned sideways. This invisibility can be detected only by means of a true seeing spell or similar methods. In addition, the Duo-Dimensional magic-user can pass through the thinnest of spaces as long as these have the proper height – going through the space between a door and its frame is a simple matter. The magic-user can perform all actions normally. He can turn and become invisible, move in this state, and appear again next round and cast a spell, disappearing on the following round. Note that when turned, the magic-user cannot be affected by any form of attack, but when visible, he is subject to double the amount of damage normal for an attack form; for example, a dagger thrust would inflict 2d4 points of damage if it struck a Duo-Dimensional magic-user. Furthermore, the magic-user has a portion of his existence in the Astral Plane when the spell is in effect, and he is subject to possible notice by creatures there. If noticed, it is 25% probable that the magic-user is pulled entirely into the Astral Plane by any attack from an astral creature. Such an attack (and any subsequent attack received on the Astral Plane) inflicts normal damage. The material components of this spell are a flat ivory likeness of the spellcaster (which must be of finest workmanship, gold filigreed and enameled and gem-studded at an average cost of 500 to 1,000 g.p.) and a strip of parchment. As the spell is uttered, the parchment is given half a twist and joined at the ends. The figurine is then passed through the parchment loop, and both disappear forever.

Finger of Death

(Necromancy)
Level: 7
Range: 60 yards
Components: V, S
Duration: Permanent
Casting Time: 5 segments
Area of Effect: 1 creature
Saving Throw: Negates

The Finger of Death spell snuffs out the victim's life force. If successful, the victim can be neither Raised nor Resurrected. In addition, in human subjects the spell initiates changes to the body such that after three days the caster can, by means of a special ceremony costing not less than 1,000 gp plus 500 gp per body, animate the corpse as a Juju Zombie under the control of the caster. The changes can be reversed before animation by a Limited Wish or similar spell cast directly upon the body and a full Wish restores the subject to life. The caster utters the Finger of Death spell incantation, points his index finger at the creature to be slain, and unless the victim succeeds in a saving throw vs. spell, death occurs. A creature successfully saving still receives 2d8+1 points of damage. If the subject dies of damage, no internal changes occur and the victim can then be revived normally.

Fireball, Delayed Blast

(Evocation)

Level: 7

Range: 100 yds. + 10 yds./level   **Components:** V, S, M

Duration: Special   **Casting Time:** 7 segments

Area of Effect: 20-ft. radius   **Saving Throw:** Half

This spell creates a Fireball, with a +1 bonus to each of its dice of damage, which releases its blast anytime from instantly to five rounds later, according to the command given by the magic-user. In other respects, the spell is the same as the 3rd level spell Fireball.

Forcecage

(Evocation)

Level: 7

Range: 10 yds./2 levels   **Components:** V, S, special

Duration: 6 turns + 1/level   **Casting Time:** 3-4 segments

Area of Effect: 20-ft. cube   **Saving Throw:** None

This powerful spell enables the caster to bring into being a cube of force, but it is unlike the magical item of that name in one important respect: The Forcecage does not have solid Walls of Force; it has alternating bands of force with 1/2-inch gaps between. Thus, it is truly a cage, rather than an enclosed space with solid walls. Creatures within the area of effect of the spell are caught and contained unless they are able to pass through the openings — and, of course, all spells and breath weapons can pass through the gaps in the bars of force of the Forcecage. A creature with magic resistance can make a single attempt to pass through the walls of the cage. If the resistance check is successful, the creature escapes. If it fails, the creature is caged. Note that a successful check does not destroy the cage, nor does it enable other creatures (save familiars) to flee with the escaping creature. The Forcecage is also unlike the solid-walled protective device, Cube of Force, in that it can be gotten rid of only by means of a Dispel Magic spell or by the expiration of the spell. By means of special preparation at the time of memorization, a Forcecage spell can be altered to a "Forcecube" spell. The cube created is 10 feet on a side, and the spell then resembles that of a Cube of Force in all respects save that of the differences between a cast spell and the magic of a device, including the methods of defeating its power. Although the actual casting of either application of the spell requires no material component, the study required to commit it to memory does demand that the magic-user powder a diamond of at least 1,000 gp value, using the diamond dust to trace the outlines of the cage or cube he desires to create via spellcasting at some later time. Thus, in memorization, the diamond dust is employed and expended, for upon completion of study, the magic-user must then toss the dust into the air and it will disappear.

Hyptor's Shimmering Sword

(Evocation)

Level: 7

Range: 30 yards   **Components:** V, S, M

Duration: 1 rd./level   **Casting Time:** 7 segments

Area of Effect: Special   **Saving Throw:** None

Upon casting this spell, the magic-user brings into being a shimmering, swordlike plane of force. The spellcaster is able to mentally wield this weapon (to the exclusion of all activities other than movement), causing it to move and strike as if it were being used by a fighter. The basic chance for Hyptor's Shimmering Sword to hit is the same as the chance for a sword wielded by a fighter of half the level of the spellcaster. For example, if cast by a 14th level magic-user, the weapon has the same hit probability as a sword wielded by a 7th level fighter. The Sword has no magical attack bonuses, but it can hit nearly any sort of opponent, even those normally struck only by +3 weapons or those who are astral, ethereal or out of phase. It hits any Armor Class on a roll of 19 or 20. It inflicts 5d4 points of damage to opponents of man size or smaller, and 5d6 points of damage to opponents larger than man size. It lasts until the spell duration expires, a Dispel Magic is used successfully upon it, or its caster no longer desires it. The material component is a miniature platinum sword with a grip and pommel of copper and zinc, which costs 500 gp to construct, and which disappears after the spell's completion.

Limited Wish

(Conjuration/Summoning, Invocation/Evocation)

Level: 7

Range: Unlimited   **Components:** V

Duration: Special   **Casting Time:** Special

Area of Effect: Special   **Saving Throw:** Special

The Limited Wish is a very potent but difficult spell. It will fulfill literally, but only partially or for a limited duration, the utterance of the spellcaster. Thus, the actuality of the past, present, or future might be altered (but possibly only for the magic-user unless the wording of the spell is most carefully stated) in some limited manner. The use of a Limited Wish will not substantially change major realities, nor will it bring wealth or experience merely by asking. The spell can, for example, restore some hit points (or all hit points for a limited duration) lost by the magic-user. It can reduce opponent hit probabilities or damage, increase duration of some magical effect, cause a creature to be favorably disposed to the spellcaster, mimic a spell of 7th level or less, and so on (see the 9th level Wish spell). Greedy desires usually end in disaster for the Wisher. Casting time is based on the time spent preparing the wording for the spell (clever players decide what they want to say before using the spell). Normally, the casting time is one round (most of it being taken up by deciding what to say). Casting this spell ages the caster one year per 100 years of regular life span.

Mass Invisibility

(Illusion/Phantasm)

Level: 7

Range: 10 yds./level   **Components:** V, S, M

Duration: Special   **Casting Time:** 7 segments

Area of Effect: 60 x 60 yds.   **Saving Throw:** None

This is a more extensive adaptation of the Invisibility spell for battlefield use. It can hide creatures in a 60-yard x 60-yard area: up to 400 man-sized creatures, 30 to 40 giants, or six to eight large dragons. The effect is mobile with the unit and is broken when the unit attacks. Individuals leaving the unit become visible. The magic-user can end this spell upon command. The material components of the Mass Invisibility spell are an eyelash and a bit of gum arabic, the former encased in the latter.

Monster Summoning V

(Conjuration/Summoning)

Level: 7

Range: Special   **Components:** V, S, M

Duration: 6 rds. + 1 rd./level   **Casting Time:** 6 segments

Area of Effect: 70-yd. radius   **Saving Throw:** None

This spell is much like the 3rd level Monster Summoning I spell, except that this spell summons 1d3 5th level monsters. These appear within the spell's area of effect and attack the caster's opponents until either he commands them to cease, the spell duration expires, or the monsters are slain. These creatures do not check morale, and they vanish when slain. If no opponent exists to fight, summoned monsters can, if the magic-user can communicate with them, and if they are physically capable, perform other services for the summoning magic-user. The material components of this spell are a tiny bag and a small (not necessarily lit) candle.

Phase Door

(Alteration)

Level: 7

Range: Touch   **Components:** V

Duration: 1 usage/2 levels   **Casting Time:** 7 segments

Area of Effect: Special   **Saving Throw:** None

When this spell is cast, the magic-user attunes his body, and a section of wall is affected as if by a Wall Passage spell. The Phase Door is invisible to all creatures save the spellcaster, and only he can use the space or passage the spell creates, disappearing when the Phase Door is entered and appearing when it is exited. If the caster desires, one other creature of man size or less can be taken through the door; this counts as two uses of the door. The door does not pass light, sound, or spell effects, nor can the caster see through it without using it.

Thus, the spell can provide an escape route, though certain creatures, such as Phase Spiders, can follow with ease. A True Seeing spell, Gem of Seeing and similar magic will reveal the presence of a Phase Door but will not allow its use. The Phase Door lasts for one usage for every two levels of experience of the spellcaster. It can be dispelled only by a casting of Dispel Magic from a higher level magic-user, or from several lower level magic-users, casting in concert, whose combined levels of experience are more than double that of the magic-user who cast the spell (this is the only instance in which dispel effects can be combined). Rumor has it that this spell has been adapted by a certain powerful magic-user (or magic-users) to create renewable (or permanent) portals, which may (or may not) be keyed to specific individuals (henchmen) or items (such as rings).

Power Word, Stun

(Conjuration/Summoning)

Level: 7

Range: 5 yds./level

Components: V

Duration: Special

Casting Time: 1 segment

Area of Effect: 1 creature

Saving Throw: None

When a Power Word, Stun spell is uttered, any creature of the magic-user's choice is stunned – reeling and unable to think coherently or act – for a duration dependent on its current hit points. Of course, the magic-user must be facing the creature, and the creature must be within the range of 5 yards per experience level of the caster. Creatures with 1 to 30 hit points are stunned for 4d4 rounds, those with 31 to 60 hit points are stunned for 2d4 rounds, those with 61 to 90 hit points are stunned for 1d4 rounds, and creatures with over 90 hit points are not affected. Note that if a creature is weakened so that its hit points are below its usual maximum, the current number of hit points is used.

Prismatic Wall

(Conjuration/Summoning)

Level: 7

Range: 10 yards

Components: V, S

Duration: 1 turn/level

Casting Time: 7 segments

Area of Effect: 4 ft./level wide x 2 ft./level high

Saving Throw: Special

This spell enables the magic-user to conjure a vertical, opaque wall – a shimmering, multicolored plane of light that protects him from all forms of attack. The Wall flashes with all colors of the visible spectrum, seven of which have a distinct power and purpose. The wall is immobile, and the spellcaster can pass through the Wall without harm. However, any creature with fewer than 8 Hit Dice that is within 20 feet of the Wall and does not shield its vision is blinded for 2d4 rounds by the colors. Each color in the Wall has a special effect. Each color can also be negated by a specific magical effect, but the colors must be negated in the precise order of the spectrum. The accompanying table shows the seven colors of the Wall, the order in which they appear, their effects on creatures trying to attack the spellcaster, and the magic needed to negate each color. The Wall's maximum proportions are 4 feet wide per level of experience of the caster and 2 feet high per level of experience. A Prismatic Wall spell cast to materialize in a space occupied by a creature is disrupted and the spell is wasted.

Prismatic Wall Effects

Color	Order	Effect of Color	Spell Negated By
Red	1st	Stops non-magical missiles –inflicts 20 points of damage, save for half	Cone of Cold
Orange	2nd	Stops magical missiles – inflicts 40 points of damage, save for half	Gust of Wind
Yellow	3rd	Stops poisons, gases, and petrification –inflicts 80 points of damage, save for half	Disintegrate
Green	4th	Stops breath weapons – save vs. poison or die; survivors suffer 20 points of damage	Wall Passage
Blue	5th	Stops location/detection and mental attacks – save vs. petrification or turn to stone	Magic Missile
Indigo	6th	Stops magical spells – save vs. wand or go insane	Continual Light
Violet	7th	Force field protection – save vs. spell or be sent to another plane	Dispel Magic

Reverse Gravity

(Alteration)

Level: 7

Range: 5 yds./level

Components: V, S, M

Duration: 1 rd./level

Casting Time: 7 segments

Area of Effect: 30 ft. x 30 ft.

Saving Throw: None

This spell reverses gravity in the area of effect, causing all unattached objects and creatures within it to "fall" upward. The Reversed Gravity lasts as long as the caster desires or until the spell expires. If some solid object is encountered in this "fall," the object strikes it in the same manner as it would during a normal downward fall. At the end of the spell duration, the affected objects and creatures fall downward. As the spell affects an area, objects tens, hundreds or even thousands of feet in the air above the area can be affected. The material components of this spell are a lodestone and iron filings.

Sequester

(Illusion/Phantasm, Abjuration)

Level: 7

Range: Touch

Components: V, S, M

Duration: 1 week + 1 day/level

Casting Time: 7 segments

Area of Effect: 2-ft. cube/level

Saving Throw: Special

When cast, this spell not only prevents detection and location spells from working to detect or locate the objects affected by the Sequester spell, it also renders the affected object(s) invisible to any form of sight or seeing. Thus, a Sequester spell can mask a secret door, a treasure vault, etc. Of course, the spell does not prevent the subject from being discovered through tactile means or through the use of devices (such as a Robe of Eyes or a Gem of Seeing). If cast upon a creature who is unwilling to be affected, the creature receives a normal saving throw. Living creatures (and even undead types) affected by a Sequester spell become comatose and are effectively in a state of suspended animation until the spell wears off or is dispelled. The material components of the spell are a basilisk eyelash, gum arabic, and a dram of whitewash.

Shadow Walk

(Illusion, Enchantment)

Level: 7

Range: Touch

Components: V, S

Duration: 6 turns/level

Casting Time: 1 segment

Area of Effect: Special

Saving Throw: None

In order to use the Shadow Walk spell, the magic-user must be in an area of heavy shadows. The caster and any creature he touches are then transported to the edge of the Prime Material Plane where it borders the Demiplane of Shadow. In this region, the magic-user can move at a rate of up to 7 miles per turn, moving normally on the borders of the Demiplane of Shadow but much more rapidly relative to the Prime Material Plane. Thus, a magic-user can use this spell to travel rapidly by stepping onto the Demiplane of Shadow, moving the desired distance, and then stepping back onto the Prime Material Plane. The magic-user knows where he will come out on the Prime Material Plane. The Shadow Walk spell can also be used to travel to other planes that border on the Demiplane of Shadow, but this requires the potentially perilous transit of the Demiplane of Shadow to arrive at a border with another plane of reality. Any creatures touched by the magic-user when Shadow Walk is cast also make the transition to the borders of the Demiplane of Shadow. They may opt to follow the magic-user, wander off through the plane, or stumble back into the Prime Material Plane (50% chance for either result if they are lost or abandoned by the magic-user). Creatures unwilling to accompany the magic-user into the Demiplane of Shadow receive a saving throw, negating the effect if successful.

Simulacrum

(Illusion/Phantasm)

Level: 7

Range: Touch

Components: V, S, M

Duration: Permanent

Casting Time: Special

Area of Effect: 1 creature

Saving Throw: None

By means of this spell, the magic-user is able to create a duplicate of any creature. The duplicate appears to be exactly the same as the original, but there are differences: the Simulacrum has only 51% to 60% (50% + 1d10%) of the hit points of the real creature, there are personality differences, there are areas of knowledge that the duplicate does not have, and a Detect Magic spell will instantly reveal it as a Simulacrum, as will a True Seeing spell.

At all times the Simulacrum remains under the absolute command of the magic-user who created it. No special telepathic link exists, so command must be exercised in some other manner. The spell creates the form of the creature, but it is only a zombie-like creation. A Reincarnation spell must be used to give the duplicate a vital force, and a Limited Wish spell must be used to empower the duplicate with 40% to 65% (35% + 5 to 30%) of the knowledge and personality of the original. The level of the Simulacrum, if any, is from 20% to 50% of that of the original creature. The duplicate creature is formed from ice or snow. The spell is cast over the rough form and some piece of the creature to be duplicated must be placed inside the snow or ice. Additionally, the spell requires powdered ruby. The Simulacrum has no ability to become more powerful; it cannot increase its level or abilities. If destroyed, it reverts to snow and melts into nothingness. Damage to the Simulacrum can be repaired by a complex process requiring at least one day, 100 gp per hit point, and a fully equipped laboratory.

Spell Turning

(Abjuration)
Level: 7
Range: 0
Duration: Up to 3 rds./level
Area of Effect: The caster
Components: V, S, M
Casting Time: 7 segments
Saving Throw: None

This powerful abjuration causes spells cast against the magic-user to rebound on the original caster. This includes spells cast from scrolls and innate spell-like abilities, but specifically excludes the following: area effects that are not centered directly upon the protected magic-user, spell effects delivered by touch, and spell effects from devices such as wands, staves, etc. Thus, a Light spell cast to blind the protected magic-user could be turned back upon and possibly blind the caster, while the same spell would be unaffected if cast to light an area within which the protected magic-user is standing. From seven to ten spell levels are affected by the turning. The exact number is secretly rolled by the GM; the player never knows for certain how effective the spell is. A spell may be only partially turned – divide the number of remaining levels that can be turned by the spell level of the incoming spell to see what fraction of the effect is turned, with the remainder affecting the caster. For example, an incoming Fireball is centered on a magic-user with one level of Spell Turning left. This means that 2/3 of the Fireball affects the protected magic-user, 1/3 affects the caster and each is the center of a Fireball effect. If the rolled damage is 40 points, the protected magic-user receives 27 points of damage and the caster suffers 13. Both (and any creatures in the respective areas) can roll saving throws vs. spell for half damage. A partially turned Hold or Paralysis spell will act as a Slow spell on those who are 50% or more affected. If the protected magic-user and a spellcasting attacker both have spell turning effects operating, a resonating field is created that has the following effects:

d100 Roll	Effect
01-70	Spell drains away without effect
71-80	Spell affects both equally at full damage
81-97	Both turning effects are rendered nonfunctional for 1d4 turns
98-00	Both casters go through a rift into the Positive Energy plane

The material component for the spell is a small silver mirror.

Statue

(Alteration)
Level: 7
Range: Touch
Duration: 1 hr./level
Area of Effect: Creature touched
Components: V, S, M
Casting Time: 7 segments
Saving Throw: Special

When a Statue spell is cast, the magic-user or other creature is apparently turned to solid stone, along with any garments and equipment worn or carried. The initial transformation from flesh to stone requires one full round after the spell is cast. During the transformation, there is an 18% chance that the targeted creature suffers a system shock failure and dies. The creature must

roll percentile dice and add its Constitution score to the roll. If the total is 18 or less, the creature dies. If the total is 19 or more, the creature survives the transformation; the creature can withstand any inspection and appear to be a stone statue, although faint magic is detected from the stone if someone checks for it. Note that a creature with a Constitution of 18 or more will always survive the transformation. Despite being in this condition, the petrified individual can see, hear and smell normally. Feeling is limited to those sensations that can affect the granite-hard substance of the individual's body — i.e., chipping is equal to a slight wound, but breaking off one of the statue's arms is serious damage. The individual under the magic of a Statue spell can return to his normal state instantly, act, and then return to the statue state, if he so desires, as long as the spell duration is in effect. The material components of this spell are lime, sand and a drop of water stirred by an iron bar, such as a nail or spike.

Teleport Without Error

(Alteration)
Level: 7
Range: Touch
Duration: Instantaneous
Area of Effect: Special
Components: V
Casting Time: 1 segment
Saving Throw: None

This spell is similar to the Teleport spell. The caster is able to transport himself, along with the material weight noted for a Teleport spell, to any known location in his home plane with no chance for error. The spell also enables the caster to travel to other planes of existence, but any such plane is, at best, "studied carefully." This assumes that the caster has, in fact, actually been to the plane and carefully perused an area for an eventual Teleportat Without Error spell. The table for the Teleport spell is used, with the caster's knowledge of the area to which transportation is desired used to determine the chance of error (for an exception, see the 9th level magic-user spell Succor.) The caster can do nothing else in the round that he appears from a Teleport.

Torment

(Evocation - Alteration)
Level: 7
Range: 1
Duration: Special
Area of Effect: One creature
Components: V, S, M
Casting Time: 1 round
Saving Throw: Special

When this spell is cast, the magic-user seeks to force submission and obedience from a captive creature from another plane from whom a service is being demanded (also see Dolor and Ensnarement spells). The initial uttering of the spell causes a link from the caster to the captive creature bound in a magic circle, thaumaturgic triangle or pentagram. An intended victim of this spell must fail a magic resistance check, if applicable, for the Torment to have any effect. Thereafter, the magic-user continues to read the balance of the specially prepared writing, and each round this continues, the captive feels progressively worse - discomfort and then pain. The first two rounds bring twinges, the third and fourth rounds of reading bring shooting pains, and the fifth and sixth rounds of reading cause aches and then cramps.

The creature refusing to submit to the performance of a service is given a straight saving throw versus spell, adjusted each round for the intensity of the dweomer. The save in the first round is made at -1 to the die roll, the second at -2, the third at -3, the fourth at -4, and the fifth and sixth at -6 and -8 respectively. Failing the saving throw indicates the creature has agreed to the mage's demands. There is no penalty following round 8 in any event. Even should the creature break loose, the Torment will have an effect on the creature. The creature is -1 on initiative for every 2 rounds the spell has been in effect, up to a maximum penalty of -4 on round 8. In addition, the creature is -1 to hit and -1 per die of damage after 3 rounds of the spell, this increasing by -1 per round to -4 in round 6, then decreasing again to -1 in round 9. It is likely that any intelligent creature with low moral standards will submit once it realizes the nature of the spell it is being subjected to. Naturally, this does not cause the creature to feel anything other than immense hatred for the caster. The forced service will be carried out to the letter, as is the case with all such agreements, but the creature will most certainly seek whatever revenge it can. Preparation for the casting of a Torment spell requires either the secret name for the type of creature or its given name to be inscribed in the text of the incantation. The caster must also identify himself. This establishes the link and allows the dweomer to be efficacious. However, for every 1 point of

Intelligence of the creature above that of the spell caster, there is a 1% chance that the captive creature will gain control, draw the caster into the confines of its prison, and carry him off to its own plane and whatever fate is thus decreed. If the magic-user is interrupted or distracted during the reading, there is a 5% chance per point of Intelligence of the captive creature that it will gain control. The material component of the spell is the aforementioned "specially prepared writing" (in the form of a scroll). Its special inks will require an expenditure of not less than 1,000 gp per Hit Die of the creature to be affected by the dweomer of the spell.

Transmute Rock to Lava

(Alteration)
Level: 7
Range: 20 ft./level　　　　　**Components:** V, S, M
Duration: Special　　　　　　**Casting Time:** 1 round
Area of Effect: 2 cubic feet/level **Saving Throw:** None

The power of Transmute Rock to Lava turns and ordinary rocky area into one filled with hot lava. The spell is permanent in the sense that the lava remains until cooled, typically 1d6 days in normal conditions. Creatures caught in the area suffer 5d10 points of damage each round until they escape by means of a successful saving throw. Characters' equipment must also save or be destroyed. The material component is a piece of obsidian.

Truename

(Enchantment/Alteration)
Level: 7
Range: 3 ft.　　　　　　　　**Components:** V, S
Duration: Special　　　　　　**Casting Time:** Special
Area of Effect: Thing named　**Saving Throw:** Negates

This spell enables the magic-user to have great power over any living thing which has a name, generic or individual, known to the spell caster. Naturally, most true names are not known (even by the creatures themselves), for the common names of most things are not their true and secret names. True names are discovered through hard work, spying, extensive use of Legend Lore and sagecraft (at the most difficult levels). The casting of a Truename spell requires the magic-user to call out the true name of the subject and then begin a recitation of verse which encompasses the nature and/or history of the subject. This will require 3 segments. Thereafter, still in verse (and preferably rhyming or near-rhyming), the caster must describe the desired result of the Truename spell. Each possible result differs in the length of time necessary to effectuate it:

Multiple Suggestion: The verses can contain from 1 to 4 Suggestion powers, just as if each were a spell. Each verse requires 1 segment to recite (see Suggestion spell). In a total of 7 segments (including the time for the initial reading), 4 Suggestions can be made.

Weakness and Surrender: The verses recited cause actual loss of 1 point of Strength (-1 to-hit and damage, -1 on movement rate) for each segment of recitation. With the loss of each point of Strength, the subject must save versus paralyzation or meekly surrender. Each verse must continue for 1 segment. Strength loss is recovered in from 2-8 rounds after the recitation ceases, and with recovery of Strength the subject regains its will to resist.

Polymorph: The verses can cause the subject to change into something else, just as if a Polymorph Any Object spell had been cast. No system shock saving throw is needed. The length of time in verses (1 segment per verse) to cause the polymorph depends on how radical the change:

mineral to animal	=	10 verses
mineral to vegetable	=	9 verses
vegetable to animal	=	8 verses
monster to normal	=	7 verses
monster to monster	=	6 verses
other to human	=	5 verses
animal to animal	=	4 verses
vegetable to vegetable	=	3 verses
mineral to mineral	=	2 verses

The reverse of the preceding cases also holds. In cases not stated, the GM is to use the closest stated case as a guide. The subject returns to its natural form in time. Duration is 6 turns per level of the spell caster minus 1 turn for every verse required to effect the polymorph. The subject will think and behave exactly as a non-polymorphed thing of the same type, but have its original hit points.

Transport: When the transport verses are recited, the subject will be Teleported Without Error or otherwise moved to some other place. The number of verses required depends on the location of the transport:

same plane/100 mile range	=	4 verses
same plane/500 mile range	=	5 verses
same plane/2,000 mile range	=	6 verses
one plane/world removed	=	7 verses
two planes/worlds removed	=	8 verses

The subject will automatically be altered so as to be able to physically survive the normal conditions of the place to which it is sent. There is no saving throw if the subjects are willing, even if they have a magic resistance.

If at any time during the recitation of the spell the caster is interrupted, the magic fails and the spell is lost.

Vanish

(Alteration)
Level: 7
Range: Touch　　　　　　　　**Components:** V
Duration: Special　　　　　　**Casting Time:** 2 segments
Area of Effect: 1 object　　　**Saving Throw:** None

When the magic-user employs this spell, he causes an object to vanish (i.e., to be teleported as if by a Teleport spell) if it weighs no more than 50 pounds per caster level. Thus, a 14th level caster can Vanish and cause to reappear at a desired location, an object up to 700 pounds in weight. The maximum volume of material that can be affected is 3 cubic feet per level of experience. Thus, both weight and volume limit the spell. An object that exceeds either limitation is unaffected and the spell fails. If desired, a vanished object can be placed deep within the Ethereal Plane. In this case, the point from which the object vanished remains faintly magical until the item is retrieved. A successful Dispel Magic spell cast on the point will bring the Vanished item back from the Ethereal Plane. Note that creatures and magical forces cannot be made to vanish. There is a 1% chance that a Vanished item will be Disintegrated instead. There is also a 1% chance that a creature from the Ethereal Plane is able to gain access to the Prime Material Plane through the Vanished item's connection.

Vision

(Divination)
Level: 7
Range: 0　　　　　　　　　　**Components:** V, S, M
Duration: Special　　　　　　**Casting Time:** 7 segments
Area of Effect: The caster　　**Saving Throw:** None

When a magic-user wishes to gain supernatural guidance, he casts a Vision spell, calling upon whatever power he desires aid from and asking a question that will be answered with a vision. Two six-sided dice are rolled. If they total 2 to 6, the power is annoyed and refuses to answer the question; instead, the power causes the magic-user to perform some service (by an ultra-powerful Geas or Quest). If the dice total 7 to 9, the power is indifferent and gives some minor vision, though it may be unrelated to the question. If the dice total 10 or better, the power grants the vision. The material component of the spell is the sacrifice of something valued by the spellcaster or by the power supplicated. The more precious the sacrifice, the better the chance of spell success. A very precious item grants a bonus of +1 to the dice roll, an extremely precious item adds +2 and a priceless item adds +3.

Volley

(Abjuration)
Level: 7
Range: Special　　　　　　　**Components:** V, S, M
Duration: Special　　　　　　**Casting Time:** 1 segment
Area of Effect: Special.　　　**Saving Throw:** Special

This highly dangerous dweomer enables the prospective recipient of a spell to turn the casting back upon its sender. Thus, the range, duration, area of effect and saving throw of this spell depend upon circumstances and the spell being volleyed. Assume that a Power Word, Kill is cast at a magic-user prepared with a Volley spell. The Volley has been cast also, so that when the Power Word, Kill is aimed at the target, the Volley causes the spell to bounce back upon its caster. Then, if the caster of the first spell fails to make a saving throw versus spell, the Power Word, Kill works upon its caster rather than its intended target. However, if the original caster does save versus spell, the spell once again flies toward the original target. The caster of the Volley spell must then save versus spell, or be affected by the attack. Again, if the caster of the Volley spell saves, then the spell is returned to its originator, who must again save or be affected. The spell will be sent back and forth until one or the other fails to save, or until the spell loses its power. The entire spell is Volleyed, such that if a Lightning Bolt were to start 10 feet before the Volleying magic-user, the full spell would be returned, leaving others in the Volleying party unscathed. Each exchange will take a single second. A spell will lose power if it passes through a number of exchanges equal to its level, counting each Volley, but not the original casting, as half of a single exchange; i.e., a 1st level spell will be cast, Volleyed the first time, (perhaps) return Volleyed, and then will dissipate; a 2nd level spell would go through four Volley portions (two complete exchanges) before being exhausted; and so on. The material component is a bit of bent willow or other flexible wood, crisscrossed with specially prepared strands of gut.

Zarba's Grasping Hand
(Evocation)
Level: 7
Range: 10 yds./level   **Components:** V, S, M
Duration: 1 rd./level   **Casting Time:** 7 segments
Area of Effect: Special   **Saving Throw:** None

Zarba's Grasping Hand is a superior version of the 6th level spell Zarba's Shoving Hand. It creates a man-sized (5 feet) to gargantuan-sized (21 feet) hand that appears and grasps a creature designated by the caster, regardless of what the spellcaster does or how the opponent tries to escape it. The Grasping Hand can hold motionless a creature or object of up to 1,000 pounds weight, slow movement to 10 feet per round if the creature weighs between 1,000 and 4,000 pounds, or slow movement by 50% if the creature weighs up to 16,000 pounds. The Hand itself inflicts no damage. The Grasping Hand has an Armor Class of 0, has as many hit points as its caster in full health, and vanishes when destroyed. The caster can order it to release a trapped opponent or can dismiss it on command. The material component is a leather glove.

Zarba's Sphere of Insanity
(Enchantment/Charm)
Level: 7
Range: 10 ft./level   **Components:** V, S, M
Duration: Special   **Casting Time:** 7 segments
Area of Effect: 1 creature   **Saving Throw:** Special

When Zarba's Sphere of Insanity is cast it causes the victim's id to attempt to assassinate his ego. The victim must make a saving throw. If he fails his id succeeds in causing him to suffer 3d6 damage and reducing his intellect to that of a babbling, hallucinating madman. The victim effectively has Intelligence and Wisdom scores of three each, which persist until the victim is cured by a Heal, Restoration, Wish or similar magic. If the target makes his saving throw his superego intervenes, preventing madness but still forcing the victim to suffer 2d6 damage and stunning him for 1d4 rounds. The material component is a silver sphere filled with smaller spheres, costing 100 gold pieces to construct.

Zargosa's Instant Summons
(Conjuration/Summoning)
Level: 7
Range: Infinite + special   **Components:** V, S, M
Duration: Instantaneous   **Casting Time:** 1 segment
Area of Effect: 1 small object **Saving Throw:** None

When this spell is cast, the magic-user teleports some desired item from virtually any location directly to his hand. The single object can be no longer in any dimension than a sword, can have no more weight than a shield (about eight pounds), and must be nonliving. To prepare this spell, the magic-user must hold a gem of not less than 5,000 gp value in his hand and utter all but the final word of the conjuration. At some point in the future, he must crush the gem and utter the final word. The desired item is then transported instantly into the spellcaster's right or left hand, as he desires. The item must have been previously touched during the initial incantation and specifically named; only that particular item is summoned by the spell. During the initial incantation, the gem becomes magically inscribed with the name of the item to be summoned. The inscription is invisible and unreadable, except by means of a Read Magic spell, to all but the magic-user who cast the summons. If the item is in the possession of another creature, the spell does not work, and the caster knows who the possessor is and roughly where he or it is located when the summons is cast. Items can be summoned from other planes of existence, but only if such items are not in the possession (not necessarily the physical grasp) of another creature. For each level of experience above the 14th, the magic-user is able to summon a desired item from one plane farther removed from the plane he is in at the time the spell is cast (one plane away at 14th level, two planes away at 15th, etc.). Thus, a magic-user of 16th level could cast the spell even if the desired item was on the second layer of one of the Outer Planes, but at 14th level the magic-user would be able to summon the item only if it were no farther than one of the Inner Planes, the Ethereal Plane or the Astral Plane. Note that special wards or barriers, or factors that block Teleport or Plane Shift spells, may also block the operation of this spell. Objects in Drayton's Hidden Stash cannot be recovered by using this spell. Note: If the item is magic-user marked, it can be summoned from anywhere on the same plane unless special local conditions apply. Furthermore, the details of the location of the item are more specific, and the item is more easily traceable with other types of scrying magic.

Zargosa's Opulent Manor House
(Alteration, Conjuration)
Level: 7
Range: 10 yards   **Components:** V, S, M
Duration: 1 hr./level   **Casting Time:** 7 rounds
Area of Effect: 300 sq. ft./level   **Saving Throw:** None

By means of this spell, the magic-user conjures up an extradimensional dwelling, entrance to which can be gained only at a single point of space on the plane from which the spell was cast. From the entry point, those creatures observing the area see only a faint shimmering in the air, in an area 4 feet wide and 8 feet high. The caster of the spell controls entry to the mansion, and the portal is shut and made invisible behind him when he enters. He may open it again from his own side at will. Once observers have passed beyond the entrance, they behold a magnificent foyer and numerous chambers beyond. The place is furnished and contains sufficient foodstuffs to serve a nine-course banquet to as many dozens of people as the spellcaster has levels of experience. There is a staff of near-transparent servants, liveried and obedient, to wait upon all who enter. The atmosphere is clean, fresh, and warm. Since the place can be entered only through its special portal, outside conditions do not affect the mansion, nor do conditions inside it pass to the plane beyond. Rest and relaxation within the place is normal, but the food is not. It seems excellent and quite filling as long as one is within the place. Once outside, however, its effects disappear immediately, and if those resting have not eaten real food within a reasonable time span, ravenous hunger strikes. Failure to eat normal food immediately results in the onset of fatigue or starvation penalties as decided by the GM. The material components of this spell are a miniature portal carved from ivory, a small piece of polished marble and a tiny silver spoon. These are utterly destroyed when the spell is cast. It is worth mentioning that this spell has been used in conjunction with a normal portal, as well as with illusion magic. There is evidence that the design and interior of the space created can be altered to suit the caster's wishes.

Eighth Level Spells

Antipathy-Sympathy
(Enchantment/Charm)
Level: 8
Range: 30 yards   **Components:** V, S, M
Duration: 2 hrs./level   **Casting Time:** 1 hour
Area of Effect: 10-ft. cube or   **Saving Throw:** Special
         one item

This spell allows the magic-user to set certain vibrations to emanate from an object or location that tend to either repel or attract a specific type of intelligent creature or characters of a particular alignment. The magic-user must decide which effect is desired with regard to what creature type or alignment before beginning the spellcasting, for the components of each application differ. The spell cannot be cast upon living creatures.

Antipathy: This spell causes the affected creature or alignment type to feel an overpowering urge to leave the area or to not touch the affected item. If a saving throw vs. spell is successful, the creature can stay in the area or touch the item, but the creature will feel very uncomfortable, and a persistent itching will cause it to suffer the loss of 1 point of Dexterity per round (for the spell's duration), subject to a maximum loss of 4 points and a minimum Dexterity of 3. Failure to save vs. spell forces the being to abandon the area or item, shunning it permanently and never willingly returning to it until the spell is removed or expires. The material component for this application of the spell is a lump of alum soaked in vinegar.

Sympathy: By casting the Sympathy application of the spell, the magic-user can cause a particular type of creature or alignment of character to feel elated and pleased to be in an area or touching or possessing an object or item. The desire to stay in the area or touch the object is overpowering. Unless a saving throw vs. spell is successfully rolled, the creature or character will stay or refuse to release the object. If the saving throw is successful, the creature or character is released from the enchantment, but a subsequent saving throw must be made 1d6 turns later. If this saving throw fails, the affected creature will return to the area or object. The material components of this spell are 1,000 gp worth of crushed pearls and a drop of honey. Note that the particular type of creature to be affected must be named specifically – for example, Red Dragons, Hill Giants, Wererats, Lammasu, Catoblepas, Vampires, etc. Likewise, the specific alignment must be named – for example, chaotic evil, chaotic good, lawful neutral, true neutral, etc. If this spell is cast upon an area, a 10-foot cube can be enchanted for each experience level of the caster. If an object or item is enchanted, only that single thing can be enchanted; affected creatures or characters save vs. spell with a -2 penalty.

Binding
(Enchantment, Evocation)
Level: 8
Range: 10 yards   **Components:** V, S, M
Duration: Special   **Casting Time:** Special
Area of Effect: 1 creature   **Saving Throw:** Special

A Binding spell creates a magical restraint to hold a creature, usually from another plane of existence. Extraplanar creatures must be confined by a circu-

lar diagram; other creatures can be physically confined. The duration of the spell depends upon the form of the Binding and the level of the caster(s), as well as the length of time the spell is actually uttered. The components vary according to the form of the spell, but they include a continuous chanting utterance read from the scroll or book page giving the spell; gestures appropriate to the form of Binding; and materials such as miniature chains of special metal (silver for lycanthropes, etc.), soporific herbs of the rarest sort, a corundum or diamond gem of great size (1,000 gp value per Hit Die of the subject creature), and a vellum depiction or carved statuette of the subject to be captured. Magic resistance applies unless the subject's true name is used. A saving throw is not applicable as long as the experience level of the caster is at least twice as great as the Hit Dice of the subject. The caster's level can be augmented by one-third of the levels of each assisting magic-user of 9th level or higher, and by one level for each assistant of 4th through 8th level. No more than six other magic-users can assist with this spell. If the caster's level is less than twice the Hit Dice of the subject, the subject gains a saving throw vs. spell, modified by the form of binding being attempted. The various forms of binding are:

Chaining: The subject is confined by restraints that generate an Antipathy spell affecting all creatures who approach the subject, except the caster. Duration is as long as one year per level of the caster(s). The subject of this form of Binding (as well as in the slumber and bound slumber versions) remains within the restraining barrier. Slumber: Brings a comatose sleep upon the subject for a duration of up to one year per level of the caster(s).

Bound Slumber: A combination of chaining and slumber that lasts for up to one month per level of the caster(s).

Hedged Prison: The subject is transported to or otherwise brought within a confined area from which it cannot wander by any means until freed. The spell remains until the magical hedge is somehow broken.

Metamorphosis: Causes the subject to change to some noncorporeal form, save for its head or face. The Binding is permanent until some prescribed act frees the subject.

Minimus Containment: The subject is shrunken to a height of 1 inch or even less and held within the hedged prison of some gem or similar object. The subject of a minimus containment, metamorphosis, or hedged prison radiates a very faint aura of magic. The subject of the chaining form of the spell receives a saving throw with no modifications. However, slumber allows the subject a +1 bonus, bound slumber a +2 bonus, hedged prison a +3 bonus, metamorphosis a +4 bonus, and minimus containment a +5 bonus to the saving throw. If the subject is magically weakened, the GM can assign a -1, -2, or even -4 penalty to the saving throw. A successful saving throw enables the subject to burst its bonds and do as it pleases.

A Binding spell can be renewed in the case of the first three forms of the spell, for the subject does not have the opportunity to break the bonds. If anything has caused a weakening of a chaining or slumber version, such as attempts to contact the subject or magically touch it, a normal saving throw applies to the renewal of the spell. Otherwise, after one year, and each year thereafter, the subject gains a normal saving throw vs. the spell. Whenever it is successful, the Binding spell is broken and the creature is free.

Clone
(Necromancy)
Level: 8
Range: Touch   **Components:** V, S, M
Duration: Permanent   **Casting Time:** 1 turn
Area of Effect: 1 clone   **Saving Throw:** None

This spell creates a duplicate of a human, demi-human or humanoid creature. This clone is in most respects the duplicate of the individual, complete to the level of experience, memories, etc. However, the duplicate really is the person, so if the original and a duplicate exist at the same time, each knows of the other's existence; the original person and the clone will each desire to do away with the other, for such an alter-ego is unbearable to both. If one cannot destroy the other, one will go insane and destroy itself (90% likely to be the clone), or possibly both will become mad and destroy themselves (2% chance). These events nearly always occur within one week of the dual existence. Note that the clone is the person as he existed at the time at which the flesh was taken for the spell component, and all subsequent knowledge, experience, etc., is totally unknown to the clone. The clone is a physical duplicate, and possessions of the original are another matter entirely. A clone takes 2d4 months to grow, and only after that time is dual existence established. Furthermore, the clone has one less Constitution point than the body it was cloned from; the Cloning fails if the clone would have a Constitution of 0. The material component of the spell is a small piece of the flesh from the person to be duplicated.

The GM may, in addition, add other stipulations to the success of a cloning effort, requiring that some trace of life must remain in the flesh sample, that some means of storing and preserving the sample must be devised and maintained, etc.

Demand
(Evocation, Enchantment/Charm)
Level: 8
Range: Unlimited   **Components:** V, S, M
Duration: Special   **Casting Time:** 1 turn
Area of Effect: 1 creature   **Saving Throw:** Special

This spell is very much like the 5th level magic-user spell Sending, allowing a brief contact with a far distant creature. However, with this spell the message can also contain a suggestion (see the 3rd level magic-user spell suggestion), which the subject will do its best to carry out if it fails its saving throw vs. spell, made with a -2 penalty. Of course, if the message is impossible or meaningless according to the circumstances that exist for the subject at the time the demand comes, the message is understood but no saving throw is necessary and the suggestion is ineffective.

The caster must be familiar with the creature contacted and must know its name and appearance well. If the creature in question is not in the same plane of existence as the spellcaster, there is a base 5% chance that the Demand does not arrive. Local conditions on other planes may worsen this chance considerably at the option of the GM. The Demand, if received, will be understood even if the creature has an Intelligence ability score as low as 1 (animal Intelligence). Creatures of demigawd status or higher can choose to come or not, as they please. The Demand message to the creature must be 25 words or less, including the suggestion. The creature can also give a short reply immediately.

The material components of the spell are a pair of cylinders, each open at one end, connected by a thin piece of copper wire and some small part of the subject creature — a hair, a bit of nail, etc.

Fireball, Death Brusher
(Evocation)
Level: 8
Range: 10 yds. + 10yds./level   **Components:** V, S, M
Duration: Instantaneous   **Casting Time:** 8 segments
Area of Effect: 20 'radius sphere   **Saving Throw:** Half

This spell is the same as the 3rd level spell Fireball, except for the above. In addition, those taking damage from the Fireball must pass a system shock roll or be instantly slain.

Fireball, Maximus
(Evocation)
Level: 8
Range: 10 yds. + 10 yds./level   **Components:** V, S, M
Duration: Instantaneous   **Casting Time:** 8 segments
Area of Effect: 20-ft. radius   **Saving Throw:** 1/2

The Maximus Fireball is similar in most respects to a normal Fireball except that the damage dealt is 1d10 per caster level.

Gandle's Spell Immunity
(Abjuration)
Level: 8
Range: Touch   **Components:** V, S, M
Duration: 1 turn/level   **Casting Time:** 1 rd/recipient
Area of Effect: Creature touched   **Saving Throw:** None

By use of this spell, the magic-user is able to confer virtual immunity to certain spells and magical attack forms upon those he touches. For every four levels of experience of the magic-user, one creature can be protected by the Gandle's Spell Immunity spell; however, if more than one is protected, the duration of the protection is divided among the protected creatures.

For example, a 16th level magic-user can cast the spell upon one creature and it will last 16 turns, or place it upon two creatures for eight turns, or four creatures for four turns. The protection gives a bonus to saving throws, according to spell type and level, as shown in the following table.

Spell Level	Magic-User Spell	Cleric Spell
1st-3rd	+9*	+7
4th-6th	+7	+5
7th-8th	+5	+3

* Includes beguiling effects.

The material component of this spell is a diamond of at least 500 gp value, which must be crushed and sprinkled over the spell recipients. Each such creature must also have in its possession a diamond of at least one carat size, intact and carried on its person.

Glassteel
(Alteration)
Level: 8
Range: Touch   **Components:** V, S, M
Duration: Permanent   **Casting Time:** 8 segments
Area of Effect: Object touched   **Saving Throw:** None

The Glassteel spell turns normal, non-magical crystal or glass into a transparent substance that has the tensile strength and sturdiness of actual steel. Only a relatively small volume of material can be affected (a maximum weight of 10 pounds per level of experience of the spellcaster), and it must form one whole object. The Armor Class of the substance is 1. The material components of this spell are a small piece of glass and a small piece of steel.

Grasping Death
(Conjuration/Summoning)
Level: 8
Range: 5 yds./2 levels   **Components:** V, S
Duration: Permanent   **Casting Time:** 3 segments
Area of Effect: one creature   **Saving Throw:** None

When a Grasping Death spell is cast, one creature of any type within the spell range is slain. In order to gain this effect, the magic-user casting the spell must sacrifice one full level of experience when casting the spell. Note that blood mages may cast this spell as a third level spell, but in that case the victim is granted a saving throw which negates the spell if the saving throw is successful.

Haarpang's Magnificent Sphere of Telekinesis
(Evocation, Alteration)
Level: 8
Range: 20 yards   **Components:** V, S, M
Duration: 2 rds./level   **Casting Time:** 4 segments
Area of Effect: sphere with diameterof 1 ft./level   **Saving Throw:** Negates

This spell is exactly the same as the 4th level magic-user spell Haarpang's Magnificent Sphere of Resiliency, with the addition that the creatures or objects inside the globe are nearly weightless – anything contained within it weighs only 1/16 its normal weight. Any subject weighing up to 5,000 pounds can be telekinetically lifted in the sphere by the caster. Range of control extends to a maximum distance of 10 yards per level after the sphere has actually succeeded in encapsulating a subject or subjects. Note that even if more than 5,000 pounds of weight is encompassed in the globe, the perceived weight is only 1/16 of the actual weight, so the Sphere can be rolled without exceptional effort. Because of the reduced weight, rapid motion or falling within the field of the sphere is relatively harmless to the object therein, although it can be disastrous should the Sphere disappear when the subject inside is high above a hard surface. The caster can dismiss the effect with a word. In addition to a hemispherical piece of diamond and a matching piece of gum arabic, the caster must also have a pair of small bar magnets as material components for this spell.

Incendiary Cloud

(Alteration, Evocation)

Level: 8

Range: 30 yards **Components:** V, S, M

Duration: 4 rds. + 1d6 rounds **Casting Time:** 2 segments

Area of Effect: Special **Saving Throw:** Half

An Incendiary Cloud spell exactly resembles the smoke effects of a Pyrotechnics spell, except that its minimum dimensions are a cloud 10 feet tall, 20 feet wide, and 20 feet long. This dense vapor cloud billows forth, and on the third round of its existence begins to flame, causing 1-2 points of damage per level of the spellcaster. On the fourth round it inflicts 1d4 points of damage per level of the caster, and on the fifth round this drops back to 1-2 points of damage per level as its flames burn out. In any successive rounds of existence, the Cloud is simply harmless smoke that obscures vision within its confines. Creatures within the Cloud need to make only one saving throw if it is successful, but if they fail the first saving throw, they roll again on the fourth and fifth rounds (if necessary) to attempt to reduce the damage sustained by one-half. In order to cast this spell, the magic-user must have an available fire source (just as with a Pyrotechnics spell), scrapings from beneath a dung pile, and a pinch of dust.

Mass Charm

(Enchantment/Charm)

Level: 8

Range: 5 yds./level **Components:** V

Duration: Special **Casting Time:** 8 segments

Area of Effect: 30-ft. cube **Saving Throw:** Negates

A Mass Charm spell affects either persons or monsters just as a Charm Person or Charm Monster spell. The Mass Charm spell, however, affects a number of creatures whose combined levels of experience or Hit Dice does not exceed twice the level of experience of the spellcaster. All affected creatures must be within the spell range and within a 30-foot cube. Note that the creatures' saving throws are unaffected by the number of recipients (see the Charm Person and Charm Monster spells), but all target creatures are subject to a penalty of -2 on their saving throws because of the efficiency and power of this spell. The Wisdom bonus against charm spells does apply.

Maze

(Conjuration/Summoning)

Level: 8

Range: 5 yds./level **Components:** V, S

Duration: Special **Casting Time:** 3 segments

Area of Effect: 1 creature **Saving Throw:** None

An extradimensional space is brought into being upon the utterance of a Maze spell. The subject vanishes into the shifting labyrinth of force planes for a period of time that is dependent upon its Intelligence. Note that Minotaurs are not affected by this spell.

Intelligence of Mazed Creature	Time Trapped in Maze
under 3	2d4 turns
3-5	1d4 turns
6-8	5d4 rounds
9-11	4d4 rounds
12-14	3d4 rounds
15-17	2d4 rounds
18+	1d4 rounds

Note that even Teleport and Dimension Door spells will not help a character escape a Maze spell, although a Plane Shift spell will.

Mimic Caster

(Enchantment)

Level: 8

Range: Touch **Components:** V, S, M

Duration: 1 turn per level **Casting Time:** 1 turn

Area of Effect: Person touched **Saving Throw:** None

By the use of this spell, the magic-user can allow the recipient the ability to cast any number of the caster's currently memorized spells. Only spellcasters (including rangers and paladins) can receive this bestowal; the Mimic Caster enchantment does not fully function for those belonging to non-spellcasting classes, for unintelligent monsters, nor for any individual with less than 1 full Hit Die. A recipient in these categories may still be enchanted with the spell and can mimic the actions of the caster for the duration of the spell but that recipient may not actually cast spells. It will be a very convincing performance but without the special effects. In addition, the person thus enchanted must have an Intelligence score of 9 or higher.

Note that the person who is enchanted with this spell cannot cast any of the original caster's retinue of spells on his own. He can only cast them at the exact same time as the original magic-user is casting them. The spell recipient must be able to see the original caster in order to properly mimic him. For example, a high level magic-user can cast Mimic Caster on a first level magic-user. This does not mean the first level magic-user can suddenly cast a Fireball at his own whim. But if the original caster of the Mimic Caster spell casts a Fireball in front of the first level magic-user, the lucky first level magic-user could then simultaneously cast a Fireball at half the strength of the original caster.

The mimicked spell's variable characteristics (range, duration, area of effect, etc.) function at 1/2 the level of the magic-user being mimicked. A cleric who casts Imbue with Spell Ability upon another character loses the number of 1st and 2nd level spells he has Imbued until the recipient uses the transferred spells or is slain. The material component for this spell is a marionette fashioned in the likeness of the caster. This item is consumed when the spell is cast.

Mind Blank

(Abjuration)

Level: 8

Range: 30 yards **Components:** V, S

Duration: 1 day **Casting Time:** 1 segment

Area of Effect: 1 creature **Saving Throw:** None

When the very powerful Mind Blank spell is cast, the creature is totally protected from all devices and spells that detect, influence or read emotions or thoughts. This protects against Augury, charm effects, Command, confusion effects, divination, empathy (all forms), ESP, fear effects, Feeblemind, Mass Suggestion, Phantasmal Killer, possession, rulership, soul trapping, suggestion, and Telepathy. Cloaking protection also extends to the prevention of discovery or information gathering by Crystal Balls or other scrying devices, Clairaudience, Clairvoyance, communing, contacting other planes, or Wish-related methods (Wish or Limited Wish). Of course, exceedingly powerful gawds can penetrate the spell's barrier.

Monster Summoning VI

(Conjuration/Summoning)

Level: 8

Range: Special **Components:** V, S, M

Duration: 7 rds. + 1 rd./level **Casting Time:** 8 segments

Area of Effect: 80-yd. radius **Saving Throw:** None

This spell is much like the 3rd level spell Monster Summoning I, except that it summons 1d3 6th level monsters. These monsters appear in 1d3 rounds within the spell's area of effect and attack the caster's opponents, until either he commands them to cease, the spell duration expires, or the monsters are slain. These creatures do not check morale, and they vanish when slain. If no opponent exists to fight, summoned monsters can, if the magic-user can communicate with them, and if they are physically capable, perform other services for the summoning magic-user. The material components of this spell are a tiny bag and a small (not necessarily lit) candle.

FRAIM

Munari's Irresistible Jig

(Enchantment/Charm)

Level: 8
Range: Touch
Duration: 1d4+1 rounds
Area of Effect: Creature touched

Components: V
Casting Time: 5 segments
Saving Throw: None

When an Munari's Irresistible Jig spell is placed upon a creature, the spell causes the recipient to begin dancing, complete with feet shuffling and tapping. This Jig makes it impossible for the victim to do anything other than caper and prance; this cavorting worsens the Armor Class of the creature by -4, makes saving throws impossible except on a roll of 20, and negates any consideration of a shield. Note that the creature must be touched, as if melee combat were taking place and the spellcaster were striking to do damage.

Permanency

(Alteration)

Level: 8
Range: Special
Duration: Permanent
Area of Effect: Special

Components: V, S
Casting Time: 2 rounds
Saving Throw: None

This spell affects the duration of certain other spells, making the duration permanent. The personal spells upon which a Permanency is known to be effective are as follows: Comprehend Languages, Protection From Evil, Detect Evil, Protection From Normal Missiles, Detect Invisibility, Read Magic, Detect Magic, Tongues, Infravision, Unseen Servant, and Protection From Cantrips. The magic-user casts the desired spell and then follows it with the Permanency spell. Each Permanency spell lowers the magic-user's Constitution by 1 point. The magic-user cannot cast these spells upon other creatures. This application of Permanency can be dispelled only by a magic-user of greater level than the spellcaster was when he cast the spell. In addition to personal use, the Permanency spell can be used to make the following object/creature or area-effect spells permanent: Enlarge, Prismatic Sphere, Fear, Stinking Cloud, Gust of Wind, Wall of Fire, Invisibility, Wall of Force, Magic Mouth, and Web.

Additionally, the following spells can be cast upon objects or areas only and rendered permanent: Alarm, Audible Glamer, Distance Distortion, Dancing Lights, Teleport, and Solid Fog. These applications to other spells allow it to be cast simultaneously with any of the latter when no living creature is the tar-

get, but the entire spell complex then can be dispelled normally, and thus negated. The Permanency spell is also used in the fabrication of magical items (see the 6th level spell Enchant an Item). At the GM's option, Permanency might become unstable or fail after a long period of at least 1,000 years. Unstable effects might operate intermittently or fail altogether. The GM may allow other selected spells to be made permanent. Researching this possible application of a spell costs as much time and money as independently researching the selected spell. If the GM has already determined that the application is not possible, the research automatically fails. Note that the magic-user never learns what is possible except by the success or failure of his research.

Polymorph Any Object

(Alteration)

Level: 8
Range: 5 yds./level
Duration: Variable
Area of Effect: Special

Components: V, S, M
Casting Time: 1 round
Saving Throw: Special

This spell changes one object or creature into another. When used as a Polymorph Other or Stone to Flesh spell, simply treat the spell as a more powerful version, with saving throws made with -4 penalties to the die roll. When it is cast in order to change other objects, the duration of the spell depends on how radical a change is made from the original state to its enchanted state, as well as how different it is in size. The GM determines the changes by using the following guidelines:

Kingdom	Animal, vegetable, mineral
Class	Mammals, bipeds, fungi, metals, etc.
Relationship	Twig is to tree, sand is to beach, etc.
Size	Smaller, equal, larger
Shape	Comparative resemblance of the original to the polymorphed state
Intelligence	Particularly with regard to a change in which the end product is more intelligent

A change in kingdom makes the spell work for hours (if removed by one kingdom) or turns (if removed by two). Other changes likewise affect spell duration. Thus, changing a lion to an Androsphinx would be permanent, but turning a turnip to a Purple Worm would be a change with a duration measured in hours. Turning a tusk into an elephant would be permanent, but turning a twig into a sword would be a change with a duration of several turns.

All polymorphed objects radiate a strong magic, and if a Dispel Magic spell is successfully cast upon them, they return to their natural form. Note that a Stone to Flesh spell or its reverse will affect objects under this spell. As with other polymorph spells, damage sustained in the new form can result in the injury or death of the polymorphed creature.

For example, it is possible to polymorph a creature into rock and grind it to dust, causing damage, perhaps even death. If the creature was changed to dust to start with, more creative methods to damage it would be needed; perhaps the magic-user could use a Gust of Wind spell to scatter the dust far and wide. In general, damage occurs when the new form is altered through physical force, although the GM will have to adjudicate many of these situations.

The system shock roll must be applied to living creatures, as must the restrictions noted regarding the Polymorph Other and Stone to Flesh spells. Also note that a polymorph effect often detracts from an item's or creature's powers, but does not add new powers, except possibly movement capabilities not present in the old form. Thus, a Vorpal Sword polymorphed into a dagger would not retain vorpal capability. Likewise, valueless items cannot be made into permanent valuable items. The material components of this spell are mercury, gum arabic and smoke.

Power Word, Blind

(Conjuration/Summoning)

Level: 8
Range: 5 yds./level
Duration: Special
Area of Effect: 15-ft. radius

Components: V
Casting Time: 1 segment
Saving Throw: None

When a Power Word, Blind spell is cast, one or more creatures within the area of effect become sightless. The spellcaster selects one creature as the target center, and the effect spreads outward from the center, affecting creatures with the lowest hit point totals first; the spell can also be focused to affect only an individual creature. The spell affects up to 100 hit points of creatures; creatures who currently have 100 or more hit points are not affected and do not count against the number of creatures affected.

The duration of the spell depends upon how many hit points are affected. If 25 or fewer hit points are affected, the blindness is permanent until cured. If 26 to 50 hit points are affected, the blindness lasts for 1d4+1 turns. If 51 to 100 hit points are affected, the spell lasts for 1d4+1 rounds. An individual creature cannot be partially affected. If all of its current hit points are affected, it is blinded; otherwise, it is not. Blindness can be removed by a Cure Blindness or Dispel Magic spell.

Screen

(Divination/Illusion)

Level: 8

Range: 0   **Components:** V, S

Duration: 1 hr./level   **Casting Time:** 1 turn

Area of Effect: 30-ft. cube/level   **Saving Throw:** Special

This spell combines several elements to create a powerful protection from scrying and direct observation. When the spell is cast, the magic-user dictates what will and will not be observed in the area of effect. The illusion created must be stated in general terms. Thus, the caster could specify the illusion of him and another playing chess for the duration of the spell, but he could not have the illusionary chess players take a break, make dinner, and then resume their game. He could have a crossroads appear quiet and empty even while an army is actually passing through the area. He could specify that no one be seen (including passing strangers), that his troops be undetected, or even that every fifth man or unit should be visible.

Once the conditions are set, they cannot be changed. Attempts to scry the area automatically detect the image stated by the caster with no saving throw allowed. Sight and sound are appropriate to the illusion created. A band of men standing in a meadow could be concealed as an empty meadow with birds chirping, etc. Direct observation may allow a saving throw (as per a normal illusion), if there is cause to disbelieve what is seen. Certainly onlookers in the area would become suspicious if the column of a marching army disappeared at one point to reappear at another! Even entering the area does not cancel the illusion or necessarily allow a saving throw, assuming the hidden beings take care to stay out of the way of those affected by the illusion.

Sink

(Enchantment, Alteration)

Level: 8

Range: 10 yds./level   **Components:** V, S

Duration: Special   **Casting Time:** 8 segments

Area of Effect: 1 creature or object, max. 1 cu. ft./level   **Saving Throw:** Special

By means of this spell, a magic-user can force a creature or object into the very earth or floor upon which it stands. When casting the spell, the magic-user must chant the spell for the remainder of the round without interruption. At that juncture, the subject creature or object becomes rooted to the spot unless a saving throw vs. spell (for a creature) or disintegration (for an object with magical properties) is successful.

Note that "magical properties" include those of magical items as listed in the Game Master Guide, those of items enchanted or otherwise of magical origin, and those of items with protection-type spells or with permanent magical properties or similar spells upon them. Items of a non-magical nature are not entitled to a saving throw. If a subject fails its saving throw, it becomes of slightly greater density than the surface upon which it stands. The spellcaster now has the option of ceasing his spell and leaving the subject as it is, in which case the spell expires in four turns, and the subject returns to normal. If the caster proceeds with the spell (into the next round), the subject begins to sink slowly into the ground. Before any actions are taken in the new round, the subject sinks one-quarter of its height; after the first group acts, another quarter; after the second group acts, another; and at the end of the round, the victim is totally sunken into the ground. This entombment places a creature or object in a state of suspended animation.

The cessation of time means that the subject does not grow older. Bodily and other functions virtually cease, but the subject is otherwise unharmed. The subject exists in undamaged form in the surface into which it was sunk, its upper point as far beneath the surface as the subject has height – a 6-foot-tall victim will be 6 feet beneath the surface, while a 60-foot-tall subject will have its uppermost point 60 feet below ground level. If the ground around the subject is somehow removed, the spell is broken and the subject returns to normal, but it does not rise up. Spells such as dig, transmute stone to mud, and freedom (the reverse of the 9th level spell imprisonment) will not harm the sunken creature or object and will often be helpful in recovering it. If a Detect Magic spell is cast over an area upon which a Sink spell was used, it reveals a faint magical aura of undefinable nature, even if the subject is beyond detection range. If the subject is within range of the detection, the spell's schools can be discovered (alteration and enchantment).

Symbol

(Conjuration/Summoning)

Level: 8

Range: Touch   **Components:** V, S, M

Duration: Special   **Casting Time:** 8 segments

Area of Effect: Special   **Saving Throw:** Special

A Symbol spell creates magical runes affecting creatures that pass over, touch, or read the runes, or pass through a portal upon which the Symbol is inscribed. Upon casting the spell, the magic-user inscribes the Symbol upon whatever surface he desires. Likewise, the spellcaster is able to place the Symbol of his choice, using any one of the following:

Death: One or more creatures, whose total hit points do not exceed 80, are slain.

Discord: All creatures are affected and immediately fall to loud bickering and arguing; there is a 50% probability that creatures of different alignments attack each other. The bickering lasts for 5d4 rounds, the fighting for 2d4 rounds.

Fear: This symbol creates an extra-strong Fear spell, causing all creatures to save vs. spell with -4 penalties to the die roll, or panic and flee as if attacked by a Fear spell.

Hopelessness: All creatures are affected and must turn back in dejection unless they save vs. spell. Affected creatures submit to the demands of any opponent – for example, surrender, get out, etc. The hopelessness lasts for 3d4 turns; during this period it is 25% probable that affected creatures take no action during any round, and 25% likely that those taking action turn back or retire from battle, as applicable.

Insanity: One or more creatures whose total hit points do not exceed 120 become insane and remain so, acting as if a Confusion spell had been placed upon them, until a Heal, Restoration, or Wish spell is used to remove the madness.

Pain: All creatures are afflicted with wracking pains shooting through their bodies, causing a -2 penalty to Dexterity and a -4 penalty to attack rolls for 2d10 turns.

Sleep: All creatures under 8+1 Hit Dice immediately fall into a catatonic slumber and cannot be awakened for 1d12+4 turns.

Stunning: One or more creatures whose total hit points do not exceed 160 are stunned and reeling for 3d4 rounds, dropping anything they are holding.

The type of Symbol cannot be recognized without being read and thus activating its effects.

The material components of this spell are powdered black opal and diamond dust, worth not less than 5,000 gp each.

Trap the Soul
(Conjuration/Summoning)

Level: 8

Range: 10 yards

Components: V, S, M

Duration: Permanent until broken

Casting Time: Special + 1

Area of Effect: 1 creature

Saving Throw: Special

This spell forces the creature's life force (and its material body) into a special prison gem enchanted by the spellcaster. The creature must be seen by the caster when the final word is uttered. The spell can be triggered in one of two ways. First, the final word of the spell can be spoken when the creature is within spell range. This allows magic resistance (if any) and a saving throw vs. spell to avoid the effect. If the creature's real name is spoken as well, any magic resistance is ignored and the saving throw vs. spell suffers a penalty of -2. If the saving throw is successful, the prison gem shatters. The second method is far more insidious, for it tricks the victim into accepting a trigger object inscribed with the final spell word, automatically placing the creature's soul in the trap. To use this method, both the creature's true name and the trigger word must be inscribed on the trigger item when the creature is enchanted. A Sympathy spell can also be placed on the trigger item. As soon as the subject creature picks up or accepts the trigger item, its life force is automatically transferred to the gem, without the benefit of magic resistance or saving throw. The gem prison will hold the trapped entity indefinitely, or until the gem is broken and the life force is released, allowing the material body to reform. If the trapped creature is a powerful creature from another plane (which could mean a character trapped by an inhabitant of another plane when the character is not on the Prime Material Plane), it can be required to perform a service immediately upon being freed. Otherwise, the creature can go free once the gem imprisoning it is broken. Before the actual casting of the Trap the Soul spell, the magic-user must prepare the prison, a gem of at least 1,000 gp value for every Hit Die or level of experience possessed by the creature to be trapped (for example, it requires a gem of 10,000 gp value to trap a 10 Hit Die or 10th level creature). If the gem is not valuable enough, it shatters when the entrapment is attempted. Note that while characters have no concept of level as such, the value of the gem needed to trap an individual can be researched. Remember that this value can change over time as characters advance.

Creating the prison gem requires an Enchant an Item spell and the placement of a Maze spell into the gem, thereby forming the prison to contain the life force.

Zarba's Fist of Rage
(Evocation)

Level: 8

Range: 5 yds./level

Components: V, S, M

Duration: 1 rd./level

Casting Time: 8 segments

Area of Effect: Special

Saving Throw: None

The Zarba's Fist of Rage spell brings forth a huge, disembodied hand that is balled into a fist. This magical member is under the mental control of the spellcaster, who can cause it to strike one opponent each round. No concentration is required once the spell is cast. The clenched fist never misses, but it can only strike as directed by the caster. Thus, it can be fooled by invisibility or other methods of concealment and misdirection. The effectiveness of its blows vary from round to round.

d20 Roll	Result
1-12	Glancing blow – 1d6 hp
13-16	Solid punch – 2d6 hp
17-19	Hard punch – 3d6 hp; opponent is stunned for next round
20	Crushing blow* – 4d6 hp; opponent is stunned for next three rounds

The magic-user adds +4 to the die rolls of subsequent attacks if the opponent is stunned, as the opponent is not capable of dodging or defending against the attack effectively.

The Fist has an Armor Class of 0, and is destroyed by damage equal to the hit points of its caster at full health.

The material component of this spell is a leather glove and a small device (similar to brass knuckles) consisting of four rings joined so as to form a slightly curved line, with an "I" upon which the bottoms of the rings rest. The device must be fashioned of an alloy of copper and zinc.

Ninth Level Spells

Astral Spell
(Evocation)

Level: 9

Range: Touch

Components: V, S

Duration: Special

Casting Time: 9 segments

Area of Effect: Special

Saving Throw: None

By means of the Astral Spell, a magic-user can project his astral body into the Astral Plane, leaving his physical body and material possessions behind in the Prime Material Plane. Only magical items can be brought into the Astral Plane (although non-magical items could be rendered temporarily magical through the use of some spells, if the GM allows). As the Astral Plane touches upon the first levels of all of the Outer Planes, the magic-user can travel astrally to any of the Outer Planes at will. The caster then leaves the Astral Plane, forming a body in the plane of existence he has chosen to enter. It is also possible to travel astrally anywhere in the Prime Material Plane by means of the Astral Spell, but a second body cannot be formed in the Prime Material Plane.

As a general rule, a person astrally projected can be seen only by creatures in the Astral Plane. At all times, the astral body is connected to the material body by a silvery cord. If the cord is broken, the affected person is killed, astrally and materially; however, normally only a psychic wind can cause the cord to break. When a second body is formed in a different plane, the silvery cord remains invisibly attached to the new body. If the astral form is slain, the cord simply returns to the original body where it rests in the Prime Material Plane, reviving it from its state of suspended animation. Although astrally projected persons are able to function in the Astral Plane, their actions do not affect creatures not existing in the Astral Plane. The spell lasts until the magic-user desires to end it, or until it is terminated by some outside means (such as a Dispel Magic spell or the destruction of the magic-user's body in the Prime Material Plane). The magic-user can project the astral forms of up to seven other creatures with him by means of the astral spell, providing the creatures are linked in a circle with the magic-user. These fellow travelers are dependent upon the magic-user and can be stranded. Travel in the Astral Plane can be slow or fast, according to the magic-user's desire. The ultimate destination arrived at is subject to the conceptualization of the magic-user. Any magical items can go into the Astral Plane, but most become temporarily non-magical therein, or in any planes removed from the Prime Material Plane. Armor and weapons of +3 or better might function in other planes, at the GM's option. Artifacts and relics function anywhere. Items drawing their power from a given plane are more powerful in that plane (for example, a Ring of Fire Resistance in the Elemental Plane of Fire or a Sword of Life Stealing in the Negative Energy plane).

Crystalbrittle
(Alteration)

Level: 9

Range: Touch

Components: V, S

Duration: Permanent

Casting Time: 9 segments

Area of Effect: 2 cu. ft./level

Saving Throw: Special

The magic of this spell causes metal, whether as soft as gold or as hard as adamantite, to turn to a crystalline substance as brittle and fragile as crystal. Thus, a sword, metal shield, metal armor or even an Iron Golem can be changed to a delicate, glasslike material easily shattered by any forceful blow. Furthermore, this change is unalterable by any means short of a Wish spell; a Dispel Magic will not reverse the spell. The caster must physically touch the item; if it is an opponent or something an opponent is using or wearing, the magic-user must get into melee and make a successful attack roll. Any single metal item can be affected by the spell. Thus, a suit of armor worn by a creature can be changed to crystal, but the creature's shield would not be affected, and vice versa. All items gain a saving throw equal to their magical bonus value or protection (the GM has this information). A +1/+3 sword would get a 10% (average of the two pluses) chance to save; +5 magical armor has a 25% chance to be unaffected; an Iron Golem has a 15% chance to save (for it is hit only by magical weapons of +3 or better quality). Artifacts and relics constructed of metal may be affected at the discretion of the GM, though it is highly unlikely. Affected items not immediately protected are shattered and permanently destroyed if struck by a normal blow from a metal tool or any weighty weapon, including a staff.

Death Rune
(Necromancy)
Level: 9

Range: 60 feet **Components:** V, S, M
Duration: Permanent **Casting Time:** 9 segments
Area of Effect: 1 creature **Saving Throw:** Negates

In order to cast this spell the magic-user must first create a special prison out of a small gem. The gem must be worth no less than 5000 gold pieces and the Death Rune must be inscribed upon it before it can be used. It may be loose or used to decorate some other item. To activate the Death Rune the magic-user must show the gem to the victim and utter the final command words. Should the victim fail his saving throw his body crumbles and his soul is drawn into the gem. The soul remains trapped inside of the gem until freed by obliterating the Death Rune, crushing the gem, or using a Wish, Hyptor's Disjunction or similar magics. A gem may contain but one soul at a time, and careful examination will reveal whether or not a gem is "full".

Demon Flame
(Conjuration/Summoning)
Level: 9

Range: Caster **Components:** V, S, M
Duration: 1 turn plus round/level **Casting Time:** 9 segments
Area of Effect: 10 foot radius **Saving Throw:** Half damage

This spell surrounds the caster with demonic flames summoned from the lower planes. The flames do not harm the caster, but any other creatures within ten feet of the caster suffer 5d6x10 points of damage (save for half). The Demon Flames are immobile and continue to burn if the caster leaves them until the end of the spell's duration. The material component is a rune-covered horn from a creature of the lower planes. The runes must be drawn using powdered sulfur.

Energy Drain
(Evocation, Necromancy)
Level: 9

Range: Touch **Components:** V, S, M
Duration: Permanent **Casting Time:** 3 segments
Area of Effect: 1 creature **Saving Throw:** None

By casting this spell, the magic-user opens a channel between the plane he is in and the Negative Energy plane, becoming the conductor between the two planes. As soon as he touches (equal to a hit if melee is involved) any living creature, the victim loses two levels (as if struck by a Spectre). A monster loses 2 Hit Dice permanently, both for hit points and attack ability. A character loses levels, Hit Dice, hit points and abilities permanently (until regained through adventuring, if applicable). The material component of this spell is essence of Spectre or Vampire dust. Preparation requires mere moments; the material component is then cast forth, and, upon touching the victim, the magic-user speaks the triggering word, causing the spell to take effect instantly. The spell remains effective for only a single round.

Humans or humanoids brought below zero energy levels by this spell can be animated as Juju Zombies under the control of the caster. The caster always has a 5% (1 in 20) chance to be affected by the dust, losing one point of Constitution at the same time as the victim is drained. When the number of Constitution points lost equals the caster's original Constitution, the caster dies and becomes a Shade.

Fawlgar's Grasping Death
(Necromancy)
Level: 9

Range: 5 ft./level **Components:** V, S, M
Duration: Instantaneous **Casting Time:** 9 segments
Area of Effect: One creature **Saving Throw:** Special

When Fawlgar's Grasping Death spell is cast the caster may force any one creature within the spell's range to make a saving throw or die. In addition the caster has the option of sacrificing one level of experience to enhance the spell. If the spell is enhanced in this fashion the victim gets no save against the spell. If cast on a creature with magic resistance, roll for the magic resistance first. If the resistance holds then the spell has no effect, if the resistance fails the victim must either make a saving throw or the caster can then opt to sacrifice a level and kill the creature without a saving throw. Creatures who are immune to death magics, undead, constructs, and extraplanar creatures are all immune to this spell. The material component is a piece of a used death shroud.

Fireball, Lava Yield
(Evocation)
Level: 9

Range: 10 yds. + 10 yds./level **Components:** V, S, M
Duration: Instantaneous **Casting Time:** 9 segments
Area of Effect: 20-ft. radius **Saving Throw:** 1/2

The Lava Yield Fireball is similar in most respects to a normal Fireball except that the damage dealt is 1d12 per caster level. Note that the fire created by means of this spell is so hot that it can melt a volume of stone equal to the area of effect of the spell.

Fireball, Nuclear Winter
(Evocation)
Level: 9

Range: 10 yds. + 10 yds./level **Components:** V, S, M
Duration: Instantaneous **Casting Time:** 9 segments
Area of Effect: 20-mile radius **Saving Throw:** 1/2

This spell has been rescinded in HackMaster 4th Edition.

Foresight
(Divination)
Level: 9

Range: 0 **Components:** V, S, M
Duration: 2d4 rds. + 1 rd./level **Casting Time:** 1 round
Area of Effect: Special **Saving Throw:** None

This spell grants the caster a powerful sixth sense in relation to himself or another. Although cast upon himself, the magic-user can specify that he or another is the beneficiary of the spell. Once the spell is cast, the magic-user receives instantaneous warnings of impending danger or harm to the object of the spell. Thus, if he were the object of the spell, the magic-user would be warned in advance if a thief were about to attempt to backstab him, or if a creature were about to leap out from an unexpected direction, or if an attacker were specifically targeting him with a spell or missile weapon. When the warnings are about him personally, the magic-user cannot be surprised and always knows the direction from which any attack on him is made. In addition, the spell gives the magic-user a general idea of what action he might take to best protect himself – duck, jump right, close his eyes, etc. – and gives him a defensive bonus of 2 to his Armor Class. When another person is the object of the spell, the magic-user receives warnings about that person. He must still communicate this to the other person to negate any surprise. Shouting a warning, yanking the person back, and even telepathically communicating through a Crystal Ball can all be accomplished before the trap is sprung, if the magic-user does not hesitate. However, the object of the spell does not gain the defensive bonus to his Armor Class. The material component for this spell is a hummingbird's feather.

Gate

(Conjuration/Summoning)

Level: 9

Range: 30 yards	**Components:** V, S
Duration: Special	**Casting Time:** 9 segments
Area of Effect: Special	**Saving Throw:** None

The casting of a Gate spell has two effects. First, it causes an interdimensional connection between the plane of existence the magic-user is on and the plane on which dwells a specific being of great power; thus, the being is able to merely step through the Gate from its plane to that of the caster. Second, the utterance of the spell attracts the attention of the sought-after dweller on the other plane. When casting the spell, the magic-user must name the entity he desires to use the Gate and come to the magic-user's aid. There is a 100% certainty that something steps through the Gate. Unless the GM has some facts prepared regarding the minions serving the being called forth by the Gate spell, the being itself comes. If the matter is trifling, the being might leave, inflict an appropriate penalty on the magic-user, or attack the magic-user. If the matter is of middling importance, the being can take some positive action to set matters right, then demand appropriate repayment. If the matter is urgent, the being can act accordingly and ask whatever is its wont thereafter, if appropriate. The actions of the being that comes through depend on many factors, including the alignments of the magic-user and the gawd, the nature of his companions, and who or what opposes or threatens the magic-user. Such beings generally avoid direct conflict with their equals or betters. The being Gated in will either return immediately (very unlikely) or remain to take action. Casting this spell ages the magic-user five years.

Hyptor's Disjunction

(Alteration, Enchantment)

Level: 9

Range: 0	**Components:** V
Duration: Instantaneous	**Casting Time:** 9 segments
Area of Effect: 30-ft. radius	**Saving Throw:** Special

When this spell is cast, all magic and magical items within the radius of the spell, except those on the person of or being touched by the spellcaster, are Disjoined. That is, spells being cast are separated into their individual components (usually spoiling the effect as a Dispel Magic spell does), and permanent and enchanted magical items must successfully save (vs. spell if actually cast on a creature, or vs. a Dispel Magic spell otherwise) or be turned into normal items. Even artifacts and relics are subject to Hyptor's Disjunction, though there is only a 1% chance per caster experience level of actually affecting such powerful items. Thus, all potions, scrolls, rings, rods, miscellaneous magical items, artifacts and relics, arms and armor, swords, and miscellaneous weapons within 30 feet of the spellcaster can possibly lose all their magical properties when the Hyptor's Disjunction spell is cast. The caster also has a 1% chance per experience level of destroying an Antimagic Shell. If the Shell survives the Disjunction, no items within it are Disjoined. Note: Destroying artifacts is a dangerous business, and 95% likely to attract the attention of some powerful being who has an interest or connection with the device. Additionally, if an artifact is destroyed, the casting magic-user must roll a successful saving throw vs. spell with a -4 penalty or permanently lose all spellcasting abilities.

Imprisonment

(Abjuration)

Reversible

Level: 9

Range: Touch	**Components:** V, S
Duration: Permanent	**Casting Time:** 9 segments
Area of Effect: 1 creature	**Saving Throw:** None

When an Imprisonment spell is cast and the victim is touched, the recipient is entombed in a state of suspended animation (see the 9th level magic-user spell Temporal Stasis) in a small sphere far beneath the surface of the earth. The victim remains there unless a reverse of the spell, with the creature's name and background, is cast. Magical search by a Crystal Ball, a Locate Object spell or similar means will not reveal the fact that a creature is Imprisoned. The Imprisonment spell functions only if the subject creature's name and background are known. The reverse spell, Freedom, cast upon the spot at which a creature was entombed and sunk into the earth, causes it to reappear at that spot. If the caster does not perfectly intone the name and background of the creature to be freed, there is a 10% chance that 1 to 100 creatures will be freed from Imprisonment at the same time. Note: The exact details of any creatures freed are up to the GM. A random method of determining this is to roll percentile dice twice (once for imprisoned creature density and once for a base number of creatures at maximum density). The rolls are multiplied and rounded to the nearest whole number. Each released creature has a 10% chance to be in the area of the spellcaster. If monsters are being generated randomly, roll 1d20 for level, with rolls of 9+ considered 9, and the exact monsters determined by the random encounter tables. For example, if the initial rolls were 22 and 60, the number of monsters released is .22 x .60 = .1320 = 13 monsters. Since only 10% of these will be in the immediate vicinity of the caster, the magic-user may encounter only one or two of them.

Meteor Swarm

(Evocation)

Level: 9

Range: 40 yds. + 10 yds./level	**Components:** V, S
Duration: Instantaneous	**Casting Time:** 9 segments
Area of Effect: Special	**Saving Throw:** Half (none)

A Meteor Swarm is a very powerful and spectacular spell which is similar to the Fireball spell in many aspects. When it is cast, either four spheres of 2-foot diameter or eight spheres of 1-foot diameter spring from the outstretched hand of the magic-user and streak in a straight line to the distance demanded by the spellcaster, up to the maximum range. Any creature in the straight-line path of these missiles receives the full effect, without benefit of a saving throw. The meteor missiles leave a fiery trail of sparks, and each bursts as a Fireball. The large spheres (2-foot diameter) inflict 10d4 points of damage, bursting in a diamond or box pattern. Each has a 30-foot diameter area of effect, and each sphere is 20 feet apart along the sides of the pattern, creating overlapping areas of effect and exposing the center to all four blasts. The smaller spheres (1-foot diameter) each have a 15-foot diameter area of effect, and each inflicts 5d4 points of damage. They burst in a pattern of a box within a diamond or vice versa, with each of the outer sides 20 feet long. Note that the center has four areas of overlapping effect, and there are numerous peripheral areas that have two overlapping areas of effect. A saving throw for each area of effect will indicate whether full damage or half damage is sustained by creatures within each area, except as already stated with regard to the missiles impacting.

Monster Summoning VII

(Conjuration/Summoning)

Level: 9

Range: Special	**Components:** V, S, M
Duration: 8 rds. + 1 rd./level	**Casting Time:** 9 segments
Area of Effect: 90-yd. radius	**Saving Throw:** None

This spell is much like the 3rd level spell Monster Summoning I, except that this spell summons one or two 7th level monsters that appear one round after the spell is cast, or one 8th level monster that appears two rounds after the spell is cast.

Power Word, Kill

(Conjuration/Summoning)

Level: 9

Range: 5 yds./2 levels	**Components:** V
Duration: Permanent	**Casting Time:** 1 segment
Area of Effect: 10-ft. radius	**Saving Throw:** None

When a Power Word, Kill spell is uttered, one or more creatures of any type within the spell range and area of effect are slain. The Power Word kills either one creature with up to 60 hit points, or multiple creatures with 10 or fewer hit points each, to a maximum of 120 hit points total. The option to attack a single creature or multiple creatures must be stated along with the spell range and center of the area of effect. The current hit points of the creatures are used.

Prismatic Sphere

(Abjuration, Conjuration/Summoning)

Level: 9

Range: 0

Duration: 1 turn/level

Area of Effect: 20 ft. diameter sphere

Components: V

Casting Time: 7 segments

Saving Throw: Special

This spell enables the magic-user to conjure up an opaque globe of shimmering, multi-colored spheres of light to surround him which give protection from all forms of attack. This scintillating Sphere flashes all the seven colors of the visible spectrum, and each of these spheres of color has a different power and purpose. Any creature with fewer than eight hit dice will be blinded for from 2 to 8 turns by the colors of the Sphere. This phenomenon is immobile and only the spell caster can pass in and out the Prismatic Sphere without harm. Note that typically the upper hemisphere of the globe will be visible, as the spell caster is at the center of the Sphere, so the lower half is usually hidden by the floor surface he is standing upon. The colors and effects of the Prismatic Sphere, as well as what will negate each globe, are:

Color of Globe	Order of Globe	Effects of Globe	Spell Negated By
red	1st	prevents all non-magical missiles - inflicts 10 hit points of damage	Cone of Cold
orange	2nd	prevents all magical missiles inflicts 20 hit points of damage	Gust of Wind
yellow-,	3rd	prevents poisons, gases, and petrification - inflicts 40 hit points of damage	Disintegrate
green	4th	prevents all breath weapons save vs. poison or dead	Wall Passage
blue	5th	prevents location/detection and psionics; - save vs. petrification or turned to stone	Magic Missile
indigo	6th	prevents all magical spells save vs. wand or insane	Continual Light
violet	7th	force field protection - save vs. magic or sent to another plane	Dispel Magic

Note that a Rod of Cancellation will destroy a Prismatic Sphere. Otherwise, anything entering the Sphere will be destroyed, any creature subject to the effects of each and every globe as indicated, i.e. 70 hit points of damage plus death, petrification, insanity and/or instantaneous transportation to another plane, and only the four latter effects are subject to saving throws. The individual globes may be destroyed by appropriate magical attacks in consecutive order, the first globe destroyed before any others, then the 2nd, etc.

Shape Change

(Alteration)

Range: 0

Duration: 1 turn/level

Area of Effect: The caster

Components: V, S, M

Casting Time: 9 segments

Saving Throw: None

With this spell, a magic-user is able to assume the form of any living thing or creature below demigawd status (greater or lesser gawd, singular dragon type, or the like). The spellcaster becomes the creature he wishes, and has all of its abilities save those dependent upon Intelligence, innate magical abilities, and magic resistance, for the mind of the creature is that of the spellcaster. Thus, he can change into a Griffon and fly away, then to an Efreeti and fly through a roaring flame, then to a Titan to lift up a wagon, etc. These creatures have whatever hit points the magic-user had at the time of the shape change. Each alteration in form requires only a second, and no system shock is incurred. For example, a magic-user is in combat and assumes the form of a Will o' Wisp. When this form is no longer useful, the magic-user changes into a Stone Golem and walks away. When pursued, the golem-shape is changed to that of a flea, which hides on a horse until it can hop off and become a bush. If detected as the latter, the magic-user can become a dragon, an ant or just about anything he is familiar with. A magic-user adopting another form also adopts its vulnerabilities. For example, a magic-user who becomes a Spectre is powerless in daylight and is subject to being turned, controlled or destroyed by opposing clerics. Unlike similar spells, a magic-user who is killed in another form does not revert to his original shape, which may disallow certain types of revivification. The material component is a jade circlet worth no less than 5,000 g.p., which shatters at the end of the spell's duration. In the meantime, the circlet is left in the wake of the Shape Change, and premature shattering ends the spell immediately.

Succor

(Alteration, Enchantment)

Reversible

Level: 9

Range: Touch

Duration: Special

Area of Effect: 1 individual

Components: V, S, M

Casting Time: 1 to 4 days

Saving Throw: None

By casting this spell, the magic-user creates a powerful magic in some specially-prepared object – a statuette, a jeweled rod, a gem, etc. This object radiates magic, for it contains the power to instantaneously transport its possessor to the abode of the magic-user who created it. Once the item is enchanted, the magic-user must give it willingly to an individual, at the same time informing him of a command word to be spoken when the item is to be used. To make use of the item, the recipient must speak the command word at the same time that he rends or breaks the item. When this is done, the individual and all that he is wearing and carrying are instantly transported to the abode of the magic-user. No other creatures can be affected. The reversed application of the spell transports the magic-user to the immediate vicinity of the possessor of the enchanted item, when it is broken and the command word spoken. The magic-user will have a general idea of the location and situation of the possessor, but has no choice whether or not to go (making this a rare casting indeed!). The material components used include gemstones totaling not less than 5,000 gp value (whether they are faceted gems or not is immaterial). The components can be enchanted only once per month (usually on a night of a clear full moon). At that time, the object is set for the type of Succor and its final destination (either the location of the spellcasting or an area well known to the magic-user).

Teleport Intercampaignia

(Alteration)

Level: 9

Range: Special

Duration: Instantaneous

Area of Effect: Special

Components: V, S

Casting Time: 1 segment

Saving Throw: None

This spell allows the magic-user to Teleport Without Error himself and/or up to six other characters holding hands and standing in a circle to the campaign world of another GM. The new GM may either randomly determine where the Teleporting characters end up or choose the location himself. The magic-user casting this spell must have firsthand knowledge of the campaign world to which he is Teleporting. All official HMPA rules for characters moving to a new campaign world apply.

Teleport Intergenre

(Alteration)

Level: 9

Range: Special

Duration: Instantaneous

Area of Effect: Special

Components: V, S

Casting Time: 1 segment

Saving Throw: None

This spell works exactly like a Teleport Intercampaignia spell except that it Teleports the targets into another Hackmaster supported game genre, such as Cattlepunk, HackNoia, Spacehack, and so on.

Temporal Stasis

(Alteration)

Reversible

Level: 9

Range: 10 yards

Duration: Permanent

Area of Effect: 1 creature

Components: V, S, M

Casting Time: 9 segments

Saving Throw: None

Upon casting this spell, the magic-user places the recipient creature into a state of suspended animation. This cessation of time means that the creature does not grow older. Its body functions virtually cease. This state persists until the magic is removed by a Dispel Magic spell or the reverse of the spell (Temporal Reinstatement) is uttered. Note that the reverse requires only a single word and no somatic or material components. The material component of a Temporal Stasis spell is a powder composed of diamond, emerald, ruby and sapphire dust, with each crushed stone worth at least 100 g.p.

Time Stop

(Alteration)

Level: 9
Range: 0
Duration: Special
Area of Effect: 15-ft. radius sphere

Components: V
Casting Time: 9 segments
Saving Throw: None

Upon casting a Time Stop spell, the magic-user causes the flow of time to stop for one round in the area of effect. Outside this area the sphere simply seems to shimmer for an instant. Inside the sphere, the caster is free to act for 1d3 rounds of apparent time. The magic-user can move and act freely within the area where time is stopped, but all other creatures, except for those of demigawd and greater status or unique creatures, are frozen in their actions, for they are literally between ticks of the time clock. The spell duration is subjective to the caster. Nothing can enter the area of effect without being stopped in time also. If the magic-user leaves the area, the spell is immediately negated. When the spell duration ceases, the magic-user is again operating in normal time. Note: It is recommended that the GM use a stopwatch or silently count to time this spell. If the caster is unable to complete the intended action before the spell duration expires, he will probably be caught in an embarrassing situation. The use of a Teleport spell before the expiration of the Time Stop spell is permissible.

Weird

(Illusion/Phantasm)

Level: 9
Range: 30 yards
Duration: Concentration
Area of Effect: 20-ft. radius

Components: V, S
Casting Time: 9 segments
Saving Throw: Special

This spell confronts those affected by it with phantasmal images of their most feared enemies, forcing an imaginary combat that seems real, but actually occurs in the blink of an eye. When this spell is cast, the magic-user must be able to converse with the victims to bring the spell into being. During the casting, the magic-user must call out to the creatures to be affected, informing one or all that their final fate, indeed their doom, is now upon them. The force of the magic is such that even if the creatures make their saving throws vs. spell, fear will paralyze them for a full round, and they will lose 1d4 Strength points from this fear (the lost Strength will return in one turn). Failure to save vs. spell causes the creature or creatures to face their nemeses, the opponents most feared and inimical to them. Actual combat must then take place, for no magical means of escape is possible. The foe fought is real for all intents and purposes; affected creatures that lose will die. If a creature's phantasmal nemesis from the Weird spell is slain, the creature emerges with no damage, no loss of items seemingly used in the combat, and no loss of spells likewise seemingly expended. The creature also gains any experience for defeating the Weird, if applicable. Although each round of combat seems normal, it takes only one-tenth of a round. During the course of the spell, the caster must concentrate fully upon maintaining it. If the combat goes beyond 10 rounds, those who saved against the spell can take action. If the caster is disturbed, the Weird spell ends immediately. Creatures attacked while paralyzed with fear are free of the paralysis immediately.

Wish

(Conjuration/Summoning)

Level: 9
Range: Unlimited
Duration: Special
Area of Effect: Special

Components: V
Casting Time: Special
Saving Throw: Special

The Wish spell is a more potent version of a Limited Wish. If it is used to alter reality with respect to damage sustained by a party, to bring a dead creature to life, or to escape from a difficult situation by lifting the spellcaster (and his party) from one place to another, it will not cause the magic-user any disability. Other forms of Wishes, however, cause the spellcaster to weaken (-3 to

Strength) and require 2d4 days of bed rest due to the stresses the Wish places upon time, space, and his body. Regardless of what is wished for, the exact terminology of the Wish spell is likely to be carried out. Casting a Wish spell ages the caster five years. Discretionary power of the GM is necessary in order to maintain game balance. For example, Wishing another creature dead is grossly unfair; the GM might well advance the spellcaster to a future period in which the creature is no longer alive, effectively putting the wishing character out of the campaign.

Zarba's Crushing Hand

(Evocation)

Level: 9
Range: 5 yds./level
Duration: 1 rd./level
Area of Effect: Special

Components: V, S, M
Casting Time: 9 segments
Saving Throw: None

The Zarba's Crushing Hand spell creates a huge, disembodied hand similar to those of the other Zarba's Hand spells. The Crushing Hand is under the mental control of the caster, and he can cause it to grasp and squeeze an opponent. No attack roll is necessary; the Hand automatically grasps and inflicts constriction damage in any round in which the magic-user concentrates. The damage inflicted depends on the number of rounds it acts upon the victim:

1st round	1d10 points
2nd & 3rd rounds	2d10 points
4th round & beyond	4d10 points

The Crushing Hand has an Armor class of 0, has as many hit points as its caster at full strength, and vanishes when destroyed. The Hand is susceptible to normal combat attacks and damaging spells, but if it is struck by an area-effect spell, the person held suffers the same fate as the Hand (i.e., if the Hand fails its saving throw, the victim automatically fails his). The Hand is not effective against noncorporeal or gaseous forms, but it does prevent creatures that are able to slip through small cracks from escaping. If the Hand grasps an item or construction, the appropriate saving throw must be made as if squeezed by a Strength of 25.

The material components of the spell are a glove of snake skin and the shell of an egg.

Appendix D

Cleric and Druid Spells

Notes Regarding Cleric Spells:

All material components required for the various spells are used upon completion of the spell in question, with the notable exceptions of standard religious items (such as religious symbols, prayer beads, or similar devices).

The reversal of some spells might well place the cleric in a questionable position with respect to alignment. The use of spells which promote healing is shunned by evil clerics in many cases. Likewise, spells which are baneful may be used only at peril by clerics of good alignment. Incautious use of spells of opposite alignment will change the cleric's alignment, if such usage continues unchecked. It is up to the player to guard his character's alignment with care.

In any event, the cleric must decide which application of a reversible spell will be used prior to praying for it - it is not possible to have one spell both ways. In like manner, the mere request for a spell (or its opposite) through prayer will not guarantee that the spell will be given to the cleric. As the spell level becomes higher, the cleric's confidence that his gawd will grant the spell will decrease.

Your GM might alter the material components of spells, require only religious adjuncts as material, or just do away with them. Consult your GM in this regard and ask for his ruling and reasoning. Then report him to the HackMaster GM Association for tampering with the rules.

Following the name of each cleric spell, a magical school is given in parentheses. The cleric spells are not really organized into magical schools, so this is provided for reference purposes only. For instance, Wisdom bonuses apply to saving throws vs. enchantment/charm spells. If the appropriate magical school were not listed with cleric spells, it would be hard to figure out which spells were considered to be enchantment/charms. There are few other reasons one might need to know this information.

First Level Cleric Spells

Befriend
(Enchantment/Charm)
Reversible
Level: 1
Range: 0   **Components:** V, S, M
Duration: 1d4 rds. + 1 rd./level   **Casting Time:** 1 segment
Area of Effect: 60-ft. radius   **Saving Throw:** Special

This is the same as the first level magic-user spell except that it is reversible. The victim of the reverse of the spell may attempt to make a saving throw to negate the effects of the spell.

Bless
(Conjuration/Summoning)
Reversible
Level: 1
Range: 60 yds.   **Components:** V, S, M
Duration: 6 rds.   **Casting Time:** 1 round
Area of Effect: 50-ft. cube   **Saving Throw:** None

Upon uttering the Bless spell, the caster raises the morale of friendly creatures and any saving throw rolls they make against fear effects by +1. Furthermore, it raises their attack dice rolls by +1. A blessing, however, affects only those not already engaged in melee combat. The caster determines at what range (up to 60 yards) he will cast the spell. At the instant the spell is completed, it affects all creatures in a 50-foot cube centered on the point selected by the caster (thus, affected creatures leaving the area are still subject to the spell's effect; those entering the area after the casting is completed are not). A second use of this spell is to bless a single item (for example, a crossbow bolt for use against a Rakshasa). The weight of the item is limited to one pound per caster level and the effect lasts until the item is used or the spell

duration ends. Multiple Bless spells are not cumulative. In addition to the verbal and somatic gesture components, the Bless spell requires holy water. This spell can be reversed by the cleric to a Curse spell that, when cast upon enemy creatures, lowers their morale and attack rolls by -1. The Curse spell requires the sprinkling of unholy water.

Ceremony
(Invocation)
Level: 1
Range: Touch   **Components:** V, S, M
Duration: Permanent   **Casting Time:** 1 hour
Area of Effect: One creature, one item, or area (see below)   **Saving Throw:** Special

Ceremony has a number of applications in the religious organization, depending on the level of the cleric. The effect of a Ceremony spell does not leave behind an aura of magic, although in some cases an aura of good or evil might be present (and thus detectable). The specific Ceremony spells can vary from religion to religion, but usually encompass:

> 1st-level cleric: *coming of age, burial, marriage*
> 3rd-level cleric: *dedication, investiture, consecrate item*
> 5th-level cleric: *ordination, special vows*
> 7th-level cleric: *consecrate ground*
> 9th-level cleric: *anathematize*

Each of these varieties of the Ceremony spell requires a cleric of the indicated level or higher, with additional restrictions as described below. For all Ceremony spells except anathematize (see below), no saving throw is called for, since the recipient is either inanimate or presumed to be willing to be affected by the magic; any version of the spell except for anathematize will simply fail if it is cast on a person who (for some reason) is unwilling to receive the benefit. Briefly, the ceremonies listed do the following things:

> **Coming of Age:** is a limited form of the Bless spell which is cast upon a young man (and in some cultures a young woman) at some point relatively early in life, often the age of 12. A young person who receives this spell gets a +1 bonus to any single saving throw, which can be taken at any time after the coming of age ceremony is completed. In some cultures, the coming of age ceremony has a symbolic significance, such that an adolescent must receive this blessing before he can enjoy the rights and privileges of adulthood.
> **Burial:** magically protects a corpse, and bestows it with the blessing of the religious organization. The body is shielded for one week as if by a Protection From Evil spell, and anyone trying to disinter the corpse within that time must make a saving throw versus spell or stop and flee in fear for one turn.
> **Marriage:** has no tangible after-effect (i.e., it does not guarantee happiness or harmony), but it usually carries a moral or legal significance, not dissimilar in nature to the various rites of marriage that are performed in our real world.
> **Dedication:** allows the recipient of the spell to be taken into the ranks of the casting cleric's religion, making that person a sanctioned worshiper of the cleric's gawd. The effect of a dedication is permanent, unless the worshiper demonstrates a desire to change allegiance to a different gawd. In such a case, the earlier dedication can be overridden by a new dedication cast by a cleric of a higher level than the one who performed the previous dedication.
> The rite of **Investiture** must be performed on any aspiring cleric before that character can achieve the status of a first-level cleric.
> **Consecrate item:** must be performed on any object to be placed on an altar or in some other location within a religious edifice. To prevent it from losing its potency, holy (or unholy) water must be kept in a properly consecrated container.

Ordination: must be performed on a cleric before the character can become the priest of a congregation or assume similar sorts of duties, and even an adventuring cleric must be ordained before he can gain followers and establish a following or other sort of group. In all cases, the cleric performing the ordination must be of higher level than the recipient; this ceremony is often conducted as part of the training a cleric receives in order to advance from second to third level.

Special vows: can be received by a would-be cavalier, dark knight or paladin before that character embarks upon a career in the desired profession. The effects of this spell persist for as long as it takes the character to accumulate enough experience points to rise to the upper limit of his current level. The special vows can then be renewed as part of the character's training between levels, or at any time during advancement through the next higher level. A cavalier, dark knight or paladin who has received special vows is immune to the effects of Bestow Curse spells (but not cursed items) for as long as the special vows remain in effect. Additionally, this ceremony renders the subject more susceptible (-4 on saving throw) to any Quest spell cast upon him by a cleric of the same alignment as the caster of the special vows.

Consecrate ground: should be performed upon an area before any holy (unholy) structure is built on the site. A religious edifice constructed on ground that has not been Consecrated will slowly but irrevocably fall into a state of disrepair and has a 1% chance per year, cumulative, of actually collapsing as a result of this oversight. This spell must be cast before the area in question is altered in any way (e.g., landscaping) and before any construction materials are brought to the site; it will have no effect if it is done as an afterthought.

Consecrate ground: can also be used on a plot of land destined for use as a graveyard, and in such a case the graveyard itself automatically turns undead each round with the same effectiveness as a 3rd-level cleric. Or, if the consecration of a would-be graveyard is performed by an evil cleric, any undead creatures occupying the area are treated as if they were being protected and controlled by an evil cleric of 3rd level.

Anathematize: is a form of excommunication where the offender is literally branded on the cheek, forehead, arm or hand with a symbol, sigil or sign that identifies the subject (to those who understand the symbol) as someone who has committed a serious offense in the eyes of his gawd. An unwilling subject of this spell is allowed a saving throw versus spell, at -4, to escape its effects. If the recipient is not truly deserving of the telling brand, the spell fails when cast.

A successful **Atonement** causes the brand to fade, and possibly vanish. If the offending actions were caused magically or by some other external force, the brand utterly disappears. If the offending actions were natural, the brand cannot be completely removed.

The components for the various Ceremony spells vary from religion to religion, but the material component always involves the use of the cleric's holy symbol in one way or another. Standard costs for the casting of these spells are as follows: *coming of age*, 5-15 sp; *burial*, 5-50 gp; *marriage*, 1-20 gp; *dedication*, 1-10 sp (or sometimes free); *investiture*, 1-100 gp (or sometimes free); *item consecration*, usually free; *ordination*, usually free put possibly as much as 200 gp; *special vows*, 1 -100 gp (or sometimes free); *consecrate ground*, 100-600 gp depending on the size of the area to be affected and the level of the cleric performing the spell; and *anathematize* is always performed at no charge, since the casting of this spell is always deemed to be in the best interests of the cleric's religion.

Combine

(Evocation)
Level: 1
Range: Touch **Components:** V, S
Duration: Special **Casting Time:** 1 round
Area of Effect: Circle of clerics **Saving Throw:** None

Using this spell, three to five clerics combine their abilities so that one of them casts spells and turns undead at an enhanced level. The highest-level cleric (or one of them, if two or more are tied for highest) stands alone, while the others join hands in a surrounding circle. The central cleric casts the Combine spell. He temporarily gains one level for each cleric in the circle, up to a maximum gain of four levels. The level increase affects turning undead and spell details that vary with the caster's level.

Note that the central cleric gains no additional spells and that the group is limited to his currently memorized spells. The encircling clerics must concentrate on maintaining the combine effect. They lose all Armor Class bonuses for shield and Dexterity.

If any of them has his concentration broken, the Combine spell ends immediately. If the Combine spell is broken while the central cleric is in the act of casting a spell, that spell is ruined just as if the caster were disturbed.

Spells cast in combination have the full enhanced effect, even if the Combine is broken before the duration of the enhanced spell ends. Note that the combination is not broken if only the central caster is disturbed.

Command

(Enchantment/Charm)
Level: 1
Range: 30 yds. **Component:** V
Duration: 1 round **Casting Time:** 1 segment
Area of Effect: 1 creature **Saving Throw:** None

This spell enables the cleric to command another creature with a single word. The Command must be uttered in a language understood by the creature. The subject will obey to the best of his/its ability only as long as the command is absolutely clear and unequivocal; thus, a Command of "Suicide!" is ignored. A Command to "Die!" causes the creature to fall in a faint or cataleptic state for one round, but thereafter the creature revives and is alive and well. Typical Commands are: back, halt, flee, run, stop, fall, go, leave, surrender, sleep, rest, etc.

No Command affects a creature for more than one round; undead are not affected at all. Creatures with Intelligence of 13 (high) or more, or those with 6 or more Hit Dice (or experience levels) are entitled to a saving throw vs. spell, adjusted for Wisdom. (Creatures with 13 or higher Intelligence and 6 Hit Dice/levels get only one saving throw!)

Create Water

(Alteration)
Reversible
Level: 1
Range: 30 yds. **Components:** V, S, M
Duration: Permanent **Casting Time:** 1 round
Area of Effect: Up to 27 cu. ft. **Saving Throw:** None

When the cleric casts a Create Water spell, up to four gallons of water are generated for every experience level of the caster (for example, a 2nd-level cleric creates up to 8 gallons of water, a 3rd-level cleric up to 12 gallons, etc.). The water is clean and drinkable (it is just like rain water). The created water can be dispelled within a round of its creation; otherwise, its magic fades, leaving normal water that can be used, spilled, evaporated, etc. The reverse of the spell, Destroy Water, obliterates without trace (no vapor, mist, fog, or steam) a like quantity of water. Water can be created or destroyed in an area as small as will actually contain the liquid, or in an area as large as 27 cubic feet (1 cubic yard).

Note that water can neither be created nor destroyed within a creature. For reference purposes, water weighs about 8 pounds per gallon, and a cubic foot of water weighs approximately 62.4 pounds at 60° F. The Create Water spell requires at least a drop of water; the Destroy Water spell, at least a pinch of dust.

Cure Light Wounds

(Necromancy)

Reversible

Level: I

Range: Touch **Components:** V, S

Duration: Permanent **Casting Time:** 5 segments

Area of Effect: Creature touched **Saving Throw:** None

When casting this spell and laying his hand upon a creature, the cleric causes the creature to be healed of 1d4 points of damage per level of the cleric. This healing cannot affect creatures without corporeal bodies, nor can it cure wounds of creatures not living or of extraplanar origin. The reverse of the spell, Cause Light Wounds, operates in the same manner, inflicting 1d4 points of damage per level of the cleric. If a creature tries to avoid this touch, an attack roll is needed to determine if the cleric's hand strikes the opponent and causes such a wound. Curing is permanent only insofar as the creature does not sustain further damage; caused wounds will heal – or can be cured – just as any normal injury.

Detect Evil

(Divination)

Reversible

Level: I

Range: 0 **Components:** V, S, M

Duration: I turn + 5 rds./level **Casting Time:** I round

Area of Effect: 10 ft. x 120 yds. **Saving Throw:** None

Except as noted above, this spell is the same as the second level magic-user spell Detect Evil (q.v.).

Detect Magic

(Divination)

Level: I

Range: 0 **Components:** V, S, M

Duration: I turn **Casting Time:** I round

Area of Effect: 10 ft. x 30 yds. **Saving Throw:** None

Except as noted above, this spell is the same as the first level magic-user spell Detect Magic (q.v.).

Endure Cold/Endure Heat

(Alteration)

Level: I

Range: Touch **Components:** V, S

Duration: I hr./level **Casting Time:** I round

Area of Effect: Creature touched **Saving Throw:** None

The creature receiving this spell is protected from normal extremes of cold or heat (depending on which application the cleric selects at the time of casting). The creature can stand unprotected in temperatures as low as -30° F. or as high as 130° F. (depending on application) with no ill effect. Temperatures beyond these limits inflict 1 point of damage per hour of exposure for every degree beyond the limit.

The spell is immediately cancelled if the recipient is affected by any non-normal heat or cold, such as magic, breath weapons and so on. The cancellation occurs regardless of the application and regardless of whether a heat or cold effect hits the character (for example, an Endure Cold spell is cancelled by magical heat or fire as well as by magical cold). The recipient of the spell does not suffer the first 10 points of damage (after any applicable saving throws) from the heat or cold during the round in which the spell is broken. The spell ends instantly if either resist fire or resist cold is cast upon the recipient.

Flutter Soft

(Alteration)

Level: I

Range: 60 ft. **Components:** V, S, M

Duration: I hour **Casting Time:** I segment

Area of Effect: One creature **Saving Throw:** None

When this spell is cast upon a flying creature it allows that creature to fly in complete silence. This spell will silence the flight of anything from the size of a small bird to a dragon. The material component is an owl feather.

Invisibility to Undead

(Abjuration)

Level: I

Range: Touch **Components:** V, S, M

Duration: 6 rds. **Casting Time:** 4 segments

Area of Effect: I creature **Saving Throw:** Special

This spell causes affected undead to lose track of and ignore the warded creature for the duration of the spell. Undead of 4 or fewer Hit Dice are automatically affected, but those with more Hit Dice receive a saving throw vs. spell to avoid the effect. Note that a cleric protected by this spell cannot turn affected undead. The spell ends immediately if the recipient makes any attack, although casting spells such as Cure Light Wounds, Augury or Chant does not end the ward. The material component is the cleric's holy symbol.

Light

(Alteration)

Reversible

Level: I

Range: 120 yds. **Components:** V, S

Duration: I hr. + I turn/level **Casting Time:** 4 segments

Area of Effect: 20-ft.-radius globe **Saving Throw:** Special

Except as noted above, this spell is the same as the first level magic-user spell Light (q.v.).

Magical Stone

(Enchantment)

Level: I

Range: Touch **Components:** V, S, M

Duration: Special **Casting Time:** 4 segments

Area of Effect: 3 pebbles **Saving Throw:** None

By using this spell, the cleric can temporarily enchant up to three small pebbles, no larger than sling bullets. The Magical Stones can then be hurled or slung at an opponent. If hurled, they can be thrown up to 30 yards, and all three can be thrown in one round. The character using them must roll normally to hit, although the magic of the stones enables any character to be proficient with them.

The stones are considered +1 weapons for determining if a creature can be struck (those struck only by magical weapons, for instance), although they do not have an attack or damage bonus. Each stone that hits inflicts 1d4 points of damage (2d4 points against undead). The magic in each stone lasts only for half an hour, or until used. The material components are the cleric's holy symbol and three small pebbles, unworked by tools or magic of any type.

Protection From Evil

(Abjuration)
Reversible
Level: 1
Range: Touch	**Components:** V, S, M
Duration: 3 rds./level	**Casting Time:** 4 segments
Area of Effect: 1 creature	**Saving Throw:** None

Except as noted above, this spell is the same as the first level magic-user spell Protection From Evil (q.v.).

Purify Food & Drink

(Alteration)
Reversible
Level: 1
Range: 30 yds.	**Components:** V, S
Duration: Permanent	**Casting Time:** 1 round
Area of Effect: 1 cu. ft./level, in a 10 sq. ft. area	**Saving Throw:** None

When cast, this spell makes spoiled, rotten, poisonous, or otherwise contaminated food and water pure and suitable for eating and drinking. Up to 1 cubic foot of food and drink per level can be thus made suitable for consumption.

This spell does not prevent subsequent natural decay or spoilage. Unholy water and similar food and drink of significance is spoiled by Purify Food and Drink, but the spell has no effect on creatures of any type nor upon magical potions. The reverse of the spell is Putrefy Food and Drink. This spoils even holy water; however, it likewise has no effect upon creatures or potions.

Remove Fear

(Abjuration)
Reversible
Level: 1
Range: 10 yds.	**Components:** V, S
Duration: Special	**Casting Time:** 1 segment
Area of Effect: 1 creature/4 levels	**Saving Throw:** Special

The cleric casting this spell instills courage in the spell recipient, raising the creature's saving throw rolls against magical fear attacks by +4 for one turn. If the recipient has recently (that day) failed a saving throw against such an attack, the spell immediately grants another saving throw, with a +4 bonus to the die roll.

For every four levels of the caster, one creature can be affected by the spell (one creature at levels 1 through 4, two creatures at levels 5 through 8, etc.). The reverse of the spell, Cause Fear, causes one creature to flee in panic at maximum movement speed away from the caster for 1d4 rounds. A successful saving throw against the reversed effect negates it, and any Wisdom adjustment also applies. Of course, Cause Fear can be automatically countered by Remove Fear and vice versa. Neither spell has any effect on undead of any sort.

Sanctuary

(Abjuration)
Level: 1
Range: Touch	**Components:** V, S, M
Duration: 2 rds. + 1 rd./level	**Casting Time:** 4 segments
Area of Effect: 1 creature	**Saving Throw:** None

When the cleric casts a Sanctuary spell, any opponent attempting to strike or otherwise directly attack the protected creature must roll a saving throw vs. spell. If the saving throw is successful, the opponent can attack normally and is unaffected by that casting of the spell. If the saving throw is failed, the opponent loses track of and totally ignores the warded creature for the duration of the spell. Those not attempting to attack the subject remain unaffected.

Note that this spell does not prevent the operation of area attacks (Fireball, Ice Storm, etc.). While protected by this spell, the subject cannot take direct offensive action without breaking the spell, but may use non-attack spells or otherwise act in any way that does not violate the prohibition against offensive action. This allows a warded cleric to heal wounds, for example, or to bless, perform an Augury or Chant spell, cast a Light in the area (but not upon an opponent), and so on. The components of the spell include the cleric's holy symbol and a small silver mirror.

Walking Corpse

(Necromancy)
Level: 1
Range: Touch	**Components:** V, S
Duration: 1 week/caster level	**Casting Time:** 1 turn
Area of Effect: 1 creature	**Saving Throw:** None

A Walking Corpse spell renders a single creature ambulatory, often so his companions need not carry his body. The corpse cannot have been dead more than one day per caster level. It continues to rot, but is capable of following the caster at half its normal (living) movement rate. It does nothing else; it does not talk, think, fight, defend itself and automatically fails saving throws, etc. A walking corpse has the maximum number of hit points that it did when it was alive. The walking corpse can be turned or destroyed as a zombie. If a cleric is turning undead and a walking corpse is within his line of sight, the walking corpse can still be accidentally turned or destroyed as a Zombie, even by the raising cleric. The creature gains 2d6 rolls on Table 6A: Flaws and Quirks, but the GM rolls these and keeps them secret until such time as the creature is fully raised or resurrected. Exceptions are obvious flaws, such as losing an ear or finger. The walking corpse can be fully restored to life by a Raise Dead, Resurrection, Limited Wish or Wish spell.

Second Level Cleric Spells

Aid

(Necromancy, Conjuration)
Level: 2
Range: Touch	**Components:** V, S, M
Duration: 1 rd. + 1 rd./level	**Casting Time:** 5 segments
Area of Effect: 1 creature	**Saving Throw:** None

The recipient of this spell gains the benefit of a Bless spell (+1 to attack rolls and saving throws) and a special bonus of 1d8 additional hit points for the duration of the spell. The Aid spell enables the recipient to actually have more hit points than his full normal total. The bonus hit points are lost first when the recipient takes damage; they cannot be regained by curative magic. For example, a 1st-level fighter has 27 hit points, suffers 4 points of damage (27-4 = 23), and then receives an Aid spell that gives 7 additional hit points. The fighter now has 30 hit points, 3 of which are temporary. If he is then hit for 5 points of damage, 2 normal hit points and all 3 temporary hit points are lost. He then receives a Cure Light Wounds spell that heals 4 points of damage, restoring him to his original 27 hit points.

Note that the operation of the spell is unaffected by permanent hit point losses due to energy drain, Hit Die losses, the loss of a familiar, or the operation of certain artifacts; the temporary hit point gain is figured from the new, lower total. The material components of this spell are a tiny strip of white cloth with a sticky substance (such as tree sap) on the ends, plus the cleric's holy symbol.

Animated Corpse

(Necromancy)
Level: 2
Range: Touch.	**Components:** V, S
Duration: 1 week/caster level	**Casting Time:** 1 turn
Area of Effect: 1 creature	**Saving Throw:** None

An Animate Corpse spell brings a dead creature back to a state somewhat resembling life. The corpse cannot have been dead more than one day per caster level. It continues to rot, but is capable of following the caster at half its normal (living) movement rate. An animated corpse is effectively a two HD Zombie that retains some of its mind. While it does not retain any class or racial abilities, it can walk, talk, remember, complain, roll saving throws, etc., but it cannot attack. The walking corpse can be turned or destroyed as a zombie. If a cleric is turning undead and a walking corpse is within his line of sight, the walking corpse can still be accidentally turned or destroyed as a Zombie, even by the raising cleric. The creature gains 2d6 rolls on Table 6A: Flaws and Quirks, but the GM rolls these and keeps them secret until such time as the creature is fully raised or resurrected. Exceptions are obvious flaws, such as losing an ear or finger. The animated corpse can be fully restored by a Raise Dead, Resurrection, Limited Wish or Wish spell.

Augury

(Divination)

Level: 2

Range: 0   **Components:** V, S, M

Duration: Special   **Casting Time:** 2 rds.

Area of Effect: Special   **Saving Throw:** None

The cleric casting an Augury spell seeks to divine whether an action in the immediate future (within one-half hour) will benefit or harm the party. For example, if a party is considering the destruction of a weird seal that closes a portal, an Augury spell can be used to find if weal or woe will be the immediate result. If the spell is successful, the GM yields some indication of the probable outcome: "weal," "woe," or possibly a cryptic puzzle or rhyme. The base chance for receiving a meaningful reply is 70%, plus 1% for each level of the cleric casting the spell; for example, 71% at 1st level, 72% at 2nd, etc.

Your GM determines any adjustments for the particular conditions of each Augury. For example, if the question is "Will we do well if we venture to the third level?" and a terrible Troll guarding 10,000 sp and a shield +1 lurks near the entrance to the level (which the GM estimates the party could beat after a hard fight), the augury might be: "Great risk brings great reward." If the Troll is too strong for the party, the augury might be: "Woe and destruction await!" Likewise, a party casting several Auguries about the same action in quick succession might receive identical answers, regardless of the dice rolls.

The material component for an Augury spell is a set of gem-inlaid sticks, dragon bones, or similar tokens of at least 1,000 gp value (which are not expended in casting).

Chant

(Conjuration/Summoning)

Level: 2

Range: 0   **Components:** V, S

Duration: Time of chanting   **Casting Time:** 2 rds.

Area of Effect: 30-ft. radius   **Saving Throw:** None

By means of the Chant spell, the cleric brings special favor upon himself and his party, and causes harm to his enemies. When the Chant spell is completed, all attack and damage rolls and saving throws made by those in the area of effect who are friendly to the cleric gain +1 bonuses, while those of the cleric's enemies suffer -1 penalties. This bonus/penalty continues as long as the caster continues to chant the mystic syllables and is stationary. However, an interruption (such as an attack that succeeds and causes damage, grappling with the chanter, or a Silence spell) breaks the spell.

Multiple Chants are not cumulative; however, if the 3rd-level Prayer spell is spoken while a cleric of the same religious persuasion (not merely alignment) is chanting, the effect is increased to +2 and -2.

Cure Moderate Wounds

(Necromancy)

Reversible

Level: 2

Range: Touch   **Components:** V, S

Duration: Permanent   **Casting Time:** 5 segments

Area of Effect: 1 creature   **Saving Throw:** None

This spell is exactly like a Cure Light Wounds spell except that it heals 1d6 points of damage per level of the cleric. Its reverse, Cause Moderate Wounds, causes 1d6 points of damage per caster level.

Detect Charm

(Divination)

Reversible

Level: 2

Range: 0   **Components:** V, S

Duration: 1 turn   **Casting Time:** 1 round

Area of Effect: 1 creature/rd.   **Saving Throw:** Negates

When used by a cleric, this spell can detect if a person or monster within 30 yards is under the influence of a Charm spell or similar control, such as Hypnosis, Suggestion, Beguiling, possession, etc. The creature rolls a saving throw vs. spell and, if successful, the caster learns nothing about that particular creature from the casting. A caster who learns that a creature is being influenced has a 5% chance per level to determine the exact type of influence.

Up to 10 different creatures can be checked before the spell wanes. If the creature is under more than one such effect, only the information that the charms exist is gained. The type (since there are conflicting emanations) is impossible to determine. The reverse of the spell, Undetectable Charm, completely masks all charms on a single creature for 24 hours.

Diminished Rite

(Necromancy)

Level: 2

Range: Touch   **Components:** V, S

Duration: Permanent   **Casting Time:** 1 round

Area of Effect: One creature   **Saving Throw:** None

A Diminished Rite will bring any dead creature back to life in the same way as a Raise Dead spell. It can be used any length of time after the death of said creature, provided the body has not significantly decayed. The creature will, however, lose some of its special essence. Anyone brought back to life with a Diminished Rite spell comes back with only half of their levels or Hit Dice, rounded down (to a minimum of first level or the creature's original Hit Dice). In addition, the recipient must roll a skill check against each of their skills or they go down by 20 points and take 2d6 rolls on Table 6A: Flaws and Quirks.

A full Resurrection or Restoration can be conducted later to restore the creature's lost levels and skill points, as long as it is done within a time period of 1 month times the creature's original level or Hit Dice. Thus, an 18th level character raised with a Diminished Rite spell would be only 9th level, but could be fully restored with Resurrection or Restoration if cast within 18 months. If the creature dies again before his lost skills and levels or Hit Dice are restored to him, they are forever lost.

A cleric gains experience points for raising the dead as if he defeated that creature in individual combat.

Dust Devil

(Conjuration/Summoning)

Level: 2

Range: 30 yds.   **Components:** V, S

Duration: 2 rds./level   **Casting Time:** 2 rds.

Area of Effect: 5 x 4 ft. cone   **Saving Throw:** None

This spell enables a cleric to conjure up a weak air elemental—a dust devil of AC 4, 2 HD, MV 180 feet per round, one attack per round for 1d4 points of damage—which can be hit by normal weapons. The Dust Devil appears as a small whirlwind 1 foot in diameter at its base, 5 feet tall, and 3 to 4 feet across at the top. It moves as directed by the cleric, but dissipates if it is ever separated from the caster by more than 30 yards. Its winds are sufficient to put out torches, small campfires, exposed lanterns, and other small, open flames of nonmagical origin.

The Dust Devil can hold a gas cloud or a creature in gaseous form at bay or push it away from the caster (though it cannot damage or disperse such a cloud). If skimming along the ground in an area of loose dust, sand, or ash, the Dust Devil picks up those particles and disperses them in a 10-foot-diameter cloud centered on itself. The cloud obscures normal vision, and creatures caught within are blinded while inside and for one round after they emerge.

A spellcaster caught in the Dust Devil or its cloud while casting must make a saving throw vs. spell to keep his concentration, or the spell is ruined. Any creature native to the Elemental Plane of Air—even another Dust Devil—can disperse a Dust Devil with a single hit.

Enthrall
(Enchantment/Charm)
Level: 2
Range: 0   **Components:** V, S
Duration: Special   **Casting Time:** 1 round
Area of Effect: 90-ft. radius   **Saving Throw:** Negates

A cleric using this spell can enthrall an audience that can fully understand his language. Those in the area of effect must successfully save vs. spell or give the caster their undivided attention, totally ignoring their surroundings. Those of a race or religion unfriendly to the caster's have a +4 bonus to the roll. Any Wisdom adjustment also applies. Creatures with 4 or more levels or Hit Dice, or with a Wisdom of 16 or better, are unaffected.

To cast the spell, the caster must speak without interruption for a full round. Thereafter, the enchantment lasts as long as the cleric speaks, to a maximum of one hour. Those enthralled take no action while the cleric speaks, and for 1d3 rounds thereafter while they discuss the matter. Those entering the area of effect must also successfully save vs. spell or become enthralled. Those not enthralled are 50% likely every turn to hoot and jeer in unison. If there is excessive jeering, the rest are allowed a new saving throw. The speech ends (but the 1d3 round delay still applies) if the cleric is successfully attacked or performs any action other than speaking. If the audience is attacked, the spell ends and the audience reacts immediately, rolling a reaction check with respect to the source of the interruption, at a penalty of -10.

Note: When handling a large number of saving throws for similar creatures, the GM can assume an average to save time; for example, a crowd of 20 men with a base saving throw of 16 (25% success chance) will have 15 men enthralled and five not.

Find Traps
(Divination)
Level: 2
Range: 0   **Components:** V, S
Duration: 3 turns   **Casting Time:** 5 segments
Area of Effect: 10 ft. x 30 yds.   **Saving Throw:** None

When a cleric casts a Find Traps spell, all traps—concealed normally or magically, of magical or mechanical nature—become apparent to him. Note that this spell is directional, and the caster must face the desired direction in order to determine if a trap is laid in that particular direction. A trap is any device or magical ward that meets three criteria: it can inflict a sudden or unexpected result, the spellcaster would view the result as undesirable or harmful, and the harmful or undesirable result was specifically intended as such by the creator. Thus, traps include alarms, glyphs, and similar spells or devices.

The caster learns the general nature of the trap (magical or mechanical) but not its exact effect, nor how to disarm it. Close examination will, however, enable the caster to sense what intended actions might trigger it. Note that the caster's divination is limited to his knowledge of what might be unexpected and harmful. The spell cannot predict actions of creatures (hence, a concealed murder hole or ambush is not a trap), nor are natural hazards considered traps (a cavern that floods during a rain, a wall weakened by age, a naturally poisonous plant, etc.). If the GM is using specific glyphs or sigils to identify magical wards (see the 3rd-level spell Glyph of Warding), this spell shows the form of the glyph or mark. The spell does not detect traps that have been disarmed or are otherwise inactive.

Heal Light Wounds
(Necromancy)
Level: 2
Range: 5 ft./level   **Components:** V, S
Duration: Permanent   **Casting Time:** 5 segments
Area of Effect: 1 creature   **Saving Throw:** None

By using this spell a cleric can restore 1d4 lost hit points per level to any one creature within the range of the spell. The hit points are healed in the same way as a Cure Light Wounds spell and are subject to the same limitations.

Know Alignment
(Divination)
Reversible
Level: 2
Range: 10 yds.   **Components:** V, S
Duration: 1 turn   **Casting time:** 1 round
Area of Effect: 1 creature or object   **Saving Throw:** Negates

Except as noted above, this spell is the same as the second level magic-user spell Know Alignment (q.v.).

Premonition
(Divination)
Level: 2
Range: Touch   **Components:** V, S, M
Duration: 2 rounds/level   **Casting Time:** 2 segments
Area of Effect: One creature   **Saving Throw:** Negates

The recipient of this spell begins to get a "bad feeling" whenever something bad is about to happen to him. While the spell lasts the recipient is immune to being surprised, cannot be the victim of a backstab and should get a moment's warning if he approaches something dangerous.

Note that this spell does not give specific information, so while it would make a character feel uneasy about a trapped chest it wouldn't tell him that there was a gas trap inside. A character would get a bad feeling about a mountain pass, but wouldn't immediately know that there was a band of Ogres waiting to ambush him. The spell component is the cleric's holy or unholy symbol.

Resist Fire/Resist Cold
(Alteration)
Level: 2
Range: Touch   **Components:** V, S, M
Duration: 1 rd./level   **Casting Time:** 5 segments
Area of Effect: 1 creature   **Saving Throw:** None

When this spell is placed upon a creature by a cleric, the creature's body is toughened to withstand heat or cold, as chosen by the caster. The spell grants the creature complete immunity to mild conditions (standing naked in the snow or reaching into an ordinary fire to pluck out a note). The recipient can somewhat resist intense heat or cold (whether natural or magical in origin), such as red-hot charcoal, a large amount of burning oil, flaming swords, fire storms, Fireballs, Meteor Swarms, Red Dragon's breath, frostbrand swords, Ice Storms, Wands of Frost or White Dragon's breath. In all of these cases, the temperature affects the creature to some extent.

The recipient of the spell gains a bonus of +3 to saving throws against such attack forms and all damage sustained is reduced by 50%; therefore, if the saving throw is failed, the creature sustains one-half damage, and if the saving throw is successful, the creature sustains only one-quarter damage. Resistance to fire lasts for one round for each experience level of the cleric placing the spell. The caster needs a drop of mercury as the material component of this spell.

Rigor Mortis

(Necromancy)

Level: 2

Range: 120 yds.	**Components:** V, S
Duration: 2 rds./level	**Casting Time:** 5 segments
Area of Effect: 1 creature	**Saving Throw:** Negates

When this spell is cast upon a creature it causes its muscles to stiffen up, making the victim rigid and immobile. This works exactly like paralyzation, except that the spell will also work on undead creatures who have physical bodies. Creatures without muscles or physical bodies are immune to this spell, as are extraplanar creatures.

Silence, 15' Radius

(Alteration)

Level: 2

Range: 120 yds.	**Components:** V, S
Duration: 2 rds./level	**Casting Time:** 5 segments
Area of Effect: 15 ft. radius	**Saving Throw:** None

Upon casting this spell, complete silence prevails in the affected area. All sound is stopped: conversation is impossible, spells cannot be cast (or at least not those with verbal components), and no noise whatsoever issues from or enters the area. The spell can be cast into the air or upon an object, but the effect is stationary unless cast on a mobile object or creature.

The spell lasts two rounds for each level of experience of the cleric. The spell can be centered upon a creature, and the effect then radiates from the creature and moves as it moves. An unwilling creature receives a saving throw against the spell. If the saving throw is successful, the spell effect is centered about 1 foot behind the position of the subject creature at the instant of casting. This spell provides a defense against sound-based attacks, such as harpy singing, Horns of Blasting, etc.

Slow Poison

(Necromancy)

Level: 2

Range: Touch	**Components:** V, S, M
Duration: 1 hr./level	**Casting Time:** 1 segment
Area of Effect: 1 creature	**Saving Throw:** None

When this spell is placed upon a poisoned individual, it greatly slows the effects of venom, if cast upon the victim before the poison takes full effect. (This period, known as the onset time, is known to the GM.) While this spell does not neutralize the venom, it does prevent it from substantially harming the individual for the duration of its magic in the hope that, during that spell period, the poison can be fully cured. The material components of the Slow Poison spell are the cleric's holy symbol and a bud of garlic that must be crushed and smeared on the wound (or eaten if poison was ingested).

Snake Charm

(Enchantment/Charm)

Level: 2

Range: 30 yds.	**Components:** V, S
Duration: Special	**Casting Time:** 5 segments
Area of Effect: 30-ft. cube	**Saving Throw:** None

When this spell is cast, a hypnotic pattern is set up that causes one or more snakes to cease all activity except a semi-erect, swaying movement. If the snakes are charmed while in a torpor, the duration of the spell is 1d4+2 turns; if the snakes are not torpid, but are not aroused and angry, the charm lasts 1d3 turns; if the snakes are angry or attacking, the spell lasts 1d4+4 rounds. The cleric casting the spell can charm snakes whose total hit points are less than or equal to those of the cleric.

On the average, a 1st-level cleric could charm snakes with a total of 24 or 25 hit points; a 2nd-level cleric could charm 29 hit points, etc. The hit points can be those of a single snake or those of several of the reptiles, but the total hit points cannot exceed those of the cleric casting the spell. A 29-hit point caster charming fifteen 2-hit point snakes would charm 14 of them.

This spell is also effective against any ophidian or ophidianoid monster, such as Naga, Couatl, etc., subject to magic resistance, hit points and so forth. Variations of this spell may exist, allowing other creatures significant to a particular mythos to be affected. Your GM will inform you if such spells exist.

Speak With Animals

(Alteration)

Level: 2

Range: 0	**Components:** V, S
Duration: 2 rds./level	**Casting Time:** 5 segments
Area of Effect: 1 animal within 30 ft.	**Saving Throw:** None

This spell empowers the cleric to comprehend and communicate with any warm or cold-blooded normal or giant animal that is not mindless. The cleric is able to ask questions of and receive answers from the creature, although friendliness and cooperation are by no means assured. Furthermore, terseness and evasiveness are likely, especially in basically wary and cunning creatures (the more stupid ones will instead make inane comments). If the animal is friendly or of the same general alignment as the cleric, it may do some favor or service for the cleric (as determined by the GM).

Note that this spell differs from the Speak With Monsters spell, for this spell allows conversation only with normal or giant non-fantastic creatures such as apes, bears, cats, dogs, elephants and so on.

Spiritual Hammer

(Invocation)

Level: 2

Range: 10 yds./level	**Components:** V, S, M
Duration: 3 rds. + 1 rd./level	**Casting Time:** 5 segments
Area of Effect: Special	**Saving Throw:** None

By calling upon his gawd, the caster of a Spiritual Hammer spell brings into existence a field of force shaped vaguely like a hammer. As long as the caster concentrates upon the hammer, it strikes at any opponent within its range, as desired. Each round the caster can choose to attack the same target as the previous round or switch to a new target that he can see anywhere within his maximum range.

The Spiritual Hammer's chance to successfully hit is equal to that of the caster, without any Strength bonuses. In addition, it strikes as a magical weapon with a bonus of +1 for every six experience levels (or fraction) of the spellcaster, up to a total of +3 to the attack roll and +3 to the damage roll for a 13th-level caster. The base damage inflicted when it scores a hit is exactly the same as a normal war hammer (1d4+1 points on opponents of man size or smaller, or 1d4 on larger opponents, plus the magical bonus). The hammer strikes in the same direction as the caster is facing, so if he is behind the target, all bonuses for rear attack are gained along with the loss of any modifications to the target's AC for shield and Dexterity.

As soon as the caster ceases concentration, the Spiritual Hammer spell ends. A Dispel Magic spell that includes either the caster or the force in its area of effect has a chance to dispel the spiritual hammer. If an attacked creature has magic resistance, the resistance is checked the first time the Spiritual Hammer strikes. If the hammer is successfully resisted, the spell is lost. If not, the hammer has its normal full effect for the duration of the spell.

The material component of this spell is a normal war hammer that the cleric must hurl toward opponents while uttering a plea to his gawd. The hammer disappears when the spell is cast.

Withdraw

(Alteration)

Level: 2

Range: 0	**Components:** V, S
Duration: Special	**Casting Time:** 5 segments
Area of Effect: The caster	**Saving Throw:** None

By means of a Withdraw spell, the cleric in effect alters the flow of time with regard to himself. While but one round of time passes for those not affected by the spell, the cleric is able to spend two rounds, plus one round per level, in contemplation. Thus, a 5th-level cleric can withdraw for seven rounds to cogitate on some matter while one round passes for all others. (The GM should allow the player one minute of real time per round withdrawn to ponder some problem or question. No discussion with other players is permitted.)

Note that while affected by the Withdraw spell, the caster can use only the following spells: any divination spell or any curing or healing spell, the latter on himself only. The casting of any of these spells in different fashion (for example, a Cure Light Wounds spell bestowed upon a companion) negates the Withdraw spell. Similarly, the withdrawn caster cannot walk or run, become invisible, or engage in actions other than thinking, reading, and the like. He can be affected by the actions of others, losing any Dexterity or shield bonus. Any successful attack upon the caster breaks the spell.

Wyvern Watch

(Evocation)
Level: 2
Range: 30 yds.   **Components:** V, S, M
Duration: Up to 8 hrs.   **Casting Time:** 5 segments
Area of Effect: 10-ft. radius   **Saving Throw:** Negates

This spell is known as Wyvern Watch because of the insubstantial haze brought forth by its casting, which vaguely resembles a Wyvern. It is typically used to guard some area against intrusion. Any creature approaching within 10 feet of the guarded area may be affected by the "wyvern."

Any creature entering the guarded area must roll a successful saving throw vs. spell or stand paralyzed for one round per level of the caster, until freed by the spellcaster, by a Dispel Magic or Remove Paralysis spell. A successful saving throw indicates that the subject creature was missed by the attack of the wyvern-form, and the spell remains in place. As soon as a subject creature is successfully struck by the wyvern-form, the paralysis takes effect and the force of the spell dissipates. The spell force likewise dissipates if no intruder is struck by the wyvern-form for eight hours after the spell is cast.

Any creature approaching the space being guarded by the wyvern-form may be able to detect its presence before coming close enough to be attacked; this chance of detection is 90% in bright light, 30% in twilight conditions, and 0% in darkness. The material component is the cleric's holy symbol.

Third Level Cleric Spells

Animate Dead

(Necromancy)
Level: 3
Range: 10 yds.   **Components:** V, S, M
Duration: Permanent   **Casting Time:** 1 round
Area of Effect: Special **Saving Throw:** None

This spell creates the lowest of the undead monsters, Skeletons or Zombies, usually from the bones or bodies of dead humans, demi-humans or humanoids. The spell causes these remains to become animated and obey the simple verbal commands of the caster, regardless of how they communicated in life. The Skeletons or Zombies can follow the caster, remain in an area and attack any creature (or just a specific type of creature) entering the place, etc. The undead remain animated until they are destroyed in combat or are turned; the magic cannot be dispelled.

The cleric can animate one Skeleton or one Zombie for each experience level he has attained. If creatures with more than 1 Hit Die are animated, the number is determined by the monster Hit Dice. Skeletal forms have the Hit Dice of the original creature, while Zombie forms have 1 more Hit Die. Thus, a 12th-level cleric could animate 12 dwarven Skeletons (or six Zombies), four Zombie Gnolls, or a single Zombie Fire Giant.

Note that this is based on the standard racial Hit Die norm; thus, a high-level adventurer would be animated as a Skeleton or Zombie of 1 or 2 Hit Dice, and without special class or racial abilities. The caster can, alternatively, animate two small animal skeletons (1-1 Hit Die or less) for every level of experience he has achieved. The spell requires a drop of blood, a piece of flesh of the type of creature being animated, and a pinch of bone powder or a bone shard to complete the spell. Casting this spell is not a good act, and only evil clerics use it frequently.

Cloudburst (Alteration)

Level: 3
Range: 1 ft./level   **Components:** V, S, M
Duration: 1 round   **Casting Time:** 5 segments
Area of Effect: 3 ft. diameter   **Saving Throw:** None
         cylinder up to 6 ft high   (special)

Except as noted above, this spell is essentially the same as the 3rd level magic-user spell of the same name.

Continual Light

(Alteration)
Reversible
Level: 3
Range: 120 yds.   **Components:** V, S
Duration: Permanent   **Casting Time:** 6 segments
Area of Effect: 60-ft. radius   **Saving Throw:** Special

Except as noted above, this spell is the same as the second level magic-user spell Continual Light.

Create Food & Water

(Alteration)
Level: 3
Range: 10 yds.   **Components:** V, S
Duration: Special   **Casting Time:** 1 turn
Area of Effect: 1 cu. ft./level   **Saving Throw:** None

When this spell is cast, the cleric causes food and water to appear. The food thus created is highly nourishing if rather bland; each cubic foot of the material sustains three human-sized creatures or one horse-sized creature for a full day. The food decays and becomes inedible within 24 hours, although it can be restored for another 24 hours by casting a Purify Food and Water spell

upon it. The water created by this spell is the same as that created by the 1st-level cleric spell Create Water.

For each experience level the cleric has attained, 1 cubic foot of food or water is created by the spell. For example, a 2nd-level cleric could create 1 cubic foot of food and 1 cubic foot of water.

Cure Blindness or Deafness

(Abjuration)
Reversible
Level: 3
Range: Touch   **Components:** V, S
Duration: Permanent   **Casting Time:** 1 round
Area of Effect: 1 creature   **Saving Throw:** Special

By touching the creature afflicted, the cleric employing the spell can permanently cure some forms of blindness or deafness. This spell does not restore or repair visual or auditory organs damaged by injury or disease. Its reverse, Cause Blindness or Deafness, requires a successful touch (successful attack roll) on the victim. If the victim rolls a successful saving throw, the effect is negated. If the saving throw is failed, a non-damaging magical blindness or deafness results.

A deafened creature can react only to what it can see or feel, and suffers a -1 penalty to surprise rolls, a +1 penalty to its initiative rolls, and a 20% chance of spell failure for spells with verbal components. A blinded creature suffers a -4 penalty to its attack rolls, a +4 penalty to its Armor Class, and a +2 penalty to its initiative rolls.

Cure Disease

(Abjuration)
Reversible
Level: 3
Range: Touch   **Components:** V, S
Duration: Permanent   **Casting Time:** 1 round
Area of Effect: 1 creature   **Saving Throw:** None

This spell enables the caster to cure most diseases by placing his hand upon the diseased creature. The affliction rapidly disappears thereafter, making the cured creature whole and well in from one turn to 10 days, depending on the type of disease and the state of its advancement when the cure took place. (The GM must adjudicate these conditions.) The spell is also effective against parasitic monsters such as Green Slime, Rot Grubs, and others. When cast by a cleric of at least 12th level, this spell cures lycanthropy if cast within three days of the infection.

Note that the spell does not prevent reoccurrence of a disease if the recipient is again exposed. The reverse of the Cure Disease spell is cause disease. To be effective, the cleric must touch the intended victim, and the victim must fail a saving throw vs. spell. The severity of the disease is decided by the cleric (debilitating or fatal). The inflicted disease can be cured by the Cure Disease spell. Lycanthropy cannot be caused. The exact details of the disease are decided by the GM, but the following are typical:

Debilitating: The disease takes effect in 1d6 turns, after which the creature loses 1 point of Strength per hour until his Strength is reduced to 2 or less, at which time the recipient is weak and virtually helpless. If a creature has no Strength rating, it loses 10% of its hit points per Strength loss, down to 10% of its original hit points. If the disease also affects hit points, use the more severe penalty. Recovery requires a period of 1d3 weeks.

Fatal: This wasting disease is effective immediately. Infected creatures receive no benefit from curing spells while the disease is in effect; wounds heal at only 10% of the natural rate. The disease proves fatal within 1d6 months and can be cured only by magical means. Each month the disease progresses the creature permanently loses 2 points of Charisma.

Cure Nasty Wounds

(Necromancy)
Reversible
Level: 3
Range: Touch   **Components:** V, S
Duration: Permanent   **Casting Time:** 5 segments
Area of Effect: 1 creature   **Saving Throw:** None

This spell is exactly like a Cure Light Wounds spell except that it heals 1d8 points of damage per level of the cleric. Its reverse, Cause Nasty Wounds, causes 1d8 damage per caster level.

Dispel Magic

(Abjuration)
Level: 3
Range: 60 yds   **Components:** V, S
Duration: Special   **Casting Time:** 6 segments
Area of Effect: 30-ft. cube   **Saving Throw:** None
                  or 1 item

Except as noted above, this spell is the same as the third level magic-user spell Dispel Magic (q.v.).

Feign Death

(Necromancy)
Level: 3
Range: Touch   **Components:** V
Duration: 1 turn + 1 rd./level   **Casting Time:** 1/2 segment
Area of Effect: Person touched   **Saving Throw:** None

Except as noted above, this spell is the same as the third level magic-user spell Feign Death (q.v.).

Flame Walk

(Alteration)
Level: 3
Range: Touch   **Components:** V, S, M
Duration: 1 rd. + 1/level   **Casting Time:** 5 segments
Area of Effect: Creature(s) **Saving Throw:** None
                  touched

By means of this spell, the caster empowers one or more creatures to withstand nonmagical fires of temperatures up to 2,000° F (enabling them to walk upon molten lava). It also confers a +2 bonus to saving throws against magical fire and reduces damage from such fires by one-half, even if the saving throw is failed. For every experience level above the minimum required to cast the spell (5th), the cleric can affect an additional creature.

This spell is not cumulative with Resist Fire spells or similar protections. The material components of the spell are the cleric's holy symbol and at least 500 gp of powdered ruby per affected creature.

Glyph of Warding

(Abjuration, Evocation)
Level: 3
Range: Touch   **Components:** V, S, M
Duration: Until discharged   **Casting Time:** Special
Area of Effect: Special   **Saving Throw:** Special

A Glyph of Warding is a powerful inscription magically drawn to prevent unauthorized or hostile creatures from passing, entering, or opening. It can be used to guard a small bridge, to ward an entry, or as a trap on a chest or box. The cleric must set the conditions of the ward; typically any creature violating the warded area without speaking the name of the glyph is subject to the magic it stores. A successful saving throw vs. spell enables the creature to escape the effects of the glyph.

Glyphs can be set according to physical characteristics, such as creature type, size, and weight. Glyphs can also be set with respect to good or evil, or to pass those of the caster's religion. They cannot be set according to class, Hit Dice or level. Multiple glyphs cannot be cast on the same area; although if a cabinet had three drawers, each could be separately warded.

When the spell is cast, the cleric weaves a tracery of faintly glowing lines around the warding sigil. For every 5 square feet of area to be protected, one round is required to trace the warding lines of the glyph. The caster can affect an area equal to a square the sides of which are the same as his level, in feet. The glyph can be placed to conform to any shape up to the limitations of the caster's total square footage. Thus, a 6th-level caster could place a glyph on a 6-foot x 6-foot square, a 4-foot x 9-foot rectangle, a 2-foot x 18- foot band, or a 1-foot by 36-foot strip.

When the spell is completed, the glyph and tracery become invisible. The cleric traces the glyph with incense, which, if the area exceeds 50 square feet, must be sprinkled with powdered diamond (at least 2,000 gp worth). Typical glyphs shock for 1d4 points of electrical damage per level of the spellcaster, explode for a like amount of fire damage, paralyze, blind, deafen, and so forth.

The GM may allow any harmful cleric spell effect to be used as a glyph, provided the caster is of sufficient level to cast the spell. Successful saving throws either reduce effects by one-half or negate them, according to the glyph employed. Glyphs cannot be affected or bypassed by such means as physical or magical probing, though they can be dispelled by magic and foiled by high-level thieves using their find-and-remove-traps skill. The GM may decide that the exact glyphs available to a cleric depend on his religion, and he might make new glyphs available according to the magical research rules.

Heal Moderate Wounds

(Necromancy)

Level: 3

Range: 5 ft./level

Duration: Permanent

Area of Effect: 1 creature

Components: V, S

Casting Time: 5 segments

Saving Throw: None

By using this spell a cleric can restore 1d6 lost hit points per level to any one creature within the range of the spell. The hit points are healed in the same way as a Cure Light Wounds spell and are subject to the same limitations.

Lesser Reanimation

(Necromancy)

Level: 3

Range: Touch

Duration: Permanent

Area of Effect: 1 creature

Components: V, S, M

Casting Time: 1 round

Saving Throw: None

This spell functions exactly like the 5th level Raise Dead spell, except that raised characters lose one level and must take 1d4+1 rolls on Table 6A: Flaws and Quirks. A Restoration, Heal, Wish or Limited Wish can remove the flaws and quirks, but the lost level is permanent. The character can earn EP to advance again, but not even a Wish spell will restore the lost level. A character cannot be reduced to less than first level (or their initial Hit Dice) with this spell. The material components are two platinum coins.

A cleric gains experience points for raising the dead as if he defeated that creature in individual combat.

Locate Object

(Divination)

Reversible

Level: 3

Range: 60 yds. + 10 yds./level

Duration: 8 hrs.

Area of Effect: 1 object

Components: V, S, M

Casting Time: 1 turn

Saving Throw: None

Except as noted above, this spell is the same as the second level magic-user spell Locate Object (q.v.).

Magic Vestment

(Enchantment)

Level: 3

Range: 0

Duration: 5 rds./level

Area of Effect: The caster

Components: V, S, M

Casting Time: 1 round

Saving Throw: None

This spell enchants the caster's vestment, providing protection at least the equivalent of chain mail (AC 5). The vestment gains a +1 enchantment for each three levels of the cleric beyond 5th level, to a maximum of AC 1 at 17th level. The magic lasts for five rounds per level of the caster, or until the caster loses consciousness.

If the vestment is worn with other armors, only the best AC (either the armor or the vestment) is used; this protection is not cumulative with any other AC protection. The material components are the vestment to be enchanted and the cleric's holy symbol, which are not expended.

Meld Into Stone

(Alteration)

Level: 3

Range: 0

Duration: 8 rds. + 1d8 rds.

Area of Effect: The caster

Components: V, S, M

Casting Time: 6 segments

Saving Throw: None

This spell enables the cleric to meld his body and possessions into a single block of stone. The stone must be large enough to accommodate his body in all three dimensions. When the casting is complete, the cleric and not more than 100 pounds of nonliving gear merge with the stone. If either condition is violated, the spell fails and is wasted.

While in the stone, the cleric remains in contact, however tenuous, with the face of the stone through which he melded. The cleric remains aware of the passage of time. Nothing that goes on outside the stone can be seen or heard, however. Minor physical damage to the stone does not harm the cleric, but its partial destruction, if enough so that the caster no longer fits, expels the cleric with 4d8 points of damage. The stone's destruction expels the cleric and slays him instantly, unless he rolls a successful saving throw vs. spell.

The magic lasts for 1d8+8 rounds, with the variable part of the duration rolled secretly by the GM. At any time before the duration expires, the cleric can step out of the stone through the stone surface he entered. If the duration runs out, or the effect is dispelled before the cleric exits the stone, he is violently expelled and suffers 4d8 points of damage.

The following spells harm the cleric if cast upon the stone that he is occupying: Stone to Flesh expels the cleric and inflicts 4d8 points of damage; Stone Shape causes 4d4 points of damage, but does not expel the cleric; Transmute Rock to Mud expels and slays him instantly unless he rolls a successful saving throw vs. spell; and Wall Passage expels the cleric without damage.

Negative Plane Protection

(Abjuration)

Level: 3

Range: Touch

Duration: Special

Area of Effect: 1 creature

Components: V, S

Casting Time: 1 round

Saving Throw: None

This spell affords the caster or touched creature partial protection from undead monsters with Negative Energy plane connections (such as Shadows, Wights, Wraiths, Spectres, or Vampires) and certain weapons and spells that drain energy levels. The Negative Plane Protection spell opens a channel to the Positive Energy plane, possibly offsetting the effect of the negative energy attack.

A protected creature struck by a negative energy attack is allowed a saving throw vs. death magic. If successful, the energies cancel with a bright flash of light and a thunderclap. The protected creature suffers only normal hit point damage from the attack and does not suffer any drain of experience or Strength, regardless of the number of levels the attack would have drained.

An attacking undead creature suffers 2d6 points of damage from the positive energy; a draining magic-user or weapon receives no damage. This protection is proof against only one such attack, dissipating immediately whether or not the saving throw was successful. If the saving throw is failed, the spell recipient suffers double the usual physical damage, in addition to the loss of experience or Strength that normally occurs. The protection lasts for one turn per level of the cleric casting the spell, or until the protected creature is struck by a negative energy attack. This spell cannot be cast on the Negative Energy plane.

Prayer
(Conjuration/Summoning)

Level: 3
Range: 0 | **Components:** V, S, M
Duration: 1 rd./level | **Casting Time:** 6 segments
Area of Effect: 60-ft. radius | **Saving Throw:** None

By means of the Prayer spell, the cleric brings special favor upon himself and his party and causes harm to his enemies. Those in the area at the instant the spell is completed are affected for the duration of the spell. When the spell is completed, all attack and damage rolls and saving throws made by those in the area of effect who are friendly to the cleric gain +1 bonuses, while those of the cleric's enemies suffer -1 penalties.

Once the Prayer spell is uttered, the cleric can do other things, unlike a Chant, which he must continue to make the spell effective. If another cleric of the same religious persuasion (not merely the same alignment) is chanting when a Prayer is cast, the effects combine to +2 and -2, as long as both are in effect at once. The cleric needs a silver holy symbol, prayer beads, or a similar device as the material component of this spell.

Remove Curse
(Abjuration)
Reversible

Level: 3
Range: Touch | **Components:** V, S
Duration: Permanent | **Casting Time:** 6 segments
Area of Effect: Special | **Saving Throw:** Special

Except as noted above, this spell is the same as the fourth level magic-user spell Remove Curse (q.v.).

Remove Paralysis
(Abjuration)

Level: 3
Range: 10 yds./level | **Components:** V, S
Duration: Permanent | **Casting Time:** 6 segments
Area of Effect: 1d4 creatures in 20-ft. cube | **Saving Throw:** None

By the use of this spell, the cleric can free one or more creatures from the effects of any paralyzation or from related magic (such as a Ghoul's touch, or a Hold or Slow spell). If the spell is cast on one creature, the paralyzation is negated. If cast on two creatures, each receives another saving throw vs. the effect that afflicts it, with a +4 bonus. If cast on three or four creatures, each receives another saving throw with a +2 bonus. There must be no physical or magical barrier between the caster and the creatures to be affected, or the spell fails and is wasted.

Speak to the Dead
(Necromancy)

Level: 3
Range: 0 | **Components:** V, S, M
Duration: Special | **Casting Time:** 1 turn
Area of Effect: 1 creature | **Saving Throw:** Special

Upon casting a Speak to the Dead spell, the cleric is able to ask several questions of a dead creature in a set period of time and receive answers according to the knowledge of that creature. Of course, the cleric must be able to converse in the language that the dead creature once used. The length of time the creature has been dead is a factor, since only higher level clerics can converse with a long-dead creature. The number of questions that can be answered and

the length of time in which the questions can be asked depend on the level of experience of the cleric.

Even if the casting is successful, such creatures are as evasive as possible when questioned. The dead tend to give extremely brief and limited answers, often cryptic, and to take questions literally. Furthermore, their knowledge is often limited to what they knew in life. A dead creature of different alignment or of higher level or Hit Dice than the caster's level receives a saving throw vs. spell. A dead creature that successfully saves can refuse to answer questions, ending the spell.

At the GM's option, the casting of this spell on a given creature might be restricted to once per week. The cleric needs a holy symbol and burning incense in order to cast this spell upon the body, remains, or a portion thereof. The remains are not expended. This spell does not function under water.

Caster's Level of Experience	Max. Length of Time Dead	Time Questioned	No. of Questions
1-6	1 week	1 round	2
7-8	1 month	3 rounds	3
9-12	1 year	1 turn	4
13-15	10 years	2 turns	5
16-20	100 years	3 turns	6
21+	1,000 years	1 hour	7

Stirring Sermon
(Enchantment/Charm)

Level: 3
Range: 0 | **Components:** V
Duration: 1 turn + 1 round/level | **Casting Time:** 1 round
Area of Effect: 20 ft. radius/level | **Saving Throw:** None

With this spell the caster can deliver an impassioned sermon that touches the minds and hearts of all who hear it. Creatures in the area who can understand the caster may re-roll any failed morale checks or fear saves, and treat the caster as if he had a Charisma score of four points higher than he actually does. Player characters can always make up their own minds as to whether or not they want to be influenced by this spell.

Ward Off Evil
(Abjuration)
Reversible

Level: 3
Range: Touch | **Components:** V, S, M
Duration: 2 rds./level | **Casting Time:** 3 segments
Area of Effect: 10-ft. radius around creature touched | **Saving Throw:** None

The globe of protection of this spell is identical in all respects to a Protection From Evil spell, except that it encompasses a much larger area and its duration is greater. The effect is centered on and moves with the creature touched. Any protected creature within the circle can break the warding against enchanted or summoned monsters by engaging in melee with them. If a creature too large to fit into the area of effect is the recipient of the spell, the spell acts as a normal Protection From Evil spell for that creature only. To complete this spell, the caster must trace a circle 20 feet in diameter using blessed chalk. The material component for the reverse is powdered iron.

Water Walk
(Alteration)

Level: 3
Range: Touch | **Components:** V, S, M
Duration: 1 turn + 1 turn/level | **Casting Time:** 6 segments
Area of Effect: Special | **Saving Throw:** None

By means of this spell, the caster is able to empower one or more creatures to tread upon any liquid as if it were firm ground; this includes mud, quicksand, oil, running water, and snow. The recipient's feet do not touch the surface of the liquid, but oval depressions of his appropriate foot size and 2 inches deep are left in the mud or snow. The recipient's rate of movement remains normal.

If cast under water, the recipient is borne toward the surface. For every level of the caster above the minimum required to cast the spell (5th level), he can affect another creature. The material components for this spell are a piece of cork and the cleric's holy symbol.

White Hot Metal
(Alteration)
Level: 3
Range: 10 yds.
Duration: 1 round/level
Area of Effect: Up to one pound of metal

Components: V, M
Casting Time: 2 segments
Saving Throw: None (neg.)

This spell makes up to one pound of metal white hot almost instantly. The heat is sufficient to melt softer metals such as gold, silver or lead, and harder metals are ruined if they are subject to any stress (such as combat). Magical metals, mithral items and adamantite alloys may make a saving throw vs. crushing blow to avoid being warped and ruined.

If the spell is cast upon a creature's equipment, that creature is entitled to a saving throw to avoid the spell, otherwise contact with White Hot Metal causes 2d6 points of damage each round. The material component is the metal being heated.

Fourth Level Cleric Spells

Abjure
(Abjuration)
Level: 4
Range: 10 yds.
Duration: Special
Area of Effect: 1 creature

Components: V, S, M
Casting Time: 1 round
Saving Throw: Special

This spell can send an extraplanar creature back to its own plane of existence. The spell fails against entities of demigawd status or greater, but their servants or minions can be abjured. If the creature has a specific (proper) name, it must be known and used.

Any magic resistance of the subject must be overcome, or the spell fails. The cleric has a 50% chance of success (a roll of 11 or better on 1d20). The roll is adjusted by the difference in level or Hit Dice between the caster and the creature being abjured; the number needed is decreased if the cleric has more Hit Dice and increased if the creature has more Hit Dice. If the spell is successful, the creature is instantly hurled back to its own plane. The affected creature must survive a system shock check. If the creature does not have a Constitution score, the required roll is 70% + 2%/Hit Die or level.

The caster has no control over where in the creature's plane the abjured creature arrives. If the attempt fails, the cleric must gain another level before another attempt can be made on that particular creature. The spell requires the cleric's holy symbol, holy water, and some material inimical to the creature.

Cloak of Bravery/Cloak of Fear
(Conjuration/Summoning)
Reversible
Level: 4
Range: Touch
Duration: Special
Area of Effect: 1 creature

Components: V, S, M
Casting Time: 6 segments
Saving Throw: Negates

The Cloak of Bravery spell can be cast upon any willing creature. The protected individual gains a bonus to his saving throw against any form of fear encountered (but not awe—an ability of some lesser and greater powers).

When cast, the spell can affect one to four creatures (caster's choice). If only one is affected, the saving throw bonus is +4. If two are affected, the bonus is

+3, and so forth, until four creatures are protected by a +1 bonus. The magic of the Cloak of Bravery spell works only once and then the spell ends, whether or not the creature's saving throw is successful. The spell ends after eight hours if no saving throw is required before then.

The reverse of this spell, Cloak of Fear, empowers a single creature touched to radiate a personal aura of fear, at will, out to a 3-foot radius. All other characters and creatures within this aura must roll successful saving throws vs. spell or run away in panic for 2d8 rounds. Affected individuals may or may not drop items, at the GM's option.

The spell has no effect upon undead of any sort. The effect can be used only once, and the spell expires after eight hours if not brought down sooner. Members of the recipient's party are not immune to the effects of the spell. The material component for the Cloak of Bravery spell is the feather of an avianderthal, eagle or hawk. The reverse requires the tail feathers of a vulture, or chicken.

Cure Serious Wounds
(Necromancy)
Reversible
Level: 4
Range: Touch
Duration: Permanent
Area of Effect: 1 creature

Components: V, S
Casting Time: 5 segments
Saving Throw: None

This spell is exactly like a Cure Light Wounds spell except that it heals 1d10 points of damage per level of the cleric and its reverse causes 1d10 damage per caster level.

Detect Lie
(Divination)
Reversible
Level: 4
Range: 30 yards
Duration: 1 rd./level
Area of Effect: 1 creature

Components: V, S, M
Casting Time: 7 segments
Saving Throw: Negates

A cleric who casts this spell is immediately able to determine if the subject creature deliberately and knowingly speaks a lie. The subject must be within 30 yards of the caster and using a form of the communication the caster can understand (magical aid such as Comprehend Languages or Tongues will work). It does not reveal the truth, uncover unintentional inaccuracies, or necessarily reveal evasions. The subject receives a saving throw vs. spell, which is adjusted only by the Wisdom of the caster—for example, if the caster has a Wisdom of 18, the subject's saving throw roll is reduced by 4.

The material component for the Detect Lie spell is one gold piece worth of gold dust. The spell's reverse, Undetectable Lie, prevents the magical detection of lies spoken by the creature for 24 hours. The reverse requires brass dust as its material component.

Divination
(Divination)
Level: 4
Range: 0
Duration: Special
Area of Effect: Special

Components: V, S, M
Casting Time: 1 turn
Saving Throw: None

A Divination spell is used to garner a useful piece of advice concerning a specific goal, event, or activity that will occur within a one-week period. This can be as simple as a short phrase, or it might take the form of a cryptic rhyme or omen. Unlike the augury spell, this gives a specific piece of advice. For example, if the question is "Will we do well if we venture to the third level?" and a terrible troll guarding 10,000 gp and a shield +1 lurks near the entrance to the level (the GM estimates the party could beat the troll after a hard fight), the divination response might be: "Ready oil and open flame light your way to wealth."

In all cases, the GM controls what information is received and whether additional divinations will supply additional information. Note that if the information is not acted upon, the conditions probably change so that the information is no longer useful (in the example, the Troll might move away and take the treasure with it). The base chance for a correct Divination spell is 60%, plus 1% for each experience level of the cleric casting the spell. The GM makes adjustments to this base chance considering the actions being divined (if, for example, unusual precautions against the spell have been taken). If the dice roll is failed, the caster knows the spell failed, unless specific magic yielding false information is at work.

The material components of the Divination spell are a sacrificial offering, incense, and the holy symbol of the cleric. If an unusually important divination is attempted, sacrifice of particularly valuable gems, jewelry, or magical items may be required.

Free Action

(Abjuration, Enchantment)

Level: 4

Range: Touch	**Components:** V, S, M
Duration: 1 turn/level	**Casting Time:** 7 segments
Area of Effect: 1 creature	**Saving Throw:** None

This spell enables the creature touched to move and attack normally for the duration of the spell, even under the influence of magic that impedes movement (such as Web or Slow spells) or while under water. It even negates or prevents the effects of Paralysis and Hold spells. Under water, the individual moves at normal (surface) speed and inflicts full damage, even with such cutting weapons as axes and swords and with such smashing weapons as flails, hammers, and maces, provided that the weapon is wielded in the hand rather than hurled.

The Free Action spell does not, however, allow water breathing without further appropriate magic. The material component is a leather thong, bound around the arm or similar appendage, which disintegrates when the spell expires.

Giant Insect

(Alteration)

Reversible

Level: 4

Range: 20 yds.	**Components:** V, S, M
Duration: Permanent	**Casting Time:** 7 segments
Area of Effect: 1 to 6 insects	**Saving Throw:** None

By means of this spell, the cleric can turn one or more normal-sized insects into larger forms resembling the giant insects described in the various volumes of the Hacklopedia of Beasts. Only one type of insect can be altered at one time (i.e., a single casting cannot affect both an ant and a fly) and all insects affected must be grown to the same size. The number of insects and the size to which they can be grown depends upon the cleric's level:

Cleric's Level	Insect Hit Dice Total	Maximum HD
7-9	3	9
10-12	4	12
13+	6	15

For example, an 8th-level cleric can grow three insects to 3 Hit Dice, four insects to 2 Hit Dice, or nine insects to 1 Hit Die. Flying insects of 3 Hit Dice or more can carry a rider of human size (assume that such can carry 80 pounds per Hit Die). If the casting is interrupted for any reason, or if the insects are currently subject to any other magical effect (including this one), the insects die and the spell is ruined.

The GM decides how many normal insects of what type are available; this is often a greater limitation on the spell than the limits above. If the insect created by this spell matches an existing monster description, use the monster description. Otherwise, unless the GM creates a special description, the giant form has an Armor Class of between 8 and 4, one attack, and inflicts 1d4 points of damage per Hit Die. For example, a 14th-level cleric uses the giant

insect spell to enlarge one beetle (all that is available) to 6 HD size. The GM decides the beetle has AC 5 and bites once for 6d4 points of damage.

Note that the spell works only on actual insects. Arachnids, crustaceans, and other types of small creatures are not affected. Any giant insects created by this spell do not attempt to harm the cleric, but the cleric's control of such creatures is limited to simple commands ("attack," "defend," "guard," and so forth). Orders to attack a certain creature when it appears or guard against a particular occurrence are too complex. Unless commanded to do otherwise, the giant insects attempt to attack whoever or whatever is near them.

The reverse of the spell, Shrink Insect, reduces any giant insect to normal insect size. The number of Hit Dice affected by the cleric is subtracted from the number of Hit Dice of the insects, and any insect reduced to 0 Hit Dice has been shrunk. Partial shrinking is ignored; an insect is either shrunk or unaffected. Thus, a 9th-level cleric attacked by giant ants could shrink three warrior ants or four worker ants to normal insect size with no saving throw. This spell has no effect on intelligent insectlike creatures. The cleric must use his holy symbol for either version of the spell.

Heal Nasty Wounds

(Necromancy)

Level: 4

Range: 5 ft./level	**Components:** V, S
Duration: Permanent	**Casting Time:** 5 segments
Area of Effect: 1 creature	**Saving Throw:** None

By using this spell a cleric can restore 1d8 lost hit points per level to any one creature within the range of the spell. The hit points are healed in the same way as a Cure Light Wounds spell and are subject to the same limitations.

Imbue With Spell Ability

(Enchantment)

Level: 4

Range: Touch	**Components:** V, S, M
Duration: Until used	**Casting Time:** 1 turn
Area of Effect: Person touched	**Saving Throw:** None

By the use of this spell, the cleric can transfer a limited number and selection of his currently memorized spells, and the ability to cast them, to another person. Only nonspellcasters (including rangers under 8th level and paladins under 9th level) can receive this bestowal; the Imbue With Spell Ability enchantment does not function for those belonging to spellcasting classes, for unintelligent monsters, nor for any individual with less than 1 full Hit Die. In addition, the person thus imbued must have a Wisdom score of 9 or higher.

Only cleric spells of an informational or defensive nature or a Cure Light Wounds spell can be transferred. Transferring any other spell type negates the entire attempt, including any allowable spells that were chosen. Higher level persons can receive more than one spell at the cleric's option:

Level of Recipient	Spells Imbued
1	One 1st-level spell
3	Two 1st-level spells
5+	Two 1st- and one 2nd-level spells

The transferred spell's variable characteristics (range, duration, area of effect, etc.) function according to the level of the cleric originally imbuing the spell. A cleric who casts Imbue With Spell Ability upon another character loses the number of 1st- and 2nd-level spells he has imbued until the recipient uses the transferred spells or is slain. For example, a 7th-level cleric with five 1st- and four 2nd-level spells imbues a 10th-level fighter with a Cure Light Wounds spell and a Slow Poison spell. The cleric now can have only four 1st-level spells memorized until the cure is cast and only three 2nd-level spells until the Slow Poison is cast, or until the fighter is killed. In the meantime, the cleric remains responsible to his ethos for the use to which the spell is put.

The material components for this spell are the cleric's holy symbol, plus some minor item from the recipient that is symbolic of his profession (a lockpick for a thief, etc.). This item, and any material component for the imbued spell, is consumed when the Imbue With Spell Ability spell is cast.

Lower Water

(Alteration)

Reversible

Level: 4

Range: 120 yds.   **Components:** V, S, M

Duration: 1 turn/level   **Casting Time:** 1 turn

Area of Effect: Special   **Saving Throw:** None

Except as noted above, this spell is the same as the sixth level magic-user spell Lower Water (q.v.).

Minor Raise Dead

(Necromancy)

Level: 4

Range: Touch   **Components:** V, S

Duration: Permanent   **Casting Time:** 1 turn

Area of Effect: 1 creature   **Saving Throw:** None

A Minor Raise Dead spell brings one creature back from the dead. The raised creature has its full Hit Dice, hit point potential, levels, abilities, etc., but must take 2 rolls on Table 6A: Flaws and Quirks. These can be removed by a Restoration, Heal, Wish or Limited Wish spell. Otherwise, it functions as the fifth level cleric spell Raise Dead.

A cleric gains experience points for raising the dead as if he defeated that creature in individual combat.

Neutralize Poison

(Necromancy)

Reversible

Level: 4

Range: Touch   **Components:** V, S

Duration: Permanent   **Casting Time:** 7 segments

Area of Effect: 1 creature or   **Saving Throw:** None
     1 cu. ft. of substance/2 levels

By means of a Neutralize Poison spell, the cleric detoxifies any sort of venom in the creature or substance touched. Note that an opponent, such as a poisonous reptile or snake (or even an envenomed weapon of an opponent) unwilling to be so touched requires the cleric to roll a successful attack in combat. This spell can prevent death in a poisoned creature if cast before death occurs. The effects of the spell are permanent only with respect to poison existing in the touched creature at the time of the touch; thus, creatures (and objects) that generate new poison are not permanently detoxified.

The reversed spell, Poison, likewise requires a successful attack roll, and the victim is allowed a saving throw vs. poison. If the latter is unsuccessful, the victim is incapacitated and dies in one turn unless the poison is magically neutralized or slowed.

No Fear

(Enchantment/Charm)

Level: 4

Range: 10 yards/level   **Components:** V

Duration: 2 rounds/level **Casting Time:** 3 segments

Area of Effect: 10 ft. radius   **Saving Throw:** None (neg.)

When this spell is cast it fills the recipients with fierce bravery, giving them a +2 bonus on to hit and damage rolls in melee combat as well as making them immune to Fear and morale checks. The spell affects everyone within a 10-foot radius from the target point when first cast, but afterwards the recipients can freely move about without losing the bonuses granted by this spell.

Spell Immunity

(Abjuration)

Level: 4

Range: Touch   **Components:** V, S, M

Duration: 1 turn/level   **Casting Time:** 1 round

Area of Effect: 1 creature   **Saving Throw:** None

By means of this spell, the cleric renders a creature touched immune to the effects of a specified spell of 4th level or lower. It protects against spells, spell-like effects of magical items, and innate spell-like abilities of creatures. It does not protect against breath weapons or gaze attacks of any type.

The spell has several additional limitations. First, the caster must have directly experienced the effect of the specified spell. For example, if the caster has been attacked by a fireball spell at some time, he can use the spell immunity spell to provide protection from a Fireball. Second, the spell cannot affect a creature already magically protected by a potion, protective spell, ring, or other device. Third, only a particular spell can be protected against, not a certain sphere of spells or a group of spells that are similar in effect; thus, a creature given immunity to the lightning bolt spell is still vulnerable to a shocking grasp spell. The material component for spell immunity is the same as that for the spell to be protected against.

Spike Stones

(Alteration, Enchantment)

Level: 4

Range: 30 yds.   **Components:** V, S, M

Duration: 3d4 turns +1/level   **Casting Time:** 6 segments

Area of Effect: 10 ft. sq./level,   **Saving Throw:** None
     1 spike/sq. ft.

The Spike Stones spell causes rock to shape itself into long, sharp points that tend to blend into the background. It is effective on both natural rock and worked stone. The spike stones serve to impede progress through an area and to inflict damage. If an area is carefully observed, each observer is 25% likely to notice the sharp points of rock. Otherwise, those entering the spell's area of effect suffer 1d4 points of damage per round.

The success of each attack is determined as if the caster of the spell were actually engaging in combat. Those entering the area are subject to attack immediately upon setting foot in the area and for each round spent in the area thereafter. The initial step enables the individual to become aware of some problem only if the initial attack succeeds; otherwise movement continues and the spike stones remain unnoticed until damage occurs. Charging or running victims suffer two attacks per round.

Those falling into pits affected by Spike Stones suffer six such attacks for every 10 feet fallen, each attack having a +2 bonus to the attack roll. In addition, the damage inflicted by each attack increases by +2 for every 10 feet fallen. Finally, the creatures also suffer normal falling damage. The material component of this spell is four tiny stalactites or stalagmites.

Sticks to Snakes

(Alteration)

Reversible

Level: 4

Range: 30 yds.   **Components:** V, S, M

Duration: 2 rds./level   **Casting Time:** 7 segments

Area of Effect: 1d4 sticks + 1   **Saving Throw:** None
     stick/level in a 10-ft. cube

By means of this spell, the caster can change 1d4 sticks, plus one stick per experience level, into snakes; thus, a 9th-level cleric can change 10-13 sticks into an equal number of snakes. These snakes attack as commanded by the cleric.

There must, of course, be sticks or similar pieces of wood (such as torches, spears, etc.) to turn into snakes. Such a stick cannot be larger than a staff. Sticks held by creatures are allowed a saving throw equal to that of the possessor (i.e., a spear held by an orc must roll the orc's saving throw vs. polymorph). Magical items, such as staves and enchanted spears, are not affected by the spell. Only sticks within the area of effect are changed.

The type of snake created varies, but a typical specimen has 2 Hit Dice, Armor Class 6, a movement rate of 9, and either constricts for 1d4+1 points of damage per round or bites for 1 point plus poison (if any). The chance of a snake thus changed being venomous is 5% per caster level, if the spellcaster desires. Thus, an 11th-level cleric has a maximum 55% chance that any snake created by the spell is poisonous.

The spell lasts for two rounds for each experience level of the spellcaster. The material components of the spell are a small piece of bark and several snake scales. The reverse spell changes normal-sized snakes to sticks for the same duration, or it negates the Sticks to Snakes spell according to the level of the cleric countering the spell (for example, a 10th-level cleric casting the reverse spell can turn 11-14 snakes back into sticks).

Tongues

(Alteration)
Reversible
Level: 4
Range: 0
Duration: 1 turn
Area of Effect: The caster

Components: V, S
Casting Time: 7 segments
Saving Throw: None

Except as noted above, this spell is the same as the third level magic-user spell Tongues (q.v.).

Touch of Death

(Necromancy)
Level: 4
Range: Touch
Duration: Permanent
Area of Effect: One living creature

Components: V, S
Casting Time: 5 segments
Saving Throw: Negates

Touch of Death allows the caster to immediately make a special touch attack against one victim. If the attack is successful the victim must make a successful saving throw vs. death magic or instantly die. If the save is successful the victim still suffers 2D8+1 damage, which may still be enough to slay them.

Note that victims can still be Raised or Reincarnated, and that the spell only works on living creatures, not on extraplanar beings, undead, constructs and the like.

Fifth Level Cleric Spells

Air Walk

(Alteration)
Level: 5
Range: Touch
Duration: 1 hour + 1 turn/level
Area of Effect: 1 creature

Components: V, S, M
Casting Time: 8 segments
Saving Throw: None

This spell enables a creature, which can be as big as the largest giant, to tread upon air as if it were walking on solid ground. Moving upward is similar to walking up a hill. A maximum upward angle of 45 degrees is possible at one-half the creature's movement rate, as is a maximum downward angle of 45 degrees at the normal movement rate. An air-walking creature is in control of its movement, except when a strong wind is blowing. In this case, the creature gains or loses 10 feet of movement for every 10 miles per hour of wind velocity.

The creature can, at the GM's option, be subject to additional penalties in exceptionally strong or turbulent winds, such as loss of control of movement or suffering physical damage. The spell can be placed upon a trained mount,

so it can be ridden through the air. Of course, a mount not accustomed to such movement would certainly need careful and lengthy training, the details for which are up to the GM. The material components for the spell are the cleric's holy symbol and a bit of thistledown.

Atonement

(Abjuration)
Level: 5
Range: Touch
Duration: Permanent
Area of Effect: 1 person

Components: V, S, M
Casting Time: 1 turn
Saving Throw: None

This spell is used by the cleric to remove the burden of unwilling or unknown deeds from the person who is the subject of the atonement. The spell removes the effects of magical alignment changes as well. The person seeking the Atonement spell must either be truly repentant or not have been in command of his own will when the acts to be atoned for were committed.

The GM will judge this spell in this regard, noting any past instances of its use upon the person. Deliberate misdeeds and acts of knowing and willful nature cannot be atoned for with this spell (see the quest spell). A character who refuses to accept an atonement is automatically considered to have committed a willful misdeed. The cleric needs his religious symbol, prayer beads or wheel or book, and burning incense.

Break Hex

(Abjuration)
Level: 5
Range: 30 ft.
Duration: Permanent
Area of Effect: Special

Components: V, S, M
Casting Time: 1 round
Saving Throw: None

This spell is a more powerful form of the Remove Curse spell. It will automatically remove any curse or hex short of a Death Hex or Divine Curse. The material component is the cleric's holy or unholy symbol.

Commune

(Divination)
Level: 5
Range: 0
Duration: Special
Area of Effect: Special

Components: V, S, M
Casting Time: 1 turn
Saving Throw: None

By use of a Commune spell, the cleric is able to contact his gawd—or agents thereof— and request information in the form of questions that can be answered by a simple "yes" or "no." The cleric is allowed one such question for every experience level he has attained. The answers given are correct within the limits of the entity's knowledge. "I don't know" is a legitimate answer, as powerful outer planar beings are not necessarily omniscient. Optionally, the GM may give a single short answer of five words or less. The spell will, at best, provide information to aid character decisions. Entities communed with structure their answers to further their own purposes.

It is probable that the GM will limit the use of Commune spells to one per adventure, one per week, or even one per month, for the greater powers dislike frequent interruptions. Likewise, if the caster lags, discusses the answers, or goes off to do anything else, the spell immediately ends. The material components necessary for a Commune spell are the cleric's religious symbol, holy (unholy) water, and incense.

If a particularly potent Commune is needed, a sacrifice proportionate with the difficulty of obtaining the information is required. If the offering is insufficient, no information or only partial information is gained.

Cure Critical Wounds

(Necromancy)
Reversible
Level: 5
Range: Touch
Duration: Permanent
Area of Effect: 1 creature
Components: V, S
Casting Time: 5 segments
Saving Throw: None

This spell is exactly like a Cure Light Wounds spell except that it heals 1d12 points of damage per level of the cleric and its reverse causes 1d12 damage per caster level.

Detect Ulterior Motives

(Divination)
Level: 5
Range: 0
Duration: 1 round/level
Area of Effect: 10 ft./level
Components: V, S, M
Casting Time: 1 round
Saving Throw: None

This spell allows the caster to determine the true intentions of any creature within the spell's area of effect. The caster will know if a creature is lying, what his general plans are, and what his true feelings are while the spell lasts. The cleric may broaden or narrow his focus as needed, so he could gauge a mob's motives before moving on to determine the leader's plans. The cleric must have his holy (or unholy) symbol in order to cast this spell.

Dispel Evil

(Abjuration)
Reversible
Level: 5
Range: Touch
Duration: 1 rd./level
Area of Effect: 1 creature
Components: V, S, M
Casting Time: 8 segments
Saving Throw: Negates

The cleric using this spell causes a summoned creature of evil nature, an evil creature from another plane, or a creature summoned by an evil caster, to return to its own plane or place when the caster successfully strikes it in melee combat. Examples of such creatures are Aerial Servants, djinn, Efreet, elementals, and Invisible Stalkers.

An evil enchantment (such as a charm spell cast by an evil creature) that is subject to a normal Dispel Magic spell can be automatically dispelled by the Dispel Evil spell. This spell lasts for a maximum of one round for each experience level of the caster, or until expended. While the spell is in effect, all creatures that could be affected by it fight with a -7 penalty to their attack rolls when engaging the spellcaster.

The reverse of the spell, Dispel Good, functions against summoned or enchanted creatures of good alignment or creatures that have been sent to aid the cause of good. The material components for this spell are the cleric's religious object and holy (or unholy) water.

Flame Strike

(Evocation)
Level: 5
Range: 60 yds.
Duration: Instantaneous
Area of Effect: 5 ft. x 30 ft. column
Components: V, S, M
Casting Time: 8 segments
Saving Throw: Half

When the cleric evokes a Flame Strike spell, a vertical column of fire roars downward in the location called for by the caster. Any creatures within the area of effect must roll a saving throw vs. spell. Failure means the creature sustains 6d8 points of damage; otherwise, the damage is halved. The material component of this spell is a pinch of sulphur.

Heal Serious Wounds

(Necromancy)
Level: 5
Range: 5 ft./level
Duration: Permanent
Area of Effect: 1 creature
Components: V, S
Casting Time: 5 segments
Saving Throw: None

By using this spell a cleric can restore 1d10 lost hit points per level to any one creature within the range of the spell. The hit points are healed in the same way as a Cure Light Wounds spell and are subject to the same limitations.

Insect Plague

(Conjuration/Summoning)
Level: 5
Range: 120 yds.
Duration: 2 rds./level
Area of Effect: 180 ft. x 60 ft. cloud
Components: V, S, M
Casting Time: 1 turn
Saving Throw: None

When this spell is cast by the cleric, a horde of creeping, hopping, and flying insects gather and swarm in a thick cloud. In an environment free of normal insects, the spell fails. The insects obscure vision, limiting it to 10 feet. Spellcasting within the cloud is impossible. Creatures in the Insect Cloud suffer 1 point of damage each round they remain within, regardless of Armor Class, due to the bites and stings of the insects. Invisibility is no protection. All creatures with 2 or fewer Hit Dice will automatically move at their fastest possible speed in a random direction until they are more than 240 yards away from the insects. Creatures with fewer than 5 Hit Dice must check morale; failure means they run as described above.

Heavy smoke drives off insects within its bounds. Fire also drives insects away. For example, a Wall of Fire in a ring shape keeps a subsequently cast Insect Plague outside its confines, but a Fireball spell simply clears insects from its blast area for one round. A single torch is ineffective against this vast horde of insects. Lightning, cold, or ice are likewise ineffective, while a strong wind that covers the entire plague area disperses the insects and ends the spell.

The plague lasts two rounds for each level of the caster, and thereafter the insects disperse. The insects swarm in an area that centers around a summon-

ing point determined by the spellcaster. The point can be up to 120 yards away from the cleric. The insect plague does not move thereafter for as long as it lasts. Note that the spell can be countered by a Dispel Magic spell. The material components of this spell are a few granules of sugar, some kernels of grain and a smear of fat.

Magic Font

(Divination)

Level: 5

Range: Touch	**Components:** V, S, M
Duration: Special	**Casting Time:** I hour
Area of Effect: Special	**Saving Throw:** None

The spell causes a holy water font to serve as a scrying device. The spell does not function unless the cleric is in good standing with his gawd. The basin of holy water becomes similar to a Crystal Ball. For each vial of capacity of the basin, the cleric may scry for one round, up to a maximum of one hour. Thus, the duration of the magic font spell is directly related to the size of the holy water receptacle. The GM will know the chances of a character being able to detect scrying. The cleric's holy symbol and the font and its trappings are not consumed by the spell.

Plane Shift

(Alteration)

Level: 5

Range: Touch	**Components:** V, S, M
Duration: Permanent	**Casting Time:** 8 segments
Area of Effect: I creature	**Saving Throw:** Neg. (special)

When the Plane Shift spell is cast, the cleric moves himself or some other creature to another plane of existence. The recipient of the spell remains in the new plane until sent forth by some like means. If several persons link hands in a circle, up to eight can be affected by the Plane Shift at the same time.

The material component of this spell is a small, forked metal rod. The size and metal type dictates to which plane of existence (including sub-planes and alternate dimensions) the spell sends the affected creatures. The GM will determine specifics regarding how and what planes are reached. An unwilling victim must be touched (successful attack roll) to be sent. In addition, the creature is also allowed a saving throw. If the saving throw is successful, the effect of the spell is negated.

Note that pinpoint accuracy is rarely achieved; arriving at a random distance from an intended destination is common. The metal rod is not expended when the spell is cast. Forked rods keyed to certain planes may be difficult to come by, as decided by the GM.

Quest

(Enchantment/Charm)

Level: 5

Range: 60 yds.	**Components:** V, S, M
Duration: Until fulfilled	**Casting Time:** 8 segments
Area of Effect: I creature	**Saving Throw:** Negates

The Quest spell enables the cleric to require the affected creature to perform a service and return to the cleric with proof that the deed was accomplished. The quest can, for example, require that the creature locate and return some important or valuable object, rescue a notable person, release some creature, capture a stronghold, slay a person, deliver some item, and so forth.

If the quest is not properly followed, due to disregard, intentional delay, or perversion, the creature affected by the spell loses 1 from its saving throw rolls for each day of such action. This penalty is not removed until the quest is properly pursued or the cleric cancels it. There are certain circumstances that will temporarily suspend a Quest, and others that will discharge or cancel it. The GM will give you appropriate information as the need to know arises. If cast upon an unwilling subject, the victim is allowed a saving throw. However, if the person quested agrees to a task—even if the agreement is gained by force or trickery—no saving throw is allowed. If a quest is just and deserved, a crea-

ture of the cleric's religion cannot avoid it, and any creature of the cleric's alignment saves with a -4 penalty to the saving throw.

A Quest spell cannot be dispelled, but it can be removed by a cleric of the same religion or of higher level than the caster. Some artifacts and relics might negate the spell, as can direct intervention by a gawd. Likewise, an unjust or undeserved quest grants bonuses to saving throws, or might even automatically fail. The material component of this spell is the cleric's holy symbol.

Rainbow

(Evocation, Alteration)

Level: 5

Range: 120 yds.	**Components:** V, S, M
Duration: I rd./level	**Casting Time:** 7 segments
Area of Effect: Special	**Saving Throw:** None

To cast this spell, the cleric must be in sight of a rainbow, or have a special component (see below). The Rainbow spell has two applications, and the cleric can choose the desired one at the time of casting. These applications are as follows:

Bow: The spell creates a shimmering, multi-layered short composite bow of rainbow hues. It is light and easy to pull, so that any character can use it without penalty for non-proficiency. It is magical: Each of its shimmering missiles is the equivalent of a +2 weapon, including attack and damage bonuses. Magic resistance can negate the effect of any missile fired from the bow. The bow fires seven missiles before disappearing. It can be fired up to four times per round. Each time a missile is fired, one hue leaves the bow, corresponding to the color of arrow that is released. Each color of arrow has the ability to cause double damage to certain creatures, as follows:

Red - fire dwellers/users and fire elementals

Orange - creatures or constructs of clay, sand, earth, stone or similar materials, and earth elementals

Yellow - vegetable opponents (including fungus creatures, Shambling Mounds, Treants, etc.)

Green - aquatic creatures, electricity-using creatures, and Air Elementals

Indigo - acid-using or poison-using creatures

Violet - metallic or regenerating creatures

When the bow is drawn, an arrow of the appropriate color magically appears, nocked and ready. If no color is requested, or a color that has already been used is asked for, then the next arrow (in the order of the spectrum) appears.

Bridge: The caster causes the rainbow to form a seven-hued bridge up to 3 feet wide per level of the caster. It must be at least 20 feet long and can be as long as 120 yards, according to the caster's desire. It lasts as long as the spell's duration or until ordered out of existence by the caster. The components for this spell are the cleric's holy symbol and a vial of holy water. If no rainbow is in the vicinity, the caster can substitute a diamond of not less than 1,000 gp value, specially prepared with Bless and Prayer spells while in sight of a rainbow. The holy water and diamond disappear when the spell is cast.

Raise Dead

(Necromancy)

Reversible

Level: 5

Range: 30 yds.	**Components:** V, S
Duration: Permanent	**Casting Time:** I round
Area of Effect: I person	**Saving Throw:** Special

When the cleric casts a Raise Dead spell, he can restore life to a dwarf, gnome, half-elf, halfling, or human (other creatures may be allowed, at the GM's option). The length of time that the person has been dead is important, as the cleric can raise persons dead only up to a limit of one day for each experience level of the cleric (i.e., a 9th-level cleric can raise a person who has been dead for up to nine days).

Note that the body of the person must be whole, or otherwise missing parts are still missing when the person is brought back to life. Likewise, other ills, such as poison and disease, are not negated. The raised person must roll a successful resurrection survival check to survive the ordeal and loses 1 point of

Constitution. Further, the raised person is weak and helpless, needing a minimum of one full day of rest in bed for each day or fraction of a day he was dead. The person has 1 hit point when raised and must regain the rest by natural healing or curative magic.

A cleric gains experience points for raising the dead as if he defeated that creature in individual combat.

A character's starting Constitution is an absolute limit to the number of times he can be revived by this means. The somatic component of the spell is a pointed finger. The reverse of the spell, Slay Living, grants the victim a saving throw vs. death magic. If the saving throw is successful, the victim sustains damage equal to that of a cause serious wounds spell—i.e., 2d8+1 hit points. Failure means the victim dies instantly.

Rigor Mortis, 10' Radius

(Necromancy)

Level: 5

Range: 120 yds.

Duration: 2 rds./level

Area of Effect: 10 ft. radius

Components: V, S

Casting Time: 5 segments

Saving Throw: Negates

This spell works exactly like the 2nd level spell Rigor Mortis, except that it affects all creatures within a 10-foot radius.

Spike Growth

(Alteration, Enchantment)

Level: 5

Range: 60 yds.

Duration: 3d4 turns + 1/level

Area of Effect: 10 ft. sq./level

Components: V, S, M

Casting Time: 6 segments

Saving Throw: None

Wherever any type of plant growth of moderate size or density is found, this spell can be used. The ground-covering vegetation or roots and rootlets in the area becomes very hard and sharply pointed. In effect, the ground cover, while appearing to be unchanged, acts as if the area were strewn with caltrops.

In areas of bare ground or earthen pits, roots and rootlets act in the same way. For each 10 feet of movement through the area, the victim suffers 2d4 points of damage. He must also roll a saving throw vs. spell. If this saving throw is failed, the victim's movement rate is reduced by 1/3 of its current total (but a creature's movement rate can never be less than 1). This penalty lasts for 24 hours, after which the character's normal movement rate is regained.

Without the use of a spell such as True Seeing, similar magical aids, or some other special means of detection (such as Detect Traps or Detect Snares and Pits), an area affected by Spike Growth is absolutely undetectable as such until a victim enters the area and suffers damage. Even then, the creature cannot determine the extent of the perilous area unless some means of magical detection is used. The components for this spell are the cleric's holy symbol and either seven sharp thorns or seven small twigs, each sharpened to a point.

True Seeing

(Divination)

Reversible

Level: 5

Range: Touch

Duration: 1 rd./level

Area of Effect: 1 creature

Components: V, S, M

Casting Time: 8 segments

Saving Throw: None

Except as noted above, this spell is the same as the sixth level magic-user spell True Seeing (q.v.).

Sixth Level Cleric Spells

Aerial Servant

(Conjuration/Summoning)

Level: 6

Range: 10 yds.

Duration: 1 day/level

Area of Effect: Special

Components: V, S

Casting Time: 9 segments

Saving Throw: None

This spell summons an invisible AerialSservant to find and bring back an object or creature described to it by the cleric. Unlike an elemental, an Aerial Servant cannot be commanded to fight for the caster. When it is summoned, the cleric must have cast a Protection From Evil spell, be within a protective circle, or have a special item used to control the aerial servant. Otherwise, it attempts to slay its summoner and return from whence it came.

The object or creature to be brought must be such as to allow the Aerial Servant to physically bring it to the cleric (an Aerial Servant has a 23 Strength). If prevented, for any reason, from completing the assigned duty, the aerial servant returns to its own plane whenever the spell lapses, its duty is fulfilled, it is dispelled, the cleric releases it, or the cleric is slain.

The spell lasts for a maximum of one day for each level of experience of the cleric who cast it. If the creature to be fetched cannot detect invisible objects, the Aerial Servant attacks, automatically gaining surprise. If the creature involved can detect invisible objects, it still suffers a -2 penalty to all surprise rolls caused by the aerial servant. Each round of combat, the Aerial Servant must roll to attack. When a hit is scored, the Aerial Servant can grab the item or creature it was sent for in lieu of dealing damage.

Most people who are caught in the grasp of an Aerial Servant will be unable to escape. Only those with a Strengths of greater than 18 will have any chance of escaping. For each Strength point score (not Fractional) past 18, the character has a 20% chance of breaking free. A character with a strength of 20, for instance, will have a 40 percent chance of gaining his freedom. If the first attempt to break free fails, the creature cannot free itself and is flown to the cleric forthwith.

Animate Object

(Alteration)

Level: 6

Range: 30 yds.

Duration: 1 rd./level

Area of Effect: 1 cu. ft./level

Components: V, S

Casting Time: 9 segments

Saving Throw: None

This powerful spell enables the cleric casting it to imbue inanimate objects with mobility and a semblance of life. The animated object, or objects, then attacks whomever or whatever the cleric first designates. The animated object can be of any nonmagical material whatsoever (wood, metal, stone, fabric, leather, ceramic, glass, etc).

Attempting to animate an object in someone's possession grants that person a saving throw to prevent the spell's effect. The speed of movement of the object depends on its means of propulsion and its weight. A large wooden table would be rather heavy, but its legs would give it speed. A rug could only slither along. A jar would roll. Thus a large stone pedestal would rock forward at 10 feet per round, a stone statue would move at 40 feet per round, a wooden statue 80 feet per round, an ivory stool of light weight would move at 120 feet per round. Slithering movement is about 10 feet to 20 feet per round; rolling is 30 feet to 60 feet per round.

The damage caused by the attack of an animated object depends on its form and composition. Light, supple objects can only obscure vision, obstruct movement, bind, trip, smother, etc. Light, hard objects can fall upon or otherwise strike for 1d2 points of damage or possibly obstruct and trip, as do light, supple objects. Hard, medium-weight objects can crush or strike for 2d4 points of damage, while larger and heavier objects may inflict 3d4, 4d4, or even 5d4 points of damage.

The frequency of attack of animated objects depends on their method of locomotion, appendages, and method of attack. This varies from as seldom as once every five melee rounds to as frequently as once per round. The Armor Class of the object per round. The Armor Class of the object animated is basically a function of material and movement ability. Damage depends on the type of weapon is effective against fabric, leather, wood, and like substances. Heavy smashing and crushing weapons are useful against wood, stone, and metal objects. Your GM will determine all of these factors, as well as how much damage the animated object can sustain before being destroyed.

The cleric can animate one cubic foot of material for each experience level he has attained. Thus, a 14th-level cleric could animate one or more objects whose total solid volume did not exceed 14 cubic feet (for example, a large statue, two rugs, three chairs, or a dozen average crocks).

Blade Barrier

(Evocation)

Level: 6

Range: 30 yds. **Components:** V, S
Duration: 3 rds./level **Casting Time:** 9 segments
Area of Effect: 5-60 ft. sq. **Saving Throw:** Special

The cleric employs this spell to set up a wall of circling, razor-sharp blades. These whirl and flash around a central point, creating an immobile barrier. Any creature attempting to pass through the blade barrier suffers 8d8 points of damage. The plane of rotation of the blades can be horizontal, vertical, or in between.

Creatures within the area of the barrier when it is invoked are entitled to a saving throw vs. spell. If this is successful, the blades are avoided and no damage is suffered; the creature escapes the area of the Blade Barrier by the shortest possible route. The barrier remains for three rounds for every experience level of the cleric casting it. The Blade Barrier can cover an area from as small as 5 feet square to as large as 60 feet square.

Conjure Animals

(Conjuration/Summoning)

Level: 6

Range: 30 yds. **Components:** V, S
Duration: 2 rds./level **Casting Time:** 9 segments
Area of Effect: Special **Saving Throw:** None

Except as noted above, this spell is the same as the sixth level magic-user spell Conjure Animals (q.v.).

Cure-All

(Necromancy)

Reversible

Level: 6

Range: Touch **Components:** V, S
Duration: Permanent **Casting Time:** 1 round
Area of Effect: 1 creature **Saving Throw:** None

The very potent Cure-All spell enables the cleric to wipe away disease and injury in the creature who receives the benefits of the spell. It completely cures all diseases or blindness in the recipient and heals all points of damage suffered due to wounds or injury. It dispels a Feeblemind spell. It cures those mental disorders caused by spells or injury to the brain, including quirks and flaws. It removes those nasty guilt feelings and nightmares associated with a character foolishly falling asleep on night watch and allowing one or more of his close comrades to die a horrible painful death.

Naturally, the effects can be negated by later wounds, injuries, diseases and psychoses. The reverse, Harm, infects the victim with a disease and causes loss of all but 1d4 hit points, if a successful touch is inflicted. For creatures that are not affected by the Cure-All or Harm spell, see the Cure Light Wounds spell.

Find the Path

(Divination)

Reversible

Level: 6

Range: Touch **Components:** V, S, M
Duration: 1 turn/level **Casting Time:** 3 rds.
Area of Effect: 1 creature **Saving Throw:** None

The recipient of this spell can find the shortest, most direct physical route that he is seeking, be it the way into or out of a locale. The locale can be outdoors or under ground, a trap, or even a Maze spell. Note that the spell works with respect to locales, not objects or creatures within a locale. Thus, the spell could not find the way to "a forest where a Green Dragon lives" or to the location of "a hoard of platinum pieces." The location must be in the same plane as the caster.

The spell enables the subject to sense the correct direction that will eventually lead him to his destination, indicating at the appropriate times the exact path to follow or physical actions to take. For example, with concentration the spell enables the subject to sense trip wires or the proper word to bypass a glyph. The spell ends when the destination is reached or when one turn for each caster level has elapsed. The spell frees the subject, and those with him, from a Maze spell in a single round, and will continue to do so as long as the spell lasts.

Note that this divination is keyed to the caster, not his companions, and that, like the Find Traps spell, it does not predict or allow for the actions of creatures. The spell requires a set of divination counters of the sort favored by the cleric—bones, ivory counters, sticks, carved runes, or whatever. The reverse spell, lose the path, makes the creature touched totally lost and unable to find its way for the duration of the spell—although it can be led, of course.

Forbiddance

(Abjuration)

Level: 6

Range: 30 yds. **Components:** V, S, M
Duration: Permanent **Casting Time:** 6 rds.
Area of Effect: 60-ft. cube/level **Saving Throw:** Special

This spell can be used to secure a consecrated area (see the GMG). The spell seals the area from teleportation, plane shifting, and ethereal penetration. At the option of the caster, the ward can be locked by a password, in which case it can be entered only by those speaking the proper words. Otherwise, the effect on those entering the enchanted area is based on their alignment, relative to the caster's. The most severe penalty is used.

Alignment identical: No effect. If password locked, cannot enter area unless password is known (no saving throw).

Alignment different with respect to law and chaos: Save vs. spell to enter the area; if failed, suffer 2d6 points of damage. If password locked, cannot enter unless password is known.

Alignment different with respect to good and evil: Save vs. spell to enter this area; if failed, suffer 4d6 points of damage. If word locked, cannot enter unless password is known. The attempt does cause damage if the save is failed. Once a saving throw is failed, an intruder cannot enter the forbidden area until the spell ceases. The ward cannot be dispelled by a caster of lesser level than the one who established it. Intruders who enter by rolling successful saving throws feel uneasy and tense, despite their success. In addition to the cleric's holy symbol, components include holy water and rare incenses worth at least 1,000 gp per 60-foot cube. If a password lock is desired, this also requires the burning of rare incenses worth at least 5,000 gp per 60-foot cube.

Heal Critical Wounds

(Necromancy)

Level: 6

Range: 5 ft./level **Components:** V, S
Duration: Permanent **Casting Time:** 5 segments
Area of Effect: 1 creature **Saving Throw:** None

By using this spell a cleric can restore 1d12 lost hit points per caster level to any one creature within the range of the spell. The hit points are healed in the same way as a Cure Light Wounds spell and are subject to the same limitations.

Heroes' Feast

(Evocation)
Level: 6
Range: 10 yds.   **Components:** V, S, M
Duration: 1 hour   **Casting Time:** 1 turn
Area of Effect: 1 feaster/level   **Saving Throw:** None

This spell enables the cleric to bring forth a great feast that serves as many creatures as the cleric has levels of experience. The spell creates a magnificent table, chairs, service, and all the necessary food and drink. The feast takes one full hour to consume, and the beneficial effects do not set in until after this hour is over.

Those partaking of the feast are cured of all diseases, are immune to poison for 12 hours, and are healed of 1d4+4 points of damage after imbibing the nectar-like beverage that is part of the feast. The ambrosia-like food that is consumed is equal to a Bless spell that lasts for 12 hours. Also, during this same period, the people who consumed the feast are immune to fear, hopelessness, and panic.

If the feast is interrupted for any reason, the spell is ruined and all effects of the spell are negated. The material components of the spell are the cleric's holy symbol and specially fermented honey taken from the cells of bee larvae destined for royal status.

Part Water

(Alteration)
Level: 6
Range: 20 yds./level   **Components:** V, S, M
Duration: 1 turn/level   **Casting Time:** 1 turn
Area of Effect: 3 ft./level x   **Saving Throw:** None
         20 yds./level x 30 yds.

Except as noted above, this spell is the same as the sixth level magic-user spell Part Water (q.v.).

Speak With Monsters

(Alteration)
Level: 6
Range: 30 yds.   **Components:** V, S
Duration: 2 rd./level   **Casting Time:** 9 segments
Area of Effect: The caster   **Saving Throw:** None

When cast, the Speak With Monsters spell enables the cleric to converse with any type of creature that has any form of communicative ability (including empathic, tactile, pheromones, etc.). That is, the monster understands, in its own language or equivalent, the intent of what is said to it by the cleric and vice versa. The creature thus spoken to is checked by the GM to determine a reaction.

All creatures of the same type as that chosen by the cleric can likewise understand if they are within range. The cleric can speak to different types of creatures during the spell duration, but he must speak separately to each type. The spell lasts for two rounds per caster level.

Stone Tell

(Divination)
Level: 6
Range: Touch   **Components:** V, S, M
Duration: 1 turn   **Casting Time:** 1 turn
Area of Effect: 1 cu. yd.   **Saving Throw:** None

When the cleric casts a Stone Tell spell upon an area, the very stones speak and relate to the caster who or what has touched them as well as revealing what is covered, concealed, or simply behind them. The stones relate complete descriptions, if asked. Note that a stone's perspective, perception, and knowledge may hinder this divination. Such details, if any, are decided by the GM. The material components for this spell are a drop of mercury and a bit of clay.

Word of Recall

(Alteration)
Level: 6
Range: 0   **Components:** V
Duration: Special   **Casting Time:** 1 segment
Area of Effect: The caster   **Saving Throw:** None

The Word of Recall spell takes the cleric instantly back to his sanctuary when the word is uttered. The sanctuary must be specifically designated in advance by the cleric and must be a well-known place. The actual point of arrival is a designated area no larger than 10 ft. x 10 ft. The cleric can be transported any distance, from above or below ground.

Transportation by the Word of Recall spell is safe within a plane, but for each plane the cleric is removed, there is a 10% cumulative chance that the cleric is irrevocably lost. The cleric is able to transport, in addition to himself, 25 pounds of weight per experience level. Thus, a 15th-level cleric could transport his person and an additional 375 pounds. This extra matter can be equipment, treasure, or even living material, such as another person. Exceeding this limit causes the spell to fail.

Note that unusually strong physical fields, such as magnetic or gravitational forces, or even magical applications can, at the GM's option, make the use of this spell hazardous or impossible.

Seventh Level Cleric Spells

Astral Spell

(Alteration)
Level: 7
Range: Touch   **Components:** V, S
Duration: Special   **Casting Time:** 9 segments
Area of Effect: Special   **Saving Throw:** None

Except as noted above, this spell is the same as the ninth level magic-user Astral Spell.

Control Weather

(Alteration)

Level: 7

Range: 0	**Components:** V, S, M
Duration: 4d12 hours	**Casting Time:** I turn
Area of Effect: 4d4 sq. miles	**Saving Throw:** None

Except as noted above, this spell is the same as the sixth level magic-user spell Control Weather.

Earthquake

(Alteration)

Level: 7

Range: 120 yds.	**Components:** V, S, M
Duration: I round	**Casting Time:** I turn
Area of Effect: 5 ft. diameter/ level	**Saving Throw:** None

When this spell is cast by a cleric, a local tremor of fairly high strength rips the ground. The shock is over in one round. The earthquake affects all terrain, vegetation, structures, and creatures in its area of effect. The area of effect of the Earthquake spell is circular, with a diameter of 5 feet for every experience level of the cleric casting it. Thus a 20th-level cleric casts an earthquake spell with a 100-foot-diameter area of effect.

Solidly built structures with foundations reaching down to bedrock sustain one-half damage; one-quarter damage if they score above 50% on a saving throw. An Earth Elemental opposed to the caster in the area of effect can negate 10% to 100% (roll 1d10, 0 = 100%) of the effect. Other magical protections and wards allowed by the GM may also reduce or negate this effect. If cast undersea, this spell may, at the discretion of the GM, create a tsunami or tidal wave.

The material components for this spell are a pinch of dirt, a piece of rock, and a lump of clay.

Earthquake Effects

TERRAIN and CREATURES	Result
Cave or cavern	Collapses roof
Cliffs	Crumble, causing landslide
Ground	Cracks open, causing the following fractions of creatures to fall in and die:
Creatures Size S:	I in 4
Creatures Size M:	I in 6
Creatures Size L:	I in 8
Marsh	Drains water to form muddy, rough ground.
Tunnel	Caves in
VEGETATION	**Result**
Small growth	No effect
Trees	I in 3 are uprooted and fall
STRUCTURES	**Result**
All structures	Sustain 5d12 points of structural damage; those suffering full damage are thrown down in rubble

Exaction

(Evocation, Alteration)

Level: 7

Range: 10 yds.	**Components:** V, S, M
Duration: Special	**Casting Time:** I round
Area of Effect: I creature	**Saving Throw:** None

When this spell is employed, the cleric confronts some powerful creature from another plane (including devas and other powerful minions, for instance, but not demigawds or gawds of any sort) and requires of it some duty or quest. A creature of an alignment opposed to the cleric (e.g., evil if the cleric is good, chaotic if the cleric is lawful) cannot be ordered around unless it is willing. Note that an absolute (true) neutral creature is effectively opposed to both good and evil, and both law and chaos.

The spellcaster must know something about the creature to exact service from it, or else he must offer some fair trade in return for the service. That is, if the cleric is aware that the creature has received some favor from someone of the cleric's alignment, then the Exaction spell can name this as cause. If no

balancing reason for service is known, then some valuable gift or service must be pledged in return for the exaction.

The service exacted must be reasonable with respect to the past or promised favor or reward, and with the being's effort and risk. The spell then acts, subject to a magic resistance roll, as a quest upon the being that is to perform the required service. Immediately upon completion of the service, the being is transported to the vicinity of the cleric, and the cleric must then and there return the promised reward, whether it is irrevocable cancellation of a past debt or the giving of some service or other material reward. After this is done, the creature is instantly freed to return to its own plane.

The GM adjudicates when an equitable arrangement has been reached. If the caster requests too much, the creature is free to depart or to attack the cleric (as if the agreement were breached) according to its nature. If circumstances leave the situation unbalanced (for example, the creature dies while achieving a result that was not worth dying for), then this might create a debt owed by the caster to the creature's surviving kith and kin, making the caster vulnerable to a future Exaction spell from that quarter. Agreeing to a future exaction or release in the event of catastrophic failure or death are common caster pledges in securing an exaction.

Failure to fulfill the promise to the letter results in the cleric being subject to exaction by the subject creature or by its master, liege, etc., at the very least. At worst, the creature can attack the reneging cleric without fear of any of his spells affecting it, for the cleric's failure to live up to the bargain gives the creature immunity from the cleric's spell powers.

The material components of this spell are the cleric's holy symbol, some matter or substance from the plane of the creature from whom an exaction is expected, and knowledge of the creature's nature or actions that is written out on a parchment that is burned to seal the pledge.

Gate

(Conjuration/Summoning)

Level: 7

Range: 30 yds.	**Components:** V, S
Duration: Special	**Casting Time:** 5 segments
Area of Effect: Special	**Saving Throw:** None

Except as noted above, this spell is the same as the ninth level magic-user spell Gate.

Holy Word

(Conjuration/Summoning)

Reversible

Level: 7

Range: 0	**Components:** V
Duration: Special	**Casting Time:** I segment
Area of Effect: 30 ft. radius	**Saving Throw:** None

Uttering a Holy Word spell creates magic of tremendous power. It drives off creatures from other planes, forcing them to return to their own planes of existence, provided the speaker is in his home plane. Creatures so banished cannot return for at least a day. The spell further affects creatures of an alignment different from that of the caster as shown on the following table:

Effects of Holy Word

Creatures Hit Dice or Level	General	Move	Attack Dice	Spells
Less than 4	Kills	—	—	—
4 to 7+	Paralyzes 1d4 turns	—	—	—
8 to 11+	Slows 2d4 rounds	-50%	-4* -	-
12 or more	Deafens 1d4 rounds	-25%	-2	50% chance of failure

* Slowed creatures attack only on even-numbered rounds until the effect wears off. Affected creatures are those within the 30-foot-radius area of effect, which is centered on the cleric casting the spell. The side effects are negated for deafened or silenced creatures, but such are still driven off if other-planar.

The reverse of this spell, Unholy Word, operates exactly the same way but affects creatures of good alignment.

Regenerate

(Necromancy)
Reversible
Level: 7
Range: Touch
Duration: Permanent
Area of Effect: Creature touched
Components: V, S, M
Casting Time: 3 rounds
Saving Throw: None

When a Regenerate spell is cast, body members (fingers, toes, hands, feet, arms, legs, tails, or even heads of multi-headed creatures), bones, and organs grow back. The process of regeneration requires but one round if the severed member(s) is (are) present and touching the creature, or 2d4 turns otherwise.

The creature must be living to receive the benefits of this spell. If the severed member is not present, or if the injury is older than one day per caster level, the recipient must roll a successful system shock check to survive the spell. The reverse of this spell, Wither, causes the member or organ touched to cease functioning in one round, dropping off into dust in 2d4 turns. Creatures must be touched for the harmful effect to occur. The material components of this spell are a prayer device and holy water (or unholy water for the reverse).

Restoration

(Necromancy)
Reversible
Level: 7
Range: Touch
Duration: Permanent
Area of Effect: 1 creature
Components: V, S
Casting Time: 3 rounds
Saving Throw: None

When this spell is cast, the life energy level of the recipient creature is raised by one. This reverses any previous life energy level drain of the creature by a force or monster. Thus, if a 10th-level character had been struck by a Wight and drained to 9th level, the Restoration spell would bring the character up to exactly the number of experience points necessary to restore him to 10th level once again, restoring additional Hit Dice (or hit points) and level functions accordingly.

Restoration is effective only if the spell is cast within one day of the recipient's loss of life energy, per experience level of the cleric casting it. A Restoration spell restores the intelligence of a creature affected by a Feeblemind spell. It also negates all forms of insanity. Casting this spell ages both the caster and the recipient by two years. The reverse, Energy Drain, draws away one life energy level (see such undead as Spectre, Wight, and Vampire, in the Hacklopedia of Beasts). The Energy Drain requires the victim to be touched. Casting this form of the spell does not age the caster.

Restorative Cure-All

(Necromancy)
Level: 7
Range: Touch
Duration: Permanent
Area of Effect: 1 creature
Components: V, S
Casting Time: 1 round
Saving Throw: None

This spell works exactly like a Cure-All spell except that it heals all damage that the creature has suffered, leaving them well rested as if they had just received eight hours of sleep, removing any curses affecting the creature, and leaving their mouth feeling minty fresh.

Resurrection

(Necromancy)
Reversible
Level: 7
Range: Touch
Duration: Permanent
Area of Effect: 1 creature
Components: V, S, M
Casting Time: 1 turn
Saving Throw: None

The cleric is able to restore life and complete strength to any living creature, including elves, by bestowing the Resurrection spell. The creature can have been dead up to 10 years per level of the cleric casting the spell. Thus, a 19th-level cleric can resurrect the bones of a creature dead up to 190 years.

The creature, upon surviving a Resurrection survival check, is immediately restored to full hit points and can perform strenuous activity. The spell cannot bring back a creature that has reached its allotted life span (i.e., died of natural causes). Casting this spell makes it impossible for the cleric to cast further spells or engage in combat until he has had one day of bed rest for each experience level or Hit Die of the creature brought back to life. The caster ages three years upon casting this spell.

The reverse, Destruction, causes the victim of the spell to be instantly dead and turned to dust. A Wish spell or equivalent is required for recovery. Destruction requires a touch, either in combat or otherwise, and does not age the caster. In addition, the victim is allowed a saving throw (with a -4 penalty). If the save is successful, the victim receives 8d6 points of damage instead.

A cleric gains experience points for raising the dead as if he defeated that creature in individual combat.

The material components of the spell are the cleric's religious symbol and holy water (unholy water for the reverse spell). The GM may reduce the chances of successful resurrection if little of the creature's remains are available.

Succor

(Alteration, Enchantment)
Reversible
Level: 7
Range: Touch
Duration: Special
Area of Effect: 1 person
Components: V, S, M
Casting Time: 1 day
Saving Throw: None

Except as noted above, this spell is the same as the ninth level magic-user spell Succor (q.v.).

Sunray

(Evocation, Alteration)
Level: 7
Range: 10 yds./level
Duration: 1+1d4 rds.
Area of Effect: 5-ft. radius (special)
Components: V, S, M
Casting Time: 4 segments
Saving Throw: Special

With this spell, the caster can evoke a dazzling beam of light each round in which no action other than movement is performed. The Sunray is like a ray of natural sunlight. All creatures in the 10-foot-diameter area of effect must roll successful saving throws vs. spell or be blinded for 1d3 rounds, those using infravision at the time for 2d4 rounds.

Creatures to whom sunlight is harmful or unnatural suffer permanent blindness if the saving throw is failed, and are blinded for 2d6 rounds if the saving throw is successful. Those within its area of effect, as well as creatures within 20 feet of its perimeter, lose any infravision capabilities for 1d4+1 rounds. Undead caught within the sunray's area of effect receive 8d6 points of damage, one-half if a saving throw vs. spell is successful. Those undead 20 feet to either side of the Sunray's area of effect receive 3d6 points of damage, no damage if a save is successful. In addition, the ray may result in the total destruction of those undead specifically affected by sunlight, if their saving throws are failed.

The ultraviolet light generated by the spell inflicts damage on fungoid creatures and subterranean fungi just as if they were undead, but no saving throw is allowed.

The material components are an aster seed and a piece of adventuring feldspar (sunstone).

Symbol

(Conjuration/Summoning)
Level: 7
Range: Touch
Duration: 1 turn/level
Area of Effect: 60 ft. radius
Components: V, S, M
Casting Time: 3 segments
Saving Throw: Negates

Except as noted above, this spell is the same as the eighth level magic-user spell Symbol (q.v.).

Wind Walk
(Alteration)
Level: 7
Range: Touch
Duration: 1 hour/level
Area of Effect: Caster + 1 person/8 levels

Components: V, S, M
Casting Time: 1 round
Saving Throw: None

This spell enables the cleric (and possibly one or two other persons) to alter the substance of his body to a cloud-like vapor. A magical wind then wafts the cleric along at a movement rate of 60, or as slow as 6, as the spellcaster wills. The Wind Walk spell lasts as long as the cleric desires, up to a maximum duration of six turns (one hour) per experience level of the caster. For every eight levels of experience the cleric has attained, up to 24, he is able to touch another person and carry that person, or those persons, along on the Wind Walk.

Persons wind walking are not invisible, but rather appear misty and translucent. If fully clothed in white, they are 80% likely to be mistaken for clouds, fog, vapors, etc. The cleric can regain his physical form as desired, each change to and from vaporous form requiring five rounds.

While in vaporous form, the cleric and companions are hit only by magic or magical weaponry, though they may be subject to high winds at the GM's discretion. No spellcasting is possible in vaporous form. The material components of this spell are fire and holy water.

Druid Spells

Notes Regarding Druid Spells:

The religious symbol of druids is mistletoe. Of lesser importance is holly, and some magical power resides in oak leaves. All of the druid spells with a material component assume the use of mistletoe, as gathered by the druid character in the manner described hereafter. Lesser mistletoe, as well as holly and oak leaves, will reduce spell effectiveness as follows:

Use of Lesser Mistletoe vs. Spell Effectiveness

ITEM	SPELL RANGE	SPELL DURATION	AREA OF EFFECT
Lesser mistletoe	100%	75%*	100%
Borrowed mistletoe	75%*	50%-	100%
Holly	75%*	50%*	75%*
Oak leaves	50%*.	50%**	50%**

*or + 1 on saving throws, if any, if the category is not applicable.
**or +2 on saving throw, if any, if category is not applicable.

Greater mistletoe, that is, mistletoe that is properly harvested by the druid, must be gathered as follows: on Midsummer's Eve, the druid must locate his mistletoe, cut it with a gold or silver sickle and catch it in a bowl before it touches the ground.

Lesser mistletoe is that which is not harvested on the eve of midsummer, or that which the druid takes in a way which is not prescribed (such as picking by hand).

Borrowed mistletoe is any mistletoe which is not personally harvested by the druid.

Holly and oak leaves may be picked or gathered in any manner, as long as they are not borrowed.

Following the name of each druid spell, a magical school is given in parentheses. The druid spells are not really organized into magical schools – these schools are for reference purposes only. For instance, Wisdom bonuses apply to saving throws vs. enchantment/charm spells. If the appropriate magical school were not listed with druid spells, it would be hard to figure out which spells were considered to be enchantment/charms. There are few other reasons one might need to know this information.

First Level Druid Spells

Animal Friendship
(Enchantment/Charm)
Level: 1
Range: 10 yds.
Duration: Permanent
Area of Effect: 1 animal

Components: V, S, M
Casting Time: 1 hr.
Saving Throw: Negates

By means of this spell, the caster is able to show any animal of animal intelligence to semi-intelligence (i.e., Intelligence 1-4) that he desires friendship. If the animal does not roll a successful saving throw vs. spell immediately when the spell is begun, it stands quietly while the caster finishes the spell. Thereafter, it follows the caster about.

The spell functions only if the caster actually wishes to be the animal's friend. If the caster has ulterior motives, the animal always senses them (for example, the caster intends to eat the animal, send it ahead to set off traps, etc.). The caster can teach the befriended animal three specific tricks or tasks for each point of Intelligence it possesses. Typical tasks are those taught to a dog or similar pet (i.e., they cannot be complex). Training for each such trick must be done over a period of one week, and all must be done within three months of acquiring the creature. During the three-month period, the animal will not harm the caster, but if the creature is left alone for more than a week, it will revert to its natural state and act accordingly.

The caster can use this spell to attract up to 2 Hit Dice of animal(s) per experience level he possesses. This is also the maximum total Hit Dice of the animals that can be attracted and trained at one time: no more than twice the caster's experience level. Only unaligned animals can be attracted, befriended, and trained. The material components of this spell are the caster's holy symbol and a piece of food liked by the animal.

Ceremony
(Invocation)
Level: 1
Range: Touch
Duration: Permanent
Area of Effect: One creature, item, or area

Components: V, S, M
Casting Time: 1 hour
Saving Throw: Special

The druidic Ceremony spell is similar to the cleric spell of the same name. It has a number of applications within the hierarchy of druids. The effect of a Ceremony spell does not leave behind an aura of magic, although a Know Alignment spell or similar magic might reveal the force of true neutrality involved in the magic. Druidic ceremonies include the following, which can be cast by a druid of the indicated or lower level:

1st-level druid: coming of age, rest eternal, marriage

3rd-level druid: dedication, investiture

7th-level druid: initiation, special vows

9th-level druid: hallowed ground

12th-level druid: cast out

The characteristics of the various types of Ceremony spells are as follows:

Coming of Age: is performed upon young people in druidic societies, usually when they reach the age of 14, and is symbolic of the young man's or young woman's entrance into adulthood. Effects of the spell are the same as for the cleric version (+1 bonus to a single saving throw); see the cleric text for other details.

Rest Eternal: is cast upon the body of a deceased being, by means of which the soul/spirit of the creature is hastened in its journey to its final resting place. The spells Raise Dead and Resurrection will not restore life to a character who has been the object of this spell, although a Wish spell would serve that purpose.

Marriage: is essentially identical to the cleric ceremony of the same name.

Dedication: allows the recipient of the spell to be taken into the ranks of the druid's followers/worshipers, provided that the character is true neutral in alignment. A recipient of this spell is charged, as are druids, with the responsibility to preserve and protect nature and the balance of forces in the world. In other respects it is similar to the cleric ceremony of the same name.

Investiture: is a rite that must be performed upon a character before he can become an Aspirant (1st-level druid). It conveys no other benefit.

Initiation: imbues the druid with the shape-changing and immunity to woodland charm powers that become available to the character upon attaining 7th level. This ceremony must be performed upon a druid immediately after he begins to advance upward through the 7th level of experience; if cast earlier than this, it will not work, and the druid will not have the benefit of the above-mentioned special powers until receiving initiation. Usually a druid must seek out another druid of 7th or higher level to perform the rite, but in unusual cases a druid may cast it upon himself.

Special Vows: is a ceremony that operates in the same fashion as the cleric rite of the same name. It does not work upon paladins, but will function upon cavaliers of any alignment.

Hallowed Ground: is cast by the druid on his permanent grove. This ceremony ensorcels the trees of the grove so that they will never be affected by disease or other natural disasters. The ground remains hallowed for as long as the druid maintains this grove as his permanent base.

Cast Out: is a form of excommunication or punishment that can be performed by a druid upon someone who has committed sacrilege upon the natural environment or in some other way violated the principles and standards of druidism. Its effects may be lessened at a later date by the casting of a reversed version of this ceremony, either by the same druid or another one of at least as high a level as the original caster, but the casting out can never be completely neutralized except by a Hierophant Druid of any level. A character who has been cast out exudes a powerful negative aura, causing any natural creature encountered to react negatively to the character. This includes all normal (non-magical) animals, monsters native to the woodlands, domesticated beasts such as horses and dogs, and all druids and their followers.

Casting Out is a very powerful form of punishment, and can only be performed by a druid who has received permission from his Archdruid to do so. Similarly, an Archdruid must get permission from the Great Druid, and the Great Druid from the Grand Druid. The Grand Druid does not need to obtain permission, but his actions may be reversed by a Hierophant Druid at any time.

This ceremony is usually only used on occasions where the severity of an offense warrants such extreme punishment. A druid who asks for and is denied permission to perform it, or one who later has his actions offset by another druid, may be subject to punishment by higher-ranking members of the hierarchy. An intended recipient of this ceremony who is unwilling receives a saving throw versus spell, at -4, to negate its effects.

The components of a ceremony spell always include mistletoe, and the rite (of any sort) must be performed in a druid grove or some other natural, healthy patch of forest. Such ceremonies are normally conducted at either dawn or dusk, the times when night and day are in balance.

Cure Minor Injury

(Necromancy)
Reversible
Level: 1
Range: Touch
Duration: Permanent
Area of Effect: Creature touched
Components: V, S
Casting Time: 5 segments
Saving Throw: None

This spell is exactly the same as a Cure Light Wounds spell except that it only heals 1d4-2 hit points per level of the druid, to a minimum of 1 point per level. The reverse, Cause Minor Injury, will cause 1d4-2 points of damage per level of the druid, with a minimum of 1 point of damage done per level.

Detect Balance

(Divination)
Level: 1
Range: 60 ft.
Duration: 1 round/level
Area of Effect: One object or creature per round
Components: V, S, M
Casting Time: 1 segment
Saving Throw: None

This spell allows the druid to determine if non-neutral forces and alignments are at work in the area of effect (upon or in the object or creature being scanned). An alignment that is partly neutral (such as that of a neutral good cleric) will radiate a mild aura, while an alignment that has no neutral component (such as that of a chaotic good fighter) will give off a strong aura.

The spell does not determine exact alignment, but only tells the druid if the object or creature being examined is something other than true neutral; a paladin and a chaotic evil thief, for instance, will radiate the same aura at the same strength. The spell will not function upon non-living items that do not have a natural aura (such as a vial of poison), but will work upon an object such as an aligned magical sword. Creatures that are under the effect of an Unknowable Alignment spell or similar magic will not radiate any aura when this spell is used upon them. If the magic is used upon something or someone that exudes a true neutral alignment (such as another druid), it will produce a smooth, well-balanced aura identifiable as one of neutrality.

Detect Magic

(Divination)
Level: 1
Range: 0
Duration: 1 turn
Area of Effect: 10 ft. x 30 yds.
Components: V, S, M
Casting Time: 1 round
Saving Throw: None

Except as noted above, this spell is the same as the first level magic-user spell Detect Magic (q.v.).

Detect Poison

(Divination)
Level: 1
Range: 0
Duration: 1 turn + 1 rd./level
Area of Effect: Special
Components: V, S, M
Casting Time: 4 segments
Saving Throw: None

This spell enables the druid to determine if an object has been poisoned or is poisonous. One object, or one 5-foot cubic mass, can be checked per round. The druid has a 5% chance per level of determining the exact type of poison. The material component is a strip of specially blessed vellum, which turns black if poison is present.

Detect Snares & Pits

(Divination)
Level: 1
Range: 0
Duration: 4 rds./level
Area of Effect: 10 ft. x 40 ft.
Components: V, S, M
Casting Time: 4 segments
Saving Throw: None

Upon casting this spell, the caster is able to detect snares, pits, deadfalls and similar hazards along a path 10 feet wide and 40 feet long. Such hazards include simple pits, deadfalls, snares of wilderness creatures (for example, trapdoor spiders, giant sundews, ant lions, etc.), and primitive traps constructed of natural materials (mantraps, missile trips, hunting snares, etc.). The spell is directional—the caster must face the desired direction to determine if a pit exists or a trap is laid in that direction.

The caster experiences a feeling of danger from the direction of a detected hazard, which increases as the danger is approached. The caster learns the general nature of the danger (pit, snare, or deadfall) but not its exact operation, nor how to disarm it. Close examination, however, enables the caster to sense what intended actions might trigger it.

The spell detects certain natural hazards—quicksand (snare), sinkholes (pit), or unsafe walls of natural rock (deadfall). Other hazards, such as a cavern that floods during rain, an unsafe construction, or a naturally poisonous plant, are not revealed. The spell does not detect magical traps (save those that operate by pit, deadfall, or snaring; see the 2nd-level spell trip and the 3rd-level spell snare), nor those that are mechanically complex, nor those that have been rendered safe or inactive. The caster must have his holy symbol to complete the spell.

Entangle

(Alteration)

Level: I

Range: 80 yds.	**Components:** V, S, M
Duration: I turn	**Casting Time:** 4 segments
Area of Effect: 40 ft. cube	**Saving Throw:** None

By means of this spell, the caster is able to cause plants in the area of effect to entangle creatures within the area. The grasses, weeds, bushes, and even trees wrap, twist, and entwine about the creatures, holding them fast for the duration of the spell. Any creature entering the area is subject to this effect. A creature that rolls a successful saving throw vs. spell can escape the area, moving at only 10 feet per round until out of the area. Exceptionally large (gargantuan) or strong creatures may suffer little or no distress from this spell, at the GM's option, based on the strength of the entangling plants. The material component is the caster's holy symbol.

Faerie Fire

(Alteration)

Level: I

Range: 80 yds.	**Component:** V, M
Duration: 4 rds./level	**Casting Time:** 4 segments
Area of Effect: 10 sq. ft/level	**Saving Throw:** None

This spell enables the caster to outline one or more objects or creatures with a pale glowing light. The number of subjects outlined depends upon the number of square feet the caster can affect. Sufficient footage enables several objects or creatures to be outlined by the Faerie Fire spell, but one must be fully outlined before the next is begun, and all must be within the area of effect.

Outlined objects or creatures are visible at 80 yards in the dark and 40 yards if the viewer is near a bright light source. Outlined creatures are easier to strike; thus, opponents gain a +2 bonus to attack rolls in darkness (including moonlit nights) and a +1 bonus in twilight or better. Note that outlining can render otherwise invisible creatures visible. However, it cannot outline noncorporeal, ethereal, or gaseous creatures. Nor does the light come anywhere close to sunlight. Therefore, it has no special effect on undead or dark-dwelling creatures.

The Faerie Fire can be blue, green, or violet according to the word of the caster at the time of casting. The faerie fire does not cause any harm to the object or creature thus outlined. The material component is a small piece of foxfire.

Fog Vision

(Divination)

Level: I

Range: Touch	**Components:** V, S, M
Duration: I turn/level	**Casting Time:** I segment
Area of Effect: One person	**Saving Throw:** None

This spell enables the caster or someone he touches the ability to see in even the thickest fog as if it were a clear sunny day. If the spell is cast within fog at night, the vision granted will still become that of a clear sunny day.

Invisibility to Animals

(Alteration)

Level: I

Range: Touch	**Components:** S, M
Duration: I turn + I rd./level	**Casting Time:** 4 segments
Area of Effect: I creature/level	**Saving Throw:** None

When an Invisibility to Animals spell is cast, the creature touched becomes totally undetectable by a normal animal with an Intelligence under 6. Normal animals include giant-sized varieties, but it excludes any with magical abilities or powers. The enchanted individual is able to walk among such animals or pass through them as if he did not exist. For example, this individual could stand before the hungriest of lions or a Tyrannosaurus Rex and not be molested or even noticed. However, a Nightmare, Hell Hound or Winter Wolf would certainly be aware of the individual.

For every level the caster has achieved, one creature can be rendered invisible. Any such invisible creature attacking while this spell is in effect ends the spell immediately (should more than one creature be under an Invisibility to Animals spell, only those who attack will become visible). The material component of this spell is holly rubbed over the recipient's body.

Locate Animals (Locate Plants)

(Divination)

Level: I

Range: 100 yds. + 20 yds./level	**Components:** V, S, M
Duration: I rd./level	**Casting Time:** I round
Area of Effect: 20 yds./level x 20 ft. wide	**Saving Throw:** None

The caster can find the direction and distance of any one type of animal or plant he desires. The caster, facing in a direction, thinks of the animal or plant, and then knows if any such animal or plant is within range. If so, the exact distance and approximate number present is learned. During each round of the spell's duration, the caster can face in only one direction (i.e., only a 20-foot-wide path can be known).

The spell lasts one round per level of experience of the caster, while the length of the path is 100 yards plus 20 yards per level of experience. At the GM's option, some casters may be able to locate only those animals (or plants) associated closely with their own mythos. While the exact chance of locating a specific type of animal or plant depends on the details and circumstances of the locale, the general frequency of the subject can be used as a guideline: common = 50%, uncommon = 30%, rare = 15%, and very rare = 5%. Most herbs grow in temperate regions, while most spices grow in tropical regions. Most plants sought as spell components or for magical research are rare or very rare. The results of this spell are always determined by the GM.

The material component is the caster's holy symbol.

Pass Without Trace

(Enchantment/Charm)

Level: I

Range: Touch	**Components:** V, S, M
Duration: I turn/level	**Casting Time:** I round
Area of Effect: I creature	**Saving Throw:** None

When this spell is cast, the recipient can move through any type of terrain—mud, snow, dust, etc.—and leave neither footprints nor scent. The area that is passed over radiates magic for 1d6 turns after the affected creature passes. Thus, tracking a person or other creature covered by this spell is impossible by normal means. Of course, intelligent tracking techniques, such as using a spiral search pattern, can result in the trackers picking up the trail at a point where the spell has worn off.

The material component of this spell is a sprig of pine or evergreen, which must be burned and the ashes powdered and scattered when the spell is cast.

Precipitation (Alteration)

Level: I
Range: 10 ft./level
Duration: I segment/level
Area of Effect: 3-foot-diameter cylinder up to 12 ft. high
Components: V, S, M
Casting Time: 3 segments
Saving Throw: None

Except as noted above, this spell is the same as the first level magic-user spell Precipitation (q.v.).

Predict Weather

(Divination)
Level: I
Range: 0
Duration: 2 hours/level
Area of Effect: Nine square miles
Components: V, S, M
Casting Time: I round
Saving Throw: None

When a predict weather spell is cost by a druid he gains 100% accurate knowledge of the weather (sky, temperature, precipitation) in a 9 square mile area centering on the druid. For each level of experience of the druid casting the spell, two hours advance weather can be forecast. Thus, at 1st level the druid knows what the weather will be for two hours; at second level he knows the weather for 4 hours in advance, etc.

Purify Water

(Alteration)
Reversible
Level: I
Range: 40 yds.
Duration: Permanent
Area of Effect: I cubic foot/lvl., I foot square area
Components: V, S
Casting Time: I round
Saving Throw: None

This spell makes dirty, contaminated water clean and pure, suitable for consumption. Up to one cubic foot per level of the druid casting the spell can be thus purified. The reverse of the spell, contaminate water, works in exactly the same manner, and its effects can spoil even holy (or unholy) water.

Shillelagh

(Alteration)
Level: I
Range: Touch
Duration: 4 rds. + I rd./level
Area of Effect: I oak club
Components: V, S, M
Casting Time: 2 segments
Saving Throw: None

This spell enables the caster to change his own oak cudgel or unshod staff into a magical weapon that gains a +1 bonus to its attack roll and inflicts 2d4 points of damage on opponents up to man size, and 1d4+1 points of damage on larger opponents. The spell inflicts no damage to the staff or cudgel. The caster must wield the shillelagh, of course. The material components of this spell are a shamrock leaf and the caster's holy symbol.

Speak With Animals

(Alteration)
Level: I
Range: 0
Duration: 2 rds./level
Area of Effect: I animal within 30 ft.
Components: V, S
Casting Time: 5 segments
Saving Throw: None

Except as noted above, this spell is the same as the second level cleric spell Speak With Animals (q.v.).

Second Level Druid Spells

Barkskin

(Alteration)
Level: 2
Range: Touch
Duration: 4 rds. + I rd./level
Area of Effect: I creature
Components: V, S, M
Casting Time: 5 segments
Saving Throw: None

When a druid casts the Barkskin spell upon a creature, its skin becomes as tough as bark, increasing its base Armor Class to AC 6, plus 1 AC for every four levels of the druid: Armor Class 5 at 4th level, Armor Class 4 at 8th, and so on. This spell does not function in combination with normal armor or any magical protection. In addition, saving throw rolls vs. all attack forms except magic gain a +1 bonus.

This spell can be placed on the caster or on any other creature he touches. In addition to his holy symbol, the caster must have a handful of bark from an oak as the material component for the spell.

Charm Person or Mammal

(Enchantment/Charm)
Level: 2
Range: 80 yds.
Duration: Special
Area of Effect: I person or mammal
Components: V, S
Casting Time: 5 segments
Saving Throw: Negates

This spell affects any single person or mammal it is cast upon. The creature then regards the caster as a trusted friend and ally to be heeded and protected. The term person includes any bipedal human, demihuman or humanoid of man size or smaller, including Brownies, Dryads, dwarves, elves, Gnolls, gnomes, Goblins, half-elves, halflings, half-orcs, hobgoblins, humans, Kobolds, Lizard Men, Nixies, Orcs, Pixies, Sprites, Troglodytes and others. Thus, a 10th-level fighter is included, while an Ogre is not.

The spell does not enable the caster to control the charmed creature as if it were an automaton, but any word or action of the caster is viewed in the most favorable way. Thus, a charmed creature would not obey a suicide command, but might believe the caster if assured that the only chance to save the caster's life is for the creature to hold back an onrushing Red Dragon for "just a minute or two" and if the charmed creature's view of the situation suggests that this course of action still allows a reasonable chance of survival.

The subject's attitudes and priorities are changed with respect to the caster, but basic personality and alignment are not. A request that a victim make itself defenseless, give up a valued item, or even use a charge from a valued item (especially against former associates or allies) might allow an immediate saving throw to see if the charm is thrown off. Likewise, a charmed creature does not necessarily reveal everything it knows or draw maps of entire areas.

Any request may be refused, if such refusal is in character and does not directly harm the caster. The victim's regard for the caster does not necessarily extend to the caster's friends or allies. The victim does not react well to the charmer's allies making suggestions such as, "Ask him this question. . .," nor does the charmed creature put up with verbal or physical abuse from the charmer's associates, if this is out of character.

Note also that the spell does not empower the caster with linguistic capabilities beyond those he normally has. The duration of the spell is a function of the charmed creature's Intelligence, and it is tied to the saving throw. A successful saving throw breaks the spell. This saving throw is checked on a periodic basis according to the creature's Intelligence, even if the caster has not overly strained the relationship.

Intelligence Score	Period Between Checks
3 or less	3 months
4-6	2 months
7-9	I month
10-12	3 weeks
13-14	2 weeks
15-16	I week
17	3 days
18	2 days
19 or more	I day

If the caster harms, or attempts to harm, the charmed creature by some overt action, or if a Dispel Magic spell is successfully cast upon the charmed creature, the charm is broken automatically.

If the subject of the Charm Person or Mammal spell successfully rolls its saving throw vs. the spell, the effect is negated. This spell, if used in conjunction with the Animal Friendship spell, can keep the animal near the caster's home base, if the caster must leave for an extended period.

Create Water

(Alteration)

Reversible

Level: 2

Range: 30 yds.   **Components:** V, S, M

Duration: Permanent   **Casting Time:** 1 round

Area of Effect: Up to 27 cu. ft.   **Saving Throw:** None

Except as noted above, this spell is the same as the seventh level cleric spell Create Water (q.v.).

Cure Light Wounds

(Necromancy)

Reversible

Level: 2

Range: Touch   **Components:** V, S

Duration: Permanent   **Casting Time:** 5 segments

Area of Effect: Creature touched   **Saving Throw:** None

Except as noted above, this spell is the same as the first level cleric spell Cure Light Wounds (q.v.).

Feign Death

(Necromancy)

Level: 2

Range: Touch   **Components:** V

Duration: 1 turn + 1 rd./level   **Casting Time:** 1/2 segment

Area of Effect: Person touched   **Saving Throw:** None

Except as noted above, this spell is the same as the third level magic-user spell Feign Death (q.v.).

Fire Trap

(Abjuration, Evocation)

Level: 2

Range: Touch   **Components:** V, S, M

Duration: Permanent until discharged   **Casting Time:** 1 turn

Area of Effect: Object touched   **Saving Throw:** Half

Except as noted above, this spell is the same as the fourth level magic-user spell Fire Trap (q.v.).

Flame Blade

(Evocation)

Level: 2

Range: 0   **Components:** V, S, M

Duration: 4 rds. + 1 rd./2 levels   **Casting Time:** 4 segments

Area of Effect: 3-ft. long blade   **Saving Throw:** None

With this spell, the caster causes a blazing ray of red-hot fire to spring forth from his hand. This bladelike ray is wielded as if it were a scimitar. If the caster successfully hits with the Flame Blade in melee combat, the creature struck suffers 1d4+4 points of damage, with a damage bonus of +2 (i.e., 7-10 points) if the creature is undead or is especially vulnerable to fire. If the creature is protected from fire, the damage inflicted is reduced by 2 (i.e., 1d4+2 points). Fire dwellers and those using fire as an innate attack form suffer no damage from the spell.

The Flame Blade can ignite combustible materials such as parchment, straw, dry sticks, cloth, etc. However, it is not a magical weapon in the normal sense of the term, so creatures (other than undead) struck only by magical weapons are not harmed by it. This spell does not function under water. In addition to the caster's holy symbol, the spell requires a leaf of sumac as a material component.

Goodberry

(Alteration, Evocation)

Reversible

Level: 2

Range: Touch   **Components:** V, S, M

Duration: 1 day + 1 day/level   **Casting Time:** 1 round

Area of Effect: 2d4 fresh berries   **Saving Throw:** None

Casting a Goodberry spell upon a handful of freshly picked berries makes 2d4 of them magical. The caster (as well as any other caster of the same faith and 3rd or higher level) can immediately discern which berries are affected. A detect magic spell discovers this also.

Berries with the magic either enable a hungry creature of approximately man size to eat one and be as well-nourished as if a full normal meal were eaten, or else cure 1 point of physical damage from wounds or other similar causes, subject to a maximum of 8 points of such curing in any 24-hour period.

The reverse of the spell, Badberry, causes 2d4 rotten berries to appear wholesome, but each actually delivers 1 point of poison damage (no saving throw) if ingested. The material component of the spell is the caster's holy symbol passed over the freshly picked, edible berries to be ensorceled (blueberries, blackberries, raspberries, currants, gooseberries, etc.).

Heat Metal

(Alteration)

Reversible

Level: 2

Range: 40 yds.   **Components:** V, S, M

Duration: 7 rds.   **Casting Time:** 5 segments

Area of Effect: Special   **Saving Throw:** Special

By means of the Heat metal spell, the caster is able to make ferrous metal (iron, iron alloys, steel) extremely hot. Elven chain mail is not affected, and magical metal armor receives an item saving throw vs. magical fire to avoid being heated. The material component is a holy symbol.

On the first round of the spell, the metal merely becomes very warm and uncomfortable to touch (this is also the effect on the last melee round of the spell's duration). During the second and sixth (next to the last) rounds, heat causes blisters and damage; in the third, fourth, and fifth rounds, the metal becomes searing hot, causing damage to exposed flesh, as shown below:

Metal Temperature Damage per Round

very warm	none
hot	1d4 points
searing*	2d4 points

* On the final round of searing, the afflicted creature must roll a successful saving throw vs. spell or suffer one of the following disabilities: hand or foot—becomes unusable for 2d4 days; body—becomes disabled for 1d4 days; head—fall unconscious for 1d4 turns. This effect can be completely removed by the 6th-level druid spell heal spell or by normal rest.

Note also that materials such as wood, leather, or flammable cloth smolder and burn if exposed to searing hot metal. Such materials cause searing damage to exposed flesh on the next round. Fire resistance (spell, potion, or ring) or a protection from fire spell totally negates the effects of a heat metal spell, as does immersion in water or snow, or exposure to a cold or ice storm spell.

This version of the spell does not function under water. For every two experience levels of the caster, the metal of one man-sized creature can be affected (i.e., arms and armor, or a single mass of metal equal to 50 pounds of weight). Thus, a 3rd-level caster would affect one such creature, a 4th- or 5th-level caster two, etc. The reverse of the spell, Chill Metal, counters a Heat Metal spell or else causes metal to act as follows:

Metal Temperature Damage per Round

cold	none
icy	1-2 points
freezing*	1d4 points

* On the final round of freezing, the afflicted creature must roll a successful saving throw vs. spell or suffer from the numbing effects of the cold. This causes the loss of all feeling in a hand (or hands, if the GM rules the saving throw was failed badly) for 1d4 days. During this time, the character's grip is extremely weak and he cannot use that hand for fighting or any other activity requiring a firm grasp.

The Chill Metal spell is countered by a Resist Cold spell, or by any great heat—proximity to a blazing fire (not a mere torch), a magical flaming sword, a Wall of Fire spell, etc. Under water, this version of the spell inflicts no damage, but ice immediately forms around the affected metal, exerting an upward buoyancy.

Messenger

(Enchantment/Charm)
Level: 2
Range: 20 yds./level   **Components:** V, S
Duration: 1 day/level   **Casting Time:** 1 round
Area of Effect: 1 creature   **Saving Throw:** Negates

This spell enables the druid to call upon a tiny (size T) creature of at least animal intelligence to act as his messenger. The spell does not affect giant animals and it does not work on creatures of low (i.e., 5) Intelligence or higher. If the creature is within range, the druid, using some type of food desirable to the animal as a lure, can call the animal to come. The animal is allowed a saving throw vs. spell. If the saving throw is failed, the animal advances toward the druid and awaits his bidding.

The druid can communicate with the animal in a crude fashion, telling it to go to a certain place, but directions must be simple. The spellcaster can attach some small item or note to the animal. If so instructed, the animal will then wait at that location until the duration of the spell expires. (Note that unless the intended recipient of a message is expecting a messenger in the form of a small animal or bird, the carrier may be ignored.) When the spell's duration expires, the animal or bird returns to its normal activities. The intended recipient of a message gains no communication ability.

Obscurement

(Alteration)
Level: 2
Range: 0   **Components:** V, S
Duration: 4 rds./level   **Casting Time:** 5 segments
Area of Effect: (level x 10 ft.)^2   **Saving Throw:** None

This spell causes a misty vapor to arise around the caster. It persists in this locale for four rounds per caster level and reduces the visibility ranges of all types of vision (including infravision) to 2d4 feet. The ground area affected by the spell is a square progression based on the caster's level: a 10 ft x 10 ft area at 1st level, a 20 ft x 20 ft area at 2nd level, a 30 ft x 30 ft area at 3rd level, and so on. The height of the vapor is restricted to 10 feet, although the cloud will otherwise expand to fill confined spaces. A strong wind (such as from the 3rd-level magic-user spell gust of wind) can cut the duration of an obscurement spell by 75%. This spell does not function under water.

Produce Flame

(Alteration)
Level: 2
Range: 0   **Components:** V, S
Duration: 1 rd./level   **Casting Time:** 5 segments
Area of Effect: Special   **Saving Throw:** None

A bright flame, equal in brightness to a torch, springs forth from the caster's palm when he casts a Produce Flame spell. The flame does not harm the caster, but it is hot and it causes the combustion of flammable materials (paper, cloth, dry wood, oil, etc.). The caster is capable of hurling the magical flame as a missile, with a range of 40 yards (considered short range). The flame flashes on impact, igniting combustibles within a 3-foot-diameter of its center of impact, and then it goes out.

A creature struck by the flame suffers 1d4+1 points of damage and, if combustion occurs, must spend a round extinguishing the fire or suffer additional damage assigned by the GM until the fire is extinguished. A miss is resolved as a grenade-like missile. If any duration remains to the spell, another flame immediately appears in the caster's hand.

The caster can hurl a maximum of one flame per level, but no more than one flame per round. The caster can snuff out magical flame any time he desires, but fire caused by the flame cannot be so extinguished. This spell does not function under water.

Reflecting Pool

(Divination)
Level: 2
Range: 10 yds.   **Components:** V, S, M
Duration: 1 rd./level   **Casting Time:** 2 hrs.
Area of Effect: Special   **Saving Throw:** None

This spell enables the caster to cause a pool of normal water found in a natural setting to act as a scrying device. The pool can be of no greater diameter than 2 feet per level of the caster. The effect is to create a scrying device similar to a crystal ball. The scrying can extend only to the Ethereal Plane and the Inner Planes (which includes the para-elemental planes, the Demiplane of Shadow, etc.).

General notes on scrying, detection by the subject, and penalties for attempting to scry beyond the caster's own plane are given in the GMG, as well as a description of the Crystal Ball item. The following spells can be cast through a reflecting pool, with a 5% per level chance for operating correctly: Detect Magic, Detect Snares and Pits, and Detect Poison. Each additional detection attempt requires a round of concentration, regardless of success.

Infravision, if available, operates normally through the Reflecting Pool. The image is nearly always hazy enough to prevent the reading of script of any type. The material component is the oil extracted from such nuts as the hickory and the walnut, refined, and dropped in three measures upon the surface of the pool. A measure need be no more than a single ounce of oil. At the GM's option, the casting of this spell may be limited to once per day.

Slow Poison

(Necromancy)
Level: 2
Range: Touch   **Components:** V, S, M
Duration: 1 hr./level   **Casting Time:** 1 segment
Area of Effect: 1 creature   **Saving Throw:** None

Except as noted above, this spell is the same as the second level cleric spell Slow Poison (q.v.).

Trip

(Enchantment/Charm)
Level: 2
Range: Touch   **Components:** V, S
Duration: 1 turn/level   **Casting Time:** 5 segments
Area of Effect: 1 object up to   **Saving Throw:** Negates
                 10 ft. long

This magic must be cast upon a normal object—a length of vine, a stick, a pole, a rope, or a similar object. The spell causes the object to rise slightly off the ground or floor it is resting on to trip most creatures crossing it, if they fail their saving throws vs. spell.

Note that only as many creatures can be tripped as are actually stepping across the enchanted object. Thus, a 3-foot-long piece of rope could trip only one man-sized creature. Creatures moving at a very rapid pace (running) when tripped suffer 1 point of damage and are stunned for 1d4+1 rounds if the surface they fall upon is very hard (if it is turf or other soft material, they are merely stunned for the rest of that round).

Very large creatures, such as elephants, are not affected at all by a Trip spell. The object continues to trip all creatures passing over it, including the spellcaster, for as long as the spell duration lasts. A creature aware of the object and its potential adds a +4 bonus to its saving throw roll when crossing the object.

The enchanted object is 80% undetectable unless a means that detects magical traps is employed or the operation of the spell is observed. This spell does not function under water.

Warp Wood

(Alteration)
Reversible
Level: 2

Range: 10 yds./level	**Components:** V, S
Duration: Permanent	**Casting Time:** 5 segments
Area of Effect: Special	**Saving Throw:** Special

When this spell is cast, the druid causes a volume of wood to bend and warp, permanently destroying its straightness, form, and strength. The range of a Warp Wood spell is 10 yards for each level of experience of the caster. It affects approximately a 15-inch shaft of wood of up to 1-inch diameter per level of the caster. Thus, at 1st level, a caster might be able to warp a hand axe handle or four crossbow bolts; at 5th level, he could warp the shaft of a typical spear.

Note that boards or planks can also be affected, causing a door to be sprung or a boat or ship to leak. Warped missile weapons are useless; warped melee weapons suffer a -4 penalty to their attack rolls. Enchanted wood is affected only if the spellcaster is of higher level than the caster of the prior enchantment. The spellcaster has a 20% cumulative chance of success per level of difference (20% if one level higher, 40% if two levels higher, etc.). Thus, a door magically held or Mage Locked by a 5th-level magic-user is 40% likely to be affected by a Warp Wood spell cast by a 7th-level druid. Wooden magical items are considered enchanted at 12th level (or better). Extremely powerful items, such as artifacts, are unaffected by this spell.

The reversed spell, Straighten Wood, straightens bent or crooked wood, or reverses the effects of a Warp Wood spell, subject to the same restrictions.

Third Level Druid Spells

Call Lightning

(Alteration)
Level: 3

Range: 360 yds.	**Components:** V, S
Duration: 1 turn/level	**Casting Time:** 1 turn
Area of Effect: 10-ft. radius	**Saving Throw:** Half

When a Call Lightning spell is cast, there must be a storm of some sort in the area—a rain shower, clouds and wind, hot and cloudy conditions, or even a tornado (including a whirlwind formed by a Djinn or Air Elemental of 7 Hit Dice or more). The caster is then able to call down bolts of lightning. The caster can call down one bolt per turn.

The caster need not call a bolt of lightning immediately—other actions, even spellcasting, can be performed; however, the caster must remain stationary and concentrate for a full round each time a bolt is called. The spell has a duration of one turn per caster level. Each bolt causes 2d8 points of electrical damage, plus an additional 1d8 points for each of the caster's experience levels. Thus, a 4th-level caster calls down a 6d8 bolt (2d8+4d8).

The bolt of lightning flashes down in a vertical stroke at whatever distance the spellcaster decides, up to 360 yards away. Any creature within a 10-foot radius of the path or the point where the lightning strikes suffers full damage unless a successful saving throw vs. spell is rolled, in which case only one-half damage is taken. Because it requires a storm overhead, this spell can only be used outdoors. It does not function under ground or under water.

Cloudburst

(Alteration)
Level: 3

Range: 10 ft./level	**Components:** V, S, M
Duration: 1 round	**Casting Time:** 5 segments
Area of Effect: 30-foot-diameter cylinder up to 60 feet high	**Saving Throw:** None (Special)

This spell is essentially the same as the 3rd level magic-user spell of the same name, with the following special notations and additions: lightning cannot be called by the use of a Cloudburst spell, and a Call Lightning spell cannot be used in the same area at the same time. Also, the druid must use mistletoe as an additional material component.

Cure Disease

(Abjuration)
Reversible
Level: 3

Range: Touch	**Components:** V, S
Duration: Permanent	**Casting Time:** 1 round
Area of Effect: 1 creature	**Saving Throw:** None

Except as noted above, this spell is the same as the third level cleric spell Create Disease (q.v.).

Heal Light Wounds

(Necromancy)
Level: 3

Range: 5 ft./level	**Components:** V, S
Duration: Permanent	**Casting Time:** 5 segments
Area of Effect: 1 creature	**Saving Throw:** None

Except as noted above this spell is the same as the second level cleric spell Heal Light Wounds.

Hold Animal

(Enchantment/Charm)
Level: 3

Range: 80 yds.	**Components:** V, S
Duration: 2 rds./level	**Casting Time:** 6 segments
Area of Effect: 1-4 animals in 40-ft. cube	**Saving Throw:** Negates

By means of this spell, the caster holds one to four animals rigid. Animals affected are normal or giant-sized mammals, birds, or reptiles, but not monsters such as Centaurs, Gorgons, Harpies, Naga, etc. Apes, bears, crocodiles, dogs, eagles, foxes, giant beavers, and similar animals are subject to this spell.

The hold lasts for two rounds per caster level. The caster decides how many animals can be affected, but the greater the number, the better chance each has to successfully save against the spell. Each animal gets a saving throw: If only one is the subject of the spell, it has a penalty of -4 on its roll; if two are subject, each receives a penalty of -2 on its roll; if three are subject, each receives a penalty of -1 on its roll; and if four are subject, each gets an unmodified saving throw.

A maximum body weight of 400 pounds (100 pounds for non-mammals) per animal per caster level can be affected—for example, an 8th-level caster can affect up to four 3,200-pound mammals or a like number of 800-pound non-mammals such as reptiles or giant insects.

Know Alignment

(Divination)
Reversible
Level: 3

Range: 10 yds.	**Components:** V, S
Duration: 1 turn	**Casting time:** 1 round
Area of Effect: 1 creature or object	**Saving Throw:** Negates

Except as noted above, this spell is the same as the second level magic-user spell Know Alignment (q.v.).

Neutralize Poison

(Necromancy)
Reversible
Level: 3

Range: Touch	**Components:** V, S
Duration: Permanent	**Casting Time:** 7 segments
Area of Effect: 1 creature or 1 cubic ft. of substance/2 levels	**Saving Throw:** None

By means of a Neutralize Poison spell, the cleric detoxifies any sort of venom in the creature or substance touched. Note that an opponent, such as a poisonous reptile or spider (or even an envenomed weapon wielded by an opponent) unwilling to be so touched requires the cleric to roll a successful attack in combat.

This spell can prevent death in a poisoned creature if cast before death occurs. The effects of the spell are permanent only with respect to poison existing in the touched creature at the time of the touch; thus, creatures (and objects) that generate new poison are not permanently detoxified.

The reversed spell, Poison, likewise requires a successful attack roll, and the victim is allowed a saving throw vs. poison. If the latter is unsuccessful, the victim is effectively incapacitated and dies in one turn unless the poison is magically neutralized or slowed.

Plant Growth

(Alteration)
Level: 3

Range: 160 yds.	**Components:** V, S, M
Duration: Permanent	**Casting Time:** 1 round
Area of Effect: Special	**Saving Throw:** Special

Except as noted above, this spell is the same as the fourth level magic-user spell Plant Growth (q.v.).

Protection From Fire

(Abjuration)
Level: 3

Range: Touch	**Components:** V, S, M
Duration: Special	**Casting Time:** 6 segments
Area of Effect: 1 creature	**Saving Throw:** None

The effect of a Protection From Fire spell differs according to whether the recipient of the magic is the caster or some other creature. In either case, the spell lasts no longer than one turn per caster level. If the spell is cast upon the caster, it confers complete invulnerability to: normal fires (torches, bonfires, oil fires, and the like); exposure to magical fires such as fiery dragon breath; spells such as Burning Hands, Fireball, Fire Seeds, Fire Storm, Flame Strike, and Meteor Swarm; Hell Hound or Pyrohydra breath, etc. The invulnerability lasts until the spell has absorbed 12 points of heat or fire damage per level of the caster, at which time the spell is negated. If the spell is cast upon another creature, it gives invulnerability to normal fire, gives a bonus of +4 to saving throw die rolls vs. fire attacks, and reduces damage sustained from magical fires by 50%. The caster's holy symbol is the material component.

Pyrotechnics

(Alteration)
Level: 3

Range: 160 yds.	**Components:** V, S, M
Duration: Special	**Casting Time:** 6 segments
Area of Effect: 10 or 100 times fire source	**Saving Throw:** Special

Except as noted above, this spell is the same as the second level magic-user spell Pyrotechnics (q.v.).

Snare

(Enchantment/Charm)
Level: 3

Range: Touch	**Components:** V, S, M
Duration: Until triggered	**Casting Time:** 3 rds.
Area of Effect: 2-ft. diameter + 2 in./level	**Saving Throw:** None

This spell enables the caster to make a snare that is 90% undetectable without magical aid. The snare can be made from any supple vine, a thong, or a rope. When the Snare spell is cast upon it, the cordlike object blends with its surroundings. One end of the snare is tied in a loop that contracts around one or more of the limbs of any creature stepping inside the circle (note that the head of a worm or snake could be thus ensnared). If a strong and supple tree is nearby, the snare can be fastened to it.

The magic of the spell causes the tree to bend and then straighten when the loop is triggered, inflicting 1d6 points of damage to the creature trapped, and lifting it off the ground by the trapped member(s) (or strangling it if the head/neck triggered the snare). If no such sapling or tree is available, the cordlike object tightens upon the member(s), then wraps around the entire creature, causing no damage, but tightly binding it. Under water, the cord coils back upon its anchor point. The snare is magical, so for one hour it is breakable only by cloud giant or greater Strength (23); each hour thereafter, the snare material loses magic so as to become 1 point more breakable per hour—22 after two hours, 21 after three, 20 after four—until six full hours have elapsed. At that time, 18 Strength will break the bonds. After 12 hours have elapsed, the materials of the snare lose all magical properties and the loop opens, freeing anything it held.

The snare can be cut with any magical weapon, or with any edged weapon wielded with at least a +2 attack bonus (from Strength, for example). The caster must have a snake skin and a piece of sinew from a strong animal to weave into the cordlike object from which he will make the snare. Only the caster's holy symbol is otherwise needed.

Spike Growth

(Alteration, Enchantment)
Level: 3

Range: 60 yds.	**Components:** V, S, M
Duration: 3d4 turns + 1/level	**Casting Time:** 6 segments
Area of Effect: 10-ft. sq./level	**Saving Throw:** None

Except as noted above, this spell is the same as the fifth level cleric spell Spike Growth (q.v.).

Starshine

(Evocation, Illusion/Phantasm)
Level: 3

Range: 10 yds./level	**Components:** V, S, M
Duration: 1 turn/level	**Casting Time:** 6 segments
Area of Effect: 10-ft. sq./level	**Saving Throw:** None

A Starshine spell enables the caster to softly illuminate an area as if it were exposed to a clear night sky filled with stars. Regardless of the height of the open area in which the spell is cast, the area immediately beneath it is lit by starshine. Vision ranges are the same as those for a bright moonlit night—movement noted out to 100 yards; stationary creatures seen up to 50 yards; general identifications made at 30 yards; and recognition at 10 yards.

The spell creates shadows and has no effect on infravision. The area of effect actually appears to be a night sky, but disbelief of the illusion merely enables the disbeliever to note that the "stars" are actually evoked lights. This spell does not function under water. The material components are several stalks from an amaryllis plant (especially Hypoxis) and several holly berries.

Stone Shape

(Alteration)

Level: 3

Range: Touch

Duration: Permanent

Area of Effect: 9 cu. ft. + 1 cu. ft./level

Components: V, S, M

Casting Time: 1 round

Saving Throw: None

Except as noted above, this spell is the same as the fifth level magic-user spell Stone Shape (q.v.).

Summon Insects

(Conjuration/Summoning)

Level: 3

Range: 30 yds.

Duration: 1 rd./level

Area of Effect: 1 creature

Components: V, S, M

Casting Time: 1 round

Saving Throw: None

The Summon Insects spell attracts a cloud or swarm of normal insects to attack the foes of the caster. Flying insects appear 70% of the time, while crawling insects appear 30% of the time. The exact insects called are bees, biting flies, hornets, or wasps, if flying insects are indicated; biting ants or pinching beetles, if crawling insects are indicated.

A cloud of the flying type, or a swarm of the crawling sort, appears after the spell is cast. This gathers at a point chosen by the caster, within the spell's range, and attacks any single creature the caster points to. The attacked creature sustains 2 points of damage if it does nothing but attempt to flee or fend off the insects during the time it is attacked; it suffers 4 points of damage per round otherwise.

If the insects are ignored, the victim fights with a -2 penalty to his attack roll and a +2 penalty to his Armor Class. If he attempts to cast a spell, an initiative roll should be made for the insects to see if their damage occurs before the spell is cast. If it does, the victim's concentration is ruined and the spell is lost.

The insects disperse and the spell ends if the victim enters thick smoke or hot flames. Besides being driven off by smoke or hot flames, the swarm might possibly be outrun, or evaded by plunging into a sufficient body of water. If evaded, the summoned insects can be sent against another opponent, but there will be at least a 1 round delay while they leave the former opponent and attack the new victim. Crawling insects can travel only about 10 feet per round (maximum speed over smooth ground) and flying insects travel 60 feet per round.

The caster must concentrate to maintain the swarm; it dissipates if he moves or is disturbed. It is possible, in underground situations, that the caster might summon 1d4 giant ants by means of the spell, but the possibility is only 30% unless giant ants are nearby. This spell does not function under water. The materials needed for this spell are the caster's holy symbol, a flower petal, and a bit of mud or wet clay.

Tree

(Alteration)

Level: 3

Range: 0

Duration: 6 turns + 1 turn/level

Area of Effect: The caster

Components: V, S, M

Casting Time: 6 segments

Saving Throw: None

By means of this spell, the caster is able to assume the form of a small living tree or shrub or that of a large dead tree trunk with only a few limbs. Although the closest inspection cannot reveal that this plant is actually a person, and for all normal tests he is, in fact, a tree or shrub, the caster is able to observe all that goes on around him just as if he were in normal form.

The Armor Class and hit points of the plant are those of the caster. The caster can remove the spell at any time, instantly changing from plant to his normal form and having full capability for any action normally possible (including spellcasting). Note that all clothing and gear worn or carried change with the caster. The material components of this spell are the druid's holy symbol and a twig from a tree.

Water Breathing

(Alteration)

Reversible

Level: 3

Range: Touch

Duration: 1 hr./level

Area of Effect: 1 creature

Components: V, S

Casting Time: 6 segments

Saving Throw: None

The recipient of a Water Breathing spell is able to breathe under water freely for the duration of the spell—i.e., one hour for each experience level of the caster. The druid can divide the base duration between multiple characters. Thus, an 8th level druid can confer this ability to two characters for four hours, four for two hours, eight for one hour, etc., to a minimum of one half-hour per character.

The reverse, Air Breathing, enables water-breathing creatures to survive comfortably in the atmosphere for an equal duration. Note that neither version prevents the recipient creature from breathing in its natural element.

White Hot Metal

(Alteration)

Level: 3

Range: 10 yds.

Duration: 1 round/level

Area of Effect: Up to one pound of metal

Components: V, M

Casting Time: 2 segments

Saving Throw: None (neg.)

This spell makes up to one pound of metal white hot almost instantly. The heat is sufficient to melt softer metals such as gold, silver, or lead and harder metals are ruined if they are subject to any stress (such as combat).

Magical metals, mithral items and adamantite alloys may make a saving throw vs. crushing blow to avoid being warped and ruined. If the spell is cast upon a creature's equipment they are entitled to a saving throw to avoid the spell, otherwise contact with White Hot Metal causes 2d6 points of damage each round. The material component is the metal to be heated.

Wood Shape

(Alteration)

Level: 3

Range: Touch

Duration: Permanent

Area of Effect: 9 cu. ft. + 1 cu. ft./level

Components: V, S, M

Casting Time: 1 round

Saving Throw: None

By means of this spell the caster can work a volume of natural wood into any shape that suits his fancy. The material component of the spell is a giant beaver tail or a bit of a Black Pudding. Except as noted above, this spell is the same as the fifth level magic-user Stone Shape (q.v.).

Fourth Level Druid Spells

Animal Summoning I

(Conjuration, Summoning)

Level: 4

Range: 1 mi. radius   **Components:** V, S
Duration: Special   **Casting Time:** 7 segments
Area of Effect: Special   **Saving Throw:** None

By means of this spell, the caster calls up to eight animals that have 4 Hit Dice or less, of whatever sort the caster names when the summoning is made. Only animals within range of the caster at the time the spell is cast will come.

The caster can try three times to summon three different types of animals. For example, a caster first tries to summon wild dogs to no avail, then unsuccessfully tries to call hawks, and finally calls wild horses that may or may not be within summoning range. The GM must determine the chance of a summoned animal type being within the range of the spell.

The animals summoned aid the caster by whatever means they possess, staying until a fight is over, a specific mission is finished, the caster is safe, he sends them away, etc. Only normal or giant animals can be summoned; fantastic animals or monsters cannot be summoned by this spell (no Chimerae, dragons, Gorgons, Manticores, etc.).

Call Woodland Beings

(Conjuration/Summoning)

Level: 4

Range: 100 yds./level   **Components:** V, S, M
Duration: Special   **Casting Time:** Special
Area of Effect: Special   **Saving Throw:** Negates

By means of this spell, the caster is able to summon certain woodland creatures to his location. Naturally, this spell works only outdoors, but not necessarily only in wooded areas. The caster begins the incantation and continues uninterrupted until some called creature appears or two turns have elapsed. (The verbalization and somatic gesturing are easy, so this is not particularly exhausting to the spellcaster.)

Only one type of the following sorts of beings can be summoned by the spell. They come only if they are within the range of the call. The caster can call three times, for a different type each time. Once a call is successful, no other type can be called without another casting of the spell. The GM will consult his outdoor map or base the probability of any such creature being within spell range upon the nature of the area the caster is in at the time of spellcasting.

The creature(s) called by the spell are entitled to a saving throw vs. spell (with a -4 penalty) to avoid the summons. Any woodland beings answering the call are favorably disposed to the spellcaster and give whatever aid they are capable of. However, if the caller or members of the caller's party are of evil alignment, the creatures are entitled to another saving throw vs. spell (this time with a +4 bonus) when they come within 10 yards of the caster or another evil character with him. These beings immediately seek to escape if their saving throws are successful.

In any event, if the caster requests that the summoned creatures engage in combat on his behalf, they are required to roll a loyalty reaction check based on the caster's Charisma and whatever dealings he has had with them. This spell works with respect to neutral or good woodland creatures, as determined by the GM. Thus, the GM can freely add to or alter the list as he sees fit. If the caster personally knows a certain individual woodland being, that being can be summoned at double the normal range. If this is done, no other woodland creatures are affected. If a percentage chance is given in the accompanying table, druids and other nature-based clerics add 1% per caster level. These chances can be used if no other campaign information on the area is available. The material components of this spell are a pine cone and eight holly berries.

Percentage Chance for Type of Woodland Being

Creature Type Called	Type of Woodlands		
	Light	Moderate/Sylvan	Dense/Virgin
2d8 Brownies	30%	20%	10%
1d4 Centaurs	5%	30%	5%
1d4 Dryads	1%	25%	15%
1d8 Pixies	10%	20%	10%
1d4 Satyrs	1%	30%	10%
1d6 Sprites	0%	5%	25%
1 Treant	—	5%	25%
1 Unicorn	—	15%	20%

Control Temperature, 10' Radius

(Alteration)

Level: 4

Range: 0   **Components:** V, S, M
Duration: 4 turns + 1 turn/level   **Casting Time:** 7 segments
Area of Effect: 10 ft. radius   **Saving Throw:** None

When this spell is cast, the temperature surrounding the caster can be altered by 10 degrees F., either upward or downward, per level of experience of the spellcaster. Thus, a 10th level caster could raise or lower the surrounding temperature from 1 to 100° F. The spell can be used to ensure the comfort of the caster and those with him in extreme weather conditions. The party could stand about in shirt sleeves during the worst blizzard (although it would be raining on them) or make ice for their drinks during a scorching heat wave.

The spell also provides protection from intense normal and magical attacks. If the extreme of temperature is beyond what could be affected by the spell (a searing blast of a Fireball or the icy chill of White Dragon's breath), the spell reduces the damage caused by 5 points for every level of the caster. Normal saving throws are still allowed, and the reduction is taken after the saving throw is made or failed. Once struck by such an attack, the spell immediately collapses.

The material component for this spell is a strip of willow bark (to lower temperatures) or raspberry leaves (to raise temperatures).

Cure Serious Wounds

(Necromancy)

Reversible

Level: 4

Range: Touch   **Components:** V, S
Duration: Permanent   **Casting Time:** 7 segments
Area of Effect: 1 creature   **Saving Throw:** None

Except as noted above, this spell is the same as the fourth level cleric spell Cure Serious Wounds (q.v.).

Dispel Magic

(Abjuration)

Level: 4

Range: 60 yds

Components: V, S

Duration: Special

Casting Time: 6 segments

Area of Effect: 30-ft. cube or 1 item

Saving Throw: None

Except as noted above, this spell is the same as the third level magic-user spell Dispel Magic (q.v.).

Summary of Dispel Effects

Source of Effect	Resists As	Result of Dispel
Caster	None	Dispel automatic
Other caster/ innate ability other caster	Level/HD of other caster	Effect negated
Wand	6th level	Effect negated
Staff	8th level	Effect negated
Potion	12th level	Potion destroyed
Other magical item	12th, unless special	*
Artifact	GM discretion	GM discretion

* Effect negated; if cast directly on item, item becomes nonoperational for 1d4 rounds.

Grow

(Alteration)

Level: 4

Range: 3 yards/level

Components: V, S, M

Duration: Instantaneous

Casting Time: 3 segments

Area of Effect: one creature

Saving Throw: Negates

This spell enables the caster to age a living creature by one year within a matter of seconds. If the target does not wish to be aged, he may attempt a saving throw to avoid the effect. A Grow spell may be cast on any living being. The spell affects the target's physical body only. Intelligence and Wisdom bonuses due to aging are not conferred as a result of this spell. Additionally, a child aged in this way would still behave as a child though he might have the body of an adult.

Hallucinatory Forest

(Illusion/Phantasm)

Reversible

Level: 4

Range: 80 yds.

Components: V, S

Duration: Permanent

Casting Time: 7 segments

Area of Effect: 40-ft. sq./level

Saving Throw: None

When this spell is cast, a hallucinatory forest comes into existence. The illusionary forest appears to be perfectly natural and is indistinguishable from a real forest. Clerics attuned to the woodlands—as well as such creatures as Centaurs, Dryads, Green Dragons, Nymphs, Satyrs and Treants—recognize the forest for what it is. All other creatures believe it is there, and movement and order of march are affected accordingly.

Touching the illusory growth neither affects the magic nor reveals its nature. The hallucinatory forest remains until it is magically dispelled by a reverse of the spell or a Dispel Magic spell. The area shape is either roughly rectangular or square, in general, and at least 40 feet deep, in whatever location the caster desires. The forest can be of less than maximum area if the caster wishes. One of its edges can appear up to 80 yards away from the caster.

Hold Plant

(Enchantment/Charm)

Level: 4

Range: 80 yds.

Components: V, S

Duration: 1 rd./level

Casting Time: 7 segments

Area of Effect: 1d4 plants in 40-ft. sq.

Saving Throw: Negates

The Hold Plant spell affects vegetable matter as follows:

1) it causes ambulatory vegetation to cease moving;

2) it prevents vegetable matter from entwining, grasping, closing, or growing;

3) it prevents vegetable matter from making any sound or movement that is not caused by wind.

The spell effects apply to all forms of vegetation, including parasitic and fungoid types, and those magically animated or otherwise magically empowered. It affects such monsters as Green Slime, molds of any sort, Shambling Mounds, Shriekers, Treants, etc.

The duration of a Hold Plant spell is one round per level of experience of the caster. It affects 1d4 plants in a 40-foot x 40-foot area, or a square 4 to•16 yards on a side of small ground growth such as grass or mold. If only one plant (or 4 yards square) is chosen as the target for the spell, the saving throw of the plant (or area of plant growth) is made with a -4 penalty to the die roll; if two plants (or 8 yards square) are the target, saving throws suffer a -2 penalty; if three plants (or 12 yards square) are the target, saving throws suffer a -1 penalty; and if the maximum of four plants (or 16 yards square) are the target, saving throws are unmodified.

Plant Door

(Alteration)

Level: 4

Range: Touch

Components: V, S, M

Duration: Special

Casting Time: 7 segments

Area of Effect: Special

Saving Throw: None

The Plant Door spell opens a magical portal or passageway through trees, undergrowth, thickets, or any similar growth—even growth of a magical nature. The Plant Door is open to the spell caster, casters of a higher level, or Dryads; others must be shown the location of the door. The door even enables the caster to enter a solid tree trunk and remain hidden there until the spell ends. The spell also enables the passage (or hiding) of any man-sized or smaller creature; hiding is subject to space considerations. If the tree is cut down or burned, those within must leave before the tree falls or is consumed, or else they are killed also.

The duration of the spell is one turn per level of experience of the caster. If the caster opts to stay within an oak, the spell lasts nine times longer than normal; if within an ash tree, it lasts three times longer. The path created by the spell is up to 4 feet wide, 8 feet high, and 12 feet long per level of experience of the caster.

This spell does not function on plant-based monsters (Shambling Mounds, molds, slimes, Treants, etc.) or plants with an Intelligence greater than 1. The material components for this spell are a piece of charcoal and the caster's holy symbol.

Produce Fire

(Alteration)

Reversible

Level: 4

Range: 40 yds.

Components: V, S, M

Duration: 1 round

Casting Time: 7 segments

Area of Effect: 12-ft. sq.

Saving Throw: None

By means of this spell, the caster creates a common fire of up to 12 feet per side in area. Though it lasts only a single round (unless it ignites additional flammable material), the fire produced by the spell inflicts 1d4 points of damage plus 1 point per caster level (1d4 + 1/level) upon creatures within its area. It ignites combustible materials, such as cloth, oil, paper, parchment, wood, and the like, so as to cause continued burning.

The reversal spell, Quench Fire, extinguishes any normal fire (coals, oil, tallow, wax, wood, etc.) within the area of effect. The material component for either version is a paste of sulfur and wax, formed into a ball and thrown at the target.

Protection From Lightning

(Abjuration)

Level: 4

Range: Touch	**Components:** V, S, M
Duration: Special	**Casting Time:** 7 segments
Area of Effect: 1 creature	**Saving Throw:** None

The effect of a Protection From Lightning spell changes depending on who is the recipient of the magic—the caster or some other creature. In either case, the spell lasts no longer than one turn per caster level. If the spell is cast upon the caster, it confers complete invulnerability to electrical attacks such as dragon breath, and magical lightning such as Lightning Bolt, Shocking Grasp, Storm Giant, Will o' Wisp, etc., until the spell has absorbed 10 points of electrical damage per level of the caster, at which time the spell is negated.

If the spell is cast upon another creature, it gives a bonus of +4 to the die roll for saving throws made vs. electrical attacks, and it reduces the damage sustained from such attacks by 50%. The caster's holy symbol is the material component.

Repel Insects

(Abjuration, Alteration)

Level: 4

Range: 0	**Components:** V, S, M
Duration: 1 turn/level	**Casting Time:** 1 round
Area of Effect: 10-ft. radius	**Saving Throw:** None

When this spell is cast, the druid creates an invisible barrier to all sorts of insects, and normal insects do not approach within 10 feet of the caster while the spell is in effect. Giant insects with Hit Dice less than 1/3 of the caster's experience level are also repelled (for example, 2 Hit Dice for 7th to 9th-level casters, 3 Hit Dice at 10th through 12th level, etc.). Insects with more Hit Dice can enter the protected area if the insect is especially aggressive and, in addition, rolls a successful saving throw vs. spell. Those that do sustain 1d6 points of damage from passing through the magical barrier.

Note that the spell does not in any way affect arachnids, myriapods, and similar creatures—it affects only true insects. The material components of the Repel Insects spell include any one of the following: several crushed marigold flowers, a whole crushed leek, seven crushed stinging nettle leaves, Aardvarkian fur or a small lump of resin from a camphor tree.

Speak With Plants

(Alteration)

Level: 4

Range: 0	**Components:** V, S, M
Duration: 1 rd./level	**Casting Time:** 1 turn
Area of Effect: 30-ft. radius	**Saving Throw:** None

When cast, a Speak With Plants spell enables the druid to converse, in very rudimentary terms, with all sorts of living vegetables (including fungi, molds, and plantlike monsters, such as shambling mounds) and to exercise limited control over normal plants (i.e., not monsters or plantlike creatures). Thus, the caster can question plants as to whether or not creatures have passed near them, cause thickets to part to enable easy passage, require vines to entangle pursuers, and command similar services.

The spell does not enable plants to uproot themselves and move about, but any movements within the plant's normal capabilities are possible. Creatures entangled by the 1st-level spell Entangle can be released. The power of the spell lasts for one round for each experience level of the casting druid. All vegetation within the area of effect is affected by the spell. The material components for this spell are a drop of water, a pinch of dung, and a flame.

Stone Passage

(Alteration)

Level: 4

Range: Touch	**Components:** V, S
Duration: 1 turn	**Casting Time:** 4 segments
Area of Effect: 1 creature	**Saving Throw:** None

This spell allows the recipient and all of its equipment to move through stone as if it were dense pudding (at about 1 foot per round). The recipient can choose to put only parts of its body into stone, or may completely enter their whole body. Note that he cannot see or hear if his head is inside a rock, and if Stone Passage is used to travel to a specific location the traveler must be very careful not to get lost!

If the spell runs out while the spell's target is still completely in stone he is instantly slain with his body entombed in the stone. If partially inside, the victim must make a system shock roll or die. If successful, any body parts left inside of the stone are trapped and a way must be found to free them. Note that movement is exhausting and difficult, and the GM may rule that characters with a Strength of 11 or lower may not move through the stone at all.

Fifth Level Druid Spells

Animal Growth

(Alteration)

Reversible

Level: 5

Range: 80 yds.	**Components:** V, S, M
Duration: 2 rds./level	**Casting Time:** 8 segments
Area of Effect: Up to 8 animals in a 20-ft. sq.	**Saving Throw:** None

Except as noted above, this spell is the same as the fifth level magic-user spell Animal Growth (q.v.).

Animal Summoning II

(Conjuration/Summoning)

Level: 5

Range: 60 yds./level	**Components:** V, S
Duration: Special	**Casting Time:** 8 segments
Area of Effect: Special	**Saving Throw:** None

By means of this spell, the caster calls up to six animals of 8 Hit Dice or less, or 12 animals of 4 Hit Dice or less—of whatever sort the caster names. Only animals within range of the caster at the time the spell is cast will come.

The caster can try three times to summon three different types of animals. For example, suppose that wild dogs are first summoned to no avail, then hawks are unsuccessfully called, and finally the caster calls for wild horses. The GM determines the chance of a summoned animal type being within range of the spell.

The animals summoned aid the caster by whatever means they possess, staying until a fight is over, a specific mission is finished, the caster is safe, he sends them away, etc. Only normal or giant animals can be summoned; fantastic animals or monsters cannot be effected by this spell (no Chimerae, dragons, Gorgons, Manticores, etc.).

Anti-Plant Shell

(Abjuration)

Level: 5

Range: 0	**Components:** V, S
Duration: 1 turn/level	**Casting Time:** 8 segments
Area of Effect: 15-ft. diameter	**Saving Throw:** None

The Anti-Plant Shell spell creates an invisible, mobile barrier that keeps all creatures within the shell protected from attacking plants or vegetable creatures such as Shambling Mounds or Treants. Any attempt to force the barrier against such creatures shatters the barrier immediately. The spell lasts for one turn for each experience level of the caster.

Commune With Nature

(Divination)
Level: 5
Range: 0 **Components:** V, S
Duration: Special **Casting Time:** 1 turn
Area of Effect: Special **Saving Throw:** None

This spell enables the caster to become one with nature, thus being empowered with knowledge of the surrounding territory. For each level of experience of the caster, he can "know" one fact—ahead, left, or right, about the following subjects: the ground, plants, minerals, bodies of water, people, general animal population, presence of woodland creatures, etc.

The presence of powerful unnatural creatures also can be detected, as can the general state of the natural setting. The spell is most effective in outdoor settings, operating in a radius of one-half mile for each level of the caster. In natural underground settings—caves, cavern, etc.—the range is limited to 10 yards per caster level. In constructed settings (dungeons and towns), the spell will not function. The GM may limit the casting of this spell to once per month.

Control Winds

(Alteration)
Level: 5
Range: 0 **Components:** V, S
Duration: 1 turn/level **Casting Time:** 8 segments
Area of Effect: 40 ft. radius/lvl. **Saving Throw:** None

By means of a Control Winds spell, the caster is able to alter wind force in the area of effect. For every three levels of experience, the caster can increase or decrease wind force by one level of strength. Wind strengths are as follows:

Wind Force	Miles Per Hour
Light Breeze	2-7
Moderate Breeze	8-18
Strong Breeze	19-31
Gale	32-54
Storm	55-72
Hurricane	73-176

Winds in excess of 18 miles per hour drive small flying creatures—those eagle-sized and under—from the skies, severely affect missile accuracy, and make sailing difficult. Winds in excess of 32 miles per hour drive even man-sized flying creatures from the skies and cause minor ship damage. Winds in excess of 55 miles per hour drive all flying creatures from the skies, uproot small trees, knock down wooden structures, tear off roofs, and endanger ships. Winds in excess of 73 miles per hour are of hurricane force. An "eye" of 40-foot radius, in which the wind is calm, exists around the caster.

Note that while the spell can be used underground, if the spell is cast in an area smaller than the area of effect, the eye shrinks 1 foot for every foot of confinement. For example, if the area of effect is a 360-foot area, the eye shrinks by 10 feet to a 30-foot radius; a space under 320 feet in a radius would eliminate the eye and subject the spellcaster to the effects of the wind.

Once the spell is cast, the wind force increases or decreases by 3 miles per hour per round until the maximum or minimum speed is attained. The caster, with one round of complete concentration, can stabilize the wind at its current strength, or set it to increase or decrease. However, the rate of the change cannot be altered.

The spell remains in force for one turn for each level of experience of the caster. When the spell is exhausted, the force of the wind wanes or waxes at the same rate, until it reaches the level it was at before the spell took effect. Another caster can use a control winds spell to counter the effects of a like spell up to the limits of his own ability.

Heal Serious Wounds

(Necromancy)
Level: 5
Range: 5 ft./level **Components:** V, S
Duration: Permanent **Casting Time:** 5 segments
Area of Effect: 1 creature **Saving Throw:** None

Except as noted above, this spell is the same as the fifth level cleric spell Heal Serious Wounds.

Insect Plague

(Conjuration/Summoning)
Level: 5
Range: 120 yds. **Components:** V, S, M
Duration: 2 rds./level **Casting Time:** 1 turn
Area of Effect: 180 ft. x 60 ft. cloud **Saving Throw:** None

Except as noted above, Insect Plague is the same as the fifth level cleric spell Insect Plague (q.v.).

Lesser Reincarnation

(Necromancy)
Level: 5
Range: Touch **Components:** V, S
Duration: Permanent **Casting Time:** 1 turn
Area of Effect: 1 person **Saving Throw:** None

With this spell, the druid can bring a dead person back to life, albeit in another body, if death occurred no more than one week before the casting of the spell. Reincarnation does not require any saving throw, system shock or resurrection survival roll. The corpse is touched, and a new incarnation of the person appears in the area in 1d6 turns. The person reincarnated recalls the majority of his former life and form, but the character class, if any, of the new incarnation might be very different indeed. The new incarnation is determined on the following table or by GM choice.

At the GM's option, certain special (expensive) incenses can be used that can increase the chance for a character to return as a specific race or species. A Wish spell can restore a reincarnated character to his original form and status.

Reincarnation (d100)

Roll	Incarnation
01-03	Badger
04-08	Bear, black
09-12	Bear, brown
13-16	Boar, wild
17-19	Cow
20-23	Chipmunk
24-28	Eagle
29-31	Mountain Lion
32-34	Bat
35-36	Fox
37-40	Adder
41-44	Hawk
45-58	Monkey
59-61	Lynx
62-64	Owl
65-68	Woodchuck
69-70	Raccoon
71-72	Otter
73-75	Stag
76-80	Wolf
81-85	Wolverine
86-00	Bestial Soul*

* The creature returns in the same type of body that it had before, but its soul has been merged with that of an animal. By day the character retains its normal form, but by night he changes into a normal version of an animal. Determine the type of animal by rolling again on the above table, re-rolling a result of 86-00. In both forms the character retains his memory and intelligence, but at times instinct may take over when in animal form (GM's discre-

tion). A Wish, Limited Wish, Restoration or similar magics will remove the bestial part of the character's soul.

If an unusual creature form is indicated, the GM can (at his option only) use the guidelines for new player character races to allow the character to earn experience and advance in levels, although this may not be in the same class as before.

Moonbeam

(Evocation, Alteration)
Level: 5
Range: 60 yds. + 10 yds./level   **Components:** V, S, M
Duration: 1 rd./level   **Casting Time:** 7 segments
Area of Effect: 5 ft. radius +   **Saving Throw:** None
             special

By means of this spell, the caster is able to cause a beam of soft, pale light to strike down from overhead and illuminate whatever area he is pointing at. The light is exactly the same as moonlight, so that colors other than shades of black, gray, or white are vague. The spellcaster can easily make the Moonbeam move to any area that he can see and point to. This makes the spell an effective way to spotlight something such as an opponent, for example. While the Moonbeam spell does not eliminate all shadows, a creature within its area of effect is most certainly visible.

The reflected light from this spell enables dim visual perception 10 yards beyond the area of effect, but it does not shed a telltale glow that would negate surprise. The light does not adversely affect infravision. The caster can dim the beam to near darkness if desired. The beam has, in addition, all the properties of true moonlight and can induce a lycanthropic change (of a creature in the beam), unless the GM rules otherwise. The material components are several seeds of any moonseed plant and a piece of opalescent feldspar (moonstone).

Pass Plant

(Alteration)
Level: 5
Range: Touch   **Components:** V, S, M
Duration: Special   **Casting Time:** 8 segments
Area of Effect: Special   **Saving Throw:** None

By using this spell, the caster is able to enter a tree and move from inside it to inside another tree. The second tree must lie in approximately the direction desired by the spell user and must be within the range shown in the following table.

Type of Tree	Range of Area of Effect
Oak	600 yards
Ash	540 yards
Yew	480 yards
Elm	420 yards
Linden	360 yards
deciduous	300 yards
coniferous	240 yards
other	180 yards

The tree entered and that receiving the caster must be of the same type, must both be living, and of girth at least equal to that of the caster. Note that if the caster enters a tree, an ash, for example, and wishes to pass north as far as possible (540 yards), but the only appropriate ash in range is to the south, the caster will pass to the ash in the south. The Pass Plant spell functions so that the movement takes only one round. The caster can, at his option, remain within the receiving tree for a maximum of one round per level of experience. Otherwise, he can step forth immediately.

Should no like tree be in range, the caster simply remains within the first tree, does not pass elsewhere, and must step forth in the appropriate number of rounds. If the occupied tree is chopped down or burned, the caster is slain if he does not exit before the process is complete.

Protection From Acid

(Abjuration)
Level: 5
Range: Touch   **Components:** V, S, M
Duration: Special   **Casting Time:** 8 segments
Area of Effect: 1 creature   **Saving Throw:** None

The effects of the Protection From Acid spell change depending on who is the recipient of the spell - the caster or another creature. In either case the spell lasts for no longer than one turn per caster level. If the caster casts the spell upon himself it provides him with complete protection from all forms of acid damage, such as that from a Black Pudding's attack, a Black Dragon's breath weapon, or a Wall of Acid.

The spell can absorb a maximum of 10 points of damage per caster level before it is negated. If the spell is used on another creature it confers a +4 bonus on saves made against acid attacks and reduces the damage sustained from such attacks by 50%. The material component is a piece of shell from a Bombardier Beetle.

Protection From Petrification

(Abjuration)
Level: 5
Range: Touch   **Components:** V, S, M
Duration: 1 turn/level   **Casting Time:** 5 segments
Area of Effect: one person   **Saving Throw:** None

The recipient of this spell becomes immune to attacks that turn a creature to stone such as the gaze of a Basilisk or the spell Flesh to Stone. The material component of the spell is powdered Basilisk eyes.

Spike Stones

(Alteration, Enchantment)
Level: 5
Range: 30 yds.   **Components:** V, S, M
Duration: 3d4 turns +1/level   **Casting Time:** 6 segments
Area of Effect: 10 ft. sq./level,   **Saving Throw:** None
             1 spike/sq. ft.

Except as noted above, this spell is the same as the fourth level cleric spell Spike Stones (q.v.).

Sticks to Snakes

(Alteration)
Reversible
Level: 5
Range: 30 yds.   **Components:** V, S, M
Duration: 2 rds./level   **Casting Time:** 7 segments
Area of Effect: 1d4 sticks + 1   **Saving Throw:** None
             stick/level in a 10-ft. cube

Except as noted above, this spell is the same as the fourth level cleric spell Sticks to Snakes (q.v.).

Transmute Rock to Mud

(Alteration)
Reversible
Level: 5
Range: 160 yds.   **Components:** V, S, M
Duration: Special   **Casting Time:** 8 segments
Area of Effect: 20-ft. cube/level   **Saving Throw:** None

Except as noted above, this spell is the same as the fifth level magic-user spell Transmute Rock to Mud (q.v.).

Wall of Fire

(Conjuration/Summoning)

Level: 5

Range: 80 yds.	**Components:** V, S, M
Duration: Special	**Casting Time:** 8 segments
Area of Effect: Special	**Saving Throw:** None

The Wall of fire spell brings forth an immobile, blazing curtain of magical fire of shimmering color—yellow-green or amber (different from the 4th-level magic-user version). The spell creates an opaque sheet of flame up to one 20 foot square per level of the spellcaster, or a ring with a radius of up to 10 feet + 5 feet for every two levels of experience of the magic-user, and 20 feet high.

The Wall of Fire must be cast so that it is vertical with respect to the caster. One side of the wall, selected by the caster, sends forth waves of heat, inflicting 2d4 points of damage upon creatures within 10 feet and 1d4 points of damage upon those within 20 feet. In addition, the wall inflicts 4d4 points of damage, plus 1 point of damage per level of the spellcaster, to any creature passing through it.

Creatures especially subject to fire may take additional damage, and undead always take twice normal damage. Note that attempting to directly catch moving creatures with a newly created Wall of Fire is difficult. A successful saving throw enables the creature to avoid the wall, while its rate and direction of movement determine which side of the created wall it is on.

The Wall of Fire lasts as long as the druid concentrates on maintaining it, or one round per level of experience of the druid in the event he does not wish to concentrate upon it. The material component of the spell is phosphorus.

Sixth Level Druid Spells

Animal Summoning III

(Conjuration, Summoning)

Level: 6

Range: 100 yds./level	**Components:** V, S
Duration: Special	**Casting Time:** 9 segments
Area of Effect: Special	**Saving Throw:** None

This spell is the same in duration and effect as the 4th-level Animal Summoning I spell, except that up to four animals of no more than 16 Hit Dice each can be summoned, or eight of no more than 8 Hit Dice, or 16 creatures of no more than 4 Hit Dice.

Only animals within range of the caster at the time the spell is cast will come. The caster can try three times to summon three different types of animals (for example, suppose that wild dogs are first summoned to no avail, then hawks are unsuccessfully called, and finally the caster calls for wild horses that may or may not be within summoning range). Your GM will determine the chance of a summoned animal type being within range of the spell.

The animals summoned will aid the caster by whatever means they possess, staying until a fight is over, a specific mission is finished, the caster is safe, he sends them away, etc. Only normal or giant animals can be summoned; fantastic animals or monsters cannot be summoned by this spell (no chimerae, dragons, gorgons, manticores, etc.).

Anti-Animal Shell

(Abjuration)

Level: 6

Range: 0	**Components:** V, S, M
Duration: 1 turn/level	**Casting Time:** 1 round
Area of Effect: 10-ft. radius	**Saving Throw:** None

By casting this spell, the caster brings into being a hemispherical force field that prevents the entrance of any sort of living creature that is wholly or partially animal (not magical or extraplanar). Thus a Sprite, a giant, or a Chimera would be kept out, but undead or conjured creatures could pass through the shell of force, as could such monsters as Aerial Servants, Imps, Quasits, golems, elementals, etc.

The Anti-Animal Shell functions normally against crossbreeds, such as cambions, and lasts for one turn for each level of experience the caster has attained. Forcing the barrier against creatures strains and ultimately collapses the field. The spell requires the caster's holy symbol and a handful of pepper.

Conjure Fire Elemental

(Conjuration/Summoning)

Reversible

Level: 6

Range: 80 yds.	**Components:** V, S
Duration: 1 turn/level	**Casting Time:** 6 rds.
Area of Effect: Special	**Saving Throw:** None

Upon casting a Conjure Fire Elemental spell, the caster opens a special gate to the Elemental Plane of Fire, and a Fire Elemental is summoned to the vicinity of the spellcaster. It is 65% likely that a 12 Hit Dice elemental appears, 20% likely that a 16 Hit Dice elemental appears, 9% likely that two to four salamanders appear, 4% likely that an efreeti appears, and 2% likely that a huge fire elemental of 21 to 24 Hit Dice appears.

The caster need not fear that the elemental force summoned will turn on him, so concentration upon the activities of the Fire Elemental (or other creatures summoned) or protection from the creature is not necessary. The elemental summoned helps the caster however possible, including attacking the caster's opponents. The Fire Elemental or other creature summoned remains for a maximum of one turn per level of the caster, or until it is slain, sent back by a Dispel Magic spell, the reverse of this spell, dismiss Fire Elemental, or similar magic.

Cure Critical Wounds

(Necromancy)

Reversible

Level: 6

Range: Touch	**Components:** V, S
Duration: Permanent	**Casting Time:** 7 segments
Area of Effect: 1 creature	**Saving Throw:** None

Except as noted above, this spell is the same as the fifth level cleric spell Cure Critical Wounds (q.v.).

Feeblemind

(Enchantment/Charm)

Level: 6

Range: 10 yds./level	**Components:** V, S, M
Duration: Permanent	**Casting Time:** 5 segments
Area of Effect: 1 creature	**Saving Throw:** Negates

Except as noted above, this spell is the same as the sixth level magic-user spell Feeblemind (q.v.).

Fire Seeds

(Conjuration)

Level: 6

Range: Touch	**Components:** V, S, M
Duration: Special	**Casting Time:** 1 rd./seed
Area of Effect: Special	**Saving Throw:** Half

The Fire Seeds spell creates special missiles or timed incendiaries that burn with great heat. The spell can be cast to create either fire seed missiles or fire seed incendiaries, as chosen when the spell is cast.

Fire seed missiles: This casting turns up to four acorns into special grenadelike missiles that can be hurled up to 40 yards. An attack roll is required to strike the intended target, and proficiency penalties are considered. Each acorn bursts upon striking any hard surface, causing 2d8 points of damage and igniting any combustible materials within a 10-foot diameter of the point of impact. If a successful saving throw vs. spell is made, a creature within the burst area receives only one-half damage, but a creature struck directly suffers full damage (i.e., no saving throw).

Fire seed incendiaries: This casting turns up to eight holly berries into special incendiaries. The holly berries are most often placed, being too light to make effective missiles. They can be tossed only up to 6 feet away. They burst into flame if the caster is within 40 yards and speaks a word of command. The berries instantly ignite, causing 1d8 points of damage to any creature and igniting any combustible within a 5-foot-diameter burst area. Creatures within the area that successfully save vs. spell suffer half damage. All fire seeds lose their power after a duration equal to one turn per experience level of the caster (for example, the seeds of a 13th-level caster remain potent for a maximum of 13 turns after their creation).

No other material components beyond acorns or holly berries are needed for this spell.

Liveoak

(Enchantment)

Level: 6

Range: Touch **Components:** V, S, M
Duration: 1 day/level **Casting Time:** 1 turn
Area of Effect: 1 oak tree **Saving Throw:** None

This spell enables the caster to charm a healthy oak tree (or other type if the GM allows) to cause it to serve as a protector. The spell can be cast on a single tree at a time. While a Liveoak spell cast by a particular caster is in effect, he cannot cast another such spell. The tree upon which the spell is cast must be within 10 feet of the caster's dwelling place, within a place sacred to the caster, or within 100 yards of something that the caster wishes to guard or protect.

The Liveoak spell can be cast upon a healthy tree of small, medium, or large size, according to desire and availability. A triggering phrase of up to maximum of one word per level of the spellcaster is then placed upon the targeted oak. For instance, "Attack any persons who come near without first saying sacred mistletoe" is an 11-word trigger phrase that could be used by a caster of 11th level or higher casting the spell. The Liveoak spell triggers the tree into animating as a Treant of equivalent size, an Armor Class of 0 and with two attacks per round, but with only a 30-feet-per-round movement rate.

Tree Size	Height	Hit Dice	Damage per Attack
Small	12 ft. – 14 ft.	7-8	2d8
Medium	16 ft. – 19 ft.	9-10	3d6
Large	20 ft. – 23 ft.+	11-12	4d6

A tree enchanted by this spell radiates a magical aura (if checked for), and can be returned to normal by a successful casting of a Dispel Magic spell, or upon the desire of the caster who enchanted it. If dispelled, the tree takes root immediately. If released by the caster, it tries to return to its original location before taking root. Damage to the tree can be healed with a Plant Growth spell, which restores 3d4 points of damage. A Plant Growth spell used in this fashion does not increase the size or hit points of the liveoak beyond the original value. The caster needs his holy symbol to cast this spell.

Transmute Water to Dust

(Alteration)
Reversible

Level: 6

Range: 60 yds. **Components:** V, S, M
Duration: Permanent **Casting Time:** 8 segments
Area of Effect: 1 cu. yd./level **Saving Throw:** Special

Except as noted above, this spell is the same as the sixth level magic-user spell Transmute Water to Dust (q.v.).

Transport Via Plants

(Alteration)

Level: 6

Range: Touch **Components:** V, S
Duration: Special **Casting Time:** 4 segments
Area of Effect: Special **Saving Throw:** None

By means of this spell, the caster is able to enter any plant (human-sized or larger) and pass any distance to a plant of the same species in a single round, regardless of the distance separating the two. The entry plant must be alive. The destination plant need not be familiar to the caster, but it also must be alive. If the caster is uncertain of the destination plant, he need merely determine direction and distance, and the Transport Via Plants spell moves him as close as possible to the desired location.

There is a 20% chance, reduced by 1% per level of experience of the caster, that the transport delivers the caster to a similar species of plant from 1 to 100 miles away from the desired destination plant. If a particular destination plant is desired, but the plant is not living, the spell fails and the caster must come forth from the entrance plant within 24 hours.

Note that this spell does not function with plantlike creatures such as Shambling Mounds, Treants, etc. The destruction of an occupied plant slays the caster (see the Plant Door spell).

Turn Wood

(Alteration)

Level: 6

Range: 0 **Components:** V, S
Duration: 1 rd./level **Casting Time:** 9 segments
Area of Effect: 20 ft./level by 120 ft. **Saving Throw:** None

When this spell is cast, waves of force roll forth from the caster, moving in the direction he faces and causing all wooden objects in the path of the spell to be pushed away from the caster to the limit of the area of effect. Wooden objects above 3 inches in diameter that are fixed firmly are not affected, but loose objects (movable mantles, siege towers, etc.) move back.

Fixed objects less than 3 inches in diameter splinter and break, and the pieces move with the wave of force. Thus, objects such as wooden shields, spears, wooden weapon shafts and hafts, and arrows and bolts are pushed back, dragging those carrying them with them. If a spear is planted to prevent this forced movement, it splinters. Even magical items with wooden sections are turned, although an anti-magic shell blocks the effects.

A successful Dispel Magic spell ends the effect. Otherwise, the Turn Wood spell lasts for one round for each experience level of the caster. The waves of force continue to sweep down the set path for the spell's duration, pushing back wooden objects in the area of effect at a rate of 40 feet per melee round.

The length of the path is 20 feet per level of the caster. Thus if a 14th-level druid casts a turn wood spell, the area of effect is 120 feet wide by 280 feet long, and the spell lasts 14 rounds. After casting the spell, the path is set and the caster can then do other things or go elsewhere without affecting the spell's power.

Wall of Thorns

(Conjuration/Summoning)

Level: 6

Range: 80 yds. **Components:** V, S
Duration: 1 turn/level **Casting Time:** 9 segments
Area of Effect: One 10-ft. cube/level **Saving Throw:** None

This spell causes a barrier of tough, tangled brush with very sharp thorns to come into being. Any creature crashing into or passing through the area suffers 8 points of damage, plus the creatures AC (negative ACs actually subtract damage). Dexterity modifiers do NOT apply to AC for this purpose. Any creature caught in the area when the spell is cast is trapped. Creatures suffer damage for each 10-foot thickness of the wall they move through.

If characters chop at the Wall of Thorns, it takes four turns to cut through a 10-foot thickness. The wall cannot be harmed by normal fire, but magical fire will burn it away in two turns. During this time the wall is treated as the fourth level magic-user spell Wall of Fire.

The nearest edge of the wall appears up to 80 yards away from the caster. The spell lasts one turn for each level of experience the caster has attained and covers one 10-foot cube per caster level. The caster can shape these cubes as desired. This a 12th level caster can make a Wall of Thorns 120 feet long and ten feet wide, 40 feet long and 30 feet wide, or 60 feet wide and 20 feet long.

The druid may cast a wall at only 5-feet thickness in order to double another dimension, but the wall will only inflict half damage. Thus the 12th level druid could make a wall 240 feet thick and only 5 feet wide (and ten feet tall).

Note that those able to pass through overgrown areas do not suffer damage. The caster can dismiss the wall with a word.

Weather Summoning
(Conjuration/Summoning)
Level: 6
Range: 0
Duration: Special
Area of Effect: Special
Components: V, S
Casting Time: 1 turn
Saving Throw: None

By this spell, the caster calls forth weather appropriate to the climate and season of the area he is in. Thus, in spring a tornado, thunderstorm, sleet storm or hot weather could be summoned. In summer a torrential rain, heat wave, hail storm, etc., can be called for. In autumn, hot or cold weather, fog, sleet, etc., could be summoned. Winter enables great cold, blizzard, or thaw conditions to be summoned. Hurricane-force winds can be summoned near coastal regions in the later winter or early spring.

The summoned weather is not under the control of the caster. It might last but a single turn, in the case of a tornado, or for hours or even days in other cases. The area of effect likewise varies from about 1 square mile to 100 square miles. Note that several casters can act in concert to greatly affect weather, controlling winds, and working jointly to summon very extreme weather conditions.

Within four turns after the spell is cast, the trend of the weather to come is apparent— e.g., clearing skies, gusts of warm or hot air, a chill breeze, overcast skies, etc. Summoned weather arrives 1d12+5 turns after the spell is cast. Note that the new weather condition cannot be changed by the caster once it has been summoned. Once the weather is fully summoned, it cannot be dispelled. If the summoning is successfully dispelled before it has been completed, the weather slowly reverts to its original condition.

Seventh Level Druid Spells

Animate Rock
(Alteration)
Level: 7
Range: 40 yds.
Duration: 1 rd./level
Area of Effect: 2 cu. ft./level
Components: V, S, M
Casting Time: 1 round
Saving Throw: None

By employing an Animate Rock spell, the caster causes a stone object of up to the indicated size to move (see the 6th-level Animate Object spell.). The animated stone object must be separate (not a part of a huge boulder or the like). It follows the desire of the caster—attacking, breaking objects, blocking—while the magic lasts. It has no intelligence or volition of its own, but it follows instructions exactly as spoken.

Only one set of instructions for one single action can be given to the animated rock, and the directions must be brief, about a dozen words or so. The rock remains animated for one round per experience level of the caster. The volume of rock that can be animated is also based on the experience level of the caster - 2 cubic feet of stone per level, such as 24 cubic feet, a mass of about man-sized, at 12th level. While the exact details of the animated rock are decided by the GM, its Armor Class is no worse than 5, and it has 1d3 hit points per cubic foot of volume. It uses the attack roll of the caster. The maximum damage it can inflict is 1d2 points per caster level. Thus, a 12th-level caster's rock might inflict 12-24 points of damage. Movement for a man-sized rock is 60 feet per round. A rock generally weighs from 100 to 300 pounds per cubic foot. The material components for this spell are a stone and drop of the caster's blood.

Cause Inclement Weather
(Alteration)
Level: 7
Range: 0
Duration: 2d12 hours
Area of Effect: 4d4 sq. miles
Components: V, S, M
Casting Time: 1 turn
Saving Throw: None

This spell works like a Control Weather spell except that only extremely bad weather can be created in the area. The weather must still be appropriate to the climate, i.e. a sandstorm could not be created in the middle of a lush forest.

Some examples of inclement weather that could be created by this spell include tornadoes, thunder storms, blizzards, monsoons, extreme heat, or hail storms. Once the weather is created it is under the control of the elements, not the druid, unless further magics are used. The material component is the caster's holy symbol.

Changestaff
(Evocation, Enchantment)
Level: 7
Range: Touch
Duration: Special
Area of Effect: The caster's staff
Components: V, S, M
Casting Time: 4 segments
Saving Throw: None

By means of this spell, the caster is able to change a specially prepared staff into a treantlike creature of the largest size, about 24 feet tall. When the druid plants the end of the staff in the ground and speaks a special command and invocation, the staff turns into a treantlike creature with 12 Hit Dice, 40 hit points, and Armor Class 0. It attacks twice per round, inflicting 4d6 points of damage with every successful attack.

The staff-treant defends the caster and obeys any spoken commands. However, it is by no means a true treant; it cannot converse with actual treants or control trees. The transformation lasts either for as many turns as the caster has experience levels, until the caster commands the staff to return to its true form, or until the staff is destroyed, whichever occurs first. If the staff-treant is reduced to 0 hit points or less, it crumbles to a sawdustlike powder and the staff is destroyed. Otherwise, the staff can be used again after 24 hours and the staff-treant is at full strength.

To cast a Changestaff spell, the caster must have either his holy symbol or leaves (ash, oak, or yew) of the same sort as the staff. The staff for the Changestaff spell must be specially prepared. The staff must be a sound limb cut from an ash, oak, or yew tree struck by lightning no more than 24 hours before the limb is cut. The limb must then be cured by sun drying and special smoke for 28 days. Then it must be shaped, carved, and polished for another 28 days. The caster cannot adventure or engage in other strenuous activity during either of these periods.

The finished staff, engraved with woodland scenes, is then rubbed with the juice of holly berries, and the end of it is thrust into the earth of the caster's grove while he casts a Speak With Plants spell, calling upon the staff to assist in time of need. The item is then charged with a magic that will last for many changes from staff to treant and back again.

Chariot of Sustarre
(Evocation)
Level: 7
Range: 10 yds.   **Components:** V, S, M
Duration: 12 hours   **Casting Time:** 1 turn
Area of Effect: Special **Saving Throw:** None

When this spell is cast, it brings forth a large, flaming chariot pulled by two fiery horses from the Elemental Plane of Fire. These appear in a clap of thunder amid a cloud of smoke. The vehicle moves at 24 on the ground, 48 flying, and can carry the caster and up to seven other creatures of man-size or less.

The passengers must be touched by the caster to protect them from the flames of the chariot. Creatures other than the caster and his designated passengers sustain 2d4 points of fire damage each round if they come within 5 feet of the horses or chariot. Such creatures suffer no damage if they evade the area by rolling successful saving throws vs. petrification, with Dexterity adjustments.

The caster controls the chariot by verbal command, causing the flaming steeds to stop or go, walk, trot, run or fly, and turn left or right as he desires. Note that the Chariot of Sustarre is a physical manifestation and can sustain damage. The vehicle and steeds are struck only by magical weapons or by water (one quart of which inflicts 1 point of damage). They are AC 2, and each requires 30 points of damage to dispel. Naturally, fire has no effect upon either the vehicle or its steeds, but magical fires other than those of the chariot can affect the riders.

Other spells, such as a successful Dispel Magic or Holy Word, will force the chariot back to its home plane, without its passengers. The chariot can be summoned only once per week. The material components are a small piece of wood, two holly berries, and a fire source at least equal to a torch.

Confusion
(Enchantment/Charm)
Level: 7
Range: 80 yds.   **Components:** V, S, M
Duration: 1 rd./level   **Casting Time:** 1 round
Area of Effect: 1d4 creatures in **Saving Throw:** Special
40-ft. sq.

Except as noted, this spell is the same as the fourth level magic-user spell Confusion (q.v.).

d10	Reaction
1	Wander away (unless prevented) for duration of spell
2-6	Stand confused one round (then roll again)
7-9	Attack nearest creature for one round (then roll again)
10	Act normally for one round (then roll again)

The spell lasts one round for each level of the caster. Those who fail their saving throws are checked by the GM for actions each round, for the duration of the spell, or until the "wander away for the duration of the spell" result occurs. Wandering creatures move as far from the caster as possible in their most typical mode of movement (characters walk, fish swim, bats fly, etc.). This is not panicked flight.

Wandering creatures also have a 50% chance of using any special innate movement abilities (plane shift, burrowing, flight, etc.). Saving throws and actions are checked at the beginning of each round. Any confused creature that is attacked perceives the attacker as an enemy and acts according to its basic nature. The material component of this spell is a set of three nut shells.

Note that if there are many creatures involved, the GM may decide to assume average results. For example, if there are 16 orcs affected and 25% could be expected to successfully roll the saving throw, then four are assumed to have succeeded, one wanders away, four attack the nearest creature, six stand confused and the last acts normally but must check next round. Since the Orcs are not near the party, the GM decides that two who are supposed to attack the nearest creature attack each other, one attacks an Orc that saved, and one attacks a confused orc, which strikes back. The next round, the base is 11 orcs, since four originally saved and one wandered off. Another one wanders off, five stands confused, four attack, and one acts normally.

Conjure Earth Elemental
(Conjuration/Summoning)
Reversible
Level: 7
Range: 40 yds.   **Components:** V, S
Duration: 1 turn/level   **Casting Time:** 1 turn
Area of Effect: Special **Saving Throw:** None

A caster who performs a Conjure Earth Elemental spell summons an earth elemental to do his bidding. The elemental is 60% likely to have 12 Hit Dice, 35% likely to have 16 Hit Dice, and 5% likely have 21 to 24 Hit Dice (20 + 1d4). Further, the caster needs but to command it, and it does as desired.

The elemental regards the caster as a friend to be obeyed. The elemental remains until destroyed, dispelled, sent away by a Holy Word spell or similar magic (see the Conjure Fire Elemental spell), or the spell duration expires.

Control Weather
(Alteration)
Level: 7
Range: 0   **Components:** V, S, M
Duration: 4d12 hours   **Casting Time:** 1 turn
Area of Effect: 4d4 sq. miles **Saving Throw:** None

Except as noted above, this spell is the same as the sixth level magic-user spell Control Weather (q.v.).

Creeping Doom

(Conjuration/Summoning)

Level: 7

Range: 0

Duration: 4 rds./level

Area of Effect: Special

Components: V, S

Casting Time: 1 round

Saving Throw: None

When the caster utters the spell of Creeping Doom, he calls forth a mass of from 500 to 1,000 ([1d6 + 4] x 100) venomous, biting and stinging arachnids, insects, and myriapods. This carpetlike mass swarms in an area 20 feet square.

Upon command from the caster, the swarm creeps forth at 10 feet per round toward any prey within 80 yards, moving in the direction in which the caster commands. The Creeping Doom slays any creature subject to normal attacks, as each of the small horrors inflicts 1 point of damage (each then dies after its attack), so that up to 1,000 points of damage can be inflicted on creatures within the path of the Creeping Doom.

If the Creeping Doom travels more than 80 yards away from the summoner, it loses 50 of its number for every 10 yards beyond 80 yards. For example, at 100 yards, its number has shrunk by 100. There are a number of ways to thwart or destroy the creatures forming the swarm. The solutions are left to the imaginations of players and GMs.

Finger Of Death

(Enchantment/Charm)

Level: 7

Range: 60 ft.

Duration: Permanent

Area of Effect: One creature

Components: V, S, M

Casting Time: 5 segments

Saving Throw: Negates

The Finger of Death spell causes the victim's heart to stop. The druid utters the incantation, points his index finger at the creature to be slain, and unless the victim succeeds in making the appropriate saving throw, death occurs. A successful saving throw negates the spell.

Fire Storm

(Evocation)

Reversible

Level: 7

Range: 160 yds.

Duration: 1 round

Area of Effect: Two 10-ft. cubes/level

Components: V, S

Casting Time: 1 round

Saving Throw: Half

When a Fire Storm spell is cast, the whole area is shot through with sheets of roaring flame that equal a wall of fire spell in effect. Creatures within the area of fire and 10 feet or less from the edge of the affected area receive 2d8 points of damage plus additional damage equal to the caster's level (2d8 +1/level).

Creatures that roll successful saving throws vs. spell suffer only one-half damage. The damage is inflicted each round the creature stays in the area of effect. The area of effect is equal to two 10-foot x 10-foot cubes per level of the caster—e.g., a 13th-level caster can cast a Fire Storm measuring 130 feet x 20 feet x 10 feet. The height of the storm is 10 or 20 feet; the imbalance of its area must be in length and width.

The reverse spell, Fire Quench, smothers twice the area of effect of a Fire Storm spell with respect to normal fires, and the normal area of effect with respect to magical fires. Fire-based creatures, such as elementals, salamanders, etc., of less than demigawd status have a 5% chance per experience level of the caster of being extinguished.

If cast only against a Flame Tongue sword, the sword must roll a successful saving throw vs. crushing blow or be rendered non-magical. Such a sword in the possession of a creature first receives the creature's saving throw, and if this is successful, the second saving throw is automatically successful.

Heal Critical Wounds

(Necromancy)

Level: 7

Range: 5 ft./level

Duration: Permanent

Area of Effect: 1 creature

Components: V, S

Casting Time: 5 segments

Saving Throw: None

Except as noted above, this spell is the same as the sixth level cleric spell Heal Critical Wounds.

Reincarnate

(Necromancy)

Level: 7

Range: Touch

Duration: Permanent

Area of Effect: 1 person

Components: V, S

Casting Time: 1 turn

Saving Throw: None

With this spell, the druid can bring back a dead person in another body, if death occurred no more than one week before the casting of the spell. Reincarnation does not require any saving throw, system shock, or resurrection survival roll. The corpse is touched, and a new incarnation of the person appears in the area in 1d6 turns. The person reincarnated recalls the majority of his former life and form, but the character class, if any, of the new incarnation might be very different indeed.

The new incarnation is determined on the following table or by GM choice. If a player character race is indicated, the character must be created. At the GM's option, certain special (expensive) incenses can be used that may increase the chance for a character to return as a specific race or species. A Wish spell can restore a reincarnated character to its original form and status.

Reincarnation (d100)

Roll	Incarnation
01-03	Badger
04-08	Bear, black
09-12	Bear, brown
13-16	Boar, wild
17-19	Centaur
20-23	Dryad
24-28	Eagle
29-31	Grunge Elf
32-34	Faun/satyr
35-36	Fox
37-40	Gnome
41-44	Hawk
45-58	Human
59-61	Lynx
62-64	Owl
65-68	Pixie Faerie
69-70	Raccoon
71-72	Rotgrub
73-75	Stag
76-80	Wolf
81-85	Wolverine
86-00	GM's choice

If an unusual creature form is indicated, the GM can (at his option only) use the guidelines for new player character races to allow the character to earn experience and advance in levels, although this may not be in the same class as before. If the reincarnated character returns as a creature eligible to be the same class as he was previously (i.e., a human fighter returns as an elf), the reincarnated character has half his previous levels and hit points.

If the character returns as a new character class, his hit points are half his previous total, but he must begin again at 1st level. If the character returns as a creature unable to have a class, he has half the hit points and saving throws of his previous incarnation.

Repel Living Creatures and Plants

(Abjuration)
Level: 7
Range: Caster
Duration: 1 turn/level
Area of Effect: 10 ft. dia. circle
Components: V, S, M
Casting Time: 1 round
Saving Throw: None

Except where noted above this spell works exactly like a combination of the Anti-Animal Shell and an Anti-Plant Shell spells. The material component is the caster's holy symbol.

Sunray

(Evocation, Alteration)
Level: 7
Range: 10 yds./level
Duration: 1+1d4 rds.
Area of Effect: 5-ft. radius
(special)
Components: V, S, M
Casting Time: 4 segments
Saving Throw: Special

With this spell, the caster can evoke a dazzling beam of light each round in which no action other than movement is performed. The Sunray spell is like a ray of natural sunlight. All creatures in the 10-foot-diameter area of effect must roll successful saving throws vs. spell or be blinded for 1d3 rounds, those using infravision at the time for 2d4 rounds.

Creatures to whom sunlight is harmful or unnatural suffer permanent blindness if the saving throw is failed, and are blinded for 2d6 rounds if the saving throw is successful. Those within its area of effect, as well as creatures within 20 feet of its perimeter, lose any infravision capabilities for 1d4+1 rounds. Undead caught within the sunray's area of effect receive 8d6 points of damage, one-half if a saving throw vs. spell is successful. Those undead 20 feet to either side of the sunray's area of effect receive 3d6 points of damage, no

damage if a save is successful. In addition, the ray may result in the total destruction of those undead specifically affected by sunlight, if their saving throws are failed.

The ultraviolet light generated by the spell inflicts damage on fungoid creatures and subterranean fungi just as if they were undead, but no saving throw is allowed. The material components are an aster seed and a piece of adventuring feldspar (sunstone).

Transmute Metal to Wood

(Alteration)
Level: 7
Range: 80 yds.
Duration: Permanent
Area of Effect: 1 metal object
Components: V, S, M
Casting Time: 1 round
Saving Throw: Special

The Transmute Metal to Wood spell enables the caster to change an object from metal to wood. The volume of metal cannot exceed a maximum weight of 10 pounds per experience level of the druid. Magical objects made of metal are 90% resistant to the spell, and those on the person of a creature receive the creature's saving throw as well. Artifacts and relics cannot be transmuted.

Note that only a Wish spell or similar magic can restore a transmuted object to its metallic state. Otherwise, for example, a metal door changed to wood would be forevermore a wooden door.

Transmute Rock to Lava

(Alteration)
Level: 7
Range: 20 ft./level
Duration: Special
Area of Effect: 2 cubic feet/level
Components: V, S, M
Casting Time: 1 round
Saving Throw: Special

The power of Transmute Rock to Lava turns an ordinary rocky area into one filled with hot lava. The spell is permanent in the sense that the lava remains until cooled, typically 1d6 days in normal conditions.

Creatures caught in the area suffer 5d10 points of damage each round until they escape by means of a successful saving throw. Each time a character fails a save, his equipment must save or be destroyed. The material component is a piece of obsidian.

Appendix E:

SPELL PLANNER

Spells Available by Level:

1___ 2___ 3___ 4___ 5___ 6___ 7___ 8___ 9___

10_____ 11_____ 12_____ 13_____ 14_____ 15_____

Cantrips, Useful

Memorized	Name	Type	Range	Components	Duration	Casting Time	Area of Effect	Saving Throw
☐☐☐☐☐	Chill	Evocation	I ft	V, S	--	1/2 segment	I ft. cube	None
☐☐☐☐☐	Clean	Abjuration	I ft	V, S	--	1/2 segment	4 sq. yards	None
☐☐☐☐☐	Color	Evocation	I ft	V, S	30 days	1/2 segment	I cubic yd.	None
☐☐☐☐☐	Dampen	Evocation	I ft	V, S	--	1/2 segment	I cubic yd.	None
☐☐☐☐☐	Dibs	Alteration	--	V, S	--	1/10 segment	I object	Special
☐☐☐☐☐	Dry	Abjuration	I ft	V, S	--	1/2 segment	I cubic yd.	None
☐☐☐☐☐	Dust	Abjuration	I ft	V, S	--	1/2 segment	10 ft. Radius	None
☐☐☐☐☐	Exterminate	Abjuration	I ft	V, S	--	1/10 segment	I small creature	None
☐☐☐☐☐	Flavor	Enchantment	I ft	V, S	--	1/2 segment	I object	None
☐☐☐☐☐	Freshen	Enchantment	I ft	V, S	I hour	1/2 segment	I object	None
☐☐☐☐☐	Gather	Alteration	I ft	V, S	--	1/6 segment	I sq. yard	None
☐☐☐☐☐	Polish	Alteration	I ft	V, S	--	1/2 segment	I object	None
☐☐☐☐☐	Salt	Evocation	I ft	V, S	--	1/6 segment	I object	None
☐☐☐☐☐	Shine	Alteration	I ft	V, S	--	1/2 segment	I object	None
☐☐☐☐☐	Spice	Evocation	I ft	V, S	--	1/2 segment	I object	None
☐☐☐☐☐	Sprout	Alteration	I ft	V, S	--	1/2 segment	I cubic yd.	None
☐☐☐☐☐	Stitch	Alteration	I ft	V, S	--	1/2 segment	Special	None
☐☐☐☐☐	Sweeten	Evocation	I ft	V, S	--	1/2 segment	I object	None
☐☐☐☐☐	Tie	Alteration	I ft	V, S	--	1/2 segment	I object	None
☐☐☐☐☐	Warm	Evocation	I ft	V, S	--	1/2 segment	I ft. cube	None
☐☐☐☐☐	Wrap	Alteration	I ft	V,S	--	1/2 segment	I cubic yd.	None

* = Reversible   Underline all Spells appearing in your Spellbook   Check a box for each Spell Memorized.

Cantrips, Reversed

Memorized	Name	Type	Range	Components	Duration	Casting Time	Area of Effect	Saving Throw
☐☐☐☐☐	Curdle	Enchantment	I ft	V,S	--	1/6 segment	I object	None
☐☐☐☐☐	Dirty	Evocation	I ft	V,S	--	1/6 segment	4 sq. yds.	None
☐☐☐☐☐	Dusty	Evocation	I ft	V,S	--	1/6 segment	10 foot radius	None
☐☐☐☐☐	Hairy	Alteration	I ft	V,S	--	1/10 segment	I object	None
☐☐☐☐☐	Knot	Alteration	I ft	V,S	--	1/2 segment	I object	None
☐☐☐☐☐	Ravel	Alteration	I ft	V,S	--	1/10 segment	Special	None
☐☐☐☐☐	Sour	Evocation	I ft	V,S	--	1/2 segment	I object	None
☐☐☐☐☐	Spill	Alteration	I ft	V,S	--	1/6 segment	I container	None
☐☐☐☐☐	Tangle	Alteration	I ft	V,S	--	1/6 segment	I object	None
☐☐☐☐☐	Tarnish	Alteration	I ft	V,S	--	1/2 segment	I object	None
☐☐☐☐☐	Untie	Alteration	I ft	V,S	--	1/3 segment	I object	None
☐☐☐☐☐	Wilt	Enchantment	I ft	V,S	--	1/2 segment	I object	None

* = Reversible   Underline all Spells appearing in your Spellbook   Check a box for each Spell Memorized.

Cantrips, Legerdemain

Memorized	Name	Type	Range	Components	Duration	Casting Time	Area of Effect	Saving Throw
☐☐☐☐☐	Air of Legitimacy	Illusion/Phatasm	I ft	V,S	I round	1/3 segment	I object	Special
☐☐☐☐☐	Change	Alteration	I ft	V,S	Special	1/10 segment	I object	Special
☐☐☐☐☐	Distract	Enchantment	I ft	V,S	--	1/3 segment	Special	None
☐☐☐☐☐	Hide	Illusion	I ft	V,S	Special	1/10 segment	I object	None
☐☐☐☐☐	Mute	Alteration	I ft	V,S	I round	1/10 segment	I object	Negates
☐☐☐☐☐	Palm	Illusion	I ft	V,S	I segment	1/10 segment	I small item	None
☐☐☐☐☐	Present	Alteration	2 ft radius	V,S	--	1/6 segment	I small item	Special

* = Reversible   Underline all Spells appearing in your Spellbook   Check a box for each Spell Memorized.

Cantrips, Person-Affecting

Memorized	Name	Type	Range	Components	Duration	Casting Time	Area of Effect	Saving Throw
☐☐☐☐☐	Aura/Vulnerability	Illusion/Phantasm	I ft per level	V, S	I round	1/3 segment	I creature	Special
☐☐☐☐☐	Belch	Evocation	I ft per level	V, S	--	1/10 segment	I person	Special
☐☐☐☐☐	Blink	Evocation	I ft per level	V, S	--	1/10 segment	I person	Special
☐☐☐☐☐	Cough	Evocation	I ft per level	V, S	1-3 seconds	1/3 segment	I person	Negates
☐☐☐☐☐	Coy Smile	Enchant/Charm	I ft per level	V, S	I round	1/6 segment	I person	Negates
☐☐☐☐☐	Double Take	Enchant/Charm	I ft per level	V, S	--	1/3 segment	I person	None
☐☐☐☐☐	Exude Fear	Enchant/Charm	I ft per level	V, S	I turn	1/3 segment	I person	None
☐☐☐☐☐	Feign Toughness	Illusion/Phantasm	I ft per level	V, S	I round	1/3 segment	I creature	Negates
☐☐☐☐☐	Flinch	Enchant/Charm	I ft per level	V, S	--	1/3 segment	I creature	Negates
☐☐☐☐☐	Giggle	Charm	I ft per level	V, S	2 to 3 seconds	1/3 segment	I person	Negates
☐☐☐☐☐	Indian Burn	Illusion/Phantasm	I ft per level	V, S	I round	1/3 segment	I person	Negates
☐☐☐☐☐	Knowing Look	Alteration	I ft per level	V, S	I round	1/6 segment	I person	None
☐☐☐☐☐	Lazy Eye	Alteration	I ft per level	V, S	I to 2 seconds	1/6 segment	I person	Negates
☐☐☐☐☐	Menacing Scowl	Alteration	I ft per level	V, S	I round	1/3 segment	I person	None
☐☐☐☐☐	Nod	Evocation	I ft per level	V, S	--	1/10 segment	I person	Negates
☐☐☐☐☐	Noogie	Enchant/Charm	I ft per level	V, S	I round	1/10 segment	I person	Negates
☐☐☐☐☐	Poker Face	Alteration	I ft per level	V, S	I rnd + I rnd/level	1/10 segment	caster	None
☐☐☐☐☐	Remote Gouge Eye	Evocation	I ft per level	V, S	2 rounds	1/6 segment	I creature	Negates
☐☐☐☐☐	Scratch	Evocation	I ft per level	V, S	I second	1/6 segment	I creature	Negates

Memorized	Name	Type	Range	Components	Duration	Casting Time	Area of Effect	Saving Throw
❑❑❑❑❑	Sheepish Grin	Enchant/Charm	I ft per level	V, S	--	1/3 segment	I creature	None
❑❑❑❑❑	Sneeze	Evocation	I ft per level	V, S	--	1/2 segment	I creature	Negates
❑❑❑❑❑	Twitch	Evocation	I ft per level	V, S	--	1/3 segment	I creature	Negates
❑❑❑❑❑	Veiled Threat	Evocation	Touch	V, S	--	1/6 segment	I creature	Negates
❑❑❑❑❑	Weak Bladder	Enchantment	I ft per level	V, S	6 turns	1/10 segment	I person	Negates
❑❑❑❑❑	Wet Willie	Evocation	I ft per level	V, S	--	1/3 segment	I person	None
❑❑❑❑❑	Wink	Enchantment	I ft per level	V, S	--	1/10 segment	I person	Special
❑❑❑❑❑	Yawn	Evocation	I ft per level	V, S	--	1/6 segment	I creature	Negates

* = Reversible   Underline all Spells appearing in your Spellbook   Check a box for each Spell Memorized.

Cantrips, Personal

Memorized	Name	Type	Range	Components	Duration	Casting Time	Area of Effect	Saving Throw
❑❑❑❑❑	Bee	Summoning	I ft	V, S	--	1/2 segment	I bee	None
❑❑❑❑❑	Bluelight	Conjuration	I ft	V, S	Special	1/2 segment	Special	None
❑❑❑❑❑	Bug	Summoning	I ft	V, S	--	1/2 segment	I bug	None
❑❑❑❑❑	Firefinger	Alteration	I ft	V, S	I segment	1/3 segment	1/2 ft. line	None
❑❑❑❑❑	Gnats	Summoning	I ft	V, S	I to 4 segments	1/2 segment	I ft. cube	Special
❑❑❑❑❑	Mouse	Summoning	I ft	V, S	--	1/2 segment	I mouse	None
❑❑❑❑❑	Smokepuff	Evocation	I ft	V, S	--	1/3 segment	Special	None
❑❑❑❑❑	Spider	Summoning	I ft	V, S	I segment	1/2 segment	I spider	Special
❑❑❑❑❑	Tweak	Conjuration	I ft	V, S	--	1/3 segment	I creature	Special
❑❑❑❑❑	Unlock	Conjuration	I ft	V, S	--	1/2 segment	I lock	None

* = Reversible   Underline all Spells appearing in your Spellbook   Check a box for each Spell Memorized.

Cantrips, Haunting

Memorized	Name	Type	Range	Components	Duration	Casting Time	Area of Effect	Saving Throw
❑❑❑❑❑	Creak	Evocation	I ft per level	V,S	Special	1/6 segment	Special	None
❑❑❑❑❑	Footfall	Illusion	I ft per level	V,S	--	1/6 segment	Special	None
❑❑❑❑❑	Groan	Illusion	I ft per level	V,S	--	1/6 segment	Special	Negates
❑❑❑❑❑	Moan	Illusion	I ft per level	V,S	--	1/10 segment	Special	None
❑❑❑❑❑	Rattle	Illusion	I ft per level	V,S	I to 2 seconds	1/10 segment	Special	Negates
❑❑❑❑❑	Tap	Evocation	I ft per level	V,S	--	1/6 segment	I sq. ft.	None
❑❑❑❑❑	Thump	Illusion	I ft per level	V,S	--	1/10 segment	Special	Negates
	Whistle	Evocation	I ft per level	V,S	--	1/6 segment	Special	None

* = Reversible   Underline all Spells appearing in your Spellbook   Check a box for each Spell Memorized.

Cantrips, Minor Illusions

Memorized	Name	Type	Range	Components	Duration	Casting Time	Area of Effect	Saving Throw
❑❑❑❑❑	Colored Lights	Alteration	I ft	V,S	Special	1/2 segment	Special	None
❑❑❑❑❑	Dim	Alteration	I ft	V,S	I round	1/2 segment	Special	None
❑❑❑❑❑	Haze	Alteration	I ft	V,S	I round	1/2 segment	I ft. cube	None
❑❑❑❑❑	Mask	Illusion	I ft	V,S	3 to 6 rounds	1/6 segment	I person	None
❑❑❑❑❑	Mirage	Illusion	I ft	V,S	Special	1/2 segment	2 sq. feet	Special
❑❑❑❑❑	Noise	Illusion	10 ft	V,S	--	1/6 segment	I ft. radius	Negates
❑❑❑❑❑	Rainbow	Alteration	I ft	V,S	I round	1/3 segment	Special	None
	Two-D'lusion	Illusion	I ft	V,S	--	1/6 segment	4 sq. feet	None

* = Reversible   Underline all Spells appearing in your Spellbook   Check a box for each Spell Memorized.

Cantrips, Social Engagement

Memorized	Name	Type	Range	Components	Duration	Casting Time	Area of Effect	Saving Throw
❑❑❑❑❑	Blather *	Enchant/Charm	10 feet	V,S	I turn	1/3 segment	I person	None
❑❑❑❑❑	Conceal Gas	Illusion/Phantasm	I ft per level	V,S	I round	1/10 segment	I person	None
❑❑❑❑❑	Dispel Body Odor*	Alteration	I ft per level	V,S	--	1/3 segment	I person	Special
❑❑❑❑❑	Gristle Teleportation	Alteration	I ft per level	V,S	--	1/6 segment	caster's mouth	None
❑❑❑❑❑	Hide Food	Illusion/Phantasm	I ft per level	V,S	6 turns	1/2 segment	I plate	None
❑❑❑❑❑	Illusion of Courtesy	Illusion/Phatasm	I ft per level	V,S	--	1/6 segment	I person	None
❑❑❑❑❑	Interject Witty Comment	Alteration	I ft per level	V,S	--	1/10 segment	I person	None
❑❑❑❑❑	Neutralize Alcohol*	Alteration	10 feet	V,S	--	1/3 segment	I quart	None
❑❑❑❑❑	Numb Tongue	Illusion	I ft per level	V,S	I turn	1/6 segment	caster	None
❑❑❑❑❑	Pass Salt	Alteration	I ft per level	V,S	--	1/6 segment	I container	None
❑❑❑❑❑	Personal Zephyr	Evocation	I ft per level	V,S	6 turns	1/3 segment	caster	None
❑❑❑❑❑	Protection from Sneezes	Abjuration	I ft per level	V,S	I round	1/10 segment	caster	None
❑❑❑❑❑	Set Table*	Alteration	I ft per level	V,S	--	1/2 segment	I table	None
❑❑❑❑❑	Strengthen Smile Muscles	Alteration	10 feet	V,S	I day	1/3 segment	I person	None
❑❑❑❑❑	Wash Hands	Alteration	I ft per level	V,S	--	1/2 segment	2 hands	None
❑❑❑❑❑	Wipe Face	Alteration	I ft per level	V,S	--	1/2 segment	I person	None

* = Reversible   Underline all Spells appearing in your Spellbook   Check a box for each Spell Memorized.

Magic User Spells
Magic-User 1st level

Memorized	Name	Type	Range	Components	Duration	Casting Time	Area of Effect	Saving Throw
☐☐☐☐☐	Affect Normal Fires	Alteration	5 yds/level	V, S, M	2 yds/level	1 segment	10 ft. radius	None
☐☐☐☐☐	Alarm	Abjur./Evocat.	10 yards	V, S, M	4 hrs+1/2 hr./level	1 round	Special	None
☐☐☐☐☐	Armor	Conjuration	Touch	V, S, M	Special	1 round	1 creature	None
☐☐☐☐☐	Audible Glamer	Illusion/Phantasm	60 yds.+10 yds/lvl	V, S, M	3 rounds/level	1 segment	hearing range	Special
☐☐☐☐☐	Aura of Innocence	Enchant/Charm	1 yd/level	V, S, M	3 rounds/level	1 segment	1 person	Negates
☐☐☐☐☐	Bash Door	Evocation	30 yards	V, S	Instantaneous	1 segment	1 door	None
☐☐☐☐☐	Befriend	Enchant/Charm	0	V, S, M	1d4 rnds+1 rnd/lvl	1 segment	60 ft. radius	Special
☐☐☐☐☐	Burning Hands	Alteration	5 feet	V, S	Instantaneous	1 segment	5 ft., 120° arc	1/2 damage
☐☐☐☐☐	Change Self	Illusion/Phantasm	0	V, S	2d6 rnds+2 rnd/lvl	1 segment	caster	None
☐☐☐☐☐	Charm Person	Encant/Charm	120 yds.	V, S	Special	1 segment	1 person	Negates
☐☐☐☐☐	Chill Touch	Necromancy	0	V, S	3 rnds+1 rnd/level	1 segment	caster	Negates
☐☐☐☐☐	Chromatic Orb	Alteration/Evocat.	30 feet	V, S, M	Special	1 segment	1 creature	Special
☐☐☐☐☐	Color Spray	Alteration	0	V, S, M	Instantaneous	1 segment	5x20x20 ft. wedge	Special
☐☐☐☐☐	Comprehend Languages *	Alteration	Touch	V, S, M	5 rounds per level	1 round	Special	None
☐☐☐☐☐	Conjure Mount	Conjur./Summon.	10 yards	V, S, M	2 hours+1 hr./level	1 turn	1 mount	None
☐☐☐☐☐	Dancing Lights	Alteration	40 yds.+10 yds/lvl	V, S, M	2 rounds/level	1 segment	Special	None
☐☐☐☐☐	Detect Magic	Divination	0	V, S	2 rounds/level	1 segment	10 ft. x 60 ft.	None
☐☐☐☐☐	Detect Undead	Divin./Necrom.	0	V, S, M	3 turns	1 round	60 ft.+10 ft./level	None
☐☐☐☐☐	Enlarge *	Alteration	5 yds./level	V, S, M	5 rounds/level	1 segment	1 creature/object	Negates
☐☐☐☐☐	Erase	Alteration	30 yards	V, S	Permanent	1 segment	1 scroll or 2 pages	Special
☐☐☐☐☐	Faerie Phantoms	Illusion/Phantasm	60 yds.+10 yds/lvl	V, S, M	Special	1 segment	1d6 phantoms/level	None
☐☐☐☐☐	Feather Fall	Alteration	10 yds./level	V	1 rd./level	1 segment	Special	None
☐☐☐☐☐	Find Familiar	Conjur./Summon.	1 mile/level	V, S, M	Special	2d12 hours	1 familiar	Special
☐☐☐☐☐	Fireball, Barrage	Alteration	50 yds. + 10 yds/lvl	V, S, M	1 round/level	1 segment	1+ creatures in rng	None
☐☐☐☐☐	Fireball, Sidewinder (FI)	Evocation	1 mile maximum	V, S, M	1 round/level	1 segment	10 ft. radius	1/2
☐☐☐☐☐	Firewater	Alteration	10 feet	V, S, M	1 round	1 segment	1 pint of water	None
☐☐☐☐☐	Fluttersoft	Alteration	60 feet	V, S, M	1 hour	1 segment	one creature	None
☐☐☐☐☐	Fog Vision	Divination	Touch	V, S, M	1 turn/level	1 segment	one person	None
☐☐☐☐☐	Gabal's Magic Aura	Illusion/Phantasm	Touch	V, S, M	1 day/level	1 round	Special	Special
☐☐☐☐☐	Gaze Reflection	Alteration	0	V, S	2 rds + 1 rd./lvl	1 segment	Special	None
☐☐☐☐☐	Grease	Conjuration	10 yards	V, S, M	3 rds. + 1 rd./lvl	1 segment	10 x 10 ft.	Special
☐☐☐☐☐	Haarpang's Floating Cart	Evocation	20 yards	V, S, M	6 hours + 1 hr./lvl	1 segment	Special	None
☐☐☐☐☐	Hold Portal	Alteration	20 yards/level	V	1 rd./level	1 segment	20 sq. ft./level	None
☐☐☐☐☐	Hypnotism	Enchant./Charm	5 yards	V, S	1 rd. + 1 rd./level	1 segment	30 ft. cube	Negates
☐☐☐☐☐	Identify	Divination	0	V, S, M	1 rd./level	Special	1 item/level	None
☐☐☐☐☐	Jump	Alteration	Touch	V, S, M	1d3 rds. + 1 rd/lvl	1 segment	creature touched	None
☐☐☐☐☐	Light	Alteration	60 yards	V, M	1 turn/level	1 segment	20 ft. radius	Special
☐☐☐☐☐	Magic Missile	Evocation	60 yds. + 10 yds/lvl	V, S	Instantaneous	1 segment	1-5 targets/10 ft. sq.	None
☐☐☐☐☐	Magic Shield	Evocation	0	V, S	5 rds./level	1 segment	Special	None
☐☐☐☐☐	Melt	Alteration	30 yards	V, S, M	1 round/level	1 segment	Special	Special
☐☐☐☐☐	Mend	Alteration	30 yards	V, S, M	Permanent	1 segment	1 object	None
☐☐☐☐☐	Merge Coin Pile	Alteration	10 yards	V, S, M	Permanent	1 segment	10 ft. x 10 ft. area	Special
☐☐☐☐☐	Message	Alteration	0	V, S, M	5 rds./level	1 segment	Special	None
☐☐☐☐☐	Minor Sphere/Perturbation	Alteration	60 yards	V, M	1 turn/level	1 segment	20 ft. radius	Negates
☐☐☐☐☐	Phantasmal Fireball	Illusion./Phantasm	60 yds.+10 yds/lvl	V, S, M	Instantaneous	1 segment	20 ft. radius	Special
☐☐☐☐☐	Phantasmal Force	Illusion./Phantasm	60 yds.+10 yds/lvel	V, S, M	Special	1 segment	Special	Special
☐☐☐☐☐	Phantom Armor	Alteration/Illusion	Touch	V, S, M	Special	1 round	one person	None
☐☐☐☐☐	Pool Gold	Alteration	20 feet	V, S, M	1 round	1 segment	20 ft. radius	Special
☐☐☐☐☐	Precipitation	Alteration	10 ft./level	V, S, M	1 segment/level	3 segments	Special	None
☐☐☐☐☐	Protection from Evil	Abjuration	Touch	V, S, M	2 rds./level	1 segment	creature touched	None
☐☐☐☐☐	Push	Conjur./Summon.	1 ft./level	V, S, M	Instantaneous	1 segment	Special	Negates
☐☐☐☐☐	Read Magic	Divination	0	V, S, M	2 rds./level	1 round	Special	None
☐☐☐☐☐	Run	Enchantment	Touch	V, S, M	5 to 8 hours	1 round	Special	None
☐☐☐☐☐	Shift Blame	Enchant./Charm	Touch	V, S, M	3 rds./level	1 segment	creature touched	Negates
☐☐☐☐☐	Shocking Grasp	Alteration	Touch	V, S	Special	1 segment	creature touched	None
☐☐☐☐☐	Sleep	Enchant./Charm	30 yards	V, S, M	5 rds./level	1 segment	Special	None
☐☐☐☐☐	Smell Immunity	Illusion/Phantasm	60 feet	V, S, M	1 turn/level	1 segment	1 creature	Negates
☐☐☐☐☐	Spider Climb	Alteration	Touch	V, S, M	3 rds. + 1 rd./level	1 segment	creature touched	Negates
☐☐☐☐☐	Spook	Illusion/Phantasm	30 feet	V, S	Special	1 segment	1 creature	Negates
☐☐☐☐☐	Taunt	Enchantment	60 yards	V, S, M	1 round	1 segment	30 ft. radius	Negates
☐☐☐☐☐	Throw Voice	Illusion/Phantasm	10 yds./lvl	V, M	4 rds + 1 rd./level	1 segment	1 creature or object	Negates
☐☐☐☐☐	Unseen Servant	Conjurat./Summon.	0	V, S, M	4 hr. + 1 hour/level	1 segment	30 ft. radius	None
☐☐☐☐☐	Wall of Fog	Evocation	30 yards	V, S, M	2d4 rds. + 1 rd./lvl	1 segment	Special	None
☐☐☐☐☐	Wizard Mark	Alteration	Touch	V, S, M	Permanent	1 segment	Up to 1 sq. foot	None
☐☐☐☐☐	Write	Evocation	0	V, S, M	1 hour/level	1 round	1 spell inscription	Special
☐☐☐☐☐	Wrygal's Delic/Deception	Illus/Phantasm	100 feet	V, S, M	1 turn	1 segment	60 yard radius	None
☐☐☐☐☐	Yudder's Whistle of Hell's Gate	Evocation	5 yds radius/lvl	V, S, M	1 round/level	1 segment	5 yard radius/level	Special/Neg

* = Reversible Underline all Spells appearing in your Spellbook Check a box for each Spell Memorized.

Magic User 2nd Level

Memorized	Name	Type	Range	Components	Duration	Casting Time	Area of Effect	Saving Throw
☐☐☐☐☐	Alter Self	Alteration	0	V, S	3d4 rds./+2 rds./lvl	2 segments	the caster	None
☐☐☐☐☐	Bind	Enchantment	30 yards	V, S, M	1 rd./level	2 segments	50 ft. + 5 ft./level	None
☐☐☐☐☐	Blindness	Illusion/Phantasm	30 yds.+10 yds./lvl	V	Special	2 segments	1 creature	Negates
☐☐☐☐☐	Blur	Illusion/Phantasm	0	V, S	3 rds. + 1 rd./level	2 segments	the caster	None
☐☐☐☐☐	Chain of Fire	Evocation	30 yards	V, S, M	Special	2 segments	Special	None
☐☐☐☐☐	Cheetah Speed	Alteration	Touch	V, S, M	3 rds. + 1 rd./lv	2 segments	1 creature/level	None

Memorized	Name	Type	Range	Components	Duration	Casting Time	Area of Effect	Saving Throw
☐☐☐☐☐	Cloud of Pummeling Fists	Evocation	1 yd./level	V, S, M	2 rounds	2 segments	10 ft. radius	None
☐☐☐☐☐	Continual Light *	Alteration	60 yards	V, S	Permanent	2 segments	60 ft. radius	Special
☐☐☐☐☐	Darkness, 15' R.	Alteration	10 yds./level	V, S, M	1 turn + 1 rd./level	2 segments	15 ft. radius	None
☐☐☐☐☐	Deafness	Illusion/Phantasm	60 yards	V, S, M	Special	2 segments	1 creature	Negates
☐☐☐☐☐	Deeppockets	Alterat./Enchant.	Touch	V, S, M	12 hrs. + 1 hr./level	1 turn	1 garment	None
☐☐☐☐☐	Detect Evil *	Divination	0	V, S	5 rds./level	2 segments	10 x 180 ft.	None
☐☐☐☐☐	Detect Invisibility	Divination	0	V, S, M	5 rds./level	2 segments	10 yds./level	None
☐☐☐☐☐	ESP	Divination	0	V, S, M	1 rd./level	2 segments	5 yds./level	None
☐☐☐☐☐	Fascinate	Illusion/Phantasm	30 yards	V, S	Special	2 segments	1 creature	Negates
☐☐☐☐☐	Fireball, Skipping Betty	Evocation	1 mile	V, S, M	1 rd./level	2 segments	10 ft. radius	1/2
☐☐☐☐☐	Fireball, S.W. (F2)	Evocation	1 mile max	V, S, M	1 rd./level	2 segments	10 ft. radius	1/2
☐☐☐☐☐	Fire Telekinesis	Alteration	30 yards	V, S	2 rnds/level	2 segments	Special	Special
☐☐☐☐☐	Flaming Sphere	Evocation	10 yards	V, S, M	1 rd./level	2 segments	3 ft. radius	Negates
☐☐☐☐☐	Fog Cloud	Alteration	10 yards	V, S	4 rds. + 1 rd./level	2 segments	Special	None
☐☐☐☐☐	Fool's Gold	Alterat./Illusion	10 yards	V, S, M	1 hr./level	1 round	10 cu. in./level	Special
☐☐☐☐☐	Forget	Enchant/Charm	30 yards	V, S	Permanent	2 segments	Special	Negates
☐☐☐☐☐	Gandle's Fble. Trap	Illusion/Phantasm	Touch	V, S, M	Permanent	3 rounds	object touched	None
☐☐☐☐☐	Glitterdust	Conjur./Summon	10 yds./level	V, S, M	Special	2 segments	20 ft. cube	Special
☐☐☐☐☐	Heat Seeking FoT	Evocation	100 feet	V, S, M	Instantaneous	2 segments	30 ft. cube	1/2
☐☐☐☐☐	Hypnotic Pattern	Illusion/Phantasm	30 yards	S, M	Special	2 segments	30 ft. cube	Negates
☐☐☐☐☐	Imprv. Phant. Force	Illusion/Phantasm	60 yds.+10 yds./lvl	V, S, M	Special	2 segments	Special	Special
☐☐☐☐☐	Invisibility	Illusion/Phantasm	Touch	V, S, M	Special	2 segments	creature touched	None
☐☐☐☐☐	Irritation	Alteration	10 yds./level	V, S, M	Special	2 segments	Special	Negates
☐☐☐☐☐	Knock *	Alteration	60 yards	V	Special	1 segment	10 sq. ft./level	None
☐☐☐☐☐	Know Alignment	Divination	10 yards	V, S	1 rd./level	1 round	Special	Negates
☐☐☐☐☐	Levitate	Alteration	20 yds./level	V, S, M	1 turn/level	2 segments	1 creature/object	Negates
☐☐☐☐☐	Locate Object *	Divination	0	V, S, M	1 rd./level	2 segments	20 yds./Level	Negates
☐☐☐☐☐	Magic Missile/Skewering	Evocation	60 ft. + 10 ft./lvl	V, S	Instantaneous	2 segments	Special	None ☐☐☐☐
☐☐☐☐☐	Magic Mouth	Alteration	10 yards	V, S, M	Special	2 segments	1 object	None
☐☐☐☐☐	Mirror Image	Illusion/Phantasm	0	V, S	3 rds./level	2 segments	6 ft. radius	None
☐☐☐☐☐	Misdirection	Illusion/Phantasm	30 yards	V, S	8 hours	2 segments	1 creature/object	Negates
☐☐☐☐☐	Munz's Bolt/Acid	Conjuration	180 yards	V, S	Special	2 segments	1 target	Special
☐☐☐☐☐	Murgain's Muster Str.	Enchant./Charm	Touch	V, S	Permanent	2 segments	1 creature	None (neg.)
☐☐☐☐☐	Premonition	Divination	Touch	V, S, M	2 rds./level	2 segments	1 creature	None (neg.)
☐☐☐☐☐	Preserve	Abjuration	Touch	V, S, M	Permanent	2 rounds	Special	None
☐☐☐☐☐	Proadus' U.F.L.	Enchantment	60 yards	V, S, M	1 rd./level	2 segments	1 or more	Negates
☐☐☐☐☐	Protection/Cantrips	Abjuration	Touch	V, S	5 hrs. + 1 hr./lvl	1 round	1 creature/object	None
☐☐☐☐☐	Pyrotechnics	Alteration	120 yards	V, S, M	Special	2 segments	1 fire source	None
☐☐☐☐☐	Ray/Enfeeblement	Enchant./Charm	10 yds.+5 yds./lvl	V, S	1 rd./level	2 segments	1 creature	Negates
☐☐☐☐☐	Reveal Secret Portal	Divination	0	V, S, M	5 rds./level	2 segments	10 yds./level	None
☐☐☐☐☐	Rope Trick	Alteration	Touch	V, S, M	2 turns/level	2 segments	Special	None
☐☐☐☐☐	Scare	Enchant./Charm	30 yds.+10 yds./lvl	V, S, M	1d4 rds. + 1 rd./lvl	2 segments	15 foot radius	Special
☐☐☐☐☐	Shatter	Alteration	30 yds.+10 yds./lvl	V, S, M	Instantaneous	2 segments	3 ft. radius	Negates
☐☐☐☐☐	Spectral Hand	Necromancy	30 yds. + 5 yds./lvl	V, S	2 rds./level	2 segments	1 opponent	None
☐☐☐☐☐	Stinking Cloud	Evocation	30 yards	V, S, M	1 rd./level	2 segments	20 ft. cube	Special
☐☐☐☐☐	Strength	Alteration	Touch	V, S, M	1 hr./level	1 turn	person touched	None
☐☐☐☐☐	Summon Swarm	Conjur./Summon	60 yards	V, S, M	Special	2 segments	10 ft. cube	Negates
☐☐☐☐☐	Tattoo of Shame	Alteration	Touch	V, S, M	Permanent	1 round	Up to 1 sq. ft.	Negates
☐☐☐☐☐	Telepathic Mute	Alteration	10 ft./level	V, S, M	2 rnds/level	2 segments	1 creature	None
☐☐☐☐☐	Total Control	Enchant./Charm	10 yds./level	V	2 rnds/level	2 segments	1 creature	None (neg.)
☐☐☐☐☐	Web	Evocation	5 yds./level	V, S, M	2 turns/level	2 segments	8,000 cubic feet	Neg or 1/2
☐☐☐☐☐	Whip	Evocation	1 ft.	V, S, M	1 rnd/level	2 segments	Special	Special
☐☐☐☐☐	Whispering Wind	Alterat./Phantasm	1 mile/level	V, S	Special	2 segments	2 ft. radius	None
☐☐☐☐☐	White Hot Metal	Alteration	10 feet	V, M	1 round/level	2 segments	up to 1 lb. metal	None (neg.)
☐☐☐☐☐	Wizard Lock	Alteration	Touch	V, S	Permanent	2 segments	30 sq. ft./level	None

* = Reversible   Underline all Spells appearing in your Spellbook   Check a box for each Spell Memorized.

Magic-User 3rd Level

Memorized	Name	Type	Range	Components	Duration	Casting Time	Area of Effect	Saving Throw
☐☐☐☐☐	Bash Face	Evocation	10 ft. + 1 ft./level	V, S, M	Instantaneous	3 segments	1 target	None
☐☐☐☐☐	Blink	Alteration	0	V, S	1 rd./level	1 segment	the caster	None
☐☐☐☐☐	Charm Undead	Necromancy	10 ft./level	V, S, M	Permanent	3 segments	1 undead creature	None
☐☐☐☐☐	Clairaudience	Divination	Unlimited	V, S, M	1 rd./level	3 segments	60 ft. radius	None
☐☐☐☐☐	Clairvoyance	Divination	Unlimited	V, S, M	1 rd./level	3 segments	line of sight	None
☐☐☐☐☐	Cloudburst	Alteration	10 ft./level	V, S, M	1 round	5 segments	Special	Special
☐☐☐☐☐	Cont. Darkness	Alteration	60 yards	V, M	Permanent	3 segments	30 ft. radius globe	Negates
☐☐☐☐☐	Delude	Alteration	0	V, S	1 turn/level	3 segments	30 ft. radius	Negates
☐☐☐☐☐	Dispel Magic	Abjuration	120 yards	V, S	Instantaneous	3 segments	30 ft. cube	None
☐☐☐☐☐	Explosive Runes	Alteration	Touch	V, S	Special	3 segments	10 ft. radius	None or 1/2
☐☐☐☐☐	Feign Death	Necromancy	Touch	V, S	1 hr. + 1 turn/lvl	1 segment	creature touched	None
☐☐☐☐☐	Fireball	Evocation	10 yds.+10 yds./lvl	V, S, M	Instantaneous	3 segments	20 ft. radius	1/2
☐☐☐☐☐	Fireball, S-Blast	Evocation	10 yds.+10 yds./lvl	V, S, M	Instantaneous	3 segments	1d6 10 ft. rad. sph.	1/2
☐☐☐☐☐	Fireball, S.W (F3)	Evocation	1 mile max.	V, S, M	1 rd./level	3 segments	10 ft. radius	1/2
☐☐☐☐☐	Flame Arrow	Conjur./Summon.	30 yds+10 yds./lvl	V, S	1 round	3 segments	Special	None
☐☐☐☐☐	Fly	Alteration	Touch	V, S, M	1 turn/lvl+1d6 trns	3 segments	creature touched	None
☐☐☐☐☐	Gandle's H. Hut	Alteration	0	V, S, M	4 hrs. + 1 hr./level	3 segments	15 ft. diameter sph.	None
☐☐☐☐☐	Grow	Alteration	3 yds./level	V, S, M	Instantaneous	3 segments	1 creature	Negates
☐☐☐☐☐	Gust of Wind	Alteration	0	V, S, M	1 round	3 segments	10 ft. x 10 yds./lvl	None
☐☐☐☐☐	Haste	Alteration	60 yards	V, S, M	3 rds. + 1 rd./level	3 segments	Special	None
☐☐☐☐☐	Hold person	Enchant./Charm	120 yds.	V, S, M	2 rds./level	3 segments	Special	Negates
☐☐☐☐☐	Hold Undead	Necromancy	60 feet	V, S, M	1d4 rds. + 1 rd./lvl	5 segments	1d3 undead	Negates
☐☐☐☐☐	Illusionary Script	Illusion/Phantasm	Touch	V, S, M	1 day/level	Special	script reader	Special

Memorized	Name	Type	Range	Components	Duration	Casting Time	Area of Effect	Saving Throw
☐☐☐☐☐	Infravision	Alteration	Touch	V, S, M	2 hrs+1 hr./level	1 round	creature touched	None
☐☐☐☐☐	Invisibility, 10' R	Illusion/Phantasm	Touch	V, S, M	Special	3 segments	10 ft. radius	Special
☐☐☐☐☐	Item	Alteration	Touch	V, S, M	4 hrs./level	3 segments	2 cu. ft./level	Special
☐☐☐☐☐	Lightning Bolt	Evocation	40 yds.+10 yds./lvl	V, S, M	Instantaneous	3 segments	Special	1/2
☐☐☐☐☐	Material	Evocat./Conjur.	1 ft.	V, S	Permanent	1 round	1 cu. ft./level	None
☐☐☐☐☐	Monster Sum. I	Conjur./Summon.	Special	V, S, M	2 rds.+1 rd. lvl	3 segments	30 yd. radius	None
☐☐☐☐☐	Murgain's Migraine	Necromancy	30 yards	V, S	Until Dispelled	3 segments	1 creature	Negates
☐☐☐☐☐	No Fear	Enchant./Charm	10 yds./level	V	2 rounds/level	3 segments	10 ft. radius	None (neg.)
☐☐☐☐☐	Non-Detection	Abjuration	Touch	V, S, M	1 hr./level	3 segments	1 creature/item	None
☐☐☐☐☐	Paralyzation	Illusion/Phantasm	10 ft./level	V, S	Special	3 segments	20 ft. x 20 ft. area	Negates
☐☐☐☐☐	Perceived Malign.	Enchant./Charm	50 feet	V	Special	3 segments	1 creature	None (neg.)
☐☐☐☐☐	Phantom Steed	Conjur./Phantasm	Touch	V, S	1 hr./level	1 turn	Special	None
☐☐☐☐☐	Phantom Wind	Alterat./Phantasm	1 rd./level	V, S	1 rd/level	3 segments	1 ft. broad path	None
☐☐☐☐☐	Polymorph/Amph.	Alteration	5 ft./level	V, S, M	Permanent	3 segments	1 creature	Negates
☐☐☐☐☐	Polymorph/Primate	Alteration	5 ft./level	V, S, M	Permanent	3 segments	1 creature	Negates
☐☐☐☐☐	Preemptive Strike	Evocation	Caster	V, S, M	1 hr./level	1 round	5 ft. radius	1/2 damage
☐☐☐☐☐	Prot./Normal Miss.	Abjuration	Touch	V, S, M	1 turn/level	3 segments	creature touched	None
☐☐☐☐☐	Runes/Eyeball Imp.	Alteration	Touch	V, S	Special	3 segments	1 creature	None
☐☐☐☐☐	Secret Page	Alteration	Touch	V, S, M	Until dispelled	1 turn	1 page/2 ft. square	None
☐☐☐☐☐	Sepia Snake Sigil	Conjur./Summon.	5 yds	V, S, M	Special	3 segments	1 sigil	None
☐☐☐☐☐	Slow	Alteration	90 yds.+10 yds./lvl	V, S, M	3 rds. + 1 rd./level	3 segments	40 ft. cube	Negates
☐☐☐☐☐	Spectral Force	Illusion/Phantasm	60 yds.+1 yd./level	V, S	Special	3 segments	Special	Special
☐☐☐☐☐	Suggestion	Enchant./Charm	30 yards	V, M	1 hr. + 1hr./level	3 segments	1 creature	Negates
☐☐☐☐☐	Sure Grip Snare	Evocation	10 feet	V, S, M	1 hr./level	1 round	Special	Negate
☐☐☐☐☐	Tongues*	Alteration	0	V, M	1 rd./level	3 segments	30 ft. radius	None
☐☐☐☐☐	Vampiric Touch	Necromancy	0	V, S	1 touch	3 segments	the caster	None
☐☐☐☐☐	Ward Off Evil*	Abjuration	Touch	V, S, M	2 rds./level	3 segments	10 ft. radius	None
☐☐☐☐☐	Water Breathing*	Alteration	Touch	V, S, M	6 turns/level	5 segments	creature touched	None
☐☐☐☐☐	Wind Wall	Alteration	10 yds./level	V, S, M	1 rd./level	3 segments	Special	Special
☐☐☐☐☐	Wraithform	Alteration/Illus.	0	S, M	2 rds./level	1 segment	the caster	None
☐☐☐☐☐	Zargosa's F.S.of T.	Evocat./Alterat.	70 yds./+10 yds./lvl	V, S, M	Special	3 segments	1 target/meteor	None

* = Reversible Underline all Spells appearing in your Spellbook Check a box for each Spell Memorized.

Magic-User 4th Level

Memorized	Name	Type	Range	Components	Duration	Casting Time	Area of Effect	Saving Throw
☐☐☐☐☐	Charm Monster	Enchant./Charm	60 yds.	V, S	Special	4 segments	Special	Negates
☐☐☐☐☐	Close Portal	Alteration	120 feet	V, S	1 round/level	4 segments	1 creature	Negates
☐☐☐☐☐	Confusion	Enchant./Charm	120 yards	V, S, M	2 rds. + 1 rd./lvl	4 segments	Up to 60 ft. cube	Special
☐☐☐☐☐	Contagion	Necromancy	30 yards	V, S	Permanent	4 segments	1 creature	Negates
☐☐☐☐☐	Detect Scrying	Divination	0	V, S, M	1d6 trns+1 trn/lvl	3 segments	120 ft. radius	Special
☐☐☐☐☐	Dig	Evocation	30 yards	V, S, M	1 rd./level	4 segments	5 ft. cube/level	Special
☐☐☐☐☐	Dimension Door	Alteration	0	V	Instantaneous	1 segment	the caster	None
☐☐☐☐☐	Dispel Exhaust.	Illusion/Phantasm	Touch	V, S	3 turns/level	4 segments	1 to 4 persons	None
☐☐☐☐☐	Emergency Teleport/Rnd	Alteration	0	V	Instantaneous	1 round	the caster	None
☐☐☐☐☐	Emotion	Enchant./Charm	10 yds./level	V, S	Special	4 segments	20 ft. cube	Negates
☐☐☐☐☐	Enchant. Weapon	Enchantment	Touch	V, S, M	5 rds/level	1 turn	weapon(s) touched	None
☐☐☐☐☐	Enervation	Necromancy	10 yds./level	V, S	1d4 hrs.+1 hr./lvl	4 segments	1 creature	Negates
☐☐☐☐☐	Extension I	Alteration	0	V	Special	2 segments	Special	None
☐☐☐☐☐	Fear	Illusion/Phantasm	0	V, S, M	Special	4 segments	60 ft. cone	Negates
☐☐☐☐☐	Fireball, Lnd Scrpr	Evocation	10 yds.+10 yds./lvl	V, S, M	Instantaneous	4 segments	Special	1/2
☐☐☐☐☐	Fireball, S.W. (F4)	Evocation	1 mile maxlum	V, S, M	1 rd./level	4 segments	10 ft. radius	1/2
☐☐☐☐☐	Fireball, Volley	Evocation	10 yrds.+10 yrds/lvl	V, S, M	Special	4 segments	10 ft. radius	1/2
☐☐☐☐☐	Fire Charm	Enchant./Charm	10 yds.	V, S, M	2 rds./level	4 segments	15 ft. radius	Negates
☐☐☐☐☐	Fire Shield	Evocat./Alterat.	0	V, S, M	2 rds. + 1 rd./lvl	4 segments	the caster	None
☐☐☐☐☐	Fire Trap	Abjuration/Evocat.	Touch	V, S, M	Until discharged	1 turn	object touched	1/2
☐☐☐☐☐	Fumble	Enchant./Charm	10 yds./level	V, S	1 rd./level	4 segments	30 ft. cube	Special
☐☐☐☐☐	Haarpang's Mag. S.R.	Alterat./Evocat.	20 yards	V, S, M	1 rd./level	4 segments	1 ft. diameter/lvl	Negates
☐☐☐☐☐	Haarpang's Mem. K.	Alteration	0	V, S, M	1 day	1 turn	the caster	None
☐☐☐☐☐	Hallucinatory Terrain	Ilusion/Phantasm	20 yds./level	V, S, M	1 hr./level	1 turn	10 yds./lvl. cube	None
☐☐☐☐☐	Hurl Animal	Alteration	10 yds./level	V, S, M	Instantaneous	4 segments	10 yds./level	Negates
☐☐☐☐☐	Ice Storm	Evocation	10 yds./level	V, S, M	Special	4 segments	20 or 40 ft. radius	None
☐☐☐☐☐	Illusionary Wall	Illusion/Phantasm	30 yds.	V, S	Permanent	4 segments	1x10x10 ft.	None
☐☐☐☐☐	Improved Invis.	Illusion/Phantasm	Touch	V, S	4 rds.+ 1 rd./lvl	4 segments	creature touched	None
☐☐☐☐☐	Mage Lock	Enchant/Charm	Touch	V, S, M	Permanent	1 turn	1 item	None
☐☐☐☐☐	Magic Mirror	Enchant./Divinat.	Touch	V, S, M	1 rd./level	1 hour	Special	None
☐☐☐☐☐	Massmorph	Alteration	10 yds./level	V, S, M	Special	4 segments	10 ft. cube/lvl	None
☐☐☐☐☐	Minor Creation	Illusion/Phantasm	Touch	V, S, M	1 hr./level	1 turn	1 cubic ft./lvl	None
☐☐☐☐☐	Minor Globe/Invuln.	Abjuration	0	V, S, M	1 rd./level	4 segments	5 ft. radius	None
☐☐☐☐☐	Mist of Corralling	Evocation	10 ft./level	V, S, M	1 turn + 1 rnd/lvl	1 round	Special	None
☐☐☐☐☐	Monster Sum. II	Conjur./Summon.	Special	V, S, M	3 rds. + 1 rd/lvl	4 segments	40 yd. radius	None
☐☐☐☐☐	Perpetual S. Grasp	Alteration	Touch	V, S, M	Permanent	4 segments	Special	None
☐☐☐☐☐	Phantasmal Killer	Illusion/Phantasm	5 yds./lvl	V, S, M	1 rd./level	4 segments	1 creature	Special
☐☐☐☐☐	Plant Growth	Alteration	10 yds./lvl	V, S	Permenant	4 segments	100 ft. sq. per lvl	None
☐☐☐☐☐	Polymorph Other	Alteration	5 yds./lvl	V, S, M	Permanent	4 segments	1 creature	Negates
☐☐☐☐☐	Polymorph Self	Alteration	0	V	2 turns/level	4 segments	the caster	none
☐☐☐☐☐	Rainbow pattern	Alter./Ill./Phant.	10 yds	S, M	Special	4 segments	30 ft. cube	Negates
☐☐☐☐☐	Remove Curse *	Abjuration	Touch	V, S	Permanent	4 segments	Special	Special
☐☐☐☐☐	Shadow Monsters	Illus./Phantasm	30 yards	V, S	1 rd./level	4 segments	20 ft. cube	Special
☐☐☐☐☐	Shout	Evocation	0	V, M	Instantaneous	1 segment	10 x 30 ft. cone	Special
☐☐☐☐☐	Solid Fog	Alteration	30 yards	V, S, M	2d4 rds.+1 rd./lvl	4 segments	20 x 10 x 10 ft.	None
☐☐☐☐☐	Stirring Oration	Enchant./Charm	0	V	1 turn + 1 rnd./lvl	1 round	20 ft. radius/level	None
☐☐☐☐☐	Stone Passage	Alteration	Touch	V, S	1 turn	4 segments	1 creature	None

Memorized	Name	Type	Range	Components	Duration	Casting Time	Area of Effect	Saving Throw
☐☐☐☐☐	Stoneskin	Alteration	Touch	V, S, M	Special	1 segment	1 creature	None
☐☐☐☐☐	Ultravision	Alteration	Touch	V, S, M	6 trns+6 trns/lvl	4 segments	1 creature	None
☐☐☐☐☐	Vacancy	Alter./Ill./Phant.	10 yds./level	V, S, M	1 hr./level	4 segments	10 ft. radius/level	None
☐☐☐☐☐	Wall of Acid	Evocation	40 yards	V, S, M	Special	4 segments	Special	None
☐☐☐☐☐	Wall of Fire	Evocation	60 yards	V, S, M	Special	4 segments	Special	None
☐☐☐☐☐	Wall of Ice	Evocation	10 yds./level	V, S, M	1 turn/level	4 segments	Special	None
☐☐☐☐☐	Wizard Eye	Alteration	0	V, S, M	1 rd./level	1 turn	Special	None
☐☐☐☐☐	Zargosa's Lodge/Prot.	Alterat./Enchant.	20 yards	V, S, M	1d4+1 hrs+1 hr/lvl	4 turns	30 sq. ft./level	None
☐☐☐☐☐	Zargosa's Tent. Fury	Conjur./Summon.	30 yards	V, S, M	1 hr./level	1 round	30 sq. ft./level	None
☐☐☐☐☐	Zombie Slave	Necromancy	30 feet	V, S, M	1 hr./level	4 segments	Special	None

* = Reversible   Underline all Spells appearing in your Spellbook   Check a box for each Spell Memorized.

MAGIC-USER 5th Level

Memorized	Name	Type	Range	Components	Duration	Casting Time	Area of Effect	Saving Throw
☐☐☐☐☐	Advanced Illusion	Illusion/Phantasm	60 yds.+10 yds./lvl	V, S, M	1 rd./level	1 round	Special	Special
☐☐☐☐☐	Airy Water	Alteration	0	V, S, M	1 trn/level	5 segments	Special	None
☐☐☐☐☐	Animal Growth*	Alteration	60 yds	V, S, M	1 rd./level	5 segments	Special	None
☐☐☐☐☐	Animate Dead	Necromancy	10 yds.	V, S, M	Permanent	5 rounds	Special	None
☐☐☐☐☐	Avoidance*	Abjuration/Alterat.	10 yds.	V, S, M	Until dispelled	5 segments	Up to 3 ft. cube	Special
☐☐☐☐☐	Chaos	Enchant./Charm	5 yds./level	V, S, M	1 rd./level	5 segments	Up to 40 ft. cube	Special
☐☐☐☐☐	Cloudkill	Evocation	10 yds.	V, S	1 rd. / level	5 segments	40 x 20 x 20 st.	None
☐☐☐☐☐	Conjure Elemental	Conjur./Summon.	60 yards	V, S, M	1 trn/level	1 turn	Special	None
☐☐☐☐☐	Contact Other Plane	Divination	0	V	Special	1 turn	Special	None
☐☐☐☐☐	Containment	Abjuration	10 ft./level	V, S, M	5 rounds/level	5 segments	10 ft. sq. wall/lvl	None
☐☐☐☐☐	Demi-Shadow Mon.	Illusion/Phantasm	30 yards	V, S	1 rd./level	5 segments	20 ft. cube	Special
☐☐☐☐☐	Dismissal	Abjuration	10 yards	V, S, M	Permanent	1 round	1 creature	Negates
☐☐☐☐☐	Distance Distortion	Alteration	10 yds./level	V, S, M	2 turns/level	5 segments	10 ft. cube/lvl	None
☐☐☐☐☐	Dolor	Enchant./Charm	1 ft.	V, S	2 rounds	5 segments	1 creature	Special
☐☐☐☐☐	Domination	Enchant./Charm	10 yds./level	V, S	Special	5 segments	1 person	Negates
☐☐☐☐☐	Drayton's Eng. Con.	Enchant./Evocat.	10 yds.	V	Special	5 segments	Special	Special
☐☐☐☐☐	Drayton's Hid. Stsh.	Alter./Conur/Sum.	Special	V, S, M	60 days	1 turn	1 chest: 2x2x3 ft.	None
☐☐☐☐☐	Dream	Invoc./Illus./Phant	Touch	V, S	Special	1 turn	1 creature	None
☐☐☐☐☐	Extension II	Alteration	0	V	Special	4 segments	Special	None
☐☐☐☐☐	Fabricate	Enchant./Alterat.	5 yds./level	V, S, M	Permanent	Special	1 cu. yd./level	None
☐☐☐☐☐	False Vision	Divination	0	V, S, M	1d4 rds./+1 rd./lvl	5 segments	30 ft. radius	None
☐☐☐☐☐	Feeblemind	Enchant./Charm	10 yds./level	V, S, M	Permanent	5 segments	1 creature	Negates
☐☐☐☐☐	Fireball, S.W. (F5)	Evocation	1 mile max	V, S, M	1 rd./level	5 segments	10 ft. radius	1/2
☐☐☐☐☐	Fireball, Torrential	Evocation	10 yds.+10 yds./lvl	V, S, M	Instantaneous	5 segments	40 ft. radius	1/2
☐☐☐☐☐	Hold Monster	Enchant./Charm	5 yds./level	V, S, M	1 rd./level	5 segments	Special	Negates
☐☐☐☐☐	Hyptor's F. B-Hnd	Conjur./Summon.	10 yards	V, S, M	Special	5 segments	Special	None
☐☐☐☐☐	Lyggl's Cone/Cold	Evocation	0	V, S, M	Instantaneous	5 segments	Special	1/2
☐☐☐☐☐	Magic Jar	Necromancy	10 yds./level	V, S, M	Special	1 round	1 creature	Special
☐☐☐☐☐	Major Creation	Illus./Phantasm	10 yds	V, S, M	Special	1 turn	Special	None
☐☐☐☐☐	Monster Sum. III	Conjur./Summon.	Special	V, S, M	4 rds.+1 rd./lvl	5 segments	50 yd. radius	None
☐☐☐☐☐	Seeming	Illusion/Phantasm	10 ft. radius	V, S	12 hours	5 segments	1 person/2 levels	None
☐☐☐☐☐	Sending	Evocation	Unlimited	V, S, M	Special	1 turn	1 creature	None
☐☐☐☐☐	Shadow Door	Illusion/Phantasm	10 yds.	S	1 rd./level	2 segments	Special	None
☐☐☐☐☐	Shadow Magic	Illusion/Phantasm	50 yds.+10 yds./lvl	V, S	Special	5 segments	Special	Special
☐☐☐☐☐	Stone Shape	Alteration	Touch	V, S, M	Permanent	1 round	1 cu. ft./level	None
☐☐☐☐☐	Stone Sphere	Evocation	1 yd./level	V, S, M	Permanent	5 segments	Special	Special
☐☐☐☐☐	Summon Shadow	Conjur./Sum./Nec.	10 yds.	V, S, M	1 rd+1 rd/level	5 segments	10 ft. cube	None
☐☐☐☐☐	Telekinesis	Alteration	10 yds./level	V, S	Special	5 segments	10 yds./level	Negates
☐☐☐☐☐	Teleport	Alteration	Touch	V	Instantaneous	2 segments	Special	None
☐☐☐☐☐	Tempus Fugit*	Illusion/Phantasm	0	V, S	5 trns/level	5 segments	10 ft. radius	None
☐☐☐☐☐	Touch of Death	Necromancy	Touch	V, S	Permanent	5 segments	1 living creature	Negates
☐☐☐☐☐	Transm. Rock/Mud*	Alteration	10 yds./level	V, S, M	Special	5 segments	20 ft. cube/level	None
☐☐☐☐☐	Wall of Force	Evocation	30 yds.	V, S, M	1 turn + 1 rd./lvl	5 segments	10 ft. sq./level	None
☐☐☐☐☐	Wall of Iron	Evocation	5 yds./level	V, S, M	Permanent	5 segments	Special	None
☐☐☐☐☐	Wall of Stone	Evocation	5 yds./level	V, S, M	Permanent	5 segments	Special	None
☐☐☐☐☐	Wall Passage	Alteration	30 yds.	V, S, M	1 hr.+ 1 turn/lvl	5 segments	5x8x10 ft.	None
☐☐☐☐☐	Zarba's Guardian H.	Evocation	10 yds./level	V, S, M	1 rd./level	5 segments	Special	None

* = Reversible   Underline all Spells appearing in your Spellbook   Check a box for each Spell Memorized.

MAGIC-USER 6th Level

Memorized	Name	Type	Range	Components	Duration	Casting Time	Area of Effect	Saving Throw
☐☐☐☐☐	Anti-Magic Shell	Abjuration	0	V, S	1 turn/level	1 segment	1ft./level diameter	None
☐☐☐☐☐	Body Heat Act. Sp.	Evocation	20 ft./level	V, S	1 day/level	1 turn	10 ft. cube/level	Special
☐☐☐☐☐	Break Hex	Abjuration	20 feet	V, S	Permanent	1 round	Special	None
☐☐☐☐☐	Chain Lightning	Evocation	40 yds.+5 yds./lvl	V, S, M	Instantaneous	5 segments	Special	1/2
☐☐☐☐☐	Charm/Undy. Dev.	Enchant./Charm	5 yds./level	V, S	Special	6 segments	1 person	Negates
☐☐☐☐☐	Conjure Animals	Conjur./Summon.	Special	V, S	1 rd./level	6 segments	30 yrd. radius	None
☐☐☐☐☐	Contingency	Evocation	0	V, S, M	1 day/level	1 turn	the caster	None
☐☐☐☐☐	Control Weather	Alteration	0	V, S, M	4d6 hours	1 turn	4d4 sq. miles	None
☐☐☐☐☐	Death Fog	Alteration/Evocat.	30 yds.	V, S, M	1d4 rds.+1/level	6 segments	two 10 ft. cubes/lvl	None
☐☐☐☐☐	Death Spell	Necromancy	10 yds./level	V, S, M	Instantaneous	6 segments	30 ft. cube/level	None
☐☐☐☐☐	Demi-Shadow Magic	Illusion/Phantasm	60 yds.+10 yds./lvl	V, S	Special	6 segments	Special	Special
☐☐☐☐☐	Disintegrate	Alteration	5 yds./level	V, S, M	Instantaneous	6 segments	Special	Negates
☐☐☐☐☐	Enchant an Item	Enchant./Invoc.	Touch	V, S, M	Special	Special	1 item	Negates
☐☐☐☐☐	Ensnarement	Conjur./Summon.	10 yrds.	V, S, M	Special	1 turn	Special	Negates

Memorized	Name	Type	Range	Components	Duration	Casting Time	Area of Effect	Saving Throw
☐☐☐☐☐	Extension III	Alteration	0	V	Special	6 segments	Special	None
☐☐☐☐☐	Eyebite	Ench./Char./Ill./Phant.	20 yards	V, S	I rnd/3 levels	6 segments	I creature	Special
☐☐☐☐☐	Fireball, S. N. Mercy	Evocation	10 yds+10 yds./lvl	V, S, M	Instantaneous	6 segments	20 ft. radius	1/2
☐☐☐☐☐	Fireball, Prox. Fused	Evocation	10 yds.+10 yds./lvl	V, S, M	I rd./level	6 segments	20 ft. radius	1/2
☐☐☐☐☐	Geas	Enchant/Charm	10 yds.	V	Special	4 segments	I creature	None
☐☐☐☐☐	Glassee	Alteration	Touch	V, S, M	I rd./level	I round	Special	None
☐☐☐☐☐	Globe/Invulnerab.	Abjuration	0	V, S, M	I rd./level	I round	5 ft. radius	None
☐☐☐☐☐	Guards and Wards	Evoc./Alt./Ench./Char.	0	V, S, M	I hr./level	3 turns	Special	None
☐☐☐☐☐	Haarpang's M.SoF	Alterat./Evocat.	Special	V, S, M	Special	6 segments	Special	Special
☐☐☐☐☐	Hyptor's Ttl. Recall	Alteration	0	V, S	Instantaneous	I segment	the caster	None
☐☐☐☐☐	Invisible Stalker	Conjur./Summon.	10 yards	V, S, M	Special	I round	Special	None
☐☐☐☐☐	Karnaac's Transf.	Alteration/Evoc.	0	V, S, M	I rd./level	6 segments	the caster	None
☐☐☐☐☐	Legend Lore	Divination	0	V, S, M	Special	Special	Special	None
☐☐☐☐☐	Lower Water	Alteration	80 yds.	V, S, M	5 rds./level	I turn	10 ft./lvl sq.	None
☐☐☐☐☐	Mass Suggestion	Enchant./Charm	30 yds.	V, M	4 turns + 4/level	6 segments	I creature/level	Negates
☐☐☐☐☐	Mirage Arcana	Illus./Phant./Alter.	10 yds./level	V, S (M)	Special	Special	10 ft./lvl radius	None
☐☐☐☐☐	Mislead	Illusion/Phantasm	10 yards	S	I rd./level	I segment	Special	None
☐☐☐☐☐	Monster Sum. IV	Conjur./Summon.	Special	V, S, M	5 rds.+I rd./lvl	6 segments	60 yd. radius	None
☐☐☐☐☐	Move Earth	Alteration	10 yds/level	V, S, M	Permanent	Special	Special	None
☐☐☐☐☐	Part Water	Alteration	10 yds./level	V, S, M	5 rds./level	I turn	Special	None
☐☐☐☐☐	Perpetual Illusion	Illusion/Phantasm	10 yds./level	V, S, M	Permanent	6 segments	Special	Special
☐☐☐☐☐	Phantasmagoria	Illusion/Phantasm	6 ft.	V, S	I round/level	6 segments	Special	Negates
☐☐☐☐☐	Prog. Illusion	Illusion/Phantasm	10 yds./level	V, S, M	Special	6 segments	Special	Special
☐☐☐☐☐	Project Image	Alter./Illus./Phant.	10 yds./level	V, S, M	I rd./level	6 segments	Special	None
☐☐☐☐☐	Reincarnation	Necromancy	Touch	V, S, M	Permanent	I turn	person touched	None
☐☐☐☐☐	Repulsion	Abjuration	0	V, S, M	I rd./2 levels	6 segments	10 ft. x 10 ft.	None
☐☐☐☐☐	Shades	Illusion/Phantasm	30 yards	V, S	I rd./level	6 segments	20 ft. cube	Special
☐☐☐☐☐	Spiritwrack	Evocat./Abjurat.	I ft. + I ft./level	V, M	Special	Special	Special	Special
☐☐☐☐☐	Stone to Flesh*	Alteration	10 yds./level	V, S, M	Permanent	6 segments	I creature	Special
☐☐☐☐☐	Trans. Water/Dust	Alteration	60 yards	V, S, M	Permanent	5 segments	10 ft. cube/level	Special
☐☐☐☐☐	True Seeing	Divination	Touch	V, S, M	I rd./level	I round	line of sight	None
☐☐☐☐☐	Veil	Illusion/Phantasm	10 yds./level	V, S	I turn./level	6 segments	20 ft. cube/level	None
☐☐☐☐☐	Zarba's Shvng Hnd	Evocation	10 yds./level	V, S, M	I rd./level	6 segments	Special	None
☐☐☐☐☐	Zarba's SoP Incl. W.	Alteration	10 ft./level	V, S	2 hours/level	I round	10 ft. radius	Negates

* = Reversible   Underline all Spells appearing in your Spellbook   Check a box for each Spell Memorized.

Magic-User 7th Level

Memorized	Name	Type	Range	Components	Duration	Casting Time	Area of Effect	Saving Throw
☐☐☐☐☐	Anger Deity	Enchant./Charm	Infinite	V	Instantaneous	I round	I gawd	None
☐☐☐☐☐	Banishment	Abjuration	20 yards	V, S, M	Instataneous	7 segments	60 ft. radius	Special
☐☐☐☐☐	Cacodemon	Conjur./Summon.	10 ft.	V, S, M	Special	Special	creature summoned	Special
☐☐☐☐☐	Charm Plants	Enchant./Charm	30 yards	V, S, M	Permanent	I turn	10 x 30 ft.	Negates
☐☐☐☐☐	Control Undead	Necromancy	60 ft.	V, S, M	3d4 rnds+I rd/lvl	I rd.	Id6 undead	Special
☐☐☐☐☐	Duo-Dimension	Alteration	0	V, S, M	3 rds + I rd./level	7 segments	the caster	None
☐☐☐☐☐	Finger of Death	Necromancy	60 yds.	V, S	Permanent	5 segments	I creature	Negates
☐☐☐☐☐	Fireball, Dlyd Blst	Evocation	100 yds+10 yds./lvl	V, S, M	Special	7 segments	20 ft. radius	1/2
☐☐☐☐☐	Forcecage	Evocation	10 yds./2 lvls	V, S, (special)	6 turns + I/lvl	3 to 4 segments	20 ft. cube	None
☐☐☐☐☐	Hyptor's Sh. Sw.	Evocation	30 yds.	V, S, M	I rd./level	7 segments	Special	None
☐☐☐☐☐	Limited Wish	Con./Sum./Invo./Evoc.	Unlimited	V	Special	Special	Special	Special
☐☐☐☐☐	Mass Invisibility	Illusion/Phantasm	10 yds./level	V, S, M	Special	7 segments	60 x 60 yds	None
☐☐☐☐☐	Monster Sum. V	Conjur./Summon.	Special	V, S, M	6 rds.+I rd/lvl	6 segments	70 yd. radisu	None
☐☐☐☐☐	Phase Door	Alteration	Touch	V	I usage/2 levels	7 segments	Special	Special
☐☐☐☐☐	Power Word, Stun	Conjur./Summon.	5 yds./level	V	Special	I segment	I creature	None
☐☐☐☐☐	Prismatic Wall	Conjur./Summon.	10 yrds.	V, S	I turn/level	7 segments	Special	Special
☐☐☐☐☐	Reverse Gravity	Aleration	5 yds./lvl	V, S, M	I rd./level	7 segments	30 ft. x 30 ft.	None
☐☐☐☐☐	Sequester	Illus./Phant./Abjur.	Touch	V, S, M	I week+I day/lvl	7 segments	2 ft. cube/level	Special
☐☐☐☐☐	Shadow Walk	Illusion/Enchant.	Touch	V, S	6 turns/level	I segment	Special	None
☐☐☐☐☐	Simulacrum	Illusion/Phantasm	Touch	V, S, M	Permanent	Special	I creature	None
☐☐☐☐☐	Spell Turning	Abjuration	0	V, S, M	Up to 3 rds./lvl	7 segments	the caster	None
☐☐☐☐☐	Statue	Alteration	Touch	V, S, M	I hr./level	7 segments	creature touched	Special
☐☐☐☐☐	Teleport w/o Error	Alteration	Touch	V	Instantaneous	I segment	Special	None
☐☐☐☐☐	Torment	Evocation/Alterat.	I ft.	V, S, M	Special	I round	I creature	Special
☐☐☐☐☐	Transm. Rock/Lava	Alteration	20 ft./level	V, S, M	Special	I round	2 cubic feet/lvl	None
☐☐☐☐☐	Truename	Enchant/Alterat.	3 ft.	V, S	Special	Special	Thing named	Negates
☐☐☐☐☐	Vanish	Alteration	Touch	V	Special	2 segments	I object	None
☐☐☐☐☐	Vision	Divination	0	V, S, M	Special	7 segments	the caster	None
☐☐☐☐☐	Volley	Abjuration	Special	V, S, M	Special	I segment	Special	Special
☐☐☐☐☐	Zarba's Grspng Hnd	Evocation	10 yds./level	V, S, M	I rd./level	7 segments	Special	None
☐☐☐☐☐	Zarba's Sol	Enchant./Charm	10 ft./level	V, S, M	Special	7 segments	I creature	Special
☐☐☐☐☐	Zargosa's Inst. Sum.	Conjur./Summon.	Infinite + Special	V, S, M	Instantaneous	I segment	I small object	None
☐☐☐☐☐	Zargosa's Oplnt Mnr H.	Alteration	10 yards	V, S, M	I hr./level	7 rounds	300 sq. ft./level	None

* = Reversible   Underline all Spells appearing in your Spellbook   Check a box for each Spell Memorized.

Magic-User 8th Level

Memorized	Name	Type	Range	Components	Duration	Casting Time	Area of Effect	Saving Throw
☐☐☐☐☐	Antipathy-Sympathy	Enchant./Charm	30 yards	V, S, M	2 hrs./level	1 hour	10 ft. cube/1 item	Special
☐☐☐☐☐	Binding	Enchant./Evocat.	10 yards	V, S, M	Special	Special	1 creature	Special
☐☐☐☐☐	Clone	Necromancy	Touch	V, S, M	Permanent	1 turn	1 clone	None
☐☐☐☐☐	Demand	Evoc./Ench./Chrm	Unlimited	V, S, M	Special	1 turn	1 creature	Special
☐☐☐☐☐	Fireball, Dth. Brsher	Evocation	10 yds.+10 yds./lvl	V, S, M	Instantaneous	8 segments	20 ft. radius sph.	1/2
☐☐☐☐☐	Fireball, Maximus	Evocation	10 yds.+10 yds./lvl	V, S, M	Instantaneous	8 segments	20 ft. radius	1/2
☐☐☐☐☐	Gandle's Sp. Imnty.	Abjuration	Touch	V, S, M	1 turn/level	1 rd./recipient	creature(s) touched	None
☐☐☐☐☐	Glassteel	Alteration	Touch	V, S, M	Permanent	8 segments	Object Touched	None
☐☐☐☐☐	Grasping Death	Conjur./Summon.	5 yds/2 lvls	V, S	Permanent	3 segments	1 creature	None
☐☐☐☐☐	Haarpang's Mag. SoT	Evoc./Alterat.	20 yds.	V, S, M	2 rnds./level	4 segments	Special	Negates
☐☐☐☐☐	Incendiary Cld.	Alterat./Evoc.	30 yds	V, S, M	4 rds.+1d6 rnds.	2 segments	Special	1/2
☐☐☐☐☐	Mass Charm	Enchant./Charm	5 yds./level	V	Special	8 segments	30 ft. cube	Negates
☐☐☐☐☐	Maze	Conjur./Summon.	5 yds./level	V, S	Special	3 segments	1 creature	None
☐☐☐☐☐	Mimic Caster	Enchantment	Touch	V, S, M	1 turn/level	1 turn	Person Touched	None
☐☐☐☐☐	Mind Blank	Abjuration	20 yards	V, S	1 day	1 segment	1 creature	None
☐☐☐☐☐	Monster Summ. VI	Conjur./Summon.	Special	V, S, M	7 rds + 1 rd./lvl	8 segments	80 yd. radius	None
☐☐☐☐☐	Munari's Irresist. Jig	Enchant./Charm	Touch	V	1d4+1 rnds	5 segments	creature touched	None
☐☐☐☐☐	Permanency	Alteration	Special	V, S	Permanent	2 rounds	Special	None
☐☐☐☐☐	Polymph Any Object	Alteration	5 yds./level	V, S, M	Variable	1 round	Special	Special
☐☐☐☐☐	Power Word, Blind	Conjur./Summon.	5 yds/level	V	Special	1 segment	15 ft. radius	None
☐☐☐☐☐	Screen	Divination/Illusion	0	V, S	1 hr./level	1 turn	30 ft. cube/level	Special
☐☐☐☐☐	Sink	Enchant./Alteration	10 yds./level	V, S	Special	8 segments	Special	Special
☐☐☐☐☐	Symbol	Conjur./Summon.	Touch	V, S, M	Special	8 segments	Special	Special
☐☐☐☐☐	Trap the Soul	Conjur./Summon.	10 yards	V, S, M	Until Broken	Special +1	1 creature	Special
☐☐☐☐☐	Zarba's Fist of Rage	Evocation	5 yds./level	V, S, M	1 rd./level	8 segments	Special	None

* = Reversible   Underline all Spells appearing in your Spellbook   Check a box for each Spell Memorized.

Magic-User 9th Level

Memorized	Name	Type	Range	Components	Duration	Casting Time	Area of Effect	Saving Throw
☐☐☐☐☐	Astral Spell	Evocation	Touch	V, S	Special	9 segments	Special	None
☐☐☐☐☐	Crystalbrittle	Alteration	Touch	V, S	Permanent	9 segments	2 cu. ft./level	Special
☐☐☐☐☐	Death Rune	Necromancy	60 ft.	V, S, M	Permanent	9 segments	1 creature	Negates
☐☐☐☐☐	Demon Flame	Conjur./Summon.	Caster	V, S, M	1 turn + 1 rnd./lvl	9 segments	10 foot radius	1/2
☐☐☐☐☐	Energy Drain	Evocation/Necrom.	Touch	V, S, M	Permanent	3 segments	1 creature	None
☐☐☐☐☐	Fawlgar's Grspng Dth	Necromancy	5 ft./Level	V, S, M	Instantaneous	9 segments	1 creature	Special
☐☐☐☐☐	Fireball, Lava Yield	Evocation	10 yds. + 10 yds/lvl	V, S, M	Instantaneous	9 segments	20 ft. radius	1/2
☐☐☐☐☐	Fireball, Nuclear Winter		[Rescinded in HackMaster 4th Edition]					
☐☐☐☐☐	Foresight	Divination	0	V, S, M	2d4 rds.+1 rd./lvl	1 round	Special	None
☐☐☐☐☐	Gate	Conjur./Summon.	30 yards	V, S	Special	9 segments	Special	None
☐☐☐☐☐	Hyptor's Disjunction	Alterat./Enchant.	0	V	Instantaneous	9 segments	30 ft. radius	Special
☐☐☐☐☐	Imprisonment *	Abjuration	Touch	V, S	Permanent	9 segments	1 creature	None
☐☐☐☐☐	Meteor Swarm	Evocation	40 yds.+10 yds./lvl	V, S	Instantaneous	9 segments	Special	1/2 (None)
☐☐☐☐☐	Monster Summ. VII	Conjur./Summon.	Special	V, S, M	8 rds.+1 rd./level	9 segments	90 yd. radius	None
☐☐☐☐☐	Power Word, Kill	Conjur./Summon.	5 yds./2 levels	V	Permanent	1 segment	10 ft. radius	None
☐☐☐☐☐	Prismatic Sphere	Abjur./Conjur./Summ.	0	V	1 turn/level	7 segments	20 ft. diameter sph.	Special
☐☐☐☐☐	Shape Change	Alteration	0	V, S, M	1 turn/level	9 segments	the caster	None
☐☐☐☐☐	Succor	Alterat./Enchant.	Touch	V, S, M	Special	1 to 4 days	1 individual	None
☐☐☐☐☐	Tele. Intercampaignia	Alteration	Special	V, S	Instantaneous	1 segment	Special	None
☐☐☐☐☐	Tele. Intragenre	Alteration	Special	V, S	Instantaneous	1 segment	Special	None
☐☐☐☐☐	Temporal Stasis*	Alteration	10 yards	V, S, M	Permanent	9 segments	1 creature	None
☐☐☐☐☐	Time Stop	Alteration	0	V	Special	9 segments	15 ft. radius sph.	None
☐☐☐☐☐	Weird	Illusion/Phant.	30 yards	V, S	Concentration	9 segments	20 ft. radius	Special
☐☐☐☐☐	Wish	Conjur./Summon.	Unlimited	V	Special	Special	Special	Special
☐☐☐☐☐	Zarba's Crushing Hnd	Evocation	5 yds./lvl	V, S, M	1 rd./lvl	9 segments	Special	None

* = Reversible   Underline all Spells appearing in your Spellbook   Check a box for each Spell Memorized.

Character:_____

Cleric Spells

Spells Available by Level:

1____ 2____ 3____ 4____ 5____ 6____ 7____ 8____ 9___

10_____ 11_____ 12_____ 13_____ 14____ 15_____

Cleric 1st level

Memorized	Name	Type	Range	Components	Duration	Casting Time	Area of Effect	Saving Throw
☐☐☐☐☐	Befriend*	Enchant./Charm	0	V, S, M	1d4 rds./+1 rd./lvl	1 segment	60 ft. radius	Special
☐☐☐☐☐	Bless*	Conj./Summon.	60 yds.	V, S, M	6 rounds	1 round	50 ft. cube	None
☐☐☐☐☐	Ceremony	Invocation	Touch	V, S, M	Permanent	1 hour	Special	Special
☐☐☐☐☐	Combine	Evocation	Touch	V, S	Special	1 round	Circle of clerics	None
☐☐☐☐☐	Command	Enchant./Charm	30 yds.	V	1 round	1 segment	1 creature	None
☐☐☐☐☐	Create Water*	Alteration	30 yds.	V, S, M	Permanent	1 round	up to 27 cu. ft.	None
☐☐☐☐☐	Cure L. Wnds*	Necromancy	Touch	V, S	Permanent	5 segments	Creature touched	None
☐☐☐☐☐	Detect Evil*	Divination	0	V, S, M	1 turn+ 5 rd./lvl	1 round	10 ft. x 120 yds.	None
☐☐☐☐☐	Detect Magic	Divination	0	V, S, M	1 turn	1 round	10 ft. x 30 yds.	None
☐☐☐☐☐	Endure Cold/Heat	Alteration	Touch	V, S	1 hr./lvl	1 round	Creature touched	None
☐☐☐☐☐	Flutter Soft	Alteration	60 ft.	V, S, M	1 hour	1 segment	1 creature	None
☐☐☐☐☐	Invisible to Undead	Abjuration	Touch	V, S, M	6 rds.	4 segments	1 creature	Special
☐☐☐☐☐	Light*	Alteration	120 yds.	V, S	1 hr. + 1 turn/lvl.	4 segments	20 ft. radius globe	Special

Memorized	Name	Type	Range	Components	Duration	Casting Time	Area of Effect	Saving Throw
☐☐☐☐☐	Magical Stone	Enchantment	Touch	V, S, M	Special	4 segments	3 pebbles	None
☐☐☐☐☐	Protect. from Evil*	Abjuration	Touch	V, S, M	3 rds./lvl.	4 segments	1 creature	None
☐☐☐☐☐	Purify Food/Drink*	Alteration	30 yds.	V, S	Permanent	1 round	1 cu. ft./lvl in 10 sq. ft.	None
☐☐☐☐☐	Remove Fear*	Abjuration	10 yds.	V, S	Special	1 segment	1 creature/4 lvls.	Special
☐☐☐☐☐	Sanctuary	Abjuration	Touch	V, S, M	2 rds.+1 rd./lvl.	4 segments	1 creature	None
☐☐☐☐☐	Walking Corpse	Necromancy	Touch	V, S	1 week/caster lvl.	1 turn	1 creature	None

* = Reversible   Underline all Spells appearing in your Spellbook   Check a box for each Spell Memorized.

Cleric 2nd level

Memorized	Name	Type	Range	Components	Duration	Casting Time	Area of Effect	Saving Throw
☐☐☐☐☐	Necro./Conj.	Touch	V, S, M	1 rd. +1 rd./lvl.	5 segments	1 creature	None	
☐☐☐☐☐	Animate Corpse	Necromancy	Touch	V, S	1 week/caster lvl.	1 turn	1 creature	None
☐☐☐☐☐	Augury	Divination	0	V, S, M	Special	2 rounds	Special	None
☐☐☐☐☐	Chant	Conj./Summon.	0	V, S	Time of chanting	5 segments	30 ft. radius	None
☐☐☐☐☐	Cure Moderate Wounds *	Necromancy	Touch	V, S	Permanent	5 segments	1 creature	None
☐☐☐☐☐	Detect Charm *	Divination	0	V, S	1 turn	1 round	1 creature/rd.	Negates
☐☐☐☐☐	Diminished Rite	Necromancy	Touch	V, S	Permanent	1 round	1 creature	None
☐☐☐☐☐	Dust Devil	Conj./Summon.	30 yds.	V, S	2 rds./lvl.	2 rounds	5 x 4 ft. cone	None
☐☐☐☐☐	Enthrall	Enchant./Charm	0	V, S	Special	1 round	90 ft. radius	Negates
☐☐☐☐☐	Find Traps	Divination	0	V, S	3 turns	5 segments	10 ft. x 30 yds.	None
☐☐☐☐☐	Heal Light Wounds	Necromancy	5 ft./lvl.	V, S	Permanent	5 segments	1 creature	None
☐☐☐☐☐	Know Alignment *	Divination	10 yds.	V, S	1 turn	1 round	1 creature/object	Negates
☐☐☐☐☐	Premonition	Divination	Touch	V, S, M	2 rds./lvl.	2 segments	1 creature	Negates
☐☐☐☐☐	Resist Fire/Cold	Alteration	Touch	V, S, M	1 rd./lvl.	5 segments	1 creature	None
☐☐☐☐☐	Rigor Mortis	Necromancy	120 yds.	V, S	2 rds./lvl.	5 segments	1 creature	Negates
☐☐☐☐☐	Silence, 15' Radius	Alteration	120 yds.	V, S	2 rds./lvl.	5 segments	15 ft. radius	None
☐☐☐☐☐	Slow Poison	Necromancy	Touch	V, S, M	1 hr./lvl.	1 segment	1 creature	None
☐☐☐☐☐	Snake Charm	Enchant./Charm	30 yds.	V, S	Special	5 segments	30 ft. cube	None
☐☐☐☐☐	Speak w/Animals	Alteration	0	V, S	2 rds./lvl.	5 segments	1 animal w/in 30 ft.	None
☐☐☐☐☐	Spiritual Hammer	Invocation	10 yds./lvl.	V, S, M	3 rds.+1 rd./lvl.	5 segments	Special	None
☐☐☐☐☐	Withdraw	Alteration	0	V, S	Special	5 segments	Caster	None
	Wyvern Watch	Evocation	30 yds.	V, S, M	up to 8 hrs.	5 segments	10 ft radius	Negates

* = Reversible   Underline all Spells appearing in your Spellbook   Check a box for each Spell Memorized.

CLERIC 3rd level

Memorized	Name	Type	Range	Components	Duration	Casting Time	Area of Effect	Saving Throw
☐☐☐☐☐	Animate Dead	Necromancy	10 yds.	V, S, M	Permanent	1 round	Special	None
☐☐☐☐☐	Cloudburst	Alteration	1 ft./lvl.	V, S, M	1 round	5 segments	3 ft diam. cyl./6 ft. high	Special
☐☐☐☐☐	Continual Light *	Alteration	120 yds.	V, S	Permanent	6 segments	60 ft radius	Special
☐☐☐☐☐	Create Food/Water	Alteration	10 yds.	V, S	Special	1 turn	1 cu. ft./lvl.	None
☐☐☐☐☐	Cure Blind/Deaf *	Abjuration	Touch	V, S	Permanent	1 round	1 creature	Special
☐☐☐☐☐	Cure Disease *	Abjuration	Touch	V, S	Permanent	1 round	1 creature	None
☐☐☐☐☐	Cure Nasty Wnd *	Necromancy	Touch	V, S	Permanent	5 segments	1 creature	None
☐☐☐☐☐	Dispel Magic	Abjuration	60 yds.	V, S	Special	6 segments	30 ft. cube/1 item	None
☐☐☐☐☐	Feign Death	Necromancy	Touch	V	1 turn +1 rd./lvl.	1/2 segment	Person touched	None
☐☐☐☐☐	Flame Walk	Abjuration	Touch	V, S, M	1 rd. +1 rd./lvl	5 segments	Creature touched	None
☐☐☐☐☐	Glyph of Warding	Abjur./Evocation	Touch	V, S, M	Until discharged	Special	Special	Special
☐☐☐☐☐	Heal Moderate Wounds *	Necromancy	5 ft./lvl.	V, S	Permanent	5 segments	1 creature	None
☐☐☐☐☐	Lesser Reanimation	Necromancy	Touch	V, S, M	Permanent	1 round	1 creature	None
☐☐☐☐☐	Locate Object *	Divination	60 yds. + 10 yds./lvl.	V, S, M	8 hours	1 turn	1 object	None
☐☐☐☐☐	Magical Vestment	Enchantment	0	V, S, M	5 rds./lvl.	1 round	Caster	None
☐☐☐☐☐	Meld into Stone	Alteration	0	V, S, M	8 rds. + 1d8 rds.	6 segments	Caster	None
☐☐☐☐☐	Neg. Plane Protect.	Abjuration	Touch	V, S	Special	1 round	1 creature	None
☐☐☐☐☐	Prayer	Conj./Summon.	0	V, S, M	1 rd./lvl.	6 segments	60 ft. radius	None
☐☐☐☐☐	Remove Curse *	Abjuration	Touch	V, S	Permanent	6 segments	Special	Special
☐☐☐☐☐	Remove Paralysis	Abjuration	10 yds./lvl.	V, S	Permanent	6 segments	1d4 creatures/20 ft. cube	None
☐☐☐☐☐	Speak to the Dead	Necromancy	0	V, S, M	Special	1 turn	1 creature	Special
☐☐☐☐☐	Stirring Sermon	Enchant./Charm	0	V	1 turn +1 rd./lvl.	1 round	20 ft. radius/lvl.	None
☐☐☐☐☐	Ward Off Evil *	Abjuration	Touch	V, S, M	2 rds./lvl.	3 segments	10 ft. radius	None
☐☐☐☐☐	Water Walk	Alteration	Touch	V, S, M	1 turn +1 turn/lvl.	6 segments	Special	None
☐☐☐☐☐	White Hot Metal	Alteration	10 yds.	V, M	1 rd./lvl.	2 segments	up to 1 lb. metal	None

* = Reversible   Underline all Spells appearing in your Spellbook   Check a box for each Spell Memorized.

Cleric 4th level

Memorized	Name	Type	Range	Components	Duration	Casting Time	Area of Effect	Saving Throw
☐☐☐☐☐	Abjure	Abjuration	10 yds.	V, S, M	Special	1 round	1 creature	Special
☐☐☐☐☐	Cloak of Bravery *	Conj./Summon.	Touch	V, S, M	Special	6 segments	1 creature	Negates
☐☐☐☐☐	Cure Serious Wounds *	Necromancy	Touch	V, S	Permanent	5 segments	1 creature	None
☐☐☐☐☐	Detect Lie *	Divination	30 yds.	V, S, M	1 rd./lvl.	7 segments	1 creature	Negates
☐☐☐☐☐	Divination	Divination	0	V, S, M	Special	1 turn	Special	None
☐☐☐☐☐	Free Action	Abj./Enchant.	Touch	V, S, M	1 turn/lvl.	7 segments	1 creature	None
☐☐☐☐☐	Giant Insect *	Alteration	20 yds.	V, S, M	Permanent	7 segments	1 to 6 insects	None
☐☐☐☐☐	Heal Nasty Wounds *	Necromancy	5 ft./lvl.	V, S	Permanent	5 segments	1 creature	None
☐☐☐☐☐	Imbue w/Spell Ability	Enchantment	Touch	V, S, M	Until used	1 turn	Person touched	None
☐☐☐☐☐	Lower Water *	Alteration	120 yds.	V, S, M	1 turn/lvl.	1 turn	Special	None

Memorized	Name	Type	Range	Components	Duration	Casting Time	Area of Effect	Saving Throw
☐☐☐☐☐	Minor Raise Dead	Necromancy	Touch	V, S	Permanent	1 turn	1 creature	None
☐☐☐☐☐	Neutralize Poison *	Necromancy	Touch	V, S	Permanent	7 segments	Special	None
☐☐☐☐☐	No Fear	Enchant./Charm	10 yds./lvl.	V	2 rds./lvl.	3 segments	10 ft. radius	None
☐☐☐☐☐	Spell Immunity	Abjuration	Touch	V, S, M	1 turn/lvl.	1 round	1 creature	None
☐☐☐☐☐	Spike Stones	Alt./Enchant.	30 yds.	V, S, M	3d4 turns +1/lvl	6 segments	10 sq.ft./lvl, 1 spike/sq.ft.	None
☐☐☐☐☐	Sticks to Snakes *	Alteration	30 yds.	V, S, M	2 rds./lvl	7 segments	1d4 +1/lvl in 10 ft. cube	None
☐☐☐☐☐	Tongues *	Alteration	0	V, S	1 turn	7 segments	Caster	None
☐☐☐☐☐	Touch of Death	Necromancy	Touch	V, S	Permanent	5 segments	1 living creature	Negates

* = Reversible   Underline all Spells appearing in your Spellbook   Check a box for each Spell Memorized.

Cleric 5th level

Memorized	Name	Type	Range	Components	Duration	Casting Time	Area of Effect	Saving Throw
☐☐☐☐☐	Air Walk	Alteration	Touch	V, S, M	1 hr. +1 turn/lvl.	8 segments	1 creature	None
☐☐☐☐☐	Atonement	Abjuration	Touch	V, S, M	Permanent	1 turn	1 person	None
☐☐☐☐☐	Break Hex	Abjuration	30 ft.	V, S, M	Permanent	1 round	Special	None
☐☐☐☐☐	Commune	Divination	0	V, S, M	Special	1 turn	Special	None
☐☐☐☐☐	Cure Critical Wounds *	Necromancy	Touch	V, S	Permanent	5 segments	1 creature	None
☐☐☐☐☐	Detect Ulterior Motives	Divination	0	V, S, M	1 rd./lvl.	1 round	10 ft./lvl.	None
☐☐☐☐☐	Dispel Evil *	Abjuration	Touch	V, S, M	1 rd./lvl.	1 round	1 creature	Negates
☐☐☐☐☐	Flame Strike	Evocation	60 yds.	V, S, M	Instantaneous	8 segments	5 ft. x 30 ft. column	1/2
☐☐☐☐☐	Heal Serious Wounds	Necromancy	5 ft./lvl.	V, S	Permanent	5 segments	1 creature	None
☐☐☐☐☐	Insect Plague	Conj./Summon.	120 yds.	V, S, M	2 rds./lvl.	1 turn	180 ft. x 60 ft. cloud	None
☐☐☐☐☐	Magic Font	Divination	Touch	V, S, M	Special	1 hour	1 creature	None
☐☐☐☐☐	Plane Shift	Alteration	Touch	V, S, M	Permanent	8 segments	1 creature	Negates
☐☐☐☐☐	Quest	Enchant./Charm	60 yds.	V, S, M	Until fulfilled	8 segments	1 creature	Negates
☐☐☐☐☐	Rainbow	Evoc./Alteration	120 yds.	V, S, M	1 rd./lvl.	7 segments	Special	None
☐☐☐☐☐	Raise Dead *	Necromancy	30 yds.	V, S	Permanent	1 round	1 person	Special
☐☐☐☐☐	Rigor Mortis 10' R.	Necromancy	120 yds.	V, S	2 rds./lvl.	5 segments	10 ft. radius	Negates
☐☐☐☐☐	Spike Growth	Alt./Enchant.	60 yds.	V, S, M	3d4 turns +1/lvl.	6 segments	10 ft. sq./lvl.	None
☐☐☐☐☐	True Seeing *	Divination	Touch	V, S, M	1 rd./lvl.	8 segments	1 creature	None

* = Reversible   Underline all Spells appearing in your Spellbook   Check a box for each Spell Memorized.

Cleric 6th level

Memorized	Name	Type	Range	Components	Duration	Casting Time	Area of Effect	Saving Throw
☐☐☐☐☐	Aerial Servant	Conj./Summon	10 yds.	V, S	1 day/lvl.	9 segments	Special	None
☐☐☐☐☐	Animate Object	Alteration	30 yds.	V, S	1 rd./lvl.	9 segments	1 cu. ft./lvl.	None
☐☐☐☐☐	Blade Barrier	Evocation	30 yds.	V, S	3 rds./lvl.	9 segments	5-60 sq. ft.	Special
☐☐☐☐☐	Conjure Animals	Conj./Summon.	30 yds.	V, S	2 rds./lvl.	9 segments	Special	None
☐☐☐☐☐	Cure-All *	Necromancy	Touch	V, S	Permanent	1 round	1 creature	None
☐☐☐☐☐	Find the Path *	Divination	Touch	V, S, M	1 turn/lvl.	3 rounds	1 creature	None
☐☐☐☐☐	Forbiddance	Abjuration	30 yds.	V, S, M	Permanent	6 rounds	60 ft. cube/lvl.	Special
☐☐☐☐☐	Heal Critical Wounds	Necromancy	5 ft./lvl.	V, S	Permanent	5 segments	1 creature	None
☐☐☐☐☐	Heroes' Feast	Evocation	10 yds.	V, S, M	1 hour	1 turn	1 feaster/lvl.	None
☐☐☐☐☐	Part Water	Alteration	20 yds./lvl.	V, S, M	1 turn/lvl.	1 turn	3 ft/lvl x20 yds/lvl x30 yds	None
☐☐☐☐☐	Speak w/Monsters	Alteration	30 yds.	V, S	2 rds./lvl.	9 segments	Caster	None
☐☐☐☐☐	Stone Tell	Divination	Touch	V, S, M	1 turn	1 turn	1 cu. yd.	None
☐☐☐☐☐	Word of Recall	Alteration	0	V	Special	1 segment	Caster	None

* = Reversible   Underline all Spells appearing in your Spellbook   Check a box for each Spell Memorized.

Cleric 7th level

Memorized	Name	Type	Range	Components	Duration	Casting Time	Area of Effect	Saving Throw
☐☐☐☐☐	Astral Spell	Alteration	Touch	V, S	Special	9	Special	None
☐☐☐☐☐	Control Weather	Alteration	0	V, S, M	4d12 hours	1 turn	4d4 sq. miles	None
☐☐☐☐☐	Earthquake	Alteration	120 yds.	V, S, M	1 round	1 turn	5 ft. diam./lvl.	None
☐☐☐☐☐	Exaction	Evoc./Alt.	10 yds.	V, S, M	Special	1 round	1 creature	None
☐☐☐☐☐	Gate	Conj./Summon.	30 yds.	V, S	Special	5 segments	Special	None
☐☐☐☐☐	Holy Word *	Conj./Summon.	0	V	Special	1 segment	30 ft. radius	None
☐☐☐☐☐	Regenerate *	Necromancy	Touch	V, S, M	Permanent	3 rounds	Creature touched	None
☐☐☐☐☐	Restoration *	Necromancy	Touch	V, S	Permanent	3 rounds	1 creature	None
☐☐☐☐☐	Restorative Cure-All	Necromancy	Touch	V, S	Permanent	1 round	1 creature	None
☐☐☐☐☐	Resurrection *	Necromancy	Touch	V, S, M	Permanent	1 turn	1 creature	None
☐☐☐☐☐	Succor *	Alt./Enchant.	Touch	V, S, M	Special	1 day	1 person	None
☐☐☐☐☐	Sunray	Evoc./Alt.	10 yds./lvl	V, S, M	1 +1d4 rds.	4 segments	5 ft radius	Special
☐☐☐☐☐	Symbol	Conj./Summon.	Touch	V, S, M	1 turn/lvl.	3 segments	60 ft. radius	Negates
☐☐☐☐☐	Wind Walk	Alteration	Touch	V, S, M	1 hr./lvl.	1 round	Caster +1 person/8 lvls.	None

* = Reversible   Underline all Spells appearing in your Spellbook   Check a box for each Spell Memorized.

Character:_____

Druid Spells

Spells Available by Level:

1___ 2___ 3___ 4___ 5___ 6___ 7___ 8___ 9___

Druid 1st level

Memorized	Name	Type	Range	Components	Duration	Casting Time	Area of Effect	Saving Throw
☐☐☐☐☐	Animal Friend.	Enchant./Charm	10 yds.	V, S, M	Permanent	1 hour	1 animal	Negates
☐☐☐☐☐	Ceremony	Invocation	Touch	V, S, M	Permanent	1 hour	1 creature/item/area	Special
☐☐☐☐☐	Cure Minor Injury *	Necromancy	Touch	V, S	Permanent	5 segments	Creature touched	None
☐☐☐☐☐	Detect Balance	Divination	60 feet	V, S, M	1 rd./lvl.	1 segment	1 object/creature/rd.	None
☐☐☐☐☐	Detect Magic	Divination	0	V, S, M	1 turn	1 round	10 ft. x 30 yds.	None
☐☐☐☐☐	Detect Poison	Divination	0	V, S, M	1 turn +1 rd./lvl.	4 segments	Special	None
☐☐☐☐☐	Detect Snares/Pits	Divination	0	V, S, M	4 rds./lvl.	4 segments	10 ft. x 40 ft.	None
☐☐☐☐☐	Entangle	Alteration	80 yds.	V, S, M	1 turn	4 segments	40 ft. cube	None
☐☐☐☐☐	Faerie Fire	Alteration	80 yds.	V, M	4 rds./lvl.	4 segments	10 sq. ft./lvl.	None
☐☐☐☐☐	Fog Vision	Divination	Touch	V, S, M	1 turn/lvl.	1 segment	1 person	None
☐☐☐☐☐	Invis. to Animals	Alteration	Touch	S, M	1 turn +1 rd./lvl.	4 segments	1 creature/lvl.	None
☐☐☐☐☐	Locate Animals/Plants	Divination	100 yds. +20 yds./lvl.	S, M	1 rd./lvl.	1 round	20 yds./lvl. x 20 ft. wide	None
☐☐☐☐☐	Pass w/o Trace	Enchant./Charm	Touch	V, S, M	1 turn/lvl.	1 round	1 creature	None
☐☐☐☐☐	Precipitation	Alteration	10 ft./lvl.	V, S, M	1 segment/lvl.	3 segments	3 ft. wide/12 ft. high cyl.	None
☐☐☐☐☐	Predict Weather	Divination	0	V, S, M	2 hrs./lvl.	1 round	9 sq. mi.	None
☐☐☐☐☐	Purify Water *	Alteration	40 yds.	V, S	Permanent	1 round	1 cu. ft./lvl., 1 ft. sq.	None
☐☐☐☐☐	Shillelagh	Alteration	Touch	V, S	4 rds. +1 rd./lvl.	2 segments	1 oak club	None
☐☐☐☐☐	Speak w/Animals	Alteration	0	V, S	2 rds./lvl.	5 segments	1 animal w/in 30 ft.	None

* = Reversible   Underline all Spells appearing in your Spellbook   Check a box for each Spell Memorized.

Druid 2nd level

Memorized	Name	Type	Range	Components	Duration	Casting Time	Area of Effect	Saving Throw
☐☐☐☐☐	Barkskin	Alteration	Touch	V, S, M	4 rds +1 rd./lvl.	5 segments	1 creature	None
☐☐☐☐☐	Charm Person	Enchant./Charm	80 yds.	V, S	Special	5 segments	1 person/mammal	Negates
☐☐☐☐☐	Create Water *	Alteration	30 yds.	V, S, M	Permanent	1 round	up to 27 cu. ft.	None
☐☐☐☐☐	Cure Light Wounds *	Necromancy	Touch	V, S	Permanent	5 segments	Creature touched	None
☐☐☐☐☐	Feign Death	Necromancy	Touch	V	1 turn +1 rd./lvl.	1/2	Person touched	None
☐☐☐☐☐	Fire Trap	Abj./Evocation	Touch	V, S, M	Until discharged	1 turn	Object touched	Half
☐☐☐☐☐	Flame Blade	Evocation	0	V, S, M	4 rds/ +1 rd./2 lvls.	4 segments	3 ft. long blade	None
☐☐☐☐☐	Goodberry *	Alt./Evocation	Touch	V, S, M	1 day +1 day/lvl.	1 round	2d4 fresh berries	None
☐☐☐☐☐	Heat Metal *	Alteration	40 yds.	V, S, M	7 rds.	5 segments	Special	Special
☐☐☐☐☐	Messenger	Enchant./Charm	20 yds./lvl.	V, S	1 day/lvl.	1 round	1 creature	Negates
☐☐☐☐☐	Obscurement	Alteration	0	V, S	4 rds./lvl.	5 segments	lvl. x 10 ft. sq.	None
☐☐☐☐☐	Produce Flame	Alteration	0	V, S	1 rd./lvl.	5 segments	Special	None
☐☐☐☐☐	Reflecting Pool	Divination	10 yds.	V, S, M	1 rd./lvl.	2 hrs.	Special	None
☐☐☐☐☐	Slow Poison	Necromancy	Touch	V, S, M	1 hr./lvl.	1	1 creature	None
☐☐☐☐☐	Trip	Enchant./Charm	Touch	V, S	1 turn/lvl.	5 segments	1 object up to 10 ft. long	Negates
☐☐☐☐☐	Warp Wood *	Alteration	10 yds./lvl.	V, S	Permanent	5 segments	Special	Special

* = Reversible   Underline all Spells appearing in your Spellbook   Check a box for each Spell Memorized.

Druid 3rd level

Memorized	Name	Type	Range	Components	Duration	Casting Time	Area of Effect	Saving Throw
☐☐☐☐☐	Call Lightning	Alteration	360 yds.	V, S	1 turn/lvl.	1 turn	10 ft. radius	Half
☐☐☐☐☐	Cloudburst	Alteration	10 ft./lvl.	V, S, M	1 round	5 segments	30 ft. diam/60 ft. high	None
☐☐☐☐☐	Cure Disease *	Abjuration	Touch	V, S	Permanent	1 round	1 creature	None
☐☐☐☐☐	Heal Light Wounds	Necromancy	5 ft./lvl.	V, S	Permanent	5 segments	1 creature	None
☐☐☐☐☐	Hold Animal	Enchant./Charm	80 yds.	V, S	2 rds./lvl.	6 segments	1-4 animals/40 ft. cube	Negates
☐☐☐☐☐	Know Alignment *	Divination	10 yds.	V, S	1 turn	1 round	1 creature/object	Negates
☐☐☐☐☐	Neutralize Poison *	Necromancy	Touch	V, S	Permanent	7 segments	1 creature/1 cu. ft./2 lvls.	None
☐☐☐☐☐	Plant Growth	Alteration	160 yds.	V, S, M	Permanent	1 round	Special	Special
☐☐☐☐☐	Protect. from Fire	Abjuration	Touch	V, S, M	Special	6 segments	1 creature	None
☐☐☐☐☐	Pyrotechnics	Alteration	160 yds.	V, S, M	Special	6 segments	10x/100x fire source	Special
☐☐☐☐☐	Snare	Enchant./Charm	Touch	V, S, M	Until triggered	3 rds.	2 ft. diam + 2 in./lvl.	None
☐☐☐☐☐	Spike Growth	Alt./Enchantment	60 yds.	V, S, M	3d4 turns +1/lvl.	6 segments	10 ft. sq./lvl.	None
☐☐☐☐☐	Starshine	Evoc./Illus./Phant.	10 yds./lvl.	V, S, M	1 turn/lvl.	6 segments	10 ft. sq./lvl.	None
☐☐☐☐☐	Stone Shape	Alteration	Touch	V, S, M	Permanent	1 round	9 cu. ft. +1 cu. ft./lvl.	None
☐☐☐☐☐	Summon Insects	Conj./Summoning	30 yds.	V, S, M	1 rd./lvl.	1 round	1 creature	None
☐☐☐☐☐	Tree	Alteration	0	V, S, M	6 turns +1 turn/lvl.	6 segments	Caster	None
☐☐☐☐☐	Water Breathing *	Alteration	Touch	V, S	1 hr./lvl.	6 segments	1 creature	None
☐☐☐☐☐	White Hot Metal	Alteration	10 yds.	V, M	1 rd./lvl.	2 segments	up to 1 lb. metal	None
☐☐☐☐☐	Wood Shape	Alteration	Touch	V, S, M	Permanent	1 round	9 cu. ft. +1 cu. ft./lvl.	None

* = Reversible   Underline all Spells appearing in your Spellbook   Check a box for each Spell Memorized.

Druid 4th level

Memorized	Name	Type	Range	Components	Duration	Casting Time	Area of Effect	Saving Throw
☐☐☐☐☐	Animal Summoning I	Conj./Summoning	1 mi. radius	V, S	Special	7 segments	Special	None
☐☐☐☐☐	Call Wood. Beings	Conj./Summoning	100 yds./lvl.	V, S, M	Special	Special	Special	Negates
☐☐☐☐☐	Control Temp, 10' R	Alteration	0	V, S, M	4 turns +1 turn/lvl.	7 segments	10 ft. radius	None
☐☐☐☐☐	Cure Serious Wounds *	Necromancy	Touch	V, S	Permanent	7 segments	1 creature	None
☐☐☐☐☐	Dispel Magic	Abjuration	60 yds.	V, S	Special	6 segments	30 ft. cube/1 item	None
☐☐☐☐☐	Grow	Alteration	3 yds./lvl.	V, S, M	Instantaneous	3	1 creature	Negates
☐☐☐☐☐	Halluc. Forest *	Illusion/Phant.	80 yds.	V, S	Permanent	7 segments	40 ft. sq./lvl.	None
☐☐☐☐☐	Hold Plant	Enchant./Charm	80 yds.	V, S	1 rd./lvl.	7 segments	1d4 plants in 40 sq. ft.	Negates
☐☐☐☐☐	Plant Door	Alteration	Touch	V, S, M	Special	7 segments	Special	None
☐☐☐☐☐	Produce Fire *	Alteration	40 yds.	V, S, M	1 round	7 segments	12 sq. ft.	None
☐☐☐☐☐	Protect. from Lightning	Abjuration	Touch	V, S, M	Special	7 segments	1 creature	None
☐☐☐☐☐	Repel Insects	Abj./Alteration	0	V, S, M	1 turn/lvl.	1 round	10 ft. radius	None
☐☐☐☐☐	Speak w/ Plants	Alteration	0	V, S, M	1 rd./lvl.	1 turn	30 ft. radius	None
☐☐☐☐☐	Stone Passage	Alteration	Touch	V, S	1 turn	4 segments	1 creature	None

* = Reversible   Underline all Spells appearing in your Spellbook   Check a box for each Spell Memorized.

Druid 5th level

Memorized	Name	Type	Range	Components	Duration	Casting Time	Area of Effect	Saving Throw
☐☐☐☐☐	Animal Growth *	Alteration	80 yds.	V, S, M	2 rds./lvl.	8	up to 8 in a 20 ft. sq.	None
☐☐☐☐☐	Animal Summon. II	Conj./Summoning	60 yds./lvl.	V, S	Special	8	Special	None
☐☐☐☐☐	Anti-Plant Shell	Abjuration	0	V, S	1 turn/lvl.	8	15 ft. diameter	None
☐☐☐☐☐	Commune w/Nature	Divination	0	V, S	Special	1 turn	Special	None
☐☐☐☐☐	Control Winds	Alteration	0	V, S	1 turn/lvl.	8	40 ft. radius/lvl.	None
☐☐☐☐☐	Heal Serious Wounds	Necromancy	5 ft./lvl.	V, S	Permanent	5 segments	1 creature	None
☐☐☐☐☐	Insect Plague	Conj./Summoning	120 yds.	V, S, M	2 rds./lvl.	1 turn	180 ft. x 60 ft. cloud	None
☐☐☐☐☐	Lesser Reincarnation	Necromancy	Touch	V, S	Permanent	1 turn	1 person	None
☐☐☐☐☐	Moonbeam	Evoc./Alteration	60 yds. +10 yds./lvl.	V, S, M	1 rd./lvl.	7 segments	5 ft. radius + special	None
☐☐☐☐☐	Pass Plant	Alteration	Touch	V, S, M	Special	8	Special	None
☐☐☐☐☐	Protection from Acid	Abjuration	Touch	V, S, M	Special	8	1 creature	None
☐☐☐☐☐	Protect. from Petrifi.	Abjuration	Touch	V, S, M	1 turn/lvl.	5 segments	1 person	None
☐☐☐☐☐	Spike Stones	Alt./Enchantment	30 yds.	V, S, M	3d4 turns +1/lvl.	6 segments	10 ft.sq./lvl, 1 spike/sq.ft.	None
☐☐☐☐☐	Sticks to Snakes *	Alteration	30 yds.	V, S, M	2 rds./lvl.	7 segments	1d4 +1/lvl. in 10 ft. cube	None
☐☐☐☐☐	Trans. Rock to Mud *	Alteration	160 yds.	V, S, M	Special	8	20 ft. cube/lvl.	None
☐☐☐☐☐	Wall of Fire	Conj./Summoning	80 yds.	V, S, M	Special	8	Special	None

* = Reversible

Druid 6th level

Memorized	Name	Type	Range	Components	Duration	Casting Time	Area of Effect	Saving Throw
☐☐☐☐☐	Animal Summon. III	Conj./Summoning	100 yds./lvl.	V, S	Special	9	Special	None
☐☐☐☐☐	Anti-Animal Shell	Abjuration	0	V, S, M	1 turn/lvl.	1 round	10 ft. radius	None
☐☐☐☐☐	Conjure Fire Elem. *	Conj./Summoning	80 yds.	V, S	1 turn/lvl.	6 rds.	Special	None
☐☐☐☐☐	Cure Crit. Wnds*	Necromancy	Touch	V, S	Permanent	7 segments	1 creature	None
☐☐☐☐☐	Feeblemind	Enchant./Charm	10 yds./lvl.	V, S, M	Permanent	5 segments	1 creature	Negates
☐☐☐☐☐	Fire Seeds	Conjuration	Touch	V, S, M	Special	1 rd./seed	Special	Half
☐☐☐☐☐	Liveoak	Enchantment	Touch	V, S, M	1 day/lvl.	1 turn	1 oak tree	None
☐☐☐☐☐	Trans. Water to Dust *	Alteration	60 yds	V, S, M	Permanent	8	1 cu. yd./lvl.	Special
☐☐☐☐☐	Transport via Plants	Alteration	Touch	V, S	Special	4 segments	Special	None
☐☐☐☐☐	Turn Wood	Alteration	0	V, S	1 rd./lvl.	9	20 ft./lvl by 120 ft.	None
☐☐☐☐☐	Wall of Thorns	Conj./Summoning	80 yds.	V, S	1 turn/lvl.	9	10 ft. cube/lvl.	None
☐☐☐☐☐	Weather Summon.	Conj./Summoning	0	V, S	Special	1 turn	Special	None

* = Reversible   Underline all Spells appearing in your Spellbook   Check a box for each Spell Memorized.

Druid 7th level

Memorized	Name	Type	Range	Components	Duration	Casting Time	Area of Effect	Saving Throw
☐☐☐☐☐	Animate Rock	Alteration	40 yds.	V, S, M	1 rd./lvl.	1 round	2 cu. ft./lvl.	None
☐☐☐☐☐	Cause Incl. Weather	Alteration	0	V, S, M	2d12 hours	1 turn	4d4 sq. miles	None
☐☐☐☐☐	Changestaff	Evoc., Enchant.	Touch	V, S, M	Special	4 segments	Caster's staff	None
☐☐☐☐☐	Chariot of Sustarre	Evocation	10 yds.	V, S, M	12 hours	1 turn	Special	None
☐☐☐☐☐	Confusion	Enchant./Charm	80 yds.	V, S, M	1 rd./lvl.	1 round	1d4 creatures/40 sq. ft.	Special
☐☐☐☐☐	Conjure Earth Elem. *	Conj./Summon.	40 yds.	V, S	1 turn/lvl.	1 turn	Special	None
☐☐☐☐☐	Control Weather	Alteration	0	V, S, M	4d12 hours	1 turn	4d4 sq. miles	None
☐☐☐☐☐	Creeping Doom	Conj./Summon.	0	V, S	4 rds./lvl.	1 round	Special	None
☐☐☐☐☐	Finger of Death	Enchant./Charm	60 ft.	V, S, M	Permanent	5 segments	1 creature	Negates
☐☐☐☐☐	Fire Storm *	Evocation	160 yds.	V, S	1 round	1 round	Two 10 ft. cubes/lvl.	Half
☐☐☐☐☐	Heal Crit. Wnds	Necromancy	5 ft./lvl.	V, S	Permanent	5 segments	1 creature	None
☐☐☐☐☐	Reincarnate	Necromancy	Touch	V, S	Permanent	1 turn	1 person	None
☐☐☐☐☐	Repel L. Creat./Plants	Abjuration	Caster	V, S, M	1 turn/lvl.	1 round	10 ft. diam. circle	None
☐☐☐☐☐	Sunray	Evoc., Alteration	10 yds./lvl.	V, S, M	1 +1d4 rds.	4 segments	5 ft radius	Special
☐☐☐☐☐	Trans. Metal to Wood	Alteration	80 yds.	V, S, M	Permanent	1 round	1 metal object	Special
☐☐☐☐☐	Trans. Rock to Lava	Alteration	20 ft./lvl.	V, S, M	Special	1 round	2 cu. ft./lvl.	Special

Appendix F

Skills, Talents and Proficiencies List

Table Explanations:

BP Cost: Building Point Cost

This entry indicates the number of appropriate Building Points (or slots) which must be spent to acquire the skill. The listed BP cost is ONLY used during the character creation process. Characters do not have to pay course costs or worry about course difficulty when acquiring skills/proficiencies with Building Points. They DO, however, have to follow course prerequisites (i.e. a character must spend a BP to buy a weapon proficiency before he can buy the weapon specialization for the same weapon.

Note that BP costs are cumulative. For example, it would cost 3 BPs total for a character to pick the Plant Identification: Holistic skill, because he must spend 1 BP for the prerequisite skill, Botany, and 2 BPs for Plant Identification.

Relevant Ability:

Indicates which primary attributes are used as the character's **base skill mastery** for the indicated skill. Those skills with an asterisk beside their name indicate that the character must buy the skill or successfully complete one block of instruction before the relevant ability can be used as a base skill mastery for that skill (i.e. the character would have zero percent chance of using such a skill unless he possessed it). For those skills which show a combination of relevant abilities (for example (CON+WIS)/2) the player should add the abilities and divide them by the indicated number. The result should be rounded down and recorded.

Mastery Die:

Indicates what type of die is rolled upon buying the skill or proficiency and/or after successfully completing each block of instruction for that skill. The die type gives an indication of just how difficult it is to progress in that skill. Thus, a character taking Engineering would only improve his skill 1d4 percent after taking a block of instruction whereas a character taking Art Appreciation would advance 1d20 percent. The result is added to his base skill mastery for that skill. During the character creation process, the character rolls the mastery die once for each expenditure of the BP cost of the skill. There is no limit to the number of mastery die rolls that can be purchased, but the skill level cannot exceed 125%.

Skill Mastery: What do the numbers mean?

Your base skill mastery gives you an indication of just how much you may have mastered a specific skill. The ranges given on the following table give you a rough indication of what your base skill mastery means.

Skill Mastery Table

Master Range	Skill Level
00	Unskilled
01–25	Beginner (Novice, Untrained) (SB)
26–50	Apprentice (Schooled, Trained) (SS)
51–75	Advanced (SA)
76–100	Expert (SE)
101–125	Master (SK)

Beginner: A novice, the character is untrained, with basic knowledge only. No real training. Dabbling. Backyard mechanic. This is the range of most skill mastery scores when only the basic relevant abilities are being used.

Apprentice: Through schooling, the character has a working knowledge of the skill. He can perform routine tasks involving the skill. However, he is unable to teach what he knows.

Advanced: Detailed knowledge and experience, character is typically troubled only by the most complex aspects of the skill. The character may be able to teach basic elements of the skill to others.

Expert: Character is expert at the skill. Can teach the skill to others.

Master: Character has gone beyond what his teachers/mentor were able to teach him and has learned on his own. Is considered a master on the subject/topic. Is capable of expanding the field by coming up with new ideas and techniques.

Course Prerequisite:

This entry shows a Y (yes), N (NO) or NA (Not Applicable) and indicates if mastery of another skill (or skills) is needed before the character can take the course/block of instruction. A character must have each prerequisite skill at 50 or higher before taking the new course. For example a character must take basic Engineering and raise it to 50 or higher before taking the course for Engineering: Fortification.

Course Cost:

The Course Cost entry indicates the fees that must be paid to learn one block of instruction for the indicated skill. Note that the costs may be greatly modified depending on the method of training (school, University, mentor, etc). Mentors tend to charge more than universities because their training is more intensive and one-on-one in nature.

Course Length:

Each course (block of instruction) takes one week to complete. Only one course can be studied a time.

Course Difficulty:

There are no guarantees in life and so it is with training. Just because a character has the smarts (and gold) to sign up for a Skill Course doesn't mean he will successfully complete the training. It may be the instructor was a poor teacher. It may be the character couldn't quite grasp what was being taught and was unable to use what was presented. When a course is completed the player makes a check against their Learning Ability, as determined by their Intelligence, for that skill. The course difficulty lists a modifier, which is added to the die roll. If the player rolls equal to or less than his learning ability he successfully masters the course and earns a roll of the Mastery Die.

Notes:

- "R" for Building Point cost indicates the skill is class restricted. Only characters of the appropriate character class can choose the skill.

- * "P" Psionics are only available to characters with certain inherent special abilities. Having the ability to do psionics is useless to a character until he is properly trained/mentored how to focus and use those powers.

- Some 'Tasks' have no BP costs and represent mundane tasks which any character could reasonably perform without any special training or expert knowledge.

PROFICIENCIES

Weapon Proficiencies

Weapon (Per Weapon)	BP Cost	Relevant* Ability	Mastery Die	Course Prerequisite	Course Cost	Course Difficulty
Basic Proficiency	I	NA	NA	N	600 gp	+5%
Specialize (only one)	I	NA	NA	Y	850 gp	+10%
Weapon Mastery (only one)	I	NA	NA	Y	1500 gp	+15%

Weapon proficiencies are handled under the combat rules and thus have no relevant abilities or skill check modifiers.

SKILLS

Arcane Skills

Arcane Knowledge	BP Cost	Relevant Ability	Mastery Die	Course Prerequisite	Course Cost	Course Difficulty
Arcane Lore	5	INT	1d6	N	500 gp	+4
Divine Lore	5	WIS	1d6	Y	450 gp	+4
Spellcraft	2	INT	1d4	Y	500 gp	+5

Academia

Subject Matter	BP Cost	Relevant Abilities	Mastery Die	Course Prerequisite	Course Cost	Course Difficulty
Administration	I	(INT+WIS)/2	1d6	Y	475 gp	+10%
Agriculture	I	WIS	1d10	N	250 gp	0
Alchemy	7	INT	1d6	N	400 gp	+5%
Anatomy, Basic	3	(INT+WIS)/2	1d8	N	500 gp	+5%
Anatomy, Vital (specific animal)	I	(INT+WIS)/2	1d8	Y	750 gp	+5%
Ancient History	I	INT	1d12	N	650 gp	0
Animal Lore	2	INT	1d10	N	200 gp	+5%
Appraisal: Gemstone	3	INT	1d6	Y	500 gp	+5%
Appraising	6	INT	1d8	N	400 gp	0
Art Appraisal: Subset: Painting	3	INT	1d6	Y	275 gp	+15%
Art Appraisal: Subset: Sculpture	3	INT	1d6	Y	250 gp	+15%
Art Appreciation: Subset: Painting	I	WIS	1d20	N	350 gp	0
Art Appreciation: Subset: Sculpture	I	WIS	1d20	N	300 gp	0
Astrology	I	(INT+WIS)/2	1d8	N	550 gp	+5%
Botany	I	INT	1d8	N	250 gp	+10%
Campaign Logistics	I	INT	1d6	Y	1200 gp	+15%
Civil Administration	2	(INT+WIS+CHA)/3	1d4	Y	500 gp	+20%
Culinary Arts	I	WIS	1d10	N	300 gp	+10%
Culture (race specific)	I	WIS	1d6	N	175 gp	+10%
Current Affairs	I	INT	1d6	N	100 gp	0
Customs and Etiquette (culture specific)	I	WIS	1d8	N	275 gp	+15%
Engineering	2	(INT+WIS)/2	1d4	N	1750 gp	+20%
Engineering, Fortifications	2	(INT+WIS)/2	1d6	Y	950 gp	+15%
Engineering, Public Works	2	(INT+WIS)/2	1d4	Y	650 gp	+10%
Forestry	I	INT	1d6	N	300 gp	0
Geology	I	INT	1d6	N	300 gp	+5%
Heraldry	I	INT	1d6	N	165 gp	0
Herbalism (Prepare Poison)	6	INT	1d6	Y	250 gp	+5%
History, Local	I	(CHA+WIS)/2	1d6	N	100 gp	0
History, World	I	WIS	1d6	Y	150 gp	+5%
Leadership, Basic	3	(CHA+WIS)/2	1d5	N	225 gp	+5%
Leadership, Committee	2	(CHA+WIS)/2	1d5	Y	275 gp	+5%
Military: Battle Sense	9	(INT+WIS)/2	1d4	N	350 gp	+10%
Military: Leadership	4	(INT+WIS+CHA)/3	1d4	Y	275 gp	+5%
Military: Operations	2	(INT+WIS)/2	1d4	Y	325gp	+10%
Military: Small Unit Tactics	5	(INT+WIS)/2	1d6	Y	375 gp	+15%
Plant Identification: Holistic	2	(INT+WIS)/2	1d8	Y	300 gp	+5%
Religion (general)	I	WIS	1d12	N	100 gp	0
Religion (specific)	2	WIS	1d8	Y	250 gp	+5%
Weather Sense	I	(INT+WIS)/2	1d4	N	150 gp	+5%
Woodland Lore	I	(INT+WIS)/2	1d8	Y	200 gp	0

Languages/Communication

Language	BP Cost	Relevant Abilities	Mastery Die	Course Prerequisite	Course Cost	Course Difficulty
Dimple Runes (Braille)	2	DEX	1d3	N	200 gp	+5%
Dragon Speak	10	INT+CHA/2	1d2	N	800 gp	+5
Evil Speak	5	INT	1d4	N	450 gp	+15%
Glersee (Trail Markers)	2	INT	1d6	N	275 gp	+5%
Languages, Ancient/Dead	2	INT	1d6	N	200 gp	+10%
Languages, Modern	1	INT	1d10	N	150 gp	0
Languages, Undead	2	INT	1d8	N	300 gp	+5%

Musical Instrument Skills

Musical Instrument	BP Cost	Relevant Ability	Mastery* Die	Course Prerequisite	Course Cost	Course Difficulty
Brass Instruments	2	(WIS+DX)/2	1d8	N	600 gp	+5%
Exotic Instruments	2	(WIS+DX)/2	1d8	N	500 gp	+5%
Percussion Instruments	1	(WIS+DX)/2	1d8	N	300 gp	+0%
Stringed Instruments	2	(WIS+DX)/2	1d8	N	600 gp	+5%
Wind Instruments	2	(WIS+DX)/2	1d8	N	500 gp	+5%

Tasks/Arts

Tasks: Mundane

Mundane Task	BP Cost	Relevant Ability	Mastery Die	Monthly Cost	Course Prerequisite	Course Cost	Course Difficulty
Armor Maintenance	1	(INT+DEX)/2	Automatic*	75 gp	N	75 gp	-5%
Maintenance /Upkeep (General)	1	WIS	Automatic*	50 gp	N	50 gp	-20%
Shaving/Grooming	1	INT	Automatic*	25 gp	N	25 gp	-15%
Weapon Maintenance	1	WIS	Automatic*	10 gp	N	75 gp	-5%

*Denotes task is automatically successful as long as the costs of upkeep/maintenance are paid along with any required investment of time to perform the task.

Tasks: Combat Procedures

Combat Procedure	BP Cost	Relevant Ability	Mastery Die	Course Prerequisite	Course Cost	Course Difficulty
Angawa Battle Cry	2	(STR+CHA)/2	1d6	N	225 gp	0
Art of Beating	2	(STR+INT)/2	1d4	N	275 gp	+5%
Attitude Adjustment	1	(STR+CHA)/2	1d8	N	200 gp	+5%
Brawler	2	(STR+DEX)/2	1d8	N	175 gp	+5%
Crane	2	DEX	1d4	N	215 gp	+10%
Cricket-in-the-Pea Pod	1	DEX	1d5	N	275 gp	+15%
Dirty Fighting	2	INT	1d6	N	225 gp	0
Entrenchment Construction	4	WIS	1d6	N	425 gp	+5%
Establish Ambush Zone	8	WIS	1d6	N	225 gp	+5%
Eye Gouge	1	DEX	1d8	N	125 gp	+5%
Eye of the Tiger Advantage	5	DEX	1d5	N	325 gp	+10%
Groin Punch	10	STR	1d4	N	75 gp	+5%
Jugular Swipe	10	DEX	1d4	N	275 gp	+5%
Kidney Bruiser	15	STR	1d6	N	255 gp	+5%
Mortal Combat	9	CON	1d4	N	435 gp	+5%
Muster Resolve	8	CON	1d6	N	325 gp	+10%
Pimp Slap (Wuss Slap)	1	STR	1d6	N	95 gp	+5%
Pugilism	7	(STR+DEX+INT)/3	1d6	N	125 gp	+5%
Round House Groin Kick	10	DEX	1d6	N	125 gp	+5%
Who's Yer Mamma Ankle Wrench	6	(STR+DEX)/2	1d6	N	225 gp	+5%

Tasks: Artisan and Performing Arts

Art	BP Cost	Relevant Abilities	Mastery Die	Course Prerequisite	Course Cost	Course Difficulty
Artistic Ability	1	(DEX+WIS)/2	1d6	N	500 gp	+5%
Dancing (Ballroom)	1	DEX	1d6	N	400 gp	+10%
Interpret/Perform Mime (secondary language)	1	INT	1d12	N	240 gp	0
Juggling	1	DEX	1d8	N	100 gp	+10%
Manu Weasel Dance	5	DEX	1d12	N	250 gp	+5%
Mocking Jig	10	DEX	1d10	N	120 gp	+5%
Musical Instrument	1 each	(DEX+INT)/2	1d6	N	500 gp	+15%
Poetry, Writing and Comprehension/Interpretation	1	(INT+WIS)/2	1d8	N	200 gp	+10%
Singing	1	CHA	1d4	N	500 gp	+15%

Tasks: Sophisticated

Task	BP Cost	Relevant Ability	Mastery Die	Course Prerequisite	Course Cost	Course Difficulty
Animal Handling	1	WIS	1d10	Y	300 gp	+5%
Animal Training	2	(INT+WIS)/2	1d10	Y	500 gp	+10%
Armorer	10	INT	1d6	Y	600 gp	+5%
Armor Repair, Basic	3	(INT+DEX)/2	1d10	Y	375 gp	+5%
Armor Repair, Advanced	4	(INT+DEX)/2	1d8	Y	575 gp	+10%
Armor Repair, Expert	8	(INT+DEX)/2	1d6	Y	875 gp	+10%
Bargain Sense	5	WIS	1d8	N	100 gp	0
Bartering	1	WIS	1d8	N	100 gp	0
Blacksmithing	1	STR	1d8	Y	100 gp	0
Bowyer/Fletcher	1	DEX	1d8	N	450 gp	+5%
Brewing	1	INT	1d12	N	75 gp	0
Carpentry	1	STR	1d10	Y	150 gp	+5%
Cartography: Dungeon	2	INT	1d8	Y	200 gp	+5%
Cartography: Hasty Mapping	2	INT	1d10	Y	75 gp	0
Cartography: Overland	2	INT	1d6	Y	225 gp	+10%
Charioteering	1	DEX	1d8	N	165 gp	+5%
Clever Packer	3	WIS	1d8	N	80 gp	0
Cobbling	1	DEX	1d12	N	85 gp	+5%
Coin Pile Numerical Approximation	2	INT	1d6	N	200 gp	+10%
Complex Geometric Estimation	2	INT	1d4	N	350 gp	+10%
Construction: Defense Works	2	(STR+DEX+WIS)/3	1d6	N	400 gp	+5%
Construction: Fortifications	2	(STR+DEX+WIS)/3	1d6	N	450 gp	+5%
Construction: Hasty Defense Works	4	(STR+DEX+WIS)/3	1d10	N	300 gp	0
Construction: Siege Works	2	(STR+DEX+WIS)/3	1d4	N	500 gp	+5%
Cooking	1	INT	1d12	Y	75 gp	0
Dig Hasty Grave	1	STR	Automatic	N	5 gp	-2
Dig Proper Grave	1	WIS	1d20	N	15 gp	0
Endurance	4	(WIS+CON)/2	1d6	N	400 gp	+10%
Farming	1	WIS	1d8	Y	100 gp	+5%
Fire-building	1	WIS	1d6	N	75 gp	+5%
First Aid Skill Suite	5 for all	INT	1d6	N	1000 gp	+10%
First Aid: Cauterize Wound	2	INT	1d8	N	350 gp	+5%
First Aid: Sew Own Wounds	2	INT	1d4	N	200 gp	+5%
First Aid: Sew Wounds	2	INT	1d6	Y	350 gp	0
Fishing	1	WIS	1d10	N	100 gp	+5%
Fondling (Covert Appraisal Technique)	3	(DEX+WIS)/2	1d4	N	325 gp	+10%
Forage for Food (By Climate)	1	WIS	1d6	N	245 gp	+10%
Forgery	10	(DEX +INT)/2	1d4	N	350 gp	+20%
Gaming	3	CHA	1d6	N	200 gp	+10%
Gem Cutting	2	DEX	1d4	Y	700 gp	+10%
Glean Information	3	CHA	1d8	N	300 gp	+10%
Haggle	2	(CHA+INT)/2	1d6	N	375 gp	0
Healing	2	WIS	1d4	Y	400 gp	+5%
Hunting	1	WIS	1d6	Y	370 gp	+5%
Identify Animal by Tracks	1	WIS	1d6	N	230 gp	+15%
Intelligence Gathering	4	(INT+WIS)/2	1d6	Y	575 gp	+10%
Interrogation	4	(STR+WIS)/2	1d6	Y	400 gp	+10%
Jeweler	2	INT	1d6	Y	670 gp	+5%
Jumping	1	STR	1d4	N	200 gp	+5%
Laborer, General	1	(STR + WIS)/2	Automatic	N	50 gp	-20%
Leatherworking	3	(STR+INT)/2	1d8	N	300 gp	0
Liar, Skilled	3	(INT+CHA)	1d6	N	400 gp	+10%
Looting, Advanced	4	WIS	1d4	Y	550 gp	+10%
Looting, Basic	2	WIS	1d6	N	350 gp	+5%
Maintain Self-Discipline	2	WIS	1d4	N	300 gp	+5%
Map Sense (was direction sense)	1	WIS	1d6	N	200 gp	+5%
Mapless Travel	3	WIS	1d8	N	150 gp	+10%
Metalworking	2	(STR+DEX+WIS)/3	1d6	Y	500 gp	+5%
Mimic Dialect	2	INT	1d4	Y	200 gp	+10%
Mining	2	WIS	1d6	N	500 gp	+5%
Mountaineering	1	(STR+DEX+INT)/3	1d8	N	400 gp	+5%
Navigation, Nautical	2	INT	1d6	N	300 gp	+10%
Orchestrate Task	3	(INT+CHA)/2	1d6	N	400 gp	+15%
Pinch (Pocket/Lift - variant of Pick Pocket)	R	DEX	NA	NA	NA	NA
Pottery	1	DEX	1d10	N	75 gp	-1
Reading Lips	2	INT	1d4	N	400 gp	+15%
Reading/Writing	2	INT	1d6	N	350 gp	+10%
Recruit Army	2	CHA	1d8	N	300 gp	+5%
Riding, Airborne	2	(DEX+WIS)/2	1d6	Y	550 gp	+10%
Riding, Land-based	1	(DEX+WIS)/2	1d8	N	350 gp	+5%
Riding, Warhorse (Dwarven)	2	(DEX+CHA)/2	1d4	N	400 gp	+10%
Rope Use	1	DEX	1d8	N	85 gp	-5%
Running	1	CON	1d8	N	100 gp	0
Seamanship Suite	5	DEX	1d6	N	700 gp	+10%
Seamstress/Tailor	2	DEX	1d12	N	200 gp	0
Seduction, Art of	1	(COM+CHA)/2	1d6	N	750 gp	+15%
Set Snares	1	DEX	1d8	N	250 gp	+5%
Shield Repair, Metal	3	(INT+DEX)/2	1d8	Y	275 gp	+15%
Shield Repair, Wood	3	(INT+DEX)/2	1d10	Y	175 gp	+10%
Skinning	1	(STR+WIS)/2	1d8	N	650 gp	+5%

Slaughter: Game Animal	I	(STR+WIS)/2	1d8	N	300 gp	+5%
Slaughter: Livestock	I	(STR+WIS)/2	1d10	N	385 gp	0
Slip Away into Shadows	I	DEX	1d6	N	450 gp	+10%
Stealthy Movement	4	DEX	1d6	Y	370 gp	+10%
Stonemasonry	I	(STR+INT)/2	1d10	N	170 gp	+5%
Survival Skill Suite	10	(INT+CON+WIS)/3	1d6	N	1500 gp	+5%
Survival, Desert	3	(INT+CON+WIS)/3	1d6	N	450 gp	+10%
Survival, Jungle	2	(INT+CON+WIS)/3	1d8	N	250 gp	+5%
Survival, Underground	3	(INT+CON+WIS)/3	1d4	N	275 gp	+5%
Survival, Winter	3	(INT+CON+WIS)/3	1d4	N	450 gp	+10%
Swimming	3	(STR+ DEX+CON)/3	1d6	Y	175 gp	+5%
Swimming: Dog Paddle	I	(STR+CON)/2	1d10	N	50 gp	0
Tightrope Walking	I	DEX	1d4	N	375 gp	+15%
Torture	3	(STR+INT)/2	1d6	N	250 gp	+5%
Track Game	I	WIS	1d6	Y	300 gp	+10%
Tracking	2	WIS	1d4	N	350 gp	+10%
Trap Sweep (Full Sweep)	R	(DEX+WIS)/2	1d8	N	375 gp	+20%
Tumbling	2	DEX	1d6	N	125 gp	+10%
Vandalism/Desecration	2	STR	1d12	N	200 gp	+5%
Ventriloquism	3	INT	1d4	N	300 gp	+15%
Weaponsmithing	4	(DEX+INT)/2	1d6	Y	700 gp	+10%
Weaving	2	(DEX+INT)/2	1d8	N	100 gp	+5%

Social Interaction Skills

Social Skill	BP Cost	Relevant Ability	Mastery Die	Course Prerequisite	Course Cost	Course Difficulty
Berate	I	CHA	1d6	N	200 gp	+5%
Calling Dibs	3	WIS	1d8	N	100 gp	+15%
Diplomacy	2	CHA	1d8	N	150 gp	+10%
Feign Toughness	2	CHA	1d10	N	250 gp	+5%
Flex Muscle	2	STR	1d8	N	170 gp	0
Graceful Entrance/Exit	I	CHA	1d6	N	100 gp	+10%
Idle Gossip	I	CHA	1d12	N	185 gp	0
Intimidation	2	WIS	1d4	Y	250 gp	+5%
Joke Telling	I	(INT+CHA)/2	1d4	N	50 gp	+10%
Knowledge of Courtly Affairs	2	WIS	1d8	N	100 gp	+5%
Mingling (Balls, Parties)	2	CHA	1d6	N	300 gp	+10%
Oration	I	(INT+CHA)/2	1d4	Y	190 gp	+20%
Parley	4	CHA	1d4	N	150 gp	+15%
Poker Face	3	WIS	1d6	N	80 gp	+10%
Resist Persuasion	I	WIS	1d8	N	90 gp	+5%
Rousing Speech	3	CHA	1d6	N	270 gp	+20%
Rules of Fair Play	I	WIS	1d6	N	150 gp	+5%
Secret Persona	2	WIS	1d4	N	600 gp	+5
Social Etiquette	I	(WIS+CHA)/2	1d6	N	170 gp	+5%
Street Cred	I	(STR+WIS+CHA)/3	1d8	N	150 gp	+10%
Taunting, Major	3	WIS	1d6	Y	200 gp	+10%
Taunting: Minor	2	WIS	1d8	N	100 gp	+5%
Threat Gesture (Nonverbal gestures - body and hand)	I	WIS	1d8	N	175 gp	+5%
Ulterior Motive	2	CHA	1d4	N	100 gp	+10%

Skills, Tools

In order to perform certrain skills effectively you need to master the tools. Just about anyone can saw a board and hammer a nail, for example, but only someone skilled in the such tools can produce quality, professional looking results.

Tool	BP Cost	Relevant Ability	Mastery Die	Course Prerequisite	Course Cost	Course Difficulty
Assaying/Surveying Tools	I	(DEX+INT)/2	1d8	N	4200 gp	0%
Blacksmith Tools	I	(STR+DEX+INT)/3	1d6	N	600 gp	+5%
Carpentry Tools (Wood Working)	I	(STR+DEX+INT)/3	1d8	N	4200 gp	0%
Construction Tools	I	(STR+DEX+INT)/3	1d8	N	4200 gp	0%
Drafting Tools	I	DEX	1d6	N	4200 gp	0%
Jeweler Tools	I	(DEX+WIS)/2	1d8	N	4200 gp	0%
Leather Working Tools	I	DEX	1d6	N	400 gp	+5%
Mining Tools (stone working)	I	STR	1d8	N	400 gp	+5%
Peg Leg (per leg – left/right)	I	DX	NA	N	Free*	+10%
Surgery Tools/Suture Kit	I	DEX+INT/2	1d8	N	4200 gp	0%

* Peg Legs are mastered through daily use. A character with a peg leg skill suffers no movement penalty. Once fitted with a peg leg the character must make a check vs. his Dexterity plus the course difficulty modifier to determine if he's skilled at walking on his new peg leg. He may automatically check once per game month with an additional +5% modifier (cumulative) until he succeeds. Note that characters who begin the game fitted with peg legs are automatically skilled.

TALENTS

Restricted by Race/Class

Talent	BP Cost	Restrictions
Acrobatic Skill Suite	5	Elves (incl. Grunge & Dark), Half-Elves, Humans, Pixie Fairies
Active Sense of Smell	5	Half-Orcs (innate), Half-Ogres
Acute (high) Alertness	5	Any but Half-Ogres
Acute Taste	0	Half-Orcs (innate)
Ambidextrous	5	Any, (innate for Elves incl. Grunge and Dark)
Animal Companion	10	Elves (incl. Grunge)
Animal Friendship	10	Gnomes (incl. Gnome Titans), Gnomelings
Astute Observation	5	Any but Half-Orcs and Half-Ogres
Attack Bonus	5	Half-Orc, Humans, Pixie Fairies
Axe Bonus	5	Dwarves
Balance Bonus	10	Half-Elves, Halflings, Humans
Blind-fighting	10	Any
Bow Bonus	5	innate for Elves (incl. Grunge), Half-Elves
Brewing	5	Dwarves, Gnomes (incl. Gnome Titans), Halflings
Close to the Earth	5	Dwarves, Dark Elves, Gnomes (incl. Gnome Titans)
Cold resistance	5	Elves (incl. Grunge & Dark), Half-Elves
Constitution/Health bonus	10	Dwarves, Dark Elves
Crossbow Bonus	5	Dwarves, Dark Elves
Dagger Bonus	5	Elves (incl. Grunge & Dark, Gnomes (incl. Gnome Titans), Gnomelings, Halflings (innate if thrown)
Damage Bonus	5	Half-Orcs, Half-Ogres
Dart Bonus	5	Gnomes (incl. Gnome Titans), Gnomelings
Defensive Bonus	5	Gnomes (incl. Gnome Titans), Gnomelings
Dense Skin	10	Dwarves, Half-Orcs, Half-ogres (innate)
Detect Evil	5	Dwarves, Halflings
Detect Poison	5	Dwarves
Detect Secret doors	5	innate for Elves (incl. Grunge & Dark) and Half-Elves, Humans
Determine Age	5	Dwarves
Determine Stability	5	Dwarves, Dark Elves
Endurance	5	Dwarves, Half-Orcs, Half-Ogres, Humans
Engineering Bonus	5	Gnomes (incl. Gnome Titans), Gnomelings
Evaluate Gems	5	Dwarves
Experience Bonus	10	Gnomelings, Humans
Expert Haggler	5	Dwarves, Halflings
Faerie Kind Martial Arts	5	Pixie Fairies
Flutter	2	Pixie Fairies
Forest Movement	10	Elves (incl. Grunge), Gnomes (incl. Gnome Titans), Gnomelings
Freeze	5	Gnomes (incl. Gnome Titans)
Grace Under Pressure	5	Elves (incl. Grunge & Dark), Humans
Heat Resistance	5	Elves (incl. Grunge & Dark), Half-Elves
Hide	10	Gnomes (incl. Gnome Titans), Gnomelings, Halflings
Hit Point Bonus	10	Dwarves, Humans, Pixie Fairies
Illusion Resistant	5	Dwarves
Javelin Bonus	5	Elves (incl. Grunge & Dark)
Keen Sight (Long Distance)	5	Elves (incl. Grunge & Dark), Half-Elves, Humans, Pixie Fairies
Less Sleep	5	Elves (incl. Grunge & Dark), Half-Elves, Humans
Mace Bonus	5	Dwarves, Half-Orcs, Half-Ogres
Magic Bonus	5	Pixie Fairies
Magic Identification	10	Elves (incl. Grunge & Dark)
Meld into Stone	10	Dwarves
Mining Sense	5	Dwarves, Dark Elves, Gnomes (incl. Gnome Titans), Gnomelings
Opportunist (skill/Trait)	5	Gnomes (incl. Gnome Titans), Halflings, Humans
Photographic Memory	5	Elves (incl. Grunge & Dark), Half-Elves, Humans
Pick Bonus	5	Dwarves
Potion Identification	5	Gnomes (incl. Gnome Titans), Gnomelings
Reaction Bonus	5	Halflings
Resistance	5	Dwarves, innate for Half-Elves, Humans
Seeking Grasping Hands	5	Elves (incl. Grunge & Dark), Humans
Short Sword Bonus	5	Dwarves, Gnomes (incl. Gnome Titans)
Sibling Empathy	10	Any
Sixth Sense	5	Any but Half-Orc or Half-Ogre
Sling Bonus	5	Gnomes (incl. Gnome Titans), Gnomelings, innate for Halflings
Speak with Plants	10	Elves (incl. Grunge & Dark)
Spear Bonus	5	Elves, innate for Grunge Elves
Spell Abilities	15	Elves (incl. Grunge), innate for Dark Elves
Stealth	10	Dwarves, Gnomes (incl. Gnome Titans), Gnomelings
Stone Tell	10	Dwarves
Sword Bonus	5	innate for Elves (incl. Dark), Half-Elves
Taunt	5	Halflings
Touched by Yurgain	NA*	Dwarves
Tough hide	10	innate for Half-Ogre, Humans
Track Game Animal	5	Grunge Elves
Trident Bonus	5	Elves
Warhammer Bonus	5	Dwarves

* Talents can only be purchased with Building Points during the character creation process. Restricted talents are available ONLY to certain races or classes. Unrestricted talents can be purchased by anyone.

Unless otherwise noted, sub-races have access to talents generally available to their kind. They only have their own listings for talents they have access to that the more general race does not (i.e. drow have access to Constitution/Health Bonus but elves in general do not).

Skill Descriptions

The following skill descriptions are arranged alphabetically by type. Each description gives a general outline of what a character with the skill knows and can do. Furthermore, some descriptions include rules to cover specific uses or situations, or exact instructions on the effects of the skill if successfully used.

ARCANE SKILLS

Arcane Lore:
[Intelligence/Arcane/5 B.P.s]

A person versed in arcane lore knows the basic principles behind magic. He's tuned in to secrets about the world around him that most others do not and knows how to read magic scrolls or writings. He may not be able to cast spells, but he can read magical writing and generally tell what it's all about.

Prerequisite: None.

Divine Lore:
[Wisdom/Arcane/5 B.P.s]

A person versed in divine lore knows the basic principles behind most religions. He knows secrets about most religious orders and practices that many others do not. He knows how to read clerical writings and scrolls He may not be able to cast clerical spells, but he can read the writing and generally tell what it's all about.

Prerequisite: Religion.

Spellcraft:
[Intelligence/Arcane/2 B.P.]

Although this skill does not grant the character any spell casting powers, it does give him a familiarity with the different forms and rites of spell casting. If he observes and overhears someone who is casting a spell, or if he examines the material components used, he can attempt to identify the spell being cast. A skill check must be rolled to make a correct identification. Specialist magic-users gain a +15% bonus to the check when attempting to identify magic of their own school. Note that since the spell caster must be observed until the very instant of casting, the spellcraft skill does not grant an advantage against combat spells. The skill is quite useful, however, for identifying spells that would otherwise have no visible effect.

Those talented in this skill also have a chance (equal to half of their normal skill check) of recognizing magical or magically endowed constructs for what they are.

Prerequisites: Arcane Lore.

ACADEMIA

Administration:
[(Intelligence+Wisdom)÷2/Acamdemia/1 B.P.]

The character with this skill knows the basics of how government and civic organizations operate. He can use such knowledge to his advantage when he wants to function well within a known governmental system, run for public office or take a position of power or leadership within any social structure.

Prerequisite: Leadership, Basic and Leadership, Committee.

Agriculture:
[Wisdom/Acamdemia/1 B.P.]

This character knows the basics of farming, including planting, harvesting and storing of crops, tending animals, butchering and other typical farm chores.

Prerequisite: None.

Alchemy:
[Intelligence/Academia/7 B.P.]

Alchemy gives a character the ability to mix compounds and to know what those compounds do. An alchemist can mix up medicines and healing potions. He can even mix up a mean Long Island Iced Tea. Alchemists have long sought to know the secret of turning lead into gold, but so far, that is an ability beyond their reach. For most other chemical mixtures, an alchemist can do the trick. He cannot create magical potions, however. The healing potions mixed by alchemists are based on natural medicinal components. Even though they cannot recreate magical potions using this skill, alchemists can identify magical potions about 50% of the time.

Prerequisite: None.

Anatomy, Basic:
[(Intelligence+Wisdom)÷2/Academia/3 B.P.]

Characters with the anatomy skill have a basic knowledge of how the body functions. They know where major organs are located on most species. They do not know much about the anatomy of rare creatures or monsters, but they can make an educated guess in certain circumstances. This skill can help a character know how to harvest organs and other body parts for spell components or other uses, including selling them to others. This particularly useful in getting all the E.P.s possible from a slain creature's yield as listed in the Hacklopedia of Beasts.

Prerequisite: None.

Anatomy, Vital (specific animal):
[(Intelligence+Wisdom)÷2/Academia/1 B.P.s]

A character with this skill knows in detail the inner workings of a specific type of animal or creature. He knows where specific organs are located that are useful as spell components and how the vital organs function. He can also perform basic first aid on an animal he is knowledgeable about. A player can choose one specific animal, with GM approval. If a player wants his character to know the vital anatomy of more than one creature, he will need to purchase this skill for each additional animal at a cost of 1 B.P. per animal. The lower cost denotes the fact that most animal anatomy is similar, and once a character gains insight into one animal, it will take him less effort to understand the anatomy of other animals. This particularly useful in getting all the E.P.s possible from a slain creature's Yield as listed in the Hacklopedia of Beasts.

Prerequisite: Anatomy, Basic.

Ancient History:
[Intelligence/Academia/1 B.P.]

The character has learned of certain specific legends, lore, and history of some ancient time and place. The knowledge must be specific (i.e. a modern historian might specialize in the Late Roman Empire, the Akkadians or the European High Middle Ages). Thus, a player character could know details about the Night of Long Shadows or the War Between the Gawds or whatever else the GM allows.

This skill gives the character familiarity with the principal historical events, legends, personalities, conflicts, places, battles, developments (scientific, cultural, and magical), unsolved mysteries, crafts and oddities of the time period chosen. The character can recognize things he encounters from that age with a successful skill check. For example, Thorg knows quite a bit about the Gnome Uprisings. While moving through some deep caverns, he and his companions stumble across a sealed portal. After rolling a successful skill check, he realizes that it bears the battle crest of Lord Flataroy's Gnome Protectorate Army.

Prerequisite: None.

Animal Lore:
[Intelligence/Academia/2 B.P.]

This skill enables a character to observe the actions or habitat of an animal and interpret what is going on. Actions can show how dangerous the creature is, whether it is hungry, protecting its young, or defending a nearby den. Furthermore, careful observation of signs and behaviors can even indicate the location of a water hole, animal herds, predators, or impending danger, such as a forest fire. The GM will secretly roll a skill check. A successful check means the character understood the basic actions of the creature.

A character may also imitate the calls and cries of animals that he is reasonably familiar with, based on his background. This ability is limited by volume. The roar of a Scoria Dragon would be beyond the abilities of a normal character. A successful skill check means that only magical means can distinguish the character's call from that of the true animal. The cry is sufficient to fool animals, perhaps frightening them away or luring them closer. Finally, animal lore increases the chance of successfully setting snares and traps (for hunting) since the character knows the general habits of the creature hunted. The GM will determine this bonus (usually +5 to +25).

Prerequisite: None.

Appraisal: Gemstone:
[Intelligence/Academia/3 B.P.]

This skill is similar to the general appraising skill described below. It is highly useful for thieves and adventurers, or others who wish to avoid being taken advantage of. A character with this skill can appraise cut or uncut gems and accurately estimate their value and authenticity most of the time. The character must handle the item in proper lighting conditions to properly examine it. A successful skill check (rolled by the GM) enables the character to estimate the value of the gem to the nearest 10% of its true value and to identify fakes. Dwarves with this skill get an additional 15% bonus to their skill check because of their racial familiarity with gems.

Prerequisite: Appraising.

Appraising:
[Intelligence/Academia/6 B.P.]

This skill is highly useful for thieves and adventurers, as it allows characters to estimate the value and authenticity of antiques, art objects, jewelry, cut gemstones, or other crafted items they find (although the GM can exclude those items too exotic or rare to be well known). The character must examine the item to be appraised in good lighting conditions. A successful skill check (rolled by the GM) enables the character to estimate the value of the item to the nearest 20% of it's true value and to identify fakes.

Prerequisite: None.

Art Appraisal: Subset: Painting
[Intelligence/Academia/3 B.P.s]

Characters with this skill have the ability to estimate the value of painted artwork. They are well versed in technique and history, enough to be able to spot fakes. A character who wants to estimate the value of a painting need not hold the painting, but he must be able to view it under adequate lighting for close inspection. He must also be uninterrupted for two rounds while examining it. A character who wants to use this skill must make a successful skill check (rolled by the GM). A successful roll means the character has estimated the worth of a painting within 10% of its true value. He will also be able to tell if the painting is a forgery.

Prerequisite: Art Appreciation: Subset: Painting.

Art Appraisal: Subset: Sculpture
[Intelligence/Academia/3 B.P.s]

This skill is similar to the painting appraisal skill described above. It allows characters to estimate the value of sculpted art and to spot forgeries of great masterpieces. A character employing this skill must be sufficiently close to the sculpture in question as to be able to touch it. He must be able to closely examine the sculpture [with proper illumination] for two uninterrupted rounds. A successful skill check (rolled by the GM) means the character has estimated the value of a sculpture to within 10% of its true value. He is also able to tell whether the sculpture is authentic or a forgery.

Prerequisite: Art Appreciation: Subset: Sculpture.

Art Appreciation: Subset: Painting
[Wisdom/Academia/1 B.P.]

Characters with this ability are well versed in the general history of the great painters and their works. A character with this skill will specialize in one particular style, artist or period of painting, having more extensive knowledge about their specialization. A character with this skill can estimate the worth of other works, but without a great deal of certainty or accuracy. They can generally tell who painted it and what style and time period it was painted in. A success skill check will allow a character to spot a forgery.

Prerequisite: None.

Art Appreciation: Subset: Sculpture
[Wisdom/Academia/1 B.P.]

This skill is similar to the painting appreciation skill subset described above. A successful skill check will allow a character to spot a forgery. They can also usually tell if a stone figure is actually a sculpture, or whether it is a person or creature that has been petrified. They are well versed in the history of great sculptors and their works and usually specialize in one particular style, sculptor or time period.

Prerequisite: None.

Astrology:
[(Intelligence+Wisdom)÷2/Academia/1 B.P.s]

This skill gives the character some understanding of the influences of the stars. Knowing the birth date and time of any person, the astrologer can study the stars and celestial events and subsequently prepare a forecast of the person's future. The astrologer's insight into the future is limited to the next 30 days, and his knowledge is vague at best. If a successful skill check is made, the astrologer can foresee some general event - a great battle, a friend lost, a new friendship made, etc. The GM decides the exact prediction.

Characters with the astrology skill gain a +5 bonus to all navigation skill checks, provided the stars can be seen.

Prerequisite: None.

Botany
[Intelligence/Academia/1 B.P.s]

A character with this skill has a basic knowledge of plants and how they grow. They know how to tell various species of plants apart and under what conditions each type of plant grows best. Most of the time they can tell poisonous plants from non-poisonous plants.

Prerequisite: None.

Campaign Logistics
[Intelligence/Academia/1 B.P.s]

Through their knowledge of how to keep troops properly supplied, characters with this skill can keep a military campaign going smoothly. A character knowledgeable in this area also knows the fastest, safest and most direct routes for getting troops and their equipment from point A to point B. A person with this skill is invaluable in any military operation. A successful skill check means everything is running smoothly.

Prerequisite: Military: Operations.

Civil Administration
[(Intelligence+Wisdom+Charisma)÷3/Academia/2 B.P.s]

This skill allows characters to be able to successfully run a city, town or village. Characters with this skill have what it takes to become a mayor, governor or town leader. They know how to hire staff, keep a budget and provide for sanitation and serviceable roadways. They know how to keep things running smoothly. A successful skill check means the character is doing well, and the people he governs are happy (or at least not rioting in the streets).

Prerequisite: Leadership, Basic and Leadership, Committee.

Culinary Arts
[Wisdom/Academia/1 B.P.]

A character with this skill knows how to prepare sumptuous meals fit for a king. He can make tasty delights out of just about any edible substance.

Prerequisite: None.

Culture (race specific)
[Wisdom/Academia/1 B.P.]

Characters with this skill know the customs and traditions of one specific race or creature. The player character may select the race or creature he is an expert on, but his selection must be approved by the GM. Among other things, the character with this skill will be able to recognize artifacts, writings and rituals of the creature or race about which he is an expert. It is possible for a character with this skill to positively influence those whose culture he is an expert on when encountering them.

Prerequisite: None.

Current Affairs
[Intelligence/Academia/1 B.P.]

A character with this skill knows on detail the goings on in the world around him. He is up on all of the latest developments in any area he has spent at least a day in. He knows who is in power, the political ambitions of those vying for power, the state of any military campaign in progress, and other such information. He has a knack for asking questions and finding answers about the local area.

Prerequisite: None.

Customs and Etiquette (culture specific)
[Wisdom/Academia/1 B.P.]

This skill allows characters to interact with members of a specific culture (chosen by the player with GM approval) smoothly and adroitly. This enables a character to deftly mingle in the chosen culture without offending anyone.

Prerequisite: None.

Engineering:
[(Intelligence+Wisdom)÷2/Academia/2 B.P.s]

The character with this skill is trained as a designer of both great and small things. Engineers can prepare plans for everything from machines (catapults, river locks, gristmills) to large buildings (fortresses, dams). A skill check is required only when designing something particularly complicated or unusual. An engineer must still find competent workmen to carry out his plans, but he is trained to supervise and manage their work.

An engineer is also familiar with the principles of siege craft and can detect flaws in the defenses of a castle or similar construction. He knows how to construct and supervise the use of siege weapons and machines such as catapults, rams, and screws

Prerequisite: None.

Engineering, Fortifications
[(Intelligence+Wisdom)÷2/Academia/2 B.P.s]

Characters with this skill are experts in designing fortresses, towers, walls and castles. They know how to construct almost indestructible fortifications. In an emergency, they can quickly erect some sort of makeshift protection as well. A skill check is required only when designing something particularly complicated or unusual. Although this character can construct simple, temporary structures himself, he needs talented workmen to complete any major project. He has the skill to supervise and manage a crew of such workers such that the project is completed properly and in the shortest amount of time possible.

Prerequisite: Engineering.

Engineering, Public Works
[(Intelligence+Wisdom)÷2/Academia/2 B.P.s]

Characters with this skill can design and oversee the construction of such things as dams, roads, bridges and sewer and irrigation systems. As with the other types of engineering skills available, a skill check is only needed when the character is designing something particularly complicated or unusual. He must have quality workmen to complete any undertaking, but he is trained to be able to supervise and manage such a workforce.

Prerequisite: Engineering.

Forestry
[Intelligence/Academia/1 B.P.]

Characters with a forestry skill are extremely knowledgeable about timber and the forests. They are familiar with how to navigate through forests, how to grow and harvest trees and how to prevent forest fires. They also know some techniques for fighting forest fires, although being able to actually do so would depend on the size of the fire and how much water, equipment and manpower is available. They know how to dig fire breaks, for instance, but this would only be useful in putting out small forest fires because large fires would require a great many fire breaks to be dug in a short amount of time. Foresters can tell a person about the nature and qualities of any tree in the forest, including the species and what the wood is good for.

Prerequisite: None.

Geology
[Intelligence/Academia/1 B.P.]

This skill gives characters a basic scientific knowledge of the planet and its structure (including subterranean caverns) as well as types of rocks. It can help a character identify potential veins of gems or safely spelunk (navigate through natural caves). Dwarves and gnomes gain a bonus for this skill due to their natural racial knowledge of rocks, caverns and gem locations.

Prerequisite: None.

Heraldry:
[Intelligence/Academia/1 B.P.]

The knowledge of heraldry enables the character to identify the crests and symbols that represent various persons and groups. Heraldry comes in many forms and is used for many different purposes. It can be used to identify noblemen, families, guilds, sects, legions, political factions and castes. The symbols may appear on flags, shields, helmets, badges, embroidery, standards, clothing, coins and more. The symbols used may include geometric patterns, lines of calligraphy, fantastic beasts, religious symbols, and magical seals (made for the express purpose of identification). Heraldry can, for example, vary from the highly formalized rules and regulations of late medieval Europe to the knowledge of different shield patterns and shapes used by African tribesmen.

The character automatically knows the different heraldic symbols of his homeland and whom they are associated with. In addition, if the character makes a successful skill check, he can correctly identify the signs and symbols of other lands, provided he has at least a passing knowledge of the inhabitants of that area. This skill is of little use upon first entering a foreign territory.

Prerequisite: None.

Herbalism:
[Intelligence/Academia/6 B.P.]

Those with herbalist knowledge can identify plants and fungi and prepare non-magical potions, poultices, powders, balms, salves, ointments, infusions and plasters for medicinal purposes. They can also prepare natural plant poisons and purgatives. The GM must decide the exact strength of such poisons based on the poison rules in the GMG. A character with both herbalism and healing skills gains bonuses when using his healing talent (see the Healing skill).

Prerequisite: Botany.

History, Local
[(Charisma+Wisdom)÷2/Academia/1 B.P.]

The character with this skill is a storehouse of facts about the history of a region the size of a large county or small province. For example, the character will know when the ruined tower on the hill was built and who built it (and what happened to him). He knows what great heroes and villains fought and fell at the old battlefield and what great treasure is supposed to be kept in a local temple. He even knows how the mayor of the next town miraculously grew hair on his balding pate.

The GM will provide information about local sites and events as the character requests it. Furthermore, the character can try to retell these events as entertaining stories. Once the subject is chosen, he can attempt a skill check and, if successful, add that tale to his repertoire. The character can tell these stories to entertain others, granting him a +2 bonus to his Charisma for the encounter. However, telling stories to hostile beings is probably not going to do any good.

Prerequisite: None.

History, World
[Wisdom/Academia/1 B.P.]

A character with this skill is a real history buff. He's studied all of the major historical events that have occured in the world. He can accurately recount stories of the rise and fall of major kingdoms and rulers. He possesses detailed knowledge about the major wars and battles fought in the past and knows something about the histories of major cities around the world. He also knows the life stories of most major historical figures.

Prerequisite: History, Local.

Leadership, Basic
[(Charisma+Wisdom)÷2/Academia/3 B.P.]

Characters with skill know how to take charge of a group of people to get a job done. If a character with this skill takes the leadership role in his party, the group will be better able to make the right decisions and avoid many mistakes. If this character faces a tough choice and wants to know what to do, he can inform the GM that he wants to make a leadership check. The GM rolls the dice, and if the skill check is a success, will attempt to point out the most advantageous options open to the character. This character also gets a +5 loyalty modifier for hirelings and henchmen.

Prerequisite: None.

Leadership, Committee
[(Charisma+Wisdom)÷2/Academia/2 B.P.]

Characters with this skill can successfully lead a group of between 8-20 people in order to help them complete a task, make a decision, or govern a political body. This character has a good chance of being able to run for public office or be selected by a lord or noble to help govern his affairs. A successful skill check means the character has made a correct decision and led his group to a successful completion of their task. It could also mean that someone important has noticed the character's finesse and tries to hire him. It also could mean that the character has been nominated to run for office. A character with this skill gets a +5 loyalty modifier when dealing with any hirelings or henchmen.

Prerequisite: Leadership, Basic.

Military: Battle Sense:
[(Intelligence+Wisdom)÷2/Academia/9 B.P.s]

This allows a character to be skilled in the art of war. He truly knows how to conduct himself on the battlefield and is apt to become a war hero. He can spot breaks in the enemies' defenses, opportunities to perform heroic deeds to save the day and any weaknesses in his enemy. If this character is in a battle, he can inform the GM that he is looking for opportunities to exploit his enemies' weaknesses, or for a chance to do a heroic deed. If he makes his skill check, the GM must tell him some secret about the enemy forces, or reveal something that is happening in the battle near him where he may have the opportunity to perform an heroic act. The player with this skill who has performed a successful skill check gets +2 to hit and damage, but only in a set-piece battle, not in single combat or brawls.

Prerequisite: None.

Military: Leadership:
[(Intelligence+Wisdom+Charisma)÷3/Academia/4 B.P.s]

A character with this skill knows how to lead men in battle. He is able to plan successful strategies to defeat enemy troops. He knows when to advance and when to retreat. He knows how to keep the morale of his men high and how to get the most out of them. When this character is leading an army, and his skill check is successful, all men under his command get a +10% to their Morale while fighting under him in battle.

Prerequisite: Leadership, Military: Battle Sense, Military: Operations, Military: Small Unit Tactics.

Military: Operations:
[(Intelligence+Wisdom)÷2/Academia/2 B.P.s]

This skill gives a character the knowledge of how military organizations work best. This character will know how to organize an efficient army. He knows how many pikemen he needs, how many archers, how many infantry and how many cavalry. He also knows how to train his army to get the best out of them. He is an expert the tactical employment of weaponry (though not necessarily proficient in their use). He is indispensable to any military campaign. This character gives everyone under his command +1 to hit and damage because they're so well trained. This character's armies also gain a 20% bonus to overland movement rates.

Prerequisite: Military: Small Unit Tactics.

Military: Small Unit Tactics:
[(Intelligence+Wisdom)÷2/Academia/5 B.P.s]

A character with this skill can organize and maneuver a small group of combatants, between 2-20 individuals. He can take charge of his adventuring party in regular combat and devise the best plan for victory. He knows how to use the advantages of each member of his force to gain the best possible outcome. He can also use hand signals to convey intent to other members fighting with him. An individual with this skill, if a successful check is made may halt the action during combat and give other players (if they are within line of sight or hearing range) directions and even suggest tactics for the situation. For example, if the GM announced the party is being attacked by a group of Bugbears and informs the party they cannot communiate but must immediately state their actions, a player with this skill could demand to make a skill check and if successful the party would have 1-2 minutes to discuss what each of them should do.

Prerequisite: Leadership, Military: Battle Sense.

Plant Identification: Holistic:
[(Intelligence+Wisdom)÷2/Academia/2 B.P.s]

A character with this skill can identify plants which may heal certain diseases, animal bites (claw damage) and poisonings. He can not use the plants he finds, however. To do that he needs the herbalist skill. This skill simply allows him to find the plants he needs in the wild.

Prerequisite: Botany.

Religion, general
[Wisdom/Academia/1 B.P.]:

Characters with religion skill know the common beliefs and cults of their homeland and the major faiths of neighboring regions. Ordinary information (type of religious symbol used, basic attitude of the faith, etc.) of any religion is automatically known by the character. Special information, such as how the clergy is organized or the significance of particular holy days, requires a skill check.

Prerequisite: None.

Religion, specific
[Wisdom/Academia/2 B.P.s]:

Additional skills gained in religion enable the character either to expand his general knowledge into more distant regions (using the guidelines above) or to gain precise information about a single faith. If the latter is chosen, the character is no longer required to make a skill check when answering questions about that religion. Such expert knowledge is highly useful to priest characters when dealing with their own and rival faiths. It can also come in handy when trying to identify religious artifacts or writings.

Prerequisite: Religion, general.

Weather Sense:
[(Intelligence+Wisdom)÷2/Academia/1 B.P.]

This skill enables the character to make intelligent guesses about upcoming weather conditions. A successful skill check means the character has correctly guessed the general weather conditions in the next six hours. A skill check can be made once every six hours. However, for every six hours of observation, the character gains a +5% bonus to skill mastery (as he watches the weather change, the character gets a better sense of what is coming). This modifier is cumulative, although sleep or other activity that occupies the attention of the character for a long period negates any accumulated bonus.

Sometimes impending weather conditions are so obvious that no skill check is required. It is difficult not to notice the tornado funnel tearing across the plain or the mass of dark clouds on the horizon obviously headed the character's way.

Prerequisite: None.

Woodland Lore:
[(Intelligence+Wisdom)÷2/Academia/1 B.P.]

This skill allows a character to know legends and specific information about woodland areas, such as where to find certain types of animals, caverns or other notable landmarks. Characters with this skill know about trees and plant life and how they survive. They know that moss always grows on the north of a tree or rock, and are therefore able to navigate through even unknown woodland territories with some degree of accuracy.

Prerequisite: Forestry.

LANGUAGES/COMMUNICATION

Dimple Runes (Braille):
[Dexterity/Languages/Communication/2 B.P.s]

Dimple Runes are a type of ancient writing using raised markings which can be read by the blind or persons unable to see for other reasons, such as being in the dark or blindfolded. This secretive type of writing was developed by a group of mages who had been blinded in punishment for using forbidden magic. As a result, there are many ancient magic scrolls and writings written in this language hidden away in secret locations around Garweeze Wurld. This skill also lets the character use Dimple Runes in their writing.

Prerequisite: None.

Dragon Speak:
[(Intelligence+Charisma)÷2/Languages/Communication/10 B.P.s]

This is a very special ability. To be able to learn this form of communication, a player character must have at least a 19 Intelligence and a 15 Charisma. Dragon Speak is not necessarily another language, the way we commonly think of languages. A character who is able to employ this skill has learned to speak with others in the manner of dragons, not necessarily the tongue. He knows the subtleties that gives dragons power when they speak.

When a dragon speaks, it uses subtle nuances, tactical pauses, and a smooth, lilting vocal tone to lure a person into revealing himself. A person who spends time speaking with a dragon soon finds himself in a trance-like state, almost as if the dragon has put a spell on him. He coaxes and entices his conversational partner to reveal far more than he had ever intended. If a dragon spends enough time with someone, he soon knows everything, from whether the person is truthful to what he had for breakfast and the name of his pet cat. A good example of this type of skill is the fictional character Hannibal Lecter. He was able to learn very intimate details about FBI agent Clarice Starling as he prompted her into telling him all about herself. That is what a person with Dragon Speak can do. For every round a character with this skill has to talk with another person, the chance increases that he will learn more and more.

In the first round of using this skill on a person, the character will be able to tell whether his subject is lying or not. On the second round, he will be able to tell what the general intent of the person is. On the third round, he will be able to find out just what his subject is planning to do next. On the fourth, he will know how much gold and treasure the subject has. On the fifth, he will know where his subject keeps his valuables. On the sixth, he will know the names of all of his companions. On the seventh, he will know whom, if anyone, is employing the subject. On the eighth, he will know if the character has any other useful information, such as maps, the location to any important sites, or his mother's maiden name. If a character with Dragon Speak spends eight rounds with a subject, he will know everything there is to know about his subject. Of course, all of this is contingent on successful skill rolls, which the GM will roll. However, if the first roll is successful, each subsequent roll will have a 5% better chance of success than the last.

Characters with this skill are immune to the effects of Dragon Speak. By the same token, a character with this skill will not be able to successfully use it on another character, or creature, with this skill.

Prerequisite: None.

Evil Speak:
[Intelligence/Languages/Communication/1 B.P.]

A character with this skill has the sinister power to corrupt the morals of others with sly conversation. Evil Speak is not a language of its own, but a seductive way of speaking. If a character with this skill has access to another person long enough to hold an ongoing conversation over at least three days time, he has a chance of forcing that person to make an alignment shift. The person who is the target of this character's skill must save vs. Charm or be forced to shift his alignment toward evil by 5 points. This shift can force a complete alignment change if the shift moves the person's alignment infraction points to 9, or if the person is subjected to an Alignment Audit. The success of this skill is contingent on a successful skill check, rolled by the GM.

Prerequisite: None.

Glersee (Trail Markers):
[Intelligence/Languages/Communication/2 B.P.]

This is a special skill, enabling a character to interpret and communicate by using trail markings. Glersee is a unique form of communication developed by rangers and grel scouts, combining symbols and the use of stones, sticks, etc. to mark trails. They are able to pass vital information to comrades without letting the enemy know what's being said. Those conversant in Glersee can interpret the signs left by others before them, and they can leave signs for others. In addition to these symbols, stones, sticks and other natural material are used. For instance, two stones placed on top of one another means that a steep mountain or cliff is straight ahead. Two stones placed side by side means the trail is relatively unobstructed. Sticks placed in the form of a cross means that the road branches off ahead and is safe. Two sticks placed in the form of an X means that enemy troops are up ahead and that it is dangerous. A pile of stones means there is a cave nearby that can be used for shelter. A pile of stones with a stick on top means that a cave is nearby, but that there is danger in the cave.

Prerequisite: None.

Languages, Ancient/Dead:
[Intelligence/Languages/Communication/2 B.P.]

The character with this skill has mastered a difficult and obscure tongue that has long since passed into the mists of time and is now primarily found in the writings of pedantic sages and sorcerers or tomes of ancient secrets written by long-dead mystics. A character with this skill easily reads scrolls, books, signs, carvings or other writings in that tounge and can also speak said language. If a player wants his character to know more than one ancient language, he must purchase this skill for each language desired.

Prerequisite: None.

Languages, Modern:
[Intelligence/Languages/Communication/1 B.P.]

The character with this skill has learned to speak a language of the known world. To do so there must be a teacher available. This could be another player character, an NPC hireling, or simply a local townsman. For each modern language known, this skill must be purchased. A character cannot, however, know more languages than his Intelligence allows.

Prerequisite: None.

Languages, Undead:
[Intelligence/Languages/Communication/2 B.P.]

The character with this skill can communicate with the undead. He can read inscriptions on crypts, coffins and other undead haunts, as well. Necromancers and clerics especially covet this skill.

Prerequisite: None.

Musical Instrument Skills

Brass Instruments:
[(Wisdom + Dexterity)÷2/Musical/2 B.P.]

This skill gives the character the ability to play one specific brass instrument and can play other brass instruments with only a minimal amount of practice and instruction. Brass instruments include trumpets, French horns, trombones, etc. When this skill is aquired, the character can choose a specific type of brass instrument. Each time he repeats the course he can add another brass instrument.

Basic skill indicates the musician can play simple tunes. Specialization means the character can play more complex tunes and compose simple tunes. Mastery indicates the character is a virtuoso and can play any piece written for his instrument, if he has enough time to practice. He can also write exquisite and intricate musical pieces for his instrument. Those without this skill cannot play any instrument instrument of this type.

Prerequisite: None.

Exotic Instruments:
[(Wisdom + Dexterity)÷2/Musical/2 B.P.]

This skill indicates that a character can play one exotic or unusual instrument such as a ram's horn, saw, washboard, etc. Once this skill is aquired, the character can choose a specific type of exotic instrument. Each time he repeats the course he can add another exotic instrument. Basic skill indicates the musician can play simple tunes. Specialization means the character can play more complex tunes and compose simple tunes. Mastery indicates the character is a virtuoso and can play any piece written for his instrument, if he has enough time to practice. He can also write exquisite and intricate pieces for his instrument. Those without this skill cannot play any instrument instrument of this type.

Prerequisite: None

Percussion Instruments:
[(Wisdom + Dexterity)÷2/Musical/1 B.P.]

This skill indicates the player knows how to play at least one percussion instrument. Once this skill is aquired, the character can choose a specific type of percussion instrument. Each time he repeats the course he can add another percussion instrument. Percussion instruments include gourds, bongos, all sorts of drums, etc.

Basic skill indicates the musician can play just some simple rhythms. Specialization means the character can play more complex rhythms. Mastery indicates the character is a virtuoso. Those without this skill cannot play any instrument of this type.

Prerequisite: None.

Stringed Instruments:
[(Wisdom + Dexterity)÷2/Musical/2 B.P.]

This skill indicates the player knows how to play at least one stringed instrument. Once this skill is aquired, the character can choose a specific type of stringed instrument. Each time he repeats the course he can add another stringed instrument. Stringed instruments include violins, lyres, harps, lutes, guitars, etc.

Basic skill indicates the musician can play simple tunes. Specialization means the character can play more complex tunes and compose simple tunes. Mastery indicates the character is a virtuoso and can compose intricate pieces for his instrument. Those without this skill cannot play any instrument of this type.

Prerequisite: None.

Wind Instruments:
[(Wisdom + Dexterity)÷2/Musical/2 B.P.]

This skill gives the player knowledge of how to play at least one wind instrument. Once this skill is aquired, the character can choose a specific type of wind instrument. Each time he repeats the course he can add another wind instrument. Wind instruments include such instruments as flutes, recorders, clarinets, etc.

Basic skill indicates the musician can play simple tunes. Specialization means the character can play more complex tunes and compose simple tunes. Mastery indicates the character is a virtuoso and can compose intricate pieces for his instrument. Those without this skill cannot play any instrument of this type.

Prerequisite: None.

MUNDANE TASKS

Mundane tasks are just that, those little things which need to be done day to day. Mundane tasks never required a skill check (unless special circumstances call for it). A character with a mundane task proficiency is assumed to have the skill AND discipline to perform the task day to day or as needed. If a character does NOT have a mundane task (such as armor maintenance for example) it is assumed the character is not routinely performing the task and any penalties for not doing so may apply. For example, a character who fails to maintain his armor or weapons may find that they wear out much faster than those characters who diligently perform such maintenance. Because it assumed the characer is performing these tasks daily he needs only to pay the monthly costs associated with the task to prove that he's been faithfully employing his mundane skills.

Armor Maintenance:
[(Intelligence+Dexterity)÷2/Mundane Task/1 B.P.]

A person with this skill can keep his (and others) armor in good working order, provided he has access to the tools he needs. There is no skill check required to successfully perform this skill, so long as the character has appropriate equipment to work the material. Maintenance does not replace armor points or repair damage sustained in battle. (You need the skill armor repair for that). This skill assumes you are waterproofing the leather straps and parts, polishing the metal and doing routine preventative maintenance which would otherwise degrade the armor's effectiveness.

Monthly Cost: 75 gp per suit of armor used on a regular basis.

Prerequisite: None.

Maintenance/Upkeep (General):
[Wisdom/Mundane Task/1 B.P.]

A person with this task is generally handy with tools. He is a general all-around fix-it man. He can keep dwellings in good repair, as well as most equipment needed for adventuring. He can also make minor repairs to wagons and carts. This is all dependent, of course, on whether he has the proper tools or not. So long as the character has this equipment, time and money, no skill check is needed to successfully complete this task (unless the GM requires it for unusual circumstances).

Monthly Cost: 50 gp.

Prerequisite: None.

Shaving/Grooming:
[Intelligence/Mundane Task/1 B.P.]

A person who is skilled in this area knows how to maintain his personal hygene. Even while on the trail, this person can make himself look presentable. The character must have access to some sort of equipment (razor, comb, etc.) to perform this task. A person with this skill can add 1 to his Comeliness score and reduces the chance of contracting diseases by 5%. No skill check is needed to properly perform this task (unless the GM requires it for unusual circumstances).

Monthly Cost: 25 gp.

Prerequisite: None.

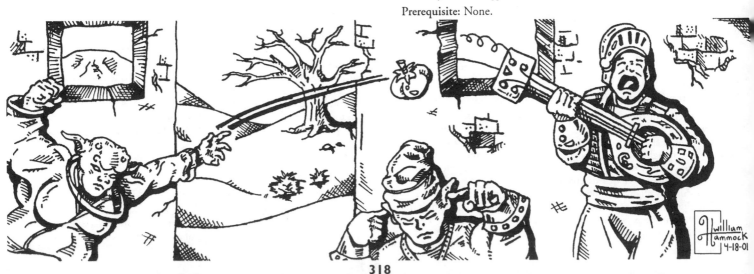

Weapon Maintenance:
[Dexterity/Mundane Task/1 B.P.]

In HackMaster, weapons take a lot of wear and tear. A person with the weapon maintenance skill is able to keep blades sharpened to their best hacking ability. He can also keep bowstrings and wooden shafts from rotting by applying the neccesary oils and waxes. He can do this for his own weapons or those of others. Of course, he needs the proper equipment in order to perform this task: oils, buffing materials, polishing cremes, a whetstone etc. So long as the character has the equipment, time and money, no skill check is needed to successfully complete this task (unless the GM requires it for unusual circumstances).

Monthly Cost: 10 gp per weapon.

Prerequisite: None.

COMBAT PROCEDURES

Angawa Battle Cry:
[(Strength+Charisma)÷2/Combat Procedure/2 B.P.s]

A bone-chilling war whoop, the Angawa Battle Cry was first used in combat by the Angawa, a race of barbarians now practically extinct. The cry was adopted by the race of pixie fairies who use this skill quite often. Characters who learn this skill are taught the closely guarded technique by some of the few descendents of the Angawa people. Letting loose this cry (sounds like Hoo-DE-Hoo) in battle forces all opponents within a 25 foot radius to save vs. fear or receive -1 to their to-hits for the duration of the encounter. Because this skill strains the vocal cords it can only be used once per day.

Prerequisite: None.

Art of Beating:
[(Strength+Intelligence)÷2/Combat Procedure/2 B.P.s]

This skill was developed by the King's Elite Guard, who were skillfully trained in the art of beating. Those who learn this skill are able to administer blows that cause damage and pain, but do not kill. They can administer blows until their victim has 1/2 of a hit point left. Usually, this is done to force a person to confess to a deed or crime, or reveal secret information. Once a victim heals up a few points, the beating can continue until the victim confesses, or reveals his secret, or until he again reaches 1/2 a hit point. Characters with this skill can interrogate a prisoner in this way almost indefinitely if they have to.

Prerequisite: None.

Attitude Adjustment:
[(Strength+Charisma)÷2/Combat Procedure/1 B.P.]

This skill is useful in keeping hirelings and henchmen in line. In a perfect world, simply treating a henchman or hireling well, keeping him fed, healthy and well paid would be enough. However, in reality, henchmen and hirelings can be a fickle lot. Disgruntled employees can wreak havoc for an adventuring party. Dissension in the ranks, if left unchecked, could spread until the characters are facing an all-out mutiny - a dangerous situation. Therefore, on occasion, it is necessary for employers to administer what is known as an attitude adjustment to unruly or defiant henchmen or hirelings. Characters with this skill know when to perform this function and how to do it effectively. The punishment must be severe enough to make others think twice about crossing the character, but not be so severe that it would further embitter the subject. A skill check performed successfully would swing any negative loyalty modifiers for henchmen and hirelings back one category in favor of the PC rendering the adjustment. Your GM will determine the exact modifiers.

Prerequisite: None.

Brawler:
[(Strength+Dexterity)÷2/Combat Procedure/2 B.P.]

A character with this skill is experienced in the art of good old-fashioned bar fighting. He gets +1 to hit and damage when engaged in any type of baroom brawl. He is also able to improvise weapons at no penalty. This is contingent on a successful skill check, rolled by the GM.

Prerequisite: None.

Crane:
[Dexterity/Combat Procedure/2 B.P.]

This maneuver is quite unique. It is graceful in appearance and a strange, but deliberate, tactic. To successfully perform the crane, the character must win initiative, and then he must decline to take it. The character stands in a crane-like pose in front of his opponent, motionless. The opponent gets +2 to hit the character and the first strike. If the opponent hits, the character's crane maneuver is ruined. If, by some stroke of luck, the opponent misses, the character then gets +4 to hit. One might wonder why anyone would want to purchase this skill, or practice it. However, this skill is primarily a matter of Honor. Any character who practices this skill automatically gets +2 to his Honor, even if he is unsuccessful. If he is successful, that Honor bonus skyrockets to +5.

Prerequisite: None.

Cricket-in-the-Pea Pod:
[Dexterity/Combat Procedure/1 B.P.s]

This method, taught by many famous fighting experts, including Master Sing Hu'Chek, lets a character gain a tactical advantage. This can be used to gain a rear attack or to bypass an opponent's shield. The character who is the master of the cricket-in-the-pea pod maneuver can roll around an opponent's body, or through his legs, if they are spread wide enough, or if the opponent is tall enough. If successful, he receives a +2 to his next initiative roll and if he attacks prior to his target, he receives a +2 to hit for a rear attack.

Prerequisite: None.

Dirty Fighting:
[Intelligence/Combat Procedure/2 B.P.s]

This skill enables a character to gain hefty to-hit and damage modifiers as long as he forgoes all defensive actions, effectively lowering his Armor Class. No skill check is necessary. The character's AC goes down by 2 but he recieves a +2 to-hit and damage. He also forces critical hits on his opponent on a 19-20. Gnome titans are able to use this skill without purchasing it only in cases where they are enraged. Using this skill reduces Honor by 1 each time it is used.

Prerequisite: None.

Entrenchment Construction:
[Wisdom/Combat Procedure/4 B.P.s]

A character with this skill can successfully dig a foxhole or other defensive position provided the ground isn't solid stone. When fighting from this defensive position, a character lowers his AC by 1d6. There is no skill check, but the character must have something to dig with and at least two uninterrupted turns to dig.

Prerequisite: None.

Establish Ambush Zone:
[Wisdom/Combat Procedure/8 B.P.s]

This character knows how to successfully establish an ambush zone. If a successful skill check is made, rolled by the GM, anyone travelling through this zone has a double chance of being surpised.

Prerequisite: None.

Eye Gouge:
[Dexterity/Combat Procedure/1 B.P.]

Being an expert in this maneuver gives a character the ability to effectively blind his opponent in combat. Any successful skill check, along with a successful to-hit roll, means the character has been able to jam a thumb or finger into the eye sockets of his opponent. The opponent is unable to see for two rounds and suffers a -4 penalty to his to-hit and damage rolls during that time. Of course, this skill is impossible to use if the opponent has any sort of eye protection.

Prerequisite: None.

Eye of the Tiger Advantage:
[Dexterity/Combat Procedure/5 B.P.]

A character who has this skill is able to discipline himself to wait and strike at just the right moment. To employ this tactic, one must voluntarily sacrifice their option to roll initiative and automatically go last. They then gain a +1 bonus to hit and damage. This character knows what Master Sing Hu'Chek teaches, that it is not necessarily he who strikes first who wins, but it is he who strikes best. There is no skill check to make for success in this skill. This character only needs to sacrifice initiative to use it.

Prerequisite: None.

Groin Punch:
[Strength/Combat Procedure/10 B.P.]

This is a very specific called shot. Unlike the groin stomp, which can only be used by gnome titans, the groin punch can be used by anyone. Female characters are particularly adept at this skill, gaining +1 to hit when using it. Male characters can take this skill, but they get no to-hit bonuses and lose 1d4 points of Honor if they use it. All other benefits of this skill, however, are available equally.

A character with this skill can disable any opponent with one blow. The damage inflicted is not great, only 1d4, but the effect is the victim must make a save vs. his Constitution at -5 or fall prone. A person in this position, obviously, is an easy target for further attacks. Female opponents can also be harmed by this attack, but they only suffer a -2 to their save vs. Constitution. Of course, all of this depends on a successful skill check, rolled by the GM, followed up with a successful to-hit roll. If the check fails, so does the punch, simple as that.

Prerequisite: None.

Jugular Swipe:
[Dexterity/Combat Procedure/10 B.P.]

This is a deadly attack. A character with this skill must also have a weapon proficiency in dagger or a sword and must be able to get behind his opponent. (Thieves can use their backstab ability in conjunction with this skill to wreak additional havoc. Assassins also love using this deadly attack.) Once a character is behind his opponent, he must grab his head with his free hand, and with the other slash his throat (-3 to his to-hit). This attack does whatever damage the weapon does, plus 1d6 points of bleeding damage per round. This person can bleed to death and must immediately apply pressure to the wound (no two-handed fighting or use of a shield). He must also attempt to break off combat, if practical, and seek immediate attention for his wounds. This skill is only effective against man-sized or smaller humans or demi-humans and is ineffective against opponents wearing any type of armor on their necks. A successful skill check is needed to perform this act as well as a successful to-hit. An unsuccessful skill roll means the opponent is able to squirm out of the grasp of his attacker.

Prerequisite: None.

Kidney Bruiser:
[Strength/Combat Procedure/15 B.P.]

Characters who are able to successfully perform this procedure can deliver a massive kidney punch that adds several points of damage to their normal damage roll. This punch adds 1d6 points to the damage roll if a successful skill check is made (rolled by the GM). Of course, this attack is not successful against armored opponents.

Prerequisite: None.

Mortal Combat:
[Constitution/Combat Procedure/9 B.P.]

A character with the ability of engaging in mortal combat suffers -2 to hit, but gains +2 to damage. A person with this skill who uses it becomes enraged during combat and strikes fast and furiously. He doesn't hit quite as often, but when he does, watch out! By using this skill successfully the character has committed himself to taking out his opponent(s) and is pressing home the attack. He must declare how many combat rounds he is going to fight in such a manner before attempting his skill check. Mortal combat can only be declared once per opponent. Breaking off before fulfilling his declaration results in the loss of 1d10 Honor points.

Prerequisite: None.

Muster Resolve:
[Constitution/Combat Procedure/8 B.P.s]

This skill enables a character to, in a sense, snatch victory from the jaws of defeat. A character with this skill shouldn't be counted out of any fight even if he has been brought to 0 hit points. A successful skill check means the character has been able to temporarily regain 1d8 hit points in order to rally and save the day. An unsuccessful skill check means he has failed to rally. This skill may only be employed once per encounter. Temporary hit points are lost after 10 rounds so the character may well die if he cannot be cured.

Prerequisite: None.

Pimp Slap (Wuss Slap):
[Strength/Combat Procedure/1 B.P.]

This skill, also known as a wuss slap, gives a character the ability to keep another person from getting uppity. A successful skill check means the character was able to deliver a degrading slap to his opponent. This slap promptly removes 3 points of Honor from the opponent.

Prerequisite: None.

Pugilism:
[(Strength+Dexterity+Intelligence)÷3/Combat Procedure/7 B.P.s]

A character skilled in pugilism is an expert in the field of unarmed combat and fighting according to established rules and protocol. He knows what punches to throw and when to throw them. He has been trained in the classic unarmed fighting technique. If an opponent drops from a punch he must allow him a chance to recover and stand back up. A character with this skill must make a successful skill check, rolled by the GM. If successful, and he is engaged in unarmed combat, he gets +3 to-hit and to damage when using his fists. Note: pugilism is an honorable sport. Anyone who has the Pugilism skill and is attacked by another pugilist is Honor bound to adhere to the code. Refusal to fight bare fisted and according to the rules of pugilism results in the loss of 1d6 points of Honor. Any characters who respond to a pugilist attack with Dirty Fighting suffer -1 to their Honor.

Prerequisite: None.

Round House Groin Kick:
[Dexterity/Combat Procedure/10 B.P.]

This maneuver is often used by shorter demi-humans such as dwarves, gnomes and halflings. It is also called a "Meat Tenderizer". The maneuver involves a very fast spinning kick targeting the groin of an opponent. If a successful skill check is made, rolled by the GM, the character gets +2 to-hit the intended body part and +3 to damage because the victim never sees it coming. This tactic is ineffective against opponents wearing groin protection. Use of this skill is considered dishonorable. (-1 Honor per use)

Prerequisite: None.

Who's Yer Mamma Ankle Wrench:
[(Strength+Dexterity)÷2/Combat Procedure/6 B.P.]

This move enables characters to drop to the ground and grab one of his opponent's feet so that he can then twist the ankle of his opponent. This is a disabling attack. If the characters skill check is successful (rolled by the GM), the character's opponent takes 1d4 points of damage and will be unable to put any weight on the injured ankle thereby reducing his movement rate by half as well suffering -2 to his to-hit rolls.

Characters attempting this procedure open themselves up to attack while doing so. Opponents get a +2 to hit and the character's AC drops by 1 temporarily. This attack is ineffective against opponents with armored ankles or wearing foot protection.

Prerequisite: None.

ARTISAN AND PERFORMING ARTS

Artistic Ability:
[(Dexterity+Intelligence)÷2/Artisan and Performing Arts/1 B.P.]

Player characters with artistic ability are naturally accomplished in various forms of the arts. They have an inherent understanding of color, form, space, flow, tone, pitch and rhythm. Characters with artistic ability must select one art form (painting, sculpture, etc.) to be proficient in. Thereafter, they can attempt to create art works in their given field. Although it is not necessary to make a skill check, one can be made to determine the quality of the work. If a 5 or lower is rolled on the check, the artist has created a work with some truly lasting value. Artistic ability also confers a +10 bonus to all skill checks requiring artistic skill (such as music or dance) and to attempts to appraise objects of art.

Prerequisite: None.

Dancing, Ballroom:
[Dexterity/Artisan and Performing Arts/1 B.P.]

A character with this skill is the personification of grace on the dance floor. He can waltz and tango with the best of them. He can perform any type of ballroom dancing with ease. While dancing, this character's Charisma goes up by 1 point. There is no skill check required for this skill. Once a character learns it, it's like riding a bicycle, he doesn't forget.

Prerequisite: None.

Interpret/Perform Mime (secondary language):
[Intelligence/Artisan and Performing Arts/1 B.P.]

In Garweeze Wurld pantomime, or mime as it is more commonly known, is sometimes a valuable form of communication. Characters with this skill can perform mime, and interpret it with ease. Because it is a silent form of communication, mime can come in handy when characters are in a situation where they want to communicate with each other in a stealthy manner. Also, mimes often perform in public or for nobles and even kings, getting paid for their efforts. A skill check is only needed if the character is attempting to communicate with another person in a difficult situation, such as being under guard. If the skill check succeeds, he is able to communicate the message he desired. Of course, communication between people using mime requires that all parties involved in the conversation be skilled in mime.

Prerequisite: None.

Juggling:
[Dexterity/Artisan and Performing Arts/1 B.P.]

The character with this skill can juggle - a talent useful for entertainment, diversions, and certain rare emergencies. When juggling normally (to entertain or distract), no skill check is required. A check is made when trying spectacular tricks ("Watch me eat this apple in mid-air!"). However, juggling also enables the character to attempt desperate moves. On a successful attack roll vs. AC 0 (not a skill check), the character can catch small items thrown to harm him (as opposed to items thrown for him to catch). Thus, the character could catch a dagger or a dart before it hits. If this attack roll fails, however, the character automatically suffers damage (sticking your hand in the path of a dagger is likely to hurt).

Prerequisite: None.

Manu Weasel Dance:
[Dexterity/Artisan and Performing Arts/5 B.P.]

A character with this skill can perform a particularly revolting dance designed to distract and mesmerize. Also known as the "showing yer ass dance", the Manu Weasel Dance is designed to taunt, humiliate and degrade another character or group. By bearing your bottom and exposing it (AC 10 for the bare bottom) to your opponent(s) within missile range and performing this dance you can steal 1d10 points of Honor from the target and add half of those Honor points to your own Honor. The dance must last a full combat round or it automatically fails. If you are struck by any weapon or missile while performing this dance, it automatically fails and you lose face (-1d10 your Honor).

Prerequisite: None.

Mocking Jig:
[Dexterity/Artisan and Performing Arts/10 B.P.]

A character with this skill is able to perform a dance that is so insulting that its intended target loses 1d4+1 points of Honor. This is often done after a character has defeated his opponent in combat. A successful skill check is needed to perform this jig so as to be properly humiliating (rolled by the GM).

Prerequisite: None.

Poetry, Writing and Comprehension/Interpretation:
[(Intelligence+Wisdom)÷2/Artisan and Performing Arts/1 B.P.]

A character skilled in poetry can write poems that can make all who hear or read them weep. They can also comprehend and interpret the writings of other poets. This allows them to ferret out clues, secret messages or riddles that are sometimes hidden in poetry. No skill check is necessary to perform this skill, unless the GM feels there are unusual circumstances.

Prerequisite: None.

Singing:
[Charisma/Artisan and Performing Arts/1 B.P.]

The character with this skill is an accomplished singer and can use this ability to entertain others and perhaps earn a small living. No skill check is required to sing in most circumstances. The character can also create choral works on a successful skill check.

Prerequisite: None.

SOPHISTICATED

Animal Handling:
[Wisdom/Sophisticated/1 B.P.]

Skill in this area enables a character to exercise a greater than normal degree of control over pack animals and beasts of burden. A successful skill check indicates that the character has succeeded in calming an excited or agitated animal. (If handling a Pack Ape you must add 10% to the die roll.)

Prerequisite: Animal Lore.

Animal Training (specify animal type):
[(Intelligence+Wisdom)÷2/Sophisticated/2 B.P.s]

Characters with this skill can train one type of creature (declared when the skill is chosen) to obey simple commands and perform tricks.

A character may acquire additional animal training skills to train other types of creatures or can improve his skill with a type already chosen. Creatures typically trained include dogs, horses, falcons, pigeons, elephants, ferrets and parrots. A character can choose more exotic creatures and monsters with animal intelligence (although these are difficult to control).

A trainer can work with up to three creatures at one time. The trainer may choose to teach general tasks or specific tricks. A general task gives the creature the ability to react to a number of nonspecific commands to do its job. Examples of general tasks include guard and attack, carry a rider, perform heavy labor, hunt, track, or fight alongside soldiers (such as a war horse or elephant). A specific trick involves the trained creature doing one specific action. A horse may rear on command, a falcon may pluck a designated object, a dog may attack a specific person, a Pack Ape may play cards or a rat may run through a particular maze. With enough time, a creature can be trained to do both general tasks and specific tricks.

Training for a general task requires three months of uninterrupted work. Training for a specific trick requires 2d6 weeks. At the end of the training time, a skill check is made. If successful, the animal is trained. If the die roll fails, the beast is untrainable. An animal can be trained in 2d4 general tasks or specific tricks, or any combination of the two.

An animal trainer can also try to tame wild animals (preparing them for training later on). Wild animals can be tamed only when they are very young. The taming requires one month of uninterrupted work with the creature. At the end of the month, a skill check is made. If successful, the beast is suitable for training. If the check fails, the creature remains too wild to train. It can be kept, though it must be leashed or caged. Note that if the character is attempting to train a normally dangerous exotic animal, such as an Owlbear, a failed skill check can be serious. It can mean the creature turns on its trainer, and the GM is justified in declaring that the character must engage the beast in combat. (The beast automatically wins initiative the first round.)

Prerequisite: Animal Lore, Animal Handling.

Armorer:
[Intelligence/Sophisticated/10 B.P.s]

This character can make and repair all of the types of armor listed in the Player's Handbook, given the proper materials and facilities, (blacksmith tool skill is also needed to perform any armorer-related tasks. Otherwise a -20 modifier applies to the skill check). When making armor, the skill check is rolled at the end of the normal construction time.

The time required to make armor is equal to two weeks per level of AC below 10. For example, a suit of full plate armor would require 18 weeks of work.

If the skill check indicates failure, the armorer may have created usable, but flawed, armor (shoddy workmanship). Your GM has specific details. Only a character with armorer skill can detect the flaws, and this requires careful and detailed inspection.

If an armorer is creating a suit of field plate or full plate armor, the character who will use the armor must be present at least once a week during the creation of the armor, since such types of armor require very exact fitting.

Prerequisite: Leatherworking and Metalworking.

Armor Repair, Basic :
[(Intelligence+Dexterity)÷2/Sophisticated Task/3 B.P.]

A person with this skill can make minor repairs and replace lost armor points to battle damaged armor. It takes two uninterrupted turns to complete a minor repair, (1-2 armor points) such as repairing a small dent, tightening a loose rivet or two, or patching a minor hole. It takes at least four uninterrupted turns to complete a medium-sized repair (3-5 points), replacing a handful of rivets or repairing a large dent. It takes eight uninterrupted turns to complete major repairs, (6-10 points) such as patching many large holes, dents that have caved in a whole side, or reattaching major parts.

A character with basic armor maintenance can fix 1d4 armor hit points per skill check. A failed skill check indicates that he can no longer make repairs on that particular suit of armor. (The armorer skill or one of the advanced armor repair skills is necessary for substantial repair.) Basic Armor repair can restore a maximum of 1 lost armor class to a damaged suit of armor. For example, if a set of damaged armor was originally AC 5 in new condition and was reduced to AC 7 through combat damage, armor repair basic could only bring it back up to AC 6 at the highest. In order for the Armor to be restored to its orginal state (AC 5), you would need Armor Repair, Advanced or the Armorer Skill. Each skill check requires the 1d100 gp in materials.

Prerequisite: Leather Working, Metal Working. BlackSmith Tools.

Armor Repair, Advanced :
[(Intelligence+Dexterity)/2/Sophisticated Task/4 B.P.]

This skill works exactly like Basic Armor Repair except that the character rolls a 1d6 hit points per skill check. Advanced Armor Repair can restore 2 levels of lost AC to damaged armor.

Prerequisite: Armor Repair, Basic.

Armor Repair, Expert :
[(Intelligence+Dexterity)÷2/Sophisticated Task/8 B.P.]

Works exactly like Basic and Advanced Armor Repair but the character rolls a 1d8 hit points per skill check. Expert Armor Repair can fully restore all lost AC to damaged armor.

Prerequisite: Armor Repair, Advanced.

Bargain Sense:
[Wisdom/Sophisticated/5 B.P.]

A character with this skill knows a good bargain when he sees one. He's the one who always comes to you with some sweet piece of merchandise (the same merchandise you just bought) and somehow he's managed to pay five gps less than you. This character can always smell a bargain. He knows where to get the best stuff for the least price. Therefore, on a successful skill check (after negotiation has arrived at a price), this character will pay 1d20% gp less for any item.

Prerequisite: None.

Bartering:
[Wisdom/Sophisticated/1 B.P.]

At first glance, this skill might appear to be similar to haggling, but it isn't. Bartering means knowing how to trade items for things other than money. A character skilled at barter is adept at trading and making the best deal possible for himself. He will be able to trade something of lesser value for something of more value every time. No skill check is necessary unless the GM decides there are extraordinary circumstances or the character is attempting to trade his item for something worth twice as much or more.

Prerequisite: None.

Blacksmithing:
[Strength/Sophisticated/1 B.P.]

A character with the blacksmithing skill is capable of making simple tools and implements from iron and steel. Use of the skill requires a forge with a coal-fed fire and bellows, as well as a hammer and anvil. The character cannot make armor or most weapons, (he needs the appropriate skills for that) but can craft crowbars, grappling hooks, horseshoes, nails, hinges, plows, and most other iron objects. (Blacksmith tools is required to do any blacksmith or metal working related tasks. Otherwise a -20 modifier applies to those skill checks).

Prerequisites: Black Smithing Tools.

Bowyer/Fletcher:
[Dexterity/Sophisticated/1 B.P.]

This character can make bows and arrows of the types given in Tables 9T and 9V. One exception: only a master elven bowyer/fletcher can make an elven Great Long bow or arrows.

A weaponsmith is required to fashion arrowheads, but the bowyer/fletcher can create arrow shafts and the bows that fire them. The construction time for a long or short bow is one week, while composite bows require two weeks, and 1d6 arrows can be made in one day.

At the end of the construction time, the player makes a skill check. If the check is successful, the weapon is of fine quality and will last for many years of normal use without breaking. If the check fails, the weapon is still usable, but not to full effect (your GM has rules regarding substandard bows and arrows).

If the character wishes to create a weapon of truly fine quality and the GM allows it, the GM has further rules pertaining its creation.

Prerequisite: None.

Brewing:
[Intelligence/Sophisticated/1 B.P.]

The character is trained in the art of brewing beers and other strong drink. This makes him very popular. The character can prepare brewing formulas, select quality ingredients, set up and manage a brewery, control fermentation, and age the finished product. A skill check is performed after each batch.

Prerequisite: None.

Carpentry:
[Strength/Sophisticated/1 B.P.]

The carpentry skill enables the character to do woodworking jobs: building houses, cabinetry, joinery, etc. Tools and materials must be available, of course. The character can build basic items from experience, without the need for plans. Unusual and more complicated items (a catapult, for example) require plans prepared by an engineer and may require a skill check. (Carpentry Tool Skill is also needed for any carpentry-related tasks. Otherwise a -20 modifier applies to the skill check). Truly unusual or highly complex items (wooden clockwork mechanisms, for example) require a skill check.

Prerequisite: Carpentry Tools.

Cartography: Dungeon:
[Intelligence/Sophisticated/2 B.P.s]

A character with this skill knows how to map a dungeon and draw it with almost perfect accuracy. This character doesn't get lost in dungeons, either. Of course, this is contingent on a successful skill check, rolled by the GM. If a player buys this skill for his character and his party is having trouble navigating a dungeon, he can ask the GM to roll his skill check. If the skill check is successful, the GM will tell him where he is in general, and, if he's looking for his way back out, how to get there. He may tell the player how far from the exit he is, or how far from a specific level he is.

Prerequisite: Map Sense.

Cartography: Hasty Mapping:
[Intelligence/Sophisticated/2 B.P.s]

This skill allows a character to draw quick, relatively accurate maps. This skill is useful if the character is forced to move quickly, and needs to be able to find his way back the way he came. This character can map while he travels with no movement penalty. If the skill check is successful, rolled by the GM, the GM has to tell the character where he is, in general. He will give him some sort of landmark or other identifying location to help the character navigate.

Prerequisite: Map Sense.

Cartography: Overland:
[Intelligence/Sophisticated/2 B.P.s]

A character with this skill has the ability to create maps of anywhere he travels. He can find his way through woods, mountains or any wilderness terrain. If a successful skill check (rolled by the GM) is made, the character can ask the GM a question about where he is, or which way he needs to go.

Prerequisite: Map Sense.

Charioteering:
[Dexterity/Sophisticated/1 B.P.]

A character with this skill is able to safely guide a chariot over any type of terrain that can normally be negotiated, at a rate 1/3 faster than the normal movement rate for a chariot driven by a character without this skill. No skill check is needed to do this. Note that this skill does not impart the ability to move a chariot over terrain that it cannot traverse; even the best charioteer in the world cannot take such a vehicle into the mountains.

Prerequisite: None.

Clever Packer:
[Wisdom/Sophisticated/3 B.P.]

A clever packer is someone who knows how to maximize space and carefully distribute weight in his pack for travel. If his skill check is successful, the pack is so well put together that the total weight is considered to be 10% less than actual, for encumbrance purposes. Thus a clever packer can carry 100 pounds as if it were 90 pounds. Whether successful or not, it takes twice as long to pack carefully as it does to pack normally.

Prerequisites: None.

Cobbling:
[Dexterity/Sophisticated/1 B.P.]

The character with this skill can fashion and repair shoes, boots and sandals. No skill check is necessary to perform this skill, however, the character must have the proper tools and materials.

Prerequisite: None.

Coin Pile Numerical Approximation:
[Intelligence/Sophisticated/2 B.P.s]

A character with this skill can look at a pile of coins and tell how many are there, within 1d10 percent. This is dependent on a skill check. Dwarves, because of their natural racial abilities, get +15 on their skill checks for this approximation. For purposes of this skill, the GM may rule what constitutes a 'pile'. (Of course, clever players will realize that there is no limit to the number of piles they can estimate.)

Prerequisite: None.

Complex Geometric Estimation:
[Intelligence/Sophisticated/2 B.P.s]

This highly technical skill gives a character the ability to look at any construct and accurately estimate the dimensions and details of the object's form. The estimate can apply to anything from a massive pyramid-shaped tomb to a miniscule orb. This can help spell casters and those firing missile weapons figure out the ricochet paths of lobbed items. It can aid thieves in casing potential treasure troves to more accurately plan a burglary. Any character with this skill is also able to play a mean game of pool. If the GM rolls a successful skill check, a character can call on this skill to help him perform a variety of tasks. He can find a place to hide out of the line of sight of roving patrols, shoot a crossbow bolt that will ricochet off of a wall so precisely that he can shoot an opponent in the back or avoid causing collateral damage from Fireballs. Generally, a successful skill check means a +50 bonus on checks related to whatever the character has approximated. It is up to the player to come up with imaginative ways to use this skill. And it is up to the GM to approve these plans.

Prerequisite: None.

Construction: Defense Works:
[(Strength+Dexterity+Wisdom)÷3/Sophisticated/2 B.P.s]

A character with this skill can construct watch towers, walls, drawbridges, moats, barricades and anything designed for the defense of a castle or town. A successful skill check means that the construction is sturdy and will last for decades.

Prerequisite: None.

Construction: Fortifications:
[(Strength+Dexterity+Wisdom)÷3/Sophisticated/2 B.P.s]

A character with this skill is able to construct fortresses and defensive earthen works, as well as walls and castles. Of course, he must have the proper tools, a skill in Construction Tools and help for large projects. A successful skill check means that the character's construction is sturdy and well built. An unsuccessful skill check means that the character's construction is usable, but flawed in some way. It may collapse if under heavy attack.

Prerequisite: None.

Construction: Hasty Defense Works:
[(Strength+Dexterity+Wisdom)÷3/Sophisticated/4 B.P.s]

This skill will enable a character to build barricades under extreme conditions, using whatever material he can find, and when he must work quickly. His construction, although done hastily, will be sturdy and well built. The GM may require a skill check if the situation involve something more than hurried efforts.

Prerequisite: None.

Construction: Siege Works:
[(Strength+Dexterity+Wisdom)÷3/Sophisticated/2 B.P.s]

This skill makes a character an expert in constructing the weapons needed to lay siege to a castle or other fortified structure. These include catapults and trebuchets. A successful skill check (rolled by the GM, of course) means that the weapons constructed function normally. An unsuccessful skill check means the weapons suffer penalties to hit and damage (determined by the GM, usually -1 to -5).

Prerequisite: None.

Cooking:
[Intelligence/Sophisticated/1 B.P.]

Although all characters have rudimentary cooking skills, the character with this skill is an accomplished cook. A skill check is required only when attempting to prepare a truly magnificent meal worthy of a master chef.

Prerequisite: Culinary Arts.

Dig Hasty Grave:
[Strength/Sophisticated/1]

It enables the character to quickly dig a grave for burying a dead body. This is especially useful for assassins. No skill check is needed to perform this task, but some sort of digging tool is necessary. It's okay to hastily bury enemies on the field of battle but hastily burying comrades and loyal NPC hirelings can cause the loss of Honor and possible hauntings until the disrespectful act is remedied.

Prerequisite: None.

Dig Proper Grave:
[Wisdom/Sophisticated/1]

Characters with this skill can give anyone a proper burial. No skill check is normally required, but the character needs appropriate tools.

Prerequisite: None.

Endurance:
[(Wisdom+Constitution)÷2/Sophisticated/4 B.P.s]

Players who wish their characters to have endurance even though they don't have a high Constitution can purchase this skill. People who have endurance are not always those with the best physiques. There are some people who have an inner strength that they draw from in times of crisis, and these are the kind of people that you can't keep down. This skill gives a character that inner reserve, so that they can keep going longer, carry more and fight even when they feel like giving up. They can automatically perform any continually strenuous activity 1 1/2 times as long as without this skill before suffering from fatigue or exhaustion. (Note that this skill does not affect how long the character can go without food or water.) A person with this skill, who makes a successful skill check, gets +10% to his movement rate, and is able to carry 1d10 more pounds without being encumbered. When in battle, he can continue to fight when he's down to -1 hit point, after which he passes out.

Prerequisite: None.

Farming:
[Wisdom/Sophisticated/1 B.P.]

A character with this skill can work a tract of land to produce the most crops, and he can manage a farm as if it were a business, working with livestock, foremen and farm hands. A character with this skill can make a profit of 1d100 gp every year, provided he makes his skill checks each year.

Prerequisite: Agriculture.

Fire-building:
[Wisdom/Sophisticated/1 B.P.]

A character with fire-building skill does not normally need a tinderbox to start a fire. Given some dry wood and small pieces of tinder, he can start a fire in 2d20 minutes. Flint and steel are not required. Wet wood, high winds, or other adverse conditions increase the time to 3d20 minutes, and a successful skill check must be rolled.

Prerequisite: None.

First Aid Skill Suite:
[Intelligence/Sophisticated/5 B.P.s]

A player who buys this skill set can get the cauterize wound skill, the sew own wounds skill and the sew wounds skill all together. See descriptions below for each of these skills. Characters who buy the suite pay one less Building Point, than if they bought each skill separately.

Prerequisite: None.

First Aid: Cauterize Wound:
[Intelligence/Sophisticated/2 B.P.s]

A character with this ability can use a hot poker or other hot metal object to stop the bleeding in a wound, thereby preventing additional bleeding damage. The process does, however, render further damage from the hot poker or piece of metal used to cauterize the wound (1d4 points of damage). The process also leaves a visible, ugly scar. The person with this skill can perform it on himself or to others.

Prerequisite: None.

First Aid: Sew Own Wounds:
[Intelligence/Sophisticated/2 B.P.s]

This skill allows a character to sew his own wounds which promotes faster healing. He must have a needle and thread and all any bleeding wounds must first be cauterized thereby stopping any bleeding damage. Thread can usually

be scrounged in emergencies, usually by tearing garments. A successful skill check must be made to succeed. Successfully sewing one's own wounds allows natural healing to progress at twice the normal rate. (Notice that damage from the sewing needle applies. See Weapons Chart)

Prerequisite: None.

First Aid: Sew Wounds:
[Intelligence/Sophisticated/2 B.P.s]

This skill allows a character to sew the wounds of others. He must have a needle and thread and all any bleeding wounds must first be cauterized thereby stopping any bleeding damage. Thread can usually be scrounged in emergencies, usually by tearing garments. A successful skill check must be made to succeed. Successfully sewing wounds allows natural healing to progress at twice the normal rate. (Notice that damage from the sewing needle applies. See Weapons Chart).

Prerequisite: Sew Own Wounds.

Fishing:
[Wisdom/Sophisticated/1 B.P.]

The character is skilled in the art of fishing, be it with hook and line, net, or spear. Each hour the character spends fishing, roll a skill check. If the roll is failed, no fish are caught that hour. Otherwise, a hook and line or a spear will land fish based on the following table.

Of course, no fish can be caught where no fish are found. On the other hand, some areas teem with fish, such as a river or pool during spawning season. The GM may modify the results according to the situation. For characters without a Fishing Skill there is a 25% base chance of landing 1d2 fish every hour.

Prerequisite: None.

Table G1	
Fishing Table	
1d20 Roll	Result
01	Character has snagged a water-dwelling monster (treat as random encounter).
02-05	1d4 Fish Caught (Edible)
06-10	2d4 Fish Caught (Edible)
11-15	2d4+2 Fish Caught (Edible)
16-17	2d4+3 Fish Caught (Edible)
19	3d4 Fish Caught (Edible)
20+	5d4 Fish Caught (Edible)

Check once per hour ONLY if skill check is successful.
Add +1 for fresh water
Add +1 for temperate waters
A net will catch three times the amounts listed above.

Fondling (Covert Appraisal Technique):
[(Dexterity+Wisdom)÷2/Sophisticated/3 B.P.]

This skill allows a person to appraise any item by touch alone, without having to see the item. It also allows the character to feel a purse and estimate the value of what's inside and how many coins are in it. A successful skill check means the character has correctly estimated the value of any item in question to within 1d10 percent.

Prerequisite: None.

Forage for Food (by Climate):
[Wisdom/Sophisticated/1 B.P.]

A character with this skill is able to find sustenance even in the most dire circumstances. This skill is limited to one particular climate of the player's choice: temperate, tropical, arctic, etc. If the player wants his character to have this skill for more than one climate he must purchase this skill for each climate. To be able to find food, a successful skill check must be made.

Prerequisite: None.

Forgery:
[(Dexterity+Intelligence)÷2/Sophisticated/10 B.P.]

This skill enables the character to create duplicates of documents and handwriting and to detect such forgeries created by others. To forge a document (military orders, local decrees, etc.) where the handwriting is not specific to a person, the character needs only to have seen a similar document before. To forge a name, an autograph of that person is needed, and a skill check with a -10% penalty must be successfully made.

To forge a longer document written in the hand of some particular person, a large sample of his handwriting is needed and a -15% penalty is applied to the check. If the check succeeds, the work will pass examination by all except those intimately familiar with that handwriting or by those with the forgery skill who examine the document carefully. Furthermore, those with the forgery skill may examine a document to learn if it is a forgery. On a successful skill roll, the authenticity of any document can be ascertained.

Prerequisite: None.

Gaming:
[Charisma/Sophisticated/3 B.P.]

The character knows most common games of chance and skill, including cards, dice, bones, draughts, and chess. When playing a game, the character may either play out the actual game (which may take too much time for some) or make a skill check, with success indicating victory. If two characters with gaming skill play each other, the one with the highest successful die roll wins. A character with the gaming skill can also attempt to cheat, thus gaining a +10 bonus to his skill check.

Prerequisite: None.

Gem Cutting:
[Dexterity/Sophisticated/2 B.P.s]

A character with this skill can finish the rough gems that are discovered through mining at a rate of 1d10 stones per day. A gem cutter derives no benefit from the assistance of non-proficient characters. A gem cutter must work with a good light source and must have an assortment of chisels, small hammers, and specially hardened blades. He must also have proficiency with gem-cutting tools.

Uncut gems, while still of value, are not nearly as valuable as the finished product. If the cutting is successful (as determined by a skill check), the gem cutter increases the value of a given stone to the range appropriate for its type. The work may be exceptionally brilliant causing the value of the gem falls into the range for the next most valuable gem (the GM has the relevant tables).

Prerequisite: Appraisal: Gemstone.

Glean Information:
[Charisma/Sophisticated/3 B.P.]

A character with this skill is able to listen to others talking and hone in on important information. He can do this by talking directly to the person he would like to get information from, perhaps even questioning him, or he can listen to conversations being held by other people. He is able to pick up clues from this trained listening that may help him find out such things as where a treasure-laden dungeon is located, critical facts about an adversary, or the weaknesses of a particular fortress or castle. The possibilities are endless. A skill check (rolled by the GM) needs to be made only if the character wishes to find out something specific. He need make no skill check to find out general information.

Prerequisite: None.

Haggle:
[(Charisma+Intelligence÷/2/Academia/2 B.P.s]

Characters with the haggle skill know how to get the best deals. They are well versed in the subtle art of obtaining the best quality items for the least amount of money, and how to sell what they have at the biggest profit.

There are two ways to handle haggling in HackMaster. The fastest way is to simply make a skill check. Using this method, the GM rolls a skill check for the character. If successful, the character with haggling skill will roll his check and pay one-third of said roll as a percentage less per item than others. For example, if he rolls a 6, he will pay 2% percent less. If he succeeds with a 50, he will pay 83.3% of the normal "list" price. He will also be able to find items more easily than others. For example, if the GM says that two-handed swords are at a low availability in some little one-horse town, the character with the haggle skill can consider them to be of medium availability.

When selling items, a character who makes a successful skill check can get between 1d100/2 percent more for any item. Characters who use the seduction skill when haggling get +7% added to their haggle roll.

If, however, a player would rather role-play his haggling attempt he may be able to get even better deals. Characters who wish to role-play haggling should keep in mind that there are strict protocols for haggling on Garweeze Wurld. Sticking to the proper protocol is very important when haggling. If a character breaks protocol, he could offend the person he's haggling with. There are several things a character can do to improve his chances. Showing hard coin often helps seal a deal, convincing the person being haggled with that the character is serious about his offer and has what it takes to back it up. Sometimes the tactic of turning around and walking away can help a character convince the person he's bargaining with that he could lose the sale if he isn't more accommodating. The first impression is often the most important thing about haggling. Refusing to exchange pleasantries and sticking to a no-nonsense business attitude can make a merchant think you're an easy mark. Once you're pegged as an easy mark, it can make all future deals more difficult. Word spreads quickly when there's an easy mark in the neighborhood.

Prerequisite: None.

Healing:
[Wisdom/Sophisticated/2 B.P.s]

A character with the healing skill knows how to use natural medicines and basic principles of first aid and doctoring. If the character tends another within one round of their wounding (and makes a successful skill check), his ministrations restore 1d3 hit points (but no more hit points can be restored than

were lost in the previous round). Only one healing attempt can be made on a particular character per day. If a wounded character remains under the care of someone with healing skill, that character can recover lost hit points at the rate of 1 per day even when traveling or engaging in non-strenuous activity. If the wounded character gets complete rest, he can recover 2 hit points per day while under such care. Characters with both healing and herbalism skills can help others recover at the rate of 3 hit points per day of rest.

This care does not require a skill check, only the regular attention of the skilled character. Up to six patients can be cared for at any time. A character with healing skill can also attempt to aid a poisoned individual, provided the poison entered through a wound. If the poisoned character can be tended to immediately (the round after the character is poisoned) and the care continues for the next five rounds, the victim gains a +2 bonus to his saving throw (delay his saving throw until the last round of tending). No skill check is required, but the poisoned character must be tended to immediately (normally by sacrificing any other actions on the part of the care giver). If the care is interrupted, the poisoned character must immediately roll a normal saving throw for the poison. This result is unalterable by normal means (i.e., more healing doesn't help). Only characters with both healing and herbalism skills can attempt the treatment for poisons the victim has either swallowed or touched (the character uses his healing to diagnose the poison and his herbalist knowledge to prepare a purgative).

A character with the healing skill can also attempt to diagnose and treat diseases. When dealing with normal diseases, a successful skill check automatically reduces the disease to its mildest form and shortest duration. Those who also have herbalism knowledge gain a +10 bonus to this check. A skilled character can also attempt to deal with magical diseases, whether caused by spells or creatures. In this case, a successful skill check diagnoses the cause of the disease. However, since the disease is magical in nature, it can be treated only by magical means.

Prerequisite: First Aid Skill Suite.

Hunting:
[Wisdom/Sophisticated/1 B.P.]

When in wilderness settings, the character can attempt to stalk and bring down game. A skill check must be made with a -5% penalty to the ability score for every non-skilled hunter in the party. If the die roll is successful, the hunter (and those with him) has come within 101 to 200 yards (100+1d100) of his prey. The group can then attempt to close the range, but a skill check must be made for each 20 yards closed. If the stalking is successful, the hunter automatically surprises the game. The type of animal stalked depends on the nature of the terrain and the whim of the GM.

Prerequisite: Identify Animal by Tracks.

Identify Animal by Tracks:
[Wisdom/Sophisticated/1 B.P.]

A character with this skill can tell, when he runs across animal tracks, if they were made by a deer, a horse, a mule with a heavy pack, or a camel with a sore foot. He can precisely identify any normal animal by their footprints. No check is needed for this skill when performing a routine identification. A skill check is needed if the character wants to try to identify precise facts, such as those mentioned above (the fact that the mule's pack is heavy or that the camel's foot is sore, etc.)

Prerequisite: None.

Intelligence Gathering:
[(Intelligence+Wisdom)÷2/Sophisticated/4 B.P.s]

A character with this skill can perform a number of tasks related to gathering information covertly, if a successful skill check is made, of course. This character is able to tail people without being caught. He can listen in on conversations without being noticed. He can sneak into secret places and blend in until he gets what he's after. He can steal documents, and pass them off without being noticed. He can also relay secret messages to comrades. In a word, he can be a spy.

Prerequisite: At least two of the following: Disguise, Stealthy Movement, Tracking, Skilled Liar.

Interrogation:
[Wisdom/Sophisticated/4 B.P.s]

A character with this skill can "convince" uncooperative people to tell them information they don't want to relate. This may involve the use of threats, coercion, seduction or other such methods. A successful skill check is necessary. If the roll is successful, the person tells what the character wants to know, that is, if he actually knows. Only one attempt may be made.

Prerequisite: Glean Information.

Jeweler
[Intelligence/Sophisticated/2 B.P.s]

Characters with this skill know how to appraise, design and work with jewelry. They can create rings, necklaces and other ornamental jewelry. Their work can fetch prices from 50-1,000 gp each, depending on the material used. A successful skill check means that the work is very well done, and worth the expected amount. They can also accurately appraise the value and quality of gems that have been set into jewelry.

Prerequisite: Appraisal: Gemstone, Metalworking, Gemcutting.

Jumping:
[Strength/Sophisticated/1 B.P.]

The character with this skill can attempt exceptional leaps both vertically and horizontally. If the character has at least a 20-foot running start, he can leap (broad jump) 2d6+his level in feet. No character can broad jump more than six times his height, however. With the same start, he can leap vertically (high jump) 1d3 plus half his level in feet. No character can high jump more than one and a half times his own height.

From a standing start, a character with this skill can broad jump 1d6 plus half his level in feet and high jump only three feet.

The character can also attempt vaults using a pole. A vault requires at least a 30-foot running start. If a pole is used, it must be four to 10 feet longer than the character's height, and sufficiently sturdy to support his weight. The vault spans a distance equal to one and a half times the length of the pole. The character can clear heights equal to the height of the pole. He can also choose to land on his feet if the vault carries him over an obstacle no higher than half the height of his pole. Thus, using a 12-foot pole, the character could either vault through a window 12 feet off the ground (tumbling into the room beyond), land on his feet in an opening six feet off the ground, or vault across a moat 18 feet wide. In all cases, the pole is dropped at the end of the vault.

Note: All the distances are reduced if the character is wearing armor. Deduct 10x(base AC bonus of armor worn)% from the figure. For example, a 6th level fighter could theoretically broad jump 8-20 feet. However, if he's wearing banded mail (base AC 4 - six better than no armor) his broad jump is limited to 3.2 - 8 feet. He attempts to jump over a 7 foot trench and rolls a 9 on two die six. His jump is calculated to be [(9+6) - 60% =] 6 feet and falls short.

Prerequisite: None.

Laborer, General:
[(Strength+Wisdom)/2/Sophisticated/1 B.P.]

Persons with this skill are able to meaningfully contribute to some labor-intensive group task such as constructing a castle wall, harvesting a crop or mining ore. They need not be familiar with the task as long as they are supervised by someone who is.

Note: persons WITHOUT this skill cannot add their labor to group tasks (they simply get in the way, ask too many questions and distract those actually doing something useful) although they will THINK that they are actually helping – usually more than anyone else! For example, the party has captured a vessel laden with papayas and brought it into port. They wish to offload their cargo to sell it. The GM rules that it's a forty man-hour job. One party member has taken the seamanship suite and so can act as a supervisor. However, of the four other party members, only one has the laborer, general skill. Consequently, instead of being able to unload the bananas in eight hours (as a group), it ends up taking two full ten-hour days.

Prerequisite: None.

Leatherworking:
[(Strength+Intelligence)÷2/Sophisticated/3 B.P.]

This skill enables a character to tan and treat leather to make clothing and other leather objects. The character can make leather armor, as well as backpacks, saddlebags, saddles, and all sorts of harnesses. No skill check is needed for this skill, but the character must have the proper tools and be skilled with those tools.

Prerequisite: None.

Liar, Skilled:
[(Intelligence+Charisma)÷2/Sophisticated/3 B.P.]

This character is smooth. He can practically talk a dwarf into believing that giving away gold is a good thing. A skilled liar can tell untruths in such a convincing manner that those who don't believe him look like idiots. Of course, this is dependent on a skill check, and a little common sense. No matter how skilled he is, he can't convince people of absurdities, such as the sky is polka dotted or a halfling is as tall as an Ogre. A successful skill check means people believe his "stories".

Prerequisite: None.

Looting, Advanced:
[Wisdom/Sophisticated/4 B.P.]

The advanced looter is so efficient that he actually has time to consider each item and still takes only 1d10 minutes to accomplish the job. Successfully employing this skill means the GM must give the player a list of the most valuable items in the room. The character can add his basic and advanced looting skills together for this roll. Furthermore, the character has a percentage chance (equal to his advanced looting skill alone) to determine what might be fake (a glass gem or an item with magic aura) even as he's stuffing his pack.

Prerequisite: Looting, Basic.

Looting, Basic:
[Wisdom/Sophisticated/2 B.P.]

A character with this skill can loot a town, village, dungeon, etc. and get items of fine quality. If the looter makes a successful skill check, he grabs the most valuable combination of items. He can even find the 'good stuff' if it is hidden: in a hollow table leg, under a loose floorboard, etc. In game terms, the GM must give the player a list of all of the apparently valuable items so the character can choose which to take. Typically a character can loot an area in 2d6 minutes.

Prerequisite: None.

Maintain Self-Discipline:
[Wisdom/Sophisticated/2 B.P.]

A character with this skill is a paragon of self-discipline. He will never go off half-cocked. In stressful situations, he will not react rashly, but will remain calm and able to perform the most rational action. He will also never make alignment violations. If he is on a quest, he will not stop until he has succeeded. If he is in a battle and things are going against him, he will not break and run out of panic, but may retreat if he thinks it is the most sound tactic. All of this, of course, is dependent on whether or not he is successfully when having to make a check against this skill.

When facing a stressful or confusing situation, the player may tell the GM that his character wishes to use this skill, and the GM will roll the skill check. If the roll is successful, the character maintains his composure, and performs the most beneficial action, guided by the GM. As an added bonus, the character receives a +2 bonus to all saves versus charm spells (provided a skill check is successful).

Prerequisite: None.

Map Sense:
[Wisdom/Sophisticated/1 B.P.]

A character with this skill has an innate sense of direction. By concentrating for 1d6 rounds, the character can try to determine the direction the party is headed. Furthermore, when traveling in the wilderness, a character with map sense has the chance of becoming lost reduced by 5%.

Prerequisite: None.

Mapless Travel:
[Wisdom/Sophisticated/3 B.P.]

There are people who always seem to know where they're going as if they had an inner compass. The character with this skill is just such a person. He has an innate sense about which direction is north, south, east, west, etc. He needs no compass. He also can read the stars and use them to navigate by, although he knows nothing about navigating on the seas. He can read signs as well, using such information as the direction a river flows or which side of a tree moss is growing on, in order to get a sense of where he is. A skill check is necessary only in the most difficult of circumstances. This skill is not useable underground.

Prerequisite: None.

Metalworking:
[(Strength+Dexterity+Wisdom)÷3/Sophisticated/2 B.P.]

This skill allows a character to be able to fashion objects out of any metal. This character cannot make armor or weapons, but he can make attractive and useful items such as simple jewlery, brass keys, or lockpicks. A skill check is not needed, but a player should ask his GM whenever he wants to make an item to see if it falls into this category. There are a variety of items that could be made using this skill.

Prerequisite: Blacksmithing.

Mimic Dialect:
[Intelligence/Sophisticated/2 B.P.]

A character with this skill can pass himself off as a member of a community with a different style of speaking than his own, but not a different language. If he is an elf, for example, he can speak in the way of a drow, grey elf, grel, sylvan elf, etc. Of course, this skill works best if the character is either unseen, or is using a disguise skill. No skill check is needed, only common sense. A dwarf who knows the speech and dialect of elves cannot pass himself off as one, unless he has some sort of polymorph ability.

Prerequisite: Language, Modern.

Mining:
[Wisdom/Sophisticated/2 B.P.s]

A character with mining skill is needed to establish and supervise the operations of any mine. First, the character can attempt to determine what type(s) of ore or gems can be found in a given area. To do this, he must spend at least a week searching a four square mile area. The GM may rule that a larger area must be searched to find anything of value and may thus increase the amount of time required. At the end of the search, the character has learned what is likely to be found in this area. After this, the character can establish the mine. On a successful skill check, the character has found a good site to begin mining for any minerals that may be in the area. The check does not guarantee a successful mine, only that a particular site is the best choice in a given area. The GM must determine what minerals, if any, are to be found in the region of the mine.

Once the mine is in operation, a character with mining skill must remain on site to supervise all work. Although this is a steady job, most player characters will find it better to hire an NPC for this purpose. A successful mine can produce quite a hefty income. Dwarves get +15% to skill checks for this skill.

Prerequisite: None.

Mountaineering:
[(Strength+Dexterity+Intelligence)÷3/Sophisticated/1 B.P.]

A character with this skill can make difficult and dangerous climbs up steep slopes and cliffs with the aid of spikes, ropes, etc. If a character with mountaineering skill leads a party, placing the pitons (spikes) and guiding the others, all in the party can gain the benefit of his knowledge. A mountaineer can guide a party up a cliff face it could not otherwise climb. Note that mountaineering is not the same as the thief's climbing ability, since the latter does not require aids of any sort.

Prerequisite: None.

Navigation, Nautical:
[Intelligence/Sophisticated/2 B.P.]

The character knows how to guide ships at sea by using the stars, how to observe currents and how to spot signs of land, reefs and hidden danger. The navigator can reduce the percentage chance of his ship getting lost by 30 percent, provided he makes a successful skill check.

Prerequisite: None.

Orchestrate Task:
[(Intelligence + Charisma)÷2/Sophisticated/3 B.P.]

A character with this skill is able to more easily facilitate the completion of any project with the help of two or more skilled workers. He can direct two or more characters, combining their skills and areas of expertise in order to perform a task that they would not be able to do individually.

Prerequisite: N

Pinch (Pocket/Lift):
[Dexterity/Sophisticated/R]

This variant of the pick pocket skill is restricted to thieves. It involves picking up an item that's just sitting around and slipping into a pocket without being detected. Shoplifting is one example of pinching.

Prerequisite: None.

Pottery:
[Dexterity/Sophisticated/1 B.P.]

A character with this skill can create any type of clay vessel or container commonly used in the campaign world. The character requires a wheel and a kiln, as well as a supply of clay and glaze. The character can generally create two small or medium-sized items or one large-sized item per day. The pieces of pottery must then be fired in the kiln for an additional day.

The raw materials involved cost 3 cp to make a small item, 5 cp to make a medium-sized item, and 1 sp to make a large item. The character need not make a skill check to perform this task.

Prerequisite: None.

Reading Lips:
[Intelligence/Sophisticated/2 B.P.s]

The character can understand the speech of those he can see but not hear. When this skill is chosen, the player must specify what language the character can lip read (it must be a language the character can already speak). To use the skill, the character must be within 30 feet of the speaker and able to see him speak. If the skill check fails, nothing is learned. If the check is successful, 70% of the conversation is understood. Since certain sounds are impossible to differentiate, the understanding of a lip-read conversation is never better than this.

Prerequisite: None.

Reading/Writing:
[Intelligence/Sophisticated/2 B.P.]

The character can read and write a modern language that he can speak. There must be someone available to teach the character (another PC, a hireling or an NPC). This skill does not enable the character to learn ancient languages (see Languages, Ancient/Dead). Nor does it mean that he can write sonnets. This ability gives a character the ability to write well enough to be understood, to write letters and such. A skill check may by required in unusual circumstances, if comprehension is in question: the character is rushed, the document is burned, partial or damaged or the penmanship is horrendous.

Prerequisite: Languages, Modern

Recruit Army:
[Charisma/Sophisticated/2 B.P.]

The character with this skill is able to recruit an army for any purpose. Of course, an army must be paid, so it doesn't depend solely on the character's skill. However, if the pay is good and terms are fair, this character is able to recruit the best soldiers for his army and convince them to swear an oath of loyalty to him. Any army recruited by this character, if he makes his skill check, gets +5% to their morale to reflect their higher level of discipline and sense of obligation.

Prerequisite: None.

Riding, Airborne:
[(Dexterity+Wisdom)÷2/Sophisticated/2 B.P.s]

The character with this skill is trained in handling a flying mount. Each time the skill is taken it applies to one particular type of creature (Griffon, Hippogriff, Pegasus, etc.), which must be chosen when the skill is purchased. Unlike land-based riding, a character must have this skill (or ride with someone who does) to handle a flying mount. In addition, a skilled character can do the following:

-Leap onto the saddle of the creature (when it is standing on the ground) and spur it airborne as a single action. This requires no skill check.

- Leap from the back of the mount and drop 10 feet to the ground or onto the back of another mount (land-based or flying). Those with only light encumbrance can drop to the ground without a skill check. In all other situations, a skill check is required. A character who is dropping to the ground can attempt an immediate melee attack, if his skill check is made with a -20% penalty.

-Spur his mount to greater speeds on a successful check, adding 1d4 to the movement rate of the mount. This speed can be maintained for four consecutive rounds. If the check fails, an attempt can be made again the next round. If two checks fail, no attempt can be made for a full turn. After the rounds of increased speed, the mount's movement drops to 2/3 its normal rate and its Maneuverability Class becomes one class worse. These conditions last until the mount lands and is allowed to rest for at least one hour.

-The rider can guide the mount with his knees and feet, keeping his hands free. A skill check is made only after the character suffers damage. If the check is failed, the character is knocked from the saddle. A second check is allowed to see if the character manages to catch himself (thus hanging from the side by one hand or in some equally perilous position). If this fails, the rider falls. Of course a rider can strap himself into the saddle, although this could be a disadvantage if his mount is slain and plummets toward the ground.

Prerequisite: Riding, Land-Based.

Riding, Land-Based:
[(Dexterity+Wisdom)÷2/Sophisticated/1 B.P.]

Those skilled in land riding are proficient in the art of riding and handling horses or other types of land-based mounts. When the skill is acquired, the character must declare which type of mount he is skilled in. Possibilities include Camels, Unicorns, Dire Wolves or virtually any creatures used as mounts by humans, demi-humans or humanoids.

A character with riding skill can perform all of the following feats. Some of them are automatic, while others require a skill check for success.

-The character can vault onto a saddle whenever the horse or other mount is standing still, even when the character is wearing armor. This does not require a skill check. The character must make a check, however, if he wishes to get the mount moving during the same round in which he lands in its saddle. He must also make a skill check if he attempts to vault onto the saddle of a moving mount. Failure indicates that the character falls to the ground - presumably quite embarrassed.

-The character can urge the mount to jump tall obstacles or leap across gaps. No check is required if the obstacle is less than three feet tall or the gap is less than 12 feet wide. If the character wants to roll a skill check, the mount can be urged to leap obstacles up to five feet high, or jump across gaps up to 20 feet wide. Success means that the mount has made the jump. Failure indicates that it balks, and the character must make another skill check to see whether he retains his seat or falls to the ground.

-The character can spur his steed on to great speeds, adding 6 feet per round to the animal's movement rate for up to four turns. This requires a skill check each turn to see if the mount can be pushed this hard. If the initial check fails, no further attempts may be made, but the mount can move normally. If the second or subsequent check fails, the mount immediately slows to a walk, and the character must dismount and lead the animal for a turn. In any event, after four turns of racing, its dismounted rider must walk the steed for one turn.

-The character can guide his mount with his knees, enabling him to use weapons that require two hands (such as bows and two-handed swords) while mounted. This feat does not require a skill check unless the character takes damage while so riding. In this case, a check is required and failure means that the character falls to the ground and sustains an additional 1d6 points of damage.

-The character can drop down and hang alongside the steed, using it as a shield against attack. The character cannot make an attack or wear armor while performing this feat.

The character's Armor Class is lowered by 6 while this maneuver is performed. Any attacks that would have struck the character's normal Armor Class are considered to have struck the mount instead. No skill check is required.

-The character can leap from the back of his steed to the ground and make a melee attack against any character or creature within 10 feet. The player must roll a successful skill check with a -20% penalty to succeed. On a failed roll, the character fails to land on his feet, falls clumsily to the ground, and suffers 1d3 points of damage.

Prerequisite: None.

Riding, Warhorse (Dwarven):
[(Dexterity+Charisma)÷2/Sophisticated/2 B.P.]

A character with this skill is able to ride a dwarven warhorse at no penalty as long as he makes his skill check. Dwarven warhorses do not let just anyone ride them, and all who try without having the benefit of this skill will get -3" to their movement rate (or worse). There is an 80% chance the warhorse will buck off and attack anyone who tries to ride them without this skill. These beasts are rare, since most dwarves hate to ride horses. This skill allows a character to find such a horse on a successful skill check. A skill check must be made at the first meeting with the warhorse. A successful check means the horse has accepted him. An unsuccessful check means the horse requires some coaxing, usually in the form of bribery with food. Note: coaxing in the form of threats or abuse will only cause the animal to become hostile.

Once the character and the warhorse have bonded, no skill check needs to be made in order for the character to be able to ride the beast in normal conditions. A skill check is only needed when the character wants to perform a complicated stunt. Below are some of the stunts possible when a character has a dwarven warhorse for a mount. Some require skill checks, others do not.

The character can vault onto a saddle whenever the horse is standing still, even when the character is wearing armor. This does not require a skill check. The character must make a check, however, if he wishes to get the mount moving during the same round in which he lands in its saddle. He must also make a skill check if he attempts to vault onto the saddle of a moving mount. Failure indicates that the character falls to the ground - presumably quite embarrassed. By the way, because of the nature of dwarven warhorses, skill checks to perform the above stunt are made at -5%.

-The character's mount will fight alongside him, with no skill check required. Dwarven warhorses are naturally cantankerous and look for opportunities to display this attitude.

-The character can spur his steed on to great speeds, adding 6 feet per round to the animal's movement rate for up to four turns. This requires a skill check each turn to see if the mount can be pushed this hard. If the initial check fails, no further attempts may be made, but the dwarven warhorse can move nor-

mally. If the second or subsequent check fails, the mount immediately slows to a walk, and the character must dismount and lead the animal for a turn. In any event, after four turns of racing, its dismounted rider must walk the steed for one turn.

-The character can guide his mount with his knees, enabling him to use weapons that require two hands (such as bows and two-handed swords) while mounted. This feat does not require a skill check unless the character takes damage while so riding. In this case, a check is required and failure means that the character falls to the ground and sustains an additional 1d6 points of damage.

-The character can drop down and hang alongside the steed, using it as a shield against attack. The character cannot make an attack or wear armor while performing this feat.

The character's Armor Class is lowered by 6 while this maneuver is performed. Any attacks that would have struck the character's normal Armor Class are considered to have struck the mount instead. No skill check is required. If this stunt is successful however, and the mount survives the attack, he will refuse to let the character ride him again.

-The character can leap from the back of his steed to the ground and make a melee attack against any character or creature within 10 feet. The player must roll a successful skill check with a -20% penalty to succeed. On a failed roll, the character fails to land on his feet, falls clumsily to the ground, and suffers 1d3 points of damage.

-The character can ride his warhorse into any structure where the animal will fit. The beast is able to travel underground with no fear whatsoever. No skill check is needed here.

-The character can pack his animal with 1d100 pounds more equipment and other items than he could pack on the back of a regular horse, without suffering an encumbrance penalty. Dwarven warhorses are known for their strong backs.

Prerequisite: None.

Rope Use:
[Dexterity/Sophisticated/1 B.P.]

This character can accomplish amazing feats with rope. He is able to tie all manner of knots, including the single Blackwall hitch, single bowknot, sheep shank, bowline, single carrick bend, figure-eight knot, etc. He can tie knots that slip, hold tightly, slide slowly or loosen with a quick tug. These can be used in all manner of circumstances, from lashing down rigging on a ship to making sure a captured enemy can't get free. If the character's hands are bound with a knot, he can roll a skill check (with a -30 penalty) to escape the bonds.

A character with rope use gains a +2 to-hit bonus to all attacks made with a lasso. He also receives a +10 bonus to all climbing checks made while he is using a rope, including attempts to belay (secure the end of a climbing rope to) companions.

Prerequisite: None.

Running:
[Constitution/Sophisticated/1 B.P.]

The character with this skill can move at twice his normal movement rate for a day. At the end of the day he must sleep for eight hours. After the first day's movement, the character must roll a skill check for success. If the die roll succeeds, the character can continue his running movement the next day. If the die roll fails, the character cannot use his running ability the next day. If involved in a battle during a day he spent running, he suffers a -1 penalty to all his attack rolls.

Prerequisite: None.

Seamanship Suite:
[Dexterity/Sophisticated/5 B.P.]

The character with this skill is familiar with boats and ships. He is qualified to work as a crewman, although he cannot actually navigate. Crews of trained seamen are necessary to manage any ship, and they improve the movement rates of inland boats by 50 percent.

Prerequisite: None.

Seamstress/Tailor:
[Dexterity/Sophisticated/2 B.P.]

The character with this skill can sew, mend and design clothing. He can also do all kinds of embroidery and ornamental work. Although no skill check is required, the character must have at least a needle and thread to work, as well as some cloth.

Prerequisite: None.

Seduction, Art of:
[(Comeliness+Charisma)÷2/Sophisticated/1 B.P.]

A character with this skill can seduce members of the opposite sex in order to curry favor or get help from them in some way. For instance, a female character might try her seduction skill on a guard at the gate in order to get him to let her and her companions inside. Seduction can work in many ways. It can act either as a distraction, allowing other characters to perform actions without being noticed, or as an attempt to sway the will of a person. A skill check can be made on any encounter with a member of the opposite sex, and if it is successful, the character advances one step higher on the reaction table. Most of the time, a skill check doesn't need to be made, as long as what is being attempted is reasonable. A character cannot talk a guard into killing himself, of course, no matter how sexy she is. By the same token, seduction is more difficult, if not impossible, to use on members of hostile races or on members of cultures with differing standards of beauty. For instance, a human male, no matter how handsome and charming, would probably not be considered good looking to a female Ogre. A skill check can still be made in such instances, but it is at -10.

Prerequisite: None.

Set Snares:
[Dexterity/Sophisticated/1 B.P.]

The character can make simple snares and traps, primarily to catch small game. These can include rope snares and spring traps. A skill check must be rolled when the snare is first constructed and every time the snare is set. The character can also attempt to set traps and snares for larger creatures: tiger pits and net snares, for example. A skill check must be rolled, this time with a -20 penalty. In both cases, setting a successful snare does not ensure that it catches anything, only that the snare works if triggered. The GM must decide if the trap is triggered.

Thief characters (and only thieves) with this skill can also attempt to rig man-traps. These can involve such things as crossbows, deadfalls, spiked springboards, etc. The procedure is the same as that for setting a large snare. The GM must determine the amount of damage caused by a man-trap.

Setting a small snare or trap takes one hour of work. Setting a larger trap requires two to three people (only one need have the skill) and 2d4 hours of work. Setting a man-trap requires one or more people (depending on its nature) and 1d8 hours of work.

To prepare any trap, the character must have appropriate materials on hand. Characters with the animal lore skill gain a +10 bonus when attempting to set a snare for the purposes of catching game. Their knowledge of animals and the woods serves them well for this purpose. They gain no benefit when attempting to trap monsters or intelligent beings.

Prerequisite: None.

Shield Repair (Metal):
[(Intelligence+Dexterity)÷2/Sophisticated Task/3 B.P.]

A person with this skill can make minor repairs and replace lost armor points to shields made of metal. It takes two uninterrupted turns to complete a minor repair (1-2 armor points) such as repairing a small dent, tightening a loose rivet or two, or patching a minor hole. It takes at least four uninterrupted turns to complete a medium-sized repair (3 -5 points) such as replacing a handful of rivets or repairing a large dent. It takes eight uninterrupted turns to complete major repairs (6 to 10 points) such as patching many large holes and dents or reattaching major parts. A character with this skill can fix 1d4 armor hit points per skill check. A failed skill check indicates he can no longer make repairs on that particular shield. Each skill check requires 2d20 gp in materials.

Prerequisite: Leather Working, Metal Working, BlackSmith Tools.

Shield Repair (Wood):
[(Intelligence+Dexterity)÷2/Sophisticated Task/3 B.P.]

This skill is exactly like Shield Repair, Metal but only works with shields made of wood with simple metal or leather bindings. Each skill check requires the 1d20 gp in materials.

Prerequisite: Leather Working, Wood Working (Carpenter Skill).

Skinning:
[(Strength+Wisdom)÷2/Sophisticated Task/1 B.P.]

A character with this skill knows the proper procedure for obtaining the hide from a dead animal or beast. He knows what skills to use, how to treat and store the hide, and which part of the hides are the most valuable or usable. He can also estimate the amount of hide needed for various items such as boots, gloves, cloaks, etc. The character must have a sharp knife and an animal to skin in order to get the hide. Treating the hide takes more tools.

Prerequisite: None.

Slaughter: Game Animal:
[(Strength+Wisdom)÷2/Sophisticated/1 B.P.]

A character with this skill knows the proper procedure to slaughter game animals, and to cut up the carcass so as to provide the most meat. He knows how to trim away the fat, if desired, and get rid of everything that is inedible. He must have a sharp knife and a game animal in order to perform this skill. The formula for determining the yield of edible flesh when slaughtering livestock is: Hit points/10xSize= pounds of edible flesh.

Where Size is as follows;

Tiny = .25, Small = 2, Medium=4, Large = 6 and Huge = 10, Giant = 25.

The size of individual game animals is listed in the Hacklopedia of Beasts, which is available only to a GM. Characters with the slaughter, game animal skill are able to increase the yield of edible meat by 25% if they make a successful skill check. They can carve the choicest cuts, trim away the fat and get rid of any inedible portions

Prerequisite: None.

Slaughter, Livestock:
[(Strength+Wisdom)÷2/Sophisticated/1 B.P.]

A character with this skill is an expert on slaughtering and butchering farm animals. The formula for determining the yield of edible flesh when slaughtering livestock is: Hit points/10xSize= pounds of edible flesh.

Where Size is as follows:

Tiny = .25, Small = 2, Medium=4, Large = 6 and Huge = 10, Giant = 25.

The size of individual livestock is listed in the Hacklopedia of Beasts, which is available only to a GM. Characters with slaughter, livestock skill can increase the yield by 50% if they make a successful skill check. He can carve the choicest cuts, trim away the fat and get rid of any inedible portions. He must have the proper tools, the exact nature of which depends on the animal to be butchered. Large livestock such as cattle require the availability of a large hammer, or similar large tool, and a sharp knife. Smaller animals, such as chickens, require only a sharp knife.

Prerequisite: None.

Slip Away into the Shadows:
[Dexterity/Sophisticated/1 B.P.]

This character is able to slip away quietly, unnoticed, in most situations. He can meld into crowds as well, without being seen. However, he cannot perform this skill if his feet are bound or he is incarcerated. A skill check is necessary to successfully perform this skill. A successful skill check means the character is able to use the cover around him (shadows, stacks of boxes, a crowd, etc.) to slip away unseen. A character in metal armor gets -10% to his skill check.

Prerequisite: None.

Stealthy Movement:
[Dexterity/Sophisticated/4 B.P.]

A character with this skill can successfully follow another person while remaining unseen and unnoticed. He can also sneak into buildings, boats or any other structure unbeknownst to the occupants. A skill check must be rolled for the character to be successful. A character in metal armor gets -10% to his skill check.

Prerequisite: Slip Away into the Shadows.

Stonemasonry:
[(Strength+Intelligence)÷/Sophisticated/1 B.P.]

A stonemason is able to build structures from stone so that they last many years. The stone can be mortared, carefully fitted without mortar, or loosely fitted and chinked with rocks and earth. A stonemason equipped with his tools (hammers, chisels, wedges, block and tackle) can build a plain section of wall one foot thick, ten feet long, and five feet high in one day, provided the stone has already been cut. A stonemason can also supervise the work of unskilled laborers to quarry stone. One stonemason is needed for every five laborers. Dwarves are among the most accomplished stonemasons in the world, they receive a +10% bonus when using this skill. No skill check is needed for this skill, but the character must have the proper tools available, and a proficiency in using those tools. A stonemason can also create simple stone carvings, such as lettering, columns, and flourishes.

Prerequisite: None.

Survival Skill Suite:
[(Intelligence+Constitution+Wisdom)÷3/Sophisticated/10 B.P.s]

This skill suite includes survival skills for arctic, desert and jungle climates as well as underground. A player who purchases this suite for his character gives his character a good chance to survive, if lost, in any of these environments. He knows the hazards he might face in each and understands the effects of the weather. He knows the proper steps to lessen the risk of exposure and the methods to locate and gather potable water and how to find basic food (whether it's appetizing is not guaranteed). Furthermore, a character with survival skill can instruct and aid others in the same situation. When using this skill to find food or water, the character must roll a skill check. If the check fails, no more attempts can be made that day.

The survival skill in no way releases the player characters from the hardships and horrors of being lost in the wilderness. At best, it alleviates a small portion of the suffering. The food found is barely adequate and water is discovered in miniscule amounts. It is still quite possible for a character with survival knowledge to die in the wilderness. Indeed, the little knowledge the character has may lead to overconfidence and doom! Descriptions of the various climates follow for those who don't wish to purchase the entire suite.

Prerequisite: None.

Survival, Desert:
[(Intelligence+Constitution+Wisdom)÷3/Sophisticated/3 B.P.s]

This skill allows a character to have a better than average chance to survive when lost in the desert. He can find water, although in miniscule amounts. He can find food, although the food may be less than tasty. He knows to travel in the cool of the evening and where to seek shelter during the full heat of the day (or how to construct said if not naturally available). A skill check must be rolled in order for the character to find food, water or shelter. If the check fails, no more attempts can be made that day. He can also teach and aid his comrades, or others, in the same situation.

As stated above in the description of the survival skill suite, this skill does not release the character from suffering during his ordeal. It is still possible for a character with this skill to die in the desert. However, this skill will lessen the chances, provided the character doesn't get too cocky.

Prerequisite: None.

Survival, Jungle:
[(Intelligence+Constitution+Wisdom)÷3/Sophisticated/2 B.P.s]

This skill allows characters to have a better than average chance to survive when lost in the jungle. The character with this skill should be able to find potable water and edible (if not necessarily appetizing) food. He knows what dangers he might face in the form of wildlife or insects and he can usually find or construct shelter. He can help others with him do the same. He must successfully make a skill check rolled to find food, water and shelter. An unsuccessful check means that he was unable to find what he was looking for. No more attempts can be made that day.

Characters with this skill can still die in the jungle, and they still suffer the effects of their ordeal, even if they do survive.

Prerequisite: None.

Survival, Underground:
[(Intelligence+Constitution+Wisdom)÷3/Sophisticated/3 B.P.s]

A character with this skill has a good chance of surviving when lost underground. He is able to find pockets of air, as well as food and water. However, a successful skill check must be rolled. If the check fails, the character has been unable to find what he needs that day, and no other skill checks can be made until the next day. This character can teach and aid others in the same situation.

As stated before, this skill does not guarantee survival. It simply gives the character the knowledge, and the chance of surviving in conditions that would be sure to kill the unskilled.

Prerequisite: None.

Survival, Arctic:
[(Intelligence+Constitution+Wisdom)÷3/Sophisticated/3 B.P.s]

This skill gives a character a better than average chance of surviving in wintery conditions. This character should be able to find food, warmth and shelter in this environment. A skill check must be rolled (by the GM) in order for the character to be able to find food, shelter and warmth. If it fails, the necessary item cannot be found, and no other skill check can be made that day. This character can help others in the same situation.

This skill, as with the other survival skills, does not guarantee the character's survival in this harsh environment. He will also still suffer from some of the effects of his ordeal, including a 60% chance of frostbite, even if warmth and shelter are found. The chance for frostbite goes up to 80% without shelter. If more than three days go by with no success in finding warmth or shelter, the character is guaranteed to suffer frostbite damage. Water is not a problem if there is plenty of snow around, although the character knows to boil the water to prevent hypothermia. The character suffers all of the effects of the deprivation involved in such an ordeal.

Prerequisite: None.

Swimming:
[(Strength+Dexterity+Constitution)÷3/Sophisticated/3 B.P.]

A character with swimming skill knows how to swim. He can move according to the rules given in the Swimming section (Chapter 16: Time and Movement). Those without this skill cannot swim. They can hold their breath and float, but they cannot intentionally move about in the water.
Prerequisite: Swimming, Dog Paddle.

Swimming Dog Paddle:
[(Strength + Constitution)÷2/Sophisticated/1 B.P.]

A character with this skill can dog paddle and move according to the rules given in the Swimming section of Chapter 16.

Prerequisite: None

Tightrope Walking:
[Dexterity/Sophisticated/1 B.P.]

The character with this skill can attempt to walk across narrow ropes or beams with greater than normal chances of success. He can negotiate any narrow surface not angled up or down greater than 45 degrees. Each round the character can walk 60 feet, if encumbered. One skill check is made every 60 feet (or part thereof), with failure indicating a fall.

The check is made with a -50% penalty to the ability score if the surface is one inch or less in width (a rope), a -25% penalty if two inches to six inches wide, and unmodified if seven inches to 12 inches wide. Wider than one foot requires no check for the skilled characters under normal circumstances. Every additional Building Point spent on tightrope walking reduces these penalties by 5%. Use of a balancing rod reduces the penalties by 10%. Winds or vibrations in the line increase the penalties by 10 to 30%.

The character can attempt to fight while on a tightrope, but he suffers a -1 penalty to his attack roll and must roll a successful skill check at the beginning of each round to avoid falling off. Since the character cannot maneuver, he gains no adjustments to his Armor Class for Dexterity. If he is struck while on the rope, he must roll an immediate skill check to retain his balance.

Prerequisite: None.

Torture:
[(Strength+Intelligence)÷2/Sophisticated/3 B.P.]

A character with this skill has the ability to cause pain and to make that pain last. Torture is usually conducted to retrieve information, though there may be other reasons for the use of such force. A character with this skill knows where and how to hurt a person so that they feel tremendous pain, but do not die. A skilled torturer can bring his victim down to within 2 hit points of death and then revive him for bout. No skill check is needed unless the tormentor wishes to learn some specific information. In such a case, the character must make a successful skill check in order for him to learn anything the victim knows. Keep in mind that the victim may not know what the character wants to know. No tools are necessary to perform this skill, but they can be used. Note that good-aligned characters are not normally allowed to purchase this skill, as even knowing how to use it violates their alignment. However, the GM may be persuaded in special circumstances to allow it. A knight errant might be successful in presenting such an argument.

Prerequisite: None.

Tracking Game:
[Wisdom/Type/1 B.P.]

A character with this skill can follow the trail of any game animal in order to hunt it for food. No skill check is needed unless the character is tracking the game across a river, shifting sand or shifting snow. In the latter cases, the character must make a skill check at -10. If the check is successful, the character is able to track the game in spite of the obstacles. Otherwise, the trail is lost.

Prerequisite: Identify Animal by Tracks.

Tracking:
[Wisdom/Sophisticated/2 B.P.s]

Characters with tracking skill are able to follow the trail of creatures and characters across most types of terrain. Characters who are not rangers must roll skill checks with a -30 penalty to their ability scores; rangers suffer no such penalty. In addition, other modifiers are also applied to the attempt, according to Table G2.

The modifiers in Table G2 are cumulative - total the modifiers for all conditions that apply and combine that with the tracker's level of mastery to get the modified chance to track.

For example, if Renorian's tracking mastery is 80 and he is trying to track through mud (+20%), at night (-30%), during a sleet storm (-25%), his net adjusment is -35%. (Being a ranger, Renorian does not suffer the -30% penalty for non-rangers tracking.)

For tracking to succeed, the creature tracked must leave some type of trail. Thus, it is virtually impossible to track flying or non-corporeal creatures. The GM may allow this in rare instances, but he should also assign substantial penalties to the attempt.

To track a creature, the character must first find the trail. Indoors, the tracker must have seen the creature in the last 30 minutes and must begin tracking from the place last seen. Outdoors, the tracker must either have seen the creature, have eyewitness reports of its recent movement ("They went thaddaway!") or must have obvious evidence that the creature is in the area (such as a well-used game trail). If these conditions are met, a skill check is rolled. Success means a trail has been found. Failure means no trail has been found. Another attempt cannot be made until the above conditions are met again under different circumstances.

Once the trail is found, additional skill checks are rolled for the following situations:

-The chance to track decreases (terrain, rain, creatures leaving the group, darkness, etc.).

-A second track crosses the first.

Table G2
Tracking Modifiers

Terrain	Modifier
Soft or muddy ground	+20%
Thick brush, vines, or reeds	+15%
Occasional signs of passage, dust	+10%
Normal ground, wood floor	0
Rocky ground or shallow water	-50%
Every two creatures in the group	+5%
Every 12 hours since trail was made	-5%
Every hour of rain, snow, or sleet	-25%
Poor lighting (moon or starlight)	-30%
Tracked party attempts to hide trail	-25%

Table G3
Movement While Tracking

Chance to Track	Movement Rate
Up to 30%	1/4 normal
Up to 70%	1/2 normal
71% or greater	3/4 normal

-The party resumes tracking after a halt (to rest, eat, fight, etc.).

Once the tracker fails a skill check, another check can be rolled after spending at least one hour searching the area for new signs. If this check is failed, no further attempts can be made. If multiple trackers are following a trail, a +5% bonus is added to the check which is made by the most adept tracker. Once he loses the trail, it is lost to all.

If the modifiers lower the chance to track below 0, the trail is totally lost to that character and further tracking is impossible (even if the chance later improves). Other characters may be able to continue tracking, but that character cannot.

A tracking character can also attempt to identify the type of creatures being followed and the approximate number by rolling a skill check. All the normal tracking modifiers apply. One identifying check can be rolled each time a check is rolled to follow the trail. A successful check identifies the creatures (provided the character has some knowledge of that type of creature) and gives a rough estimate of their numbers. Just how accurate this estimate is depends on the GM.

When following a trail, the tracking character (and those with him) must slow down, their speed depending on the character's modified chance to track as found from Table G3.

In the earlier example, Renorian has a modified tracking chance of 45, so he moves at half his normal movement rate.

Prerequisite: None.

Trap Sweep, Full Sweep:
[(Dexterity+Wisdom)÷2/Sophisticated/R]

This skill involves more than the typical check for traps. It is a big picture check, with a wider area than a simple trap check. When performing this task, the skilled thief checks every area of a room (approximately 20' x 20') quickly but carefully in just 2d12 rounds. The GM rolls a skill check for each area of the room and/or item that is checked. If the check is successful, the character has accurately determined whether there is a trap in that area or item. A character can perform this task as many times as he wants, and need not be able to touch the area in question.

Prerequisite: None.

Tumbling:
[Dexterity/Sophisticated/2 B.P.]

The character is practiced in all manner of acrobatics - dives, rolls, somersaults, handstands, flips, etc. Tumbling can only be performed while lighty encumbranced or less. Aside from being entertaining, the character with a tumbling skill can improve his Armor Class by 4 against attacks directed solely at him in any round of combat, provided he has the initiative and foregoes all attacks that round.

Additionally, on a successful skill check, he suffers only one-half the normal damage from falls of 60 feet or less and none falls of 10 feet or less. Falls from greater heights result in normal damage.

Prerequisite: None.

Vandalism/Desecration:
[Dexterity/Sophisticated/2 B.P.]

The character with this skill wreaks havoc on property. He can desecrate enemy temples, lay waste to a town or destroy the grave of a defeated nemesis. There are a variety of uses for this skill. It is most commonly used to take Honor from an individual enemy. Any enemy who has personal property desecrated by a character with this skill loses 1d8 Honor points, depending on the type of vandalism performed. Use of excrement or other foul substances adds a +2 modifier to the die roll for Honor taking. No skill check is necessary for this skill.

Prerequisite: None.

Ventriloquism:
[Intelligence/Sophisticated/3 B.P.]

The character with this skill has learned the secrets of "throwing his voice". Although not actually making sound come from somewhere else (like the Throw Voice spell), the character can deceive others into believing this to be so. When using ventriloquism, the supposed source of the sound must be relatively close to the character. The nature of the speaking object and the intelligence of those watching can modify the character's chance of success. If the character makes an obviously inanimate object talk (a book, mug, etc.), a -25 penalty is applied to his check. If a believable source (a PC or NPC) is made to appear to speak, a +10 bonus is added to his check. The observer's intelligence modifies this as shown in Table G4.

Table G4	
Ventriloquism Modifiers	
Target's Intelligence	Modifier
less than 3	+30%
3-5	+20%
6-8	+10%
9-14	0
15-16	-5%
17-18	-10%
19+	-20%

A successful skill check means the character has successfully deceived his audience. One check must be made for every sentence or response. The character is limited to sounds he could normally make (thus, the roar of a lion is somewhat beyond him). He is also limited to speaking only languages he knows.

Since ventriloquism relies on deception, people's knowledge of speech, and assumptions about what should and shouldn't talk, it is effective only on intelligent creatures. Thus, it has no effect on animals and the like. Furthermore, the audience must be watching the character since part of the deception is visual ("Hey, his lips don't move!"). Using ventriloquism to get someone to look behind him does not work, since the voice is not actually behind him (this requires the Throw Voice spell). All but those with the gullibility of children or the extremely dense realize what is truly happening. They may be amused - or they may not be.

Prerequisite: None.

Weaponsmithing:
[(Dexterity+Intelligence)÷2/Sophisticated/4 B.P.s]

This highly specialized skill enables a character to perform the difficult and highly exacting work involved in making metal weapons, particularly those with blades. The character blends some of the skill of the blacksmith with an ability to create strong, sharp blades. A fully equipped smithy is necessary to use this skill. The time and cost to make various types of weapons are listed on Table G5. Use the table as a guideline for similar weapons

A character must be skilled in using the proper tools for this task. A skill mastery check must be made upon the completion of each weapon. Failure may not be immediately obvious.

Prerequisite: Metalworking or Blacksmithing.

Table G5		
Weapon Construction		
Weapon	Construction Time	Material Cost
Arrowhead	10/day	1 c.p.
Battle Axe	10 days	10 s.p.
Hand Axe	5 days	5 s.p.
Dagger	5 days	2 s.p.
H. Crossbow	20 days	10 s.p.
L. Crossbow	15 days	5 s.p.
Fork, Trident	20 days	10 s.p.
Spear, Lance	4 days	4 s.p.
Short Sword	20 days	5 s.p.
Long Sword	30 days	10 s.p.
2-hd Sword	45 days	2 g.p.

Weaving:
[(Dexterity+Intelligence)÷2/Sophisticated/2 B.P.]

A character with a weaving skill is able to create garments, tapestries, and draperies from wool or cotton. The character requires a spinning apparatus and a loom. A weaver can create two square yards of material per day.

Prerequisite: None.

SOCIAL INTERACTION SKILLS

Berate:
[Wisdom/Social Interaction/1 B.P.]

A character with this skill can make even a giant feel 2 feet tall when he's done with him. This skill may used to keep unruly henchmen and hirelings in line as well as to rob a person of 2 Honor points. No skill check is needed to perform this task on one's own henchmen and hirelings. If the berating character's Honor is equal to or higher than the target's Honor, a check is necessary. Failure simply means the target loses no Honor. If the target's Honor is higher than the berating characters Honor by 10 or fewer points, a failed check means the target loses no Honor and the berater loses 2 Honor points. If the target's Honor is 11 points or more higher than the berater's, a failed check results in the loss of 4 Honor points.

Prerequisite: None.

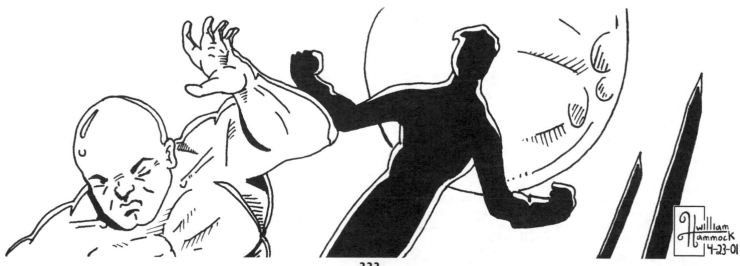

Calling Dibs:
[Wisdom/Social Interaction/3 B.P.]

Characters with this skill have an advantage when calling dibs for treasure. In accordance with the Dibs Protocol in Chapter 8, whenever there is a dispute over who gets what, a roll-off takes place. A character with this skill at 50% or less who makes a successful skill check also gets +1 on his roll-off score. If he is successful with his skill check and has the dibs protocol skill at 51% or more, he gets +2 to his roll-off score.

Prerequisite: None.

Diplomacy:
[Charisma/Social Interaction/2 B.P.s]

A character with this skill is able to negotiate treaties, conduct relations between political entities, nations and/or races, and establish trade between such groups. He is able to deal effectively with people. He knows when to compromise and when to take a hard line in order to get what he wants. A skill check is required, of course, whenever a character wants to establish diplomatic relations with any person or group. A successful roll means the person being negotiated with reacts favorably to the character and his offer. A skill check is also required every year after relations have been established. A successful check means that relations are still favorable.

Prerequisite: None.

Feign Toughness:
[Charisma/Social Interaction/2 B.P.]

A character with this skill knows how to put on his game face. He can use this skill to intimidate others. It works well in conjunction with other skills, such as flex muscles and interrogation. A person with the feign toughness will appear to be 1d4 levels of higher experience than he actually is.

Prerequisite: None.

Flex Muscle:
[Strength/Social Interaction/2 B.P.]

A character with this skill is able to flex his muscles to make himself appear to be 1d4 points stronger than he really is. It is used to intimidate others by exaggerating the apparent strength of a character.

Prerequisite: None.

Graceful Entrance/Exit:
[Charisma/Social Interaction/1 B.P.]

A character with this skill knows how to make an entrance. He can better any initial reaction by one when he encounters a person or group of people. He also knows how to leave a room so that people will talk about him afterwards. He leaves an impression in most social situations. When this skill is successful, the characer recieves +5 to his Honor in that social situation. As soon as he leaves the room his Honor drops back to normal. This is useful when in social gatherings and the Honor pecking order is being established.

Prerequisite: None.

Idle Gossip:
[Charisma/Social Interaction/1 B.P.]

A person with this skill can spread rumors about another person and have those rumors be believed. A character can use this skill to ruin the reputation of someone, thereby lowering that person's Honor by 1d6 points. A skill check is required. If it is successful, the rumors he spreads are believed and passed on down the line.

Prerequisite: None.

Intimidation:
[Wisdom/Social Interaction/2 B.P.]

Characters with this skill can cause others to back down in a contest of wills. He can make others afraid to fight him or use his skill to help in interrogation. No skill check is needed unless the character wants to use intimidation in conjunction with the interrogation skill. If the skill check is successful, the character can force an Honor Check between himself and his intended target with a +10% modifier. If unsuccessful, no bonus is added.

Prerequisite: Feign Toughness.

Joke Telling:
[(Intelligence+Charisma)÷2/Social Interaction/1 B.P.]

A character with this skill is the life of the party. He can tell a good joke that can help him get a good reaction on initial encounters. He can entertain others. The GM rolls a skill check whenever a character wants to tell a joke. A successful skill check means the joke is very funny and everyone laughs. Sometimes, a character may want to use a joke to insult someone, causing that person to lose 1d4 points of Honor if they fail an honor check between themselves and the joke teller.

Prerequisite: None.

Knowledge of Courtly Affairs:
[Wisdom/Social Interaction/2 B.P.s]

This skill allows a character to know the inner workings of local royalty and nobility. He also knows how to behave among such company so that he fits in well and is accepted by these people. He can move about freely in these circles, an ability which may make him privy to certain information that few others have. How he uses such information is up to the character. No skill check is necessary when the character simply wants to fit in among the elite. One is required if he attempts to glean information. A successful check means that someone in the know has taken the character into his confidence.

Success in this skill also depends on how the character behaves and dresses. No one of any stature in a government or kingdom will accept a scruffy-looking or rude person into his inner circle.

Prerequisite: None.

Mingling (Balls, Parties):
[Charisma/Social Interaction/2 B.P.]

A character with this skill is able to use balls and parties to make beneficial connections with powerful people. He is able to strike up conversations with desirable people not only to court their favor, but often to gather useful tidbits of information. A successful skill check need only be made if the character attempts to gain a favor from someone. If the check is successful, the person agrees to grant the character a favor.

Prerequisite: None.

Oration:
[(Intelligence+Charisma)÷2/Social Interaction/1 B.P.]

A character with this skill is a powerful speaker with the ability to hold the attention of a crowd and sway public opinion. A skill check is required. If it succeeds, the character is able to convince a crowd to do something he wants them to do.

Prerequisite: Rousing speech.

Parley:
[Charisma/Social Interaction/4 B.P.]

A character with this skill can use his conversational skills to smooth over potentially difficult or contentious encounters in order to avoid bloodshed. A character with this skill, who makes a successful skill check (rolled by the GM), causes those he encounters to react to him one step more favorably than they normally would.

Prerequisite: None.

Poker Face:
[Wisdom/Social Interaction/3 B.P.]

A character with this skill is able to mask his emotions. This is especially helpful in playing games of chance. Provided he makes a successful skill check, the character can add a +5% bonus to any skill checks related to gaming. This skill can be used in other ways, such as when being interrogated or tortured, when attempting to bluff an opponent in combat or when trying to intimidate someone. The uses of this skill are varied. Skill checks are not needed except when using the skill to bluff in games of chance. A successful roll means the character gets his bonus.

Prerequisite: None.

Resist Persuasion:
[Wisdom/Social Interaction/1 B.P.]

This skill could be considered somewhat the opposite of poker face; it makes a character less susceptible to the orations, parleying or other persuasive efforts of others. Any time such persuasion would alter the character's attitude, he can make a resist persuasion check. If successful, he is immune to forcible attitude changes.

The above only applies to non-magical efforts. If magic is involved, as with a Charm Person spell, the character gets a +2 bonus to his saving throw provided he makes a successful resist persuasion check.

Prerequisites: None.

Rousing Speech:
[Charisma/Social Interaction/3 B.P.]

This skill gives a character the ability to affect morale in a positive way. For instance, if the character's hirelings or henchmen are getting discouraged, he could give a speech so inspiring that they'd walk over their own mothers to help the character. This can also be used in battle to reinvigorate the morale of beleaguered troops, effectively rallying them. A skill check is necessary. If successful, the character gets +5% to his loyalty modifiers for his workers or he is able to rally his troops. There may be other circumstances where the player thinks he can use this skill to help his character and his party, and most need no skill check. However, if the intent of the speech is something unusual or very difficult the GM may require a skill check.

Prerequisite: None.

Rules of Fair Play:
[Wisdom/Social Interaction/1 B.P.]

A character with this skill knows the proper ways to do just about anything, from playing a game to waging war, and he sticks to those rules. Such a character is known for his Honor, and as such gets 2 points of Honor every time he engages in any activity where fair play can be used - provided his skill check is successful.

Prerequisite: None.

Secret Persona:
[Wisdom/Social Interaction/2 B.P.s]

A person with this skill can pass himself off as a member of another class if he makes a successful skill check. He knows the talk and walks the walk so well that others are fooled. Of course, the GM rolls this check. This can be useful if an assassin character wants to pass himself off as a fighter for some nefarious reason.

Prerequisite: None.

Social Etiquette:
[(Wisdom+Charisma)÷2/Social Interaction/1 B.P.]

This skill gives the character a basic understanding of the proper forms of behavior and address required in many different situations, especially those involving nobility and persons of rank. Thus, the character will know the correct title to use when addressing a duke, the proper steps of ceremony to greet visiting diplomats, gestures to avoid in the presence of dwarves, etc. For extremely unusual occurrences, a skill check must be made for the character to know the proper etiquette for the situation (an imperial visit, for example, is such a rare event). However, having the character know what is correct and actually doing it are two different matters. The encounters must still be role-played by the character. Knowledge of etiquette does not give the character protection from a gaffe or faux pas.

Prerequisite: None.

Street Cred:
[(Strength+Wisdom+Charisma)/3/Social Interaction/1 B.P.]

A character with this skill can be accepted into the earthy, life-hardened ranks of the street. This character has a reputation in the seediest parts of town as someone not to be messed with. He also is known for his useful skills and may be "recruited" by members of certain unsavory groups to do "jobs". Whenever a character with this skill ventures into an area of any town where such types hang out the GM needs to make a skill check. If the check is successful, the character's street cred holds up, and he has earned their respect. If his cred holds up, the character may be able to glean valuable information from his new buddies.

Prerequisite: None.

Taunting, Major:
[Wisdom/Social Interaction/3 B.P.]

This skill imbues the character with the knowledge of exactly how to best hurt a person with his words. He can use his major taunting skill to reduce another person's Honor by 1d4 points or to goad another person into a fight. No skill check is needed for starting a fight, but one is needed to reduce a person's Honor. This check is rolled by the GM. Success means he has reduced his target's Honor by 1d4.

Prerequisite: Taunting, Minor.

Taunting, Minor:
[Wisdom/Social Interaction/2 B.P.]

This skill means a person has the ability to taint someone's Honor with his words or to goad them into a fight. A successful skill check is needed only when the character attempts to reduce the Honor of another. If successful, the target of the taunting loses 1 point of Honor.

Prerequisite: None.

Threat Gestures (nonverbal-body and hand):
[Wisdom/Social Interaction/1 B.P.]

A character with this skill knows how to use body language to intimidate others, including animals. Two successful skill checks must be made (rolled by the GM). If the first roll succeeds, the character's gestures cause the potentially dangerous person or creature to back down temporarily and to reevaluate the situation. If a subsequent successful check is made, it means the person or creature might actually leave.

Prerequisite: None.

Ulterior Motive:
[Charisma/Social Interaction/2 B.P.]

A person with this skill could be planning to kill you, and you'd never guess it by talking to him. This is a person with the ability to hide his true intentions. A character with this skill ensures that those who meet him think he's an extremely nice guy, even if he's evil to the core. A good-aligned person could also pass himself off as evil in a crowd of evil aligned beings. A successful skill check (rolled by the GM) is necessary to pull off this charade. If it succeeds, the character's motives are hidden. If this skill is used in conjunction with secret persona, the character gets +5 to his skill check to ensure his true class is not uncovered.

Prerequisite: None.

Tool Skills

Assaying/Surveying Tools:
[(Dexterity+Intelligence)÷2/Tool/1 B.P.]

This skill indicates the character knows how to use tools (including plumb lines and viewing glasses) for surveying and assaying properties. Without this skill any character attempting a task related to assaying/surveying suffers a -20 penalty on his skill check (in addition to any other modifiers which may apply).

Prerequisite: None.

Blacksmith Tools:
[(Strength+Dexterity+Intelligence)÷3/Tool/1 B.P.]

This skill indicates the character knows how to use all the tools related to the job of working metal. This includes using a forge, bellows, anvil, sledge, tongs, etc. Without this tool skill any character attempting to do any sort of metal working task (including blacksmith, armorer, weaponsmith, etc) suffers a -20 on his skill check (in addition to any other modifiers which may apply).

Prerequisite: None.

Carpentry Tools:
[(Strength+Dexterity+Intelligence)÷3/Tool/1 B.P.]

This skill indicates the character knows how to use all the tools related to the job of carpentry. This includes using a saw, hammer, plane, nails, etc. Without this tool skill any character attempting to do a carpentry-related task suffers a -20 penalty on his skill check (in addition to any other modifiers which may apply).

Prerequisite: None.

Construction Tools:
[(Strength+Dexterity+Intelligence)÷3/Tool/5 B.P.]

This skill indicates the character knows how to use all the tools related to the job of construction. This includes the use of carpentry tools, as well as tools related to masonry and heavy construction tools such as levers and winches. Anyone without this tool skill who tries to perform a construction-related task suffers a -20 penalty on his skill check (in addition to any other modifiers which may apply).

Prerequisite: Carpentry Tools, Mining Tools.

Drafting Tools:
[Dexterity/Tool/1 B.P.]

This skill indicates the character knows how to use tools related to drafting plans for engineering projects: straight edges, right angle markers, and so forth. There's no penalty for not having this skill but anyone with this skill who is mapping, doing engineering design, etc, recieves a +10% modifier.

Prerequisite: None.

Jeweler Tools:
[(Dexterity + Wisdom)÷2/Tool/1 B.P.]

This skill indicates the character knows how to use all the tools related to the job of gem cutting and jewelry making. This includes an assortment of chisels, small hammers, and specially hardened blades. Without this tool skill any character attempting to do any sort of tasks related to gem cutting suffers a -20 penalty on his skill check (in addition to any other modifiers which may apply).

Prerequisite: None.

Leather Working Tools:
[Dexteriity/Tool/1 B.P.]

This skill indicates the character knows how to use tools need to work leather. Without this tool skill any character attempting to do any task involving the working of leather suffers a -20 on his skill check (in addition to any other modifiers which may apply).

Prerequisite: None.

Mining Tools:
[Strength/Tool/1 B.P.]

This skill indicates the character knows how to use all the tools related to the job of mining. This includes using a pick, mattock, shovel, wheelbarrow, chisels, etc. Without this tool skill any character attempting to do any sort of mining suffers a -20 penalty on his skill check (in addition to any other modifiers which may apply). In addition, his progress will be significantly slowed.

Prerequisite: None.

Peg Legs:
[Dexterity/Tool/1 B.P.]

Peg Legs are mastered through daily use. A character with a peg leg skill suffers no movement penalty. Once fitted with a peg leg the character must make a check vs. his Dexterity plus the Course Difficulty modifier to determine if he's proficient walking on his new peg leg. He may automatically

check once per game month with an additional +1 modifier (cumulative) until he succeeds. Note that a character who begins the game fitted with peg legs is automatically proficient. Without this skill, any character attempting to walk on a peg leg suffers a -20 penalty to any skill check that involves moving that leg (in addition to any other modifiers which may apply).

Prerequisite: None.

Surgery Tools/Suture Kit:
[(Dexterity + Intelligence)÷2/Tool/1 B.P.]

This skill indicates the character knows how to use the tools necessary to perform surgery. This includes scalpels for cutting out unwanted bits, scissors for fine work and needle and thread for stitching up wounds. Without this skill, any character attempting to perform any type of surgery suffers a -20 penalty to his skill check (in addition to any other modifiers which may apply).

Prerequisite: None.

Appendix H

Talent Descriptions

The following descriptions are arranged alphabetically by name. The bold heading for each talent gives the name of the talent and the Building Point (BP) cost, followed by the race(s) to which that talent is restricted. For example, Acute Alertness costs 5 Building Points and any race except Half-ogres can have this talent.

The description text gives a general outline of what a character with that particular talent knows and can do. Furthermore, some talent descriptions include rules to cover specific uses or situations, or exact instructions on the effects of the talent if successfully used.

Acrobatic Skill Suite: (5)
[Elves (incl. Grunge & Dark), Half-Elves, Humans, Pixie Fairies]

A character with this talent can tumble, walk a tightrope, and attempt many types of difficult maneuvers with his body. This talent gives the character a +1 AC bonus in melee. When falling, the character suffers 5 points less damage than characters without this talent.

Active Sense of Smell: (5)
[Half-Orcs (innate), Half-Ogres]

An Active Sense of Smell will grant the character a nose sensitive enough to give him a +1 bonus to surprise rolls.

Acute (high) Alertness: (5)
[Any but Half-Ogres]

Persons with this talent are almost impossible to surprise in any situation (they are only surprised on a 1 in 10 chance.). Even when such a character is asleep, he has an 8 out of 10 chance of knowing when something is amiss in his immediate vicinity.

Acute Taste: (0)
[Half-Orcs (innate)]

The character's sense of taste is so sensitive, thanks to this talent, that he gains a +2 bonus to saving throws vs. imbibed poisons. He may also complain twice as often if forced to eat iron rations for weeks at a time, and will relish the chance to feast at any quality eating establishment.

Ambidextrous: (5)
[Any, (innate for Elves incl. Grunge and Dark)]

A character with this talent can use either his left or right hand equally well for weapons, writing, etc. In combat situations, a character with this talent can change weapon hands in one action. Because of his flexibility, this character can attack with two weapons with no penalty.

Animal Companion: (10)
[Elves (incl. Grunge)]

The character fortunate enough to have this talent gains the constant, loyal companionship of an Elven Wardawg (See your GM for the correct details from the Hacklopedia of Beasts, Volume 3).

Animal Friendship: (10)
[Gnomes (incl. Gnome Titans), Gnomelings]

Once a day the character gains an Animal Friendship spell ability, as the druid spell, with respect to burrowing animals. See the Hacklopedia of Beasts for more information on animals that burrow.

Astute Observation: (5)
[Any but Half-Orcs and Half-Ogres]

Characters with this talent notice what's going on around them. They are quick to notice details that could be important. This character is surprised only on a 1 in 10 chance. Thieves can use this talent to gain a +10 bonus on their checks for picking pockets and +10% to notice anything that might help in performing a successful burglary.

Attack Bonus: (5)
[Half-Orc, Humans, Pixie Fairies]

A character with this talent gets +1 attack bonus with any one weapon of the player's choice.

Axe Bonus: (5)
[Dwarves]

A character with this talent gets +1 to attack rolls with hand or battle axes.

Balance Bonus: (10)
[Half-Elves, Halflings, Humans]

A character with this talent gets +5% to any check involving balance-related feats including climbing, tumbling, tightrope walking, etc..

Blind Fighting: (10)
[Any]

A character with a talent for blind-fighting is capable of fighting in conditions of poor or no light (but this talent does not allow spell use). In total darkness, the character suffers only a -2 penalty to his attack roll (as compared to a -4 penalty without this skill). Under starlight or moonlight, the character incurs only a -1 penalty. The character suffers no penalties to his AC because of darkness or inability to see.

Furthermore, the character retains special abilities that would normally be lost in darkness, although the effectiveness of these are reduced by one-half (skill checks are made at half the normal score, etc.). This talent is effective only against opponents or threats within melee distance of the character. Blind-fighting does not grant any special protection from missile fire or anything outside the immediate range of the character's melee weapon. Thus, AC penalties remain for missile fire. (By the time the character hears the whoosh of the arrow, for example, it is too late for him to react.)

While moving in darkness, the character suffers only half the normal movement penalty of those without this talent.

Furthermore, this talent aids the character when dealing with invisible creatures, reducing the attack penalty to -2. However, it does not enable the character to discover invisible creatures; he has only a general idea of their location and cannot target them exactly.

Bow Bonus: (5)
[innate for Elves (incl. Grunge), Half-Elves]

An elven character with this talent gets +1 to attack rolls with any type of bow other than a crossbow.

Brewing: (5)
[Dwarves, Gnomes (incl. Gnome Titans), Halflings]

A character with this talent gets +10 to all his brewing skill checks. (The character must have the skill to gain this benefit.)

Close to the Earth: (5)
[Dwarves, Dark Elves, Gnomes (incl. Gnome Titans)]

Characters with this ability heal faster in subterranean settings. When this character is underground, he heals twice as fast as he would on the surface. If the character merely goes into a cave, he must rest there a full day to gain any significant benefit.

Cold Resistance: (5)
[Elves (incl. Grunge & Dark), Half-Elves]

A character with this talent gets +1 bonus on all his saving throws vs. cold- and ice-based attacks, as the character's body is less susceptible to extremely low temperatures.

Constitution/Health Bonus: (10)
[Dwarves, Dark Elves]

A character with this talent gets a Constitution bonus of +1 when underground, because he is accustomed to the cold and often damp Underwurld.

Crossbow Bonus: (5)
[Dwarves, Dark Elves]

Because dwarven characters favor crossbows, they gain a +1 attack bonus with any crossbow. (Hurled weapons are limited in tunnels, and other bows require large pieces of wood which are not readily accessible.)

Dagger Bonus: (5)
[Elves (incl. Grunge & Dark, Gnomes (incl. Gnome Titans), Gnomelings, Halflings (innate if thrown)]

Characters with this talent get +1 attack roll bonus with daggers.

Damage Bonus: (5)
[Half-Orcs, Half-Ogres]

Characters with this talent get a +1 bonus to damage with one weapon of the player's choice.

Dart bonus: (5)
[Gnomes (incl. Gnome Titans), Gnomelings]

Characters with this talent get +1 to attack rolls with darts, their preferred missile weapon.

Defensive bonus: (5)
[Gnomes (incl. Gnome Titans), Gnomelings]

Characters with this talent get +1 to Armor Class when in their native underground environment.

Dense Skin: (10)
[Dwarves, Half-Orcs, Half-ogres (innate)]

If the character is struck by a blunt weapon, he suffers only half the damage the attack would normally inflict, thanks to this talent.

Detect Evil: (5)
[Dwarves, Halflings]

Once a day a character with this ability can detect evil in creatures or individuals. This talent does not function on items or locations.

Detect Poison: (5)
[Dwarves]

By sniffing any food or drink, the character with this talent can determine if it has been poisoned. He successfully detects any poison on a result of 1–4 rolled on 1d6.

Detect Secret Doors: (5)
[innate for Elves (incl. Grunge & Dark) and Half-Elves, Humans]

The character with this talent is quick to spot concealed doors and hidden entranceways. Merely passing within 10' of a concealed door allows an elf a one-in-six chance (a 1 on 1d6) to notice it. If actively searching, an elf's chances improve to a two-in-six chance (1 or 2 on 1d6) to find secret doors, and a three-in-six (1, 2, or 3 on 1d6) to notice a concealed door.

Determine Age: (5)
[Dwarves]

By examining a building or ruins, the character with this talent stands an excellent chance of determining the approximate age of the structure. The chance of success is 1–5 on 1d6.

Determine Stability: (5)
[Dwarves, Dark Elves]

The character with this talent is an expert at determining if the ground is stable. By concentrating for one round, the character can determine if there will be a dangerous tremor, collapse, rock fall or rockslide when the character enters an area. The chance of success is 1–4 on 1d6.

Endurance: (5)
[Dwarves, Half-Orcs, Half-Ogres, Humans]

A character with Endurance is able to perform continual strenuous physical activity for twice as long as a normal character before becoming subject to the effects of fatigue and exhaustion. In those cases where extreme endurance is required, a check against Constitution must be made.

Note that this talent does not enable a character to extend the length of time that he can remain unaffected by a lack of food or water.

Engineering Bonus: (5)
[Gnomes (incl. Gnome Titans), Gnomelings]

If the character with this talent also has the engineering skill, he gains a +10 bonus to any engineering skill checks he must make.

Evaluate Gems: (5)
[Dwarves]

A character with this ability can determine the value of any given gem within 10%, given a full 1d4 minutes of examination.

Experience Bonus: (10)
[Gnomelings, Humans]

A character with this talent gets a +5% experience point bonus. This is cumulative with the 10% experience point bonus certain classes get for high primary attributes, if the character has them.

Expert Haggler: (5)
[Dwarves, Halflings]

This talented character drives a hard bargain. Anything he purchases costs 10% less than the listed price. Unlike the haggling skill, no check is necessary.

Faerie Kind Martial Arts: (5)
[Pixie Fairies]

A character with this talent knows the special fighting style of the wee folk. He gets +2 to-hit and damage in any combat situation.

Flutter: (2)
[Pixie Fairies]

Flutter allows a pixie fairy to use the move silently skill while flying, and without penalty.

Forest Movement: (10)
[Elves (incl. Grunge), Gnomes (incl. Gnome Titans), Gnomelings]

This talent affords the character the ability to pass without trace through his native woodlands, as per the druid ability.

Freeze: (10)
[Gnomes (incl. Gnome Titans)]

This is the ability to "freeze" in place, anytime this gnomish character wishes, in a gnome's native underground environment. This gives such a character a 60% chance to remain unnoticed by any who pass by.

Grace Under Pressure: (5)
[Elves (incl. Grunge & Dark), Humans]

This talent gives human and elven characters the ability to perform under even the most stressful of circumstances. Characters with this talent are less likely to crack under interrogation or torture. This gives the character a 60% chance not to break and run in battle, and the same percentage chance to not divulge any information under duress (regardless of the torturer's skill check).

Heat Resistance: (5)
[Elves (incl. Grunge & Dark), Half-Elves]

Elven and half-elven characters with this talent get a +1 bonus on saving throws vs. heat and fire-based attacks, as the character's body is far less susceptible to extremely high temperatures.

Hide: (10)
[Gnomes (incl. Gnome Titans), Gnomelings, Halflings]

This is the ability to hide in woods with a chance equal to a barbarian of the same level's hide in natural surroundings ability.

Hit Point Bonus: (10)
[Dwarves, Humans, Pixie Fairies]

The dwarven, human, or pixie fairy character with this talent gains an additional hit point each time the character rolls a hit die for attaining a new level.

Illusion Resistant: (5)
[Dwarves]

The dwarven character with this talent will gain a +2 bonus on any attempts to disbelieve illusions.

Javelin Bonus: (5)
[Elves (incl. Grunge & Dark)]

These elven characters get +1 attack roll bonus when using a javelin.

Keen Sight (Long Distance): (5)
[Elves (incl. Grunge & Dark), Half-Elves, Humans, Pixie Fairies]

People who possess this talent have superior eyesight, enabling them to see great distances. Player characters who have keen sight can use ranged weapons at much greater accuracy, giving them +1 to all ranged to-hit rolls.

These characters notice things many others would miss. They can see 25% farther than normal characters in any given light condition (see Chapter 17: Vision and Light).

Less Sleep: (5)
[Elves (incl. Grunge & Dark), Half-Elves, Humans]

The character with this talent requires only four hours' worth of sleep to be fully rested. This is especially valuable to adventuring spell casters.

Mace Bonus: (5)
[Dwarves, Half-Orcs, Half-Ogres]

Characters with this talent get +1 to attack rolls with the footman's mace.

Magic Bonus: (5)
[Pixie Fairies]

A character with this talent receives a plus one to all saving throws against spells or other magical effects.

Magic Identification: (10)
[Elves (incl. Grunge & Dark)]

This talent gives a character a 5% chance per experience level of identifying the general purpose and function of any magical item, reflecting their special interest in knowledge of the arcane.

Meld Into Stone: (10)
[Dwarves]

Once a day a dwarven character with this ability can meld into stone as a cleric of the same level.

Mining Sense: (5)
[Dwarves, Dark Elves, Gnomes (incl. Gnome Titans), Gnomelings]

A character with this talent is familiar with mining, tunneling and stonework. By concentrating for one round the character can: Detect grade or slope in passage (1-5 on 1d6); Detect new tunnel/passage construction (1-5 on 1d6); Detect sliding/shifting walls or rooms (1-4 on 1d6); Detect stonework traps, pits, and deadfalls (1-3 on 1d6); Determine approximate depth underground (1-4 on 1d6); Detect unsafe walls, ceiling, and floors (1-7 on 1d10); Determine approximate direction underground (1-3 on 1d6). If the character already possesses one of the above talents, i.e. it was granted as a bonus racial talent, they instead receive a +1 modifier to all checks of that type. However, a maximum result on the die always fails in these instances.

Opportunist: (5)
[Gnomes (incl. Gnome Titans), Halflings, Humans]

A human, gnomish, or halfling character with this talent is quick to spot any opportunity which would benefit him. He is a capable wheeler and a dealer. Therefore, this character gets a +5% bonus to any percentile die rolls for any purpose.

Photographic Memory: (5)
[Elves (incl. Grunge & Dark), Half-Elves, Humans]

A character with this talent can remember anything he has read. This gives spell casters the ability to memorize one additional spell per level.

Pick Bonus: (5)
[Dwarves]

This talent gives a dwarven character a +1 to attack rolls with military picks.

Potion Identification: (5)
[Gnomes (incl. Gnome Titans), Gnomelings]

A gnomish or gnomeling character with this ability has a percentage chance equal to his Wisdom score of identifying a potion by appearance and scent. He can make an attempt once per level per potion.

Reaction Bonus: (5)
[Halflings]

This talent grants a +1 to reaction rolls for other races' acceptance of the character when first meeting him.

Resistance: (5)
[Dwarves, innate for Half-Elves, Humans]

This talent gives a character a 30% resistance to Sleep and charm-related spells.

Seeking, Grasping Hands: (5)
[Elves (incl. Grunge & Dark), Humans]

This talent allows a character to reach out telepathically and give the mind of another person a "push." This allows him to plant one single suggestion into another person's mind. The target must roll a save vs. spell or treat the suggestion as favorably as is reasonable. (Attempting to suggest that a paladin steal something is far more likely to send the paladin to prayer than to get him to start a life of crime.) This talent can be used once per day, and may affect any creature only once ever.

Short Sword Bonus: (5)
[Dwarves, Gnomes (incl. Gnome Titans)]

A character with this talent gets +1 to attack rolls with short swords.

Sibling Empathy: (10)
[Any]

Characters with this ability share a special link with a brother or sister that is beyond the norm. They can actually feel what their sibling is feeling as if they were there. Such empathy usually kicks in whenever a sibling is experiencing strong emotions, such as fear or anger.

It can warn of danger. Also, a person with this talent can concentrate for one full round and communicate any single emotion to a sibling, or read any single emotion from a sibling. This talent works no matter how far away the brother or sister is.

Sixth Sense: (5)
[Any but Half-Orc or Half-Ogre]

This is the ability to "see" things that can't normally be seen. Players with this talent can sense invisible or hidden people or items with a fair degree of accuracy. This does not mean that the character has a detailed picture of that which is invisible or hidden, he only knows that something is there. This sense also helps characters that happen to be blind, blindfolded or in the dark find their way around safely.

Characters with this ability can sense only things or people that are in front of them. Objects to the sides or rear are undetectable by means of this talent. The basic chance of success is 50%, though the GM may adjust this (for example, -20 if an object is in a lead-lined box or +25 if the character holds something strongly linked to the person hiding).

Sling Bonus: (5)
[Gnomes (incl. Gnome Titans), Gnomelings, innate for Halflings]

This character gets a +1 bonus to-hit when using a sling.

Speak with Plants: (10)
[Elves (incl. Grunge & Dark)]

Once a day, the elven character who has this talent can use the Speak with Plants ability, as a druid of the same level.

Spear Bonus: (5)
[Elves, innate for Grunge Elves]

This elven character gets a +1 attack roll bonus when using a spear.

Spell Abilities: (15)
[Elves (incl. Grunge), innate for Dark Elves]

Once a day the elven character with this talent can choose to cast Faerie Fire, Dancing Lights and Darkness as a cleric or magic-user of the same level. When the character reaches 4th level, he can add the following spells to his list of possibilities: Levitate, Detect Magic and Know Alignment.

Stealth: (10)
[Dwarves, Gnomes (incl. Gnome Titans), Gnomelings]

If the character with this talent is not in metal armor, a −2 penalty is applied to opponent's surprise rolls. The stealthy character must be at least 90 feet ahead of a party of characters without this ability or accompanied only by characters with equivalent stealth skills. The character is also difficult to surprise and receives a +2 bonus to his own surprise rolls.

Stone Tell: (10)
[Dwarves]

Once a day a dwarven character with this talent can use the Stone Tell ability, as a cleric of the same level.

Sword Bonus: (5)
[innate for Elves (incl. Dark), Half-Elves]

These half-elven characters get +1 to attacks with either long swords or short swords.

Taunt: (5)
[Halflings]

Once per day the halfling character with this talent can taunt someone, as per the 1st level magic-user spell.

Touched by Yurgain: (—)
[Dwarves]

Dwarves born 'touched' are able to become battle mages. There is a price, however. Such characters do not suffer the penalties for using magic items that their brethren suffer but they lose the bonuses on saves vs. magic. Touched characters also lose the to-hit modifiers/defense adjustments other dwarves get when attacking or being attacked by certain races.

There is no Building Point cost for this talent but the dwarf gives up any chance of being a fighter or multi-classing.

Tough Hide: (10)
[innate for Half-Ogre, Humans]

A few rare human characters (and all half-ogres) have a natural Armor Class of 8. If the character wears armor that would improve his AC to better than 8, this ability has no effect. If the character wears armor that gives him an AC of 8 or worse, he may add a +1 bonus to his Armor Class.

Track Game Animal: (5)
[Grunge Elves]

A character with this Talent receives a +10 bonus to the track game and identify animal by tracks skills. The character must possess these skills to gain the benefits.

Trident Bonus: (5)
[Elves]

A character with this talent gets +1 on attack rolls when using a trident.

Warhammer Bonus: (5)
[Dwarves]

Characters with this talent get +1 to attack rolls with the warhammer.

Appendix I

Step-by-Step Character Creation Procedure

This appendix was included to help players through the process of creating characters and equipping them for the campaign. It will guide you step by step through this process.

Player Character Generation

Okay, the moment to gird up your loins has arrived. It's time to create your character. To create your HackMaster character, simply follow the steps in sequential order and refer to the appropriate chapters/appendices as instructed (Remember to return to this Appendix and continue to the next step after finishing the previous step). Most GameMasters require characters to be created under the watchful eye of a sanctioned/accredited GM, although the 'honor system' is acceptable if the GM deems the player(s) trust-worthy. Be sure to check with your GM on his policy before rolling up your character.

If you encounter terms you don't understand, just check the glossary in the back or re-read the appropriate section/chapter. Everything should be fully explained. If it isn't, then it's probably something you're not ready to embrace, in which case you should consult your GM for guidance. Once you've worked through this list, and your GM has signed off on your character, you are ready to jump into the fray.

Step 1: Proper mindset

Creating a character shouldn't be taken lightly. Not only can it be time-intensive (Your first character could take up to 45 minutes to complete), but there are a lot of critical decisions to be made throughout the process. If you're not in the proper frame of mind, you're going to make mistakes. I recommend sitting in a quiet place for ten to fifteen minutes to clear your mind. Take the phone off the hook, put the cat outside - do whatever it takes to shake off the worries of the day so you can think clearly. Some meditate, others use yoga and special breathing techniques, while some listen to soothing music or watch the final few scenes of Excalibur. You'll need to find your own personal method to get into your zone.

If your GM has insisted on observing while you create your character you should accept the fact that it is his right (and responsibility) to do so. Just tell him you need to step out of the room to gather your thoughts. He should fully understand.

Step 2: Proper setting

It's also important that you have a proper setting that is conducive to the process. Make sure you have a sharpened pencil, an eraser, a calculator, several sheets of scrap paper and a pencil sharpener. You should also have some extra character sheets on hand just in case you need them. A cold tasty beverage of your preference is a good idea as well. Other important aspects of the setting to consider include adequate lighting, comfortable seating and a good flat surface free of obstructions on which you can roll your dice. Most importantly you need to make sure you're dice are game-ready. You should never use virgin dice to roll up a character. See Appendix L for procedures on how to properly fine tune and ready your dice for play.

Step 3: Roll ability scores (Chapter 1)

Your character needs scores for Strength, Dexterity, Constitution, Intelligence, Wisdom, Charisma and Comeliness. The base ability scores are determined by rolling 3 six-sided dice. For each ability, a player also needs to roll a d100 for fractional abilities. These "fractional" ability scores represent how close a character is to attaining the next integer ability score. (You'll have a chance of raising fractional scores as you go up levels. You can also raise them in later steps with building points).

If you don't like the results you rolled you can try to adjust them to suit your needs. Consult Table 3D for class ability requirements. You can adjust Ability Scores by burning off two (2) points from one ability and adding one (1) point to another (however, comeliness may be adjusted neither up nor down). You can also deduct points from your Ability Scores to generate building points (BPs) at this stage (you'll use these later). See Chapter 1 for the exact procedure and rules for doing this. Record the final results on scrap paper.

Step 4: Choose a race (Chapter 2)

It's now time to choose what race your character will be. Your options will be somewhat dictated by the Ability Scores you rolled. Each race has its own maximum or minimum limitations on certain abilities. Consult Table 2A for a compiled list of racial ability score requirements. Then adjust the character's scores as indicated on the table for the race you've chosen.

Step 5: Record racial abilities and talents (Chapter 2)

Now flip back to Chapter 2 and find the description for the race you've chosen. Consult the 'At a Glance' listings and record the character's special racial abilities. It's also a good idea to read through the descriptions for any additional racial abilities which were not listed. Record the racial BP bonus on your scratch paper.

Step 6: Character priors and particulars (Chapter 4)

Now flip back to Chapter 4 and roll up your background in the following order:
- Table 4A: Character Starting Age (roll according to race)
- Table 4D: Determine Character Handedness.
- Table 4E: Determine Character Height and Weight.
- Table 4F: Roll for Character Social Class and Rank.
- Table 4G: Roll for Circumstances of Birth.
- Table 4H: If Table 4G indicated an Illegitimate Birth determine the nature of the illegitimacy.
- Determine Status of Parents (d100)
- Table 4I: Determine Quality of Parent
- Table 4J: Determine Family Heritage
- Table 4K: Determine Number of Siblings
- Table 4L: Determine Order of Birth (if necessary based on result of Table 4L)
- Determine Status of Sibling(s) (1d20)

Note that you are allowed to burn a building point and reroll if you don't like the results of a die roll on any table in Chapter 4 or Chapter 6. This process could result in unwanted quirks and flaws and possible Ability Score adjustments. Be sure to keep track of these (if any) on your scrap piece of paper.

Step 7: Earning BPs with additional quirks and flaws (Chapter 6)

Now you have an opportunity to earn more building points (BPs) by voluntarily taking on quirks and flaws. You have two options:

7a: Cherry Picking: You may pick up to two minor quirks or flaws from Chapter 6 and gain 2 BPs for each one you choose. You can also pick 1 major quirk or flaw to gain an additional 4 BPs. Therefore using this method could earn you a maximum of 8 additional BPs.

7b: Rolling Randomly for Quirks/Flaws: With this method you must declare how many rolls you are going to make on the quirk and flaw tables in Chapter 6 (Table 6A). You can roll a maximum nine times. The catch is you must roll at least as many times as you had declared. The tables might require you to roll additional times beyond those you had declared but if not, you must roll the exact number of times you declared. BP earnings for quirks/flaws randomly rolled are listed in their descriptions in Chapter 6.

Once you have chosen or rolled for all of your quirks and flaws, you should record them on your character sheet and total the number of building points you have. Also, don't forget to adjust any abilities that may have been affected by a quirk or flaw.

Step 8: Record final ability scores and relevant data (Chapter 1)

Now that you've chosen your race and made any necessary adjustments to your ability scores for quirks or flaws you have the opportunity to adjust your fractional Ability Scores by spending as many building points as you want on them. One BP can increase a fractional Ability Score by 25. Any fractional ability Score that is increased beyond 100 by this method allows the main Ability Score (those that were determined by 3d6) to be increased to the next highest integer. Once you have spent as many BPs as you want for this, record your final Ability Scores on your character sheet. Once that's done consult tables 1(A) thru 1(G) and record the various bonuses and penalties the character receives for having particularly high or low scores. There should be a specific box for each bonus/penalty on your character sheet.

Step 9: Select a class and Record your class abilities and bonuses (Chapter 3)

Consult the 'At a Glance' listings in the racial descriptions section of Chapter 2, and select a class that is available to your character's race and one that you qualify for with your current Ability Scores. This information is also compiled for all of the races on Table 2C.

Consult the description for the class you've chosen, and record any abilities and bonuses derived from that profession. For example, if your character is a thief, record his base thieving skills. Add your BP bonus for the class you've chosen to your current BP total.

Step 10: Finish background (Chapter 4)

At this time, you can determine how long it took your character to make it through school and/or training for his chosen class and what money he has left over. Turn back to Chapter 4 and roll on the following tables:
- Table 4B: Modify Character Starting Age (roll according to race)
- Table 4C: Determine Aging Effects if any. (by racial type)
- Table 4M: Determine Starting Money

Step 11: Calculating your starting Honor (Chapter 1)

Now add the seven ability scores from Step 3 together, and divide that sum by seven (round down any fractions). Adjust the result by any modifiers for your Charisma score, character class, background or quirks and flaws. This is your starting Honor. Record the result on your character sheet. Check Table 1H to see if any adjustments to your current total of BPs are in order.

Step 12: Purchase beginning skills, proficiencies and talents
(Chapter 7 and Appendixes F thru I)

Now you can spend your building points on any skills, proficiencies or talents from any of the lists in Appendix F, subject of course to any racial/class restrictions and skill progression requirements. Each skill you purchase allows you one (1) roll of the mastery die for that skill, which can be added to your base skill mastery for that skill. You cannot buy a progression skill until you have at least a 50% in the pre-requisite skill(s) for that skill. Note that you must spend the BP cost to gain weapon proficiencies. They are not automatic.

Step 13: Cash in any remaining BPs for money

Each BP you have remaining can be cashed in for 25 gp. Any BPs not converted are lost.

Step 14: Choose an Alignment (Chapter 5)

Abide by class restrictions when choosing your alignment.

Step 15: Record Saving Throws (Chapter 12)

See Table 12G.

Step 16: Roll Hit Points (Chapter 3)

Roll the appropriate hit die for your character, as indicated on the class progression table for the class you've chosen.

Step 17: Record base movement (Chapter 16)

Find the character' base movement rate on Table 16A and record it. Also record the encumbrance categories from Table 9Y as well as modified movement rates and combat abilities.

Step 18: Name your Character

Give your character an appropriate name and record it on your character sheet.

Step 19: Equip your character.

Check with your GM and determine if you're allowed to equip your character out-of-game. (i.e. choosing what you want from the equipment lists in Chapter 9, rolling for availability and making your purchases.) Some GMs require beginning characters to make all their purchases in the game (i.e. you must actually role-play your interactions with the merchants).

Don't forget to determine your character's armor class rating for any armor worn. Also be sure to modify your base AC by your defensive adjustment.

Record the weight, size, damage, rate of fire, and range information for each weapon carried. Include type and speed factors also.

Step 20: Have GameMaster review Character and certify.

Obtain your GM's approval and get his signature. Be sure to make him two copies of your character-one for his files, and one for the local chapter of the HMPA Registry.

Well, that's it. You now have a character ready for battle. Now be off with you and good gaming!

Class Building Point Bonuses	
Class	Bonus Points
Cleric	10
Druid	10
Fighter	10
Barbarian	7
Beserker	8
Cavalier	10
Dark Knight	12
Knight Errant	5
Monk	12
Paladin	12
Ranger	10
Magic-User	9
Battlemage	8
Bloodmage	11
Illusionist	9
Thief	12
Assassin	9
Bard	8

Racial Building Point Bonuses	
Race	Bonus Points
Dwarf	10
Elf, High	12
Elf, Grunge	13
Elf, Dark	13
Gnome	10
Gnome Titan	15
Gnomeling	10
Half-Elf	11
Halfling	11
Half-Orc	8
Half-Ogre	8
Human	10
Pixie-Faire	14

Building Point Expenditures:

Appendix J

Step-by-Step Advancement Procedure

This appendix was included to help players through the process of advancing your characters through experience levels. It will guide you step by step through this process.

Eventually, when you gain enough experience points, you come to a juncture where your character is eligible to rise to the next level. Your GM will assist you when this moment arrives, but there are certain things you should be aware of so you don't unintentionally get shorted.

Things that can affect your rate of advancment.

There are several things which can cause you to go up to the next level quicker or even to be held back. You should be aware of these, since in the heat of the game your GM is likely to overlook them. And let's face it, you need to look out for number one.

Primary ability scores: Most character classes have primary ability scores. If these scores are above a certain level the character may qualify for a 10% experience point bonus. (i.e. he can obtain the next level with less experience points). For example a fighter's primary ability score is a 16 or higher Strength. Make sure you add the 10% bonus EACH TIME your GM awards experience points.

Great Honor/Dishonor: Your character's Honor can make it easier to go up the next level, or hold him back. If your character's Honor places him in the Great Honor Bonus Window (See Chapter 5 Table 5A) category, he will earn an additional 5% to any experience point award given while he remains in that window.

Experience point awards/penalties: During the course of the game your GM may award you with extra EPs for outstanding behavior/achievements above and beyond those earned normally. Likewise he may slap you with an EP penalty bad role-playing, disruptive behavior, etc. Such awards/penalties can affect your rate of advancement to the next level.

Advancing to the next level

Immediately inform your GM once you've broken the EP barrier to the next level. At the end of the game session the two of you will proceed through the necessary steps to prepare your character for advancement

Step 1: Verification and GM Rating

GM verifies the character has the required number of EPs to advance and rates your character by assigning a rating between 1 and 4.

Step 2: Schooling: Basic block of instruction (BBI)

Now your character must attend schooling, either in a formal school or under the tutelage of a qualified mentor or teacher, and complete the BBI (basic block of instruction) for the level he's advancing to. BBI is an abstract collection of teachings and procedures which your character needs to apply his knowledge and experience and rise in level. It's what gives him any new abilities/powers associated with his new level.

The rating number you were assigned by your GM in Step 1 indicates the number of weeks it will take for your character to complete his BBI. Each week of BBI studies costs him 1,500 gold pieces (payable in advance) in fees. Advancement does not take place until the character has completed his training. Completing BBI is the qualifier for advancement in levels. Other than any abilities/powers associated with the new level there are no other awards or benefits in completing training.

Step 3: Advanced training.

During your BBI schooling, you have an opportunity to learn new skills or improve those you already have. This is handled in two different ways:

A. Concurrent Training: During your BBI, you may sign up for up to one (1) additional Skill course. You must pay the fees listed in Appendix F prior to taking the class. At the end of your BBI you must roll to see if you passed the course, using your % Chance to Learn for your Intelligence and adding in the Course Difficulty Modifier. If you succeed you may roll the Skill Mastery Die listed for that skill, along with your Honor Die, and add the total to your current Skill Mastery for that skill (or to the relevant abilities for that skill if this is a NEW skill you've just learned).

If you fail the course the fees are lost, no new skills/improvement takes place and you lose a point of Honor.

B. Prolonged Training: After your BBI is completed you may choose to stay at school and continue your studies. For each week you stay in school you can attempt to learn/improve two skills. You must pay 1,500 gold pieces per week plus any course fees. At the end of each week you must roll to see if you passed the course (See step **A** above).

There is no limit to how long a character can stay in school so long as he has the money to pay for his classes, however, for each week beyond the BBI the character loses one (1) point of Honor. After all, you're an adventurer by the gawds, not a backpack-toting full-time student at Urbana-Champaign!

Step 4: Increasing Hit Points.

After you've completed your training, and have advanced to the next level, you roll the hit die indicated on the progression table for your character's class and add the result to your hit points. This is your 'new' maximum hitpoint level.

Step 5: Improving Fractional Ability Scores

You may now roll your Honor Die and the appropriate polyhedron based on your class for each of your fractional ability scores and add the result to the former number. If a fractional score is pushed above 100 you should raise that ability score by 1 and record the balance of the fractional score. For example if you had a 12/87 Dexterity and rolled a twenty on your Honor Die your new Dexterity would be 13/07.

Once you are finished rolling these fractional ability scores, check the Tables in Chapter 1 to see if any of your ability modifiers have changed and make the necessary changes on your character sheet.

Table 11A Fractional Ability Die Roll by Class			
	Fighter	Magic User	Cleric	Thief
Strength	d20	d4	d12	d8
Intelligence	d4	d20	d6	d10
Wisdom	d6	d12	d20	d4
Dexterity	d10	d8	d4	d20
Constitution	d12	d10	d10	d6
Charisma	d8	d6	d8	d12
Comeliness	d4	d4	d4	d4

Step 6: Improve Your Saving Throws (see Chapter 12)

Your Saving Throw numbers change (for the better) as your character goes up in level, so check the appropriate for your class (Tables 12G-12J) in Chapter 12, and mark any changes on your character sheet for easy reference during combat. (When you'll need it!)

Step 7: Choose New Proficiencies (Chapter 7)

Be sure to check Table 7A in Chapter 7 to see if you have earned any new Proficiencies, and record any changes or new information on your character sheet.

Step 8: Record any new abilities/powers of your Class for your new level.

Refer to Chapter 3 to see if you have gained any new spells, skills, abilities or powers from your increase in level.

Character _____

HackMaster

Player Character Record

Alignment _____ Race _____ Class _____ Level _____

Player's Name _____ Family/Clan _____

Homeland _____ Patron Gawd _____

Liege/Patron _____ Social Class _____

Appearance _____ Birth Date _____ Birth Rank _____ # Siblings _____

Sex _____ Age _____ Height _____ Family History _____

Hair _____ Eyes _____ Weight _____ Appearance _____

Character Quirks & Flaws. _____

_____ Handedness _____

BASE %

STRength
DEXterity
CONstitution
INTelligence
WISdom
CHArisma
COMeliness
HONor

BASE   TEMP

ABILITIES

Hit Prob.	Dam. Adj.	Wt. All.	Max. Press	Open Doors	Bend Bars Lift Gates
Defense Adj.		Reaction Adj.		Missile Adj.	
HP Adj.	System Shock	Resurrect Survival	Poison Save	Imm. to Dis./Alc.	Regen./ Heal
# of Lang.	Spell Lvl.	Learn. Ability	Max. # Spells/Lvl.	Illus. Imm.	Chance Spell Mis.
Magical Def. Adj.	Bonus Spells	Chance Spell Fail.	Spell Imm.	Chance Imp. Skill	
Max. # Hench.	Loyalty Base	React. Adj.	COM. Mod.	HON. Mod.	

Fame:

MOVEMENT

Base Rate

Unencumb. _____

Light ( ) _____

Mod ( ) _____

Hvy ( ) _____

Svr ( ) _____

Jog (x2) _____

Run (x3) _____

Run (x4) _____

Run (x5) _____

Total Melee _____ to hit / _____ dam.

SAVING THROWS

Paralyzation, Poison, Death Magic _____

Rod, Staff, or Wand _____

Petrifaction, HackFrenzy, HackLust, Polymorph _____

Breath Weapon _____

Apology _____

Spells _____

Modifier   Save

ARMOR

AC

Adjusted AC

Surprised _____

Shieldless _____

Rear _____

Defenses _____

Armor Type (Pieces)

_____

_____

_____

_____

Armor Hit Points

☐☐☐☐ ☐☐☐☐
☐☐☐☐ ☐☐☐☐
☐☐☐☐ ☐☐☐☐

Shield Hit Points

☐☐☐☐ ☐☐☐☐
☐☐☐☐ ☐☐☐☐

HIT POINTS | CON Adj.:

HD type:

Wounds

COMBAT

Weapon	Mag. Adj.	Space Req./Ranges	Speed	10	9	8	7	6	5	4	3	2	Damage vs. Size S-M/L

Weapons Adj. vs. AC

Special Attacks _____

Ammunition: _____ ☐☐☐☐☐
☐☐☐☐☐ ☐☐☐☐☐ _____ ☐☐☐☐☐
☐☐☐☐☐ ☐☐☐☐☐ _____ ☐☐☐☐☐

Special Abilities _____

_____
_____
_____
_____
_____
_____
_____

☐ I certify that this character is HMA/Tournament legal.

Skills/Languages

(/) _____
(/) _____
(/) _____
(/) _____
(/) _____
(/) _____
(/) _____

(/) _____
(/) _____
(/) _____
(/) _____
(/) _____
(/) _____
(/) _____

GameMaster: _____ HMGA Membership # _____ Revision #: _____

Gear

Item	Location	Wt.	Item	Location	Wt.	Item	Location	Wt.

Supplies

Water/Wine
☐☐☐☐☐ ☐☐☐☐☐
☐☐☐☐☐ ☐☐☐☐☐
☐☐☐☐☐ ☐☐☐☐☐

Rations
☐☐☐☐☐ ☐☐☐☐☐
☐☐☐☐☐ ☐☐☐☐☐
☐☐☐☐☐ ☐☐☐☐☐

Feed
☐☐☐☐☐ ☐☐☐☐☐
☐☐☐☐☐ ☐☐☐☐☐

Experience

For Next Level

Treasure

Coins

Gems

Other Valuables _____

Miscellaneous Information (Personal notations, Magical Items, Command Words, Spells, etc.)

Hereditary Grudges

Henchmen/Cronies/Sidekicks/Animal Companions

Name	AC	Race/Class	HD/Lvl	#AT	Dmg/Effects	HP	Skills/Abilities
Background							
Name	AC	Race/Class	HD/Lvl	#AT	Dmg/Effects	HP	Skills/Abilities
Background							

Last Will and Testament: *I,* _____ *do hereby* _____

Appendix L

All Things Dice

This appendix is devoted solely to the topic of dice — the tools of the trade for every player and gamemaster. It is highly recommended that you read this section thoroughly and refer to it often. Also known as polyhedrons, dice are to the gamer what the assault rifle is to the combat soldier. Those little odd shaped lumps of hard impact plastic, along with your sharp wit, are often the only things standing between you and character death. If you become intimately familiar with your dice and learn to use and care for them properly, they will serve you well.

Dice Etiquette

There are a few rules of protocol concerning dice and the sooner you learn them (and put them to use) the better.

1. Dice Rolling Zones. (DRZ)

Every Player should have plenty of room to roll their dice properly. The minimum area for a dice rolling zone is 17 3/4 inches wide and 11 7/8 inches deep. Note also, that all "public table areas" are officially free rolling zones (FRZ). These are the battle/miniatures area and free spaces between zones. Using an FRZ is the only way to create the Distance-Dramatic Roll (such a roll being made famous by little Isaac Goldstein while slaying the Swak Iron Dragon with a desperate crit in the closing seconds of the HackMaster Finals at GaryCon '82). But take care when rolling in the battle area not to disturb any miniatures. If you find your assigned dice rolling zone at the gaming table insufficient you should bring it to the attention of your GM.

Enough space must be provided so when the dice are rolled, none of them touch each other. The DRZ should be free of obstacles so that the dice get plenty of tumble-action and roll freely without interference or inhibition. Also, clear DRZs are necessary to avoid any disputes between players who do not care to have another person's dice intrude upon their own DRZ. This is critical for those who believe in the possible transference of (bad) luck between dice in close proximity to one another. Indeed, invading another's dice zone with a poor roll of your own is akin to the infraction of touching another's dice as described below. Because some players don't respect the DRZs of other players it is within the GM's power to apply a modifier to any die/dice which violate another player's zone as a penalty.

There has been some speculation about training an area of the table for high numbers. Let me say, unequivocally, that this is nothing more than a myth. Norman Bowzer's popular articles in the Hack Journal were flawed and his figures fudged. We have taken the opportunity with the publication of this edition, to publicly refute them, and thus cleanse HackMaster of confusing and highly-speculative information. Let me also state here, for the record, that we at Hard Eight dispute the claim that a die can be rolled on the outstretched surface of an open palm. The open palm is NOT a sufficient rolling surface for properly resolving die rolls.

2. Hands to Yourself.

Another thing to remember, especially for neophytes, is that most experienced gamers are somewhat possessive, even superstitious, when it comes to their dice. As a general rule, one player should never, EVER touch another player's dice. It just isn't done, not without the shedding of blood. The surest way of ostracizing yourself from the fellowship of other gamers is to be a dice-squirrel and put your paws on dice that don't belong to you.

3. A Moment of Silence, Please!

When a player is in the actual act of rolling his dice, shut the hell up. Before he rolls, feel free to cheer him on, hex him, whatever, but when his arm begins that forward motion, you'd better pipe down. As his fingers glide open and the die springs free, the table should hush and watch and listen. There's nothing like the drama and expectation of an important roll rat-a-tat-tatting across the table and tumbling to a stop. Speaking when one is rolling, even to cheer him on is rude and should be avoided as the poorest of etiquette. Furthermore, if the die roll is poor, the player has a valid gripe that you ruined his concentration.

4. High Color Convention

Some old school gamers still like to use the antiquated twenty siders which were made in the 70s and 80s. These dice were manufactured with no distinction made between results of 1-10 versus results of 11-20. They were simply numbered 1 to 10 twice. It is perfectly acceptable to use such out-dated dice but certain conventions must be adhered to. Half of the numbers appearing on a die of this type must be colorized by some method, usually a colored wax crayon or a mascara pen. When a player uses a die of this type, it is essential that the color of the higher numbers be declared publicly and agreed upon for that session (and recorded in a verifiable place, such as on a character record sheet). Under no circumstances are players to be allowed to "call" the color of the higher numbers after a roll has been made. Similarly, it is considered poor etiquette to try to switch the convention of high-color once a gaming session has begun. Breaching this etiquette, is acceptable in extreme extenuating circumstances, such as when your character is getting decimated and you're rolling consistently poor all session. A final method to use these dice (or a ten sider) to generate rolls of 1-20 is to roll a d6 along with the d10. On a 4-6 you add 10 to the d10 result. This method eliminates the color issue, and is an alternative for those who have lost their d20, or were too dim to use two different colored crayons on their d20.

5. Open and Closed Rolling

All rolls required of player characters during a HackMaster game session must be made publicly such that all other attending players and the GM may view the roll. Under no circumstances shall a player be allowed to hide his dice rolls. The GM on the other hand may use "closed" die rolling at his discretion. In fact, it is the normal procedure for a GM to secretly make die rolls from behind the safety of his official HackMaster GM shield. However, the GM is allowed to intrude upon any other die rolling zone on the table at will (this is the only exception to the normal protocol) with no penalty. This is often done during those dramatic moments when letting the players see the fearsome result of a 20 coming up on a to-hit roll is just too much to pass up.

6. Let the Dice Fall Where They May

Dice rolls are sacred. In my campaigns, I let the dice fall where they may — period. I don't cotton to fudging die rolls and other such nonsense and I despise those who practice such foolishness or allow it to take place at their table. But that's a matter for the GameMaster, so I have addressed this issue in the GM's Guide.

Die Nomenclature

Before any further discussion on dice can take place, let us define the proper nomenclature for the various forms they take. In the HackMaster rules the die is symbolized by "d", and its number of sides is shown immediately thereafter. A six-sided die is therefore "d6", d8 is an eight-sided die, and so on.

Two four-sided dice are expressed by 2d4, five eight-sided dice are 5d8, etc. Any additions to or subtractions from the die or dice are expressed after the identification, thus: d8 + 8 means a linear number grouping between 9 and 16, while 3d6 -2 means a bell-shaped progression from 1 to 16, with the greatest probability group in the middle (8, 9). This latter progression has the same median numbers as 2d6, but it has higher and lower ends and a greater probability of a median number than if 2d12 were used.

On a d10 and d20 a zero result (0) is read as a result of 10.

The d20 is the most versatile die in your dice arsenal. It can be used as d10 and d20. Two d20s can also be used to simulate a d100. More typically, however, rolling two ten-siders of different colors generates percentages (numbers ranging from 1 to 100). Before rolling, the player announces which color is high (tens) and which color is low (single digits). When percentage dice are to be used, it is indicated by d100.

Sometimes you will need to use various dice to simulate dice of another type. For example a d6 can be used to simulate a d3 (generating a random number from 1 to 3). In this case the result of rolling a d6 would be read as follows; 1-2 = 1, 3-4 = 2, 5-6 = 3. Likewise a d10 could be used to simulate

Dice Recognition Chart

The players first line of offense/defense — his dice arsenal.

four sider (d4), six sider (d6), eight sider (d8), ten sider (d10), twelve sider (d12), twenty sider (d20)

Top View

3/4 View

Side View

a d5 (1-2 = 1, 3-4 = 2, 5-6 = 3, 7-8 = 4, 9-0 = 5) and a d4 could be used as a d2 (1-2=1 3-4=2).

The Nature of Dice

Dice in HackMaster are akin to the Fates of mythology. And you might as well know one sad fact up front — like the Fates, dice are fickle, friend to neither GameMaster nor Player. The player who appears to be on a lucky streak one week and rolling one critical hit after another is often the same guy rolling an endless stream of fumbles the next session.

Now there are those misguided individuals out there who would have you believe the outcome of any given die/dice roll is governed by the cold, blind tenets of probability. "There is no such thing as luck!" they assure you as they go on and on about bell curves, the law of mathematical averages, and other such nonsense in an attempt to hammer their point of view into your skull.

To be honest, they are partly correct — dice are designed to do one thing — generate truly random numbers that dictate the outcome of various actions during the course of the game in a fair and impartial manner. The random numbers they generate are ultimately what keeps the GM's power over his players in check. He may design the adventure and chart the course of the action but at the end of the day it's the dice which decide the outcome. But to say there is no 'luck' involved in the tumble of the die is folly.

Ask anyone who has bellied up to the game table and they will swear that this die or that favors (or disfavors) them. If you press the subject most gamers will produce one or more of their lucky dice. (I myself have a blue benzene polyfibre d20 model 5 called Nat Faithful which has served me well for twenty three years). We've all witnessed the player on a 'hot streak' who inexplicably pulls nat' twenties out of his butt like some Easter Bunny doling out eggs to a schoolyard full of preschoolers. There's little doubt that luck exists and to say it doesn't simply reeks of denial. The notion of luck (and bad luck) is very real to most players and they take it seriously. You'd be advised to do the same.

Having said that, let me warn you not to fall into the trap of attempting to live by the good graces of Lady Luck. Those who use luck as a crutch soon find themselves falling flat on their faces. Lady Luck has a wandering eye and she dances with many partners. One moment she may be at your side and the next moment she's nowhere to be found. When it comes to hacking it's best to rely on your own wits and mettle.

Choosing/Purchasing your Dice

Great care and attention should be given when purchasing/selecting your dice. I recommend going with dice produced by a reliable manufacturer. Examine each die for imperfections such as misshapen appearance, flawed edges or mold marks/extra material which protrudes. Ask the shopkeeper if

you can test-roll your dice selections prior to purchase. Any die which rolls a "1" should be returned to the dice bin on the spot (unless you're looking for an "init" 10-sider). You may even want to refrain from buying any other dice from that same bin since unlucky dice usually come in groups.

Pay special attention to the numbers/pips on each face of the die. Are they clearly legible? Is the die made of high impact plastic? Is it used? Don't be afraid to ask questions. Most game shopkeepers understand the importance of dice selection and will cheerfully cater to you.

You may also want to ask what the store's policy is on returning dice that fail to perform properly. Note: Special care should be taken with virgin dice (new dice that have never been used in a game). Whenever you buy new dice be sure not to mix them with your battle-hardened dice until you've properly primed them. This is important since any bad luck may be transferred to your battle-hardened dice arsenal.

Assembling your Dice Arsenal (Battle Line Dice)

When you first begin playing you'll probably be content just to buy the basic dice required to play and throw them in a dice bag without much more thought or consideration. This is typical for the neophyte. As your gaming experience grows, however, you will want to give more serious thought to maintaining and building a proper Dice Arsenal. This involves weeding out dice which under-perform or which show the slightest signs of being under-performers (or perhaps unlucky). You'll also want to begin taking note of any die which demonstrates the early signs of being a 'lucky die' (A very rare thing indeed).

For example, over the course of several game sessions you'll probably notice that one twenty-sider seems to be rolling more than its share of high numbers. It's entirely possible you have a 'lucky' one in the making. You may want to consider assigning this die a specific task/purpose (such as making back stab rolls only).

Let's not forget the ever-important Honor Dice. It is of utmost importance that you purchase a separate set of dice for Honor rolls. In fact, I recommend you use ONLY official HackMaster™ Honor Dice™ brand polyhedrons, but hey, it's your funeral. Remember that it is a dishonorable act to use a die not designated as an honor die.

Dice Priming

You should never play with virgin dice (new dice which have never been used in a game) without properly priming them. The process is simple and if you diligently follow it for each and every new die you purchase you'll save yourself a world of headaches and problems.

When you purchase a new die it should be segregated from your active Dice Arsenal until it's properly primed and its status is known.

Take the virgin die and roll it 25 times. Count the number of rolls which result in a maximum result as well as those which result in the minimum possible result. If the number of minimum results is more than the number of maximum results repeat the process. I use the 'three strikes yer out' rule. If the die fails the Min/Max test three times in a row throw it away. You could try to purge it of any bad luck but it's just a virgin die — why take chances?

Once a virgin die has passed the Min/Max test you need to trial-test it in active play. You should still keep it segregated, however, from your main dice arsenal. Wait 'til an opportunity comes up in the game when a die roll of some type is needed. Then, and only then, produce the die and roll it. If the result is a critical failure (i.e. fumble) dispose of the die immediately. If the die roll is a simple failure try it again when the opportunity rises. If the die produces a failed result a third time toss it out.

If the die rolls a successful result, however, it shows promise. You should still keep it segregated until it has produced three successful in-game results. Then, and only then, should you move it to your active Dice Arsenal.

Care and Maintenance

When not using your dice, you should keep them stored in a special bag (leather, neoprene, suede or vinyl bags are best). Care should be taken that any suspect dice or untested dice are segregated. Studies conducted at the Hard Eight A.C.T. labs have suggested that dice stored together tend to maintain their luck-levels for longer periods of time than dice stored individually or in open containers. These studies further suggest that low-rolling dice tend to benefit from being stored with more robust dice and that their luck-levels may actually be pulled up. But a single unlucky die can bring down the luck-level of every die in the bag it's stored in. It is my recommendation that you take no chances. If the status of a die is in question— segregate it.

Lucky Dice

You should always name any dice that are lucky. There is power in a name, as many cultures know, and this name should not be given lightly. You should never name it a dishonorable name, as it may rebel. The name should reflect your hopes, or the positive characteristics of the die. You may also want to name your die according to a specific task you assign to it.

That is the next step. Once a die has been found lucky, you may want to assign it to perform some specific task. For instance, a dice that consistently rolls high numbers might end up being your to-hit or damage die. An appropriate name will seal this deal. A dice that rolls consistently low may be useful for saving throws.

Whatever happens, use lucky dice wisely. Don't overuse them. Don't abuse them. Don't use them for such trivialities as rolling for supply availability unless there's something you can't live without. Treat them with respect. Then they will rarely let you down.

When Good Dice Go Bad —

Dice Cleansing and other Rituals

Sometimes, after many campaigns of faithful service, a die will somehow start rolling badly. It should be obvious when that occurs, that it has fallen into a bad-luck slump. You might want to simply toss the die in the trash and write it off. However, sometimes it's tough turning your back on a die which has served you so well for so long. In cases like this you might attempt to purge it of the tainted influence of bad luck.

There are hundreds of dice cleansing rituals out there being promoted by every two-bit hack jockey and dice shaman in the gaming world. Some of them work. Most don't and are unproven. We support only the following time-proven methods.

The Fame-Rub

The fame rub is a tactic with some merit. A person who wants to quickly transfer good luck into his dice can do so by rubbing the dice on the person, or some personal effect, of a popular game designer. Rubbing a die across ol' Gar's signature, from left to right, for example, has been reported to yield wondrous results. (Remember: Always left to right for higher numbers. Right to left for lower numbers). This practice can also be used to prime new dice and many game designers at conventions and store signings are more than glad to oblige fans. As a rule of thumb you should do a minimum of six swipes of the

The Fame-Rub

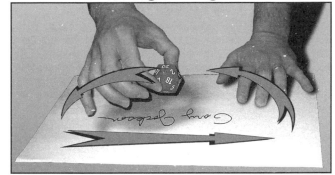

Left to Right = Higher #s

Right to Left = Lower #s

die across the signature. (But no more than ten as that can sometimes have the opposite effect of what is desired.)

You can also gather something a game designer has used, such as a napkin, paper cup, soda can, etc. and rub your dice on it. (Again — from left to right to yield higher numbers). If you're lucky, you might even be able to rub your dice on the designer himself, or even get one kissed or blessed!!! You might want to check the game designer's credentials before going this route, however. Has he had any hit games? Has he won at least three Origins Awards? Make sure his stuff is up to snuff before rubbing your dice on him.

There are even those who suggest if you rub a die on a dead game designer's tombstone, the bad luck will immediately be discharged only to be replaced by good luck. Such a charged-die is said to be luckiest of all dice. According to Norman Bowzer, who has tried this approach on numerous occasions it simply doesn't work. He recommends leaving the die on the tombstone for two nights under a full moon in order to give the bad luck time to dissipate. Since this particular method is the subject of dispute we present it here with proper notice that it may, or may not useful.

One thing is certain. If you have a die that starts rolling badly, you need to quickly get it away from all your other dice. DON'T under ANY circumstance place it back in your dice bag with the rest of your dice. Such an act is sheer folly. You need to keep it sequestered from the rest of your dice, or you're just begging for trouble. Until you have been able to purge the bad luck from a die, and instill it with good luck, there's no use taking any chances.

Emergency Purge

There may be times when you as a player are unsure about the luck of your dice. Or what if you're in the middle of a Hacktournament and you feel your luck has dropped out of your dice bag? There is one way to infuse a little luck back into your dice bag which may just save your game. First, you must empty out your dice bag. Roll each one until it yields a maximum result. Set it aside. Rub each die across Gary's signature (or, a less affective option, across his byline on any HackMaster product) as stated earlier, from left to right. Put all the dice back in the bag and shake it 100 times to redistribute the luck.

Cocky Dice

Sometimes a die simply rolls badly because it has gotten a bad attitude. Some lucky dice suddenly become cocky and think they can't roll a bad number. Then Lady Luck steps in and demands alimony. In such instances, it may be in the best interest of that die, your other dice, and your game, if you make an example of this particular bad apple. An attitude adjustment could be just what the dice doctor ordered. There are several methods of punishing dice, but the best ones are the simplest. Simply refuse to use the die, or even touch it. Ostracize it. Ignore it.

GMs and players alike need to keep a particular eye on the luck the dice at their table. Bad luck can spread from dice bag to dice bag. Players should be aware that if they don't deal with their bad luck dice on their own, their GM will be forced to intervene. After all, there is a risk of one player's bad luck being transferred to another player, and if that happens, chaos could soon ensue.

Dice Rolling Procedure

Every gamer has his own approach when it comes to rolling the dice. Some gamers take it in stride, content with tossing the dice and accepting the results. Most gamers, however, take the rolling of the dice very seriously. The act of rolling dice is crucial to such people. It is the one aspect of the game where you, as players have some power over how the game is played and its outcome. The more energy and focus you put into the process of rolling dice, the better your chances of success.

Now, over the years, I've seen hundreds of gamers toss the bones. It seems every individual has his own technique, but here are a few tips to getting the most out of each and every die roll.

Before rolling the dice, 'prep' them. Every gamer has his own method of doing this. A good way to prepare a die to do its best is to kiss it. Yes, I said KISS it. The transfer of psychic energy from this process can do wonders and often makes a nat-twenty pop up just when you need it.

Others blow on their dice, but the rationale for this is unclear. Some rub them between their palms, which may work if the person rolling the dice is a very lucky person. It may transfer from the hands to the die. Other people talk to their dice, encouraging them to roll high. I've seen people who have had such a close relationship with their dice that they have been able to tell the dice what numbers they need, and they get them!

Some people feel that rattling the dice for a prolonged period of time prepares them for the rigors of battle. However, it is a well-known fact in more enlightened gaming circles that the longer you shake a die, the more random the result. If you want to control the dice results, I have a little saying that helps. "Hold 'em tight, the roll ain't right. Let 'em fly, the roll will be high."

The Standard Roll

1. After shaking the die vigorously in a clenched fist, the palm is opened and thrust toward the designated dice rolling zone.
2. The momentum of the open hand causes the die to roll forward off the extended fingers.
3. A slight twist to the wrist as the die is released gives the dice a bit more tumble-action.
4. The die is released and the results are read when the die comes to a complete stop.

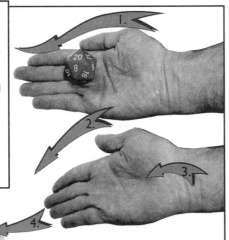

Now as to the actual roll, the best practice is to put a "back-roll" spin on the die when releasing. This is a really good technique when the dice have been luke warm and you're in a pinch. My old friend Gar' liked to simply open his palm and let the dice gently roll off and onto the table. Another good maneuver, to be used ONLY when your dice are already performing well is the "confidence roll." Give some topspin as you push them forcefully from your palm in a violent manner. I usually precede this type of roll with an insolent statement directed at my foe, such as: "OK you scumbag! Wanna DANCE!!!" The cockier and more defiant the verbal attack, the better. Then rub it in real good when you roll the damage. A word of warning, though. Confidence rolls can

The Confidence Roll

Some gamers find that having an attitude when rolling the dice works best for them. The Confidence Roll is just that — stepping up to the plate and letting the dice fly without any begging or tip of the hat to Lady Luck.

1. After shaking the die vigorously in a clenched fist, the palm is opened and tipped as it is thrust toward the designated dice rolling zone.
2. Just as the die is about to leave the hand the palm is inverted with a quick twist of the wrist for added thrust.
3. The die is projected toward the table at a sharp angle to give it a 'bounce.'

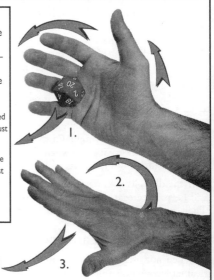

raise your luck to an uncanny level, but they draw grudge monsters like you wouldn't believe.

Among gamers, there is some dispute as to what constitutes an official roll. Most groups have house rules which all players have agreed to comply with. Some groups consider a roll to be void if it leaves the table or playing surface. Other groups consider all rolls valid, including those that land on the floor, in the pizza, in a cup of soda, etc.

I've heard of a group of players in the South Carolina H.M.P.A. chapter that have a special 'cat clause' to their house die-rolling rules. If the family cat intercepts the dice during a roll, the cat is allowed to play with the dice until he's bored and breaks off his attack. The results of the abandoned dice are considered official!

As for a die that lands in such a way that it is leaning, (cocked) with only part of its surface on the table, the general rule is this: if you can insert two pennies underneath the cocked edge of the die, the roll is invalid and the die must be re-rolled.

Whatever the house rules, the GM has the final say on whether a die roll is acceptable or not.

Let me say this, as a final word on the importance of dice to HackMaster, and a personal note. Most gamers will agree, there's nothing more beautiful than a handful of multi-colored, jewel-like dice glistening in the warm light over the gaming table. There is no better sound than that of the hard plastic patter of dice hitting a gaming table. There is no greater thrill than having a character standing toe to toe with death, and seeing that impossible number pop up on the dice to save him. So, treasure those little gems, my friends. Treat 'em right. You won't be sorry.

The Backspin Roll

The backspin is best left to veteran role-players. It takes years to master and doing it improperly could result in a disasterous die-roll or even invading the DRZ of another player.
Still, it doesn't hurt to practice and some players do have a natural talent for picking it up.

1. After shaking the die vigorously in a clenched fist, the palm is inverted face down. The die/dice are cradled in the curl of the fingers and the wrist is snapped forward.
2. Just as the 'snap' reaches a point where the hand is fully extended, the fingers are straightened and waved/twirled away from the thumb to give the die a slight spin.
3. At the point of release the wrist is twisted in an outward motion to give additional spin to the die/dice.
4. The die is released with a combination sliding/tumbling action.

HackMaster Official Dungeon Map Symbols

1. Altar		36. Gate, Iron
2. Archway		37. Gate, Wood
3. Balcony		38. Hole, Ceiling
4. Barred Opening		39. Hole, Floor
5. Barrel		40. Illusionary Wall
6. Campsite, Cold		41. Lair
7. Cauldron		42. Mosaic
8. Chasm (Depth)		43. Murder Holes
9. Chute		44. Pillars
10. Cleared Out		45. Pit (with depth in feet)
11. Coal Bin		46. Pit, Covered
12. Collapsed Ceiling		47. Pit, Spiked
13. Curtain		48. Portcullis
14. Danger Here		49. Pressure Switch
15. Debris		50. Railing
16. Door, Locked		51. Rallying Point
17. Door, One Way		52. Resupply Point
18. Door, Secret		53. Sconce
19. Door, Spiked Closed		54. Sloping Passage/Corridor (Ascending)
20. Door, Spiked Open		55. Sloping Passage/Corridor (Descending)
21. Double Door		56. Spiral Staircase
22. False Door		57. Spring/Pool
23. Flooded		58. Stairs Down
24. Furnace/ Fireplace		59. Stairs Up
25. Furnishing: Armoire		60. Stash (Loot)
26. Furnishing: Bed		61. Stash (Party Member Corpse)
27. Furnishing: Bench		62. Structure Unsound
28. Furnishing: Chair		63. Sub-passageway
29. Furnishing: Chest, locked		64. Tapestry
30. Furnishing: Chest, unlocked		65. Trap Door (Floor)
31. Furnishing: Desk/Bureau		66. Trap Door (Ceiling)
32. Furnishing: Pew		67. Trap, Mechanical
33. Furnishing: Statue		68. Trap, Spell
34. Furnishing: Table		69. Treasure
35. Furnishing: Urn		70. Unexplored Beyond This Point

HackMaster Official Wilderness Map Symbols

1. Border, Disputed	33. Pass, Mountain (Snow Locked)
2. Border, Patrolled	34. Pond/Lake
3. Border, Unpatrolled	35. Rapids/White Water
4. Bridge	36. Rocks, Boulders
5. Bridge, Toll	37. Rocks, Broken
6. Bushes	38. River, Deep
7. Campsite, Cold	39. River, Intermittent
8. Campsite, Seasonal	40. Road, Patrolled
9. Chasm	41. Road, Paved
10. City	42. Road, Unpatrolled
11. Cliff	43. Ruins
12. Crops/Field	44. Seasonal Village/Settlement
13. Dam	45. Spring, Manmade
14. Desert	46. Spring, Natural
15. Ferry, Toll	47. Stash (Loot)
16. Ford	48. Stash (Party Member Corpse)
17. Forest, Deep	49. Stream
18. Forest, Sparse	50. Swamp
19. Gully/Ravine	51. Town
20. Hamlet	52. Tracks (animal)
21. Herd Animals	53. Tracks (humanoid)
22. Hills	54. Trail, Footpath
23. Ice	55. Trail, Game
24. Lair, abandoned	56. Trail, Deer/Goat
25. Lair, occupied	57. Tundra
26. Livestock	58. Village
27. Marsh	59. Waterfall
28. Meadow	60. Waystation, Patrolled
29. Mountains, High	61. Waystation, Unpatrolled
30. Mountains, Low	62. Well
31. Pass, Mountain (Guarded)	63. Whirlpool
32. Pass, Mountain (Open)	64. Wilderness

Appendix N

Glossary

Ability check— a 1d20 roll against one of your character's ability scores (modifiers may be added to or subtracted from the die roll). A result that is equal to or less than your character's ability score indicates that the attempted action succeeds.

Ability— any of the seven natural traits that represent the basic definition of a player character: Strength, Dexterity, Constitution, Intelligence, Wisdom, Charisma and Comeliness. A player character's abilities are determined at the beginning of a game by rolling 3d6. The scores continue to be used throughout the game as a means of determining success or failure of many actions.

AC— abbreviation for Armor Class.

Accelerated Campaign Testing (ACT Lab)— a division of Hard Eight Enterprises concentrating on statistics and testing of game mechanics.

Adventuring Company— a company formed to help cash-strapped parties of adventurers equip themselves properly. The party becomes a company with investors backing them by covering the party's expenses under contract. These take many forms. (See Chapter 13 under Sponsored Adventuring Parties.)

Alignment— a factor in defining a player character that reflects his basic attitude toward society and the forces of the universe. Basically there are nine categories demonstrating the character's relationship to order vs. chaos and good vs. evil. A player character's alignment is selected by the player when the character is created.

Alignment Audit— scrutiny by any number of authorities into a character's adherence to his professed alignment.

Alignment Infraction Points— the number of deviations from a character's professed alignment.

Apology die roll— a roll made when a person apologizes, which may force a wronged person to forgive him. It may also restore any honor lost due to a wrong action.

Area of effect— the area in which a magical spell or a breath weapon works on any creatures unless they make a saving throw.

Armor Class (abbr. AC)— a rating for the protective value of a type of armor, figured from 10 (no armor at all) to 0 or even -10 (the best magical armor). The higher the AC, the more vulnerable the character is to attack.

Armor Hit Points— the amount of damage armor absorbs without passing the damage on to the wearer.

Attack Roll— the 1d20 roll used to determine if an attack is successful.

Availability Index— a table which indicates if a desired item for purchase is available in a given locale and the chance for finding that item. It gives information on whether the chance for purchasing any item in a particular place is high, medium or low.

BPs— an abbreviation for Building Points, which are used to purchase skills, raise attributes, and any number of other purposes.

Basic Block of Instruction (abbr. BBI)— a formal training session, used to enhance player's skills and abilities.

Bend Bars/Lift Gates Roll— the roll of percentile dice to determine whether a character succeeds in bending metal bars, lifting a heavy portcullis, or similar task. The result needed is a function of Strength and can be found in Table 1A.

Body Count Maximus— gamer slang for an extremely bloody engagement or session, in which many lives were lost.

Bonus Spells— extra spells at various spell levels that a priest is entitled to because of high Wisdom; shown in Table 1E.

Breath Weapon— the ability of a dragon or other creature to spew a substance out of its mouth just by breathing, without making an attack roll. Those in the area of effect must roll a saving throw.

Building Points (abbr. BP)— points a player uses to buy skills or abilities for his character during the character creation process.

Carcass Boy— gamer slang for a character who has just died, usually in a particularly humiliating or devastating fashion. A term of derision.

Cardboard Curtain— gamer slang for the GM's screen. It signifies the separation between GM and player.

Casually Depart— gamer slang used when an adventuring party is planning to run like hell due to being obviously outnumbered. Many gamers contend that this term sounds less cowardly than "retreat" or "run like hell." Variations include Tactical Withdrawal or Retrograde Advance.

CHA— abbreviation for Charisma.

Chance of Spell Failure— the percentage chance that a priest spell will fail when cast. Based on Wisdom, it is shown in Table 1E.

Chance to Know Spell— the percentage chance for a wizard to learn a new spell. Based on Intelligence, it is shown in Table 1D.

Character Baiting— a tactic some players accuse GMs of. It consists of using treasure or some other goodie to lure characters into foolish and/or dangerous, actions.

Character Demise Studies— research conducted by the Hack Master Player's Association into character deaths. This research is used to determine what actions and/or scenarios are the most lethal for characters.

Charisma (abbr. CHA)— an ability score representing a character's persuasiveness, personal magnetism, and ability to lead.

Clanger— gamer slang for anyone wearing a lot of noisy armor.

Class— A character's primary profession or career.

COM— abbreviation for Comeliness.

Comeliness— an ability score that represents a character's physical attractiveness, social grace and personal beauty.

Common— the language that all player characters in the HackMaster game world speak. Other languages may require the use of proficiency slots.

CON— abbreviation for Constitution.

Constitution (abbr. Con)— an ability score that represents a character's general physique, hardiness, and state of health.

d100— either an actual 100-sided die or two different-colored ten-sided dice to be rolled

d20— a twenty-sided die.

d12— a twelve-sided die.

d10— a ten-sided die. Two d10s can be used as percentile dice.

d8— an eight-sided die.

d6— a six-sided die.

d4— a four-sided die.

d3— since there is no such thing as a three-sided die, a roll calling for d3 means to use a d6, making 1 and 2 be a 1, 3 and 4 be a 2, and 5 and 6 be a 3.

d— abbreviation for dice or die. A roll that calls for 2d6, for example, means that the player rolls two six-sided dice.

Damage— the effect of a successful attack or other harmful situation, measured in hit points.

Demihuman— a player character who is not human: a dwarf, elf, gnome, half-elf, or halfling.

DEX— abbreviation for Dexterity.

Dexterity (abbr. Dex)— an ability score representing a combination of a character's agility, reflexes, hand-eye coordination, and the like.

Dibs (Dibs Protocol)— the acceptable method of claiming treasure.

Dice Grunts— gamer slang for role players.

Dice Heads— gamer slang for role players.

Dice Priming— the method of preparing virgin (new) dice for play, determining each die's potential for good luck.

Dice Squirrel— gamer slang for a person who touches, takes and/or uses someone else's dice. A term of derision.

Dicequake— gamer slang for what happens just after someone has bumped the playing table.

Dip Dice— gamer slang for a player who's acting stupidly.

Don't Get Yer Dice Bag In A Wad— gamer slang meaning not to worry or over react.

Dual-class character— a human who switches character class after having already progressed several levels. Only humans can be dual-classed.

Emergency Purge (Dice)— the method of quickly purging bad luck from a player's dice.

Encumbrance— the amount, in pounds, that a character is carrying. How much he can carry and how being encumbered affects his movement rate are based on Strength and are shown in Tables 9Y. Encumbrance is an optional rule.

Encumbrance Audit— at a Game Master's discretion a player may be required to hand over his character sheet to be checked for encumbrance violations. The random nature of these audits ensures that players do not fudge on the encumbrance rules, and that they carefully monitor the amount of weight their characters are carrying. Infractions can cause penalties.

Energy drain— the ability of a creature, especially undead, to drain energy in the form of class levels from a character, in addition to the normal loss of hit points.

EP— abbreviation for experience points.

EP-Moochers— gamer slang for players who will do anything to get easy experience points. A term of derision.

Experience Point Leaching Wuss!— gamer slang for a player who deceptively takes experience points that other players feel are rightfully theirs. A term of derision.

Experience Points (abbr. EP)— points a character earns (determined by the Game Master) for completing an adventure, for doing something related to his class particularly well, or for solving a major problem. Experience points are accumulated, enabling the character to rise in level in his class (See Chapter 3).

Fame (Infamy)— an indication of how widely known (and spoken of) a character's deeds and exploits are in the campaign milieu he's adventuring in.

Flavor Text— gamer slang for anything that comes out of the GM's mouth that isn't immediately useful to the players. Includes descriptions of the weather, random dungeon dressing, etc.

Flaws— physical imperfections and disabilities.

Follower— a nonplayer character who works for a character for money but is initially drawn to his reputation.

Fractional Ability Score— These scores are determined by rolling a d100 for each ability score.—the percentage, rolled on 1d100, which augments each of a character's ability scores. These scores can help raise base ability scores as experience and honor is gained.

Fringe-Gamer (Bush-Leaguer)— gamer slang for someone new to gaming, or someone who plays infrequently. Sometimes a term of derision.

Gamer Slang— jargon used by gamers which makes up a sort of language all its own. Those outside of gaming circles, or those new to RPGs may not be able to understand these terms without translation. Also referred to as Gamer Speak.

Gaze Attack— the ability of a creature, such as a basilisk, to attack simply by making eye contact with the victim.

Glory-Hound— gamer slang meaning a player who tries to take all of the glory for an adventure for himself. A term of derision.

GMG— a reference to the Game Master Guide.

Goon— gamer slang for characters that seem to be designed strictly for combat.

Grudge Monsters— gamer slang for creatures, usually extremely powerful, used by the GM to get revenge on a player for some real, or imagined, slight. Such tactics are not endorsed by Hard Eight or the HMPA

Grudge Trap— Similar to grudge monsters, this is gamer slang for traps, usually unavoidable, designed by a GM to exact revenge on players in retaliation for some real, or imagined, slight. Again, such tactics are not endorsed by Hard Eight or the HMPA

Hack Jockey— gamer slang for a role player.

Hack Monger— gamer slang for players who are especially bloodthirsty in their methods of gaming.

Handedness— a term meaning the preferred hand used by a character during combat, or for other tasks.

Henchmen— nonplayer characters who work for a character mainly out of loyalty and love of adventure. The number of henchmen a character can have is based on Charisma and is shown in Table 1F. The GM and the player share control of the henchmen.

Hireling— nonplayer characters who work for a character just for money. Hirelings are completely under the control of the GM.

Hit Dice— the dice rolled to determine a character's hit points. Up to a certain level, one or more new Hit Dice are rolled each time a character attains a new class level. A fighter, for example, has only one 10-sided Hit Die (1d10) at 1st level, but when he rises to the 2nd level, the player rolls a second d10, increasing the character's hit points.

Hit Points— a number representing: 1. How much damage a character can suffer before being killed, determined by Hit Dice. The hit points lost to injury can usually be regained by rest or healing; 2. How much damage a specific attack does, determined by weapon or monster statistics, and subtracted from a player's total.

Home Table— gamer slang referring to a gaming group's usual playing location.

Honor Checks— checks made of a character's honor made under varying circumstances. GMs can always call for such checks whenever they feel situations warrant such checks. Checks are also made at such times as alignment audits, when new characters join a game or when characters encounter extremely powerful or honorable NPCs.

Honor Die/Dice— a die used to supplement various die/dice rolls which depend on a character's honor.

Honor Duels— a contest whereby characters pit their honor against each other, or against NPCs.

Honor Factor— this is the measure of how well respected your character is and how he is viewed by others. It is based upon a number of varying factors, such as accomplishments, parentage and family heritage as well as courage and reputation.

Honor, Group— an average of the Honor Factors of all of the characters in an adventuring group. It is the way in which a group is viewed by the public.

Honor, Individual— the measure of an individual character's reputation and the amount of respect he commands from others.

Hot-To-Plot— gamer slang for GMs who try to rush characters into the storyline of his adventure. Players sometimes resent being prodded into doing anything other than what they want to do.

HP— abbreviation for Hit Points.

Infravision— the ability of certain character races or monsters to see in the dark. Infravision generally works up to 60 feet in the darkness.

Initiative— the right to attack first in a combat round, usually determined by the lowest roll of a 10-sided die. The initiative roll is eliminated if surprise is achieved.

INT— abbreviation for Intelligence.

Intelligence (abbr. Int)— an ability score representing a character's memory, reasoning, and learning ability. Italic type—used primarily to indicate spells and magical items.

Level— any of several different game factors that are variable in degree, especially: 1. Class level, a measure of the character's power, starting at the 1st level as a beginning adventurer and rising through the accumulation of experience points to the 20th level or higher. At each level attained, the character receives new powers. 2. Spell level, a measure of the power of a magical spell. A magic-using character can use only those spells for which his class level qualifies him.

Like An Anchor With A Dice Bag— gamer slang for a player who slows the party down. A term of derision.

Lint-Fer-Brians— gamer slang for a player who fails to pay attention to the game around him and acts in stupid ways, endangering himself and/or his party. A term of derision.

Loyalty Base— a bonus added to or a penalty subtracted from the probability that henchmen are going to stay around when the going gets tough. Based on the character's Charisma, it is shown in Table 1F.

M— abbreviation for material component.

Magical Defense Adjustment— a bonus added to or a penalty subtracted from saving throws vs. spells that attack the mind. Based on Wisdom, it is shown in Table 1E.

Maneuverability Class— a ranking for flying creatures that reflects their ability to turn easily in aerial combat. Each class—from a top rank of A to a bottom rank of E—has specific statistical abilities in combat.

Map-Monkey— gamer slang for the player chosen to map a group's progress through dungeons and other locales.

Material Component (abbr. M)— any specific item that must be handled in some way during the casting of a magical spell.

Maximum Press— the most weight a character can pick up and raise over his head. It is a function of Strength and may be found in Table 1A.

Melee— combat in which characters are fighting in direct contact, such as with swords, claws, or fists, as opposed to fighting with missile weapons or spells.

Missile Combat— combat involving the use of weapons that shoot missiles or items that can be thrown. Because the combat is not "toe-to-toe," the rules are slightly different than those for regular combat.

Movement Rate— a number used in calculating how far and how fast a character can move in a round. This number is in units of 10 yards per round outdoors, but it represents 10 feet indoors. Thus, an MR of 6 is 60 yards per round in the wilderness, but only 60 feet per round in a dungeon.

Monty Haul— possibly the oldest gamer slang term of all, referring to dungeons that are packed with treasure, but relatively unguarded and easy to loot. Usually the sign of an immature GM who uses such devices so his players will "like" him.

MR— abbreviation for movement rate.

Mulligans— a die re-roll awarded for having optimal honor.

Multi-class Character— a demihuman who improves in two or more classes at the same time by dividing experience points between the different classes. Humans cannot be multi-classed.

Mythos (pl. mythoi)— a complete body of belief particular to a certain time or place, including the pantheon of its gods.

NetherDeep — name given for the complex underground network of caverns, and dungeon passages which lie beneath the surface of Garweeze Wurld.

Neutrality— a philosophical position, or alignment, of a character that is between belief in good or evil, order or chaos.

Nonhuman— any humanoid creature that is neither a human nor a demihuman.

Nonplayer Character (abbr. NPC)— any character controlled by the GM instead of a player.

No-Want-Ems— gamer slang for treasure items that are less than desirable, such as helmets with holes in them, balls of lint, broken arrows, etc.

NPC— abbreviation for non-player character.

Numb Dice— gamer slang for a stupid player. It is a term of derision.

Oath, Blood— a promise made when a character wants to indicate he's making a binding pact. A character who makes a blood oath is literally swearing by his Honor. If he breaks his word he loses honor.

Oath, Gawd— the most solemn of all oaths, it is when a character swears by his patron deity. Breaking such oaths brings severe penalty in the form of the loss of a level of experience.

One-Hitpoint-Wonders— gamer slang for NPCs and monsters who can be defeated easily.

Open Doors Roll— the roll of a 20-sided die to see if a character succeeds in opening a heavy or stuck door or performing a similar task. The die roll at which the character succeeds can be found in Table 1.

Opposition School— a school of magic that is directly opposed to a specialist's school of choice, thus preventing him from learning spells from that school, as explained in Chapter 3: Magic-Users.

Orc-Wipe— gamer slang, it is an extremely derisive term, indicating a player who has invoked the wrath of one or more of his fellow players. A player labeled with this term has just been compared to an item of personal hygiene used by orcs.

PC— abbreviation for player character.

Pencil Death— gamer slang referring to a character who has died so many times there are holes in the character sheet from all of the erasures and updates made.

Percentage (or percent) Chance— a number between 1 and 100 used to represent the probability of something happening. If a character is given an X percentage chance of an event occurring, the player rolls percentile dice.

Percentile Dice— either a 100-sided die or two 10-sided dice used in rolling a percentage number. If 2d10 are used, they are of different colors, and one represents the tens digit while the other is the ones.

PizzaMan-Speak— gamer slang referring to a player skill, and NOT a character skill. Only one player per group may possess this skill at a time, and one who has this skill may only rid himself of it by passing it on to a newbie. The player who has pizzaman-speak is the guy who has to call in any pizza orders and collect the money to pay the pizza dude.

Player Character (abbr. PC)— the characters in a role-playing game who are under the control of the players.

Plot Hammering— gamer slang for GMs who are extremely heavy handed in ensuring players stay on track with the adventure he has planned, allowing for little, if any, deviation.

Plot Stick— gamer slang, similar to the above mentioned plot hammering. It is a term used for methods a GM uses to keep players from straying from his adventure story line.

Plot Wagon— gamer slang, which is a minor variation on Plot Hammering. It refers to heavy handed methods used by GMs to prevent deviation from planned adventures.

Point Mooch— gamer slang for players who try to get easy experience points.

Point Whore— gamer slang, similar to the above, referring to players who will do just about anything to get the most, and easiest amount of experience points.

Poison Save— a bonus or a penalty to a saving throw vs. poison. Based on Constitution, it is shown in Table 1C.

Presence Factor— a score indicating a character's ability to influence the reactions of others towards himself. It is arrived at by adding the character's Honor Die to his Charisma. It affects skills such as Oration, Haggle, etc.

Prime Requisite— the ability score that is most important to a character class; for example, Strength to a fighter.

Proficiency— a character's learned skill not defined by his class but which gives him a greater percentage chance to accomplish a specific type of task during an adventure. Weapon and nonweapon proficiency slots are acquired as the character rises in level, as explained in Chapter 7. The use of proficiencies in the game is optional.

Quirks— character qualities that make them unique, but often present problems in game situations.

Race— a player character's species, either a human, elf, dwarf, gnomeling, half-elf, half-orc, half ogre, halfling or pixie fairy. Race puts some limitations on the PC's class.

Rate of Fire (abbr. ROF)— number of times a missile-firing or thrown weapon can be shot in a round.

Reaction Adjustment— a bonus added to or penalty subtracted from a die roll used in determining the success of a character's action. Such an adjustment is used especially in reference to surprise (shown on Table 1B as a function of Dexterity) and the reaction of other intelligent beings to a character (shown on Table 1F as a function of Charisma).

Regeneration— a special ability to heal faster than usual, based on an extraordinarily high Constitution, as shown in Table 1C.

Resistance— the innate ability of a being to withstand attack, such as by magic. Gnomes, for example, have a magic resistance that adds bonuses to their saving throws against magic. See Chapter 2.

Resurrection Survival— the percentage chance a character has of being magically raised from death. Based on Constitution, it is shown in Table 1C.

Reversible— of a magical spell, able to be cast "backwards," so that the opposite of the usual effect is achieved.

ROF— abbreviation for rate of fire.

Round— in combat, a segment of time approximately 1 minute long, during which a character can accomplish one basic action. Ten combat rounds equal one turn.

Rounds, Melee— 6 seconds, 10 melee rounds make up one standard round.

Rule Stomp(ing)— gamer slang for when a player seems to be constantly, or heavy-handedly, correcting other players' interpretations of the rules and bringing such supposed infractions to the attention of the GM.

Rule Tweakers— gamer slang usually referring to GMs who adjust the rules of HackMaster to their liking. Such tactics are discouraged by Hard Eight.

Rules Lawyering— gamer slang, usually referring to players who are well versed in the rules, and who use their knowledge to regularly challenge GM decisions. Again, such tactics are discouraged by Hard Eight.

S— abbreviation for somatic component.

Saving Throw— a measure of a character's ability to resist (to "save vs.") special types of attacks, especially poison, paralyzation, magic, and breath weapons. Success is usually determined by the roll of 1d20.

School of Magic— One of nine different categories of magic, based on the type of magical energy utilized. Wizards who concentrate their work on a single school are called specialists. The specific school of which a spell is a part is shown after the name of the spell in the spell section at the end of the book.

Screen Grunt— a derogatory term for a GameMaster.

Screen Monkey— a derogatory term for a GameMaster

Shield Hit Points— the amount of damage a shield can take before it becomes useless.

Sidekick— the term for an NPC who is extremely loyal to a character. A sidekick is a special friend who will provide help, expecting little, if anything, in return.

Skill Check— the roll of a d100 to see if a character succeeds in doing a skill or task by comparing the die roll to the character's skill mastery score for the appropriate skills, plus or minus any modifiers (the modified die roll must be equal to or less than the ability score for the action to succeed. A 01 to 05 always succeeds. A result of 98 to 00 always fails regardless of mastery). See Chapter 7 and Appendix F.

Skills, Academia— these skills are those which involve "head" knowledge, such as Administration, Botany, Forestry and Weather Sense.

Skills, Arcane— these are skills which are generally restricted and known by only a few. They tend to be magical in nature and include such knowledge as Cleric Discipline, Magic Discipline and Arcane Lore.

Skills, Language— these skills are those that help characters communicate. They include such languages as Alignment Speak, Dimple Runes and Modern Languages.

Skills, Musical Instrument— skills that deal with the ability to play and master musical instruments. These include Brass Instruments, Percussion Instruments and Woodwind Instruments.

Skills, Task Oriented— skills that require some sort of hands-on action and/or set of procedural actions in order to successfully use them. Examples include painting a portrait, making a boat, etc.

Somatic Component (abbr. S)— the gestures that a spellcaster must use to cast a specific spell. A bound wizard cannot cast a spell requiring somatic components.

Specialist— a wizard who concentrates on a specific school of magic, as opposed to a magic-user, who studies all magic in general.

Spell Immunity— protection that certain characters have against illusions or other specific spells, based on high Intelligence (Table 1D) or Wisdom (Table 1E) scores.

Spell Jacking— an ability usable only by illusionists, giving them the chance to push the envelope in spell memorization. It allows them to hold more spells in memory, but also increases the chance for spell mishaps.

Spell Jockey— gamer slang for a magic user or other type of spell caster.

Sphere of Influence— any of sixteen categories of priest spells to which a priest may have major access (he can eventually learn them all or minor access (he can learn only the lower level spells). The relevant sphere of influence is shown as the first item in the list of characteristics in the priest spells.

Spinectomy— gamer slang for an attempt at backstabbing, usually referring to such an act performed by a high-level thief. It usually means the attempt will be a sure kill.

Starting Honor— the amount of honor a character begins his adventuring career with.

STP— the abbreviation for skills, talents and proficiencies.

STR— abbreviation for Strength.

Strength (abbr. Str)— an ability score representing a character's muscle power, endurance, and stamina.

Surprise Roll— the roll of a ten-sided die by the Game Master to determine if a character or group takes another by surprise. Successful surprise (a roll of 1, 2, or 3) cancels the roll for initiative on the first round of combat.

Sympathy Monsters— gamer slang for monsters that players suspect are introduced by a GM to help a character who seems to be down on his luck gain easy experience points.

Sympathy Whore— gamer slang for a player who attempts to gain the GMs sympathy in hopes of gaining favors. A term of derision.

System Shock— a percentage chance that a character survives major magical effects, such as being petrified. Based on Constitution, it is shown in Table 1C.

Temporal Honor— the honor gained and lost during individual gaming sessions, which cause adjustments to the character's overall Honor.

To-hit Roll— another name for attack roll.

Tossing the Stiff— gamer slang for throwing a dead body into a room to check for traps.

Turn Undead— an ability of a cleric or paladin to turn away an undead creature, such as a skeleton or a vampire.

Turn— in game time, approximately 10 minutes; used especially in figuring how long various magic spells may last. In combat, a turn consists of 10 rounds.

V— abbreviation for verbal component.

Verbal Component (abbr. V)— specific words or sounds that must be uttered while casting a spell.

Weapon Grand Mastery— the highest level of weapon specialization, this proficiency is attainable only by fighters of 6th level or higher.

Weapon High Mastery— the next level of weapon specialization above Weapon Mastery, this proficiency is attainable only by fighters that are already Weapon Masters.

Weapon Mastery— the next level of weapon specialization, this proficiency is attainable only by fighters of 5th level or higher.

Weapon Specialization— a fighter can hone his skills on a particular weapon and 'specialize' in it by taking this proficiency. Gives bonuses to attack and damage.

Weapon Speed— an initiative modifier used in combat that accounts for the time required to properly position a weapon for attack or parry.

Who Put A Burr In His Dice Bag— gamer slang used when referring to a player who seems to be abnormally irritable.

WIS— abbreviation for Wisdom.

Wisdom (abbr. Wis)— an ability score representing a composite of a character's intuition, judgment, common sense, and will power.

Wuss of Heart— gamer slang for players who seem to avoid dangerous situations at all costs, also called cowards. A term of derision.

Zero Level Trash (Zero Level NPC Trash)— gamer slang referring to NPCs who are of no interest to them because they are not worth many experience points.

Appendix O

HMA Bylaws
Version 4.20 (supercedes the erroneously listed version 41.36 in all previously published HackMaster Player's Handbooks)

I. Membership

Why Should I Become a Member?

The Hackmaster Elite. One of the best reasons to become a member is the opportunity to face heroic challenges and high adventure in the HackMaster tradition. Many will start down the road to glory, but few will achieve the legendary status of the HackMaster Elite. These proud few will be able to boast of their famous (or infamous) world-shaking deeds throughout the land.

Friendships. HMA members are part of an exclusive worldwide organization of gamers, all with a common interest: the HackMaster universe. The potential to meet new friends in your local area, at tournaments, and even online, is expanded hundreds of times. When you get together to play HackMaster, you're developing friendships that will last a lifetime (or at least until you find a HackMaster +12).

Tournaments. As a registered HMA member, you are able to participate in sanctioned HackMaster tournaments. At tournaments you can win treasure and experience points for your character, and proud memories of your hacking success.

Sanctioned characters. All members of the HackMaster Player's Association (HMPA) and the HackMaster GameMaster's Association (HMGMA) are permitted to have up to three sanctioned characters registered with the HMA.

Constant Self-Improvement. The HMA encourages its members to be (to coin a phrase) the best that they can be. Through statewide and local area tournaments, HMA members can compete to prove their role-playing excellence. As one of these members, you're competing with some of the best players in the world – something that can only improve your role-playing skills.

What Types of Memberships are Available?

Members must be registered in either the HMPA or the HMGMA, depending on their preference and qualifications. There is a minimum age requirement of 14 to become a sanctioned GM, but there is no age restriction for becoming a player. A HackMaster Retailer's Association (HMRA) membership is available to qualified stores. Contact hma@kenzerco.com for information on the HMRA.

The HMPA offers two types of memberships: Trial and Full. All HMGMA members must be full members of the HMPA.

Trial. A trial membership is free, just sign up! Trial members can create one sanctioned character and participate in tournaments. Trial members' characters cannot advance past 1st level.

Full. For the low annual cost of $ 20.00, full members gain access to a wide range of benefits and services. A 3-year membership is available at a discount rate of $50.00. Benefits include:

- **Membership Card.** Your HackMaster membership card, containing your name, group name (for members in named groups only), and your current level, proves to others that you are a force to be reckoned with. Cards are specially marked and color-coded to distinguish between Players and GameMasters. You will automatically receive a new, updated card when your membership is renewed.
- **HMA Pin.** You will receive a HMA pewter pin when you sign up. This pin lets the whole world know you are a proud member of the HMA.
- **Website Access.** The HMA website is your official online meeting place for all things HackMaster. The website maintains statistics for sanctioned characters, as well as a message board where you can post your thoughts for other members.
- **Playtesting.** As an authorized, confidential KenzerCo playtester, you'll be one of the first people to see our products still in production. You'll have the opportunity to play the modules before anyone else even knows they exist, and contribute your thoughts on how they might be improved. Only named groups may be considered for playtesting.

Other Benefits:

1. Hospitality suites at major conventions for HMA members,
2. Reserved up-front seating, among other benefits, at such illustrious evenst as the KODT live readings,
3. 'Dibs' certificates for treasure, drinks, or snacks during game sessions,
4. HackMaster-certified game effect cards,
5. Special offers and coupons for KenzerCo products,
6. Character Pardons for alignment violations,
7. Seminars open to HMA members only,
8. PAC (Player Advantage Code) listings – available to Players only,
9. Dice bumps of various (+1, +2) calibers,
10. Clue cards, for various adventures, and
11. Bonuses earned against specific creatures.

More benefits coming soon...

How Do I Become a Member?

There are two ways to join the HMA. The preferred method is by signing up at your local HMRA (HackMaster Retailers Association) games store. If you are not near a HMRA store, then you can send in an application form (available on the HMA website) directly to the HackMaster HQ.

1. Player Registration.

You should register yourself as a Player or GM separately from your group, though you can register your group at the same time (on a different form). If you're doing this, you should include all of the appropriate forms and dues in the same envelope. That will make it much simpler for us to enter your information in our database.

2. Character Registration

A full member may have up to three HMA-sanctioned characters at the same time. A member may register new characters at any time by filling out the appropriate form and sending it in to the HMA. *Do not include a copy of your character sheet. We don't need it and will only abuse him or her as a lowly torch bearer in our in-house games.* Newly sanctioned characters must begin at 1st level, with a standard amount of starting equipment and money as defined in chapter 4 of the *HackMaster Player's Handbook*. If you want to start a new character, but you already have three registered, you may retire one of your existing characters from the sanctioned list and replace it with the new one. Be sure you think carefully, for once a character is retired from sanctioned play, it cannot be re-registered at a later date. Your character has retired for good. Trying to roust their tired bones back into the wild life of the HackMaster would make them grumpy, and no one likes a grumpy adventurer.

What if I Want to be a GM and a Player?

If you registered as a player and want to GM, you must e-mail HMA HQ (hma@kenzerco.com) to have your membership converted to the HMGMA. You will then have 90 days to pass your level 1 GM test or be permanently converted back to HMPA.

For the purpose of playing characters, GMs are treated as registered players, and are able to register 3 characters at any time, which they may play in sanctioned adventures and tournaments. GMs may not participate as a player in any sanctioned adventure they have run previously.

GMs accrue ONLY player UPS points (see section VI) when participating as a player, which are added to any UPS points they accrue while acting as a GM. Note that a GM participating in two tournaments as a player DOES NOT meet that part of the Level Three certification requirements (see section IV).

II. HMA Organization

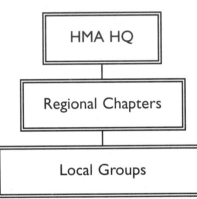

HMA Headquarters

The headquarters of the HMA is at an undisclosed, secret location far below a dormant volcano. All of our mail can be sent to Kenzer and Company and will be diligently forwarded to us. We are responsible for making sure that all HackMaster GMs are hacking through characters and that players are toppling over their GMs' most clever dungeons.

We track the activities of all members of the HMRA, HMGMA and HMPA including new members, tournament sanctioning, sanctioned characters, chapter formation, group formation and even home games! We are always watching. The buck stops here. We are the ultimate authority for all HMA-related events. We may or may not have our hands in other, non-gaming matters of political intrigue and world domination but that is far beyond the scope of this document.

The HMA can be reached through our minions at KenzerCo:

> HackMaster Association
> Kenzer & Company
> 25667 Hillview Court
> Mundelein IL 60060
> hma@kenzerco.com

Regional Chapters

Regional chapters are responsible for organizing HMA activities for their local gaming groups and HMRA stores. By electing officers and maintaining a treasury (the HMA recommends a high tech, electronically guarded vault with cybernetic attack dogs and laser weapons to guard all chapter funds!!!), regional chapters can do things such as coordinate local tournaments, host an annual regional tournament and possibly even earn the privilege of hosting a state championship or the coveted national championship!

The exact "coverage area" of a regional chapter will be determined on a case-by-case basis with an eye toward keeping regions spread out. In order to form a chapter, you must meet the following minimum requirements:

1. The proposed chapter must have at least three officers. Officers must be HMA (either HMRA, HMGMA or HMPA) members in good standing. Officers can be Pro Tempore for 90 days. All new chapters must have regular officers installed within 90 days of formation.
2. The proposed chapter must have a minimum of three local groups in good standing who will be member groups within that chapter.
3. The proposed chapter must be in an area that HMA HQ deems is in dire need of a chapter.

To remain in good standing with the HMA, each chapter must:
1. Maintain an accurate database of all its members.
2. Submit that database to HMA HQ twice annually: by January 1st and July 1st of each year.
3. Run at least one local tournament every two months. If there is at least one local HMRA store in your region which has on-site gaming space, you must hold your local tournaments at an HMRA store.
4. Run a regional championship tournament each year.
5. Promote and recruit for the HMRA, HMGMA and HMPA. If there is at least one local HMRA store in your region, new HMGMA and HMPA memberships must be processed through an HMRA store.

The benefits of running a regional chapter include:
1. Keep $5.00 of the membership fee for each new HMRA store you sign up.
2. Keep 50% of all fees collected at your annual HMA regional championship tournament.
3. May bid for the right to hold the state HMA championship tournaments. You must be located in that state. If a state has no regional chapters then any out-of-state chapter may bid to hold that state's championship.
4. May bid for the right to hold the HMA national championship tournament.
5. Once per year, each chapter will be mentioned in a Kenzer & Company co-op ad in KODT.
6. Upon formation, each chapter will receive a single-frame, customized KODT strip.

To form a chapter, the interested individuals should obtain an *HMA Chapter Formation Form* from their local HMRA store. If there is no local HMRA store, the applicants may obtain one from the HMA web site or by contacting HMA Headquarters directly. The cost of maintaining chapter status is $20.00 per year. If there is an HMRA store within the proposed chapter's region, the application must be processed through that store. If not, the application can be processed through HMA Headquarters directly.

Local Groups

Local groups lie at the very heart of the HMA. They are the backbone of HackMaster gaming and it is from their exploits which sagas are written! Such legendary groups as the *Knights of the Dinner Table* or the *Black Hand Gaming Society* have permanently left their footprints upon the road of high adventure. Can you too take up the flag of valor and the banner of honor and march alongside them? Or are you just a little wuss-monkey who brings low-fat potato chips to the gaming table?

In order to qualify as a local group:
1. There must be one HMGMA GameMaster in good standing.
2. There must be a minimum of three HMPA and/or HMRA members in good standing in the group. Non-HMPA members may never be in an official local group. An HMGMA member in good standing may be a player in a local group but may never be that group's GM!
3. The group must submit a minimum of one "HMA Home Game Reporting Form" per month. After three months of inactivity, the

group will be dissolved and the name of that group *permanently retired*!

An HMGMA member may only be the GameMaster of one group at a time. That place behind the shield – the Loneliest Seat of All – is just too demanding. However, HMGMA, HMPA and HMRA members may be players in any number of local groups.

In order to form a local group, interested members must obtain an "HMA Group Application" from a local HMRA store. If no HMRA store is available, interested members may obtain the form from the HMA web site or from HMA Headquarters directly. There is no charge to form a group.

III. Players

All HMPA members are nationally ranked based on their level as a player and the Universal Point Scale (UPS) points they have earned. There are seven levels through which a player can ascend if they meet the minimum requirements for that level and have earned enough UPS points. Levels 6 and 7 are special levels and are available by HMA Headquarters appointment only.

In order to advance in level a player must contact HMA Headquarters by e-mail (hma@kenzerco.com) and petition for advancement. HQ will review the petition and if the player has met all the requirements for the next level he will be advanced. If HQ finds that the petitioning player has not met the requirements for the next level, he will lose 10% of his UPS points. *DISHONOR IS NOT TOLERATED IN THE HMA!*

The levels and their requirements are:

Level 1: New HMPA members are automatically level 1. There are no requirements other than joining. HMPA members should be warned that level 1 players have not been tested, they have not walked through the flames of virtue and lofted the banner of honor. Though they are brothers, these wuss bags should be given a minimum of responsibility until they have proven themselves.

Level 2: *UPS point requirement: 20*

Other requirements: Must have played in at least one local tournament.

Level 3: *UPS point requirement: 100*

Other requirements: Must have played in at least three local tournaments. Must have submitted at least one approved article to the HackJournal.

Level 4: *UPS point requirement: 500*

Other requirements: Must have played in at least one regional level or higher tournament. Must have submitted at least three approved articles to the HackJournal.

Level 5: *UPS Point requirement: 1000*

Other requirements: Must have played in at least one state level or higher tournament. Must have submitted at least five approved articles to the HackJournal.

Level 6: Hack boys and girls, don't even *think* about achieving this level. No mere dice monkey can simply belly up to the table and become a level 6 player. Level 6 players will be appointed by the HMA Headquarters directly. The mere act of requesting advancement to level 6 will cost you 25% of your earned UPS points and one experience level a piece from each of your sanctioned characters! There will only be five level 6 players worldwide and they will receive Very Special Treatment at conventions and tournaments.

Level 7: There will only ever be one level 7 player worldwide. The details of how that player is selected and advanced are so secret that even knowing that those details exist somewhere in some dark, hidden place puts your life in peril! *FORGET THAT YOU HAVE READ THIS PART!*

UPS Points for Players

UPS (Universal Point Scale) points are used as a means of comparing players and GMs and HMRA members. Let's face it, if being an honorable hero was easy then anybody could do it! There has to be some method of separating the cheesebags and chumps from the HackMasters and heroes! And the UPS system is how it's done.

Players can earn UPS points as follows:

Universal Point Scale – Players	
UPS Points	Activity
1	home game session*
5	approved monster or special item creation
5	each year as a chapter officer**
10	each year of membership (processed January 1st)
10	sign up new HMRA member
25	Hall of Fame character acceptance
5/10/15/20	playing in a local/regional/state/national level tournament
variable	HackJournal submission accepted for print
variable	special certificates earned during HackMaster tournaments

*Regardless of how many home games a player plays in, he may only receive points for one each week. Only members of an approved local group may earn these points.

** Chapters are responsible for e-mailing HMA HQ (hma@kenzerco.com) with a list of the names and HMA numbers of its officers by no later than December 1 of each year or their officers will not receive points for that year. Points are awarded January 1.

Hall of Fame

Every year the HMA selects one character for the Hall of Fame. In addition to receiving Very Special Treatment at conventions, the player whose character is selected receives 25 UPS points.

Hall of Fame selections are announced on July 1 of each year. Submissions must reach the HMA no later than June 1 or they will not be considered. Only official groups may submit characters for consideration in the Hall of Fame. The GM of the group must make the submission and each group may submit only one character each year.

The group's GM must complete an *HMA Character Hall of Fame Submission Form* and include a complete and legible copy of the character sheet.

IV. GameMasters

There's the elite and then there's the elite. Sure, the HMA would be nothing without its players, but the players would have nothing to do without GameMasters. Take care, though, lest you recklessly and thoughtlessly enter the GM's world only to find it's not what you thought. Then you would join those sad, tired souls who populate the realm of Retired GMs.

Often called the Loneliest Seat of All, that honored place behind the GameMaster Shield is at once a sanctuary, a resource center and a final fallback position. The GM is the final authority on his game world but that is both a blessing and a curse.

GMs advance in level by earning UPS (Universal Point Scale) points and meeting other requirements. There are seven levels of GM but only the first five can be advanced through by normal means. HMA Headquarters appoints level 6 and 7 GMs.

Like players, a GM must contact HMA Headquarters via e-mail (hma@kenzerco.com) and petition for level advancement when he has met all the requirements for the next level. Be warned, though! The HMA tolerates dishonor in GMs even less than in players. Requesting advancement when he has not met the requirements will cost a GM 25% of his earned UPS points.

The level requirements are:

Level 1: All new HMGMA members are considered level 1 GameMasters Pro Tempore. In order to maintain level 1 status, new GMs have 90 days to pass the written level 1 test. Tests can be taken at HMRA stores or conventions at which HMA staff are in attendance. If there are no HMRA stores in his area and no upcoming conventions, a new GM can request a test from HMA HQ directly. Tests will also be available on the HMA member web site.

Privileges: Level 1 GMs can run local tournament adventures.

Level 2: *UPS point requirement: 20*

Other requirements: Must be a level 1 GM in good standing. Must pass the level 2 test. Must have run at least one local tournament adventure as a level 1 GM. The level 2 test can be taken in the same manner as the level 1 test.

Privileges: Level 2 GMs can run local and regional tournament adventures. They may write local tournament adventures and submit them to the HMA for approval.

Level 3: *UPS point requirement: 100*

Other requirements: Must be a level 2 GM in good standing. Must have run at least three local and/or regional tournament adventures as a level 2 GM. Must have submitted an approved local tournament to the HMA.

Privileges: Level 3 GMs can run local, regional and state tournaments. They may write local and regional tournament adventures and submit them to the HMA for approval.

Level 4: *UPS point requirement: 500*

Other requirements: Must be a level 3 GM in good standing. Must pass the level 4 test. Must have run at least five local, regional and/or state tournament adventures as a level 3 GM. Must have submitted at least two approved local and/or regional tournament adventures to the HMA.

Privileges: Level 4 GMs can run all HMA tournament adventures. They may write local, regional and state tournament adventures and submit then to the HMA for approval.

Level 5: *UPS point requirement: 1000*

Other requirements: Must be a level 4 GM in good standing. Must have run at least 10 tournament adventures as a level 4 GM including at least one regional tournament adventure. Must have submitted at least three approved local, regional and/or state tournament adventures to the HMA.

Privileges: Level 5 GMs can run all HMA tournament adventures. They write any level tournament adventures and submit them to the HMA for approval.

Level 6: An intern at HMA HQ once accidentally read the Secret Internal Document detailing how the HMA selects level 6 GMs (there can only be five of them worldwide at any time). Donations may be sent in his memory to the charity of your choice.

Level 7: There can only be one level 7 GM worldwide. Don't ask how he is selected. If HMA revealed that information to you, you would become insane from the very knowledge! (We have.)

UPS Points for GMs

Sure it would be nice if all GMs were skilled in the art of character death. It would be great if all them had perfected the sinister art of trap setting. We would love it if every last GM was a dark master of monster creation. But sadly that's not how things are. So to separate the Shield Shysters from the Dungeon Doctors, we use the UPS point system.

GMs earn UPS points as follows:

Universal Point Scale – GameMasters	
UPS Points	**Activity**
1	home game session*
1	each character death in a sanctioned HMA tournament
5	each year as a chapter officer**
5	approved monster or special item creation
10	each year of membership
10	sign up new HMRA member
5/10/15/20	run a local/regional/state/national tournament
10/20/30/40	write an approved local/regional/state/national tournament
variable	HackJournal submission accepted for print

* Regardless of how many home game sessions a GM runs, he may only receive points for one each week. Only members of an approved local group may earn these points.

**Chapters are responsible for e-mailing HMA HQ (hma@kenzerco.com) with a list of the names and HMA numbers of its officers by no later than December 1 of each year or their officers will not receive points for that year. Points are awarded January 1.

V. Items

From time to time, the HMA will make available certain rare and powerful magic items. Such items will be assigned a serial number and will be tracked by the HMA. The item name, item serial number, basic powers of the item and the owner of the item will be public information available on the HMA web site. *Beware, dice monkies! Falsely creating numbered magic items is grounds for immediate expulsion from the HMA.* And one you're expelled, then the real pain begins.

Items with serial numbers may be freely given away, traded or sold at the owner's discretion. He is free to do so at cons, at local gaming stores or even over the internet via online auction sites. Most larger cons will host HackMaster auctions.

VI. Sanctioned vs. Non-Sanctioned Play

Of course, any self-respecting HMA member worth his salt will want to test himself in as many sanctioned HMA tournaments as possible. The only way to become tempered is to jump into the fire. However, waiting for only sanctioned tournaments to play is just not acceptable so the HMA awards points to local groups for playing home games.

Sanctioned Play

Sanctioned play is any official HMA tournament run by an approved HMGMA member during a time approved by the HMA. This includes everything from official local tournaments at the game store down the street to the coveted National Championship.

Non-Sanctioned Local Group Play

Members of officially sanctioned local groups can earn points for playing home games with some restrictions. GMs and players may only earn points for playing with a group of which they are a member. They may only earn points for one game a week regardless of how many they play. No points will be awarded unless the HMGMA member running the game properly submits an "HMA Home Game Reporting Form" for the session.

Non-Group Play

If you are not playing as part of a sanctioned HMA group then your game is not recognized by the HMA. Whatever trials, tribulations and rewards your character received in such a shoddy, amateurish game are of no concern to us because as far as we're concerned it never happened. Card carrying HMA members should be wary of such games. Why isn't the group a sanctioned HMA group? Is the GM too chicken to be sanctioned? Is a blind eye being turned to the rules?

Magic Items in Home Games

Well of course GMs in home games are going to give out magic items. If they didn't, their players would rise up against them and slam their fingers in a car door over and over again. However, it is necessary to place limits on how much magic a sanctioned HMA character may have otherwise an unscrupulous group might be tempted to cheat the system.

In order for a character to be considered a legal, sanctioned HMA character it may not have more EPs worth of magic item than shown on the table entitled "Maximum Allowable Magic Item EPs per Character Level. Your GM has information on how many EPs each magic item is worth.

Maximum Allowable Magic Item EPs per Character Level	
Character Level	Max EP in Magic Items
1	1,000
2	2,000
3	4,000
4	6,000
5	8,000
6	10,000
7	14,000
8	18,000
9	22,000
10	26,000
>10	+4,000 EP per level >10

VII. Tournaments

The tournament should be the goal of any decent gamer worth his dice. Not only does it give you a chance to meet other people with similar interests as your own, but it gives you a chance to kick their asses! In any tournament there are exactly two groups: the guy who won and everyone who wishes they won. In order to separate the piddling pandas from the roaming ravagers, the HMA has categorized their tournaments into the following divisions:

Local tournament: A local tournament is any tournament with an open invitation run by a sanctioned HMGMA GM and played by sanctioned HMPA players. It's irrelevant whether it takes place in the musty basement of your neighborhood hobby store or in one of the brightly lit halls of GaryCon, they are all classified as local tournaments.

Regional tournament: Once a year each regional chapter is required to host a championship tournament open to any groups in their region. These tournaments fall under the classification of regional championships.

State tournament: Every year the HMA will take bids from regional chapters to run an annual state championship. State tournaments will ultimately culminate in a single victor who is declared that state's champion.

National tournament: And of course every year the HMA will sponsor the mighty national championship! The bragging rights of the victor are almost immeasurable.

Tournament event schedules are available both online at the HMA web site and in the HackJournal. All HMA members are encouraged to test themselves and their group against others and some tournament participation is required to advance to the higher GM and player levels.

Individual and Group Tournaments

Most tournaments are individual tournaments. You bring your character, get together with some other players who traveled to the tournament and go at it. Some tournaments, as announced by the HMA, will have a special group status. Only sanctioned groups can play and the players not only compete for status within their game, but the group as a whole competes for status among other groups.

Requesting Local Tournaments

Any HMRA store, HMGMA member or regional chapter member can request a tournament. A minimum of 30 days advance notice is required in order to request sanctioned tournaments. Standard tournament entry fee is $5.00 per player and tournament organizers must submit justification to the HMA if they wish to charge more (e.g., awesome prizes, expensive tournament site, etc.).

Requesting Regional Tournaments

Regional chapter officers must arrange annual regional championship tournaments a minimum of 90 days in advance of the event.

Requesting State and National Tournaments

All state and national championship tournaments are arranged by HMA HQ.

Submitting HMA tournaments.

All active HMGMA GameMasters are encouraged to write tournaments for sanctioning by the HMA. In fact, it's required in order to reach the higher levels of HMGMA membership. Tournaments should be submitted to:

HMA Tournament Submission
Kenzer & Company
25667 Hillview Ct
Mundelein IL 60060

Or e-mailed to:

hma@kenzerco.com

Tournaments should be written to a specific level range and based on six PCs. For example, 6 characters levels 1-4, or 6 characters level 10-14. All tournaments are based on a four hour time block. The beginning 30 minutes and the last 30 minutes should be reserved for administrative and scorekeeping activities, which leaves approximately three hours of play time.

VIII. HackJournal

In order to get the word out to fellow HMA members, HQ will print the HackJournal on a quarterly basis. All HMA members will receive a printed copy in the mail. Members may request to receive a PDF electronic copy instead of a paper copy by e-mailing orders@kenzerco.com. The HMA encourages all members to switch to electronic circulation. Non-HMA members may purchase HackJournals at any HMRA store.

The HackJournal is strongly player supported. HMRA, HMGMA and HMPA members can earn UPS points by submitting articles which are accepted for print. *All submissions become the property of Kenzer & Company. By submitting your article, you hereby assign all right title and interest in and of the story to Kenzer and Company, and agree to be bound by these terms.*

IX. Online Play

Although there is simply no substitute for sitting around a table with your gaming group and laying waste to monsters and hoarding treasure, the HMA recognizes that the modern age brings modern changes to our hobby. An HMA group does not need to be located in the same geographic area. They can register as a group and play exclusively online, only getting together in person perhaps at larger conventions.

At this time, this applies only to the type of games described under the "Non-Sanctioned Local Group Play" section of part VI of this document. The HMA is exploring options for electronic tournaments and conventions but is not currently allowing them.

X. HackMaster Retailers' Association

Essential to the foundation of gaming is the local retail store. Who doesn't have glorious stories about treasure won, creatures slain and fair damsels rescued during all-nighters down at the local shop! The local retail store provides GameMasters with all the tools they need to mow down players, and players all the tools they need to stand united against the GM's tyranny (and from a little bit of backstabbing between friends).

The HMA strongly encourages its members to support their local hobby shops. Remember the importance of spending your money at local businesses and supporting your favorite industry. Let's face it, though, not every store has the perspicaciousness to be elite. That's exactly why we offer a HackMaster Retailer Association membership to stores that do the right stuff!

HMRA stores manage memberships, sanction groups, run tournaments and are often the first stores to receive new HMA sanctioned materials. So

get down to your local non-HMRA hobby shop and politely but firmly show them the error of their ways. Interested retailers can contact the HMA directly at:

HackMaster Association
Kenzer & Company
25667 Hillview Court
Mundelein, IL 60060
(847) 540-0029
hma@kenzerco.com

XI. Word from the HMA Manager

As I look out over the HackMaster Association, I can only think about the power I have gained by taking its helm. I have single-handedly accomplished the biggest coup in the histo…. [Editor's note: At this point, Jamie was sedated and rushed to an area hospital.]

As I look out over the HackMaster Association, I can only think about the opportunity I have to serve its membership. I'm brought back to high school D&D games in my friend Mike Watt's basement. Games where all that mattered was the spirit of the fight, the allure of the treasure and the glory that came with success. To me, that's what fantasy role-playing is all about: setting aside your briefcase or backpack, picking up your HackMaster +12 and seeing just what the heck is around that next corner in the dungeon. Political intrigue and complex diplomatic errands be damned! Strap on my shield, hand me my weapon and I'm going to stride boldly into the dungeon (with the torchbearer in the lead, of course) and stomp some ass.

I hope all of you will see some of those same things in the HackMaster Association. I hope many legends will be written, many Dragons will be slain and many treasure hoards will be plundered by every one of you. As the HMA develops and grows, it's going to be one hell of a ride. I hope you'll come along!

Hoody hoo!

Jamie LaFountain

Jamie LaFountain
HMA Manager

Appendix P

Index

ADVENTURE COMPANY LOG

HackMaster

COMPANY CREST/SYMBOL

Company Name_____

STATUS:　　❑ Freelance　　❑ Sponsored　　❑ Charted

Charter filed at:_____　Terms:_____

Sponsor:_____　Buy Out:_____

GROUP HONOR	GROUP FAME	GROUP LEVEL

GROUP ALIGNMENT:

COMPANY MEMBERS:

	Position	Name	Class	Race	Level	% of Ownership	Shares	Bonus Shares	Honor
1									
2									
3									
4									
5									
6									
7									
8									
9									
10									

Member/Owner Position Codes -- SP: Sponsor　　OW: Owner　　PL: Party Leader　　TR: Treasurer　　QU: Quarterly　　SE: Secretary

HIRELINGS (INCLUDING HENCHMEN, CRONIES, SIDEKICKS ETC.):

	Position	Name	Class	Race	Level	Terms of Employment	Shares	Bonus Shares	Loyalty
1									
2									
3									
4									
5									
6									
7									
8									
9									
10									

Hireling Position Codes -- TB: Torch Bearer　　PB: Pack Bearer　　AH: Animal Handling　　WS: Weaponsmith
AR: Armorer　　MA: Men at Arms　HNCH: Henchman　　HIRL: Hireling　　SDK: SideKick

NOTES

Marching Order

INVENTORY OF LOOT TAKEN

Coins, Gems, etc.

Magic Items

Misc. Items of Value

LIGHT SOURCE	
TYPE	TIME REMAINING

COMPANY FINANCES/ASSETS

Company Treasury (Stashed)

Location:_____

Company Emergency Funds (Stashed)

Location:_____

Petty Cash (Carried)

Carried by: _____

Monies Owed to Company

OWED BY:	AMOUNT	TERMS

Debts Company Owes

OWED TO:	AMOUNT	TERMS

Communal/Company Property

CONTRACTED SERVICES:

	Service	Name (Contact)	Terms/Fees
1	Healing		
2	Fencing of Goods		
3	Legal/Contract		
4	Magic Item Identify		
5	Money Changing		
6	Storage of Goods		
7			
8			
9			
10			

Favors to call in

Scores to Settle

NOTES

Compiled Equipment Tables

Table 9A: Alcohol/Beverages

Item	Cost	Hi	Med	Low
Ale (per gallon)	2 sp	95	85	75
Ale, Dead Viking (Cut Ale) (pint)	1 sp	95	95	95
Ale, Kromian	5 gp	85	70	60
Ale, Pint	5 cp	95	85	75
Beer, Cut, (pint)	5 cp	90	85	75
Beer, Heavy (pint)	1 sp	95	85	75
Bitter Broth (pint)	5 gp	65	70	80
Brandy, Orluian (pint)	5 gp	70	50	35
Grog (pint)	3 sp	95	85	75
Gut Bruiser (pint)	1 gp	75	65	55
Finch-Yager (Amber Brew)	7 gp	70	60	50
Honey Brew (pint) (medicinal)	1 gp	80	70	60
Liver Squeezings	2 gp	85	70	60
Mead, Baker's Thicke (pint)	10 sp	95	90	85
Mead, Common (pint)	5 sp	95	85	80
Mead, Dwarven, Keg	300 gp	30	20	10
Mead, Nordlar (gallon)	10 gp	75	60	45
Mead, Orluian (gallon)	100 gp	65	50	40
Rum (pint)	5 sp	75	65	55
Stout Brown Grevan (pint)	7 sp	90	85	80
Whiskey, Bitter-Korn	2 gp	90	80	70
Wine, Blackberry (pint)	1 gp	85	70	60
Wine, Good (pint)	10 sp	75	65	55
Wine, Gutberry (pint)	4 gp	85	70	60
Wine, Watered (pint)	1 cp	95	85	75
Wine, Watered (pitcher)	2 sp	95	85	75
Wine, Elderberry (pint)	40 gp	60	40	20

To compute weight for any liquids carried allow 1 lb. per pint (8 lbs. per gallon). Don't forget to buy a container as well, GMs always get you with that one. And remember to include the weight for the type of container being used to transport the liquid so you won't fail a dreaded encumbrance audit.

Note also that each type of alcohol has its own inherent effects on the imbiber. Your GM knows this information and will share it when or if appropriate.

Table 9C: Containers: Packs, Bags, Bottles etc.

Item	Cost	Weight	Hi	Med	Low
Backpack	2 gp	2 lbs.	95	85	75
Barrel, small	2 gp	30 lbs.	95	90	85
Basket	—				
Large	3 sp	1 lbs.	95	85	75
Small	5 cp	*	95	90	85
Belt pouch					
Large	1 gp	1 lbs.	95	90	85
Small	7 sp	.5 lbs.	95	90	85
Bolt case	1 gp	1 lbs.	90	85	80
Bucket	5 sp	3 lbs.	95	90	85
Chest					
Large	2 gp	25 lbs.	95	90	85
Small	1 gp	10 lbs.	95	90	85
Flask, metal (pint)	10 sp	.25 lbs.	90	80	70
Glass bottle (pint)	1 gp	*	85	75	65
Iron pot/kettle (gallon)	5 sp	2 lbs.	95	90	85
Sack	—				
Large	2 sp	.5 lbs.	95	90	85
Small	5 cp	*	95	90	85
Map or scroll case	8 sp	.5 lbs.	90	85	80
Wineskin	8 sp	1 lbs.	95	90	85

* These items weigh little individually. Ten of these items weigh one pound.

Table 9E: Light Sources

Item	Cost	Weight	Hi	Med	Low
Candle	1 cp	*	95	90	85
Lantern	—				
Beacon	150 gp	50 lbs.	85	75	60
Bullseye	12 gp	3 lbs.	90	85	80
Hooded	7 gp	2 lbs.	90	85	80
Oil (per flask)	—				
Greek fire	10 gp	2 lbs.	60	40	25
Lamp	6 cp	1 lbs.	90	85	80
Torch	1 cp	1 lbs.	95	90	85

* These items weigh little individually. Ten of these items weigh one pound.

Table 9B: Clothing

Item	Cost	Weight	Hi	Med	Low
Belt	3 sp	.5 lbs.	95	85	75
Boots	—				
Riding	3 gp	2.5 lbs.	90	85	75
Soft	1 gp	2 lbs.	95	85	75
Snakeskin	25 gp	2 lbs.	65	45	35
Breeches	2 gp	.5 lbs.	95	85	75
Cap, Hat	—				
Fine, Formal	3 gp	.25 lbs.	90	80	70
Common, Utilitarian	1 sp	.25 lbs.	95	85	75
Beret, Upper Class	6 gp	.5 lbs.	75	70	65
Cloak	—				
Good cloth	8 sp	3 lbs.	95	85	75
Fine fur	50 gp	6 lbs.	90	80	70
Garments (matching outfit)					
Fine, Leather	20 gp	5 lbs.	90	80	70
Fine, Silk	50 gp	2 lbs.	75	65	55
Fine, Embroidered	75 gp	3 lbs.	85	75	65
Common	2 cp	3 lbs.	95	85	75
Shoddy	1 cp	3 lbs.	95	85	75
Girdle	3 gp	.5 lbs.	95	85	75
Gloves	1 gp	.5 lbs.	95	85	75
Gown, common	12 sp	2 lbs.	95	85	75
Hose	2 gp	.5 lbs.	90	80	70
Jerkin, Laced	1 gp	.5 lbs.	90	80	70
Knife sheath	3 cp	.5 lbs.	95	85	75
Mittens, Winter	3 sp	.5 lbs.	95	85	75
Pin/Brooch, gold	6 gp	—	85	75	65
Pin/Brooch, brass/iron	5 sp	—	95	85	75
Robe	—				
Common	9 sp	3 lbs.	95	85	75
Embroidered	20 gp	4 lbs.	90	75	65
Sandals	5 cp	1 lbs.	95	85	75
Sash	2 sp	.5 lbs.	95	85	75
Shirt, wool	5 cp	.5 lbs.	90	80	70
Shoes	5 sp	2 lbs.	95	85	75
Silk jacket	80 gp	1 lbs.	70	60	50
Surcoat	6 sp	4 lbs.	95	85	75
Sword scabbard, hanger, baldric	4 gp	3 lbs.	95	85	75
Tabard	6 sp	3 lbs.	95	85	75
Toga, coarse	8 cp	3 lbs.	90	80	70
Tunic	8 sp	1 lbs.	95	85	75
Vest	6 sp	.5 lbs.	95	85	75

Table 9D: Daily Food and Lodging

Item	Cost	Weight	Hi	Med	Low
Banquet (per person)	10 gp	—	90	85	80
Bath	3 cp	—	95	85	75
Bear Fat Dumplings	6 cp	—	70	60	50
Bread	5 cp	—	95	85	75
Cheese	4 sp	—	95	85	75
Cheese, Rank (hard)	10 sp	—	80	75	60
City rooms (per month)	—				
Opulent	100 gp	—	90	85	80
Common	20 gp	—	95	85	75
Poor	6 sp	—	95	90	85
Egg or fresh vegetables	1 gp	—	95	90	85
Grain and stabling for horse (daily)	5 sp	—	95	90	85
Grouse Onion Stew	3 cp	—	95	90	85
Honey	5 sp	—	95	90	85
Inn lodging (per day/week)					
Opulent Lodging	50 gp	—	90	85	80
Common	5 sp/3 gp	—	95	90	85
Poor	5 cp/2 sp	—	95	90	85
Meat for one meal	1 sp	—	95	90	85
Meals (per day)	—				
Gourmet	5 gp	—	90	85	80
Good	5 sp	—	95	90	85
Common	3 sp	—	95	90	85
Poor	1 sp	—	95	90	85
Scratch-Root Stew	1 sp	—	95	90	85
Separate latrine for rooms (per month)	2 gp	—	85	75	60
Soup	5 cp	—	95	90	85

Table 9F:
Livestock (Including Mounts and Beasts of Burden)

Item	Cost	Weight	Hi	Med	Low
			Base Availability*		
Ape, Pack (trained)	1,500 gp	400 lbs.	50	30	10
Boar	10 gp	var.	90	85	80
Bull	20 gp	var.	85	75	60
Cow, Calf	5 gp	var.	90	85	80
Cow, Milk	10 gp	var.	90	85	80
Camel	50 gp	var.	90	85	80
Capon	3 cp	var.	90	85	80
Cat, Big, Hunting (jaguar…)	1,500 gp	var.	40	30	20
Cat, Domestic	1 sp	var.	95	90	85
Chicken, Hen, Laying	5 cp	var.	95	90	85
Chicken, Hen, Roasting Kind	2 cp	var.	95	90	85
Cow	10 gp	var.	90	85	80
Dawg	—				
Guard (per skill)	50 gp	var.	80	70	60
Hunting (game specific)	25 gp	var.	85	75	65
Pitbull, Untrained	5 sp	var.	95	80	80
Pitbull, Trained	500 gp	var.	75	65	50
Rottweiler, Untrained	10 sp	var.	90	80	70
Rottweiler, Trained	800 gp	var.	85	75	65
War	100 gp	var.	75	65	55
Dolphin, Mount (trained)	2,000 gp	var.	40	30	20
Dolphin, War (trained)	4,000 gp	var.	30	20	10
Donkey, mule, or ass	8 gp	var.	90	85	80
Elephant	—	—			
Labor	200 gp	var.	75	65	50
War	500 gp	var.	50	40	20
Saber-Toothed	1,500 gp	var.	30	25	15
Falcon, Trained	1,000 gp	var.	80	60	40
Ferret, Trained	70 gp	var.	60	40	20
Goat, Common	1 gp	var.	90	85	80
Goat, Unblemished	8 gp	var.	70	50	40
Goat, Pack, Trained	10 gp	var.	70	50	40
Goose	5 cp	var.	90	85	80
Guinea Hen	2 cp	var.	90	85	80
Hawk, Trained	800 gp	var.	80	60	40
Horse	—				
Draft	200 gp	var.	90	85	80
Draft, Team	500 gp	var.	80	60	40
Dwarven war	1,300 gp	var.	30	20	10
Heavy war	400 gp	var.	70	50	40
Light war	150 gp	var.	70	50	40
Medium war	225 gp	var.	70	50	40
Riding	75 gp	var.	90	85	80
Shirkmare	2,500 gp	var.	40	30	20
Killer Whale, War (trained)	6,000 gp	var.	25	15	5
Killer Whale, Mount	4,000 gp	var.	30	20	10
Monkey, Trained (per skill)	500 gp	var.	60	40	20
Otter	70 gp	var.	60	40	20
Ox	15 gp	var.	95	90	85
Oxen, Matched Pair	50 gp	var.	85	75	65
Partridge	5 cp	var.	90	85	80
Peacock	5 sp	var.	90	85	80
Pig, Suckling	1 gp	var.	95	90	85
Pig, Sow	3 gp	var.	95	90	85
Pigeon	1 cp	var.	95	90	85
Pigeon, Homing	100 gp	var.	70	50	40
Pigeon, Carrier	150 gp	var.	60	40	30
Pony	30 gp	var.	95	90	85
Ram	4 gp	var.	70	50	40
Rooster	8 cp	var.	95	90	85
Sheep	2 gp	var.	95	90	85
Songbird	10 sp	var.	95	90	85
Swan	5 sp	var.	80	75	70
Weasel, Trained	75 gp	var.	65	45	25

* Quantity Available. If availability check determines the type of livestock desired is available then take the base availability index and divide by ten (round down). The result indicates the number of d20s you should roll to determine how many such animals are available for sale. [In third edition this footnote read 'd100' above. This was a typo as reported in Unearthed Errata volume 6 number 4 and now permanently corrected here.].

A note on slaughtering livestock for meat: The beauty of livestock is that first they're beasts of burden, then later as food stores run low, they're actually self-propelled rations. The formula for determining the yield of edible flesh when slaughtering livestock is: Hit points/10*Size= pounds of edible flesh. Where Size is as follows: Tiny = .25, Small = 2, Medium=4, Large = 6 and Huge =10, Giant=25. The size of individual livestock is listed in the Hacklopedia of Beasts, which is available only to a GM. Barbarians, rangers and characters with the "Slaughter, Game Animal" skill are able to increase the yield of edible meat by 25%. Characters with "Slaughter, Livestock" skill can increase the yield by 50%.

Table 9G:
Miscellany

Item	Cost	Weight	Hi	Med	Low
			Base Availability		
Book, Used	5 cp(c)	.5	90	80	60
Cloth (per 10 sq. yds.)	—				
Common	7 gp	10 lbs.	95	85	80
Fine	50 gp	10 lbs.	90	80	75
Rich	100 gp	10 lbs.	85	75	70
Canvas (per sq. yard)	4 sp	1 lbs.	95	85	80
Ring, Poison Container	1 gp	—	65	50	45
Water clock	1,000 gp	200 lbs.	80	75	60
Withering Blue (poison) 8 oz.	50 gp	—	30	20	10

Price listed is base price for a used book. The actual buying or selling price will vary considerably depending on the subject matter and date of publication. For every year that's passed since the date of publication on a book add 1 copper piece to the value. If the subject is history multiply the base price by a factor of 2. If the subject of the book is arcane in nature multiply the base price by a factor of 10.

Table 9H:
Musical Instruments

Item	Cost	Weight	Hi	Med	Low
			Base Availability		
Bagpipes	60 gp	20 lbs.	70	60	50
Bandore	15 gp	10 lbs.	75	65	55
Chime	2 gp	3 lbs.	90	85	80
Drum	4 gp	8 lbs.	90	85	80
Fife	5 gp	1 lbs.	90	85	80
Flute	15 gp	2 lbs.	85	80	75
Gong	5 gp	10 lbs.	90	85	80
Harp	75 gp	25 lbs.	95	90	85
Horn	6 gp	4 lbs.	80	75	70
Lute	25 gp	1 lbs.	90	85	80
Lyre, Darnetian	200 gp	15 lbs.	70	60	50
Mandolin	28 gp	10 lbs.	90	85	80
Pan Flute	5 gp	1 lbs	95	90	85
Rebec and Bow	30 gp	5 lbs.	90	85	80
Recorder	6 gp	1 lbs.	95	90	85
Whistle	1 gp	.25 lbs.	95	90	85

Table 9J:
Provisions: Rations

Item	Cost	Weight	Hi	Med	Low
			Base Availability		
Barrel of pickled fish	3 gp	500 lbs.	90	85	80
Butter (per lb.)	2 sp	1 lbs.	85	80	75
Coarse sugar (per lb.)	1 gp	1 lbs.	70	60	50
Corn dodgers (2 weeks rations)	5 gp	75 lbs.	90	85	80
Eggs (per 100)	8 sp	15 lbs.	90	85	80
Eggs (per two dozen)	2 sp	3 lbs.	90	85	80
Figs (per lb.)	3 sp	1 lbs.	85	80	75
Fish, Parvum (1 day's rations)	1 sp	2 lbs.	70	60	50
Fish, Salted (1 day's rations)	5 cp	3 lbs.	85	80	75
Herbs (per lb.)	5 cp	1 lbs.	90	85	80
Belladonna, sprig	4 sp	1 lbs.	90	85	80
Garlic, bud	5 cp	1 lbs.	90	85	80
Wolvesbane, sprig	1 gp	1 lbs.	90	85	80
Nuts (per lb.)	1 gp	1 lbs.	90	85	80
Preserves, Fruit (1 day's rations)	5 cp	1 lbs.	85	80	75
Raisins (per lb.)	2 sp	1 lbs.	90	85	80
Rations, Dry (1 week's rations)	10 gp	65 lbs.	85	80	75
Rations, Iron (1 week's rations)	5 gp	25 lbs.	90	85	80
Rations, Standard (1 week's rations)	3 gp	50 lbs.	85	80	75
Rice (per lb.)	2 sp	1 lbs.	90	85	80
Salt, 1 lb bag	1 gp	1 lbs.	85	80	75
Sausage, Blood (1 meal)	1 sp	.5 lbs.	90	85	80
Sausage, Peppered (1 meal)	2 sp	1 lbs.	85	80	75
Sausage, Sailor's (1 week's rations)	2 gp	15 lbs.	90	85	80
Spice (per lb.)	—				
Exotic (saffron, clove)	15 gp	.5 lbs.	80	75	65
Rare (pepper, ginger)	2 gp	.5 lbs.	70	60	50
Uncommon (cinnamon)	1 gp	.5 lbs.	75	65	55
Venison, Smoked (1 meal)	1 gp	.5 lbs.	90	85	80
Tun of cider (250 gal.)	8 gp	2500 lbs.	90	85	80
Tun of good wine (250 gal.)	20 gp	2500 lbs.	95	85	70

Table 9I:
Outfitting Bundles (Pre-Packs)

Outfitting bundles are pre-packed assortments of provisions and equipment which characters can buy with a single purchase. This is to help save time so players don't have to meticulously re-provision themselves every few days of game time. Each bundle is tailored for a specific adventure type. They are lettered A to G and list the number of days/weeks the bundle will feed/provision one character. The player simply enters the bundle type on his character sheet followed by the number of days/weeks which he checks off accordingly. This will aid the GM in monitoring player activity. For instance, if a player states he is trying to coax a wild horse into coming closer, and says that he is pulling out a carrot from his pack, the GM can note what bundle type the character is carrying. Then, he can look up the bundle on the following list to determine if the player is indeed, actually carrying a carrot.

Type	Lasts	Cost	Weight
A. Basic Excursion	3 days	25 gp	30 lb.

1 flask of water, 1 loaf of bread, dried fish, sausage, 3 pieces of fruit, 3 vegetables, needle/thread, 10 feet/rope, whetstone

B. Extended Excursion	7 days	50 gp	75 lb.

3 flasks of water, 4 loaves of bread, sausage, 6 pieces of fruit, 5 potatoes, 3 carrots, 1 onion, needle/thread, 10 feet/rope, 1 flask lampoil, whetstone, wool blanket

C. Prolonged Excursion	14 days	120 gp	140 lb.

3 flasks of water, 1 flask of cut ale, 8 loaves of bread, 2 blocks hard cheese, pickled fish, blood sausage, 10 lbs. of corn dodgers, 1 jar of honey, 1 jar jam, pressed dates, 1 dozen eggs, 5 lbs. of smoked venison, needle/thread, 10 feet/rope, whetstone, tender and flint, 2 flasks of lamp oil

D. Basic Dungeon Crawl	1 day	50 gp	50 lb.

1 flask of water, 1 loaf of bread, sausage links, 1 wedge of cheese, 1 apple, needle/thread, 10 feet/rope, whetstone, 5 iron spikes, 10 torches

E. Extended Dungeon Crawl	3 days	100 gp	85 lb.

1 flask of water, 2 loaves of bread, 1 jar of honey, 1 jar of nuts, 3 lbs. of corn dodgers, 3 potatoes 1 radish, smoked beef, whetstone, 10 iron spikes, 20 torches, 2 flasks of lamp oil, a piece of chalk

F. Basic Overland Excursion	2 days	35 gp	50 lb.

1 flask of water, 1 wedge of cheese, smoked venison, 1 loaf of bread, peppered sausage, 1 apple, 2 carrots, 1 bag of oats (horse feed), 1 woolen blanket, 1 machette, 10 feet of rope.

G. Extended Overland Excursion	7 days	80 gp	100 lb.

2 flasks of water, 2 loaves of bread, 5 pickled eggs, smoked sausage, 5 pieces of fruit, 5 vegetables, 10 feet/rope, whetstone, 3 bag of oats (horsefeed)

NOTES: Campaign Particulars

Table 9K:
Provisions: Outfitting

Item	Cost	Weight	Base Availability		
			Hi	Med	Low
Chain (per ft.)	—	—			
Heavy	4 gp	3 lbs.	95	85	70
Light	3 gp	1 lbs.	95	85	70
Chalk	1 cp	*	95	85	70
Firewood (per day)	1 cp	200 lbs.	95	90	85
Fishhook	1 sp	**	95	90	85
Fishing net, 10 ft. sq.	4 gp	5 lbs.	90	85	80
Hourglass	25 gp	1 lbs.	85	75	65
Ladder, 10 ft.	5 cp	20 lbs.	95	90	85
Lock	—				
Good	100 gp	1 lbs.	90	85	80
Poor	20 gp	1 lbs.	90	85	80
Mirror, small metal	10 gp	*	90	85	80
Perfume (per vial)	5 gp	*	90	85	80
Piton	3 cp	.5 lbs.	90	85	80
Rope (per 50 ft.)	—	—			
Hemp	1 gp	20 lbs.	90	85	80
Silk	10 gp	8 lbs.	70	60	50
Signal whistle	8 sp	*	90	85	80
Soap (per lb.)	5 sp	1 lbs.	90	85	80
Tent	—	—			
Large	25 gp	20 lbs.	80	75	70
Pavilion	100 gp	50 lbs.	80	75	70
Small	5 gp	10 lbs.	80	75	70
Winter blanket	5 sp	3 lbs.	90	85	80

* These items weigh little individually. Ten of these items weigh one pound.
** These items have no appreciable weight and should not be considered for encumbrance unless hundreds are carried.

Table 9L:
Tools

Item	Cost	Weight	Base Availability		
			Hi	Med	Low
Block and tackle	5 gp	5 lbs.	90	85	80
Carpentry Tools (set)	50 gp	60 lbs.	90	85	80
Crampons	4 gp	2 lbs.	90	85	80
Crowbar/Pry bar	10 sp	10 lbs.	90	85	80
Flint and steel	5 sp	*	90	85	80
Grappling hook	8 sp	4 lbs.	90	85	80
Mining Tools (set)	2 gp	30 lbs.	90	85	80
Magnifying glass	100 gp	*	85	75	70
Merchant's scale	2 gp	1 lbs.	90	85	80
Portable Forge	400 gp	500 lbs.	80	75	70
Repair Kit, Armor	—				
Banded mail	20 gp	10 lbs.	80	70	60
Brigandine	10gp	5 lbs.	85	80	75
Bronze Plate mail	20 gp	10 lbs.	80	70	60
Chain mail	12gp	10 lbs.	85	80	75
Field plate	50 gp	15 lbs.	65	45	25
Full Plate	100 gp	20 lbs.	50	30	10
Hide	6 gp	3.5 lbs.	90	85	80
Leather	5gp	3 lbs.	90	85	80
Padded	1gp	2 lbs.	90	85	80
Plate mail	25 gp	10 lbs.	80	70	60
Ring mail	5 gp	5 lbs.	85	80	75
Robes	10 sp	.25 lb.	90	85	80
Scale mail	5 gp	10 lbs.	90	85	80
Splint	17 gp	10 lbs.	80	70	60
Studded Leather	10 gp	6 lbs.	85	80	75
Repair Kit, Sail/Nautical	50 gp	50 lbs.	90	85	80
Spyglass	1,000 gp	1 lbs.	80	65	50
Surgeon's Kit	100 gp	20 lbs.	85	75	70
Thieves' Tools**	—				
Coin Sharpened (Cut Purse)	5 sp	.25 lbs.	95	90	85
Hacksaw (hardened)	5 sp	3 lbs.	85	75	70
Key Making set	50 gp	3 lbs.	75	65	55
Lockpick set	30 gp	1 lbs.	70	65	60
Locksmithing Tools	100 gp	5 lbs.	85	75	70
Salimic Acid, Vial	150 gp	*	65	55	45
Soot/Face Black	10 sp	—	95	95	95
Whetstone	2 cp	1 lbs.	95	90	85

* These items weigh little individually. Ten of these items weigh one pound.
** Thieves and assassins may add +20 to the base availability chance when searching for thieves' tools due to their connections with the thieves' guild and underground.

Table 9M:
Religious Items and Accouterments

Item	Cost	Weight	Hi	Med	Low
Beads, Prayer	1 gp	—	95	85	80
Incense, Burner	1 gp	—	95	85	80
Incense, Stick (per dozen)	5 cp	—	95	85	80
Robes, Clerical	25 to 500 gp	—	85	80	75
Snake, Bond	100 gp	—	70	65	60
Symbol, Holy/Unholy gold	50 gp	1 lbs.	95	85	80
Symbol, Holy/Unholy iron	5 gp	1 lbs.	95	85	80
Symbol, Holy/Unholy silver	10 gp	1 lbs.	95	85	80
Symbol, Holy/Unholy wood	1 gp	.5 lbs.	95	85	80
Water, Holy/Unholy gold	25 gp	1 lbs.	95	85	80

Table 9N:
Scribe Materials

Item	Cost	Weight	Hi	Med	Low
Ink Pot/Vial	8 gp	*	95	85	80
Journal, Blank 100 pages	75 gp	1 lb	80	75	70
Paper (per sheet)	2 gp	**	85	80	75
Papyrus (per sheet)	8 sp	**	80	75	70
Parchment (per sheet)	1 gp	**	90	85	80
Pen, Bone/Ivory/Wood	8 sp	.25 lbs.	95	85	80
Pen, Quill	2 cp	.25 lbs.	95	85	80
Sealing/candle wax (per lb.)	1 gp	1 lbs.	90	85	80
Signet ring or personal seal	5 gp	.25 lbs.	95	85	80
Stylus, Wood	5 cp	.25 lbs.	95	85	80
Tablet, Silted Clay	1 gp	1 lbs.	95	85	80
Tablet, Wax	10 sp	1 lbs.	95	85	80
Vellum, (per sheet)	8 gp	**	80	75	70

* These items weigh little individually. Ten of these items weigh one pound.
** These items have no appreciable weight and should not be considered for encumbrance unless hundreds are carried.

Table 9O:
Services

Item	Cost	Weight	Hi	Med	Low
Bath	3 cp	—	95	85	80
Doctor, Leech, or Bleeding	3 gp	—	90	85	80
Doctor, Sew Wounds	10 gp	—	90	85	80
Guide, in city (per day)	2 sp	—	90	85	80
Lantern or torchbearer (per night)	1 sp	—	90	85	80
Laundry (by load)	1 cp	—	85	80	70
Massage	1 gp	—	90	85	80
Messenger, 10 to 50 miles	1 gp	—	95	85	80
Messenger, 51 to 100 miles	5 gp	—	90	85	80
Messenger, in city (per message)	10 cp	—	85	80	75
Messenger, per 100 miles	5 gp	—	80	75	70
Minstrel (per performance)	3 gp	—	90	85	80
Mourner (per funeral)	2 sp	—	90	85	80
Scout, Wilderness (per day)	1 gp	—	90	85	80
Scribe, Legal document/contract	10 sp	—	90	85	80
Scribe, Letter	2 sp	—	90	85	80
Tattoo (per design)	1 gp	—	95	85	80
Teamster w/wagon	1 sp/mile	—	90	85	80

Table 9Q:
Transport, Land*

Item	Cost	Weight	Hi	Med	Low
Cart, Small	5 gp	—	90	85	80
Carriage	—				
Common	150 gp	—	90	85	80
Coach, ornamented	7,000 gp	—	75	70	65
Chariot	—				
Riding	200 gp	—	80	75	70
War	500 gp	—	75	70	65
Sedan chair	100 gp	—	90	85	80
Wagon, Two-Wheeled	60 gp	—	90	85	80
Wagon, Four Wheeled	125 gp	—	85	80	75
Wheel, Replacement (spoked)	5 gp	65 lbs.	90	85	80
Wheel, Replacement (planked)	1 gp	125 lbs.	90	85	80

*Movement rates for this equipment are given in the GMG

Table 9P:
Tack and Harness

Item	Cost	Weight	Hi	Med	Low
Barding Horse**	—				
Chain	500 gp	70 lbs.	85	80	75
Full plate	2,000 gp	85 lbs.	70	65	60
Full scale	1,000 gp	75 lbs.	75	70	65
Half brigandine	500 gp	45 lbs.	85	80	75
Half padded	100 gp	25 lbs.	90	85	80
Half scale	500 gp	50 lbs.	85	80	75
Leather or padded	150 gp	60 lbs.	95	90	85
Barding, Dolphin					
Chain	1,000 gp	30 lbs.	35	25	10
Leather	500 gp	20 lbs.	45	35	30
Barding, Killer Whale					
Chain	1,700 gp	60 lbs.	35	25	10
Leather	900 gp	50 lbs.	45	35	30
Bit and bridle	15 sp	3 lbs.	95	85	80
Blinders, Horse	05 sp	3 lbs.	95	85	80
Cart harness	2 gp	10 lbs.	95	85	80
Fort, Elephant	400 gp	300 lbs.	55	50	45
Halter	5 cp	*	95	85	80
Horseshoes & shoeing	1 gp	10 lbs.	95	85	80
Saddle	—	—			
Pack	5 gp	15 lbs.	95	85	80
Riding	10 gp	35 lbs.	95	85	80
Saddle bags	—	—			
Large	4 gp	8 lbs.	95	85	80
Small	3 gp	5 lbs.	95	85	80
Saddle blanket	3 sp	4 lbs.	95	85	80
Yoke	—	—			
Horse	5 gp	15 lbs.	95	85	80
Ox	3 gp	20 lbs.	95	85	80

* These items weigh little individually. Ten of these items weigh one pound.
** For barding for Elephants multiply price by 3 and weight by four.
Bonding with a new mount takes 1d20 days. Until bonding period is complete any new mount is likely to be skittish and have lower morale.

Table 9R:
Transport, Water*

Item	Cost	Weight	Hi	Med	Low
Barge, River	500 gp	—	90	85	80
Boat, Collapsible	300 gp	—	90	85	80
Canoe					
Small	30 gp	—	90	85	80
War	50 gp	—	90	85	80
Caravel	10,000 gp	—	60	50	40
Coaster	5,000 gp	—	70	65	60
Cog	10,000 gp	—	60	50	40
Currach	500 gp	—	85	80	75
Drakkar	25,000 gp	—	45	35	25
Dromond	15,000 gp	—	60	50	40
Galleon	50,000 gp	—	40	30	20
Galley, Great	30,000 gp	—	45	35	25
Galley, War	45,000 gp	—	40	30	20
Galley, Trireme	80,000 gp	—	40	30	20
Galley, Duceres	1,000,000 gp	—	35	25	10
Knarr	3,000 gp	—	65	60	55
Longship	10,000 gp	—	60	50	40
Oar, Replacement					
Common	2 gp	25 lbs.	90	85	80
Galley	10 gp	120 lbs.	80	70	60
Raft or small keelboat	100 gp	—	90	85	80
Sail, Standard size	20 gp	—	90	85	80
Sail, Made to spec.	150 gp+	—	90	85	80
Ship, Merchant, Large	15,000 gp	—	60	50	40
Ship, Merchant, Small	7,500 gp	—	65	60	55

*Movement rates for this equipment are given in the GMG

Table 9S:
Armor and Related Items

Item	Cost	AC	HP	Weight	Bulk	Hi	Med	Low
Robes/Garments	Varies	9	1	Varies	non	Varies (see Table 9B)		
Leather	5 gp	8	2	15 lbs.	non	95	90	85
Padded	4 gp	8	2	10 lbs.	fairly	95	90	85
Ring mail	65 gp	7	6	30 lbs.	fairly	90	85	80
Studded leather	40 gp	7	4	25 lbs.	fairly	95	90	85
Scale mail	120 gp	6	7	40 lbs.	fairly	90	85	80
Hide	75 gp	6	5	35 lbs.	fairly	95	90	85
Brigandine	120 gp	6	6	35 lbs.	fairly	90	85	80
Chain mail	350 gp	5	8	40 lbs.	fairly	95	90	85
Chain mail, Elven	700gp	5	8	20 lbs.	non	30	20	10
Bronze plate mail	1,000 gp	4	12	45 lbs.	bulky	85	80	75
Banded mail	900 gp	4	9	35 lbs.	bulky	90	85	80
Splint mail	600 gp	4	8	40 lbs.	bulky	95	90	85
Plate mail	2,000 gp	3	12	50 lbs.	bulky	85	80	75
Field plate	4,000 gp	2	24**	60 lbs.	bulky	70	65	60
Full plate	6,000-10,000 gp	1	36**	70 lbs.	bulky	65	60	55
Helmet								
Great helm	30 gp	—	—	10 lbs.	bulky	70	65	60
Basinet	8 gp	—	—	5 lbs.	fairly	95	90	85
Shield								
Buckler	5 gp	+1	3	3 lbs.	non	90	85	80
Buckler, Spiked	15 gp	+1	3	4 lbs.	non	90	85	80
Small	20 gp	+2	4	5 lbs.	non	90	85	80
Medium	30 gp	+3	5	10 lbs.	fairly	90	85	80
Body*	100 gp	+4 (+6)	6	25 lbs.	bulky	90	85	80

* A body shield affords +6 AC against missile weapons.
** Field and full-plate absorb 2 hit points per die.

Table 9X:
Shield Hit Points

Item\AC modifier	+4	+3	+2	+1
Buckler	—	—	—	3
Small	—	—	4	3
Medium	—	5	4	3
Body	6	5	4	3

NOTES: Campaign Particulars

Table 9W:
Hit Point Absorption Regression for Damaged Armor

Item	1	2	3	4	5	6	7	8	9
Robes/Garments	—	—	—	—	—	—	—	—	1
Leather	—	—	—	—	—	—	—	2	1
Padded	—	—	—	—	—	—	—	2	1
Ring mail	—	—	—	—	—	—	6	2	1
Studded leather	—	—	—	—	—	—	4	2	1
Scale mail	—	—	—	—	—	7	4	2	1
Hide	—	—	—	—	—	5	4	2	1
Brigandine	—	—	—	—	—	6	4	2	1
Chain mail	—	—	—	—	8	6	4	2	1
Bronze plate mail	—	—	—	12	8	6	4	2	1
Banded mail	—	—	—	9	8	6	4	2	1
Splint mail	—	—	—	8	8	6	4	2	1
Plate mail	—	—	12	10	8	6	4	2	1
Field plate	—	24*	12	10	8	6	4	2	1
Full plate	36*	24*	12	10	8	6	4	2	1

*Field and full-plate absorb 2 hit points per die.

Table 9U:
Weapons: Ammo

Item	Cost	Weight	Size	Damage Type	Speed Factor	S	M	L	Hi	Med	Low
Blowgun											
Barbed Dart	1 sp	*	S	P	—	1d6-1	1d6-2	1d6-4	95	90	85
Needle	2 cp	*	S	P	—	1	1	1	95	90	85
Bow											
Arrow, Flight	3sp/12	*	S	P	—	1d6	1d6	1d6	90	85	80
Arrow, Sheaf	3 sp/6	*	S	P	—	1d8	1d8	1d8	85	80	75
Crossbow											
Quarrel, Hand	1 gp	*	S	P	—	1d6-1	1d6-3	1d6-4	90	85	80
Quarrel, Hard Silver Jack.1	50 gp	*	S	P	—	+1	+1	+1	50	30	15
Quarrel, Heavy	2 sp	*	S	P	—	1d8	2d4+1	3d4	90	85	80
Quarrel, Light	1 sp	*	S	P	—	1d6	1d8	2d4+1	90	85	80
Quarrel, Peashooter	10 sp	*	S	P	—	1d6-3	1d6-4	1	90	85	80
Quarrel, Silver Jacketed	25 gp	*	S	P	—	—	—	—	60	40	30
Sling											
Sling bullet	1 cp	.5 lbs.	S	C	—	1d6-1	1d6	1d6+1	95	95	95
Sling stone	—	.5 lbs.	S	C	—	1d6-1	1d6-1	1d6-1	95	95	95

1. Hard silver coating adds a +1 damage to the standard missile weapon damage.
* These items weigh little individually. Ten of these weigh one pound.

Table 9T
Weapons

Item	Cost	Weight (lb.)	Size	Damage Type[6]	Speed Factor	S	M	L	H	Med	Low
Battle axe	5 gp	7	M	H	2	2d4	2d4	2d4	90	85	80
Blowgun	5 gp	2	L	—	—	Δ	Δ	Δ	90	85	80
Bow	—	—	—	—	—	Δ	Δ	Δ	—	—	—
Composite long bow	100 gp	3	L	—	—	Δ	Δ	Δ	85	80	75
Composite short bow	75 gp	2	M	—	—	Δ	Δ	Δ	80	75	70
Great Long bow (elven)	800gp	4	L	—	—	Δ	Δ	Δ	20	10	5
Long bow	75 gp	3	L	—	—	Δ	Δ	Δ	90	85	80
Short bow	30 gp	2	M	—	—	Δ	Δ	Δ	90	85	80
Club	—	3	M	C	-1	1d8	1d6	1d6-2	95	90	85
Crossbow	—	—	—	—	—	Δ	Δ	Δ	—	—	—
Hand crossbow	300 gp	3	S	—	—	Δ	Δ	Δ	75	70	65
Heavy crossbow	50 gp	14	M	—	—	Δ	Δ	Δ	85	80	75
Light crossbow	35 gp	7	M	—	—	Δ	Δ	Δ	80	75	70
Peashooter crossbow	350 gp	1/2	S	—	—	Δ	Δ	Δ	55	40	25
Dagger or dirk	2 gp	1	S	P	-3	1d6	1d6-1	1d6-2	95	90	85
Dart	5 sp	1/2	S	P	—	1d6-1	1d6-2	1d6-4	95	90	85
Footman's flail	15 gp	15	M	C	2	1d6	1d6+1	2d4	90	85	80
Footman's mace	8 gp	10	M	C	2	1d8	1d6+1	1d6	90	85	80
Footman's pick	8 gp	6	M	P	2	1d6	1d6+1	2d4	95	90	85
Hand or throwing axe	1 gp	5	M	H	-1	1d8	1d6	1d6-1	95	90	85
Harpoon	20 gp	6	L	P	2	1d6	2d4	2d6	95	90	85
Horseman's flail	8 gp	5	M	C	1	1d4+1	1d4+1	1d4+1	90	85	80
Horseman's mace	5 gp	6	M	C	1	1d8	1d6	1d6-1	90	85	80
Horseman's pick	7 gp	4	M	P	0	1d6	1d6-1	1d6-2	90	85	80
Hurled Tankard, Full[8]	—	3 lb	S	C	—	1d6	1d6-1	1d6-2	90	85	80
Hurled Tankard, Empty	—	2 lb	S	C	—	1d6-1	1d6-2	1d6-4	90	85	80
Javelin	5 sp	2	M	P	—	1d6	1d6	1d6	95	90	85
Knife	5 sp	1/2	S	P/H	-3	1d6-1	1d6-2	1d6-4	95	90	85
Lance[4]	—	—	—	—	—	—	—	—	—	—	—
Heavy horse lance	15 gp	15	L	P	3	1d6	1d8+1	3d6	85	80	75
Light horse lance	6 gp	5	L	P	1	1d6-1	1d6	1d8	85	80	75
Jousting lance	20 gp	20	L	P	2	1d6-3	1d6-2	1d6-4	85	80	75
Medium horse lance	10 gp	10	L	P	2	1d4+1	1d6+1	2d6	85	80	75
Mancatcher[2]	30 gp	8	L	—	2	—	—	—	95	90	85
Morning star	10 gp	12	M	C	2	2d4+1	2d4	1d6+1	85	80	75
Polearm	—	—	—	—	—	—	—	—	—	—	—
Awl pike[5]	5 gp	12	L	P	8	1d4	1d6	1d12	90	85	80
Bardiche	7 gp	12	L	H	4	1d6	2d4	2d6	95	90	85
Bec de corbin	8 gp	10	L	P/C	4	1d10	1d8	1d6	95	90	85
Bill-guisarme	7 gp	15	L	P/H	5	1d8	2d4	1d10	95	90	85
Fauchard	5 gp	7	L	P/H	3	1d4	1d6	1d8	90	85	80
Fauchard-fork	8 gp	9	L	P/H	3	1d6	1d8	1d10	95	90	85
Glaive[1]	6 gp	8	L	H	3	1d4	1d6	1d10	95	90	85
Glaive-guisarme[1]	10 gp	10	L	P/H	4	1d6	2d4	2d6	85	80	75
Guisarme	5 gp	8	L	H	3	1d10	2d4	1d8	90	85	80
Guisarme-voulge	8 gp	15	L	P/H	5	2d4	2d4	2d4	95	90	85
Halberd	10 gp	15	L	P/H	4	1d8	1d10	2d6	85	80	75
Hook fauchard	10 gp	8	L	P/H	4	1d4	1d4	1d4	85	80	75
Lucern hammer[5]	7 gp	15	L	P/C	4	2d6	2d4	1d6	90	85	80
Military fork[1]	5 gp	7	L	P	2	1d6	1d8	2d4	95	90	85
Partisan[5]	10 gp	8	L	P	4	1d4	1d6	1d6+1	85	80	75
Ranseur[5]	6 gp	7	L	P	3	2d4	2d4	2d4	90	85	80
Spetum[5]	5 gp	7	L	P	3	1d4+1	1d6+1	2d6	95	90	85
Voulge	5 gp	12	L	H	5	2d4	2d4	2d4	90	85	80
Quarterstaff	—	4	L	C	-1	1d6	1d6	1d6	95	90	85
Sewing needle[7]	5 sp	**	S	P	-4	.125 pts	.125 pts	.125 pts.	95	90	85
Scourge	1 gp	2	S	—	0	1d6	1d6-2	1d6-4	95	90	85
Sickle	6 sp	3	S	H	-1	1d6	1d6-1	1d6-2	95	90	85
Sling	5 cp.	*	S	—	—	—	—	—	95	90	85
Spear[5]	8 sp	5	M	P	1	1d6-1	1d6	1d8	90	85	80
Spear, Great[5]	1 gp	8	L	P	3	1d6	1d8	1d10	90	85	80
Staff sling	2 sp	2	M	—	—	—	—	—	85	80	75
Stilleto, Bloodthorn	12 gp	1/2	S	P	-4	1d6-2	1d6-2	1d6-2	75	70	65
Sword	—	—	—	—	—	—	—	—	—	—	—
Bastard sword	25 gp	10	M	H	—	—	—	—	90	85	80
One-handed	—	—	—	—	1	1d6	1d8	1d12	95	90	85
Two-handed	—	—	—	—	3	1d4	2d4	2d8	85	80	75
Broad sword	10 gp	4	M	H	0	1d10	2d4	1d6+1	90	85	80
Khopesh	10 gp	7	M	H	4	1d10+1	2d4	1d6	95	90	85
Long sword	15 gp	4	M	H	0	1d6	1d8	1d12	90	85	80
Rapier, Petite	15 gp	1/2	S	P	-4	1d6-2	1d6-1	1d6	80	75	70
Scimitar	15 gp	4	M	H	0	1d8	1d8	1d8	95	90	85
Short sword	10 gp	3	S	P	-2	1d6-1	1d6	1d6	90	85	80
Two-handed sword	50 gp	15	L	H	5	1d6-1	1d10	3d6	85	80	75
Trident	15 gp	5	L	P	2	1d4	1d6+1	3d4	90	85	80
Warhammer	2 gp	6	M	C	-1	1d8	1d6	1d4	95	90	85
Whip	1 sp	2	M	—	3	1d6-2	1d6-4	1	95	90	85

Notes for Weapon Table (Table 9T)

1. This weapon inflicts double damage against charging creatures of L or greater size.
2. This weapon can dismount a rider on a successful hit.
4. This weapon inflicts double damage when used from the back of a charging mount.
5. This weapon inflicts double damage when firmly set to receive a charge.
6. The "Type" category is divided into Crushing (C), Puncturing (P), and Hacking (H). Note that the Edged Weapon categories; honed and serrated from 3rd edition have been combined into the Hacking category. This indicates the type of attack made, which may alter the weapon's effectiveness against different types of armor.
7. Sewing needles do a flat .25 (one quarter) hit point of damage.
8. If a hurled tankard (full) hits its target, roll to see if the victim is temporarily blinded from alcohol.
* These items weigh little individually. Ten of these weigh one pound.
** These items weigh little individually. Ten of these weigh two grams.
Δ The damage for these missle weapons is dependent upon the ammo used. They are detailed on Table 9U, Weapons: Ammo.

Table 9V: Missile Weapon Ranges

Weapon	ROF	S	M	L
		Range (yards)		
Blowgun	2	10	20	30
Comp. long bow, flight arrow	2	60	120	210
Comp. long bow, sheaf arrow	2	40	80	170
Comp. short bow	2	50	100	180
Great Longbow, flight arrow	1/2	80	160	230
Great Longbow, sheaf arrow	1/2	70	140	210
Longbow, flight arrow	2	70	140	210
Longbow, sheaf arrow	2	50	100	170
Short bow	2	50	100	150
Club	1	10	20	30
Hand crossbow	1	20	40	60
Heavy crossbow	1/2	80	160	240
Light crossbow	1	60	120	180
Peashooter crossbow	2	10	20	30
Dagger	2	10	20	30
Dart	3	10	20	40
Hammer	1	10	20	30
Hand axe	1	10	20	30
Harpoon	1	10	20	30
Javelin	1	20	40	60
Knife	2	10	20	30
Sling bullet	1	50	100	200
Sling stone	1	40	80	160
Spear	1	10	20	30
Staff sling bullet	2	30	60	90
Staff sling stone	2	30	60	90

"ROF" is the rate of fire (how many shots that weapon can fire off in one round.) This is independent of the number of melee attacks a character can make in a round.

Each range category (Short, Medium, or Long) includes attacks from distances equal to or less than the given range. Thus, a heavy crossbow fired at a target 136 yards away uses the medium range modifier. The attack roll modifiers for range are -2 for medium range and -5 for long range.

Table 9Z: Carrying Capacities of Animals

Mount	Base Move	2/3 Move	1/3 Move
Camel	0-330 lbs.	331-500 lbs.	501-660 lbs.
Dawg	0-15 lbs.	16-20 lbs.	21-30 lbs.
Elephant	0-500 lbs.	501-750 lbs.	751-1,000 lbs.
Horse, draft	0-260 lbs.	261-390 lbs.	391-520 lbs.
Horse, heavy	0-260 lbs.	261-390 lbs.	391-520 lbs.
Horse, light	0-170 lbs.	171-255 lbs.	256-340 lbs.
Horse, medium	0-220 lbs.	221-330 lbs.	331-440 lbs.
Horse, riding	0-180 lbs.	181-270 lbs.	271-360 lbs.
Llama	0-165 lbs.	166-250 lbs.	251-335 lbs.
Mule	0-250 lbs.	251-375 lbs.	376-500 lbs.
Ox	0-220 lbs.	221-330 lbs.	331-440 lbs.
Pack Ape	0-170 lbs.	171-255 lbs.	256-340 lbs.
Yak	0-220 lbs.	221-330 lbs.	331-440 lbs.

Table 9AA: Stowage Capacity

Item	Weight Cap.	Volume
Backpack	50 lbs.	3'x2'x1'
Basket, large	20 lbs.	2'x2'x2'
Basket, small	10 lbs.	1'x1'x1'
Belt pouch, large	8 lbs.	6"x8"x2"
Belt pouch, small	5 lbs.	4"x6"x2"
Chest, large	100 lbs.	3'x2'x2'
Chest, small	40 lbs.	2'x1'x1'
Sack, large	30 lbs.	2'x2'x1'
Sack, small	15 lbs.	1'x1'x8"
Saddle bags, large	30 lbs.	18"x1'x6"
Saddle bags, small	20 lbs.	1'x1'x6"

NOTES: Campaign Particulars

Table 9Y:
Character Encumbrance

Character Strength	Unencum.	Light	Encumbrance Moderate	Heavy Laden	Severe	Max.Car. Weight
1	0-1	2-3	4-5	6-7	8-9	9
1/51	0-2	3-4	5-6	7-8	9-10	10
2	0-3	4-5	6-7	8-9	10-11	11
2/51	0-4	5-6	7-8	9-10	11-12	12
3	0-5	6-7	8-9	10-11	12-15	15
3/51	0-7	8-9	10-11	12-14	15-21	21
4	0-9	10-11	12-14	15-18	19-27	27
4/51	0-11	12-14	15-17	18-22	23-33	33
5	0-13	14-16	17-20	21-26	27-39	39
5/51	0-15	16-19	20-23	24-30	31-45	45
6	0-18	19-23	24-27	28-36	37-54	54
6/51	0-21	22-26	27-32	33-42	43-63	63
7	0-24	25-30	31-36	37-48	49-72	72
7/51	0-27	28-34	35-41	42-54	55-81	81
8	0-30	31-38	39-45	46-60	61-90	90
8/51	0-33	34-41	42-50	51-66	67-99	99
9	0-36	37-45	46-54	55-72	73-108	108
9/51	0-39	40-49	50-59	60-78	79-117	117
10	0-43	44-54	55-65	66-86	87-129	129
10/51	0-47	48-59	60-71	72-94	95-141	141
11	0-51	52-64	65-77	78-102	103-153	153
11/51	0-55	56-69	70-83	84-110	111-165	165
12	0-59	60-74	75-89	90-118	119-177	177
12/51	0-63	64-79	80-95	96-126	127-189	189
13	0-67	68-84	85-101	102-134	135-201	201
13/51	0-71	72-89	90-107	108-142	143-213	213
14	0-76	77-95	96-114	115-152	153-228	228
14/51	0-81	82-101	102-122	123-162	163-243	243
15	0-86	87-108	109-129	130-172	173-258	258
15/51	0-91	92-114	115-137	138-182	183-273	273
16	0-97	98-121	122-146	147-194	195-291	291
16/51	0-103	104-129	130-155	156-206	207-309	309
17	0-109	110-136	137-164	165-218	219-327	327
17/51	0-115	116-144	145-173	174-230	231-345	345
18	0-130	131-163	164-195	196-260	261-390	390
18/51	0-160	161-200	201-240	241-320	321-480	480
19	0-200	201-250	251-300	301-400	401-600	600
19/51	0-300	301-375	376-450	451-600	601-900	900
20	0-400	401-500	501-600	601-800	801-1200	1200
20/51	0-500	501-625	626-750	751-1000	1001-1500	1500
21	0-600	601-750	751-900	901-1200	1201-1800	1800
21/51	0-700	701-875	876-1050	1051-1400	1401-2100	2100
22	0-800	801-1000	1001-1200	1201-1600	1601-2400	2400
22/51	0-900	901-1125	1126-1350	1351-1800	1801-2700	2700
23	0-1,000	1001-1250	1251-1500	1501-2000	2001-3000	3000
23/51	0-1,100	1101-1375	1376-1650	1651-2200	2201-3300	3300
24	0-1,200	1201-1500	1501-1800	1801-2400	2401-3600	3600
24/51	0-1,300	1301-1625	1626-1950	1951-2600	2601-3900	3900
25	0-1,500	1501-1875	1876-2250	2251-3000	3001-4500	4500

Table 16A:
Base Movement Rate

Race	Rate/Points
Human	12
Dwarf	6
Elf	12
Half-elf	12
Gnome	6
Gnomeling	4
Halfling	6
Half-Orc	12
Half-Ogre	13
Pixie-Fairy	4/18*

* unencumbered flying rate.

Character Notes

Encumbrance Worksheet

Table 17B:
Light Sources

Source	Radius	Burning time
Beacon lantern	240 ft.*	30 hrs./pint
Bonfire	50 ft.	1/2 hr./armload
Bullseye lantern	60 ft.*	2 hrs./pint
Campfire	35 ft.	1 hr./armload
Candle	5 ft.	10 min./inch
Continual light	60 ft.	Indefinite
Hooded lantern	30 ft.	2 hrs./pint
Light spell	20 ft.	Variable
Torch	15 ft.	30 min.
Weapon**	5 ft.	As desired

* Light from these is not cast in a radius, but rather in a cone-shaped beam. At its far end, the cone of light from a beacon lantern is 90 feet wide. A bullseye lantern has a beam 20 feet wide at its far end.

** Some magical weapons shed light. Your GM has details on which ones do so.

Appendix S

Compiled Character Tables

Table 1B:
Dexterity

Ability Score	Defense Adjustment	Reaction Adjustment	Missile Adjustment
1	+5	-5	-6
1/51	+5	-5	-5
2	+4	-5	-5
2/51	+4	-4	-5
3	+4	-4	-4
3/51	+3	-4	-4
4	+3	-3	-4
4/51	+3	-3	-3
5	+2	-3	-3
5/51	+2	-2	-3
6	+2	-2	-2
6/51	+1	-2	-2
7	+1	-1	-2
7/51	+1	-1	-1
8	0	-1	-1
8/51	0	0	-1
9 - 9/99	0	0	0
10 - 10/99	0	0	0
11 - 11/99	0	0	0
12	0	0	0
12/51	0	0	+1
13	0	+1	+1
13/51	-1	+1	+1
14	-1	+1	+2
14/51	-1	+2	+2
15	-2	+2	+2
15/51	-2	+2	+3
16	-2	+3	+3
16/51	-3	+3	+3
17	-3	+3	+4
17/51	-3	+4	+4
18	-4	+4	+4
18/51	-4	+4	+5
19	-4	+5	+5
19/51	-5	+5	+5
20	-5	+5	+6
20/51	-5	+6	+6
21	-6	+6	+6
21/51	-6	+6	+7
22	-6	+7	+7
22/51	-7	+7	+7
23	-7	+7	+8
23/51	-7	+8	+8
24	-8	+8	+8
24/51	-8	+8	+9
25	-8	+9	+9

Table 1F:
Charisma

Ability Score	Maximum # Henchmen Cronies/S-kicks	Loyalty Base	Reaction Adjustment	Comeliness Modifier	Starting Honor Modifier
1	0*	-8	-7	-8	-9
2	1	-7	-6	-8	-8
3	1	-6	-5	-5	-7
4	1	-5	-4	-3	-6
5	2	-4	-3	-3	-5
6	2	-3	-2	-1	-4
7	3	-2	-1	-1	-3
8	3	-1	0	-1	-2
9	4	0	0	0	-1
10	4	0	0	0	0
11	4	0	0	0	0
12	5	0	0	0	+1
13	5	0	+1	+1	+2
14	6	+1	+2	+1	+3
15	7	+3	+3	+1	+4
16	8	+4	+5	+2	+5
17	10	+6	+6	+2	+6
18	15	+8	+7	+3	+7
19	18	+10	+8	+4	+8
20	20	+12	+9	+4	+9
21	25	+14	+10	+5	+10
22	30	+16	+11	+5	+11
23	35	+18	+12	+6	+12
24	40	+20	+13	+7	+13
25	45	+20	+14	+8	+14

* Note that a character is ALWAYS entitled to have one (1) sidekick no matter how low his Charisma is.

WARNING: Be sure to consult the appropriate chapters when rolling on these tables. Some tables, especially the Background Tables (Chapter 4), have several modifiers which can be applied.

Table 1A:
Strength

Ability Score	Hit Prob.	Damage Adj.	Weight Allowance	Max. Press	Open Doors	Bend Bars/ Lift Gates
1	-3	-8	1	3	1	0%
1/51	-3	-8	2	4	1	0%
2	-3	-7	3	5	1	0%
2/51	-3	-7	4	7	1	0%
3	-3	-6	5	10	2	0%
3/51	-3	-6	7	20	2	0%
4	-2	-5	9	25	3	0%
4/51	-2	-5	11	35	3	0%
5	-2	-4	13	30	3	0%
5/51	-2	-4	15	40	4	0%
6	-2	-3	18	55	4	0%
6/51	-2	-3	21	60	4	0%
7	-1	-2	24	70	4	0%
7/51	-1	-2	27	80	5	0%
8	-1	-1	30	90	5	1%
8/51	-1	-1	33	95	5	1%
9	Normal	-1	36	100	5	1%
9/51	Normal	-1	39	110	6	1%
10	Normal	None	43	115	6	2%
10/51	Normal	None	47	125	6	3%
11	Normal	None	51	130	6	4%
11/51	Normal	None	55	135	7	4%
12	Normal	+1	59	140	7	5%
17/51	Normal	+1	63	145	7	5%
13	+1	+1	67	150	7	6%
13/51	+1	+1	71	160	8	6%
14	+1	+2	76	170	8	7%
14/51	+1	+2	81	175	8	8%
15	+1	+3	86	185	9	9%
15/51	+1	+3	91	190	9	10%
16	+2	+4	97	195	10	11%
16/51	+2	+4	103	220	10	12%
17	+2	+5	109	255	11	15%
17/51	+2	+5	115	290	11	20%
18	+3	+6	130	350	12(3)	25%
18/51	+3	+6	160	480	14(6)	35%
19	+3	+7	200	640	15(8)	50%
19/51	+3	+7	300	660	16(9)	55%
20	+3	+8	400	700	17(10)	60%
20/51	+3	+8	500	625	17(11)	65%
21	+4	+9	600	810	17(12)	70%
21/51	+4	+9	700	865	18(13)	75%
22	+4	+10	800	970	18(14)	80%
22/51	+4	+10	900	1050	18(15)	85%
23	+5	+11	1000	1,130	18(16)	90%
23/51	+5	+11	1,100	1,320	19(16)	95%
24	+6	+12	1,200	1,440	19(16)	97%
24/51	+6	+12	1,300	1,540	19(17)	98%
25	+7	+14	1,500	1,750	19(18)	99%

Table 2B:
Demi-human Ability Adjustments

Race	Adjustments
Dwarf	+1 Constitution; -1 Charisma; -1 Comeliness
Elf	+1 Dexterity; -1 Constitution; +1 Comeliness (sylvan elves only); +2 Comeliness (gray and high elves only); -1 Comeliness (grunge elves only);-2 Comeliness (drow only)
Gnome	+1 Intelligence; -1 Wisdom; -1 Comeliness; +2 Strength (Gnome Titans only)
Gnomeling	+1 Intelligence; +1 Dexterity; -1 Strength; -1 Wisdom; -1 Constitution
Halfling	+1 Dexterity; -1 Strength
Half Elves	+1 Comeliness
Half-orc	+1 Strength; +1 Constitution; -2 Charisma; -3 Comeliness
Half-Ogre	+2 Strength; +2 Constitution; -1 Wisdom; -2 Intelligence; -3 Charisma; -5 Comeliness
Pixie Fairy	-6 Strength, +2 Dexterity; +1 Intelligence, +1 Wisdom, +2 Charisma; +3 Comeliness

Table 1C:
Constitution

Ability Score	Hit Point Adjustment	System Shock	Resurrection Survival	Poison Save	Immunity to Disease/Alcohol	Regeneration/Healing
1	-5	25%	30%	-2	+30%	Nil / 1 HP every 2 weeks
2	-4	30%	35%	-1	+25%	Nil / 1 HP every week
3	-4	35%	40%	0	+20%	Nil / 1 HP every 2 days
4	-3	40%	45%	0	+15%	Nil / 1 HP every 2 days
5	-3	45%	50%	0	+10%	Nil / 1 HP every 2 days
6	-2	50%	55%	0	+5%	Nil / 1 HP every 2 days
7	-2	55%	60%	0	no modifier	Nil / 1 HP every day
8	-1	60%	65%	0	-5%	Nil / 1 HP every day
9	-1	65%	70%	0	-10%	Nil / 1 HP every day
10	0	70%	75%	0	-20%	Nil / 1 HP every day
11	0	75%	80%	0	-25%	Nil / 1 HP every day
12	+1	80%	85%	0	-30%	Nil / 1 HP every day
13	+1	85%	90%	0	-35%	Nil / 1 HP every day
14	+2	88%	92%	0	-40%	Nil / 1 HP every day
15	+2	90%	94%	0	-45%	Nil / 1 HP every day
16	+3	95%	96%	0	-50%	Nil / 1 HP every day
17	+3	97%	98%	0	-55%	Nil / 1 HP every day
18	+4	99%	100%	0	-60%	Nil / 1 HP every 18 hours
19	+4	99%	100%	+1	-65%	1 HP every 12 hours
20	+5*	99%	100%	+1	-70%	1 HP/6 turns
21	+5**	99%	100%	+2	-75%	1 HP/5 turns
22	+6**	99%	100%	+2	-85%	1 HP/4 turns
23	+6***	99%	100%	+3	-90%	1 HP/3 turns
24	+7***	99%	100%	+3	-95%	1 HP/2 turns
25	+7***	100%	100%	+4	-99%	1 HP/1 turn

* All 1s rolled for Hit Dice are automatically considered 2s.
** All 1s and 2s rolled for Hit Dice are automatically considered 3s.
*** All 1s, 2s, and 3s rolled for Hit Dice are automatically considered 4s.

Building Point Expenditures

WARNING: Be sure to consult the appropriate chapters when rolling on these tables. Some tables, especially the Background Tables (Chapter 4), have several modifiers which can be applied.

Table 1E:
Wisdom

Ability Score	Magical Defense Adjustment	Bonus Spells	Chance of Spell Failure	Spell Immunity	Chance to Improve Skill
1	-6	—	80%	—	—
2	-4	—	60%	—	—
3	-3	—	50%	—	01%
4	-2	—	45%	—	02%
5	-1	—	40%	—	03%
6	-1	—	35%	—	03%
7	-1	—	30%	—	04%
8	0	—	25%	—	04%
9	0	0	20%	—	05%
10	0	0	15%	—	05%
11	0	0	10%	—	05%
12	0	0	5%	—	05%
13	0	1st	0%	—	05%
14	0	1st	0%	—	06%
15	+1	2nd	0%	—	07%
16	+2	2nd	0%	—	08%
17	+3	3rd	0%	—	09%
18/01-50	+4	4th	0%	—	10%
18/51-00	+4	5th	0%	Befriend	11%
19	+4	1st, 3rd	0%	Cause Fear, Charm Person, Command, Hypnotism	12%
20	+4	2nd, 4th	0%	Forget, Hold Person, Ray of Enfeeblement, Scare	13%
21	+4	3rd, 5th	0%	Fear	14%
22	+4	4th, 5th	0%	Charm Monster, Confusion, Emotion, Fumble, Suggestion	
23	+4	1st, 6th	0%	Chaos, Feeblemind, Magic Jar, Quest	15% 16%
24	+4	5th, 6th	0%	Geas, Mass Suggestion, Rod of Rulership	18%
25	+4	6th, 7th	0%	Antipathy/Sympathy, Death Spell, Mass Charm	20%

Table 1D:
Intelligence

Ability Score	# 0f Lang.	Spell Level	Learning Ability	Max. # of Spells/Level	Illusion Immunity	Chance of Spell Mishap
1	0*	—	01%**	—	—	—
2	1	—	05%**	—	—	—
3	1	—	10%**	—	—	—
4	1	—	15%**	—	—	—
5	1	—	20%**	—	—	—
6	1	—	25%**	—	—	—
7	1	—	30%**	—	—	—
8***	1	Cantrips	30%***	5	—	35%
9 ****	2	4th	35%****	6	—	20%
10	2	5th	40%	7	—	15%
11	2	5th	45%	7	—	10%
12	3	6th	50%	7	—	05%
13	3	6th	55%	9	—	0%
14	4	7th	60%	9	—	0%
15	4	7th	65%	11	—	0%
16	5	8th	70%	11	—	0%
17	6	8th	75%	14	—	0%
18/01-50	7	9th	85%	18	Cantrips	0%
18/51-00	7	9th	90%	20	Cantrips	0%
19	8	9th	95%	All	1st-level	0%
20	9	9th	96%	All	2nd-level	0%
21	10	9th	97%	All	3rd-level	0%
22	11	9th	98%	All	4th-level	0%
23	12	9th	99%	All	5th-level	0%
24	15	9th	100%	All	6th-level	0%
25	20	9th	100%	All	7th-level	0%

* While unable to speak a language, the character can still communicate by grunts and gestures.
** Learning Ability for this level of intelligence is for Skills/Proficiencies only. Learning spells is impossible.
*** 8 is the minimum Intelligence required for a gnome titan to learn/cast spells though such a character, as indicated, would be limited to the use of cantrips.
**** 9 is the minimum Intelligence required to learn/cast spells for all races except for the gnome titan

Table 1G:
Effects of Comeliness

Comeliness	How others view the Character
-16 or lower:	Those viewing a character with Comeliness this low are repulsed and horrified, so as to turn away or attempt to destroy the creature that is so offensive to the sight. If the individual with low Comeliness is powerful, his appearance will make others tend to want to escape, or they will experience a reinforcement of a previously determined awe (horror) reaction. If both viewer and creature are of evil alignment, the effect is that of a positive Comeliness of the same total.
-15 to -9:	Those viewing creatures with Comeliness in this range display disgust, evidenced by a tendency to look away. They will revile the individual, and act hostile in general. Under no circumstances will the viewers accept this character unless all are of evil alignment, so that the negative Comeliness can be regarded as positive.
-8 to 0:	All viewers will evidence aversion and a desire to be away from so ugly a creature. If given an excuse, those near the individual will be hostile and openly aggressive; otherwise they will merely tend toward rejection.
+ 1 to + 6:	Such an individual is simply ugly. The reaction evidenced will tend toward unease and a desire to get away from such brutishness as quickly as possible. If given the opportunity, the character's Charisma can offset ugliness, but this requires a fair amount of conversation and interaction to take place.
+ 7 to + 9:	The homeliness of the individual will be such that initial contact will be of a negative sort. This negative feeling will not be strongly evidenced. High Charisma will quickly overcome it if any conversation and interpersonal interaction transpires. (Consider a dwarf with a 16 Charisma and a base Comeliness roll of 9; he will be at 8 when viewed by all creatures except other dwarves - who will see him with Comeliness adjusted by + 2 for Charisma.)
+ 10 to + 13:	Plain to average Comeliness; no effect on the viewer.
+ 14 to + 17:	Interest in viewing the individual is evidenced by those in contact, as he is good-looking. The reaction adjustment is increased by a percentage equal to the Comeliness score of the character. Individuals of the opposite sex will seek out such characters, and they will be affected as if under a Fascinate spell unless the Wisdom of such individuals exceeds 50% of the character's Comeliness total.
+ 18 to + 21:	The beauty of the character will cause heads to turn and hearts to race. Reaction for initial contact is at a percent equal to 150% of the Comeliness score. Individuals of the opposite sex will be affected as if under a Fascinate spell unless their Wisdom exceeds two-thirds of the character's Comeliness total. Individuals of the same sex will do likewise unless Wisdom totals at least 50% of the other character's Comeliness score. Rejection of harsh nature can cause the individual rejected to have a reaction as if the character had a negative Comeliness of half the actual (positive) score.
+ 22 to + 25:	The stunning beauty and gorgeous looks of a character with so high a Comeliness will be similar to that of those of lesser beauty (18-21). However, individuals will actually flock around the character, follow him and generally behave foolishly or in some manner so as to attract the attention of the character. The reaction adjustment is double the score of Comeliness: i.e., 22 Comeliness equals 44%. Fascinate-like power will affect all those with Wisdom of less than two-thirds the Comeliness score of the character. If an individual of the opposite sex is actually consciously sought by a character with Comeliness of 22-25, that individual will be effectively Fascinated unless his Wisdom is 18 or higher. Rejection is as above.
+ 26 to + 30:	Only creatures from other planes - demi-gawds, demi-gawddesses and otherworldly beings of unusual sort, can possess unearthly beauty of this sort. Reaction adjustment is double the Comeliness score. Fascinate-like power affects all except those with Wisdom equal to at least 75% of Comeliness, except that 19 or higher Wisdom always allows a saving throw versus the power. An individual of the opposite sex who is consciously sought by the possessor of such unearthly beauty and Comeliness will always be under the "spell" of the individual with such beauty unless he has Wisdom of 20 or more. The Fascinate-like power of high Comeliness is similar to the 2nd-level spell of the same name. Those subject to this power will be captivated by the user, and treat him as a trusted friend, mentor and companion. A saving throw versus spell will negate the effect but if the Comeliness is not magical in nature, then Dispel Magic, Antimagic Shell and similar spells will not affect the Fascination effect. Fascinated creatures will follow the orders of characters with high Comeliness, provided a roll of 3d6 does not exceed the Comeliness of the character. Requests that are not in the best interest of the creature get a + 1 to the die, while those that are hazardous can add up to + 6 or more to this roll. If the roll is higher than the user's Comeliness, the Fascinate-effect is broken. If a once-Fascinated creature has been badly treated and breaks free of this enrapturement, the creature will react as if the character's Comeliness was a negative amount. If the creature has been well treated, it may still be friendly to the character even after the Fascination has worn off.

Table 1H:
Beginning Honor Adjustment to Building Points

Honor Score	Building Point Bonus
1	-9
2	-8
3	-7
4	-6
5	-5
6	-4
7	-3
8	-2
9	-1
10	0
11	0
12	0
13	0
14	+1
15	+2
16	+3
17	+4
18	+5
19	+6
20	+7
21	+8
22	+9
23	+10
24	+11
25	+12

Racial Building Point Bonuses

Race	Bonus Points
Dwarf	10
Elf, High	12
Elf, Grunge	13
Elf, Dark	13
Gnome	10
Gnome Titan	15
Gnomeling	10
Half-Elf	11
Halfling	11
Half-Orc	8
Half-Ogre	8
Human	10
Pixie-Faire	14

Class Building Point Bonuses

Class	Bonus Points
Cleric	10
Druid	10
Fighter	10
Barbarian	7
Beserker	8
Cavalier	10
Dark Knight	12
Knight Errant	5
Monk	12
Paladin	12
Ranger	10
Magic-User	9
Battlemage	8
Bloodmage	11
Illusionist	9
Thief	12
Assassin	9
Bard	8

Table 2E:
Dwarven Con Saving Throw Bonuses

Constitution Score	Saving Throw Bonus
4-6	+1
7-10	+2
11-13	+3
14-17	+4
18-20	+5
21-24	+6
25	+7

Humans At a Glance:

The Upside

Racial Bonuses:
- Can rise to any level in chosen class.
- Can choose any character class.

Initial Languages:
Common, human*

Talents:
Must be purchased

Allowable Classes:
Any

Allowable Multi-Classes:
None. Humans may only dual-class

Attribute Modifiers:
Humans are the norm and receive no modifiers for attributes.

Building Point Bonus: 10

Additional Talents Which May be Purchased:
Acrobatic Skill Suite, Acute Alertness, Ambidextrous, Astute Observation, Attack Bonus, Balance Bonus, Blind Fighting, Detect Secret Doors, Endurance, Experience Bonus, Grace Under Pressure, Hit Point Bonus, Keen Sight, Less Sleep, Opportunist, Photographic Memory, Resistance, Seeking Grasping Hands, Sibling Empathy, Sixth Sense, Tough Hide

The Downside
None

*The number of languages a human can learn is limited by his Intelligence (see Table 1D) or by the Building Points/training he devotes to languages.

Table 2A:
Ability Prerequisites for Demi-human Characters

Ability	Dwarf M/F	Elf M/F	Gnome M/F	Gnomeling M/F	Half-Elf M/F	Halfling M/F	Half-Orc M/F	Half-Ogre M/F	Pixie Fairy M/F
STR									
MIN	8/8	3/3	6/6	6/6	3/3	6/6	6/18	14/14	1/1
MAX	18/17	18/17	18/15	17/15	18/17	17/14	18/19	19/19	14/14
DEX									
MIN	3/4	7/7	3/3	5/5	6/6	7/8	3/4	3/3	12/12
MAX	17/18	19/19	18/18	18/18	18/18	18/18	17/17	17/17	19/19
CON									
MIN	12/12	6/7	8/8	9/9	6/6	10/10	13/13	14/14	6/7
MAX	19/19	18/18	18/18	18/18	19/19	19/19	19/19	19/19	14/14
INT									
MIN	3/3	8/8	7/8	6/7	4/6	6/6	3/3	3/3	8/8
MAX	18/18	18/18	18/18	18/18	18/18	18/18	17/17	17/17	19/19
WIS									
MIN	3/3	3/3	3/3	3/3	3/3	3/3	3/3	3/3	3/3
MAX	18/18	18/18	18/18	17/17	18/18	17/16	14/14	15/15	19/19
CHA									
MIN	3/3	8/8	3/3	3/3	3/3	3/3	3/3	2/2	8/8
MAX	16/15	18/19	18/18	18/18	18/18	18/18	12/12	11/11	19/19
COM									
MIN	3/2	5/6	3/3	3/3	5/5	3/3	3/2	-/-	8/8
MAX	15/14	18/19	17/17	17/17	17/18	18/18	12/11	12/12	19/19

Table 2C:
Demi-human Class Restrictions and Level Limitations[1]

Racial Stock of Character

Class	Dwarf	Elf	Gnome	Gnomeling	Half-elf	Halfling	Half-orc	Half-ogre	Pixie Fairy	Human
Cleric	10	13	9	7	14	8	4	5	10	U
Druid	no	13	no	6	14	6	no	no	no	U
Fighter	15	12	11	9	14	9	U	U	9	U
Barbarian	no	no[4]	no	no	no	U	U	U	no	U
Berserker	16	13	no[3]	9	14	9	U	U	9	U
Cavalier	no	13[7]	no	no	no	no	no	no	9	U
Dark K.	no	no	no	no	no	no	no	no	no	U
Knight E.	15	12	11	9	14	9	U	U	9	U
Monk	no	no	no	no	no	no	no	no	no	U
Paladin	no	no	no	no	no	no	no	no	no	U
Ranger	no	15	no	no	16	no	no	no	no	U
Magic-User	no	15	no	no	12	no	no	no	U	U
Battle Mage	U	15	no[5]	no	10	no	no	no	no	U
Blood Mage[6]	no	15	no	no	11	no	no	no	no	U
Illusionist	no	no	15	U	no	no	no	no	U	U
Thief	U	12	13	U	U	U	8	7	15	U
Assassin	12	10	8	U	11	10[2]	U	7	no	U
Bard	no	no	no	no	U	no	no	no	no	U

1) The numbers on the chart are increased by 2 for demi-humans that are not multi-classed.

2) Thugs only.

3) The sub-race gnome titans may become berserkers. Such characters are restricted to 12th level max.

4) Grunge and wood elves only. Level Limitation 12

5) Gnome titans only. Level limitation 10.

6) The blood mage is a restricted magic-user specialist. Check with your GM for more information on this class.

7) The cavalier is not permitted for Grunge and Dark Elves.

Table 2D:
Racial Preferences

Basic Acceptability of Racial Type

RACE	Dwarf	Elf	Gnome	Gnomeling	Half-elf	Halfling	Half-orc	Half-ogre	Pixie Fairy	Human
Dwarf	P	A	G	H	N	G[1]	H	H	A	N
Elf	A	P	T	T	G	T	A	N	G[4]	N
Gnome	G	T	P	T	T	G	H	H	A	N
Gnomeling	G	T	T	P	T	N	A	A	H	N
Half-Elf	N	P	T	T	P	N	N	A	G	T
Halfling	G[2]	G[2]	T	G	N	P	N	T	T	N
Half-Orc	H	A	H	A	A	N	N	A	H	T
Half-ogre	H	N	H	A	A	T	A	N[5]	H	T
Pixie Fairy	A	G[4]	A	H	G	T	H	H	P	T
Human	N	N	N	N	T	N	T	N	T	P

1. Only with regard to tallfellows and stouts, other halflings are regarded with tolerance (T).

2. Only stouts regard dwarves as acceptable, other halflings tolerate them (T).

3. Tallfellows regard elves as good company, other halflings are tolerant (T).

4. Drow and grunge elves are not as tolerant of pixie fairies as other elves. (H)

5. Half-ogres generally don't get along with anyone – not even members of their own kind.

P: indicates that the race is generally preferred, and dealings with the members of the race will be reflected accordingly.

N: shows that the race is thought of neutrally, although some suspicion will be evidenced.

G: means that considerable goodwill exists towards the race.

A: means that the race is greeted with antipathy.

T: indicates that the race is viewed with tolerance and generally acceptable, if not loved.

H: tokens a strong hatred for the race in question.

Dwarves At a Glance:

The Upside

Racial Bonuses:
- Infravision. Dwarves can see 60 feet in the dark
- Saving throw bonus on saves vs. magic* (See Table 2E)
- Saving throw bonus save vs. poison (See Table 2E)
- +1 on to-hits vs. Orcs, half-orcs, Goblins, and Hobgoblins**
- Ogres, Trolls, Ogre Magi, giants, and Titans suffer a -4 to hit dwarves**

Initial Languages:
Common, dwarf, gnome, gnomeling, goblin, kobold, orc***

Talents:
- Detect grade or slope in passage 1-5 on 1d6
- Detect new tunnel/passage construction 1-5 on 1d6
- Detect sliding/shifting walls or rooms 1-4 on 1d6
- Detect stonework traps, pits, and deadfalls 1-3 on 1d6
- Determine approximate depth underground 1-3 on 1d6

Allowable Classes:
Cleric, fighter, berserker, knight errant, battle mage, thief, assassin (Level restrictions apply. See Table 2C)

Allowable Multi-Classes:
Fighter/assassin, cleric/assassin, fighter/cleric or fighter/thief

Attribute Modifiers:
Dwarves gain/suffer the following bonuses/penalties: +1 Constitution; -1 Charisma; -1 Comeliness

Building Point Bonus: 10

Additional Talents Which May be Purchased:
Acute Alertness, Ambidextrous, Astute Observation, Axe Bonus, Blind Fighting, Brewing, Close to the Earth, Constitution/Health Bonus, Crossbow Bonus, Dense Skin, Detect Evil, Detect Poison, Determine Age, Determine Stability, Endurance, Evaluate Gems, Expert Haggler, Hit Point Bonus, Illusion Resistant, Mace Bonus, Meld Into Stone, Mining Sense, Pick Bonus, Resistance, Short Sword Bonus, Sibling Empathy, Sixth Sense, Stealth, Stone Tell, Touched by Yurgain***, Warhammer Bonus

The Downside
Dwarves suffer a 20% chance for failure every time they use any magical item except weapons, armor, shields, and (if the character is a thief) items that duplicate thieving abilities. This penalty does not apply if the character is a battle mage or a cleric using a cleric item.

* Bonus for save vs. spells is lost if the dwarven character chooses to become a battle mage.
** This advantage is lost if the character chooses to become a battle mage.
*** The number of languages a dwarf can learn is limited by his Intelligence (see Table 1D) or by the Building Points/training he devotes to languages.
**** The talent, Touched by Yurgain, is free. Dwarves choosing the battle mage class MUST take this talent.

Dark Elves (Drow) At a Glance:

The Upside

Racial Bonuses:
- Infravision. Drow can see 120 feet in the dark
- 90% resistance to Sleep and all charm-related spells
- Only surprised on a 1 on 1d10
- Chance of starting with drow boots/cloak (see text)
- Chance of starting with drow chainmail (see text)
- Spell Ability (see text)
- Base resistance to magic of 50%. Increases by 2% for each level of experience.
- +2 bonus on saves vs. all forms of magical attack (including devices)

Initial Languages:
Common, drow, drow silent language, elf, dwarf, gnome, undercommon, kuo-toa, bugbear, and orcish *

Talents:
- +1 bonus on to-hits when using a crossbow, dart or a short/long sword.
- Move Silently. Opponents suffer a -4 penalty to their surprise die rolls. If the drow must open a door or screen to attack, this penalty is reduced to -2.
- Detect secret doors when passing by: 1 on 1d6
- Detect secret doors when searching: 1 or 2 on 1d6
- Detect concealed doors when searching: 1, 2 or 3 on 1d6
- Detect grade or slope in passage 1-5 on 1d6
- Detect new tunnel/passage construction 1-5 on 1d6
- Detect sliding/shifting walls or rooms 1-4 on 1d6
- Detect stonework traps, pits, and deadfalls 1-3 on 1d6
- Determine approximate depth underground 1-3 on 1d6

Allowable Classes:
Cleric, druid, fighter, berserker, knight errant, ranger, magic-user, battle mage, bloodmage, thief, assassin (Level restrictions apply. See Table 2C)

Allowable Multi-Classes:
Fighter/magic-user, fighter/thief, fighter/magic-user/thief, or magic-user/thief

Attribute Modifiers:
Elves gain/suffer the following bonuses/penalties: +1 Dexterity; -1 Constitution; -2 Comeliness

Building Point Bonus: 13

Additional Talents Which May be Purchased:
Acrobatic Skill Suite, Acute Alertness, Astute Observation, Blind Fighting, Close to the Earth, Cold Resistance, Constitution/Health Bonus, Crossbow Bonus, Dagger Bonus, Determine Stability, Grace Under Pressure, Heat Resistance, Javelin Bonus, Keen Sight, Less Sleep, Magic Identification, Mining Sense, Photographic Memory, Seeking Grasping Hands, Sibling Empathy, Sixth Sense, Speak With Plants, Sword Bonus

The Downside
- Dark elves suffer a -1 penalty on all rolls when exposed to bright sunlight or Continual Light spells. Lesser light sources do not bother them.
- All other elves hate dark elves, resulting in an initial reaction roll penalty of -2.

* The number of languages a drow can learn is limited by his Intelligence (see Table 1D) or by the Building Points/training he devotes to languages.

High Elves (incl. Sylvan Elves and Grey Elves) At a Glance:

The Upside
Racial Bonuses:
- Infravision. Elves can see 60 feet in the dark
- 90% resistance to Sleep and all charm-related spells

Initial Languages:
Common, elf, gnome, gnomeling, halfling, goblin, hobgoblin, orc, and gnoll*

Talents:
- +1 bonus on to-hit rolls when using a bow of any sort (except crossbow) or when using a short or long sword.
- Move Silently. Opponents suffer a -4 penalty to their surprise die rolls. If the elf must open a door or screen to attack, this penalty is reduced to -2.
- Detect secret doors when passing by: 1 on 1d6
- Detect secret doors when searching: 1 or 2 on 1d6
- Detect concealed doors when searching: 1, 2 or 3 on 1d6
- Move through undergrowth as if in open terrain

Allowable Classes:
Cleric, druid, fighter, berserker, cavalier, knight errant, ranger, magic-user, battle mage, bloodmage, thief, assassin (Level restrictions apply. See Table 2C)

Allowable Multi-Classes:
Fighter/magic-user, fighter/thief, fighter/magic-user/thief, or magic-user/thief

Attribute Modifiers:
Elves gain/suffer the following bonuses/penalties: +1 Dexterity; -1 Constitution; +1 Comeliness (sylvan elves only) +2 Comeliness (gray elves and high elves only)

Building Point Bonus: 12

Additional Talents Which May be Purchased:
Acrobatic Skill Suite, Acute Alertness, Animal Companion, Astute Observation, Blind Fighting, Cold Resistance, Dagger Bonus, Forest Movement, Grace Under Pressure, Heat Resistance, Javelin Bonus, Keen Sight, Less Sleep, Magic Identification, Photographic Memory, Seeking Grasping Hands, Sibling Empathy, Sixth Sense, Speak With Plants, Spear Bonus, Spell Abilities, Trident Bonus

The Downside
Except for some attribute penalties and class restrictions, none.

* The number of languages an elf can learn is limited by his Intelligence (see Table 1D) or by the Building Points/training he devotes to languages.

Gnome Titans At a Glance:

The Upside
Racial Bonuses:
- Infravision. Gnome titans can see 60 feet in the dark
- Saving Throw Bonus on Saves vs. Magic (See Table 2E)
- +1 on to-hits vs. Kobolds or Goblins
- Gnolls, Bugbears, Ogres, Trolls, Ogre Magi, giants, and Titans suffer a -4 to hit gnomish characters
- Gnome titans attack at one level higher than their current experience level
- Gnome titans only pay half Building Point/training costs for any skill of a military or combat nature. (Talents still have full BP costs, regardless of their nature)
- Gnome titans fighting along side with other gnome titans receive a +1 to their to-hit and damage rolls because of the incredible boost in morale they receive.
- Gnome titans fighting as a group cannot be broken or routed.

Initial Languages:
Common, dwarf, gnome, gnomeling, halfling, goblin, kobold, and the simple common speech of burrowing mammals (moles, badgers, weasels, shrews, ground squirrels, etc.)*

Talents:
- Detect grade or slope in passage 1-5 on 1d6
- Detect unsafe walls, ceiling, and floors 1-7 on 1d10
- Determine approximate depth underground 1-4 on 1d6
- Determine approximate direction underground 1-3 on 1d6
- Groin Stomp Attack (Special Combat Maneuver)

Allowable Classes:
Cleric, fighter, berserker, knight errant, battle mage, illusionist, thief, assassin. (Level restrictions apply. See Table 2C.)

Allowable Multi-Classes:
Fighter/assassin, fighter/cleric, fighter/illusionist, fighter/thief

Attribute Modifiers:
Gnomes gain/suffer the following bonuses/penalties: +2 Strength; +1 Intelligence; -1 Wisdom; -1 Comeliness

Building Point Bonus: 15

Additional Talents Which May be Purchased:
Acute Alertness, Ambidextrous, Animal Friendship, Astute Observation, Blind Fighting, Brewing, Close to the Earth, Dagger Bonus, Dart Bonus, Defensive Bonus, Engineering Bonus, Forest Movement, Freeze, Hide, Mining Sense, Opportunist, Potion Identification, Short Sword Bonus, Sibling Empathy, Sixth Sense, Sling Bonus, Stealth

The Downside
- Gnomes suffer a 20% chance for failure every time they use any magical item except weapons, armor, shields, illusionist items, and (if the character is a thief) items that duplicate thieving abilities.
- Gnome titans only earn 50% of any experience points awarded.
- Gnome titans must choose the gnomish gawd of war, Pangrus, as their patron gawd, and pay a tithe of 20% of all their income.
- Gnome titans only receive 50% of any hit points (rounded down) rolled on the hit dice for their class/level. This does not apply to the 20 hit point 'kicker'.

* The number of languages a gnome titan can learn is limited by his Intelligence (see Table 1D) or by the Building Points/training he devotes to languages.

Gnomes At a Glance:

The Upside
Racial Bonuses:
- Infravision. Gnomes can see 60 feet in the dark.
- Saving throw bonus on saves vs. magic (See Table 2E)
- +1 on to-hits vs. Kobolds or Goblins.
- Gnolls, Bugbears, Ogres, Trolls, Ogre magi, giants, and Titans suffer a -4 to hit gnomish characters.

Initial Languages:
Common, dwarf, gnome, gnomeling, halfling, goblin, kobold, and the simple common speech of burrowing mammals (moles, badgers, weasels, shrews, ground squirrels, etc.)*

Talents:
- Detect grade or slope in passage 1-5 on 1d6
- Detect unsafe walls, ceiling, and floors 1-7 on 1d10
- Determine approximate depth underground 1-4 on 1d6
- Determine approximate direction underground 1-3 on 1d6

Allowable Classes:
Cleric, fighter, knight errant, illusionist, thief, assassin (Level restrictions apply. See Table 2C)

Allowable Multi-Classes:
Cleric/illusionist, cleric/thief, fighter/cleric, fighter/illusionist, fighter/thief, illusionist/thief

Attribute Modifiers:
Gnomes gain/suffer the following bonuses/penalties: +1 Intelligence; -1 Wisdom; -1 Comeliness

Building Point Bonus: 10

Additional Talents Which May be Purchased:
Acute Alertness, Ambidextrous, Animal Friendship, Astute Observation, Blind Fighting, Brewing, Close to the Earth, Dagger Bonus, Dart Bonus, Defensive Bonus, Engineering Bonus, Forest Movement, Freeze, Hide, Mining Sense, Opportunist, Potion Identification, Short Sword Bonus, Sibling Empathy, Sixth Sense, Sling Bonus, Stealth

The Downside
Gnomes suffer a 20% chance for failure every time they use any magical item except weapons, armor, shields, illusionist items, and (if the character is a thief) items that duplicate thieving abilities.

*The number of languages a gnome can learn is limited by his Intelligence (see Table 1D) or by the Building Points/training he devotes to languages.

Gnomelings At a Glance:

The Upside
Racial Bonuses:
- Infravision. Gnomelings can see 30 feet in the dark
- Saving throw bonus on saves vs. magic (see Table 2E)
- +1 on to-hits vs. Kobolds or Goblins
- Gnolls, Bugbears, Ogres, Trolls, Ogre Magi, giants, and Titans suffer a -4 on to-hits gnomish characters
- Have special stealth abilities. Are able to hide and move about unnoticed. There is only a 5% chance of noticing a gnomeling who is hiding, and the person noticing must concentrate for one round.

Initial Languages:
Common, dwarf, gnome, gnomeling, halfling, goblin, kobold*

Talents:
- Detect grade or slope in passage 1-5 on 1d6
- Detect unsafe walls, ceiling, and floors 1-7 on 1d10
- Determine approximate depth underground 1-4 on 1d6
- Determine approximate direction underground 1-3 on 1d6
- +1 bonus on to-hits when using a dagger

Allowable Classes:
Cleric, druid, fighter, berserker, knight errant, illusionist, thief, assassin, (Level restrictions apply. See Table 2C.)

Allowable Multi-Classes:
Cleric/illusionist, cleric/thief, fighter/cleric, fighter/illusionist, fighter/thief, illusionist/thief

Attribute Modifiers:
Gnomelings gain/suffer the following bonuses/penalties: +1 Intelligence; +1 Dexterity; -1 Strength; -1 Wisdom; -1 Constitution

Building Point Bonus: 10

Additional Talents Which May be Purchased:
Acute Alertness, Ambidextrous, Animal Friendship, Astute Observation, Blind Fighting, Dagger Bonus, Dart Bonus, Defensive Bonus, Engineering Bonus, Experience Bonus, Forest Movement, Hide, Mining Sense, Potion Identification, Sixth Sense, Sling Bonus, Stealth

The Downside
Gnomelings suffer a 10% chance for failure every time they use any magical item except weapons, armor, shields, illusionist items, and (if the character is a thief) items that duplicate thieving abilities.

*The number of languages a gnomeling can learn is limited by his Intelligence (see Table 1D) or by the Building Points/training he devotes to languages.

Pixie Fairies At a Glance:

The Upside
Racial Bonuses:
- Fly at 18" per round
- Can use Giant Moth and Butterfly mounts
- a +2 bonus to hit in mounted combat or flying combat
- Heal an extra hit point per day
- Never surprised
- Telepathic linking
- When a fairy dies he is reincarnated within 1d4 months
- May cast a Faerie Phantom spell once per day
- At fifth level they may cast a Minor Sphere of Perturbation spell once per day

Initial Languages:
Common, elvish, gnomish, butterfly, bird, pixie fairy*

Talents:
- Turn invisible once per day.

Allowable Classes:
Cleric, fighter, berserker, cavalier, knight errant, magic-user, illusionist, or thief (Level restrictions apply. See Table 2C.)

Allowable Multi-Classes:
Fighter/magic-user

Attribute Modifiers:
+1 Intelligence, +1 Wisdom, +2 Dexterity; -6 Strength; +2 Charisma; +3 Comeliness

Building Point Bonus: 14

Additional Talents Which May be Purchased:
Acrobatic Skill Suite, Acute Alertness, Ambidextrous, Astute Observation, Attack Bonus, Blind Fighting, Faerie Kind Martial Arts, Flutter, Hit Point Bonus, Keen Sight, Magic Bonus

The Downside
- Pixie fairies must pay 3 times the gp value for their daily food requirements unless they forage for their food
- They have a very short life span — generally only ten to fifteen years
- Pixie fairies don't get the twenty hit point-kicker other characters receive at first level, instead they receive only a 10 hit point kicker
- They also only get half the hit points rolled for each level (rounded up)

*The number of languages a pixie fairy can learn is limited by his Intelligence (see Table 1D) or by the Building Points/training he devotes to language.

Half-Ogres At a Glance:

The Upside
Racial Bonuses:
- Infravision with a 30' range
- Half-ogres receive a +1 to saving throws versus poison
- Starting Hit Dice are doubled at 1st level

Initial Languages:
Common, ogre, orc, troll, stone giant, and gnoll*

Talents:
- +1 attack and damage bonus with one melee weapon
- Dense Skin
- Tough Hide

Allowable Classes:
Cleric, fighter, barbarian, berserker, knight errant, thief, assassin (Level restrictions apply. See Table 2C.)

Allowable Multi-Classes:
none

Attribute Modifiers:
Half-ogres gain/suffer the following bonuses/penalties: +2 Strength; +2 Constitution; -1 Wisdom, -2 Intelligence, -3 Charisma; -5 Comeliness

Building Point Bonus: 8

Additional Talents Which May be Purchased:
Active Sense of Smell, Ambidextrous, Blind Fighting, Damage Bonus, Endurance, Mace Bonus, Sibling Empathy

The Downside
- Half-ogres qualify as large creatures and suffer more damage from many weapons.
- Certain smaller races enjoy combat bonuses against half-ogres.
- -2 penalty to attack rolls against dwarves.
- -4 penalty to attack rolls against gnomes.
- Their armor and other garb costs 200% that of humans.

*The number of languages a half-ogre can learn is limited by his Intelligence (see Table 1D) or by the Building Points/training he devotes to languages.

WARNING: Be sure to consult the appropriate chapters when rolling on these tables. Some tables, especially the Background Tables (Chapter 4), have several modifiers which can be applied.

Halflings At a Glance:

The Upside

Racial Bonuses:
- Possible Infravision: 15% of halflings have normal infravision (60-foot range)
  Failing that, 25% have limited infravision (30-foot range)
  Otherwise, halflings has normal vision
- Saving throw bonus on saves vs. magic (See Table 2E)
- Saving throw bonus on saves vs. poison (See Table 2E)
- Surprise Bonus. Opponents suffer a -4 penalty to their surprise die rolls. If the halfling must open a door or screen to attack, this penalty is reduced to -2.

Initial Languages:
  Common, halfling, dwarf, elf, gnome, gnomeling, goblin, and orc*

Talents:
- +1 bonus to attack rolls when using thrown weapons and slings
- If stout or partially stout blood, character can detect if a passage is an up or down grade with 75% accuracy
- If stout or partially stout blood, character can determine direction half the time

Allowable Classes:
  Cleric, druid, fighter barbarian, berserker knight errant, thief assassins (thugs only), (Level restrictions apply. See Table 2C.)

Allowable Multi-Classes:
  Fighter/thief

Attribute Modifiers:
  Halflings gain/suffer the following bonuses/penalties: +1 Dexterity, -1 Strength

Building Point Bonus: 11

Additional Talents Which May be Purchased:
  Acute Alertness, Ambidextrous, Astute Observation, Balance Bonus, Blind Fighting, Brewing, Dagger Bonus, Detect Evil, Expert Haggler, Hide, Opportunist, Reaction Bonus, Sibling Empathy, Sixth Sense, Taunt

The Downside
  Halflings are highly valued in the slave market.

*The number of languages a halfling can learn is limited by his Intelligence (see Table 1D) or by the Building Points/training he devotes to languages.

Grunge Elves (Grels) At a Glance:

The Upside

Racial Bonuses:
- Infravision. Grel can see 60 feet in the dark
- 90% resistance to Sleep and all charm-related spells
- Only surprised on a 1 on 1d10

Initial Languages:
  Common, grel, elf, dwarf, orc, ogre, glersee, gnomish, brownie, pixie faerie*

Talents:
- War Cry: Enemies must save vs. fear at −5 or lose their first attack
- +1 bonus on to-hits when using a spear or bow
- Move Silently. Opponents suffer a -4 penalty to their surprise die rolls. If the Grel must open a door or screen to attack, this penalty is reduced to -2.
- Detect secret doors when passing by: 1 on 1d6
- Detect secret doors when searching: 1 or 2 on 1d6
- Detect concealed doors when searching: 1, 2 or 3 on 1d6
- Tracking (automatically gain this Sophisticated Task)
- Move through undergrowth as if in open terrain (per High Elves)

Allowable Classes:
  Cleric, druid, fighter, barbarian, berserker, knight errant, ranger, magic-user, battle mage, bloodmage, thief, assassin (Level restrictions apply. See Table 2C.)

Allowable Multi-Classes:
  Fighter/magic-user, fighter/thief, fighter/magic-user/thief, or magic-user/thief

Attribute Modifiers:
  Grunge elves gain/suffer the following bonuses/penalties: +1 Dexterity; -1 Constitution; -1 Comeliness

Building Point Bonus: 13

Additional Talents Which May be Purchased:
  Acrobatic Skill Suite, Acute Alertness, Animal Companion, Astute Observation, Blind Fighting, Cold Resistance, Constitution/Health Bonus, Dagger Bonus, Forest Movement, Grace Under Pressure, Heat Resistance, Javelin Bonus, Keen Sight, Less Sleep, Magic Identification, Mining Sense, Photographic Memory, Seeking Grasping Hands, Sibling Empathy, Sixth Sense, Speak With Plants, Spell Abilities, Track Game Animal

The Downside
  The Grel must suffer the jealousy of the other races.

*The number of languages a grunge elf can learn is limited by his Intelligence (see Table 1D) or by the Building Points/training he devotes to languages.

Half-Elves At a Glance:

The Upside

Racial Bonuses:
- Infravision enables half-elves to see up to 60 feet in darkness
- 30% resistance to Sleep and all charm-related spells

Initial Languages:
  Common, elf, gnome, gnomeling, halfling, goblin, hobgoblin, orc and gnoll*

Talents:
- Detect secret doors when passing by: 1 on 1d6
- Detect secret doors when searching: 1 or 2 on 1d6
- Detect concealed doors when searching: 1, 2 or 3 on 1d6

Allowable Classes:
  Cleric, druid, fighter, berserker, knight errant, ranger, magic-user, battle mage, bloodmage, thief, assassin, bard (Level restrictions apply. See Table 2C.)

Allowable Multi-Classes:
  Cleric (or druid)/fighter, cleric (or druid)/fighter/magic-user, cleric (or druid)/ranger, cleric (or druid)/magic-user, fighter/magic-user, fighter/thief, fighter/magic-user/thief and magic-user/thief

Attribute Modifiers:
  Half-elves gain/suffer the following bonuses/penalties: +1 Comeliness

Building Point Bonus: 11

Additional Talents Which May be Purchased:
  Acrobatic Skill Suite, Acute Alertness, Ambidextrous, Astute Observation, Balance Bonus, Blind Fighting, Bow Bonus, Cold Resistance, Heat Resistance, Keen Sight, Less Sleep, Photographic Memory, Sibling Empathy, Sixth Sense, Sword Bonus

The Downside
  None.

*The number of languages a half elf can learn is limited by his Intelligence (see Table 1D) or by the Building Points/training he devotes to languages.

Half-Orcs At a Glance:

The Upside

Racial Bonuses:
- Infravision. Half-orcs can see 60 feet in the dark

Initial Languages:
  Common, orc, dwarf, goblin, hobgoblin, and ogre*

Talents:
- Active Sense of Smell
- Acute Taste

Allowable Classes:
  Cleric, fighter, barbarian, berserker, knight errant, thief, assassin (Level restrictions apply. See Table 2C.)

Allowable Multi-Classes:
  Fighter (or berserker)/cleric, fighter (or berserker)/thief, fighter (or berserker)/assassin

Attribute Modifiers:
  Half-orcs gain/suffer the following bonuses/penalties: +1 Strength; +1 Constitution; -2 Charisma, -3 Comeliness

Building Point Bonus: 8

Additional Talents Which May be Purchased:
  Acute Alertness, Ambidextrous, Attack Bonus, Blind Fighting, Damage Bonus, Dense Skin, Endurance, Mace Bonus, Sibling Empathy

The Downside
- In human and halfling societies, half-orcs suffer a −2 reaction roll penalty.
  In dwarven, elven and gnomish societies, they suffer a −4 reaction roll penalty.

*The number of languages a half-orc can learn is limited by his Intelligence (see Table 1D) or by the Building Points/training he devotes to languages.

Table 3A:
Character Class Groupings

Fighter Group	Magic-User Group	Cleric Group	Thief Group	HackMaster Class*
Fighter	Magic-user	Cleric	Thief	HackFighter
Barbarian	Illusionist	Druid	Bard	HackMage
Berserker	Battle mage		Assassin	HacKleric
Cavalier	Blood mage			Hackssassin
Dark knight				
Knight errant				
Monk				
Paladin				
Ranger				

* HackMaster is a progression class and is restricted. Beginning characters cannot choose to be HackMaster class characters.

Table 3B:
Hit Dice, Spell Ability, and Class Level Limit

Class of Character	Hit Die Type	Maximum # Hit Dice	Spell Ability	Class Level Limit	BP Bonus
CLERIC	d8	9	yes	none	10
Druid	d8	14	yes	23 (Hierophant of the Cabal)	10
FIGHTER	d10	9	no	none	10
Barbarian	d12	8	no	none	7
Berserker	d12	8	no	none	8
Cavalier	d12	10	no	none	10
Dark Knight	d10	9	yes	none	12
Knight Errant	d10	9	no	none	5
Monk	d6	22	no	21 (S.G.D.M.otF.S.W.)	12
Paladin	d10	9	yes*	none	12
Ranger	d8	11	yes**	none	10
MAGIC-USER	d4	11	yes	none	9
Battle Mage	d4	10	yes	none	8
Blood Mage	d4	11	yes	none	11
Illusionist	d4	10	yes	none	9
THIEF	d6	10	no***	none	12
Assassin	d6	15	no***	none	9
Bard	d6	10	yes****	none	8
HACKMASTER*****					
HackFighter	Special	Special	Special	none	NA
HackMage	Special	Special	Special	none	NA
HacKleric	Special	Special	Special	none	NA
Hackssassin	Special	Special	Special	none	NA

* Clerical spell ability up to 4th level spells, first gained at 9th level.
** Druid spell ability up to 3rd level spells, first gained at 8th level; and magic-user spell ability up to 2nd level, first gained at 9th level.
*** At 10th level (12th level with regard to assassins) thieves gain the ability to read magic-user (and illusionist) spells from scrolls.
**** Some of the affects of bard songs resemble the effects of spells.
***** Information on the HackMaster Classes is player restricted.

Table 3C:
Armor and Weapons Permitted by Class

Class of Character	Armor	Shield	Weapons*	Oil
CLERIC	any	any	club, flail, hammer, mace, staff****	yes
Druid	leather/padded	wooden	club, dagger, dart, hammer, scimitar, sling, spear, staff	yes
FIGHTER	any	any	any	yes
Berserker	any	none	any	yes
Barbarian	any	any	any	yes
Cavalier	any	any	any	no
Dark Knight	any	any	any	yes
Knight Errant	any	none	only melee weapons	seige use only
Monk	robes/garments	none	club, crossbow, dagger, hand axe, javelin, pole arm, spear, staff	no
Paladin	any	any	any	no
Ranger	any	any,	any**	yes
MAGIC-USER	robes/garments	none	dagger, dart, staff	yes
Battle Mage	any	none	dagger, short sword, staff	yes
Blood Mage	robes/garments	none	dagger, dart, staff	yes
Illusionist	robes/garments	none	dagger, dart, staff	yes
THIEF	any up to studded leather or elven chain mail	none	club, dagger, dart, sling, sword***	yes
Assassin	leather	any	any	yes
Bard	any up to chainmail	none	club, dagger, dart, javelin, sling, scimitar, spear, staff, bastard sword, broad sword, long sword, short sword	yes
HACKMASTER				
HackFighter	any	none	any	yes
HackMage	any	none	dagger, dart, short sword, staff	yes
HackKleric	any	any	club, flail, hammer, mace, staff	yes
HackSsassin	leather	any	any	yes

* This heading includes any magical weapons of the type named unless use by the class in question is specifically proscribed in the description of the magic weapon.
** Characters under 5' height cannot employ the longbow or any weapon over 12' in length. Those under 100 pounds of body weight cannot use the heavy crossbow or pole arms in excess of 200 gold piece weight equivalent, including two-handed swords.
*** A thief may use a short sword, broadsword, or longsword but not a bastard sword or a two-handed sword.
**** Clerics might be allowed different weapons depending upon their deity.

Berserker
Ability Requirements:
Str 17+, Con 15+
Prime Requisite:
Strength and Constitution
Hit Dice Type:
d12
Allowed Races:
any
Allowed Alignments:
any chaotic
Building Point Bonus:
8 BP

The Assassin
Ability Requirements:
Strength 12+, Intelligence 11+ Dexterity 12+
Prime Requisite(s):
Dexterity, Intelligence, Strength
Hit Dice Type:
d6
Allowed Races:
Any except pixie fairy
Allowed Alignments:
evil
Building Point Bonus:
9 BP

Dark Knight
(aka Anti-Paladin)
Ability Requirements:
Str 12+, Con 9+, Wis 13+, Cha 17
Prime Requisite(s):
Wisdom and Charisma
Hit Dice Type:
d10
Allowed Races:
Human
Allowed Alignments:
chaotic evil
Building Point Bonus
12 BP

Monk
Ability Requirements:
Str 12+, Dex 15+, Con 11+, Wis 15+, Int 12+
Prime Requisite(s):
None
Hit Dice Type:
d6
Allowed Races:
Human
Allowed Alignments:
lawful
Building Point Bonus:
12 BP

Ranger
Ability Requirements:
Str 13+, Dex 13, Con 14+, Wis 14+
Prime Requisite(s):
Strength, Dexterity, Wisdom
Hit Dice Type:
d8
Allowed Races:
Human, Elf, Half-elf
Allowed Alignments:
any good
Building Point Bonus:
10 BP

Cavalier
Ability Requirements:
Str 15+, Con 15+, Dex 15+, Int 10+, Wis 10+, Com 9+
Prime Requisite:
None
Hit Dice Type:
d12
Allowed Races:
Human, Elves, Half-elves, Gnome Titans, Pixie Fairy
Allowed Alignments:
any good alignment initially
Building Point Bonus:
10BP

Thief
Ability Requirements:
Dexterity 9+
Prime Requisite(s):
Dexterity
Hit Dice Type:
d6
Allowed Races:
All
Allowed Alignments:
any
Building Point Bonus:
12 BP

Knight Errant
(aka Rogue Knight)
Ability Requirements:
Str 14+, Con 10+, Wis 13+, Cha 17+ Comeliness 15+
Prime Requisite(s):
Strength and Charisma
Hit Dice Type:
d10
Allowed Races:
Any
Allowed Alignments:
any good
Building Point Bonus:
5 BP

Paladin
Ability Requirements:
Str 12+, Con 9+, Wis 13+, Cha 17
Prime Requisite(s):
Strength and Charisma
Hit Dice Type:
d10
Allowed Races:
Human
Allowed Alignments:
lawful good
Building Point Bonus:
12 BP

Table 3D:
Class Ability Requirements

Character Class	Str	Dex	Con	Int	Wis	Cha	Com
Fighter	9	--	--	--	--	--	--
Barbarian	15	14	15	--	<17	--	--
Berserker	17	--	15	--	--	--	--
Cavalier	15	15	15	10	10	--	9
Dark Knight	12	--	12	--	13	17	--
Knight Errant	14	--	--	--	13	17	15
Monk	12	15	11	12	15	--	--
Paladin	12	--	9	--	13	17	--
Ranger	13	13	14	--	14	--	--
Magic-User	--	--	--	9	--	--	--
Battle Mage	12	12	12	9	--	--	--
Blood Mage	--	--	16	9	15	--	--
Illusionist	--	16	--	9	--	--	--
Cleric	--	--	--	--	9	--	--
Druid	--	--	--	--	12	15	--
Thief	--	9	--	--	--	--	--
Assassin	12	12	--	11	--	--	--
Bard	--	12	--	13	--	15	12
HackFighter*	18	--	--	--	--	16	--
HackMage*	--	--	--	18	--	16	--
HacKleric*	--	--	--	--	18	16	--
HackSsassin*	12	18	11	12	15	16	--

* The HackMaster classes are a progression-class and are restricted. A character must progress to the required levels and meet all prerequisites as well as make a successful 'called' roll before obtaining study in these classes.

Fighter
Ability Requirements:
Strength 9
Prime Requisite:
Strength [gain 10% ep bonus if Str is 16 or higher]
Hit Dice Type:
d10
Allowed Races:
All
Allowed Alignments:
Any (as long as chosen racial type allows it)
Building Point Bonus:
10 BP

Barbarian
Ability Requirements:
Strength 15+, Constitution 15+, Dexterity 14+, Wisdom <17
Prime Requisite:
None
Hit Dice Type:
d12
Allowed Races:
Human, Grel, Half-orcs, Half-ogres, Halflings
Allowed Alignments:
any non-lawful alignment
Building Point Bonus:
7 BP

Table 3H:
Barbarian Progression Table

Experience Points	Exp. Level	12-Sided Dice for Accumulated Hit Points	Level Title
0-6,000	1	20+1d12*	Barbarian
6,001-12,000	2	2	Barbarian
12,001-24,000	3	3	Barbarian
24,001-48,000	4	4	Barbarian
48,001-80,000	5	5	Barbarian
80,001-150,000	6	6	Barbarian
150,001-275,000	7	7	Barbarian
275,001-500,000	8	8**	Barbarian
500,001-1,000,000	9	8+4	Barbarian
1,000,001-1,500,000	10	8+8	Barbarian
1,500,001-2,000,000***	11	8+12	Chairman of the Horde

* At first level barbarians receive 20 points + 1d12. This twenty point 'kicker' is received at first level only.
** Barbarians gain 4 hps per level after the 8th.
*** 500,000 experience points per level for each additional level above the 11th.

Table 3E:
Fighter Melee Attacks per Round

Fighter Level	Barbarian, Berserker, Cavalier Level	Dark Knight, Knight Errant Paladin Level	Ranger Level	Attacks/Round
1-6	1-5	1-6	1-7	1/round
7-12	6-10	7-11	8-14	3/2 rounds
13-18	11-15	11-17	15+	2/round
19+	16+	18+		5/2 rounds

Table 3F:
Fighter Progression Table

Experience Points	Experience Level	10-Sided Dice for Accumulated Hit Points	Level Title
0-2,000	1	20 +1d10*	Veteran
2,001--4,000	2	2	Warrior
4,001 --8,000	3	3	Swordsman
8,001-18,000	4	4	Hero
18,001-35,000	5	5	Swashbuckler
35,001-70,000	6	6	Myrmidon
70,001-125,000	7	7	Champion
125,001-250,000	8	8	Superhero
250,001-500,000	9	9**	Lord
500,001-750,000	10	9+3	Lord (10th Level)
750,001-1,000,000***	11	9+6	Lord (11th Level)

* At first level fighters receive 20 points + 1d10. This twenty-point 'kicker' is received at first level only.
** Fighters gain 3 h.p. per level after the 9th.
*** 250,000 experience points per level for each additional level beyond the 11th.

Table 3G:
Fighter's Followers

Roll percentile dice and add your Honor die on each of the following sub-tables of Table 3G: once for the leader of the troops, once for troops, and once for a bodyguard (elite) unit.

Die Roll	Leader (and suggested magical items)
01-40	5th-level fighter, plate mail, shield, battle axe +2
41-75	5th-level fighter, plate mail, shield +1, spear +1, dagger +1
76-90	6th-level fighter, plate mail +1, shield, spear +1, dagger +1, plus 3rd-level fighter, splint mail, shield, Crossbow of Distance
91-99	7th-level fighter, plate mail +1, shield +1, broad sword +2, heavy war horse with Horseshoes of Speed
00	GM's Option

Die Roll	Troops/Followers (all 0th-level)
01-50	20 cavalry with ring mail, shield, 3 javelins, long sword, hand axe; 100 infantry with scale mail, polearm*, club
51-75	20 infantry with splint mail, morning star, hand axe; 60 infantry with leather armor, pike, short sword
76-90	40 infantry with chain mail, heavy crossbow, short sword; 20 infantry with chain mail, light crossbow, military fork
91-99	10 cavalry with banded mail, shield, lance, bastard sword, mace; 20 cavalry with scale mail, shield, lance, long sword, mace; 30 cavalry with studded leather armor, shield, lance, long sword
00	GM's Option (Barbarians, headhunters, armed peasants, extra-heavy cavalry, etc.)

*Player selects type.

Die Roll	Elite Units
01-10	10 mounted knights; 1st-level fighters with field plate, large shield, lance, broadsword, morning star, and heavy war horse with full barding
11-30	10 1st-level elven fighter/magic-users with chain mail, longsword, long bow, dagger
31-40	20 Berserkers: 2nd-level fighters with leather armor, shield, battle axe, broadsword
41-65	20 expert archers: 1st-level fighters with studded leather armor, long bows or crossbows (+2 to hit, or bow specialization)
66-99	30 infantry: 1st-level fighters with plate mail, body shield, spear, short sword
00	GM's Option (pegasi cavalry, eagle riders, demi-humans, siege train, etc.)

WARNING: Be sure to consult the appropriate chapters when rolling on these tables. Some tables, especially the Background Tables (Chapter 4), have several modifiers which can be applied.

Table 3I
Barbarian Power/Ability Acquisitions

Level	Actions and Abilities
2	May associate freely with clerics
3	May use magic potions
4	May use magic weapons. May strike creatures hit only by + 1 weapons. Gains + 1 on saving throws versus spell.
5	May use magic armor
6	May associate with magic-users - if necessary! May strike creatures hit only by + 3 weapons
7	May use weapon-like miscellaneous magic items
8	May associate with magic-users - occasionally. May strike creatures hit only by + 5 weapons. Gains + 2 on saving throws versus spell. May summon a barbarian horde (see the Barbarian Horde section)
9	May use protection scrolls.
10	May use most magic items available to fighters. May strike creatures hit only by + 7 weapons.
12	Gains + 3 on saving throws versus spell. May strike creatures hit only by + 9 weapons.

Table 3K:
Berserker Lack of Hack Table

Number of Days without Combat	Penalty
1	none
2	-1d4 hit points
3	-1 Str
4	-1 Dex
5	add a minor mental quirk
6	-20% to all skill and proficiency checks
7	-1 Con
8	-1d8 hit points
9	-1 Wis
10	-1 Con and -1 Wis
11	add a major mental quirk
12	-1 Str and -1 Dex
13	-20% to Honor
14	-50% to Honor

Table 3J:
Berserker Progression Table

Experience Points	Exp. Level	12-Sided Dice for Accum. Hit Points	Level Title
0-6,000	1	20+1d12*	RageWarrior
6,001-12,000	2	2	RageMonger
12,001-24,000	3	3	RageMaster
24,001-48,000	4	4	BattleBane
48,001-80,000	5	5	BaneLord
80,001-150,000	6	6	BaneMaster
150,001-275,000	7	7	BattleDancer
275,001-500,000	8	8**	BattleRager
500,001-1,000,000	9	8+4	Berserker
1,000,001-1,500,000	10	8+8	Berserker Lord
1,500,001-2,000,000***	11	8+12	Master Berserker

* At first level berserkers receive 20 points + 1d12. This twenty point 'kicker' is received at first level only.

** Berserkers gain 4 h.p. per level after the 8th.

*** 500,000 experience points per level for each additional level above the 11th.

Table 3N:
Dark Knight Progression Table

Experience Points	Experience Level	10 Sided Dice for Accumulated Hit Points	Level Title
0-2,750	1	20+1d10*	Knave
2,751-5,500	2	2	Dread Knight
5,501-12,000	3	3	Shade Knight
12,001-24,000	4	4	Shadow Knight
24,001-45,000	5	5	Knight of Twilight
45,001-95,000	6	6	Knight of Midnight
95,001-175,000	7	7	Knightmare
175,001-350,000	8	8	Knight Terminus
350,001-700,000	9	9**	Knight Terminus Master
700,001-1,050,000	10	9+3	Lord Terminus
1,050,001-1,400,000***	11	9+6	Lord Terminus Rogue
1,400,001 – 1,750,000	12	9+9	Lord Terminus Master
1,750,001 – 2,100,000	13	9+12	Lord Terminus Supreme
2,100,001 – 2,450,000	14	9+15	Lord of the Pit
2,450,001 – 2,800,000	15	9+18	Dark Lord of the Pit (15th level)
2,800,001 – 3,150,000	16	9+21	D.L.o.t.P. (16th level)
3,150,001 – 3,500,000	17	9+24	D.L.o.t.P. (17th level)
3,500,001 – 3,850,000	18	9+27	D.L.o.t.P. (18th level)
3,850,001 – 4,200,000	19	9+30	D.L.o.t.P. (19th level)
4,200,001 – 4,550,000	20	9+33	D.L.o.t.P. (20th level, etc.)

* At first level dark knights receive 20 points + 1d10. This twenty point 'kicker' is received at first level only.

** Dark knights gain 3 hps per level after the 9th.

*** 350,000 experience points per level for each additional level above the 11th.

Table 3L:
Cavalier Progression Table

Experience Points	Exp. Level	12-Sided Dice for Accum. Hit Points	Level Title
(-1,500- -501)	0	21 + 1d4*	(Horseman)
(-501- -1)	0	2d4	(Lancer)
0-2,500	1	1**	Armiger,
2,501-5,000	2	2	Scutifer
5,001-10,000	3	3	Esquire
10,001-18,500	4	4	Knight Plebe
18,501-37,000	5	5	Knight Bachelor
37,001-85,000	6	6	Knight
85,001-140,000	7	7	Grand Knight
140,001-220,000	8	8	Banneret
220,001-300,000	9	9	Chevalier
300,001-600,000	10	10***	Cavalier
600,001-900,000	11	10+3	Cavalier, 11th
900,001-1,200,000	12	10+6	Cavalier, 12th
1,200,001-1,500,000	13	10+9	Cavalier Commander
1,500,001-1,800,000	14	10+12	Cavalier Commander
1,800,001-2,100,000	15	10+15	Cavalier Commander
2,100,001-2,400,000	16	10+18	Cavalier Commander
2,400,001-2,700,000	17	10+21	Cavalier Commander
2,700,001-3,000,000	18	10+24	Cavalier Commander
3,000,001-3,300,000	19	10+27	Cavalier Commander
3,300,001-3,600,000****	20	10+30	Cavalier Commander

* If qualification for 1st level required progression through the two 0-level grades, then hit dice for 1st level are 3d4 + 21, but in all other cases 1d12+20 applies.

** A character whose social standing qualifies him or her for immediate entrance into the cavalier class begins as a 1st-level Armiger with 1d10 + 2 hit points. He rolls 1d12 per level thereafter until 10th level.

*** Cavaliers gain 3 hps per level after the 10th.

**** 300,000 experience points per level for each level beyond the 20th

Table 3P:
Dark Knight's Followers

Roll percentile dice and add your Honor die on each of the following sub-tables of Table 3P: once for the leader of the troops and once for troops.

Die Roll	Leader (and suggested magical items)
01-40	5th-level fighter, plate mail, shield, battle axe +2
41-75	5th-level dark knight, plate mail, shield +1, spear +1, dagger +1
76-90	6th-level dark knight, plate mail +1, shield, spear +1, dagger +1, plus 3rd-level fighter, splint mail, shield, Crossbow of Distance
91-99	7th-level dark knight, plate mail +1, shield +1, broad sword +2, heavy war horse with Horseshoes of Speed
00	GM's Option (or lesser demon)

Die Roll	Troops/Followers
01-50	20 Warg mounted goblins with ring mail, small shield, 3 javelins, long sword, & hand axe; 100 goblins with scale mail, small shield, short sword & club
51-76	20 orcs with splint mail, morning star, & hand axe; 60 orcs with scale mail, halberd & short sword
76-91	20 gnolls with chain mail, heavy crossbow, & longsword; 20 gnolls with chain mail, light crossbow & guisarme-voulge
91-99	25 bugbears with medium shield & bastard sword; 30 hobgoblin cavalry with light warhorse, banded mail, medium shield, lance & long sword
00	GM's Option (giants, trolls)

*Player selects type.

Table 3M:
Cavalier Follower Gear

Die roll	Follwers equipped with:
01-50	Light cavalry in ring mail and shield, each with 3 javelins, long sword, and hand axe; or, heavy infantry in scale mail, with pole arm of choice and club.
51-75	Heavy infantry in splint mail with morning star and hand axe; or, heavy infantry in leather armor with pike and short sword.
76-90	Crossbowmen in chain mail with heavy crossbow and short sword; or, crossbowmen in chain mail with light crossbow and military fork.
91-00	Cavalry in banded mail and shield with lance and horseman's mace; or, cavalry in studded leather with long sword and horseman's flail. Either type will be mounted on medium warhorses.

Table 3O:
Dark Knight Communicable Disease Table

d100	Disease
01-10	rotting flesh
11-20	orc shingles
21-30	goblin pox
31-40	black plague
41-50	rotting death
51-60	blue death
61-70	dancing death
71-80	burning death
81-90	common cold
91-00	other

Table 3R:
Knight Errant Progression Table

Experience Points	Experience Level	10 Sided Dice for Accumulated Hit Points	Level Title
0-2,750	1	20+1d10*	Wayward Warrior
2,751-5,500	2	2	Misguided Militant
5,501-12,000	3	3	Knight of the Whispering Wind
12,001-24,000	4	4	Knight of Drifting
24,001-45,000	5	5	Knight of the Shooting Stars
45,001-95,000	6	6	Knight of Shifting Sands
95,001-175,000	7	7	Rogue Knight
175,001-350,000	8	8	Rogue Knight Master
350,001-700,000	9	9**	Knight Errant
700,001-1,050,000	10	9+3	Knight Errant (10th level)
1,050,001-1,400,000***	11	9+6	K.E.(11th level)
1,400,001 – 1,750,000	12	9+9	K.E.(12th level)
1,750,001 – 2,100,000	13	9+12	K.E.(13th level)
2,100,001 – 2,450,000	14	9+15	K.E.(14th level)
2,450,001 – 2,800,000	15	9+18	K.E.(15th level)
2,800,001 – 3,150,000	16	9+21	K.E.(16th level)
3,150,001 – 3,500,000	17	9+24	K.E.(17th level)
3,500,001 – 3,850,000	18	9+27	K.E.(18th level)
3,850,001 – 4,200,000	19	9+30	K.E.(19th level)
4,200,001 – 4,550,000	20	9+33	K.E.(20th level, etc.)

* At first level knight errants receive 20 points + 1d10. This twenty point 'kicker' is received at first level only.

** Knight errants gain 3 hps per level after the 9th.

*** 350,000 experience points per level for each additional level above the 20th.

Table 3Q:
Dark Knight Spell Progression

Dark Knight Level	Casting Level	Spell Level 1	2	3	4
9	1	1	--	--	--
10	2	2	--	--	--
11	3	2	1	--	--
12	4	2	2	--	--
13	5	2	2	1	--
14	6	3	2	1	--
15	7	3	2	1	1
16	8	3	3	2	1
17	9*	3	3	3	1
18	9*	3	3	3	1
19	9*	3	3	3	2
20*	9*	3	3	3	3

* Maximum spell ability

Table 3T:
Monk Ability Table

Level	Effective Armor Class	Move	Open Hand Attacks per Melee Round*	Open Hand Damage
1	7	15"	5/4	1-4
2	6	15"	5/4	1-6
3	5	16"	5/4	2-7
4	4	16"	3/2	2-7
5	3	17"	3/2	2-8
6	2	17"	3/2	2-8
7	2	18"	3/2	3-9
8	1	18"	2	2-12
9	1	19"	2	3-12
10	0	20"	2	3-13
11	0	21"	5/2	4-13
12	0	22"	5/2	4-16
13	-1	23"	5/2	5-17
14	-1	24"	3	5-20
15	-2	25"	3	2-24
16	-2	26"	3	4-24
17	-3	27"	4	4-24
18	-4	28"	4	6-24
19	-5	29"	4	5-30
20	-6	30"	4	8-32
21	-7	31"	4	8-32

* Listings with a slash indicate extra attacks after the appropriate number of rounds, i.e. 5/4 means 5 attacks per 4 rounds, with the additional attack coming at the end of the round sequence.

Table 3S:
Monk Progression Table

Experience Points	Experience Level	6 Sided Dice for Accumulated Hit Points	Level Title
0-1,000	1	20+2d6*	Grasshopper
1,001-3,000	2	3	Brother
3,001-6,000	3	4	Brother of the Winds
6,001-10,000	4	5	Brother of Secrets
10,001-22,000	5	6	Brother of Mysteries
22,001-40,000	6	7	Disciple
40,001-70,000	7	8	Sub-Master
70,001-110,000	8	9	Master
110,001-160,000	9	10	Superior Master
160,001-220,000	10	11	Master of the North Wind
220,001-400,000	11	12	Master of the West Wind
400,001-650,000	12	13	Master of the South Wind
650,001-890,000	13	14	Master of the East Wind
890,001-1,150,000	14	15	Master of Winter
1,150,001-1,300,000	15	16	Master of Autumn
1,300,001-1,600,000	16	17	Master of Spring
1,600,001-2,000,000	17	18	Master of Summer
2,000,001-2,250,000	18	19	Grand Master of Blood
2,250,001-2,500,000	19	20	Grand Master of Venom
2,500,001-3,000,000	20	21	Grand Master of Dragons
3,000,001+	21	22	**Superior Grand Dragon Master of the Four Seasonal Winds**

* At first level monks receive 20 points + 2d6. This twenty point 'kicker' is received at first level only.

Table 3U:
Paladin Progression Table
10 Sided
Dice for

Experience Points	Experience Level	Accumulated Hit Points	Level Title
0-2,750	1	20 +1d10*	Gallant
2,751-5,500	2	2	Keeper
5,501-12,000	3	3	Protector
12,001-24,000	4	4	Defender
24,001-45,000	5	5	Warder
45,001-95,000	6	6	Guardian
95,001-175,000	7	7	Chevalier
175,001-350,000	8	8	Justiciar
350,001-700,000	9	9**	Paladin
700,001-1,050,000	10	9+3	Paladin (10th level)
1,050,001-1,400,000	11	9+6	Paladin (11th level)
1,400,001-1,750,000	12	9+9	Paladin (12th level)
1,750,001-2,100,000	13	9+12	Paladin (13th level)
2,100,001-2,450,000	14	9+15	Shinning Knight
2,450,001-2,800,000	15	9+18	Holy Knight
2,800,001-3,150,000	16	9+21	Angelic Knight
3,150,001-3,500,000	17	9+24	Arch Angelic Knight
3,500,001-3,850,000	18	9+27	Holy WarLord of the 1st Order
3,850,001-4,200,000	19	9+30	Holy WarLord of the 2nd Order
4,200,001***	20	9+33	Holy WarLord of the 3rd Order

* At first level paladins receive 20 points + 1d10. This twenty point 'kicker' is received at first level only.

** Paladins gain 3 hps per level after the 9th

*** 350,000 experience points per level for each additional level above the 20th.

Table 3V:
Paladin Spell Progression

Paladin Level	Casting Level	Cleric Spell Level 1	2	3	4
9	1	1	--	--	--
10	2	2	--	--	--
11	3	2	1	--	--
12	4	2	2	--	--
13	5	2	2	1	--
14	6	3	2	1	--
15	7	3	2	1	1
16	8	3	3	2	1
17	9*	3	3	3	1
18	9*	3	3	3	1
19	9*	3	3	3	2
20	9*	3	3	3	3

* Maximum spell ability

Table 3W:
Ranger Progression Table
8 Sided
Dice for

Experience Points	Experience Level	Accumulated Hit Points	Level Title
0-2,250	1	20+2d8*	Runner
2,251-4,500	2	3	Strider
4,501-10,000	3	4	Scout
10,001-20,000	4	5	Courser
20,001-40,000	5	6	Tracker
40,001-90,000	6	7	Guide
90,001-150,000	7	8	Pathfinder
150,001-225,000	8	9	Ranger
225,001-325,000	9	10	Ranger Knight
325,001-650,000	10	11**	Ranger Lord
650,001-975,000	11	11+2	Ranger Lord (11th level)
975,001-1,300,000	12	11+4	R.L. (12th level)
1,300,001-1,625,000	13	11+6	R.L. (13th level)
1,625,001-1,950,000	14	11+8	R.L. (14th level)
1,950,001-2,275,000	15	11+10	R.L. (15th level)
2,275,001-2,600,000	16	11+12	R.L. (16th level)
2,600,001-2,925,000	17	11+14	R.L. (17th level)
2,925,001-3,250,000	18	11+16	R.L. (18th level)
3,250,001-3,575,000	19	11+18	R.L. (19th level)
3,575,001***	20	11+20	R.L. (20th level, etc.)

* At first level rangers receive 20 points + 2d8. This twenty point 'kicker' is received at first level only.

** Rangers gain 2 hps per level after the 11th.

*** 325,000 experience points per level for each additional level above the 20th.

Table 3X:
Ranger's Followers

Die Roll	Follower
01-10	Bear, black
11-20	Bear, brown
21	Pixie fairy*
22-26	Cleric (human)
27-38	Dog/wolf
39-40	Druid
41-50	Falcon
51-53	Fighter (elf)
54-55	Fighter (gnome)
56-57	Fighter (halfling)
58-65	Fighter (human)
66	Fighter/magic-user (elf)*
67-72	Great cat (tiger, lion, etc.)*
73	Hippogriff
74	Pegasus*
75	Pixie*
76-80	Ranger (half-elf)
81-90	Ranger (human)
91-94	Raven
95	Satyr*
96	Thief (halfling)
97	Thief (human)
98	Treant*
99	Werebear/weretiger*
00	Other wilderness creature (chosen by the GM)

*If the ranger already has a follower of this type, ignore this result and roll again.

Cleric
Ability Requirements:
  Wisdom 9+
Prime Requisite(s):
  Wisdom
Hit Dice Type:
  d8
Allowed Races:
  All
Allowed Alignments:
  any
Building Point Bonus:
  10 BP
Spell Jacking?
  No

Illusionist
(aka Spell-Jacker)
Ability Requirements:
  Intelligence 9+, Dexterity 16+
Prime Requisite(s):
  Intelligence
Hit Dice Type:
  d4
Allowed Races:
  Human, Gnome, Gnomeling, Pixie Fairy
Allowed Alignments: any
Building Point Bonus: 9 BP
Spell Jacking? Yes

Table 3Y:
Ranger Abilities

Ranger Level	Hide in Shadows	Move Silently	Casting Level	Druid Spell Levels 1	2	3
1	10%	15%	--	--	--	--
2	15%	21%	--	--	--	--
3	20%	27%	--	--	--	--
4	25%	33%	--	--	--	--
5	31%	40%	--	--	--	--
6	37%	47%	--	--	--	--
7	43%	55%	--	--	--	--
8	49%	62%	1	1	--	--
9	56%	70%	2	2	--	--
10	63%	78%	3	2	1	--
11	70%	86%	4	2	2	--
12	77%	94%	5	2	2	1
13	85%	99%*	6	3	2	1
14	93%	99%	7	3	2	2
15	99%*	99%	8	3	3	2
16	99%	99%	9**	3**	3**	3**

* Maximum percentile score
** Maximum spell ability.

Table 3Z:
Armor Effect on Spell Mishaps

Armor Used*	Chance of Spell Mishap**
none	0
buckler	+5%
small shield	+15%
medium shield	+10%
padded	+20%
elven chain mail	+20%
leather	+25%
studded leather	+30%
brigandine	+35%
scale mail	+35%
hide	+40%
ring mail	+40%
chain mail	+50%
body shield	+55%
splint mail	+60%
banded mail	+80%
bronze plate mail	+90%
platemail	+100%
field plate	+120%
full plate	+150%

* Magic armor results in the same spell mishap % as normal armor of the same type.

** This percentage chance is added to the character's Chance of Spell Mishap % for his Intelligence as listed on Table 1D.

Magic-User
(aka Spell Lobber, Spell Jockey)

Ability Requirements:
Intelligence 9+
Prime Requisite(s):
Intelligence
Hit Dice Type:
d4
Allowed Races:
Human, Elf, Half-elf, Pixie Fairy
Allowed Alignments:
any
Building Point Bonus:
9 BP
Spell Jacking?
No

Battle Mage

Ability Requirements:
Intelligence 9+ Strength 12, Dexterity 12, Constitution 12
Prime Requisite(s):
Intelligence
Hit Dice Type:
d4
Allowed Races:
Human, Elf, Half-elf, Dwarf
Allowed Alignments:
any
Building Point Bonus:
8 BP
Spell Jacking?
Yes

Table 3BB:
Magic-User Spell Progression*

Magic-user Level	Magic-User Spell Level								
	1	2	3	4	5	6	7	8	9
1	3	--	--	--	--	--	--	--	--
2	4	--	--	--	--	--	--	--	--
3	4	1	--	--	--	--	--	--	--
4	5	2	--	--	--	--	--	--	--
5	6	2	1	--	--	--	--	--	--
6	6	2	2	--	--	--	--	--	--
7	6	3	2	1	--	--	--	--	--
8	6	3	3	2	--	--	--	--	--
9	6	3	3	2	1	--	--	--	--
10	6	4	3	2	2	--	--	--	--
11	6	4	4	3	3	--	--	--	--
12	6	4	4	4	4	1	--	--	--
13	7	5	5	4	4	2	--	--	--
14	7	5	5	4	4	2	1	--	--
15	7	5	5	5	5	2	1	--	--
16	7	5	5	5	5	3	2	1	--
17	7	5	5	5	5	3	3	2	--
18	7	5	5	5	5	3	3	2	1
19	7	5	5	5	5	3	3	3	1
20	7	5	5	5	5	4	3	3	2

* This table indicates the number of spells of each level a magic-user can memorize at one time. For example a fifth level mage could memorize six first level spells, two second level spells and one third level spell.

Table 3EE:
Battle Mage Simul-Casting

Level of Battle Mage	Number of Simul-cast Spells
1 – 4	NA
5 – 7	2
8 – 9	3
10 – 12	4
13+	5

Table 3CC:
Battle Mage Progression Table

Experience Points	Experience Level	4-Sided Dice for Accumulated Hit Points	Level Title
0 – 3000	1	16+1d4*	Second
3001– 6000	2	2	MinuteMage
6001– 12,000	3	3	Doughboy
12001 – 24,000	4	4	Dawgface
24001 – 48,000	5	5	WitchRanger
48,001 – 90,000	6	6	SpellSoldier
90,001 – 130,000	7	7	Artillerist
130,001 – 175,000	8	8	MeleeMage
175,001 – 275,000	9	9	SkirmishMage
275,001 – 400,000	10	10**	WarLock
400,001 – 800,000	11	10+1	BattleMage, junior grade
800,001 – 1,300,000	12	10+2	BattleMage
1,300,001 – 1,600,000	13	10+3	Arch BattleMage, junior grade
1,600,001 – 1,900,000	14	10+4	Arch BattleMage
1,900,001 – 2,300,000	15	10+5	WarMage, junior grade
2,300,00 – 2,700,000	16	10+6	Brigadier WarMage
2,700,001 – 3,300,000	17	10+7	WarMage
3,300,001 – 3,600,000	18	10+8	Arch WarMage, junior grade
3,600,001 – 4,000,000	19	10+9	Brigadier Arch WarMage
4,000,001***	20	10+10	Arch WarMage

* At first level battle mages receive 16 points + 1d4. This sixteen point 'kicker' is received at first level only.

** Battle mages gain 1 hp per level after the 10th.

*** 300,000 experience points per level of experience beyond the 20th.

Table 3AA:
Magic-User Progression Table

Experience Points	Experience Level	4 Sided Dice for Accumulated Hit Points	Level Title
0-2,500	1	20+1d4*	Prestidigitator
2,501-5,000	2	2	Evoker
5,001-10,000	3	3	Conjuror
10,001-22,500	4	4	Theurgist
22,501-40,000	5	5	Thaumaturgist
40,001-60,000	6	6	Magician
60,001-90,000	7	7	Enchanter
90,001-135,000	8	8	Warlock
135,001-250,000	9	9	Sorcerer
250,001-375,000	10	10	Necromancer
375,001-750,000	11	11**	Wizard
750,001-1,125,000	12	11+1	Wizard (12th level)
1,125,001-1,500,000	13	11+2	Wizard (13th level)
1,500,001-1,875,000	14	11+3	Wizard (14th level)
1,875,001-2,250,000	15	11+4	Wizard (15th revel)
2,250,001-2,625,000	16	11+5	Mage
2,625,001-3,000,000	17	11+6	Mage (17th level)
3,000,001-3,375,000	18	11+7	Arch-Mage
3,375,-001-3,750,000	19	11+8	Arch Mage (19th level)
3,750,001+	20***	11+9	Arch-Mage (20th level)

* At first level magic-users receive 20 points + 1d4. This twenty point 'kicker' is received at first level only.

** Magic-users gain 1 hp per level after the 11th.

*** 375,000 experience points per level for each additional level beyond the 20th.

Bard

Ability Requirements:
Charisma 15+, Intelligence 13+, Dexterity 12+, Comeliness 12+
Prime Requisite(s):
Dexterity, Charisma
Hit Dice Type:
d6
Allowed Races:
Human, Half-elf
Allowed Alignments:
any neutral
Building Point Bonus:
8 BP

Druid

Ability Requirements:
Wisdom 12, Charisma 15
Prime Requisite(s):
Wisdom, Charisma
Hit Dice Type:
d8
Allowed Races:
Human, half-elf, halfling, elf, gnomeling
Allowed Alignments:
any
Building Point Bonus:
10 BP
Spell Jacking?
No

WARNING: Be sure to consult the appropriate chapters when rolling on these tables. Some tables, especially the Background Tables (Chapter 4), have several modifiers which can be applied.

Table 3DD:
Battle Mage Spell Progression*

Battle Mage Level	1	2	3	4	5	6	7	8	9	Spell-Jack**
1	3	--	--	--	--	--	--	--	--	--
2	4	--	--	--	--	--	--	--	--	--
3	4	1	--	--	--	--	--	--	--	--
4	5	2	--	--	--	--	--	--	--	1.5X
5	5	2	1	--	--	--	--	--	--	1.5X
6	6	2	2	--	--	--	--	--	--	1.5X
7	6	2	2	1	--	--	--	--	--	1.5X
8	6	3	3	2	--	--	--	--	--	1.5X
9	6	3	3	2	1	--	--	--	--	2X
10	6	4	3	3	2	--	--	--	--	2X
11	6	4	4	3	3	--	--	--	--	2X
12	7	4	4	4	4	1	--	--	--	2X
13	7	5	5	4	4	2	--	--	--	2X
14	7	5	5	4	4	2	1	--	--	2X
15	7	5	5	4	5	2	1	--	--	2X
16	7	5	5	5	5	3	2	1	--	2.5X
17	7	5	5	5	5	3	3	2	--	2.5X
18	7	5	5	5	5	3	3	2	1	2.5X
19	7	5	5	5	5	3	3	3	1	2.5X
20	7	5	5	5	5	4	3	3	2	2.5X

Column header: Magic-User Spell Level (columns 1–9)

* This table indicates the number of spells of each level a battle mage can memorize at one time. For example a fifth level battle mage could memorize four first level spells, two second level spells and one third level spell.
** Indicates how many spells the battle mage can spell-jack (memorize) at the indicated level. Multiplier is applied to each spell level with results rounded down. For example, a 5th level battle mage could memorize five 1st level spells, two 2nd level spells and one 3rd level spell If the same mage spell-jacks he can memorize seven 1st level spells, 3 2nd level spells and 1 third level spell. (See Spell-Jacking)

Table 3 GG:
Illusionist Spell Progression*

Illusionists Level	1	2	3	4	5	6	7	8	9	Spell Jack**
1	3	--	--	--	--	--	--	--	--	--
2	4	--	--	--	--	--	--	--	--	--
3	4	1	--	--	--	--	--	--	--	1.5X
4	5	2	--	--	--	--	--	--	--	1.5X
5	6	2	1	--	--	--	--	--	--	1.5X
6	6	2	2	--	--	--	--	--	--	1.5X
7	6	3	2	1	--	--	--	--	--	1.5X
8	6	3	3	2	--	--	--	--	--	2X
9	6	3	3	2	1	--	--	--	--	2X
10	6	4	3	2	2	--	--	--	--	2X
11	6	4	4	3	3	--	--	--	--	2X
12	6	4	4	4	4	1	--	--	--	2X
13	7	5	5	4	4	2	--	--	--	2X
14	7	5	5	4	4	2	1	--	--	2X
15	7	5	5	4	5	2	1	--	--	2.5X
16	7	5	5	5	5	3	2	1	--	2.5X
17	7	5	5	5	5	3	3	2	--	2.5X
18	7	5	5	5	5	3	3	2	1	2.5X
19	7	5	5	5	5	3	3	3	1	2.5X
20	7	5	5	5	5	4	3	3	2	3X

Column header: Illusionist Spell Level (columns 1–9)

* This table indicates the number of spells of each level an illusionist can memorize at one time. For example a fifth level illusionist could memorize six first level spells, two second level spells and one third level spell.
** Indicates how many spells the illusionist can spell-jack (memorize) at the indicated level. Multiplier is applied to each spell level with results rounded down. For example a 5th level illusionist could memorize six 1st level spells, two 2nd levels spells and one 3rd level spell (see Spell-Jacking). The same illusionist who is spell-jacking could memorize nine 1st level spells, three 2nd level spells and one 3rd level spell (See Spell-Jacking)

Table 3FF:
Illusionist Progression Table

Experience Points	Experience Level	4-Sided Dice for Accumulated Level Hit Points	Title
0--2,250	1	20+1d4*	Prestidigitator
2,251--4,500	2	2	Minor Trickster
4501--9,000	3	3	Trickster
9,001-18,000	4	4	Master Trickster
18,001-35,000	5	5	Cabalist
35,001---60,000	6	6	Visionist
60,001-95,000	7	7	Phantasmist
-1,95,001--145,000	8	8	Apparitionist
145,001-220,000	9	9	Spellbinder
220,001-440,000	10	10**	Illusionist
440,001-660,000	11	10+1	Illusionist (11th level)
660,001-880,000	12	10+2	Illusionist (12th level)
1,100,001-1,300,000	13	10+3	Illusionist (13th level)
1,300,001-1,520,000	14	10+4	Illusionist (14th level)
1,520,001-1,740,000	15	10+5	Illusionist (15th level)
1,740,001-1,960,000	16	10+6	Illusionist (16th level)
1,960,001-2,180,000	17	10+7	Illusionist (17th level)
2,180,001-2,400,000	18	10+8	Illusionist (18th level)
2,400,001-2,620,000	19	10+9	Illusionist (19th level)
2,620,001-	20***	10+10	Illusionist (20th level)

* At first level illusionists receive 20 points + 1d4. This twenty point 'kicker' is received at first level only.
** Illusionists gain 1 hp per level after the 10th.
*** 220,000 experience points per level of experience beyond the 20th.

Table 3HH:
Cleric Progression Table

Experience Points	Experience Level	8-Sided Dice for Accumulated Level Hit Points	Title
0-1,500	1	20+1d8*	Altar Boy
1,501-3,000	2	2	Acolyte
3001-6000	3	3-	Brother
6,001-13,000	4	4	Layman
13,001-27,500	5	5	Adept
27,501-55,000	6	6	Friar
55,001-110,000	7	7	Curate
110,001-225,000	8	8	Preacher
225,001-450,000	9	9**	Priest
450,001-675,000	10	9+2	Perfect
675,001-900,000	11	9+4	Canon
900,001-1,125,000	12	9+6	Deacon
1,125,001-1,350,000	13	9+8	Abbott
1,350,001-1,575,000	14	9+10	Evangelist
1,575,001-1,800,000	15	9+12	Prior
1,800,001-2,025,000	16	9+14	Prelate
2,025,001-2,250,000	17	9+16	Rector
2,250,001-2,475,000	18	9+18	Vicar
2,475,001-2,700,000	19	9+20	Patriarch
2,700,001-2,925,000	20***	9+22	High Priest

* At first level clerics receive 20 points + 1d8. This twenty point 'kicker' is received at first level only.
** Clerics gain 2 hps per level after the 9th.
*** 225,000 experience points per level for each additional level beyond the 20th.

Character Advancement Notes

Table 3II:
Cleric Spell Progression

Cleric Level	Spell Level 1	2	3	4	5	6*	7**
1	3	--	--	--	--	--	--
2	4	--	--	--	--	--	--
3	4	1	--	--	--	--	--
4	5	2	--	--	--	--	--
5	5	3	1	--	--	--	--
6	5	3	2	--	--	--	--
7	5	3	2	1	--	--	--
8	5	3	3	2	--	--	--
9	6	4	3	2	1	--	--
10	6	4	3	3	2	--	--
11	7	4	4	3	2	1	--
12	8	5	5	3	2	2	--
13	8	6	6	4	2	2	--
14	8	6	6	5	3	2	1
15	8	6	6	6	4	2	1
16	9	7	7	6	4	3	1
17	9	7	7	7	5	3	2
18	9	8	8	8	6	4	2
19	9	9	8	8	6	4	2
20	9	9	9	8	7	5	2

* Usable only by clerics with 17 or greater Wisdom.
** Usable only by clerics with 18 or greater Wisdom.

Table 3JJ:
Druid Progression Table

Experience Points	Level	8-Sided Dice for Accumulated Hit Points	Level Title
0-2,000	1	20+1d0*	Aspirant
2,001-4,000	2	2	Ovate
4,001-7,500	3	3	Initiate of the 1st Circle
7,501-12,500	4	4	Initiate of the 2nd Circle
12,501-20,000	5	5	Initiate of the 3rd Circle
20,001-35,000	6	6	Initiate of the 4th Circle
35,001-60,000	7	7	Initiate of the 5th Circle
60,001-90,000	8	8	Initiate of the 6th Circle
90,001-125,000	9	9	Initiate of the 7th Circle
125,001-200,000	10	10	Initiate of the 8th Circle
200,001-300,000	11	11	Initiate of the 9th Circle
300-750,000	12	12	Druid
750:001-1,500,000	13	13	Archdruid
1,500,001-3,000,000	14	14	The Great Druid
3,000,001-3,500,000	15	15**	The Grand Druid***
3,500,001-500,000	16	15+1	Hierophant Druid****
500,001-1,000,000	17	15+2	Hierophant Initiate
1,000,001-1,500,000	18	15+3	Hierophant Adept
1,500,001-2,000,000	19	15+4	Hierophant Master
2,000,001-2,500,000	20	15+5	Numinous Hierophant
2,500,001-3,000,000	21	15+6	Mystic Hierophant
3,000,001-3,500,000	22	15+7	Arcane Hierophant
3,500,001+	23	15+8	Hierophant of the Cabal

* At first level druids receive 20 points + 1d8. This twenty point 'kicker' is received at first level only.
** Druids gain 1 hp per level after the 15th.
*** See the description of druids concerning 15th level and the Grand Druid.
**** See hierophant druids in the druid description. At 16th Level druids start over at 0 experience points.

Table 3KK:
Druid Spell Progression

Druid Level	Spell Level 1	2	3	4	5	6	7
1	4	-	-	-	-	-	-
2	4	1	-	-	-	-	-
3	5	2	1	-	-	-	-
4	6	2	2	-	-	-	-
5	6	3	2	-	-	-	-
6	6	3	2	1	-	-	-
7	6	4	3	1	-	-	-
8	6	4	3	2	-	-	-
9	6	4	3	2	1	-	-
10	6	4	3	3	2	-	-
11	6	5	3	3	2	1	-
12	6	5	4	4	3	2	1
13	6	5	5	5	4	3	2
14	6	6	6	6	5	4	3
15	6	6	6	6	6	6	6

Table 3LL:
Thief Experience Levels

Experience Points	Experience Level	6-Sided Dice for Accumulated Hit Points	Level Title
0-1,250	1	20+1d6*	Apprentice
1,251-2,500	2	2	Footpad
2,501-5,000	3	3	Cutpurse
5,001-10,000	4	4	Larcenist
10,001-20,000	5	5	Scout
20,001-42,500	6	6	Treasure Hunter
42,501-70,000	7	7	Fingersmith
70,001-110,000	8	8	Filcher
110,001-160,000	9	9	Burglar
160,001-220,000	10	10**	Highwayman
220,001-440,000	11	10+2	Robber
440,001-660,000	12	10+4	Expert Treasure Hunter
660,001-880,000	13	10+6	Guild Thief
880,001-1,100,000	14	10+8	Guild Soldier
1,100,001-1,320,000	15	10+10	Thief
1,320,001-1,540,000	16	10+12	Master Thief
1,540,001-1,760,000	17	10+14	Captain Thief
1,760,001-1,980,000	18	10+16	Guild Master Thief
1,980,001-2,200,000	19	10+18	Guild Captain
2,200,001-2,420,000	20***	10+20	Guild Boss

* At first level thieves receive 20 points + 1d6. This twenty point 'kicker' is received at first level only.
** Thieves gain 2 hps per level after the 10th.
*** 220,000 experience points per level for each additional level beyond the 20th.

Table 3MM:
Thieving Skill Base Scores

Skill	Base Score
Pick Pockets	15%
Open Locks	10%
Find Traps	5%
Remove Traps	5%
Move Silently	10%
Hide in Shadows	5%
Detect Noise	15%
Climb Walls	60%
Read Languages	0%

Notes:

Table 3NN:
Thieving Skill Racial Adjustments

Skill	Dwarf	Elf*	Gnome	Gnomeling	Half-elf	Halfling	Pixie fairy	Half-orc	Half-ogre
Pick Pockets	--	+5%	--	--	+5%	+5%	+10%	-5%	-10%
Open Locks	+10%	-5%	+5%	+5%	--	+5%	-15%	+5%	+5%
Find Traps	+10%	+5%	+10%	+5%	--	+10%	-15%	--	+5%
Remove Traps	+15%	--	+10%	+5%	--	--	-15%	+5%	+5%
Move Silently	-10%	+5%	+5%	+5%	--	+10%	+20%	--	-5%
Hide in Shadows	-5%	+10%	+5%	+10%	+5%	+15%	+30%	--	-20%
Detect Noise	--	+5%	+10%	+5%	--	+5%	+10%	+5%	+10%
Climb Walls	+5%	--	-15%	-15%	--	-15%	-50%	+5%	+20%
Read Languages	--	--	--	--	--	-5%	-10%	-10%	-20%

* includes Grel, Drow and other sub-races as well.

Table 3OO:
Thieving Skill Dexterity Adjustments

Dexterity	Pick Pockets	Open Locks	Find/Remove Traps	Move Silently	Hide in Shadows
7	-25%	-20%	-20%	-30%	-20%
8	-20%	-15%	-15%	-25%	-15%
9	-15%	-10%	-10%	-20%	-10%
10	-10%	-5%	-10%	-15%	-5%
11	-5%	--	-5%	-10%	--
12	--	--	--	-5%	--
13-15	--	--	--	--	--
16	--	+5%	--	--	--
17	+5%	+10%	--	+5%	+5%
18	+10%	+15%	+5%	+10%	+10%
19	+15%	+20%	+10%	+15%	+15%
20	+20%	+25%	+15%	+20%	+20%
21	+25%	+30%	+20%	+25%	+25%
22	+30%	+35%	+25%	+25%	+30%
23	+35%	+40%	+30%	+30%	+35%
24	+40%	+45%	+35%	+35%	+40%
25	+45%	+50%	+40%	+40%	+45%

Table 3PP:
Thieving Skill Armor Adjustments

Skill	No Armor	Elven Chain	Chainmail (Bards only)	Studded Leather, Ring mail or Padded
Pick Pockets	+5%	-20%	-25%	-25%
Open Locks	--	-5%	-10%	-10%
Find/Remove Traps	--	-5%	-10%	-10%
Move Silently	+10%	-10%	-15%	-15%
Hide in Shadows	+5%	-10%	-15%	-15%
Detect Noise	--	-5%	-10%	-5%
Climb Walls	+10%	-20%	-25%	-25%
Read Languages	--	--	--	--

A thief character uses the "No Armor" column if wearing Bracers of Defense or a cloak without large or heavy protective clothing.

Table 3QQ:
Backstab Damage Multipliers

Thief's Level	Extra Damage Dice
1-4	+1
5-8	+2
9-12	+3
13+	+4

Table 3TT:
Bard Experience Levels

Experience Points	Experience Level	6-Sided Die* for Accumulated Hit Points	Level Title
0-2,000	1	20+1d6*	Tramp
2,001-4,000	2	2	Face-man
4,001-8,000	3	3	Drifter
8,001-16,000	4	4	Fraud
16,001-25,000	5	5	Circus Performer
25,001-40,000	6	6	Jongleur
40,001-60,000	7	7	Troubadour
60,001-85,000	8	8	Scoundrel
85,001-110,000	9	9	Skald
110,001-150,000	10	10**	Scheister
150,001-200,000	11	10+1	Swindler
200,001-400,000	12	10+2	Fast Talker
400,001-600,000	13	10+3	Artist
600,001-800,000	14	10+4	Bunko Artist
800,001-1,000,000	15	10+5	Con Artist
1,000,001-1,200,000	16	10+6	Scam Artist
1,200,001-1,400,000	17	10+7	Scammer
1,400,001-1,600,000	18	10+8	Grifter
1,600,001-1,800,000	19	10+9	Bard
1,800,001-2,000,000***	20	10+10	Master Bard

* At first level bards gain 20 points + 1d6. This twenty point 'kicker' is received at first level only.
** Bards gain 2 hps per level after the 10th.
*** 200,000 experience points per level for each additional level beyond the 20th.

Table 3RR:
Thief's Followers

D100 Roll	Follower	Level Range
01-03	Dwarf fighter/thief	1-4
04-08	Dwarf thief	1-6
09-13	Elf thief	1-6
14-15	Elf thief/fighter/magic-user	1-3
16-18	Elf thief/magic-user	1-4
19-24	Gnome thief	1-6
25-27	Gnome thief/fighter	1-4
28-30	Gnome thief/illusionist	1-4
31-35	Half-elf thief	1-6
36-38	Half-elf thief/fighter	1-4
39-41	Half-elf thief/fighter/magic-user	1-3
42-46	Halfling thief	1-8
47-50	Halfling thief/fighter	1-6
51-98	Human thief	1-8
99	Human dual-class thief/fighter	1-8/1-4
00	Other (GM selection)	--

Table 3SS:
Assassin Experience Levels

Experience Points	Experience Level	6-Sided Dice for Accumulated Hit Points	Level Title
0 – 1,500	1	20+1d6*	Bravo (Apprentice)
1,501 – 3,000	2	2	Rutterkin
3,001 – 6,000	3	3	Waghalter
6,001 – 12,000	4	4	Murderer
12,001 – 25,000	5	5	Thug
25,001 – 50,000	6	6	Killer
50,001 – 1000,000	7	7	Cutthroat
100,001 – 200,000	8	8	Executioner
200,001 – 300,000	9	9	Assassin
300,001 – 425,000	10	10	Expert Assassin
425,001 – 575,000	11	11	Senior Assassin
575,001 – 750,000	12	12	Chief Assassin
750,001 – 1,000,000	13	11	Prime Assassin
1,000,001 – 1,500,000	14	14	Guild Soldier
1,500,001 – 2,000,000	15	15**	Guild Assassin
2,000,001 – 2,500,000	16	15+2	Guild Capo
2,500,001 – 3,000,000-	17	15+4	GuildMaster Assassin
3,000,001 – 3,500,000	18	15+6	Guildfather of Assassins
3,500,001 – 4,000,000	19	15+8	Grandfather of Assassins
4,000,001 – 4,500,000	20 ***	15+10	Gawdfather of Assassins

* At first level assassins receive 20 points + 1d6. This twenty point 'kicker' is received at first level only.
** Assassins gain 2 hps per level after the 15th.
*** 500,000 experience points per level for each additional level beyond the 20th.

Table 3UU:
Bard Spell Progression

Bard Level	Spell Level 1	2	3	4	5	6
1	--	--	--	--	--	--
2	1	--	--	--	--	--
3	2	--	--	--	--	--
4	2	1	--	--	--	--
5	3	1	--	--	--	--
6	3	2	--	--	--	--
7	3	2	1	--	--	--
8	3	3	1	--	--	--
9	3	3	2	--	--	--
10	3	3	2	1	--	--
11	3	3	3	1	--	--
12	3	3	3	2	--	--
13	3	3	3	2	1	--
14	3	3	3	3	1	--
15	3	3	3	3	2	--
16	4	3	3	3	2	1
17	4	4	3	3	3	1
18	4	4	4	3	3	2
19	4	4	4	4	3	2
20	4	4	4	4	4	3

Table 3VV:
Bard Abilities

Climb Walls	Detect Noise	Pick Pockets	Read Languages
50%	20%	10%	5%

These abilities are described in the thief section, above.

Table 4A:
Age

Race	Starting Age Base Age	Variable	Maximum Age Range* (Base+Variable)
Dwarf (all types)	40	5d6	250+2d100
Elf (all types)	100	5d6	350+4d100
Gnome (all types)	60	3d12	200+3d100
Gnomeling	40	2d12	150+2d100
Half-elf	15	1d6	125+3d20
Halfling (all types)	20	3d4	100+1d100
Half-ogre	13	2d4	100+1d10
Half-orc	15	1d3	60+1d20
Human	15	1d4	90+2d20
Pixie fairy	2	1d3	6+1d4

* Add half the character's Constitution to the result.

Table 4B:
Age Modifier by Class Table*

Class	Modifier
assassin	none
barbarian	none
bard	1d2
battlemage	2d8
berserker	1d4
cavalier	1d4
cleric	1d6
dark knight	1d3
druid	1d6
fighter	1d4
illusionist	2d8
knight errant	1d4
magic-user	2d8
monk	1d3
paladin	1d6
ranger	1d4
thief	1d2

* Pixie fairies do not receive this modifier

Table 4C:
Aging Effects

Race	Middle Age* (1/2 Base Max.)	Old Age** (2/3 Base Max.)	Venerable*** (Base Max.)
Dwarf (all)	125 years	167 years	250 years
Elf (all)	175 years	233 years	350 years
Gnome (all)	100 years	133 years	200 years
Gnomeling	75 years	100 years	150 years
Half-elf	62 years	83 years	125 years
Halfling (all)	50 years	67 years	100 years
Half-orc	30 years	40 years	60 years
Half-ogre	55 years	73 years	98 years
Human	45 years	60 years	90 years
Pixie fairies****	6 years	11 years	14 years

* -1 Str/Con; +1 Int/Wis
** -2 Str/Dex, -1 Con; +1 Wis
*** -1 Str/Dex/Con; +1 Int/Wis
**** Pixie fairies' Ability Scores do not adjust with age.

It is important to remember that adjustments cannot cause an Ability Score to exceed racial maximums. Likewise, any adjustments cannot lower an Ability Score below racial or class minimums.

Table 4D:
Handedness of Character

Roll	Handedness
01 - 12	Left-handed
13 - 22	Ambidextrous*
23 - 00	Right-handed

* All elves are ambidextrous.
** Dwarves and gnomes may add or subtract 10% to their roll to reflect their tendency to be ambidextrous.
*** Characters with 16 Dex or higher may add or subtract 5% to their roll.

Table 4E:
Average Height and Weight

Race	Height in Inches Base*	Modifier	Weight in Pounds Base*	Modifier
	M/F		M/F	
Dwarf	43/41	1d10	130/105	4d10
Elf	55/50	1d10	90/70	3d10
Gnome	38/36	1d6	72/68	5d4
Gnomeling	32/33	1d6	46/44	2d4
Half-elf	60/58	2d6	110/85	3d12
Halfling	32/30	2d8	52/48	5d4
Half-ogre	84/82	2d6	315/310	1d100
Half-orc	66/62	1d4	150/120	4d10
Human	60/59	2d10	140/100	6d10
Pixie fairy	18/18	1d4	24/24	1d6

* Females tend to be lighter and shorter than males. Thus, the base numbers for height and weight are divided into male/female values. Note that the modifier still allows for a broad range in each category.

Character Description/Family Heritage:

WARNING: Be sure to consult the appropriate chapters when rolling on these tables. Some tables, especially the Background Tables (Chapter 4), have several modifiers which can be applied.

Table 4F:
Social Class Table

Dice roll	Social (/Economic) Class	Typical Members of the Social Class
01	Slave Class (SLC) *	Slaves, indentured servants, prisoners, banished individuals
02-06	Lower Lower Class (LLC)	Freed slaves, peasants, tinkers, vagabonds, beggars, criminals, low-level thieves, low-level and mid-level assassins
07-11	Middle Lower Class (MLC)	Herdsmen, laborers, peddlers, actors, jugglers, men-at-arms, low-level barbarians, mid-level thieves, high-level assassins, low-level bards
12-20	Upper Lower Class (ULC)	Freemen, tradesmen, petty officers, money changers, fences, low-level fighters, high-level thieves
21-35	Lower Middle Class (LMC)	Artisans, craftsmen, petty merchants, junior officers, bankers, landless knights, druids, rangers
36-55	Middle Middle Class (MMC)	Landed gentry, merchants, petty officials, senior officers, landless petty nobles, mid-level fighters, low-level magic-users, low-level illusionists
56-87	Upper Middle Class (UMC)	Guild masters, great merchants, military commanders, officials, landless nobles, lesser clerics, high-level fighters, mid-level magic-users, mid-level illusionists
88-96	Lower Upper Class (LUC)	Great landed gentry, generals and marshals, greater officials, knights, mid-level clerics, cavaliers, paladins, high-level magic-users, high-level illusionists
97-99	Middle Upper Class (MUC)**	Knights, commanders, great clerics, nobles, high-level paladins, very high-level magic-users and illusionists
00	Upper Upper Class (UUC)***	Great nobles, sovereign nobility, royalty

* On SLC results roll a 1d20. 1-5 indicates character is a runaway slave. 06-15 indicates the character is an escaped criminal (GM to determine the crime) 16-20 indicates character was stripped of all rank and title by his native culture and banished.
** On a result of MUC check with your GM. Character may have a title, chain-of-office or position.
*** On a result of UUC check with your GM. Character may have properties, titles and other family/royal house entitlements.

Table 4G:
Circumstances of Birth (d100)

Roll	Circumstance of Birth
<01 - 90	Character's birth was legitimate. Parents were married at time of character's birth.
91 – 00+*	Character's birth was illegitimate. Parents were not married at time of character's birth. Roll again on Illegitimate Birth Table.

*The child of unmarried parents is typically one social class lower than the social class of the father (85% percent of the time).

Racial Modifiers to Circumstances of Birth

	Table 4G	Table 4H
Dwarves, all	+5	+15
Elves		
Drow	+5	+15
Gray	-8	+25
Grunge	+10	-20
High	-5	+20
Wood	-5	+10
all others	-5	+20
Gnomes		
Gnone Titan	+5	0
all others	-5	+15
Half-elves	+15	0
Halflings, all	-5	+10
Half-orcs	+25	-30
Half-ogres	+35	-40
Humans	0	0
Pixie fairies	+15	+50

Table 4H:
Illegitimate Birth Table (d100)

Roll	Nature of Illegitimacy
<01 – 05	Character was abandoned at birth. Parents unknown. [-3 to beginning Honor]
06 - 30	Birth was a result of rape. Father unknown. [-5 to beginning Honor]
31 – 60	Mother was a prostitute. Father unknown. [-10 to beginning Honor]
61 – 90	Birth was the result of an adulterous affair. 75% chance father's identity is known. [-3 to beginning Honor]
91 – 00+	Birth was arranged through a surrogate mother. 25% chance birth mother's identity is known. [-1 to beginning Honor]

Table 4I:
Quality of Parent Table (1d100)*

Result	Parental Quality	Effect
01–60	Loving parent.	Character grew up well nurtured and properly cared for. Five (5) Building Point bonus
61–80	Ill-Equipped Parent.	Parent was well intentioned but poor at raising children.
81–91	Indifferent Parent.	Character was viewed as a burden. Character grew up with feelings of inadequacy and felt unloved. (Roll on Minor Quirk Table - player choice of which one)*
92–00+	Abusive Parent.	Character was abused by parents. (Roll on Major Quirk Table - player choice of which one)*

* Roll twice – once for each parent. If character is an illegitimate child, roll only once for mother.
Modifiers: Orphans add +20   Bastards add +35

Table 4J:
Family Heritage (d100)

Roll	Heritage	Effect
01	Great dishonor	[–5 to beginning Honor]
02 – 15	Dishonor	[-2 to beginning Honor]
16 – 45	No Honor	[No modifier]
46 – 76	Honorable	[+2 to beginning Honor]
77 – 00	Great Honor	[+5 to beginning Honor]

Table 4K:
Number of Siblings (d100)

Dice Roll	Number of Siblings
01-15	None – Only child
16-35	1 sibling
36-50	2 siblings
51-60	3 Siblings
61-68	4 siblings
69-75	5 siblings
76-81	6 siblings
82 –86	7 siblings
86 – 90	8 siblings
91 – 95	9 siblings
96 – 00	Character has 1d4 illegitimate siblings. Roll on table 4H with a –10 modifier to determine nature of illegitimate siblings (honor modifiers only effect them). Roll for order of birth - your character is first born if he is legitimate himself.

Table 4L:
Order of Birth (d100)

Roll	Order of Birth	Effect
01 - 20	First born	[+ 5 to starting money roll]
21 – 40	2nd born	[+2 to starting money roll]
41 – 60	Middle born (roll randomly)[no effect]*	
61 – 80	2nd to last born	[-2 to starting money roll]
81 – 00	Last born	[-5 to starting money roll]

* Roll once on Minor Personality Quirk Table

WARNING: Be sure to consult the appropriate chapters when rolling on these tables. Some tables, especially the Background Tables (Chapter 4), have several modifiers which can be applied.

Table 4M:
Character Starting Money

Roll	Starting Funds
01-05	Hereditary Debt[1]
06-10	Flat Broke
11-15	20 + 1d4 gps
16-20	25 + 1d4 gps
21-25	30 + 1d4 gps
26-30	35 + 1d4 gps
31-35	45 + 1d6 gps
36-40	50 + 1d6 gps
41- 45	55 + 1d6 gps
46-50	60 + 1d6 gps
51-55	70 + 1 d8 gps
56-60	80 + 1d8 gps
61-65	90 + 1d8 gps
66-70	100 + 1d8 gps
71-75	110 + 1d10 gps
76-80	120 + 1d10 gps
81-85	130 + 1d10 gps
86-90	140 +1d10 gps
91-95	145 + 1d20 gps
96-100	150 + 1d20 gps
101-105	160 + 1d20 gps[2]
106-110	170 + 1d20 gps[3]
111-115	180 + 2d20 gps[4]
116+	190 + 2d20 gps[5]

1. Character has inherited a debt from his parents/family, which is responsible for repaying. Re-roll on table above and multiply the results by 10. This is the amount that must be repaid in d12 game months. The GM must decide exactly to whom the debt is owed and repercussions for defaulting payment. (Note there is ALWAYS a hit to Honor for failure to repay a loan.)
2. Character has also inherited his father's weapon (see GM).
3. Character has inherited his father's weapon and armor (see GM).
4. Character has inherited his father's weapon, armor and horse (w/basic tack) (see GM).
5. Character has inherited all of the items in #4, plus the deed to some land. (see GM)

Table 5A:
Honor Standards for Level Progression

Current Level	GREAT HONOR (Bonus Window*)	DISHONORABLE (Penalty Window**)
1	17-20	<6
2	25-30	<9
3	33-40	<12
4	41-50	<15
5	49-60	<18
6	57-70	<21
7	65-80	<24
8	73-90	<27
9	81-100	<30
10	89-110	<33
11	97-120	<36
12	105-130	<39
13	113-140	<42
14	121-150	<45
15	129-160	<48
16	137-170	<51
17	145-180	<54
18	153-190	<57
19	161-200	<60
20	169-210	<63

* Characters with Honor in the 'bonus window' get a +1 to ALL their die rolls.
** Characters with low Honor (penalty window) receive a –1 to ALL their die rolls.

Table 5B:
Breaking a Blood Oath (1d20)

Roll	% of Honor Lost
01	75%
02-05	65%
06-09	50%
10-13	40%
14-17	30%
18-19	20%
20	10%

Note that keeping/making good on a blood oath has no benefit whatsoever. A person is expected to keep his word so no incentive is given. If breaking an oath results in a negative Honor it is recorded as such.

Table 5D:
Cleric/Paladin Atonement Table

Roll	Atonement
1	Character must voluntarily inflict 1d4 points of damage upon himself per day and may only seek healing for these if he has fewer than 10 hit points.[1]
2	Character must voluntarily inflict 1d6 points of damage upon himself per day and may only seek healing for these if he has fewer than 10 hit points.[1]
3	Character must voluntarily inflict 1d8 points of damage upon himself per day and may only seek healing for these if he has fewer than 10 hit points.[1]
4	Pay 1d20*100 in gps to church/temple of character's faith
5	Pay 2d20*100 in gps to church/temple of character's faith
6	Sacrifice most cherished possession and pilgrimage to holy site 1d10 days away.
7-8	Sacrifice most cherished possession and pilgrimage to holy site 1d20+10 days away.
9-10	Sacrifice most cherished possession and 2 points from ability scores.[2]
11	Sacrifice most cherished possession and 3 points from ability scores.[2]
12	Character must purge his Honor.
13	Continuously bear an enormous Holy Symbol of character's faith for 1d20 months.
14	Pay monthly tithe of 100 gps to church/temple of character's faith for 1 year.
15-16	Temporarily retire from adventuring to perform community service for 1 month.
17-18	Temporarily retire from adventuring to perform community service for 6 months.
19-20+	Temporarily retire from adventuring to perform community service for 1 year.

[1] - duration is determined by the GM.
[2] - points sacrificed may be taken from one or more abilities

Character Advancement Notes

Table 11A:
Stat Percentile Die Roll by Class

	Fighter	Magic User	Cleric	Thief
Strength	d20	d4	d12	d8
Intelligence	d4	d20	d6	d10
Wisdom	d6	d12	d20	d4
Dexterity	d10	d8	d4	d20
Constitution	d12	d10	d10	d6
Charisma	d8	d6	d8	d12
Comeliness	d4	d4	d4	d4

Table 6A:
Flaws and Quirks d100

Roll	Table
01-14	Roll on Table 6B
15-28	Roll on Table 6C
29-42	Roll on Table 6D
43-50	Roll on Table 6E
51-66	Roll on Table 6F
67-76	Roll on Table 6G
77-93	Roll on Table 6H
94-100	Roll on Table 6I

Table 6B:
Flaws, Minor (Physical) d100

Roll	Flaw	BP Bonus
01 - 09	Albino	5
10 - 14	Animal [type] Antipathy*	7
15 - 23	Anosmia (loss of the sense of taste)	5
24 - 26	Asthmatic	10
27 - 35	Blind, Color	5
36 - 40	Chronic Nose Bleeds	8
41 - 49	Excessive Drooling	5
50 - 58	Flatulent	5
59 - 61	Hearing Impaired	10
62 - 70	Lisp	5
71 - 85	Roll again on this table and an extra time on Table 6C	
86 - 100	Roll again on this table and an extra time on Table 6D	

* See flaw description for roll for specifics

Table 6C:
Flaws, Minor (Physical) d100

Roll	Flaw	BP Bonus
01 - 07	Loss of Ear	6
08 - 13	Loss of Eye	7
14 - 21	Male Pattern Baldness	5
22 - 26	Migraines	8
27 - 34	Missing Finger(s)*	5
35 - 42	Nervous Tic	5
43 - 47	Scar, Facial	8
48 - 54	Sleep Chatter	6
55 - 61	Sound, Sleeper	6
62 - 70	Strange Body Odor	6
71 - 85	Roll again on this table and an extra time on Table 6E	
86 - 100	Roll Twice more on this table. (If this result comes up again, roll again on this table, and an extra time on Table 6E)	

*See Flaw description for roll for specifics

Table 6D*:
Flaws, Minor (Physical) d100

Roll	Flaw	BP Bonus
01 - 10	Stutter	8
11 - 20	Tone Deaf	5
21 - 31	Vision Impaired, Far Sighted	7
32 - 37	Blind, one eye	5
38 - 70	Vision Impaired, Near Sighted	7
71 - 90	Roll once on Table 6B and once on Table 6C	
91 - 100	Roll on Table 6E (Flaws, Major)	

The version of this table appearing on page 92 is incorrectly printed.

Table 6E:
Flaws, Major (Physical) d100

Roll	Flaw	BP Bonus
01 - 06	Accident Prone	11
07 - 12	Acute Allergies*	11
13 - 17	Amputee, Arm	15
18 - 20	Amputee, Double, Arm	20
21 - 23	Amputee, Double, Leg	20
24 - 28	Amputee, Leg	15
29 - 31	Blind	20
32 - 40	Deaf	20
41 - 45	Hemophiliac	15
46 - 50	Low Threshold for Pain (LTP)	15
51 - 56	Maimed*	11
57 - 62	Mute	11
63 - 67	Narcolepsy	15
68 - 73	No Depth Perception	11
74 - 78	Seizure, Disorders (Epilepsy)*	12-20
79 - 84	Sleep Walker	11
85 - 90	Trick Knee	12
91 - 100	Roll once on this table and once on Table 6B	

* See flaw description for roll for specifics

Table 6F:
Quirks, Minor (Mental) d100

Roll	Flaw	BP Bonus
01 - 05	Absent Minded	9
06 - 08	Acrophobia (fear of heights)	10
09 - 11	Agoraphobia (fear of open spaces)	10
12 - 17	Alcoholic	8
18 - 22	Animal Phobia*	9
23 - 28	Chronic Nightmares	6
29 - 32	Claustrophobia (fear of closed spaces)	8
33 - 35	Delusional (Minor)*	10
36 - 41	Depression (Minor)*	8
42 - 47	Gambling Addiction	8
48 - 53	Inappropriate Sense of Humor	7
54 - 56	Kleptomaniac (compelled to steal)	10
57 - 59	Obsessive Compulsive*	10
60 - 70	Nagging Conscience	5
71 - 73	Paranoid	10
74 - 79	Short Term Memory Loss	8
80 - 82	Superstitious	10
83 - 90	Temper*	7
91 - 95	Roll again on this table and an extra time on Table 6G	
96 - 100	Roll again on this table and an extra time on Table 6H	

* See quirk description for roll for specifics

Table 6G:
Quirks, Major (Mental) d100

Roll	Flaw	BP Bonus
01 - 04	Delusional (Major)*	15
05 - 07	Depression (Major)*	16
08 - 13	Enmity toward Class*	13
14 - 19	Enmity toward Monster*	13
20 - 25	Enmity toward Race*	13
26 - 29	HackFrenzy	15
30 - 33	HackLust	15
34 - 41	Psychotic Aversion to Class*	11
42 - 50	Psychotic Aversion to Monster*	11
51 - 58	Psychotic Aversion to Race*	11
59 - 65	Pyromaniac	12
66 - 72	Sadistic	12
73 - 80	Wuss-of-Heart	11
81 - 90	Roll again on this table and an extra time on Table 6F	
91 - 100	Roll again on this table and an extra time on Table 6H	

* See quirk description for roll for specifics

Table 6H:
Quirks, Minor (Personality) d100

Roll	Flaw	BP Bonus
01 - 08	Chronic Liar	6
09 - 17	Clingy	5
18 - 30	Glutton	5
31 - 35	Greedy	8
36 - 42	Gullible	7
43 - 48	Jerk	8
49 - 55	Loud Boor	7
56 - 67	Misguided	5
68 - 72	Obnoxious	6
73 - 76	Pack Rat	5
77 - 82	Self Absorbed	8
83 - 88	Socially Awkward	7
89 - 95	Value Privacy (Reclusive)	9
96 - 100	Roll again on this table and an extra time on Table 6G	

Table 6(I):
Quirks, Major (Personality) d100

Roll	Flaw	BP Bonus
01 - 35	Multiple Personalities (per personality)	special*
36 - 70	Truthful*	11
71 - 85	Roll twice on Table 6H	
86 - 100	Roll twice on Table 6G	

* See quirk description for roll for specifics

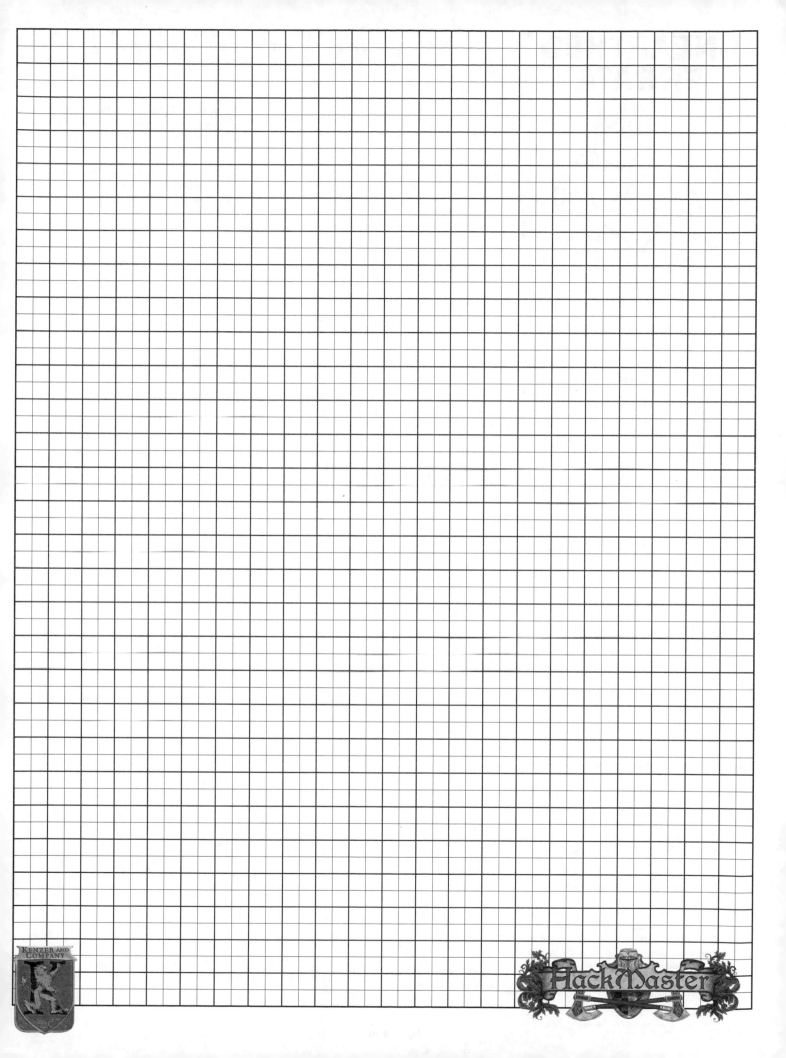

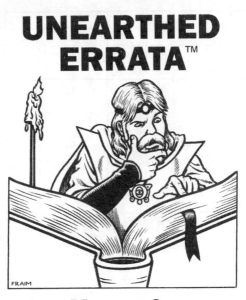

UNEARTHED ERRATA™

HackMaster Official Errata & Clarifications

p. 28 - Ambidextrous and Bow Bonus should not be listed under **Additional Talents Which May be Purchased** for High Elves (incl. Sylvan Elves and Grey Elves). These are already possessed as innate Talents.

p. 30 - Ambidextrous, Bow Bonus and Spear Bonus should not be listed under **Additional Talents Which May be Purchased** for Grunge Elves (Grels). These are already possessed as innate Talents. Track Game Animal should be added whereas Constitution/Health Bonus and Mining Sense should not be listed as they are NOT additional talents which may be purchased. Additionally, the cavalier is not one of the allowable classes for the Grunge Elf.

p. 31 - Ambidextrous should not be listed under **Additional Talents Which May be Purchased** for Dark Elves (Drow). This is already possessed as an innate Talent. Animal Companion should not be listed as it is NOT an additional talent which may be purchased. Additionally, the cavalier is not one of the allowable classes for the Dark Elf (Drow).

Errors on pages 28, 30-31 are corrected in Appendix S.

p. 85 - The numbers listed in the honor column are the upper limit for that row. Thus, the row labeled fifteen is for honor values of 11-15.

p. 92 - Table 6D: **Flaws, Minor (Physical)** is itself flawed. The version of this table appearing on p. 398 is correct.

p. 94 - The following sentence should be inserted into the description of the Male Pattern Baldness flaw, after the first sentence: "If a female character rolls this flaw, she must immediately re-roll on Table 6C, and once on the minor mental quirk table 6F, because of the trauma."

CHANGE Buying Initial Skills: When you purchase a skill during the character generation process, you pay the building point cost and record the skill on your character sheet. You then reference Appendix F: Skills, Talents and Proficiencies to find the relevant ability and mastery die. In some cases, the relevant ability is the average of two or more abilities. You roll the mastery die, add a roll of your honor die and add the result to the relevant ability. This is your skill mastery. If you choose, you can

spend the building point cost of the skill again. Each additional time you pay the cost of the skill, you get to roll the mastery die and your honor die and add the result to your skill mastery. When you buy a skill during the character creation process, you DO add your Honor die.

For example, Garrison the fighter wants to purchase the task skill armor repair: basic. Armor repair: basic has a building point cost of three (3), a relevant ability of (Dex+Int)/2, and a mastery die of 1d10. Initially, Garrison's player pays three points for the skill and records it on his character sheet. The he calculates the relevant ability. His Dexterity is 15, but his intelligence is only 4, so the relevant ability is 9 [(15+4)/2 rounded down = 9]. He then rolls 1d10 and gets a 7. Garrison has average honor, so he rolls a d3, and gets a 1. Garrison's base skill percentage for armor repair: basic is 17% (9+7+1). His player marks this on the character sheet next to the skill. After purchasing the rest of the skills he wanted, Garrison's player has six (6) building points left over. He decides to improve his armor repair: basic skill. He spends the six (6) building points to get two more rolls of the mastery die, one for each cost of the skill spent. He rolls a 4 and a 9 on his mastery die, and a 2 and a 4 (3+2-1 for penetration). His final skill mastery is 35% (16+4+9+2+4).

Racial Talents: There are two types of talents available to each race, those that are free, and those that need to be purchased with Building Points. The talents that each race receives free are listed on the racial At a Glance tables under Talents. Some of these talents are unique, and some are available to be purchased by other races. The talents which need to be purchased are also listed on the racial At a Glance tables under Restricted Talents Which May be Purchased. These talents are described in Appendix H.

Weapon Proficiencies: A distinction must be made between a weapon proficiency slot and the weapon proficiency itself. The slots are free and are determined by Table 7A Proficiency Slots on page 101. The actual weapon proficiencies are the weapons you choose to fill these slots. In order to fill the slot with a weapon proficiency, you must pay the one (1) BP cost of the weapon proficiency. Garrison the Fighter gets four weapon proficiency slots at first level. Since he is a fighter, his first weapon proficiency is free, so he chooses the bastard sword. He also wants to be proficient in the long bow, so he pays 1 BP to get a long bow proficiency. Garrison spends one more BP to become specialized in the bastard sword, filling his third slot, and one BP to be proficient in the morning star. Garrison has filled all four of his initial proficiency slots and spent 3 BP to do so (fighters get the first weapon proficiency free, otherwise he would have spent 4 BP).

"Impossible" Classes: Some races have racial ability limits and/or adjustments that make it seem impossible for them to qualify for certain classes that they are allowed to qualify for. However, you can spend building points after having chosen your race to raise your abilities. You can use building points to raise abilities above the racial maximums and thus qualify for the "impossible" classes.

Hit Point Bonus Talent: This talent gives you 1 extra hitpoint anytime you roll a hit die, in any situation and for any reason. This includes the cavalier sub-levels and multiple hit dice instances.

Untrained Skills: The complete list of skills that can be used without paying the BP cost or taking a block of instruction is in the GMG. Ask your GM for details.

CHANGE Ranger/Druid: Because of alignment conflicts, the Ranger/Druid is NOT and eligible multi-class combination for any race.

Thief Abilities for the Assassin: When the an assassin character reaches third level, he gains the thieving abilities of a first level thief. He is granted 65 discretionary points to distribute amongst the thieving abilities, adhering to the same restrictions as a first level thief.

Building Points for Multi-Classed Characters: A multi-classed character gets the higher of the two building point totals for his classes, not both.

Dual-Classed Characters: Dual-classes characters do not gain any building points when they take on a new class, nor do they get an ability score adjustments until the new class level surpasses that of the old class.

Specialist Mages: The information on specialist mages will be included in the GMG and future supplements.

Skill Suites: Skill suites can be bought at first level, even if some of the suite skills have prerequisites that aren't at the normally required level of 50%. When recording the mastery level for the skill suite, a level is calculated for the suite as a whole and for the individual skills. At any time a character can choose to use either the individual skill value or the suite skill value for a particular skill.

CHANGE Free Skills: Anytime a skill is gotten for free, because of a class or other reason, any prerequisites for that skill are also received free. These prerequisite skills are gained at a mastery level of 50%.

Social Class and Illegitimate Children: The statement on table 4G on p. 78 of the PHB has caused some confusion. The statement reads, "The child of unmarried parents is typically one social class lower than the social class of the father (85% of the time)." This does not effect the social class you rolled; the social class you roll is your social class. If you are illegitimate, it means the social class of your parents could be higher. Thus an illegitimate human who rolls MMC might have parents of UMC or higher (85% of the time).

CHANGE Armorer Skill: The Armorer skill grants the ability to repair armor as the armor repair: basic skill. However, unlike the armor repair: basic skill, the armorer may attempt to repair a piece of armor again after failing his skill check the first time.